TEACHER'S EDITION

**Houghton
Mifflin
Harcourt**

D0123845

collections

GRADE 7

Program Consultants:

Kylene Beers

Martha Hougen

Carol Jago

William L. McBride

Erik Palmer

Lydia Stack

Houghton
Mifflin
Harcourt

collections

Teacher's Edition Table of Contents

Kylene Beers Nationally known lecturer and author on reading and literacy; 2011 recipient of the Conference on English Leadership Exemplary Leader Award; coauthor of *Notice and Note: Strategies for Close Reading*; former president of the National Council of Teachers of English. Dr. Beers is the nationally known author of *When Kids Can't Read: What Teachers Can Do* and coeditor of *Adolescent Literacy: Turning Promise into Practice*, as well as articles in the *Journal of Adolescent and Adult Literacy*. Former editor of *Voices from the Middle*, she is the 2001 recipient of NCTE's Richard W. Halley Award, given for outstanding contributions to middle school literacy. She recently served as Senior Reading Researcher at the Comer School Development Program at Yale University as well as Senior Reading Advisor to Secondary Schools for the Reading and Writing Project at Teachers College.

Martha Hougen National consultant, presenter, researcher, and author. Areas of expertise include differentiating instruction for students with learning difficulties, including those with learning disabilities and dyslexia; and teacher and leader preparation improvement. Dr. Hougen has taught at the middle school through graduate levels. Recently her focus has been on working with teacher educators to enhance teacher and leader preparation to better meet the needs of all students. Currently she is working with the University of Florida at the Collaboration for Effective Educator Development, Accountability, and Reform Center (CEEDAR Center) to improve the achievement of students with disabilities by reforming teacher and leader licensure, evaluation, and preparation. She has led similar efforts in Texas with the Higher Education Collaborative and the College & Career Readiness Initiative Faculty Collaboratives. In addition to peer-reviewed articles, curricular documents, and presentations, Dr. Hougen has published two college textbooks: *The Fundamentals of Literacy Assessment and Instruction Pre-K–6* (2012) and *The Fundamentals of Literacy Assessment and Instruction 6–12* (2014).

Carol Jago Teacher of English with 32 years of experience at Santa Monica High School in California; author and nationally known lecturer; and former president of the National Council of Teachers of English. Currently serves as Associate Director of the California Reading and Literature Project at UCLA. With expertise in standards assessment and secondary education, Ms. Jago is the author of numerous books on education, including *With Rigor for All* and *Papers, Papers, Papers*, and is active with the California Association of Teachers of English, editing its scholarly journal *California English* since 1996. Ms. Jago also served on the planning committee for the 2009 NAEP Framework and the 2011 NAEP Writing Framework.

William L. McBride Curriculum specialist. Dr. McBride is a nationally known speaker, educator, and author who now trains teachers in instructional methodologies. He is coauthor of *What's Happening?*, an innovative, high-interest text for middle-grade readers, and author of *If They Can Argue Well, They Can Write Well*. A former reading specialist, English teacher, and social studies teacher, he holds a master's degree in reading and a doctorate in curriculum and instruction from the University of North Carolina at Chapel Hill. Dr. McBride has contributed to the development of textbook series in language arts, social studies, science, and vocabulary. He is also known for his novel *Entertaining an Elephant*, which tells the story of a veteran teacher who becomes reinspired with both his profession and his life.

Erik Palmer Veteran teacher and education consultant based in Denver, Colorado. Author of *Well Spoken: Teaching Speaking to All Students* and *Digitally Speaking: How to Improve Student Presentations*. His areas of focus include improving oral communication, promoting technology in classroom presentations, and updating instruction through the use of digital tools. He holds a bachelor's degree from Oberlin College and a master's degree in curriculum and instruction from the University of Colorado.

Lydia Stack Internationally known teacher educator and author. She is involved in a Stanford University project to support English Language Learners, *Understanding Language*. The goal of this project is to enrich academic content and language instruction for English Language Learners (ELLs) in grades K–12 by making explicit the language and literacy skills necessary to meet the Common Core State Standards (CCSS) and Next Generation Science Standards. Her teaching experience includes twenty-five years as an elementary and high school ESL teacher, and she is a past president of Teachers of English to Speakers of Other Languages (TESOL). Her awards include the TESOL James E. Alatis Award and the San Francisco STAR Teacher Award. Her publications include *On Our Way to English, Visions: Language, Literature, Content,* and *American Themes,* a literature anthology for high school students in the ACCESS program of the U.S. State Department's Office of English Language Programs.

Additional thanks to the following Program Reviewers

Rosemary Asquino
Sylvia B. Bennett
Yvonne Bradley
Leslie Brown
Haley Carroll
Caitlin Chalmers
Emily Colley-King
Stacy Collins
Denise DeBonis
Courtney Dickerson
Sarah Easley
Phyllis J. Everette
Peter J. Foy Sr.

Carol M. Gibby
Angie Gill
Mary K. Goff
Saira Haas
Lisa M. Janeway
Robert V. Kidd Jr.
Kim Lilley
John C. Lowe
Taryn Curtis MacGee
Meredith S. Maddox
Cynthia Martin
Kelli M. McDonough
Megan Pankiewicz

Linda Beck Pieplow
Molly Pieplow
Mary-Sarah Proctor
Jessica A. Stith
Peter Swartley
Pamela Thomas
Linda A. Tobias
Rachel Ukleja
Lauren Vint
Heather Lynn York
Leigh Ann Zerr

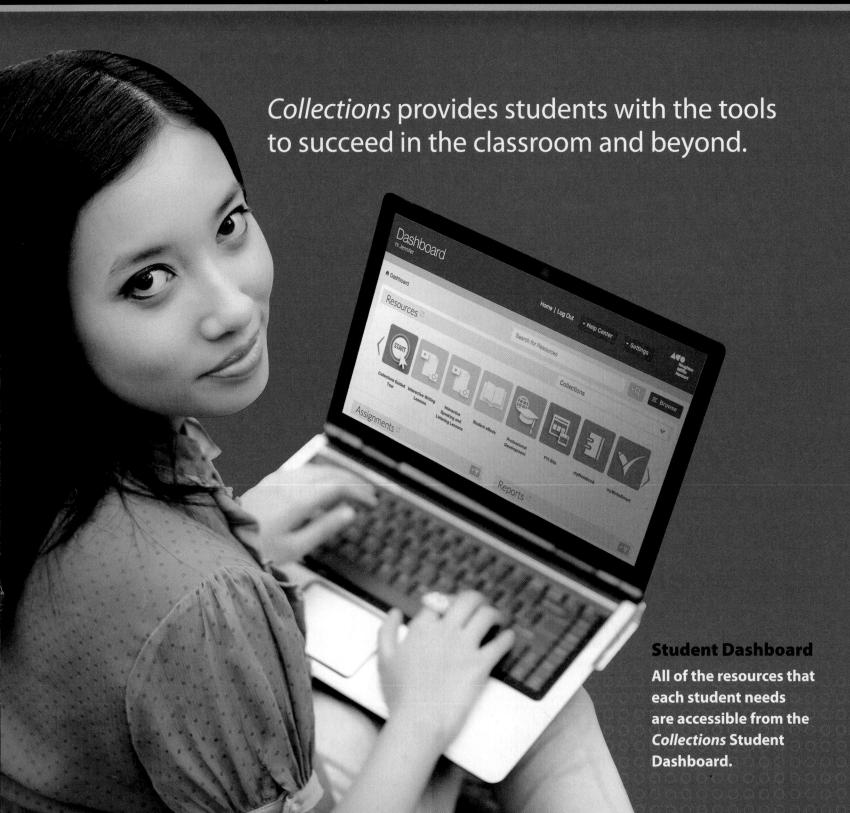

Living and Learning . . .

Collections provides students with the tools to succeed in the classroom and beyond.

Student Dashboard

All of the resources that each student needs are accessible from the *Collections* Student Dashboard.

HMH Player App provides innovative features supporting instruction both in class and outside of class, synchronizing online and offline work.
available in iOS® and Google Chrome™ formats

Teachers can plan lessons, customize content, present instruction, assign assessments and activities, and review student progress.

Students can download content to their devices and fully use *Collections* without an Internet connection. When back online, all student work is saved and available.

Supporting students' individual strengths, *Collections* integrates scaffolds that build competencies.

 Text in FOCUS **Videos enhance understanding of each anchor text by using graphic elements to explain figurative language, sentence structure, and main ideas.**

Integrated English Language Development

Integrated ELD instruction is woven seamlessly throughout *Collections*, providing directions for teachers and scaffolding for students.

Designated English Language Development

***Language Workshop* provides instruction and the opportunity for students to master collaboration, interaction, and language production as they develop English language skills.**

Level Up Interactive Tutorials

Tutorials escalate learning with new digital instruction and feedback for critical learning objectives.

Making Meaning

Collections' digital annotation and note-taking tools are essential for text analysis and for writing to sources.

Online Annotation Tools allow students to make meaning and draw conclusions supported by text evidence.

myNotebook stores students' annotations and notes for use in Performance Tasks.

Close Read Screencasts provide modeled conversations about text at point of use in your eBook.

Contents

Resources

Bookmarks

Notes

Page View

Audio

Help

Standards

53

Play

Background *The Hmong (hmông) are an ethnic group from southern China, Laos, Vietnam, and Thailand. In the 1970s, war and conflict caused many of the Hmong people in Laos to flee to refugee camps in Thailand. Author* **Kao Kalia Yang** *(b. 1980) was born in one of these camps. She moved with her family, including her older sister Dawb, to Minnesota in 1987. Four other siblings were born in the United States, where all the Yang children received their educations.*

from

The Latehomecomer

Memoir by Kao Kalia Yang

SETTING A PURPOSE As you read, notice the challenges and the opportunities that life in a new country presents Kao Kalia Yang and her family. How does Yang react to her situation?

Close Read

We had been in America for almost ten years. I was nearly fifteen, and Dawb had just gotten her driver's license. The children were growing up. We needed a new home—the apartment was too small. There was hardly room to breathe when the scent of jasmine rice and fish steamed with ginger mingled heavily with the scent of freshly baked pepperoni pizza—Dawb's favorite food. We had been looking for a new house for nearly six months.

10   It was in a poor neighborhood with houses that were ready to collapse—wooden planks falling off, colors chipping away, sloping porches—and huge, old trees. There was a realty sign in the front yard, a small patch of green in front of the white house. It was one story, with a small open patio and a single wide window framed by black panels beside a black door. There was a short driveway that climbed up a

Credits

Annotation   ✕

✉ **Add Recipient**

Narrator describing the poor condition of the neighborhood and home she was to live in

Enter Tag   +

☑ Save to myNotebook   **Delete**   **Save**

I was feeling a strong push to reinvent myself. Without my realizing, by the time high school began, I had a feeling in the pit of my stomach that I had been on simmer for too long. I wanted to bubble over the top and douse the confusing fire that burned in my belly. Or else I wanted to turn the stove off. I wanted to sit cool on the burners of life, lid on, and steady. I was ready for change, but there was so little in my life that I could adjust. So life took a blurry seat.

These images give the impression the narrator is uncomfortable.

Close Read

Does love
look with the eyes. . .

Stream to Start

Stream to Start Videos delight and instruct with engaging digital explanations of each collection's theme.

Close Reader allows students to apply standards and practice close-reading strategies in a digital or consumable print format.

Anchor Texts drive each collection and have related selections in the **Close Reader**.

Background *A member of the Standing Rock Sioux,* **Susan Power** *was born in 1961 and grew up in Chicago. She spent her childhood listening to her mother tell stories about their American Indian heritage. These stories later served as inspiration for Power's writing. As a young girl, Power made frequent visits with her mother to local museums—trips that inspired her memoir "Museum Indians."*

Museum Indians

Memoir by Susan Power

CLOSE READ
Notes

1. **READ ▶** As you read lines 1–16, begin to cite text evidence.

• Underline a metaphor in the first paragraph that describes the mother's braid.

• Underline a metaphor in the second paragraph that describes the mother's braid differently.

• In the margin, note the adjectives the narrator uses to describe the braid.

coils in my mother's dresser drawer; it is thick and black, as sequins. My mother cut her hair several years ago, born, but she kept one heavy braid. It is the three-foot from its nest and handle as if it were alive.

why did you cut your hair?" I ask. I am a little girl lifting a river into the light that streams through the kitchen om turns to me.

me headaches. Now put that away and wash your hands

n't cut *my* hair, will you?" I'm sure this is a whine. t a little trim now and then to even the ends."

the dark snake to its nest among my mother's slips, so that its thin tail hides beneath the wide mouth sheared

thick
black
glossy

13

Background *A member of the Standing Rock Sioux,* **Susan Power** *was born in 1961 and grew up in Chicago. She spent her childhood listening to her mother tell stories about their American Indian heritage. These stories later served as inspiration for Power's writing. As a young girl, Power made frequent visits with her mother to local museums—trips that inspired her memoir "Museum Indians."*

Museum Indians

Memoir by Susan Power

Creating Knowledge

COMPARE ANCHOR TEXTS AND MEDIA

HISTORY VIDEO

The March on Washington

I Have a Dream
Speech by Martin Luther King Jr.

from Nobody Turn Me Around: A History of the 1963 March on Washington
History Writing by Charles Euchner

MEDIA

AMERICA The Story of Us: March on Washington
Video by HISTORY®

Background *On August 28, 1963, thousands of Americans marched on Washington, D.C., to urge Congress to pass a civil rights bill. Martin Luther King Jr. delivered his "I Have a Dream" speech on the steps of the Lincoln Memorial before more than 250,000 people. After you read and analyze the speech, you will read an excerpt from a history text which describes the historic speech in detail and includes first-hand accounts from people who were on the National Mall that day. Then you will watch a short video about the march and compare the two accounts.*

Martin Luther King Jr. *(1929–1968) became a catalyst for social change in the 1950s and 1960s. Preaching a philosophy of nonviolence, he galvanized people of all races to participate in boycotts, marches, and demonstrations against racial injustice. His moral leadership stirred the conscience of the nation and helped bring about the passage of the Civil Rights Act of 1964. In that same year, he was awarded the Nobel Peace Prize. King continued his work for justice and equality until he was assassinated in 1968.*

Compare Anchor Texts

Transcending time and place, media resources enrich informational and literary text throughout *Collections*.

Voices and images from A&E®, Bio®, and HISTORY® transport students to different times and places.

Informational text on *FYI* is linked to each collection topic and is curated and updated monthly.

Channel One News®

Channel One helps students become global citizens in a digital world.

Media Lessons prompt students to read news reports, literary adaptations, ads, and websites as complex texts.

Communicating Effectively

Today's students practice the skills of communication in speaking, listening, and writing with interactive lessons that provide models, feedback, and practice.

Using Textual Evidence
Put your research into writing.

W 7, W 8, W 9

Interactive Lessons

1. Introduction
2. Synthesizing Information
3. Writing an Outline
4. Summarizing, Paraphrasing, and Quoting
5. Attribution

Interactive Lessons for writing, speaking, and listening provide opportunities for in-depth instruction and practice in key 21st century skills.

✓**my WriteSmart** provides a collaborative tool for students to use to revise and edit Performance Tasks with peers and teachers.

Types of Planning Activities ⌄

Researching

Taking Notes

Organizing Your Notes

Getting Feedback

Speaking and Listening

Interactive lessons provide audio and video speeches and class discussions for students to critique using rubrics for each activity.

Writing

Models, rubrics, direct instruction, and ongoing feedback provide quality interactive instruction in each of the primary writing types.

Performance Tasks for each collection provide explicit writing process instruction and links to *my*Notebook and to related Interactive Lessons.

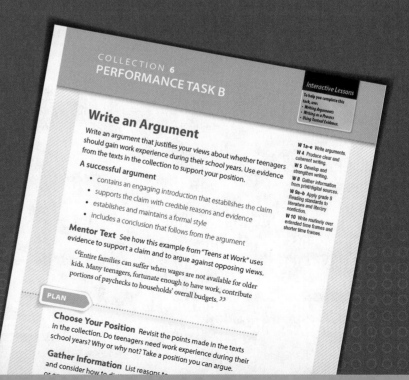

COLLECTION 6
PERFORMANCE TASK B

Interactive Lessons
To help you complete this task, use:
• *Writing Arguments*
• *Writing as a Process*
• *Using Textual Evidence.*

Write an Argument

Write an argument that justifies your views about whether teenagers should gain work experience during their school years. Use evidence from the texts in the collection to support your position.

A successful argument

- contains an engaging introduction that establishes the claim
- supports the claim with credible reasons and evidence
- establishes and maintains a formal style
- includes a conclusion that follows from the argument

W 1a–e Write arguments.
W 4 Produce clear and coherent writing.
W 5 Develop and strengthen writing.
W 8 Gather information from print/digital sources.
W 9a–b Apply grade 8 Reading standards to literature and literary nonfiction.
W 10 Write routinely over extended time frames and shorter time frames.

Mentor Text See how this example from "Teens at Work" uses evidence to support a claim and to argue against opposing views.

"Entire families can suffer when wages are not available for older kids. Many teenagers, fortunate enough to have work, contribute portions of paychecks to households' overall budgets."

PLAN

Choose Your Position Revisit the points made in the texts in the collection. Do teenagers need work experience during their school years? Why or why not? Take a position you can argue.

Gather Information List reasons to
and consider how to d

Collections provides 21st century resources supporting teachers and students in achieving their learning goals.

Performance Assessment

Guided instruction and practice performance tasks prepare students for reading and writing tasks in state and national assessments. Three detailed steps—Analyze the Model, Practice the Task, and Perform the Task—lead students to confidence and success.

HMH Close Reads App engages learners with appealing digital instruction in close reading, informing learning with instant feedback as students practice.

HMH Professional Development Website provides teachers with instructional videos by our authors and with podcasts, teaching resources, and more to enhance classroom success.

Assessment Drives Informed Instruction

- **Diagnostic tests with Lexile® scores**
- **Selection and collection tests**
- **ExamView® customization**
- **Selection and collection performance tasks**
- **Benchmark tests**
- **Summative evaluation**

Foundational Skills and Intervention

System 44 provides intensive intervention and support to help students master foundational reading skills through explicit instruction in phonics, comprehension, and writing.

READ 180 provides a personalized learning experience for students reading two or more years below grade level.

COLLECTION 1
Bold Actions

Collection Overviews

Each collection provides overviews of digital resources, key learning objectives, instructional topics for selections, and student support.

COLLECTION PERFORMANCE TASKS

Annotated Student Edition Table of Contents

Topical Organization

Each collection reflects an engaging topic that connects selections for discussion and analysis, so students can integrate and synthesize evidence as they explore several dimensions of the topic.

COLLECTION **1**

Bold Actions

Close Reader

Image credits: ©Kevin C. Downs/Photolibrary/Getty Images

KEY LEARNING OBJECTIVES
Make inferences.
Determine theme.
Analyze plot, conflict, and setting.
Analyze myths.
Analyze alliteration.
Analyze poetic form.
Cite evidence.
Determine central idea and details.
Analyze and compare news stories.
Determine author's purpose.

eBook *Explore It!*

▶ **Video Links**

Visit hmhfyi.com for current articles and informational texts.

Standards Coverage

Each collection addresses a range of standards, ensuring coverage of the Reading Literature and Reading Informational Texts standards.

Close Reader

The **Close Reader** provides selections related to the collection topic for additional practice and application of close reading skills and annotation strategies.

COLLECTION 2
Perception and Reality

COLLECTION PERFORMANCE TASKS

Student Edition + Close Reader

In each collection, the collection topic is explored in both the **Student Edition** and **Close Reader** selections. This page shows how the two components are integrated.

Annotated Student Edition Table of Contents

Anchor Texts

Complex and intellectually challenging, the anchor texts provide a cornerstone for exploring the collection topic and completing the Collection Performance Task. Close Reader selections relate to the Student Edition anchor texts.

Variety of Genres

Both the Student Edition and the Close Reader include a variety of genres of literary texts, informational texts, and media. The genre of each selection is clearly labeled.

COLLECTION **2**

Perception and Reality

COLLECTION PERFORMANCE TASKS

Close Reader

Image credits: ©Todd Davidson/Images.com/Corbis

 eBook *Explore It!*

 Video Links   **Visit hmhfyi.com** for current articles and informational texts.

KEY LEARNING OBJECTIVES

Summarize a story.
Identify elements of a folk tale.
Analyze influence of setting on characters.
Analyze use of figurative language.
Analyze use of sound devices.
Analyze poetic form.

Identify and analyze drama elements.
Compare script and performance.
Summarize informational text.
Analyze text features.
Analyze visual media.

Collection Performance Tasks

One or two Collection Performance Tasks present a cumulative task in which students draw on their reading and analysis of the collection's selections as well as on additional research.

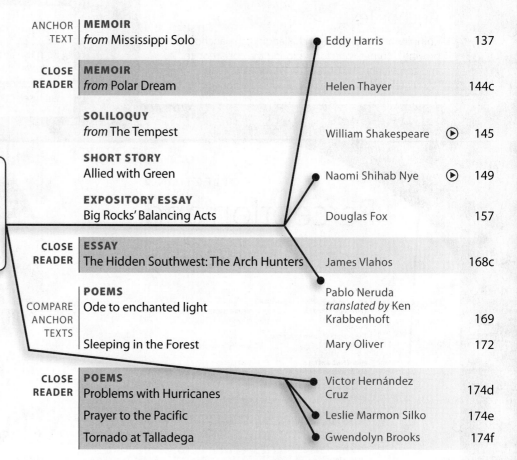

Cultural Diversity

To enrich students' perspectives, both the Student Edition and the Close Reader include selections by writers from diverse cultures.

COLLECTION PERFORMANCE TASKS

Annotated Student Edition Table of Contents

Classic and Contemporary Texts

Students read the works of world-renowned masters and current popular authors.

Text-Dependent Questions

Both the Student Edition and the Close Reader include a range of text-dependent questions that require students to engage with the text, make inferences, and cite text evidence to support their claims.

COLLECTION **3**

Nature at Work

Close Reader

eBook *Explore It!*

▶ Video Links   H HISTORY   A&E   ① Channel One News®   fyi hmhfyi.com   **Visit hmhfyi.com** for current articles and informational texts.

Image credits: ©Franz Pritz/Picture Press/Getty Images

KEY LEARNING OBJECTIVES	Identify elements of Shakespearean language.	Compare and contrast poetic forms.
	Analyze a soliloquy.	Identify features of a memoir.
	Determine theme.	Analyze author's style.
	Analyze figurative language.	Analyze structure in an expository essay.

eBook

The eBook, both Student Edition and Teacher's Edition, is your entryway to a full complement of digital resources that promote 21st century skills.

COLLECTION **4**
Risk and Exploration

Focus on Argument

Through a range of content-rich informational texts—including speeches, commentaries, and essays—students analyze claims and supporting evidence.

Image Credit: ©PhotoSpin/Alamy

Annotated Student Edition Table of Contents

Complex Texts

Complex texts from a variety of genres and content areas include rich themes, sophisticated concepts, and high knowledge demands that challenge students to make meaning as readers and thinkers.

COLLECTION 4

Risk and Exploration

Close Reader

ONLINE ESSAY
Is Space Exploration Worth the Cost?   Joan Vernikos

NEWSPAPER ARTICLE
Stinging Tentacles Offer Hint of Oceans' Decline   Elisabeth Rosenthal

KEY LEARNING OBJECTIVES
Analyze extended metaphor.
Analyze imagery.
Determine central ideas and details.
Analyze sound reasoning.

Analyze tone.
Analyze cause-and-effect relationships.
Trace and evaluate an argument.

Image credits: ©PhotoSpin, Inc/Alamy; (bg) ©Corbis

eBook *Explore It!*

▶ Video Links   Channel One News®

Visit hmhfyi.com
for current articles and
informational texts.

Digital Resources

From video links to additional selections and informational texts, a range of digital resources in the eBook enriches students' reading and supports technology skills..

The Stuff of Consumer Culture

Informational Texts

A variety of challenging informational texts offer opportunities for close reading, analysis, and meaning making.

COLLECTION PERFORMANCE TASK

Compare Texts

To enrich the analysis and discussion of each text, students compare and contrast selections, evaluating elements such as authors' choices, themes, and the structure of arguments.

COLLECTION 5

The Stuff of Consumer Culture

Close Reader

Image credits: ©Michael Blann/Getty Images and Guy Jarvis/Houghton Mifflin Harcourt

KEY LEARNING OBJECTIVES
Determine theme.
Analyze elements of science fiction.
Compare and contrast poetic forms.
Make inferences.

Draw conclusions about graphic aids.
Analyze author style.
Analyze cause-and-effect organization.

eBook *Explore It!*

   ▶ **Video Links**

Visit hmhfyi.com
for current articles and informational texts.

  ## HISTORY® and A&E®

Adding the images and voices that make selections and historical periods come alive, these video assets are available at point of use in the eBook.

COLLECTION 6
Guided by a Cause

Contemporary Selections

21st-century selections offer current perspectives on how to improve society.

Grade 7

Annotated Student Edition Table of Contents

Media Analysis

Lessons based on media provide opportunities for students to apply analysis and techniques of close reading to other kinds of texts.

COLLECTION **6**

Guided by a Cause

Close Reader

eBook *Explore It!*

▶ Video Links   Visit **hmhfyi.com** for current articles and informational texts.

Image credits: ©Mohd Shahrizan Hussin/Shutterstock

Collection Performance Tasks

Collection Performance Tasks require students to develop a variety of writing and speaking products, working through the process of planning, producing, revising, and presenting for each task.

fyi

The fyi website at hmhfyi.com provides additional contemporary informational texts to enhance each collection. Updated regularly, this site expands background knowledge, discussion, and research.

Student Resources

Word Knowledge

The Glossaries provide definitions for selection, academic, and domain-specific vocabulary, conveniently compiled in a single location.

Connecting to Your World

Every time you read something, view something, write to someone, or react to what you've read or seen, you're participating in a world of ideas. You do this every day, inside the classroom and out. These skills will serve you not only at home and at school but eventually in your career.

The digital tools in this program will tap into the skills you already use and help you sharpen those skills for the future.

Start your exploration at my.hrw.com

Start with the Dashboard
Get one-stop access to the complete digital program for *Collections* and to management and assessment tools.

Close Read

fyi
hmhfyi.com
Research Explore

eBook Read Annotate

WriteSmart
Produce Collaborate

Text in **FOCUS**

myNotebook
Cite Organize

1 Channel One News®
HISTORY A&E
View Extend

Stream to Start

Interactive Lessons
Write Communicate

Writing and Speaking & Listening

Communication in today's world requires quite a variety of skills. To express yourself and win people over, you have to be able to write for print, for online media, and for spoken presentations. To collaborate, you have to work with people who might be sitting right next to you or at the other end of an Internet connection.

Comprehensive Standards Coverage

Twelve interactive lessons provide thorough coverage of all Writing standards and Speaking and Listening standards.

Available Only in Your eBook

Interactive Lessons

These interactive lessons will help you master the skills needed to become an expert communicator.

Choosing Relevant Evidence

Choose the pieces of evidence that support the reason shown and drag them into the box.

Tip

Reality stars are often placed in situations that cause them to grow or change in a positive way.

One contestant who participated in a fashion reality show remarked, "The show made me a better designer." ✓

The winner of one cooking show won a million dollars.

According to Nielsen ratings for this season, 17 of the top 50 most popular TV shows for viewers between the ages of 18-49 were reality shows.

68% of former contestants on a popular weight-loss show have maintained their goal weight for five years post-show.

You've got it! This quotation shows how one contestant experienced personal growth.

Writing Arguments

Learn how to build a strong argument.

W 1, W 10

Interactive Lessons

1. Introduction
2. What Is a Claim?
3. Support: Reasons and Evidence
4. Building Effective Support
5. Creating a Coherent Argument
6. Persuasive Techniques
7. Formal Style
8. Concluding Your Argument

Student-Directed Lessons

Though primarily intended for individual student use, these interactive lessons also offer opportunities for whole-class and small-group instruction and practice.

Writing Informative Texts

Shed light on complex ideas and topics.

W 2, W 10

Interactive Lessons

1. Introduction
2. Developing a Topic
3. Organizing Ideas
4. Introductions and Conclusions
5. Elaboration
6. Using Graphics and Multimedia
7. Precise Language and Vocabulary
8. Formal Style

Writing Narratives

A good storyteller can always capture an audience.

W 3, W 10

Interactive Lessons

1. Introduction
2. Narrative Context
3. Point of View and Characters
4. Narrative Structure
5. Narrative Techniques
6. The Language of Narrative

Writing as a Process

W 4, W 5, W 10

Get from the first twinkle of an idea to a sparkling final draft.

Interactive Lessons

1. Introduction
2. Task, Purpose, and Audience
3. Planning and Drafting
4. Revising and Editing
5. Trying a New Approach

Teacher Support

Each lesson in your teacher eBook includes

- support for English language learners and less-proficient writers
- instructional and management tips for every screen
- a rubric
- additional writing applications

Producing and Publishing with Technology

W 6

Learn how to write for an online audience.

SUBMIT

Interactive Lessons

1. Introduction
2. Writing for the Internet
3. Interacting with Your Online Audience
4. Using Technology to Collaborate

Conducting Research

W 6, W 7, W 8

There's a world of information out there. How do you find it?

Interactive Lessons

1. Introduction
2. Starting Your Research
3. Types of Sources
4. Using the Library for Research
5. Conducting Field Research
6. Using the Internet for Research
7. Taking Notes
8. Refocusing Your Inquiry

Evaluating Sources
Don't believe everything you read!

W 8

Interactive Lessons

1. Introduction
2. Evaluating Sources for Usefulness
3. Evaluating Sources for Reliability

Authentic Practice of 21st Century Skills

Students have ample opportunities to evaluate real websites, engage in digital collaboration, conduct Web research, and critique student discussions.

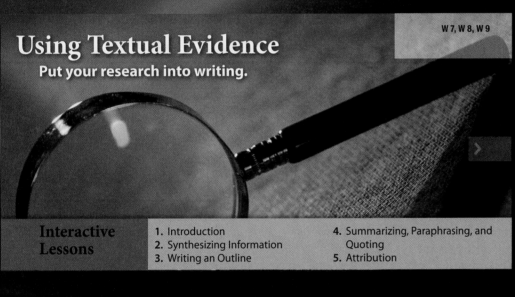

Using Textual Evidence
Put your research into writing.

W 7, W 8, W 9

Interactive Lessons

1. Introduction
2. Synthesizing Information
3. Writing an Outline
4. Summarizing, Paraphrasing, and Quoting
5. Attribution

Participating in Collaborative Discussions

SL 1

There's power in putting your heads together.

Interactive Lessons

1. Introduction
2. Preparing for Discussion
3. Establishing and Following Procedure
4. Speaking Constructively
5. Listening and Responding
6. Wrapping Up Your Discussion

SL 2, SL 3, SL 6

Analyzing and Evaluating Presentations

**Media-makers all want your attention.
What are they trying to tell you?**

Interactive Lessons	1. Introduction	4. Tracing a Speaker's Argument
	2. Analyzing a Presentation	5. Rhetoric and Delivery
	3. Evaluating a Speaker's Reliability	6. Synthesizing Media Sources

---

SL 4, SL 6

Giving a Presentation

**Learn how to talk to a
roomful of people.**

Interactive Lessons	1. Introduction	3. The Content of Your Presentation
	2. Knowing Your Audience	4. Style in Presentation
		5. Delivering Your Presentation

SL 5

Using Media in a Presentation

**If a picture is worth a thousand words,
just think what you can do with a video.**

| **Interactive Lessons** | 1. Introduction | 3. Using Presentation Software |
| | 2. Types of Media: Audio, Video, and Images | 4. Practicing Your Presentation |

Assessments in *my*WriteSmart

Test students' mastery of the standards covered in each interactive lesson by assigning the accompanying assessment in *my*WriteSmart.

DIGITAL SPOTLIGHT

| eBook | myNotebook | fyi hmhfyi.com | my WriteSmart |

Supporting 21st Century Skills

The amount of information people encounter each day keeps increasing. Whether you're working alone or collaborating with others, it takes effort to analyze the complex texts and competing ideas that bombard us in this fast-paced world. What can allow you to succeed? Staying engaged and organized. The digital tools in this program will help you to think critically and take charge of your learning.

Integrated Digital Suite

The digital resources and tools in *Collections* are designed to support students in grappling with complex text and formulating interpretations from text evidence.

Stream to Start

Ignite your Investigation

You learn best when you're engaged. The **Stream to Start** video at the beginning of each collection is designed to inspire interest in the topics being explored. Watch it and then let your curiosity lead your investigations.

Videos to Motivate and Engage

Spark student curiosity and conversation by viewing short, engaging videos at the start of each collection.

Learn How to Do a Close Read

Close Read

An effective close read is all about the details; you have to examine the language and ideas a writer includes. See how it's done by accessing the **Close Read Screencasts** in your eBook. Hear modeled conversations about anchor texts.

Close Read Screencasts

For each anchor text, students can access modeled conversations in which readers analyze and annotate key passages.

long after we got here, Papa got a job driving a cab, and Mama worked cleaning people's houses. It was hard for them not to have the respect they were used to from holding government teaching jobs, but they had high regard for the food they could now easily buy at the store.

Six months after we got here, the Boeing Company moved to Chicago and Mr. Bob Campbell got transferred there. When Aunt Madina left with him, it broke Mama's heart. Aunt Madina was the only person we knew from Kazakhstan, and it felt like our family just huddled together on a tiny island in the middle of a great American sea.

I looked at the permission slip, wishing there were some special words I could say to get Mama and Papa to sign it. Around me, everyone in my homeroom was talking excitely about the Spring Fling. Mama says she thinks the school is

Text in Focus Videos

These engaging videos will help students better comprehend the anchor texts. Each video targets a particular passage or element of the text and then provides students with concrete tips for fixing their comprehension.

Increase Your Understanding

Text in FOCUS

TEXT IN FOCUS helps you dig deeper into complex texts by offering visual explanations of potential stumbling blocks. Look for **TEXT IN FOCUS** videos in anchor texts.

"sank our roots"

Annotate the Texts

Practice close reading by utilizing the powerful annotation tools in your eBook. Mark up key ideas and observations using highlighters and sticky notes. Tag unfamiliar words to create a personal word list in *my*Notebook.

Digital Tools for Close Reading

Annotation tools allow students to note central ideas and details as they gather evidence from the text.

Find More Text Evidence on the Web

Tap into the *fyi* website for links to high-interest informational texts about collection topics. Synthesize information and connect notes and text evidence from any Web source by including it in *my*Notebook

High-Interest Informational Text

Updated monthly, *FYI* features links to reputable sources of informational text.

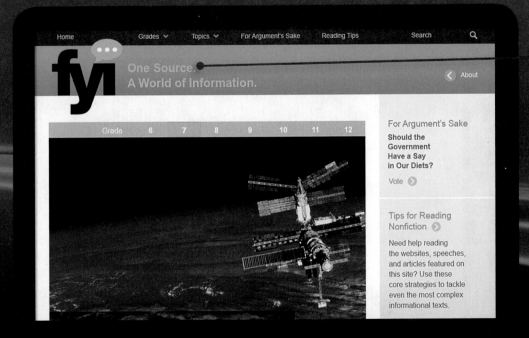

myNotebook

Save and Organize Your Notes

Save your annotations to *my*Notebook, where you can organize them to use as text evidence in performance tasks and other writing assignments. You can also organize the unfamiliar words you tagged by creating word lists, which will help you grow your vocabulary.

Digital Notebook

Students can save their annotations to *my*Notebook, tag them to particular performance tasks, and create word lists for vocabulary development.

Create, Communicate, and Collaborate

Use the technology provided by the **myWriteSmart** tool to keep track of your writing assignments, create drafts, and collaborate and communicate with peers and your teacher. Use the evidence you've gathered in *my*Notebook to support your ideas.

Tools for Writing

Assign and manage performance tasks in *my*WriteSmart. Students can use the annotations they've gathered and tools for writing and collaboration to complete each task.

Digital Spotlight **xxix**

Correlation of *Collections*, Grade 7, to the English Language Arts Common Core Standards

The grade 7 standards on the following pages define what students should understand and be able to do by the end of the grade. They correspond to the College and Career Readiness (CCR) anchor standards below by number. The CCR and grade-specific standards are necessary complements—the former providing broad standards, the latter providing additional specificity—that together define the skills and understandings that all students must demonstrate. In the following pages, Teacher's Edition page references are boldfaced.

College and Career Readiness Anchor Standards for Reading

Common Core State Standards
KEY IDEAS AND DETAILS
1. Read closely to determine what the text says explicitly and to make logical inferences from it; cite specific textual evidence when writing or speaking to support conclusions drawn from the text.
2. Determine central ideas or themes of a text and analyze their development; summarize the key supporting details and ideas.
3. Analyze how and why individuals, events, and ideas develop and interact over the course of a text.
CRAFT AND STRUCTURE
4. Interpret words and phrases as they are used in a text, including determining technical, connotative, and figurative meanings, and analyze how specific word choices shape meaning or tone.
5. Analyze the structure of texts, including how specific sentences, paragraphs, and larger portions of the text (e.g., a section, chapter, scene, or stanza) relate to each other and the whole.
6. Assess how point of view or purpose shapes the content and style of a text.
INTEGRATION OF KNOWLEDGE AND IDEAS
7. Integrate and evaluate content presented in diverse media and formats, including visually and quantitatively, as well as in words.
8. Delineate and evaluate the argument and specific claims in a text, including the validity of the reasoning as well as the relevance and sufficiency of the evidence.
9. Analyze how two or more texts address similar themes or topics in order to build knowledge or to compare the approaches the authors take.
RANGE OF READING AND LEVEL OF COMPLEXITY
10. Read and comprehend complex literary and informational texts independently and proficiently.

Reading Standards for Literature

Standard	Where Taught

KEY IDEAS AND DETAILS

RL 1
Cite several pieces of textual evidence to support analysis of what the text says explicitly as well as inferences drawn from the text.

INSTRUCTION
Student Edition/**Teacher's Edition:**
3, **4**, **5**, **6**, **7**, **8**, **9**, **10**, **11**, **12**, **13**, **14**, 15, **15**, 16, **16**, **18a**, **31**, **32**, **33**, **34**, 36, **36**, **40**, **42**, **63**, **65**, **67**, **69**, **72**, 73, **73**, **74**, **95**, **96**, **97**, **98**, **99**, **100**, **103**, 108, **108**, **112**, **113**, **114**, **115**, **116**, **118**, **119**, **121**, **124**, 126, **126**, **146**, **149**, **150**, **151**, 154, **154**, **170**, 171, **171**, **172**, 173, **173**, 174, **174**, **213**, 214, **214**, **214a**, 242, 243, 244, **244**, 245, 246, **246**, 249, 250, 252, 253, 254, 256, **256**, 284, 285, 287, 288, 289, 291, 292, 294, 296, 297, 299, 300, 302, 322, 323, 324, 325, **325**, **327**, **328**, **330**, **331**, **332**, 334, **334**

APPLICATION
Student Edition/**Teacher's Edition:**
3–14, 3–14, 31–34, **31–34**, 63–67, 71–72, 74, 93–96, 145–146, 149–152, 169–170, 172, 213, **214a**, 241–245, 249–254, 321–323, 327–332

Close Reader/**Teacher's Edition:**
3–12, **18b–18i**, 17–22, **38b–38g**, 25–30, **70b–70g**, 35–42, **126b–126g**, 55–60, **174b–174g**, 87–92, **258b–258g**, 103–106, **306b–306e**

ASSESSMENT
Student Edition/**Teacher's Edition:**
16, **16**, 36, **36**, 69, **69**, 73, **73**, 108, **108**, 126, **126**, 127–130, **127–130**, 131–134, **127–134**, 154, **154**, 171, **171**, 173, **173**, 214, **214**, 244, **244**, 246, **246**, 248, **248**, 256, **256**, 325, **325**, 334, **334**

RL 2
Determine a theme or central idea of a text and analyze its development over the course of the text; provide an objective summary of the text.

INSTRUCTION
Student Edition/**Teacher's Edition:**
31, **31**, **32**, **33**, **34**, 35, **35**, 36, **36**, **38a**, 42, **42**, **63**, **64**, **66**, **67**, 68, **68**, 69, **69**, 75, **75**, 76, **76**, 108, **108**, 126, **126**, 148, **148**, **149**, **151**, **152**, 153, **153**, **156a**, **172**, 173, **173**, **174a**, 214, **214**, 244, **244**, 246, **246**, 247, **247**, **248a**, 250, 251, 252, 253, 254, 255, **255**, **321**, **322**, **323**, 324, **324**, **325**, **331**, **332**, 333, **333**, **336a**, **337a**

APPLICATION
Student Edition/**Teacher's Edition:**
31–34, **31–34**, **38a**, 63–68, 63–**68**, 71–72, 74, 93–106, 145–146, 149–152, **156a**, 169–170, 172, 213, 241–243, 245, 249–254, 321–323, 327–332, **336a**, **337a**

Close Reader/**Teacher's Edition:**
17–22, **38b–38g**, 25–30, **70b–70g**, 87–92, **258b–258g**

ASSESSMENT
Student Edition/**Teacher's Edition:**
36, **36**, 42, **42**, 75, **75**, 76, **76**, 108, **108**, 126, **126**, 148, **148**, 154, **154**, 171, **171**, 174, **174**, 214, **214**, 244, **244**, 246, **246**, 248, **248**, 256, **256**, 304, **304**, 325, **325**, 334, **334**

Standard	Where Taught
RL 3 Analyze how particular elements of a story or drama interact (e.g., how settings shape the characters or plot).	**INSTRUCTION** Student Edition/**Teacher's Edition:** **3, 4, 6, 7, 9,10, 12, 13, 14,** 15, **15,** 16, **16, 18a,** 31, **31, 33,** 35, **35, 38a, 63, 64, 67,** 68, **68, 70a, 93, 94, 96, 97, 99, 100, 101, 103, 105, 106,** 107, **107, 110a, 113, 114, 115, 116, 117, 118, 119, 120, 121, 122, 123, 124,** 125, **125, 146, 156a, 249, 250, 252, 253, 254,** 255, **255, 258a, 284, 286, 292, 296, 297, 298, 300, 302,** 303, **303, 328, 329, 330, 331, 332,** 333, **333, 336a, 336b** **APPLICATION** Student Edition/**Teacher's Edition:** 3–14, **18a,** 31–34, **38a,** 63–67, **70a,** 93–106, 111–124, **156a,** 249–254, 283–302, 327–332, **336a, 336b** Close Reader/**Teacher's Edition:** 3–12, **18b–18i,** 17–22, **38b–38g,** 25–30, **70b–70g,** 35–42, **126b–126g,** 87–92, **258b–258g,** 103–106, **306b–306e** **ASSESSMENT** Student Edition/**Teacher's Edition:** 16, **16,** 36, **36,** 69, **69,** 108, **108,** 126, **126,** 154, **154,** 256, **256,** 304, **304,** 334, **334**
CRAFT AND STRUCTURE	
RL 4 Determine the meaning of words and phrases as they are used in a text, including figurative and connotative meanings; analyze the impact of rhymes and other repetitions of sounds (e.g., alliteration) on a specific verse or stanza of a poem or section of a story or drama.	**INSTRUCTION** Student Edition/**Teacher's Edition:** **6,** 36, **36, 40,** 41, **41, 42a, 45, 65, 72,** 73, **73, 74,** 75, **75,** 76, **76, 76a, 95, 97, 98, 103,** 107, **107, 117, 119,** 147, **147, 148, 148a, 150, 151, 152,** 153, **153, 170,** 171, **171, 172,** 173, **173,** 174, **174, 213,** 214, **214, 214a, 242, 243,** 244, **244,** 246, **246,** 247, **247, 249, 289, 299, 321, 322, 323,** 324, **324, 326a, 327, 332** **APPLICATION** Student Edition/**Teacher's Edition:** 39–40, **42a,** 71–72, 74, **76a,** 145–146, **148a,** 149–152, 169–170, 172, 213, **214a, 214b,** 241–243, 245, 321–323, **326a** Close Reader/**Teacher's Edition:** 55–60, **174b–174g,** 87–92, **258b–258g** **ASSESSMENT** Student Edition/**Teacher's Edition:** 36, **36,** 42, **42,** 69, **69,** 73, **73,** 75, **75,** 76, **76,** 108, **108,** 148, **148,** 154, **154,** 171, **171,** 173, **173,** 174, **174,** 214, **214,** 244, **244,** 246, **246,** 248, **248,** 256, **256,** 325, **325**

Standard	Where Taught
RL 5 Analyze how a drama's or poem's form or structure (e.g., soliloquy, sonnet) contributes to its meaning.	**INSTRUCTION** Student Edition/**Teacher's Edition:** 40, **40**, 41, **41**, **42a**, **72**, 73, **73**, **74**, 75, **75**, 76, **76**, 111, **112**, 113, **114**, 115, **116**, 117, **118**, **119**, **121**, **122**, **124**, 125, **125**, **126a**, **146**, 147, **147**, **148a**, **170**, 171, **171**, **172**, 173, **173**, 174, **174**, 175, **175**, **214b**, 242, 243, 244, **244**, **245**, 246, **246**, 247, **247**, **321**, **323**, 324, **324**, **326a** **APPLICATION** Student Edition/**Teacher's Edition:** 39–40, **42a**, 71–72, 74, 111–124, **126a**, 145–146, **148a**, 169–170, 172, **214b**, 241–243, 245, 321–323, **326a** Close Reader/**Teacher's Edition:** 55–60, **174b–174g** **ASSESSMENT** Student Edition/**Teacher's Edition:** 42, **42**, 73, **73**, 75, **75**, 76, **76**, 108, **108**, 126, **126**, 148, **148**, 171, **171**, 173, **173**, 174, **174**, 244, **244**, 246, **246**, 248, **248**, 325, **325**
RL 6 Analyze how an author develops and contrasts the points of view of different characters or narrators in a text.	**INSTRUCTION** Student Edition/**Teacher's Edition:** 154, **154**, **156a**, **172**, **174**, **174a**, **283**, **287**, **290**, **291**, **292**, **295**, **298**, 303, **303**, **306a** **APPLICATION** Student Edition/**Teacher's Edition:** **156a**, **174a**, 283–302, **306a** **ASSESSMENT** Student Edition/**Teacher's Edition:** 304, **304**, 334, **334**

Standard	Where Taught

INTEGRATION OF KNOWLEDGE AND IDEAS

RL 7
Compare and contrast a written story, drama, or poem to its audio, filmed, staged, or multimedia version, analyzing the effects of techniques unique to each medium (e.g., lighting, sound, color, or camera focus and angles in a film).

INSTRUCTION
Student Edition/**Teacher's Edition:**
126, **126, 126a**

APPLICATION
Student Edition/**Teacher's Edition:**
111–124, **126a**

Close Reader/**Teacher's Edition:**
35–42, **126b–126g**

ASSESSMENT
Student Edition/**Teacher's Edition:**
126, **126**

RL 8
(Not applicable to literature)

N/A

RL 9
Compare and contrast a fictional portrayal of a time, place, or character and a historical account of the same period as a means of understanding how authors of fiction use or alter history.

INSTRUCTION
Student Edition/**Teacher's Edition:**
284, 285, 288, 289, 290, 294, 296, 297, 300, 301, 303, **303, 306a**

APPLICATION
Student Edition/**Teacher's Edition:**
265–273, 275–277, 283–302, **306a**

Close Reader/**Teacher's Edition:**
103–106, **306b–306e**

ASSESSMENT
Student Edition/**Teacher's Edition:**
304, **304**

RANGE OF READING AND LEVEL OF TEXT COMPLEXITY

RL 10
By the end of the year, read and comprehend literature, including stories, dramas, and poems, in the grades 6–8 text complexity band proficiently, with scaffolding as needed at the high end of the range.

APPLICATION
Student Edition/**Teacher's Edition:**
3A, 3–16, **3–16, 63A, 69, 93A,** 93–108, **93–108, 111A,** 111–126, **111–126, 169A,** 169–174, **169–174, 241A,** 241–248, **241–248, 249A,** 249–256 **249–256**

Close Reader/**Teacher's Edition:**
17–22, **38b–38g,** 35–42, **126b–126g**

Reading Standards for Informational Text

Standard	Where Taught

KEY IDEAS AND DETAILS

RI 1
Cite several pieces of textual evidence to support analysis of what the text says explicitly as well as inferences drawn from the text.

INSTRUCTION
Student Edition/**Teacher's Edition:**
20, 21, 22, 24, **24, 26,** 43, **43, 44, 45, 46, 47, 48,** 49, **49, 77, 78, 81, 137, 138, 139,** 142, **142, 157, 159, 161, 162, 163,** 166, **166, 185, 186, 187, 188, 189, 194, 195, 196, 203, 204, 205, 207, 208, 221, 222, 223, 224, 225, 226, 227, 228,** 229, **229, 232a, 233, 234, 236, 237, 237, 240a, 266, 267, 268, 269, 270, 271, 272, 273,** 274, **274, 275, 276, 307, 308, 309, 310, 311, 312,** 313, **313, 316a, R16, R23**

APPLICATION
Student Edition/**Teacher's Edition:**
43–48, 157–164, 221–228, **232a,** 233–236, **240a,** 265–273, 275–277, 307–312, **316a**

Close Reader/**Teacher's Edition:**
13–16, **30b–30e,** 31–34, **88b–88e,** 45–50, **144b–144g,** 51–54, **168b–168e,** 63–66, **192b–192e,** 67–74, **212b–212g,** 77–82, **232b–232g,** 83–86, **240b–240e,** 95–102, **282b–282g,** 107–112, **320b–320g**

ASSESSMENT
Student Edition/**Teacher's Edition:**
26, **26,** 50, **50,** 142, **142,** 190, **190,** 198, **198,** 210, **210,** 230, **230,** 238, **238,** 274, **274,** 278, **278,** 280, **280,** 314, **314**

RI 2
Determine two or more central ideas in a text and analyze their development over the course of the text; provide an objective summary of the text.

INSTRUCTION
Student Edition/**Teacher's Edition:**
20, 21, 23, **23, 24, 25, 26,** 27, **27,** 29, **29,** 30, **30, 52a, 79, 80, 82, 83, 84,** 85, **85, 163,** 165, **165,** 198, **198, 202, 205, 206,** 209, **209, 222, 223, 226, 227,** 229, **229, 232a, 235,** 238, **238, 240a, 266, 267, 268, 269, 270, 271, 272, 273,** 274, **274, 282a, 307, 308, 309, 310, 311, 312,** 313, **313, 316a,** R16–R22, **R16, R18, R19, R21, R22, R23,** R23–R29

APPLICATION
Student Edition/**Teacher's Edition:**
19–22, 24–26, 28, 77–84, 167–164, 201–208, 221–228, **232a, 240a, 282a,** 265–273, 275–277, 307–312, **316a**

Close Reader/**Teacher's Edition:**
13–16, **30b–30e,** 31–34, **88b–88e,** 51–54, **168b–168e,** 63–66, **192b–192e,** 67–74, **212b–212g,** 77–82, **232b–232g,** 83–86, **240b–240e,** 95–102, **282b–282g,** 107–112, **320b–320g**

ASSESSMENT
Student Edition/**Teacher's Edition:**
23, **23,** 27, **27,** 29, **29,** 30, **30, 52a,** 86, **86,** 142, **142,** 148, **148,** 166, **166,** 198, **198,** 210, **210,** 230, **230,** 238, **238,** 274, **274,** 278, **278,** 280, **280,** 314, **314**

Standard	Where Taught
RI 3 Analyze the interactions between individuals, events, and ideas in a text (e.g., how ideas influence individuals or events, or how individuals influence ideas or events).	**INSTRUCTION** Student Edition/**Teacher's Edition:** 30, **30**, **137**, **138**, **140**, 141, **141**, **144a**, 157, **159**, **160**, **161**, **162**, **163**, **164**, 165, **165**, **168a**, **202**, **203**, **204**, **205**, **206**, **208**, 209, **209**, **212a**, **223**, **224**, **225**, **226**, **227**, **228**, **232a**, 279, **279**, **308**, **311**, 313, **313**, **316a**, R16–R22, **R16**, **R18**, **R19**, **R21**, **R22**, **R23** **APPLICATION** Student Edition/**Teacher's Edition:** 28, 137–140, **144a**, 157–164, **168a**, 201–208, **212a**, **231a**, 265–273, **316a**, **R22** Close Reader/**Teacher's Edition:** 45–50, **144b–144g**, 51–54, **168b–168e**, 67–74, **212b–212g**, 77–82, **232b–232g**, 95–102, **282b–282g**, 107–112, **320b–320g** **ASSESSMENT** Student Edition/**Teacher's Edition:** 30, **30**, 50, **50**, 142, **142**, 166, **166**, 210, **210**, 280, **280**, 314, **314**

CRAFT AND STRUCTURE

Standard	Where Taught
RI 4 Determine the meaning of words and phrases as they are used in a text, including figurative, connotative, and technical meanings; analyze the impact of a specific word choice on meaning and tone.	**INSTRUCTION** Student Edition/**Teacher's Edition:** **45**, **77**, **78**, **81**, **83**, 85, **85**, **137**, **138**, **139**, 141, **141**, **144a**, 157, **162**, **193**, **196**, 197, **197**, **200a**, 206, **225**, **231**, **232a**, **233**, **235**, **236**, 237, **237**, **240a**, 312, **R16**, **R23**, R23–R29 **APPLICATION** Student Edition/**Teacher's Edition:** 77–84, 137–140, **144a**, 193–196, **200a**, **232a**, 233–236, **240a** Close Reader/**Teacher's Edition:** 31–34, **88b–88e**, 45–50, **144b–144g**, 67–74, **212b–212g**, 83–86, **240b–240e**, 95–102, **282b–282g**, 107–112, **320b–320g** **ASSESSMENT** Student Edition/**Teacher's Edition:** 86, **86**, 142, **142**, 166, **166**, 190, **190**, 198, **198**, 238, **238**

Standard	Where Taught

RI 5
Analyze the structure an author uses to organize a text, including how the major sections contribute to the whole and to the development of the ideas.

INSTRUCTION
Student Edition/**Teacher's Edition:**
20, 21, 22, 23, **23, 24, 25, 26,** 27, **27,** 29, **29,** 30, **30, 77, 78, 81, 83,** 85, **85, 88a, 157, 158, 159, 160, 161, 162, 163, 164,** 165, **165, 168a, 186, 187, 188,** 189, **189, 192a, 193,** 197, **197, 201, 203, 204, 207, 208,** 209, **209, 212a, 221, 223, 224, 225, 226,** 229, **229, 240a, 271, 275, 276, 277,** 278, **278, 282a, 307, 308, 310, 311,** 313, **313, 316a,** R16–R22, **R16–R22, R16, R18, R19, R21, R22, R23, R26,** R23–R29

APPLICATION
Student Edition/**Teacher's Edition:**
20–22, 24–26, 77–84, **88a,** 157–164, **168a, 192a,** 193–196, **212a,** 221–228, **240a,** 265–273, **282a, 316a**

Close Reader/**Teacher's Edition:**
13–16, **30b–30e,** 31–34, **88b–88e,** 51–54, **168b–168e,** 67–74, **212b–212g,** 77–82, **232b–232g,** 95–102, **282b–282g,** 107–112, **320b–320g**

ASSESSMENT
Student Edition/**Teacher's Edition:**
23, **23,** 27, **27,** 29, **29,** 30, **30,** 86, **86,** 166, **166,** 190, **190,** 198, **198,** 210, **210,** 230, **230,** 238, **238,** 278, **278,** 314, **314**

RI 6
Determine an author's point of view or purpose in a text and analyze how the author distinguishes his or her position from that of others.

INSTRUCTION
Student Edition/**Teacher's Edition:**
30, **30, 30a, 43, 44, 47, 48,** 49, **49, 52a, 185, 186, 267, 268, 269, 271, 273,** 274, **274, 275, 276,** 279, **279, 282a, 308, 309, 312,** 313, **313,** R23–R29, **R23**

APPLICATION
Student Edition/**Teacher's Edition:**
19–22, 24–26, 28, **30a,** 43–48, **52a, 282a,** 265–273, 275–277, 307–312

Close Reader/**Teacher's Edition:**
45–50, **144b–144g,** 95–102, **282b–282g**

ASSESSMENT
Student Edition/**Teacher's Edition:**
30, **30,** 50, **50,** 166, **166,** 210, **210,** 274, **274,** 280, **280,** 314, **314,** 320, **320**

Standard	Where Taught

INTEGRATION OF KNOWLEDGE AND IDEAS

RI 7
Compare and contrast a text to an audio, video, or multimedia version of the text, analyzing each medium's portrayal of the subject (e.g., how the delivery of a speech affects the impact of the words).

INSTRUCTION
Student Edition/**Teacher's Edition:**
192a

APPLICATION
Student Edition/**Teacher's Edition:**
185–188, **192a**, 317–318

ASSESSMENT
Student Edition/**Teacher's Edition:**
190, **190**, 320, **320**

RI 8
Trace and evaluate the argument and specific claims in a text, assessing whether the reasoning is sound and the evidence is relevant and sufficient to support the claims.

INSTRUCTION
Student Edition/**Teacher's Edition:**
24, 25, 26, 27, **27,** 30, **30, 186, 187, 188,** 189, **189, 192a, 193, 194, 195, 196,** 197, **197, 316a,** R23–R29, **R23, R24, R26, R28, R29**

APPLICATION
Student Edition/**Teacher's Edition:**
24–26, 185–188, **192a,** 193–196, **316a**

Close Reader/**Teacher's Edition:**
13–16, **30b–30e,** 63–66, **192b–192e**

ASSESSMENT
Student Edition/**Teacher's Edition:**
27, **27,** 30, **30,** 190, **190,** 198, **198,** 238, **238,** 314

RI 9
Analyze how two or more authors writing about the same topic shape their presentations of key information by emphasizing the different evidence or advancing different interpretations of facts.

INSTRUCTION
Student Edition/**Teacher's Edition:**
30, **30, 30a,** 279, **279, 280, 282a,** 303, **303, 306a**

APPLICATION
Student Edition/**Teacher's Edition:**
19–22, 24–26, 28, 265–273, 275–277, 283–302, **282a, 306a**

Close Reader/**Teacher's Edition:**
95–102, **282b–282g**

ASSESSMENT
Student Edition/**Teacher's Edition:**
30, **30,** 280, **280,** 303, **303**

Standard	Where Taught

RANGE OF READING AND LEVEL OF TEXT COMPLEXITY

RI 10
By the end of the year, read and comprehend literary nonfiction in the grades 6–8 text complexity band proficiently, with scaffolding as needed at the high end of the range.

APPLICATION
Student Edition/**Teacher's Edition:**
43A, 43–50, **43–50, 157A**, 157–166, **157–166, 265A**, 275–280, **275–280, 307A**, 307–314 **307–314, R16, R23**

Close Reader/**Teacher's Edition:**
13–16, **30b–30e**, 45–50, **144b–144g**, 63–66, **192b–192e**, 67–74, **212b–212g**, 83–86, **240b–240e**, 107–112, **320b–320g**

College and Career Readiness Anchor Standards for Writing

Common Core State Standards

TEXT TYPES AND PURPOSES

1. Write arguments to support claims in an analysis of substantive topics or texts, using valid reasoning and relevant and sufficient evidence.

2. Write informative/explanatory texts to examine and convey complex ideas and information clearly and accurately through the effective selection, organization, and analysis of content.

3. Write narratives to develop real or imagined experiences or events using effective technique, well-chosen details, and well-structured event sequences.

PRODUCTION AND DISTRIBUTION OF WRITING

4. Produce clear and coherent writing in which the development, organization, and style are appropriate to task, purpose, and audience.

5. Develop and strengthen writing as needed by planning, revising, editing, rewriting, or trying a new approach.

6. Use technology, including the Internet, to produce and publish writing and to interact and collaborate with others.

RESEARCH TO BUILD AND PRESENT KNOWLEDGE

7. Conduct short as well as more sustained research projects based on focused questions, demonstrating understanding of the subject under investigation.

8. Gather relevant information from multiple print and digital sources, assess the credibility and accuracy of each source, and integrate the information while avoiding plagiarism.

9. Draw evidence from literary and/or informational texts to support analysis, reflection, and research.

RANGE OF WRITING

10. Write routinely over extended time frames (time for research, reflection, and revision) and shorter time frames (a single sitting or a day or two) for a range of tasks, purposes, and audiences.

Writing Standards

Standard	Where Taught
TEXT TYPES AND PURPOSES	

Standard	Where Taught
W 1 Write arguments to support claims with clear reasons and relevant evidence.	**INSTRUCTION/APPLICATION** **Interactive Lessons:** Writing Arguments • Introduction • What Is a Claim? • Support: Reasons and Evidence • Building Effective Support • Creating a Coherent Argument • Persuasive Techniques • Formal Style • Concluding Your Argument Student Edition/**Teacher's Edition:** 57–60, **57–60**, 127–130, **127–130**, 215–218, **215–218**, R2–R3, R2, **R2** **ASSESSMENT** Student Edition/**Teacher's Edition:** 30, **30**, 57–60, **57–60**, 127–130, **127–130**, 154, **154**, 210, **210**, 215–218, 280, **280**, 314, **314**, 334, **334**
a. Introduce claim(s), acknowledge alternate or opposing claims, and organize the reasons and evidence logically.	**INSTRUCTION/APPLICATION** **Interactive Lessons:** Writing Arguments • What Is a Claim? • Creating a Coherent Argument Student Edition/**Teacher's Edition:** 57–60, **57–60**, 127–130, **127–130**, 215–218, **215–218**, R2–R3, **R2, R2** **ASSESSMENT** Student Edition/**Teacher's Edition:** 57–60, **57–60**, 127–130, **127–130**, 154, **154**, 210, **210**, 215–218, **215–218**
b. Support claim(s) with logical reasoning and relevant evidence, using accurate, credible sources and demonstrating an understanding of the topic or text.	**INSTRUCTION/APPLICATION** **Interactive Lessons:** Writing Arguments • What Is a Claim? • Support: Reasons and Evidence Building Effective Support Student Edition/**Teacher's Edition:** 57–60, **57–60**, 127–130, **127–130**, 215–218, **215–218**, R2–R3, **R2** **ASSESSMENT** Student Edition/**Teacher's Edition:** 57–60, **57–60**, 127–130, **127–130**, 154, **154**, 210, **210**, 215–218, **215–218**, 230, **230**

Standard	Where Taught
c. Use words, phrases, and clauses to create cohesion and clarify the relationships among claim(s), reasons, and evidence.	**INSTRUCTION/APPLICATION** **Interactive Lessons:** Writing Arguments • Creating a Coherent Argument Student Edition/**Teacher's Edition:** 57–60, **57–60,** 127–130, **127–130,** 215–218, **215–218,** R2–R3, **R2** **ASSESSMENT** Student Edition/**Teacher's Edition:** 57–60, **57–60,** 127–130, **127–130,** 154, **154,** 210, **210,** 215–218, **215–218**
d. Establish and maintain a formal style.	**INSTRUCTION/APPLICATION** **Interactive Lessons:** Writing Arguments • Formal Style Student Edition/**Teacher's Edition:** 57–60, **57–60,** 127–130, **127–130,** 215–218, **215–218,** R2–R3, **R2** **ASSESSMENT** Student Edition/**Teacher's Edition:** 57–60, **57–60,** 127–130, **127–130,** 154, **154,** 210, **210,** 215–218, **215–218**
e. Provide a concluding statement or section that follows from and supports the argument presented.	**INSTRUCTION/APPLICATION** **Interactive Lessons:** Writing Arguments • Concluding Your Argument Student Edition/**Teacher's Edition:** 57–60, **57–60,** 127–130, **127–130,** 215–218, **215–218,** R2–R3, **R2** **ASSESSMENT** Student Edition/**Teacher's Edition:** 57–60, **57–60,** 127–130, **127–130,** 154, **154,** 210, **210,** 215–218, **215–218**
W 2 Write informative/explanatory texts to examine a topic and convey ideas, concepts, and information through the selection, organization, and analysis of relevant content.	**INSTRUCTION/APPLICATION** **Interactive Lessons:** Writing Informative Texts • Developing a Topic • Organizing Ideas • Introductions and Conclusions • Elaboration • Formal Style Student Edition/**Teacher's Edition:** 131–134, 179–182, 259–262, 280, 337–340, 341–344, R4–R5, **R4** **ASSESSMENT** Student Edition/**Teacher's Edition:** 42, **42,** 50, **50,** 126, **126,** 131–134, **131–134,** 179–182, **179–182,** 190, **190,** 214, **214,** 230, **230,** 248, **248,** 259–262, **259–262,** 337–340, **337–340,** 341–344, **341–344**

Standard	Where Taught
a. Introduce a topic clearly, previewing what is to follow; organize ideas, concepts, and information, using strategies such as definition, classification, comparison/contrast, and cause/effect; include formatting (e.g., headings), graphics (e.g., charts, tables), and multimedia when useful to aiding comprehension.	**INSTRUCTION/APPLICATION** **Interactive Lessons:** Writing Informative Texts • Developing a Topic • Organizing Ideas • Introductions and Conclusions • Using Graphics and Multimedia Student Edition/**Teacher's Edition:** 131–134, **131–134**, 179–182, **179–182**, 259–262, **259–262**, 337–340, **337–340**, 341–344, **341–344**, 337–340, **337–340**, 341–344, **341–344**, R4–R5, **R4** **ASSESSMENT** Student Edition/**Teacher's Edition:** 131–134, **131–134**, 179–182, **179–182**, 259–262, **259–262**, 337–340, **337–340**, 341–344, **341–344**
b. Develop the topic with relevant facts, definitions, concrete details, quotations, or other information and examples.	**INSTRUCTION/APPLICATION** **Interactive Lessons:** Writing Informative Texts • Elaboration Student Edition/**Teacher's Edition:** 131–134, **131–134**, 179–182, **179–182**, 259–262, 337–340, **337–340**, R4–R5, **R4** **ASSESSMENT** Student Edition/**Teacher's Edition:** 131–134, **131–134**, 179–182, **179–182**, 259–262, **259–262**, 337–340, **337–340**, 341–344, **341–344**
c. Use appropriate transitions to create cohesion and clarify the relationships among ideas and concepts.	**INSTRUCTION/APPLICATION** **Interactive Lessons:** Writing Informative Texts • Organizing Ideas Student Edition/**Teacher's Edition:** 131–134, **131–134**, 179–182, **179–182**, 259–262, **259–262**, 337–340, **337–340**, 341–344, **341–344**, R4–R5, **R4** **ASSESSMENT** Student Edition/**Teacher's Edition:** 131–134, **131–134**, 179–182, **179–182**, 259–262, **259–262**, 337–340, **337–340**, 341–344, **341–344**
d. Use precise language and domain-specific vocabulary to inform about or explain the topic.	**INSTRUCTION/APPLICATION** **Interactive Lessons:** Writing Informative Texts • Precise Language and Vocabulary Student Edition/**Teacher's Edition:** 131–134, **131–134**, 179–182, **179–182**, 259–262, **259–262**, 337–340, **337–340**, 341–344, **341–344**, R4–R5, **R4** **ASSESSMENT** Student Edition/**Teacher's Edition:** 131–134, **131–134**, 179–182, **179–182**, 259–262, **259–262**, 337–340, **337–340**, 341–344, **341–344**

Standard	Where Taught
e. Establish and maintain a formal style.	**INSTRUCTION/APPLICATION** **Interactive Lessons:** Writing Informative Texts • Formal Style Student Edition/**Teacher's Edition:** 131–134, **131–134**, 179–182, **179–182**, 337–340, **337–340**, R4–R5, **R4** **ASSESSMENT** Student Edition/**Teacher's Edition:** 131–134, **131–134**, 179–182
f. Provide a concluding statement or section that follows from and supports the information or explanation presented.	**INSTRUCTION/APPLICATION** **Interactive Lessons:** Writing Informative Texts • Introductions and Conclusions Student Edition/**Teacher's Edition:** 131–134, **131–134**, 179–182, 259–262, **259–262**, 337–340, **337–340**, 341–344, **341–344**, R4-R5 **ASSESSMENT** Student Edition/**Teacher's Edition:** 131–134, **131–134**, 179–182, 259–262, **259–262**, 337–340, **337–340**, 341–344, **341–344, R4**
W 3 Write narratives to develop real or imagined experiences or events using effective technique, relevant descriptive details, and well-structured event sequences.	**INSTRUCTION/APPLICATION** **Interactive Lessons:** Writing Narratives • Introductions • Narrative Context • Point of View and Characters • Narrative Structure • Narrative Techniques • The Language of Narrative Student Edition/**Teacher's Edition:** 16, **16**, 36, **36**, 53–56, **53–56**, 174, 175–178, **175–178**, 256, **256**, 304, **304**, 325, **325**, R6–R7, **R6** **ASSESSMENT** Student Edition/**Teacher's Edition:** 53–56, **53–56**, 174, 175–178, **175–178**, 256, **256**, 304, **304**, 325, **325**
a. Engage and orient the reader by establishing a context and point of view and introducing a narrator and/or characters; organize an event sequence that unfolds naturally and logically.	**INSTRUCTION/APPLICATION** **Interactive Lessons:** Writing Narratives • Narrative Context • Point of View and Characters • Narrative Structure Student Edition/**Teacher's Edition:** 53–56, **53–56**, 175–178, **175–178**, R6–R7, **R6** **ASSESSMENT** Student Edition/**Teacher's Edition:** 53–56, **53–56**, 175–178, **175–178**

Standard	Where Taught
b. Use narrative techniques, such as dialogue, pacing, and description, to develop experiences, events, and/or characters.	**INSTRUCTION/APPLICATION** **Interactive Lessons:** Writing Narratives • Narrative Techniques • The Language of Narrative Student Edition/**Teacher's Edition:** 53–56, **53–56,** 175–178, **175–178,** R6–R7 **ASSESSMENT** Student Edition/**Teacher's Edition:** 53–56, **53–56,** 175–178, **175–178**
c. Use a variety of transition words, phrases, and clauses to convey sequence and signal shifts from one time frame or setting to another.	**INSTRUCTION/APPLICATION** **Interactive Lessons:** Writing Narratives • Narrative Structure Student Edition/**Teacher's Edition:** 53–56, **53–56,** 175–178, **175–178, R6–R7** **ASSESSMENT** Student Edition/**Teacher's Edition:** 53–56, **53–56,** 175–178, **175–178**
d. Use precise words and phrases, relevant descriptive details, and sensory language to capture the action and convey experiences and events.	**INSTRUCTION/APPLICATION** **Interactive Lessons:** Writing Narratives • The Language of Narrative Student Edition/**Teacher's Edition:** 53–56, **53–56,** 175–178, **175–178,** R6–R7 **ASSESSMENT** Student Edition/**Teacher's Edition:** 53–56, **53–56,** 175–178, **175–178**
e. Provide a conclusion that follows from and reflects on the narrated experiences or events.	**INSTRUCTION/APPLICATION** **Interactive Lessons:** Writing Narratives • Narrative Structure Student Edition/**Teacher's Edition:** 53–56, **53–56,** 175–178, **175–178,** R6–R7 **ASSESSMENT** Student Edition/**Teacher's Edition:** 53–56, **53–56,** 175–178, **175–178**

Standard	Where Taught

PRODUCTION AND DISTRIBUTION OF WRITING

W 4
Produce clear and coherent writing in which the development, organization, and style are appropriate to task, purpose, and audience. (Grade-specific expectations for writing types are defined in Standards 1–3 above.)

INSTRUCTION/APPLICATION
Interactive Lessons:
Writing as a Process
• Task, Purpose, and Audience

Student Edition/**Teacher's Edition:**
53–56, **53–56**, 57–60, **57–60**, 127–130, **127–130**, 131–134, **131–134**, 175–178, **175–178**, 179–182, **179–182**, 215–218, 259–262, **259–262**, 337–340, **337–340**, 341–344, **341–344**, R2–R3, **R2**, R4-R5, **R4**, R6–R7, **R6**

ASSESSMENT
Student Edition/**Teacher's Edition:**
30, **30**, 30a, 53–56, **53–56**, 57–60, **57–60**, 126, **126**, 127–130, **127–130**, 131–134, **131–134**, 154, **154**, 175–178, **175–178**, 179–182, **179–182**, 210, **210**, 215–218, 248, **248**, 256, **256**, 259–262, **259–262**, 304, **304**, 314, **314**, 325, **325**, 334, **334**, 337–340, **337–340**, 341–344, **341–344**

W 5
With some guidance and support from peers and adults, develop and strengthen writing as needed by planning, revising, editing, rewriting, or trying a new approach, focusing on how well purpose and audience have been addressed. (Editing for conventions should demonstrate command of Language standards 1–3 up to and including grade 7.)

INSTRUCTION/APPLICATION
Interactive Lessons:
Writing as a Process
• Introduction
• Task, Purpose, and Audience
• Planning and Drafting
• Revising and Editing
Trying a New Approach

Student Edition/**Teacher's Edition:**
53–56, **53–56**, 127–130, **127–130**, 175–178, **175–178**, 179–182, **179–182**, 215–218, **215–218**, 259–262, **259–262**, 337–340, **337–340**, 341–344, **341–344**

ASSESSMENT
Student Edition/**Teacher's Edition:**
36, **36**, 53–56, **53–56**, 127–130, **127–130**, 175–178, **175–178**, 179–182, **179–182**, 215–218, **215–218**, 259–262, **259–262**, 304, **304**, 337–340, **337–340**, 341–344, **341–344**

W 6
Use technology, including the Internet, to produce and publish writing and link to and cite sources as well as to interact and collaborate with others, including linking to and citing sources.

INSTRUCTION/APPLICATION
Interactive Lessons:
Producing and Publishing with Technology
• Introduction
• Writing for the Internet
• Interacting with Your Online Audience
• Using Technology to Collaborate

Student Edition/**Teacher's Edition:**
30, **30**, 30a, 50, **52b**, 92, **92**, 131–134, **131–134**, 179–182, **179–182**, 230, **230**, 259–262, **259–262**, 337–340, **337–340**, 341–344, **341–344**

ASSESSMENT
Student Edition/**Teacher's Edition:**
131–134, **131–134**, 179–182, **179–182**, 259–262, **259–262**, 337–340, **337–340**, 341–344, **341–344**

Standard	Where Taught

RESEARCH TO BUILD AND PRESENT KNOWLEDGE

W 7
Conduct short research projects to answer a question, drawing on several sources and generating additional related, focused questions for further research and investigation.

INSTRUCTION/APPLICATION
Interactive Lessons:
Conducting Research
- Introduction
- Starting Your Research
- Types of Sources
- Using the Library for Research
- Conducting Field Research
- Using the Internet for Research
- Taking Notes
- Refocusing Your Inquiry

Using Textual Evidence
- Synthesizing Information

Student Edition/**Teacher's Edition:**
166, **166,** 190, **190,** 198, **198,** 215–218, **215–218, 230,** 259–262, **259–262,** 337–340, **337–340,** R8–R9, **R8**

ASSESSMENT
Student Edition/**Teacher's Edition:**
36, **36,** 86, **86, 88a,** 166, **166,** 190, **190,** 198, **198,** 215–218, **215–218, 230,** 259–262, **259–262,** 337–340, **337–340**

W 8
Gather relevant information from multiple print and digital sources, using search terms effectively; assess the credibility and accuracy of each source; and quote or paraphrase the data and conclusions of others while avoiding plagiarism and following a standard format for citation.

INSTRUCTION/APPLICATION
Interactive Lessons:
Conducting Research
- Types of Sources
- Using the Library for Research
- Using the Internet for Research

Evaluating Sources
- Introduction
- Evaluating Sources for Usefulness
- Evaluating Sources for Reliability

Using Textual Evidence
- Summarizing, Paraphrasing, and Quoting
- Attribution

Student Edition/**Teacher's Edition:**
52b, 57–60, **57–60, 88a,** 190, **190,** 198, **198,** 210, **210,** 215–218, **215–218, 230,** 259–262, **259–262, 280,** 337–340, **337–340,** R8–R11, **R8**

ASSESSMENT
Student Edition/**Teacher's Edition:**
57–60, **57–60,** 190, **190,** 198, **198,** 210, **210,** 215–218, **215–218, 230,** 259–262, **259–262, 280,** 337–340, **337–340**

Standard	Where Taught
W 9 Draw evidence from literary or informational texts to support analysis, reflection, and research.	**INSTRUCTION/APPLICATION** **Interactive Lessons:** Writing Informative Texts • Elaboration Conducting Research • Taking Notes Using Textual Evidence • Introduction • Synthesizing Information • Summarizing, Paraphrasing, and Quoting Student Edition/**Teacher's Edition:** 57–60, **57–60,** 69, **69,** 108, **108,** 126, **126,** 127–130, **127–130,** 142, 179–182, 214, **214,** 304, **304,** 314, 334, **334** **ASSESSMENT** Student Edition/**Teacher's Edition:** 57–60, **57–60,** 127–130, **127–130,** 179–182
a. Apply *grade 7 Reading Standards* to literature (e.g., "Compare and contrast a fictional portrayal of a time, place, or character and a historical account of the same period as a means of understanding how authors of fiction use or alter history").	**INSTRUCTION/APPLICATION** Student Edition/**Teacher's Edition:** 108, **108,** 126, **126,** 127–130, **127–130,** 179–182, **179–182,** 214, **214,** 334, **334** **ASSESSMENT** Student Edition/**Teacher's Edition:** 127–130, **127–130,** 179–182, **179–182**
b. Apply *grade 7 Reading Standards* to literary nonfiction (e.g. "Trace and evaluate the argument and specific claims in a text, assessing whether the reasoning is sound and the evidence is relevant and sufficient to support the claims").	**INSTRUCTION/APPLICATION** Student Edition/**Teacher's Edition:** 314, **314** **ASSESSMENT** Student Edition/**Teacher's Edition:** 314, **314**

Standard	Where Taught

RANGE OF WRITING

W 10
Write routinely over extended time frames (time for research, reflection, and revision) and shorter time frames (a single sitting or a day or two) for a range of discipline-specific tasks, purposes, and audiences.

INSTRUCTION/APPLICATION
Interactive Lessons:
Writing as a Process
• Task, Purpose, and Audience
Writing Arguments
Writing Informative Texts
Writing Narratives
Using Textual Evidence

Student Edition/**Teacher's Edition:**
53–56, **53–56**, 57–60, **57–60**, 127–130, **127–130**, 131–134, **131–134**, 175–178, **175–178**, 179–182, **179–182**, 215–218, **215–218**, 259–262, **259–262**, 337–340, **337–340**, 341–344, **341–344**

ASSESSMENT
Student Edition/**Teacher's Edition:**
50, **50**, 53–56, **53–56**, 57–60, **57–60**, 126, **126**, 127–130, **127–130**, 131–134, **131–134**, 154, **154**, 174, **174**, 175–178, **175–178**, 179–182, **179–182**, 210, **210**, 215–218, **215–218**, 248, **248**, 256, **256**, 259–262, **259–262**, 304, **304**, 314, **314**, 325, **325**, 334, **334**, 337–340, **337–340**, 341–344, **341–344**

College and Career Readiness Anchor Standards for Speaking and Listening

Common Core State Standards

COMPREHENSION AND COLLABORATION

1. Prepare for and participate effectively in a range of conversations and collaborations with diverse partners, building on others' ideas and expressing their own clearly and persuasively.

2. Integrate and evaluate information presented in diverse media and formats, including visually, quantitatively, and orally.

3. Evaluate a speaker's point of view, reasoning, and use of evidence and rhetoric.

PRESENTATION OF KNOWLEDGE AND IDEAS

4. Present information, findings, and supporting evidence such that listeners can follow the line of reasoning and the organization, development, and style are appropriate to task, purpose, and audience.

5. Make strategic use of digital media and visual displays of data to express information and enhance understanding of presentations.

6. Adapt speech to a variety of contexts and communicative tasks, demonstrating command of formal English when indicated or appropriate.

Speaking and Listening Standards

Standard	Where Taught
COMPREHENSION AND COLLABORATION	

SL 1

Engage effectively in a range of collaborative discussions (one-on-one, in groups, and teacher-led) with diverse partners on *grade 7 topics, texts, and issues,* building on others' ideas and expressing their own clearly.

INSTRUCTION/APPLICATION
Interactive Lessons:
Participating in Collaborative Discussions
- Introduction
- Preparing for Discussion
- Establishing and Following Procedure
- Speaking Constructively
- Listening and Responding
- Wrapping Up Your Discussion

Student Edition/Teacher's Edition:
14, **14,** 28, **28,** 34, **34,** 40, **40, 42a,** 43, **43,** 48, **48,** 67, **67,** 74, **74,** 76, **76,** 84, **84,** 91, **91,** 106, **106,** 124, **124,** 140, **140,** 146, **146,** 148, **148,** 152, **152,** 172, **172, 174a,** 188, **188, 192a,** 196, **196,** 198, **198, 200a,** 208, **208,** 213, **213,** 228, **228,** 236, **236,** 238, **238,** 245, **245,** 254, **254,** 277, **277,** 302, **302,** 312, **312,** 318, **318,** 323, **323,** 332, **332,** 341–344, **341–344,** R12–R13, **R12**

Close Reader/Teacher's Edition:
3–12, **18b–18i,** 13–16, **30b–30e,** 25–30, **70b–70g,** 45–50, **144b–144g,** 51–54, **168b–168e,** 63–66, **192b–192e**

ASSESSMENT
Student Edition/Teacher's Edition:
76, **76,** 148, **148, 174a, 192a,** 198, **198, 200a,** 238, **238,** 341–344, **341–344**

---

a. Come to discussions prepared, having read or researched material under study; explicitly draw on that preparation by referring to evidence on the topic, text, or issue to probe and reflect on ideas under discussion.

INSTRUCTION/APPLICATION
Interactive Lessons:
Participating in Collaborative Discussions
- Preparing for Discussion

Student Edition/Teacher's Edition:
14, **14,** 28, **28,** 172, **172,** 318, **318,** 198, 238, 341–344, **341–344,** R12–R13

Close Reader/Teacher's Edition:
3–12, **18b–18i,** 13–16, **30b–30e,** 25–30, 45–50, 51–54, **70b–70g, 144b–144g, 168b–168e,** 63–66, **192b–192e**

ASSESSMENT
Student Edition/Teacher's Edition:
76, **76,** 341–344, **341–344**

Standard	Where Taught
b. Follow rules for collegial discussions, track progress toward specific goals and deadlines, and define individual roles as needed.	**INSTRUCTION/APPLICATION** **Interactive Lessons:** Participating in Collaborative Discussions • Establishing and Following Procedure Student Edition/**Teacher's Edition:** 198, 238, 341–344, **341–344**, R12–R13 **ASSESSMENT** Student Edition/**Teacher's Edition:** 76, **76**, 341–344, **341–344**
c. Pose questions that elicit elaboration and respond to others' questions and comments with relevant observations and ideas that bring the discussion back on topic as needed.	**INSTRUCTION/APPLICATION** **Interactive Lessons:** Participating in Collaborative Discussions • Speaking Constructively • Listening and Responding Student Edition/**Teacher's Edition:** 198, 238, 341–344, **341–344**, R12–R13 Close Reader/**Teacher's Edition:** 3–12, **18b–18i**, 13–16, **30b–30e**, 25–30, **70b–70g**, 45–50, **144b–144g**, 51–54, **168b–168e**, 63–66, **192b–192e** **ASSESSMENT** Student Edition/**Teacher's Edition:** 76, **76**, 341–344, **341–344**
d. Acknowledge new information expressed by others and, when warranted, modify their own views and understanding.	**INSTRUCTION/APPLICATION** **Interactive Lessons:** Participating in Collaborative Discussions • Wrapping Up Your Discussion Student Edition/**Teacher's Edition:** 198, 238, 341–344, **341–344**, R12–R13 Close Reader/**Teacher's Edition:** 51–54, **168b–168e**, 63–66, **192b–192e** **ASSESSMENT** Student Edition/**Teacher's Edition:** 76, **76**, 341–344, **341–344**

Standard	Where Taught
SL 2 Analyze the main ideas and supporting details presented in diverse media and formats (e.g., visually, quantitatively, orally) and explain how the ideas clarify a topic, text, or issue under study.	**INSTRUCTION/APPLICATION** **Interactive Lessons:** Analyzing and Evaluating Presentations • Introduction • Analyzing a Presentation Student Edition/**Teacher's Edition:** 20, **21**, **22**, 23, **23**, 29, **29**, 30, **30**, 90, **90**, 91, **91**, **92a**, 319, **319**, **320a** **ASSESSMENT** Student Edition/**Teacher's Edition:** 23, **23**, 29, **29**, 30, **30**, 92, **92**, 126, **126**, 320, **320**
SL 3 Delineate a speaker's argument and specific claims, evaluating the soundness of the reasoning and the relevance and sufficiency of the evidence.	**INSTRUCTION/APPLICATION** **Interactive Lessons:** Analyzing and Evaluating Presentations • Identifying a Speaker's Claim • Tracing a Speaker's Argument Student Edition/**Teacher's Edition:** 23, **23**, 29, **29**, 30, **30**, 190, **190**, **192a**, **200a**, R14–R15, **R14** **ASSESSMENT** Student Edition/**Teacher's Edition:** 23, **23**, 29, **29**, 30, **30**, 320, **320**

PRESENTATION OF KNOWLEDGE AND IDEAS

Standard	Where Taught
SL 4 Present claims and findings, emphasizing salient points in a focused, coherent manner with pertinent descriptions, facts, details, and examples; use appropriate eye contact, adequate volume, and clear pronunciation.	**INSTRUCTION/APPLICATION** **Interactive Lessons:** Giving a Presentation • Introduction • The Content of Your Presentation • Style in Presentation • Delivering Your Presentation Student Edition/**Teacher's Edition:** 16, **16**, 42, **42**, 57–60, **57–60**, 131–134, **131–134**, 175–178, **175–178**, 179–182, **179–182**, 215–218, **215–218**, 259–262, **259–262**, 280, **280**, 320, **320**, R14–R15 **ASSESSMENT** Student Edition/**Teacher's Edition:** 57–60, **57–60**, 76, **76**, 86, **86**, 131–134, **131–134**, 154, **154**, 166, **166**, 175–178, **175–178**, 179–182, **179–182**, 198, **198**, 215–218, **215–218**, 259–262, **259–262**, 280, **280**, 320, **320**

Standard	Where Taught
SL 5 Include multimedia components and visual displays in presentations to clarify claims and findings and emphasize salient points.	**INSTRUCTION/APPLICATION** **Interactive Lessons:** Using Media in a Presentation • Introduction • Types of Media: Audio, Video, and Images • Using Presentation Software • Building and Practicing Your Presentation Student Edition/**Teacher's Edition:** 57–60, **57–60**, 215–218, **215–218**, 259–262, **259–262** **ASSESSMENT** Student Edition/**Teacher's Edition:** 57–60, **57–60**, 92, **92**, 215–218, **215–218**, 259–262, **259–262**, 320, **320**
SL 6 Adapt speech to a variety of contexts and tasks, demonstrating command of formal English when indicated or appropriate. (See grade 7 Language standards 1 and 3 for specific expectations.)	**INSTRUCTION/APPLICATION** **Interactive Lessons:** Participating in Collaborative Discussions • Speaking Constructively Giving a Presentation • Style in Presentation Student Edition/**Teacher's Edition:** 57–60, **57–60**, 70a, 215–218, **215–218**, 259–262, **259–262** **ASSESSMENT** Student Edition/**Teacher's Edition:** 57–60, **57–60**, 69, **69**, 76, **76**, 148, **148**, 215–218, **215–218**, 259–262, **259–262**, 280, **280**

College and Career Readiness Anchor Standards for Language

Common Core State Standards

CONVENTIONS OF STANDARD ENGLISH

1. Demonstrate command of the conventions of standard English grammar and usage when writing or speaking.

2. Demonstrate command of the conventions of standard English capitalization, punctuation, and spelling when writing.

KNOWLEDGE OF LANGUAGE

3. Apply knowledge of language to understand how language functions in different contexts, to make effective choices for meaning or style, and to comprehend more fully when reading or listening.

VOCABULARY ACQUISITION AND USE

4. Determine or clarify the meaning of unknown and multiple-meaning words and phrases by using context clues, analyzing meaningful word parts, and consulting general and specialized reference materials, as appropriate.

5. Demonstrate understanding of figurative language, word relationships, and nuances in word meanings.

6. Acquire and use accurately a range of general academic and domain-specific words and phrases sufficient for reading, writing, speaking, and listening at the college- and career-readiness level; demonstrate independence in gathering vocabulary knowledge when encountering an unknown term important to comprehension or expression.

Language Standards

Standard	Where Taught
CONVENTIONS OF STANDARD ENGLISH	
L 1 Demonstrate command of the conventions of standard English grammar and usage when writing or speaking.	**INSTRUCTION/APPLICATION** Student Edition/**Teacher's Edition:** 18, 52, **52,** 88, **88,** 156, **156,** 168, **168,** 200, **200,** 212, **212,** 240, **240,** 306, **306,** 316, **316,** 326, **326,** 336, **336,** R30–R54, **R30, R38, R40**
a. Explain the function of phrases and clauses in general and their function in specific sentences.	**INSTRUCTION/APPLICATION** Student Edition/**Teacher's Edition:** 18, **18,** 52, **52,** 88, **88,** 168, **168,** 200, **200,** 212, **212,** 240, **240,** 306, **306,** 326, **326,** R30, R47–R50, **R38, R40, R50**
b. Choose among simple, compound, complex, and compound-complex sentences to signal differing relationships among ideas.	**INSTRUCTION/APPLICATION** Student Edition/**Teacher's Edition:** 18, 18, 156, **156,** R30, **R30,** R32, R44–R45, R46, R50–R51
c. Place phrases and clauses within a sentence, recognizing and correcting misplaced and dangling modifiers.	**INSTRUCTION/APPLICATION** Student Edition/**Teacher's Edition:** 316, **316,** 326, **326,** 336, **336,** R30, **R30,** R44–R45, **R46,** R47–R50
L 2 Demonstrate command of the conventions of standard English capitalization, punctuation, and spelling when writing.	**INSTRUCTION/APPLICATION** Student Edition/**Teacher's Edition:** 38, **38,** 110, **110,** 192, **192,** 258, **258,** 282, **282,** R30, **R30,** R33–R36, R60–R63
a. Use a comma to separate coordinate adjectives (e.g., *It was a fascinating, enjoyable movie* but not *He wore an old[,] green shirt*).	**INSTRUCTION/APPLICATION** Student Edition/**Teacher's Edition:** 38, **38,** R30, **R30**
b. Spell correctly.	**INSTRUCTION/APPLICATION** Student Edition/**Teacher's Edition:** 110, **110,** 258, **258,** R30, **R30,** R55, **R55,** R60–R63

Standard	Where Taught

KNOWLEDGE OF LANGUAGE

L 3
Use knowledge of language and its conventions when writing, speaking, reading, or listening.

INSTRUCTION/APPLICATION

Student Edition/**Teacher's Edition:**
53–56, **53–56,** 57–60, **57–60,** 144, **144,** 192, 232, **232,** R30, **R30**

a. Choose language that expresses ideas precisely and concisely, recognizing and eliminating wordiness and redundancy.

INSTRUCTION/APPLICATION

Student Edition/**Teacher's Edition:**
53–56, **53–56,** 57–60, **57–60,** 144, **144,** 232, **232**

VOCABULARY ACQUISITION AND USE

L 4
Determine or clarify the meaning of unknown and multiple-meaning words and phrases based on *grade 7 reading and content,* choosing flexibly from a range of strategies.

INSTRUCTION/APPLICATION

Student Edition/**Teacher's Edition:**
17, **17,** 37, **37,** 51, **51,** 70, **70, 78, 81,** 87, **87,** 109, **109, 117,** 155, **155,** 167, **167,** 191, **191,** 199, **199, 206, 211,** 211, **212a,** 231, **231,** 239, **239,** 257, **257,** 281, **281,** 315, **315,** 335, **335,** R55, **R55,** R57, R59

a. Use context (e.g., the overall meaning of a sentence or paragraph; a word's position or function in a sentence) as a clue to the meaning of a word or phrase.

INSTRUCTION/APPLICATION

Student Edition/**Teacher's Edition:**
17, **17,** 51, **51, 78, 81,** 87, **87,** 109, **109, 117,** 191, **191, 206, 212a,** 231, **231,** 315, **315,** R55–R56, **R55**

b. Use common, grade-appropriate Greek or Latin affixes and roots as clues to the meaning of a word (e.g., *belligerent, bellicose, rebel*).

INSTRUCTION/APPLICATION

Student Edition/**Teacher's Edition:**
17, **17,** 37, **37,** 70, **70,** 87, **87,** 167, **167,** 109, **109,** 199, **199,** 211, **211,** 281, **281,** R55, **R55,** R56–R57

Standard	Where Taught
c. Consult general and specialized reference materials (e.g., dictionaries, glossaries, thesauruses), both print and digital, to find the pronunciation of a word or determine or clarify its precise meaning or its part of speech.	**INSTRUCTION/APPLICATION** Student Edition/**Teacher's Edition:** 17, 87, **87**, 109, **109**, **117**, 155, **155**, 191, **191**, 211, **211**, **212a**, 315, **315**, 335, **335**, R55, **R55**, R59–R60
d. Verify the preliminary determination of the meaning of a word or phrase (e.g., by checking the inferred meaning in context or in a dictionary).	**INSTRUCTION/APPLICATION** Student Edition/**Teacher's Edition:** 70, **70**, 191, **191**, **212a**, 239, **239**, 257, **257**, 281, **281**, 315, **315**, R55, **R55**, R59–R60
L 5 Demonstrate understanding of figurative language, word relationships, and nuances in word meanings.	**INSTRUCTION/APPLICATION** Student Edition/**Teacher's Edition:** 51, **51**, 109, **109**, 143, **143**, 239, **239**, **289**, **299**, 305, **305**, R55–R59, **R55**
a. Interpret figures of speech (e.g., literary, biblical, and mythological allusions) in context.	**INSTRUCTION/APPLICATION** Student Edition/**Teacher's Edition:** 143, **143**, R55, **R55**
b. Use the relationship between particular words (e.g., synonym/antonym, analogy) to better understand each of the words.	**INSTRUCTION/APPLICATION** Student Edition/**Teacher's Edition:** 109, **109**, **203**, 239, **239**, 305, **305**, R55, **R55**, R58–R59
c. Distinguish among the connotations (associations) of words with similar denotations (definitions) (e.g., *refined, respectful, polite, diplomatic, condescending*).	**INSTRUCTION/APPLICATION** Student Edition/**Teacher's Edition:** 51, **51**, R55, **R55**, R58

Standard	Where Taught
L 6 Acquire and use accurately grade-appropriate general academic and domain-specific words and phrases; gather vocabulary knowledge when considering a word or phrase important to comprehension or expression.	**INSTRUCTION/APPLICATION** Student Edition/**Teacher's Edition:** 2, **2**, **8**, **20**, **24**, **33**, **47**, 53, **53**, 57, **57**, 62, **62**, **65**, **72**, **78**, **91**, **94**, 109, **109**, **115**, 127, **127**, 136, **136**, **139**, **152**, **161**, 167, **167**, 175, **175**, 179, **179**, 184, **184**, **187**, 199, **199**, **203**, 211, **211**, 215, **215**, 220, **220**, **225**, 231, **231**, **235**, 239, **239**, **242**, **252**, **255**, 257, **257**, 259, **259**, 264, **264**, **269**, **286**, **309**, 315, **315**, **318**, **322**, **330**, 335, **335**, 337, **337**, 341, **341**, R55, **R55**, R55–R63, **R55–R63**

Making Meaning
in the 21st Century ... or
Don't Let Complex Texts Get You Down

By Carol Jago

Do you sometimes think that what your teacher asks you to read is too hard? Let me tell you a secret. Those poems and passages can be tough for your teacher as well. Just because a text isn't easy doesn't mean there is something wrong with it or something wrong with the reader. It means you need to do more than skim across the words on the page or screen. You will need to think critically at every turn. Problem solving isn't only needed for math. Complex texts demand the same kind of effort and focused attention. Do you sometimes wish writers would just say what they have to say simply? I assure you that writers don't use long sentences and unfamiliar words to annoy their readers or make readers feel dumb. They employ complex syntax and rich language in order to express complex ideas.

Excellent literature and nonfiction—the kind you will be reading over the course of the year—challenges readers in various ways. Sometimes the background of a story or the content of an essay is so unfamiliar that it is difficult to understand why characters are behaving as they do or to follow the argument a writer is making. By persevering, reading like a detective, and following clues in the text, you will find that your store of background knowledge grows. As a result, the next time you read about global issues, financial matters, political events, environmental news (like the California drought) or health research, the text won't seem nearly as hard. The more you read, the better a reader you will become.

Good readers aren't put off by challenging text. When the going gets rough, they know what to do. Let's take vocabulary, a common measure of text complexity, as an example. Learning new words is the business of a lifetime. Rather than shutting down when you meet a word you don't know, take a moment to think about the word. Is any part of the word familiar to you? Is there something in the context of the sentence or paragraph that can help you figure out its meaning? Is there someone or something that can provide you with a definition? When reading literature or nonfiction from a time period other than our own, the text is often full of words we don't know. Each time you meet those words in succeeding readings you will be adding to your understanding of the word and its use. Your brain is a natural word-learning machine. The more you feed it complex text, the larger a vocabulary you'll have.

Have you ever been reading a long, complicated sentence and discovered that by the time you reached the end you had forgotten the beginning? Unlike the sentences we speak or dash off in a note to a friend, complex text is often full of sentences that are not only lengthy but also constructed in intricate ways. Such sentences require readers to slow down and figure out how phrases relate to one another as well as who is doing what to whom. Remember, rereading isn't cheating. It is exactly what experienced readers know to do when they meet dense text on the page. On the pages that follow you will find stories and articles that challenge you at the sentence level. Don't be intimidated. With careful attention to how those sentences are constructed, their meaning will unfold right before your eyes.

That same kind of attention is required for reading the media. Every day you are bombarded with messages— online, offline, everywhere you look. These, too, are complex texts that you want to be able to see through; that is, to be able to recognize the message's source, purpose, context, intended audience, and appeals. This is what it takes to be a 21st century reader.

> **"Your brain is a natural word-learning machine. The more you feed it complex text, the larger a vocabulary you'll have."**

Another way text can be complex involves the density of the ideas in a passage. Sometimes a writer piles on so much information that you think your head might explode if you read one more detail or one more qualification. At times like this talking with a friend can really help. Sharing questions and ideas, exploring a difficult passage together, can help you tease out the meaning of even the most difficult text. Poetry is often particularly dense and for that reason it poses particular challenges. A seemingly simple poem in terms of vocabulary and length may express extremely complex feelings and insights. Poets also love to use mythological and Biblical allusions which contemporary readers are not always familiar with. The only way to read text this complex is to read it again and again.

You are going to notice a range of complexity within each collection of readings. This spectrum reflects the range of texts that surround us: some easy, some hard, some seemingly easy but in fact hard, some seemingly hard but actually easy. Whatever their complexity, I think you will enjoy these readings tremendously. Remember, read for your life!

Understanding the Common Core State Standards

What are the English Language Arts Common Core State Standards?

The Common Core State Standards for English Language Arts indicate what you should know and be able to do by the end of your grade level. These understandings and skills will help you be better prepared for future classes, college courses, and a career. For this reason, the standards for each strand in English Language Arts (such as reading informational text or writing) directly relate to the College and Career Readiness Anchor Standards for each strand. The Anchor Standards broadly outline the understandings and skills you should master by the end of high school so that you are well-prepared for college or for a career.

How do I learn the English Language Arts Common Core State Standards?

Your textbook is closely aligned to the English Language Arts Common Core State Standards. Every time you learn a concept or practice a skill, you are working on mastering one of the standards. Each collection, each selection, and each performance task in your textbook connects to one or more of the standards for English Language Arts listed on the following pages.

The English Language Arts Common Core State Standards are divided into five strands: Reading Literature, Reading Informational Text, Writing, Speaking and Listening, and Language.

©Blend/Getty Images

Strand	What It Means to You
Reading Literature (RL)	This strand concerns the literary texts you will read at this grade level: stories, drama, and poetry. The Common Core State Standards stress that you should read a range of texts of increasing complexity as you progress through high school.
Reading Informational Text (RI)	Informational text encompasses a broad range of literary nonfiction, including exposition, argument, and functional text, in such genres as personal essays, speeches, opinion pieces, memoirs, and historical and technical accounts. The Common Core State Standards stress that you will read a range of informational texts of increasing complexity as you progress from grade to grade.
Writing (W)	For the Writing strand you will focus on generating three types of texts—arguments, informative or explanatory texts, and narratives—while using the writing process and technology to develop and share your writing. The Common Core State Standards also emphasize research and specify that you should write routinely for both short and extended time frames.
Speaking and Listening (SL)	The Common Core State Standards focus on comprehending information presented in a variety of media and formats, on participating in collaborative discussions, and on presenting knowledge and ideas clearly.
Language (L)	The standards in the Language strand address the conventions of standard English grammar, usage, and mechanics; knowledge of language; and vocabulary acquisition and use.

Common Core Code Decoder

The codes you find on the pages of your textbook identify the specific knowledge or skill for the standard addressed in the text.

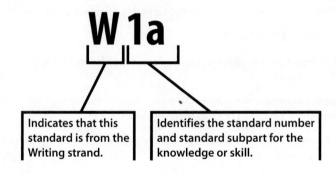

Indicates that this standard is from the Writing strand.

Identifies the standard number and standard subpart for the knowledge or skill.

English Language Arts
Common Core State Standards

Listed below are the English Language Arts Common Core State Standards that you are required to master by the end of grade 7. We have provided a summary of the concepts you will learn on your way to mastering each standard. The CCR anchor standards and grade-specific standards for each strand work together to define college and career readiness expectations—the former providing broad standards, the latter providing additional specificity.

College and Career Readiness Anchor Standards for Reading

Common Core State Standards

KEY IDEAS AND DETAILS

1. Read closely to determine what the text says explicitly and to make logical inferences from it; cite specific textual evidence when writing or speaking to support conclusions drawn from the text.

2. Determine central ideas or themes of a text and analyze their development; summarize the key supporting details and ideas.

3. Analyze how and why individuals, events, and ideas develop and interact over the course of a text.

CRAFT AND STRUCTURE

4. Interpret words and phrases as they are used in a text, including determining technical, connotative, and figurative meanings, and analyze how specific word choices shape meaning or tone.

5. Analyze the structure of texts, including how specific sentences, paragraphs, and larger portions of the text (e.g., a section, chapter, scene, or stanza) relate to each other and the whole.

6. Assess how point of view or purpose shapes the content and style of a text.

INTEGRATION OF KNOWLEDGE AND IDEAS

7. Integrate and evaluate content presented in diverse media and formats, including visually and quantitatively, as well as in words.

8. Delineate and evaluate the argument and specific claims in a text, including the validity of the reasoning as well as the relevance and sufficiency of the evidence.

9. Analyze how two or more texts address similar themes or topics in order to build knowledge or to compare the approaches the authors take.

RANGE OF READING AND LEVEL OF TEXT COMPLEXITY

10. Read and comprehend complex literary and informational texts independently and proficiently.

Reading Standards for Literature, Grade 7 Students

The College and Career Readiness Anchor Standards for Reading apply to both literature and informational text.

Common Core State Standards	What It Means to You
KEY IDEAS AND DETAILS	
1. Cite several pieces of textual evidence to support analysis of what the text says explicitly as well as inferences drawn from the text.	You will use information from the text to support its main ideas—both those that are stated directly and those that are suggested.
2. Determine a theme or central idea of a text and analyze its development over the course of the text; provide an objective summary of the text.	You will analyze a text's main ideas and themes by showing how they unfold throughout the text. You will also summarize the main idea of the text as a whole without adding your own ideas or opinions.
3. Analyze how particular elements of a story or drama interact (e.g., how setting shapes the characters or plot).	You will analyze how different parts of a story or drama affect each other.
CRAFT AND STRUCTURE	
4. Determine the meaning of words and phrases as they are used in a text, including figurative and connotative meanings; analyze the impact of rhymes and other repetitions of sounds (e.g., alliteration) on a specific verse or stanza of a poem or section of a story or drama.	You will analyze specific words, phrases, and patterns of sound in the text to determine what they mean and how they contribute to the text's larger meaning.
5. Analyze how a drama's or poem's form or structure (e.g., soliloquy, sonnet) contributes to its meaning.	You will analyze how the form of a drama or poem affects its meaning.
6. Analyze how an author develops and contrasts the points of view of different characters or narrators in a text.	You will analyze how an author contrasts the perspectives of different characters or the points of view of narrators in a text.
INTEGRATION OF KNOWLEDGE AND IDEAS	
7. Compare and contrast a written story, drama, or poem to its audio, filmed, staged, or multimedia version, analyzing the effects of techniques unique to each medium (e.g., lighting, sound, color, or camera focus and angles in a film).	You will compare and contrast how events and information are presented in visual and non-visual texts.

Common Core State Standards **XXXV**

Common Core State Standards	What It Means to You
8. (Not applicable to literature)	
9. Compare and contrast a fictional portrayal of a time, place, or character and a historical account of the same period as a means of understanding how authors of fiction use or alter history.	You will recognize and analyze how an author draws from and uses historical source material.
RANGE OF READING AND LEVEL OF TEXT COMPLEXITY	
10. By the end of the year, read and comprehend literature, including stories, dramas, and poems, in the grades 6–8 text complexity band proficiently, with scaffolding as needed at the high end of the range.	You will read and understand grade-level appropriate literary texts by the end of grade 7.

Reading Standards for Informational Text, Grade 7 Students

Common Core State Standards	What It Means to You
KEY IDEAS AND DETAILS	
1. Cite several pieces of textual evidence to support analysis of what the text says explicitly as well as inferences drawn from the text.	You will cite information from the text to support its main ideas—both those that are stated directly and those that are suggested.
2. Determine two or more central ideas in a text and analyze their development over the course of the text; provide an objective summary of the text.	You will analyze the development of at least two of a text's main ideas by showing how they progress throughout the text. You will also summarize the text as a whole without adding your own ideas or opinions.
3. Analyze the interactions between individuals, events, and ideas in a text (e.g., how ideas influence individuals or events, or how individuals influence ideas or events).	You will analyze the ways in which individuals, events, and ideas in the text interact with one another.

Common Core State Standards	What It Means to You
CRAFT AND STRUCTURE	
4. Determine the meaning of words and phrases as they are used in a text, including figurative, connotative, and technical meanings; analyze the impact of a specific word choice on meaning and tone.	You will analyze specific words and phrases in the text to determine both what they mean and how they affect the text's tone and meaning as a whole.
5. Analyze the structure an author uses to organize a text, including how the major sections contribute to the whole and to the development of the ideas.	You will examine the major sections of a text and analyze how each one contributes to the whole.
6. Determine an author's point of view or purpose in a text and analyze how the author distinguishes his or her position from that of others.	You will understand the author's point of view and analyze how the author sets his or her position apart from others.
INTEGRATION OF KNOWLEDGE AND IDEAS	
7. Compare and contrast a text to an audio, video, or multimedia version of the text, analyzing each medium's portrayal of the subject (e.g., how the delivery of a speech affects the impact of the words).	You will compare and contrast text to an audio, video, or multimedia version of the text.
8. Trace and evaluate the argument and specific claims in a text, assessing whether the reasoning is sound and the evidence is relevant and sufficient to support the claims.	You will evaluate the strength of the author's claims and reasoning and identify any faults or weaknesses in them.
9. Analyze how two or more authors writing about the same topic shape their presentations of key information by emphasizing different evidence or advancing different interpretations of facts.	You will compare and contrast at least two different authors' treatments of the same subject.

Common Core State Standards	What It Means to You

RANGE OF READING AND LEVEL OF TEXT COMPLEXITY

10. By the end of the year, read and comprehend literary nonfiction in the grades 6–8 text complexity band proficiently, with scaffolding as needed at the high end of the range.	You will demonstrate the ability to read and understand grade-level appropriate literary nonfiction texts by the end of grade 7.

College and Career Readiness Anchor Standards for Writing

Common Core State Standards

TEXT TYPES AND PURPOSES

1. Write arguments to support claims in an analysis of substantive topics or texts, using valid reasoning and relevant and sufficient evidence.

2. Write informative/explanatory texts to examine and convey complex ideas and information clearly and accurately through the effective selection, organization, and analysis of content.

3. Write narratives to develop real or imagined experiences or events using effective technique, well-chosen details, and well-structured event sequences.

PRODUCTION AND DISTRIBUTION OF WRITING

4. Produce clear and coherent writing in which the development, organization, and style are appropriate to task, purpose, and audience.

5. Develop and strengthen writing as needed by planning, revising, editing, rewriting, or trying a new approach.

6. Use technology, including the Internet, to produce and publish writing and to interact and collaborate with others.

RESEARCH TO BUILD AND PRESENT KNOWLEDGE

7. Conduct short as well as more sustained research projects based on focused questions, demonstrating understanding of the subject under investigation.

8. Gather relevant information from multiple print and digital sources, assess the credibility and accuracy of each source, and integrate the information while avoiding plagiarism.

9. Draw evidence from literary and/or informational texts to support analysis, reflection, and research.

RANGE OF WRITING

10. Write routinely over extended time frames (time for research, reflection, and revision) and shorter time frames (a single sitting or a day or two) for a range of tasks, purposes, and audiences.

Writing Standards, Grade 7 Students

Common Core State Standards	What It Means to You
TEXT TYPES AND PURPOSES	
1. Write arguments to support claims with clear reasons and relevant evidence.	You will write and develop arguments with clear reasons and strong evidence that include
a. Introduce claim(s), acknowledge alternate or opposing claims, and organize the reasons and evidence logically.	a clear organization of claims and counterclaims
b. Support claim(s) with logical reasoning and relevant evidence, using accurate, credible sources and demonstrating an understanding of the topic or text.	strong, accurate support for claims
c. Use words, phrases, and clauses to create cohesion and clarify the relationships among claim(s), reasons, and evidence.	use of cohesive words, phrases, and clauses to link information
d. Establish and maintain a formal style.	a formal style
e. Provide a concluding statement or section that follows from and supports the argument presented.	a strong concluding statement that summarizes the argument
2. Write informative/explanatory texts to examine a topic and convey ideas, concepts, and information through the selection, organization, and analysis of relevant content.	You will write clear, well-organized, and thoughtful informative and explanatory texts with
a. Introduce a topic clearly, previewing what is to follow; organize ideas, concepts, and information, using strategies such as definition, classification, comparison/contrast, and cause/effect; include formatting (e.g., headings), graphics (e.g., charts, tables), and multimedia when useful to aiding comprehension.	a clear introduction and organization, including headings and graphic organizers (when appropriate)
b. Develop the topic with relevant facts, definitions, concrete details, quotations, or other information and examples.	sufficient supporting details and background information

Common Core State Standards	What It Means to You
c. Use appropriate transitions to create cohesion and clarify the relationships among ideas and concepts.	cohesive transitions to link ideas
d. Use precise language and domain-specific vocabulary to inform about or explain the topic.	precise language and relevant vocabulary
e. Establish and maintain a formal style.	a formal style
f. Provide a concluding statement or section that follows from and supports the information or explanation presented.	a strong conclusion that restates the importance or relevance of the topic
3. Write narratives to develop real or imagined experiences or events using effective technique, relevant descriptive details, and well-structured event sequences.	You will write clear, well-structured, detailed narrative texts that
a. Engage and orient the reader by establishing a context and point of view and introducing a narrator and/or characters; organize an event sequence that unfolds naturally and logically.	draw your readers in with a clear topic that unfolds logically
b. Use narrative techniques, such as dialogue, pacing, and description, to develop experiences, events, and/or characters.	use narrative techniques to develop and expand on events and/or characters
c. Use a variety of transition words, phrases, and clauses to convey sequence and signal shifts from one time frame or setting to another.	use a variety of transition words to clearly signal shifts between time frames or settings
d. Use precise words and phrases, relevant descriptive details, and sensory language to capture the action and convey experiences and events.	use precise words and sensory details that keep readers interested
e. Provide a conclusion that follows from and reflects on the narrated experiences or events.	have a strong conclusion that reflects on the topic

PRODUCTION AND DISTRIBUTION OF WRITING

4. Produce clear and coherent writing in which the development, organization, and style are appropriate to task, purpose, and audience. (Grade-specific expectations for writing types are defined in standards 1–3 above.)	You will produce writing that is appropriate to the task, purpose, and audience for whom you are writing.

Common Core State Standards	What It Means to You
5. With some guidance and support from peers and adults, develop and strengthen writing as needed by planning, revising, editing, rewriting, or trying a new approach, focusing on how well purpose and audience have been addressed.	With help from peers and adults, you will revise and refine your writing to address what is most important for your purpose and audience.
6. Use technology, including the Internet, to produce and publish writing and link to and cite sources as well as to interact and collaborate with others, including linking to and citing sources.	You will use technology to share your writing and to provide links to other relevant information.

RESEARCH TO BUILD AND PRESENT KNOWLEDGE

7. Conduct short research projects to answer a question, drawing on several sources and generating additional related, focused questions for further research and investigation.	You will conduct short research projects to answer a question using multiple sources and generating topics for further research.
8. Gather relevant information from multiple print and digital sources, using search terms effectively; assess the credibility and accuracy of each source; and quote or paraphrase the data and conclusions of others while avoiding plagiarism and following a standard format for citation.	You will effectively conduct searches to gather information from different sources and assess the strength of each source, following a standard format for citation.
9. Draw evidence from literary or informational texts to support analysis, reflection, and research. a. Apply *grade 7 Reading standards* to literature (e.g., "Compare and contrast a fictional portrayal of a time, place, or character and a historical account of the same period as a means of understanding how authors of fiction use or alter history"). b. Apply *grade 7 Reading standards* to literary nonfiction (e.g. "Trace and evaluate the argument and specific claims in a text, assessing whether the reasoning is sound and the evidence is relevant and sufficient to support the claims").	You will paraphrase, summarize, quote, and cite primary and secondary sources to support your analysis, reflection, and research.

RANGE OF WRITING

10. Write routinely over extended time frames (time for research, reflection, and revision) and shorter time frames (a single sitting or a day or two) for a range of discipline-specific tasks, purposes, and audiences.	You will write for many different purposes and audiences both over short and extended periods of time.

College and Career Readiness Anchor Standards for Speaking and Listening

Common Core State Standards

COMPREHENSION AND COLLABORATION

1. Prepare for and participate effectively in a range of conversations and collaborations with diverse partners, building on others' ideas and expressing their own clearly and persuasively.

2. Integrate and evaluate information presented in diverse media and formats, including visually, quantitatively, and orally.

3. Evaluate a speaker's point of view, reasoning, and use of evidence and rhetoric.

PRESENTATION OF KNOWLEDGE AND IDEAS

4. Present information, findings, and supporting evidence such that listeners can follow the line of reasoning and the organization, development, and style are appropriate to task, purpose, and audience.

5. Make strategic use of digital media and visual displays of data to express information and enhance understanding of presentations.

6. Adapt speech to a variety of contexts and communicative tasks, demonstrating command of formal English when indicated or appropriate.

Speaking and Listening Standards, Grade 7 Students

Common Core State Standards	What It Means to You
COMPREHENSION AND COLLABORATION	
1. Engage effectively in a range of collaborative discussions (one-on-one, in groups, and teacher-led) with diverse partners on grade 7 topics, texts, and issues, building on others' ideas and expressing their own clearly.	You will actively participate in a variety of discussions in which you
a. Come to discussions prepared, having read or researched material under study; explicitly draw on that preparation by referring to evidence on the topic, text, or issue to probe and reflect on ideas under discussion.	have read any relevant material beforehand and have come to the discussion prepared
b. Follow rules for collegial discussions, track progress toward specific goals and deadlines, and define individual roles as needed.	work with others to establish goals and processes within the group

Common Core State Standards	What It Means to You
c. Pose questions that elicit elaboration and respond to others' questions and comments with relevant observations and ideas that bring the discussion back on topic as needed.	ask and respond to questions and make observations that bring the discussion back to topic as needed
d. Acknowledge new information expressed by others and, when warranted, modify their own views.	respond to different perspectives and adjust your own views if necessary
2. Analyze the main ideas and supporting details presented in diverse media and formats (e.g., visually, quantitatively, orally) and explain how the ideas clarify a topic, text, or issue under study.	You will analyze main ideas and details of various media and relate them to a topic under study.
3. Delineate a speaker's argument and specific claims, evaluating the soundness of the reasoning and the relevance and sufficiency of the evidence.	You will evaluate a speaker's argument and identify any false reasoning or evidence.

PRESENTATION OF KNOWLEDGE AND IDEAS

Common Core State Standards	What It Means to You
4. Present claims and findings, emphasizing salient points in a focused, coherent manner with pertinent descriptions, facts, details, and examples; use appropriate eye contact, adequate volume, and clear pronunciation.	You will organize and present information to your listeners in a logical sequence and engaging style that is appropriate to your task and audience.
5. Include multimedia components and visual displays in presentations to clarify claims and findings and emphasize salient points.	You will use digital media to enhance and add interest to presentations.
6. Adapt speech to a variety of contexts and tasks, demonstrating command of formal English when indicated or appropriate.	You will adapt the formality of your speech appropriately.

College and Career Readiness Anchor Standards for Language

Common Core State Standards

CONVENTIONS OF STANDARD ENGLISH

1. Demonstrate command of the conventions of standard English grammar and usage when writing or speaking.

2. Demonstrate command of the conventions of standard English capitalization, punctuation, and spelling when writing.

KNOWLEDGE OF LANGUAGE

3. Apply knowledge of language to understand how language functions in different contexts, to make effective choices for meaning or style, and to comprehend more fully when reading or listening.

VOCABULARY ACQUISITION AND USE

4. Determine or clarify the meaning of unknown and multiple-meaning words and phrases by using context clues, analyzing meaningful word parts, and consulting general and specialized reference materials, as appropriate.

5. Demonstrate understanding of figurative language, word relationships, and nuances in word meanings.

6. Acquire and use accurately a range of general academic and domain-specific words and phrases sufficient for reading, writing, speaking, and listening at the college- and career-readiness level; demonstrate independence in gathering vocabulary knowledge when encountering an unknown term important to comprehension or expression.

Language Standards, Grade 7 Students

Common Core State Standards	What It Means to You
CONVENTIONS OF STANDARD ENGLISH	
1. Demonstrate command of the conventions of standard English grammar and usage when writing or speaking.	You will correctly understand and use the conventions of English grammar and usage, including
a. Explain the function of phrases and clauses in general and their function in specific sentences.	explaining the function of phrases and clauses
b. Choose among simple, compound, complex, and compound-complex sentences to signal differing relationships among ideas.	using a variety of sentence structures
c. Place phrases and clauses within a sentence, recognizing and correcting misplaced and dangling modifiers.	correctly placing phrases and clauses in sentences

Common Core State Standards	What It Means to You
2. Demonstrate command of the conventions of standard English capitalization, punctuation, and spelling when writing.	You will correctly use the conventions of English capitalization, punctuation, and spelling, including
a. Use a comma to separate coordinate adjectives (e.g., *It was a fascinating, enjoyable movie* but not *He wore an old[,] green shirt*).	commas
b. Spell correctly.	spelling

KNOWLEDGE OF LANGUAGE

3. Use knowledge of language and its conventions when writing, speaking, reading, or listening.	You will apply your knowledge of language in different contexts by
a. Choose language that expresses ideas precisely and concisely, recognizing and eliminating wordiness and redundancy.	choosing precise and concise language to avoid wordiness or stating the same thing more than once

VOCABULARY ACQUISITION AND USE

4. Determine or clarify the meaning of unknown and multiple-meaning words and phrases based on *grade 7 reading and content,* choosing flexibly from a range of strategies.	You will understand the meaning of grade-level appropriate words and phrases by
a. Use context (e.g., the overall meaning of a sentence or paragraph; a word's position or function in a sentence) as a clue to the meaning of a word or phrase.	using context clues
b. Use common, grade-appropriate Greek or Latin affixes and roots as clues to the meaning of a word (e.g., *belligerent, bellicose, rebel*).	using Greek or Latin roots
c. Consult general and specialized reference materials (e.g., dictionaries, glossaries, thesauruses), both print and digital, to find the pronunciation of a word or determine or clarify its precise meaning or its part of speech.	using reference materials
d. Verify the preliminary determination of the meaning of a word or phrase (e.g., by checking the inferred meaning in context or in a dictionary).	inferring and verifying the meanings of words in context

Common Core State Standards	What It Means to You
5. Demonstrate understanding of figurative language, word relationships, and nuances in word meanings.	You will understand figurative language, word relationships, and slight differences in word meanings by
a. Interpret figures of speech (e.g., literary, biblical, and mythological allusions) in context.	interpreting figures of speech in context
b. Use the relationship between particular words (e.g., synonym/antonym, analogy) to better understand each of the words.	analyzing relationships between words
c. Distinguish among the connotations (associations) of words with similar denotations (definitions) (e.g., *refined, respectful, polite, diplomatic, condescending*).	distinguishing among words with similar definitions
6. Acquire and use accurately grade-appropriate general academic and domain-specific words and phrases; gather vocabulary knowledge when considering a word or phrase important to comprehension or expression.	You will learn and use grade-appropriate vocabulary.

©Kevin C. Downs/Photolibrary/Getty Images

Bold Actions

❝ Be bold, take courage . . . and be strong of soul. ❞

—Ovid

STREAM TO START

Motivate students to read the collection texts and spark their curiosity about the collection by playing the video and watching it in class. After students view the video, ask them to think about two things they hope to learn about taking bold actions and risking failure. Call on volunteers to share their responses.

PERFORMANCE TASK PREVIEW

Point out to students that they will complete two performance tasks at the end of the collection. The performance tasks will require them to further analyze the selections in the collection and to synthesize ideas about these analyses. Students will present their findings in a variety of products.

ACADEMIC VOCABULARY

View It!

Professional Development Podcast:
Academic Vocabulary

Students can acquire facility with the academic vocabulary words through frequent, repeated exposure as they analyze and discuss the selections in the collection. Academic vocabulary words can be used in the instructional contexts shown below. This will enable students to incorporate the academic vocabulary words into their working vocabulary.

- Collaborative Discussion sections at the end of each selection
- Analyzing the Text questions for each selection
- Selection-level Performance Tasks
- Vocabulary instruction exercises (for Critical Vocabulary and/or for Vocabulary Strategy)
- Language Conventions
- End-of-collection Performance Tasks for all selections in the collection

ASK STUDENTS to review the Academic Vocabulary word list for this collection. You may wish to pronounce each word aloud so students hear the correct pronunciation. Then, discuss the definitions and the related forms for each word. Remind students that they will encounter these five academic vocabulary words throughout the collection.

Bold Actions

In this collection, you will explore what it means to face challenges fearlessly, even if it means failing in the attempt.

Stream to Start

fyi hmhfyi.com

Channel One News®

COLLECTION
PERFORMANCE TASK Preview

After reading the selections in this collection, you will have the opportunity to complete two performance tasks:

- In one, you will write a fictional narrative with a main character who boldly attempts to overcome a tremendous challenge.
- In the second, you will write and present an argument about the rewards and risks of undertaking bold actions.

ACADEMIC VOCABULARY

Study the words and their definitions in the chart below. You will use these words as you discuss and write about the texts in this collection.

Word	Definition	Related Forms
aspect (ăs´pĕkt) *n.*	a characteristic or feature of something	aspectual
cultural (kŭl´chər-əl) *adj.*	of or relating to culture or cultivation	agriculture, culture, cultured, multicultural
evaluate (ĭ-văl´yōō-āt´) *v.*	to examine something carefully to judge its value or worth	evaluation, evaluator, evaluative
resource (rē´sôrs´) *n.*	something that can be used for support or help	resources, resourceful, natural resources
text (tĕkst) *n.*	a literary work that is regarded as an object of critical analysis	textbook, textual, texture, textile

2

myNotebook

As students read, analyze, and discuss the texts in this collection, encourage them to create a **my**WordList folder in **my**Notebook to build their own personal word lists.

- **Annotate** Students can highlight vocabulary terms and other unfamiliar words and save each highlighted term to **my**Notebook.
- **Organize** Within **my**Notebook, students can drag each word into the **my**WordList folder.
- **Elaborate** Ask students to add details to the entry for each word, such as a definition, other forms of the word, and a sample sentence.

English Language Support

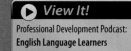
ENGAGE WITH THE COLLECTION TOPIC

Draw students' attention to the title of the collection: Bold Actions. Explain that *bold* means "confident and courageous." Tell students that this collection focuses on people who faced challenges with courage and determination.

ACCESS PRIOR KNOWLEDGE Ask students why people take risks to face challenges. Discuss the rewards and the costs of facing challenges.

TAKING NOTES

Use this strategy to help students learn how to take notes as they read or discuss a text. Explain that taking good notes will not only help them remember, review, and organize important ideas and details, but will also help them better understand a complex text.

- *First*, provide students with a graphic organizer they can use for notetaking, such as a story map, timeline, character chart, or argument frame. Explain the purposes of each section of the organizer.
- *Then*, display a passage from a text and ask students to take notes in the graphic organizer. Remind them to write down important and memorable ideas and details in their appropriate locations.

- *Next*, have students in small groups present each point on their graphic organizers and explain why they included each. Tell groups that their task is to determine which notes are accurate, significant, and useful.
- *Finally*, distribute one blank graphic organizer to each group; have the groups complete it together using the conclusions they reached in their discussions.

 Collection 1 Digital Resources for English Language Support

LANGUAGE WORKSHOP
Designated English Learners

You may use the digital Teacher Resources > Language Workshop to support English learners in summarizing texts, applying an understanding of language resources, and exchanging information by asking and answering questions.

Text in FOCUS **VIDEOS**

These videos will help students learn how to build background and how to analyze an important idiom. Have students use **Zoom In Practice** to apply those skills.

my SmartPlanner | **eBook** | **myNotebook** | **myWriteSmart** | **fyi** hmhfyi.com

Collection 1 Lessons	Media	Teach and Practice
Student Edition | **eBook**	▶ Video Links **HISTORY** **A&E** **Channel One News**	**Close Reading and Evidence Tracking**
ANCHOR TEXT Short Story by Theodore Taylor **"Rogue Wave"**	🔊 **Audio** "Rogue Wave"	**Close Read Screencasts** · Modeled Discussion 1 (lines 75–82) · Modeled Discussion 2 (lines 154–161) · Close Read application PDF (lines 351–362) — **Text in Focus** · Building Background (line 67) **Strategies for Annotation** · Make Inferences · Analyze Story Elements: Plot and Setting · Latin Roots
CLOSE READER Short Story by Eleanora E. Tate **"Big Things Come in Small Packages"**	🔊 **Audio** "Big Things Come in Small Packages"	
Online News Article by Paul Harris **"Parents of Rescued Teenage Sailor Abby Sunderland Accused of Risking Her Life"**	🔊 **Audio** "Parents of Rescued Teenage Sailor Abby Sunderland Accused of Risking her Life"	**Strategies for Annotation** · Analyze Structure · Trace and Evaluate an Argument
Editorial by Joanna Weiss **"Ship of Fools"**	🔊 **Audio** "Ship of Fools"	
TV News Interview by CBS News **"Was Abby Too Young to Sail?"**		
CLOSE READER Essay by Robert Medina **"Finding Your Everest"**	🔊 **Audio** "Finding Your Everest"	
ANCHOR TEXT Greek Myth retold by Sally Benson **"The Flight of Icarus"**	🔊 **Audio** "The Flight of Icarus"	**Close Read Screencasts** · Modeled Discussion (lines 35–47) · Close Read application PDF (lines 63–75) — **Text in Focus** · Analyzing Language (line 95) **Strategies for Annotation** · Determine Theme · Analyze Story Elements: Myth · Noun Suffixes -ty and -ity
CLOSE READER Greek Myth retold by Olivia E. Coolidge **"Arachne"**	▶ **HISTORY®** "Greek Gods" ▶ **HISTORY®** "Spartans Deconstructed" 🔊 **Audio** "Arachne"	
Poem by Stephen Dobyns **"Icarus's Flight"**	🔊 **Audio** "Icarus's Flight"	**Strategies for Annotation** · Meaning of Words and Phrases: Alliteration
Informational Text by Patricia and Fredrick McKissack **"Women in Aviation"**	▶ **HISTORY®** "Bessie Coleman" 🔊 **Audio** "Women in Aviation"	**Strategies for Annotation** · Text Evidence and Draw Conclusions · Determine Author's Purpose · Connotations and Denotations
Collection 1 Performance Tasks: **A** Write a Fictional Narrative **B** Present an Argument	**fyi** hmhfyi.com	**Interactive Lessons** **A** Writing Narratives — **B** Writing Arguments **B** Giving a Presentation **B** Using Media In a Presentation

	For Systematic Coverage of Writing and Speaking & Listening Standards	**Interactive Lessons** Writing as a Process Participating in Collaborative Discussions

	Assess		Extend	Reteach
Performance Task		✓ *Assess It Online!*	**Teacher eBook**	**Teacher eBook**
Writing Activity: Movie Outline		Selection Test	**Analyze Story Elements: Plot and Conflict > Interactive Whiteboard Lesson** > Plot and Conflict	**Analyze Story Elements: Plot and Setting > Level Up Tutorial >** Setting: Effect on Plot
Media Activity: Blogs		Selection Test	**How to Create a Blog > Interactive Lessons** > Producing and Publishing with Technology	**Analyze Presentations of Information**
Writing Activity: Graphic Comic		Selection Test	**Analyze Story Elements: Characterization >Interactive Whiteboard Lesson >** Character Development **Interactive Graphic Organizer** > Freeform Web	**Determine Theme >Level Up Tutorial >** Theme
Speaking Activity: Oral Response		Selection Test	**Analyze Form: Scansion >Level Up Tutorial** > Rhythm	**Analyze Form: Poetry >Interactive Whiteboard Lessons >** Form in Poetry **Interactive Graphic Organizer >** Comparison-Contrast Chart
Writing Activity: Report		Selection Test	**Determine Facts and Opinions**	**Determine Author's Purpose > Level Up Tutorials >** Author's Purpose
A Write a Fictional Narrative **B** Present an Argument		Collection Test		

Lesson Assessments Writing as a Process Participating in Collaborative Discussions	**Standards Support and Enrichment** **For Designated English Language Instruction**	For more standards instruction and practice, see Teacher Resources > Standards Support and Enrichment. To provide support for English Learners during Designated English Language instruction, use the lessons found in Teacher Resources > Language Workshop.

Collection 1 Lessons	Key Learning Objective	Performance Task	Vocabulary Strategy
ANCHOR TEXT **Short Story by Theodore Taylor** "Rogue Wave," p. 3A **Lexile 980L**	**The student will be able to . . .** identify, analyze, and make inferences about the elements of plot in a short story.	Writing Activity: Movie Outline	Latin Roots
Online News Article by Paul Harris **Lexile 1110L** "Parents of Rescued Teenage Sailor Abby Sunderland Accused of Risking Her Life," p. 19A	**The student will be able to . . .** analyze and compare news stories about the same event from various sources.	Media Activity: Blogs	
Editorial by Joanna Weiss **Lexile 1120L** "Ship of Fools," p. 19A			
TV News Interview by CBS News "Was Abby Too Young to Sail?" p. 19A			
ANCHOR TEXT **Greek Myth retold by Sally Benson** **Lexile 1110L** "The Flight of Icarus," p. 31A	**The student will be able to . . .** analyze the elements of a myth and to determine two or more themes.	Writing Activity: Graphic Comic	Noun Suffixes -ty and -ity
Poem by Stephen Dobyns "Icarus's Flight," p. 39A	**The student will be able to . . .** understand how the elements of form and the use of alliteration emphasize ideas and meaning in a poem.	Speaking Activity: Oral Response	
Informational Text by Patricia and Fredrick McKissack **Lexile 1150L** "Women in Aviation," p. 43A	**The student will be able to . . .** identify, analyze, and draw conclusions about an author's purpose for writing informational texts.	Writing Activity: Informative Report	Connotations and Denotations

Collection 1 Performance Tasks:

A Write a Fictional Narrative
B Present an Argument

Language Conventions	English Language Support	Differentiated Instruction	CLOSE READER Selection
Sentence Structure	• Analyze Language • Read Closely • Improve Reading Fluency • Support Opinions • Combine Sentences	**For Students with Disabilities:** Sequence of Events **For Standard English Learners:** Past-Tense Verbs **When Students Struggle:** Plot and Suspense **To Challenge Students:** Discuss Themes	Short Story by Eleanora E. Tate "Big Things Come in Small Packages," p. 18b **Lexile 900L**
	• Analyze Language • Analyze Structure • Take Notes	**When Students Struggle:** • Reasons For/Against • Claims and Reasons	Essay by Robert Medina "Finding Your Everest," p. 30b **Lexile 1160L**
Commas and Coordinate Adjectives	• Analyze Language: Description • Use Coordinate Adjectives		Greek Myth retold by Olivia E. Coolidge "Arachne," p. 38b **Lexile 1250L**
	• Analyze Language	**When Students Struggle:** Rhythm in Poetry **For Standard English Learners:** Pronunciation	
Subordinate Clauses	• Analyze Language • Support Opinions • Combine Clauses • Determine Facts and Opinions	**When Students Struggle:** Author's Purpose **For Standard English Learners:** • Contractions • Prepositions **For Students with Disabilities:** Cite Text Evidence	
A Active and Passive Voice **B** Noun Phrases	**A** Plan a Fictional Narrative Plot Sequence Text Structure **B** Plan to Present an Argument Link Ideas Adapt Speech Use Language Resources	**A** **For Standard English Learners:** Add Dialogue **When Students Struggle:** Add Sensory Details **For Students with Disabilities:** Create Storyboards **To Challenge Students:** Change the Point of View **B** **When Students Struggle:** Integrate Visuals **For Standard English Learners:** Use Stress Patterns **For Students with Disabilities:** Use Visual Cues **To Challenge Students:** Debate the Topic	

ANCHOR TEXT # Rogue Wave

my **Smart**Planner — Create lesson plans and access resources online.

Short Story by Theodore Taylor

Why This Text?

Understanding the elements of plot and learning to make inferences to "read between the lines" helps students experience fiction more fully and deepens their experience with all great works of literature. This lesson explores the interaction of plot elements in an adventure story.

▶ **View It!**

Professional Development Podcast:

Text-Dependent Analysis

Key Learning Objective: The student will be able to identify, analyze, and make inferences about the elements of plot in a short story.

For practice and application:

Close Reader selection:
"Big Things Come in Small Packages"
Short Story by Eleanora E. Tate

RL 1 Cite textual evidence.

RL 3 Analyze how elements of a story interact.

RL 4 Determine meanings of words and phrases as they are used in a text.

SL 4 Present claims and findings.

W 3 Write narratives.

L 1b Choose among simple, compound, complex, and compound-complex sentences.

L 4a Use context as a clue to the meaning of a word or phrase.

L 4b Use Greek or Latin affixes and roots as clues to word meanings.

L 4c Consult general reference materials.

▲ ## Text Complexity Rubric

Quantitative Measures	**Rogue Wave** **Lexile:** 980L
Qualitative Measures	**Levels of Meaning/Purpose** ●—●—⬤—●—→ multiple levels of meaning
	Structure ●—●—⬤—●—→ some unconventional story structure elements
	Language Conventionality and Clarity ●—●—⬤—●—→ increased unfamiliar, academic, or domain-specific words
	Knowledge Demands ●—●—●—⬤—→ distinctly unfamiliar situation
Reader/Task Considerations	• Teacher determined • Vary by individual reader and type of text • See the Text X-Ray for suggested Reader/Task Considerations.

English Language Support Before teaching, use the Text X-Ray below for an overview of the text's complexity. The Text X-Ray and the supports and scaffolds in the Teacher's Edition will help you guide students of different skill levels.

Meaning Making

Language Development

Effective Expression

Content Knowledge

Foundational Skills

Text Complexity: Qualitative Measures

Levels of Meaning/Purpose

multiple levels of meaning

Help students make inferences.

- Teacher's Edition side notes, pp. 5, 7, 8, 11, 12, 14, 15
- English Language Support, pp. 8, 11
- Close Read Screencasts, p. 3
- Strategies for Annotation, p. 7
- Make Inferences, p. 15

To reteach how to make inferences, see

▶ *Use It! Level Up* Tutorial: Making Inferences

***ZOOM IN ON* MAKING INFERENCES** Explain that authors present details to describe characters and events. Tell students that they can use these details to **make inferences**, or logical guesses, about characters and the situations they face.

- Read aloud lines 11–16 and 37–50 as students follow along. Pause to clarify nautical terms as necessary.
- Guide students to identify details that hint at Scoot's abilities.
- Have small groups use these details to make inferences about Scoot's skill as a sailor.
- Summarize findings in a whole-class discussion and list inferences on the board. *(Scoot is careful and comfortable below deck. She has experience with smaller vessels and she has sailed the* Sea Dog *alone at night. Although she's on her first extended trip, she's no beginner.)*

Structure

some unconventional story structure elements

Help students analyze story elements.

- Teacher's Edition side notes, pp. 3, 4, 6, 7, 9, 10, 12, 13, 14, 15
- English Language Support, pp. 4, 9, 10
- Close Read Screencasts, p. 3
- Strategies for Annotation, pp. 12, 15
- When Students Struggle, p. 11
- Analyze Story Elements: Plot and Conflict, p. 15

To reteach plot and setting, see

- Analyze Story Elements: Plot and Setting, p. 18a

▶ *Use It! Level Up* Tutorial: Setting: Effect on Plot
Interactive Whiteboard Lesson: Plot and Conflict

***ZOOM IN ON* ANALYZING SETTING AND PLOT** Explain that the **plot** is a series of related events in a story. **Setting** is the time and place of these events. Note that the setting often presents **conflicts**, or problems that characters must overcome. Point out that because Scoot is inside the boat and Sully is outside, they must solve different problems.

- Have small groups read the story and use a two-column chart to keep track of plot events and the settings in which they occur.
- Monitor each group's progress.
- After groups finish, have them discuss how the author's presentation of plot events builds suspense in the story.

Language Conventionality and Clarity

increased unfamiliar, academic, or domain-specific words

Teach unfamiliar vocabulary in context.

- Teacher's Edition Critical Vocabulary notes, pp. 4, 5, 17
- English Language Support, pp. 3, 8
- Applying Academic Vocabulary, p. 8
- Strategies for Annotation, p. 17
- Vocabulary Strategy: Latin Roots, p. 17

Guide students to analyze the language and sentence structure of the short story.

- Teacher's Edition side notes, pp. 6, 18
- English Language Support, pp. 4, 9, 18
- Language Conventions: Sentence Structure, p. 18

ZOOM IN ON **USING CONTEXT** Remind students that when they encounter unfamiliar words or phrases, they can look for context clues in the surrounding sentences to help explain the meaning. Have pairs locate each of the terms below, find context clues in the surrounding text, and suggest a definition.

- *trough*, line 7 (clues: *bottom, crest*)
- *schooner*, line 10 (clues: *boats, aboard*)
- *pitch-poled*, line 79 (clue: *violently, end-over-end*)

Ask pairs to share their definitions. Point out that often it is not as important to know the exact definition as it is to comprehend the overall meaning of the sentence.

Knowledge Demands

distinctly unfamiliar situation

Help students understand the geographical and physical context of the story.

- Teacher's Edition Background note, p. 3

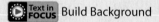 Build Background

ZOOM IN ON **VISUALIZING SETTING** Help students understand and **visualize,** or make mental pictures of, the setting in which the story takes place. Explain that Scoot and Sully are sailing in the Pacific Ocean, 15 miles west of the Mexican coast. When students encounter the lines below, read them aloud and ask students to describe what they visualize.

- Lines 83–91 and lines 120–129 describe Scoot's location after the accident. She is trapped inside the upside-down boat as the cabin fills with seawater.
- Lines 92–101 describe how Sully is thrown into the sea when the wave hits.

Suggested Reader/Task Considerations

Consider the following before assigning this short story to students.

- Do students have the attention necessary to read and comprehend a story of this length?
- Do students have the necessary vocabulary to understand the plot and setting?

ZOOM IN ON **SUPPORTING COMPREHENSION**

- Break the story into manageable chunks. Have students in mixed-ability groups read the story. Provide opportunities for students to discuss the text after reading.
- The text makes extensive use of nautical terminology to describe the setting and plot. In addition to the terms cited in the footnotes and sidebars, list and help students define the following common terms: *hatch* (line 14), *starboard* (line 41), *watch* (line 49), *belay* (line 52), *hull* (line 53), *tack* (line 68), *port* (line 70), *bulkhead* (line 84).

CLOSE READ

Background Have students read the Background note. Explain that this short story contains many nautical terms specific to recreational sailing. Point out that while knowing all the terms is not necessary, it may be helpful for students to consult a dictionary or manual of nautical terms as they read. Finally, explain that the custom among sailors is to refer to boats using the female pronouns *she* and *her*, which Theodore Taylor follows in the story.

SETTING A PURPOSE Direct students to use the Setting a Purpose prompt to focus their reading. Remind them to write any questions they have as they read.

Analyze Story Elements: Plot and Setting (LINES 1–10, 11–16)
RL 1, RL 3

Explain to students that most stories follow a series of events, called the **plot.** The first part of a plot is called the **exposition,** where the author introduces the **setting,** or time and place of the action, and the characters. Point out that in this story, the author provides background information before introducing the first character.

A **ASK STUDENTS** to reread lines 1–10. Why might the author include this information? *(It reveals possible impending danger to sailors near Baja California.)*

Note that the second paragraph introduces a main character and adds details that hint at the setting.

B **CITE TEXT EVIDENCE** Have students reread lines 11–16 to cite text evidence that identifies the setting. *(The author uses nautical terms, such as* galley *and* companionway, *and the phrase "always a good idea in offshore sailing." These suggest that the setting is the ocean on the* Old Sea Dog, *a "thirty-foot Baba type" sailboat.)*

English Language Support

Read Closely Pronounce the word *rogue*. Tell students that a *rogue* wave is one that differs from others in a dangerous way. Explain that *rogue* can be used as an adjective or a noun. Have small groups discuss the following questions.

- How might a rogue wave be dangerous?
- How can a person be a rogue? Would you trust a rogue to treat you fairly?

Background *This adventure story features a cutter-rigged sailboat. Cutter-rigged boats are small sailing yachts, each with a single mast for the main sail and smaller sails up front. Cutters can be equipped with a cabin that usually includes a small kitchen, called a galley. Author* **Theodore Taylor** *(1921–2006) wrote many stories about self-reliant characters who face great challenges. His best-known book,* The Cay, *depicts the struggles of a young shipwrecked sailor.*

Rogue Wave

Short Story by Theodore Taylor

SETTING A PURPOSE Pay attention to the details and events that make this story an adventure. As you read, think about how the author builds a sense of excitement and anticipation throughout the short story.

As you read, save new words to *my*WordList.

A killer wave, known to mariners as a "rogue wave," was approaching a desolate area of Baja California below Ensenada. It had been born off the east coast of Australia during a violent storm; it had traveled almost 7,000 miles at a speed of 20.83 miles an hour. Driven by an unusual pattern of easterly winds, it was a little over 800 feet in length and measured about 48 feet from the bottom of its trough to its crest. On its passage across the Pacific, it had already killed thirteen people, mostly fishermen in small boats, but also an
10 *entire French family of five aboard a 48-foot schooner . . .*

Melissa "Scoot" Atkins went below into the *Old Sea Dog's* tiny galley, moving down the three steps of the companionway, closing the two solid entry doors behind her, always a good

(t) ©Don Romero/Romero Fine Portraiture

Rogue Wave   **3**

Close Read Screencasts

Modeled Discussions

Have students click the *Close Read* icons in their eBooks to access two screencasts in which readers discuss and annotate the following key passages:

- It was already too late . . . (lines 75–82)
- He fought back tears of frustration . . . (lines 154–161)

As a class, view and discuss at least one of these videos. Then have students pair up to do an independent close read of an additional passage—"A big sailboat, beating south . . ." (lines 351–362).

Analyze Story Elements: Plot and Setting (LINES 17–36)

RL 1,
RL 3

Explain that details help readers picture the setting and can also influence events and characters.

C **CITE TEXT EVIDENCE** Have students find details in lines 17–36 that describe the setting. Why is the setting potentially dangerous? *(Sunlight glitters off the waves as the boat glides over the swells. But the characters are all alone on the ocean, a powerful force.)*

English Language Support

Point out the italic type in lines 17–31. Ask how the details in this paragraph fit into the narrative.

ASK STUDENTS why different type is used for this paragraph. *(It interrupts the story to provide facts.)* Have students identify the main idea of this paragraph. *(Rogue waves are dangerous and unpredictable.)*

CRITICAL VOCABULARY

swell: The author uses *swells* to describe the motion of the ocean's surface. *Swells* are longer, rolling waves that cover a vast area.

ASK STUDENTS how the swells might affect the *Old Sea Dog*. *(The boat is probably gently rising and falling on the swells as it moves through the water.)*

deck: Scoot is in the galley, which is part of the boat's interior cabin below deck.

ASK STUDENTS what Scoot would see if she were on deck. *(From the boat's open upper surface, Scoot would see the sails, sun, sky, and ocean swells.)*

---

idea in offshore sailing. The three horizontal hatch boards that were on top of the doors were also firmly in place, securing the thirty-foot Baba type against sudden invasion of seawater.

Rogues and sneakers have been around since the beginning of the oceans, and the earliest sea literature makes note of "giant" waves. The U.S. Navy manual Practical Methods for Observing and Forecasting Ocean Waves *says, "In any wave system, after a long enough time, an exceptional high one will occur. These monstrous out-sized waves are improbable but still possible and the exact time of occurrence can never be predicted." Naval hydrography[1] studies indicate that waves 15 to 25 feet high qualify for "sneaker" or "sleeper" status; the freak rogue is up to 100 feet or over. As waters slowly warm they seem to be occurring more frequently. In 1995 the* Queen Elizabeth 2 *(the QE2), the great British passenger liner, encountered a 95-foot rogue south of Newfoundland. More than 900 feet long, the QE2 rode over it, but her captain said it looked like they were sailing into the White Cliffs of Dover.*

Sullivan Atkins, Scoot's oldest brother, was steering the cutter-rigged boat on a northerly course about fifteen miles off desolate Cabo Colnett, south of Ensenada. Under a brilliant sun, the glittering blue Pacific rose and fell in long, slick **swells,** a cold light breeze holding steady.

Below **deck** Scoot was listening to Big Sandy & His Fly-Rite Boys doing "Swingin' West," and singing along with them while slicing leftover steak from last night's meal. They'd grilled it on a small charcoal ring that was mounted outboard on the starboard side[2] at the stern, trailing sparks into the water. The *Sea Dog* had every blessed thing, including a barbecue pit, she marveled.

Scoot was learning how to be a deep-water sailor. She was fourteen years old and pretty, with dark hair. Though small in size, not even five feet, she was strong. She'd started off with eight-foot Sabots. On this trip, her first aboard the *Sea Dog,* she'd manned the wheel for most of the three days they'd been under way. She'd stood four-hour watches at night. Sully was a good teacher.

swell
(swĕl) *n.*
A *swell* is a long, unbroken wave.

deck
(dĕk) *n.* The *deck* is the platform on a ship or boat where people stand.

---

[1] **hydrography:** the scientific description and analysis of the earth's surface waters.

[2] **outboard on the starboard side:** positioned outside and on the right side of the boat.

English Language Support

Analyze Language Using a whiteboard, project lines 1–10 and highlight in yellow the following: *killer wave,* "*rogue wave,*" *800 feet in length* and *measured about 48 feet from the bottom of its trough to its crest.*

- Underline *killer wave* and "*rogue wave*" and explain that both name the same thing. Guide students to understand that although *killer* and *rogue* are not synonyms, in this context both express danger to mariners, or sailors.

- Ask pairs to identify how the third highlighted phrase modifies the underlined terms. *(It describes the size of the wave.)* Tell them to use context clues to define *trough* and *crest* and then to confirm their definitions in a dictionary. Encourage volunteers to describe the danger a wave of this size presents to boaters.

- Highlight the next sentence in green. Have students use context clues to define *passage* and *schooner.* Then ask them to rewrite the sentence in their own words.

It was one of those perfect days to be out, Sully thought: the three Dacron sails belayed and whispering, white bow waves singing pleasant songs as the fiberglass hull, tilting to starboard, sliced through the ocean. It was a day filled with goodness, peace, and beauty. They'd come south as far as Cabo Colnett, turning back north only an hour ago. They'd sailed from Catalina Island's Avalon Harbor, the *Sea Dog's* home port, out in the channel off Los Angeles. Sully had borrowed the boat from a family friend, Beau Tucker,
60 a stockbroker with enough money to outfit it and maintain it properly. Built by Ta-Shing, of Taiwan, she was heavy and sturdy, with a teakwood deck and handsome teakwood interior, and the latest in **navigation** equipment. Sully had sailed her at least a dozen times. He'd been around boats, motor and sail, for many of his nineteen years. He thought the *Old Sea Dog* was the best, in her category, that he'd ever piloted.

As he was about to complete a northeast tack, Sully's attention was drawn to a squadron of seagulls diving on
70 small fish about a hundred yards off the port bow, and he did not see the giant wave that had crept up silently behind the *Sea Dog.* But a split second before it lifted the boat like a carpenter's chip, he sensed something behind him and glanced backward, toward the towering wall of shining water.

It was already too late to shout a warning to Scoot so she could escape from the cabin; too late to do anything except hang on to the wheel with both hands; too late even to pray. He did manage a yell as the *Sea Dog* became vertical. She rose up the surface of the wall stern first and then pitch-poled
80 violently, end over end, the bow **submerging** and the boat going upside down, taking Sully and Scoot with it, the forty-foot mast, sails intact, now pointing toward the bottom.

Scoot was hurled upward, legs and arms flying, her head striking the after galley bulkhead and then the companionway steps and the interior deck, which was now the ceiling. She instantly blacked out.

Everything loose in the cabin was scattered around what had been the overhead. Water was pouring in and was soon lapping at Scoot's chin. It was coming from a four-inch
90 **porthole** that had not been dogged securely and a few other smaller points of entry.

D navigation
(năv´ĭ-gā´shən) *n.* The *navigation* of a ship or boat is the act of guiding it along a planned course.

submerge
(səb-mûrg´) *v.* When something *submerges,* it becomes covered by water.

porthole
(pôrt´hōl) *n.* A *porthole* is a circular window on a boat or ship.

Rogue Wave 5

A killer wave, known to mariners as a "rogue wave," was approaching . . . it was a little over 800 feet in length and measured about 48 feet from the bottom of its trough to its crest. On its passage across the Pacific, it had already killed thirteen people, mostly fishermen in small boats, but also an entire French family of five aboard a 48-foot schooner . . .

CLOSE READ

Make Inferences (LINES 63–67)   RL 7

Explain to students that as they read they can make **inferences,** or logical guesses based on details in the text and their own knowledge. Making inferences helps them to understand aspects of a story that are not directly described by the author. To support their inferences, they should **cite textual evidence,** or provide specific information from the text.

D CITE TEXT EVIDENCE Have students reread lines 63–67 and use the textual evidence to support an inference about Sully's abilities as a sailor. *(Sully had sailed the* Old Sea Dog *many times already and been around boats most of his life. People with a lot of experience at something are usually experts. So, Sully seems to be an expert sailor. He'd be very capable of handling trouble at sea.)*

CRITICAL VOCABULARY

navigation: The *Old Sea Dog* is an impressive sailing vessel with the "latest in navigation equipment."

ASK STUDENTS why this feature would make Sully feel confident and safe in the middle of the ocean. *(A boat with good navigation equipment is easy to navigate, or reliably steer and direct its course.)*

submerge: The front end, or bow, of the *Old Sea Dog* is submerged when the rogue wave hits.

porthole: Water is pouring into the galley from a porthole that has not been locked, or "dogged."

ASK STUDENTS to explain why an open porthole would be a problem for a boat that is submerged. *(Portholes are windows in a boat's cabin. If the boat is submerged and a porthole is open, then water will come into the boat's cabin.)*

 English Language Support

Building Background (LINE 67)

Have students view the **Text In Focus** video on this page of their eBook to build background that will help them better comprehend the story. Then have students use **Text In Focus Practice** to apply what they have learned.

Analyze Story Elements: Plot and Conflict (LINES 94–107)

RL 1, RL 3

Explain to students that in most stories, characters must solve or deal with a problem. This problem is called the **conflict,** a struggle between opposing forces. The sudden appearance of the rogue wave has created an **external conflict**—a struggle with an outside force.

 CITE TEXT EVIDENCE Have students reread lines 94–107 and use text evidence to identify the external conflict. *(The rogue wave has tipped over the* Sea Dog. *Judging by the locked cabin doors that Sully can't open, Scoot is trapped inside the cabin. He concludes that the cabin is probably filling with water. So, the external conflict is Sully's struggle to get inside the cabin to free his sister. For Scoot, the conflict is the same—she must find a way out.)*

Determine Meanings

RL 1, RL 4

(LINES 94–101)

Explain to students that a **simile** is a figure of speech that makes a comparison between two unlike things using the word *like* or *as.* Point out that the author uses a number of similes in this story to help create vivid images for the reader.

 CITE TEXT EVIDENCE Have students reread lines 94–101 and identify the simile. Then ask them to explain the effect this choice of words creates in describing the setting. *(The simile "like a cork" suggests that the* Sea Dog *is now a small object floating helplessly in the water. It has the effect of underscoring how alone and helpless Sully and Scoot are now.)*

Sully's feet were caught under forestay sailcloth, plastered around his face, but then he managed to shove clear and swim upward, breaking water. He looked at the mound of upside-down hull, bottom to the sky, unable to believe that the fine, sturdy *Sea Dog* had been flipped like a cork, perhaps trapping Scoot inside. Treading water, trying to collect his thoughts, he yelled, "Scoot," but there was no answer. Heart pounding, unable to see over the mound of the hull, he circled 100 it, thinking she might have been thrown clear. But there was no sign of her.

> ❝ *Maneuvering his body, he pulled on the handles. The doors were jammed.* ❞

He swam back to the point of cabin entry, took several deep breaths, and dove. He felt along the hatch boards and then opened his eyes briefly to see that the doors were still closed. She *was* still inside. Maneuvering his body, he pulled on the handles. The doors were jammed, and he returned to the surface for air.

He knew by the way the boat had already settled that there was water inside her. Under usual circumstances, the hull 110 being upright, there would be four feet, nine inches of hull below the waterline. There would be about the same to the cabin overhead, enabling a six-foot-person to walk about down there.

Panting, blowing, Sully figured there was at least a three-foot air pocket holding the *Sea Dog* on the surface, and if Scoot hadn't been knocked unconscious and drowned, she could live for quite a while in the dark chamber. How long, he didn't know.

In the blackness, water continued to lap at Scoot's chin. She 120 had settled against what had been the deck of the galley alcove, her body in an upright position on debris. Everything

FOR STUDENTS WITH DISABILITIES

As the narrative swings from Scoot's location to Sully's location, students with learning disabilities may struggle to follow the sequence of events. To guide comprehension, have students use a chart like the one shown to list the actions of each character. Explain that the chart will help them keep track of events.

Have pairs fill in the chart as they reread lines 83–137. Then check comprehension by asking students to summarize each character's actions.

Scoot/Inside Boat	Sully/Outside Boat

not tied down or in a locker was now between the overhead ribs. Wooden hatch covers[3] from the bilges were floating in the water and the naked bilges were exposed. Just aft of her body, and now above it, was the small diesel engine as well as the batteries. Under the water were cans of oil, one of them leaking. Battery acid might leak, too. Few sailors could imagine the nightmare that existed inside the *Sea Dog.* Scoot's pretty face was splashed with engine oil.

130 Over the next five or six minutes, Sully dove repeatedly, using his feet as a fulcrum, and using all the strength that he had in his arms, legs, and back, in an effort to open the doors. The pressure of the water defeated him. Then he thought about trying to pry the doors open with the wooden handle of the scrub brush. Too late for that, he immediately discovered. It had drifted away, along with Scoot's nylon jacket, her canvas boat shoes—anything that could float.

Finally he climbed on top of the keel, catching his breath, resting a moment, trying desperately to think of a way to enter 140 the hull. Boats of the Baba class, built for deep-water sailing, quite capable of reaching Honolulu and beyond, were almost sea-tight unless the sailors made a mistake or unless the sea became angry. The side ports were supposed to be dogged securely in open ocean. Aside from the cabin doors, there was no entry into that cabin without tools. He couldn't very well claw a hole through the inch of tough fiberglass.

He thought about the hatch on the foredeck, but it could only be opened from inside the cabin. Then there was the skylight on the top of the seventeen-foot cabin, used for 150 ventilation as well as a sun source; that butterfly window, hinged in the middle, could be opened only from the inside. Even with scuba gear, he couldn't open that skylight unless he had tools.

He fought back tears of frustration. There was no way to reach Scoot. And he knew what would happen down there. The water would slowly and inevitably rise until the air pocket was only six inches; her head would be trapped between the surface of the water and the dirty bilge. The water would torture her, then it would drown her. Seawater has no heart,

---

[3] **Wooden hatch covers:** door-like coverings made of wood that fit over openings on the deck or hull of a boat.

CLOSE READ

Analyze Story Elements: Plot and Setting (LINES 119–137)
RL 1, RL 3

Point out now that while the overall setting is still the middle of the ocean, Scoot and Sully are each in their own settings.

G CITE TEXT EVIDENCE Ask students to reread lines 119–137, which begin on the previous page, and identify the two settings. Have them explain how these two settings now impact the plot. *(Sully is outside the capsized boat, where there is plenty of light and air. But he wants to get into the boat to free his sister. Scoot is below in the darkness with limited air. She wants to get out to the surface. So, the settings separate the two characters, underscoring the external conflict.)*

Make Inferences
RL 1, RL 3

(LINES 124–129)

The author directly describes the scene inside the cabin, where an unconscious Scoot rests, as a "nightmare." He includes details that suggest that Scoot has more to worry about than just the flooding water and dwindling oxygen.

H CITE TEXT EVIDENCE Have students reread lines 124–129 and identify evidence in the text that suggests the added danger. *(The water is becoming toxic. Oil is dripping into it, and the battery could leak acid. These liquids are poisonous, so Scoot is threatened by these additional, unseen dangers.)*

Strategies for Annotation   *Annotate it!*

Make Inferences
RL 1

Have students locate the five sentences in lines 124–129. Encourage them to use their eBook annotation tools to do the following:

- Highlight in yellow the text that directly describes Scoot's situation.
- Underline clues that help you make inferences about other dangers.
- Review your annotations and use them to make inferences about these details. *(Scoot is trapped with oil and possibly battery acid leaking into the water. These are harmful chemicals, so they add to the danger.)*

her body, and now above it, was the small diesel engine as well as the batteries. Under the water were cans of oil, one of them leaking. Battery acid might leak, too. Few sailors could imagine the nightmare that existed inside the *Sea Dog.* Scoot's pretty face was splashed with engine oil.

Make Inferences RL 1

(LINES 175–185)

Explain that the author provides details that hint at Scoot's ability to take care of herself in tough situations.

ⓘ CITE TEXT EVIDENCE Ask students to reread lines 175–185 and identify details that support an inference about how Scoot might deal with the situation she is in. *(The author tells us Scoot was always "spunky." Her reaction to Sully's teasing and her determination to go offshore sailing show she is persistent, fearless, and unflinching. Although she is small, she is energetic and strong. People like this often persevere and overcome challenges, so Scoot will use her strength and spunk to get out and won't stop trying until she does.)*

English Language Support

Use Morphology Make sure students know what *spunky* means. Explain that the noun *spunk* means "spirit, courage, and determination." Adding a *y* to the end of the word makes it an adjective that means "having spirit, courage, and determination."

ASK STUDENTS to find details in lines 175–185 that show Scoot is spunky. *(She expresses disapproval of Sully's girlfriends. She wants to take an adventurous cruise for her fourteenth birthday. She's a competitive athlete.)*

160 no brain. The *Sea Dog* would then drop to the ocean floor, thousands of feet down, entombing her forever.

Maybe the best hope for poor Scoot was that she was already dead, but he had to determine whether she was still alive. He began pounding on the hull with the bottom of his fist, waiting for a return knock. At the same time, he shouted her name over and over. Nothing but silence from inside there. He wished he'd hung on to the silly scrub brush. The wooden handle would make more noise than the flesh of his fist.

Almost half an hour passed, and he finally broke down
170 and sobbed. His right fist was bloody from the constant pounding. Why hadn't *he* gone below to make the stupid sandwiches? Scoot would have been at the wheel when the wave grasped the *Sea Dog*. His young sister, with all her life to live, would be alive now.

They'd had a good brother-sister relationship. He'd teased her a lot about being pint-sized and she'd teased back, holding her nose when he brought one girl or another home for display. She'd always been spunky. He'd taken her sailing locally, in the channel, but she'd wanted an offshore cruise for
180 her fourteenth birthday. Now she'd had one, unfortunately.

Their father had nicknamed her Scoot because, as a baby, she'd crawled so fast. It was still a fitting name for her as a teenager. With a wiry body, she was fast in tennis and swimming and already the school's champion in the hundred-yard dash.

Eyes closed, teeth clenched, he kept pounding away with the bloody fist. Finally he went back into the ocean to try once more to open the doors. He sucked air, taking a half-dozen deep breaths, and then dove again. Bracing his feet against the
190 companionway frames, he felt every muscle straining, but the doors remained jammed. He was also now aware that if they did open, more water would rush in and he might not have time to find Scoot in the blackness and pull her out. But he was willing to take the gamble.

Scoot awakened as water seeped into her mouth and nose. For a moment she could not understand where she was, how she got there, what had happened …Vaguely, she remembered the boat slanting steeply downward, as if it were suddenly diving, and she remembered feeling her body going up.

APPLYING ACADEMIC VOCABULARY

evaluate	resource	text

THINK-PAIR-SHARE Have students turn to a partner and discuss the following questions. Guide students to include the academic vocabulary words *evaluate*, *resource*, and *text* in their responses. Ask volunteers to share their responses with the class.

- What **resource** can help you understand nautical terms in the **text**?
- How would you **evaluate** the effectiveness of the solutions that the characters try?

That's all she remembered, and all she knew at the moment
was that she had a fierce headache and was in chill water in
total darkness. It took a little longer to realize she was trapped
in the *Sea Dog's* cabin, by the galley alcove. She began to feel
around herself and to touch floating things. The air was thick
with an oil smell. Then she ran her hand over the nearest solid
thing—a bulkhead. *That's strange,* she thought—her feet were
touching a pot. She lifted her right arm and felt above her—the
galley range. The galley range above her? *The boat was upside
down.* She felt for the companionway steps and found the
entry doors and pushed on them; that was the way she'd come
in. The doors didn't move.

Sully crawled up on the wide hull again, clinging to a faint
hope that a boat or ship would soon come by; but the sun
was already in descent, and with night coming on, chances
of rescue lessened with each long minute. It was maddening
to have her a few feet away and be helpless to do anything.
Meanwhile the hull swayed gently, in eerie silence.

Scoot said tentatively, "Sully?" Maybe he'd been drowned.
Maybe she was alone and would die here in the foul water.
She repeated his name, but much more loudly. No answer.
She was coming out of shock now and fear icier than the water
was replacing her confusion. To die completely alone? It went
that way for a few desperate moments, and then she said to
herself, *Scoot, you've got to get out of here! There has to be some
way to get out . . .*

CLOSE READ

Analyze Story Elements: Plot and Setting (LINES 200–211)

RL 1, RL 3

Explain to students that once the conflict has been introduced, the **rising action** that follows presents additional obstacles for the characters. Trapped inside the cabin, Scoot must face a number of obstacles that make her situation more dangerous.

J CITE TEXT EVIDENCE Have students reread lines 200–211 and identify details that create obstacles for Scoot. *(Scoot is in total darkness, so she can't see what she's doing or where things are. She has a headache. She finally realizes that the cabin where she is trapped is upside down, which makes her disoriented. Finally, when she tries to open the entry doors, she can't.)*

English Language Support

Make sure students understand the idiom *upside down*. Explain that the wave has overturned the boat, and what was the cabin's ceiling is now its floor.

ASK STUDENTS to review lines 200–211 to find details that confuse Scoot when she awakens. *(She's in water and darkness. Things are floating, she smells oil, and the stove is above her.)*

FOR STANDARD ENGLISH LEARNERS

Remind students that most past-tense verbs end in the suffix *-ed*. Read aloud lines 200–203 to point out the examples *remembered* and *trapped*. Then provide the following sentences for students to complete:

- After the accident, Sully *(hope, hoped)* that a ship would come by.
- When Scoot woke up, her head *(ache, ached)*.
- Finally, Scoot understood that she was *(trap, trapped)*.

Have students check their answers with a partner.

English Language Support

Read Closely Point out the dashes in lines 205–208. Explain that dashes signal an interruption or a break in thought. An author uses a dash to call particular attention to the words that follow it.

- Read aloud the sentence in lines 205–206. Ask students to explain the purpose of the dash. What does Scoot touch?
- Organize students into pairs and have them take turns reading lines 205–208 to each other, pausing at the dashes.
- Ask partners to explain the purpose of each of the dashes in lines 205–208.

Analyze Story Elements: Plot and Conflict

RL 1,
RL 3

(LINES 239–258, 245–249)

Explain to students that the introduction of obstacles in the rising action helps build **suspense,** or the growing feeling of tension and excitement that readers feel as they follow a character's struggle with the conflict. Explain further that there are two kinds of conflicts: **external conflicts,** which are struggles with outside forces, such as another character or a force of nature, and **internal conflicts,** which are struggles characters have with their own thoughts.

K **CITE TEXT EVIDENCE** Have students reread lines 239–258 and identify how Sully and Scoot have overcome the first big obstacle in their way. *(Neither Scoot nor Sully was sure that the other person was still alive. Now that they know this, they've overcome one hurdle in their way.)*

L **ASK STUDENTS** to reread lines 245–249 and explain how this quick exchange between the characters helps build suspense. *(The urgent back and forth between Scoot and Sully, who are suddenly energized and hopeful, creates a feeling of excitement. The reader is suddenly excited for the characters.)*

English Language Support

Point out that the paragraphs alternate between two points of view: Sully's and Scoot's. Discuss how this structure adds suspense. Guide students to see that as Sully becomes more desperate, Scoot grows more confident.

ASK STUDENTS to read aloud lines 231–271 in pairs, with one partner reading descriptions of Sully and the other reading descriptions of Scoot. To begin, model how to use volume and voice modulation to convey suspense. When pairs finish, have partners exchange roles and reread the paragraphs. If time allows, let volunteers present a staged reading.

Sully clung to the keel with one hand, his body flat against the smooth surface of the hull. There was ample room on either side of the keel before the dead-rise, the upward slope of the hull. The *Sea Dog* had a beam of ten feet. Unless a wind and 230 waves came up, he was safe enough in his wet perch.

Scoot again wondered if her brother had survived and if he was still around the boat or on it. With her right foot she began to probe around the space beneath her. The pot had drifted away, but her toes felt what seemed to be flatware. That made sense. The drawer with the knives and forks and spoons had popped out, spilling its contents. She took a deep breath and ducked under to pick out a knife. Coming up, she held the knife blade, reaching skyward with the handle . . .

Eyes closed, brain mushy, exhausted, Sully heard a faint 240 tapping and raised up on his elbows to make sure he wasn't dreaming. No, there was a tapping from below. He crawled back toward what he thought was the source area, the galley area, and put an ear to the hull. *She was tapping!* He pounded the fiberglass, yelling, "Scoot, Scooot, Scooot . . ."

K

Scoot heard the pounding and called out, "Sully, I'm here, I'm here!" Her voice seemed to thunder in the air pocket.

L

Sully yelled, "Can you hear me?"

Scoot could only hear the pounding.
   "Help me out of here . . ."

250 Ear still to the hull, Sully shouted again, "Scoot, can you hear me?" No answer. He pounded again and repeated, "Scoot, can you hear me?" No answer. The hull was too thick and the slop of the sea, the moan of the afternoon breeze, didn't help.

Though she couldn't hear his voice, the mere fact that he was up there told her she'd escape. Sully had gotten her out of jams before. There was no one on earth that she'd rather have as a rescue man than her oldest brother. She absolutely knew she'd survive.

Though it might be fruitless, Sully yelled down to the galley 260 alcove, "Listen to me, Scoot. You'll have to get out by yourself. I can't help you. I can't break in. Listen to me, I know you're in water, and the best way out is through the skylight. You've got to dive down and open it. You're small enough to go through it . . ." She could go through either section of the butterfly window. "Tap twice if you heard me!"

She did not respond, and he repeated what he'd just said, word for word.

No response. No taps from below.

270 Scoot couldn't understand why he didn't just swim down and open the doors to the cabin, release her. That's all he needed to do, and she'd be free.

> # No response.
> # No taps from below.

Sully looked up at the sky. "Please, God, help me, help us." It was almost unbearable to know she was alive and he was unable to do anything for her. Then he made the decision to keep repeating: "Listen to me, Scoot. You'll have to get out by yourself. I can't break in. Listen to me, the best way out is through the skylight. You've got to dive down and open it. You're small enough to go through it . . ."

He decided to keep saying it the rest of the day and into
280 the night or for as long as it took to penetrate the hull with words. *Skylight! Skylight!* Over and over.

He'd heard of mental telepathy but had not thought much about it before. Now it was the only way to reach her.

Scoot finally thought that maybe Sully was hurt, maybe helpless up on that bottom, so that was why he couldn't open the doors and let her out. That had to be the reason—Sully up there with broken legs. *So I'll have to get out on my own,* she thought.

Over the last two days, when she wasn't on the wheel she
290 had been exploring the *Sea Dog,* and she thought she knew all the exits. Besides the companionway doors, which she knew she couldn't open, there was the hatch on the foredeck for access to the sails; then there was the skylight, almost

CLOSE READ

Make Inferences
RL 1
(LINES 272–281)

Explain to students that Sully is making a decision to do something by repeating the same words over and over.

Ⓜ **ASK STUDENTS** to reread lines 272–281 and make an inference about how Sully's actions might help both Scoot and Sully himself. *(Sully thinks that his repeating the words to Scoot might reach her through mental telepathy. But, the repetition of words is also likely helping Sully because it makes him feel less powerless. Earlier in the paragraph, Sully actually prays. This repetition of words may comfort him like a prayer.)*

English Language Support

Point out the quotation marks in the text and make sure students understand who is speaking.

ASK STUDENTS to read lines 272–278 and identify to whom Sully is speaking. Then have pairs discuss what these quotations tell us about Sully and his situation. *(Sully first asks God for help and then speaks to Scoot, though he knows she can't hear him. Although Sully realizes that there's nothing he can do, he refuses to do nothing.)*

WHEN STUDENTS STRUGGLE . . .

To guide students' comprehension of plot elements that create tension, have students work in pairs to fill out a chart like the one shown. Explain that the chart will help them to link feelings of tension or excitement to story events.

Have pairs fill in the chart as they reread lines 245–249, and discuss their reactions to the story event. Explain that as they read they can ask questions, such as *What parts of the story are most exciting? Why do they make me feel that way?*

WHEN I READ . . .	I FELT . . .
Sully hears Scoot tapping and starts trying to yell to her. She yells back, but they can't hear each other's voices.	excited, frustrated

CLOSE READ

Make Inferences   RL 1
(LINES 303–312)

Explain to students that the author is providing many details about Scoot's thought process and abilities in an emergency.

 CITE TEXT EVIDENCE Have students reread lines 303–312 and cite evidence that supports an inference about Scoot's abilities. *(Scoot is levelheaded, calm, and resourceful, even in an emergency situation. She clearly thinks through a number of solutions to her problem. She remembers the emergency flashlight and reasons that it's waterproof. She calculates how much time she will have to unscrew the dogs. She even has the presence of mind to let Sully know she is still alive.)*

Analyze Story Elements: Plot and Setting   RL 3
(LINES 314–319)

Explain to students that the author is using an aspect of the outdoor, ocean setting to reinforce a continually worsening obstacle.

O **ASK STUDENTS** to reread lines 314–319 and identify the obstacle and how it is related to the setting. *(Sully is noting that there are three hours until sundown. The approaching nighttime is like a deadline for him and Scoot. If she doesn't get out by then, they could be in much worse trouble.)*

---

in the middle of the long cabin. Sully had opened it, she remembered, to air out the boat before they sailed. As she clung to a light fixture by the alcove, in water up to her shoulders, something kept telling her she should first try the butterfly windows of the skylight. The unheard message was compelling—*Try the skylight.*

300   Sully's voice was almost like a recording, a mantra, saying the same thing again and again, directed down to the position of the galley.

Scoot remembered that an emergency flashlight was bracketed on the bulkhead above the starboard settee, and she assumed it was waterproof. From what Sully had said, Beau Tucker took great care in selecting emergency equipment. It might help to actually see the dogs on the metal skylight frame. She knew she wouldn't have much time to spin them loose. Maybe thirty or forty seconds before she'd have to surface for breath. Trying 310 to think of the exact position of the upside-down flashlight, she again tapped on the hull to let her brother know she was very much alive.

He pounded back.

Sully looked at his watch. Almost four-thirty. About three hours to sundown. Of course, it didn't make much difference to Scoot. She was already in dank night. But it might make a difference if she got out after nightfall. He didn't know what kind of shape she was in. Injured, she might surface and drift away.
320   The mantra kept on.

Scoot dove twice for the boxy flashlight, found it, and turned it on, suddenly splitting the darkness and immediately feeling hopeful. But it was odd to see the *Sea Dog's* unusual overhead, the open hatchways into the bilge and the debris floating on the shining water, all streaked with lubricants; odd to see the toilet upside down. She held the light underwater and it continued to operate.

Every so often, Sully lifted his face to survey the horizon, looking for traffic. He knew they were still within sixteen or 330 seventeen miles of the coast, though the drift was west. There was usually small-boat activity within twenty miles of the shore—fishermen or pleasure boats.

12   Collection 1

Strategies for Annotation   *Annotate it!*

Analyze Story Elements: Plot and Setting   RL 1, RL 3

Have students locate lines 314–319. Encourage them to use their eBook annotation tools to do the following:

- Highlight in yellow the text that describes the obstacle.
- Underline the text that explains why this detail poses a threat to Sully and Scoot.
- Review your annotations and explain how this text evidence helps build suspense. *(Time is running out for Scoot and Sully. If it gets dark, Scoot may never get rescued.)*

Sully looked at his watch. Almost four-thirty. About three hours to sundown. Of course, it didn't make much difference to Scoot. She was already in dank night. But it might make a difference if she got out after nightfall. He didn't know what kind of shape she was in. Injured, she might surface and drift away.

Scoot worked herself forward a few feet, guessing where the skylight might be, and then went down to find the butterfly windows, the flashlight beam cutting through the murk. It took a few seconds to locate them and put a hand on one brass dog. She tried to turn it, but it was too tight for her muscles and she rose up to breathe again.

340 Not knowing what was happening below or whether Scoot was trying to escape, Sully was getting more anxious by the moment. He didn't know whether or not the crazy telepathy was working. He wished she would tap again to let him know she was still alive. It had been more than twenty minutes since she'd last tapped.

Scoot had seen a toolbox under the companionway steps and went back to try to find it. She guessed there'd be wrenches inside it, unless they'd spilled out. Using the flashlight again, she found the metal box and opened it. Back to the surface to breathe again, and then back to the toolbox to extract a wrench.
350 With each move she was becoming more and more confident.

A big sailboat, beating south, came into Sully's view; but it was more than two miles away and the occupants—unless he was very lucky—would not be able to spot the *Sea Dog's* mound and the man standing on it, waving frantically.

Four times Scoot needed to dive, once for each dog; and working underwater was at least five times as difficult as trying to turn them in usual circumstances. She'd aim the light and rest it to illuminate the windows. Finally, all the dogs

Rogue Wave **13**

Analyze Story Elements: Plot and Setting (LINES 339–354)

RL 1, RL 3

Explain to students that now the rising action is moving at a faster pace, as time is running out for Scoot and Sully. The author jumps back and forth between the two settings, showing what each character is experiencing.

P **ASK STUDENTS** to reread lines 339–354 to identify details that are increasing the suspense, and have the students explain how these details create tension and excitement for the reader. *(Sully is getting very anxious. Meanwhile, Scoot is working away, growing more confident. The situation is getting very bad, although there is some hope. But the hope caused by the sighting of the other boat fades, adding to Sully's frustration. These details seem to make the plot move more quickly because we want to find out what will happen.)*

English Language Support

Improve Reading Fluency Model how to use a tone that creates suspense. Read aloud the paragraph on page 12, lines 321–327, and have students follow along in their books. Then have students pair-read the paragraphs starting on page 12, line 328, and ending on page 13, line 354. One partner will read about Scoot and the other will read about Sully. Encourage students to provide feedback. Then have pairs switch paragraphs and read the passage again.

Analyze Story Elements:
Plot and Setting (LINES 363–372)

RL 1,
RL 3

Explain that suspense in a story often builds to a breaking point, called the **climax**—the story's most interesting moment, which resolves the conflict.

Q **CITE TEXT EVIDENCE** Have students reread lines 363–372 and cite evidence that indicates this is the **climax** of the story. *(Sully is finally giving up hope. Scoot is on her sixth dive. She gives one final push "with all her strength" and the skylight finally opens. Scoot is almost out of breath—about to lose consciousness— but she has resolved her conflict.)*

Make Inferences
(LINES 383–387)

RL 1,
RL 3

Explain that in the moments of the story right after the climax, called the **resolution,** Sully has one last exchange with the captain of the *Red Rooster*.

R **ASK STUDENTS** to reread the exchange and explain why Stevens responds as he does. *(Sully answers Stevens's question with two words: "rogue wave." Stevens winces and nods because he understands that a rogue wave is so sudden and destructive, it goes without saying that it causes massive problems.)*

COLLABORATIVE DISCUSSION Have pairs discuss the specific details and events in the plot that made this story so exciting. Then have them share their ideas with the class and discuss others' reactions to the story.

ASK STUDENTS to share any questions they generated in the course of reading and discussing the selection.

English Language Support

Support Opinions Provide students with the following sentence stems to aid discussion.

For clarification: What do you mean by _____?

To affirm or agree: That's a good point because _____.

To disagree respectfully: I see your point, but _____.

---

360 were loose and she rose once again. This time, after filling her lungs to bursting, she went down and pushed on the starboard window. It cracked a little, but the outside sea pressure resisted and she had to surface again.

Q Sully sat down, almost giving up hope. How long the air pocket would hold up was anybody's guess. The boat had settled at least six inches in the last two hours. It might not last into the night.

370 On her sixth dive Scoot found a way to brace her feet against the ceiling ribs. She pushed with all her strength, and this time the window opened. Almost out of breath, she quickly pushed her body through and the *Old Sea Dog* released her. Treading water beside the hull, she sucked in fresh air and finally called out, "Sully …"

He looked her way, saw the grin of triumph on the oil-stained imp face, and dived in to help her aboard the derelict.

Shivering, holding each other for warmth all night, they rode and rocked, knowing that the boat was sinking lower each hour.

Just after dawn, the *Red Rooster,* a long-range sports fishing boat out of San Diego bound south to fish for wahoo 380 and tuna off the Revilla Gigedo Islands, came within a hundred yards of the upside-down sailboat and stopped to pick up its two chattering survivors.

R The *Red Rooster's* captain, Mark Stevens, asked, "What happened?"

"Rogue wave," said Sully. That's what he planned to say to Beau Tucker as well.

Stevens winced and nodded that he understood.

The *Old Sea Dog* stayed on the surface for a little while longer, having delivered her survivors to safety; then her air 390 pocket breathed its last and she slipped beneath the water, headed for the bottom.

COLLABORATIVE DISCUSSION How and when did this adventure tale "hook" you? As it unfolded, what events helped to keep you anxious about what would happen? With a partner, review "Rogue Wave" to point out and discuss the parts that helped to create excitement and anticipation.

TO CHALLENGE STUDENTS . . .

Theme Explain to students that a story's theme is a message or lesson about life that a writer shares with the reader. Have students work in small groups and use examples from the text to discuss the unpredictability of and devastation caused by the rogue wave.

Analyze Story Elements: Plot and Setting

RL 3

The power of a story, such as "Rogue Wave," comes from its action and events. Most stories follow a series of events, also known as the **plot.** A story centers around the **conflict,** the struggle between opposing forces. As the characters struggle to resolve a conflict, the plot builds **suspense,** the growing tension and excitement felt by the reader. Most plots have five stages:

- The **exposition** introduces the characters and presents the setting and conflict.
- The **rising action** presents complications that intensify.
- The **climax** is the story's moment of greatest interest—the point where the conflict is resolved.
- In the **falling action,** the story begins to draw to a close.
- The **resolution** reveals the final outcome of the conflict.

Often the plot is influenced by the **setting,** or the time and place of the action. For example, the setting can cause plot complications. In "Rogue Wave," Sully notes that as evening comes, the fading light could hamper his rescue efforts. To understand the influence of setting on the plot in "Rogue Wave," find details that tell where and when the events are happening. Use those details to visualize the setting and follow the action.

Make Inferences

RL 1

Authors do not always fully describe every aspect of a story, setting, or character. They do, however, provide clues that help you to make **inferences,** logical guesses based on facts and one's own knowledge and experience. You make an inference by combining evidence with what you know.

To support your inferences, you may need to **cite textual evidence,** or provide specific information from the text. For example, you can identify story details that indicate a character's feelings, as shown in the chart. Using a chart like this one can help you make inferences throughout a text.

Detail from the Text

In lines 37–39, Scoot is listening to music and singing along.

My Own Experience

When I sing along to a song, I usually feel happy.

My Inference

Scoot feels happy to be sailing with her brother.

CLOSE READ

Analyze Story Elements: Plot and Setting

RL 3

Discuss the terms and the five stages of a plot. Have volunteers name at least one example of each stage from the story. Then discuss the information about how setting can influence plot.

Work with students to analyze the plot and identify how suspense is created. Explain that

- with each additional obstacle, the suspense is usually heightened.
- details of setting, such as the oncoming sundown and the flooding cabin, build suspense.
- as students read a story, they should notice each time they wonder "What happens next?"

Make Inferences

RL 1

Help students understand that making inferences is a way to figure out things that are not directly described in a text. To demonstrate making an inference, point out that when you see someone crying, you can infer that the person is sad. You don't need to be told. Discuss the chart and how to use details from the text and your own experiences to make an inference about Scoot. Then work with students to use a chart, like the one shown, to make additional inferences about other plot elements.

Strategies for Annotation *Annotate it!*

Analyze Story Elements: Plot and Setting

RL 1, RL 3

Share these strategies for guided or independent analysis:

- Highlight in yellow details about the setting that prove to be an obstacle.
- Underline details that show how the character deals with the obstacle.

Over the next five or six minutes, Sully dove repeatedly, <u>using his feet as a fulcrum,</u> and <u>using all the strength that he had in his arms, legs, and back, in an effort to open the doors.</u> The pressure of the water defeated him. Then <u>he thought about trying to pry the doors open with the wooden handle of the</u>

Analyzing the Text

RL 1, RL 3

Possible answers:

1. *Scoot has scary thoughts about whether Sully is okay. Fear takes over her, but only for a few moments. Then she turns her attention to getting out. People who act like this in the face of disaster are brave and resilient.*

2. *By providing details of the dangers of rogue waves, it underscores the threat to Scoot and Sully and suggests the conflict that they will soon have to resolve—surviving the sudden strike of a rogue wave.*

3. *Sully has just been thinking about his sister and their loving relationship. He has pounded his fists bloody, trying to contact her. He jumps in the water for one final time. He is scared and desperate.*

4. *Sully knows roughly their location in the ocean. He also knows that small boats might be in the area. This shows that he is knowledgeable and that rescue might be close. There is still hope for Sully and Scoot.*

5. *Scoot's complications: 1. the flooding, upturned, dark cabin; 2. a headache; 3. concern about Sully and inability to hear him; 4. dwindling air; 5. the locked skylight. Sully's complications: 1. his inability to see or hear Scoot; 2. his inability to get inside the capsized cabin; 3. fears of what could happen to Scoot; 4. guilt about putting Scoot in danger; 5. the sinking hull and the oncoming sunset.*

6. *The two settings are outside on the Sea Dog's upturned hull, and below in the upturned cabin. Shifting between these settings builds suspense by alternating between the obstacles each character encounters.*

7. *The climax is the moment when Scoot finally unfastens the dogs of the skylight and pushes through to the ocean. It's suspenseful because we know she is exhausted and running out of air. Meanwhile, up above, Sully has almost given up hope. The situation seems desperate.*

English Language Support

Guide students to work in small groups to answer the questions on page 16. Have each group answer one question. When all the groups are finished, let them take turns presenting their answers to the class. Encourage students to provide their classmates with useful feedback.

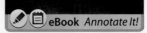

Analyzing the Text

RL 1, RL 3, W 3, SL 4

Cite Text Evidence   Support your responses with evidence from the text.

1. **Infer** Reread lines 218–225. What inference can you make about Scoot's personality, based on these lines?

2. **Connect** How does the information in lines 17–31 help establish the conflict?

3. **Infer** Reread lines 186–194. Describe Sully's emotions at this point.

4. **Infer** Reread lines 328–332. What inference does the author want you to make at this point?

5. **Compare** Fill out a chart like this one to trace the conflicts or complications Scoot and Sully encounter in the story. Review the story events in the text, expanding the chart as necessary to cover the key happenings.

Complication	1	2	3	4	5
Scoot's					
Sully's					

6. **Analyze** Identify the two settings in this story. How does the author's shifting between these settings help build suspense?

7. **Evaluate** Describe the climax of the story. What makes this moment so suspenseful? Explain.

PERFORMANCE TASK

Writing Activity: Movie Outline
Think about how "Rogue Wave" could be adapted as an action movie. Write a four-paragraph movie outline showing how it could be done. Use your completed outline to "pitch"—or present persuasively—your movie idea to a partner or group. In your outline, be sure to include:

- a description of the opening scene that establishes the characters, setting, and conflict.
- a description of each important scene in the plot.
- suggestions for how to shoot each scene to convey the suspense.

Assign this performance task.

PERFORMANCE TASK

W 3, SL 4

Writing Activity: Movie Outline Have students work independently. Direct them to review "Rogue Wave" and use the main plot elements to organize their outlines. Suggest that they search online for sample movie outlines, or treatments, to use as examples of how to describe movie scenes. When finished, encourage students to use their completed outlines to pitch their idea to a partner or small group, explaining why the movie should be made.

Critical Vocabulary

L 4a, L 4b, L 4c

swell   deck   navigation   submerge   porthole

Practice and Apply Complete each sentence to show that you understand the meaning of the boldfaced vocabulary word.

1. I can see the water's motion by watching how a **swell** . . .
2. One reason to be on the **deck** of a boat is . . .
3. Sailors need tools for **navigation,** such as . . .
4. When the tide comes in on the beach, it could **submerge** . . .
5. There was a **porthole** in our room on the boat, so we . . .

Vocabulary Strategy: Latin Roots

A **root** is a word part that came into English from an older language. Roots from the ancient language of Latin appear in many English words. Often, by identifying Latin roots, you can figure out the meanings of words that seem unfamiliar. For example, the chart shows two words from "Rogue Wave." Each contains a Latin root having to do with the sea.

Word	Latin Root	Root's Meaning
mariners	mar	sea
navigation	nav	ship

Mariners, which comes from the Latin root *mar*, are sea sailors. The Latin root *nav*, from which *navigation* comes, appears in words having to do with ships and sailing, such as *navy* (a fleet of ships) and *naval* (having to do with navies). By identifying the roots *mar* and *nav*, you can make a good guess about the meanings of longer words that include them. Relying on a resource such as a print or online dictionary also can help you confirm your ideas.

Practice and Apply Read each sentence. Identify the words with the Latin roots *mar* and *nav*. Tell what each word means. Use a print or online dictionary to check your ideas.

1. Sailors in the navy may spend time in submarines.
2. Mariners long ago navigated using the stars.
3. Using navigation equipment, fishermen found a region of rich marine life.
4. Boats set out from the marina to sail up the river, which is navigable to the waterfalls.

Critical Vocabulary

L 4a, L 4b, L 4c

Possible answers:

1. *rises and falls on the ocean.*
2. *to move the boat's wheel or rudder to steer it.*
3. *a map and a compass.*
4. *any sand castles that have been built near the water.*
5. *could see the other boats in the harbor.*

Vocabulary Strategy: Latin Roots

Answers:

1. *navy:* fleet of ships; *submarines:* sea vessels that travel underwater
2. *mariners:* sea sailors; *navigated:* directed a ship's course
3. *navigation:* the act of directing a ship's course; *marine:* having to do with the sea
4. *marina:* docks by the sea for boats and supplies; *navigable:* able to be sailed through

---

Strategies for Annotation 🖊️ 📖 *Annotate it!*

Latin Roots

L 4b

Have students locate the sentences containing *navy* and *naval* in lines 19–26. Encourage them to use their eBook annotation tools to do the following:

- Highlight each word.
- Underline the Latin root in each word.
- Use the Latin root in each word to make a good guess about its meaning and write an annotation.

"giant" waves. The U.S. Navy manual Practical Methods for Observing and Forecasting Ocean Waves *says, "In any wave system, after a long enough time, an exceptional high one will . . . still possible and the exact time of occurrence can never be predicted."* Naval *hydrography studies indicate that wave*

navy: a fleet of military ships

Language Conventions: Sentence Structure

L 1b

Tell students that the examples in the chart show the building blocks of a simple sentence—the basic type of sentence. Invite volunteers to come up with examples of other simple sentences and identify the complete subject and complete predicate in each. *(Sample answers: Rogue waves are very destructive. Complete subject: Rogue waves; Complete predicate: are very destructive. Sully and Scoot almost died in a serious maritime accident. Complete subject: Sully and Scoot; Complete predicate: almost died in a serious maritime accident.)* Then have volunteers use these simple sentences to form compound sentences, using either conjunctions or a semicolon. *(Rogue waves are very destructive, so Sully and Scoot almost died in a serious maritime accident.)*

Sample answers:

1. *Rogue waves are frightening, and they are unpredictable giants.*

2. *A rogue wave can be very tall, and it can travel thousands of miles.*

3. *Sailors know about the sea's dangers, so they follow safety rules.*

4. *Life at sea has its risks, but it also has beauty.*

5. *Sailors prepare for dangerous weather, or they risk dying at sea.*

✓ *Assess It Online!*

Online Selection Test
- Download an editable ExamView bank.
- Assign and manage this test online.

Language Conventions: Sentence Structure

L 1b

A **clause** is a group of words that has the two main parts of a sentence—a complete subject and a complete predicate. A **complete subject** includes all the words that identify the person, place, thing, or idea that the sentence is about. The **complete predicate** includes all the words that tell or ask something about the subject.

Complete Subject	Complete Predicate
The *Sea Dog*	had every blessed thing.
Sully	was a good teacher.

A **simple sentence** contains just one main clause.

Sully looked at his watch.

In this sentence, the complete subject is *Sully* and the complete predicate is *looked at his watch*.

A **compound sentence** contains two or more main clauses that are joined either by a comma and coordinating conjunction, such as *and*, *but*, *or*, *for*, *so*, *yet*, and *nor*, or are joined by a semicolon.

She pushed with all her strength, and this time the window opened.

In this compound sentence, the simple sentence *She pushed with all her strength* is combined with the sentence *this time the window opened*, using a comma and the coordinating conjunction *and*.

She found the entry doors; they were closed.

In this compound sentence, a semicolon is used to connect two simple sentences.

Practice and Apply Create a compound sentence by joining the two simple sentences with either a comma and a coordinating conjunction or a semicolon.

1. Rogue waves are frightening. They are unpredictable giants.

2. A rogue wave can be very tall. It can travel thousands of miles.

3. Sailors know about the sea's dangers. They follow safety rules.

4. Life at sea has its risks. It also has beauty.

5. Sailors prepare for dangerous weather. They risk dying at sea.

English Language Support

Combine Sentences Point out that coordinating conjunctions signal different kinds of relationships between ideas. On a whiteboard, display the conjunctions *and, but, or, for, so, yet, nor.*

- Tell students that the coordinating conjunction *and* signals additional information, *but* signals a contrast, and *so* signals a cause-and-effect relationship. Give students simple sentences to combine using *and* or *but* (for example: Sailing is a lot of fun. It can also be very dangerous.). Have them work with a partner to practice combining the sentences.

- Have pairs explain how the ideas in each pair of Practice and Apply sentences are connected. Then work with students to choose appropriate coordinating conjunctions.

- Ask students to write four compound sentences about the sea and sailing, using a different coordinating conjunction for each one.

INTERACTIVE WHITEBOARD LESSON
Analyze Story Elements: Plot and Conflict

RL 1,
RL 3

Learn the Skill ▶ What Is Conflict?

What Is Conflict?
Click to explore different types of conflicts.

Conflict in Literature

A **conflict** is a struggle between two opposing forces in the plot of a story. A conflict can be external (against an outside force) or internal (within the character).

Conflict in Literature | External: Against Character(s) | External: Against Nature

TEACH

Before having students complete their outlines as part of the Performance Task, review these points about conflict:

- Every story centers around a **conflict,** a struggle between opposing forces.
- An **external conflict** is a struggle against an outside force, such as nature, a physical obstacle, or another character.
- Ask volunteers to name examples of a few external conflicts, such as a knight fighting against an evil king or characters trying to survive a tornado.
- An **internal conflict** is one that occurs within a character. An internal conflict is a struggle inside a character's mind.
- Ask volunteers to name examples of a few internal conflicts, such as deciding to keep a found wallet or deciding to turn it in to the police, or a character struggling with a choice between helping a friend and doing the right thing.

COLLABORATIVE DISCUSSION

Have students work in pairs to review the story "Rogue Wave" and identify examples of both kinds of conflict. Ask students to cite evidence from the text to discuss how the author establishes each conflict and how these conflicts help build suspense in the story.

Analyze Story Elements: Plot and Setting

RL 3

RETEACH

Use a story map to review the five stages of a plot (Exposition, Rising Action, Climax, Falling Action, and Resolution), filling in the map with events from "Rogue Wave."

- Then give an example of another story in which the setting has an effect on the plot, such as "A lava flow from an erupting volcano threatens the lives of the people in the village below."
- Ask students to name other ways in which the sample setting could affect the plot. *(Sample answer: Ash falling from the erupting volcano covers the roads, making escape more difficult.)*
- Discuss how obstacles like this create suspense, making the reader want to find out what happens next.

LEVEL UP TUTORIALS Assign the following *Level Up* tutorial: **Setting: Effect on Plot**

Setting: Effect on Plot | TUTORIAL | PRACTICE

Setting: Effect on Plot

Say you're writing a story about someone throwing the game-winning touchdown pass. Would it be important to discuss the time and place of a story? How about the events that led up to the winning pass?

The **setting**, or the time and place in which the story occurs, helps shape stories. Often, the setting can also affect the **plot**, or the series of events that make up a story.

The setting of a story is important.

The setting sometimes affects the plot.

1 2 3 4 5 6 7 8 9 ..9

INDEPENDENT READING

Students can apply the skill to another short story of their own choosing. Have them work independently to identify the main plot elements. Then have them list ways in which the setting has an effect on the plot. Ask: *How does the writer use aspects of the setting to introduce obstacles? How do these obstacles help create suspense?*

Big Things Come in Small Packages

Short Story by Eleanora E. Tate

Why This Text

Students often read a short story without understanding that the elements of a story interact. The setting of a story, for example, may shape the characters or plot—or both. Stories such as this one by Eleanora E. Tate may explicitly describe the setting, characters, and plot, or they may provide clues to help the reader make inferences, supported by textual evidence. With the help of the close-reading questions, students will recognize how the setting influences the characters and plot. This close reading will lead students to develop their understanding of how particular elements of a short story interact.

Background Have students read the background information about the author. Introduce the selection by telling students that Eleanora E. Tate is a powerful storyteller who writes books and short stories "so that everyone of every ethnic group can read about the proud history and culture of African Americans." As a folklorist, Tate imbues her writing with African American lore and sayings, as seen in her popular book *Don't Split the Pole: Tales of Down-Home Folk Wisdom*.

SETTING A PURPOSE Ask students to pay close attention to how the elements of the story interact. When do they first understand the conflict that needs to be resolved in the story?

Standards Support

- cite several pieces of textual evidence
- make inferences drawn from the text
- analyze how particular elements of a story interact
- analyze how setting shapes the characters or plot

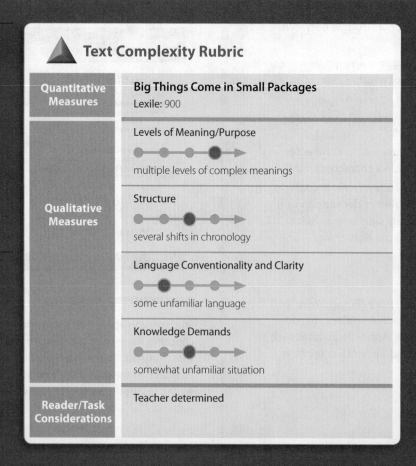

Text Complexity Rubric

Quantitative Measures	**Big Things Come in Small Packages** Lexile: 900
Qualitative Measures	Levels of Meaning/Purpose multiple levels of complex meanings
	Structure several shifts in chronology
	Language Conventionality and Clarity some unfamiliar language
	Knowledge Demands somewhat unfamiliar situation
Reader/Task Considerations	Teacher determined

Strategies for CLOSE READING

Analyze Story Elements: Plot and Setting

Students should read this short story carefully all the way through. Close-reading questions at the bottom of the page will help them focus on a thorough analysis of how particular story elements interact, specifically on how the setting influences the characters and plot. As they read, students should record comments about the text in the side margins.

WHEN STUDENTS STRUGGLE . . .

To help students understand the major structural elements in a fictional narrative, have them work in a small group to fill out a story map, such as the one shown below, as they analyze the story.

CITE TEXT EVIDENCE For practice in tracking how the particular story elements interact, have students cite text evidence to complete the story map.

> *Setting:*
> *Where: Morehead City, North Carolina*
> *When: 1970s and present*

> *Major Characters: Tucker Willis ("Tugboat"), narrator (LaShana Mae), and Richard Etheridge*
> *Minor Characters: Mr. Nibbles, narrator's mother, Tucker's parents*

> *Plot/Problem: Tucker is called names by the other kids because of his small size.*

> *Event 1:*
> *Tucker meets Richard, who nicknames him "Tugboat."*

> *Event 2:*
> *Tucker tries to save Mr. Nibbles from drowning, but thinks he is going to die.*

> *Event 3:*
> *Richard helps in the rescue, and he and Tucker save Mr. Nibbles.*

> *Outcome: Tucker becomes a hero for having saved Mr. Nibbles, and the name-calling stops. Tucker discovers that Richard actually died in 1900 and was the Keeper of the Pea Island Lifesaving Service.*

Background **Eleanora E. Tate** *was born in Canton, Missouri, and spent her first year of school in a one-room schoolhouse for students in the first through eighth grades. She wrote her first story when she was in the third grade. Tate says she writes books and stories so that all people can read about the proud history and culture of African Americans.*

Big Things
Come in Small Packages

Short Story by Eleanora E. Tate

CLOSE READ
Notes

1. **READD** As you read lines 1–77, begin to collect and cite text evidence.

- Underline details in lines 1–5 that describe the story's setting.
- Circle several events that depend on the setting.
- Circle the narrator's name and underline three things she reveals about herself and Tucker.

(A) I want to tell you about a boy I knew who lived in Morehead City, North Carolina, some years ago named Tucker Willis. He lived by Calico Creek where it narrows down to marsh grass, flounder, and fiddler crabs. It's not far from the back side of the Morehead City Port **Terminal**, where the big ships come in from the Atlantic Ocean.

Everybody liked him, and he was good at almost everything he put his hand to. But when Tucker turned eleven or twelve, he was still so short he looked like an elf. And you know how it is when you're a little different from other folks in even some harmless kind of way.

10 Kids called him Tom Thumb, squirt, midget, inchworm, dwarf.

I thought Tucker was the cutest little thing in the world. But to him back then I was ole knock-kneed LaShana Mae, the girl who lived down the street. I was a couple years younger than him. We were friends, though, and went to the same church—St. Luke's Missionary Baptist—and the same school.

People tease him for being small, and he does not like it.

terminal:
end of a transportation line

3

---

1. **READ AND CITE TEXT EVIDENCE** Explain to students that Tate explicitly identifies the setting at the beginning of the story, establishing how the time and place will shape the characters and plot.

(A) **ASK STUDENTS** to determine how Tate establishes the setting to shape the characters and plot by citing specific textual evidence in lines 1–77. *Responses may include references to evidence in lines 1–5, 12, 19–21, 27–30, 34–36, 39–40, and 53.*

Critical Vocabulary: terminal (line 5) Have students explain the meaning of *terminal* as it is used here. Ask students what means of transportation have terminals at the end of their lines. *Students should be able to cite these modes of transportation: bus, train, and subway lines.*

Back in those days, in the 1970s, young boys and girls didn't hang out as boyfriend and girlfriend like kids do now. Plus, I was just a skinny girl with braids and braces. Kids called me Wires because of those braces, and boy, did it ever make me mad! So Tucker and I had a
20 lot in common, and lots of times we talked about the things kids called us, especially when we went fishing.

Even though being called those names hurt, Tucker gave up fighting the kids who said them. Fighting didn't help. The name-callers were all too big for him to beat up. So after a while, he learned to ignore the teasing. Most times he laughed it off. He was a tough little dude. But oh mercy, how he hated those names!

B One day Tucker did something that made everybody stop calling him names he didn't like. I think it helped him grow a few inches, too.

You need to know a few things about this boy before I tell you
30 what changed things around. Tucker could do almost anything that any other kid his age could do. He was a hotshot shortstop on the Little League baseball team. He could jump like a flea on the basketball court. He was smart in school. He was in the Boy Scouts. He could swim like a fish—and even surf!

He looked like a Tootsie Roll to me in that big ocean. Yeah, I had a name for him, too. I called him Tootsie Roll, but never to his face. I just kept it to myself. And when I called him that in my head, I didn't mean it in a bad way.

Tucker could do some fishing. He especially liked to fish his folks'
40 little **pier** alongside their house. In the summertime he'd lie on his stomach on the pier and catch some of the biggest flounder to come out of Calico Creek. Instead of a rod and reel, he used a handful of fishing line, a hook baited with shrimp, and a sinker to keep the bait from floating on the surface.

He'd dangle that shrimp an inch or two off the bottom, right in front of a flounder's nose. Sometimes we'd fish together on his pier, and I wouldn't catch diddlysquat, not even a pinfish, not even a lizard fish, nothing. But ole Tootsie Roll could catch 'em.

I tried fishing the way he did, but most of the time I used a rod
50 and reel 'cause I thought the way Tucker did it was country. I still couldn't catch anything, not in Calico Creek. I did all right when I fished at the pier in Atlantic Beach.

pier:
a platform
over the water

That's how I'd see Tucker surfing. He even got teased about surfing, because not many black kids we knew surfed. Shoot, as much as we all loved the water, not a whole lot of us even knew how to swim. I didn't. Not until Tucker taught me later on.

He and his dad or mom would fish out on their own little pier all night sometimes with a Coleman lantern[1] for light. His folks used regular rods and reels. I never fished out there at night with them
60 because the mosquitoes and the gnats would about eat me up.

Plus, my momma liked to tell me that they used to do baptizing in that creek, which was okay. But then Momma'd say, "LaShana Mae, you watch out about being around that creek by yourself at night. The people who got baptized there and who've passed on come back to that creek as spirits in the middle of the night when the moon's full. They'll be singing and celebrating and shouting and praising, and they don't want to be **disturbed**. Unless you wanna join in with 'em."

Me being a scared little kid, you can believe that Momma didn't have to worry about me going out to *nobody's* Calico Creek by myself
70 at night. But sometimes I'd go to my window at night and look out to see if anybody was celebrating the way she said. All I ever saw were grown folks fishing. Sometimes somebody would holler when they caught a big one. After I got grown I understood that Momma told me that story to try to help me stay out of trouble. She was worried I'd drown or get into some kind of foolishness. Well, it worked. I knew that it was easy to get into trouble when you're out someplace where you're not supposed to be.

disturbed:
bothered

[1] **Coleman lantern:** a lamp that burns pressurized kerosene to give light.

2. **◀ REREAD** Reread lines 6–26. In the margin, describe the conflict Tucker faces. Circle the text that foreshadows a future event.

3. **READ ▶** As you read lines 78–116, continue to cite textual evidence.
- Circle text that creates suspense about a major event in the plot that will take place.
- Underline text that suggests that his meeting with Richard was important to Tucker.
- In the margin, make an inference about Tucker's attitude toward Richard.

Critical Vocabulary: pier (line 40) Have students share their definitions of "pier." Ask them to provide a homophone (a word that sounds the same but has a different meaning and spelling) for the word. *Students should be able to cite the word "peer," but not "pear," which has a slightly different pronunciation.*

FOR ELL STUDENTS It will be difficult for ELL students to understand the central idea of this section if they do not know the meaning of a few key words and phrases. Make sure that they understand that "calling someone names" actually means to call the person bad names. Describe what "braids," "braces," and "wires" are.

ASK STUDENTS to make the connection between the narrator's braces and her nickname, *Wires*.

2. **REREAD AND CITE TEXT EVIDENCE** Remind students that writers include textual details that foreshadow, or hint at, future events.

B **ASK STUDENTS** to point out the text that foreshadows an event that will resolve the conflict.

3. **READ AND CITE TEXT EVIDENCE**

C **ASK STUDENTS** to make inferences drawn from the text and from their margin notes that suggest why the meeting with Richard is important to Tucker and what Tucker's attitude is toward Richard. *Students should cite examples in lines 97–98, 103–104, and 115–116.*

Critical Vocabulary: disturbed (line 67) Have students share their definitions of *disturbed* as Tate uses it here. What does the narrator's mother mean when she says that the spirits "don't want to be disturbed"? *She means that they don't want to be bothered, or annoyed, by her daughter.*

Anyway, what happened to change all the name-calling started when Tucker was on his pier trying to catch a flounder. He noticed a
80 man standing on the Moten Motel dock just a few yards from him. The man had a thick white mustache and Vandyke beard and wore a blue-and-gold military-style jacket and cap. I wasn't there, so I didn't see him, but that's what Tucker told me.

When the man waved, Tucker, being a friendly kind of kid, waved back. They struck up a conversation. The man said his name was Richard and that he was staying at the motel for a few days. His home was in Manteo, on Roanoke Island, not far from the Outer Banks, where he worked with the U.S. Lifesaving Service.

Tucker figured what he meant was that he was with the U.S. Coast
90 Guard. Tucker was pretty knowledgeable about the coast guard, but he had never heard of this lifesaving service. Tucker asked the man if he liked to fish. Richard said yes. He'd been a commercial fisherman before he became a captain in the lifesaving service. As a lifesaver, he said, he and his men went into the ocean in the middle of hurricanes and nor'easters[2] to save passengers and crew members whose ships were sinking.

C Of course, anything about water fascinated Tucker, so he must have asked this Richard a million questions. Richard didn't seem to mind, though. He said he didn't get to talk to kids much anymore.
D 100 Richard said a good crewman had to be strong, an excellent swimmer, a quick thinker, and in good physical health, have good eyesight, and understand how dangerous the sea can be. He told so many stories about lifesaving that Tucker wished he could enlist right away, and said so. He had the right **qualifications**—other than being too young, of course. And too short.

Richard told him it wasn't the size of a person that got the job done. It was how bad the person wanted to do it. How were those huge ships two and more stories high able to move into the Morehead City port and back out to sea? Most couldn't do it without little
110 tugboats pushing and pulling them in, Richard said. A tugboat could bring in a ship many times its size.

Richard said that Tucker would make a good tugboat and one day might even grow to be a big ship. He thanked Tucker for the conversation, said maybe they'd meet again, and then the man

qualifications:
abilities and accomplish-ments

Tucker is fascinated by Richard's knowledge and reassured by his kindness.

---
[2] **nor'easters:** storms with winds blowing from the northeast.

wandered off back toward the motel. Tucker said for the rest of the afternoon, he thought over what Richard had said.

A few days later, Tucker decided to go with his dad to the Atlantic Beach pier to fish. His daddy worked there as a cook. For some reason I couldn't go that day. I've always wished I had. Tucker said he took
120 his surfboard too, in case fishing got slow. It was early morning, but a hot July wind blew in from the southwest, making the waves choppy and sandy. The tide was going out. Hardly anybody was on the pier, which was another hint that the fish might not be biting. Tucker said only one guy was in the water, floating on a red raft like a huge jellyfish.

After a good hour had passed and he hadn't got a bite, Tucker left his rod and reel with his father in the pier restaurant's kitchen and went surfing. After he swam out far enough, he climbed onto his surfboard and rode a wave in. When he glanced back at the pier,
130 guess who he saw? His new friend, Richard, on the pier, clapping for him. At least this time he had on shorts and a regular shirt. Tucker said he bet Richard had about burnt up in that heavy uniform the other day.

Richard hollered, "Do it, Tugboat! Pull that ole wave in!"

Tugboat? Tucker said he frowned until he remembered Richard's story about tugboats. So he waved back and swam out to pull in another one, passing the man on the raft. The man said, "You're

---

4. ◀ **REREAD** Reread lines 100–116. Explain the significance of Richard's statement that "Tucker would make a good tugboat and one day might even grow to be a big ship." Cite specific text evidence to support your explanation.

Richard is reassuring Tucker that his size would not interfere with his ability to save someone's life at sea. He explained that Tucker has the main requirement for the job, strong desire. He is also giving Tucker hope that he may grow taller someday.

5. **READ ▶** As you read lines 117–183, continue to cite textual evidence.

• In the margin, take notes about how suspense is built in this section.
• Circle the paragraph that is most likely the story's climax.

Critical Vocabulary: qualifications (line 104) Have students give examples of *qualifications* that team members need to have to be on a basketball or soccer team. *Students should be able to draw on their own knowledge and experience to brainstorm a list of qualifications, such as strength and coordination, that members of these teams need to have.*

4. **REREAD AND CITE TEXT EVIDENCE**

D **ASK STUDENTS** to explain how Richard's statement that "Tucker would make a good tugboat and one day might even grow to be a big ship" reveals Richard's attitude about Tucker. *Students should cite specific textual evidence as they point out that Richard believes Tucker has great potential. He is trying to reassure Tucker that he is qualified for the job and that his ability to rescue someone at sea would not be impaired by his size.*

5. **READ AND CITE TEXT EVIDENCE**

E **ASK STUDENTS** to read their margin notes to a partner and then work together to find and cite specific text examples of how suspense is built into this section, leading to the climax of the story. *Students should note that the possibility of drowning, the worsening storm, and the man's falling into the water all build suspense, leading to the climax, the moment before the rescue when Tucker thinks he is going to die.*

" *He thrashed around in the water screaming that he couldn't swim.* "

kinda little to be way out here, ain't ya, squirt?" Tucker just shook his head and kept going.

(F) 140   Tucker pulled in four more waves until he noticed a tall purple thunderhead rising up on the southwest horizon. That cloud meant a storm was probably on its way, but Tucker figured he had at least half an hour before the wind kicked up the waves and blew the cloud in and the rain began. Tucker wasn't afraid of a thing, but his common sense and his folks had told him to always leave away from water when storms and lightning came along. It's hard to get grown without having common sense, because being stupid can get you killed sometimes.

The possibility of drowning builds suspense.

(E) 150   Keeping an eye on the horizon, Tucker went on pulling in those waves until a huge one arched up behind his back and crashed down on him. Tucker disappeared.

Wipeout. No big deal for Tucker, though. He popped right up in the water and grabbed his board, which was tied to his ankle. He was all right. But the man on the raft wasn't. He thrashed around in the water screaming that he couldn't swim.

Now someone's life is in real danger.

As that big black cloud spread across the sky toward them, the wind and waves grew rougher. Wanting to help the man, but concerned about his own safety, Tucker hesitated, then straddled his surfboard and, using his hands for oars, paddled toward the raft.

160   He'd have time to get the guy's raft back to him and then head in. But as Tucker passed, the man lunged at the surfboard, knocking Tucker off.

Now Tucker is in danger.

And then this guy grabbed hold of Tucker! Wrapped up in that big bear's arms and legs, with the sea getting choppier, Tucker said he knew he was about to die. He began to pray.

But something lifted Tucker up through the water and onto his surfboard, where he was able to catch his breath. That's when he saw his friend Richard in the water, too! Have mercy! Richard was hauling that raft toward the man. With two big heaves, Richard snatched that **170** guy straight up out of the water and onto the raft.

Richard yelled, "Let's push and pull it, Tugboat! Push and pull it in!"

Somehow Tucker and Richard pushed and pulled that raft—with the guy glued to it—close enough to shore that the man was able to wade in the rest of the way. Four or five people splashed into the water and helped them onto the beach and into the pier house. One of the helpers was a reporter on vacation.

As soon as everybody was inside the pier house, the rain poured down. An arrow of lightning whizzed across the pier into the water **180** and lit up the whole ocean. That's when Tucker said he got scared, seeing that lightning. He'd have been fried alive, you know. The guy Tucker rescued was named Nibbles. Mr. Nibbles was so grateful that he gave Tucker a hundred dollars right on the spot.

The reporter interviewed everybody and took pictures of Tucker, Nibbles, and Tucker's dad, who almost had a heart attack when he heard what happened. When the reporter asked how such a small boy was able to rescue a big, grown man, Tucker said, "'Cause I'm a tugboat, like Richard said. We pull the big ones in."

But when Tucker turned around to point out Richard, he couldn't **190** find him.

Getting help releases some of the suspense.

We know the man is okay.

---

6. ◀ **REREAD AND DISCUSS**   Reread lines 140–148. With a partner, discuss the details that build suspense. What do you think these details foreshadow? Support your answer with explicit textual evidence.

7. **READ** ▶   As you read lines 184–237, continue to cite textual evidence.

- In the margin, explain how Tucker's conflict is resolved.
- Then, summarize what Tucker learns about Richard in lines 216–237.

8

9

FOR ELL STUDENTS   Direct students to lines 140–148. Ask them to reread this passage and to point out the storm-related vocabulary: *thunderhead, cloud* (line 141); *storm* (line 142); *wind, blew* (line 143); *rain* (line 144); and *lightning* (line 146). Ask students to define these weather words by using the context of the story. If students have difficulty explaining the meaning of the words, invite them to draw pictures or to use gestures to define them.

6.   **REREAD AND DISCUSS USING TEXT EVIDENCE**

(F) ASK STUDENTS   to work with a partner to cite specific text evidence that builds suspense and might foreshadow the climax. *Students should cite textual evidence from lines 140–148 to show that the approaching storm builds tension, creating suspense, and foreshadows the "stormy weather ahead," in the form of near-drowning, for Tucker and Mr. Nibbles.*

7.   **READ AND CITE TEXT EVIDENCE**

(G) ASK STUDENTS   to read their margin notes to a partner and then create one summary that briefly states what Tucker learns about Richard. *Students should cite textual evidence from lines 206–207 and 216–237.*

Tucker is a local hero when he rescues a grown man from the sea.

The reporter's story about Tucker's rescue was in the local paper, then got picked up by the Associated Press and went all over the world. CBS TV even flew him and his folks to New York to be on its morning show. Afterwards, back home in Morehead City, strangers stopped Tucker on the street, in stores, even came to his home. They wanted to see the little "tugboat" that hauled in that big man, and get his autograph.

200 Businesses up and down Arendell Street put up WELCOME HOME, TUGBOAT! posters in their windows. And there was a parade. Tucker was a hero! He and the mayor rode on the back of a big ole white Cadillac convertible and waved at everybody. I was so proud that I almost forgot and hollered out, "Way to go, Tootsie Roll!" but I caught myself in time.

Everybody—even local folks—called Tucker Tugboat after that, including us kids. We'd never seen a real live hero close up before, especially one our age. It wasn't cool anymore to tease him with those other names. Funny how things can turn right around, isn't it?

No one makes fun of Tucker anymore.

Plus, he grew tall after all.

And you know what? Tucker grew to be six feet five. He played on 210 the North Carolina Central University Eagles basketball team, joined the U.S. Coast Guard, and lives in Kill Devil Hills, North Carolina, on the Outer Banks.

But there's something Tucker never figured out. When he first told people that Richard was the real hero, nobody believed him. Apparently nobody but Tucker had seen Richard—not even Mr. Nibbles.

There's more. When Tucker went into the pier gift shop to spend some of his rescue money, he picked up a book about the coast guard. He was thumbing through it when he stopped at an old-timey picture of some black men wearing jackets like Richard's. They were standing 220 in front of a building on the Outer Banks. Below it was a picture of— yes, Richard! Mustache, beard, jacket, everything!

Tucker read, "History of the Pea Island Lifesaving Service. Captain Richard Etheridge was Keeper of the Pea Island Lifesaving Service, a forerunner of part of what is now the U.S. Coast Guard. This unique, all African American, courageous lifesaving crew, and those who followed, saved hundreds of shipwrecked passengers' lives by plunging into the stormy seas and bringing their charges back to safety."

Richard was the head of a lifesaving service and died in 1900.

10

230 Tucker said he shot out of that gift shop toward the restaurant to show his dad the book to prove his case, but what he read next made him stop: "Captain Etheridge, born in 1844 on Roanoke Island in North Carolina, died in 1900."

Tucker said he read that date fifteen or twenty times before it started to sink in. Nineteen hundred? Richard Etheridge had been dead for almost one hundred years. How was it possible a dead man helped him save that guy? Unless Richard was a ghost. He'd been talking to, and swimming with—a ghost?

You can believe Tucker hit up the library that very next day and 240 searched for as much information as he could find on Richard Etheridge. There wasn't much, but what he read was that Richard Etheridge was all those great things he had read about and that he still died in 1900.

A few years later, when Tucker's folks visited the North Carolina Aquarium on Roanoke Island, Tucker found Richard Etheridge's grave and monument. Etheridge's headstone was marked 1844–1900. That's when Tucker stopped talking about Richard being involved in the rescue. Unless somebody asked.

So now, if you run into Tucker "Tugboat" Willis, ask him about the rescue, and he'll tell you. Then, real carefully, ask if he ever met 250 Richard Etheridge. He'll tell you yes, he did, and what he learned. What he learned was that it pays to be polite to everybody you meet, like Tucker was to a man named Richard. You never know when that person might help you.

And every time Tucker tells me the story, he tells it to me the same way I told it to you. Seeing how Tucker turned out proves that some mighty things that help folks out in some mighty big ways can come in some mighty small packages.

It also proves that good things come to those who wait, like I did. I know, because I'm Mrs. LaShana Mae Willis, Tugboat's wife.

8. **READ** ▶ As you read lines 238–275, continue to cite textual evidence.

- Underline the reason Tucker stops talking about Richard's involvement in the rescue (lines 243–247).
- Circle what you learn about the narrator.

11

WHEN STUDENTS STRUGGLE . . .

To help students understand how the setting shapes the events and the role Richard plays in the story, ask them to reread lines 212–237. Invite them to work with a small group to discuss how this passage gives insight into the setting, characters, and plot of the story.

FOR ELL STUDENTS A phrasal verb (a verb that is followed by a preposition, which gives the verb another meaning) may be difficult for ELL students to comprehend. Make sure that students understand the actual meaning of "shot out" (left very quickly), "hit up" (went to), and "run into" (meet by coincidence).

ASK STUDENTS to use each of these phrasal verbs in a sentence.

8. **READ AND CITE TEXT EVIDENCE** Although Tucker most likely believes that Richard Etheridge participated in the rescue, he stops including Richard's involvement in the rescue until somebody asks about him.

Ⓗ ASK STUDENTS to cite textual evidence that suggests why Tucker stops talking about Richard's involvement in the rescue of Mr. Nibbles. *Students should cite that when Tucker sees Richard Etheridge's grave and monument, confirming that Richard had died in 1900, he stops talking about Richard's participation in the rescue because people might doubt Tucker's sanity if he says he was helped by someone who has been dead for a century.*

260   *There really was a man named Richard Etheridge, a professional fisherman who was born in 1844 on Roanoke Island off North Carolina. A member of the Thirty-sixth U.S. Colored Troops of the Union Army, he fought at the Battle of New Market Heights in Virginia during the Civil War. And in 1880, Etheridge was hired as the Keeper of the Pea Island Lifesaving Station on the Barrier Islands (the Outer Banks) of North Carolina. The station continued to set a high standard of performance with its all-black personnel until 1947, when the Coast Guard closed down the facilities.*

   No one made any formal recognition of the Pea Island surfmen's *270* *daring sea rescues until 1996. In March of that year, Etheridge and his men were finally acknowledged* **posthumously** *in formal ceremonies in Washington, D.C., with a Gold Lifesaving Medal from the United States Coast Guard. Etheridge and his wife and daughter are buried on the grounds of the North Carolina Aquarium in Manteo, which maintains an exhibit on these brave men.*

posthumously:
after death

9. ◀ **REREAD AND DISCUSS** Reread lines 260–275. With a partner, discuss the inclusion of the historical facts at the end of a fictional story. Does it add anything to the story or is it unnecessary?

SHORT RESPONSE

Cite Text Evidence   Was Tucker the hero that everyone thought him to be, or was Richard mostly responsible for the rescue? **Cite text evidence** to support your opinion.

Tucker was a hero. He decided to save Mr. Nibbles, despite knowing he was in danger himself. Even if Richard was really there, Tucker "wasn't afraid of a thing." He still had to fight the storm and struggle hard to help rescue Mr. Nibbles. If Richard was only in Tucker's imagination, then Tucker certainly was a hero and accomplished an amazing feat.

12

---

9. **REREAD AND DISCUSS USING TEXT EVIDENCE**

ASK STUDENTS to cite specific text evidence and line numbers to support what interest historical facts add to the story. *Students should cite text evidence from lines 260–275.*

Critical Vocabulary: posthumously (line 271) Discuss why the author uses the word "posthumously" when discussing the awards given to the Pea Island surfmen. *The surfmen were only recognized for their service many years after their death.*

SHORT RESPONSE

Cite Text Evidence   Student responses will vary, but students should cite evidence from the text to support their positions. Students should

- explain whether Tucker or Richard was truly the hero
- give reasons for their point of view
- cite specific evidence from the text to support their reasons

TO CHALLENGE STUDENTS . . .

For more context about Richard Etheridge and the Pea Island Lifesaving Service, students can conduct print, online, or multimedia research to write a report about Etheridge and his all–African American Pea Island lifesavers and their daring rescues on North Carolina's Outer Banks.

ASK STUDENTS to do some preliminary research to find an aspect of the topic that interests them. Possible topics for their research might include

- Etheridge's role as the keeper of the Pea Island station
- the rescue of the *E.S. Newman* by the Pea Island lifesavers in 1896
- the Roanoke Island Freedmen and the Pea Island Lifesaving Station

With the class, discuss the following elements of a research report after students have chosen a topic.

Plan Your Research

- Write questions about your topic.
- Research your topic and take notes.
- Organize your notes.
- Write an outline based on your notes.

Write Your Report

- Keep your purpose and audience in mind.
- Write a first draft, revise your report, and proofread it.
- Reread your report and check that your bibliography is accurate.

Publish and Share

- Make a final copy of your report.
- Publish and share it.

ASK STUDENTS what they hope to discover as they research their report. How is the information they find similar to, yet different from, the story and facts shared by Tate?

DIG DEEPER

1. With the class, return to Question 6, Reread and Discuss. Have students share the results of their discussion.

   ASK STUDENTS whether they were pleased with the outcome of their partner discussions. Have each pair share the details they chose that created suspense in the plot. How did these details create tension and excitement for the reader? Then ask each pair to share their discussion about a future event these details foreshadowed. What textual evidence did pairs cite to support their opinion about this future plot development?

   - Guide each pair to tell whether his or her partner cited any textual details (or evidence) with which he or she did not agree. If so, what was it? How did the partners resolve their differences of opinion?

   - Encourage partners to explain how they decided on the event (or plot development) in the story that was foreshadowed by the details of the growing storm. What compelling evidence did they find to support their choice?

   - After partners have shared the results of their discussion, ask whether another pair shared any ideas they wish they had thought of.

2. With the class, return to Question 9, Reread and Discuss. Have students share the results of their discussion.

   ASK STUDENTS whether they were satisfied with the outcome of their partner discussions. Have each pair share their agreed-upon opinion about the inclusion of the historical facts at the end of the fictional story. What convincing evidence did pairs cite from the story to support their opinion?

   - Encourage pairs to tell whether their partner cited any compelling textual evidence to support the opposite position. If so, why wasn't the evidence strong enough to become the agreed-upon opinion? How did the pairs resolve any conflicts or disagreements?

   - After partners have shared the results of their discussion, ask whether another pair's findings convinced them that the opposite opinion had merit. Did it change their opinion?

   ASK STUDENTS to return to their Short Response answer and to revise it based on the class discussion about citing convincing textual evidence to support an opinion.

CLOSE READING NOTES

COMPARE MEDIA

MEDIA **Covering Issues in the News**

Online News Article, Editorial, and TV News Interview

Why These Texts?

Students regularly encounter news stories in their daily lives. This lesson explores the same news story as covered in three different forms of media, offering a variety of perspectives and opinions. By learning to analyze news stories in different media, students will become more savvy consumers of news.

Key Learning Objective: The student will be able to analyze and compare news stories about the same event from various sources.

For practice and application:

Finding Your Everest

Essay by Robert Medina

Close Reader selection:
"Finding Your Everest"
Essay by Robert Medina

RI 1 Cite textual evidence.
RI 2 Determine central ideas and details.
RI 3 Analyze interactions between individuals, events, and ideas.
RI 5 Analyze the structure an author uses to organize a text.
RI 6 Determine an author's point of view or purpose.
RI 8 Trace and evaluate an argument.
RI 9 Analyze how two or more authors write about the same topic.
SL 2 Analyze main ideas and details presented in diverse media.
W 1 Write arguments.
W 4 Produce clear and coherent writing.
W 6 Use technology to produce and publish writing.

▲ Text Complexity Rubric

	Parents of Rescued Teenage Sailor . . . **Lexile:** 1110L	Ship of Fools **Lexile:** 1120L	Was Abby Too Young to Sail? **Lexile:** N/A
Quantitative Measures			
Qualitative Measures	Levels of Meaning/Purpose — single level of simple meaning	Levels of Meaning/Purpose — single level of simple meaning	Levels of Meaning/Purpose — more than one purpose; implied, easily identified from context
	Structure — organization of main ideas and details complex, but clearly stated and generally sequential	Structure — implicit problem-solution text structure	Structure — largely simple graphics, supplementary to understanding of the media
	Language Conventionality and Clarity — some unfamiliar language	Language Conventionality and Clarity — more complex sentence structure	Language Conventionality and Clarity — mainly conversational language
	Knowledge Demands — some specialized knowledge required	Knowledge Demands — some specialized knowledge required	Knowledge Demands — some specialized knowledge required
Reader/Task Considerations	• Teacher determined • Vary by individual reader and type of text • See the Text X-Ray for suggested Reader/Task Considerations.		

Meaning Making

Language Development

Effective Expression

Content Knowledge

Foundational Skills

English Language Support Before teaching, use the Text X-Ray below for an overview of the texts' complexity. The Text X-Ray and the supports and scaffolds in the Teacher's Edition will help you guide students of different skill levels.

Text Complexity: Qualitative Measures

▲ Levels of Meaning/Purpose

Help students identify the author's purpose and central idea or claim.

- Teacher's Edition side notes, pp. 24, 29, 30
- English Language Support, pp. 19, 24, 26
- When Students Struggle, p. 25
- Strategies for Annotation, pp. 21, 27
- Analyze Ideas in Diverse Media, p. 30

To help students determine the claim, see

- Trace and Evaluate an Argument, pp. 25, 26, 27

To reteach how to analyze diverse media, see

- Analyze Presentations of Information, p. 30a

▶ *Use It! Level Up* Tutorials: Reading for Details and Main Idea and Supporting Details
Interactive Whiteboard Lesson: Author's Purpose and Perspective

ZOOM IN ON **ANALYZING IDEAS IN DIVERSE MEDIA** Explain that news stories can be presented on different types of media (for example, newspapers, the Internet, TV). Point out that the same news event may be covered differently depending on the **author's purpose,** or reason for writing or producing. Explain that an author chooses a format that best suits his or her purpose.

As a class, discuss the most likely purpose for writing in these formats:

- a news article *(to provide information)*
- an editorial *(to present opinions)*
- a television program *(to entertain and inform)*

▲ Structure

Help students analyze the structure of a news article, an editorial, and a TV interview.

- Teacher's Edition side notes, pp. 20, 21, 22, 23, 25, 26, 27, 28, 29
- English Language Support, pp. 20, 28
- When Students Struggle, p. 22
- Strategies for Annotation, pp. 21, 23, 26
- Analyze Structure, pp. 23, 29

▶ *Use It!* **Interactive Graphic Organizer:** 5 Ws and H Questions

ZOOM IN ON **ANALYZING STRUCTURE** Tell students that the main purpose of a **news report** is to convey facts and details. Introduce students to the **5 Ws and H Questions** chart on page 23. Explain that journalists use these questions to organize facts and details.

- After students read the news story and the editorial, have pairs fill in a 5 Ws and H Questions chart for each piece.
- Remind them to include only the most important facts and details.
- Have pairs join small groups and compare their charts.

After students watch the TV interview, have groups discuss how it differs from the print pieces.

▲ Language Conventionality and Clarity

Teach unfamiliar academic vocabulary in context.

• Applying Academic Vocabulary, pp. 20, 24

Guide students to analyze the language and sentence structure of the news pieces.

• English Language Support, pp. 19, 20, 22, 25

ZOOM IN ON **USE OF VERBS** Read aloud lines 13–18 on page 20 and point out the use of verbs in the present, past, and past perfect tenses. Explain that the past perfect tense indicates something that happened before another past action or before a specific time in the past.

• Ask students to identify the past perfect verb. *(had destroyed)*
• Have them identify the tense of each other verb in the paragraph.
• Then have pairs work together to create a timeline of the events described in the paragraph.

Explain that when they read news stories, paying attention to tenses will help them keep track of the sequence of events.

▲ Knowledge Demands

Help students understand the background of the news story.

• Teacher's Edition Background note, p. 19

ZOOM IN ON **BUILDING BACKGROUND** Note that Abby Sunderland is one of many young people who have put themselves at risk to break a record or achieve fame. Before reading, discuss these questions:

• Why might a young person want to break a world record?
• How young is too young when breaking a record involves danger?
• Why might people object to allowing young people to try to break records?

After students have read and viewed the news pieces, revisit these questions to see if their responses have changed.

▲ Suggested Reader/Task Considerations

Consider the following before assigning these pieces to students:

• Do students have the analytical thinking skills to understand the relationships between the different news formats and types of media?
• Do students have questioning skills to evaluate the ideas presented in these pieces?

ZOOM IN ON **SUPPORTING COMPREHENSION**

• Form mixed-ability groups to read and view the news pieces. After reading, have them fill in a chart like the one on page 30. Students can then refer to the charts as they discuss news formats.
• Read aloud the title, subtitle, and first paragraph of "Ship of Fools" and model questioning techniques. *(What is the author's attitude toward the topic? The first paragraph presents facts, but the title and subtitle indicate a very critical view of the Sunderlands. As I read on, I'll ask more questions to evaluate the evidence the author presents.)*

TEACH

CLOSE READ

Background Have students read the background information about news pieces. Explain that students are going to read and watch news pieces about Abby Sunderland, a 16-year-old American girl who in 2010 attempted to sail around the world by herself. Abby's trip was cut short when her sailboat was hit by a storm in the Indian Ocean. Abby's story raised a range of emotions around the world, from admiration to fear to anger.

SETTING A PURPOSE Direct students to use the Setting a Purpose text to focus their reading and viewing. Remind them to generate questions as they read and view.

English Language Support

Read Closely After students read the Background note, discuss the title of each piece and note the different formats (a news article, an editorial, and a TV news interview).

ASK STUDENTS what each title might indicate about the author's **purpose,** or reason for writing or producing the piece. Guide students to understand that the news article title states a fact, the editorial title states an opinion, and the interview title asks a question. Tell students that the title of a piece often gives a clue to the author's purpose.

English Language Support

Analyze Language In a word web, display words and phrases from the two news articles that are all related to the danger Abby Sunderland faced, such as *risking her life, save her life, sink, emergency beacon, search and rescue,* and *difficult conditions*. Discuss the meaning of each word and phrase. Then explain how these words are related.

ASK STUDENTS what kinds of dangers a teenager might meet on a solo sailboat trip around the world.

Background *A compelling event in the news can trigger controversy. Through television, the Internet, and print articles, journalists and the general public voice their opinions and ask heated questions that may not have easy answers.*

SETTING A PURPOSE In this lesson, you'll analyze media about a 16-year-old's attempt to become the youngest person to sail solo around the world, an event that sparked worldwide controversy.

MEDIA ANALYSIS

Covering Issues in the News

Parents of Rescued Teenage Sailor Abby Sunderland Accused of Risking Her Life
Online News Article by Paul Harris

Ship of Fools
Editorial by Joanna Weiss

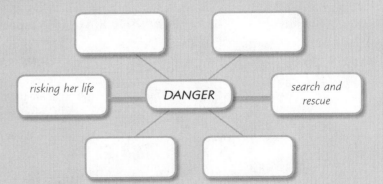

Was Abby Too Young to Sail?
TV News Interview by CBS News

(t) ©Richard Hartog/AP Images; (tc) ©Eric Hoarau/TAAF/AFP/Getty Images; (bc) ©Charles Krupa/AP Images; (b) ©BBC Motion Gallery

---

risking her life — DANGER — search and rescue

CLOSE READ

Analyze Structure

RI 1,
RI 2,
RI 5,
SL 2

(LINES 1–4)

Explain to students that journalists use the **5 Ws and H** questions as an outline for writing a news story. The questions are *who, what, when, where, why,* and *how.* Journalists then use this information to organize their writing. Answering each question contributes to the development of the article.

Ⓐ CITE TEXT EVIDENCE Have students reread lines 1–4 and tell who and what the online news article is about. *(It is about a teenage girl who was rescued after she attempted to sail around the world by herself.)*

English Language Support

Read Closely Tell students that some words or expressions have a meaning that is different from what the words actually say. Have students read lines 8–12 and discuss why Abby's father says that she got out of the boat "with the clothes on her back."

Help them understand the phrase: Abby had to leave everything behind, taking nothing from the boat except the clothes she was wearing. Encourage students to visualize Abby leaving the boat.

ASK STUDENTS what the expression suggests about the condition of the boat and Abby's reaction to being rescued. *(It indicates the difficulty of getting off the boat and suggests that many items aboard the battered boat had been ruined.)*

MEDIA

Parents of Rescued Teenage Sailor Abby Sunderland Accused of Risking Her Life

Sailing experts condemn family for allowing 16-year-old American girl to attempt a solo round-the-world voyage

Paul Harris, New York
The Observer, June 12, 2010

A teenage girl attempting to sail solo around the world was rescued yesterday in a remote spot of the Indian Ocean, bringing to a successful conclusion the dramatic bid to save her life.

Ⓐ

Sixteen-year-old American Abby Sunderland was picked up from her stricken vessel by a dinghy[1] launched from the French fishing boat *Ile de la Reunion*.[2]

Her father, Laurence Sunderland, speaking to reporters outside their California home, said his daughter was safe and
10 well: "She got out of her vessel with the clothes on her back, and we are just really excited and ecstatic that Abigail is in safe hands. She was in good spirits . . . she talked to her mother."

However, the same cannot be said of Sunderland's yacht, *Wild Eyes.* The vessel was apparently pounded by gigantic waves that had destroyed its mast,[3] which in turn knocked out her satellite communications equipment. The yacht was then effectively left floundering midway between Africa and Australia. It is likely to be allowed to sink.

Sunderland had activated an emergency beacon[4] which
20 started a huge search and rescue operation involving Australia, America, and France. Numerous ships became involved in the hunt, as well as a chartered jet which spotted the teenager late on Thursday. Sunderland was able to radio the plane and report that she was fit and had food and water supplies.

---

[1] **dinghy:** a small open boat carried as a lifeboat on a larger boat.
[2] **Ile de la Reunion:** the French fishing boat carrying the dinghy that picked up Abby is a large ocean-going ship, 180 feet long, 23 feet wide, and weighing 1295 tons.
[3] **mast:** the tall, vertical pole that supports the sail and rigging of a ship.
[4] **beacon:** a radio or transmitter that emits a guidance signal.

20 Collection 1

APPLYING ACADEMIC VOCABULARY

aspect	resource

THINK-PAIR-SHARE Have partners discuss the questions below. Encourage them to include the vocabulary words *aspect* and *resource* in their responses. Let volunteers share their responses with the class.

- What **aspect** of Abby's trip was most concerning to you?
- What **resources** did Abby have on board to help keep her safe?

The rescue itself was not without incident as rough seas saw the captain of the French boat fall into the water. "He was fished out in difficult conditions," said a statement from the French territory of Reunion Island.

Though the search for Sunderland ended happily, it has caused a debate on the wisdom of such young sailors making dramatic and dangerous journeys. Sunderland was following the achievement of her brother, Zac, who had made the solo journey around the world at the age of 17, becoming the youngest person in the world to do so.

Abby Sunderland on her sailboat *Wild Eyes* in Ensenada, Mexico, during her attempt at a solo round-the-world voyage

Many critics of Sunderland—and her parents—have criticized the decision to let her go on such a journey. "It's not something that a 16-year-old should be able to decide—whether they're capable of doing it. It's potentially irresponsible for the parents," Michael Kalin, junior director of San Francisco's St Francis Yacht Club, told the Associated Press.

Other top figures from the world of sailing joined in the criticism. "In Abby's case she was lucky. It's only a matter of time until we end up with a tragedy on our hands," said Derrick Fries, a world sailing champion and author of *Learn to Sail.*

CLOSE READ

Analyze Structure

RI 1, RI 2, RI 5, SL 2

(LINES 30–35, 36–47)

At this point in the news article, the focus shifts from the recounting of Abby Sunderland's rescue to the debate in the media her voyage created. Here the **central idea,** or the most important idea about a topic, shifts from focusing on Abby's voyage to reactions to Abby's voyage.

B **ASK STUDENTS** to reread lines 30–35 and identify the central idea introduced in this section of the article. *(This section introduces the debate sparked by Abby's voyage over the wisdom of young sailors making "dramatic and dangerous journeys.")*

Explain to students that **supporting details** can be facts, statistics, and anecdotes that tell more about, or support, a central idea.

C **CITE TEXT EVIDENCE** Have students reread lines 36–47 and identify supporting details that provide more information about the central idea. *(Many critics, including experts, criticized the decision to let Abby go on the voyage. The director of a yacht club suggested it wasn't Abby's decision to make, and a world sailing champion thought Abby was lucky to survive.)*

Strategies for Annotation   🖉 📖 *Annotate it!*

Analyze Structure

RI 2, RI 5, SL 2

Have students locate lines 43–47. Encourage them to use their eBook annotation tools to do the following:

- Highlight in yellow *What* this paragraph is about—the central idea.
- Highlight in green a *Who* detail that supports this idea.
- On a note, write the central idea in your own words.

Other top figures from the world of sailing joined in the criticism. "In Abby's case she was lucky. It's only a matter of time until we end up with a tragedy on our hands," said Derrick Fries, a world sailing champion and author of *Learn to Sail.*

CLOSE READ

Analyze Structure

RI 1,
RI 5,
SL 2

(LINES 57–62)

Point out that news stories often tell about why something happened.

D CITE TEXT EVIDENCE Ask students to reread lines 57–62 and tell why Abby's family believed that she should have been allowed to go on the sailing trip. *(Abby's family believed that Abby was highly experienced and skilled; they believe challenge is healthy for an adventurous child; they believe many parents are overprotective.)*

English Language Support

Have students consider the family's use of the adjective phrases "highly experienced" and "highly skilled" to describe Abby in lines 57–59. What does the repetition of the word "highly" suggest about the family's viewpoint? *(The repetition of "highly" adds emphasis and shows that the family feels very strongly that they were right to allow Abby to go on the sailing trip.)*

Such opinions by professionals have been echoed on blogs and comments on news articles as members of the public
50 have called the Sunderlands irresponsible and careless. One commentator on the *Los Angeles Times* website summed up the view of many: "Abby Sunderland was on the wrong type of boat (a racing yacht) in the wrong location (the southern Indian Ocean) at the wrong time of year (winter in the southern hemisphere). Other than those minor details, it was a well-planned voyage."

But the family have robustly defended themselves. They have pointed out that Abby is a highly experienced and highly skilled sailor. They have even used the debate to criticize the
60 too-careful tendency of much modern parenting advice and said that a certain amount of risky challenge was healthy for an adventurous child.

"I never questioned my decision in letting her go. In this day and age we get overprotective with our children," Laurence Sunderland said. "Look at how many teenagers die in cars every year. Should we let teenagers drive cars? I think it'd be silly if we didn't."

WHEN STUDENTS STRUGGLE ...

To guide students' understanding of the information presented in the news piece, have pairs of students work together to make a two-column chart to list reasons given in the text that explain why Abby should and should not have been allowed to make the solo sailboat trip. Students can then look at their chart and discuss their own opinions.

Reasons For	Reasons Against
She had a radio.	It's not something a child should be able to decide.
She had food and water supplies.	

LEVEL UP TUTORIALS For additional support, assign the following *Level Up* tutorials: **Analyzing Arguments, Evidence.**

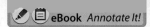
Analyze Structure

RI 2, RI 5, SL 2

In a **news report,** whether it's online, in print, or broadcast on television, journalists commonly use the **5 *Ws* and *H* questions**—*who, what, when, where, why,* and *how*—as an outline for writing the news story. Following this structure helps to ensure that writers have covered the necessary details. In turn, readers can use the 5 *Ws* and *H* questions to determine the main idea and supporting details of a news story. The **central idea** is the most important idea about a topic that a writer conveys, and the **supporting details** are the examples, facts, statistics, and anecdotes that provide a basis for the central idea.

Analyzing the Media

RI 2, RI 5, SL 2

Cite Text Evidence Support your responses with evidence from the text.

1. **Summarize** Review the news story and fill out a chart like this one to record the story's 5 *Ws* and *H*.

5 Ws and H Questions

Who is the story about?	
What happened to this person?	
When did it happen?	
Where did it happen?	
Why did it happen?	
How did it happen?	

2. **Infer** What is the central idea of this article? Cite details from the article to support your answer.

PRACTICE & APPLY

Analyze Structure

RI 2, RI 5, SL 2

Help students understand the terms. Discuss whether the news report they just read answers all of the 5 *Ws and H* questions. Then have them explain how answering these questions helped the journalist to write the story. *(Answering all of these questions makes sure that the reader understands everything about the news event and what people thought of it.)*

Analyzing the Media

RI 2, RI 5, SL 2

Possible answers:

1. **Who:** *A 16-year-old girl and her family;* **What:** *She gets rescued while attempting to sail around the world by herself;* **When:** *In 2010;* **Where:** *In the Indian Ocean;* **Why:** *Her sailboat was disabled by a big storm;* **How:** *A fishing boat picked her up.*

2. *The central idea of this article is that many people do not think that Abby should have been able to go on this trip by herself, but her parents disagree. Details that support this idea include the following: experts and other members of the public said that the girl should not have been able to go by herself; her parents said that she was skilled enough to sail alone and that risky challenges are good for adventurous children.*

Strategies for Annotation   🖉 🗐 *Annotate it!*

Analyze Structure

RI 2, RI 5, SL 2

Have students locate lines 8–12. Encourage them to use their eBook annotation tools to do the following:

- Highlight in yellow *Who* this paragraph is about.
- Highlight in green *Where* this person is.
- Review annotations and, in a note, tell how this paragraph supports the article's central idea.

Her father, Laurence Sunderland, speaking to reporters outside their California home, said his daughter was safe and well: "She got out of her vessel with the cl[...] and we are just really excited and ecstatic[...] hands. She was in good spirits . . . she tal[...]

> That her parents were happy Abby made the trip even though others may disagree with their choice is supported here by showing that they were relieved she was safe.

Trace and Evaluate an Argument (LINES 7–9, 19–23)

RI 1,
RI 2,
RI 5,
RI 8

Explain to students that an **editorial** is an opinion piece that appears in the part of a newspaper that has other opinions. An **opinion** is a statement of belief or feeling. It is not a fact. A **fact** is a statement that can be proved. Facts can be used to support a person's opinions.

F **ASK STUDENTS** to reread the sentence on lines 7–9 and identify whether the statement is a fact or an opinion. *(It is an opinion because it cannot be proved. It is a statement of the writer's beliefs.)*

Explain that an editorial can include a claim. A **claim** is the writer's position or opinion. To prove a claim, a writer must provide reasons and evidence. **Reasons** are statements that explain a person's beliefs or actions. **Evidence** includes the facts, statistics, quotations, or anecdotes that support each reason.

G **CITE TEXT EVIDENCE** Have students reread lines 19–23, state the writer's claim, and identify reasons that support that claim. *(The writer's claim is that letting Abby go on her solo voyage was a foolish and dangerous decision by Abby's parents. The writer gives reasons, such as the danger the rescue workers were exposed to, and talks about the "uninspiring" image of Abby alone surrounded by threatening waves.)*

English Language Support

Have pairs complete the activity above. Model how to identify reasons and evidence the author uses to support her opinion of the Sunderlands. Note that the editorial's title is one piece of evidence. Provide students with sentence frames to help them organize their responses.

- The writer's claim, or opinion, is that the Sunderlands _____.
- One reason the writer gives to support this opinion is _____.
- Another reason that supports the writer's opinion is _____.

Ship of Fools

Protecting a 16-year-old sailor, not enabling dangerous dreams, is a parent's responsibility

Joanna Weiss, Globe Columnist
The Boston Globe, June 15, 2010

'I THINK it's a parent's job to realize their kids' dreams," Abby Sunderland's father told the *Los Angeles Times* last winter. This was just before he waved his 16-year-old daughter off on what was to be a six-month voyage alone on a small boat, her effort to become the youngest person to sail around the world nonstop and unassisted.

F Here's a proposed rule of thumb: any record that requires more than 10 syllables to explain does not need to be broken. At any rate, Abby did not succeed. A massive storm 10 in the Indian Ocean knocked out her mast, launching a massive international rescue effort. She has since abandoned her 40-foot boat and boarded a French fishing vessel, from where she has resumed her blog.

Actually, she has a panoply of interlinked blogs,[1] set up to track and promote her journey, including one that sold T-shirts and shoes with an "Abby 16" logo. They're flooded now with comments offering gratitude and praise, calling her a role model and an inspiration.

G So this is the definition of bravery now? Embarking[2] on 20 unnecessary risk that jeopardizes the lives of rescue workers? When I thought of a 16-year-old bobbing alone in the Indian Ocean, surrounded by 25-foot waves, I didn't feel inspired. I felt sad. And when I thought about her parents, I felt furious.

Abby's fans would call me a naysayer,[3] I gather from their posts, and tell me I lack a spirit of adventure. And I'll admit that parenthood requires one to overcome a certain intolerance[4] for risk. I can't watch my 5-year-old daughter climb the monkey bars without feeling like I'm going to have a coronary. God knows what I'll do when she starts driving.

---

[1] **panoply (păn´ə plē) of interlinked blogs:** an array of blogs that are linked together.
[2] **Embarking:** setting out.
[3] **naysayer:** one who opposes or takes a negative view.
[4] **intolerance:** condition or quality of not accepting.

APPLYING ACADEMIC VOCABULARY

cultural	evaluate	text

THINK-PAIR-SHARE Have students turn to a partner to discuss the following questions. Guide students to include the vocabulary words *cultural*, *evaluate*, and *text* in their responses. Ask volunteers to share their responses with the class.

- How might **cultural** influences affect decisions like the one Abby's parents made? What examples of these influences appear in the **text**?
- How would you **evaluate** the writer's overall claim?

30 But parenthood also requires you to invoke[5] maturity where your child lacks it, whether it's telling her that she's too small to slide down the fireman's pole or that her sailing journey will have to wait until she's old enough to come to her senses. It involves helping her figure out the difference between a dream and a fantasy.

Perhaps someone should have stepped in to impose some parenting standards on the Sunderlands; last summer, a court in the Netherlands stopped a 13-year-old girl from making her own unadvised solo sail. Better yet, we could give up a
40 culture that treats accomplishment as a race and turns risk into its own reward. Abby Sunderland couldn't drive without a learner's permit, but her journey on the high seas got her fawning press[6] and endorsement deals. Now, some fans on her site have offered their own money to recover her lost boat. One pledged to play an extra $5 a day in the lottery, just in case.

> "Perhaps someone should have stepped in to impose some parenting standards."

When will he realize he's simply a pawn in the Sunderlands' audience-building scheme? From onboard the French fishing vessel, Abby has declared, *quelle surprise*,[7] that she's writing a book. Her father also disclosed that he's been
50 shopping a reality show with the working title "Adventures in Sunderland." (What good fortune this family has, to have a name that lends itself to puns.)

---

[5] **invoke:** to call (a higher power) for assistance or support.
[6] **fawning press:** favor-seeking press.
[7] *quelle surprise*: What a surprise!

Ship of Fools **25**

CLOSE READ

Trace and Evaluate an Argument (LINES 36–45)

RI 2,
RI 5,
RI 8

The writer is suggesting that society has a certain responsibility to intercede in situations like Abby's.

H **CITE TEXT EVIDENCE** Have students reread lines 36–45 and name a reason that the writer presents to support her claim that someone should have stepped in to impose some parenting standards on Abby Sunderland's parents. (*A court in the Netherlands stopped another teenage girl from making her own unadvised solo sail; Abby couldn't drive without a learner's permit, but she could sail without conforming to any rules.*)

English Language Support

Determine Meaning Point to the verb *shopping* in line 50 and tell students that it has several meanings. Write these definitions on the board: (1) examining goods or services with the intention to buy; (2) trying to get a company to produce or purchase something; (3) seeking multiple options to try out. Have pairs of students choose the correct meaning of *shopping* based on the context of the paragraph. (*definition 2*)

WHEN STUDENTS STRUGGLE . . .

To guide students' understanding of claims and reasons, have pairs of students reread lines 30–35. Have them work together to make a two-column chart to list the claim the author makes about parenthood and the reasons she provides. Have students continue to use the chart as they read and view.

LEVEL UP TUTORIALS For additional support, assign the following *Level Up* tutorials: **Analyzing Arguments, Evidence.**

Claim	Reasons
Parents need to be invoking maturity where children lack it.	*It helps children figure out the difference between a dream and a fantasy.*

Trace and Evaluate an Argument (LINES 63–69)

RI 1,
RI 2,
RI 5,
RI 8

Tell students that a writer may also make counterarguments. A **counterargument** is a response to a differing opinion. By presenting a counterargument, the writer more fully develops his or her opinion and ideas.

 CITE TEXT EVIDENCE Have students reread lines 63–69 and cite a counterargument to some people's opinion that Abby was a hero. *(The writer argues that being the youngest person to do something shouldn't be confused with being the first to do something; she feels that Abby was very lucky to have survived.)*

English Language Support

Point out the author's use of the coordinating conjunction *But* to begin sentences on lines 63 and 67. Explain that the word signals a contrast or objection to something that has already been mentioned. Discuss ways in which we can use *but* to state a counterargument, and ask volunteers to suggest examples. Then have pairs summarize the counterarguments the word introduces in the text. *(Being the youngest to do something isn't very important. Developing skills at an early age isn't heroic.)*

Childhood fame is always some mix of the child's dream and the parents'; so it was with Jessica Dubroff, the 7-year-old who died in 1996, trying to pilot a plane across the country.

With the growing temptations of book deals and TV series, the balance may be shifting even more. We'll surely hear more from Jordan Romero, the 13-year-old who just became the youngest person to climb Mount Everest. We
60 probably haven't heard the last of the Heenes of Colorado,[8] who at least had the sense not to actually put their child inside the Mylar balloon.

But while there's clearly a market for immature stars, we shouldn't confuse "youngest" with significant "first," and we shouldn't call these publicity stunts anything but what they are. Abby Sunderland may find a way to convert her misadventures into lingering fame. But while she seems to be a skilled junior sailor, calm in the face of danger, that doesn't make her a hero. It just makes her very, very lucky.

---

[8] **Heenes of Colorado:** a reference to a widely reported incident in 2009 in which a six-year-old boy was said to have floated away in a helium balloon. The report turned out to be false.

Strategies for Annotation *Annotate it!*

Analyze Structure

RI 2,
RI 5

Have students locate lines 63–69. Encourage them to use their eBook annotation tools to do the following:

- Highlight in yellow an opposing viewpoint the writer cites.
- Highlight in green the writer's counterargument.
- Underline reasons the writer includes to show the opposing viewpoint is wrong.

> But while there's clearly a market for immature stars, we shouldn't confuse "youngest" with significant "first," and we shouldn't call these publicity stunts anything but what they are. Abby Sunderland may find a way to convert her misadventures into lingering fame. But while she seems to be a skilled junior sailor, calm in the face of danger, that doesn't make her a hero. It just makes her very, very lucky.

Trace and Evaluate an Argument

RI 2, RI 5, RI 8

An **editorial** is an opinion piece that usually appears in the opinion and commentary section of a newspaper. An editorial is a type of argument in which the writer expresses one or more opinions about an issue and uses facts to support those opinions. A **fact** is a statement that can be proved. An **opinion** is a statement of belief or feeling. Like an argument, an editorial can include a **claim,** which is the writer's position or opinion; **reasons and evidence** that support the claim; and **counterarguments,** or responses to differing opinions.

Analyzing the Media

Cite Text Evidence   Support your responses with evidence from the text.

1. **Cite Evidence** Reread the editorial and fill in a chart like this one to cite the facts and opinions you find.

Type of Evidence	Examples
Facts	
Opinions	

2. **Identify** Which sentence in the editorial represents the writer's claim?

3. **Analyze** In the first quote, Abby's father says, "I think it's a parent's job to realize their kids' dreams." What is the editorial writer's counterargument to this statement?

4. **Summarize** What point does the editorial writer make in lines 41–62?

5. **Evaluate** How effectively does the editorial writer convey her opinion? Evaluate how clearly and convincingly the writer presents her evidence and ideas and concludes the editorial.

Ship of Fools   **27**

Trace and Evaluate an Argument

RI 2, RI 5, RI 8

Help students with the terms. Discuss whether the editorial made a convincing counterargument to Abby's father's statement that it is "a parent's job to realize their kids' dreams." Have students cite three reasons the author of "Ship of Fools" gives to support her claim that letting Abby take a solo voyage was foolish and dangerous. *(Parenting requires invoking maturity where a child lacks it. The Sunderlands used Abby's voyage to create an audience for media projects. Being the youngest to do something is not as significant as being the first.)*

Analyzing the Media

RI 1, RI 2, RI 5, RI 8

Possible answers:

1. ***Facts:*** *Abby tried a solo voyage; A storm knocked out her mast; She abandoned her boat; A court in the Netherlands stopped a teen from taking a solo sailing trip.* ***Opinions:*** *It's a parent's job to realize their kids' dreams; Parents must invoke maturity where their child lacks it; Someone should have imposed parenting standards on the Sunderlands.*

2. *Protecting a 16-year-old sailor, not enabling dangerous dreams, is a parent's responsibility.*

3. *The writer's counterargument is that parenthood requires you to invoke maturity where your child lacks it.*

4. *The writer points out that Abby and her family were trying to get endorsement, book, and TV deals.*

5. *The writer conveys her opinion well. Her arguments are supported with facts. She concludes with the strong point that despite her skills, Abby was not a hero.*

Trace and Evaluate an Argument

RI 5, RI 8

Have students locate lines 46–52. Encourage them to use their eBook annotation tools to do the following:

- Highlight opinions in yellow.
- Highlight facts in green.
- Review the annotations and explain how this text evidence helps readers understand the editorial.

The examples support the opinion that the Sunderlands were trying to get publicity.

...ize he's simply a pawn in the Sunderlands' audience-building scheme? From onboard the French fishing vessel, Abby has declared, *quelle surprise,* that she's writing a book. Her father also disclosed that he's been shopping a reality show with the working title "Adventures in Sunderland." (What good fortune this family has, to have a

Ship of Fools   **27**

TEACH

CLOSE READ

AS YOU VIEW Direct students to use the information in this section to help them understand the TV interview they are about to watch. Remind them to generate questions as they view.

COLLABORATIVE DISCUSSION Have students work in small groups to view and discuss the director's use of the different onscreen techniques and how they affect the viewer. Then have them compare the information with the other news pieces and discuss what is accomplished in the news report that cannot be done in the two print texts. Students may want to make a three-column chart to help them compare the information and insights they gathered from each news piece.

ASK STUDENTS to share any questions they generated in the course of viewing and discussing the TV interview.

English Language Support

Explain Ideas Before students begin their discussions, provide the following sentence stems.

- The video of Abby is important because _____.
- The words of Abby's family are important because _____.
- Compared with the information and emotions in the newspaper article, the television interview is _____.

Was Abby Too Young to Sail?

TV News Interview by Harry Smith, CBS News

Running Time: 3:40 minutes

AS YOU VIEW The news interview you are about to view was first broadcast June 11, 2010, on the CBS Morning News as news broke that Abby Sunderland had been found in the Indian Ocean and was being rescued. In the segment you are about to view, journalist Harry Smith interviews the Sunderland family. Video clips of Abby and her sailboat before the trip are included.

▶ NEW YORK ▶ THOUSAND OAKS, CA
EARLY SHOW BREAKING NEWS
FOUND ALIVE!
BOATS HEADING TO RESCUE TEEN SAILOR

©BBC Motion Gallery

COLLABORATIVE DISCUSSION Consider the choices the director makes about arranging the split-screen and including media features such as video clips. What is the effectiveness and impact of using video segments while the interviewees are speaking? What new information or insights do you learn from the interview about Abby's voyage and her preparedness? Discuss these choices and questions with your group and cite segments from the newscast to support your ideas.

English Language Support

Analyze Structure Remind students of the main purpose of a news report: to give facts and details about an event. Explain that different media have different strengths and weaknesses in meeting this goal. Ask volunteers to suggest some advantages and disadvantages of TV news, and list them on the board.

- Have partners watch the interview and identify information the print stories did not contain. As volunteers share examples, guide the class to identify the kinds of information in each medium.

- As pairs view the video, have them complete a "5 *Ws* and *H*" chart like the one on page 23. Encourage them to first watch the interview without interruption, and then view it again, pausing to list and evaluate their answers. Next, help the whole group decide which questions the interview answered best.

- Have students view the interview and complete a "5 *Ws* and *H*" chart. Then have them join small groups to compare and contrast the facts and details in the video with the information in the two print articles.

Analyze Structure

RI 2, RI 5, SL 2

In a **TV news interview,** a journalist asks questions of and discusses issues with one or more people who may be experts, eyewitnesses, informed persons, or others close to the subject of the news interview. An interview includes video of the discussion between the interviewer and interviewee and may also include video or visuals of related information that tell the viewer more about the subject. The visual elements usually illustrate or emphasize important information by showing rather than telling what happened. These images can create positive or negative views of the topic or individuals.

When gathering information from a television interview, note the questions and listen carefully to the information provided in each interviewee's response.

Analyzing the Media

RI 2, RI 5, SL 2

Cite Text Evidence   Support your responses with evidence from the media.

1. **Identify** As you view the interview, use a chart like the one shown below to record information provided by each interviewee.

2. **Interpret** What overall impression of the Sunderland family does the interview create? Cite specific examples from the interview to support your response.

3. **Analyze** The video segments of Abby that appear at certain points during the interview were recorded before her trip. How do these video segments and the video overall characterize Abby?

Analyze Structure

RI 2, RI 5, SL 2

Discuss the elements and structure of TV news interviews with students. Have them point out who is being interviewed in "Was Abby Too Young to Sail?" Then have them tell why the interviewees were good choices for the TV interview. *(They are members of Abby's family. They know her very well and know about the trip she was making.)*

Analyzing the Media

RI 2, RI 5, SL 2

Possible answers:

1. *Interviewee: Abby's father; Statement: He believed Abby is relieved that the rescue mission had found her; He believed that Abby had proven to him that she was qualified to do what she set out to do; Interviewee: Abby's mother; Statement: Abby is very resilient; The storm was just another challenge for her to meet; Interviewee: Abby's brother; Statement: Abby had the correct safety gear for this trip.*

2. *The interview makes them seem very confident about Abby's abilities and supportive of her trip. They told about how she had proven that she was qualified, how she was ready and equipped for challenges, and that she had the right safety gear to protect her in case of emergency.*

3. *The video segments of Abby show her sailing. They give the viewer the feeling that she is a very competent sailor.*

English Language Support

Exchange Information and Ideas Have students work in small groups to answer the questions on page 29. Let each group answer one question. When all the groups are finished, they can take turns presenting their answers to the class. Encourage classmates to provide useful feedback.

PRACTICE & APPLY

Analyze Ideas in Diverse Media

RI 2, RI 3, RI 5, RI 6, RI 8, RI 9, SL 2

Remind students that news can be reported in a variety of different media. Each type has special characteristics that make it different and able to achieve its purpose.

Have students explain what advantage the TV interview had over the news article and editorial. *(The TV interview included footage that showed what Abby's family is like in person, including their reactions to the questions, so that viewers could see it for themselves and form their own opinions. It also included footage of Abby sailing that gave the viewer a good idea about her abilities.)*

Analyzing the Media

RI 2, RI 3, RI 5, RI 6, RI 8, RI 9, SL 2, W 6

Possible answers:

1. **News Article:** *Purpose: to inform; Central Idea: There is a debate about whether Abby should have been allowed to go on her trip; Support: The article provides quotes from experts and Abby's parents;* **Editorial:** *Purpose: to persuade and to express thoughts or feelings; Claim: It is a parent's responsibility to protect his or her child; Evidence: The editorial provides counterarguments to Abby's parents' claim that she was capable of making the trip;* **TV News Interview:** *Purpose: to inform and to entertain; Central Idea: Abby's family thinks that she was capable of making the trip; Support: The answers include reasons such as that she was a capable and proven sailor and that she had the proper safety equipment.*

2. *The editorial emphasized the idea that it is a parent's responsibility to protect a child from dangerous dreams. It attempted to change a reader's view from thinking that Abby was a hero to thinking she was reckless.*

3. *The TV interview let us know what Abby's family looked like and gave some more information on the reasons they let her go. The footage also showed what Abby's boat looked like and her ability as a sailor.*

30   Collection 1

COMPARE MEDIA

Analyze Ideas in Diverse Media

RI 2, RI 3, RI 5, RI 6, RI 8, RI 9, SL 2

You've just read coverage of a single topic in three different formats—a news article, an editorial, and a television interview—by different writers who provide their own unique evidence and interpretations of Abby Sunderland's rescue.

To analyze the information from these varied sources, examine the purpose and the ideas presented in each. The writer's purpose is his or her reason for writing the report or story: to inform, to persuade, to entertain, or to express thoughts or feelings. Often there is more than one purpose.

Analyzing the Media

RI 2, RI 3, RI 5, RI 6, RI 8, RI 9, SL 2, W6

Cite Text Evidence   Support your responses with evidence from the media.

1. **Analyze** Use a chart like this one to analyze the purpose and key information presented in each of the selections.

Type	News Article	Editorial	TV News Interview
Purpose			
Central Idea(s) or Claim(s)			
Support or Evidence			

2. **Synthesize** What idea about Abby's trip is emphasized in the editorial but not in the other two reports? How does this emphasis change your view of Abby's story?

3. **Analyze** What did you learn from the news interview that you did not learn from the articles? Cite specific evidence from each media piece to support your answer.

PERFORMANCE TASK

Media Activity: Blog With your classmates, create a class blog to discuss what you think would be an appropriate age to pursue such an undertaking. To build the blog, map out your home page and plan one or more discussion threads.

Begin the blog by writing your own opinion of Abby's solo adventure. Was it foolish or wise for someone her age to attempt such a trip alone? Refer to any of the three news pieces for evidence. Encourage classmates to post to the blog.

Assign this performance task.

PERFORMANCE TASK

W1, W4, W6

Media Activity: Blogs Have students work in teams.

- Explain that a good blog is visually appealing, with an easy-to-navigate structure. Teams should collaborate to choose the best structure.
- Remind students that when they respond to blog posts or comments, they should maintain a respectful tone and support their ideas with evidence.

Analyze Presentations of Information

RETEACH

Explain to students that different authors can write about the same topic, but often these authors have different reasons for writing, or **author's purposes.** Depending on the author's purpose, a writer will choose different types of texts, each with its own goals and structure. Review the following to illustrate the differences between two types of texts.

- **Informative/Explanatory** The goal of informative or explanatory text is to present facts about a topic. The facts are used as evidence to support a central idea. Authors of this kind of text want to inform, for example, by presenting facts about Abby Sunderland's voyage, or to explain, by reporting why Abby's voyage stirred up a lot of debate.

- **Argument** The goal of texts that present an argument is to provide reasons and evidence to support a claim. An opinion essay is an example of this type of writing. In "Ship of Fools," the author argued that Abby Sunderland's parents used poor judgment.

- To compare two different texts about the same topic, look at the structure of each text, as well as the author's purpose for writing it. Is one author presenting an opinion while the other author is reporting facts? What does each author want the reader to take away from the text?

COLLABORATIVE DISCUSSION

Work with students to develop a chart that tells about the similarities and differences between a news article and an editorial on the same subject. Have them discuss the different purposes for each type of text, as well as the different kinds of information provided in each one.

English Language Support

Take Notes Have students use the Collaborative Discussion chart to take notes about each piece.

1. Display a passage from the text, and ask students to take notes in the chart. Remind them to write down only important ideas.

2. Have students gather in small groups to present each point in their charts. Group members should work together to determine which notes are accurate, significant, and useful.

3. Finally, distribute one blank chart to each group; have the groups complete it together using the conclusions they reached in their discussions.

How to Create a Blog

TEACH

Explain to students that a **blog** enables writers to share their ideas about a topic over the Internet with a broad audience. It can also enable blog writers to benefit from readers' comments on their writing.

Before students begin working on their blog in the Performance Task, discuss the following:

- **Determine discussion threads.** Include a separate **discussion thread**—a chain of related posts—for each different idea discussed. Take notes on all the team's ideas before voting to select the best ones.

- **Map out a home page.** Sketch the home page, visually representing how users will link to the different threads. Discuss and vote on what other information to include.

- **Assign roles.** Make a plan to complete all the team's goals by specific deadlines. Divide the work equally. One person might research websites that can host the blog. Another might make a logo for the home page. Make sure any images used are not copyrighted. In addition, one person should be responsible for writing the first post within each thread.

- **Build the blog.** With the assistance of a school technology coordinator, assemble and launch the blog on a school or blogging website.

PRACTICE AND APPLY

Students can work with a team to plan and produce their blog. Once they have launched their blog, have students take turns posting messages several times a week. After a few weeks, have students evaluate what they might add or change to make their blog more user-friendly and current.

 INTERACTIVE LESSON Have students complete the tutorials in this lesson: **Producing and Publishing with Technology.**

Finding Your Everest

Essay by Robert Medina

Why This Text

Students often read the text of an argumentative essay without a complete grasp of the author's ideas and evidence. Arguments such as this one by Robert Medina may have several central ideas and reasoning that become clear only with careful study. With the help of the close-reading questions, students will trace and evaluate the argument about the risks and rewards of mountain climbing for a 13-year-old boy. This close reading will lead students to develop a coherent understanding of the argument as well as the counterargument that Medina presents.

Background Have students read the background information about Mount Everest, the highest peak on Earth. Introduce the selection by sharing this anecdote: When asked why he kept trying to climb Mount Everest, the English mountaineer George Mallory is said to have replied, "Because it was there." Whether or not this is the main reason for the more than five thousand climbs to the summit of Mount Everest since the first successful ascent in 1953 by Edmund Hillary and Tenzing Norgay, one thing is clear. Mount Everest is there to challenge its climbers.

SETTING A PURPOSE Ask students to pay close attention to the structure of this essay. How soon into the essay does Medina present the argument "for" Jordan's climb and the counterargument "against" it?

Standards Support

- cite several pieces of textual evidence
- determine two or more central (or main) ideas in a text
- trace and evaluate an argument
- assess claims, reasoning, and evidence in a text

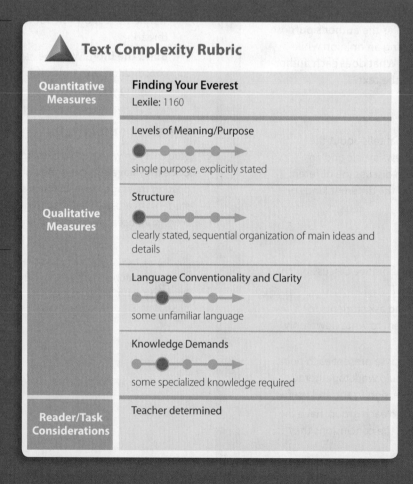

Text Complexity Rubric

Quantitative Measures

Finding Your Everest

Lexile: 1160

Qualitative Measures

Levels of Meaning/Purpose

single purpose, explicitly stated

Structure

clearly stated, sequential organization of main ideas and details

Language Conventionality and Clarity

some unfamiliar language

Knowledge Demands

some specialized knowledge required

Reader/Task Considerations

Teacher determined

Trace and Evaluate an Argument

Students should read this essay carefully all the way through. Close-reading questions at the bottom of the page will help them focus on a thorough analysis of the argument as well as the counterargument. As they read, students should record comments or questions about the text in the side margins.

WHEN STUDENTS STRUGGLE . . .

To help students follow the reasons Medina cites to support a claim made by Paul Romero and a counterclaim made by several mountaineers and medical experts, have students work in a small group to fill out charts, such as the ones shown below, as they analyze the essay.

CITE TEXT EVIDENCE For practice in tracing an argument and counterargument, ask students to cite evidence that Medina gives to support each reason.

CLAIM: *The risks of climbing Everest are not too great for 13-year-old Jordan.*

SUPPORT:

Reason 1: *He is up to the challenge physically and mentally.*

Reason 2: *He is well prepared for the climb.*

Reason 3: *His parents will be climbing with him.*

Reason 4: *His young brain is more resilient, according to some medical experts.*

COUNTERCLAIM: *The risks are too great for 13-year-old Jordan.*

SUPPORT:

Reason 1: *He does not have the cognitive ability to make life-and-death decisions or to truly understand what he is signing on for.*

Reason 2: *Such a high climb will harm his body.*

Reason 3: *He has his whole life to climb Everest.*

Reason 4: *It is just a publicity stunt and not worth the risk.*

Background *At approximately 29,000 feet above sea level, Mount Everest is the highest mountain in the world. More than five thousand people have reached the summit of Mount Everest since the first successful climb in 1953 by Edmund Hillary and Tenzing Norgay. However, the climb is extremely dangerous; more than 200 people have died attempting to reach the top.*

Finding Your Everest

Essay by Robert Medina

CLOSE READ
Notes

1. **READ ▶** As you read lines 1–33, begin to collect and cite text evidence.

- Circle the most important information you learn about Jordan Romero in lines 1–13.
- Explain in the margin what is meant by "the seven summits."
- Underline details in lines 22–33 that explain what Jordan achieved.

A *C*an parents go too far in supporting their children's dreams? This is a question people sometimes ask when they hear the story of the teenage mountain climber, Jordan Romero. Between the ages of 10 and 15, Jordan climbed the highest mountain on every continent— and his father and stepmother climbed them with him. They call themselves Team Jordan.

Paul Romero, Jordan's father, was taken by surprise when his 9-year-old son firmly announced his intention to climb "the seven summits." Jordan had seen a mural at school, showing the seven 10 peaks that made up this **pantheon** of mountains. When he told his father what he wanted to do, Paul Romero's jaw dropped. Paul Romero is an experienced mountaineer, so he knew what was involved. He also knew his son.

"The seven summits" refers to the tallest mountain on each continent.

pantheon: a very famous group

13

---

1. **READ AND CITE TEXT EVIDENCE** Explain that Medina poses a question ("Can parents go too far in supporting their children's dreams?") to open his essay. Such a provocative question "grabs" the reader's attention, and in this case, states the topic of the essay's argument.

A **ASK STUDENTS** to determine how Medina begins to answer his question by citing specific textual evidence in lines 1–33. *Responses may include references to evidence in lines 1–6, 14–21, 22–33.*

Critical Vocabulary: pantheon (line 10) Have students share their definitions of *pantheon*. Ask how *pantheon* fits into Jordan's "dream." *His "dream" is to climb "the seven summits," the highest and most famous mountains on each continent.*

Climbing mountains is not just fun. It's hard work.

B "We've always taught him to just think big and we'll try to make it happen," Paul Romero said. But, as Romero later noted, there was a fine line between encouraging his son and pushing him too far. The father began by training his son so that he could "begin to even understand what mountaineering was—that there's this long, hard, dirty, un-fun hours and days and weeks of carrying packs and long, extensive, brutal travel, and all this type of stuff just before you can even think of climbing a mountain."

persevered:
continued in spite of difficulties

Jordan **persevered**, though, and in July 2006, when he was 10 years old, Jordan and his family climbed 19,300-foot-high Mount Kilimanjaro, the highest peak on the African continent. This was the first rung in the amazing ladder that Jordan Romero had set out to climb. Over the next five and a half years, Team Jordan climbed Mount Elbrus in Russia (2007), Mount Aconcagua in South America (2007), Mount McKinley in North America (2008), Mount Carstensz Pyramid in Indonesia (2009), Mount Everest in Asia (2010), and Vinson Massif in Antarctica (2011). In many of these climbs, Jordan set a world record as the youngest ever to climb the peak. When he completed the seven summits at 15, he was the youngest person ever to accomplish that feat.

controversy:
a dispute between opposing sides

C It was the Mount Everest ascent—when Jordan was only 13 years old—that has created the greatest **controversy.** Jordan's feat as the youngest person to reach "the top of the world" was publicized

around the world. "How Young Is Too Young?" asked one newspaper headline. Many mountain climbers and medical experts questioned whether a 13-year-old boy could climb so high (Mount Everest is almost 30,000 feet high) without physically harming his body. Dr. Michael Bradley, a psychologist and expert on teen behavior, noted, "Most 13-year-olds don't have the wiring to make **cognitive** life-and-death decisions and are not truly able to understand what they're signing on for." Another physician, Dr. Peter Hackett, reported that there are conflicting opinions about the effects on a young brain. Some theories say that a young brain is more resilient; others say that it may be more vulnerable.

cognitive:
using reason to understand and make judgments

D Many climbers take exception to the publicity surrounding Team Jordan. Everest climber Todd Burleson summed it up by saying, "He's got his whole life to climb Everest. Being the youngest boy to climb is a fashionable, celebrity-oriented sort of thing. But it's not about the mountains. It's like trying to get your PhD at ten."

E Paul Romero claims that he is fully aware of the risks. There is a fine line between encouraging Jordan and pushing him too far, he says. He talked about the point where Jordan might have "reached his maximum mentally, physically, and where the risk has become too high." He said, "Jordan has just not even come close to that point yet."

Paul Romero claims that Jordan is up to the challenge and not at risk.

And what about Jordan, now that he has accomplished his goal of climbing the seven summits before his 16th birthday? Unsurprisingly,

2. ◀ **REREAD** Reread lines 14–21. In the margin, restate in your own words what Paul Romero says about mountaineering.

3. **READ** ▶ As you read lines 34–52, continue to cite textual evidence.
- Underline the medical claim (a position or opinion) about the dangers of mountain climbing to a 13-year-old.
- Circle the medical claim that offers a counterargument, or response, to the dangers of mountain climbing to a 13-year-old.
- Underline the opinion given by another mountain climber.

4. ◀ **REREAD AND DISCUSS** Reread lines 49–52. With a small group, discuss whether the evidence Todd Burleson cites is sufficient to support his opinion that Jordan and his family are just publicity seekers.

5. **READ** ▶ As you read lines 53–68, continue to cite textual evidence.
- In the margin, restate the claim that Paul Romero makes in lines 53–57.
- Circle the main idea in lines 58–65.
- Underline the details that support the main idea.

2. **REREAD AND CITE TEXT EVIDENCE**

B **ASK STUDENTS** to explain the reason for Romero's statement about the difficulties of mountaineering. *He is trying to inject some reality into his son's dream.*

3. **READ AND CITE TEXT EVIDENCE**

C **ASK STUDENTS** to find and cite specific examples of the risks involved for a 13-year-old boy. *Students should cite examples in lines 34–52.*

Critical Vocabulary: persevered (line 22) Have students share examples of times when they have persevered in a situation. *Students should cite examples of learning a difficult subject, sport, or musical instrument.*

Critical Vocabulary: controversy (line 35) Why does Medina use the word *controversy* to introduce the counterargument? *It is the perfect word to use to present the opposing claim.*

4. **REREAD AND DISCUSS USING TEXT EVIDENCE**

D **ASK STUDENTS** to appoint a reporter for each group to cite specific text evidence and line numbers to support their position about the sufficiency of Todd Burleson's evidence. *Students should cite evidence from lines 49–52.*

5. **READ AND CITE TEXT EVIDENCE**

E **ASK STUDENTS** to read their margin notes to a partner and then write one response that summarizes Paul Romero's viewpoint in lines 53–57, incorporating his central idea. *Students should see that he says that he realizes the risks but is encouraging Jordan, not pushing him beyond his mental and physical limits.*

Critical Vocabulary: cognitive (line 42) Have students explain *cognitive* as it is used here. Ask how it fits in with the counterargument given by a medical expert. *The doctor says, "'Most 13-year-olds don't have the wiring'" to make judgments about "'life-and-death decisions.'"*

Some may say that Jordan and his family are only trying to attract attention.

F 60 he has a new mission. He calls it Find Your Everest. In 2012 Team Jordan set out to encourage young people to be active and healthy and to pursue their own adventures. In the process, he is inviting young people to join him in climbing the highest peak in each state. (They range from Denali or Mount McKinley at 20,320 feet to Florida's greatest height—345-foot-high Britton Hill!)

"I feel good about what my parents have taught me about setting goals," Jordan says. And now he wants to spread that message to others.

6. **◀ REREAD** Reread lines 58–68. Make a note in the margin about how people might react to Jordan's new mission, considering the response to his earlier climbs.

SHORT RESPONSE

Cite Text Evidence The article opens with the question, "Can parents go too far in supporting their children's dreams?" Review your reading notes, and answer the question as it relates to the Romeros, evaluating the strength of the claims offered. Be sure to **cite text evidence** in your response.

Answers will vary. Some students may believe that Jordan Romero's parents have gone too far in allowing him to realize his dream of climbing the highest mountains on all seven continents. The claims made by many medical experts suggest that most 13-year-olds do not have the ability to make "cognitive life-and-death decisions." While some doctors claim that a young brain is more resilient, many doctors think that climbing the highest summits will damage a young body. Furthermore, some climbers suggest that Jordan and his parents are just publicity seekers hoping to gain celebrity status.

16

---

6. **REREAD AND CITE TEXT EVIDENCE**

F **ASK STUDENTS** to write a response that states why some people might be in favor of Jordan's new mission and why others might not be. *Students should cite textual evidence from lines 58–68 to offer a "for" and "against" position.*

FOR ELL STUDENTS (line 60) Explain that *mission* is a multiple-meaning word. Ask students if they know at least two meanings of the word. *One meaning is that of a goal or special task; another is that of a church.* Have students tell which meaning is used here. *Here, it means "a goal or special task."*

SHORT RESPONSE

Cite Text Evidence Students should

- explain whether or not they believe that the Romeros have gone too far in supporting Jordan's dream
- give reasons for their point of view
- cite specific evidence from the text to support their reasons

---

TO CHALLENGE STUDENTS . . .

For additional information about Mount Everest, students can conduct print, online, or multimedia research on what makes it such a difficult and dangerous mountain to climb.

ASK STUDENTS what they have learned about why Mount Everest is such a forbidding mountain. *Students might say that Mount Everest is a risky mountain for anyone to climb because it is the world's tallest peak, rising 29,000 feet above sea level.*

DIG DEEPER

With the class, return to Question 4, Reread and Discuss. Have students share the results of their discussion.

ASK STUDENTS whether they were satisfied with the outcome of their small-group discussions. Have each group share whether or not they agreed with the claim made by Todd Burleson, an Everest climber, that Jordan and his family are just publicity seekers looking to achieve celebrity status. Invite each group to share the majority opinion of the group. What compelling evidence from the essay did each group cite to support its opinion?

- Encourage students to tell whether there was any compelling textual evidence cited by Burleson to support his position and how that evidence (or lack of it) may have prompted them to agree (or disagree) with his point of view.
- Have groups disclose how they decided whether or not the evidence was sufficient. Did everyone in the group agree as to what made the evidence sufficient? How did the group resolve any conflicts or differing opinions?
- Invite groups to reveal whether there was any convincing evidence cited by group members holding the minority opinion. If so, why didn't it sway the group's opinion?
- After students have shared the results of their group's discussion, ask whether another group shared any findings they wished they had brought to the table.

ASK STUDENTS to return to their Short Response answer and to revise it based on the class discussion.

ANCHOR TEXT

The Flight of Icarus

Greek Myth retold by Sally Benson

Why This Text?

Students often encounter universal themes that have their roots in mythology—lessons about human nature that were important not only to the ancient peoples but also to people of today. After reading the myth of Icarus, students will better understand references to someone who "flies too close to the sun."

Key Learning Objective: The student will be able to analyze the elements of a myth and to determine two or more themes.

For practice and application:

Close Reader selection
"Arachne"
a Greek myth retold by Olivia Coolidge

RL 1 Cite textual evidence.
RL 2 Determine a theme and analyze its development.
RL 3 Analyze how elements of a story interact.
RL 4 Determine the meaning of words and phrases.
W 3 Write narratives.
W 5 Develop and strengthen writing by revising.
W 7 Conduct short research projects.
L 2a Use a comma to separate coordinate adjectives.
L 4c Consult general and specialized reference materials.

▲ Text Complexity Rubric

Quantitative Measures	**The Flight of Icarus** Lexile: 1110L
Qualitative Measures	**Levels of Meaning/Purpose** multiple levels of meaning (multiple themes)
	Structure somewhat complex story concepts
	Language Conventionality and Clarity some figurative language
	Knowledge Demands increased amount of cultural and literary knowledge useful
Reader/Task Considerations	• Teacher determined • Vary by individual reader and type of text • See the Text X-Ray for suggested Reader/Task Considerations.

English Language Support Before teaching, use the Text X-Ray below for an overview of the text's complexity. The Text X-Ray and the supports and scaffolds in the Teacher's Edition will help you guide students of different skill levels.

Meaning Making

Language Development

Effective Expression

Content Knowledge

Foundational Skills

Text Complexity: Qualitative Measures

Levels of Meaning/Purpose

multiple levels of meaning (multiple themes)

Help students identify the theme of the myth.

- Teacher's Edition side notes, pp. 31, 32, 34
- English Language Support, p. 34
- Close Read Screencasts, p. 31
- Determine Theme, p. 35

 Analyzing Language

To reteach how to determine theme, see

- Determine Theme, p. 38a

 Use It! *Level Up* Tutorial: Theme

ZOOM IN ON **DETERMINING THEME** Explain that a **theme** is a message about life or human nature. Display the following sentences and ask students to identify the sentence that best expresses a literary theme.

- The story is about the two people who go mountain climbing.
- It is a story about how facing challenges makes a person stronger.

Lead a discussion about the two choices. Guide students to recognize that "mountain climbing" is the topic of the story, while "facing challenges makes a person stronger" expresses the author's message about life.

Structure

somewhat complex story concepts

Help students analyze the elements of a myth.

- Teacher's Edition side notes, pp. 31, 33, 35
- Strategies for Annotation, p. 35
- Analyze Story Elements: Myth, p. 35

To teach how to analyze characterization, see

- Analyze Story Elements: Characterization, p. 38a

 Use It! Interactive Whiteboard Lesson: Character Development

ZOOM IN ON **ANALYZING THE STORY ELEMENTS OF A MYTH** Tell students that a **myth,** like a short story, contains a **plot, characters,** a **setting,** and a **theme.** Review the elements that make a story a myth:

- characters who have special abilities or are gods
- setting in ancient or prehistoric times
- events that defy physical reality

Organize students into small, mixed-ability groups. Have each group use a story map to track important details and events. Circulate to monitor each group's progress.

After groups have finished the story, have them present to the class the details they recorded that identify the story as a myth.

Language Conventionality and Clarity

some figurative language

Teach unfamiliar academic vocabulary in context.

- Teacher's Edition Critical Vocabulary notes, pp. 32, 33, 37
- Applying Academic Vocabulary, p. 33
- Strategies for Annotation, p. 37
- Vocabulary Strategy: Noun Suffixes, p. 37

Guide students to analyze language and sentence structure.

- Teacher's Edition side notes, p. 38
- English Language Support, pp. 32, 38
- Language Conventions: Commas and Coordinate Adjectives, p. 38

***ZOOM IN ON* PREVIEWING CRITICAL VOCABULARY** Preview the vocabulary for this selection with students.

- Write the Critical Vocabulary terms on the board.
- As a class, identify familiar affixes and roots and record them next to the corresponding words.
- Use each word in a sentence.
- Guide students to define the words based on their context.
- Have pairs use the words to write sentences and share them with the class.

Knowledge Demands

increased amount of cultural and literary knowledge useful

Help students clarify the cultural contexts of the myth.

- Teacher's Edition Background note, p. 31

***ZOOM IN ON* CULTURAL CONTEXT** Explain that the mythological character Daedalus has inspired artists and writers through the ages.

- Explain that Daedalus was a craftsman and inventor who built a labyrinth, or maze, for King Minos to hold the Minotaur, the king's pet monster. When it was killed, Minos imprisoned Daedalus and his son, but Daedalus used his ingenuity to escape.
- Note that characters in myths helped people understand life. A character like Icarus was intended to teach a lesson. Discuss these questions to help students understand Icarus's behavior: *How do playful children behave? Are they always sensible? Do children always obey their parents?*

Suggested Reader/Task Considerations

Consider the following before assigning this myth to students:

- Do students have the visualization skills to imagine what is being described in the myth?
- Will students be able to make inferences that help them connect the ideas in the myth and come to an understanding of the theme?

***ZOOM IN ON* SUPPORTING COMPREHENSION**

- Model how sensory details aid visualization. Read aloud lines 15–23, noting sensory details and how they bring the scene to life. Have small groups read and discuss how they visualize the scene.
- Display these questions to help students identify the theme: *What do the characters want? What do the characters do to reach that goal? How well do they succeed, and why?* As students read, have them record text details that help answer the questions.

CLOSE READ

Background Have students read the background information about myths and their role in ancient Greek civilization. Tell students that Greek myths have also become an important part of our culture. In their reading or in viewing other media, students are likely to come across references to mythological characters like Icarus. Also point out that the first lines of this myth refer to another mythological character called Theseus. Theseus escaped from a fierce monster in King Minos's labyrinth, setting the stage for the myth students are about to read.

SETTING A PURPOSE Direct students to use the Setting a Purpose question to focus their reading. Remind them to also write any questions they have as they read.

Analyze Story Elements: Myth (LINES 10–12)

RL 1, RL 3

Tell students that a **myth** is a traditional story that attempts to answer basic questions about human nature or the natural world. In a myth, events occur that cannot happen in real life, and characters also have unusual or even supernatural powers.

A **CITE TEXT EVIDENCE** Ask students what we have learned so far about Daedalus. What evidence in the text hints that he may have unusual or supernatural powers? (*We have learned that Daedalus is resourceful and ingenious. The lines "but he does not control the air. I will try that way" hint at unusual powers, since there was no air travel in the time of the ancient Greeks.*)

Determine Theme

RL 1, RL 2

(LINES 4–12)

Explain that the **theme** of a literary text is a message about life or human nature. In a myth, the theme often reveals what is important to a culture. The first step in determining the theme of a myth is to determine what the characters want.

B **ASK STUDENTS** to reread lines 4–12 and to identify what Daedalus and Icarus want. (*They want to escape from the island of Crete.*)

Background *Today we think of myths as stories that have been passed down through countless generations. In the ancient civilization of Greece, myths were the basis of an elaborate system of beliefs. Myths explained their mystifying world and offered wisdom on how to live in it. The myth of Daedalus and his son Icarus is one example.*

The Flight of Icarus

Greek Myth retold by Sally Benson

SETTING A PURPOSE As you read, pay close attention to the choices Icarus and his father make. What do these choices reveal? Write down any questions you may have while reading.

When Theseus escaped from the labyrinth, King Minos flew into a rage with its builder, Daedalus, and ordered him shut up in a high tower that faced the lonely sea. In time, with the help of his young son, Icarus, Daedalus managed to escape from the tower, only to find himself a prisoner on the island. Several times he tried by bribery to stow away on one of the vessels sailing from Crete, but King Minos kept strict watch over them, and no ships were allowed to sail without being carefully searched. **B**

10 Daedalus was an ingenious artist and was not discouraged by his failures. "Minos may control the land and sea," he said, "but he does not control the air. I will try that way." **A**

He called his son, Icarus, to him and told the boy to gather up all the feathers he could find on the rocky shore.

Image Credits: (cl) ©zoev/Shutterstock; (cr) ©Igor Zh/Shutterstock

---

Close Read Screencasts Close Read

Modeled Discussions

Have students click the *Close Read* icons in their eBooks to access a screencast in which readers discuss and annotate the passage about Icarus's first flight and Daedalus's warning to him (lines 35–47).

As a class, view and discuss this video. Then have students pair up to do an independent close read of an additional passage—Icarus flies too high and begins to lose his feathers (lines 63–75).

Determine Theme

RL 1,
RL 2

(LINES 15–29, 39–47)

Tell students that, once they have discovered what the characters want, the next step in determining the theme of a myth is to learn what they do to reach that goal.

C **ASK STUDENTS** to reread lines 15–29 and summarize what Daedalus does to help himself and his son escape from the island. *(He makes two sets of wings from melted wax and feathers. He intends that he and his son will fly away from the island.)*

The final step in determining the theme is to analyze how well the characters succeed at reaching their goal, and why.

D **CITE TEXT EVIDENCE** Have students reread lines 39–47 and cite the specific evidence that suggests Daedalus's plan will not go well. *("Daedalus watched him proudly but with misgivings"; "No human being has ever traveled through the air before"; "if you fly too low, the fog and spray will clog your wings, and if you fly too high, the heat will melt the wax that holds them together.")*

CRITICAL VOCABULARY

moderate: Daedalus warned his son to keep at a moderate height, neither too high nor too low.

ASK STUDENTS why Daedalus gave his son this warning to be moderate. What does this suggest about one theme of the myth? *(If Icarus flew too low, his wings would clog; if he flew too high, the wax would melt. The warning suggests that one theme of the myth is the value of moderation.)*

prowess: Point out that Icarus and Daedalus wanted to test their prowess before setting out across the sea.

ASK STUDENTS to describe the prowess that this flight required. *(It required the ability to control height and direction and the strength to keep flying for as long as it took to cross the sea.)*

C As thousands of gulls soared over the island, Icarus soon collected a huge pile of feathers. Daedalus then melted some wax and made a skeleton in the shape of a bird's wing. The smallest feathers he pressed into the soft wax and the large ones he tied on with thread. Icarus played about on the beach happily while his father worked, chasing the feathers that blew away in the strong wind that swept the island and sometimes taking bits of the wax and working it into strange shapes with his fingers.

It was fun making the wings. The sun shone on the bright feathers; the breezes ruffled them. When they were finished, Daedalus fastened them to his shoulders and found himself lifted upwards, where he hung poised in the air. Filled with excitement, he made another pair for his son. They were smaller than his own, but strong and beautiful.

Finally, one clear, wind-swept morning, the wings were finished, and Daedalus fastened them to Icarus's shoulders and taught him how to fly. He bade him watch the movements of the birds, how they soared and glided overhead. He pointed out the slow, graceful sweep of their wings as they beat the air steadily, without fluttering. Soon Icarus was sure that he, too, could fly and, raising his arms up and down, skirted over the white sand and even out over the waves, letting his feet touch the snowy foam as the water thundered and broke over the sharp rocks. Daedalus watched him proudly but **D** with misgivings. He called Icarus to his side and, putting his arm round the boy's shoulders, said, "Icarus, my son, we are about to make our flight. No human being has ever traveled through the air before, and I want you to listen carefully to my instructions. Keep at a **moderate** height, for if you fly too low, the fog and spray will clog your wings, and if you fly too high, the heat will melt the wax that holds them together. Keep near me and you will be safe."

He kissed Icarus and fastened the wings more securely to his son's shoulders. Icarus, standing in the bright sun, the shining wings dropping gracefully from his shoulders, his golden hair wet with spray, and his eyes bright and dark with excitement, looked like a lovely bird. Daedalus's eyes filled with tears, and turning away, he soared into the sky, calling to Icarus to follow. From time to time, he looked back to see that the boy was safe and to note how he managed his wings in his flight. As they flew across the land to test their **prowess** before

moderate
(mŏd´ər-ĭt) *adj.* When something is kept moderate, it is kept within a certain limit.

prowess
(prou´ĭs) *n.* Prowess is the strength and courage someone has.

32 Collection 1

English Language Support

Analyze Language: Description Paying attention to the author's vivid descriptive language will help English learners visualize events in the myth. Project lines 15–19, and invite volunteers to highlight the details that help them picture how Daedalus made the wings.

ASK STUDENTS to describe in their own words how the wings were made.

setting out across the dark wild sea, plowmen below stopped their work and shepherds gazed in wonder, thinking Daedalus and Icarus were gods.

60   Father and son flew over Samos and Delos, which lay on their left, and Lebinthus,[1] which lay on their right. Icarus, beating his wings in joy, felt the thrill of the cool wind on his face and the clear air above and below him. He flew higher and higher up into the blue sky until he reached the clouds. His father saw him and called out in alarm. He tried to follow him, but he was heavier and his wings would not carry him. Up and up Icarus soared, through the soft, moist clouds and out again toward the glorious sun. He was bewitched by a sense of freedom and beat his wings **frantically** so that they
70 would carry him higher and higher to heaven itself. The blazing sun beat down on the wings and softened the wax. Small feathers fell from the wings and floated softly down, warning Icarus to stay his flight and glide to earth. But the enchanted boy did not notice them until the sun became so hot that the largest feathers dropped off and he began to sink. Frantically he fluttered his arms, but no feathers remained to hold the air. He cried out to his father, but his voice was submerged in the blue waters of the sea, which has forever after been called by his name.
80   Daedalus, crazed by **anxiety**, called back to him, "Icarus! Icarus, my son, where are you?" At last he saw the feathers

frantic
(frăn´tĭk) *adj.* If you do something in a frantic way, you do it quickly and nervously.

anxiety
(ăng-zī´ĭ-tē) *n.* Anxiety is an uneasy, worried feeling.

---

[1] **Samos . . . Delos . . . Lebinthus:** (sā´mŏs´… dē´lŏs´… lubĭn´thus´): small Greek islands in the eastern Aegean Sea.

APPLYING ACADEMIC VOCABULARY

aspect	cultural

THINK-PAIR-SHARE Let students turn to a partner and discuss the questions below. Guide them to include the academic vocabulary words *aspect* and *cultural* in their responses. Ask volunteers to share their responses with the class.

- What **aspects** of the characters and plot are typical of myths?
- What can we learn from this myth about the **cultural** values of the ancient Greeks?

CLOSE READ

Analyze Story Elements: Myth

RL 1,
RL 2,
RL 3

(LINES 57–63, 60–79)

Remind students that myths typically include events that cannot happen in real life and characters with unusual abilities.

E   **CITE TEXT EVIDENCE** Ask students to cite specific evidence in the text that illustrates these two aspects of a myth. *(Daedalus and Icarus are able to fly. The people watching from below think they are gods.)*

Recall also that myths often show the values of the culture in which the myth was first told.

F   **ASK STUDENTS** to reread lines 60–79 and ask them to identify the cause of Icarus's fall and what his failure reveals about the cultural values of the ancient Greeks. *(He falls because he flies higher and higher, "bewitched by a sense of freedom." Finally, the sun melts the wax on his wings, just as his father had warned. This tells us that the Greeks valued moderation and knowing your place—not trying to be like the gods.)*

CRITICAL VOCABULARY

frantic: The author tells us that Icarus beat his wings frantically in order to fly higher and higher.

ASK STUDENTS how the author's use of the word *frantically* helps us to picture the scene. *(It helps us to visualize Icarus in a very excited state, beating his wings faster and faster.)*

anxiety: Earlier in the text (line 65) Daedalus "called out in alarm." Now, after seeing his son fly too high, he is "crazed by anxiety."

ASK STUDENTS to describe the change in Daedalus's feelings. How does *alarm* differ from *anxiety*? *(Alarm is a sudden feeling that something may be wrong or a warning; anxiety is a nervous state—an intense worry or fear that something will go wrong.)*

Determine Theme

RL 1,
RL 2

(LINES 88–95)

Remind students that, to determine the theme of a myth, they should consider whether the characters succeeded or failed at achieving their goal—and why.

 CITE TEXT EVIDENCE Have students reread lines 88–95, keeping Daedalus's original goal in mind. Ask them whether he succeeded or failed and what this might reveal about a life lesson or theme. *(His original goal was to escape from Crete. He succeeded at that goal but "his victory over the air was bitter to him" because he had lost his son. This suggests the theme "know your place"—don't soar too high or try to be like the gods.)*

 English Language Support

Analyzing Language (LINE 95)

Have students view the **Text In Focus** video on this page of their eBook to analyze an idiom and consider how it relates to the theme of the myth. Then have students use **Text In Focus Practice** to apply what they have learned.

COLLABORATIVE DISCUSSION Have students work in small groups to discuss the "bold and risky moves" made by both Daedalus and Icarus. Suggest that they consider whether each character's actions were worth the risk he took. Then have each group share their ideas with the class.

ASK STUDENTS to share any questions they generated in the course of reading and discussing the selection.

---

floating from the sky, and soon his son plunged through the clouds into the sea. Daedalus hurried to save him, but it was too late. He gathered the boy in his arms and flew to land, the tips of his wings dragging in the water from the double burden they bore. Weeping bitterly, he buried his small son and called the land Icaria in his memory.

Then, with a flutter of wings, he once more took to the air, but the joy of his flight was gone and his victory over the air was bitter to him. He arrived safely in Sicily, where he built a temple to Apollo and hung up his wings as an offering to the god, and in the wings he pressed a few bright feathers he had found floating on the water where Icarus fell. And he mourned for the birdlike son who had thrown caution to the winds in the exaltation of his freedom from the earth.

90

COLLABORATIVE DISCUSSION In the last sentence, the author says that Icarus "had thrown caution to the winds"—he had made a bold and risky move. How had both Icarus and Daedalus made bold and risky moves? Share your ideas with your group.

RL 2

CONTENT-AREA CONNECTION

Fine Arts Tell students that over the centuries the story of Daedalus and Icarus has inspired artists around the world. Both well-known and unknown artists have depicted the story in a variety of media, including oil paintings, mosaics, stone carvings, collage, and sculpture. Work with your school's visual arts teacher to gather images of a variety of representations of this myth, including works by the Dutch Renaissance painter Pieter Breughel, the influential twentieth-century artist Henri Matisse, and the modern American sculptor Peter Calaboyias.

Activity After reading the story, have students work in small groups to research additional images of Daedalus and Icarus. Suggest that groups organize the images they find—for example, according to chronology, types of media, style, or another organizing principle that they determine. Have students present a summary of their findings to the class.

Analyze Story Elements: Myth

RL 3

"The Flight of Icarus" is a **myth,** a traditional story that attempts to answer basic questions about human nature, origins of the world, mysteries of nature, and social customs. A myth is also a form of entertainment that people have enjoyed since ancient times. Most myths share these elements:

- gods and other supernatural beings with special powers
- supernatural events and settings
- a lesson about life or human nature

Myths may also explain the origins of natural phenomena, such as volcanoes or constellations, or warn against the consequences of human error. Often, myths reveal the values that are of greatest cultural importance to a society, such as honesty, cleverness, and moderation, which means acting within reasonable limits. Myths were used to guide ancient people's behavior in a way that reflected these values and beliefs.

Explain how each of these statements is true for "The Flight of Icarus":

- In a myth, events occur that cannot happen in real life.
- A mythical character has unusual abilities.
- A myth shows the values of a culture.

Determine Theme

RL 2

A **theme** is a message about life or human nature that a writer shares with the reader. An example of a theme might be "beauty fades" or "greed can lead to ruined lives." Authors might state a theme directly. More often, however, a reader must analyze the story events and characters' actions to infer, or make logical guesses about, the theme.

A myth often contains more than one theme, and often the theme reflects the cultural values of the society in which the myth was first told. By analyzing the behavior of mythic characters in unusual situations, we can learn lessons about the traits that mattered to a culture. This chart provides helpful questions for determining a myth's likely themes.

Your answers to the third question can lead you to ideas about life lessons or other big ideas—the themes—in a myth.

Finding the Theme of a Myth

1. What do the characters want?	2. What do the characters do to reach that goal?	3. How well do they succeed, and why?

CLOSE READ

Analyze Story Elements: Myth

RL 3

Help students understand the definition and characteristics of a myth. Then discuss their responses to the activity at the end of the lesson.

- In a myth, events occur that cannot happen in real life. *(Possible answer: In this myth, a man and his son are able to fly, using wings that the man made of wax and feathers.)*
- A mythical character has unusual abilities. *(Possible answer: Both Icarus and Daedalus are able to fly.)*
- A myth shows the values of a culture. *(Possible answer: The lesson seems to be to stay in the middle and not fly too high or too low. Flying high would make Icarus too much like a god, which was probably seen as being against the laws of nature to the Greeks. It also seems to be saying "don't get ahead of yourself," suggesting the Greeks prized humility and good sense.)*

Determine Theme

RL 2

Review the definition of a theme, emphasizing that in a myth the theme often reflects the cultural values of the society in which it was told.

Review the three steps for finding the theme shown in the chart. Have students review the myth to answer the questions, and share their responses.

Strategies for Annotation   🖉 🗐 *Annotate it!*

Analyze Story Elements: Myth

RL 3

Have students use their eBook annotation tools to analyze the text. Ask them to do the following:

- Reread lines 56–59 and highlight in yellow the evidence that shows supernatural abilities.
- Highlight in blue the evidence that suggests the values of the ancient Greek culture.

As they flew across the land to test their prowess before setting out across the dark wild sea, plowmen below stopped their work and shepherds gazed in wonder, thinking Daedalus and Icarus were gods.

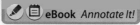
PRACTICE & APPLY

Analyzing the Text

RL 1, RL 2, RL 3, RL 4

Possible answers:

1. *Daedalus is reacting with frustration, because he has tried every way possible, including bribery, to escape from the island with no success.*

2. *The advice suggests that the ancient Greeks valued moderation.*

3. *The sentence suggests that the people watching from below thought that Daedalus and Icarus were gods. It suggests that one theme of the myth is, "Don't get above yourself and try to be like the gods."*

4. *When Icarus first tries the wings, he riskily "lets his feet touch the snowy foam," and his father watches "with misgivings." Daedalus offers specific instructions about not flying too high or too low, which are hints that his son, whose eyes show excitement, may be too thrilled to obey.*

5. *The words and phrases* up and up, soared, glorious, sense of freedom, higher and higher, *and* heaven *suggest the thrill that Icarus experiences. The words* bewitched *and* frantically *suggest that he cannot control his urge to fly higher.*

6. *Someone who flies too close to the sun reaches for thrills, power, or a goal in a self-destructive way. Like Icarus, the person reaches for greatness and is punished for his or her misguided ways.*

Analyzing the Text

RL 1, RL 2, RL 3, RL 4, W 3, W 7

Cite Text Evidence Support your responses with evidence from the text.

1. **Infer** Reread lines 1–9. How do you think Daedalus is reacting to his situation at this point?

2. **Interpret** Think about Daedalus's advice to Icarus in lines 41–47. What do these lines suggest about the kind of behavior that ancient Greeks valued?

3. **Interpret** Reread lines 56–59. What does the sentence suggest about one of the themes of this myth?

4. **Cite Evidence** What text clues does the author provide to hint at the outcome of Icarus's flight?

5. **Analyze** Reread lines 67–71, and identify descriptive words and phrases. What do these descriptions suggest about Icarus's experience?

6. **Connect** People today may refer to someone "who flew too close to the sun" as a cautionary tale. What does this expression mean and what does it have to do with the myth of Icarus? Explain.

PERFORMANCE TASK

Writing Activity: Graphic Comic
"The Flight of Icarus" begins with references to Theseus and his escape from the labyrinth built by Daedalus. Retell your own version of the myth in the form of a graphic comic. In this kind of text, both verbal and visual elements work together.

- Research retellings of the myth of Theseus and the Minotaur.

- Redo the text of the myth in your own words. Try to keep any character speeches or descriptions as brief as possible.

- Make sure that the words don't crowd the art space.

- Plan how your characters will look. Use any descriptions you find in the text version of the myth to help you.

- Do a rough sketch of your ideas before creating finished pages.

English Language Support

Exchange Information and Ideas Guide students to work in small groups to answer the questions. Have each group answer one question. When all the groups are finished, let them take turns presenting their answers to the class. Encourage students to provide their classmates with useful feedback.

Assign this performance task.

PERFORMANCE TASK

W 3, W 5, W 7

Writing Activity: Graphic Comic Have students work independently to research retellings and sketch their ideas.

- Suggest that they look at a variety of graphic novels as examples of the format.

- Have pairs of students review and comment on each other's sketches before they create final pages.

Critical Vocabulary

L 4c

moderate	prowess	frantic	anxiety

Practice and Apply Answer each question with *yes* or *no*. With your group, use examples and reasons to explain your answers.

1. Are most professional basketball players of **moderate** height?

2. Is **prowess** related to pride?

3. Is it possible to speak in a **frantic** way?

4. Would you look forward to having **anxiety**?

Vocabulary Strategy: Noun Suffixes -ty and -ity

A **suffix** is a word part that appears at the end of a word or root. Readers can use their knowledge of suffixes to figure out word meanings. Some suffixes signal that a word is a naming word, or **noun.** Notice the word with a noun suffix in this sentence from "The Flight of Icarus."

> Daedalus, crazed by anxiety, called back to him, "Icarus! Icarus, my son, where are you?"

The word *anxiety* ends with the suffix *-ty*, which signals that *anxiety* is a noun. Another form of the suffix is *-ity*. These suffixes add the meaning "state or condition of" to a word.

Anxiety means "the state of feeling anxious."

The suffix *-ty* changes the adjective into a noun.

> The word *anxious* is an **adjective,** a word that modifies a noun or a pronoun.

Practice and Apply The bold words in these items are adjectives. Change each adjective into its noun form by using the suffix *-ty* or *-ity*. Consult a resource, such as a print or online dictionary, for words that are unfamiliar.

1. Things that are **similar** are alike. A likeness is a _____ .

2. Something that is **frail** may break. It has _____ .

3. A **loyal** friend can be trusted. Friends share _____ .

4. **Cruel** words hurt. Their speaker shows _____ .

5. To be free from danger is to feel **secure.** This freedom is called _____ .

Critical Vocabulary

L 4c

Possible answers:

1. *No. Most professional basketball players are extremely tall.*

2. *Yes, because if you have prowess, you have great skill and the ability to accomplish things, which would make most people proud.*

3. *Yes. If you're upset, you might speak very quickly and erratically.*

4. *No. I don't like the feeling of being worried or scared, which is how anxiety makes me feel.*

Vocabulary Strategy: Noun Suffixes -ty and -ity

Answers:

1. *similarity*

2. *frailty*

3. *loyalty*

4. *cruelty*

5. *security*

Strategies for Annotation   🖊 🗐 *Annotate it!*

Vocabulary Strategy: Noun Suffixes -ty and -ity

L 4c

Have students locate the sentence on lines 80–81. Encourage them to use their eBook annotation tools to do the following:

- Highlight the word that contains the ending *-ty* or *-ity*.
- Underline the ending.
- In a note, write the meaning of the word.
- Consult a resource, such as a print or online dictionary, to confirm the answer.

> Daedalus, crazed by anxiety, called back to him, "Icarus! Icarus, my son, where are you?"

> anxiety: state of feeling anxious or nervous

Language Conventions: Commas and Coordinate Adjectives

Tell students that the left side of the chart in the lesson shows examples of phrases with coordinate adjectives, or adjectives of equal effect, which are set apart by a comma. The examples in the right side are phrases containing adjectives that do not have an equal effect and therefore do not require a comma. Ask volunteers to come up with additional examples, such as the ones shown here, for each side of the chart. Use the tests suggested in the lesson to confirm each example.

Comma Needed	No Comma Needed
tall, dark stranger; *slow, easy* pace; *shallow, murky* water	*great big* smile; *angry old* man; *silly little* girl

Possible Answers:

1. *bright, sparkling sun*

2. *shining, feathery wings*

3. *golden, flowing hair*

4. *bright, intelligent eyes*

5. *lovely, soaring bird*

Assess It Online!

Online Selection Test
- Download an editable ExamView bank.
- Assign and manage this test online.

Language Conventions: Commas and Coordinate Adjectives

Writers use **adjectives** to modify, or describe, nouns. Often, a writer will use more than one adjective to modify the same noun, such as in this phrase from "The Flight of Icarus": *one clear, wind-swept morning.*

Notice that the adjectives *clear* and *wind-swept* are separated by a comma. These are called **coordinate adjectives,** adjectives of equal effect that modify the same noun. Here is another example from the story: *the slow, graceful sweep of their wings.*

The comma acts like the word *and* between the coordinate adjectives. When you write, you can use a comma to replace *and.* Sometimes, however, two or more adjectives that modify the same noun do not have equal effect. Then no comma is needed.

✔ Comma Needed	✘ No Comma Needed
dark, stormy night	**little red** schoolhouse
fierce, angry cries	**usual afternoon** nap
crowded, noisy city	**tired old** dog

You can determine whether adjectives modify equally with these tests:
- Swap the position of the adjectives. If the sentence makes sense, the adjectives modify equally: *the stormy, dark night*
- Insert the word *and* between the adjectives. If the sentence still reads well, the adjectives modify equally: *the dark **and** stormy night*

Practice and Apply Find the nouns *sun, wings, hair, eyes,* and *bird* in this sentence from "The Flight of Icarus." Write two coordinate adjectives to describe each noun, using commas where needed. Consult resources such as a print or online dictionary for words that are unfamiliar to you.

> Icarus, standing in the bright sun, the shining wings dropping gracefully from his shoulders, his golden hair wet with spray, and his eyes bright and dark with excitement, looked like a lovely bird.

English Language Support

Use Coordinate Adjectives Clarify the definition of coordinate adjectives and the tests that determine whether adjectives modify equally.

- Read the Practice and Apply sentence aloud. Then display the following nouns: *sun, wings, hair, eyes,* and *bird.* Provide students with a list of adjectives and help them choose two adjectives that describe each noun. Guide students to determine where commas are needed.

- As a class, list at least two adjectives for every noun in the Practice and Apply sentence (*sun, wings, hair, eyes,* and *bird*). Ask pairs to choose two adjectives for each noun, use the tests of swapping positions and inserting the word ***and,*** and decide whether to use a comma.

- Display a list of adjectives and a list of nouns. Have students use words from the lists to write sentences that contain nouns modified by two or more adjectives. Ask volunteers to read their sentences and explain why they did or did not use a comma between adjectives.

INTERACTIVE WHITEBOARD LESSON
Analyze Story Elements: Characterization

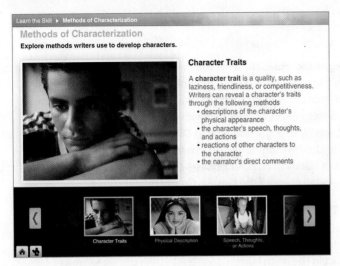

TEACH

Use the whiteboard lesson to review the methods that writers use to develop characters. Discuss how the author of "The Flight of Icarus" used these methods to develop the character of Icarus.

- **Description of physical appearance** (*his golden hair wet with spray, and his eyes bright and dark with excitement; looked like a lovely bird*)
- **Character's speech, thoughts, and actions** (*beating his wings in joy, felt the thrill of the cool wind on his face*)
- **Reactions of other characters** (*Daedalus watched him proudly but with misgivings.*)
- **Narrator's direct comments** (*…the birdlike son who had thrown caution to the winds in the exaltation of his freedom from the earth.*)

PRACTICE AND APPLY

As students apply what they have learned about character development in their graphic comics for the Performance Task, suggest that they use an Interactive Graphic Organizer, such as a Freeform Web, to list the traits of Theseus they want to show. Have them work with partners to plan the best ways to show these traits.

INTERACTIVE GRAPHIC ORGANIZER Have students use this interactive graphic organizer: **Freeform Web**

Determine Theme

RETEACH

Review the definition of **theme:** a message about life or human nature that a writer shares with the reader. Explain that the theme of a story is not just what the story is about. Use this example:

- **What "The Flight of Icarus" is about:** A man and his son attempt to escape from an island by flying.
- **Theme of "The Flight of Icarus":** Practice moderation; do not aspire to be like the gods.

Review the chart on Student Edition page 35. Discuss how the answer to the third question, "How well do they succeed, and why?" leads to the theme of the myth. (*Icarus does not succeed because he ignores his father's warning to be moderate and flies toward heaven, like a god. Daedalus succeeds in escaping the island, but his success is bitter because he has lost his son.*)

LEVEL UP TUTORIALS To give students additional practice in determining theme, assign the following *Level Up* tutorial: **Theme**

INDEPENDENT READING

Students can apply the skill to another myth of their choice. Have them work independently to use the three questions for finding the theme of a myth to guide them.

Arachne

Greek Myth retold by Olivia E. Coolidge

Why This Text

Students may read the text of a myth without a thorough grasp of the theme or of the way in which the elements of the myth interact. For example, a myth such as this one will share a message about life or human behavior, but students may not understand that this is the theme. With the help of the close-reading questions, students will see how the theme reflects the cultural values of the ancient Greeks, who first told the myth. This close reading will help students develop an awareness of the elements of a myth and of how these elements interact.

Background Have students read the background of this Greek myth and explain that Greek mythology is filled with stories about mortals who pit themselves against the gods and about the consequences of their behavior or defiance. Introduce the selection by telling students that Olivia E. Coolidge (1908–2006) is a famous mythographer. An expert on Greek mythology, some of her most popular books—*Greek Myths* and *The Trojan War*—retell many of the famous Greek stories.

SETTING A PURPOSE Ask students to pay attention to the theme and to how the elements of the myth interact. When do they first start to understand how the theme grows out of the conflict in the myth?

Standards Support

- cite several pieces of textual evidence
- determine a theme and analyze its development over the course of a text
- analyze how particular elements of a story interact

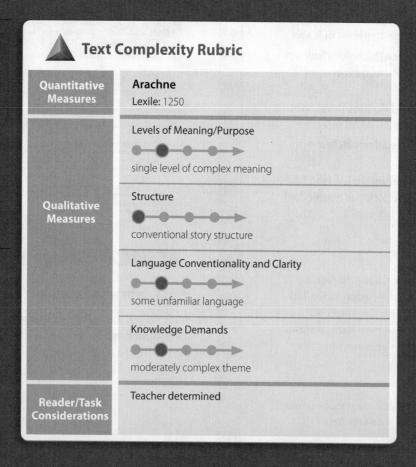

Text Complexity Rubric

Quantitative Measures	**Arachne** Lexile: 1250
Qualitative Measures	**Levels of Meaning/Purpose** single level of complex meaning
	Structure conventional story structure
	Language Conventionality and Clarity some unfamiliar language
	Knowledge Demands moderately complex theme
Reader/Task Considerations	Teacher determined

Strategies for CLOSE READING

Determine Theme

Students should read this myth carefully all the way through. Close-reading questions at the bottom of the page will help them determine the theme (the message about life or human nature) and analyze the way elements of a myth interact, including how characters influence plot events. As they read, students should record comments or questions about the text in the side margins.

WHEN STUDENTS STRUGGLE . . .

To help students determine the theme of the myth, have them work in a small group to fill out a chart such as the one shown below as they analyze the myth.

CITE TEXT EVIDENCE The theme of a Greek myth, such as this one about Arachne, is the central idea that expresses an important message about life or human nature. In a myth or story, the theme is an idea, such as "pride goes before a fall," that is revealed through the writer's presentation of characters or plot events. For practice in determining the theme of this myth, track the goal of the characters, what they do to reach that goal, how well they succeed, and why.

Finding the Theme of a Myth

What do the characters want?	What do the characters do to reach that goal?	How well do they succeed, and why?
Arachne wants to be viewed as being as great a weaver as Athene, a god. Athene does not want Arachne to put herself on a pedestal with the gods.	They engage in a contest to see who is the better weaver—a mortal or a god.	They prove to be nearly equal in skill, but Arachne remains proud and arrogant, insulting Athene. Athene transforms Arachne into a spider because her pride and disdain have caused her to overstep her bounds.

Background *Many Greek myths are about characters who stray beyond the limits set by Greek gods and goddesses or who ignore their warnings. In this myth, Arachne (ə-răk´nē), a weaver, pits herself against Athene (ə-thē´nē), the goddess of wisdom and all crafts, particularly weaving.*

Arachne

Greek Myth retold by Olivia E. Coolidge

CLOSE READ
Notes

1. **READ ▶** As you read lines 1–37, begin to collect and cite text evidence.

   • Underline details that describe Arachne's skill.
   • Circle details that reveal Arachne's personality.

A Arachne was a maiden who became famous throughout Greece, though she was neither wellborn nor beautiful and came from no great city. She lived in an **obscure** little village, and her father was a humble dyer of wool. In this he was very skillful, producing many varied shades, while above all he was famous for the clear, bright scarlet which is made from shellfish, and which was the most glorious of all the colors used in ancient Greece. Even more skillful than her father was Arachne. It was her task to spin the fleecy wool into a fine, soft thread and to weave it into cloth on the high-standing loom[1]

10 within the cottage. Arachne was small and pale from much working. Her eyes were light and her hair was a dusty brown, yet she was quick and graceful, and her fingers, roughened as they were, went so fast that it was hard to follow their flickering movements. So soft and even

obscure:

not well-known

---

[1] **high-standing loom:** a tall frame used to hold threads in a vertical position as other threads are woven through horizontally.

17

---

1. **READ AND CITE TEXT EVIDENCE** Explain to students that Coolidge opens her retelling of the myth with details that describe Arachne's skill at weaving and also reveal her personality, or character traits, which will shape events in the myth.

A ASK STUDENTS to determine how Coolidge describes Arachne's skill and character traits, both positive and negative, by citing specific textual evidence in lines 1–37. *Responses may include references to evidence in lines 1–4, 7–16, and 17–37.*

Critical Vocabulary: obscure (line 3) Have students explain the meaning of *obscure* as it is used here. Ask how *obscure* plays a role in the setting and how it contrasts with Arachne's character traits. *Although Arachne comes from a little-known village, she becomes known all over Greece because of her skill. Her fame becomes so great that it shapes her disdainful attitude and leads to the conflict and contest between Arachne and Athene.*

was her thread, so fine her cloth, so gorgeous her embroidery, that soon her products were known all over Greece. No one had ever seen the like of them before.

At last Arachne's fame became so great that people used to come from far and wide to watch her working. Even the graceful nymphs would steal in from stream or forest and peep shyly through the dark
20 doorway, watching in wonder the white arms of Arachne as she stood at the loom and threw the shuttle² from hand to hand between the hanging threads, or drew out the long wool, fine as a hair, from the distaff³ as she sat spinning. "Surely Athene herself must have taught her," people would murmur to one another. "Who else could know the secret of such marvelous skill?"

B Arachne was used to being wondered at, and she was immensely proud of the skill that had brought so many to look on her. Praise was all she lived for, and it displeased her greatly that people should think anyone, even a goddess, could teach her anything. Therefore when she
30 heard them murmur, she would stop her work and turn round **indignantly** to say, "With my own ten fingers I gained this skill, and by hard practice from early morning till night. I never had time to stand looking as you people do while another maiden worked. Nor if I had, would I give Athene credit because the girl was more skillful than I. As for Athene's weaving, how could there be finer cloth or

indignantly:

in a manner that expresses anger over an injustice

---

² **shuttle:** a piece of wood holding the thread that is to be woven horizontally through the vertical threads on a loom.
³ **distaff:** a short rod for holding wool that is to be spun into a thread.

---

2. ◀ **REREAD** Reread lines 26–37. Explain why Arachne is so indignant. What character traits does Arachne reveal with this behavior? Support your answer with explicit textual evidence.

Arachne is angered when people say Athene taught her to weave.

Arachne's behavior indicates that she is proud and ungrateful.

---

3. **READ** ▶ As you read lines 38–67, continue to cite textual evidence.
   • Underline the advice the old woman gives Arachne.
   • In the margin, restate Arachne's response to the woman's advice.
   • In the margin, describe Arachne's reaction when she finds out she's speaking to Athene.

18

> **Reckless girl, how dare you claim to be equal to the immortal gods themselves?**

more beautiful embroidery than mine? If Athene herself were to come down and compete with me, she could do no better than I."

One day when Arachne turned round with such words, an old woman answered her, a grey old woman, bent and very poor, who
40 stood leaning on a staff and peering at Arachne amid the crowd of onlookers. "Reckless girl," she said, "how dare you claim to be equal to the immortal gods themselves? I am an old woman and have seen much. Take my advice and ask pardon of Athene for your words. Rest content with your fame of being the best spinner and weaver that mortal eyes have ever beheld."

"Stupid old woman," said Arachne indignantly, "who gave you a right to speak in this way to me? It is easy to see that you were never good for anything in your day, or you would not come here in poverty and rags to gaze at my skill. If Athene resents my words, let her
50 answer them herself. I have challenged her to a contest, but she, of course, will not come. It is easy for the gods to avoid matching their skill with that of men."

At these words the old woman threw down her staff and stood erect. The wondering onlookers saw her grow tall and fair and stand clad in long robes of dazzling white. They were terribly afraid as they realized that they stood in the presence of Athene. Arachne herself flushed red for a moment, for she had never really believed that the goddess would hear her. Before the group that was gathered there she would not give in; so pressing her pale lips together in **obstinacy** and
60 pride, she led the goddess to one of the great looms and set herself before the other. Without a word both began to thread the long

D

C

Arachne rejects the woman's advice and insults her.

obstinacy:

unwillingness to change one's behavior or attitude

19

---

2. **REREAD AND CITE TEXT EVIDENCE**

B ASK STUDENTS to "unpack" Arachne's prideful behavior and indignation. How does it reveal her disdainful attitude? *Instead of being humbled by all the praise she receives, she has become indignant toward those who say that Athene has taught her to spin and weave.*

3. **READ AND CITE TEXT EVIDENCE**

C ASK STUDENTS to read their margin notes to a partner and then create one response that describes Arachne's reaction when she discovers that she is speaking to Athene in lines 53–67, citing textual evidence.

Critical Vocabulary: indignantly (line 31) Have students share their definitions of *indignantly*. Ask how *indignantly* reveals Arachne's character traits. *It shows her haughty attitude toward her skill and her anger toward those who would say that Athene taught her.*

Critical Vocabulary: obstinacy (line 59) Encourage students to cite textual examples of Arachne's obstinacy and to describe what this behavior says about her. *Students should be able to point to her refusal to take the old woman's advice about begging Athene's forgiveness for her prideful speech and behavior.*

FOR ELL STUDENTS Explain to students that *poor* (line 39), *right* (line 47), *threw* (line 53), *red* (line 57), *hear, there* (line 58), *would,* and *pale* (line 59) are examples of homophones, words that sound alike but have different meanings and spellings. Ask students if they know what each of these words means. Then have them make a list of the words, writing the homophone beside each word. *Students should be able to list these homophones: pour, write, through, read, here, their, wood, and pail.*

Arachne challenges Athene to a competition to see who is a more talented weaver.

woolen strands that hang from the rollers, and between which the shuttle moves back and forth. Many skeins lay heaped beside them to use, bleached white, and gold, and scarlet, and other shades, varied as the rainbow. Arachne had never thought of giving credit for her success to her father's skill in dyeing, though in actual truth the colors were as remarkable as the cloth itself.

Soon there was no sound in the room but the breathing of the onlookers, the whirring of the shuttles, and the creaking of the wooden frames as each pressed the thread up into place or tightened the pegs by which the whole was held straight. The excited crowd in the doorway began to see that the skill of both in truth was very nearly equal, but that, however the cloth might turn out, the goddess was the quicker of the two. A pattern of many pictures was growing on her loom. There was a border of twined branches of the olive, Athene's favorite tree, while in the middle, figures began to appear. As they looked at the glowing colors, the spectators realized that Athene was weaving into her pattern a last warning to Arachne. The central figure was the goddess herself competing with Poseidon for possession of the city of Athens; but in the four corners were mortals who had tried to **strive** with gods and pictures of the awful fate that had overtaken them. The goddess ended a little before Arachne and stood back from her marvelous work to see what the maiden was doing.

strive:
compete

70

80

An ancient Greek statue of Athene

Never before had Arachne been matched against anyone whose skill was equal, or even nearly equal to her own. As she stole glances from time to time at Athene and saw the goddess working swiftly, calmly, and always a little faster than herself, she became angry instead of frightened, and an evil thought came into her head. Thus as Athene stepped back a pace to watch Arachne finishing her work, she saw that the maiden had taken for her design a pattern of scenes which showed evil or unworthy actions of the gods, how they had deceived fair maidens, resorted to trickery, and appeared on earth from time to time in the form of poor and humble people. When the goddess saw this insult glowing in bright colors on Arachne's loom, she did not wait while the cloth was judged, but stepped forward, her grey eyes blazing with anger, and tore Arachne's work across. Then she struck Arachne across the face. Arachne stood there a moment, struggling with anger, fear, and pride. "I will not live under this insult," she cried, and seizing a rope from the wall, she made a noose and would have hanged herself.

90

100

F

4. ◀ REREAD Reread lines 38–45. What does the old woman's advice suggest about the theme, or central idea, of the myth?

The old woman's advice suggests that human beings should not overstep their bounds.

5. READ ▶ As you read lines 68–112, continue to cite textual evidence.

• Underline the warning that Athene weaves into her cloth for Arachne.
• Circle the insult Arachne weaves into her cloth for Athene.
• In the margin, explain what happens to Arachne at the end of the myth.

4. **REREAD AND CITE TEXT EVIDENCE**

D **ASK STUDENTS** to explain how the old woman's advice to Arachne may express the theme of the myth. How does it signify a message about human behavior? *Students should cite textual evidence from lines 38–45 as they point out that the advice suggests that human beings should not be proud, nor overstep their bounds.*

5. **READ AND CITE TEXT EVIDENCE**

E **ASK STUDENTS** to read their margin notes to a partner and then collaborate to find and cite text examples from lines 68–112 to explain what happens to Arachne at the end of the myth. *Students should recognize that Arachne's disdainful, insulting behavior causes Athene to transform her into a spider.*

Critical Vocabulary: strive (line 81) Encourage students to explain *strive* as it is used here. Why does Coolidge use this word? *She may wish to emphasize the theme of not overstepping one's bounds.*

FOR ELL STUDENTS Explain that *from time to time* (line 87) is an idiomatic phrase (or expression), in which the words together have a meaning that differs from the dictionary definition of the individual words. Ask students if they know what this idiomatic expression means. *Students should be able to point out that it means "at intervals," "occasionally," or "once in a while."* Ask students to look for other idiomatic phrases (or expressions) and cite them in the margin. *Possible answers include* **from far and wide** *(line 18) and* **steal in** *(line 19).*

CLOSE READ
Notes

descendants:

people who come after

Arachne is turned into a spider.

The goddess touched the rope and touched the maiden. "Live on, wicked girl," she said. "Live on and spin, both you and your **descendants.** When men look at you they may remember that it is not wise to strive with Athene." At that the body of Arachne shriveled up, and her legs grew tiny, spindly, and distorted. There before the eyes of the spectators hung a little dusty brown spider on a slender thread.

110   All spiders descend from Arachne, and as the Greeks watched them spinning their thread wonderfully fine, they remembered the contest with Athene and thought that it was not right for even the best of men to claim equality with the gods.

6. ◀ REREAD AND DISCUSS With a small group, discuss what Arachne does to so enrage Athene and whether or not her punishment is justified. Cite text evidence in your discussion.

SHORT RESPONSE

Cite Text Evidence   What lessons about human behavior does this myth teach? Review your reading notes, and be sure to **cite text evidence** from the myth in your response.

The myth teaches that humans should not be prideful and arrogant. Arachne does not listen to the advice to "Rest content with your fame of being the best spinner and weaver that mortal eyes have ever beheld." Arachne's boasting and rude treatment of Athene lead Athene to accept Arachne's challenge. Arachne's pride causes her to insult Athene and causes Athene to turn her into a spider.

22

---

6. **REREAD AND DISCUSS USING TEXT EVIDENCE**

F **ASK STUDENTS** to appoint a reporter for each group to cite specific textual evidence and line numbers to support their position about whether or not Arachne's punishment is justified. *Students should cite specific textual evidence from lines 68–112.*

Critical Vocabulary: descendants (line 105) Have students share their definitions of *descendants*. Then ask them to compare the meanings of the words *descendants* and *ancestors*.

SHORT RESPONSE

Cite Text Evidence   Students should

- explain the larger lesson about human behavior this myth teaches
- give reasons for their point of view
- cite specific evidence from the text to support their reasons

---

TO CHALLENGE STUDENTS . . .

For more context about the Greek myth of Arachne, and for additional information about Greek mythology, history, or culture, students can do print, online, or multimedia research to write a chapter for a book about the context in which the ancient Greek myths were created and told.

ASK STUDENTS to work with a small group to do some preliminary research to find an interesting topic for their chapter, explaining that the completed chapters will be combined into a class book. Possible topics might include

- special heroes of Greek mythology and their attributes, including the goddess Athene
- how Greek myths expressed the values and beliefs of ancient Greek culture and society
- heroes, gods, and monsters of Greek myths
- brief history of ancient Greece, perhaps focusing on conflicts or culture

With the class, discuss the elements of writing a chapter after students have chosen a topic, eliciting the following points.

Plan your group research:

- choose a group recorder
- make a list of questions about your topic
- research your topic and take notes
- organize your notes
- write an outline based on your notes

Write your group chapter:

- keep your purpose and audience in mind
- write a first draft and title your chapter
- illustrate your chapter
- revise your writing and proofread the revision
- make a final copy and combine it with the other groups' chapters to publish and share a class book

Students might also wish to view the following videos: "Greek Gods" or "Spartans Deconstructed," which are part of the program *Ancient Greece*, in their eBooks.

DIG DEEPER

With the class, return to Question 6, Reread and Discuss. Have students share the results of their discussion.

ASK STUDENTS whether they were satisfied with the outcome of their group discussions. Have each group share what the majority opinion was of the group. What convincing evidence did the group cite from the myth to support its opinion?

- Encourage students to tell whether there was any convincing evidence cited by group members holding the minority opinion. If so, why didn't it sway the group's position on the judgment meted out by Athene?
- Have groups explain how they decided that the punishment was (or was not) justified. Did everyone in the group agree? How did the group use the skills of conflict resolution to clear up any disagreements or disputes?
- After students have shared the results of their individual group's discussion, ask whether another group shared any findings that would have swayed their opinion.

ASK STUDENTS to return to their Short Response answer and to revise it based on the class discussion, revising their specific textual evidence if needed.

CLOSE READING NOTES

Icarus's Flight

Poem by Stephen Dobyns

Why This Text?

Students will often encounter poetry in their studies and, from time to time, in their own reading. Understanding poetic form and elements will deepen their appreciation of the poet's art. This lesson focuses on poetic form and on how alliteration contributes to a poem's meaning.

Key Learning Objectives: The student will understand how the elements of form and the use of alliteration emphasize ideas and meaning in a poem.

RL 1 Cite textual evidence.

RL 2 Determine a theme or central idea.

RL 4 Analyze the impact of repetitions of sounds of a poem.

RL 5 Analyze how a poem's form contributes to its meaning.

W 2 Write informative/explanatory texts.

SL 1 Engage in collaborative discussions.

SL 4 Present claims and findings; use appropriate eye contact, adequate volume, and clear pronunciation.

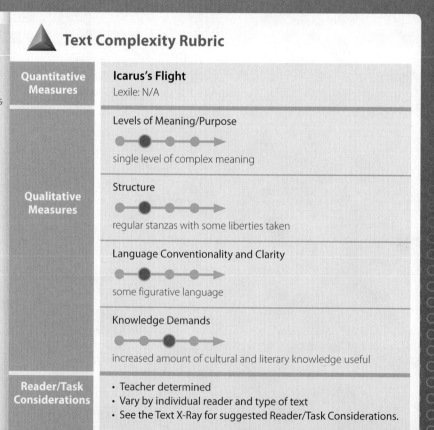

Text Complexity Rubric

Quantitative Measures

Icarus's Flight
Lexile: N/A

Qualitative Measures

Levels of Meaning/Purpose

single level of complex meaning

Structure

regular stanzas with some liberties taken

Language Conventionality and Clarity

some figurative language

Knowledge Demands

increased amount of cultural and literary knowledge useful

Reader/Task Considerations

• Teacher determined
• Vary by individual reader and type of text
• See the Text X-Ray for suggested Reader/Task Considerations.

TEXT X-RAY

English Language Support Before teaching, use the Text X-Ray below for an overview of the text's complexity. The Text X-Ray and the supports and scaffolds in the Teacher's Edition will help you guide students of different skill levels.

Meaning Making

Language Development

Effective Expression

Content Knowledge

Foundational Skills

Text Complexity: Qualitative Measures

Levels of Meaning/Purpose

single level of complex meaning

Help students understand how poetic elements contribute to meaning.

- Teacher's Edition side notes, pp. 40, 41
- Strategies for Annotation, p. 41

ZOOM IN ON **ANALYZING POETIC ELEMENTS** Tell students that poets use **alliteration,** the repetition of consonant sounds at the beginning of words, to add rhythm and sound effects to poetry.

- Read aloud lines 3–6 of the poem, from "But how" to "he fell," putting emphasis on the *f* consonant sound.
- Have small groups complete these sentence frames:
  - Three words that create alliteration in these lines are _____, _____, _____.
  - The repetition of the consonant sound suggests that the speaker feels _____.
- Discuss students' responses as a class.

Structure

regular stanzas with some liberties taken

Help students analyze the poetic form.

- Teacher's Edition side notes, pp. 40, 41
- English Language Support, p. 39
- When Students Struggle, p. 40

To reteach poetic form, see

- Analyze Form: Scansion, p. 42a
- Analyze Form: Poetry, p. 42a

▶ *Use It! Level Up* Tutorial: Rhythm
Interactive Whiteboard Lesson: Form in Poetry

ZOOM IN ON **UNDERSTANDING POETIC FORM** Explain that poets use a variety of **forms** to arrange words and lines on the page and group ideas. Tell students that in this poem, the end of a **stanza,** or group of lines, does not always signal the end of a sentence. Instead, sentences continue on to the next stanza.

- Demonstrate this by reading aloud the first two stanzas, stopping at the end of line 8.
- Discuss why the poet chose to end each stanza in the middle of a thought. Guide students to the understanding that it helps to create a feeling of suspense that pushes the reader along.

Language Conventionality and Clarity

some figurative language

Help students recognize figurative language in the poem.

▶ *Use It!* **Interactive Whiteboard Lesson:** Figurative Language and Imagery

ZOOM IN ON **RECOGNIZING METAPHORS** Explain that a **metaphor** is figurative language that directly compares two things that are unlike but have some quality or characteristic in common.

- Direct students to lines 12–14.
- Point out the word "flutter" and help them to identify the creature that the sentence describes. *(a butterfly)*
- Have them state the comparison the poet makes between the flight of a butterfly and that of Icarus. *(Icarus is purposeful, the butterfly aimless.)*

Knowledge Demands

increased amount of cultural and literary knowledge useful

Help students clarify the cultural and literary contexts of the poem.
- Teacher's Edition Background note, p. 39
- Performance Task, p. 42

ZOOM IN ON **UNDERSTANDING CONTEXT** As a class, review the myth of Daedalus and Icarus (pp. 31–34) and then share information from the Background note on Teacher's Edition page 39.

- Have volunteers provide details about the characters, plot, setting, and theme of the myth. List them on the board.
- Ask students to make predictions about how telling the myth through a poem might be different from the story they already read. *(shorter, fewer details, focused on the main idea or theme)* List predictions on the board.
- As students read the poem, encourage them to list more differences between the poem and the myth.

Suggested Reader/Task Considerations

Consider the following before assigning this poem to students:
- Do students have adequate inferencing skills to grasp the meaning of this poem?
- Do students have the questioning skills to challenge ideas presented in the poem and consider ideas from multiple points of view?

ZOOM IN ON **SUPPORTING COMPREHENSION**

- Have pairs read the poem, focusing on the questions in each stanza. For each question, have students write a sentence explaining how it challenges popular ideas about Icarus.
- Point out that the poet's portrayal of Icarus differs from the usual depiction in literature and art. As a class, discuss whether students agree with the poet's ideas about Icarus. Encourage them to ask questions that challenge ideas in the poem.

CLOSE READ

Background Have students read the background and poet information. Explain that the story of Icarus has been the subject of many other poems, stories, songs, and paintings. Icarus is usually depicted as a young teen, who, like most young people, possesses a naïve and bold confidence about his own mortality. In this poem, Stephen Dobyns depicts Icarus as having a great deal more insight into his actions during his fatal flight than is commonly found in traditional retellings of the myth. To share more about the poet, Stephen Dobyns, point out that not only does Dobyns feel he must work at the craft of poetry every day, but that being a poet also requires a love of reading of all kinds of books, but especially "good books." As for his own writing, he says that poems can begin for him at any time or place during a day. An idea might wake him in the middle of the night, or it might come to him while swimming laps in a pool.

SETTING A PURPOSE Direct students to use the Setting a Purpose prompt to focus their reading. Tell students to write any questions they generate during reading.

Background *From ancient times to present, writers have been fascinated by the characters of myths. They have featured famous mythic characters in such forms as dramas, stories, and poetry. Whether powerful or weak, noble or flawed, these characters have a hold on writers' imaginations. "Icarus's Flight" is a poem that reflects a poet's fascination with the myth of Icarus, the son of Daedalus who flew too close to the sun.*

Icarus's Flight

Poem by Stephen Dobyns

Stephen Dobyns (b. 1941) *has written numerous, critically acclaimed poetry collections. While he is also the author of other popular works of fiction, including novels and mysteries, he considers himself first and foremost a poet. In fact, he has claimed that he thinks of poetry twenty-four hours a day and that being a successful poet requires constant focus on the craft. Dobyns has also taught writing at a number of colleges throughout the United States.*

SETTING A PURPOSE As you read this poem, think about the way the poet portrays Icarus and his true intention.

English Language Support

Analyze Language Explain to students that the use of alliteration, or the repetition of consonant sounds at the beginning of words, can help give a poem rhythm. Display and read aloud lines 9–10. Highlight in yellow the words that stand out because of the alliterative sounds.

- Work with students to read lines 9–10, emphasizing the rhythm that the alliterative sounds give to the lines.
- Have pairs of students read lines 9–10 aloud to hear the rhythm. Then ask them to read lines 9–12 and identify another alliterative word in the stanza. *(flutter)*

- Ask pairs of students to replace one instance of *flew* with *soared*, and one instance of *far* with *high*. Then have them reread the lines aloud and describe how the rhythm and pace of the poem change.

> his liberty. You say he flew too far?
>
> He flew just far enough. He flew precisely

Analyze Form: Poetry (LINES 1–8)

RL 1, RL 5

Explain that a poem's **form** is the way in which words and lines are arranged on the page, including the way in which lines are organized into **stanzas,** the groups of two or more lines that form a unit in a poem.

 CITE TEXT EVIDENCE Have students identify the number of lines in each stanza, whether the lines rhyme, and how end punctuation is used in each line. What is the effect of these elements of form on the meaning? *(Stanzas have four lines. The lines do not rhyme. The sentences extending across lines and stanzas pull the reader along, from one line to the next.)*

Determine Meaning of Words and Phrases: Alliteration (LINES 10–16)

RL 1, RL 4

Inform students that **alliteration** is the repetition of consonant sounds at the beginning of words. Poets use alliteration to give the poem **rhythm,** the pattern of sounds similar to beats in music. Alliteration also helps direct attention to certain words.

 CITE TEXT EVIDENCE Have students reread from line 10 to "around him" in line 16. Ask them to identify the alliterative words *(flew, flutter, flight, far, forever)* and explain how these words affect the poem. *(The repeating consonant sounds emphasize these words, helping to create the image of flight and distance.)*

COLLABORATIVE DISCUSSION Have partners discuss their ideas about what Icarus really wanted and whether he achieved it. Remind them to cite evidence from the text to support their ideas.

ASK STUDENTS to share any questions they generated in the course of reading and discussing this selection.

Icarus's Flight

What else could the boy have done? Wasn't
flight both an escape and a great uplifting?
And so he flew. But how could he appreciate
his freedom without knowing the exact point

5 where freedom stopped? So he flew upward
and the sun dissolved the wax and he fell.
But at last in his anticipated plummeting
he grasped the confines of what had been

his liberty. You say he flew too far?
10 He flew just far enough. He flew precisely
to the point of wisdom. Would it
have been better to flutter ignorantly

from petal to petal within some garden
forever? As a result, flight for him was not
15 upward escape, but descent, with his wings
disintegrating around him. Should it matter

that neither shepherd nor farmer with his plow
watched him fall? He now had his answer,
laws to uphold him in his downward plunge.
20 Cushion enough for what he wanted.

COLLABORATIVE DISCUSSION According to the poet, what did Icarus really want? Do you think Icarus achieved it? Discuss your ideas with a partner.

WHEN STUDENTS STRUGGLE . . .

Explain to students that reading a poem aloud often helps reveal the rhythm. Have students work in small groups to take turns reading the poem aloud to each other. Point out that it helps to read to the end of each thought, pausing at the end of sentences and questions rather than at the end of each line.

 LEVEL UP TUTORIALS For additional support, assign the following *Level Up* tutorial: **Rhythm.**

Image Credits: (t) ©eAlisa/Shutterstock

Analyze Form: Poetry

RL 5

Poetry is a type of literature in which words are carefully chosen and arranged to create certain effects. **Form** in poetry is the way the words are arranged on the page. Here are two basic elements of form in poetry:

- The **line** is the main unit of all poems. Poets play with line length to emphasize meaning and to create rhythm. **Rhythm** is a pattern of stressed and unstressed syllables in a line of poetry, similar to the rhythmic beats in music.
- Lines are arranged in a group called a **stanza**. A single stanza may express a separate idea or emotion, but each stanza contributes to the overall meaning of a poem.

Crafting a poem's form involves careful choices of words, rhythms, and sounds. To understand how form can help create an effect such as rhythm in a poem, ask yourself these questions.

How long are the lines?   Do the lines rhyme?   Do the sentences always end at the end of a line?   How many lines are in each stanza?

Determine Meaning of Words and Phrases: Alliteration

RL 4

Poetry is often created to be spoken and heard. Reading a poem aloud can give readers a better sense of the feeling and sounds that the poet intended.

Poets often choose different words for their sounds. **Alliteration** is the repetition of consonant sounds at the beginning of words. It can establish rhythms in a poem that create feelings or emphasize ideas and images.

Read aloud these lines from "Icarus's Flight." Listen for the alliterative sounds. What do the repeated sounds suggest to you? How do they create rhythm and add emphasis to ideas or images in text?

> As a result, flight for him was not
> upward escape, but descent, with his wings
> disintegrating around him. Should it matter

Notice how the alliterative words of *descent* and *disintegrating* not only emphasize similar sounds, but they create a sense of falling *downward*— another word that begins with the same sound.

CLOSE READ

Analyze Form: Poetry
RL 5, SL 1

Have students work with a partner to examine the poem's form and answer the questions. Have them describe how the form affects the poem. *(Possible answer: There are four lines in each stanza. Each line is about the same length. There is a pattern of asking questions that introduces ideas, helps organize the speaker's thoughts, and gives the poem rhythm.)*

Determine Meaning of Words and Phrases: Alliteration
RL 4

Have partners take turns reading the poem aloud. As one partner reads, have the other jot down repeated consonant sounds at the beginning of words. Ask how this use of language contributes to the meaning and feeling of the poem. *(Possible answer: Repeated words and sounds provide rhythm and emphasize the actions described in the poem. They help the reader understand the poet's view of Icarus's flight.)*

English Language Support

Guide students to work in small groups to answer the questions on page 42. Each group should answer one question. When all the groups are finished, they can take turns presenting their answers to the class. Encourage students to provide their classmates with useful feedback.

Strategies for Annotation   🖉 📄 *Annotate it!*

Determine Meaning of Words and Phrases: Alliteration
RL 4

Have students use their eBook annotation tools to analyze the text. Ask them to do the following:

- Highlight in yellow the questions.
- Underline alliterative words.
- On a note, record difficult or confusing words or phrases.
- Review their annotations and explain how alliteration contributes to the meaning of the poem.

What else could the boy have done? Wasn't flight both an escape and a great uplifting? And so he flew. But how could he appreciate his freedom without knowing the exact point

confusing words and phrases: great uplifting

Analyzing the Text
RL 1, RL 2,
RL 4, RL 5

Possible answers:

1. *It pulls the reader along, connecting the stanzas and giving the poem an almost vertical motion downward. This seems to suggest the downward descent of Icarus's flight.*

2. *The exact point where freedom stopped is the moment in which Icarus's wings failed, and he was about to begin his descent.*

3. ~~*The words flew and flutter are alliterative, the poet chose*~~ *those words to emphasize the contrast between strong and weak flight.*

4. *The poet means that Icarus succeeded because by flying to that point, he learned what freedom was. He achieved "precisely" the "wisdom" of understanding both freedom and mortality at the same time.*

5. *Alliterative words:* him, he, had, his. *The poet uses these words to emphasize the idea that Icarus has finally attained what he wanted.*

6. *This poem changed my perception of Icarus from thinking of him as a young boy who forgot to heed his father's warning and loses his life, to someone who becomes fully aware of his actions and in failure actually gains wisdom and freedom.*

---

eBook *Annotate It!*

Analyzing the Text
RL 2, RL 4, RL 5,
W 2, SL 4

Cite Text Evidence   Support your responses with evidence from the text.

1. **Identify** Look closely at how certain sentences of the poem extend from one stanza into the next one. What effect is created by extending a sentence into the next line or into the next stanza?

2. **Analyze** Examine the question in lines 3–5. Based on what you know about the Icarus myth, where is the "exact point where freedom stopped"? How would you answer this question?

3. **Analyze** Look at the third stanza and identify the alliterative words. What idea does this alliteration emphasize or draw attention to?

4. **Interpret** What does the poet mean by the two sentences in lines 10 and 11?

5. **Analyze** Find the sentence that begins within line 18 and read it aloud. What examples of alliteration do you see? Why do you think the poet uses alliteration here?

6. **Compare** Consider what you already knew about the mythological character, Icarus, before reading this poem. How does this poem cause your perception of Icarus to change? Explain.

PERFORMANCE TASK
 WriteSmart

Speaking Activity: Response to Literature The poet asks a number of questions throughout the poem, as if speaking directly to readers. What is the purpose of these questions? Do they cause you to consider Icarus's actions in a new light? Share your views in an oral response.

- Think about the questions and views the poet presents.
- Identify evidence from the poem to support your views.
- Make sure your points are clear and convincing. Use verbal and nonverbal techniques to enhance your points.

FOR STANDARD ENGLISH LEARNERS

Pronunciation Some students may have trouble voicing the final /r/, as in *flutter* (line 12), *forever* (line 14), or *farmer* (line 17) in "Icarus's Flight." Write line 10 on the board, "He flew just far enough. He flew precisely. . . ." Read the sentence aloud with students echo reading. Emphasize the sound of the final /r/ in *far*. As students are working on the Performance Task, have them underline words with the final /r/ in their answers to the questions included in the poem. Ask student pairs to practice their oral responses, checking their pronunciation.

Assign this performance task.   ✓ WriteSmart

PERFORMANCE TASK
W 2, SL 4

Speaking Activity: Response to Literature Have students review the poem.

- Ask them to list the questions the poet includes in the poem. Then, have them try to answer each question, citing examples from the poem.

- Have them organize their ideas, using a hierarchy chart, to support their views on the effectiveness of these questions.

- Remind them to use appropriate eye contact, volume, and clear pronunciation when speaking.

Analyze Form: Scansion

RL 4,
RL 5

TEACH

Explain to students that **rhythm** in a poem is like the beat in music. It is a regular pattern of sound that is created by stressing some words or syllables and not others. Poets intentionally arrange words into rhythms that convey feelings and meaning.

- Explain that **scansion** is the process of marking the stressed and unstressed words or syllables in a poem to find its rhythm. Display and read aloud the following sentence, pointing out that the boldfaced words are stressed:

    The **time** to **act** is **now!**

- Explain that a repeated pattern of rhythm is called **meter.** Point out that in the meter in the example sentence, every other word is stressed.

- Explain that another way to mark up the rhythm of a line of poetry is by placing an acute accent (´) over the stressed syllables and a breve (˘) over the unstressed syllables.

- Display the sentence again, marking it as shown.

    The time to act is now!

 LEVEL UP TUTORIALS Assign the following *Level Up* tutorial: **Rhythm**

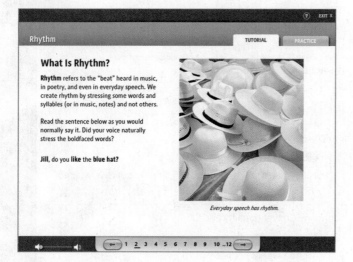

What Is Rhythm?

Rhythm refers to the "beat" heard in music, in poetry, and even in everyday speech. We create rhythm by stressing some words and syllables (or in music, notes) and not others.

Read the sentence below as you would normally say it. Did your voice naturally stress the boldfaced words?

Jill, do you **like** the **blue hat?**

Everyday speech has rhythm.

PRACTICE AND APPLY

Have partners work together to mark the stressed and unstressed syllables in the first stanza of "Icarus's Flight." Have them identify its rhythm and meter, and discuss how they affect the poem's meaning.

RL 5,
SL 1

INTERACTIVE WHITEBOARD LESSON
Analyze Form: Poetry

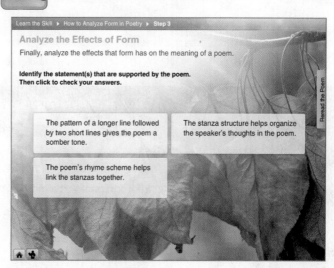

Learn the Skill ▸ How to Analyze Form in Poetry ▸ Step 3

Analyze the Effects of Form

Finally, analyze the effects that form has on the meaning of a poem.

Identify the statement(s) that are supported by the poem. Then click to check your answers.

> The pattern of a longer line followed by two short lines gives the poem a somber tone.

> The stanza structure helps organize the speaker's thoughts in the poem.

> The poem's rhyme scheme helps link the stanzas together.

RETEACH

Review with students that the **form,** or structure, of a poem is the way in which the words and **lines,** the main units of a poem, are arranged on the page. Form also includes the way in which related ideas are grouped together into **stanzas.**

- Poets use different forms to suit the types of thoughts and feelings they wish to convey.

- For example, a poet might use many short lines with no stanzas to create a feeling of energy and movement. They might alternate between long and short lines to play with rhythm and to emphasize some ideas over others.

- By analyzing the lengths of lines and the organization of the poem into stanzas, readers can understand and better appreciate a poet's ideas.

COLLABORATIVE DISCUSSION

Have pairs of students pick three poems by the same poet, either in a book or in an online collection. Have partners use an Interactive Graphic Organizer, such as a Comparison-Contrast Chart, to list how the poet uses lines and stanzas in each poem. Then have students discuss the effects that the different forms have on rhythm and meaning in each poem.

 INTERACTIVE GRAPHIC ORGANIZER Have students use this interactive graphic organizer: **Comparison-Contrast Chart**

Women in Aviation

Informational Text by Patricia and Fredrick McKissack

Why This Text?

Students encounter informational text almost daily. Understanding why an author writes a particular piece and how the author's choices reveal that purpose helps students be more analytical readers. This lesson explores an author's purpose for writing and has students support the conclusions they draw as they read.

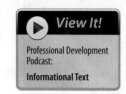

▶ **View It!**

Professional Development Podcast:

Informational Text

Key Learning Objective: Students will be able to identify, analyze, and draw conclusions about an author's purpose for writing informational texts.

RI 1 Cite textual evidence.

RI 2 Determine two or more central ideas.

RI 3 Analyze interactions between individuals, events, and ideas.

RI 4 Determine the meaning of words and phrases.

RI 6 Determine an author's purpose.

W 2 Write informative/explanatory texts.

W 6 Use technology to produce/publish writing.

W 8 Gather information from print and digital sources.

W 10 Write routinely.

L 1a Explain the function of phrases and clauses.

L 4a Use context as a clue to the meaning of a word or phrase.

L 5c Distinguish among connotations of words with similar denotations.

▲ Text Complexity Rubric

Quantitative Measures	**Women in Aviation** Lexile: 1150L
Qualitative Measures	**Levels of Meaning/Purpose** single purpose, explicitly stated
	Structure organization of main ideas and details complex, but clearly stated and generally sequential
	Language Conventionality and Clarity less straightforward sentence structure
	Knowledge Demands somewhat complex social studies concepts
Reader/Task Considerations	• Teacher determined • Vary by individual reader and type of text • See the Text X-Ray for suggested Reader/Task Considerations.

English Language Support
Before teaching, use the Text X-Ray below for an overview of the text's complexity. The Text X-Ray and the supports and scaffolds in the Teacher's Edition will help you guide students of different skill levels.

Meaning Making

Language Development

Effective Expression

Content Knowledge

Foundational Skills

Text Complexity: Qualitative Measures

Levels of Meaning/Purpose

single purpose, explicitly stated

Help students determine the author's purpose.

- Teacher's Edition side notes, pp. 43, 44, 47, 48, 49
- English Language Support, p. 47
- When Students Struggle, p. 44
- Strategies for Annotation, p. 49
- Determine Author's Purpose, p. 49

To reteach how to determine author's purpose, see

- Determine Author's Purpose, p. 52a

 Use It! Level Up Tutorials: Author's Purpose

***ZOOM IN ON* UNDERSTAND AUTHOR'S PURPOSE** Explain that authors have four main reasons for writing: to inform or explain, to persuade, to entertain, and to express thoughts or feelings. Write the following words and definitions on the board:

- inform; to give knowledge or learning
- explain; to make plain, to define
- persuade; to lead someone to agree to an action or idea
- entertain; give someone enjoyment

Tell students that understanding the meaning of these words will help them name the author's purpose. Ask volunteers to use each word in a sentence. If students are having difficulty, provide example sentences, such as, *A band likes to entertain with music.*

Structure

organization of main ideas and details complex, but clearly stated and generally sequential

Help students cite evidence and draw conclusions.

- Teacher's Edition side notes, pp. 46, 49
- English Language Support, pp. 46, 52a
- Strategies for Annotation, p. 46
- Cite Evidence and Draw Conclusions, p. 49

To help students determine facts and opinions, see

- Determine Facts and Opinions, p. 52a

***ZOOM IN ON* DRAWING CONCLUSIONS** Tell students that when they **draw conclusions,** they first look at facts and details, or **textual evidence,** and then they use their own knowledge and experience to make a judgment.

- Ask pairs to read the Background Note on page 43 and work together to identify facts and details.
- Ask what conclusions they can draw about why the McKissacks chose to write about women aviators.
- Have students cite the textual evidence they used to reach their conclusion.
- Ask students to share how their own knowledge and experience helped them reach their conclusion.

Language Conventionality and Clarity

less straightforward sentence structure

Teach unfamiliar academic vocabulary in context.

- Teacher's Edition Critical Vocabulary notes, pp. 44, 45, 47, 51
- Applying Academic Vocabulary, p. 47
- Vocabulary Strategy: Connotations and Denotations, p. 51
- Strategies for Annotation, p. 51

Guide students to analyze the language and sentence structure of the informational text.

- Teacher's Edition side notes, pp. 45, 52
- English Language Support, pp. 43, 45, 52
- Language Conventions: Subordinate Clauses, p. 52

ZOOM IN ON **DETERMINING MEANING** Tell students that a word's **denotation** is its dictionary definition, while its **connotation** comes from the ideas and feelings connected with the word. A word's connotation can be positive or negative. Words with strong connotations can point toward an author's message, or purpose.

- Display lines 10–11 and underline the word *daring*. Ask a volunteer to read the dictionary definition of *daring* aloud.
- Discuss the connotation of the word. Is it positive or negative? *(positive)* Why? *(because the women "gained fame" for being daring)*
- Review the idea that words and sentences around a word can help the reader understand its connotations.

Knowledge Demands

somewhat complex social studies concepts

Help students clarify the historical and political contexts of the informational text.

- Teacher's Edition Background note, p. 43
- Performance Task, p. 50

 For more historical background, students can view the video "Women in Aviation" in their eBooks.

 Use It! **Interactive Whiteboard Lesson:** Evaluating Web Sources

ZOOM IN ON **BUILDING HISTORICAL CONTEXT** Tell students that in the early 20th century, women in the U.S. did not enjoy the freedoms they have today. Many jobs were closed to women, who did not gain the right to vote until 1920. Life was even more restricted for African American women. Bessie Coleman went to Europe for pilot training because of discriminatory laws at home. These "Jim Crow" laws severely limited African Americans' freedom and opportunities for decades. Discriminatory rules affected nearly every aspect of daily life, including where people could work and live.

- As students read, have them note how restrictions affected Bessie Coleman's choices.
- Have students summarize how she dealt with these obstacles.

Suggested Reader/Task Considerations

Consider the following before assigning this informational text to students:

- Will students find the topic of this informational text engaging?
- Do students have adequate prior knowledge to understand the text?

ZOOM IN ON **SUPPORTING COMPREHENSION**

- Explain that the story of the first women pilots is filled with courage and determination. Before reading, ask small groups to discuss why these women might have decided to become pilots.
- Introduce the topic by having students read the Background Note and view the History video. Before reading, let small groups discuss any questions that arise about the topic.

Background Have students read the background and author information. Explain that aviation—the operation of aircraft—dates back to the first balloon flights in the late 1700s. In the 1890s, the first gliders, airplane-like aircraft without engines, were flown. But it was not until 1903 that the Wright brothers made the first successful flight in an engine-powered aircraft, the airplane. Airplane flight really "took off" during and after World War I (1914–1918), which saw a more widespread use of airplanes for military purposes.

SETTING A PURPOSE Direct students to use the Setting a Purpose question to focus their reading. Remind them to generate questions as they read.

Determine Author's Purpose (LINES 1–8)   RI 1, RI 6

Explain to students that authors write for a reason—the **author's purpose.** Authors of informational texts often write to inform or explain, presenting facts and other information about a topic.

 CITE TEXT EVIDENCE Ask students to reread lines 1–8 and cite evidence that helps them identify the authors' purpose. *(The purpose is to inform, because the authors include information about women aviators in the early days of aviation in America. The authors also explain that despite prejudice, some women and African Americans still dreamt of becoming aviators.)*

Cite Evidence and Draw Conclusions (LINES 9–15)   RI 1

Explain that as they read, students can **draw conclusions,** or make judgments about or take positions on a topic. They should base these conclusions on evidence, experience, and reasoning. To support their conclusions, readers should cite **textual evidence** in the form of facts and details.

 CITE TEXT EVIDENCE Ask students to reread lines 9–15 and identify evidence that supports a conclusion that the earliest women aviators were brave and accomplished. *(The detail "a number of women . . .gained fame for their skill and daring" supports this, as do the facts about Sophie Blanchard and other European women aviators.)*

Background *In the early 1900s, flying in "aeroplanes"— fixed-winged, self-propelled flying machines—was a bold undertaking. Male pilots were dashing heroes. However, female aviators—especially African American women—had to struggle for acceptance.* **Patricia and Fredrick McKissack** *(b. 1944; b. 1939) have written over 100 biographies and nonfiction books, most focusing on the achievements of African Americans.*

Women in Aviation

Informational Text by Patricia and Fredrick McKissack

SETTING A PURPOSE As you read, pay attention to the details that describe what it was like for a woman to become a pilot during this period. What obstacles did each pilot face? Write down any questions you may have while reading.

A merican aviation was from its very beginnings marred with sexist and racist assumptions. It was taken for granted that women were generally inferior to men and that white men were superior to all others. Flying, it was said, required a level of skill and courage that women and blacks lacked. Yet despite these prevailing prejudices, the dream and the desire to fly stayed alive among women and African-Americans.

The story of women in aviation actually goes back to the
10 time of the hot-air balloons. A number of women in Europe and America gained fame for their skill and daring. Sophie Blanchard made her first solo balloon flight in 1805. She grew in fame and was eventually named official aeronaut of the empire by Napoleon. By 1834, at least twenty women in Europe were piloting their own balloons.

(t) Houghton, Mifflin, Harcourt; (l) ©Tobias Helbig/Getty Images; (bg) ©Digital Vision/Getty Images; (cl) ©Apic/Hulton Archive/Getty Images; (cr) ©Fotosearch/Archive Photos/Getty Images; (r) ©Bettmann/Corbis

Women in Aviation **43**

English Language Support

Analyze Language Project lines 9–15 using a whiteboard, reading aloud as students follow. Highlight *aviation, flight, aeronaut,* and *piloting.*

- Ask students how these words are related after clarifying the definitions. Allow them to use visual clues on the page to determine that the words relate to flying aircraft.
- Would an aeronaut pilot an airplane? Have students work in pairs to explain why or why not.
- Ask pairs to create a word web. Have them choose a category for the web and add related words as they read.

CLOSE READ

For more context and historical background, students can view the video "Bessie Coleman" in their eBooks.

Determine Author's Purpose (LINES 25–33)

RI 1,
RI 6

Explain to students that authors can have more than one purpose for writing. For example, in an informational text, a writer might include fun details or interesting facts in order to entertain the reader as well as to inform.

C **ASK STUDENTS** to reread lines 25–33 and identify details that both entertain and inform. *(Sample answer: The quotation from Harriet Quimby "Flying is easier than voting" was said with "a smile and a wink." This detail adds some humor to the piece, making it both informative and fun to read.)*

CRITICAL VOCABULARY

inundate: The author is describing how Harriet Quimby was often surrounded by male reporters who found her both attractive and entertaining.

ASK STUDENTS how a woman aviator might feel to be inundated with questions by a large group of reporters. *(She might feel crowded or overwhelmed, and several people might be asking her questions at the same time.)*

Though she did not fly, Katherine Wright was a major supporter of her brothers' efforts. Orville so appreciated his sister's help that he said, "When the world speaks of the Wrights, it must include my sister. . . . She inspired much of 20 our effort."

Although Raymonde de la Roche of France was the first woman in the world to earn her pilot's license, Harriet Quimby held the distinction of being the first American woman to become a licensed pilot.

On August 1, 1911, Quimby, who was described as a "real beauty" with "haunting blue-green eyes," strolled off the field after passing her pilot's test easily. To the male reporters who **inundated** her with questions, Quimby fired back answers with self-confidence. Walking past a group of women who had 30 come to witness the historic event, Quimby was overheard to quip with a smile and a wink: "Flying is easier than voting." (The Woman's Suffrage Amendment wasn't passed until 1920.)

As difficult as it was for women to become pilots in significant numbers, it was doubly hard for African-Americans, especially black women. That's why Bessie Coleman, the first African-American to earn her pilot's license, is such an exciting and important figure in aviation.

Bessie Coleman was born in 1893 in Atlanta, Texas, 40 the twelfth of thirteen children. Her mother, who had been a slave, valued education and encouraged all of her children to attend school in order to better themselves. The encouragement paid off, because Coleman graduated from high school, a feat not too many black women were able to accomplish in the early 1900s.

Bessie Coleman refused to accept the limitations others tried to place on her. She attended an Oklahoma college for one semester but ran out of money. Accepting the offer of one of her brothers to come live with him and his family 50 in Chicago, Coleman found a job as a manicurist. She fully intended to return to school after saving enough money. But she never did. While in Chicago she learned about flying and made a new set of goals for herself. She wanted to be a pilot.

Coleman learned about flying from reading newspaper accounts of air battles during World War I. She tried to find a school that would accept her as a trainee. But no American instructor or flying school was willing to teach her.

inundate
(ĭn´ŭn-dāt´) *v.* To *inundate* is to give a huge amount of something.

WHEN STUDENTS STRUGGLE . . .

Some students may have difficulty determining authors' purposes beyond the general purpose of informing the reader. Explain that choices authors make can reveal evidence of other purposes as well. As students read, have pairs identify and record the authors' choices on a chart. Have them ask questions about each choice: *What effect does this detail create? Does it make the text fun to read? Does it help explain something?*

LEVEL UP TUTORIALS For additional support, assign the following *Level Up* tutorial: **Author's Purpose.**

THE AUTHORS' CHOICES	WHAT CHOICES REVEAL ABOUT AUTHORS' PURPOSE
The authors show male reporters crowded around Harriet Quimby as she jokes with them.	*The authors want to entertain with an interesting detail.*
	They also want to explain how Quimby dealt with sexist attitudes toward women.

When the war ended, a friend, Robert S. Abbott, the founder of the *Chicago Defender*, one of the most popular black-owned and -operated newspapers in the country, suggested that Coleman go to France, where racial prejudice was not as **restrictive** as it was in America. Even though the United States was the birthplace of flight, it was slower than other countries to develop an organized aviation program. European leaders immediately saw the commercial and military advantages of a strong national aviation program. Bessie knew from her reading that both French and German aircraft were among the best in the world.

60

restrictive
(rĭ-strĭk′tĭv) *adj.*
When something is *restrictive*, it is limiting in some way.

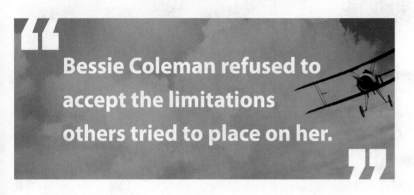

> Bessie Coleman refused to accept the limitations others tried to place on her.

Coleman had also read about Eugene Jacques Bullard, the well-decorated[1] and highly honored native of Georgia who had become the first African-American to fly an airplane in combat as a member of the French Lafayette Flying Corps during World War I. Other blacks had gone to Europe to get their training, too. Coleman realized that if she were ever going to get a chance to fly, she, too, would have to go to France. But she didn't have any money to get there, and besides, she couldn't speak a word of French.

70

D

For almost two years, Coleman worked part-time as a manicurist and as a server in a Chicago chili parlor and saved every penny to finance her trip to France. Meanwhile she learned to speak French, so when the time came, she'd be able to understand her instructors.

80

---

[1] **well-decorated:** term used to describe a person in the military who has received many awards.

CLOSE READ

Analyze the Meanings of Words and Phrases

RI 1,
RI 4

(LINES 74–77)

Tell students that an author's choice of words can affect the meaning and tone of a passage. Explain that **tone** is the author's attitude toward a topic, or the way the author sounds, such as angry, outraged, or amused.

D **CITE TEXT EVIDENCE** Have students reread lines 74–77 and identify words that suggest a more conversational, informal tone. Ask what this might reveal about the authors' attitude toward Bessie Coleman. (*The words "and besides, she couldn't speak a word of French" have a more conversational tone. This suggests a familiarity and understanding of Coleman by the authors, almost as if they were talking about someone they actually know and admire.*)

English Language Support

Contrast a conversational tone and a formal tone. Tell students that **tone** describes how an author expresses ideas and should suit the audience.

- A conversational tone can include contractions, slang, abbreviations, and simple sentences. It might be used in an entertaining story or letter.
- A formal tone may use complex sentences, without contractions or slang. It is used for academic work, such as an essay for school.

Write these expressions on the board: *Miss Coleman, Bessie, let's go flying, the instrument panel is crucial to an airplane.* Guide students to identify each expression as either formal or conversational.

CRITICAL VOCABULARY

restrictive: The authors are explaining how prejudices that held back African Americans in the United States were not as common in France.

ASK STUDENTS to describe how a restrictive policy in the United States affected Bessie Coleman. (*The unwillingness of American instructors and flying schools to teach African American women was restrictive to Coleman because it prevented her from pursuing her dream of becoming a pilot.*)

FOR STANDARD ENGLISH LEARNERS

Explain that writers often use contractions to create an informal, conversational tone. Remind students that a contraction is an abbreviated form of a word or words. Review the rules of contractions. Provide the following examples of common contractions, modeling their pronunciation for students: *it's, don't, he's he'd, I've.* Ask students to find the sentences on page 45 that contain contractions (lines 76, 77, and 81). Have students write sentences using the contractions they found and then share and check their sentences with a partner.

CLOSE READ

Cite Evidence and Draw Conclusions

RI 1

(LINES 86–88)

Point out to students that while the overall topic of this informational text is women in aviation, the authors chose to focus on just two women aviators—Harriet Quimby and Bessie Coleman.

E **ASK STUDENTS** to reread lines 86–88 and to think about the information they read earlier about Harriet Quimby. Ask them what conclusion they can draw about the significance of these two aviators. *(Both aviators were "firsts" to become aviators: Quimby was the first woman, and Coleman was the first African American woman. The conclusion can be made that the experiences of people who are "first" at something reveal the struggle and determination that it takes to succeed.)*

English Language Support

Have pairs review and discuss lines 21–24 about Harriet Quimby and lines 86–88 about Bessie Coleman. Ask students to use these sentence frames to draw a conclusion about the two aviators.

Harriet Quimby was the first _____.
Bessie Coleman was the first _____.
The authors focused on these two women because _____.

Aviator Bessie Coleman posed for this photograph in 1920.

In 1921, Coleman made it to France, where she found an instructor who was one of Tony Fokker's chief pilots. Fokker, the famous aircraft manufacturer, said Coleman was a "natural talent." On June 15, 1921, Coleman made history by becoming the first black woman to earn her wings, thus joining the ranks of the handful of American women fliers.

90 Returning to the United States determined to start a flying school where other African-American pilots could be trained, Coleman looked for ways to finance her dream. There were very few jobs in the aviation industry for women or blacks. She soon learned that there was little or no support for a black woman who wanted to start a flying school. To call attention to aviation and to encourage other women and African-Americans to take part in the new and growing field,

©Michael Ochs Archives/Getty Images

46 Collection 1

Strategies for Annotation   ✎ 🗐 *Annotate it!*

Cite Text Evidence and Draw Conclusions

RI 1

Have students locate the first paragraph on page 46. Encourage them to use their eBook annotation tools to do the following:

- Highlight in yellow the text that describes Coleman's achievements.
- Underline text that indicates why the achievements were important.
- Review your annotations and explain how this text helps you draw a conclusion. *(A person who is a first in a field is important because that person overcame obstacles that no one else had.)*

an instructor who was one of Tony Fokker's chief pilots. Fokker, the famous aircraft manufacturer, said Coleman was a "natural talent." On June 15, 1921, Coleman made history by becoming the <u>first black woman</u> to earn her wings, thus joining the ranks of the handful of American women fliers.

F Coleman gave flying **exhibitions** and lectured on aviation. She thrilled audiences with daredevil maneuvers, just as Quimby had done before her.

100   Along with racism, Coleman encountered the burden of sexism, but she made believers out of those who doubted her skill. "The color of my skin," she said, "[was] a drawback at first. . . . I was a curiosity, but soon the public discovered I could really fly. Then they came to see *Brave Bessie*, as they called me."

    The strict rules and regulations that govern aviation today didn't exist during the first three decades of flying. For example, it wasn't uncommon for aviators to ignore safety belts and fly without parachutes. One of these simple 110 safety **precautions** might have saved the lives of both Harriet Quimby and Bessie Coleman.

    On a July morning in 1912, Quimby, and a passenger named William P. Willard, set out to break an over-water speed record. When Quimby climbed to five thousand feet, the French-made Blériot monoplane[2] suddenly nosed down. Both Quimby and Willard were thrown from the plane and plunged to their deaths in the Boston Harbor.

    The *New York Sun* used the opportunity to speak out against women fliers:

120   Miss Quimby is the fifth woman in the world killed while operating an aeroplane (three were students) and their number thus far is five too many. The sport is not one for which women are physically qualified. As a rule they lack strength and presence of mind and the courage to excel as aviators. It is essentially a man's sport and pastime.

    Fourteen years later, Bessie Coleman died in a similar accident. With almost enough savings to start her school, Coleman agreed to do an air show in Florida on May Day 130 for the Negro Welfare League of Jacksonville. At 7:30 P.M. the night before, Coleman, accompanied by her publicity agent, William Wills, took her plane up for a test flight. When she reached an altitude of about five thousand feet, her plane flipped over. Coleman was thrown from the plane and

---

[2] **monoplane:** an airplane with only one pair of wings.

exhibition
(ĕk´sə-bĭsh´ən) *n.*
An *exhibition* is an organized presentation or show.

precaution
(prĭ-kô´shən) *n.*
A *precaution* is an action taken to avoid possible danger.

APPLYING ACADEMIC VOCABULARY

aspect	cultural	evaluate

THINK-PAIR-SHARE Have partners discuss the questions below. Guide students to include the academic vocabulary words *aspect*, *cultural*, and *evaluate* in their responses. Encourage volunteers to share their responses with the class.

- What **aspects** of life in America created **cultural** obstacles for women who wanted to become pilots?
- What are some factors to consider as you **evaluate** the achievements of the first women aviators?

TEACH

CLOSE READ

Determine Author's Purpose (LINES 97–99)
RI 1, RI 6

Point out that an author's choice of words often helps reveal a purpose for writing a certain section of text.

F **CITE TEXT EVIDENCE** Have students reread lines 97–99 and ask them to identify words that reveal the authors' purpose in this section. What do these word choices reveal about the authors' purpose? *(The words "thrilled audiences" and "daredevil maneuvers" suggest excitement and courageousness. The authors want to show how fearless and entertaining Coleman and Quimby were as aviators. These choices by the authors are both informative and entertaining. They also help create a more vivid description for the reader.)*

English Language Support

Explain that the words authors use can reveal their purpose, or reason for writing. Reread lines 97–99 aloud, and point out the words "thrilled audiences" and "daredevil maneuvers." Ask volunteers to define confusing words for the group with a dictionary. Then discuss what the words show about Coleman and Quimby. *(They weren't afraid and they did exciting things.)* Ask students why the authors chose these words. *(To express their strongly positive view of Coleman and Quimby.)*

CRITICAL VOCABULARY

exhibition: The authors are explaining how Bessie Coleman became well known by performing as an aviator and public speaker.

ASK STUDENTS to describe what they might have seen at one of Bessie Coleman's exhibitions. *(Sample answer: I might see Coleman flying upside down in her airplane above a large crowd on the ground.)*

precaution: Early aviation was a particularly dangerous endeavor as pilots flew in relatively unstable aircraft, sitting in open-air cockpits.

ASK STUDENTS to describe why a safety belt would be a good precaution for an aviator in an open-air cockpit. *(Sample answer: It would hold them securely to their seats so that they couldn't fall out of the aircraft.)*

CLOSE READ

Determine Author's Purpose (LINES 137–145)

Explain that Amelia Earhart was famous for being the first woman, and second person, to make a solo airplane flight across the Atlantic Ocean. This 1932 flight from Canada to France made Earhart one of the most famous people in the world. Earhart's interest in flying was sparked at age ten, when she saw an aviation exhibition much like the ones in which Bessie Coleman and Harriet Quimby performed.

G **ASK STUDENTS** to reread lines 137–145 and explain why the authors chose to quote Amelia Earhart at the end of the selection. *(The authors quoted Amelia Earhart because she was one of the most famous women aviators from the early 1900s and was a pioneer of aviation; Earhart's quotation underscores the authors' point that all women aviators had to overcome cultural obstacles to pursue their dreams.)*

COLLABORATIVE DISCUSSION Have groups of students discuss the obstacles that early female pilots overcame, using examples from the text. Further, have students consider how the history of aviation might have been different had more diverse groups been welcomed into the community of early explorers. Encourage them to jot down notes as they talk. Then have them share their ideas with the class and evaluate how effectively the women featured in the text achieved their goals.

ASK STUDENTS to share any questions they generated in the course of reading and discussing the selection.

English Language Support

Support Opinions Before students begin their discussion, provide the following sentence stems:

For clarification: Do you mean that _____?

To affirm or agree: That's a good point because _____.

To build or add on: Another thing I noticed was that _____.

To disagree respectfully: I understand, but _____.

---

plunged to her death April 30, 1926. Wills died seconds later when the plane crashed.

G Once again critics used the tragedy to assert that neither women nor blacks were mentally or physically able to be good pilots. "Women are often penalized by publicity for their every 140 mishap," said Amelia Earhart, the most famous female pilot in aviation history. "The result is that such emphasis sometimes directly affects [a woman's] chances for a flying job," Earhart continued. "I had one manufacturer tell me that he couldn't risk hiring women pilots because of the way accidents, even minor ones, became headlines in the newspapers."

Although Bessie Coleman died tragically, her plans to open a flight training school for blacks were continued by those she had inspired.

COLLABORATIVE DISCUSSION What obstacles did Quimby, Coleman, and other early female pilots face that their male counterparts did not face? In a group, share ideas about what motivated these women to achieve in spite of difficulties.

FOR STUDENTS WITH DISABILITIES

Students may struggle to scan the text for examples of obstacles that early female pilots overcame, preventing them from participating fully in collaborative activities. Prior to the Collaborative Discussion, have students work in pairs to review each page of the text. Have them take turns jotting down notes about the obstacles that female pilots overcame to use in the larger group discussion. Remind them to record the note, the page number, and the line number to help them find these pieces of evidence quickly during the discussion with the larger group.

Determine Author's Purpose

RI 6

An **author's purpose** is the reason the author wrote a particular work. Usually an author writes for one or more purposes, as shown in this chart:

Author's Purpose	Examples of Written Works
To inform or explain	encyclopedia entries, informational articles, how-to articles, biographies, and other factual, real-world examples
To persuade	editorials, opinion essays and blogs, advertisements, and other works in which the author shares an opinion and tries to persuade readers to agree
To entertain	stories, novels, plays, essays, and literary works that engage the reader with qualities such as humor, suspense, and intriguing details
To express thoughts or feelings	poems, personal essays, journals and other texts in which the author shares insights, emotions, and descriptions

To determine an author's purpose in informational texts, examine the facts and quotations. An author may have a main purpose for writing, as well as other purposes. For example, "Women in Aviation" provides facts, so it is written mainly to inform. But the authors have other purposes, too, revealed by their word choices and their examples.

Cite Evidence and Draw Conclusions

RI 1

When you **draw conclusions,** you make judgments or take a position on a topic. To support conclusions, readers cite **textual evidence**—information from the text in the form of facts and details. To draw conclusions in an informational text, follow these steps:

- Look for statements in the text that support your conclusion.
- Consider your own experience and knowledge about the topic.
- Make a judgment based on evidence and your own knowledge.

Informational texts contain details readers can use as textual evidence. For example, here's a quote from "Women in Aviation" that describes Katherine Wright, the sister of famous aviators Orville and Wilbur Wright:

> **"When the world speaks of the Wrights, it must include my sister. . . . She inspired much of our effort."**

Katherine Wright wasn't a pilot. However, based on this text, what conclusion can you draw about her contribution to the Wright brothers' achievements?

CLOSE READ

Determine Author's Purpose

RI 6

Discuss the definition of author's purpose with students, asking volunteers for reasons that writers might have for writing different types of text. Review the different author's purposes listed in the chart, and ask volunteers to name titles of the various genres listed for each author's purpose.

Help students determine an author's purpose in an informational text. Explain that

- an author usually has one main purpose for the piece as a whole, and other secondary purposes
- details, such as facts, quotations, opinions, and word choices, can reveal an author's purpose
- as students read, they should track these details to figure out an author's purpose

Cite Evidence and Draw Conclusions

RI 1

Explain that drawing conclusions is a way to add up information to make judgments or to decide how one feels about a text. To do this, readers should cite textual evidence to support their conclusions. Have students draw a conclusion about Katherine Wright's contributions to her brothers' achievements. *(Sample answer: She inspired her brothers' accomplishments.)*

Strategies for Annotation   *Annotate it!*

Determine Author's Purpose

RI 1, RI 6

Share these strategies for guided or independent analysis (lines 34–48):

- Highlight in yellow details that suggest that the authors' purpose is to inform.
- Underline details that suggest the authors' purpose is to persuade.
- Draw a conclusion about the text supported by the evidence. *(Sample answer: Because she was the first African American woman aviator, Bessie Coleman is a good example of a pioneering female aviator.)*

As difficult as it was for women to become pilots in significant numbers, it was doubly hard for African-Americans, especially black women. That's why Bessie Coleman, the first African-American to earn her pilot's license, is such an exciting and important figure in aviation.

PRACTICE & APPLY

Analyzing the Text

RI 1,
RI 3,
RI 6

Possible answers:

1. *Their purpose is to inform readers that American aviation had a history of unfairness to women and minorities. The phrase "marred with sexist and racist assumptions" supports this.*

2. *Harriet Quimby was an attractive, self-confident woman with a sense of humor. Evidence of this is the description of her appearance, her interaction with the reporters, and her comment to the other women.*

3. ***Textual Evidence:*** *Coleman worked for two years to finance her trip and also learned French.* ***Experience:*** *Reaching a goal requires making a plan and sticking to it.* ***Conclusion:*** *Coleman showed patience and determination in overcoming obstacles to reach her goal.*

4. *Both were pioneers in aviation. Both had the self-confidence to overcome male prejudice. Both were probably courageous risk takers who enjoyed the thrill of flight.*

5. *By including facts and details about prejudice and sexist attitudes of the time, the authors were primarily informing about the size of the challenges faced by early women and African American aviators. In addition, the authors were entertaining through the use of colorful details about the female pilots' experiences.*

6. *The authors want readers to see early female pilots, especially African American female pilots, as heroic. The authors provide convincing support, such as quotations from the women and from news reports. The authors also select interesting details, such as Quimby's self-confident manner and Coleman's learning French.*

FOR STANDARD ENGLISH LEARNERS

Prepositions Some students may have trouble choosing accurate prepositions as they write. In the sentence "The pilots took part in the race," they may, for example, use the preposition *of* instead of *in*. Write these prepositions on the board: *at, on, to, from, in, of, off, for, out of,* and *so.* As a group, write sentences about the selection using these prepositions. Read each sentence aloud to reinforce the correct preposition. Then challenge students to use at least five prepositions in questions they write about woman aviators in their Performance Task groups.

Analyzing the Text

RI 1, RI 3, RI 6,
W 2, W 6, W 10

Cite Text Evidence Support your responses with evidence from the text.

1. **Cite Evidence** Based on the first sentence in "Women in Aviation," what do you think the authors' purpose might be? Which words or phrases indicate this purpose?

2. **Interpret** Reread lines 26–33. What impression do the authors create of Harriet Quimby by using facts and quotations?

3. **Draw Conclusions** Reread lines 69–82. What conclusion can you draw about Bessie Coleman's personality, based on the information in these paragraphs? Fill out a chart to show how you came to your conclusion. Use chart headings like these:

Textual Evidence	My Experience	Conclusion

4. **Compare** In what ways were Harriet Quimby and Bessie Coleman probably most alike? Explain.

5. **Analyze** You've learned that authors may have more than one purpose in mind for a text. For "Woman in Aviation," it's clear that the authors' main purpose is to inform. What secondary purpose do you think is evident in the text?

6. **Evaluate** What do you think is the most important idea the authors want to convey about the efforts of women aviators in the early 20th century? Support your view with evidence from "Women in Aviation."

PERFORMANCE TASK

Writing Activity: Informative Report Do further research on one of the figures from "Women in Aviation." Then present your research in the form of a report.

- Use text, online, and digital resources such as encyclopedias, web searches, and other texts to find facts and details.

- Include details about the pilot's achievements and their importance.

- Be sure to include additional quotes either directly from or about the aviator you chose.

Assign this performance task.

PERFORMANCE TASK

W 2, W 6, W 8, W 10

Writing Activity: Informative Report Have students work in small groups to choose and research a woman aviator from the early 20th century.

- Direct them to reread the selection to generate questions they would want to answer.

- See page R8 for further instruction on evaluating credible online sources.

Critical Vocabulary

L 4a, L 5c

inundate	restrictive	exhibition	precaution

Practice and Apply Which of the two situations best matches the meaning of the vocabulary word? Explain your choice.

1. inundate
   a. More than 400 customers call the hot line one morning.
   b. One or two visitors come to a museum.

2. restrictive
   a. The gate to the park is locked at six o'clock.
   b. The gate to the park has a rusty lock.

3. exhibition
   a. A crowd gathered at a store advertising a one-day sale.
   b. The crowd watched a holiday cooking demonstration.

4. precaution
   a. The state lets voters send in their ballots before Election Day.
   b. The state requires motorcyclists to wear safety helmets.

Vocabulary Strategy: Connotations and Denotations

A word's **denotation** is its literal dictionary meaning. A word's **connotation** comes from the ideas and feelings associated with the word. The authors of "Women in Aviation" chose words based on connotation and denotation.

> On August 1, 1911, Quimby, who was described as a "real beauty" with "haunting blue-green eyes," strolled off the field after passing her pilot's test easily.

Notice how the specific word choice of *strolled* suggests an easy, confident way of walking. This paints a picture of an accomplished young pilot. Words can have a positive or a negative connotation. The context of a phrase, sentence, or paragraph can help you determine the connotation of a word.

Practice and Apply For each item that follows, choose the word you think better expresses the meaning of the sentence. Use a print or online dictionary to help you with unfamiliar words. Then write the reason for your choice.

1. Bessie Coleman refused to give up. She was (**stubborn, determined**).

2. Early pilots performed stunts. The pilots were (**daring, reckless**).

3. Women had barriers. Yet female pilots (**followed, pursued**) their dreams.

4. Coleman died as a pioneer. Her efforts (**inspired, helped**) future generations.

Critical Vocabulary

L 4a, L 5c

Answers: **1.** *a,* **2.** *a,* **3.** *b,* **4.** *b*

Vocabulary Strategy: Connotations and Denotations

Sample answers: 1. determined; Determined *has a positive connotation of working toward a goal, while* stubborn *has a slightly more negative connotation.* **2.** daring; Daring *connotes courage and bravery, while* reckless *suggests the person is foolhardy and lives carelessly.* **3.** pursued; Pursued *has a slightly stronger connotation of striving for a goal than* followed. **4.** inspired; Inspired *connotes that Coleman did more than just help. She actually motivated others.*

Strategies for Annotation   Annotate it!

Connotations and Denotations

L 4a, L 5c

Have students locate the sentence that contains *thrilled, daredevil,* and *maneuvers* in lines 97–99 of the selection. Encourage them to use their eBook annotation tools to do the following:

- Highlight each word.
- Use the context or a print or digital dictionary to determine each word's meaning.
- Make an annotation explaining why each word choice is better than other synonyms such as *entertained, exciting,* and *stunts.*

Coleman gave flying exhibitions and lectured on aviation. She thrilled audiences with daredevil maneuvers, just as Quimby had done before her.

> *Maneuvers* is a better word choice than *stunts* because it suggests that Bessie was very skillful and talented.

Language Conventions: Subordinate Clauses

L 1a

Tell students that the examples show two types of clauses: independent clauses and subordinate clauses. Point out that the word *independent* means that something can be on its own and does not need anything to help make it complete. *Subordinate* means that something is subject to the control of something else. Tell students they can think of a subordinate clause as needing the help of another clause to make it a complete thought. Point to the list of subordinate clauses and ask volunteers to use each one in a sentence with an independent clause. Discuss why the first half of the sample sentence is a subordinate clause and the second half, after the comma, is an independent clause.

Sample answers:

1. *Because flying was a new and exciting sport, crowds gathered to watch air shows.*

2. *Accidents were common until aviation was regulated.*

3. *Military pilots returned to jobs flying planes when World War I ended.*

4. *Although Bessie Coleman died tragically, her life inspired other African Americans to become pilots.*

 Assess It Online!

Online Selection Test
- Download an editable ExamView bank.
- Assign and manage this test online.

Language Conventions: Subordinate Clauses

L 1a

Think of clauses as building blocks for sentences. A sentence is an **independent clause** because it can stand alone and express a complete thought. A **subordinate clause** cannot stand alone in a sentence because it is subordinate to, or dependent on, a main clause. Subordinate clauses are also called **dependent clauses.**

Subordinate Clause	Independent Clause
Because it's stormy,	the flight is delayed.
When the skies are clear,	we'll take off.

You can recognize a subordinate clause because it begins with a **subordinating conjunction.** Common subordinating conjunctions are *after, although, as, because, before, even though, if, since, so that, though, unless, until, when, where,* and *while.*

The subordinating conjunction *even though* introduces the subordinating clause in this sentence from "Women in Aviation":

> **Even though the United States was the birthplace of flight, it was slower than other countries to develop an organized aviation program.**

When you write, be careful not to confuse a subordinate clause with a complete sentence; a subordinate clause cannot stand alone. A subordinate clause can appear anywhere in a sentence. If you position it before the independent clause, set it off with a comma.

Practice and Apply Write a complete sentence, using each of these subordinate clauses. You can review the text of "Women in Aviation" for details to include.

1. because flying was a new and exciting sport

2. until aviation was regulated

3. when World War I ended

4. although Bessie Coleman died tragically

English Language Support

Combine Clauses Clarify the definitions of subordinate and independent clauses. Explain that a subordinate clause can appear anywhere in a sentence. Remind students that a subordinate clause that begins a sentence should be set off with a comma.

- Read the subordinate clauses in Practice and Apply to students. Then list independent clauses that students could use to write complete sentences. Let pairs work together to combine independent clauses with the subordinate clauses to write complete sentences.

- As a class, create an independent clause to combine with each subordinate clause. Then have pairs decide where to place the subordinate clause and complete each sentence.

- Write a list of subordinate clauses on the board. Have students combine each one with an independent clause to form a sentence. Ask volunteers to read their sentences to the class.

Determine Facts and Opinions

TEACH

Most informational writing contains both facts and opinions. Explain to students that a **fact** is a statement that can be proved, or verified, while an **opinion** is a statement that expresses a writer's belief, feelings, or thoughts, and cannot be proved.

- Use the following example from the text (lines 108–111) to review how to distinguish fact from opinion: *For example, it wasn't uncommon for aviators to ignore safety belts and fly without parachutes. One of these simple safety precautions might have saved the lives of both Harriet Quimby and Bessie Coleman.*

- Explain that the first sentence is a fact, which can be proved by consulting sources about the use of safety equipment in the early days of airplane aviation.

- The second sentence is more of an opinion because it expresses the authors' belief that this equipment "might" have saved the two pilots' lives.

- Point out, however, that it is likely that the authors could have **substantiated** this opinion, or established it by evidence, by providing verifiable facts about the effectiveness of safety belts and parachutes.

PRACTICE AND APPLY

Display lines 34–38 of the selection. Have volunteers identify examples of facts and opinions in the passage. *(Facts: It was difficult for women to become pilots and especially difficult for African Americans to do so. Bessie Coleman was the first African American woman to earn her pilot's license. Opinion: Bessie Coleman is an exciting and important figure in aviation.)* Have students explain why these details are either facts or opinions. You might point out that the opinion in the passage is eventually substantiated by additional evidence in the rest of the selection.

English Language Support

Determine Facts and Opinions Follow these steps:

1. Read aloud lines 34–38 on page 44.
2. Stop after each clause and tell students to consider whether the statement can be proved.
3. If students say the statement can be proved, ask what sources could be consulted to verify it.
4. Together, list the facts and opinions that students identify in the passage.

Determine Author's Purpose

Review that writers always have a reason for writing a piece—the author's purpose.

- Review the four main reasons for writing: to inform or to explain; to persuade; to entertain; to express thoughts or feelings.

- Explain that clues in the text help reveal the author's purpose. For example, a text with many facts and statistics is evidence that the author's purpose is to inform. A text with jokes is likely intended to entertain.

- Select a variety of texts, such as a humorous personal narrative, how-to books or websites, news stories, textbook chapters, and editorial opinion pieces.

- Read sample passages from each text with students and ask volunteers to identify the author's purpose and cite evidence from the text that reveals this purpose.

 LEVEL UP TUTORIALS Assign the following *Level Up* tutorial: **Author's Purpose**

INDEPENDENT READING

Students can apply the skill to another piece of writing of their own choosing. Have them work independently to determine the author's purpose, citing evidence from the text.

BOLD ACTIONS

The *FYI* site provides links to online articles from a variety of magazines and newspapers. Help students choose a few articles to read to further their exploration of the topic Bold Actions.

NOVELWISE

Students can unlock the power of novels with this unique resource. Help students read through longer works with these tips:

- Find a Book
- Before You Read
- As You Read
- After You Read

Each book includes introductory material, worksheets, graphic organizers, and discussion guides.

ADDITIONAL TEXTS BY COLLECTION

Suggest students read the following:

- "The Charge of the Light Brigade" by Alfred, Lord Tennyson
- "Icarus and Daedalus" as retold by Josephine Preston Peabody

Have students read the poem and the myth and then ask them to identify the respective themes. *(Bravery in battle, Bravery versus impetuousness)* What similarities and differences do students see in the development of the themes?

NONFICTION CONNECTIONS

Suggest that students increase their reading of informational texts. The nonfiction connections include

- speeches
- diaries
- true-life accounts
- newspaper articles
- political cartoons

Creating an Independent Reading Program

BUILD A CLASSROOM LIBRARY

A classroom library full of books and other media offers students a rich and accessible reading environment.

- Designate a bookcase as the classroom library. Organize books into categories such as fiction, biography, and informational text.
- Ask your school or local librarian to recommend other trade books you could include in your classroom library.
- Create a checkout system. You may want to put an index card in a pocket at the back of each book or use a cell phone to take a photo of each student with the book he or she wants to check out. (Delete the photo when the student returns the book.)
- Designate a box or crate where students place returned books.
- Assign volunteers to take turns with library upkeep.

CREATE LIBRARY RULES

Work with students to create a list of library rules, such as these:

- Check out one book at a time.
- Return a book before you check a new one out.
- Sign the checkout card and place it in the Checkout Box.
- Use a shared digital spreadsheet to create an online catalog and to track books.

Write a Fictional Narrative

W 3a–e Write narratives.
W 4 Produce clear and coherent writing.
W 5 Develop and strengthen writing.
W 10 Write routinely.

Use the texts in the collection as models for writing your own story in which the characters take bold actions in the face of a seemingly overwhelming challenge.

A successful fictional narrative

- introduces and develops characters and a setting
- contains a plot with a well-structured and logical sequence
- establishes, develops, and resolves a conflict
- uses dialogue, pacing, and relevant descriptive details
- utilizes transitions to convey sequence
- provides a conclusion that reflects a message about life

Mentor Text See how this example from "Rogue Wave" uses descriptive details to introduce a character and the setting.

> " Sullivan Atkins, Scoot's oldest brother, was steering the cutter-rigged boat on a northerly course about fifteen miles off desolate Cabo Colnett, south of Ensenada. Under a brilliant sun, the glittering blue Pacific rose and fell in long, slick swells. . . . "

myNotebook

Use the annotation tools in your eBook to mark up key details that you might want to include. Save each detail to your notebook.

PLAN

Establish Story Elements A fictional narrative describes experiences and events that you imagine.

- Brainstorm ideas for your characters. How do the characters act, speak, and relate to each other?
- Determine the setting—the time and place the narrative occurs. How will the setting cause your character to confront his or her fear?
- Establish the conflict. How does this challenge give your main character the opportunity to take bold actions?

ACADEMIC VOCABULARY

As you plan, write, and review your draft, try to use the academic vocabulary words.

aspect
cultural
evaluate
resource
text

Collection Performance Task A **53**

WRITE A FICTIONAL NARRATIVE

W 3a–e, W 4, W 5, W 10, L 3a

Introduce students to the Performance Task by reading the introductory paragraph with them and reviewing the criteria for what makes a good fictional narrative. Remind students that a narrative becomes more interesting when the characters seem real and when their problems are ones with which readers can identify.

PLAN

ESTABLISH STORY ELEMENTS

View It!

Professional Development Podcast:

Performance Tasks

Share with students that good narratives focus on characters who face a conflict. When choosing the plot for their narratives, students can think about external and internal challenges. Point out that challenges can range from physical ones, such as struggling to survive in a disaster, to more thoughtful ones, such as overcoming a fear about speaking in front of an audience.

English Language Support

Plan a Fictional Narrative Make sure students understand that they will write imaginative text about characters who take bold actions. Have pairs use the following questions to discuss the descriptive details in the Mentor Text and in their own plans for a fictional narrative:

- What details give information about the character?
- What details tell about the setting?

- What details about setting might challenge the character?
- What bold actions will your character take?
- What challenges will your character face?
- What details will describe your character?
- What details will describe your setting?

PERFORMANCE TASK A

English Language Support

Explain that the plot diagram shows the events of a narrative in time order from left to right. Review the definitions of *exposition, rising action, climax, falling action,* and *resolution.*

- To make sure students understand the sequence, have them annotate the chart with Beginning, Middle, and End.
- Have student pairs discuss how the events in their narratives correspond to the plot diagram, making sure to use transitional expressions to link the events.

PRODUCE

WRITE YOUR NARRATIVE

Remind students that before writing they should decide upon the kind of narrator they want to use in their narratives. Students can ask themselves questions such as the following:

View It!

Professional Development Podcast:

Writing Narratives at the Secondary Level

- Should the narrative be told by one of the characters? First-person narrators give a very personal feel to a narrative but tell it from only one person's point of view.
- Or should the narrative be told by someone who is not a character? Third-person narrators have the advantage of being able to tell about all of the characters' thoughts and feelings.

FOR STANDARD ENGLISH LEARNERS

Add Dialogue Remind students of the differences between formal and informal language. Explain that their characters, just like people in real life, may speak informally. Ask students to identify each of the following examples as either formal or informal:

- "I apologize, sir. There are no more seats available." *(formal)*
- "Calm down, man. It's no big deal." *(informal)*

List Plot Events Fill out a plot diagram to plan your story.

- Use the exposition to introduce the characters, setting, and conflict.
- Introduce obstacles for the characters in the rising action.
- At the climax, tell the most important or exciting event. This is where your character is about to overcome the challenge.
- End with the falling action and resolution to show how the conflict is resolved.
- As you plan, keep pacing in mind. In a well-paced story, the action transitions smoothly from one event to the next.

Interactive Lessons
To help you plot out your narrative, use:
• Writing Narratives: Narrative Structure

Consider Your Purpose and Audience Who will read or listen to your story? What effect do you want the story to have on readers? Do you want simply to entertain them?

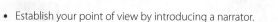

Write Your Narrative Review your plot diagram as you begin your draft.

*my*WriteSmart
Write your rough draft in *my*WriteSmart. Focus on getting your ideas down, rather than perfecting your choice of language.

- Establish your point of view by introducing a narrator.
- Create the sequence of events, building suspense with transition words and phrases that clearly show the order of events and signal any shifts in setting.
- Leave the audience with a message to reflect on.

Language Conventions: Active and Passive Voice

A verb in the **active voice** describes an action performed by the subject. A verb in the **passive voice** describes an action received by its subject, using a form of the verb *be.*

Passive Voice "Scoot *was hurled* upward, legs and arms flying. . . ."

Active Voice "Scoot *dove* twice for the boxy flashlight. . . ."

Notice how the passive voice verb "was hurled" emphasizes that Scoot was not in control of her body, while the active voice verb "dove" emphasizes that Scoot is working to escape. Consider how you can use verbs to achieve a particular effect.

English Language Support

Text Structure Display the Student Model from *Interactive Lessons: Writing Narratives.* Read it aloud, drawing attention to the verbs. Most are in the past tense, but present-tense verbs appear in dialogue. Explain that verb tenses in a narrative show when an action happens.

- Past: *He squinted*
- Present progressive: *pointing at the swings*
- Present: *Nobody comes near*
- Past perfect: *He'd studied*

REVISE

Review Your Draft Have your partner or group of peers review your draft. Use the following chart to revise your draft.

my WriteSmart

Have your partner or a group of peers review your draft in *my*WriteSmart. Ask your reviewers to note any scenes that do not help build suspense.

Questions	Tips	Revision Techniques
Does the narrative have a well-developed plot?	**Underline** each element: conflict, rising action, climax, and resolution.	**Add** or **elaborate** on plot elements. **Delete** events that do not help move the story to its climax.
Are the characters well developed and convincing? Does the story establish a specific setting?	**Underline** the descriptive details and dialogue that reveal character. **Highlight** details that describe the setting.	**Add** descriptive details, dialogue, and actions that develop characters. **Elaborate** on the setting by adding details.
Are events arranged in a logical sequence? Are transitions used to show order?	**Highlight** the main events. **Underline** transitional words and phrases.	**Rearrange** events that are out of order. **Add** a variety of transitions to show the order of events.
Is the point of view established and maintained throughout the narrative?	**Underline** pronouns that show whether the point of view is first or third person.	**Change** pronouns or details that shift point of view.
Does the story reveal a theme or message?	**Underline** clues that suggest an important idea about life or human nature.	**Add** details or sentences that clarify and reflect on the theme.

Interactive Lessons
To help you revise your draft, use:
· Writing Narratives: Narrative Techniques

PRESENT

Create a Finished Copy Finalize your story and choose a way to share it with your audience. You might submit your story to the school literary magazine or other online or print literary magazines.

PERFORMANCE TASK A

PRODUCE

LANGUAGE CONVENTIONS

Explain that in narrative writing, the active and passive voices can stress who is doing something or whether a character controls an action. If the writer wants to emphasize what a character does, the active voice works best. If the writer wants to emphasize something acting *on* the character, the passive voice is used. Have students find places in their narratives where the voice can complement meaning.

REVISE

REVIEW YOUR DRAFT

As students use the chart to evaluate their fictional narratives, remind them to think about these goals: 1) Find places to add details about the characters, including dialogue and description, and 2) make the plot more entertaining by adding sensory details and making sure that the action builds to create suspense.

PRESENT

CREATE A FINISHED COPY

Students can present their narratives to the class. Remind them that when reading a narrative aloud, it is important to deliver it in a way that helps to bring the narrative to life.

WHEN STUDENTS STRUGGLE...

Add Sensory Details Have students work with partners to revise their work. To focus on sensory details, let students brainstorm lists of sights, sounds, tastes, and smells that their characters might experience. Then have them suggest places to add details from the lists as they help each other revise.

FOR STUDENTS WITH DISABILITIES

Create Storyboards Have students work in small groups to create visual storyboards of their narratives. Let them start by creating pictures of the main characters and events. Then have them add dialogue. Stress that the pictures can be rough sketches and dialogue can be brief excerpts. The main objective is to show the main episodes of the narrative's beginning, middle, and end in visual form. If students are unfamiliar with storyboards, explain that they are similar to comics, but not as finished.

PERFORMANCE TASK A

USE THE SCORING RUBRIC

Assign pairs to score each other's narratives using the three rubric categories. Ask students to write a brief explanation of the reasons for their score using the language of the rubric.

REFLECT ON THE PROCESS

In addition to reflecting on the experience of writing their narratives, ask students to reflect on the planning, producing, and revising in this task. They should consider what they learned as well as what they might do differently in a future assignment. Ask students to discuss their answers to the following questions in small groups:

- How did you make the climax exciting?
- What is your favorite descriptive detail? What do you like about it?
- How did writing a fictional narrative help you understand the structure of stories you have read?

PERFORMANCE TASK A RUBRIC
FICTIONAL NARRATIVE

	Ideas and Evidence	Organization	Language
4	• An engaging conflict is clearly established, developed, and resolved. • The setting is skillfully established and developed and helps shape the conflict. • Characters are compelling and believable. • Dialogue and description are used effectively.	• Event sequence is smooth, is well structured, and creates suspense. • The plot builds to a strong, satisfying conclusion. • Pacing is clear and effective. • Transitions convey sequence and indicate shifts in setting. • The conclusion clearly reflects a theme.	• The story has a consistent and effective point of view. • Words, phrases, and verbs are precise and vivid. • Sensory language reveals the setting and characters. • Spelling, capitalization, and punctuation are correct. • Grammar and usage are correct.
3	• A conflict is introduced, developed, and resolved, but it could better engage the readers. • The setting is established but could be more developed to shape the characters and conflict. • Characters have some believable traits but may need development. • Dialogue and description could be more interesting.	• Event sequence is generally well structured but includes some extraneous events. • The plot builds to a conclusion. • Pacing is somewhat uneven and confusing. • Transitions convey sequence but don't indicate shifts in setting. • The conclusion could more clearly reflect a theme.	• The story has a consistent point of view. • Words, phrases, sensory language, and verbs could be more vivid. • Few spelling, capitalization, and punctuation errors occur. • Some grammatical and usage errors are repeated in the story.
2	• A conflict is introduced but not developed or resolved; it does not engage the reader. • The setting is unclear and does not affect the characters or conflict. • Characters are somewhat clear but undeveloped. • Dialogue and description are insufficient or uninteresting.	• Events are not well structured, are too numerous, or distract from the plot. • The conclusion is unsatisfying, with little suspense, and does not follow from the events. • Pacing is distracting or choppy. • Few transitions are used. • The conclusion does not reflect a theme.	• The story's point of view is inconsistent. • Precise words, sensory language, and effective verbs are mostly lacking. • Spelling, capitalization, and punctuation errors make reading the story difficult. • Grammar and usage are incorrect in many places, but the writer's ideas are still clear.
1	• A conflict is not identifiable. • The setting is not described. • Characters are unclear and underdeveloped. • Dialogue and descriptions are not included.	• Event sequence is not evident. • There is no clear conclusion. • There is no evidence of pacing. • No transitions are used.	• The story's point of view is never clearly established. • Precise words, sensory language, and effective verbs are lacking. • Spelling, capitalization, and punctuation are incorrect throughout. • Many grammatical and usage errors change the meaning of the writer's ideas.

TO CHALLENGE STUDENTS...

Change the Point of View Challenge students to rewrite their narratives from the different point of view of a different character. (If their story has only one character, let them add one.) Ask students to discuss how this might change the narrative. Have students read the original and the new version to a small group and discuss which version was more interesting and why.

Interactive Lessons

To help you complete this task, use:
- *Writing Arguments*
- *Giving a Presentation*
- *Using Media in a Presentation*

Present an Argument

This collection depicts the bold actions of daring individuals. The myth "The Flight of Icarus" presents a clear message about the risks and rewards of taking those actions. In the following activity, you will draw from "The Flight of Icarus" and other texts in the collection to prepare and present an argument, either for taking bold actions or for avoiding them.

A successful argument

- provides an introduction that clearly states your **claim**—the point your argument is making
- includes quotations or examples from the texts to support or illustrate central ideas
- uses good eye contact, volume, and pronunciation
- includes visuals to emphasize salient points
- concludes by restating the claim

> **W 1a–e** Write arguments.
> **W 8** Gather relevant information.
> **W 9** Draw evidence from literary or informational texts.
> **W 10** Write routinely.
> **SL 4** Present claims and findings.
> **SL 5** Include multimedia components and visual displays.
> **SL 6** Adapt speech to a variety of contexts and tasks.
> **L 3** Use knowledge of language and its conventions.

fyi
hmhfyi.com

Visit hmhfyi.com to explore your topic and enhance your research.

PLAN

Clarify Understanding Review the selections in this collection about people and characters that took bold actions.

- Determine the various opinions or messages expressed about the rewards and risks associated with bold actions.
- Identify the reasons and evidence given to support these opinions and messages.

Make Your Claim Decide whether you think the rewards of bold actions are worth the risks. Make a list of the reasons for your opinion. This will help you determine your claim.

Do Research Gain a better understanding of the topic.

- Search for solid, credible evidence for both sides of the argument.
- Find supporting facts, details, and examples.
- Understand the **counterclaim,** or opposing view, that might keep your audience from agreeing with you.
- Identify any visuals that illustrate your ideas.

myNotebook

Use the annotation tools in your eBook to find evidence to support your ideas. Save each piece of evidence to your notebook.

ACADEMIC VOCABULARY

As you plan and present your argument, be sure to use the academic vocabulary words.

aspect
cultural
evaluate
resource
text

PERFORMANCE TASK B

PRESENT AN ARGUMENT

> W 1a–e, W 5, W 8,
> W 9, W 10,
> SL 4, SL 5,
> SL 6, L 3

Introduce students to the Performance Task by reading the introductory paragraph with them and reviewing the criteria for what makes a good oral argument. Remind students that it is important for an oral argument to be written well, but that it is equally important for it to be delivered well.

PLAN

CLARIFY UNDERSTANDING

Remind students that claims need to be supported by reasons and evidence. Before students begin writing, they should review the evidence they have gathered.

- Does the evidence support the reasons for the claim?
- Is the evidence credible?

English Language Support

Plan to Present an Argument Make sure students understand that their arguments will support a claim about the risks and rewards of taking bold actions. Assign a pair of students to review half of the collection texts and assign the other half of the texts to another student pair. For each text that students examine, ask them to list the risks and rewards of the bold actions the people and characters took. Then have them discuss their opinions on whether the risks were worth the rewards in each instance. Students may use a chart like the one shown to record their observations and opinions about each text.

Risks	Rewards	Opinions

After student pairs have discussed their assigned texts, have them share the main points of their discussion with a pair that has discussed the other collection texts. Students can use the conversations to help them develop their claims.

PERFORMANCE TASK B

English Language Support

Link Ideas Remind students to use connecting words and phrases in their arguments to show how ideas are related. Have students work in small groups to write sentences using the transitions below. Then invite students to share their sentences and explain how each transition links ideas.

at the end	*in fact*
next	*as a result*
for example	*on the other hand*

PRODUCE

DRAFT YOUR ARGUMENT

Remind students that their presentations should present a clear, well-supported argument to their audience. As they write, tell students to "hear" the argument in their heads as if they were the people listening. Have students consider:

View It!

Professional Development Podcast:

Teaching Argument

- Is the argument well laid out?
- Is it convincing?
- Are the reasons presented in a logical manner?

PRODUCE

LANGUAGE CONVENTIONS

Tell students to add adjectives, prepositional phrases, and other modifiers to nouns where they will help enrich meaning or support ideas.

WHEN STUDENTS STRUGGLE...

Integrate Visuals Make sure students understand that visuals should support and elaborate on their ideas. Have students work with a partner to determine which elements of their arguments would be most effective to represent visually. For example, they might present numerical data in a chart or show a video clip that illustrates an example of a bold action.

Consider Your Purpose and Audience Who will listen to your report? What do you think your audience will think? Think about that audience as you prepare your commentary. Keep your audience in mind as you determine your tone and word choices.

PRODUCE ▸

myWriteSmart

Write your rough draft in *my*WriteSmart. Focus on getting your ideas down, rather than perfecting your choice of language.

Draft Your Argument
Although you will be presenting your argument orally, you will need to write it out as a full draft.

- Begin by introducing the topic and stating your claim.
- Express your reasons and support them with credible sources.
- Recognize opposing claims, and use a counterargument to show you've anticipated other viewpoints.
- Use words and phrases such as *because*, *therefore*, and *for that reason* to make your argument clearer and more cohesive.
- Conclude by summarizing your argument.

Interactive Lessons

For help in writing your draft, use:
- Writing Arguments: Creating a Coherent Argument

Language Conventions: Noun Phrases

A **noun phrase** consists of a noun and all the words that modify the noun. The modifiers in noun phrases add details. Read the following passage from the editorial "Ship of Fools."

> " A massive storm in the Indian Ocean knocked out her mast, launching a massive international rescue effort. "

Notice how the modifier *massive* adds emphasis in the two noun phrases in the sentence. Look for places in your argument in which you can add details for emphasis or to make a point more vivid.

Prepare Visuals
Consider using multimedia and visual displays to emphasize your key points.

Interactive Lessons

For help with visuals, use:
- Using Media in a Presentation

- Be sure each visual has a purpose and is interesting.
- Check that all visuals are large and clearly readable.

English Language Support

Adapt Speech Remind students that they will need to use verbal and nonverbal elements to persuade their audience to agree with their claim.

- Ask students to work in pairs to identify words they want to emphasize. Have them practice saying these passages aloud using volume, expression, and gestures to add emphasis.
- Have students read aloud their drafts to a partner. Then have the partner provide feedback on how clear and effective the delivery was.

Practice Your Argument Use your draft to practice on your own. Then practice with a partner, keeping these suggestions in mind.

- Speak loudly, varying your pitch and tone.
- Look directly at individuals in your audience.
- Use gestures and facial expressions to emphasize ideas.

Evaluate Your Argument Work with your partner to determine whether your presentation is effective. Use this chart to make adjustments to the draft based on your evaluation.

Questions	Tips	Revision Techniques
Does the introduction clearly state my claim?	**Highlight** the claim.	**Revise** the existing claim to make it clear and focused.
Are my reasons supported by effective examples?	**Underline** each reason. **Highlight** your evidence.	**Add** additional quotes or examples to support your reasons.
Have I included noun phrases to enrich sentences?	**Highlight** sensory details.	**Insert** adjectives in order to add details to your ideas.
Did I anticipate a counterargument?	**Underline** opposing claims.	**Add** any opposing claim that may not have been addressed.
Does my conclusion restate my claim and sum up my position?	**Underline** the conclusion.	**Add** a restatement, if needed, to clarify.

my WriteSmart

Have your partner or a group of peers review your draft in *my*WriteSmart. Ask your reviewers to note any reasons that do not support your argument or lack sufficient evidence.

Interactive Lessons
For help in practicing your presentation, use:
• Giving a Presentation: Delivering Your Presentation

Deliver Your Argument Finalize your argument and present it to the class. You might also want to use these additional formats to present it:

- Use a computer presentation program to create an interactive version of your argument.
- Make a video recording of yourself presenting your argument, and share it on your class or school website.

FOR STUDENTS WITH DISABILITIES

Use Visual Cues Encourage students to use highlighting as visual cues for when to pause and stress certain words and phrases in their arguments. Students may then read their arguments from a projector screen as they record a video of their presentation.

FOR STANDARD ENGLISH LEARNERS

Use Stress Patterns Remind students that in standard English, one-syllable prefixes are short, or not stressed. When giving presentations, students should use formal English stress patterns. Have partners practice pronouncing the following words without stressing the first syllable before they give their presentations, giving each other corrective feedback as needed: *today, decide, refuse, repeat, resist.*

If necessary, give examples of correct pronunciation. Have partners practice saying sentences with similar words from their own presentations.

EVALUATE YOUR ARGUMENT

Have students work with a partner to help them revise their arguments. Students can take turns listening to each other's presentations and offering suggestions to make them more effective based on the revision techniques in the chart.

DELIVER YOUR ARGUMENT

Students may want to create multimedia presentations using computer software. They can create slides to accompany and support the points they make in their presentations.

English Language Support

Use Language Resources Explain how students may make their texts more cohesive by using synonyms or different forms of a word to refer a reader backward in a text. Review the following examples.

- While bold actions may offer *excitement*, the consequences may not be as *exciting*.
- You must be aware of all the *risks*. Proper planning for *hazards* is the first step in prevention.

PERFORMANCE TASK B

USE THE SCORING RUBRIC

Assign three students to score each presentation, with each student focusing on one of the three rubric categories. Ask students to write a brief explanation of the reasons for their score.

REFLECT ON THE PROCESS

Ask students to reflect on the entire writing process as well as their final product. They should consider what they learned and what they might improve in future assignments. Have them write short responses to the following questions:

- How could you have made your argument more convincing?
- How did developing counterarguments help you better understand opposing viewpoints?
- What do you think was your most persuasive piece of evidence?

PERFORMANCE TASK B RUBRIC
ARGUMENT

	Ideas and Evidence	Organization	Language
4	• The introduction immediately grabs the audience's attention; the speaker clearly states his or her claim. • Logical reasons and relevant evidence from the texts and multiple, credible sources convincingly support the speaker's claim. • The opposing claim is anticipated and effectively addressed. • The conclusion effectively sums up the argument and leaves a lasting impression.	• The reasons and evidence are organized consistently and logically throughout. • Uses words and phrases in a cohesive manner to connect reasons and evidence. • Visuals and graphic aids are visible, well organized, and support key points.	• The argument reflects a formal speaking style. • The speaker uses precise and concise language. • Sentence beginnings, lengths, and structures vary and have a rhythmic flow. • Expands on noun phrases to enrich sentence meanings.
3	• The introduction could do more to grab the reader's attention; the speaker states a claim. • Most reasons support the speaker's claim but could be more convincing; most reasons are supported with evidence from the texts and research sources. • The opposing claim is anticipated but could be better refuted. • The conclusion restates the claim.	• The organization of reasons and evidence is confusing in some places. • A few more words and phrases are needed to connect the ideas cohesively. • Visuals and graphic aids could be clearer and more complete; they don't always support important points.	• The style becomes informal in a few places. • The speaker's use of language could be more precise and concise. • Sentence beginnings, lengths, and structures vary somewhat. • Misses one or two opportunities to expand on noun phrases.
2	• The introduction is ordinary; the speaker's claim is unclearly stated. • The reasons are not always logical or relevant. • The speaker uses poor, unclear evidence from just a few sources. • The opposing claim is anticipated but not logically addressed. • The conclusion provides an incomplete or unclear summary of the argument.	• The organization of reasons and evidence is logical in some places, but it often doesn't follow a pattern. • Many more words and phrases are needed to connect reasons and evidence cohesively. • Few visuals or graphic aids are used; those used are unclear, poorly organized, and don't support important points.	• The style frequently becomes informal. • Language used is vague, unnecessarily wordy, and unclear in many places. • Sentence structures barely vary, and some fragments or run-on sentences are present. • Grammar and usage are incorrect in many places, but the ideas are clear.
1	• The introduction is confusing and contains no claim. • Supporting reasons are missing. • The speech contains no evidence from the texts or research sources. • The opposing claim is neither anticipated nor addressed. • The concluding section is missing.	• There is no logical organization; reasons and evidence are presented randomly. • No cohesive words or phrases are used, making the argument difficult to understand. • No visuals or graphic aids are used.	• The style is inappropriate. • Language used makes the argument confusing. • Repetitive sentence structure, fragments, and run-on sentences make the argument hard to follow. • Many grammatical and usage errors change the meaning of ideas.

TO CHALLENGE STUDENTS...

Debate the Topic Challenge students to argue opposing viewpoints in a timed formal debate. Students may adapt their arguments to present opening statements, rebuttal arguments, and closing statements. Instruct students to take notes on their opponent's opening statement to help them prepare their rebuttals.

©Todd Davidson/Images.com/Corbis

Perception and Reality

Now I do not know whether it was then I dreamt I was a butterfly, or whether I am now a butterfly, dreaming I am a man.

—Chuang Tzu

STREAM TO START

Motivate students to read the collection texts and spark their curiosity by playing the video for the class. After students view the video, ask them if life would be better or worse if things were always how we perceive them to be. Call on volunteers to share their responses.

PERFORMANCE TASK PREVIEW

Point out to students that they will complete two performance tasks at the end of the collection. The performance tasks will require them to further analyze the selections in the collection and to synthesize ideas about these analyses. Students will present their findings in a variety of products.

ACADEMIC VOCABULARY

> ▶ **View It!**
>
> Professional Development Podcast:
> **Academic Vocabulary**

Students can acquire facility with the academic vocabulary words through frequent, repeated exposure as they analyze and discuss the selections in the collection. Academic vocabulary can be used in the instructional contexts shown below. This will enable students to incorporate the academic vocabulary words into their working vocabulary.

- Collaborative Discussion at the end of each selection
- Analyzing the Text questions for each selection
- Selection-level Performance Task
- Vocabulary instruction (for Critical Vocabulary and/or for Vocabulary Strategy)
- Language Conventions
- End-of-collection Performance Task for all selections in the collection

ASK STUDENTS to review the Academic Vocabulary word list for this collection. You may wish to pronounce each word aloud so students hear the correct pronunciation. Then, discuss the definitions and the related forms for each word. Remind students that they will encounter these five academic vocabulary words throughout the collection.

Perception and Reality

In this collection, you will explore how things in life are not always how we perceive them to be.

Stream to Start   hmhfyi.com   Channel One News®

COLLECTION

PERFORMANCE TASK Preview

After reading the selections in this collection, you will have the opportunity to complete two performance tasks:

- In one, you will write an argument expressing your opinion of the saying, "Seeing is believing," using evidence from the literature to support your opinion.

- In the second, you will give a summary presentation that shows an understanding of the drama *Sorry, Wrong Number*.

ACADEMIC VOCABULARY

Study the words and their definitions in the chart below. You will use these words as you discuss and write about the texts in this collection.

Word	Definition	Related Forms
abnormal (ăb-nôr´məl) *adj.*	not typical, usual, or regular; not normal	normal, normalcy, normality, normalize, paranormal, subnormal
feature (fē´chər) *n.*	a prominent or distinctive part, quality, or characteristic	feature article, featured, featureless, featuring, text feature
focus (fō´kəs) *v.*	to direct toward a specific point or purpose	autofocus, focused, refocus, unfocused
perceive (pər-sēv´) *v.*	to become aware of something directly through any of the senses	misperceive, misperception, perception, unperceived
task (tăsk) *n.*	an assignment or work done as part of one's duties	multitask, taskmaster

62

≡ myNotebook

As students read, analyze, and discuss the texts in this collection, encourage them to create a ***my*WordList** folder in ***my*Notebook** to build their own personal word lists.

- **Annotate** Students can highlight vocabulary terms and other unfamiliar words and save each highlighted term to ***my*Notebook**.
- **Organize** Within ***my*Notebook**, students can drag each word into the ***my*WordList** folder.
- **Elaborate** Ask students to add details to the entry for each word, such as a definition, other forms of the word, and a sample sentence.

English Language Support

ENGAGE WITH THE COLLECTION TOPIC

Point out the collection's title: Perception and Reality. Explain that *perception* means "a way of regarding something," or "a mental impression," and that this collection focuses on things that may not be what they seem.

ACCESS PRIOR KNOWLEDGE Ask students to think of times when their perception of a person or situation didn't match the reality. Discuss why doing a "reality check" might help in certain instances.

GENERATING INTERACTIONS BETWEEN SCHEMATA AND TEXT (GIST)

Use this strategy to help students determine the central idea of the texts in this collection.

- *First*, read aloud a section of a text. Tell students to follow along and listen closely for words and ideas that seem to be most important.
- *Then*, work together to underline ten or more words that the class identifies as "most important." List the underlined words on the board.

- *Next*, work together to write a summary statement, using as many of the underlined words as possible.
- *Finally*, work with students to create a topic sentence to precede the summary.

 Collection 2 Digital Resources for English Language Support

LANGUAGE WORKSHOP
Designated English Learners

You may use the digital Teacher Resources > Language Workshop to support English learners in planning and carrying out interviews, applying an understanding of informational text structures, and collaborating to produce and present information.

 VIDEOS

These videos will help students learn how to interpret figurative language and make predictions while reading. Have them use **Text In Focus Practice** to apply the skills.

Collection 2 Lessons	Media	Teach and Practice
Student Edition | eBook	▶ Video Links HISTORY A&E Channel One News®	**Close Reading and Evidence Tracking**
ANCHOR TEXT Folk Tale retold by Virginia Hamilton "The People Could Fly"	🔊 Audio "The People Could Fly"	**Close Read Screencasts** • Modeled Discussion (lines 23–30) • Close Read application PDF (lines 71–81) — **Text in Focus** • Interpreting Figurative Language (line 70) **Strategies for Annotation** • Analyze Story Elements: Folk Tale • Summarize Text • Latin Suffixes
CLOSE READER Short Story by David Yoo "Heartbeat"	🔊 Audio "Heartbeat"	
EXEMPLAR Poem by W. B. Yeats "The Song of Wandering Aengus"	🔊 Audio "The Song of Wandering Aengus"	**Strategies for Annotation** • Determine the Impact of Rhyme • Analyze Form: Sonnet
Poem by William Shakespeare "Sonnet 43"	▶ Video BIO® Biography: William Shakespeare 🔊 Audio "Sonnet 43"	
Magazine Article by Susana Martinez-Conde and Stephen L. Macknik "Magic and the Brain"	▶ Video HISTORY® Steve Cohen's Lost Magic 🔊 Audio "Magic and the Brain"	**Strategies for Annotation** • Analyze Structure: Text Features • Summarize Text • The Greek Prefix neuro-
CLOSE READER Science Writing by Reynaldo Vasquez "Saving the Lost"	🔊 Audio "Saving the Lost"	
Public Art by Julian Beever *Pavement Chalk Art*		
Short Story by Cory Doctorow "Another Place, Another Time"	🔊 Audio "Another Place, Another Time"	**Strategies for Annotation** • Determine Meaning of Words and Phrases • Analyze Story Elements: Character • Reference Aids
ANCHOR TEXT Drama by Lucille Fletcher *Sorry, Wrong Number*	🔊 Audio *Sorry, Wrong Number*	**Close Read Screencasts** • Modeled Discussion (lines 53–75) • Close Read application PDF (lines 872–898) — **Text in Focus** • Making Predictions (line 140) **Strategies for Annotation** • Analyze Form: Drama
CLOSE READER Novel Excerpt by Charles Dickens from *A Christmas Carol* Drama Excerpt by Israel Horovitz Graphic Story by Marvel Comics	🔊 Audio from A Christmas Carol	
Collection 2 Performance Tasks: **A** Write an Argument **B** Give a Summary Presentation	fyi hmhfyi.com	**Interactive Lessons** **A** Writing Arguments — **B** Giving a Presentation

For Systematic Coverage of Writing and Speaking & Listening Standards	**Interactive Lessons** Writing an Argument Analyzing and Evaluating Presentations

Assess		Extend	Reteach
Performance Task	✔ *Assess It Online!*	**Teacher eBook**	**Teacher eBook**
Speaking Activity: Dramatic Reading	Selection Test	**Prepare for a Dramatic Reading > Interactive Lessons >** Giving a Presentation	**Analyze Story Elements: Folk Tale >Interactive Graphic Organizer >** Comparison-Contrast Chart
Speaking Activity: Discussion	Selection Test	**Analyze Form >Interactive Whiteboard Lesson >** Form in Poetry	**Determine Meanings >Level Up Tutorial >** Figurative Language
Speaking Activity: Demonstration	Selection Test	**Conduct Online Research > Interactive Lessons >** Conducting Research, Evaluating Sources	**Analyze Structure: Text Features >Level Up Tutorial >** Informational Text
Media Activity: Poster	Selection Test	**Analyze Media: Perspective and Illusion > Interactive Graphic Organizer >** Comparison-Contrast Chart	**Analyze Diverse Media**
Writing Activity: Character Analysis	Selection Test	**Analyze Story Elements: Character and Setting >Interactive Graphic Organizer >** Comparison-Contrast Chart	**Analyze Story Elements: Character >Level Up Tutorial >** Methods of Characterization
Writing Activity: Character Analysis	Selection Test	**Compare and Contrast: Text and Media > Interactive Graphic Organizer >** Venn Diagram	**Analyze Form: Drama >Level Up Tutorial >** Elements of Drama
A Write an Argument **B** Give a Summary Presentation	Collection Test		

Lesson Assessments Writing an Argument Analyzing and Evaluating Presentations	**Standards Support and Enrichment** **For Designated English Language Instruction**	For more standards instruction and practice, see Teacher Resources > Standards Support and Enrichment. To provide support for English Learners during Designated English Language instruction, use the lessons found in Teacher Resources > Language Workshop.

Collection 2 Lessons	Key Learning Objective	Performance Task	Vocabulary Strategy
ANCHOR TEXT **Folk Tale retold by Virginia Hamilton** **Lexile 430L** **"The People Could Fly," p. 63A**	**The student will be able to . . .** identify elements of a folk tale and summarize the story.	Speaking Activity: Dramatic Reading	Latin Suffixes
EXEMPLAR **Poem by W. B. Yeats** **"The Song of Wandering Aengus," p. 71A** **Poem by William Shakespeare** **"Sonnet 43," p. 71A**	**The student will be able to . . .** learn how to analyze a poem's form as well as the use of figurative language and sound devices to understand their effects on meaning.	Speaking Activity: Discussion	
Magazine Article by Susana Martinez-Conde and Stephen L. Macknik **Lexile 1340L** **"Magic and the Brain," p. 77A**	**The student will be able to . . .** analyze how text features contribute to a text and to summarize text objectively.	Speaking Activity: Demonstration	The Greek Prefix *neuro-*
Public Art by Julian Beever *Pavement Chalk Art,* **p. 89A**	**The student will be able to . . .** analyze the purposes of public art and the techniques Beever uses to create the illusion of three-dimensionality.	Media Activity: Poster	
Short Story by Cory Doctorow **Lexile 1060L** **"Another Place, Another Time," p. 93A**	**The student will be able to . . .** identify and analyze how setting affects characters' traits, motivations, and actions.	Writing Activity: Character Analysis	Reference Aids
ANCHOR TEXT **Drama by Lucille Fletcher** *Sorry, Wrong Number,* **p. 111A**	**The student will be able to . . .** analyze the elements of a drama and make comparisons between a script and a performance.	Writing Activity: Character Analysis	

Collection 2 Performance Tasks:

A Write an Argument
B Give a Summary Presentation

Language Conventions	English Language Support	Differentiated Instruction	CLOSE READER Selection
	• Analyze Language	**When Students Struggle:** Analyze Characters	Short Story by David Yoo "Heartbeat," p. 70b **Lexile 840L**
	• Word Study • Use Adverb Clauses	**When Students Struggle:** Paraphrase Poetry	
Adverb Clauses	• Examine Affixes	**When Students Struggle:** Summarize Central Ideas **To Challenge Students:** Evaluate Ideas	Science Writing by Reynaldo Vasquez "Saving the Lost," p. 88b **Lexile 920L**
	• Summarize Information	**When Students Struggle:** Perspective	
Spell Correctly	• Explain Ideas • Understand Language Choices • Read Closely • Write a Summary • Check Capitalization and Spelling	**For Students with Disabilities:** Visual Accommodations **When Students Struggle:** • Symbols • Determine Meanings of Words and Phrases **To Challenge Students:** Analyze Theme	
	• Analyze Form: Drama • Use Verbs and Verb Phrases • Summarize • Improve Reading Fluency	**For Standard English Learners:** • Pronounce Present Participles • Informal Language **When Students Struggle:** Visualize Onstage Action **To Challenge Students:** Analyze Story Elements	from *A Christmas Carol,* p. 126b Novel Excerpt by Charles Dickens **Lexile 730L** Drama Excerpt by Israel Horovitz Graphic Story by Marvel Comics
A Connect Ideas **B** Adverbial Phrases	**A** Write Arguments Understand Text Structure Justify Opinions **B** Plan a Summary Presentation Use Adverbials	**A When Students Struggle:** Vary Word Choice **For Standard English Learners:** Use Plurals **To Challenge Students:** Create a Podcast **For Students with Disabilities:** Make a Checklist **B For Standard English Learners:** Adapt Speech **For Students with Disabilities:** Use Spoken Cues **When Students Struggle:** Practice Speaking Techniques **To Challenge Students:** Perform a Staged Reading	

ANCHOR TEXT EXEMPLAR

The People Could Fly

Folk Tale retold by Virginia Hamilton

Why This Text?

Folk tales and other folklore show students connections among history, culture, and literature. By reading folk tales, students broaden their understanding and appreciation of literature from the oral tradition. This lesson leads students to analyze and summarize the elements of a folk tale.

Key Learning Objective: The student will be able to identify elements of a folk tale and summarize the story.

For practice and application:

Close Reader selection:
"Heartbeat"
Short Story by David Yoo

RL 1 Cite textual evidence.
RL 2 Determine a theme and provide a summary.
RL 3 Analyze story elements.
RL 4 Determine the meaning of words and phrases.
RL 10 Read grade 6–8 literature proficiently.
SL 6 Adapt speech to a variety of contexts and tasks.
L 4b Use Greek or Latin affixes and roots as clues to word meanings.
L 4d Verify the meaning of a word or phrase by checking context.

Text Complexity Rubric

Quantitative Measures	**The People Could Fly** **Lexile:** 430L
Qualitative Measures	**Levels of Meaning/Purpose** single level of complex meaning
	Structure conventional story structure
	Language Conventionality and Clarity figurative, less accessible language
	Knowledge Demands some cultural and literary knowledge useful
Reader/Task Considerations	• Teacher determined • Vary by individual reader and type of text • See the Text X-Ray for suggested Reader/Task Considerations.

English Language Support Before teaching, use the Text X-Ray for an overview of the text's complexity. The Text X-Ray and the supports and scaffolds in the Teacher's Edition will help you guide students of different skill levels.

Meaning Making

Language Development

Effective Expression

Content Knowledge

Foundational Skills

Text Complexity: Qualitative Measures

Levels of Meaning/Purpose

single level of complex meaning

Help students summarize text.

- Teacher's Edition side notes, pp. 63, 64, 66, 67, 68
- English Language Support, p. 63
- When Students Struggle, p. 66
- Close Read Screencasts, p. 63
- Strategies for Annotation, p. 68

▶ *Use It!* **Level Up Tutorial:** Summarizing

ZOOM IN ON SUMMARIZING TEXT Explain that a text **summary** includes only the text's most important details. Tell students that a summary should tell *who* the text is about, *what* happens, and *when* and *where* it occurs. After students have read the folk tale, ask pairs to discuss the story and answer the following questions.

- Who is the story about?
- When and where does the story take place?
- What happens?

Then have pairs summarize the story. Ask volunteers to share their summaries with the class.

Structure

conventional story structure

Help students analyze story elements.

- Teacher's Edition side notes, pp. 63, 65, 67, 68
- English Language Support, p. 64
- Strategies for Annotation, p. 67

▶ *Use It!* **Level Up Tutorial:** Myths, Legends, and Tales

To reteach Story Elements, see

- Analyze Story Elements: Folk Tale, p. 70a

▶ *Use It!* **Interactive Graphic Organizer:** Comparison-Contrast Chart

ZOOM IN ON ANALYZING FOLK TALES Tell students that folk tales are stories passed down from generation to generation through the oral tradition. Display these special features of folk tales:

- supernatural events
- setting in the distant past
- characters with supernatural powers
- message that teaches a lesson about life

As a class, discuss examples of these features found in tales that students know. After students have finished reading the selection, have small groups discuss and cite examples of folk-tale elements they encountered.

Language Conventionality and Clarity

figurative, less accessible language

Teach unfamiliar academic vocabulary in context.

- Teacher's Edition Critical Vocabulary notes, pp. 64, 65, 66, 70
- English Language Support, p. 64
- Applying Academic Vocabulary, p. 65
- Strategies for Annotation, p. 70
- Vocabulary Strategy: Latin Suffixes, p. 70

Guide students to analyze language and sentence structure.

- Close Read Screencasts, p. 63
- English Language Support, p. 65

 Interpreting Figurative Language

ZOOM IN ON **SENTENCE STRUCTURE** Point out that in everyday speech, people do not always speak in complete sentences. Instead, they often use **sentence fragments**, or incomplete sentences, which can confuse readers of dialogue. Tell students that when they encounter a sentence fragment, they should look at the preceding sentence for clues to its meaning. Have pairs locate sentence fragments in lines 25 and 30. For each one, have them read the preceding sentence and suggest a subject and/or verb that will complete the fragment.

- line 25: *He was*
- line 30: *They*

Ask pairs to share their responses. Then discuss how the author's use of sentence fragments suits the style and purpose of the folk tale.

Knowledge Demands

some cultural and literary knowledge useful

Help students understand the cultural context of the folk story.

- Teacher's Edition Background note, p. 63
- Teacher's Edition side notes, p. 67

ZOOM IN ON **BUILDING CULTURAL KNOWLEDGE** After reading the Background note, explain that people taken from Africa and enslaved in the Americas were separated from their families, communities, and cultural histories. They were not allowed to read or write, so storytelling became a way to share experiences and pass along cultural values.

- Discuss the role of the oral tradition in creating a new sense of community.
- After students read the story, discuss the cultural values that it reflects. Consider how these values might differ from those held in Africa.

Suggested Reader/Task Considerations

Consider the following before assigning this folk tale to students:

- Will students be engaged with the style of writing and the presentation of the message of the folk tale?
- Will the folk tale maintain students' interest throughout the lesson?

ZOOM IN ON **SUPPORTING COMPREHENSION**

- Read aloud lines 1–18 to model how the dialect sounds. Use a warm, relaxed tone to engage interest. Then have pairs continue reading aloud, alternating readers for each page. Encourage them to use dramatic expression.
- Read aloud the first two paragraphs of the selection. Then model predicting techniques. (*I think that the people will fly again, even without wings. If I find that my prediction is incorrect, I'll change it based on story events.*) As students read the text, have them pause to make and adjust predictions.

CLOSE READ

Background Have students read the background and author information. Tell them that Virginia Hamilton created a narrator, the person who tells a story, who sounds like an African American storyteller from the days of slavery. Point out that folk tales come from an oral tradition—they were told aloud long before they were written. Explain that the narrator uses speech rhythms and language like that of a storyteller speaking to an audience. Students may imagine themselves as listeners as they read.

SETTING A PURPOSE Direct students to use the Setting a Purpose prompt to focus their reading. Remind them to generate questions as they read.

Analyze Story Elements:
Folk Tales (LINES 1–9)

RL 1,
RL 3

Tell students that **folk tales** are stories passed down by word of mouth from generation to generation. Explain that folk tales often feature supernatural events and characters with supernatural abilities.

(A) CITE TEXT EVIDENCE Ask students to reread lines 1–9 to identify supernatural abilities that seem likely to be important in the story. *(Some of the African people had the magical power to fly, though they shed their wings after being captured.)*

Summarize Text

(LINES 10–18)

RL 2

Tell students that a **summary** is a brief retelling of the most important details of setting, characters, and events.

(B) ASK STUDENTS to reread lines 10–18 and tell what seems most important to remember about the characters who "could no longer breathe the sweet scent of Africa." *(Once the people were in the land of slavery, some still had the secret power of flying, though they looked like everyone else.)*

English Language Support

Point out that students must tell about the characters after they were "in the land of slavery." Have pairs find two or three important details about the characters and write a sentence that summarizes them.

Background *Between the 1600s and 1800s, millions of Africans were taken forcibly to the Americas as enslaved people. Their labor spurred the growth of large-scale farming in the colonies. Despite the hardships of oppression, these people nurtured a strong sense of tradition, passing stories from generation to generation.* **Virginia Hamilton** (1934–2002) *grew up listening to such stories. As an adult, she put many of them into writing and wrote a number of her own books about African American history and culture.*

The People Could Fly

Folk Tale by Virginia Hamilton

SETTING A PURPOSE As you read, think about what this folk tale says about the importance of hope in the lives of oppressed people.

myNotebook

As you read, mark up the text. Save your work to *myNotebook*.
• Highlight details
• Add notes and questions
(A) Add new words to *myWordList*

They say the people could fly. Say that long ago in Africa, some of the people knew magic. And they would walk up on the air like climbin' up on a gate. And they flew like blackbirds over the fields. Black, shiny wings flappin' against the blue up there.

Then, many of the people were captured for Slavery. The ones that could fly shed their wings. They couldn't take their wings across the water on the slave ships. Too crowded, don't you know.

10   The folks were full of misery, then. Got sick with the up and down of the sea. So they forgot about flyin' when they could no longer breathe the sweet scent of Africa.

(B)

Say the people who could fly kept their power, although they shed their wings. They kept their secret magic in the land

The People Could Fly   **63**

Close Read Screencasts   Close Read

Modeled Discussions

Have students click the *Close Read* icons in their eBooks to access a screencast in which readers discuss and annotate the following key passage:
• The slaves labored in the fields . . . did move faster. Had to. (lines 23–30)

As a class, view and discuss the video. Then have students pair up to do an independent close read of an additional passage—"Say the next day . . . And they too rose on the air" (lines 71–81).

Summarize Text

RL 2

(LINES 33–40)

Tell students that a **conflict** is a struggle between opposing forces. Explain that the conflict sets up the story action and is important to include in a summary.

C **ASK STUDENTS** to reread the two paragraphs beginning on line 33 and sum up the conflict shown. *(The conflict is between the cruel Overseer and the young mother named Sarah. When she doesn't quiet her baby, the Overseer whips it.)*

CRITICAL VOCABULARY

croon: The young mother, Sarah, does not even try to croon to her baby to soothe it.

ASK STUDENTS how Sarah's crooning to the child might have soothed it. *(Soft singing to a young child usually calms the child, especially when the crooning is done by the child's mother.)*

English Language Support

Determine Meaning Tell students that if they continue reading after encountering an unfamiliar word, they will often find clues about its meaning in the text. Point out the author's use of informal language—language that sounds like casual conversation—in lines 33 and 39.

ASK STUDENTS to identify context clues that help them explain the meanings of *bawling* in line 33 *("cry," in line 35)* and *hollered* in line 39 *("like any hurt child," in line 40).*

---

of slavery. They looked the same as the other people from Africa who had been coming over, who had dark skin. Say you couldn't tell anymore one who could fly from one who couldn't.

20 One such who could was an old man, call him Toby. And standin' tall, yet afraid, was a young woman who once had wings. Call her Sarah. Now Sarah carried a babe tied to her back. She trembled to be so hard worked and scorned.

The slaves labored in the fields from sunup to sundown. The owner of the slaves callin' himself their Master. Say he was a hard lump of clay. A hard, glinty coal. A hard rock pile, wouldn't be moved. His Overseer[1] on horseback pointed out the slaves who were slowin' down. So the one called Driver cracked his whip over the slow ones to make them move faster. That whip was a slice-open cut of pain. So they did

30 move faster. Had to.

Sarah hoed and chopped the row as the babe on her back slept.

Say the child grew hungry. That babe started up bawling too loud. Sarah couldn't stop to feed it. Couldn't stop to soothe and quiet it down. She let it cry. She didn't want to. She had no heart to **croon** to it.

"Keep that thing quiet," called the Overseer. He pointed his finger at the babe. The woman scrunched low. The Driver cracked his whip across the babe anyhow. The babe hollered

40 like any hurt child, and the woman fell to the earth.

The old man that was there, Toby, came and helped her to her feet.

"I must go soon," she told him.

"Soon," he said.

Sarah couldn't stand up straight any longer. She was too weak. The sun burned her face. The babe cried and cried, "Pity me, oh, pity me," say it sounded like. Sarah was so sad and starvin', she sat down in the row.

"Get up, you black cow," called the Overseer. He pointed

50 his hand, and the Driver's whip snarled around Sarah's legs. Her sack dress tore into rags. Her legs bled onto the earth. She couldn't get up.

Toby was there where there was no one to help her and the babe.

croon
(krōōn) *v.* When someone *croons*, that person hums or sings softly.

---

[1] **Overseer** (ō´vər-sē´ər): a person who directs the work of others; a supervisor. During the time of slavery, the overseer was usually a white man.

English Language Support

Analyze Language Read the four sentences in lines 24–28 out loud to students. Point out that the author is describing a character in the folk tale. This helps readers understand the character and also gives readers an impression of what the author might think of the character.

- Using a whiteboard, project lines 24–28. Invite volunteers to mark up the lines, underlining the words that tell who is described, and highlighting the words that describe that person.
- Have pairs note who is being described and the phrases that are used in the description. Point out how the author has made careful

word choices in the description of the owner. Explain that **figurative language** is the use of words in imaginative ways to express or highlight ideas. Ask: *What is the owner of the slaves being compared to? Based on these comparisons the author has deliberately used, what do you understand about the owner?*

- Have students write a paragraph explaining the comparisons the author is making in lines 24–28. In their paragraphs, ask students to make a guess about how the author views the owner of the slaves and why.

"Now, before it's too late," panted Sarah. "Now, Father!"

"Yes, Daughter, the time is come," Toby answered. "Go, as you know how to go!"

He raised his arms, holding them out to her. *"Kum . . . yali, kum buba tambe,"* and more magic words, said so quickly, they sounded like whispers and sighs.

60

The young woman lifted one foot on the air. Then the other. She flew clumsily at first, with the child now held tightly in her arms. Then she felt the magic, the African mystery. Say she rose just as free as a bird. As light as a feather.

The Overseer rode after her, hollerin'. Sarah flew over the fences. She flew over the woods. Tall trees could not **snag** her. Nor could the Overseer. She flew like an eagle now, until she was gone from sight. No one dared speak about it. Couldn't believe it. But it was, because they that was there

70

saw that it was.

snag

(snăg) *v.* If you *snag* something, you catch it quickly and unexpectedly.

Say the next day was dead hot in the fields. A young man slave fell from the heat. The Driver come and whipped him. Toby come over and spoke words to the fallen one. The words of ancient Africa once heard are never remembered completely. The young man forgot them as soon as he heard them. They went way inside him. He got up and rolled over on the air. He rode it awhile. And he flew away.

APPLYING ACADEMIC VOCABULARY

feature	focus

THINK-PAIR-SHARE Have partners discuss the questions below. Encourage them to include the vocabulary words *feature* and *focus* in their responses. Allow volunteers to share their responses with the class.

- What **features** of the author's language deliver a clear, sharp storytelling voice?
- How does the author use figurative comparisons to **focus** the reader's attention on Sarah's flight?

Analyze Story Elements: Folk Tales (LINES 64–70)

RL 1, RL 3, RL 4

Tell students that a folk tale may be told in **dialect,** a style of language specific to a particular place or culture. Explain that dialect can help readers hear how the narrator and characters sound.

D **CITE TEXT EVIDENCE** Have students find dialect in lines 64–70 and explain its effect. *(The narrator says* Say *instead of* They say; *drops the final* g *in* hollering; *and says* they that was there *instead of* those who were there. *The speaker sounds natural and sincere.)*

CRITICAL VOCABULARY

snag: Even tall trees could not snag the flying woman named Sarah.

ASK STUDENTS how the word *snag* as used here contrasts with the description in lines 49–52. Have them tell how Sarah is snagged in the earlier description. *(Sarah is free and soaring, instead of on the ground because she was snagged by a whip.)*

English Language Support

Read Closely Point out the similes in lines 64 and 67. Explain that **similes,** comparisons that use the words *like* or *as*, help readers form mental pictures. Read aloud the two sentences in line 64. Model with gestures the gentle motion of a feather floating on air.

ASK STUDENTS to consider how the mental picture created in line 67 differs from the image in line 64. What change in Sarah does the simile indicate? *(Sarah has become stronger and more confident.)*

 English Language Support

Interpreting Figurative Language (LINE 70)

Have students view the **Text In Focus** video on this page of their eBook to learn how to interpret the figurative language in this folk tale. Then have students use **Text In Focus Practice** to apply what they have learned.

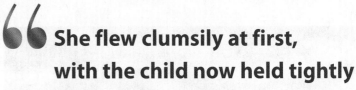

She flew clumsily at first, with the child now held tightly in her arms.

Summarize Text

RL 2

(LINES 98–109)

Tell students that when they summarize a story, they should include information about the most important characters and events.

E ASK STUDENTS to reread lines 98–109. Have them summarize what is most important to recall about old Toby and the people who could fly. *(The slave old Toby is a seer. He still remembers the ancient magical words that cause all the people who could fly to rise into the air to freedom. Old Toby flies, too.)*

CRITICAL VOCABULARY

shuffle: The slaves join hands as if in a ring-sing, but they don't shuffle in a circle. Instead, they rise into the air.

ASK STUDENTS to describe people shuffling in a ring-sing and suggest why the author included this detail. *(In a ring-sing, people join hands in a circle. They take little sliding steps while singing. This detail shows a feature of culture among slaves and contrasts it with the change that happens as the people rise to freedom.)*

plantation: The people fly above the plantation, "way over the slavery land."

ASK STUDENTS what the plantation probably represents to the African Americans who told this folk tale. *(It represents the bondage, sorrow, and pain that the people remember as part of their history.)*

Another and another fell from the heat. Toby was there. He cried out to the fallen and reached his arms out to them. *"Kum kunka yali, kum . . . tambe!"* Whispers and sighs. And they too rose on the air. They rode the hot breezes. The ones flyin' were black and shinin' sticks, wheelin' above the head of the Overseer. They crossed the rows, the fields, the fences, the streams, and were away.

"Seize the old man!" cried the Overseer.

"I heard him say the magic *words*. Seize him!"

The one callin' himself Master come runnin'. The Driver got his whip ready to curl around old Toby and tie him up. The slave owner took his hip gun from its place. He meant to kill old black Toby.

But Toby just laughed. Say he threw back his head and said, "Hee, hee! Don't you know who I am? Don't you know some of us in this field?" He said it to their faces. "We are ones who fly!"

And he sighed the ancient words that were a dark promise. He said them all around to the others in the field under the whip, ". . . *buba yali . . . buba tambe . . .*"

There was a great outcryin'. The bent backs straightened up. Old and young who were called slaves and could fly joined hands. Say like they would ring-sing. But they didn't **shuffle** in a circle. They didn't sing. They rose on the air. They flew in a flock that was black against the heavenly blue. Black crows or black shadows. It didn't matter, they went so high. Way above the **plantation**, way over the slavery land. Say they flew away to *Free-dom*.

And the old man, old Toby, flew behind them, takin' care of them. He wasn't cryin'. He wasn't laughin'. He was the seer. His gaze fell on the plantation where the slaves who could not fly waited.

shuffle
(shŭf´əl) *v.* When you *shuffle*, you move with short sliding steps.

plantation
(plăn-tā´shən) *n.* A *plantation* is a large farm or estate on which crops are raised.

WHEN STUDENTS STRUGGLE . . .

Help students focus on old Toby's significance in this folk tale. Direct partners to find each of the following descriptions in the text and decide together what the details show about old Toby:

- lines 41–42, lines 53–54
- lines 55–60, lines 72–73
- lines 78–80, lines 91–97, lines 106–109

Partners may list ideas in a chart like the one shown.

LEVEL UP TUTORIALS For additional support, assign the following Level Up tutorial: **Making Inferences About Characters.**

Character: Old Toby	
What He Is Like	**What He Does**
fatherly brave remembers the ancient ways has magical powers	recites magic words to rescue people laughs at slave owner flies to freedom takes care of the flying group

"Take us with you!" Their looks spoke it, but they were afraid to shout it. Toby couldn't take them with him. Hadn't the time to teach them to fly. They must wait for a chance to run.

"Goodie-bye!" the old man called Toby spoke to them, poor souls! And he was flyin' gone.

So they say. The Overseer told it. The one called Master said it was a lie, a trick of the light. The Driver kept his mouth shut.

The slaves who could not fly told about the people who could fly to their children. When they were free. When they sat close before the fire in the free land, they told it. They did so love firelight and *Free-dom*, and tellin'.

They say that the children of the ones who could not fly told their children. And now, me, I have told it to you.

COLLABORATIVE DISCUSSION Sarah, Toby, and the others hold onto hope in the most difficult of circumstances. With a partner, discuss what this folk tale says about the nature of hope.

CLOSE READ

Summarize Text
RL 2

(LINES 110–115)

Tell students that a story's conflict is usually resolved by its end. Explain that this part of the plot, called the **resolution,** is the final part of a story summary.

F **ASK STUDENTS** to reread lines 110–115 and suggest a final sentence of this story summary. *(The people who could fly escape to freedom, but those who couldn't remain enslaved, with only the hope of escape.)*

Analyze Story Elements:
RL 1,
RL 2,
RL 3

Folk Tale (LINES 118–123)

Tell students that a folk tale reveals what is important to the cultural group that first told it. Values such as cleverness and courage are often features of folk tales.

G **CITE TEXT EVIDENCE** Ask students to reread lines 118–123 and identify and discuss details that reveal values that are important to those who told this story. *(The sentence "They did so love firelight and* Free-dom, *and tellin'" shows that people used stories to pass down values such as hope, love of freedom, connections to one's past and future, and triumph over oppression.)*

COLLABORATIVE DISCUSSION Have student pairs discuss the message of hope in this folk tale. Then have them share their ideas with the class as a whole.

ASK STUDENTS to share any questions they generated in the course of reading and discussing the selection.

Strategies for Annotation   🖉 🗐 **Annotate it!**

Analyze Story Elements:
RL 2,
RL 3

Folk Tale

Have students locate the last two paragraphs of the story. Encourage them to use the eBook annotation tools to do the following:

- Highlight in yellow the sentences that reveal the cultural values of the people who tell this story.
- Underline specific details that support this.
- Add a note that summarizes these lines to show the most important information.

The slaves who could not fly told about the people who could fly to their children. When they were free. When they sat close before the fire in the free land, they told it. They did so love firelight and Free-dom, and tellin'.

They say that the children of the ones who could not fly told their children. And now, me, I have told it to you.

Analyze Story Elements: Folk Tale

RL 3

Talk with students about the term *oral tradition,* sharing ideas about how a story that is passed down by word of mouth differs from one that is written. Discuss the term *dialect,* and have students give ideas about why dialect is common in stories in the oral tradition.

Have students work in small groups of three. Each group member will choose one feature of folk tales and locate examples of the feature in the story. Then have the groups discuss their findings.

- supernatural events set in the past: *(The setting is a plantation during the days of slavery. Characters fly.)*
- characters with supernatural abilities: *(Old Toby can make people fly.)*
- life lesson: *(People can draw on hope and their inner strength to escape evil.)*

Summarize Text

RL 2

Help students recognize that the sample first sentence of the summary corresponds to the "Title and Genre" entry in the story map. Have them suggest a next sentence that gives information about the setting. *(It takes place on a plantation during slavery times.)*

Use the graphic organizer to point out that this folk tale, like many others, has a straightforward plot that includes these parts: conflict, events, climax, and resolution. Students should jot down the most important information that belongs in each frame.

Analyze Story Elements: Folk Tales

RL 3

Folk tales are stories passed down by word of mouth from generation to generation. "The People Could Fly" is a folk tale that would have been around a long time as an oral tradition before it was finally recorded.

Folk tales can vary from culture to culture, but often have these elements:

- supernatural events set in the distant past
- talking animals or other characters with supernatural abilities
- lessons about what is important to the culture of origin

Folk tales are often told using **dialect**—a form of language that is spoken in a particular place or by a particular group of people—to suggest real people talking. In "The People Could Fly," Virginia Hamilton uses dialect to suggest the folksy speech of the African American storyteller. The use of dialect helps to draw the reader or listener more fully into the setting.

Choose one of the listed features of folk tales. Tell how the feature is shown in "The People Could Fly."

Summarize Text

RL 2

A **summary** of a story is a brief retelling that gives only the most important details. When you summarize a story, you use your own words to answer the basic questions *who? when and where?* and *what happens?* A story map like the one shown can help you organize your answers.

Title and Genre (kind of story):	Setting:

Conflict:	

Main Events (several events in order):	

Outcome/Resolution:	

Here is a possible first sentence of a summary of the story you have read:

"The People Could Fly" is a folk tale that originated among people held captive as slaves.

What would you write as the next sentence of the summary?

Strategies for Annotation ✎ 🗐 *Annotate it!*

Summarize Text

RL 2

Share these strategies for guided or independent analysis:

- Identify a segment of the story in which an important event occurs (e.g., lines 55–64).
- Highlight in yellow the names of the characters.
- Underline details about them and their actions.
- Add a note that summarizes the information in as few words as possible.

"Now, before it's too late," panted Sarah. "Now, Father!"

"Yes, Daughter, the time is come," Toby answered. "Go, as you know how to go!"

He raised his arms, holding them out to her.
kum buba tambe," and more magic words, said so

> When Sarah asked Toby for help, he held out his arms to her and said the magic words that sent her into the air holding her baby.

Heartbeat

Short Story by David Yoo

Why This Text

Students may read a short story without a complete understanding of the story's theme or central idea, or of how particular elements of a story interact. The setting of a story, for example, may influence the characters or plot—or both—and may contribute to the shaping of the theme. Stories such as this one by David Yoo may explicitly state the theme or imply it. With the help of the close-reading questions, students will determine the theme or central idea and use it to provide an objective summary of the text.

Background Have students read the background and the biographical information about the author. Introduce the selection by telling students that David Yoo is a Korean American writer known for his true-to-life stories and his young-adult novels that mix humor with brutal honesty about being different. In his memoir, *The Choke Artist*, Yoo demonstrates his endearing ability to laugh at himself, revealing the insecurities we all feel, but hate to admit.

SETTING A PURPOSE Ask students to pay attention to the development of the theme or central idea and to the way that story elements interact. At what point do students begin to identify the theme or central idea—that of trying to pretend to be more than what they are?

Standards Support

- cite several pieces of textual evidence
- determine the theme or central idea in a text
- provide an objective summary of a text
- analyze how particular elements of a story interact

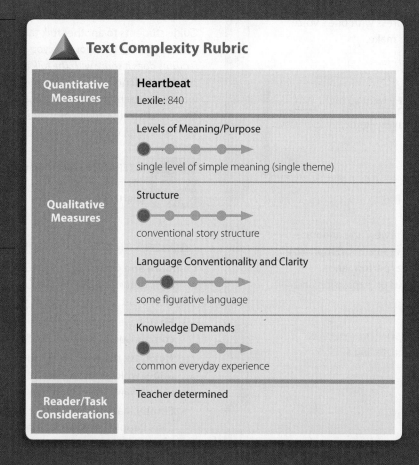

Text Complexity Rubric

Quantitative Measures	**Heartbeat** Lexile: 840
Qualitative Measures	**Levels of Meaning/Purpose** single level of simple meaning (single theme)
	Structure conventional story structure
	Language Conventionality and Clarity some figurative language
	Knowledge Demands common everyday experience
Reader/Task Considerations	Teacher determined

Prepare for a Dramatic Reading

TEACH

Use these ideas to help students prepare for the Performance Task.

Give an expressive reading of the last two paragraphs of the folk tale. Then point out that the narrator is also the storyteller, reminding listeners that this folk tale comes from the oral tradition. Help students to prepare their dramatic reading by imagining themselves as a storyteller addressing listeners sitting "close before the fire in the free land."

 Annotate it!

Together, choose one segment to analyze for an oral reading using the eBook Annotation tools.

- Have students read the segment softly to themselves while listening for the storyteller's voice.
- Together, decide on the words to emphasize, and underline them.
- Decide on the places to pause. Highlight with yellow for a short pause. Highlight with green for a longer pause.
- Add notes about the emotion to express with one's voice and face, along with any gestures to make.

For example

> or black shadows. It didn't matter, they went so high. Way above the plantation, way over the slavery land. Say they flew away to Free-dom.

PRACTICE AND APPLY

Choose another segment for students to review and annotate independently. Then invite volunteers to read aloud. Emphasize the need for multiple rehearsals for an oral performance. Repeated practice enables readers to focus on expression and also gives them confidence.

 INTERACTIVE WHITEBOARD LESSON Have students complete the tutorials in this lesson: **Giving a Presentation**.

Analyze Story Elements: Folk Tale

RETEACH

Review common features of a **folk tale** by listing each of these terms and connecting it to "The People Could Fly."

- *oral tradition* (stories passed down by speaking, not writing)
- *supernatural abilities* (abilities that no person could have)
- *supernatural events* (things that can't happen in real life)
- *life lesson* (what is important and valuable)
- *culture of origin* (the group that first told the tale)

Offer each of the following folk tale descriptions, and have students identify the common features of folk tales in each one:

- In Native American tales, Coyote is a trickster character who tries to trick people but is often tricked himself.
- Two hundred years ago, children in Italy listened to stories about a girl whose father was a wolf.
- In a folk tale from Japan, the gentleness of a servant girl so impresses a rich farmer's son that she becomes his bride.

INDEPENDENT READING

Guide students to another folk tale, and have them read it independently. Ask: *How can you tell this is a folk tale? What features does it share with the folk tale "The People Could Fly"?* Have pairs of students work together to compare and contrast the features in each tale using a Comparison-Contrast Chart. Then have students use their completed charts to discuss the two folk tales and what each one reveals about its culture of origin.

INTERACTIVE GRAPHIC ORGANIZER Have students use this Interactive Graphic Organizer: **Comparison-Contrast Chart.**

English Language Support

Compare and Contrast Help students make comparisons and contrasts between "The People Could Fly" and another folk tale they have read.

- **First,** have pairs list the basic story elements as points of comparison in their charts: Setting, Plot, Characters.
- **Next,** ask them to add a fourth category, "Other Features," under which they will list items such as theme or message, use of dialect, and cultural values.
- **Finally,** have pairs consider how each item they listed for "The People Could Fly" is similar to or different from the item listed for the other folk tale.

Critical Vocabulary L 4d

Answers:

1. *The word* croon *goes with* song, *because when you croon a song, you sing it softly.*

2. *The word* plantation *goes with* farm, *because a plantation is a big farm, particularly one in the South of the United States.*

3. *The word* snag *goes with* thorn, *because a thorn is sharp and could snag—catch or tear—something, like skin or clothing.*

4. *The word* shuffle *goes with* feet, *because shuffling is taking little steps without lifting your feet.*

Vocabulary Strategy: Latin Suffixes L 4b

1. *misery*

2. *transportation*

3. *posture*

4. *defiance*

5. *creative*

Assess It Online!

Online Selection Test
- Download an editable ExamView bank.
- Assign and manage this test online.

Critical Vocabulary L 4b, L 4d

| croon | snag | shuffle | plantation |

Practice and Apply Identify the vocabulary word that is tied in meaning to the italicized word in each question. Provide reasons for your choices.

1. Which word goes with *song*? Why?

2. Which word goes with *farm*? Why?

3. Which word goes with *thorn*? Why?

4. Which word goes with *feet*? Why?

Vocabulary Strategy: Latin Suffixes

A **suffix** is a word part added to the end of a root or base word to form a new word. Readers can use their knowledge of suffixes to analyze words and find familiar parts to determine the meaning of a word. Many suffixes in English words come from Latin. Look at the meanings of the suffixes in the chart.

Suffix	Example Words
-ure	exposure, lecture
-ery/-ary	nursery, military
-ence/-ance	violence, reliance
-ive/-ative	selective, talkative
-ion/-ation	tension, imagination

For example, notice the word with a Latin suffix in this sentence from "The People Could Fly."

> His gaze fell on the plantation where the slaves who could not fly waited.

You can see that *plantation* is made of the base word *plant* and the suffix *-ation*. The meaning of *plantation* is "a farm where crops are planted."

Practice and Apply Choose a suffix from the chart to complete each word. Use a print or online dictionary to find the meanings of unfamiliar words and to confirm your answers.

1. To be enslaved is to live in **mis**_____.

2. Human flight is an unusual form of **transport**_____.

3. The people stood up and straightened their **post**_____.

4. When confronting evil, story characters show **defi**_____.

5. The solutions in folk tales may be magical and **creat**_____.

Strategies for Annotation 🖉 📄 *Annotate it!*

Latin Suffixes L 4b

Give students practice identifying words with the Latin suffixes in a passage from the story, such as lines 6–12. Encourage them to use their eBook annotation tools to

- Highlight the suffix in yellow
- Underline the part of the word before the suffix
- Note whether the suffix is attached to a base word or a word root
- Give a meaning for the word, using the suffix as a clue

The folks were full of misery, then. Got sick with the up and down of the sea. So they forgot about flyin' when they could no longer breathe the sweet scent of Africa.

Analyzing the Text

RL 2, RL 3, RL 4,
RL 10, SL 6

Cite Text Evidence Support your responses with evidence from the text.

1. **Interpret** Folk tales often feature lessons that are important to a culture or group of people. What is the lesson of this folk tale? How would enslaved Africans have perceived the lesson as being important?

2. **Summarize** Early in the folk tale, the narrator says, "The folks were full of misery, then." Review the first half of the tale to find details about the conditions under which the slaves lived. Then in your own words, describe these conditions.

3. **Summarize** Fill out a story map for "The People Could Fly." Use your completed map to summarize the plot of the folk tale. Compare your summary with that of a classmate.

4. **Analyze** Reread lines 1–10 to identify examples of dialect. What effect does the use of dialect achieve at the beginning of the story?

5. **Analyze** Reread lines 23–30. What is the Master compared to? What is the whip compared to? Why might the author have included these figurative comparisons?

6. **Analyze Theme** Reread lines 98–105. What theme is expressed in this paragraph?

PERFORMANCE TASK

Speaking Activity: Dramatic Reading With a small group, do a dramatic reading of "The People Could Fly," using the text of the folk tale as a script. Follow these tips for preparing and performing:

- Rehearse the reading several times.
- Make sure your voices fit the personalities of the characters you portray.
- Deliver lines with the appropriate emotion.
- Keep in mind how the tale begins somberly but builds in intensity.

Analyzing the Text

RL 2, RL 3,
RL 4, RL 10

Possible answers:

1. *The lesson is that even in the worst of circumstances, people have the power within themselves to hold onto hope and the promise of freedom. This lesson would have been critical for enslaved people as they dreamed about rising above their hardships.*

2. *Slaves suffered with sickness on the ships to America. At the plantations, they did back-breaking work all day. Cruel men watched them, and the Driver whipped them when they slowed down, even while some carried hungry infants.*

3. *Story Map: **Title and Genre:** "The People Could Fly," African American folk tale. **Setting:** plantation during slavery era. **Characters:** Toby; Sarah; the Overseer; Driver. **Conflict:** Overseer and Driver treat slaves with brutality. **Main Events:** (1) African slaves lose their memory of flying. (2) Sarah hoes with the crying baby on her back. (3) The Driver whips the baby and Sarah. (4) Toby enables Sarah and the baby to fly away. (5) Toby helps more slaves to find their power of flight. **Outcome/Resolution:** Toby and the people who can fly escape to freedom. The slaves who remain tell the story of what they saw. **Sample Plot Summary:** Some of the slaves have a secret power inherited from their African ancestors, the ability to fly. After the slave driver whips a young mother, named Sarah, and her baby, she reaches her breaking point. An old man named Toby recites magic words that enable Sarah to fly away with her baby. Toby helps other slaves fly away, telling those who remain they must find their own way to freedom.*

4. *Examples of dialect:* Say that; climbin', flappin'; Too crowded, don't you know. *Use of dialect establishes the narrator's voice as a storyteller from the times of slavery.*

5. *The Master was a "hard lump of clay. A hard glinty coal. A hard rock pile." The whip was "a slice-open cut of pain." These comparisons are vivid, helping the reader experience the unfeeling, immovable Master and the hurtful whip.*

6. *The theme is soaring hope leading to freedom.*

Assign this
performance task.

PERFORMANCE TASK

RL 10,
SL 6

Speaking Activity: Dramatic Reading Here are three ideas for assigning parts:

- Students may divide the text into parts, one student reading each part.
- Several students may divide the narration, and one student may read the dialogue spoken by the different characters.
- Partners may share a segment, devising a method for giving a lively reading.

English Language Support

Form six small groups to answer the questions. Assign one question to each group. When all groups have finished, let them take turns presenting their answers to the class. Encourage the class to provide useful feedback.

Strategies for CLOSE READING

Summarize Text

Students should read this short story carefully all the way through. Close-reading questions at the bottom of the page will help them focus on the theme and on how particular elements of the story interact and will help them write an objective summary of the text after they have read it. As they read, students should record comments or questions about the text in the side margins.

WHEN STUDENTS STRUGGLE . . .

To help students write an objective summary of the story, have them work in a small group to fill out a story map such as the one shown below.

CITE TEXT EVIDENCE For practice in writing an objective summary, free of their opinions, ask students to trace the development of the theme over the course of the text and to analyze how the story elements interact.

> **Setting:** *A cold region of the United States in winter*

> **Major Characters:** *Heartbeat (Dave)*
> **Minor Characters:** *Sarah, Heartbeat's parents*

> **Plot/Problem:** *A skinny 16-year-old boy nicknamed "Heartbeat" decides to wear several layers of clothing to appear bigger and stronger in order to impress a girl.*

> **Event 1:** *Heartbeat tries everything to look bigger and stronger, but nothing works.*

> **Event 2:** *He begins to wear extra layers of clothing to look bigger. The kids stop calling him Heartbeat.*

> **Event 3:** *At a party he is so hot that he sheds his extra layers of clothing, but he leaves them behind by mistake.*

> **Outcome:** *After he sheds his clothes at the party, Heartbeat realizes that in the spring, he will have to stop wearing so many layers, so he might as well just be himself now.*

Background *Born in 1974,* **David Yoo** *has often felt like an outsider. While attending an international school in Korea, he was the only Korean American student among German and Saudi Arabian classmates. When his family moved to Connecticut, he again encountered few Asian peers. He published his first book,* Girls for Breakfast, *when he was twenty-nine. The book is a humorous account of a Korean-American teenage hero's efforts to fit in at a suburban American high school.*

Heartbeat

Short Story by David Yoo

CLOSE READ
Notes

1. **READ ▶** As you read lines 1–36, begin to collect and cite text evidence.
   - Underline adjectives that describe Heartbeat.
   - In the margin, summarize how Heartbeat tries to gain weight.
   - Circle text that reveals how Heartbeat feels when he tries to gain weight.

My nickname's "Heartbeat," because my friends swear that you can actually see the pulse on my bare chest. I've always been skinny. Everyone assumes I'm a weakling because I'm so thin (I prefer "lean and mean" or "wiry"), despite being a three-sport athlete. I decided to do something about it this fall when Sarah, the girl I have a crush on, said, "Oh my gosh . . . you are so skinny." She was visibly repulsed by my sunken chest as I stepped off the soccer bus after practice. I silently vowed to do everything within my power to become the "after" picture. I was sixteen years old, but looked like I was eleven.

10 For the rest of fall, I did countless push-ups and curled free weights until I couldn't bend my arms. I got ridiculously strong and defined, but I wasn't gaining weight. I wanted to be *thicker*. I didn't care about getting stronger if nobody could tell. I did research, and started lifting heavier weights at lower reps and supplemented my meals with weight-gainer shakes, egg whites, boiled yams, and tubs of

Heartbeat works out, eats a huge amount, and moves less.

25

---

1. **READ AND CITE TEXT EVIDENCE** Explain that as they read, students may want to note the most important idea on the page to include in a summary of Heartbeat's efforts to gain weight. Remind students that a brief objective summary answers the questions: *Who? When and Where?* and *What happens?*

Ⓐ ASK STUDENTS to read their margin notes to a partner and then write one response that objectively summarizes what Heartbeat does to try to gain weight, citing specific textual evidence from lines 11–22.

FOR ELL STUDENTS Clarify for your ELL students that *skinny* (lines 3 and 6) and *lean* (line 4) are adjectives that describe someone who is thin. Explain that these words have a similar meaning and are called synonyms.

ASK STUDENTS to look for other synonyms of *skinny* in the text and cite them in the margin.

cottage cheese. I forced myself to swallow the daily caloric intake equivalent of three overweight men and still wasn't able to increase my mass. (I have a ridiculously fast metabolism.) Over Christmas

20 break I cut out all useless movement, like Ping-Pong and staircases, because I'm like a sieve—the 83 calories in a mini-Snickers bar is **moot** because I waste 90 chewing it.

moot:
of little or no value

B   I returned to school in January (depressed) because I was still Heartbeat in everyone's eyes. I constantly weighed myself. At least once an hour, no matter where I was, I'd find a bathroom so I could take off my shirt and flex in the mirror for a couple of minutes. I was so (frustrated) that nothing was working—but the frustration didn't last. I was sitting in study hall two weeks ago when Sarah said the magic words: "Have you been working out, (Dave?) You look bigger." I

30 couldn't tell if she was being **sarcastic**. I went home and inspected myself in the mirror. I did look bigger!

sarcastic:
bitter and mocking

futile:
serving no useful purpose

     But then I realized the reason: I'd accidentally worn *two* T-shirts under my rugby shirt that day. It was just an illusion. I was **futilely** stuffing my face and religiously pumping iron and failing to alter my appearance, and now I'd stumbled on the simplest solution to looking bigger. I felt like I was reborn.

     I went to school the next day wearing <u>two</u> T-shirts under my turtleneck. I felt solid. By the end of last week, I was wearing <u>three</u>

<u>T-shirts</u> under my rugby shirt. This Monday I tucked <u>four T-shirts</u>

40 under my plaid button-down. It gave me traps that didn't exist. My

C
Q-tip-sized shoulders transformed into NBA-grapefruit deltoids.[1] I

D
could tell my classmates subtly regarded me differently. It was respect. Sarah gave me a look I'd never seen before, as if she felt . . . *safer around me.* I was walking down the hallway at the end of the day and must have twisted awkwardly because suddenly my zipper literally exploded, and all my T-shirts spilled out of my pants. Luckily, the hallway was empty and I was wearing a belt.

     I realized I had artificially outgrown my clothes. My button-downs were so tight that a few seconds after jamming the extra layers

50 into my pants, the pressure would suddenly bunch the cloth up in random places so it looked like I had a goiter[2] on my shoulder or something. I complained to my parents over dinner last night. "I don't fit into anything anymore," I said. "It reflects poorly on you guys. You could get arrested."

     "What are you talking about? You look the same as always. You're still my little boy," my dad replied, putting me in a headlock and giving me a noogie. I glared at him.

     "I need a new ski jacket," I said. It was true. I could barely clap my hands with all the layers I was wearing. I was getting out of control at

60 this point. The <u>four T-shirts</u> under my wool sweater were smushing my lungs together like a male girdle. It was a small price to pay; nobody called me Heartbeat anymore, I reminded myself.

     After dinner I went to a party. Even though it was winter, I opted to hang out on the back porch as much as possible because it was so

---

2.   **◄ REREAD**   Reread lines 23–31. Circle the narrator's real name. How does he think his classmates perceive him? Support your answer with explicit textual evidence.

Heartbeat says that everyone thinks he's a weakling. He says Sarah is "visibly repulsed" by his body. He can't tell if Sarah is being sarcastic when she says he looks bigger.

3.   **READ ►**   As you read lines 37–75, continue to cite textual evidence.

• Underline the number of T-shirts Heartbeat wears.
• Circle Heartbeat's interpretation of the way his classmates feel when they see him wearing extra layers.

26

---

[1] **traps...deltoids:** traps (short for trapezius) are large, flat upper-back muscles; deltoids are triangular muscles that connect the top of the shoulder to the arm.
[2] **goiter:** swollen thyroid gland often visible at the bottom of the neck.

27

---

2.   **REREAD AND CITE TEXT EVIDENCE**

B   **ASK STUDENTS** to infer what Heartbeat means when he thinks: "I was still Heartbeat in everyone's eyes." What does it suggest about how he thinks his classmates view him? *He thinks they still perceive him as being a scrawny weakling. Even Sarah may be using sarcasm when she says he looks bigger. Students should support their answer with evidence from lines 23–31.*

3.   **READ AND CITE TEXT EVIDENCE**

C   **ASK STUDENTS** to evaluate whether Heartbeat's interpretation of his classmates' new perception of him is accurate. *Students should recognize that he thinks that his classmates are viewing him with a newfound respect, citing evidence from lines 41–44.*

Critical Vocabulary: moot (line 22), **sarcastic** (line 30), and **futile** (line 33) Ask students to share their definitions of these words and use them in a summary of lines 19–36.

WHEN STUDENTS STRUGGLE . . .

To help students understand how particular elements of a story interact, guide them to reread lines 37–75 to recognize how the specific setting (the party) influences the main character (Heartbeat) and the events of the plot (what happens as a result of his wearing extra layers to the party). Have students work in a small group to discuss how this section highlights the interaction of story elements.

FOR ELL STUDENTS Direct ELL students to reread lines 37–75. Ask them to point out the clothing vocabulary: *T-shirts* (line 37), *turtleneck* (line 38), *rugby shirt* (line 39), *button-down* (line 40), *zipper* (line 45), *pants* (line 46), *belt* (line 47), *layers* (line 49), *ski jacket* (line 58), *girdle* (61), *long-sleeves* (line 70), *wool sweater, sweatpants* (line 71), and *tube socks* (lines 71–72).

ASK STUDENTS to define these words related to clothing. If students have difficulty, ask them to point to the articles of clothing on students who are wearing them or to draw pictures of the items.

hot inside. Being indoors was like a sauna, but Sarah was in the basement so I headed that way. We were talking and she noticed that I was dripping with perspiration. "You're trembling," she said, touching my shoulder. She thought I was nervous talking to her and probably thought it was cute, but in reality I was on the verge of passing out
70 because I was wearing four tight T-shirts and two long-sleeves under my wool sweater, not to mention the sweatpants tucked into my tube socks to add heft to my (formerly chicken-legs) quads. She squeezed my biceps.[3]

"Jeez, Dave, how many layers are you wearing?"

I couldn't even feel her squeezing them.

"I have to go," I said, excusing myself to another corner of the basement. Everyone was smushed together. It was so hot everyone except me was hanging out in T-shirts and tank tops. I was sopping and delirious and felt **claustrophobic**. My chest was cold because I
80 had four drenched T-shirts underneath my sweater. It looked like I was breaking out with Ebola[4] or something. When I coughed people turned away from me in fear. *Abandon ship, abandon ship!* I had no choice but to take some layers off. I lurched to the bathroom. My arms were ponderously heavy as I pulled off the sweater. Just lifting my arms exhausted me, and I had to stop midway and take a rest by sitting on the edge of the tub, gasping. I slowly peeled off the layers, one at a time. I took off my pants and peeled off my sweatpants, too, down to my undies. I dried myself off with a wash cloth. My red T-shirt had bled onto the three white Ts because of the sweat, so they
90 now were faded pink tie-dyes. I hoisted the bundle of clothes and was

[3] **quads...biceps:** quads (short for quadriceps) are long muscles in the front of the thigh; biceps are the large muscles in the front of the upper arm.
[4] **Ebola:** deadly virus that causes high fever and bleeding.

claustrophobic:
*uncomfortable
in closed
spaces*

4. **◄ REREAD AND DISCUSS** Reread lines 37–44. Dave says, "my classmates subtly regarded me differently. It was with respect." With a small group, discuss whether Dave's assessment of his classmates' response is reality-based or a product of his imagination.

5. **READ ▶** As you read lines 76–113, continue to cite textual evidence.
   • Underline adjectives Heartbeat uses to describe himself.
   • In the margin, summarize how Heartbeat feels when he sheds his layers at the party.

"I was sopping and delirious and felt claustrophobic.

*Heartbeat
feels happy
and free when
he takes off
his layers.*

*He wants
Sarah to like
him as he is.
He could not
wear all the
layers in the
spring.*

shocked at the weight. I jammed them into the closet. I'd retrieve them later, before I left. I put my sweater back on without anything underneath. After two weeks of constricting my air supply and range of motion by wearing upwards of six layers, I was amazed at how much freedom I had with my arms. I felt like dancing for the first time in my life. I suddenly realized what I really looked like at this party: a padded, miserable, and frustrated puffball, burning up in all my layers. All this because I hated my nickname?

I got home and realized I'd left my bundle of wet clothes back at
100 the party. I took this as a sign. My days of wearing extra layers was officially over. Had Sarah fallen for the padded me, she'd be falling for someone else. Besides, winter wasn't going to last forever, and I couldn't just revert back to wearing just one set of clothes like a normal human being come spring. The change in my outward appearance would be the equivalent of a sheared sheep. From now on, I was going to just be me.

That was last night. *I'm not disgustingly thin,* I constantly remind myself. I am wiry. I'm lean and mean.

4.

REREAD AND DISCUSS USING TEXT EVIDENCE

D ASK STUDENTS to appoint a reporter for each group to cite specific textual evidence and line numbers to support their position about Dave's (Heartbeat's) interpretation of his classmates' "subtle" change in attitude toward him. *Students should cite evidence from lines 37–44 to support their opinion.*

5.

READ AND CITE TEXT EVIDENCE

E ASK STUDENTS to read their margin notes to a partner and write one response that best summarizes the causes for Dave's shedding of his layers at the party and the effects, or results, of his actions. *Students should cite evidence from lines 77–83, 93–98, and 99–106.*

Critical Vocabulary: claustrophobic (line 79) Have students define *claustrophobic* in context. Why does the author use the word to describe why Dave sheds his layers? *Yoo may be creating an image to suggest that Dave is shedding his skin.*

FOR ELL STUDENTS Explain that *winter* (line 102) and *spring* (line 104) signify two of the four seasons of the year and that *night* (line 107) represents a time of day. Ask students to define these words, either through words or pictures. Then review the days of the week and the months of the year using a print or an online calendar as a prop. Write each day and month on the board, saying each one and having students repeat.

ASK STUDENTS to look through the text for other words that name the seasons, the times of the day, the months of the year, and holidays, citing each word in the margin.

110   Outside it's snowing again. There's a party tonight, and my friends are on their way to pick me up. I don't know what to wear, so I lay out four different outfits on the floor as if they're chalk outlines of people. A car horn honks ten minutes later and I still haven't decided on an outfit. Maybe I'll just wear all of them.

6. ◀ **REREAD**   As you reread lines 76–113, make notes in the margin about why Heartbeat decides he is done wearing extra layers. Then reread the story's final line. Do you think Heartbeat's essential personality has changed? Support your answer with explicit textual evidence.

He uses the same kind of humor and is making fun of himself, as he has throughout the story.

SHORT RESPONSE

Cite Text Evidence   Write a brief summary of the plot of "Heartbeat." Review your reading notes, and use your own words to answer *who? when and where?* and *what happens?* **Cite text evidence** to support your response.

Heartbeat is a sixteen-year-old boy who hates his nickname. He says his classmates assume he's a weakling, and Sarah is repulsed by how skinny he is. After he tries to put on weight by eating a lot and lifting weights, he wears more layers of clothing—gradually realizing that it is a ridiculous solution. He thinks his body looks strange, and he is uncomfortable all of the time. When he sheds his extra layers, he is relieved. He understands he was silly to try to change because of a nickname, and he wants people to like him the way he is.

30

6.   REREAD AND CITE TEXT EVIDENCE

F   **ASK STUDENTS**   to read their margin notes to a partner or a small group and then create one response that best states why Dave (Heartbeat) decides to stop wearing layers. *Students should cite specific textual evidence from lines 93–106.* Have students evaluate the meaning and effectiveness of the last line of the story, citing evidence and line numbers to support their position about whether or not Dave has really changed.

SHORT RESPONSE

Cite Text Evidence   Student responses will vary, but students should cite evidence from the text in order to write an objective summary of the story. Students should:

• explain the theme or central idea of the story.

• cite evidence to show the interaction of story elements.

• answer these questions in their summary: *Who? When and where?* and *What happens?*

TO CHALLENGE STUDENTS . . .

For more context about health and fitness, encourage students to conduct print, online, or multimedia research to write a "how-to" guide to fitness, including information and graphics about diet and exercise.

ASK STUDENTS to work with a small group to do some preliminary research to find an aspect of the topic that interests them. Possible topics for their "how-to" fitness guide might include:

• How to build total fitness

• How to use strength training to build lean muscle tissue

• How to use exercise and nutrition to burn calories

• How to build power, strength, and stamina

• How to use health-and-fitness equipment, step by step

After students have chosen a topic, discuss these guidelines for writing a "how-to" guide, reminding students that the purpose of such a guide is to tell the audience how to do something.

GUIDELINES FOR "HOW-TO" WRITING

• Explain your information clearly.

• Present step-by-step instructions in a logical way.

• Give directions that are easy to follow.

• Use time-order or spatial words to help your reader complete the steps of the process.

• Include graphics to help you explain.

Students might also wish to view one of the hundreds of videos about fitness, strength training, and nutrition.

ASK STUDENTS what they hope to discover as they research their "how-to" fitness guide. How is the information they find similar to, yet different from, the facts and information about nutrition and fitness shared by Yoo in his story?

DIG DEEPER

With the class, return to Question 4, Reread and Discuss. Have students share the results of their discussion.

ASK STUDENTS whether they were pleased with the outcome of their small-group discussions. Have each group share its majority opinion. How did most of the group members react to Dave's (Heartbeat's) interpretation of his classmates' newfound respect for him? Is this newfound respect Dave perceives based on reality, or is it a figment of Dave's imagination? What compelling evidence did the groups cite from the text to support their opinion, or point of view?

- Encourage groups to tell whether there was any convincing evidence cited by group members who held a different opinion from most of the group. If so, why didn't this opinion sway the group?

- Have groups explain how they decided whether or not they had found sufficient textual evidence to support their opinion. Did everyone in the group agree as to what made the evidence sufficient? How did the group resolve any conflicts or disagreements? What conflict-resolution techniques did the group use to resolve any differences?

- After students have shared the results of their group discussion, ask whether another group shared any ideas or findings they wish they had brought to the table. Did the group's findings convince them that the opposite view was reasonable and had merit? Did it change their opinion? Why or why not?

ASK STUDENTS to return to their Short Response answer and to revise it based on the class discussion. What important details or evidence can they add to their summary? What unnecessary details can they delete?

CLOSE READING NOTES

EXEMPLAR

The Song of Wandering Aengus

Sonnet 43

Poem by William Butler Yeats

Poem by William Shakespeare

Why These Texts?

The form of a poem is integral to its meaning. Understanding a poem's form deepens a reader's experience of a poem. This lesson focuses on figurative language and sound devices in poems and how they affect meaning in a poem.

▶ **View It!**

Professional Development Podcast:

Text-Dependent Analysis

Key Learning Objective: The student will learn how to analyze a poem's form, as well as the use of figurative language and sound devices, to understand their effects on meaning.

RL 1 Cite evidence to support analysis.
RL 2 Determine theme.
RL 4 Analyze the impact of rhymes and other repetitions of sounds on a specific verse or stanza of a poem.
RL 5 Analyze how a poem's form contributes to its meaning.
SL 1 Engage in a collaborative discussion.
SL 4 Present claims and findings; use appropriate eye contact, adequate volume, and clear pronunciation.
SL 6 Adapt speech.

 Text Complexity Rubric

Quantitative Measures	The Song of Wandering Aengus Lexile: N/A	Sonnet 43 Lexile: N/A
Qualitative Measures	Levels of Meaning/Purpose multiple levels of meaning (multiple themes)	Levels of Meaning/Purpose multiple levels of complex meanings
	Structure regular stanzas, predictable rhyme scheme	Structure regular stanzas, predictable rhyme scheme
	Language Conventionality and Clarity figurative, symbolic language	Language Conventionality and Clarity archaic, unfamiliar language
	Knowledge Demands distinctly unfamiliar situation	Knowledge Demands complex or sophisticated theme; multiple themes
Reader/Task Considerations	• Teacher determined • Vary by individual reader and type of text • See the Text X-Ray for suggested Reader/Task Considerations.	

Meaning Making

Language Development

Effective Expression

Content Knowledge

Foundational Skills

TEXT X-RAY

English Language Support Before teaching, use the Text X-Ray for an overview of the text's complexity. The Text X-Ray and the supports and scaffolds in the Teacher's Edition will help you guide students of different skill levels.

Text Complexity: Qualitative Measures

▲ Levels of Meaning/Purpose

Help students analyze diction.

- Teacher's Edition side notes, pp. 72, 73
- Strategies for Annotation, p. 73

***ZOOM IN ON* ANALYZING RHYME** Explain that in poetry, **diction,** the careful choice of words, often includes the element of rhyme. Remind students that **rhyme** is the repetition of sounds at the ends of words. The placement of rhyming words in a poem can create a rhythm, or musical quality. **End rhyme** is the placement of rhyming words at the ends of lines.

Read aloud "The Song of Wandering Aengus," and model for students how to identify the rhyming lines in each stanza:

- Stanza 1 *(lines 2 and 4; 6 and 8)*
- Stanza 2 *(lines 10 and 12; 14 and 16)*
- Stanza 3 *(lines 18 and 20; 22 and 24)*

Have students reread the poem aloud with a partner and discuss the feeling or mood that the rhythm creates.

▲ Structure

Help students analyze the structure of the sonnet.

- Teacher's Edition side notes, pp. 74, 75
- When Students Struggle, p. 74
- Strategies for Annotation, p. 75

To teach poetic form, see

- Analyze Form, p. 76a

▶ ***Use It!*** **Interactive Whiteboard Lesson:** Form in Poetry

***ZOOM IN ON* ANALYZING A SHAKESPEAREAN SONNET** Remind students that some poems follow a set **form,** or pattern of arranging words and lines. Explain that a Shakespearean **sonnet** develops a single message in 14 lines, which are divided into three sets of 4 lines, followed by a final pair of lines, or **couplet.** It follows a set pattern of end rhyme.

- Read aloud "Sonnet 43." Then work with students to help them identify the four parts of the sonnet.
- Help students use their own words to restate the idea or message the poet conveys in each part of the poem.

Language Conventionality and Clarity

Teach unfamiliar academic vocabulary in context.

- Teacher's Edition side notes, pp. 72, 74, 76
- English Language Support, p. 71
- Applying Academic Vocabulary, p. 72
- Performance Task, p. 76

Guide students to analyze the language of the sonnet.

- When Students Struggle, p. 74

Reteach Figurative Language.

- Determine Meanings, p. 76a

 Use It! **Level Up Tutorial:** Figurative Language
Interactive Graphic Organizer: Venn Diagram

ZOOM IN ON **ANALYZING LITERARY LANGUAGE** Explain that poets use literary devices to create special effects and emphasize their messages. Tell students that literary language often uses descriptions and comparisons that appeal to the senses. Have students focus on and identify the sensory appeal of the **figurative language** in "The Song of Wandering Aengus."

- Line 2: "a fire was in my head" *(tactile)*
- Line 6: "moth-like stars" *(visual)*

Explain that forming a mental picture of the images a poet presents can help readers better understand the poet's message.

 ## Knowledge Demands

Help students understand the cultural and literary background of the poems.

- Teacher's Edition Background note, p. 71

ZOOM IN ON **BUILDING BACKGROUND** After students read the biographies on page 71, tell them that knowing about the cultural and historical background of the poet can add layers of meaning to a poem's message.

- Explain that many images and details in Yeats's poetry relate to Irish folklore, the oral tradition of Ireland. For example, Irish folklore connects the hazel tree with wisdom, inspiration, and magic. The transformation of a sea creature into a beautiful woman also commonly occurs in Celtic folklore.
- Remind students that each poem may express meaning that goes beyond pining for a lost love.

 ## Suggested Reader/Task Considerations

Consider the following before assigning these poems to students:

- Do students have adequate experience with the syntax and diction of the poems to understand them?
- Will students be interested in the content of the poems?

ZOOM IN ON **SUPPORTING COMPREHENSION**

- Have students read aloud in mixed-ability groups, pausing after each line to paraphrase it. Let groups record the text and their paraphrase in a two-column chart. Then, as a class, discuss the meaning of each sentence.
- To motivate students, explain that much of Yeats's work was inspired by his hopeless love for Maud Gonne, an Irish revolutionary and actress. Let pairs read "The Song of Wandering Aengus" to find clues about its inspiration. Then ask them to make guesses about the possible inspiration for "Sonnet 43."

TEACH

CLOSE READ

Background Have students read the background and information about the poets. Explain that many poems are inspired by the experience of love and loss. Like the myth of Aengus, Yeats's poem "The Song of Wandering Aengus" tells of a man in search of a loved one in hopes of spending the rest of his life in happiness with her. Shakespeare's "Sonnet 43" also highlights these themes, describing the speaker's own emotional state as he longs for an absent loved one. It is a part of a series of sonnets by Shakespeare that are all connected by these same themes.

SETTING A PURPOSE Direct students to use the Setting a Purpose question to focus their reading. Remind them to write down questions as they read.

Background *"The Song of Wandering Aengus" was inspired by Aengus, the Irish god of love and inspiration. In the original myth, Aengus falls in love with a girl he has dreamed about, but when he is unable to find her, he becomes ill. His parents go searching for her, and after three years the couple is finally united.*

The Song of Wandering Aengus
Poem by W. B. Yeats

Sonnet 43
Poem by William Shakespeare

William Butler Yeats (1865–1934) *was an Irish poet and playwright, and one of the most notable literary figures of the 20th century. As a boy, Yeats lived in a rural region in Ireland called Sligo. There he enjoyed local stories about Irish heroes, heroines, and magical creatures. In Yeats's later life as a poet and playwright, the region and its folklore inspired his poetry and drama. "The Song of Wandering Aengus" is an example of this inspiration.*

William Shakespeare (1564–1616) *was an English playwright, poet, and actor. While Shakespeare is widely regarded as the greatest playwright in the English language, he was also just as influential as a poet. He began writing poetry when theaters shut down during an outbreak of the plague in London. Adapting and refining the sonnet form, he produced 154 of his own sonnets. Now the Shakespearean sonnet is itself a unique poetic form.*

SETTING A PURPOSE As you read, think about what each poem has to say about the absence of a loved one. How does each poem convey a sense of loss and longing?

English Language Support

Analyze Language Define **idiom** as a phrase with a meaning different from the meaning of its individual words. Display the idiom *once in a blue moon*, noting that it means "rarely," though the moon is never really blue. Context clues can clarify idioms, but students may need to look them up.

- Display lines 1–4, and read them aloud. Discuss the phrase *a fire was in my head*. Ask how a fire feels. (*hot, burning*) Ask what a person might be feeling if he had a fire in his head. (*uncomfortable, emotional, excited*) Ask how this feeling might fit the poem.

- Discuss the image that *a fire was in my head* suggests. Then have pairs discuss the idiom by completing this sentence frame: If a person had a fire in his head, he would probably be feeling ___.

- Ask small groups of students to discuss the image created by the idiom. Have them decide how the image helps the reader understand how the speaker feels and what he does in lines 3–4.

Determine the Impact of Rhyme (LINES 1–16)

RL 1, RL 4, RL 5

Explain to students that poets play with **diction,** or word choice, as they write. They choose words not only for their meaning, but also for their sound. Explain that one example of this is a poet's use of **rhyme,** the repetition of sounds at the end of words. Rhyme can help emphasize ideas and create a musical quality. The most common type of rhyme in a poem is **end rhyme,** in which rhyming words come at the end of lines.

A **CITE TEXT EVIDENCE** Have students reread lines 1–16 aloud. Ask students to identify examples of rhyme and explain its effect on the poem. *(Possible answers:* head/thread, out/trout, aflame/name, hair/ air *are end rhymes. The rhyming words create rhythm and help give the poem a rhythm of a folk song, which adds a mystical feel.)*

Determine Meanings

RL 4, RL 5

(LINES 17–24)

Explain to students that poets often use figurative language to compare things, emphasize ideas, or give an emotional effect. **Figurative language** uses statements that are not literally true to express the writer's ideas. Yeats uses the following types of figurative language in this poem.

- A **simile** is a comparison between two unlike things using the word *like* or *as.*
- A **metaphor** is a comparison of two unlike things without the word *like* or *as.*

B **ASK STUDENTS** to reread lines 17–24. Have them tell what the poet means by the metaphors "silver apples of the moon" and "golden apples of the sun." *(night and day)* Then have them explain the meaning of lines 17–24. *(When Aengus finds his love, they will be together until the end of time.)*

The Song of Wandering Aengus
by W. B. Yeats

A

I went out to the hazel wood,
Because a fire was in my head,
And cut and peeled a hazel wand,
And hooked a berry to a thread;
5   And when white moths were on the wing,
And moth-like stars were flickering out,
I dropped the berry in a stream
And caught a little silver trout.

When I had laid it on the floor
10   I went to blow the fire aflame,
But something rustled on the floor,
And someone called me by my name:
It had become a glimmering girl
With apple blossom in her hair
15   Who called me by my name and ran
And faded through the brightening air.

B

Though I am old with wandering
Through hollow lands and hilly lands,
I will find out where she has gone,
20   And kiss her lips and take her hands;
And walk among long dappled[1] grass,
And pluck till time and times are done,
The silver apples of the moon,
The golden apples of the sun.

---

[1] **dappled:** marked with many spotted colors or light.

(r) ©Bubica/Shutterstock

APPLYING ACADEMIC VOCABULARY

focus	perceive

THINK-PAIR-SHARE Define the word *focus* as "direct attention toward a specific point or purpose." Define the word *perceive* as "to be aware of something through the senses." Have pairs discuss the questions below, including the words *focus* and *perceive* in their responses. Allow volunteers to share responses with the class.

- How does the **focus** of the poem shift at different points?
- How does the speaker, or person who "talks" to the reader, **perceive** life with and without love?

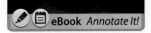

Determine the Impact of Rhyme

RL 4, RL 5

A poem is a combination of sound and meaning. Poets choose their words carefully, since word choice, or **diction,** affects a poem's meaning and the way it sounds. **Rhyme** is the repetition of sounds at the end of words, as in *more* and *roar*. Words rhyme when their accented vowels and the letters that follow have identical or similar sounds.

Poets use rhyme for a number of purposes:

to make a poem songlike or playful

to emphasize sounds that suggest feelings

to create rhythms that help convey sensory feelings, such as a sense of motion

End rhyme refers to words that rhyme at the ends of lines of poetry. For example, the second and fourth lines from "The Song of Wandering Aengus" contain end rhymes:

> I went out to the hazel wood,
> Because a fire was in my head,
> And cut and peeled a hazel wand,
> And hooked a berry to a thread;

The end rhymes are *head/thread*. Reread the first stanza of the poem to listen for and identify a second pair of end rhymes.

Analyzing the Text

RL 1, RL 4, RL 5

Cite Text Evidence   Support your responses with evidence from the text.

1. **Summarize** What are the primary actions that take place in each of the three stanzas of the poem?

2. **Identify Patterns** Find end rhymes and other examples of repetition in the second stanza. What effects do those forms of repetition have? Do they emphasize a particular meaning?

3. **Interpret** What is the quest of Aengus in this poem?

4. **Analyze** What words suggest that Aengus is chanting a song?

PRACTICE & APPLY

Determine the Impact of Rhyme

RL 4, RL 5

Review the information about the use of rhyme in a poem and its effect on meaning and **rhythm,** or the pattern of stressed and unstressed syllables in a line of poetry. Guide students to find another example of rhyme in the first stanza of "The Song of Wandering Aengus." *(out/trout)* Then have partners reread the poem and discuss the impact of the rhyme.

Analyzing the Text

RL 1, RL 4, RL 5

Possible answers:

1. *In the first stanza, Aengus makes a fishing rod and catches a silver trout. In the second stanza, the trout turns into a girl who calls his name and runs away. In the third stanza, he is old and dreams of finding the girl.*

2. *The end rhymes in the second stanza are* aflame/name *and* hair/air. *The poet repeats the word* floor; *the /f/ in* floor, fire, aflame, faded; *and the /g/ in* glimmering girl. *The sounds create a musical rhythm. They also create images of a glowing fire, suggesting a feeling of burning love and the sudden disappearance of this love, almost into thin air* (hair/air).

3. *The line "Because a fire was in my head" suggests a burning desire for something. That something turns out to be his quest for love, embodied by the trout-girl.*

4. *The lines have a repeating pattern of rhythm and rhyme, like in a chant. Every other syllable is stressed to create a steady rhythm, and end rhymes, such as* head/thread *and* out/trout, *give it the feeling of a song or chant.*

Strategies for Annotation   *Annotate it!*

Determine the Impact of Rhyme

RL 4, RL 5

Have students use their eBook annotation tools to identify rhyme in "The Song of Wandering Aengus." Ask them to do the following:

- Highlight in yellow the rhyming words in the first stanza.
- Highlight in blue the rhyming words in the second stanza.
- Highlight in green the rhyming words in the third stanza.
- Identify any patterns in rhyme.

Discuss how these rhyming patterns give the poem a chanting, folk song quality.

> Though I am old with wandering
>
> Through hollow lands and hilly lands,
>
> I will find out where she has gone,
>
> And kiss her lips and take her hands;

CLOSE READ

 For more context and historical background, students can view the video "Biography: William Shakespeare" in their eBooks.

Analyze Form: Sonnet

RL 1,
RL 4,
RL 5

(LINES 1–4)

Explain that a poem's **form** is the arrangement of words and lines. Explain that traditional forms of poetry have fixed rules for the number of lines, how the lines are grouped, and the pattern of end rhymes, called the **rhyme scheme**. A **sonnet** is a traditional form that has 14 lines, a specific rhyme scheme, and a set rhythmic pattern, or meter. **Meter** is the regular pattern of stressed and unstressed syllables.

C **CITE TEXT EVIDENCE** Reread lines 1–4 aloud. Have students count the number of syllables in each line and then describe the meter, or rhythmic pattern. *(There are 10 syllables in lines 1 and 3, and 11 syllables in lines 2 and 4. Each line follows a pattern of one unstressed syllable followed by one stressed syllable.)*

Determine Meanings

RL 1,
RL 4,
RL 5

(LINES 13–14)

Tell students that "Sonnet 43" makes use of conflicting ideas, or paradox. **Paradox** is a statement that has seemingly contradictory ideas. Point out line 1 when the speaker says he sees best when asleep, a time when our eyes are closed, and we don't "see" at all.

D **CITE TEXT EVIDENCE** Have students identify examples of paradox in lines 13–14 and explain how they deepen the poem's meaning. *("days are as dark as night and nights bright days"; The speaker's days are dark because he is sad when he cannot dream of his beloved. Nights are light because he sees his love in his dreams.)*

COLLABORATIVE DISCUSSION Have partners discuss how effectively the poets express their feelings. Then have them share their ideas with the larger group.

ASK STUDENTS to share any questions they generated in the course of reading and discussing these selections.

Sonnet 43

by William Shakespeare

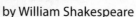

C
When most I wink, then do mine eyes best see,
For all the day they view things unrespected;[1]
But when I sleep, in dreams they look on thee,
And, darkly bright, are bright in dark directed.
5 Then thou, whose shadow shadows doth make bright,
How would thy shadow's form form happy show
To the clear day with thy much clearer light,
When to unseeing eyes thy shade shines so!
How would, I say, mine eyes be blessèd made
10 By looking on thee in the living day,
When in dead night thy fair imperfect shade
Through heavy sleep on sightless eyes doth stay!
　　All days are nights to see till I see thee,
　　And nights bright days when dreams do show thee me. **D**

COLLABORATIVE DISCUSSION Each of these two poems is, in a sense, a love poem. With a partner, discuss how effectively each poet expresses his feelings about love and loss.

---

[1] **they view things unrespected:** during the day the poet's eyes are looking at things that are insignificant or unimportant.

WHEN STUDENTS STRUGGLE . . .

To guide comprehension, work with students to paraphrase the poem line by line. Have them complete a two-column chart and use it to explain the poem's meaning.

When I most wink, then mine eyes best see,	I see best when I am asleep.
For all the day they view things unrespected;	All day, I look at things that are unimportant.

 LEVEL UP TUTORIALS For additional support, assign the following Level Up tutorial: **Figurative Language.**

Analyze Form: Sonnet

RL 4, RL 5

The deliberate arrangement of words is the mark of a well-crafted poem. The **form** of a poem is the arrangement of its words and lines on a page. One established form is a 14-line poem called a **sonnet.** The sonnet is a form that originated in Italy but was altered by English poets, especially William Shakespeare. The Shakespearean sonnet is named for the best-known user of the form.

A Shakespearean sonnet has these features:

- The whole poem develops a single idea.
- The idea is developed in three parts, each made of four lines.
- The **rhyme scheme** is the pattern of end rhymes: a-b-a-b, c-d-c-d, e-f-e-f, g-g. The matching letters refer to the pairs of end rhymes.
- The final pair of lines, called a **couplet,** completes the poet's message with a strong impact and helps focus the reader's attention on the theme.

A sonnet may also have a specified **meter,** which is a regular pattern of stressed and unstressed syllables. Notice where the stress falls in this line of the poem.

> When most I wink, then do mine eyes best see,

Look again at the sonnet you have just read. How does the punctuation at the end of the lines show how the ideas are organized?

Analyzing the Text

RL 2, RL 4, RL 5

Cite Text Evidence Support your responses with evidence from the text.

1. **Identify Patterns** Explain what you notice about the rhyme scheme of this poem.

2. **Summarize** A **paradox** is a statement that seems to contradict itself. What paradox presented in the first line is developed throughout the sonnet? (Note that the word *wink* means "to close one's eyes to sleep.")

3. **Interpret** Reread the final couplet. Restate its message in your own words.

4. **Analyze** Reread line 5. How should it be read aloud to express its meaning?

PRACTICE & APPLY

Analyze Form: Sonnet

RL 4, RL 5

Review the features of a Shakespearean sonnet. Discuss how the punctuation at the end of the lines helps the reader identify the sonnet's parts.

Then have students reread each part of "Sonnet 43" and explain the ideas developed in each. *(In the first part, the speaker declares that he is happy at night because he can see his love in his dreams. In the second part, the speaker wonders how his love would appear in the daylight, after appearing so brightly at night. In the third part, the speaker imagines how happy he would be to see his love by day.)*

Analyzing the Text

RL 2, RL 4, RL 5

Possible answers:

1. *This sonnet has the rhyme scheme a-b-a-b, c-d-c-d, e-f-e-f, g-g: see/unrespected/thee/directed; bright/show/light/so; made/day/shade/stay; thee/me.*

2. *The line "When most I wink, then do mine eyes best see" means that the speaker sees best when he is asleep. This is the paradox developed throughout the poem—that seeing is sharpest when there's darkness, which usually prevents sight. This image emphasizes the poet's longing for an absent loved one.*

3. *"All days are nights" because the speaker will be in darkness without seeing his beloved. "And nights bright days" because the speaker will see his beloved in his dreams.*

4. *When read aloud, a pause between* shadow *and* shadows *suggests the meaning that even darkness will shed bright light on the beloved.*

Strategies for Annotation   *Annotate it!*

Analyze Form: Sonnet

RL 4, RL 5

Have students use their eBook annotation tools to identify the rhyme scheme of "Sonnet 43." Ask them to do the following:

- Highlight each set of rhyming words in a different color.
- Review your highlights. On a note, assign the lines that are highlighted in yellow the letter *a*. Assign the lines highlighted in green the letter *b*.
- Continue in the same way for the remaining verses.
- Identify the pattern in the rhyme scheme.

> When most I wink, then do mine eyes best see,
>
> For all the day they view things unrespected;
>
> But when I sleep, in dreams they look on thee,
>
> And, darkly bright, are bright in dark directed.

rhyme scheme: abab

Determine Meanings

RL 4, RL 5

Review the examples of figurative language. Discuss how they contribute to the meaning and feeling of the poem. Ask students to provide additional examples of each type of figurative language in the poems. Then discuss the question, having students support their answers with evidence from the text. *("All days are nights to see till I see thee"; the speaker compares day to night because he feels lonely during the day when he cannot dream of his beloved.)*

Analyzing the Text

RL 4, RL 5

Possible answers:

1. *In the Yeats poem, not every line has an end rhyme. In each stanza, the 2nd and 4th lines and the 6th and 8th lines share end rhymes. In the sonnet, every line has an end rhyme, using the standard rhyme scheme for sonnets: a-b-a-b, c-d-c-d, e-f-e-f, g-g.*

2. *The metaphor in the Yeats poem compares true love to an elusive magical spirit. The speaker does not recognize his love until it calls his name, but then it runs off, and fades "through the brightening air." Still, he pursues his elusive love until he is "old with wandering." In "Sonnet 43," the extended metaphor of shades and shadows creates a paradox. The shadow of the loved one can "make shadows bright." The loved one's "shade shines so!"*

3. *It is easy to speak the words, as the consistent pattern of rhythm feels like regular speech. The Yeats poem almost sounds like a chant or a song. And the sonnet's meter creates a similar rhythmic pattern.*

Determine Meanings

RL 4, RL 5

Figurative language is the use of words in imaginative ways to express ideas that are not literally true. Poets use figurative language to convey meaning and achieve certain effects. This chart shows three common types of figurative language with examples from "The Song of Wandering Aengus."

Types of Figurative Language	Examples	Effect
Simile is a comparison between two unlike things using the words *like* or *as*.	*moth-like stars,* line 6	The twinkling stars look like moths fluttering.
Metaphor is a comparison of two unlike things without the words *like* or *as*.	*a fire was in my head,* line 2	A feverish, uneasy feeling is likened to a fire in the head.

The figurative language in "Sonnet 43" seems subtler than that in the Yeats poem. In Shakespeare's sonnet, which words help create a metaphor for the absence of the poet's loved one?

Analyzing the Text

RL 2

Cite Text Evidence Support your responses with evidence from the texts.

1. **Identify Patterns** What is the rhyme scheme of the Yeats poem and how does it differ from the rhyme scheme of "Sonnet 43"?

2. **Compare** An **extended metaphor** compares two unlike things at length and in a number of ways, sometimes throughout an entire work. In each poem, the poet uses an extended metaphor. What is the metaphor in each poem and what words does the poet use to extend it?

3. **Analyze** Read each poem aloud to hear and feel the unstressed and stressed syllables in each line. What qualities does the meter contribute to each poem? Explain.

PERFORMANCE TASK

Speaking Activity: Discussion With a small group, discuss which speaker of these two poems seems more affected by what he perceives. To prepare for your discussion:

- Consider what each speaker is longing for.
- Think about the words used to express the speaker's longing in each poem.

PERFORMANCE TASK

SL 1a–d, SL 4, SL 6

Assign this performance task.

Speaking Activity: Discussion As students compare and contrast how the speakers express feelings, have them record ideas in a Venn diagram.

- They can use the completed diagram as a guide for their discussion.
- Remind them to use appropriate eye contact, adequate volume, and clear pronunciation when speaking.
- Point out to students that because this is a discussion with classmates, they can use more informal language.

The Song of Wandering Aengus   **Sonnet 43**

Determine Meanings

RETEACH

Review that **figurative language** is a way of using words in nonliteral, imaginative ways to express ideas.

- A **simile** is a comparison between two unlike things using the word *like* or *as*.
- A **metaphor** is a comparison of two unlike things without the word *like* or *as*.
- **Personification** is giving human qualities to an animal, object, or idea.

Give simple examples of each, prompting students with relevant questions. For example:

- *My brother was as cold as ice.* What two things are being compared? Does the example include the word *like* or *as*? What type of figurative language is this?

 LEVEL UP TUTORIALS Assign the following *Level Up* tutorial: **Figurative Language**

INDEPENDENT READING

Student partners can work together to apply the skill to another poem or poems they have read. Have them work together to find at least two examples of each type of figurative language. They can list their examples in a three-column chart. Then have pairs explain the examples and their meanings in a group discussion.

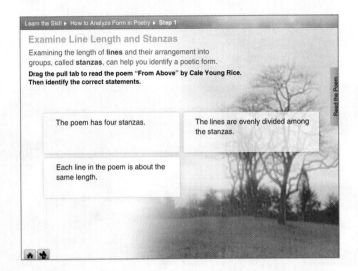

TEACH

Review with students that the form of a poem is the arrangement of its words and lines. Form may also involve patterns of rhythm and rhyme.

Explain that students can focus on these steps when analyzing form to compare and contrast two poems:

1. Examine line length and stanzas. A **line** is the core unit of a poem. A **stanza** is a group of two or more lines.

2. Look for a **rhyme scheme,** or pattern of end rhymes, in a poem.

3. Identify whether each poem is traditional or unconventional. A **traditional** poem follows fixed rules for the number of lines and stanzas and for the pattern of rhyme. An **unconventional** poem does not follow fixed rules. Its words and lines may be arranged in different ways.

4. Analyze the effects the form has on meaning in each poem. Think about how ideas are linked together, the feeling you get when reading the poem, and how the speaker's thoughts are organized into stanzas.

PRACTICE AND APPLY

Have students work in groups to apply the steps to another pair of poems: a poem with alternating end rhymes, such as the Yeats poem, and another sonnet. Have groups compare their results.

Magic and the Brain

Magazine Article by Susana Martinez-Conde and Stephen L. Macknik

Why This Text?

While this text is complex and technical, it also involves a high-interest topic. It is an example of how complex, scientific information can connect to students' lives and interests. The lesson will guide students to use organizational text features to better understand such complex texts.

▶ View It!

Professional Development Podcast:

Text Complexity

Key Learning Objective: The student will be able to analyze how text features contribute to a text and to summarize text objectively.

For practice and application:

Close Reader selection
"Saving the Lost"
Science Writing by Reynaldo Vasquez

RI 1 Cite textual evidence.

RI 2 Provide an objective summary of the text.

RI 4 Determine the meaning of technical words and phrases; analyze the impact of word choice.

RI 5 Analyze the structure used to organize a text, including text features.

W 7 Conduct short research projects.

W 8 Gather relevant information from print and digital sources.

SL 4 Present claims and findings.

L 1a Explain the function of adverb clauses.

L 4a Use context as a clue to the meaning of a word or phrase.

L 4b Use common Greek affixes as clues to the meaning of a word.

L 4c Consult print and digital reference materials to determine/clarify meaning.

L 6 Acquire and use accurately domain-specific words and phrases.

▲ Text Complexity Rubric

Quantitative Measures	**Magic and the Brain** **Lexile:** 1340L
Qualitative Measures	**Levels of Meaning/Purpose** two topics **Structure** genre traits specific to science text **Language Conventionality and Clarity** many unfamiliar, high academic, and complex domain-specific words **Knowledge Demands** complex science concepts
Reader/Task Considerations	• Teacher determined • Vary by individual reader and type of text • See the Text X-Ray for suggested Reader/Task Considerations.

Meaning Making

Language Development

Effective Expression

Content Knowledge

Foundational Skills

TEXT X-RAY

English Language Support
Before teaching, use the Text X-Ray for an overview of the text's complexity. The Text X-Ray and the supports and scaffolds in the Teacher's Edition will help you guide students of different skill levels.

Text Complexity: Qualitative Measures

Levels of Meaning/Purpose

two topics

Help students summarize text.

- Teacher's Edition side notes, pp. 80, 82, 84, 85
- English Language Support, p. 80
- When Students Struggle, p. 81
- Strategies for Annotation, p. 82

▶ **Use It! Level Up Tutorial:** Summarizing

ZOOM IN ON SUMMARIZING TEXT Tell students that an **objective summary** of a text includes only the most important ideas from the text. Explain that when students summarize, they should be careful not to include their own opinions or feelings.

- Have students read lines 110–123 in small groups.
- Then have them work together to complete these sentence frames:

  The details in this part of the article are mostly about _____

  Neuroscientists use the tools of magic to _____
- Discuss the groups' responses as a class.

Structure

genre traits specific to science text

Help students analyze text features.

- Teacher's Edition side notes, pp. 77, 78, 79, 81, 83, 85
- English Language Support, p. 83
- Strategies for Annotation, pp. 79, 85

▶ **Use It! Level Up Tutorial:** Informational Text

To reteach text features, see

- Analyze Structure: Text Features, p. 88a

ZOOM IN ON ANALYZING TEXT FEATURES Tell students that an informational article uses a variety of **text features** to help organize the information. Use the chart on page 85 to preview specific text features and describe their uses.

- After students have read the article, have them work with a partner to list each type of text feature it contains.
- Have pairs join small groups and compare their lists.
- Then have groups discuss the kind of information that each text feature conveyed.

Language Conventionality and Clarity

many unfamiliar, high academic, and complex domain-specific words

Teach unfamiliar academic vocabulary in context.

- Teacher's Edition Critical Vocabulary notes, pp. 78, 79, 80
- English Language Support, p. 82
- Applying Academic Vocabulary, p. 78
- Vocabulary Strategy: Greek Prefix *neuro–*, p. 87
- Strategies for Annotation, p. 87

Guide students to analyze the language of the informational article.

- Teacher's Edition side notes, pp. 77, 81, 84, 87, 88
- English Language Support, pp. 77, 88
- Language Conventions: Adverb Clauses, p. 88

ZOOM IN ON **PREVIEWING CRITICAL VOCABULARY** Preview the vocabulary for this selection with students.

- Display the Critical Vocabulary terms.
- Identify and discuss the meaning and derivation of the Greek prefix *neuro-*.
- Identify and highlight other affixes and roots in the vocabulary.
- Use each word in a sentence.
- Guide students to define the words based on their context.
- Have pairs write sentences using the words and share them with the class.

Knowledge Demands

complex science concepts

Help students understand the scientific context of the article.

- Teacher's Edition Background note, p. 77
- Content-Area Connection, p. 83

 For more context and historical background, students can view the video "Steve Cohen's Lost Magic" in their eBooks.

ZOOM IN ON **BUILDING SCIENCE CONTEXT** Explain that the authors use scientific words and detailed descriptions of experiments.

- Use examples on page 78 to model using such text features as definitions and footnotes to determine meaning.
- Show how sidebars, illustrations, and headings add information.

  As students read, encourage them to record their questions about the text. Then have pairs reread the text to find answers.

Suggested Reader/Task Considerations

Consider the following before assigning this article to students:

- Will the style of writing and the presentation of information in the text engage students?
- Do students have sufficient prior knowledge of the article's vocabulary to manage the material that it presents?

ZOOM IN ON **SUPPORTING COMPREHENSION**

- Engage students' interest by having them view the video "Steve Cohen's Lost Magic" in their eBook. Tell them the text will explain how magic tricks help scientists make important discoveries about how the brain functions.
- Before students read, preview the Critical Vocabulary words and the footnoted terms. Model for students how to use roots and affixes to determine the meanings of unfamiliar words.

CLOSE READ

Background Have students read the background and information about the authors. Tell students that the two scientists study the nervous system, which has to do with the nerves in the human body. Explain that nerves transmit signals to and from the brain and all of the body's muscles and organs.

SETTING A PURPOSE Direct students to use the Setting a Purpose prompt to focus their reading. Remind students to write down questions that arise as they read.

Analyze Structure: Text Features (TITLE)

RI 4, RI 5

Point out to students that the **title** is the name that is attached to a piece of writing. The title is sometimes called a **heading.** Explain that the title is just one type of **text feature,** or an element that helps organize or call attention to important information. Note that this title is accompanied by a photograph, a visual element that both clarifies the title's meaning and draws readers into the text.

 ASK STUDENTS to explain how the title and the visual elements that accompany it introduce the text. *(The title states the topic so readers know what the article is about. The photograph emphasizes the magic aspect of the article; the lines of electricity create a little excitement and raise curiosity.)*

Analyze the Meanings of Words and Phrases (LINES 1–9)

RI 1, RI 4

Explain that the authors begin the article with an **anecdote,** or a brief account of an event. Tell students that authors use anecdotes to make a point or to provide information in an entertaining and/or memorable way.

 CITE TEXT EVIDENCE Ask students to identify words and phrases that make the anecdote especially vivid. Have them tell what effect the word choices have on this opening paragraph. *(Vivid words and phrases include: "tiny white dress," "luminous beacon of beauty radiating," "burning her image," and "a blaze of red." The vivid details help make readers feel as if they are witnessing the event.)*

Background *Brain scientists* **Susana Martinez-Conde** *and* **Stephen L. Macknik** *study how the human visual system responds to and perceives the world around us. They see science at work behind magicians' techniques. A good magician relies on the inner workings of the brain to create all kinds of sensory illusions. By studying how these tricks work, scientists are learning more about the brain. Their work has led them to start a new area of science that they call* neuromagic.

Magic
and the Brain

Magazine Article by Susana Martinez-Conde and Stephen L. Macknik

SETTING A PURPOSE As you read, think about the term *neuromagic* and its usefulness as a new field of scientific study. Write down any questions you may have during reading.

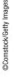 The spotlight shines on the magician's assistant. The woman in the tiny white dress is a luminous beacon of beauty radiating from the stage to the audience. The Great Tomsoni announces he will change her dress from white to red. On the edge of their seats, the spectators strain to focus on the woman, burning her image deep into their retinas. Tomsoni claps his hands, and the spotlight dims ever so briefly before reflaring in a blaze of red. The woman is awash in a flood of redness.

10   Whoa, just a moment there! Switching color with the spotlight is not exactly what the audience had in mind. The magician stands at the side of the stage, looking pleased at his little joke. Yes, he admits, it was a cheap trick; his favorite kind, he explains devilishly. But you have to agree, he did turn her dress red—along with the rest of her. Please, indulge him

©Comstock/Getty Images

Magic and the Brain   **77**

English Language Support

Word Study Project lines 36–40, highlighting *responsiveness* and *stimulus.* Help students use this strategy to define unfamiliar words:

- Look for familiar word parts, such as *respons*, which indicates that *responsiveness* is related to *respond*, or "answer."
- Find meaning in the context: a *stimulus* is something that the neural system responds to. Use a dictionary to confirm or clarify meaning.

ASK STUDENTS to apply the same strategy to another unfamiliar word.

Analyze Structure: Text Features (LINES 21–25, FOOTNOTES)

RI 1,
RI 4,
RI 5,
L 4a

Explain that words in **boldface type**—dark, heavy print—are also text features. Boldface words call attention to important words or ideas.

C **CITE TEXT EVIDENCE** Ask students to identify the words in boldface type as well as the associated definitions in the margins, and identify how they impact the reading of the text. *(The boldface words* neural *and* neuroscientists *are Critical Vocabulary words. Their definitions make the text easier to understand, as they are placed where the words first occur.)*

Tell students that **footnotes,** or notes at the bottom of a page, provide definitions or additional information.

D **CITE TEXT EVIDENCE** Have students locate the word *intuitive* on line 22. Ask them to use the context, or the words and phrases surrounding it that provide hints about its meaning, to try to determine the word's meaning. Then have them use the footnote to confirm the meaning and restate the ideas in their own words. *(Thompson has a natural ability to understand how to use science to make his trick work.)*

CRITICAL VOCABULARY

neural: The authors refer to neural processes that take place in people's brains as they watch a trick.

neuroscientist: The authors note that neuroscientists can learn from magicians.

ASK STUDENTS what kinds of neural processes engaged during a magic show might be of interest to a neuroscientist. *(The brains of spectators at a magic show would be using neural processes that send and receive signals from the eyes. Learning how this works might be of interest to a neuroscientist.)*

neuron: Neurons have a "firing rate" that scientists can measure.

ASK STUDENTS to explain what is meant by the "firing rate" of a neuron. *(Neurons send messages, so "firing rate" has to do with how many messages or how quickly neurons are sending messages back and forth to the brain.)*

and direct your attention once more to his beautiful assistant as he switches the lights back on for the next trick. He claps his hands, and the lights dim again; then the stage explodes in a supernova of whiteness. But wait! Her dress really has turned

20 red. The Great Tomsoni has done it again!

C The trick and its explanation by John Thompson (aka the Great Tomsoni) reveal a deep intuitive[1] understanding of the **neural** processes taking place in the spectators' brains—the kind of understanding that we **neuroscientists** can appropriate for our own scientific benefit. Here's how the trick works. As Thompson introduces his assistant, her skintight white dress wordlessly lures the spectators[2] into assuming that nothing—certainly not another dress—could possibly be hiding under the white one. That reasonable assumption, of course, is

30 wrong. The attractive woman in her tight dress also helps to focus people's attention right where Thompson wants it—on the woman's body. The more they stare at her, the less they notice the hidden devices in the floor, and the better adapted their retinal neurons[3] become to the brightness of the light and the color they perceive.

All during Thompson's patter after his little "joke," each spectator's visual system is undergoing a brain process called neural adaptation. The responsiveness of a neural system to a constant stimulus (as measured by the firing rate of the

40 relevant **neurons**) decreases with time. It is as if neurons actively ignore a constant stimulus to save their strength for signaling that a stimulus is changing. When the constant stimulus is turned off, the adapted neurons fire a "rebound" response known as an after discharge.

In this case, the adapting stimulus is the redlit dress, and Thompson knows that the spectators' retinal neurons will rebound for a fraction of a second after the lights are dimmed. The audience will continue to see a red afterimage in the shape of the woman. During that split second, a trap door in

50 the stage opens briefly, and the white dress, held only lightly in place with fastening tape and attached to invisible cables leading under the stage, is ripped from her body. Then the lights come back up.

neural
(nŏŏr´əl) *adj.*
Anything that is *neural* is related to the nervous system.

neuroscientist
(nŏŏr´ō-sī´ən-tĭst) *n.*
A *neuroscientist* is a person who studies the brain and the nervous system.

neuron
(nŏŏr´ŏn´) *n.* A *neuron* is a nerve cell.

[1] **intuitive** (ĭn-tōō´ĭ-tĭv): having the ability to know or understand something without evidence.

[2] **spectators:** the people who are watching the event.

[3] **retinal neurons** (rĕt´n-əl´nŏŏr´ŏnz´): the cells in the retina of the eye that convert light into images.

78 Collection 2

APPLYING ACADEMIC VOCABULARY

focus	perceive	task

THINK-PAIR-SHARE Ask pairs to discuss the questions below. Guide them to include the academic vocabulary words *focus, perceive,* and *task* in their responses. Call on volunteers to share their responses with the class.

- When people watch magic tricks, on what do they **focus**?
- When we view magic tricks, how does what we **perceive** differ from reality?
- How does giving a **task** to magic-show viewers affect what they perceive?

VISUAL ILLUSIONS
FOOLING MIND OR EYE?

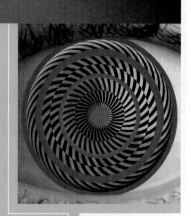

An illusion created by an image like this one often induces a false sense of flowing movement in the concentric rings (start at the center dot in the pictures). But does the illusion originate in the mind or in the eye? The evidence was conflicting until the authors and their colleagues showed in October that the illusory motion is driven by microsaccades—small, involuntary eye movements that occur during visual fixation. Knowing the roles of eye and mind in magic can be used as experimental tools **neuroscience**.

neuroscience
(nŏŏr´ō-sī´əns) *n.*
Neuroscience is any of the sciences that study the nervous system.

Two other factors help to make the trick work. First, the lighting is so bright just before the dress comes off that when it dims, the spectators cannot see the rapid motions of the cables and the white dress as they disappear underneath the stage. The same temporary blindness can overtake you when you walk from a sunny street into a dimly lit 60 shop. Second, Thompson performs the real trick only after the audience thinks it is already over. That gains him an important cognitive advantage—the spectators are not looking for a trick at the critical moment, and so they slightly relax their scrutiny.

The New Science of Neuromagic

Thompson's trick nicely illustrates the essence of stage magic. Magicians are, first and foremost, artists of attention and awareness. They manipulate the focus and intensity of human attention, controlling, at any given instant, what

Magic and the Brain **79**

CLOSE READ

HISTORY

For more context and historical background, students can view the video "Steve Cohen's Lost Magic" in their eBooks.

Analyze Structure: Text Features (SIDEBAR)   RI 5

Tell students that **sidebars** are boxes that appear alongside or within an article to provide additional information related to the text. Sidebars often contain additional **graphic aids,** such as charts, graphs, or photographs.

E ASK STUDENTS to reread the sidebar and explain how the text and graphic aid enhance the information of the main text. *(The sidebar explains how neuroscientists investigated and determined whether a visual illusion originates in the eye or in the brain. The photograph shows the image that creates the illusion.)*

CRITICAL VOCABULARY

neuroscience: The authors, who are neuroscientists, are actually studying magic to learn about how people's brains work.

ASK STUDENTS to tell what magic and neuroscience have in common. *(Both are concerned with how the brain works. In magic, people try to "fool" the brain; in neuroscience, people try to understand the brain.)*

Strategies for Annotation   Annotate it!

Analyze Structure: Text Features   RI 2, RI 5

Have students use their eBook annotation tools to analyze the text. Ask students to

- Highlight in green the central idea of the sidebar.
- Write a note that briefly states the central idea.
- Write another note that explains how this information fits in with the rest of the text.

their colleagues showed in October that the illusory motion is driven by microsaccades—small, involuntary eye movements that occur during visual fixation. Knowing the roles of

Neuroscientists were able to determine that the visual illusion originated in the eye. Studying magic in the same way can be a tool for neuroscientists.

Magic and the Brain **79**

Summarize Text (LINES 85–94)   RI 2

Explain that to **summarize** is to retell a text's central, or main, ideas in your own words. When readers summarize, they should be **objective,** or not include their own opinions or judgments about the text. Tell students that stopping to summarize a paragraph or a section as they read can help them remember information.

F **ASK STUDENTS** to reread lines 85–94 and identify the central idea. Then have them summarize the paragraph. *(Central idea: Scientists and magicians have different aims, yet they can learn from each other. Sample summary: Neuroscientists try to understand the brain's cognitive functions. Magicians try to find cognitive weaknesses. Neuroscientists could use magicians' techniques to explore brain functions further.)*

English Language Support

To help students identify the central idea and supporting details, guide them to ask and discuss the following questions:

- What do neuroscientists want to know?
- What do magicians want to know?
- What is the most important idea in the paragraph about scientists and magicians?

CRITICAL VOCABULARY

cynic: The authors say that a cynic would not approve of their research.

ASK STUDENTS why a cynic would not approve of the authors' research. *(Because a cynic is skeptical or critical of others, it would be likely that a cynic would point out that such research is unnecessary.)*

FOR STUDENTS WITH DISABILITIES

Students may struggle with an article of this length. Let them follow the text as they listen to the audio in their eBooks. Encourage them to pause regularly to ask questions and to check comprehension.

---

we are aware of and what we are not. They do so in part by
70 employing bewildering combinations of visual illusions (such as afterimages), optical illusions (smoke and mirrors), special effects (explosions, fake gunshots, precisely timed lighting controls), sleight of hand, secret devices and mechanical artifacts ("gimmicks").

Neuroscience is becoming familiar with the methods of magic.

But the most versatile instrument in their bag of tricks may be the ability to create cognitive illusions. Like visual illusions, cognitive illusions mask the perception of physical reality. Yet unlike visual illusions, cognitive illusions are not sensory in nature. Rather they involve high-level functions
80 such as attention, memory and causal inference. With all those tools at their disposal, well-practiced magicians make it virtually impossible to follow the physics of what is actually happening—leaving the impression that the only explanation for the events is magic.

Neuroscientists are just beginning to catch up with the magician's facility in manipulating attention and cognition. Of course the aims of neuroscience are different from those of magic, the neuroscientist seeks to understand the brain and neuron underpinnings of cognitive functions, whereas the
90 magician wants mainly to exploit cognitive weaknesses. Yet the techniques developed by magicians over centuries of stage magic could also be subtle and powerful probes in the hands of neuroscientists, supplementing and perhaps expanding the instruments already in experimental use.

Neuroscience is becoming familiar with the methods of magic by subjecting magic itself to scientific study—in some cases showing for the first time how some of its methods work in the brain. Many studies of magic conducted so far confirm what is known about cognition and attention from earlier
100 work in experimental psychology. A **cynic** might dismiss such efforts: Why do yet another study that simply confirms what is

cynic
(sĭn´ĭk) *n.* A *cynic* is a person who has negative opinions about other people and what they do.

already well known? But such criticism misses the importance and purpose of the studies. By investigating the techniques of magic, neuroscientists can familiarize themselves with methods that they can adapt to their own purposes. Indeed, we believe that cognitive neuroscience could have advanced faster had investigators probed magicians' intuitions earlier. Even today magicians may have a few tricks up their sleeves that neuroscientists have not yet adopted.

110   By applying the tools of magic, neuroscientists can hope to learn how to design more robust experiments and to create more effective cognitive and visual illusions for exploring the neural bases of attention and awareness. Such techniques could not only make experimental studies of cognition possible with clever and highly attentive subjects; they could also lead to diagnostic and treatment methods for patients suffering from specific cognitive deficits—such as attention deficits resulting from brain trauma, ADHD (attention-deficit hyperactivity disorder), Alzheimer's disease, and the like. The

Diagnosing a Brain Disorder Physicians and scientists use Magnetic Resonance Imaging (MRI) as shown above on the left to make detailed scans of the body's internal structures. The MRI scan on the right highlights regions of the brain most affected by Alzheimer's disease.

Brain Regions and Alzheimer's Disease

- The hippocampus is the region where the disease may start.
- In the temporal lobe, the advancing disease affects memory, hearing and language.
- The cerebral cortex thins as the disease progresses, judgement worsens and language is impaired.

CLOSE READ

Analyze Meanings of Words and Phrases

RI 1,
RI 4,
L 4a

(LINES 110–116)

Tell students that authors choose words carefully to convey certain meanings. Ask students to reread lines 110–116 and to consider the use of the word *robust*.

G **CITE TEXT EVIDENCE** Have students reread the first six lines of the paragraph and identify context clues that might help them determine the meaning of *robust*. As needed, have students confirm the meaning with a print or digital dictionary. Have them discuss the effect of the use of the word *robust*. *(The phrase "more effective" suggests that* robust *describes something better or stronger.* Robust *has a sense of being both strong and healthy, in the sense of an experiment being well thought out or very thorough.)*

Analyze Structure: Text Features (SIDEBAR)

RI 5

Direct students' attention to the sidebar.

H **ASK STUDENTS** to reread the sidebar and explain how it adds or contributes to the topic. *(The main text above the sidebar mentions using new experimental techniques that could lead to diagnosing or treating certain disorders. The sidebar gives an example of how brain research is used to explore Alzheimer's disease.)*

WHEN STUDENTS STRUGGLE...

Remind students that summarizing is a strategy that can help them understand and remember complex text. Explain that using a graphic organizer to record central ideas and supporting details will help them summarize. Model rereading the paragraph in lines 95–109 and identifying its central idea. *(Neuroscientists are studying magic to learn how its methods work in the brain.)* Have students record the central idea in a graphic organizer like the one shown. Next, have them reread the paragraph, identify details that support the central idea, and add them to the chart.

 LEVEL UP TUTORIALS For additional support, assign the following *Level Up* tutorial: **Summarizing.**

Central Idea 1

Supporting Detail 1

Supporting Detail 2

Supporting Detail 3

Summarize Text

RI 2

(LINES 124–134)

Explain that stopping to summarize a paragraph as students read can help them clarify meaning and better comprehend the central idea.

 ASK STUDENTS to summarize the paragraph. If students need support, have them first identify the central idea and then the supporting details. *(Sample summary: Misdirection is the act of turning spectators' attention away from a secret action. Overt misdirection is a direct request to spectators to focus on something.)*

English Language Support

Read Closely Help students use context to determine the definitions of *overt* and *covert*. Reread the statement about overt misdirection in lines 131–132 with students. Then reread line 135, guiding students to focus on the comparison indicated by the word *subtler*. Explain that *subtle* means "not obvious," so if something that is *covert* is not obvious, or covered, then something that is *overt* is obvious, or open. Have pairs use each word in a sentence.

---

120 methods of magic might also be put to work in "tricking" patients to focus on the most important parts of their therapy, while suppressing distractions that cause confusion and disorientation.

Magicians use the general term "misdirection" to refer to the practice of diverting the spectator's attention away from a secret action. In the lingo of magic, misdirection draws the audience's attention toward the "effect" and away from the "method," the secret behind the effect. Borrowing some terms from cognitive psychology, we have classified misdirection as 130 "overt" and "covert." The misdirection is overt if the magician redirects the spectator's gaze away from the method—perhaps simply by asking the audience to look at a particular object. When the Great Tomsoni introduces his lovely assistant, for instance, he ensures that all eyes are on her.

> ❝ *Magicians use the general term 'misdirection' to refer to the practice of diverting the spectator's attention.* ❞

"Covert" misdirection, in contrast, is a subtler technique; there, too, the magician draws the spectator's attentional spotlight—or focus of suspicion—away from the method, but without necessarily redirecting the spectator's gaze. Under the influence of covert misdirection, spectators may be looking 140 directly at the method behind the trick yet be entirely unaware of it.

Cognitive neuroscience already recognizes at least two kinds of covert misdirection. In what is called change blindness, people fail to notice that something about a scene is different from the way it was before. The change may be expected or unexpected, but the key feature is that observers

---

Strategies for Annotation ✏️ 📖 *Annotate it!*

Summarize Text

RI 2

Have students use their eBook annotation tools to analyze the text in lines 124–134. Ask students to do the following:

- Highlight in green the central idea.
- Underline one or two important details that support the central idea.
- In a note, write an objective summary of the paragraph.

Magicians use the general term "misdirection" to refer to the practice of diverting the spectator's attention away from a secret action. In the lingo of magic, misdirection draws the audience's attention toward the "effect" and away from the "method," the secret behind the effect.

> Misdirection is the act of turning spectators' attention away from a secret action. Magicians call this drawing attention to the "effect" and away from the "method."

do not notice it by looking at the scene at any one instant in time. Instead the observer must compare the postchange state with the prechange state.

150 Inattentional blindness differs from change blindness in that there is no need to compare the current scene with a scene from memory. Instead people fail to notice an unexpected object that is fully visible directly in front of them. Psychologist Daniel J. Simons invented a classic example of the genre. Simons and psychologist Christopher F. Chabris, both then at Harvard University, asked observers to count how many times a "team" of three basketball players pass a ball to each other, while ignoring the passes made by three other players. While they concentrated on counting, half of the 160 observers failed to notice that a person in a gorilla suit walks across the scene (the gorilla even stops briefly at the center of the scene and beats its chest!). No abrupt interruption or distraction was necessary to create this effect; the counting task was so absorbing that many observers who were looking directly at the gorilla nonetheless missed it.

Controlling Awareness in the Wired Brain

The possibilities of using magic as a source of cognitive illusion to help isolate the neural circuits responsible for specific cognitive functions seem endless. Neuroscientists recently borrowed a technique from magic that made 170 volunteer subjects incorrectly link two events as cause and effect while images of the subjects' brains were recorded. When event A precedes event B, we often conclude, rightly or wrongly, that A causes B. The skilled magician takes advantage of that predisposition by making sure that event A (say, pouring water on a ball) always precedes event B (the ball disappearing). In fact, A does not cause B, but its prior appearance helps the magician make it seem so. Cognitive psychologists call this kind of effect illusory correlation.

In an unpublished study in 2006 Kuhn and cognitive 180 neuroscientists Ben A. Parris and Tim L. Hodgson, both then at the University of Exeter in England, showed videos of magic tricks that involved apparent violations of cause and effect to subjects undergoing functional magnetic resonance imaging. The subjects' brain images were compared with those of a control group: people who watched videos showing no

CLOSE READ

Analyze Structure: Text Features (HEADING)

RI 2
RI 4,
RI 5

Point out that this is the second heading in this article. A **heading,** like a title, is another text feature that organizes information for readers. Headings tell what a section of text is about.

J ASK STUDENTS to reread the heading and use it to tell what the section is about and explain how it represents a new kind of information. *(The previous section was about neuromagic and how neuroscientists are using magicians' techniques to understand the brain. This heading reveals that the next section of text will deal with controlling the brain rather than just understanding it.)*

English Language Support

To guide students in analyzing the heading, have them answer the following questions.

- What is the heading of the previous section? *(The New Science of Neuromagic)*
- What was that section about? *(It was about techniques neuroscientists use to understand how the brain works.)*
- What do the words *Controlling Awareness* suggest that this section will be about? *(controlling brain functions)*
- How does the information in the second section differ from information in the first section? *(The first section is about understanding the brain; the second is about controlling it.)*

CONTENT-AREA CONNECTION

Science Tell students that the scientific method is an organized approach used to examine something, such as cause-and-effect connections. Invite a science teacher to visit your class to outline the six steps of the scientific method: (1) Ask a question about what you want to learn; (2) Do research to gather information; (3) Form a hypothesis, or a guess, about the answer to your question; (4) Do an experiment to test your hypothesis; (5) Analyze and record results of the experiment; (6) Draw a conclusion about whether your hypothesis was correct.

Activity After students read the text, have small groups research and report on how scientists have used this method to make discoveries about the brain.

Summarize Text

RI 2

(LINES 166–199)

Tell students that, in a longer article, it is sometimes useful to summarize a section instead of each paragraph. Guide students to turn the heading above line 166 into a question (*"How can we control awareness in the wired brain?"*).

(K) **ASK STUDENTS** to reread and summarize the last section of the article, using the heading-turned-question as a guide. *(Sample summary: Scientists are using the illusion techniques of magic to learn more about cognitive functions. In one study, illusory correlation causes subjects to misidentify causes and effects. In another study, scientists were able to see the particular part of the brain that was active while subjects watched magic tricks. Using the techniques of magicians may allow scientists to understand and possibly even control the brain's specific areas of function.)*

COLLABORATIVE DISCUSSION Have individuals review the text on the page where the term *neuromagic* is introduced (heading above line 65). Encourage students to jot notes about what the term means and whether it is useful or not. Then, when students discuss the term with small group members, tell them to cite text evidence to support their opinions or conclusions.

ASK STUDENTS to share any questions they generated in the course of reading and discussing the selection.

English Language Support

Paraphrase Information Provide the following sentence stems to support discussions:

- What I understand about this term is _____.
- I think the term *neuromagic* is useful because _____.
- I don't agree that the term is useful; I think that _____.

---

apparent causal violations. The investigators found greater activation in the anterior cingulate cortex among the subjects who were watching magic tricks than among the controls. The finding suggests that this brain area may be important for interpreting causal relationships.

The work of Kuhn and his colleagues only begins to suggest the power of the techniques of magic for manipulating attention and awareness while studying the physiology of the brain. If neuroscientists learn to use the methods of magic with the same skill as professional magicians, they, too, should be able to control awareness precisely and in real time. If they correlate the content of that awareness with the functioning of neurons, they will have the means to explore some of the mysteries of consciousness itself.

COLLABORATIVE DISCUSSION The authors have invented the term *neuromagic*. Why do they think it is a useful term? Talk about your ideas with other group members.

TO CHALLENGE STUDENTS . . .

Evaluate Ideas In the last section of the article, the authors state that the possibilities of using the techniques of magic in neuroscience "seem endless." They go on to suggest, "If neuroscientists learn to use the methods of magic with the same skill as professional magicians, they, too, should be able to control awareness precisely and in real time."

ASK STUDENTS to closely reread this section of the article. Challenge them to brainstorm some of the "endless" possibilities—for good or for ill—that might result from scientists being able to control human awareness. Have them sort their ideas into two categories—those that would benefit society and those that might be harmful—and share them with the class.

Analyze Structure: Text Features

RI 4, RI 5

Text features are elements of a text that help organize and call attention to important information. Informational texts such as "Magic and the Brain" often contain one or more text features, such as those shown in the chart.

Text Features in Informational Texts	
titles, headings, subheadings	The **title** of a piece of writing is the name that is attached to it. It often identifies the topic of the whole text and is sometimes referred to as a **heading. Subheadings** appear at the beginning of sections within the text and indicate the focus of that section.
sidebar	A **sidebar** is a box alongside or within an article that provides additional information that is related to the article's main text.
boldface type	**Boldface type** is dark, heavy print that is used to draw attention to unfamiliar vocabulary.
footnotes	**Footnotes,** which appear at the bottom of the page, provide definitions or additional information about terms in the text.

Graphic aids, such as maps, charts, diagrams, graphs, and pictures are visual text features that can help you understand ideas or processes.

Text features may be used to highlight **technical language**—terms used in a specialized field such as science or technology. If there is no definition for a technical term, use context to determine its meaning. You can confirm the meaning in such resources as print or online dictionaries and encyclopedias.

Look at the top of page 79 of "Magic and the Brain." Identify the text feature that appears there.

Summarize Text

RI 2

When you **summarize** a text, you briefly retell the central ideas in your own words. An **objective summary** reports what the original writer intended, without opinions or unnecessary details. Do not include opinions or commentary. Use headings and subheadings to help you organize ideas.

To summarize a paragraph, find and restate the main idea. To summarize a section, turn the heading into a question. Answer the question using the main idea and important details in the paragraph. To summarize an article, combine your section summaries. Add a sentence to sum up the central idea of the whole article.

Reread lines 1–20 of "Magic and the Brain." How would you complete a summary of that section?

TEACH

CLOSE READ

Analyze Structure: Text Features

RI 4, RI 5

Review the role and examples of text features. Have students point out examples of text features in the article and tell how or what each text feature adds to the text. Pose these questions to guide discussion:

- Does this text feature organize information, call attention to it, or both? How?
- Does this text feature emphasize information in the text or *add to* information in the text?
- Does this text feature use technical language— terms used in a special field, such as science?

Answer to final question: *sidebar*

Summarize Text

RI 2

Explain that students summarize when they relate the events of a movie, telling only main events, or "big ideas." Point out that a text summary is similar because they tell central ideas in their own words.

Sample summary of lines 1–20: *The Great Tomsoni says he will change his assistant's dress from white to red. He dims the lights, the stage is flooded in red light, and everything, including the dress, is red. He claims it was just a joke and directs the audience's attention back to the dress. Again he dims the lights. This time the stage is flooded in white light, but the dress is still red.*

Strategies for Annotation   🖊 🗐 *Annotate it!*

Analyze Structure: Text Features

RI 4, RI 5

Share these strategies for guided or independent analysis:

- Highlight headings in yellow.
- Underline boldface words, including those in footnotes.
- For each highlighted or underlined feature, write a note that restates the feature's important idea or tells briefly what the feature adds to the text. (*This section explores a new type of science called neuromagic.*)

The New Science of Neuromagic

Thompson's trick nicely illustrates the essence of stage magic. Magicians are, first and foremost, artists of attention

Analyzing the Text

RI 2,
RI 4,
RI 5

Possible answers:

1. *Stage magicians use two types of misdirection: "overt" and "covert." With overt misdirection, the magician tells the audience to look at a particular object. "Covert" misdirection is subtler because spectators may be looking unknowingly at the method behind the trick yet be totally unaware of it. One kind of covert misdirection is change blindness, in which the viewer can't compare two scenes and therefore doesn't see the change. Another kind is inattentional blindness, in which people simply don't see something because they're focusing on something else.*

2. *The authors found that the illusion of motion doesn't originate in the brain, but in tiny movements of the eye. They solved an ongoing scientific puzzle about the roles of eye and brain.*

3. *"The wired brain" refers to neural circuits in the brain, the nerve connections responsible for cognitive functions.*

4. *The aim of a magician is to use the functions of the brain and the eyes to fool and entertain people. The aim of neuroscientists is to study and understand the functions of these organs as they process illusions in order to explore the mysteries of consciousness itself.*

5. *The most surprising aspect is that the subjects did not notice the person in the gorilla suit as they counted.*

6. *A visual illusion causes people to misperceive reality by changing what they sense with their eyes. A cognitive illusion causes people to misperceive reality because of how the brain works as it attends, remembers, and thinks.*

7. *The authors believe that experiments on attention and awareness should incorporate magicians' techniques because they could help scientists understand how the brain works in both highly attentive people and in people with attention deficits. More understanding might lead to being better able to diagnose or treat people with attention deficits.*

English Language Support

Exchange Information and Ideas Guide students to work in small groups to answer the questions on page 86. Have each group answer one question. When all groups have finished, let them take turns presenting their answers to the class. Encourage classmates to provide useful feedback.

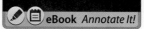 eBook *Annotate It!*

Analyzing the Text

RI 2, RI 4, RI 5,
W 7, SL 4

Cite Text Evidence Support your responses with evidence from the text.

1. **Summarize** Reread lines 124–141. Write a summary of these paragraphs to explain how magic tricks work through the techniques of "misdirection."

2. **Draw Conclusions** Reread the sidebar on page 79. What discovery did the authors make about the origin of illusion? Why is it important?

3. **Interpret** Reread the heading on page 83. Use the information in that section to explain what is meant by "the wired brain."

4. **Summarize** Reread lines 85–94. In your own words, describe how the aims of a magician might differ from those of a neuroscientist.

5. **Infer** Reread lines 154–165. What is the most surprising detail about the counting task that is performed by the test subjects?

6. **Compare** Reread lines 65–80. What is the difference between a cognitive illusion and a visual illusion?

7. **Synthesize** Reread lines 110–123. Why do the authors want neuroscientists to use "tools of magic"?

PERFORMANCE TASK

Speaking Activity: Demonstration
Do research to find an easily performed "magic trick" that is based on a science principle. Follow the step-by-step directions for the trick and practice performing it. Determine the principle that makes the trick work. Then demonstrate the trick in a performance for your classmates. Follow these suggestions during the demonstration:

- If necessary, perform the trick a second time, but more slowly, indicating whatever you're doing to distract their attention.
- At the end of the performance, explain the principle at work in the trick and how it relates to the article "Magic and the Brain."
- Invite feedback. Discuss with your classmates whether the demonstration increases their understanding of neuromagic.

Assign this performance task.

PERFORMANCE TASK

W 7, SL 4,
L 6

Speaking Activity: Demonstration Suggest that students work with partners to take the roles of magician and assistant. Provide this additional guidance:

- Encourage students to search for videos as they conduct research. Videos will help them understand the visual showmanship involved in the trick.
- When students explain their tricks, encourage them to use technical terms from the article such as "visual illusion" and "cognitive illusion."

Critical Vocabulary

L 4a, L 4b, L 4c

neural	neuroscientist	neuron	neuroscience	cynic

Practice and Apply Answer each question.

1. How is a **neural** network like and different from a computer network?

2. How is a **neuroscientist** like and different from a brain surgeon?

3. How is a **neuron** like and different from a blood cell?

4. How is **neuroscience** like and different from medical science?

5. How is a **cynic** like and different from a critic?

Vocabulary Strategy: The Greek Prefix *neuro-*

A **root** is a word part that came into English from an older language, such as ancient Latin or Greek. The Greek word for "cord" or "nerve" was *neuron*. The Greek root *neuro* appears as a prefix at the start of many English words about nerves and the nervous system.

This sentence comes from "Magic and the Brain"; notice the two words with the prefix *neuro-*:

> The responsiveness of a neural system to a constant stimulus (as measured by the firing rate of the relevant neurons) decreases with time.

Restate the sentence, replacing each word with *neuro* with another term that includes *nerve* or *nervous*.

Practice and Apply Use the context and your knowledge of the root *neuro* to write a likely meaning for each bold word. Use a print or online dictionary to look up unfamiliar words or word parts and to confirm word meanings.

1. A patient with an abnormal tingling in one arm may consult a **neurologist.**

2. Some snakes paralyze their prey by injecting a **neurotoxin.**

3. People with a **neuromuscular** disorder may have difficulty with tasks such as unscrewing a jar lid.

4. The **neurosurgeon** removed a tumor from the patient's brain.

PRACTICE & APPLY

Critical Vocabulary

L 4a, L 4c

Possible answers:

1. *A neural network is a system of nerves. A computer network is a system of electronic devices. Both handle high-speed signals to transmit messages or move data.*

2. *Both a neuroscientist and a brain surgeon work with the nervous system. A neuroscientist studies how the brain works; a brain surgeon performs surgery on the brain.*

3. *Neurons and blood cells are both cells. A neuron is a cell in the nervous system that transmits signals to and from the brain. A blood cell is a cell in the circulatory system that carries oxygen to and from the heart.*

4. *Neuroscience and medical science are both concerned with the body. Neuroscience focuses on how the brain and nervous system work; medical science focuses on the treatment of illness affecting organs and bodily functions.*

5. *A cynic and a critic both make judgments, but a cynic is less trusting and more negative than a critic.*

Vocabulary Strategy: The Greek Prefix *neuro-*

L 4b

Possible answers:

The responsiveness of a nervous system to a constant stimulus (as measured by the firing rate of the relevant nerve cells) decreases with time.

1. *neurologist: a medical doctor who treats nerve disorders*

2. *neurotoxin: a substance that damages nerves*

3. *neuromuscular: having to do with the nerves that control muscle movement*

4. *neurosurgeon: a medical doctor who operates on parts of the nervous system such as the brain*

Strategies for Annotation   *Annotate it!*

Vocabulary Strategy: The Greek Prefix *neuro-*

L 4b

Have students locate the various words in the selection that contain the Greek prefix *neuro-*. Encourage them to use their eBook tools to do the following:

- Highlight in yellow each word with the prefix *neuro-* or *neur-*.
- Underline the prefix in each.
- Write notes for each explaining how you used the root to infer the word's meaning.

The trick and its explanation by John Thompson (aka the Great Tomsoni) reveal a deep intuitive understanding of the **neural** processes taking place in the spectators' brains—the kind of understanding that we **neuroscientists** can

> A scientist is someone who studies, so a neuroscientist must study nerves.

PRACTICE & APPLY

Language Conventions: Adverb Clauses

L 1a

Review that an adverb answers the questions *When? Where? How?* or *To what extent?* about a verb, an adjective, or another adverb. Provide these examples as review:

- *When?* She went to school <u>yesterday</u>.
- *Where?* She went to school <u>somewhere</u>.
- *How?* She went to school <u>slowly</u>.
- *To what extent?* She went to school <u>rather</u> slowly. (*slowly* is also an adverb; *rather* tells to what extent she went slowly)

Emphasize that an adverb clause functions in the same way as a one-word adverb does. Point out that the subordinating conjunctions are signal words. Help students see that these are all familiar words.

Answers:

1. *adverb clause: After the magician's "little joke,"; modifies the verb* took place; *tells when*

2. *adverb clause: as any the magician had ever performed; modifies the adjective* complicated; *tells how or to what extent*

3. *adverb clause: where they usually performed their act; modifies the adverb* here; *tells where (i.e., tells where "here" is)*

4. *adverb clause: Before the assistant left the stage; modifies the verb* handed; *tells when*

 Assess It Online!

Online Selection Test
- Download an editable ExamView bank.
- Assign and manage this test online.

Language Conventions: Adverb Clauses

L 1a

An **adverb** is a part of speech that modifies a verb, an adjective, or another adverb. It answers the question *When? Where? How?* or *To what extent?* A **clause** is a group of words that contains a subject and a predicate—the two main parts of a complete sentence. An **adverb clause** is a subordinate clause that completes the same task as an adverb: it modifies a verb, an adjective, or another adverb.

Adverb clauses start with a connecting word called a **subordinating conjunction,** such as *after, although, as, because, before, even though, if, since, so that, though, unless, until, when, where, while*. Notice the subordinating conjunction and adverb clause in this sentence from "Magic and the Brain."

> **When the constant stimulus is turned off, the adapted neurons fire a "rebound" response known as an afterdischarge.**

The phrase *When the constant stimulus is turned off* modifies the verb *fire* in the rest of the sentence. The clause tells when the "neurons fire." It begins with the subordinating conjunction *when*.

When you write, be careful not to confuse an adverb clause with a complete sentence; an adverb clause cannot stand alone. If you position an adverb clause before the main clause, set it off with a comma.

Sentence Fragment	Complete Sentence
Because not enough research had been done	The science of magic could not be used in medicine because not enough research had been done.
After the lights on stage flashed	After the lights on stage flashed, a set of cables switched the dresses worn by the assistant.

Practice and Apply Identify the adverb clause in each of these sentences and tell whether it modifies a verb, an adjective, or an adverb. Tell which question the adverb clause answers: *When? Where? How?* or *To what extent?*

1. After the magician's "little joke," the real illusion took place.

2. The trick was as complicated as any the magician had ever performed.

3. The magician and his assistant stood here, where they usually performed their act.

4. Before the assistant left the stage, the magician handed her his hat.

English Language Support

Use Adverb Clauses Explain that an adverb clause **modifies,** or tells more about, a verb, an adjective, or an adverb. A subordinating conjunction connects the adverb clause to the word it modifies.

- Present a bank of paired sentences that use the same adverb clause to begin and end sentences (for example, *I walked the dog after the rain stopped. / After the rain stopped, I walked the dog.*) As students read each pair, ask a *When? Where? How?* or *To what extent?* question to help them identify the adverb clause.

- Have students work with partners to identify adverb clauses in the Practice and Apply sentences. Then have the partners form groups to discuss and check their responses.

- Ask students to write their own sentences using adverb clauses.

Conduct Online Research

TEACH

Explain to students that finding information on the Internet is easy. The hard part is weeding out the unreliable, useless, or just plain bad information from the reliable, useful, and good information. Provide these tips for conducting keyword searches for the Performance Task:

- Avoid very broad topics or keywords. For this Performance Task, the search string "magic trick" would bring an overwhelming list of results. Narrow the search string to a specific type of magic trick; perhaps "sleight of hand."

- Be specific, but not *too* specific. The search string "how-to video on sleight of hand trick with coins" would yield some good results, but you might also miss out on some good sites that don't include videos or that are about sleight of hand tricks with other materials.

As students conduct searches, provide these tips for evaluating the validity or assessing the relevance of websites:

- If the website is primarily a site that sells things, it is unlikely to be a good source of information.

- If the website is maintained by an organization or professional association, what is the group and what is its mission?

- If the website or blog is maintained by a person, check the person's credentials. For this Performance Task, if he or she is a professional magician, the information is *likely* to be valid, but readers should still use their good judgment.

PRACTICE AND APPLY

Have students apply these tips as they conduct their magic trick research. Or, you may wish to have them complete the Interactive Lessons "Conducting Research" and/or "Evaluating Sources." Monitor students' research, and ask probing questions to help shape their search strings or evaluate websites.

 INTERACTIVE LESSON Have students complete the tutorials in these lessons: **Conducting Research, Evaluating Sources**

Analyze Structure: Text Features

RETEACH

Review the following list of text features with students and talk about what each one is. As needed, point to examples of each type of text feature in "Magic and the Brain" or another magazine article or informational text.

- **titles, headings, subheadings** (organizational items that label sections of text and tell what a section is about)
- **sidebars** (a box beside or within text that provides additional information)
- **boldface type** (a text treatment that calls attention to important words or ideas)
- **footnotes** (definitions or additional information at the bottom of a page)
- **graphic aids** (visual elements such as maps, charts, diagrams, graphs, and photographs)

 LEVEL UP TUTORIALS Assign the following *Level Up* tutorial: **Informational Text**

INDEPENDENT READING

Students can apply their knowledge of text features and how to use them to other pieces of informational text. Have them work independently to fill in a chart with examples of each kind of text feature that appears in the text and how it helps them to locate and understand the information.

Text Feature	Example	What It Does
sidebar		
heading		

As students read, suggest that they ask themselves questions such as these:

- Does this feature emphasize something in the text or add information to the text?
- What important idea or information does this feature provide?
- How does this feature add or contribute to my understanding of this topic?

Saving the Lost

Science Article by Reynaldo Vasquez

Why This Text

Students may find it difficult to identify and follow the central ideas of science articles. This difficulty may be compounded if students are not familiar with scientific terms and technical concepts that are common in such articles. With the help of the close-reading questions, students will identify and then summarize some of the central ideas in this science article. This close reading will lead students to understand how the central ideas are developed, forming a coherent argument.

Background Have students read the background information about the scientist in the article. Point out that medicine has provided incredible benefits to modern society, improving the health and extending the lives of most people. However, modern medicine also presents doctors and scientists with difficult medical challenges and ethical dilemmas. People with serious brain injuries, for example, may prove to be conscious in unexpected ways.

SETTING A PURPOSE Ask students to pay attention to the major steps in Owen's research. How does the author use these as central ideas for his article?

Standards Support

- cite multiple pieces of text evidence
- determine central ideas in a text
- provide an objective summary of the text
- determine the meaning of words as they are used in the text
- analyze the structure of a text

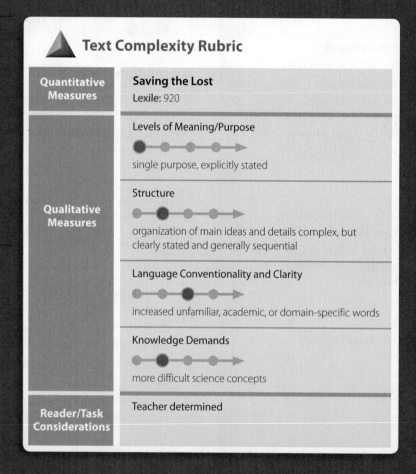

Text Complexity Rubric

Quantitative Measures	**Saving the Lost** Lexile: 920
Qualitative Measures	**Levels of Meaning/Purpose** — single purpose, explicitly stated
	Structure — organization of main ideas and details complex, but clearly stated and generally sequential
	Language Conventionality and Clarity — increased unfamiliar, academic, or domain-specific words
	Knowledge Demands — more difficult science concepts
Reader/Task Considerations	Teacher determined

Strategies for CLOSE READING

Summarize Text

Students should read this science article carefully all the way through. Close-reading questions at the bottom of the page will help them focus on a thorough analysis of central ideas. As they read, students should jot down comments or questions about the text in the margins.

WHEN STUDENTS STRUGGLE . . .

To help students summarize "Saving the Lost," have them work in small groups to fill out a chart like the one shown below.

CITE TEXT EVIDENCE For practice in summarizing text, ask students to write a central idea of the article, cite text evidence in support of the idea, and then summarize the idea.

Central Idea	Textual Evidence
Many patients in a vegetative state may in fact be conscious.	A brain scan of one patient "lit up like a Christmas tree."
	When asked to think about playing tennis, another patient's brain showed the same response as that of a healthy person.
	Five out of another 54 patients also showed a normal brain response when asked to imagine playing tennis.
	A patient was able to alter his brain activity to give yes/no answers to questions.

Summary: A scientist named Adrian Owen has used neuroimaging technology to study the brains of patients in a vegetative state. He found that some patients' brains respond to questions and directions the same way that healthy people's brains do. This proved to Owen that some of these patients are in fact conscious and capable of communication.

Background *Adrian Owen is a groundbreaking British scientist whose research has been reported in documentaries, on radio and television shows, and in newspapers and magazines. This article presents the remarkable discoveries Owen brought to light as he studied the brain activity of a special group of people.*

Saving the Lost

Science Article by Reynaldo Vasquez

CLOSE READ
Notes

1. **READ ▶** As you read lines 1–14, begin to collect and cite text evidence.
   - Circle the question at the beginning of the article.
   - Underline the central idea in the first paragraph, and paraphrase the idea in the margin.
   - Underline the central idea in the second paragraph, and restate it in the margin.

How can we understand what a person who cannot respond is thinking or feeling? People in a *vegetative state* are those who have come out of a coma and appear to be awake with open eyes and sleep patterns. However, they do not show any awareness of who they are or where they are. They cannot speak and do not respond to sounds, hunger, or pain. The actual condition of patients in a vegetative state mostly remained a secret until Adrian Owen made some startling discoveries.

A

In the late 1990s, British scientist Owen realized that the technology of *neuroimaging*—producing images of brain activity without surgery—supported what scientists already knew. Different parts of the brain process different kinds of thoughts. Owen's concern was that neuroimaging was breaking no new ground. He wanted to find a real use for it.

B

Adrian Owen discovered new facts about people who are in a vegetative state.

Owen wanted to find a way to make neuroimaging more useful.

31

---

1. **READ AND CITE TEXT EVIDENCE** Point out that the author begins the article with a simple but puzzling question that catches the reader's attention. Also, he phrases the question in "friendly," nonscientific language, thus inviting a wide audience to continue reading.

A **ASK STUDENTS** to explain how they identified the central idea of the first paragraph. What clues in the underlined sentence suggest that this sentence expresses the central idea? *The word* actual *makes it clear that the condition of patients wasn't what people expected. Also, Owen made some "startling" discoveries about the patients' condition.*

> STRANGE AS IT SOUNDS, SCIENTISTS KNOW THE
> PART OF THE BRAIN THAT SHOWS ACTIVITY IN
> HEALTHY PEOPLE WHEN THEY IMAGINE PLAYING
> TENNIS. IT IS ALWAYS THE SAME.

rehabilitation:

therapy to restore good health

Time-order words or phrases let the reader follow the events in order.

In 1997, Owen and his team began testing a patient who was in a vegetative state. They scanned her brain as they showed her familiar faces, and "it lit up like a Christmas tree." Based on these results, the patient was given intense **rehabilitation**—whereas in many cases, people in a vegetative state are simply kept alive. She has since sent a
20　letter to thank Owen, realizing that without the brain scan, she too would have been written off.

Owen continued his research, and in 2006 he made another breakthrough. He took brain scans of a woman patient as he asked her to imagine playing tennis. Strange as it sounds, scientists know the part of the brain that shows activity in healthy people when they imagine playing tennis. It is always the same. It was the same in his patient, too. He asked his patient to imagine walking through her home. Her brain showed activity in the exact same spot as healthy

---

2. ◀ **REREAD** Reread lines 9–14. Summarize Adrian Owen's challenge and the medical mystery he hoped to solve. Support your answer with explicit textual evidence.

Adrian Owen, a British scientist, looked for a real use for neuroimaging, and he wanted to find out about the actual condition of people who are in a vegetative state.

3. **READ** ▶ As you read lines 15–33, continue to cite textual evidence.

• Circle the time-order words or phrases that signal the sequence of events.
• In the margin, explain the advantage of using chronological order to organize the text.

32

30　people would if they thought of walking through the rooms of their homes. Owen believed that this showed that the patient was conscious. Some researchers agreed with Owen, while others disagreed. They believed that the response was an involuntary reaction to the final words that Owen said to the patient.

Owen did not give up. With a team from Belgium, he tested 54 other patients. Of these, five responded in the same way as his previous patient. Then they reached a huge breakthrough studying "patient 23." He had been in a vegetative state for five years following a car accident. The scientists discovered that patient 23 was able to give "yes" and "no" answers by changing his brain activity. They
40　asked him questions with answers that the **technicians** couldn't know, and that weren't given away by any clues.

"Is your father's name Thomas?"
"No."
"Is your father's name Alexander?"
"Yes."
"Do you have any brothers?"
"Yes."
"Do you have any sisters?"
"No."
50　When Owen published his discovery in 2010, there was an immediate response from the media and the scientific community. A Canadian university offered a huge amount of funding for Owen to continue his research there.

The questions Owen asked did not include clues, and the technicians could not have know the answers.

technician:

a person with training in a technical process

Owen's discovery prompted an offer from a university to fund his research.

---

4. ◀ **REREAD** Reread lines 22–33. Summarize the events that took place in 2006. Support your answer with explicit textual evidence.

Owen found that a patient reacted to a prompt the same way as a healthy person would. He believed that it proved that the patient was conscious, though some other researchers did not agree.

5. **READ** ▶ Read lines 34–60. Underline each central idea, and in the margin, write at least one supporting detail.

33

---

2. **REREAD AND CITE TEXT EVIDENCE**

B **ASK STUDENTS** to discuss Owen's implied criticism of neuroimaging in the 1990s. What was neuroimaging being used for then? *Scientists were using the technology to confirm what they already knew.* What was Owen's new idea? *He wanted to use neuroimaging to study the brains of patients in a vegetative state.*

3. **READ AND CITE TEXT EVIDENCE**

C **ASK STUDENTS** how the phrase *based on these results* establishes a sequence of events. *The phrase* based on these results *implies that the results lead to some sort of action.*

FOR ELL STUDENTS Some students will know that a *state* is a part of a country. It can also mean the condition of something.

Critical Vocabulary: rehabilitation (line 18) Have students share their definitions of *rehabilitation,* and ask volunteers to use the noun in a sentence.

4. **REREAD AND DISCUSS USING TEXT EVIDENCE**

D **ASK STUDENTS** to state the two central ideas of the paragraph. *One central idea is that the patient's brain responded to directions the same way as a healthy person's brain. Another central idea is that not everyone believed this was a sign of consciousness.*

5. **READ AND CITE TEXT EVIDENCE**

E **ASK STUDENTS** to debate whether the sentence beginning "Then they reached . . ." or the sentence beginning "The scientists discovered . . ." better states that paragraph's central idea. *Students should point out that the second sentence explains the breakthrough mentioned in the first sentence. Also, the following series of questions and answers supports the idea in the second sentence.*

Critical Vocabulary: technician (line 40) Have students name different fields in which a technician might work. Then have volunteers use the word in sentences for two or three different kinds of technicians.

Owen believes that his work could help thousands of patients in the United States.

There are neuroscientists who do not agree with Owen's conclusions and who argue about the point at which consciousness can be said to exist. Owen is not interested in such details. In the United States, there are tens of thousands of people in vegetative states. Owen thinks that perhaps one-fifth of these people could be able to communicate. He would like to see that possibility become
60 a reality.

6. ◀ REREAD AND DISCUSS Reread lines 34–49. With a small group, discuss the reasons the author includes dialogue in this passage.

SHORT RESPONSE

Cite Text Evidence Using specific details from the text, write a short summary of Owen's work and its possible consequences. **Cite text evidence** to support your response.

Owen worked with patients in a vegetative state. He discovered that neuroimaging could be used to monitor changes in brain activity— one patient was able to give answers to yes/no questions, leading Owen to believe that some patients in a vegetative state are conscious. Although some neuroscientists do not agree with his conclusions, Owen believes that his discovery could help thousands of patients in a vegetative state to communicate.

34

6. REREAD AND DISCUSS USING TEXT EVIDENCE

F **ASK STUDENTS** from each group to reach a consensus on reasons why the author might have included the dialogue. How does the author use the dialogue to structure the final section of the article? *Students should recognize that the dialogue provides an immediate, dramatic conclusion to the story of Owen's research—technicians are actually having a conversation with a person in a vegetative state.*

SHORT RESPONSE

Cite Text Evidence Students' responses should include text evidence in their summaries. They should

- explain that Owen used neuroimaging to study the brains of patients in a vegetative state
- explain that some patients' brains responded to directions and questions in the same way that healthy people's brains respond
- describe how Owen's research has been received by others

TO CHALLENGE STUDENTS . . .

To better understand the context of Owen's work, students can research the history of how patients in a vegetative state have been viewed and treated over the last century.

ASK STUDENTS to discuss why it took so long for medical researchers to apply neuroimaging technology to patients in a vegetative state. In what ways can widely accepted "truths" block the way of medical innovations and other breakthroughs? *As Owen's case shows, when the experts in a field of medicine think they know something, they may not bother to investigate whether it is in fact true. Since everyone believed that patients in a vegetative state were unconscious, nobody thought to use neuroimaging to test the hypothesis.*

DIG DEEPER

With the class, return to Question 2, Reread. Have groups share their responses to the question.

ASK STUDENTS about the challenges Owen faced.

- Ask students to describe some of the challenges presented by the patients themselves. *People in a vegetative state cannot speak or move. Nor do they respond to noises, pain, or hunger. So it seemed impossible to communicate with them.*
- Have students discuss some of the challenges that came from other scientists in Owen's field. *At the time, researchers were using neuroimaging to study the brains of healthy people, so it took a leap even to think of applying the technology to patients in a vegetative state. Later, when Owen published his results, other researchers were skeptical. Some thought that the patients' brains were showing involuntary responses to Owen's directions. Others thought Owen's results did not prove the patients were actually conscious.*

ASK STUDENTS to return to their Short Response answer and revise it based on the class discussion.

COMPARE MEDIA

MEDIA **Pavement Chalk Art**

Art by Julian Beever

Why This Media?

Students usually encounter art in museums. This lesson will explore the public pavement art created by Julian Beever. By learning about public art and the techniques Beever uses to produce it, students will be better able to appreciate an artist's purpose and messages when they see a work of art.

Key Learning Objective: The student will be able to analyze the purposes of public art and the techniques Beever uses to create the illusion of three-dimensionality.

SL 2 Analyze the main ideas and supporting details presented in diverse media.
SL 5 Integrate multimedia and visual displays into presentations.
W 6 Use technology to publish writing.

▲ Text Complexity Rubric

Quantitative Measures	**Pavement Chalk Art** **Lexile:** N/A
Qualitative Measures	**Levels of Meaning/Purpose** ●─●─●─●─➤ single topic
	Structure ●─●─●─●─➤ organization of main ideas and details complex, but clearly stated and generally sequential
	Language Conventionality and Clarity ●─●─●─●─➤ increased unfamiliar, academic, or domain-specific words
	Knowledge Demands ●─●─●─●─➤ somewhat complex visual art concepts
Reader/Task Considerations	• Teacher determined • Vary by individual reader and type of text • See the Text X-Ray for suggested Reader/Task Considerations.

TEXT X-RAY

English Language Support
Before teaching, use the Text X-Ray for an overview of the text's complexity. The Text X-Ray and the supports and scaffolds in the Teacher's Edition will help you guide students of different skill levels.

Meaning Making · Effective Expression · Foundational Skills · Content Knowledge · Language Development

Text Complexity: Qualitative Measures

Levels of Meaning/Purpose

single topic

Help students analyze art.
- Teacher's Edition side notes, pp. 90, 91, 92

To reteach analyzing media, see
- Analyze Media: Perspective and Illusion, p. 92a
- Analyze Diverse Media, p. 92a

▶ *Use It!* **Level Up Tutorials:** Analyzing Visuals

ZOOM IN ON **ANALYZING DIVERSE MEDIA** Explain that just as writers use words to convey a **message** to readers, people working in other **media** use certain tools to convey messages to an **audience**, or viewers. After students have examined the images, have small groups discuss the following questions:

- How do artists use lines to create **perspective**?
- What kinds of effects can artists create by using color and shadow?
- Why is creating a sense of three-dimensionality especially important in Beever's pavement art?

Structure

organization of main ideas and details complex but clearly stated and generally sequential

Help students focus their viewing.
- Teacher's Edition side notes, pp. 90, 91

ZOOM IN ON **VIEWING DIVERSE MEDIA** Tell students that reading the information about each piece of art can help them better appreciate its details and its message.

- Have students in small groups first focus on the art on page 90. Then have them read the text, pausing to point out examples of art techniques that the text describes.
- Let students follow the same procedure for page 91.
- Ask students to identify and discuss what the text added to their understanding of the artist's work.

Language Conventionality and Clarity

increased unfamiliar, academic, or domain-specific words

Teach unfamiliar academic vocabulary in context.

- Teacher's Edition side notes, p. 91
- Applying Academic Vocabulary, p. 91
- English Language Support, pp. 89, 91
- When Students Struggle, p. 90
- Performance Task, p. 92

***ZOOM IN ON* DETERMINING MEANING** Remind students that words that appear in boldface are defined in the text. Have pairs locate each of the following words:

- **perspective** *(page 90)*
- **audience** *(page 92)*
- **message** *(page 92)*

For each word, ask students to read aloud the definition they find in the text. Then help students use each word in a sentence.

Knowledge Demands

somewhat complex visual art concepts

Help students understand the cultural context of the sidewalk drawings.

- Teacher's Edition Background note, p. 89

***ZOOM IN ON* BUILDING CULTURAL KNOWLEDGE** Have students read and discuss the Background note on page 89.

- Discuss the pros and cons of viewing art in conventional places such as museums, galleries, public buildings and parks, and sculpture gardens.
- When students finish the lesson, have them list the advantages and disadvantages of sidewalk art such as Beever's.

Suggested Reader/Task Considerations

Consider the following before assigning this material to students:

- Will the content engage students?
- Will students recognize the purpose for reading the text that accompanies each piece of art?

***ZOOM IN ON* SUPPORTING COMPREHENSION**

- Allow students to preview the sidewalk art on pages 90 and 91 and encourage them to develop questions. Provide opportunities for students to answer and discuss their questions after they view and read about each piece.
- Ask students to explain how they determine an artist's message when they view a piece of art. What do they know about the techniques the artist uses? Explain that the images they will view and discuss are fun and easy to understand.

TEACH

CLOSE READ

Julian Beever Have students read the background about the artist Julian Beever. Point out that Beever uses a technique called "anamorphosis" to create his drawings. This technique involves doing a drawing in a distorted, stretched form so that from one particular viewpoint, the distortion is resolved into the correct shape and form. It allows Beever to create the illusion of solid or hollow forms going into, coming out of, or standing on the ground.

SETTING A PURPOSE Direct students to use the Setting a Purpose prompt to focus their viewing. Remind them to write down any questions they have as they read and view.

English Language Support

Understand Root Words Write the term *anamorphosis* on the board. Have students preview the images in the text to help them understand the term. Underline *morph* in the term, and tell students that this is a Greek root that occurs in some English words. It means "shape" or "form." As a group, discuss other words with the root, such as *metamorphosis* and *amorphous*. Remind students that one strategy to determine the meaning of an unfamiliar word is to look for Greek or Latin roots that can give clues to the meaning.

Julian Beever (b. 1959) *creates unusual chalk drawings on public sidewalks. Beever started drawing pavement art as a way to make money while traveling. Since then, he has gained international recognition. Beever chooses to draw on sidewalks so that everyone can have access to his art. He says, "My work appeals literally to the man (and woman) in the street and is not confined in galleries or limited by the gallery system."*

MEDIA ANALYSIS

Pavement Chalk Art

Public Art by Julian Beever

(bg) ©olivier/Shutterstock; (r) ©Rex Features/AP Images

SETTING A PURPOSE Beever has developed a special technique of using distortion to unequally magnify images in his work. When seen from one special angle, these images come together to create the illusion that his "anamorphic" drawings are truly three dimensional. Viewed this way, his drawings seem to come to life.

Beever's pavement art gives viewers the impression that they are entering a very real, physical place that exists in the drawings. As you view the two drawings, think about what it would be like to be a passerby who suddenly walks across—or into—one of Beever's works. Write down any questions you have as you view.

English Language Support

Examine Affixes Explain that analyzing art requires special words. Display the terms *impression, illusion, distortion, perception,* and *dimension.* Ask what these words have in common (the affix *-ion*). Explain that a suffix is added to the end of a word or word part to affect its meaning. Adding *-ion* ("act of" or "state of") makes a word a noun.

- Ask pairs of students to examine each word, saying each one aloud. Ask them to use a dictionary to find each noun and copy the definition on a sheet of paper to help them discuss the art.

- Have pairs look up each word in a dictionary. Ask them to use the entry to determine the word or word part to which *-ion* was added. Have them discuss how *-ion* changes the meaning of the word or word part and use each word in a sentence.

- Ask pairs to write a sentence using each word and then write definitions for the words *interpretation, generalization,* and *recommendation.* Have them write these words and definitions on the board for all students to use in discussing the art.

CLOSE READ

AS YOU VIEW Tell students that they will be looking at one of Beever's drawings. Explain that artists use different techniques to make their images come to life. Have students read the As You View section to help them focus their viewing on how Beever uses lines to help create his illusion. Discuss how Beever uses the technique called **perspective** to create the sense of three-dimensionality.

Analyze Diverse Media   SL 2

Explain to students that artists like Beever have an audience in mind when they create their art. The **audience** is the group of people who will view an artist's work.

ASK STUDENTS how Beever's audience differs from the audience of most artists. Then ask why he may have chosen this audience. *(Beever's audience is people who just happen to be walking along the street. Beever chose this audience because he wanted his audience to be surprised. If his art were in a museum, the audience would be expecting to see it.)*

English Language Support

Exchange Ideas Give students the opportunity to add relevant information about pavement chalk art that they have seen. Ask:

- Have you ever seen pavement chalk art on a street or in a park?
- What was shown in that art?
- How was that art like or unlike what this artist is doing?

A Slight Accident in a Railway Station

AS YOU VIEW Artists make choices about the works they produce and the techniques they use to create those works. **Perspective** is the technique that artists use to give the illusion of three-dimensional space on a two-dimensional surface, which in Beever's case is the sidewalk. One way that Beever creates this illusion is through his use of lines. Beever uses thick and thin as well as long and short lines to frame the stairway in the drawing. Notice how the lines make the stairs look thinner the farther away they seem to get from the viewer.

©Julian Beever

WHEN STUDENTS STRUGGLE...

After students read the As You View section, discuss the meaning of *perspective* with them. You may want to show students some of M. C. Escher's artwork as an example of how other artists play with perspective to create illusions.

LEVEL UP TUTORIALS For additional support, assign the following *Level Up* tutorial: **Using Context Clues.**

Meeting Mr. Frog

AS YOU VIEW In addition to lines, Beever uses colors and shadows to create the illusion that we are seeing something real. Artists can use color to create mood and to create images that imitate life. Notice how the colors Beever uses at the top of the frog seem brighter or lighter. He uses shadows, or shading, at the bottom of the drawing where the frog sits on the lily pad. Color and shadow work together to give the whole image a sense of shape and depth.

COLLABORATIVE DISCUSSION Beever's drawings focus on the sudden collision of perception and reality. With a partner, discuss your reactions to one of Beever's drawings.

Pavement Chalk Art **91**

APPLYING ACADEMIC VOCABULARY

abnormal	focus	perceive

THINK-PAIR-SHARE Ask pairs to answer and discuss the questions below. Guide students to use the academic vocabulary words *abnormal, focus,* and *perceive* in their responses. Let volunteers share their responses with the class.

- On what part of the first drawing do you **focus**?
- What do you **perceive** in that part of the drawing?
- What seems **abnormal** about Beever's art and where he creates it?

CLOSE READ

AS YOU VIEW Tell students that they will be looking at another one of Beever's drawings. Explain that artists also use color and shading to make their images come to life. Have students read the As You View section to help them focus their viewing on the ways Beever uses these elements.

Analyze Diverse Media   SL 2

Explain to students that artists like Beever also have a message in mind when they create art. The **message** is the idea or point that an artist wants to convey to the audience.

ASK STUDENTS how Beever's use of color and shadows helps him to convey the message that everything you see is not what you think it is. *(By using color and shading, Beever creates forms that seem so realistic that viewers mistake them for the real thing.)*

COLLABORATIVE DISCUSSION Have pairs work together to discuss how they reacted to Beever's drawings and why each of Beever's drawings would be confusing to a passerby. What is real about them? What is unreal? Accept all reasonable responses.

ASK STUDENTS to share any questions they generated in the course of viewing and discussing the artwork.

English Language Support

Paraphrase Information Before students begin their discussion, provide the following sentence stems:

- The drawing I like best is _____ because _____.
- The drawing of ___ might make a passerby _____.
- I like how the artist _____.

PRACTICE & APPLY

Analyze Diverse Media
SL 2

Explain to students that artists, like writers, create their works with an audience in mind. Have students compare how visual artists, such as Beever, and writers might convey a message. *(Visual artists use visual elements such as line, color, and shape to craft their messages. Writers use words to convey their messages.)* Then discuss how Beever's audience differs from the kinds of audiences most artists create their works for. *(Beever's art reaches people who are not expecting to view art. They are not necessarily people who usually go to museums—their viewing of Beever's work is usually accidental and, therefore, a surprising experience.)*

Analyzing the Media
SL 2

Possible answers:

1. *The colors are dark, forming shadows that help create a sense of depth. The shadow below the man suggests he is airborne. The vertical lines that narrow toward the train platform also create depth, giving the sense that the man, who is drawn mainly with curving and non-linear lines, is falling.*

2. *"A Slight Accident in a Railway Station" uses perspective to give the stairs the illusion that they are receding into the sidewalk; lines help to create a sense of space by making the stairs seem like they extend into a space in the sidewalk; color and shadow give the drawing a sense of realism and form; distorted forms create the illusion of three-dimensionality.*

3. *The drawings are different in several ways. "A Slight Accident in a Railway Station" recedes into the ground. It also creates a sense of motion and energy. "Meeting Mr. Frog" projects out of the ground. It is very still and whimsical.*

4. *Because he places his work in public spaces, all of Beever's work conveys the message that art should be experienced everywhere by everyone, not just by those who enter an art museum. Another message is that what we see is not always what is true reality. The drawings playfully trick the viewer.*

Analyze Diverse Media
SL 2

Art is created with an audience in mind. The **audience** is the group of people who view an exhibit or performance. Because Beever produces art that is viewed in public outdoor spaces, his audience is everyday passersby.

Artists also have a **message,** an idea or point, that they want to convey through their art. Beever uses various artistic elements and techniques, such as lines, perspective, and distortion, to convey his message and to make his illusions come to life.

Analyzing the Media
SL 2, SL 5, W 6

Cite Text Evidence   Support your responses with evidence from the media.

1. **Analyze** How do the colors and lines in "A Slight Accident in a Railway Station" create a feeling of movement and make the image seem real?

2. **Analyze** Choose one of Beever's drawings. Tell how Beever uses the elements of line, color, perspective, shadow, and distortion to create effects. As shown in the graphic below, explain what effect each element creates.

| Element | | Effect |

3. **Compare** Both drawings create the illusion of depth. What are some ways the two drawings are different?

4. **Synthesize** Why do you think Beever chooses to create this style of art to put in public spaces? What message or messages does Beever convey through his art?

PERFORMANCE TASK

Media Activity: Poster Working in small groups, create a poster or a flyer that announces an exhibit of Beever's art in a city. Use your favorite design software program to lay out your work, including images and text.

- Highlight the effectiveness of Beever's drawings as public art.

- Promote the advantages of having sidewalk art in a city.
- Present your completed flyer or poster to the other groups, explaining what you intend to communicate with it and how you accomplished that goal.

Assign this performance task.

PERFORMANCE TASK
SL 5, W 6

Media Activity: Poster Have students work in small groups. Posters should promote the art and highlight its advantages as public art. Have students

- include engaging images that convey their message, using photo editing, design/layout, and/or illustration software as appropriate
- collaborate on written elements, such as flyer text, to revise for clarity

Analyze Media: Perspective and Illusion

TEACH

Explain to students that artists use different design elements instead of words to help them convey their messages. The following basic elements are used to help give meaning to visuals:

- **Lines** are strokes or marks. They can be thick or thin, long or short, smooth or jagged. They can focus attention and create a feeling of depth. They can frame an object, direct a viewer's eye, or create a sense of motion.
- **Shape** is the external outline of an object. Shape can emphasize visual elements and add interest.
- **Color** can be used to create a mood and to make things look real. By using color and shadow together, artists can give an image a sense of shape and depth.
- **Texture** is the surface quality or appearance of an object. For example, an object's texture can be rough, wet, or shiny. Texture can also be used to make an object seem real. For example, wallpaper patterns can create a sense of depth, smoothness, or roughness, even though the texture is only visual and cannot be felt.

PRACTICE AND APPLY

Have students search online for other images created by Julian Beever. Have them tell how the artist uses the design elements you discussed to help create the illusion of reality. Students can compare and contrast two of Beever's other drawings using an interactive Comparison-Contrast Chart to list the ways the visual techniques are used in each drawing.

 INTERACTIVE GRAPHIC ORGANIZER Have students use this Interactive Graphic Organizer: **Comparison-Contrast Chart**

Analyze Diverse Media

RETEACH

Remind students that artists create art with an audience in mind. Point out that the **audience** is the person or group of people who will view an artist's work. Perhaps most often, the audience comes to a museum to see the art. But in some cases, like with Julian Beever's art, artists seek out a different audience.

Point out that artists, like writers, have **messages** they want to convey. Writers use words to convey their messages, but artists use design elements to convey their messages.

Discuss the following descriptions of pieces of art. Have students identify the likely audience and message:

- an outdoor sculpture of a baseball player in front of a ballpark
- a painting of a beautiful mountain in a museum
- a mural of a community working together on the wall of a city building

INDEPENDENT VIEWING

Students can apply the skill to other works of art. Have them work independently to find other examples of different forms of visual art online, including paintings, computer-rendered artwork, sculpture, and mixed-media installations. Ask: *Who is the artist's audience? What message does the artist want to convey to viewers?*

English Language Support

Summarize Information Have students use a four-column chart to record their questions and answers about different forms of media.

Title of art	What is the form?	Who is the audience?	What is the artist's message?

After students have recorded information about several works of art, have them compare and discuss their responses in small groups.

Another Place, Another Time

Short Story by Cory Doctorow

Why This Text?

When students understand the elements of fiction, they can analyze and discuss literature—a skill that will serve them in school, when they read for enjoyment, and when they view and discuss movies and television shows. This lesson explores the elements of character, setting, and symbolism in a science fiction story.

Key Learning Objective: The student will be able to identify and analyze how setting affects characters' traits, motivations, and actions.

RL 1 Cite text evidence.

RL 2 Determine a theme and provide a summary.

RL 3 Analyze interactions among story elements.

RL 4 Determine word meaning; analyze impact of repeated sounds.

RL 5 Analyze how structure contributes to meaning.

W 9a Apply grade 7 reading standards to literature.

L 2b Use correct spelling.

L 4a Use context as a clue to the meaning of a word or phrase.

L 4c Consult general and specialized reference materials.

L 5b Use the relationship between particular words to understand each of the words.

 Text Complexity Rubric

Quantitative Measures	**Another Place, Another Time**
	Lexile: 1060L

Qualitative Measures

Levels of Meaning/Purpose

multiple levels of complex meanings

Structure

somewhat complex story concepts

Language Conventionality and Clarity

more complex descriptions

Knowledge Demands

complex or sophisticated theme; multiple themes

Reader/Task Considerations

- Teacher determined
- Vary by individual reader and type of text
- See the Text X-Ray for suggested Reader/Task Considerations.

English Language Support

Before teaching, use the Text X-Ray for an overview of the text's complexity. The Text X-Ray and the supports and scaffolds in the Teacher's Edition will help you guide students of different skill levels.

Meaning Making

Language Development

Effective Expression

Content Knowledge

Foundational Skills

Text Complexity: Qualitative Measures

Levels of Meaning/Purpose

multiple levels of complex meaning

Help students summarize text.

- Teacher's Edition side notes, pp. 95, 97, 98, 99, 103, 107
- English Language Support, p. 99
- Strategies for Annotation, p. 95
- When Students Struggle, pp. 98, 101

▶ *Use It!* **Level Up Tutorial:** Symbol

ZOOM IN ON **UNDERSTANDING SYMBOLS** Explain that a **symbol** is something that represents, or stands for, something else. Symbols in a text add another level of meaning. Discuss common symbols and what they represent. (For example, a dove stands for peace; red roses or hearts stand for love; owls represent wisdom.) As students read, have them ask questions to identify symbols.

- What people, places, things, or actions does the writer emphasize or mention frequently?
- How are these details important to the story?

Have students use a two-column chart like the one on page 98 to track symbols as they read.

Structure

somewhat complex story concepts

Help students analyze story elements.

- Teacher's Edition side notes, pp. 96, 97, 99, 100, 101, 103, 105, 106, 107, 108
- English Language Support, p. 94
- Strategies for Annotation, pp. 97, 105, 107
- Performance Task, p. 108

▶ *Use It!* **Level Up Tutorial:** Methods of Characterization

To reteach character, see

- Analyzing Story Elements: Character, p. 110a

To help students analyze character and setting, see

- Analyze Story Elements: Character and Setting, p. 110a

ZOOM IN ON **ANALYZING CHARACTER** Explain that the **main character** in a short story is the one trying to solve a problem or reach a goal. Readers can determine what **motivates,** or moves a character to action, by analyzing what the character says, does, and thinks. Explain that the main character in this story is a boy named Gilbert. After students read the story, have pairs discuss the following questions:

- What are Gilbert's strongest qualities, or **character traits?**
- Does Gilbert change during the story? If so, how?
- What does Gilbert want? Does he achieve his goal?

Language Conventionality and Clarity

more complex descriptions

Teach unfamiliar academic vocabulary in context.

- Teacher's Edition Critical Vocabulary notes, pp. 94, 95, 96, 101, 109
- English Language Support, p. 105
- Applying Academic Vocabulary, p. 94
- Strategies for Annotation, p. 109
- Vocabulary Strategy: Reference Aids, p. 109

Guide students to analyze the language of the short story.

- English Language Support, pp. 100, 103, 110
- Language Conventions: Spell Correctly, p. 110

ZOOM IN ON **USING REFERENCE AIDS** Remind students that when they cannot define a word from its context, they can consult a **dictionary** to confirm its meaning, spelling, pronunciation, or related forms. Explain that to explore shades of meaning or find just the right word, they can find synonyms in a **thesaurus,** a reference aid that includes words in groups of synonyms.

- Have pairs of students choose two Critical Vocabulary words.
- For one Critical Vocabulary word, have pairs consult a dictionary to find related forms. Ask students to use a related form in a sentence.
- For the other Critical Vocabulary word, have the pairs find synonyms in a thesaurus. Ask them to use a synonym in a sentence.

Knowledge Demands

complex or sophisticated theme, multiple themes

Support English Learners in understanding the cultural and literary context of the short story.

- Teacher's Edition Background note, p. 93

ZOOM IN ON **BUILDING CULTURAL KNOWLEDGE** After reading the Background note, point out references to Albert Einstein in lines 36–50. Explain that Gilbert's ideas about time and space are inspired by Einstein.

- Einstein developed his theories of relativity in the early 20th century. His work explains the relationship between space and time.
- Considered a genius, he won the Nobel Prize in Physics in 1921.

Encourage students to discuss how scientific theories are reflected in the story.

Suggested Reader/Task Considerations

Consider the following before assigning this short story to students:

- Will students develop an interest in the topic?
- Do students have prior experience with the genre that will help them manage the content?

ZOOM IN ON SUPPORTING COMPREHENSION

- Before students read, ask them why the idea of time travel is so popular. Ask if they would or would not want to travel through time. As students read, have them make connections between their ideas and Gilbert's motivation.
- Let students share examples of science fiction tales and characters. Discuss the goals and motivations of these characters, as well as how the setting affects them. Explain that students will read a story that shares such elements.

TEACH

CLOSE READ

Background Have students read the background and information about the author. Explain that this short story is featured in a collection of stories titled *The Chronicles of Harris Burdick*. The collection is based on a series of text-free illustrations by Chris Van Allsburg, titled *The Mysteries of Harris Burdick*. The illustration that served as the basis of "Another Place, Another Time" is featured on page 102 in the student edition. If students enjoy this selection, suggest that they explore *The Chronicles of Harris Burdick* for further reading or *The Mysteries of Harris Burdick* to inspire their own imaginations and their own writing projects.

SETTING A PURPOSE Direct students to use the Setting a Purpose prompt to focus their reading. In addition, remind students to generate questions as they read.

Analyze Story Elements: Character (LINES 1–7)

RL 3

Explain to students that one story element can often reveal information about another story element. For instance, **setting,** the time and place of the action, can influence the **characters,** the people, animals, or other creatures who take part in the story. In this section, the character Gilbert's interpretation of each setting reveals much about him.

Ⓐ **ASK STUDENTS** to reread the first paragraph, identify the different settings that Gilbert is thinking of, and discuss what these settings reveal about Gilbert. (*Time flies by for Gilbert when he is in the summer garden setting, playing with his friends. This shows he is fun-loving and playful. Time crawls slowly by when he is waiting for his father's return in the winter setting of the beach at the bottom of the cliffs. This shows Gilbert loves his father, and he is lonely without him.*)

Background *When **Cory Doctorow** (b. 1971) first saw the movie Star Wars at the age of six, he was inspired to rewrite the entire story as a self-made book. The movie sparked his desire to be a science fiction writer. Publishing his first story at 17, Doctorow has since produced many science fiction novels, short stories, and magazine articles. The author has an online presence as a blogger and makes most of his books available online for free.*

Another Place, Another Time

Short Story by Cory Doctorow

SETTING A PURPOSE Science-based ideas are important in this story. As you read, think of the significance of these ideas to the characters—especially to Gilbert.

Gilbert hated time. What a tyrant it was! The hours that crawled by when his father was at sea, the seconds that whipped past when he was playing a brilliant game in the garden with the Limburgher children. The eternity it took for summer to arrive at the beach at the bottom of the cliffs, the flashing instant before the winter stole over them again and Father took to the sea once more.

"You can't hate *time*," Emmy said. The oldest of the three Limburghers and the only girl, she was used to talking
10 younger boys out of their foolishness. "It's just *time*."

Gilbert stopped pacing the tree house floor and pointed a finger at her. "That's where you're wrong!" He thumped the book he'd taken out of his father's bookcase, a book fetched

---

English Language Support

Explain Ideas Read aloud the first two sentences in the story with students following along. Explain that time is an important idea in this story.

- Tell students that in this story time is presented in ways that may be unfamiliar. Discuss how in different situations time seems to move more quickly or slowly. Invite students to give examples, such as time seeming to move quickly when having fun, or more slowly when waiting for something to happen.

- Have pairs of students reread lines 1–7 and write a sentence that summarizes why the character Gilbert seems to hate time.

- Ask students to reread lines 1–7 and discuss with a partner the words and phrases that the author uses to personify the "tyrant" time.

Analyze Story Elements: Character (LINES 31–44)

RL 3

Explain to students that all stories have a **main character,** the character whose problem or goal drives the plot. Point out that authors often reveal information about characters by showing how they interact with each other.

B **CITE TEXT EVIDENCE** Ask students to reread lines 31–44 and identify the main character and the problem that is being explained. Ask them to cite evidence from the text that reveals his state of mind here and what the other characters may think about him. *(The main character is Gilbert. As he struggles to explain his ideas to Emmy and the twins, their reactions show that they are at first frustrated with him. Emmy and Gilbert are both smart, but Gilbert can frustrate his friends with his ideas.)*

English Language Support

Let pairs complete the activity above. Provide the following questions to guide students' responses:

- Which character seems to have a problem?
- What is the main character trying to do?
- What words would you use to describe Emmy's response to Gilbert?

CRITICAL VOCABULARY

eloquence: The author uses the word *eloquence* to describe Emmy as she rolls her eyes.

ASK STUDENTS if Emmy's later reply to Gilbert, "That's stupid," would be an example of eloquence. Why? *(No. Eloquence suggests a way of speaking or acting that is effective and persuasive, but Emmy's words seem harsh and confrontational.)*

---

home from London, heavy and well made and swollen with the damp air of the sea-crossing home to America. He hadn't read the book, but his tutor, sour Señor Uriarte, had explained it to him the day before while he was penned up inside, watching summer whiz past the study's windows. "Time isn't just time! Time is also space! It's also a dimension." Gilbert
20 thumped the book again for emphasis, then opened it to the page he'd marked with a wide blade of sawgrass.

"See this? This is a point. That's one dimension. It doesn't have length or depth. It's just a dot. When you add another dimension, you get *lines*." He pointed at the next diagram with a chewed and dirty fingernail. "You can go back and you can go forward, you can move around on the surface, as though the world were a page. But you can't go up and down, not until you add another dimension." He pointed to the diagram of the cube, stabbing at it so hard, his finger dented the page. "That's
30 three dimensions, up and down, side to side, and in and out."

B Emmy rolled her eyes with the **eloquence** of a thirteen-year-old girl whose tutor had already explained all this to her. Gilbert smiled. Em would always be a year older than he was, but that didn't mean he would always be dumber than she was.

"And Mr. Einstein, who is the smartest man in the whole history of the world, he has proved—absolutely *proved*—that time is just *another dimension*, just like space. Time is what happens when you can go up and down, side to side, in and
40 out, and *before and after*."

Em opened her mouth and closed it. Her twin brothers, Erwin and Neils, snickered at the sight of their sister struck dumb. She glared at them, then at Gilbert. "That's stupid," she said.

"You're calling *Einstein* stupid?"

"Of course not. But you must not understand him properly. Space is space. Time is time. Everyone knows that."

Gilbert pretended he hadn't heard her. "But here's the part no one knows: why can we move through space in any
50 direction—"

"You can't go up!" Em said, quickly.

"You got up into my tree house," he said, putting a small emphasis on *my*. "And you could go back *down*, too."

eloquence
(ĕl′ə-kwəns) *n.* If someone behaves or speaks with *eloquence*, he or she uses persuasive, powerful expression.

APPLYING ACADEMIC VOCABULARY

abnormal	feature	focus

THINK-PAIR-SHARE Have partners discuss the questions below. Encourage students to use the vocabulary words *abnormal, feature,* and *focus* in their responses. Ask volunteers to share their responses with the class.

- How do characters change when **features** of the setting change?
- How does the author keep the reader's **focus** on the element of time?
- How do the **abnormal** events near the end of the story give new insight into the characters?

Emmy, who was a better fighter than any of them, put her fists on her hips and mimed *Make me*. He pretended he didn't see it.

"Why can we move through space in *almost* any direction, but time only goes in one direction, at one speed? Why can't we go faster? Slower? Backwards?"

60 "Sideways?" Neils said. He didn't speak often, but when he did, what he said was usually surprising.

"What's sideways in time?" his twin asked.

Neils shrugged. "Sideways is sideways."

"This is dumb," Emmy declared, but Gilbert could see that she was getting into the spirit of the thing—starting to understand how it had made him all so angry.

Outside Gilbert's house the summer roared past like a three-masted schooner before a gale,[1] with all sails bellied out. Inside the study, the hours crawled by. And then, in between, there 70 were the breakfasts and dinners with Gilbert's father, who was home for the summer, whose kind eyes were set into an ever-growing net of wrinkles and bags, who returned from his winter voyages each year a little thinner, a little more frail.

"And what did you learn today, my boy?" he said, as he tucked in to the mountain of lentils and beans made by the housekeeper, Mrs. Curie (who was so old that she had actually once served as Father's nanny and changed his diapers, which always made Gilbert giggle when he thought of it). Father was a strict vegetarian and swore by his diet's life-enhancing 80 properties, though that didn't seem to stop him from growing older and older and older.

Gilbert stopped fussing with his lentils, which he didn't like very much. "Geography," he said, looking at his plate. "We're doing the lowlands." He looked out at the sunset, the sun racing for the other side of the planet, dragging them all back toward the winter. "Belgium. Belgium, Belgium, Belgium."

His father laughed and smacked his hands on his thighs. "Belgium! Poor lad. I've been **marooned** there once or twice. 90 Land of bankers and cheese-makers. Like hitting your head, Belgium, because it feels so good when you stop. What else?"

maroon
(mə-rōōn´) *v.* To *maroon* is to abandon or leave someone in a place that is hard to get away from.

---
[1] **three-masted schooner before a gale:** a vessel with three sails, moving fast because of a forceful wind.

CLOSE READ

Determine Meaning of Words and Phrases

RL 1, RL 4

(LINES 82–87)

Explain to students that a **symbol** is a person, a place, an object, or an activity that stands for something beyond itself. Point out that throughout the story, the author uses different symbols to emphasize time's significance to Gilbert. Also point out that, often, symbols are open to interpretation. Two different readers might determine that the same symbol represents two different things, but as long as an interpretation is supported in the text and makes sense within the story, the interpretation can be valid.

C CITE TEXT EVIDENCE Have students reread lines 82–87 and identify a symbol that suggests the passing of time. Ask them to use text evidence to explain what it reveals about Gilbert. *(The sunset is a symbol that suggests time passing. Gilbert seems to be struggling with the idea of time—and his inability to control it. The idea that the sun is "dragging them all back toward winter" shows that he is concerned with the passing of time, as winter means his father will leave.)*

CRITICAL VOCABULARY

maroon: Gilbert's father was marooned in Belgium.

ASK STUDENTS to describe what it might feel like to be marooned somewhere. When might Gilbert feel marooned? *(Being marooned is probably lonely and frightening. Gilbert might feel marooned when he has to study on beautiful days.)*

Strategies for Annotation   🖉 ▣ *Annotate it!*

Determine Meaning of Words and Phrases

RL 4

Have students reread lines 82–87. Encourage them to use their eBook annotation tools to do the following:

- Highlight in yellow the details that suggest a symbol of time.
- Underline details that reveal Gilbert's feelings.
- Write a note to describe what the symbol reveals about Gilbert.

"We're doing the lowlands." He looked out at the sunset, the sun racing for the other side of the planet, dragging them all back toward the winter. "Belgium. Belgium, Belgium, Belgium."

Gilbert feels dread about the coming winter, so he is unhappy about time moving too quickly.

Analyze Story Elements:
Character (LINES 94–122)

RL 1,
RL 3

Explain to students that authors use many techniques to give readers an understanding of each character's **character traits**—the qualities shown by a character. Point out that a character trait might be physical, such as eye color, or a trait could be an expression of personality, such as shyness. Point out that one way to show a character's traits is through **dialogue,** or the words that the character and other characters speak.

D **CITE TEXT EVIDENCE** Have students reread lines 94–122 and cite evidence in the text that reveals some of Gilbert's and his father's character traits. *(Gilbert's words show him to be inquisitive and focused on his struggle with time. His father seems patient and loving, as he listens, asks questions, and even adds more information for Gilbert to think about. This reveals a loving relationship. The author also describes a physical character trait of Gilbert's father—"furry eyebrows.")*

CRITICAL VOCABULARY

judicious: Gilbert's father is listening to Gilbert go on and on about time—a topic that Gilbert is clearly obsessed with.

ASK STUDENTS why Gilbert's father nods judiciously when Gilbert talks about his tutor. *(Gilbert is trying to get his father to take his side. His father responds to him in a fair, even way, showing he understands Gilbert's concern while respecting the tutor's authority.)*

"I *want* to do more physics, but Señor says I don't have the math for it."

His father nodded **judiciously**. "He would know. Why physics?"

judicious
(jōō-dĭsh´əs) *adv.* If you are *judicious*, you have good judgment.

"Time," he said, simply. They'd talked of time all summer, in those few hours when Gilbert wasn't with his tutor and when Father wasn't sitting at his desk working at his accounts, or riding into town to huddle over the telephone, casting his will over place and time, trying to keep his ships and their cargos in proper and correct motion.

"Why time, Gil? You're eleven, son! You've got lots of time! You can worry about time when you're an old man."

Gilbert pretended he hadn't heard. "I was thinking of more ways that time is like space. If I was at sea, standing on the deck of a ship, I could see a certain ways before me, and if I turned around, I could see a small ways behind me. But the horizon cuts off the view in both directions. Time is like that. I can think back a certain ways, and the further back I try to remember, the fuzzier it gets, until I can't see at all. And I can see forward—we'll have cobbler soon, go to bed, wake tomorrow. But no further."

His father raised his furry eyebrows and smiled a genuine and delighted smile. "Ah, but things separated by time affect each other the way that events separated by space can't. A star dying on the other side of the universe, so far away that its light hasn't yet had time enough to crawl all the way to us, can't have any effect on us. But things that happened hundreds of years ago, like the planting of the seed that grew the oak that made this table . . ." He rattled his saucer on it, making his coffee sway like a rough chop. He waggled his eyebrows again.

"Yikes," Gilbert said. That hadn't occurred to him. "What if time moved in every direction and at every speed—could you have a space where events at the far end of the galaxy affected us?" He answered his own question. "Of course. Because the events could travel backwards in time—or, uh . . ." He fumbled, remembered Neils. "Sideways." He swallowed.

"What's sideways in time?"

He shrugged. "Sideways is sideways," he said.

FOR STUDENTS WITH DISABILITIES

To assist students with visual disabilities, help them adjust the type size in their eBooks as needed before reading. They can also listen to the audio version of the text in their eBooks.

"WHAT IF TIME MOVED IN EVERY DIRECTION AND AT EVERY SPEED?"

His father laughed until tears rolled down his cheeks, and Gilbert didn't have the heart to tell him that the phrase had been Neils's, because making his father laugh like that was like Christmas and his birthday and a day at the beach all rolled into one.

And then his father took him down to the ocean, down the rough goat trail cut into the cliff, as surefooted as a goat himself. They watched the sun disappear behind the waves, and then they moved among the tidepools, swirling their
140 hands in the warm, salty water to make the bioluminescent[2] speck-size organisms light up like fireworks. They sat out and watched the moon and the stars, lying on their backs in the sand, Gilbert's head in the crook of his father's arm, and he closed his eyes and let his father tell him stories about the sea and the places he went in the long, lonely winters, while the waves went *shhh, shhh*, like the whisper of the mother who'd died giving birth to him.

Then they picked their way back up the cliff by moonlight that was so bright, it might have been day, a blue-white noon
150 in shades of gray, and his father tucked him up into bed as if he were three years old, smoothing the covers and kissing him on the forehead with a whiskery kiss.

As he lay along a moment that stretched sleepily out like warm taffy, suspended on the edge of sleep, the thought occurred to him: *What if space moved in only one direction, in two dimensions, like time?*

---

[2] **bioluminescent** (bī´ō-lōō´mə-nĕs´ənt): visible light, caused by chemical reactions, that emits from a living organism.

CLOSE READ

Analyze Story Elements: Character (LINES 131–135)
RL 1, RL 3

Explain that a **character's motivation** is the reason for a character's behavior.

E CITE TEXT EVIDENCE Have students reread lines 131–135 and cite details that reveal one of Gilbert's motivations. *(Gilbert loves to make his father laugh. It shows how deeply he loves his father. He feels safe and cared for with his father.)*

Determine Meaning of Words and Phrases
RL 4

(LINES 136-147)

Explain to students that an author sometimes uses a **simile**—a figure of speech that makes a comparison between two unlike things using the word *like* or *as*— to make explicit comparisons.

F ASK STUDENTS how the author uses a simile to reveal the sea as a symbol. *(Gilbert is sad at this moment, thinking about his father's imminent departure. But the author is using the sea as a symbol for Gilbert's lost mother, calming him.)*

Strategies for Annotation   ✎ 🖥 **Annotate it!**

Analyze Story Elements: Character
RL 3

Have students reread lines 131–135. Encourage them to use their eBook annotation tools to do the following:

- Underline clues that reveal his father's character traits.
- Highlight the details that reveal Gilbert's motivations.
- Describe Gilbert's character traits when he is in his father's presence. *(Gilbert feels happy and secure.)*

His father laughed until tears rolled down his cheeks, and Gilbert didn't have the heart to tell him that the phrase had been Neils's, because making his father laugh like that was like Christmas and his birthday and a day at the beach all rolled into one.

CLOSE READ

Determine Meaning of Words and Phrases

RL 1,
RL 4

(LINES 157–171)

Emphasize for students that the author repeatedly describes the weather in this passage and that weather is often used in fiction to create different kinds of **moods,** or the feelings or atmosphere that a writer creates for the reader.

G CITE TEXT EVIDENCE Have students reread lines 157–171 and identify references to weather. Ask them to describe the effect the weather has on the setting and on Gilbert. *(References to weather: "while the wind and rain howled outside the window" and "adding logs against the unseasonal winds outside." The author uses the unseasonably cold, turbulent weather to symbolize that something is not quite right. This aspect of the setting creates a mood of dread—that perhaps something bad is about to happen.)*

WHEN STUDENTS STRUGGLE...

To guide students' understanding of the author's use of weather as a symbol, have students work in pairs to fill out a chart like the one shown. Explain that the chart will help them identify ways that the author uses symbols to reveal information about the plot. Have pairs fill in the chart as they read and discuss how the details help identify symbols.

 LEVEL UP TUTORIALS For additional support, assign the following *Level Up* tutorial: **Symbol.**

The year passed. For so long as Gilbert could remember, summer's first messenger had been the postmaster, Mr. Ossinger, who rode his bicycle along the sea road to the house
160 to deliver his father's telegram advising of his expected arrival in port and the preparations to be made for him. Mrs. Curie usually signed for the letter, then knocked on the study door to deliver it into Gilbert's eager hands.

But this year, while the wind and rain howled outside the window, and Señor Uriarte plodded through the formation of igneous rock,[3] Mrs. Curie did not come and deliver the letter, rescuing him from geography. She didn't come to the door, though Señor had finished rocks and moved on to algebra and then to Shakespeare. Finally, the school day ended. Gilbert left
170 Señor stirring through the coals of the study fire, adding logs against the unseasonal winds outside.

Gilbert floated downstairs to the kitchen as though trapped in a dream that compelled him to seek out the housekeeper, even though some premonition told him to hide away in his room for as long as possible.

From behind, she seemed normal, her thin shoulders working as she beat at the batter for the night's cake, cranking the mixer's handle with slow, practiced turns. But when the door clicked shut behind him, she stopped working the
180 beater, though her shoulders kept working, shuddering, rising, falling. She turned her face to him and he let out a cry and took a step back toward the door. It was as though she had been caught by an onrush of time, one that had aged her, turning her from an old woman to an animated corpse. Every wrinkle seemed to have sunk deeper, her fine floss hair hung limp across her forehead, her eyes were red and leaked steady rills of tears.

She took a step toward him, and he wanted to turn and run, but now he was frozen. So he stood, rooted to the
190 spot, while she came and took him up in her frail arms and clutched at him, sobbing dry, raspy sobs. "He's not coming home," she whispered into his ear, the whiskers on her chin tickling at him. "He's not coming home, Gilbert. Oh, oh, oh." He held her and patted her and the time around him seemed to crawl by, slow enough that he could visualize every sweet moment he'd had with his father, time enough to visualize

---

[3] **igneous rock** (ĭg′nē-əs rŏk): rock formed when melted rock, called magma, cools and solidifies above or below the earth.

Detail	What it reveals
But this year, the wind and rain howled outside.	*Unlike past happier summers, the weather suggests something bad. It seems to represent darkness and death.*

every storm his father had ever narrated to him. Had all that time and more before Señor Uriarte came downstairs for his tea and found them in the kitchen. He gathered up frozen Gilbert and carried him to his bedroom, removed his shoes, and sat with him for hours until he finally slept.

When morning dawned, the storm had lifted. Gilbert went to his window to see the stupid blue sky with its awful yellow sun and realized that his father was now gone forever and ever, to the end of time.

Emmy and her brothers were queasy of him for the first week of summer, playing with him as though he were made of china or tainted with plague. But by the second week, they were back to something like normal, scampering up the trees and down the cliffs, ranging farther and farther afield on their bicycles.

Most of all, they were playing down at the switchyards, the old rail line that ran out from the disused freight docks a few miles down the beach from their houses. Señor and Mrs. Curie didn't know what to do with him that summer, lacking any direction from Father, and so Gilbert made the most of it, taking the Limburghers out on longer and longer trips, their packs bursting with food and water and useful tools: screwdrivers, crowbars, cans of oil.

Someone probably owned the switchyard, but whoever that was, he was far away and had shown no interest in it in Gilbert's lifetime. It had been decades since the freighters came into this harbor and freight trains had taken their cargos off into the land on the rusted rails. The rusted padlocks on the utility sheds crumbled and fell to bits at the lightest touch from the crowbars; the doors squealed open on their ancient hinges.

Inside, the cobwebby, musty gloom yielded a million treasures: old time-tables, a telegraph rig, stiff denim coveralls with material as thick as the hall carpet at home, ancient whiskey bottles, a leather-bound journal that went to powder when they touched it, and . . .

A handcar.[4]

"It'll never work," said Emmy. "That thing's older than the dinosaurs. It's practically rusted through!"

---

[4] **handcar:** a small, open railroad car that is propelled by a hand pump.

CLOSE READ

Analyze Story Elements: Character (LINES 211–231)   RL 3

Reiterate for students that characters often behave differently in different settings. In addition, children behave differently when adults are not present, compared with when they are.

(H) ASK STUDENTS how the characters' freedom from adult supervision affects their behavior. How does Gilbert "make the most of" this time in his life? *(The children are very brave, and they take actions, such as breaking into the utility sheds, that they would probably not take if adults were present. Gilbert takes advantage of this time by adventuring away from home farther and for longer periods of time.)*

Make Inferences   RL 1
(LINES 230–232)

Explain to students that authors use many techniques to emphasize important ideas, such as setting ideas apart from the rest of the text. Students can use this textual evidence to support inferences, or good guesses, about information that is not directly stated in the text.

(I) CITE TEXT EVIDENCE Ask students to identify how the author sets apart text in this section. What inference about the handcar does this text evidence support? *(By placing the first mention of the handcar on a separate line preceded by an unfinished line, the author shows it will be important. It's likely that the handcar will be a significant story element.)*

English Language Support

Before students begin, review the uses of ellipses. Explain that in addition to signaling an omission of text, ellipses can also signal a hesitation or a pause. Read aloud lines 227–232, pausing dramatically at the ellipses.

ASK STUDENTS to explain the feeling the pause created for them *(a feeling of suspense or drama).* Then ask volunteers to suggest what this special emphasis helps them infer about the handcar *(the handcar will be important to the plot).*

CLOSE READ

Analyze Story Elements: Character (LINES 235–249)

RL 1,
RL 3

Explain to students that sometimes authors explicitly describe a character's traits. More often, however, they provide evidence of character traits and expect readers to **infer,** or make good guesses about, them.

Ⓙ CITE TEXT EVIDENCE Have students reread the section and identify ways in which the author shows that Gilbert's determination affects the other characters. *(Gilbert keeps trying to move the handcar, while the other children watch. He moves it a little at a time. Each time gives him more hope. He applies oil. Emmy "leans in" and "doesn't mind" that the car almost crushes her foot. They all stare at the handcar "as if to say, 'Where have you been all my life?'" This shows that Gilbert's determination has motivated the others to help get it going.)*

Gilbert pretended he hadn't heard her. He wished he could move the car a little closer to the grimy windows. It was almost impossible to make sense of in the deep shadows of the shed. He pushed hard on the handle, putting his weight into it. It gave a groan, a squeal, and another groan. Then it moved an inch. That was a magic inch! He got his oilcan and lavishly applied the forty-weight oil to every bearing he could find. Neils and Erwin held the lamp. Emmy leaned in closer. He pushed the handle again. Another groan, and a much higher squeal, and the handle sank under his weight. The handcar rumbled forward, almost crushing Emmy's foot—if she hadn't been so quick to leap back, she'd have been crippled. She didn't seem to mind. She, her brothers, and Gilbert were all staring at the handcar as if to say, "Where have you been all my life?"

> **"THE HANDCAR RUMBLED FORWARD, ALMOST CRUSHING EMMY'S FOOT."**

They christened it *Kalamazoo* and they worked with oil and muscle until they had moved it right up to the doorway. It cut their fingers to ribbons and turned their shins into fields of bruises, but it was all worth it because of what it promised: motion without end.

The track in the switchyard went in two directions. Inland, toward the nation and its hurrying progress and its infinite hunger for materials and blood and work. And out to sea, stretching out on a rockbed across the harbor, to the breakers where the great boats that were too large for the shallow harbor used to tie up to offload. Once they had bullied *Kalamazoo* onto the tracks—using blocks, winches, levers, and a total disregard for their own safety—they stood to either side of its bogey handle and stared from side to side. Each knew what the others were thinking: Do we pump for the land, or pump for the sea?

English Language Support

Understand Language Choices Project lines 255–257 for students and read them aloud as students follow along in their texts. Review the term *personification,* or giving human characteristics to something that is not human. Tell students that authors sometimes use personification to help readers understand the text and create images of the ideas the author is trying to express. Encourage students to look for other examples of personification in the text.

• With students, reread lines 255–257. Ask them to identify something that is being given human characteristics. As a group,

work through the idea that "the nation" is being personified with the phrases "hurrying progress" and "infinite hunger."

• Have pairs or small groups reread lines 255–257 and note what is being personified and what phrases are used in the personification.

• Have pairs of students discuss the personification in lines 255–257 and write several sentences explaining why using personification adds power to the author's ideas.

"Tomorrow," Gilbert said. It was the end of August now, and lessons would soon begin again, and each day felt like something was drawing to a close. "Tomorrow," Gilbert said. "We'll decide tomorrow. Bring supplies."

270 That night, by unspoken agreement, they all packed their treasures. Gilbert laid out his sailor suit—his father bought him a new one every year—and his book about time and space and stuffed a picnic blanket with Mrs. Curie's preserves, hardtack bread, jars of lemonade, and apples from the cellar. Mrs. Curie—three quarters deaf—slept through his raid. Gilbert then went to his father's study and took the **spyglass** that had belonged to his grandfather, who had also been lost at sea. He opened the small oak box holding Grandad's **sextant**, but as he'd never mastered it, he set it down. He took
280 his father's enormous silver-chased[5] turnip watch, and tried on his rain boots and discovered that they fit. The last time he'd tried them on, he could have gotten both feet into one of them. Time had passed without his noticing, but his feet had noticed.

He hauled the bundles out to the hedgerow at the bottom of the driveway, and then he put himself to bed and in an instant he was asleep. An instant later, the sun was shining on his face. He woke, put on his sailor suit, went downstairs, and shouted hello to Mrs. Curie, who smiled a misty smile to
290 see him in his sailor suit. She gave him hotcakes with butter and cherries from the tree behind Señor's shed, a glass of milk and a mountain of fried potatoes. He ate until his stomach wouldn't hold any more, said goodbye to her, and walked to the bottom of the hedgerow to retrieve his secret bundle. He wrestled it into his bike's basket and wobbled down to the Limburghers' gate to meet his friends, each with a bundle and a bike.

The half-hour ride to the switchyard took so little time that it was over even before Gilbert had a chance to think
300 about what he was doing. Time was going by too fast for thoughts now, like a train that had hit its speed and could now only be perceived as a blur of passing cars and a racket of wheels and steam.

spyglass
(spī´glăs´) *n*. A *spyglass* is a small telescope.

sextant
(sĕk´stənt) *n*. A *sextant* is an instrument used to determine location by measuring the position of the stars and sun.

---
[5] **silver-chased:** Silver-chasing is a technique used in engraving silver. The silver is moved, rather than removed, with a small pointed tool and mallet to create a design or texture.

Another Place, Another Time **101**

CLOSE READ

Analyze Story Elements: Character (LINES 270–284)
RL 3

Remind students that things rarely "just happen" in literature. Authors portray actions and events either to advance the plot or to provide insight into character traits and motivations.

K **ASK STUDENTS** to reread lines 270–284 and determine Gilbert's motivation for bringing each item. Were his motivations purely practical, or did he bring any of the items for sentimental reasons? *(The practical items that Gilbert takes include the picnic blanket full of food, the spyglass, and the turnip watch. The food will nourish him on his journey. The watch will help him keep track of time. The spyglass will help him see where he is going. However, the watch, spyglass, and sailor suit also have sentimental value. They are symbols of his lost father (sailor suit and watch) and grandfather (spyglass). So, his motivations are not purely practical.)*

CRITICAL VOCABULARY

spyglass: Gilbert brings "the spyglass that had belonged to his grandfather, who had also been lost at sea."

ASK STUDENTS to explain why the author might have chosen to use the term *spyglass* instead of the term *telescope*. *(Spyglass is more old-fashioned, underscoring the object's connection to the past, and making it another symbol of time.)*

sextant: Gilbert chose not to bring his grandfather's sextant because he had never learned to use it.

ASK STUDENTS why a sextant might have been helpful had Gilbert taken it. *(He would have been able to figure out his location during the journey.)*

WHEN STUDENTS STRUGGLE . . .

To enhance understanding of the author's use of symbols, have pairs continue to fill out the charts they began on page 98. Have students think about the purpose of a switchyard and then consider the significance of the switchyard to the plot.

LEVEL UP TUTORIALS For additional support, assign the following *Level Up* tutorial: **Symbol.**

Detail	What it reveals
switchyard	The switchyard is a place that allowed trains to go in different directions. It seems to represent Gilbert's desire to travel in a different direction through space and time.

WHEN STUDENTS STRUGGLE...

Students may be unfamiliar with what a *handcar* is. Explain that in this particular story, there are two significant clues that can help them clarify the meaning. Have students reread the footnote for the word *handcar* on page 99 of the Student Edition. Then, have them use the illustration to further clarify the meaning.

LEVEL UP TUTORIALS For additional support, assign the following *Level Up* tutorial: **Analyzing Visuals.**

Kalamazoo was still beaded with dew as they began to unload their bundles onto its platform. Gilbert set his down at the end farthest from the sea, and Emmy set hers down at the end farthest from the land, and when they stood to either side of the pump handle, it was clear that Emmy wanted to push for the land while Gilbert wanted to push them out to sea.

310 Naturally.

Emmy looked at Gilbert and Gilbert looked at Emmy. Gilbert took out his grandfather's spyglass, lifted off the leather cap from the business end, extended it, and pointed it out to sea, sweeping from side to side, looking farther than he'd ever seen. Wordlessly, he held it out to Emmy, who turned around to face the bay and swept it with the telescope. Then she handed it off to Neils and Erwin, who took their turns.

Nothing more had to be said. They leaned together into the stiff lever that controlled *Kalamazoo's* direction of travel, 320 threw it into position, and set to pumping out to sea.

What the spyglass showed: waves and waves, and waves and waves, and, farther along, the curvature of the planet itself as it warped toward Europe and Africa and the rest of the world. It showed a spit of land, graced with an ancient and crumbling sea fort, shrouded in mist and overgrown with the weeds and trees of long disuse. And beyond it, waves and more waves.

The gentle sea breeze turned into a stiff wind once they'd pumped for an hour, the handcart at first rolling slowly on the complaining wheels. Then, as the rust flaked off the axles 330 and the bearings found their old accommodations, they spun against one another easily. The pumping was still hard work, and even though they traded off, the children soon grew tired and sore and Emmy called for a rest stop and a snack.

As they munched their sandwiches, Gilbert had a flash. "We could use this for a sail," he said, nudging his picnic blanket with one toe. Neils and Erwin—whose shorter arms suffered more from the pumping labor—loved the idea, and set to rigging a mast from their fishing poles and the long crowbar they'd lashed to *Kalamazoo's* side. Emmy and Gilbert 340 let them do the work, watching with the wisdom of age, eating sandwiches and enjoying the breeze that dried their sweat.

English Language Support

Read Closely Note that authors do not always use complete sentences. Read aloud lines 321–326, guiding students to identify sentence fragments (*What the spyglass showed. . . .rest of the world.; And beyond it, waves and more waves.*). Explain that authors purposely use sentence fragments to emphasize an idea or create a mood.

ASK STUDENTS to work in pairs to rewrite the fragments as complete sentences and read the lines aloud, substituting their sentences for the fragments. Ask what mood each version conveys and which has a more dramatic feeling.

CLOSE READ

Determine Meaning of Words and Phrases
RL 1, RL 4

(LINES 304–310)

Explain to students that here the author is using the land and sea both as symbols and as literal destinations to establish what Gilbert wants.

Ⓛ CITE TEXT EVIDENCE Have students reread lines 304–310. Ask them to identify what Emmy and Gilbert each want at this moment, while keeping in mind that Emmy is the older of the two. Then ask students to explain what this may reveal about the significance of the symbols of the land and the sea in this story. *(Emmy is older and perhaps more responsible. She chooses land, as it seems to represent the safety of the adult world—a place of "hurrying progress and infinite hunger" and a place of "work," as indicated earlier in the story. Gilbert wants to go to the sea, a symbol of the lost love of his parents, of the adventures and imagination of childhood.)*

Analyze Story Elements: Character (LINES 321–333)
RL 3

Explain to students that both the spyglass and the handcar are tools that help the children see and set their course very clearly. They use each to change their setting.

Ⓜ ASK STUDENTS to reread this passage and tell how the settings of the handcar and the sea ahead of them help focus the children's motivation. *(They all want to head for the infinite possibilities of the sea on the handcar that moves more and more easily, even though it is tiring work. Through the spyglass they see the infinite waves and the last signs of the finite world—an ancient, decaying fort.)*

As they started up again, *Kalamazoo* seemed as refreshed from the rest as they were, and it rolled more easily than ever, the sail bellied out before the mast. When Gilbert and Emmy stopped to trade pumping duties back to the twins, Kalamazoo continued to roll, propelled by the stiff wind alone. All four children made themselves comfortable at the back of the pump car and allowed the time and the space to whip past them as they would.

350 "We're moving through space like time," Gilbert said.

Emmy quirked her mouth at him, a familiar no-nonsense look that he ignored.

"We are," he said. "We are moving in a straight line, from behind to in front, at a rate we can't control. Off to the sides are spaces we could move through, but we're not. We're on these rails, and we can't go sideways, can't go back, can't go up or down. We can't control our speed. We are space's slaves. This is just how we move through time."

Emmy shook her head. Neils seemed excited by the idea, 360 though, and he nudged his twin and they muttered in their curious twinnish dialect to one another.

The sea fort was visible with the naked eye now, and with the spyglass, Gilbert could make out its brickwork and the streaks of guano that ran down its cracked walls. The rails ran right up to the fort—last used as a customs inspection point— and past it to the hidden docks on the other side of the spit.

"Better hope that the wind shifts," Emmy said, holding a wetted finger up to check the breeze.

"Otherwise we're going to have a devil of a time pumping 370 ourselves home in time for supper."

Gilbert drew out the turnip watch, which he'd set this morning by the big grandfather clock in the front hall, carefully winding its spring. He opened its face and checked the second hand. It seemed to be spinning a little more slowly, but that could have been his imagination. According to the watch, it was nearly eleven, and they'd been on the rails for three hours.

"I think we'll make the fort in time for lunch," he said.

At the mention of food, Neils and Erwin clamored for 380 snacks, and Emmy found them cookies she'd snitched from the big jar in the Limburgher kitchen.

TO CHALLENGE STUDENTS ...

Analyzing Theme What is Gilbert's take on time? Cory Doctorow has Gilbert explain how time is a fourth dimension, as laid out in the theories of scientist Albert Einstein. Doctorow himself has said that he had difficulty grasping all the science in this story, so he consulted real scientists while he wrote it. Suggest that students briefly research student-friendly online sources on Einstein's theories of relativity and what they say about time. Then have students work in small groups to discuss Gilbert's grasp of the theory and how his explanation early in the story plays out in the events at the end.

Gilbert looked at the watch for a moment. The second hand had stopped moving. He held it up to his ear, and it wasn't precisely ticking any longer, but rather making a sound like a truck-wheel spinning in spring mud. He closed the lid again, and held it so tight that the intricate scrolling on the case dug into his palm.

Time passed.

And then it didn't.

390 And then it did again.

"Oh!" said Neils and Erwin together.

> # GILBERT LOOKED AT THE WATCH FOR A MOMENT. THE SECOND HAND HAD STOPPED MOVING.

To either side of the car, stretching into infinity, were more tracks, running across the endless harbor, each with its own car, its own sail, its own children. Some were edging ahead of them. Some were going backwards. A racket overhead had them all look up at once, at the tracks there, too, the rails and the cars and the Limburghers and the Gilberts in them. Some children were older. Some were younger. One Gilbert was weeping. One was a girl.

400 Gilbert waved his hand, and a hundred Gilberts waved back. One made a rude gesture.

"Oh!" said Emmy. To her right, another Emmy was offering her a sandwich. She took it and handed over the last of her cookies and Emmy smiled at herself and said thank you as politely as you could wonder.

"Sideways is sideways," Neils and Erwin said together. Emmy and Gilbert nodded.

CLOSE READ

Analyze Story Elements: Character (LINES 392–407)   RL 3

Suddenly, the setting changes significantly—to a different reality. The children are still safely on the handcar, but around them, everything extends to infinity.

(N) CITE TEXT EVIDENCE Have students reread lines 392–407 and discuss the effect that the change in setting has on the children. Ask how each child reacts and what that reveals about him or her. *(The children seem unfazed and happy to see the strange sights around them. Gilbert waves to the other children, including duplicates of his grieving self and his feminine self. Emmy also seems happy as she shares the cookie and smiles at herself. The twins stay constant, repeating the same line that they had earlier in the story.)*

English Language Support

Before students participate in the discussion, have them reread lines 392–407, pausing to use a dictionary to define terms that are confusing. Then ask them to list each character and write brief notes about how each one behaves in the new setting.

Strategies for Annotation   ✏ 🖹 Annotate it!

Analyze Story Elements: Character   RL 3

Have students reread lines 400–405. Encourage them to use their eBook annotation tools to do the following:

- Underline any clues that show how the setting has changed.
- Highlight in yellow details that reveal how Gilbert and Emmy react.
- Write a note to describe Emmy's and Gilbert's character traits.

Gilbert waved his hand, and a hundred Gilberts waved back. One made a rude gesture.

"Oh!" said Emmy. To her right, another Emmy was offering her a sandwich. She took it and handed over the last of her cookies and Emmy smiled at herself and said thank you as politely as you could wonder.

> Gilbert is intrigued and happy.
> Emmy is still polite but also happy.

Analyze Story Elements: Character (LINES 414–421)

RL 3

In the end, Gilbert makes a bold move to leave the other children behind and set out on his own.

 CITE TEXT EVIDENCE Ask students to reread the last three paragraphs and identify what Gilbert does and explain what this action reveals about him. *(Gilbert has been on a mission to fulfill a dream—to break free of the tyranny of time. That has been his motivation. He now sees his chance to step into the timeless realm of infinite possibility. Emmy responds with a playful gesture, which shows she's like a supportive big sister. Gilbert leaps onto the other handcar. It is an easy leap. He remains a dreamer and a searcher—but this time, all on his own.)*

COLLABORATIVE DISCUSSION Have groups of students discuss Gilbert's interest in the dimension of time. Point out that Gilbert's interest in time is connected to Einstein's idea that the experience of time can be relative. For Gilbert, time is relative to events, actions, and settings—his experience of it varies as these elements change. Then have them share their ideas with the class as a whole. Accept all reasonable responses.

ASK STUDENTS to share any questions they generated in the course of reading and discussing the selection.

English Language Support

Support Opinions Provide the following sentence stems to students before they begin the discussion.

- I think that _____.
- I agree that _____, but_____.
- That is a good point, but I still think _____, because _____.

Gilbert pulled out his spyglass and looked ahead at the fort. All the rails converged on it, but without ever meeting. And some stretched beyond. And out there, somewhere, there was time like space and space like time. And somewhere there was a father on a ship that weathered a storm rather than succumbed to it.

Gilbert turned to his friends and shook each of their hands in turn. Neils was crying a little. Emmy gave Gilbert a friendly punch in the shoulder and then a hug.

There was another *Kalamazoo* to the right, and Gilbert was pretty sure he could easily make the leap from his car to it. And then to the next car, and the next. And beyond, into the infinite sideways.

If there was an answer, he'd find it there.

COLLABORATIVE DISCUSSION Why is Gilbert so interested in the dimension of time? Talk about your ideas with other group members. Discuss how time interacts with and changes Gilbert.

English Language Support

Write a Summary Use the GIST method to help students write a summary of the ending events in the story. Follow these steps:

1. Display lines 392-421 of the story, and read them together.
2. After reading, help students underline ten or more words that seem "most important." List these words on the board.
3. Together, write a summary statement using as many of the underlined words as possible.
4. Work with students to create a topic sentence to precede the summary.

Analyze Story Elements: Character

RL 3

The characters of "Another Place, Another Time" bring amazingly complex happenings down to a human level. **Characters** are the people, animals, or other creatures who take part in a story. A short story often has a **main character,** whose problem or goal drives the plot. The behavior and action of all the characters affects what happens. In addition, the **setting** of the story, or the time and place of the action, can affect the characters' traits, motivations, and actions.

When you analyze how characters act and change throughout a story, consider the chart below.

Character traits are the qualities shown by a character. Traits may be physical (blond hair) or expressions of personality (fearlessness).	The writer may directly state the character's traits, or you may have to infer traits based on the character's words, thoughts, actions, appearance, or relationships.
Character motivations are the reasons for a character's behavior.	To understand a character's obvious or hidden desires and goals, notice what makes the character take or avoid action.

Think about the main character, Gilbert, in "Another Place, Another Time." Use one or two words to describe his traits. How do the setting and events change him as the story unfolds?

Determine Meaning of Words and Phrases

RL 4

A **symbol** is a person, a place, an object, or an activity that stands for something beyond itself. Often, a symbol represents an important idea or concept, such as freedom, love, or loneliness. For example, a dove is often a symbol of peace. Characters, objects, conflicts, and settings can serve as symbols for important ideas in a story.

You can identify symbols and determine their meanings by analyzing details in the text.

- Look for people, places, things, or actions that the writer emphasizes or mentions frequently.
- Think about the importance of these details to the characters.

The sea setting is a major feature in "Another Place, Another Time." The sea stands for at least one idea or feeling that is important to Gilbert. Reread lines 138–147 of the story. What might the sea represent for Gilbert here?

CLOSE READ

Analyze Story Elements: Character

RL 3

Discuss the literary terms and what to consider when analyzing characters. Have volunteers identify the main character and other characters in the story. Then, discuss examples of the characters' traits, especially in different settings. Finally, discuss the main character's motivation and how Gilbert's pursuit of his goal changes him in the story.

Determine Meaning of Words and Phrases

RL 4

Discuss the definition of the term *symbol*. Using familiar symbols in school, such as the flag, discuss what each represents. Then ask volunteers to identify symbols they encountered in the story, such as the symbol of the sea. Discuss what these symbols represent and how they make the story more compelling and satisfying to read.

English Language Support

Form small groups to answer the questions on page 108. Assign one question to each group. When all groups finish their answers, have them take turns presenting answers to the class. Encourage students to provide useful feedback.

Strategies for Annotation 📝 🖥 *Annotate it!*

Analyze Story Elements: Character

RL 3

Share these strategies for guided or independent analysis:

- Highlight in yellow details about the setting that affect a character's motivations.
- Underline details that show characters taking action.
- On a note, jot down your insights regarding the character's motivations for taking the action.

"You got up into my tree house," he said, putting a small emphasis on *my.* "And you could go back *down*, too."

Emmy, who was a better fighter than any of them, put her fists on her hips and mimed *Make me*. He pretended he didn't see it.

Analyzing the Text

RL 1, RL 2, RL 3, RL 4, RL 5

Possible answers:

1. *The title directly reveals the character's interest in time and its interplay with place. These ideas are further developed in the first paragraph of the story, when we see that Gilbert is keenly aware that time seems to move more quickly in some places than others. Gilbert's interest in the interplay between space and time is one of his primary motivations.*

2. *Words used to describe time include* tyrant, crawled, whipped, eternity, flashing instant. *These descriptions suggest that time—or at least our perception of it—is imposed upon us and entirely outside our control. It is part of the nature of humanity to be caught in time.*

3. *Einstein claimed that time was similar to space, implying that one might travel back in time. At the beginning of the story this is an interesting idea to Gilbert, but his father's death further increases its appeal. If Gilbert could travel backward in time, he might be with his father—and his mother—once more.*

4. *Gilbert feels trapped in and by time. His observation that the rails limit the children's movements through space helps reiterate his understanding of time. It also sets up a clear point of reference for the following section in which the bounds of both space and time fall away.*

5. *Gilbert is still struggling to come to terms with his father's death. He wants to see his father again, and in these lines we see his belief that this may be possible.*

6. *Symbol:* handcar; *What it represents (in outer ovals of web):* freedom, power, self-directed movement, hope, determination. *The handcar symbolizes the children's newfound ability first to determine their own direction in space from just two choices and later to determine their own direction through both time and space from an unlimited list of possibilities. The handcar symbolizes freedom from the bounds of both space and time.*

Analyzing the Text

RL 1, RL 2, RL 3, RL 4, RL 5, W 9a

Cite Text Evidence Support your responses with evidence from the text.

1. **Infer** What does the story title have to do with the setting and the main character's motivations?

2. **Interpret** Reread lines 1–7. What words or phrases describe time? What do these descriptions suggest about the story's **theme,** the message about life or human nature?

3. **Cite Evidence** How might Albert Einstein be a motivating factor in Gilbert's quest?

4. **Infer** Reread lines 353–358. What does this speech reveal about Gilbert and how he perceives reality?

5. **Interpret** Examine lines 408–413. What do these lines suggest about Gilbert's emotional state at this point of the story?

6. **Synthesize** Use a web like the one shown to explore symbolism in the story. In the central circle, write *handcar, father's watch,* or the name of something else from the story that works as a symbol. Fill out the web by recording your ideas about what the symbol represents.

PERFORMANCE TASK

Writing Activity: Character Analysis
With a partner, find and record references to the passage of time that connect to key experiences for Gilbert. For each important reference, also note what is happening to Gilbert. Together, write a one-page character profile of Gilbert, including details that answer these questions:

- What are Gilbert's personal traits?
- What motivates Gilbert's actions?
- What life-changing events occur in his life?
- When and where is he at the start of the story? At the end?
- How has he changed by the end of the story?

Assign this performance task.

PERFORMANCE TASK

RL 1, RL 2, W 9a

Writing Activity: Character Analysis Have students work with a partner to complete their character profiles of Gilbert. For this work, they should review the story and

- use each new setting as a clue that new character traits might come to the surface.
- use each new event in the story as a clue to character motivations.

Critical Vocabulary

L 4c, L 6

eloquence   maroon   judicious   spyglass   sextant

Practice and Apply Complete each sentence to show that you understand the meaning of the vocabulary word.

1. Everyone was impressed by the **eloquence** of . . .

2. The sailors were **marooned** on . . .

3. Before the travelers set out, they were **judicious** about . . .

4. The way to use a **spyglass** is to . . .

5. Sailors long ago needed a **sextant** to . . .

Vocabulary Strategy: Reference Aids

A **dictionary** is a valuable resource for anyone who is checking and expanding their vocabulary. The searching and browsing methods differ for print and digital dictionaries, but users can find the same basic information about each entry word.

- pronunciation
- part of speech label
- one or more definitions
- related forms

> in•tri•cate (ĭn′trĭ-kĭt) *adj.* **1.** Having many complexly arranged elements; elaborate. **2.** Difficult to understand, analyze, or solve for having many interconnected elements. —in′tri•cate•ly *adv.* —in′tri•cate•ness *n.*

Synonyms are words with similar meanings. The dictionary entry shown for *intricate* includes a synonym within the definition: *elaborate.* Some dictionaries provide a list of synonyms after an entry. A **thesaurus** is a reference aid that lists synonyms. Writers can use a print or digital thesaurus to help find the exact word they need.

> **intricate** *adj.* complicated, complex, elaborate, involved, convoluted

Practice and Apply Find the sentence with *judiciously* in line 94 of "Another Place, Another Time." Look up the word *judicious* and find the related form in an available dictionary and thesaurus. Use your own words to tell what the sentence means. Then rewrite the sentence using an appropriate synonym.

PRACTICE & APPLY

Critical Vocabulary

L 2b, L 4c

Sample answers:

1. *Everyone was impressed by the eloquence of the speaker, whose words moved some listeners to tears.*

2. *The sailors were marooned on an island with no fresh water, and no rescue ship was in sight.*

3. *Before the travelers set out, they were judicious about packing only the clothes they could carry in backpacks.*

4. *The way to use a spyglass is to hold it up to one eye and look through it so that distant objects appear close.*

5. *Sailors long ago needed a sextant to determine their location in the open sea.*

Vocabulary Strategy: Reference Aids

Sample answer:

The sentence His father nodded judiciously *means that his father nodded with an expression on his face that showed he was thinking wisely and agreeing with the judgment of the tutor. Sample restatement with a synonym:* His father nodded thoughtfully.

English Language Support

Using Reference Aids Explain that language resources not only help readers understand unfamiliar words; they also help writers make their texts more **cohesive,** with clearly connected ideas. Have mixed-ability pairs review each other's character analyses, watching for repeated or unclear word choices. Partners should use a thesaurus to suggest synonyms that will help avoid repetition and clearly link ideas.

Strategies for Annotation   🖉 🗐 *Annotate it!*

Reference Aids

L 4a, L 4c, L 5b

Have students locate the first two lines of the story. Encourage them to use their eBook annotation tools to do the following:

- Highlight the word *tyrant* in yellow.
- Use the context of the sentence to make a guess at the word's meaning.
- Confirm the meaning in a dictionary.
- Use a thesaurus to find a synonym and add it to a note.

Gilbert hated time. What a tyrant it was! The hours that crawled by when his father was at sea, the seconds that

Synonym
oppressor
dictator

PRACTICE & APPLY

Language Conventions: Spell Correctly

Tell students that the examples in the chart show just a few examples for each category. Invite volunteers to come up with familiar examples for each category. *(Possible answers: geographical names: your town's name, your school's name, your state's name; personal titles and names: your name, students' names, Principal Smith, President Obama; proper adjectives: Italian, French, American, Canadian; abbreviations: St., Rd., Mrs., Ms.)*

Answers:

1. *Doctorow, Kalamazoo*

2. *Limburgher, Erwin*

3. *Uriarte, Mrs., Atlantic Ocean*

4. *Professor, Newtonian*

 Assess It Online!

Online Selection Test
- Download an editable ExamView bank.
- Assign and manage this test online.

Language Conventions: Spell Correctly

When you proofread your writing for accuracy, you should check the spelling of every word. If you are using computer software to write, you will find that the spellchecker catches most misspellings—but not all. So, you still need to check the spelling in your work. In particular, be attentive to the spelling of proper nouns, proper adjectives, personal titles, and abbreviations, which are less likely to be corrected by a spellchecker.

Read these sentences from "Another Place, Another Time."

> He thumped the book he'd taken out of his father's bookcase, a book fetched home from London, heavy and well made and swollen with the damp air of the sea-crossing home to America. He hadn't read the book, but his tutor, sour Señor Uriarte, had explained it to him the day before . . .

Note the capitalization and spelling of the geographical names *London* and *America*; a personal title, *Señor*; and a proper name, *Uriarte*.

The chart shows categories of words to check for correct spelling and capitalization.

Category	Examples
geographical names	Madagascar, Kaskaskia River, Cincinnati, Sagamore Boulevard
personal titles and names	Madame Thibeau, Professor Moriarty, Señorita Madariaga
proper adjectives	Parisian, Colombian, Shakespearean, Einsteinian
abbreviations	Mme., Mr., Dr., Ave., Sq., Blvd.

Practice and Apply These sentences include errors in spelling and capitalization. In each sentence, identify the misspellings and write the words correctly. Refer to "Another Place, Another Time" and to other reference resources to check spellings.

1. Cory Docorow, the author of "Another Place, Another Time," tells how the children named the handcar *Kamalazoo*.

2. In this story, Gilbert is friends with Emmy Limberger and her twin brothers, Neils and Irwin.

3. Gilbert's tutor, Señor Uriate, and his housekeeper, Mme. Curie, care for him when his father is crossing the Altantic ocean.

4. Profesor Einstein's book leaves a deep impression on Gilbert, who wants to understand how the newtonion view of the universe has changed.

English Language Support

Check Capitalization and Spelling Point out the available resources for checking capitalization and spelling. Remind students that when a computer spell checker suggests a change, they should first confirm the correction in a dictionary or other source before accepting it.

- Read the first two Practice and Apply sentences aloud. Help students identify and correct the misspelled words. Point out that reading aloud the names helps to call attention to the misspellings. Explain that for this exercise, students can refer to

the text of "Another Place, Another Time" to confirm capitalization and spelling corrections.

- Have pairs identify and correct the capitalization and spelling errors in the Practice and Apply sentences. Remind students to use the story as a reference source.

- Dictate to students a geographical name, a title, a person's name, a proper adjective, and an abbreviation. Have partners note the words and write a sentence using each one.

Analyze Story Elements: Character and Setting

TEACH

Remind students that the **settings** in a story—or the times and places of the action—can affect the characters.

- Ask students how their own behavior and feelings can change from one place to another. For example, they'd likely feel one way on a beach on a hot summer afternoon and another way at a bus stop on a cold, rainy evening in winter. Their reasons, or **motivations,** for their behavior would be different in each setting.
- Point out that these feelings and actions are similar to the **traits** and motivations of story characters.
- As story characters encounter different settings, their traits and motivations can change. The settings affect the characters, and their reactions reveal information about them.
- In works of fiction, the evidence of these changes is revealed by the dialogue, descriptions, and details in the text.
- Discuss how in "Another Place, Another Time," Gilbert behaved differently when he was by the ocean with his father than when he was in the tree house with his friends.

INDEPENDENT READING

Have pairs of students work together to identify different settings in "Another Place, Another Time." Have them use a graphic organizer such as a Comparison-Contrast Chart to track how Gilbert changes in each setting. Have them list details about each setting that seem to affect Gilbert and list how each setting reveals different traits and motivations for Gilbert. Have students share their completed charts with another pair of students and discuss what the changes in setting reveal about Gilbert.

INTERACTIVE GRAPHIC ORGANIZERS Have students find graphic organizers for comparing and contrasting, such as the **Comparison-Contrast Chart.**

Analyzing Story Elements: Character

RETEACH

Review the terms *character, main character, character traits,* and *character motivations.* Point out that all main characters and most secondary characters have traits and motivations that can be identified in a number of ways.

- **Direct Characterization** An author might directly describe a character's traits and motivations.
- **Indirect Characterization** Often, authors reveal character traits and motivations indirectly. They include information that helps the reader **infer,** or guess, what a character is like. These indirect hints include details, such as the character's physical appearance, speech, thoughts, and actions as well as other characters' reactions to a character.

LEVEL UP TUTORIALS Assign the following *Level Up* tutorial: **Methods of Characterization**

COLLABORATIVE DISCUSSION

Have small groups of students work together to find examples of both direct and indirect characterization of three or four characters from the story. Have each group member pick a character to analyze by rereading the text and writing down examples of characterization. Then have students come together to discuss the different ways that Cory Doctorow created interesting, believable characters.

ANCHOR TEXT EXEMPLAR
Sorry, Wrong Number

Drama by Lucille Fletcher

Why This Text?

As regular viewers of dramas, students can also develop as readers of drama and enhance their understanding of how works of fiction are structured for audiences. This lesson leads students to analyze a written script for dramatic elements and explore the ways in which a play and a film are similar and different.

Key Learning Objective: Students will be able to analyze the elements of a drama and make comparisons between a script and a performance.

For practice and application:

A Christmas Carol

Close Reader selection
A Christmas Carol
Novel Excerpt by Charles Dickens; Drama Excerpt by Israel Horovitz; Graphic Story from Marvel Comics

---

RL 1 Make inferences.
RL 2 Provide a summary.
RL 3 Analyze story elements.
RL 4 Determine meanings of words and phrases.
RL 5 Analyze how a drama's structure contributes to its meaning.
RL 7 Compare and contrast a drama to its filmed version.
RL 10 Read and comprehend dramas.
W 2 Write explanatory texts.
W 4 Produce clear and coherent writing.
W 9a Apply grade 7 Reading standards to literature.
W 10 Write routinely.
L 4a Use context as a clue to meaning.
L 4c Consult reference materials to clarify meaning.
SL 2 Analyze the main ideas and supporting details in diverse media and formats.

▲ Text Complexity Rubric

Quantitative Measures	**Sorry, Wrong Number** **Lexile:** N/A
Qualitative Measures	**Levels of Meaning/Purpose** single level of simple meaning (single theme)
	Structure simple, linear chronology
	Language Conventionality and Clarity increased, clearly assigned dialogue
	Knowledge Demands some cultural and literary knowledge useful
Reader/Task Considerations	• Teacher determined • Vary by individual reader and type of text • See the Text X-Ray for suggested Reader/Task Considerations.

English Language Support
Before teaching, use the Text X-Ray for an overview of the text's complexity. The Text X-Ray and the supports and scaffolds in the Teacher's Edition will help you guide students of different skill levels.

Meaning Making

Language Development

Effective Expression

Content Knowledge

Foundational Skills

Text Complexity: Qualitative Measures

Levels of Meaning/Purpose

single level of simple meaning (single theme)

Help students summarize text.

- Teacher's Edition side notes, pp. 113, 114, 115, 116, 120, 122, 123, 124, 125, 126
- English Language Support, p. 119
- When Students Struggle, p. 120
- Close Read Screencasts, p. 111
- Strategies for Annotation, pp. 122, 125

To reteach plot, see

Analyze Form: Drama, p. 126a

 Use It! **Level Up Tutorial:** Plot Stages

ZOOM IN ON **ANALYZING PLOT** Tell students that a drama and a story share the same plot elements.

- Display a plot diagram like the one on page 126.
- Review and discuss each of the five main parts of a plot: exposition, rising action, climax, falling action, and resolution.
- Have students read the play in small groups, using a story map to keep track of events.
- Monitor each group's progress.
- After groups have finished reading, have them discuss the drama's main conflict and its resolution.

Structure

simple, linear chronology

Help students analyze story elements.

- Teacher's Edition side notes, pp. 111, 112, 113, 114, 115, 117, 118, 119, 121
- English Language Support, pp. 111, 112, 122
- Strategies for Annotation, pp. 117, 118

Guide students to compare the play with a film version.

- Compare and Contrast: Text and Media, p. 126a

 Use It! **Level Up Tutorial:** Elements of Drama
Interactive Graphic Organizer: Elements of Plot, p. 125

ZOOM IN ON **ANALYZING ELEMENTS OF DRAMA** Explain that a drama includes elements that other forms of literature usually do not have, such as

- a **cast of characters**
- assigned **dialogue**
- **stage directions**

As a class, define and discuss each of these elements. Tell students to consider, as they read the play, how these elements would or would not be included in a film version of the play. After they have read the play, have students discuss how a film version would differ from a live performance.

Language Conventionality and Clarity

increased, clearly assigned dialogue

Teach unfamiliar academic vocabulary in context.

- Teacher's Edition side notes, pp. 117, 119, 124, 126
- English Language Support, p. 121
- Applying Academic Vocabulary, p. 115

ZOOM IN ON **DETERMINING MEANINGS OF WORDS AND PHRASES** Tell students they can often use the **context,** or nearby words, to determine the meaning of an unfamiliar word or phrase. Turn to page 114 and direct students' attention to the following:

- line 176: *bridles*
- line 199: *apprehend*
- lines 217–218: *can't make head nor tail of it*

Help students to ask and answer questions about the context of each word or phrase (*What is Mrs. Stevenson's attitude? What do police do when they catch killers? What problem does the Operator have?*). Assign pairs to work together to determine meanings as they read.

Knowledge Demands

some cultural and literary knowledge useful

Help students understand the cultural and historical context of the drama.

- Teacher's Edition Background note, p. 111

ZOOM IN ON **BUILDING CULTURAL KNOWLEDGE** Have students read and discuss the Background on page 111 of their books; then share information from the Background note in the Teacher's Edition.

Have students discuss what life must have been like before cell phones and computers enhanced people's ability to contact and communicate with others. In addition to the technical capabilities, have students discuss the possible difficulties of disabled people of that earlier time, who had few places to turn for dedicated support.

Suggested Reader/Task Considerations

Consider the following before assigning this drama to students:

- Do students have the necessary attention to read and comprehend a play script of this length?
- Do students have the inference skills necessary to make connections among the various elements of the play?

ZOOM IN ON **SUPPORTING COMPREHENSION**

- Have students listen to the eBook audio as they read along. Pause as needed to make sure students follow the stage directions and understand who is speaking the lines.
- Have students read in small groups, pausing after every two or three pages to recap the action and share observations about characters. When these observations differ, have students reread to clarify their understanding.

CLOSE READ

Background Have students read the background and information about the author. Provide further explanation of mid-twentieth century communication:

- Telephone numbers were literally dialed, as in the rotary phone shown.
- There was no voice messaging. If a phone was in use, a caller heard a short series of beeps, called a busy signal.
- Each phone number began with a two-letter abbreviation; for example, the phone exchange "Murray Hill" in this play was MU.
- Callers dialed the number for Information to talk to a live operator who looked up phone numbers.

SETTING A PURPOSE Direct students to use the Setting a Purpose prompt to focus their reading. Remind them to write down any questions they have as they read.

Analyze Form: Drama
RL 5

(CAST OF CHARACTERS)

Tell students that a play, or **drama,** is a form of literature meant to be performed by actors in front of an audience. The script for a play begins with a list of all the characters in the play, called the **cast of characters.** Explain that in this play, the main character is Mrs. Stevenson, and the other characters have supporting roles.

Ⓐ ASK STUDENTS what they can predict about the action of the play based on the Operator and Information listings. *(Mrs. Stevenson will talk to seven different telephone operators over the course of the action.)*

English Language Support

Clarify that the role of "Information" listed in the Cast of Characters refers to a type of telephone operator who looks up telephone numbers.

ASK STUDENTS to count the number of operators listed in the Cast of Characters *(seven).* Then ask what this large number of operators suggests about the action of the play. *(Much of the play will involve speaking on the telephone.)*

Background *Long before cell phones, telephone service went over wires. People called the operator, who connected them to a number. Occasionally, malfunctions resulted in "crossed" wires, allowing a caller to hear other people's phone conversations.* **Lucille Fletcher** (1912–2000) *wrote novels, radio plays, stage plays, and screenplays. She is best remembered for her radio play* Sorry, Wrong Number, *which was first broadcast in 1943. The play became a sensation, capturing the imaginations of mystery fans around the world.*

Sorry, Wrong Number

Drama by Lucille Fletcher

SETTING A PURPOSE A drama is mainly intended to be performed for an audience. As you read, pay attention to the stage directions to help you imagine the plot events as if they were being performed by live actors. Write down any questions you have while reading.

Ⓐ

Cast of Characters

Mrs. Stevenson	**4th Operator**
1st Operator	**5th Operator**
1st Man	**Information**
2nd Man	**Hospital Receptionist**
Chief Operator	**Western Union**
2nd Operator	**Sergeant Duffy**
3rd Operator	**A Lunchroom-Counter Attendant**

(bg) ©PhotoHouse/Shutterstock; (cr) ©Mihai Simonia/Shutterstock

Sorry, Wrong Number **111**

Close Read Screencasts   ▶ View It!

Modeled Discussion

Have students click the *Close Read* icons in their eBooks to access a screencast in which readers discuss and annotate the following key passage:

> **Operator.** Ringing Murray Hill 4–0098. … **George.** Yes, sir. (lines 53–75)

As a class, view and discuss the video. Then have students pair up to do an independent close read of an additional passage: **Operator.** Ringing the Police Department. . . . *(the curtain falls.)* (lines 872–898)

Analyze Form: Drama

RL 1,
RL 5

(LINES 1–15, 28–29)

Point out the typography conventions used in the script:

- *Italic* type, often in parentheses, denotes **stage directions**—unspoken instructions about how the drama is to be performed. The letters *L* and *R* denote "stage left" and "stage right," when facing the audience.

- Roman type labels the characters' names within stage directions.

- Roman type is used for **dialogue,** the words spoken by the characters. The character's name in boldface type precedes his or her lines of dialogue.

B CITE TEXT EVIDENCE Have students find the descriptive details in the stage directions that tell what is lit and what is in darkness onstage. *(Mrs. Stevenson in her bed is in the center of the stage, lit by a table lamp. The left and right sections of the stage are dark.)*

Tell students that readers of a play can use the stage directions to visualize the characters and imagine how they sound.

C ASK STUDENTS to give ideas about Mrs. Stevenson's character based on the description in lines 28–29. *(She is a "querulous, self-centered neurotic." That means she is nervous, demanding, and possibly not likable.)*

B **Scene:** *As the curtain rises, we see a divided stage, only the center part of which is lighted and furnished as Mrs. Stevenson's bedroom. Expensive, rather fussy furnishings. A large bed, on which* Mrs. Stevenson, *clad in a bedjacket, is lying. A nighttable close by, with phone, lighted lamp, and pill bottles.*
10 *A mantel, with clock, R. A closed door, R. A window, with curtains closed, rear. The set is lit by one lamp on nighttable. Beyond this central set, the stage on either side is in darkness.*

Mrs. Stevenson *is dialing a number on the phone as the curtain rises. She listens to the phone, slams down the receiver in irritation. As*
20 *she does so, we hear the sound of a train roaring by in the distance. She reaches for her pill bottle, pours herself a glass of water, shakes out a pill, swallows it, then reaches for the phone again, dials the number nervously.* Sound: *Number being dialed on the phone. Busy signal.*

C **Mrs. Stevenson** (*a querulous, self-centered neurotic*). Oh, *dear!*
30 (*Slams down receiver. Dials* Operator. *A spotlight, L. of side flat, picks up out of peripheral darkness the figure of* 1st Operator *sitting with headphones at small table.*)

Operator. Your call, please?

Mrs. Stevenson. Operator? I've been dialing Murray Hill 4-0098 for the last three quarters of an hour and the line is always busy.
40 But I don't see how it *could* be busy

that long. Will you try it for me, please?

Operator. Murray Hill 4-0098? One moment, please. (*She makes gesture of plugging in call through a switchboard.*)

Mrs. Stevenson. I don't see how it could be busy all this time. It's my husband's office. He's working late
50 tonight and I'm all alone here in the house. My health is very poor and I've been feeling so nervous all day.

▶ Close Read **Operator.** Ringing Murray Hill 4-0098. (Sound: *Phone buzz. It rings three times. Receiver is picked up at the other end. Spotlight picks up a figure of a heavy-set man seated at a desk with a phone on R. side of dark periphery of stage. He is*
60 *wearing a hat. Picks up phone.*)

Man. Hello.

Mrs. Stevenson. Hello? (*a little puzzled*) Hello. Is Mr. Stevenson there?

Man (*into phone, as though he has not heard*). Hello. (*louder*) Hello. (*Spotlight on L. now moves from* Operator *to another man,* George—*a killer type, also wearing*
70 *a hat, but standing as in a phone booth.*)

2nd Man (*slow heavy quality, faintly foreign accent*). Hello.

1st Man. Hello? George?

George. Yes, sir.

Mrs. Stevenson (*louder and more imperious, to phone*). Hello. Who's this? What number am I calling, please?

English Language Support

Analyze Form: Drama Display lines 1–15, which give stage directions. Review that italic type is used to present stage directions, which tell people reading or presenting the play what the stage looks like and what the actors are doing. Ask volunteers to **highlight** in yellow the names of props on the set and underline the words that describe Mrs. Stevenson.

- Reread lines 1–5 aloud as students follow. Work with students to clarify any unfamiliar words. Draw an empty stage on the board and ask students to describe what each prop looks like and where it is located. Have volunteers add the props to the drawing.

- Have students work in pairs to draw a picture of the stage as described in lines 1–15. Ask them to label each prop with a sentence that describes the prop and its location.

- Using the information provided in lines 1–15, ask students to write their own description of what an audience would see as the curtain rose for a production of this play. Remind students to make connections between ideas by using compound and complex sentences.

D 80 **1st Man.** We have heard from our client. He says the coast is clear for tonight.

George. Yes, sir.

1st Man. Where are you now?

George. In a phone booth.

1st Man. Okay. You know the address. At eleven o'clock, the private patrolman goes around to the bar on Second Avenue for 90 a beer. Be sure that all the lights downstairs are out. There should be only one light visible from the street. At eleven-fifteen, a subway train crosses the bridge. It makes a noise in case her window is open and she should scream.

Mrs. Stevenson (*shocked*). Oh— *hello!* What number is this, please?

George. Okay. I understand.

100 **1st Man.** Make it quick. As little blood as possible. Our client does not wish to make her suffer long.

George. A knife okay?

1st Man. Yes. A knife will be okay. And remember—remove the rings and bracelets, and the jewelry in the bureau drawer. Our client wishes it to look like simple robbery.

E 110 **George.** Okay—I get—(*Spotlight suddenly goes out on* George. Sound: *A bland buzzing signal. Spotlight goes off on* 1st Man.)

Mrs. Stevenson (*clicking phone*). Oh! (*Bland buzzing signal continues. She hangs up.*) How awful! How unspeakably—(*She

lies back on her pillows, overcome for a few seconds, then suddenly 120 *pulls herself together, reaches for phone. Sound:* Dialing. Phone buzz. *Spotlight goes on at* 1st Operator's *switchboard.* 1st *and* 2nd Man *exit as unobtrusively as possible, in darkness.*)

Operator. Your call, please?

Mrs. Stevenson (*unnerved and breathless, into phone*). Operator, I—I've just been cut off.

130 **Operator.** I'm sorry, madam. What number were you calling?

Mrs. Stevenson. It was supposed to be Murray Hill 4-0098, but it wasn't. Some wires must have crossed—I was cut into a wrong number. And I've just heard the most dreadful thing—a—a murder—and (*imperiously*) you'll simply have to retrace that call at 140 once, Operator. Text in FOCUS

Operator. I beg your pardon, madam, I don't quite—

Mrs. Stevenson. Oh, I know it was a wrong number and I had no business listening, but these two men—they were cold-blooded fiends and they were going to murder somebody—some poor innocent woman who was all 150 alone—in a house near a bridge. And we've got to stop them—

Operator (*patiently*). What number were you calling, madam?

Mrs. Stevenson. That doesn't matter. This was a *wrong* number.

Scene: *As the curtain rises, we see a divided stage, only the center part of which is lighted and furnished as Mrs. Stevenson's bedroom. Expensive, rather fussy furnishings. A large bed, on which* Mrs. Stevenson, *clad in a bedjacket, is lying. A nighttable close by, with*

phone, lighted lamp, and pill bottles. A mantel, with clock, R. *A closed door,* R. *A window, with curtains closed, rear. The set is lit by one lamp on nighttable. Beyond this central set, the stage on either side is in darkness.*

CLOSE READ

Analyze Form: Drama
(LINES 80–96, 110–125)

RL 1,
RL 3,
RL 5

Tell students that, like other forms of literature, this play has a series of events called a **plot.** The first part of the plot, called the **exposition,** gives audiences the basic information about the **conflict**—the struggle between opposing forces—that will drive the rest of the plot.

D ASK STUDENTS to reread lines 80–96 to tell what the audience and Mrs. Stevenson learn at the same time. (*A murder of a woman is being planned by two men, one working for a client and the other named George, the hired killer.*)

Tell students that the lighting and dialogue help audiences understand that different characters onstage are each in a different **setting**—the time and place of the events.

E CITE TEXT EVIDENCE Have students find the details in lines 110–125 that describe what the audience sees onstage. (*Spotlights go off the two men. Then one spotlight lights the 1st Operator's switchboard. Mrs. Stevenson, still in bed, is no longer overhearing the men's phone conversation but is speaking to the Operator.*)

Text in FOCUS English Language Support

Making Predictions (LINE 140)

Have students view the **Text In Focus** video on this page of their eBook to learn how to make predictions about what might happen in the drama. Then have students use **Text In Focus Practice** to apply what they have learned.

Analyze Form: Drama

RL 1,
RL 3,
RL 5

(LINES 176–182, 194–200)

Explain that stage directions help actors know what emotions to convey and help readers visualize those emotions.

F **CITE TEXT EVIDENCE** Have students reread lines 176–182 and note the stage directions that reveal how Mrs. Stevenson feels. Ask them why she might feel that way. *(As she wipes her forehead with a handkerchief, she is "glancing uneasily for a moment toward the window." That uneasy glance reveals that she is worried about what might be happening outside.)*

Point out that the **conflict** in a drama or other fictional work is the problem that the characters try to resolve. Efforts to resolve the conflict create the action of the plot and build **suspense,** the feeling of growing tension and excitement felt by readers and viewers of a play.

G **ASK STUDENTS** to reread lines 194–200 to tell about Mrs. Stevenson's conflict and her attempts to resolve it. *(The conflict is set up when Mrs. Stevenson overhears plans for a murder. She is desperate for the operator to trace the call to find the men and apprehend them.)*

English Language Support

Read Closely Explain that some words or expressions convey a meaning different from what the words actually say. Point to the phrase "trace a call" in line 226. Model how to use the context clue "be tracked down" in line 230 to define the phrase as "finding out who made the call."

And *you* dialed it. And we've got to find out what it was—immediately!

Operator. But, madam—

160 **Mrs. Stevenson.** Oh, why are you so stupid? Look—it was obviously a case of some little slip of the finger. I told you to try Murray Hill 4-0098 for me—you dialed it but your finger must have slipped and I was connected with some other number. I could hear them, but they couldn't hear me. I simply fail to see why you couldn't make that same mistake again—on purpose.

170 Why you couldn't *try* to dial Murray Hill 4-0098 in the same careless sort of way—

Operator (*quickly*). Murray Hill 4-0098? I will try to get it for you, madam.

F **Mrs. Stevenson** (*sarcastically*). Thank you. (*She bridles, adjusts herself on her pillows, reaches for a handkerchief and wipes her* 180 *forehead, glancing uneasily for a moment toward the window. Sound of ringing and busy signal.*)

Operator. I'm sorry. Murray Hill 4-0098 is busy.

Mrs. Stevenson (*frantically clicking receiver*). Operator—Operator!

Operator. Yes, madam?

Mrs. Stevenson (*angrily*). You *didn't* try to get that wrong number 190 at all. I asked explicitly and all you did was dial correctly.

Operator. I'm sorry. What number were you calling?

G **Mrs. Stevenson.** Can't you forget what number I was calling and do something specific? I want to trace that call. It's my civic duty—it's *your* civic duty—to trace that call 200 and to apprehend those dangerous killers. And if *you* won't—

Operator (*glancing around wearily*). I will connect you with the Chief Operator.

Mrs. Stevenson. *Please!* (*Sound of ringing. Operator puts hand over mouthpiece of phone, gestures into darkness.*)

Operator (*a half whisper*). Miss Curtis, will you pick up on 210 seventeen, please? (*Miss Curtis, Chief Operator, enters. Middle-aged, efficient, pleasant. Wearing headphone.*)

Miss Curtis. Yes, dear. What's the trouble?

Operator. Somebody wanting a call traced. I can't make head nor tail of it.

Miss Curtis (*sitting down at desk* 220 *as Operator gets up*). Sure, dear. (*She makes gesture of plugging in her headphone, coolly and professionally.*) This is the Chief Operator.

Mrs. Stevenson. Chief Operator? I want you to trace a call. Immediately. I don't know where it came from, or who was making it, but it's absolutely necessary 230 that it be tracked down. It was about a murder, a terrible, cold-

114 Collection 2

FOR STANDARD ENGLISH LEARNERS

Pronounce Present Participles Explain that the telephone operators employ formal language when speaking to the public. Point out their use of present participles, or the *-ing* form of verbs.

- Model the correct pronunciation of *-ing* words, such as *calling, ringing,* and *dialing,* emphasizing the final syllable.
- Have students repeat the words after you say them. Encourage them to compare your diction with the more informal tendency of dropping the final *g* (*callin', ringin',* etc.).

blooded murder of a poor innocent woman—tonight, at eleven-fifteen.

Chief Operator. I see.

Mrs. Stevenson (*high-strung, demanding*). Can you trace it for me? Can you track down those men?

240 **Chief Operator.** It depends, madam.

Mrs. Stevenson. Depends on what?

Chief Operator. It depends on whether the call is still going on. If it's a live call, we can trace it on the equipment. If it's been disconnected, we can't.

Mrs. Stevenson. Disconnected?

Chief Operator. If the parties have 250 stopped talking to each other.

Mrs. Stevenson. Oh, but of course they must have stopped talking to each other by *now*. That was at least five minutes ago.

Chief Operator. Well, I can try tracing it. (*She takes a pencil out of her hair.*) What is your name, madam?

Mrs. Stevenson. Mrs. Elbert 260 Stevenson. But listen—

Chief Operator (*writing*). And your telephone number?

Mrs. Stevenson (*more irritated*). Plaza 4-2295. But if you go on wasting all this time—(*She glances at clock on the mantel.*)

Chief Operator. And what is your reason for wanting this call traced?

Mrs. Stevenson. My reason? Well, 270 for heaven's sake, isn't it obvious? I overhear two men planning to murder this woman—it's a matter for the police!

Chief Operator. Have you told the police?

Mrs. Stevenson. No. How could I?

Chief Operator. You're making this check into a private call purely as a private individual?

280 **Mrs. Stevenson.** Yes. But meanwhile—

Chief Operator. Well, Mrs. Stevenson, I seriously doubt whether we could make this check for you at this time just on your say-so as a private individual. We'd have to have something more official.

Mrs. Stevenson. Oh, for heaven's 290 sake! You mean to tell me I can't report a murder without getting tied up in all this red tape? It's perfectly idiotic. All right, then I *will* call the police. (*She slams down the receiver. Spotlight goes off two* Operators.) Ridiculous! (*Sound of dialing as* Mrs. Stevenson *dials phone and two* Operators *exit unobtrusively in darkness. On* R. 300 *of stage, spotlight picks up a* 2nd Operator, *seated like first, with headphone at table—same one vacated by* 1st Man.)

2nd Operator. Your call, please?

Mrs. Stevenson (*very annoyed*). The Police Department—please.

CLOSE READ

Analyze Form: Drama

RL 1, RL 3, RL 5

(LINES 235–266, 289–304)

Tell students that once the conflict sets the plot in motion, the events that occur are called the **rising action.**

H ASK STUDENTS to reread lines 235–266 and give ideas about why rising action is a fitting term to describe what is happening. (*As Mrs. Stevenson tries to explain what she wants to the Chief Operator, her panic starts to rise. The suspense builds for the audience, too, because it's clear that the call can't be traced, and precious time is passing.*)

Point out that stage directions help readers visualize how characters are entering and exiting the scene.

I CITE TEXT EVIDENCE Have students reread lines 289–304 and tell what the audience sees as Mrs. Stevenson dials the phone. (*The table to the right that was hidden in darkness is now lit with a spotlight, and a new character, 2nd Operator, is seated at it.*)

English Language Support

Before students complete the activity, read lines 289–304 aloud with students reading along. Help clarify terms that may be confusing, such as *red tape, idiotic, ridiculous,* and *unobtrusively*. Ask students to explain what "R." means. (*stage right*) Then have pairs work together to discuss what the audience sees.

APPLYING ACADEMIC VOCABULARY

perceive	task

THINK-PAIR-SHARE Have students turn to a partner and discuss the questions below. Ask them to include the vocabulary words *perceive* and *task* in their responses. Then call on students to share their responses with the class.

- How does the playwright carry out the **task** of building suspense?
- What techniques help the audience **perceive** onstage events as if they were happening in a real-life setting?

Analyze Form: Drama

RL 1,
RL 3,
RL 5

(LINES 337–349)

Explain that suspense is building as Mrs. Stevenson keeps trying to persuade others that a murder is going to occur.

J **CITE TEXT EVIDENCE** Ask students to reread lines 337–349 to identify words that show Duffy's reaction to Mrs. Stevenson's call. Ask them what effect the dramatist wants to create. *(Duffy "relaxes, sighs, starts taking lunch from bag." He says "Yes, ma'am," in a voice that shows he's not impressed. The effect is to build tension, because the audience knows that Mrs. Stevenson is right, but she can't seem to explain the situation convincingly.)*

FOR STANDARD ENGLISH LEARNERS

Informal Language Have pairs take turns reading aloud lines 316–327. Tell them to listen to the dialogue and identify examples of informal English. As a group, discuss why the characters' speech is or isn't appropriate for the scene.

2nd Operator. Ringing the Police Department. (*Ring twice. At table L. spotlight now picks up Sergeant Duffy, seated in a relaxed position. Just entering beside him is a young man in a cap and apron, carrying a large brown-paper parcel, delivery boy for a local lunch counter. Phone is ringing.*)

Lunchroom Attendant. Here's your lunch, Sarge. They didn't have no jelly doughnuts, so I got French crullers, okay?

Duffy. French crullers. I got ulcers. Whyn't you make it apple pie? (*picks up phone*) Police Department, Precinct 43, Duffy speaking.

Lunchroom Attendant (*anxiously*). We don't have no apple pie, either, Sarge.

Mrs. Stevenson. Police Department? Oh. This is Mrs. Stevenson—Mrs. Elbert Smythe Stevenson of 53 North Sutton Place. I'm calling to report a murder. (*Duffy has been examining lunch, but double-takes suddenly on above.*)

Duffy. Eh?

J **Mrs. Stevenson.** I mean, the murder hasn't been committed yet, I just overheard plans for it over the telephone—over a wrong number the operator gave me. (*Duffy relaxes, sighs, starts taking lunch from bag.*) I've been trying to trace the call myself, but everybody is so stupid—and I guess in the end

you're the only people who could *do* anything.

Duffy (*not too impressed*). Yes, ma'am. (Attendant *exits.*)

Mrs. Stevenson (*trying to impress him*). It was perfectly *definite* murder. I heard their plans distinctly. (Duffy *begins to eat sandwich, phone at his ear.*) Two men were talking, and they were going to murder some woman at eleven-fifteen tonight—she lived in a house near a bridge.

Duffy. Yes, ma'am.

Mrs. Stevenson. There was a private patrolman on the street who was going to go around for a beer on Second Avenue. And there was some third man, a client, who was paying to have this poor woman murdered. They were going to take her rings and bracelets—and use a knife. Well, it's unnerved me dreadfully—and I'm not well.

Duffy. I see. (*He wipes his mouth with a paper napkin.*) When was all this, ma'am?

Mrs. Stevenson. About eight minutes ago. Oh—(*relieved*)—then you *can* do something? You *do* understand.

Duffy. And what is your name, ma'am? (*He reaches for a pad of paper.*)

Mrs. Stevenson (*impatiently*). Mrs. Stevenson. Mrs. Elbert Stevenson.

Duffy. And your address?

English Language Support

Using Verbs and Verb Phrases Project lines 360–369, and underline the verb phrases "was going" (line 362), "was paying" (line 365), and "were going" (line 356). Explain that these verbs are in the past progressive tense: Each describes an action that was in progress in the past. Past progressive tense includes a past form of the verb *be* as a helping verb followed by the *-ing* form of a verb.

• Have pairs take turns reading these lines aloud, using the anxious tone that Mrs. Stevenson might use. Discuss how the verb tense shows she is telling about something she heard a few minutes ago.

• Write these verbs on the board: *call, talk, eat, live.* Have pairs of students write a verb phrase in the past progressive using each verb and then use each phrase in a sentence.

• Have small groups of students rewrite the lines using the present tense; for example, "There is a private patrolman on the street who goes around for a beer on Second Avenue." Help them discuss how using a different tense would change Mrs. Stevenson's report to Sergeant Duffy.

(bridge) ©DLe/Shutterstock; (curtains) ©s duffett/Shutterstock

Mrs. Stevenson. 53 North Sutton Place. *That's* near a bridge. The Queensboro Bridge, you know—and *we* have a private patrol-man on *our* street. And Second Avenue—

390 **Duffy.** And what was that number you were calling?

Mrs. Stevenson. Murray Hill 4-0098. (*Duffy writes it down.*) But that wasn't the number I overheard. I mean Murray Hill 4-0098 is my husband's office. (Duffy, *in exasperation, holds his pencil poised.*) He's working late tonight and I was trying to reach 400 him to ask him to come home. I'm an invalid, and it's the maid's night off, and I *hate* to be alone even though he says I'm perfectly safe as long as I have the telephone right beside my bed.

Sorry, Wrong Number **117**

CLOSE READ

Analyze Form: Drama
RL 3,
RL 5

(LINES 384–405)

Tell students that a dramatist uses dialogue to move the action along and to provide information to the audience.

K ASK STUDENTS to reread lines 384–405 and tell what Mrs. Stevenson is revealing to the audience as she speaks to Duffy. (*She herself lives in a place like the one described by the murder planners. She is all alone because her husband is not home and it's the maid's night off. The woman who is to be murdered is also alone in her house.*)

Determine Meaning of Words and Phrases
RL 4
L 4a
L 4c

(LINE 401)

Point out line 401, where Mrs. Stevenson says she is an invalid.

L ASK STUDENTS to use the context of surrounding words to determine the meaning of *invalid*. As needed, have students confirm the meaning in a digital or print dictionary. Then ask students what the word *invalid* suggests about how Mrs. Stevenson perceives herself. (*She sees herself as ill, helpless, and always requiring care from others.*) Point out that this usage of the word *invalid* was more common at the time that this play was first performed. Discuss how it would no longer be an appropriate way to categorize someone in a similar situation today.

Strategies for Annotation
🖊 🗐 *Annotate it!*

Analyze Form: Drama
RL 3, RL 5

Have students use their eBook annotation tools to annotate the text, focusing on what the audience hears and sees as Mrs. Stevenson and Duffy interact.

- Highlight in yellow the stage directions that tell what Duffy is doing.
- Add a note to describe Duffy's expression as he does each thing.
- Add a note to describe how Mrs. Stevenson sounds as she speaks the dialogue.

Mrs. Stevenson. Murray Hill 4-0098. (*Duffy writes it down.*) But that wasn't the number I overheard. I mean Murray Hill 4-0098 is my husband's office.

(Duffy, *in exasperation, holds his pencil poised.*) He's working late tonight and I was trying to reach him to ask him an invalid and

Duffy: bored or resigned
Mrs. Stevenson: rushing, with anxiety

Analyze Form: Drama

RL 1,
RL 3,
RL 5

(LINES 415–439)

Point out that the characters' gestures and postures onstage reveal what they are thinking and feeling.

 CITE TEXT EVIDENCE Direct students to scan lines 415–439 to identify words that show what Duffy is doing. Ask what his actions reveal about him. (*Duffy "yawns slightly"; "reaches for a paper cup of coffee"; "He begins to remove the top of the coffee container"; "puts down the phone to work on the cup." His actions show that he is unconcerned about Mrs. Stevenson's report and has no intention of getting involved.*)

ASK STUDENTS According to the emergency procedures of our time, how would Duffy's response to Mrs. Stevenson be different? (*Duffy would most likely have to dispatch an officer to investigate, no matter how he may have felt about Mrs. Stevenson's reliability. It is the job of a first responder to attempt to put a distressed person at ease so that he or she can feel safe to share information or to follow instructions. To uphold public safety in these times, all responders have to show a degree of concern.*)

Duffy (*stolidly*). Well, we'll look into it, Mrs. Stevenson, and see if we can check it with the telephone company.

410 **Mrs. Stevenson** (*getting impatient*). But the telephone company said they couldn't check the call if the parties had stopped talking. I've already taken care of that.

Duffy. Oh—yes? (*He yawns slightly.*)

Mrs. Stevenson. Personally, I feel you ought to do something far more immediate and drastic than 420 just check the call. What good does checking the call do if they've stopped talking? By the time you track it down, they'll already have committed the murder.

Duffy (*he reaches for a paper cup of coffee*). Well, we'll take care of it, lady. Don't worry. (*He begins to remove the top of the coffee container.*)

430 **Mrs. Stevenson.** I'd say the whole thing calls for a complete and thorough search of the whole city. (Duffy *puts down the phone to work on the cup as her voice continues.*) I'm very near a bridge, and I'm not far from Second Avenue. And I know I'd feel a whole lot better if you sent around a radio car to *this* neighborhood at once.

440 **Duffy** (*picks up phone again, drinks coffee*). And what makes you think the murder's going to be committed in your neighborhood, ma'am?

Mrs. Stevenson. Oh, I don't know—the coincidence is so

horrible. Second Avenue—the bridge—

Duffy. Second Avenue is a very long street, ma'am. And do you 450 happen to know how many bridges there are in the city of New York? How do you know there isn't some little house out on Staten Island— on some little Second Avenue you never heard about? (*He takes a long gulp of coffee.*) How do you know they were even talking about New York at all?

Mrs. Stevenson. But I heard 460 the call on the New York dialing system.

Duffy. How do you know it wasn't a long-distance call you overheard? Telephones are funny things. (*He sets down coffee.*) Look, lady, why don't you look at it this way? Supposing you hadn't broken in on that telephone call? Supposing you'd got your husband the way 470 you always do? Would this murder have made any difference to you then?

Mrs. Stevenson. I suppose not. But it's so inhuman—so cold-blooded—

Duffy. A lot of murders are committed in this city every day, ma'am. If we could do something to stop 'em, we would. But a clue of 480 this kind that's so vague isn't much more use to us than no clue at all.

Mrs. Stevenson. But surely—

Duffy. Unless, of course, you have some reason for thinking this call

---

Strategies for Annotation ✏️ 🗒 *Annotate it!*

Analyze Form: Drama

RL 3, RL 5

Have students use their eBook annotation tools to annotate Duffy's actions in lines 415–429.

- Highlight in yellow the words that indicate what Duffy is doing.
- Add notes to describe how his actions contradict the words he speaks.

Duffy. Oh—yes? (*He yawns slightly.*)

Mrs. Stevenson. Personally, I feel you ought to do something far more immediate and drastic…

Duffy (*he reaches for a paper cup of coffee*). Well, we'll take care of it, lady. Don't worry. (*He begins to remove the top of the coffee container.*)

Duffy isn't listening closely and has no intention to help Mrs. Stevenson.

is phony, and that someone may be planning to murder *you*?

Mrs. Stevenson. *Me?* Oh, no—I hardly think so. I mean—why should anybody? I'm alone all day and night. I see nobody except my maid Eloise—she's a big two-hundred-pound woman too lazy to bring up my breakfast tray—and the only other person is my husband Elbert. He's crazy about me—adores me—waits on me hand and foot. He's scarcely left my side since I took sick twelve years ago—

Duffy. Well, then, there's nothing for you to worry about, is there? (*The* Lunchroom-Counter Attendant *has entered. He is carrying a piece of apple pie on a plate and points it out to* Duffy *triumphantly.*) And now, if you'll just leave the rest of this to us—

Mrs. Stevenson. But what will you *do?* It's so late—it's nearly eleven o'clock.

Duffy (*firmly*). We'll take care of it, lady.

Mrs. Stevenson. Will you broadcast it all over the city? And send out squads? And warn your radio cars to watch out—especially in suspicious neighborhoods like mine. (*The* Attendant, *in triumph, has put the pie down in front of* Duffy.)

Duffy (*more firmly*). Lady, I *said* we'd take care of it. Just now I've got a couple of other matters here on my desk that require my immediate—

Mrs. Stevenson. Oh! (*She slams down the receiver hard.*) Idiot! (Duffy *listening at the phone, hangs up and shrugs, then attacks his pie as spotlight fades out. Mrs. Stevenson, in bed, looks at the phone nervously.*) Why did I do that? Now he'll think I *am* a fool. (*She sits tensely, then throws herself back against the pillows, lying there a moment, whimpering with self-pity.*) Oh, why doesn't Elbert come home? *Why* doesn't he? (*We hear sound of train roaring by in the distance. She sits up, reaching for phone. Sound of dialing operator. Spotlight picks up* 2nd Operator, *seated R.*)

Operator. Your call, please?

Mrs. Stevenson. Operator—for heaven's sake—will you ring that Murray Hill 4-0098 number again? I can't think what's keeping him so long.

Operator. Ringing Murray Hill 4-0098. (*rings—busy signal*) The line is busy. Shall I—

Mrs. Stevenson (*nastily*). I can hear it, you don't have to tell me it's busy! (*Slams down receiver. Spotlight fades off on* 2nd Operator. Mrs. Stevenson *sinks back against the pillows again, whimpering to herself fretfully. She glances at the clock, then, turning, punches her pillows up, trying to make herself comfortable. But she isn't and she whimpers to herself as she squirms restlessly in bed.*) If I could get out of this bed for a little while. If I could get a breath of fresh air—or

Sorry, Wrong Number **119**

Sorry, Wrong Number **119**

CLOSE READ

Analyze Drama: Form
RL 1, RL 3, RL 5

(LINES 487–498, 537–539)

Review that a dramatist, the person who writes a drama, uses dialogue to reveal character. The audience uses what the character says to **make inferences,** or good guesses, about what the character doesn't say.

N **ASK STUDENTS** to reread lines 487–498 and tell what they can infer about Mrs. Stevenson that she herself doesn't seem to realize. (*Mrs. Stevenson says that she can't imagine anyone wanting to kill her. Yet she goes on to name two people who might have reason to: her maid and her husband.*)

Tell students that in a staged drama, sound effects may be used to show elements of the time and place of the action—the setting.

O **CITE TEXT EVIDENCE** Direct students to identify the sound effect in lines 537–539 and tell about its significance. (*The "train roaring by in the distance" is a reminder that the murderers are planning to use the sound of a train to muffle the victim's screams.*)

Determine Meaning of Words and Phrases
RL 4

(Lines 535, 557, 562)

Draw students' attention to forms of the word *whimper* in the stage directions. Have them demonstrate whimpering.

P **ASK STUDENTS** what the word *whimper* suggests about Mrs. Stevenson. (*She feels frustrated and can't cope with setbacks. She's like a helpless child.*)

English Language Support

Summarize Guide students to summarize what Mrs. Stevenson reveals about her situation in lines 397–498.

- Read aloud these lines as students follow. Ask them to note words and ideas that seem important. Have volunteers share their important words, and lead the class to select the "top ten" words.
- Together, write a summary that uses as many of these words as possible. Have each student add a topic sentence to the summary.

CLOSE READ

Analyze Form: Drama

RL 3

(LINES 567–581, 630–643)

Tell students that as the rising action of the plot continues, the main character tries to deal with obstacles that prevent her from resolving the conflict.

Q ASK STUDENTS to describe the new obstacle Mrs. Stevenson encounters in lines 567–581 and how she handles it. *(Now the phone rings, but nobody is on the other end. She handles this problem poorly, just shouting "Hello" repeatedly and slamming down the receiver.)*

Explain that the telephone is the most important prop in the play. In some ways it is like a character interacting with Mrs. Stevenson.

R ASK STUDENTS to reread lines 630–643 to visualize how Mrs. Stevenson is interacting with the phone. Volunteers may say Mrs. Stevenson's lines as they pantomime using a telephone like hers.

English Language Support

Have students work in small groups to say and pantomime Mrs. Stevenson's lines. Encourage them to listen first to how other students are saying the lines, following along in their texts to notice both how the spelling of the words is associated with the pronunciation and the tone of Mrs. Stevenson's speech.

Q just lean out the window—and see the street. (*She sighs, reaches for pill bottle, and shakes out a pill. As she does, the phone rings and she darts for it instantly.*) Hello, Elbert? Hello. Hello. Hello. Oh—what's the *matter* with this phone? *Hello? Hello?* (*Slams down the receiver and stares at it tensely. The phone rings again. Once. She picks it up.*) Hello? Hello! Oh, for heaven's sake, who *is* this? Hello. Hello. *Hello.* (*Slamming down the receiver, she dials the operator. Spotlight comes on L. showing* 3rd Operator, *at spot vacated by* Duffy.)

3rd Operator. Your call, please?

Mrs. Stevenson (*very annoyed and imperious*). Hello, Operator, I don't know what's the matter with this telephone tonight, but it's positively driving me crazy. I've never seen such inefficient, miserable service. Now, look. I'm an invalid, and I'm very nervous, and I'm *not* supposed to be annoyed. But if this keeps on much longer—

3rd Operator (*a young, sweet type*). What seems to be the trouble, madam?

Mrs. Stevenson. *Everything's* wrong. The whole world could be murdered for all you people care! And now my phone keeps ringing!

Operator. Yes, madam?

Mrs. Stevenson. Ringing and ringing and ringing every five seconds or so, and when I pick it up there's no one there!

Operator. I'm sorry, madam. If you'll hang up, I'll test it for you.

Mrs. Stevenson. I don't want you to test it for me, I want you to put through that call—whatever it is—at once.

Operator (*gently*). I'm afraid that's not possible, madam.

Mrs. Stevenson (*storming*). Not possible? And why, may I ask?

Operator. The system is automatic, madam. If someone is trying to dial your number, there's no way to check whether the call is coming through the system or not—unless the person who is trying to reach you complains to his particular operator.

Mrs. Stevenson. Well, of all the stupid, complicated—And meanwhile *I've* got to sit here in my bed, *suffering* every time that phone rings, imagining everything!

Operator. I'll try to check it for you, madam.

Mrs. Stevenson. Check it! Check it! That's all anybody can do. Of all the stupid, idiotic—(*She hangs up.*) Oh, what's the use! (3rd Operator *fades out of spotlight as* Mrs. Stevenson's *phone rings again. She picks up the receiver.*) Hello! *Hello!* Stop ringing, do you hear me? Answer me? What do you want? Do you realize you're driving me crazy? (*Spotlight goes on* R. *We see a* Man *in eyeshade and shirtsleeves at a desk with a phone and telegrams.*) Stark, staring—

R

WHEN STUDENTS STRUGGLE . . .

To help students visualize the onstage action, guide partners to create a diagram of the stage, showing the bed in the center, a desk to the right (Stage Right), and a desk to the left (Stage Left). Suggest that they read aloud Mrs. Stevenson's spoken parts in lines 570–581 and 630–643 and label the desks to understand who is entering and exiting the stage at the same time.

LEVEL UP TUTORIALS For additional support, assign the following *Level Up* tutorial: **Elements of Drama.**

Western Union (*dull, flat voice*). Hello. Is this Plaza 4-2295?

Mrs. Stevenson (*catching her breath*). Yes. Yes. This is Plaza 4-2295.

650 **Western Union.** This is Western Union. I have a telegram here for Mrs. Elbert Stevenson. Is there anyone there to receive the message?

Mrs. Stevenson (*trying to calm herself*). I am Mrs. Stevenson.

Western Union (*reading flatly*). The telegram is as follows: "Mrs. Elbert Stevenson, 53 North Sutton Place, New York, New York. 660 Darling. Terribly sorry. Tried to get you for last hour, but line busy. Leaving for Boston eleven P.M. tonight on urgent business. Back tomorrow afternoon. Keep happy. Love. Signed, Elbert."

Mrs. Stevenson (*breathlessly, aghast, to herself.*) Oh, no—

Western Union. That's all, madam. Do you wish us to deliver a copy of 670 the message?

Mrs. Stevenson. No—no, thank you.

Western Union. Thank you, madam. Goodnight. (*He hangs up the phone. Spotlight on* Western Union *immediately out.*)

Mrs. Stevenson (*mechanically, to phone*). Goodnight. (*She hangs up slowly, suddenly bursting into*) 680 No—no—it isn't true! He couldn't do it! Not when he knows I'll be all alone! It's some trick—some fiendish—(*We hear the sound of a train roaring by outside. She half rises in bed, in panic, glaring toward the curtains. Her movements are frenzied. She beats with her knuckles on the bed, then suddenly stops and reaches for the phone.* 690 *Spotlight picks up* 4th Operator, *seated L.*)

Operator (*coolly*). Your call, please?

Mrs. Stevenson. Operator—try that Murray Hill 4-0098 number for me just once more, please.

Operator. Ringing Murray Hill 4-0098. (*Call goes through. We hear ringing at the other end, ring* 700 *after ring.*)

Mrs. Stevenson. He's gone. Oh, Elbert, how could you? How could you? (*She hangs up, sobbing pityingly to herself, turning restlessly. Spotlight goes out on* 4th Operator.) But I can't be alone tonight, I can't! If I'm alone one more second— (*She runs her hands wildly through her hair.*) I don't care what he 710 says, or what the expense is, I'm a sick woman—I'm entitled! (*With trembling fingers she picks up the receiver again and dials* Information. *The spotlight picks up* Information Operator, *seated R.*)

Information. This is Information.

Mrs. Stevenson. I want the telephone number of Henchley Hospital.

720 **Information.** Henchley Hospital? Do you have the address, madam?

CLOSE READ

Analyze Drama: Form

RL 1, RL 3, RL 5

(LINES 656–665, 683–689)

Remind students that a dramatist uses dialogue to move the action along.

Ⓢ **ASK STUDENTS** to reread what the man from Western Union says beginning in line 656 and tell what new obstacle is being presented. (*Mrs. Stevenson's husband is not coming home tonight, and she now must deal with being alone.*)

Point out that stage directions help readers visualize the action and imagine the emotions that audiences experience.

Ⓣ **CITE TEXT EVIDENCE** Direct students to reread the stage directions in lines 683–689. Have them identify the words that convey emotion. (*"Panic," "frenzied," and "beats with her knuckles on the bed" show that Mrs. Stevenson is out of control with frustration and terror. The "sound of a train roaring by outside" is like a scream that adds to the feeling of terror.*)

English Language Support

After students examine lines 683–689, have them read lines 701–715 and complete the same exercise. Have them identify the words in the stage directions that convey emotion (*sobbing pityingly, restlessly, runs her hands wildly through, trembling fingers*) and then discuss how these words and phrases help build tension in the audience. Help students understand that one purpose of a play is to build emotion in the audience by showing emotion on the stage.

English Language Support

Improve Reading Fluency Have students work in groups of three to read lines 656–700 as a Readers' Theater presentation. Model how to use an appropriate tone and expression for each character. After groups finish their performances, encourage members to provide feedback. Then have students switch roles and perform the dialogue again.

Analyze Form: Drama

RL 3,
RL 5

(LINES 759–795)

Tell students that Mrs. Stevenson is now attempting to handle the obstacle of facing the night alone.

 ASK STUDENTS to reread the conversation between Mrs. Stevenson and the Woman at Henchley Hospital and to tell how the dialogue builds suspense. *(The dialogue creates tension because Mrs. Stevenson's growing panic is contrasted with the businesslike manner of the Woman. Time is passing, the murder is about to be committed, and Mrs. Stevenson still can't get anyone to help her.)*
Invite volunteers to read the dialogue aloud to convey the contrast in emotions between the characters.

English Language Support

Have students analyze the dialogue in pairs. Model how to identify text elements that show suspense building. Provide students with sentence frames to help them organize their responses.

- Mrs. Stevenson speaks in _____ sentences.
- The dashes and exclamation points in Mrs. Stevenson's lines show that _____.
- The Woman is speaking in a _____ manner that contrasts with Mrs. Stevenson's _____ tone.

Mrs. Stevenson. No. It's somewhere in the Seventies. It's a small, private, and exclusive hospital where I had my appendix out two years ago. Henchley. H-E-N-C—

Information. One moment, please.

730 **Mrs. Stevenson.** Please—hurry. And please—what's the time?

Information. I don't know, madam. You may find out the time by dialing Meridan 7-1212.

Mrs. Stevenson (*irritated*). Oh, for heaven's sake, couldn't you—?

Information. The number of Henchley Hospital is Butterfield 7-0105, madam.

Mrs. Stevenson. Butterfield
740 7-0105. (*She hangs up before she finishes speaking and immediately dials the number as she repeats it. Spotlight goes out on* Information. *Phone rings. Spotlight picks up* Woman *in nurse's uniform, seated at desk L.*)

Woman (*middle-aged, solid, firm, practical*). Henchley Hospital, good evening.

750 **Mrs. Stevenson.** Nurses' Registry.

Woman. Who was it you wished to speak to, please?

Mrs. Stevenson (*high-handed*). I want the Nurses' Registry at once. I want a trained nurse. I want to hire her immediately. For the night.

Woman. I see. And what is the nature of the case, madam?

Mrs. Stevenson. Nerves. I'm very
760 nervous. I need soothing—and companionship. My husband is away and I'm—

Woman. Have you been recommended to us by any doctor in particular, madam?

Mrs. Stevenson. No. But I really don't see why all this catechizing is necessary. I want a trained nurse. I was a patient in your hospital
770 two years ago. And, after all, I *do* expect to pay this person—

Woman. We quite understand that, madam. But registered nurses are very scarce just now and our superintendent has asked us to send people out only on cases where the physician in charge feels it is absolutely necessary.

Mrs. Stevenson (*growing*
780 *hysterical*). Well, it is absolutely necessary! I'm a sick woman. I'm very upset! Very! I'm alone in this house—and I'm an invalid—and tonight I overheard a telephone conversation that upset me dreadfully. About a murder—a poor woman who was going to be murdered at eleven-fifteen tonight. In fact, if someone doesn't come
790 at once, I'm afraid I'll go out of my mind!

Woman (*calmly*). I see. Well, I'll speak to Miss Phillips as soon as she comes in. And what is your name, madam?

Mrs. Stevenson. When do you expect Miss Phillips in?

Strategies for Annotation ✎ 🖥 *Annotate it!*

Analyze Form: Drama

RL 3, RL 5

Have students use their eBook annotation tools to annotate Mrs. Stevenson's dialogue in lines 759–791 as if preparing to play the role.

- Highlight in yellow words to emphasize.
- Add notes to describe how she speaks and what gestures she makes.

Have students compare their annotations and take turns reading segments aloud expressively.

Mrs. Stevenson. Nerves. I'm very nervous. I need soothing—and companionship. My husband is away and I'm—. . .

almost breathless, gripping phone tightly with both hands

Mrs. Stevenson. No. But I really don't see why all this catechizing is necessary. I want a trained nurse. I was a patient in your hospital two years ago. And, after all, I do expect to pay this person—

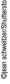

Woman. I really don't know, madam. She went out to supper at 800 eleven o'clock.

Mrs. Stevenson. Eleven o'clock. But it's not eleven yet. (*She cries out.*) Oh, my clock *has* stopped. I *thought* it was running down. What time is it? (*Woman glances at wristwatch.*)

Woman. Just fourteen minutes past eleven. (*Sound of phone receiver being lifted on same line as* 810 *Mrs. Stevenson's. A click.*)

Mrs. Stevenson (*crying out*). What's *that?*

Woman. What was what, madam?

Mrs. Stevenson. That—that click just now—in my own telephone? As though someone had lifted the receiver off the hook of the extension phone downstairs.

Woman. I didn't hear it, madam. 820 Now, about this—

Mrs. Stevenson (*scared*). But I *did.* There's someone in this house! Someone downstairs in the kitchen! And they're listening to me now—they're (*She puts hand over her mouth, hangs up the phone, and sits in terror, frozen, listening.*) I won't pick it up, I won't let them hear me. I'll be quiet—and they'll think—(*with growing terror*) But 830 if I don't call someone now while they're still down there, there'll be no time! (*She picks up the receiver. There is a bland, buzzing signal. She dials the operator. On the second ring, spotlight goes on R. We see 5th Operator.*)

Operator (*fat and lethargic*). Your call, please?

Sorry, Wrong Number **123**

CLOSE READ

Analyze Drama: Form

RL 3

(LINES 821–837)

Tell students that the rising action of the plot is almost at the point of greatest tension, called the **climax.**

Ⓥ **ASK STUDENTS** to reread Mrs. Stevenson's dialogue beginning on line 821 and tell how audiences are probably reacting at this point in the play. (*People at a live performance of this drama are probably biting their knuckles or shading their eyes because the tension is almost unbearable. They've strongly suspected that Mrs. Stevenson is the intended murder victim, and now that someone is downstairs, they know for sure.*)

TO CHALLENGE STUDENTS . . .

Analyzing Story Elements Have students work in small groups to discuss how this drama might be different if it were written today, with modern characters, a modern setting, and current technology. How could a dramatist use modern technology to create a similarly suspenseful conflict? How might changes in language and cultural sensibilities since the original version was written be reflected in the modern version? Have students refer to examples from the original version to compare and contrast a possible modern version.

Analyze Form: Drama

RL 1,
RL 3,
RL 5

(LINES 850–871, 895–898)

The play is approaching the climax. At the climax, audiences know how the conflict will be resolved.

W **ASK STUDENTS** to reread lines 850–871 and tell why this is the climax of the play. *(Mrs. Stevenson is desperately trying to overcome the final obstacle—the murderer in her house—by calling the police. Her screams and the shadow rushing in the darkness create an emotional peak. Her silence tells the audience that the conflict has been resolved with her murder.)*

Tell students that tension eases during **falling action,** the events following the climax and leading to the last event of the plot, called the **resolution.** Explain that **irony** can refer to something that the audience knows but a character doesn't know.

X **CITE TEXT EVIDENCE** Have students tell what George says and does at the resolution of the plot. Ask what is ironic about that remark and action. *(George says, "Sorry, wrong number," and hangs up. The audience knows that his victim had been trying to use the phone as a lifeline, doing nothing but calling "wrong numbers"—never finding the connection that would prevent her death.)*

COLLABORATIVE DISCUSSION Have pairs discuss how they would present this drama to be viewed, or only to be heard. Suggest that they tell what they as directors would look for when casting Mrs. Stevenson, and what would make a strong performance.

ASK STUDENTS to share any questions they generated in the course of reading and discussing the selection.

English Language Support

Support Opinions Before students begin their discussion, provide the following sentence stems:

- To cast Mrs. Stevenson, I would look for an actress who _____.
- If this drama were heard but not seen, I would emphasize _____.
- I think that I would change _____.

---

840 **Mrs. Stevenson** (*a desperate whisper*). Operator—I—I'm in desperate trouble—

Woman. I cannot hear you, madam. Please speak louder.

Mrs. Stevenson (*still whispering*). I don't dare. I—there's someone listening. Can you hear me now?

Operator. Your call, please? What number are you calling, madam?

850 **Mrs. Stevenson** (*desperately*). You've got to hear me! Oh, please! You've got to help me! There's someone in this house—someone who's going to murder me! And you've got to get in touch with the—(*Click of receiver being put down on* Mrs. Stevenson's *line. She bursts out wildly.*) Oh—there it is—he's put it down! He's coming! 860 (*She screams.*) He's coming up the stairs! (*She thrashes in the bed. The phone cord catching in the lamp wire, the lamp topples, goes out. Darkness. Hoarsely.*) Give me the Police Department (*We see on the dark* C. *stage the shadow of the door opening.* Mrs. Stevenson *screams.*) The police! (*On stage, there is the*

swift rush of a shadow advancing to 870 the bed—the sound of her voice is choked out as)

Operator. Ringing the Police Department. (*Phone is rung. We hear the sound of a train beginning to fade in. On the second ring,* Mrs. Stevenson *screams again, but the roaring of the train drowns out her voice. For a few seconds we hear nothing but the roaring of the* 880 *train, then, dying away, the phone at Police Headquarters ringing. Spotlight goes on* Duffy, L. *stage.*)

Duffy. Police Department. Precinct 43. Duffy speaking. (*Pause. Nothing visible but darkness on* C. *stage*) Police Department. Duffy speaking. (*Now a flashlight goes on, illuminating the open phone to one side of* Mrs. Stevenson's 890 *bed. Nearby hanging down, is her lifeless hand. We see the second man,* George *in black gloves, reach down and pick up the phone. He is breathing hard.*)

George. Sorry, wrong number. (*He replaces the receiver on the hook quietly and exits as* Duffy *hangs up with a shrug and the curtain falls.*)

COLLABORATIVE DISCUSSION *Sorry, Wrong Number* was originally performed as a radio play. With a partner, discuss how you would translate this drama into a radio or stage production. How would you direct the actors to bring the mystery story to life in performance?

Analyze Form: Drama

The play you have just read is a **drama,** a form of literature meant to be performed by actors in front of an audience. Like other forms of literature, a drama presents a series of events, called the **plot,** and establishes the time and place of those events, called the **setting.** The plot centers on a **conflict,** a struggle between opposing forces, and unfolds through the characters' words and actions.

Unlike other forms of literature, a drama usually includes the following elements:

- **cast of characters**—a list of all the characters in the drama; the cast appears at the beginning of the drama.
- **dialogue**—the words that the characters say; the character's name precedes his or her lines of dialogue.
- **stage directions**—instructions for how the drama is to be performed in front of an audience; the instructions are often set in parentheses.

Because dramas are primarily meant to be performed, reading the script requires you to focus on the dialogue and stage directions to picture the action and understand the drama's meaning. Use a graphic organizer to keep track of the plot as you read and to help you analyze how the elements of the drama interact.

| Setting: | Where: Mrs. Stevenson's bedroom | When: around 11 P.M. |

Major Characters: Mrs. Stevenson **Minor Characters:** various operators, two murder conspirators, Sergeant Duffy, the lunchroom attendant

Problem/Conflict: Mrs. Stevenson overhears a murder plot and wants to convince someone to stop it.

Event: (List as many as occur.) **Event: Event:**

Outcome/Resolution:

Return to *Sorry, Wrong Number* and complete the graphic organizer to show the Plot Events and Outcome/Resolution.

CLOSE READ

Analyze Form: Drama

Review the boldfaced terms by having students use each in a sentence that tells about the play *Sorry, Wrong Number.*

After students read the items in the graphic organizer, help them to review the play to summarize the main events of the plot. Suggest that they begin with Mrs. Stevenson's attempt to have operators trace the call she has overheard. For example:

Plot Events (in order)

(1) Mrs. S. learns that she can't order a trace. (2) Mrs. S. tells Police Sergeant Duffy about the call, but he doesn't take her seriously. (3) Growing ever more anxious, Mrs. S. keeps trying to call her husband, but the line is always busy. (4) Western Union tells Mrs. S. that her husband won't be home. (5) With rising panic, Mrs. S. calls a hospital to try to get a nurse. (6) Mrs. S. overhears someone in the house. In terror, she tries to call the police. (7) George murders Mrs. S.

Outcome/Resolution:

George hangs up the dead woman's phone after saying, "Sorry, wrong number."

Strategies for Annotation

 Annotate it!

Analyze Form: Drama

Share these strategies for guided or independent analysis:

- To summarize the main events, divide the play into segments based on transitions in the action.
- Highlight in yellow the start and end of each segment.
- For each segment, jot notes to sum up the action and conversation.
- Write a summarizing note to answer, "What happens?"

Department. *(Ring twice. At table L. spotlight now picks up* Sergeant Duffy, *seated in a relaxed position. Just entering beside him . . .*

. . . his pie as spotlight fades out. Mrs. Stevenson, *in bed, looks at the phone nervously.)* Why did I do that? Now he'll think I *am* a fool.

Analyzing the Text

RL 1, RL 2, RL 3, RL 5, RL 7, RL 10

Possible answers:

1. *She is lying in bed with pill bottles within reach. After slamming down the phone, she takes a pill. These actions reveal a character who is bedridden, possibly for a medical reason, and seems very nervous.*

2. *Sergeant Duffy initially reacts with interest, but he quickly loses interest. He is "not too impressed" and seems preoccupied with his food. When Mrs. Stevenson realizes that he is not going to take her fears seriously, she slams down the phone and says, "Idiot!"*

3. *Exposition: Mrs. Stevenson is bedridden and trying to call someone when she accidentally overhears a murder plot.*
   Rising Action: She makes call after call trying but failing to enlist the help of operators, the police, and a hospital.
   Climax: Mrs. Stevenson hears an intruder and knows that she is the intended murder victim. The murderer kills her.
   Falling Action: Sergeant Duffy answers Mrs. Stevenson's final call.
   Resolution: The murderer delivers the title line of the play and hangs up.

4. *The sound of the train in the opening scene foreshadows the plotters' mention of a train that will muffle screams. During Mrs. Stevenson's talk with Sergeant Duffy, she gives details about her own location, which match those of the murder victim's.*

5. *Mrs. Stevenson knows that the murder will be committed in a location very similar to her own, but she doesn't perceive herself as the victim until it's too late. She also can't imagine anyone having a reason to want her dead. No one she calls takes her fears seriously—everyone perceives her as a worrier.*

RL 7, SL 2

Speaking and Listening

Have students watch the film clip, which can be found in their eBook. Then have them locate the corresponding section of the script for the stage play. See Extend & Reteach at the end of this selection for further instruction on comparing and contrasting a stage drama to its film version.

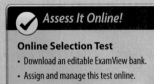

Assess It Online!

Online Selection Test
- Download an editable ExamView bank.
- Assign and manage this test online.

---

eBook *Annotate It!*

Analyzing the Text

RL 1, RL 2, RL 3, RL 5, RL 7, RL 10, W 2, W 4, W 9a, W 10, SL 2

Cite Text Evidence   Support your responses with evidence from the text.

1. **Infer**   Reread the stage directions in lines 16–27. What do Mrs. Stevenson's actions reveal about her physical condition?

2. **Cause/Effect**   Reread lines 328–531. How does Sergeant Duffy react to Mrs. Stevenson's call and how does his reaction affect Mrs. Stevenson?

3. **Summarize**   Create a plot diagram like the one shown. Then place the events of *Sorry, Wrong Number* in their correct position on the diagram.

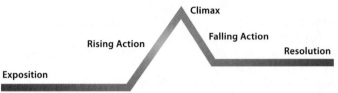

4. **Analyze**   When a writer provides hints that suggest future events in a story, it's called **foreshadowing.** Go back through the drama and find examples of foreshadowing. For each example, provide a description of what eventually happens.

5. **Analyze and Evaluate**   How do the setting and other details from the drama show that perception and reality do not always match up?

Speaking and Listening

Watch the clip from the film version of *Sorry, Wrong Number*. How is seeing the drama as a film different from reading it? With a partner, discuss the differences between the use of stage directions in the drama and the filmmakers' use of film techniques to create suspense and a feeling of terror.

PERFORMANCE TASK

Writing Activity: Character Analysis   Write a three-paragraph character analysis of Mrs. Stevenson. Support your analysis with examples of her actions, as expressed in the dialogue and stage directions. Try to answer these questions.

- How does she perceive herself?

- How does she perceive other people such as the operators, police sergeant, and hospital workers?
- What parts of her personality might have been misunderstood or allow her to be misunderstood by others?
- How do her actions affect the drama's plot?

Assign this performance task.

PERFORMANCE TASK

RL 3, W 2, W 4, W 9a, W 10

Writing Activity: Character Analysis   Provide guidance for planning the writing:

- In the center of a web graphic organizer, write the name of the main character and her role in the drama.
- In the surrounding circles, write details about her traits and qualities, how others perceive her, and how she interacts with others.

Compare and Contrast: Text and Media

TEACH

Explain to students that a play and a film share certain elements, including *settings, characters, a plot,* and *dialogue.* Review the terms, and then ask why the dramatic element of *suspense* belongs in any discussion of *Sorry, Wrong Number.* (*The suspense builds throughout the play. Suspense is the tense feeling that grows stronger as we wait for the outcome.*)

Emphasize that dramatists and filmmakers combine visual and sound techniques in different ways.

- **In a play,** the action is driven by dialogue, with help from the stage directions. The settings are usually limited to sets that would be built for a stage.
- **On film,** the action is recorded and often seems real. Audiences usually aren't aware of the sources of lighting, sound, and special effects, as they would be with a play. Settings are often in actual real-world locations, such as a city street, although often films are shot on sets, too.
- A movie version of a play is usually more detailed and realistic in presentation—it is one person's vision of the play's plot transferred to screen.

PRACTICE AND APPLY

Film Clip: 90 minutes

Encourage multiple viewings of the film clip and rereadings of the similar scene in the script. Provide these questions to prompt discussion of similarities and differences. Suggest that students jot down notes in a Venn Diagram.

- How do the settings differ?
- How is the main character in the film like and different from the character you pictured while reading?
- How is suspense created in the script? In the film?
- What do you notice about the dialogue in each form?
- What is alike and different about the visual and sound techniques used onstage and onscreen?
- What seems most different about reading a script and viewing a film?

 INTERACTIVE GRAPHIC ORGANIZER Have students use this Interactive Graphic Organizer: **Venn Diagram**.

Analyze Form: Drama

RETEACH

Help students understand the ways in which drama and other forms of fiction are alike:

- Review the names of story elements in both drama and fiction by displaying these terms and questions and having students match the term with the question it answers:
  - *characters, setting, plot*
  - *When and where? What happens? Who?*
- Define *conflict* as the struggle or problem that sets the plot in motion. Have students give examples of conflicts in stories they have recently viewed or read.
- Then use a plot diagram, such as the one in Analyzing the Text, and details from *Sorry, Wrong Number* to review the five main parts of a plot.

Ask questions that will prompt discussion of the unique features of drama; for example: *Why are stage directions needed? How does an actor know what words to say? Why is dialogue so important in a play?*

 LEVEL UP TUTORIALS Assign the following *Level Up* tutorial: **Elements of Drama**

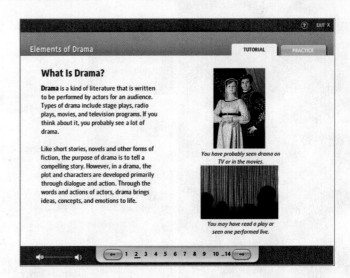

INDEPENDENT READING

Guide students to locate a script for a short drama and to read it with a partner. Possible search term: "One-act plays." Have partners identify the elements of the drama that are shared with other works of fiction and the features that are shared only with other works of drama.

Comparing Versions of A Christmas Carol

A Christmas Carol

Novel by Charles Dickens

A Christmas Carol: Scrooge and Marley

Drama by Israel Horovitz

A Christmas Carol

Graphic Story by Marvel Comics

Why This Text

Students will read the same scene from *A Christmas Carol* presented in three genres: as an excerpt from the novel, as a scene from a play, and as part of a graphic story. With the help of close-reading questions, students will analyze the characters and the benefits of each genre. This will lead students to an understanding of how different genres can present a story.

Background Have students read the background about the novel *A Christmas Carol*. Tell students that Charles Dickens was the most popular novelist of his time, and wrote 15 novels and hundreds of short stories and articles. Dickens was a social reformer. He campaigned for children's rights and for the poor. When he toured America he was a vocal opponent of slavery.

SETTING A PURPOSE Ask students to compare and contrast each genre. What advantages does each genre have?

Standards Support

- cite several pieces of textual evidence
- analyze how particular elements of a drama interact
- compare and contrast genres

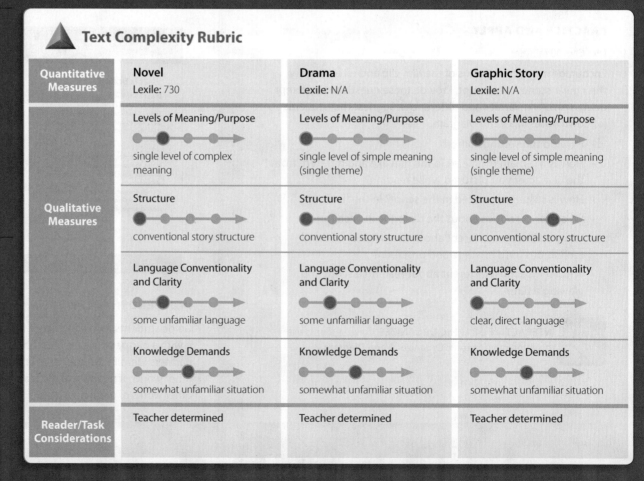

▲ Text Complexity Rubric

	Novel Lexile: 730	**Drama** Lexile: N/A	**Graphic Story** Lexile: N/A
Quantitative Measures			
Qualitative Measures	Levels of Meaning/Purpose single level of complex meaning	Levels of Meaning/Purpose single level of simple meaning (single theme)	Levels of Meaning/Purpose single level of simple meaning (single theme)
	Structure conventional story structure	Structure conventional story structure	Structure unconventional story structure
	Language Conventionality and Clarity some unfamiliar language	Language Conventionality and Clarity some unfamiliar language	Language Conventionality and Clarity clear, direct language
	Knowledge Demands somewhat unfamiliar situation	Knowledge Demands somewhat unfamiliar situation	Knowledge Demands somewhat unfamiliar situation
Reader/Task Considerations	Teacher determined	Teacher determined	Teacher determined

Compare and Contrast Genres

Students should read each version of the scene carefully all the way through. Close-reading questions at the bottom of the page will help them understand how the elements of the story interact in each genre. As they read, students should jot down comments or questions about the text in the margins.

WHEN STUDENTS STRUGGLE . . .

To help students compare and contrast how each genre presents a specific scene from *A Christmas Carol*, have them work in small groups to fill out a chart like the one shown below.

CITE TEXT EVIDENCE For practice in comparing how each genre presents the same scene, ask students to give text examples and identify the advantages of each.

Text Example	Advantage
Novel:	
"The spirit was immovable as ever." (line 14)	The reader learns a lot about the character and his previous actions.
"It shrunk, collapsed, and dwindled down into a bedpost." (lines 29–30)	This "impossible" action can be described with well-chosen words.
Drama:	
Stage directions describe the setting.	The directions are sufficient for readers to visualize the setting.
The story is told through dialogue.	Dialogue brings the story alive.
Graphic Story:	
The story is illustrated.	Each frame advances the story; the illustrations show the setting, action, and characters' expressions.
Dialogue is shown with lettering and speech balloons.	The combination of kinds of lettering and speech balloons can imply emotions and volume.

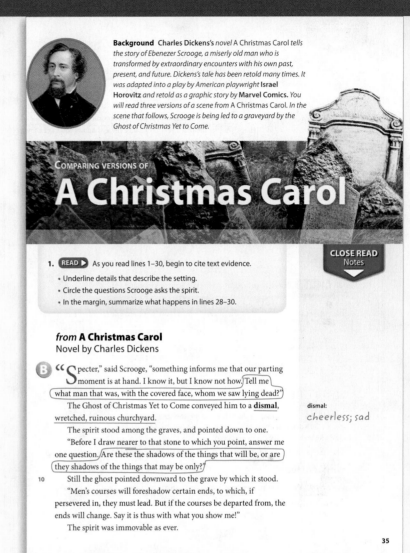

Background Charles Dickens's novel *A Christmas Carol tells the story of Ebenezer Scrooge, a miserly old man who is transformed by extraordinary encounters with his own past, present, and future. Dickens's tale has been retold many times. It was adapted into a play by American playwright* **Israel Horovitz** *and retold as a graphic story by* **Marvel Comics.** *You will read three versions of a scene from A Christmas Carol. In the scene that follows, Scrooge is being led to a graveyard by the Ghost of Christmas Yet to Come.*

Comparing Versions of

A Christmas Carol

CLOSE READ
Notes

1. **READD** As you read lines 1–30, begin to cite text evidence.
- Underline details that describe the setting.
- Circle the questions Scrooge asks the spirit.
- In the margin, summarize what happens in lines 28–30.

from **A Christmas Carol**
Novel by Charles Dickens

B   "Specter," said Scrooge, "something informs me that our parting moment is at hand. I know it, but I know not how. Tell me what man that was, with the covered face, whom we saw lying dead?"
　　　 The Ghost of Christmas Yet to Come conveyed him to a **dismal**, wretched, ruinous churchyard.
　　　 The spirit stood among the graves, and pointed down to one.
　　　 "Before I draw nearer to that stone to which you point, answer me one question. Are these the shadows of the things that will be, or are they shadows of the things that may be only?"
10　 Still the ghost pointed downward to the grave by which it stood.
　　　 "Men's courses will foreshadow certain ends, to which, if persevered in, they must lead. But if the courses be departed from, the ends will change. Say it is thus with what you show me!"
　　　 The spirit was immovable as ever.

dismal:
cheerless; sad

35

1. **READ AND CITE TEXT EVIDENCE** Scrooge has seen his own grave in the future—and it is neglected. He begs the spirit to let him change his ways, and by doing so, change the way he will be remembered.

A **ASK STUDENTS** what happens in lines 28–30. *The spirit collapsed and turned into a bedpost.* What might this tell the reader about the spirit? *Students may suggest that the spirit is no longer interacting with Scrooge, which might imply that Scrooge's words have been heeded. Students may also suggest that the spirit is simply in Scrooge's imagination and disappears after Scrooge has experienced all he needed to.*

Critical Vocabulary: dismal (line 4) Ask students to share their definitions of *dismal*. Ask them how the word choice contributes to the mood in the first paragraph.

Scrooge crept toward it, trembling as he went; and following the finger, read upon the stone of the neglected grave his own name—EBENEZER SCROOGE.

"Am I that man who lay upon the bed? No, Spirit! Oh no, no! Spirit! hear me! I am not the man I was. I will not be the man I must
20 have been but for this intercourse. Why show me this, if I am past all hope? Assure me that I yet may change these shadows you have shown me, by an **altered** life."

For the first time the kind hand faltered.

"I will honor Christmas in my heart, and try to keep it all the year. I will live in the Past, the Present, and the Future. The spirits of all three shall strive within me. I will not shut out the lessons that they teach. Oh, tell me I may sponge away the writing on this stone!"

(A)   Holding up his hands in one last prayer to have his fate reversed,
30 he saw an alteration in the phantom's hood and dress. It shrunk, collapsed, and dwindled down into a bedpost.

altered:
changed

The spirit turned into a bedpost.

---

2. **◄ REREAD** Reread lines 1–30. What effect do Scrooge's repeated questions achieve?

The questions show his desperation. He is scared of the future and wants to know how he can stop it from happening. Repeating the questions shows he wants to change.

SHORT RESPONSE

Cite Text Evidence Scrooge is the only character who speaks in the scene. Which details show that the spirit is affected by what Scrooge says? **Cite text evidence** in your response.

The descriptions of the spirit's physical reactions convey that the spirit is affected by Scrooge. First, the spirit is unmoved by Scrooge, perhaps because Scrooge is too demanding. Then, the spirit's hand falters when Scrooge announces his sincere intention to change.

36

---

3. **READ ►** As you read lines 1–28, continue to cite textual evidence.

• Underline every sentence that mentions Future's hand.
• Circle the special effects in the stage directions.
• In the margin, note an element in this drama that is not in the original story.

from **A Christmas Carol: Scrooge and Marley**
Drama by Israel Horovitz

Scrooge. Specter, something informs me that our parting moment is at hand. I know it, but I know not how I know it.

(D)   [FUTURE *points to the other side of the stage. Lights out on* CRATCHITS.[1] FUTURE *moves slowing, gliding.* SCROOGE *follows.* FUTURE *points opposite.* FUTURE *leads* SCROOGE *to a wall and a tombstone. He points to the stone.*]

Am *I* that man those ghoulish parasites[2] so gloated over? (*Pauses*) Before I draw nearer to that stone to which you point, answer me one question. Are these the shadows of things that will be, or the shadows
10 of things that MAY be, only?

(C)   [FUTURE *points to the gravestone.* MARLEY[3] *appears in light well* UPSTAGE. *He points to grave as well.* Gravestone turns front and grows to ten feet high, Words upon it: EBENEZER SCROOGE. Much smoke billows now from the grave. Choral music here. SCROOGE *stands looking up at gravestone.* FUTURE *does not at all reply in mortals' words, but points once more to the gravestone.* The stone undulates and glows. Music plays, *beckoning* SCROOGE. SCROOGE, *reeling in terror*]

The ghost of Scrooge's former partner Marley appears in this drama.

---

[1] **Crachits:** The family of Bob Crachit, Scrooge's clerk. He is mistreated and underpaid by Scrooge.
[2] **ghoulish parasites:** people who stole Scrooge's possessions and divided them up after he died.
[3] **Marley:** Scrooge's business partner, deceased at the time of the events in the drama. He appears to Scrooge as a ghost.

37

---

2. **REREAD AND CITE TEXT EVIDENCE**

(B) **ASK STUDENTS** to refer to the questions they circled. What might Scrooge want to accomplish with these questions? *Students may say that he is hoping that the spirit will give him answers. They may also point out that Scrooge wants reassurance that he can change the future, and he tells the spirit of his intentions.*

Critical Vocabulary: altered (line 22) Have students compare the words *altered* and *changed*. Ask them if there is a slight difference of meaning. *Students may suggest that the word* altered *sometimes has a connotation of intentional change.*

SHORT RESPONSE

Cite Text Evidence Students should

• cite details that explain the spirit's actions
• explain what the spirit's actions imply
• compare the spirit's gestures to infer a change in its attitude

3. **READ AND CITE TEXT EVIDENCE**

(C) **ASK STUDENTS** to consider which stage directions require special effects. What do the special effects add to the drama? *The gravestone turning and growing huge while smoke billows from the grave creates a terrifying setting, and as the gravestone undulates and glows it is clear why Scrooge is terrified.*

FOR ELL STUDENTS Encourage a volunteer student to guess the meaning of the expression *at hand*. Act out having something at hand to demonstrate why it means "near."

Spirit! Hear me! I am not the man I was.

Oh, no, Spirit! Oh, no, no!

20 [FUTURE's *finger still pointing*]

Spirit! Hear me! I am not the man I was. I will not be the man I would have been but for this intercourse. Why show me this, if I am past all hope?

[FUTURE *considers* SCROOGE's *logic. His hand wavers.*]

Oh, Good Spirit, I see by your wavering hand that your good nature intercedes for me and pities me. Assure me that I yet may change these shadows that you have shown me by an altered life!

[FUTURE's *hand trembles; pointing has stopped.*]

I will honor Christmas in my heart and try to keep it all the year.

30 I will live in the Past, the Present, and the Future. The Spirits of all Three shall strive within me. I will not shut out the lessons that they teach. Oh, tell me that I may sponge away the writing that is upon this stone!

F [SCROOGE *makes a desperate stab at grabbing* FUTURE's *hand. He holds it firm for a moment, but* FUTURE, *stronger than* SCROOGE, *pulls away.* SCROOGE *is on his knees, praying.*]

E Spirit, dear Spirit, I am praying before you. Give me a sign that all is possible. Give me a sign that all hope for me is not lost. Oh, Spirit, kind Spirit, I beseech thee: give me a sign . . .

Scrooge wants a sign that he can change his future.

4. ◀ **REREAD AND DISCUSS** Reread lines 1–28. In a small group, discuss why Future stops pointing.

5. **READ** ▶ As you read lines 29–44, continue to cite textual evidence.

• Underline the promise that Scrooge makes.
• Circle the stage directions.
• Note in the margin what Scrooge wants in lines 37–39.

38

---

40 [FUTURE *deliquesces,*⁴ *slowly, gently. The* PHANTOM's *hood and robe drop gracefully to the ground in a small heap. Music in. There is nothing in them. They are mortal cloth. The* SPIRIT *is elsewhere.* SCROOGE *has his sign.* SCROOGE *is alone. Tableau. The lights fade to black.*]

⁴ **deliquesces:** melts away; dissolves.

6. ◀ **REREAD** Reread lines 34–36. What do the stage directions reveal about Scrooge's emotions? Cite textual evidence in your answer.

Scrooge "makes a desperate stab at" Future's hand because he wants a sign from him that things can change. Scrooge also kneels and prays, which indicates that he is humble and sincere.

SHORT RESPONSE

Cite Text Evidence How is this experience of reading a dramatization of *A Christmas Carol* different from reading the original story? Analyze elements such as stage directions and dialogue. Use your reading notes and be sure to **cite text evidence** in your response.

The additional details in the drama's stage directions make it easier to visualize the setting. For example, the smoke surrounding Scrooge's grave emphasizes how somber and spooky the scene is. The description of Scrooge's and Future's physical actions help me picture certain aspects of the scene. Also, the dialogue helps me understand that Scrooge is sorry for his behavior.

39

---

4. **REREAD AND DISCUSS USING TEXT EVIDENCE** Point out to students that Future has said nothing, but only gestured using his hand.

D ASK STUDENTS to explain Future's gestures. *First, Future points to the other side of the stage and then at a tombstone. When Scrooge asks if he is seeing a possible future, the spirit simply points again at the gravestone, and keeps pointing there until Scrooge promises to change. He then asks why he is shown the future if there is no way to alter it. The spirit's hand wavers, showing that Future hears Scrooge, and then it trembles again, revealing that Future is considering Scrooge's pleas.*

5. **READ AND CITE TEXT EVIDENCE**

E ASK STUDENTS what Scrooge is feeling in the graveyard. *He desperately wants to change so that the future he sees will not happen.* Ask what Scrooge means when he says, "Give me a sign that all is possible." *Knowing that the spirit will not talk, Scrooge wants the spirit to show him a sign that he can change the future.*

6. **REREAD AND CITE TEXT EVIDENCE**

F ASK STUDENTS what Scrooge does in lines 34–36. *He makes a desperate grab at Future's hand, holds it for a moment, then kneels and prays.* What does the word *desperate* tell you? *Scrooge is frantic for some response from the spirit.* Why is Scrooge kneeling and praying? *He is showing that he is humble and that he has no pride in begging for the spirit's help.*

SHORT RESPONSE

Cite Text Evidence Students' responses should include text evidence that supports their positions. They should

• contrast the drama with the original story
• analyze the stage directions and explain their effects
• analyze the dialogue and what it reveals about Scrooge

7. **READ ▶** As you read this page, begin to collect and cite text evidence.

- Circle examples of Scrooge's facial expressions.
- Circle text that shows Scrooge trying to convince or influence the spirit.
- In the margin, explain what Scrooge wants to know from the spirit.

from **A Christmas Carol**
Graphic Story by Marvel Comics

Scrooge wants to know who the dead man is.

The Ghost has transformed into a bedpost.

8. **◀ REREAD** What do Scrooge's facial expressions tell you about his feelings about the Ghost of Christmas Future?

Scrooge's facial expressions indicate that he is afraid of the Ghost and is concerned about the news the Ghost may share with him.

9. **READ ▶** As you read this page, continue to cite textual evidence.

- Circle what Scrooge sees on the tombstone.
- Circle text that reveals that Scrooge wants to change.
- In the margin, explain what happens to the Ghost of Christmas Future.

40

41

7. **READ AND CITE TEXT EVIDENCE**

G **ASK STUDENTS** what they can infer from the frames on this page. *Scrooge has seen a dead man, and the ghost takes Scrooge to a graveyard where it is probable that the dead man is buried.* Why does Scrooge suggest that the future can be changed? *He is concerned that he himself may be the dead man.*

8. **REREAD AND CITE TEXT EVIDENCE**

H **ASK STUDENTS** to describe the expressions on Scrooge's face. *Scrooge looks terrified. In the final frame on the page, he is shocked and distressed.* What do Scrooge's expressions reveal about his feelings? *He is scared of the ghost and of what he may learn. His expression of shock reveals that he has learned something that torments him.*

FOR ELL STUDENTS Point out that the word *indeed* is used to emphasize the truth of a statement. It can be replaced with *certainly* or *without question.*

9. **READ AND CITE TEXT EVIDENCE** Scrooge has been asking the ghost to assure him that he can change his ways and therefore his future, but has had no definite response.

I **ASK STUDENTS** why Scrooge grabs the ghost's hand. *He is trying to get a response from the ghost.* What happens when Scrooge grabs the ghost's hand? *The ghost shrinks and turns into a bedpost—he is no longer present. Scrooge is holding his own bedpost, as if he has awoken from a nightmare.*

10. ◄ REREAD AND DISCUSS In a small group, discuss which was most effective in conveying the change in Scrooge: the text or the illustrations. Cite text evidence in your discussion.

SHORT RESPONSE

Cite Text Evidence Is the change in Scrooge's character most believable in the novel, the drama, or the graphic story? **Cite text evidence** in your response.

Answers may vary. Some students may say they think the change in Scrooge's character is most believable in the drama. Scrooge's dialogue, especially when he is pleading for a sign from the spirit, conveys how remorseful he feels. Likewise, the playwright reveals Scrooge's desperation for a chance to change in the stage directions.

42

10. REREAD AND DISCUSS USING TEXT EVIDENCE

ASK STUDENTS to assign a reporter for each group to present its response. *Some groups may suggest that the text is more effective as it tells the story, and devices such as the size and weight of the lettering show variations in emphasis; others may think that the illustrations tell the story adequately on their own. It's likely that some groups will point out that the text and illustrations work together to tell the story most effectively.*

SHORT RESPONSE

Cite Text Evidence Students' responses should include text evidence that supports their positions. They should

- analyze the change in Scrooge's character
- explain how the dialogue reveals Scrooge's motivations
- determine which presentation they think most effectively portrayed Scrooge's change of character

TO CHALLENGE STUDENTS . . .

It took Dickens only six weeks to write *A Christmas Carol.* When it was first published, it had a huge impact on the public. An American entrepreneur gave his employees an extra day's holiday after reading the story; within two months there were eight different theatrical productions playing in London; and two months after publication a publisher pirated the book.

ASK STUDENTS to research some of the effects Dickens's novel had. (These include the popularization of the phrase *Merry Christmas* and the use of the name *Scrooge* and the expression *Bah! Humbug!* A more meaningful effect was the change in the way Christmas was celebrated after Dickens's novel became such a hit—the importance of the holiday increased, and it was spent with family in merry moods.) Have students write a paragraph from their research, and compare what they find out.

DIG DEEPER

With the class, return to the Short Response on page 42. Have students share their responses.

ASK STUDENTS to cite the text evidence that led to their decision about the most effective presentation of the scene from *A Christmas Carol.*

- Have students explain how each genre presents the setting of the scene. *The novel describes the setting; the drama explains the setting in stage directions; the graphic story shows the setting in the illustrations.*
- Ask students how the story of Scrooge's character change is told in each genre. *The novel uses dialogue and descriptions to tell the story; the drama uses dialogue; the graphic story uses dialogue, description, and illustrations.*
- Have students describe the part of the story that had the greatest impact on them, and which of the versions was most effective.

ASK STUDENTS to return to their Short Response answer and revise it based on the class discussion.

PERCEPTION AND REALITY

The FYI site provides links to online articles from a variety of magazines and newspapers. Help students choose a few articles to read to further their exploration of the topic Perception and Reality.

NOVELWISE

Students can unlock the power of novels with this unique resource. Help students read through longer works with these tips:

- Find a Book
- Before You Read
- As You Read
- After You Read

Each book includes introductory material, worksheets, graphic organizers, and discussion guides.

ADDITIONAL TEXTS BY COLLECTION

Suggest that students read these:

- "The Artilleryman's Vision" by Walt Whitman
- "Richard Cory" by Edwin Arlington Robinson
- "Kubla Khan" by Samuel Taylor Coleridge

Read one poem aloud. Discuss how diction contributes to the mood as it relates to perception and reality. Have students read another poem and compare its diction to that of the first poem.

NONFICTION CONNECTIONS

Suggest that students increase their reading of informational texts. The nonfiction connections include

- speeches
- diaries
- true-life accounts
- newspaper articles
- political cartoons

Creating an Independent Reading Program

STUDENTS CHOOSE THEIR OWN BOOKS

Students who choose their own books will read more actively.

- Discuss with students how they already choose books. Record responses on a chart, poster, or word cloud.
- Ask students if they prefer certain types of books over others. Do they have favorite topics or authors? What would make them consider different genres, topics, or authors?
- Encourage students to choose books in pairs or trios, so they can talk about their reading with others, or have designated days when students can "shop" for books they might want to read.
- Explain that it's okay to abandon a book that doesn't fit. Model scenarios in which this might be the case.

STRATEGIES FOR SELECTING A BOOK

Help students select books of suitable difficulty, content, and interest.

- Have students preview a book by skimming its table of contents, the amount of text on a page, and any illustrations.
- Ask students to read the first two pages. How many words did they not know? (More than five means the book is too difficult; three is about right.) Can students summarize what they've read? Can they start to make predictions? (If so, the book is on level.)
- Ask students to read to page 5. They should have to think and clarify some. If not, the book is too easy. If they can't make any sense of the first five pages, the book is too hard.
- If the book meets these criteria and interests them, students may continue reading.

COLLECTION 2
PERFORMANCE TASK A

Interactive Lessons
To help you complete this task, use *Writing Arguments*.

PERFORMANCE TASK A

Write an Argument

Folk tales like "The People Could Fly" often make readers reflect on the ways we perceive our world. Consider the common saying "seeing is believing" and its meaning. After reading the texts in this collection, do you believe this saying is true? You will draw from "The People Could Fly" and other texts in the collection to write an argument that states and supports your position.

RL 1 Cite textual evidence.
W 1a–e Write arguments.
W 4 Produce clear and coherent writing.
W 5 Develop and strengthen writing.
W 9 Draw evidence from literary or informational texts.
W 10 Write routinely.

A successful argument

- contains an engaging introduction that clearly states the claim, or opinion
- supports the opinion with logical reasoning and relevant evidence
- presents and refutes opposing claims, or viewpoints
- uses language that effectively conveys ideas and adds interest
- concludes with a restatement of the claim

PLAN

myNotebook

Use the annotation tools in your eBook to find evidence to support your claim. Save each piece of evidence to your notebook.

Form a Claim Revisit the texts in the collection. Consider your answers to the following questions as you form your claim:

- How and why do the characters or people perceive the things that happen?
- How does this information relate to the meaning of the saying "seeing is believing"?

Gather Information Focus on the selection(s) that have information you can cite to support your claim.

- Consider the points of view or opinions that are expressed.
- Make a list of the reasons you have for your claim.
- Identify evidence in the texts that supports your reasons.

ACADEMIC VOCABULARY

As you plan, write, and review your draft, be sure to use the academic vocabulary words.

abnormal
feature
focus
perceive
task

PERFORMANCE TASK A

WRITE AN ARGUMENT

W 1a–e,
W 4, W 5,
W 9, W 10

Introduce students to the Performance Task by reading the introductory paragraph with them and reviewing the criteria for what makes a good argument. Remind students that an argument needs to provide evidence to support the reasons for the writer's position.

PLAN

GATHER INFORMATION

Explain to students that as they plan their writing they should anticipate readers' opposing viewpoints, or claims. Students should write down opposing claims and questions and prepare counterarguments to include in their essays. Point out that including counterarguments will make it harder for readers to disagree with students' claims.

English Language Support

Write an Argument Make sure that students understand the saying, "seeing is believing." Have students review collection texts to identify beliefs central to each selection and answer these questions in groups:

- *Do you have to see something to believe it is true?*
- *Is it easier to believe something if you can see it? Why?*
- *What beliefs do the texts express? Do they seem possible?*
- *How do characters respond to events in the text?*

After the discussion, let each group write an explanation of the phrase "seeing is believing." Encourage students to use notes from their discussions to help form claims and supporting reasons for their arguments.

PERFORMANCE TASK A

English Language Support

Understand Text Structure Help students understand that arguments are organized around reasons and evidence. Point out the structure of the graphic organizer. Tell students that their reasons should answer *Why* questions about their claim or opinion. Tell them that solid evidence for their arguments may come from both texts and background knowledge.

PRODUCE

WRITE YOUR ARGUMENT

Explain to students that before they begin writing they should think about what kind of tone would be most convincing to their likely audience. Suggest that their audience will include their fellow students and teacher, and discuss the following questions with students:

View It!

Professional Development Podcast:

Teaching Argument

- Would a light, humorous tone be convincing to this audience? Why or why not?
- Would a serious, formal tone be convincing to this audience? Why or why not?

Organize Your Ideas Think about organizing your argument. A graphic organizer like this one can help present ideas logically.

Interactive Lessons
For help in organizing your ideas, use:
• Writing Arguments: Building Effective Support

```
                    Claim
          ┌───────────┴───────────┐
        Reason                  Reason
     ┌────┼────┐            ┌────┼────┐
 Evidence Evidence Evidence Evidence Evidence Evidence
```

Consider Your Purpose and Audience Think about who will read or listen to your argument. What do you want them to understand? What will be most convincing to them? Keep these questions and your answers in mind as you prepare to write.

> **PRODUCE**

Write Your Argument Review the information in your notes as you begin your draft.

- Begin by introducing the topic and stating your claim. Include an attention-grabbing lead.
- Write your reasons and support them with evidence, such as facts and examples. Organize your argument logically.
- Be aware of any **counterclaims,** or opinions that oppose your position.
- Include words and phrases such as *because, therefore*, and *for that reason* that will link your opinion, reasons, and evidence and make your argument clearer and more coherent.
- Establish and maintain a formal style and tone.
- Summarize your argument, repeating the most important reasons and evidence, and leave a lasting impression.

Write your rough draft in *my*WriteSmart. Focus on getting your ideas down, rather than perfecting your choice of language.

Interactive Lessons
For help in developing your argument, use:
• Writing Arguments: Creating a Coherent Argument

Language Conventions: Connect Ideas

Words like *and, but,* and *or* can help to combine ideas in a sentence. Read the following example from "Magic and the Brain."

> " Tomsoni claps his hands, and the spotlight dims ever so briefly before reflaring in a blaze of red. "

English Language Support

Justify Opinions Explain that precise word choices clarify ideas.

- Have student pairs review the following sentences:

  He *can/may* walk to school.

  It is *possible/likely* that she will disappear on stage.

  They *could/would/should* complete the project.

Ask the groups to discuss the differences in sentence meaning using each word choice and to consider ways these words can help them express opinions and shades of meaning in their arguments.

- Have students break into small groups to review the following sentences:

  Eating eggs will *absolutely* help boys to gain weight.

  Eating eggs will *possibly* help boys to gain weight.

Explain that *absolutely* means definitely, or without a doubt. Therefore, the first sentence says that boys who eat eggs will definitely gain weight. *Possibly* means the boys may or may not gain weight. Have group members write and compare statements that contain *absolutely* and *possibly*.

Notice how the word *and* connects two clauses to form a compound sentence. Look for places in your argument where you can add words to make connections between ideas.

REVISE

Evaluate Your Draft Work with your partner to determine whether your argument is effective. Use this chart to help you.

Questions	Tips	Revision Techniques
Does my introduction clearly state the claim?	**Underline** the claim.	**Clarify** the claim to make it hard to miss.
Is my claim supported by reasons and evidence?	**Highlight** each reason, and **underline** your evidence.	**Add** facts, statistics, and examples to strengthen your claim.
What words or phrases are helping to make my argument clear?	**Highlight** words that help to connect your reasons and evidence.	**Use** words like *and*, *but*, *so*, and *because* to connect ideas and to create cohesion.
Have I addressed counterclaims?	**Underline** your claim. **Consider** what an opposing claim might be and how to address it.	**Include** a visible counterargument to show you understand and can address an opposing view.
Is the tone of my argument formal?	**Highlight** any contractions and use of casual wording.	**Change** the contractions. **Revise** so the tone sounds objective.
Does the conclusion restate my claim and end convincingly?	**Underline** the restatement.	**Summarize** your main points in a restatement that tells the audience what you want it to believe or understand.

my WriteSmart

Have your partner or a group of peers review your draft in *my*WriteSmart. Ask your reviewers to note any reasons or evidence that does not support your claim.

Interactive Lessons
For help in refining your argument, use:
• Writing Arguments: Concluding Your Argument

PRESENT

Create a Finished Copy Finalize your argument and choose a way to share it with your audience. Consider these options:

• Post it as a blog on a personal or school website.
• Present your ideas in a debate with someone who has an opposing claim.

PRODUCE

LANGUAGE CONVENTIONS

Tell students that the connecting word *but* shows a contrast between two opposing ideas. Read this example from "Heartbeat."

"I got ridiculously strong and defined, *but* I wasn't gaining weight."

Model another sample sentence, such as "I saw them fly, *but* I couldn't believe it." Next, have partners practice writing sentences using *but*. As students draft, they should look for opportunities to link opposing ideas.

REVISE

EVALUATE YOUR DRAFT

Tell students that they should reread their draft as if they were reading it for the first time and use the questions and tips in the chart to strengthen their arguments.

PRESENT

CREATE A FINISHED COPY

Students with differing claims can debate their positions. After listening to each other's claims, allow time for students to question each other's reasoning. Remind students to take turns asking and answering questions, and to listen to each other's responses.

FOR STANDARD ENGLISH LEARNERS

Use Plurals Encourage students to monitor the formation of regular plurals with *s* or *es* in their writing and formal speech. Review the rules and provide examples for practice: two tents, baked good*s*, miss*es*, stitch*es*.

WHEN STUDENTS STRUGGLE...

Vary Word Choice Have students work in pairs to check each partner's draft for frequently repeated words. Ask partners to highlight repeated words and to help each other find appropriate synonyms for each word in a thesaurus.

PERFORMANCE TASK A

USE THE SCORING RUBRIC

Ask students to exchange their arguments with a partner and to score it using the chart. Have each student write a brief paragraph listing what he or she liked about the work and what areas could use more attention.

REFLECT ON THE PROCESS

Invite students to reflect on the process of writing and revising their arguments. Point out that these skills they developed, such as stating claims, supplying reasons, and finding convincing evidence, can be used in many academic and career settings. Have small groups answer the following questions:

- How did the process of writing an argument affect your understanding of the text?
- Compare your first draft to your final revision. What changes are most noticeable?
- What do you like most about your argument?
- What strategies could you use to make your argument more effective?

PERFORMANCE TASK A RUBRIC
ARGUMENT

	Ideas and Evidence	Organization	Language
4	• The introduction is engaging; it clearly states the writer's claim about the statement. • Logical reasons and relevant evidence from the texts convincingly support the writer's claim. • Opposing claims are anticipated and effectively refuted. • The concluding section effectively summarizes the claim and leaves a lasting impression.	• The reasons and evidence are organized logically and consistently throughout the argument. • Words and phrases logically connect reasons and evidence to the writer's claim.	• The writing reflects a formal style and tone. • The use of clear, succinct language effectively conveys the writer's ideas. • Sentence beginnings, lengths, and structures vary and have a rhythmic flow. • Spelling, capitalization, and punctuation are correct. • Grammar and usage are correct.
3	• The introduction could do more to grab the reader's attention; the introduction states the writer's claim. • Most reasons and relevant evidence from the texts support the writer's claim, but they could be more convincing. • Opposing claims are anticipated, but they could be more effectively refuted. • The concluding section restates the claim, but it is not very memorable.	• The organization of reasons and evidence is confusing in a few places. • A few more words and phrases are needed to connect reasons and evidence to the writer's claim.	• The style and tone become informal in a few places. • Sentence beginnings, lengths, and structures vary somewhat. • Few spelling, capitalization, and punctuation mistakes occur. • Some grammatical and usage errors are repeated in the argument.
2	• The introduction is ordinary; the writer's claim is not clearly stated. • The reasons and evidence are not always relevant or logical. • Opposing claims are anticipated but not addressed logically. • The concluding section includes an incomplete summary of the claim.	• The organization of reasons and evidence is generally logical, but it frequently doesn't follow a pattern. • Many more words and phrases are needed to connect reasons and evidence to the writer's claim.	• The style and tone become informal in many places. • Sentence structures barely vary, and some fragments or run-on sentences are present. • Several spelling and capitalization mistakes occur, and punctuation is inconsistent. • Grammar and usage are incorrect in many places.
1	• The introduction is missing. • Supporting reasons and evidence are missing. • Opposing claims are neither anticipated nor addressed. • The concluding section is missing.	• A logical organization is not used; reasons and evidence are presented randomly. • Connecting words and phrases are not used.	• The style and tone are inappropriate for an argument. • Repetitive sentence structure, fragments, and run-on sentences make the writing hard to follow. • Spelling and capitalization are often incorrect, and punctuation is missing. • Many grammatical and usage errors occur.

TO CHALLENGE STUDENTS . . .

Create a Podcast Challenge students to present their arguments as a podcast, video, audio recording, or other media presentation. Have them consider ways to illustrate or support their presentations with photos, graphics, audio, and other features. If your time or resources are limited, have students simply present detailed plans for such presentations.

FOR STUDENTS WITH DISABILITIES

Make a Checklist Let pairs create a revision checklist, using the rubric as a guideline. As each student reads the draft aloud, have partners list items for revision. Then both partners may make suggestions for the checklists. Remind students to read aloud slowly and clearly and to take accurate notes, and then refer to the checklists as they revise.

COLLECTION 2
PERFORMANCE TASK B

Interactive Lessons
To help you complete this task,
use *Giving a Presentation*

Give a Summary Presentation

Sorry, Wrong Number is a drama chockful of actions and shifting perceptions. In the following activity, you will draw from *Sorry, Wrong Number* to deliver a summary presentation.

A successful summary presentation

- includes the title and author of the work being summarized
- restates in your own words the **theme,** or main idea, and its supporting details
- shows a comprehensive understanding of the source
- interests listeners through the use of effective verbal and nonverbal techniques

W 2a–f Write informative/explanatory texts.
W4 Produce clear and coherent writing.
W 5 Develop and strengthen writing.
W 6 Use technology to produce and publish writing.
W 10 Write routinely.
SL 4 Present claims and findings.

PLAN

Review and Take Notes The first step in presenting a summary is making sure you fully understand the work that you are summarizing. Review *Sorry, Wrong Number* closely to identify key details.

- Jot down notes about the setting, the characters' personalities, and the major plot events.
- Look for details that help you decide what point the writer is making. Reread for details that support this point.
- Consider that not every detail will be important enough to include.
- Sum up the details in your own words in a statement about the **theme,** or main idea, the writer has expressed.

Consider Your Purpose and Audience Think about who will see your presentation and what you want them to understand. Keep in mind the essential information you want to share and how to capture your audience's attention.

myNotebook

Use the annotation tools in your eBook to mark up key details that you might want to include. Save each detail to your notebook.

ACADEMIC VOCABULARY

As you plan your summary, try to use the academic vocabulary words.

abnormal
feature
focus
perceive
task

PERFORMANCE TASK B

W 2a–f,
W 4, W 5, W 6,
W 10, SL 4

GIVE A SUMMARY PRESENTATION

Introduce students to the Performance Task by reading the introductory paragraph with them and reviewing the criteria for what makes a good summary presentation. Remind students that the purpose for a summary presentation is to explain or inform.

PLAN

REVIEW AND TAKE NOTES

As students begin, remind them that a summary focuses on only the most important information. Also, point out that key events in a drama are usually revealed in dialogue, and that themes are not always stated directly. Encourage students to reread as necessary to identify and note the theme.

English Language Support

Plan a Summary Presentation Have students discuss their plans with a partner using the following sentence frames:

I think you should tell about _____ in your summary.

_____ is not very important. You can leave it out.

_____ is important, but you should say it in your own words. Maybe you could paraphrase it this way: _____.

I like your summary, but it could be shorter. For example, you can take out _____.

PERFORMANCE TASK B

PRODUCE

DRAFT YOUR SUMMARY

Remind students that a good summary presents information in the same order as in the text, but in a condensed, or shortened, form. It should clearly reflect the underlying meaning of the passage.

LANGUAGE CONVENTIONS

Point out that adverbial phrases indicating time contain both time words and adverbs. Other kinds of adverbial phrases contain words indicating how something was done, where something was placed, or why something happened. Encourage students to find places in their drafts where an adverbial phrase would help the audience better understand when, where, how, or why an event occurred.

REVISE

PRACTICE YOUR DELIVERY

As students practice, have them first focus on the verbal elements of their presentations. The more they become familiar with the words, the easier it will be for them to develop nonverbal elements, such as eye contact, facial expressions, and gestures. Encourage students to practice nonverbal signals in front of a mirror, as well as with a partner who can give feedback and suggestions.

PRODUCE

Draft Your Summary Review your notes as you begin a draft of your summary. Your draft should

- cite the drama's title and author
- clearly identify the theme by stating it in your own words
- include the most important details that support the theme
- present this information in a condensed, short passage
- show that you fully understand the source

Write your rough draft in myWriteSmart. Focus on getting your ideas down before condensing your summary.

Language Conventions: Modifying to Add Details

An **adverbial phrase** is a group of words that modifies much like a simple adverb. There are different categories of adverbial phrases. Adverbial phrases of time describe when an action occurs, how often, or to what extent. Read the following speech from *Sorry, Wrong Number*.

> **Mrs. Stevenson.** Operator? I've been dialing Murray Hill 4-0098 for the last three quarters of an hour and the line is always busy.

The phrase *for the last three quarters of an hour* modifies the verb *dialing*, telling how long Mrs. Stevenson has waited and revealing her impatience.

REVISE

Practice Your Delivery Once you have a firm grasp of your summary, you are ready to practice how you'll present it. Practice until you know your summary well. The tips below will help you make your summary presentation more engaging.

Have your partner or a group of peers review your draft in myWriteSmart. Ask your reviewers to suggest possible cuts.

Verbal Elements	Nonverbal Signals
Enunciation: Pronounce your words clearly.	**Eye contact:** Look into the eyes of your audience members.
Inflection: Let your voice rise and fall naturally as you speak.	**Facial expressions:** Look serious, look intense, or raise an eyebrow.
Pace: Match the speed of your delivery to the mood of what you are describing.	**Gestures:** Use your hands, shrug, nod, or shake your head.

Interactive Lessons
For help in practicing your presentation, use:
- Giving a Presentation: Delivering Your Presentation

English Language Support

Use Adverbials Remind students that an adverbial is a word or phrase that answers the question *When? Where? How?* or *Why?* in a sentence. Share the chart at right and have pairs take turns using the examples in sentences. Explain that adverbials can help students add details to summary presentations.

Adverbials	
To provide details about...	Example
time	*next week, the day after tomorrow, in the morning*
manner	*quickly, precisely, in a loud voice*
place	*in the hallway, outside, under the moon*
cause	*in order to hide the evidence, to find the killer, in return for a favor*

Evaluate Your Summary To help you smooth out any rough spots, have a partner view a practice run of your presentation. Use the following chart to help you.

Interactive Lessons
For help in refining your presentation, use:
• Giving a Presentation: Style in Presentation

Questions	Tips	Revision Techniques
Are the author and title included in your summary?	**Highlight** the author and title.	**Mention** the author and title at or near the beginning of the summary.
Does your summary state the theme of the drama in your own words?	**Underline** the theme.	**Check** to be sure you have used your own words.
How well do the details in the summary support the theme?	**Highlight** supporting details.	**Revise** the details so that the connections to the theme are clear.
How effective are your nonverbal and verbal techniques?	**Pair** with a partner to find out how you are using your body language and voice.	**Improve** your delivery by trying out any suggestions.

> **PRESENT**

Create a Finished Copy Finalize your summary presentation for a wider audience. You might present it to the class or record it as a video to post on an approved website.

PERFORMANCE TASK B

PRESENT

CREATE A FINISHED COPY

Students may want to present their summaries to the class or post them as videos. Remind students to pause slightly after making important points, speak clearly, maintain good posture, and use expressive body language while speaking.

FOR STANDARD ENGLISH LEARNERS

Adapt Speech Some students may struggle with pronouncing the /z/ and /v/ sounds. As they practice their summary presentations, encourage them to pay close attention to words that contain these sounds. Remind them that speaking slowly and clearly can help them focus on their pronunciation.

FOR STUDENTS WITH DISABILITIES

Use Spoken Cues Encourage students with visual impairments to rely on verbal cues rather than visual cues to structure their presentations. Inserting pauses, adjusting volume or tone for emphasis, and using sequence words can help an audience follow a presentation and recognize transitions and examples. Encourage students to make and review audio recordings of their presentations.

WHEN STUDENTS STRUGGLE...

Practice Speaking Techniques Give students an opportunity to view or listen to a recording of a model presentation before they deliver their own summaries. Pause the presentation intermittently to point out examples of strong speaking techniques. Note examples of maintaining eye contact and using voice modulation and inflection. Then have pairs focus on one technique at a time as they rehearse excerpts from their summaries.

PERFORMANCE TASK B

USE THE SCORING RUBRIC

Assign three students to score each presentation, with one student focusing on each of the three rubric categories. Ask students to write a brief explanation of the reasons for their score.

REFLECT ON THE PROCESS

In addition to evaluating the effectiveness of their presentations, ask students to reflect on the planning, producing, and revising required for this task. Have them consider what they learned, as well as what they might do differently in a future assignment. Form small groups to discuss answers to the following questions:

- How did writing the summary affect your interpretation of the text?
- What changes did you make as you practiced your summary presentation?
- What was the most challenging part of the process? What strategies helped you meet the challenge?

PERFORMANCE TASK B RUBRIC
SUMMARY PRESENTATION

	Ideas and Evidence	Organization	Language
4	• The summary cites the work's title and author. • The summary states the work's theme in the presenter's own words. • The summary reflects the presenter's full understanding of the work.	• The theme is supported strongly by relevant details. • The summary consists of a condensed, short passage.	• The presentation quite effectively conveys the work's theme and supporting ideas. • The presenter's verbal and nonverbal techniques engage the audience. • The summary features rich details through use of strong modifiers.
3	• The summary doesn't include both the title and author. • The summary states the theme of the work but it could be less wordy. • The summary shows a sufficient understanding of the work.	• There is sufficient support for the theme. • The summary passage, though short, could use some tightening.	• The presentation needs more work to convey the theme and supporting ideas well. • The presenter shows a decent grasp of verbal and nonverbal techniques. • Improved use of modifiers would add more detail to the summary.
2	• The title is mentioned in the summary but not the author. • The theme that is stated seems relatively minor. • The summary could do more to show a better understanding of the work.	• One or two supporting details seem randomly chosen. • The summary includes too many repeated words and phrases.	• The work's theme and supporting ideas are not evident. • The verbal and nonverbal techniques are minimal. • The summary needs modifiers in more places.
1	• Neither the title nor the author is included. • The theme is missing. • The details show no understanding of the work.	• The supporting details for the theme are missing. • Due to lack of detail, the summary shows no understanding of the work.	• There is no communication of the work's theme and supporting ideas. • The presenter uses no verbal or nonverbal techniques to engage the audience. • There is little or no use of modifiers.

TO CHALLENGE STUDENTS . . .

Perform a Staged Reading Challenge students to use insights gained from summarizing *Sorry, Wrong Number* to perform a staged reading of the play. Assign roles, with students alternately reading longer parts, such as Mrs. Stevenson. In addition, assign group members other tasks, such as director and foley artist (who produces sound effects).

© Franz Pritz/Picture Press/Getty Images

Nature at Work

❝ Those who dwell . . . among the beauties and mysteries of the earth are never alone or weary of life. ❞

—Rachel Carson

135

STREAM TO START

Motivate students to read the collection texts, and spark their curiosity by playing the video and watching it in class. After students view the video, ask them to think about two things they hope to learn from reading about nature and human interaction with it. Call on volunteers to share their responses.

PERFORMANCE TASK PREVIEW

Point out to students that they will complete two performance tasks at the end of the collection. The performance tasks will require them to further analyze the selections in the collection and to synthesize ideas about these analyses. Students will present their findings in a variety of products.

ACADEMIC VOCABULARY

View It!

Professional Development Podcast:

Academic Vocabulary

Students can acquire facility with the academic vocabulary words through frequent, repeated exposure as they analyze and discuss the selections in the collection. Academic vocabulary can be used in the instructional contexts shown below. This will enable students to incorporate the academic vocabulary words into their working vocabulary.

- Collaborative Discussion at the end of each selection
- Analyzing the Text questions for each selection
- Selection-level Performance Task
- Vocabulary instruction (for Critical Vocabulary and/or for Vocabulary Strategy)
- Language Conventions
- End-of-collection Performance Task for all selections in the collection

ASK STUDENTS to review the Academic Vocabulary word list for this collection. You may wish to pronounce each word aloud so students hear the correct pronunciation. Then, discuss the definitions and the related forms for each word. Remind students that they will encounter these five academic vocabulary words throughout the collection.

In this collection, you will explore the beauty, power, and mystery of nature.

Stream to Start   hmhfyi.com   Channel One News®

COLLECTION

PERFORMANCE TASK Preview

After reading the selections in this collection, you will have the opportunity to complete two performance tasks:

- In one, you will write a personal narrative about an experience in a natural setting that is meaningful to you.
- In the second, you will write a poetry analysis of poems about nature.

ACADEMIC VOCABULARY

Study the words and their definitions in the chart below. You will use these words as you discuss and write about the texts in this collection.

Word	Definition	Related Forms
affect (ə-fĕkt´) v.	to have an influence on or effect a change in something	affectation, affection, affective, affects, disaffected, unaffected
element (ĕl´ə-mənt) n.	a part or aspect of something	elemental, elementally, elementary, elements
ensure (ĕn-shŏŏr´) v.	to make sure or certain	ensured, ensuring
participate (pär-tĭs´ə-pāt´) v.	to be active and involved in something or to share in something	participant, participation, participator
specify (spĕs´ə-fī´) v.	to state exactly or in detail what you want or need	nonspecific, specific, specific gravity, specific heat

136

©Franz Prinz/Picture Press/Getty Images

myNotebook

As students read, analyze, and discuss the texts in this collection, encourage them to create a *my*WordList folder in *my*Notebook to build their own personal word lists.

- **Annotate** Students can highlight vocabulary terms and other unfamiliar words and save each highlighted term to *my*Notebook.
- **Organize** Within *my*Notebook, students can drag each word into the *my*WordList folder.
- **Elaborate** Ask students to add details to the entry for each word, such as a definition, other forms of the word, and a sample sentence.

English Language Support

ENGAGE WITH THE COLLECTION TOPIC

Draw attention to the title of the collection, Nature at Work. Make sure students understand that the word *nature* encompasses all living creatures and all non-living things not made by humans, such as rocks, plants, and water. Then explain that this collection focuses on the power, complexity, and beauty of nature.

ACCESS PRIOR KNOWLEDGE Invite students to identify an aspect of nature that they find awe-inspiring or mysterious, for example, rainbows or thunderstorms. Discuss the ways in which humans depend on nature and study it.

LEARNING CIRCLES

Use this strategy to deepen students' understanding of the texts in this collection and to encourage collaboration.

- **First,** arrange students into small groups of three or four.
- **Then,** have members of each group select their individual roles. For example, one student can note unfamiliar vocabulary, another can identify interesting language, and another can prepare questions about the text and take notes. Explain that each member of the group is expected to share what he or she notes about the text.

- **Next,** read aloud or present an audio recording of the text, reminding students to perform the duties associated with their selected roles as they listen. Have them take a few minutes to review and finalize their notes.
- **Finally,** explain that each group member is expected to share what he or she noted about the text, respond to others by asking clarifying questions, and build on the comments of the group member who is sharing.

 Collection 3 Digital Resources for English Language Support

LANGUAGE WORKSHOP
Designated English Learners

Use the digital Teacher Resources > Language Workshop to support English learners in using narrative text structures, incorporating adverbs to provide details, and facilitating improvement by providing useful feedback.

Text in FOCUS VIDEOS

These videos will help students learn how to visualize a scene and how to understand form in poetry. Have students use **Text In Focus Practice** to apply those skills.

Collection 3 Lessons	Media	Teach and Practice
Student Edition | eBook	▶ Video Links HISTORY A&E Channel One News®	**Close Reading and Evidence Tracking**
ANCHOR TEXT Memoir by Eddy Harris from *Mississippi Solo*	◀ **Audio** from *Mississippi Solo*	**Close Read Screencasts** • Modeled Discussion (lines 19–27) • Close Read application PDF (lines 93–100) / **Text in Focus** • Visualizing (line 84) **Strategies for Annotation** • Analyze Meanings of Words and Phrases • Precise Language
CLOSE READER Memoir by Helen Thayer from *Polar Dream*	◀ **Audio** from *Polar Dream*	
Soliloquy by William Shakespeare from *The Tempest*	▶ **Video BIO®** *Biography: William Shakespeare* ◀ **Audio** from *The Tempest*	**Strategies for Annotation** • Determine Meanings
Short Story by Naomi Shihab Nye "Allied with Green"	▶ **Video HISTORY®** *Greening Lower Manhattan* ◀ **Audio** "Allied with Green"	**Strategies for Annotation** • Determine Meanings of Words and Phrases • Determine Theme • Using a Glossary
Expository Essay by Douglas Fox "Big Rocks' Balancing Act"	◀ **Audio** "Big Rocks' Balancing Act"	**Strategies for Annotation** • Analyze Structure: Essay • Prepositional Phrases
CLOSE READER Informational Text by James Vlahos "The Hidden Southwest: The Arch Hunters"	◀ **Audio** "The Hidden Southwest: The Arch Hunters"	
ANCHOR TEXT Poem by Pablo Neruda "Ode to enchanted light" Poem by Mary Oliver "Sleeping in the Forest"	◀ **Audio** "Ode to enchanted light" ◀ **Audio** "Sleeping in the Forest"	**Close Read Screencasts** • Modeled Discussion1 "Ode to enchanted light" (lines 10–12) • Modeled Discussion2 "Sleeping in the Forest" (lines 1–5) • Close Read application PDF "Ode to enchanted light" (lines 13–15) "Sleeping in the Forest" (lines 12–18) / **Text in Focus** • Understanding Form (line 15) **Strategies for Annotation** • Analyze Form: Ode • Analyze Form: Lyric Poem
CLOSE READER Poems by Leslie Marmon Silko, Victor Hernandez Cruz, and Gwendolyn Brooks from *Poems About Nature*	▶ **Video HISTORY®** "Science of a Hurricane" ◀ **Audio** from *Poems About Nature*	
Collection 3 Performance Tasks: **A** Write a Personal Narrative **B** Write a Poetry Analysis	**fyi** hmhfyi.com	**Interactive Lessons** **A** Writing Narratives **B** Writing Informative Texts

For Systematic Coverage of Writing and Speaking & Listening Standards

Interactive Lessons

Conducting Research
Evaluating Sources

Assess		Extend	Reteach
Performance Task	✓ *Assess It Online!*	**Teacher eBook**	**Teacher eBook**
Writing Activity: Literary Analysis	Selection Test	**Determine the Meanings of Words and Phrases**	**Analyze Text: Memoir > Interactive Graphic Organizer >** Spider Map
Speaking Activity: Dramatic Reading	Selection Test	**Analyze Form**	**Determine Meanings**
Writing Activity: Argument	Selection Test	**Analyze Point of View > Interactive Whiteboard Lesson >** Point of View in Literature	**Determine Theme > Level Up Tutorial >** Theme
Speaking Activity: Summary Presentation	Selection Test	**Analyze Texts: Fact and Opinion**	**Analyze Structure: Essay > Level Up Tutorial >** Chronological Order; Cause-and-Effect Organization; Comparison-Contrast Organization
Writing Activity: Poem	Selection Test	**Determine Theme > Interactive Whiteboard Lesson >** Theme/Central Idea	**Determine Meanings of Words and Phrases > Level Up Tutorial >** Narrator and Speaker
A Write a Personal Narrative **B** Write a Poetry Analysis	Collection Test		

Lesson Assessments Conducting Research Evaluating Sources	**Standards Support and Enrichment**	For more instruction and practice in reading literary and informational texts, language, spelling, and speaking and listening, see Teacher Resources > Standards Support and Enrichment.
	For Designated English Language Instruction	To provide scaffolded support specific to the needs of English Learners during Designated English Language instruction, use the selection- and standards-aligned lessons found in Teacher Resources > Language Workshop.

Collection 3 Lessons	Key Learning Objective	Performance Task	Vocabulary Strategy
ANCHOR TEXT **Memoir by Eddy Harris** from *Mississippi Solo*, **p. 137A** Lexile 830L	**The student will be able to . . .** identify features of a memoir and analyze the author's style.	Writing Activity: Literary Analysis	Figures of Speech
Soliloquy by William Shakespeare from *The Tempest*, **p. 145A**	**The student will be able to . . .** identify elements of Shakespearean language, interpret meaning, and analyze a soliloquy.	Speaking Activity: Dramatic Reading	
Short Story by Naomi Shihab Nye **"Allied with Green," p. 149A** Lexile 900L	**The student will be able to . . .** determine the theme of a short story and to analyze word choice and style.	Writing Activity: Argument	Using a Glossary
Expository Essay by Douglas Fox **"Big Rocks' Balancing Act," p. 157A** Lexile 1060L	**The student will be able to . . .** analyze elements of an expository essay and its structure.	Speaking Activity: Summary Presentation	Latin Roots
ANCHOR TEXT **Poem by Pablo Neruda** **"Ode to enchanted light," p. 169A** **Poem by Mary Oliver** **"Sleeping in the Forest," p. 169A**	**The student will be able to . . .** analyze poetic form and learn how poets use figurative language to express feelings and ideas.	Writing Activity: Poem	

Collection 3 Performance Tasks:

A Write a Personal Narrative

B Write a Poetry Analysis

Language Conventions	English Language Support	Differentiated Instruction	CLOSE READER Selection
Precise Language	• Analyze Language • Understand Text Structure • Use Precise Language • Write Informational Texts	**To Challenge Students:** Characterization **For Standard English Learners:** Subject-Verb Agreement	Memoir by Helen Thayer from *Polar Dream,* p. 144b **Lexile 1070L**
	• Read Closely • Word Study	**For Standard English Learners:** Pronunciation	
Sentence Structure	• Culturally Responsive Instruction • Read Closely • Listen Actively • Exchange Information and Ideas • Connect Ideas	**When Students Struggle:** Figurative Language **For Standard English Learners:** Double Negatives	
Prepositional Phrases	• Understand Text Structure • Improve Reading Fluency • Read Closely • Use Knowledge of Morphology	**For Students with Disabilities:** Strategies **When Students Struggle:** Summarize **To Challenge Students:** Analyze Media	Informational Text by James Vlahos "The Hidden Southwest: The Arch Hunters," p. 168b **Lexile 1060L**
	• Read Closely • Analyze Language • Exchange Information and Ideas	**When Students Struggle:** Analyze Form **For Students with Disabilities:** Using Tablets	Poems by Leslie Marmon Silko, Victor Hernandez Cruz, and Gwendolyn Brooks from *Poems About Nature,* p. 174b
A Compound-Complex Sentences **B** Use Connecting Words	**A** Plan a Personal Narrative Understand Text Structure Use Language Effectively **B** Plan a Poetry Analysis Use Domain-specific Words Adapt Language Choices Understand Text Structure Format Text	**A** **For Standard English Learners:** Use Past-Tense Verbs **When Students Struggle:** Write a Conclusion **For Students with Disabilities:** Evaluate Drafts **To Challenge Students:** Add Dialogue **B** **When Students Struggle:** Use an Outline **For Standard English Learners:** Use Formal English **For Students with Disabilities:** Evaluate an Analysis **To Challenge Students:** Compare and Contrast Speakers	

ANCHOR TEXT *from* Mississippi Solo

Memoir by Eddy Harris

Why This Text?

Memoirs and other forms of autobiographical writing show how writers reflect on personal experiences. By analyzing a memoir, students tap into the writer's mind and build an understanding of the writer's craft. This lesson introduces students to the memoir genre and to how various choices create a writer's style.

Key Learning Objective: The student will be able to identify features of a memoir and analyze the author's style.

For practice and application:

Background: Helen Thayer is a decorated explorer and adventurer. Her achievements include being the first woman to walk across the Sahara Desert, kayaking 1,200 miles across two rivers in the Amazon, and walking 1,600 miles across the Gobi Desert in Asia. In 1988, at the age of 50, she became the first woman to walk and ski to the North Pole without a snowmobile or dogsled. She wrote about her adventure in Polar Dream.

from **Polar Dream**

Memoir by Helen Thayer

Close Reader selection
from *Polar Dream*
Memoir by Helen Thayer

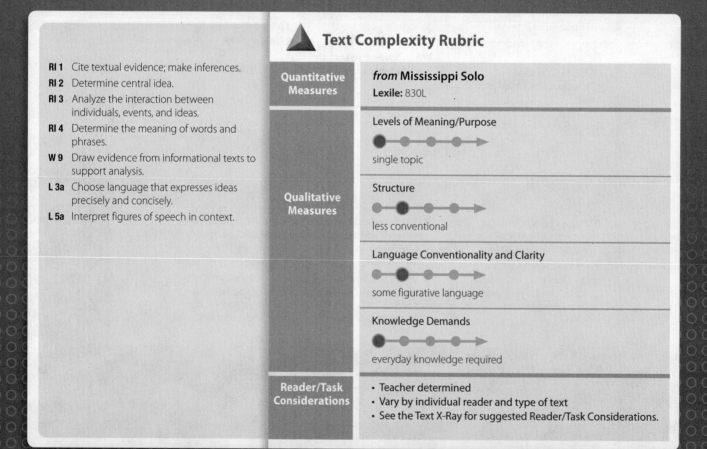

RI 1 Cite textual evidence; make inferences.

RI 2 Determine central idea.

RI 3 Analyze the interaction between individuals, events, and ideas.

RI 4 Determine the meaning of words and phrases.

W 9 Draw evidence from informational texts to support analysis.

L 3a Choose language that expresses ideas precisely and concisely.

L 5a Interpret figures of speech in context.

▲ Text Complexity Rubric

Quantitative Measures	*from* **Mississippi Solo** **Lexile:** 830L
Qualitative Measures	**Levels of Meaning/Purpose** single topic
	Structure less conventional
	Language Conventionality and Clarity some figurative language
	Knowledge Demands everyday knowledge required
Reader/Task Considerations	• Teacher determined • Vary by individual reader and type of text • See the Text X-Ray for suggested Reader/Task Considerations.

English Language Support

Before teaching, use the Text X-Ray for an overview of the text's complexity. The Text X-Ray and the supports and scaffolds in the Teacher's Edition will help you guide students of different skill levels.

Text Complexity: Qualitative Measures

Levels of Meaning/Purpose

single topic

Help students analyze the meaning of words and phrases in a memoir.

- Teacher's Edition side notes, pp. 138, 139, 140, 141
- Close Read Screencasts, p. 137
- Strategies for Annotation, p. 141
- Analyze the Meanings of Words and Phrases, p. 141

▶ **Use It!** Interactive Whiteboard Lesson: Figurative Language and Imagery

ZOOM IN ON ANALYZING FIGURATIVE LANGUAGE Explain that a **simile** is a type of figurative language that compares two unlike things using the word *like* or *as*.

- Display the following sentence: "Clouds rolled overhead in wild swirls like batter in a bowl." (lines 26–27)
- Ask students to describe what batter for an uncooked cake looks like when it is being mixed. Then ask how clouds could look like batter. (*The movement and shape of the clouds may resemble the swirling of different-colored ingredients in batter.*)
- Have students identify the simile in the paragraph that begins on line 85. Discuss the comparison it makes.

Structure

less conventional

Help students analyze the features of a memoir.

- Teacher's Edition side notes, pp. 137, 140, 141
- English Language Support, p. 139
- Analyze Text: Memoir, p. 141

To reteach analyzing a memoir, see

- Analyze Text: Memoir, p. 144a

▶ **Use It!** Interactive Graphic Organizer: Spider Map

ZOOM IN ON ANALYZING A MEMOIR Tell students that the word **memoir** is related to *memory*. Discuss how the name of the genre tells the kinds of details it normally includes.

- Display lines 26–37. Organize students into small groups. Ask them to find examples of these features of a memoir: first-person point of view; the author's thoughts and feelings about an event; informal language.
- Have groups present their examples and discuss them as a class.

Language Conventionality and Clarity

some figurative language

Teach unfamiliar vocabulary in context.

- Teacher's Edition Critical Vocabulary notes, pp. 138, 139, 140, 143
- English Language Support, pp. 138, 143
- Applying Academic Vocabulary, p. 139
- Vocabulary Strategy: Figures of Speech, p. 143

Help students analyze language in the memoir.

- Teacher's Edition side notes, pp. 137, 144
- English Language Support, pp. 138, 144
- Strategies for Annotation, p. 144
- Language Conventions: Precise Language, p. 144

To teach syntax in a memoir, see

- Determine the Meaning of Words and Phrases, p. 144a

ZOOM IN ON **USING PRECISE LANGUAGE** Explain that while some words share similar meanings, they may express different degrees of intensity. Have students read the following sentences from the memoir. Then ask them to compare the intensity of the highlighted word with the synonym in parentheses. Discuss how the author's choice of words makes his writing more precise.

- line 56: ". . . the river grabbed the end of the canoe . . ." (took)
- line 76: ". . . the river sloshed over the side . . ." (splashed)
- line 86: "I was drenched . . ." (wet)

Knowledge Demands

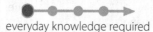

everyday knowledge required

Support English learners in understanding the necessary geographical context of the memoir.

- Teacher's Edition Author note, p. 137
- Student Edition footnotes, pp. 137, 138, 139

ZOOM IN ON **BUILDING GEOGRAPHICAL CONTEXT** Explain that the Mississippi River is one of the longest rivers in the United States. It begins as a clear stream but eventually becomes broad and muddy, with a strong current, after it joins with the Missouri and Ohio rivers. Natchez, Mississippi, the author's goal in this excerpt, is still more than 300 miles from the river's end at the Gulf of Mexico.

Suggested Reader/Task Considerations

Consider the following before assigning this memoir to students.

- Will students be able to visualize what the text describes?
- Do students have prior experience with memoirs that will help them focus on what is most meaningful?

 Visualizing

ZOOM IN ON **SUPPORTING COMPREHENSION**

- Display this sentence: "I passed from the cool moisture surrounding me and into a pocket of thin air hot and dry." (lines 30–31) Point out words that appeal to the senses: *cool moisture, pocket, thin, hot and dry*. Explain that these sensory words bring the author's experience to life. Have students look for sensory language as they read.

- Tell students that a memoir lets the author explore how an event changed his or her life. As students read, encourage them to identify what the author realizes or learns.

CLOSE READ

Eddy Harris Have students read the information about the author. Explain that the author had grown up along the Mississippi River in St. Louis and had long held a dream of canoeing its length—to experience the adventure, challenge himself, and make self-discoveries. The voyage from Lake Itasca in Minnesota to the Gulf of Mexico covers more than 2,300 miles.

SETTING A PURPOSE Direct students to use the Setting a Purpose question to focus their reading. Remind them to generate questions as they read.

Analyze Text: Memoir

RI 1, RI 3

(LINES 6–8)

Tell students that a **memoir** is a form of autobiographical writing in which the author tells about personal experiences.

Ⓐ **CITE TEXT EVIDENCE** Have students reread the full sentence in lines 6–8 and cite evidence that reveals this text to be a memoir. How have events already shaped the author's ideas about this day? *(The author uses the pronoun I and gives personal information about "hard days" and "scary times" in his past. This indicates he is writing about a personal experience. Previous events that created "hard days" make the author appreciate peaceful days.)*

Analyze the Meanings of Words and Phrases (LINE 10)

RI 1, RI 4

Tell students that **style** is *how* an author writes, rather than *what* an author writes. Explain that an author's style includes ways of shaping sentences. Point out that this author's style includes **sentence fragments,** groups of words that are only parts of sentences.

Ⓑ **CITE TEXT EVIDENCE** Direct students to locate sentence fragments in line 10 and to give ideas about why the author chose to write in this style. *("No singing, no thinking, no talking to myself. Just feeling." These fragments make a good connection to meaning—as if he's not even thinking connected thoughts.)*

Eddy Harris (b. 1956) *is a writer, adventurer, and seeker who spent his early years in New York City before moving to St. Louis. His first book,* Mississippi Solo, *chronicles the canoe trip he took down the entire length of the Mississippi River in the 1980s—a risky trip that this city dweller was unprepared for. He has also written about adventurous journeys in other southern regions and in Africa.*

from Mississippi Solo

Memoir by Eddy Harris

SETTING A PURPOSE Pay attention as you read to how the author recounts a special moment from his life while he canoed by himself down the Mississippi River. What makes his experience so meaningful for him?

▤ **myNotebook**

As you read, mark up the text. Save your work to *my***Notebook**.

· Highlight details
· Add notes and questions
· Add new words to *my***WordList**

Too many marvelous days in a row and you begin to get used to it, to think that's the way it's supposed to be. Too many good days, too many bad days—you need some break in the monotony of one to appreciate the other. If you only get sunshine, someone said, you end up in a desert.

I guess I'd had enough hard days to last me for a while, enough scary times to be able to appreciate the peaceful, easy, glorious days. On the way to Natchez,[1] I had another one, and I took full advantage of it to do absolutely nothing.
10 No singing, no thinking, no talking to myself. Just feeling. Watching the river, noticing the changes in color, seeing the way it rises and falls depending on the wind and on what lies

---

[1] **Natchez** (năch´ĭz): a city in southwest Mississippi on the Mississippi River.

Close Read Screencasts ▶ Close Read

Modeled Discussions

Have students click the *Close Read* icon in their eBooks to access the screencast in which readers discuss and annotate the following key passage:

· "The river was like that to me. . . . like batter in a bowl." (lines 19–27)

As a class, view and discuss this video. Then have students work in pairs to do an independent close read of an additional passage—"I was more amazed than anything . . . nothing could happen to me." (lines 93–100)

CLOSE READ

Analyze the Meanings of Words and Phrases

RI 1,
RI 4

(LINES 13–25)

Point out that as part of his style, Harris uses **personification,** giving human qualities to something that is not human. Explain that personification is a form of **figurative language**—the imaginative use of words to express ideas that are not literally true but add meaning and emotional impact.

C **CITE TEXT EVIDENCE** Tell students to reread lines 13–25, cite evidence of how the author personifies the river, and discuss the effect this comparison has on the text. *(The author says, "The river was talking to me"; "A comfortable buddy sharing a lazy day." "The river kept me company and kept me satisfied." "Then the river whispered, 'Get ready. Get ready.'" This language suggests a connection between the author and the river, as if the river is a human friend.)*

English Language Support

Point out the comparison in lines 27–29. Ask students to suggest why the author compares the storm to an avalanche. *(to show that it is going to be a violent, unstoppable storm; to convey the idea that there is little he can do to avoid it; to heighten the mood of dread)* Have students imagine that instead of the simile, the author had said, "The sky was getting dark and heavy." Ask volunteers to explain how the change would produce a different effect. *(It wouldn't be as ominous or threatening; it wouldn't create as much suspense.)*

CRITICAL VOCABULARY

avalanche: The author compares a distant rainstorm to an avalanche.

ASK STUDENTS what feelings are suggested by the word *avalanche* and how a rainstorm might be like an avalanche. *(power and danger; A storm could be like an avalanche of rainwater falling from the sky.)*

insulate: The author describes passing through insulated air.

ASK STUDENTS to describe what insulated air feels like. *(It's warm because it's holding onto heat.)*

C

Close Read

on the river bed. Each change had something to say, and I listened to the river. The river was talking to me, changing colors from puce[2] to brown to thick, murky green. Saying nothing. The idle chatter you get when you walk with your favorite niece or nephew going no place in particular with nothing special on your minds and the little kid just jabbers away because it's comfortable and he feels like it. The river was

20 like that to me. A comfortable buddy sharing a lazy day.

Nothing else mattered then. Going someplace or not. Arriving in New Orleans or shooting past and landing in Brazil. I didn't care about anything. The river kept me company and kept me satisfied. Nothing else mattered.

Then the river whispered, "Get ready. Get ready."

The day turned gray and strange. Clouds rolled overhead in wild swirls like batter in a bowl. I could see the rainstorm forming off in the distance but swirling rapidly toward me like a dark gray **avalanche.** I felt the river dip down and up—a

30 shallow dale[3] in the water. I passed from the cool moisture surrounding me and into a pocket of thin air hot and dry. It was as though a gap had opened in the clouds and the sun streamed through to boil the water and heat up this isolated patch of river a scant[4] thirty yards long. My first thought was to shed a shirt and stay cool, but when I passed through the far curtain of the **insulated** air, I knew I had better do just the opposite. I drifted and donned my yellow rain suit and hood. The sky above grew serious and advanced in my direction with the speed of a hurricane. Looking for a place to land, I

40 scanned the shore. There was no shore. Only trees. Because of the heavy rains and high water, the shore had disappeared, and the new shoreline of solid earth had been pushed back through the trees and beyond the woods. How far beyond, I couldn't tell. I looked across to the other side of the river half a mile away. No way could I have made it over there. Halfway across and the wind would have kicked up and trapped me in the middle.

The leading edge of the storm came, and the first sprinkles passed over like army scouts. The wooded area lasted only

50 another hundred yards or so, and I thought I could easily get there before the rains arrived. I could then turn left and find

---

[2] **puce** (pyo͞os): purplish brown.
[3] **dale:** valley.
[4] **scant:** just short of.

avalanche
(ăv´ə-lănch´) *n.* An *avalanche* is a large mass of snow, ice, dirt, or rocks falling quickly down the side of a mountain.

insulate
(ĭn´sə-lāt´) *v.* When you *insulate* something, you prevent the passage of heat through it.

English Language Support

Analyze Language Tell students that sentence fragments lack a subject, verb, or both, and they do not express a complete thought.

- Read aloud lines 14–24 as students follow along. Have them work with a partner to identify the sentence fragments.

- Have pairs identify sentence fragments in lines 14–24 and suggest ways to make them complete sentences. Assign pairs one or more fragments to rewrite.

- Have pairs rewrite fragments in lines 14–24 as complete sentences. Ask how the change affects the impact of the passage.

ground to pull out and wait out the storm. But the voice of the river came out and spoke to me teasingly but with a chill of seriousness down my spine. I could have ignored it, but as if reading my thoughts and not wanting me to fight it, the river grabbed the end of the canoe and turned me toward the trees. I thought I was looking for land. I wasn't. I was looking for shelter.

"The day turned gray and strange."

60   The urge to get into the trees came on me quite suddenly and really without thought or effort on my part. Almost an instinct.

    No sooner had I ducked into the trees than the sky split open with a loud crash and a **splintery** crackle of lightning. I was not going to make it through the trees. The wind came in at hurricane strength. The tips of the trees bent way over and aimed toward the ground, like fishing rods hooked on a big one. Water flooded like the tide rushing upstream. The trees swooshed loudly as the leaves and branches brushed hard together. Branches fell. Rains came and poured down

70 bucketfuls.

    The trees were tall and no more than three feet around. I maneuvered the canoe as best I could in the wind and rushing water, turned it to face upstream, and kept my back to the rain, which slanted in at a sharp angle. I reached out for the sturdiest tree I could get my arms around and I held on.

    Water everywhere.[5] The river sloshed over the side and into the canoe. I tried to keep the stern pointed right into the flow so the canoe could ride the waves, but it didn't work. The canoe was twisted about, and water poured over the side. The

splinter

(splĭn´tər) v. To *splinter* means to break up into sharp, thin pieces.

Ⓓ

---

[5] **Water everywhere:** The author is referring to the line "water, water, everywhere" from *The Rime of the Ancient Mariner*, a widely known poem about a sailor recounting supernatural events at sea.

APPLYING ACADEMIC VOCABULARY

affect	element	participate

THINK-PAIR-SHARE Have pairs of students discuss the questions below, using the academic vocabulary words *affect*, *element*, and *participate* in their responses. Let volunteers share their responses with the class.

- How was Eddy Harris **affected** by his experiences on the river?
- What techniques does Harris use to describe the river as a living being that is able to **participate** in these events?
- What **elements** of a memoir appear in this selection?

CLOSE READ

Analyze the Meanings of Words and Phrases

RI 1, RI 4

(LINES 65–67)

Point out that the author uses descriptive language to help the reader share the experience of the storm. Tell students that a **simile** is a kind of figurative comparison in which unlike things are shown to be alike in some way. A simile includes the word *like* or *as*.

Ⓓ **CITE TEXT EVIDENCE** Direct students to reread lines 65–67. Ask them to cite evidence of what the tips of the trees are compared to and to describe the impact this simile has on the text. (*"The tips of trees bent way over" are "like fishing rods hooked on a big one." The simile deepens the description of the bending trees, creating an image of arched branches straining against a force, like a fishing rod strains when a big fish is hooked.*)

CRITICAL VOCABULARY

splinter: The author describes the crash of thunder and the "splintery crackle" of lightning.

ASK STUDENTS what lightning made of splintery crackles might look like. (*The lines of lightning go off in different directions, like a network of cracks in crackled pottery or tree branches.*)

English Language Support

Understand Text Structure Read lines 62–75 aloud. Tell students that most memoirs are told in chronological order to enable readers to follow the sequence of events.

ASK STUDENTS to work with a partner to identify important events in this passage in the order in which they occur. Encourage them to include the following words in their responses: *first, then, next*. (*Possible responses: First, the author finds shelter in the trees. Then he moves the canoe around so that his back is toward the rain. Next, he hangs on to a sturdy tree.*)

Analyze Text: Memoir

RI 3

(LINES 85–100)

Tell students that the author of a memoir recalls particular events that have left a strong impression on him or her. A memoir describes how events have shaped the author's ideas about the experience being recounted.

E **ASK STUDENTS** to reread lines 85–100 and share ideas about why this particular episode is so memorable for the author and how events shaped his ideas about the episode. (*His reaction to the danger is surprising, even to him. He doesn't feel worried or fearful, but safe and protected, as if he's in a "cocoon." The storm has sparked a reaction in him—a feeling of calm— leading him to conclude that he is "one with this river.")*

CRITICAL VOCABULARY

ethereal: The author points out that something "so very definite" yet "so ethereal" urged him to seek safety in the trees.

ASK STUDENTS why the author contrasts the words *definite* and *ethereal*. (*He's trying to show that he doesn't know what the voice or intuition was. It was something he definitely heard or felt, but it was also something vague that he couldn't put his finger on.)*

Text in FOCUS English Language Support

Visualizing (LINE 84)

Have students view the **Text In Focus** video on this page of their eBook to learn how to use descriptive details to visualize the setting and action in this passage. Then have students use **Text In Focus Practice** to apply what they have learned.

COLLABORATIVE DISCUSSION Have student pairs reread segments of the memoir in order to talk with group members about the author's experience on the river. Suggest that students think about what new understanding Harris reached as a result of this experience.

ASK STUDENTS to share any questions they generated in the course of reading and discussing the selection.

---

80 rain was heavier than any I had ever been in or seen before. It really was more like a tropical storm. The heavy winds, the amount of water, the warmth of the air, and the cold rain. Only my neck was exposed to the rain. When the rain hit my neck, it ran under the rain suit and very cold down my back.

The wind shifted as the storm came directly overhead. Water streamed straight down. I was drenched, and the canoe was filling up quickly. Anything in the canoe that could float was floating. If the rain continued for long or if the wind kept up strong and the rain kept spilling into the canoe, I would 90 sink. But I was not worried, hardly more than concerned. In fact I enjoyed the feeling of the water all around me and on me, enveloping me like a cocoon, and despite the drama I felt no real threat. I was more amazed than anything, trying to analyze the voice I had heard or whatever instinct or intuition it was that urged me to park in these trees. It had been something so very definite that I could feel it and yet so **ethereal** that I could not put my finger on it. So I stopped trying and just sat there patiently waiting and hugging my tree. I was one with this river, and nothing could happen to 100 me.

The storm slid forward, and the rain slanted in on my face. Then it moved on farther up the river to drench someone else. It was gone as suddenly as it had arisen. Only the trailing edge was left, a light rain that lasted almost until I reached Natchez.

ethereal
(ĭ-thîr´ē-əl) *adj.* If something is *ethereal*, it is light and airy.

COLLABORATIVE DISCUSSION What do you think made this experience on the river affect the author so strongly? Talk about your ideas with other group members.

TO CHALLENGE STUDENTS . . .

Characterization Point out that readers can learn a lot about Eddy Harris as a person from what he reveals in his memoir.

ASK STUDENTS to discuss in small groups what inferences they can make about Harris's character. Have students create a brief character sketch, including supporting evidence from the memoir.

Analyze Text: Memoir

RI 3

A **memoir** is a form of autobiographical writing in which a writer shares his or her personal experiences and observations of significant events or people. Memoirs are often written in the first person. Authors of memoirs often

- "talk" to readers, using informal language and sharing personal feelings
- recall actual events and emphasize their reactions to them
- show how their experiences changed their attitudes and lives

What feature of a memoir appears in the first sentence of the excerpt from *Mississippi Solo*?

Analyze the Meanings of Words and Phrases

RI 4

The author's **style** is the manner of writing—*how* something is said rather than *what* is said. Readers can analyze an author's style by making observations about these elements:

- word choice
- sentence types
- sentence length
- sentence fragments
- repetition of one or more words
- descriptive details

An author's style can be **formal,** using complex language and sentence structures, or **informal,** using simpler language, sentences, and fragments.

Figurative language is an imaginative use of words to express ideas that are not literally true but that are meaningful and can have an emotional impact. This chart shows three common kinds of figurative comparisons.

Comparison	Example	Effect
simile: a comparison of two unlike things using the word *like* or *as*	Clouds rolled overhead in wild swirls like batter in a bowl. (lines 26–27)	vivid image of changing sky
metaphor: a comparison of two unlike things that have qualities in common, without using *like* or *as*	. . . the far curtain of the insulated air . . . (lines 35–36)	warmth that is trapped inside a barrier
personification: the giving of human qualities to an animal, object, or idea	The river was talking to me . . . (line 14)	a feeling of connectedness

Find another example of a simile in this memoir. What does it help you understand?

from Mississippi Solo **141**

Analyze Text: Memoir

RI 3

Explain that memoirs emphasize remembering particular personal experiences.

- Have students read the features of memoirs.
- Have students reread lines 1–2 of the memoir and imagine that they are listening to the author speaking.
- Have students name features of a memoir in the sentence. (*The author talks in a familiar way. He uses an informal sentence structure and the pronoun* you *to mean "everyone." He reveals a personal view that life isn't supposed to be just "marvelous days."*)

Analyze the Meanings of Words and Phrases

RI 4

Discuss Harris's use of language. Guide students to cite examples of sentence fragments, descriptive details, and word choice. Have students list words that describe his style. (*descriptive, informal, conversational, natural*)

To review figurative language, have students find the listed examples. Discuss how the examples impact the meaning and feeling, or **mood,** of the narrative.

Share ideas about additional similes students locate. (*"sprinkles passed over like army scouts;" The comparison connects sparse drops that hint at the full "army" of rain to come.*)

Strategies for Annotation

 Annotate it!

Analyze the Meanings of Words and Phrases

RI 4

Share these strategies for guided or independent analysis:

- Highlight in green figurative and descriptive language.
- Underline sentence fragments.
- Highlight any other technique you may notice in yellow.
- In a note, describe the effect of the language.

Nothing else mattered then. Going someplace or not. Arriving in New Orleans or shooting past and landing in Brazil. I didn't care about anything. The river kept me company and kept me satisfied. Nothing else mattered.

Then the river whispered, "Get ready. Get ready."

Repetition reinforces his presence in the moment. It hints at something to come.

Analyzing the Text

RI 1, RI 2,
RI 3, RI 4

Possible answers:

1. It's surprising that the author is "not worried," even though drowning or other harm seems possible. He is "more amazed than anything" at feeling protected by the river. His feeling of being "one with this river" is unexpected, because experiencing a severe storm while being vulnerable in a canoe usually creates the feeling of fear.

2. The author compares his figurative conversation with the river to a pleasant experience with a young niece or nephew jabbering away on a walk to "no place in particular." The comparison suggests a familiar, easy, friendly experience.

3. The author is in a relaxed, philosophical frame of mind, thinking about what is important in life. He reflects on "hard days" and "scary times" in the past, and he is appreciating the "peaceful, easy, glorious days" of the present.

4. The author is using personification to develop his idea that the river has human qualities. The river is talking to him and is warning him to prepare for danger.

5. In lines 81–82, the author strings together these fragments: "The heavy winds, the amount of water, the warmth of the air, and the cold rain." The author uses fragments here and elsewhere to reflect his thinking at the moment that he is experiencing events. Thoughts and images come to mind in incomplete sentences, as they often do in life. The author also uses fragments, which are more conversational, to create a more informal style.

6. Examples include "the sky split open with a loud crash"; "a splintery crackle of lightning"; the bent treetops were "like fishing rods hooked on a big one"; the rising water was "like the tide rushing upstream"; "trees swooshed loudly"; rain "poured down in bucketfuls." All of this imagery comes in a rush, suggesting a flood and conveying the sounds, sights, and feelings of the storm.

FOR STANDARD ENGLISH LEARNERS

Explain that literary analyses use the present tense. Review the rules of subject-verb agreement, focusing on third-person singular subjects and verbs with these examples:

- Harris [view, views] the river as his "buddy." *(views)*
- The memoir [describe, describes] an unforgettable trip. *(describes)*

Have pairs review subject-verb agreement in their analyses.

Analyzing the Text

RI 1, RI 2, RI 3,
RI 4, W 9

Cite Text Evidence   Support your responses with evidence from the text.

1. **Interpret**   Reread lines 85–100. What seems unexpected about the author's reactions during this experience?

2. **Compare**   Reread lines 13–20 to find what the author compares to walking with a favorite niece or nephew. What does that comparison suggest?

3. **Cite Evidence**   Reread lines 1–10. What does the author reveal about himself?

4. **Analyze**   Reread line 25. What kind of figurative language is the author using, and what does it suggest about his connection to his environment?

5. **Analyze**   Find an example of one or more sentence fragments. Why might the author have chosen to use fragments instead of complete sentences, and what does it suggest about the style of his writing?

6. **Analyze**   Reread lines 62–70. What word choices and figurative language help you picture the scene?

PERFORMANCE TASK

Writing Activity: Literary Analysis
Look back through the memoir to list examples of how the author uses similes and personifies the river. Focusing on examples from your list, write a two-to four-paragraph literary analysis that explains how the author uses figurative language in this memoir.

- Support your main points by using quotes from the text as examples.
- Explain the meanings of the examples and how they contribute to important ideas of the memoir.
- Discuss what impressions you have about the author's writing style, based on his use of figurative language.

Assign this performance task.

PERFORMANCE TASK

RI 4,
W 9

Writing Activity: Literary Analysis   Help students plan their analyses by

- starting with a central idea about the author's relationship with the river
- listing text examples of similes and personification to support that idea
- jotting down notes about the meanings of the figurative language and the effects they have on the reader

Critical Vocabulary

avalanche   insulate   splinter   ethereal

Practice and Apply Choose the situation that is the better match with the meaning of the vocabulary word. Give your reasons.

1. **avalanche**
   a. Snow fell for two days, covering the rooftops and streets.
   b. Snow on a mountainside suddenly loosened and slid.

2. **insulate**
   a. On a hot day, a car with closed windows heats up quickly.
   b. An old, drafty house is expensive to heat in winter.

3. **splinter**
   a. People stroll on the boardwalk that crosses the wetland.
   b. River water breaks up into many streams and smaller creeks.

4. **ethereal**
   a. The desert travelers came to an area with palm trees and shade.
   b. The desert travelers mistakenly thought they saw a lake ahead.

Vocabulary Strategy: Figures of Speech

An author may make an **allusion,** a reference to a famous person, place, event, or work of literature. Although an allusion is not explained, the reader may recognize its source and meaning, or may do research to learn about it. Look for the allusions in these examples:

> Poppa's shoe store closed after only a year, and he lost money. Poppa worked hard, but he just didn't have the Midas touch.

> All of my cousins were strong and good-looking; I was unhappily aware of my ugly duckling status from an early age.

In the first example, the phrase *the Midas touch* is an allusion to the Greek myth about King Midas, who was briefly able to turn everything he touched into gold. The second example includes an allusion to the fairy tale "The Ugly Duckling," by Hans Christian Andersen. In that tale, an odd-looking duckling endures abuse until it grows up to find its true family of beautiful swans.

Practice and Apply Reread the paragraph that begins on line 76 of the memoir. The first sentence of that paragraph is an allusion to a well-known quotation from the long poem *The Rime of the Ancient Mariner*, by Samuel Taylor Coleridge. Find the poem and identify the famous lines in Part II. What meaning from the poem might Harris have tried to connect to his own experience?

from Mississippi Solo **143**

Critical Vocabulary

Answers:

1. *b*

2. *a*

3. *b*

4. *b*

Vocabulary Strategy: Figures of Speech

The line "Water everywhere" in this memoir may be an allusion to the lines in stanza nine of Part II of Coleridge's poem: "Water, water everywhere, / Nor any drop to drink." In the poem, these lines come at a part where the Mariner and his crew are stuck at sea with no wind, becoming more and more desperate for drinking water in the harsh sun. The line expresses the frustration that the sailors are surrounded by ocean water, but can drink none of it. In his memoir, Harris uses the allusion to underscore his situation—being surrounded by water both below (the river) and above (the rain). He is alone in a possibly desperate situation.

English Language Support

Analyze Language Extend the explanation of allusions. Explain that well-known allusions let writers make a comparison without having to explain it. Display the following sentences containing allusions, understanding that the allusions may not be familiar to all students: *(1) George was like Pinocchio when it came to telling a lie. (2) Bella was generous when buying gifts but a Scrooge toward herself.*

- Explain that Pinocchio is a fictional wooden puppet whose nose grows when he tells a lie. Ask students what this allusion tells them about George. *(It is obvious when he lies.)*

- Elicit from students what they know about Pinocchio or Scrooge, prompting them as needed. Then have them work with partners to explain what each allusion tells them about the subject of the sentence. *(George cannot lie without giving himself away; Bella dislikes spending money on herself.)*

- Have pairs explain each allusion in the two sentences on the board. Then have them work together to complete the Practice and Apply activity.

Language Conventions: Precise Language

L 3a

Tell students that strong writing is concise—it has no unnecessary words. It is also precise, or sharply written—with concrete nouns and vivid verbs.

Possible answers:

1. *Cottony clouds sailed slowly overhead like ships.*

2. *A streak of lightning suddenly zigzagged from a gigantic cloud to the ground.*

3. *Thunder boomed, and the ground shook.*

4. *I scanned the area for shelter and dashed into a nearby building.*

English Language Support

Use Precise Language Have students in mixed-ability groups rewrite the Practice and Apply sentences. Before they begin, discuss and circle the words and phrases in each sentence that could be replaced with more descriptive language or more powerful parts of speech. Prompt students with examples as needed, or provide fill-in-the-blank sentences drawn from the possible answers above.

Language Conventions: Precise Language

L 3a

When you write, choose words carefully to ensure that readers picture what you see and understand what you mean. Use precise words to express exact meanings and to be concise, using only necessary words. Compare these two sentences:

> I moved the canoe in the water, which was rushing very fast.

> I maneuvered the canoe in the rushing water.

You can tell that the second sentence is the stronger one. The word *maneuvered* is more precise than *moved*. In the clause *which was rushing very fast*, the words *very fast* are unnecessary because they repeat the meaning of *rushing*. The single word *rushing* conveys the same meaning.

This sentence appears in the excerpt from *Mississippi Solo*. Note how the author has used vivid language and precise words—*gap, streamed, boil, isolated patch, a scant thirty yards long*—to help the reader participate in the scene.

> It was as though a gap had opened in the clouds and the sun streamed through to boil the water and heat up this isolated patch of river a scant thirty yards long.

Practice and Apply Each of these sentences is not as strong as it could be. Rewrite the sentence to make it more precise and concise.

1. The clouds in the sky overhead moved very slowly and looked interesting.

2. All at once, a streak of lightning suddenly traveled down from a big cloud.

3. I heard the thunder, which was loud and shook the ground under my feet a lot.

4. I looked around for a place that would be safe and went into a building that was nearby.

Strategies for Annotation   ✐ 🖺 *Annotate it!*

Language Conventions: Precise Language

L 3a

Have students use their eBook annotation tools to analyze the Practice and Apply sentences. Ask them to do the following:

- Underline words that repeat meaning.
- Highlight in green other unnecessary words.
- Highlight in yellow words that could be made more precise.

The clouds in the sky overhead moved very slowly and looked interesting.

Determine the Meaning of Words and Phrases

RI 4

TEACH

Explain that examining authors' sentences can help students shape their own sentences. Define **syntax** as "the ways in which words, phrases, and clauses are put together to form grammatical sentences." Note that word order is a main feature of syntax.

Tell students that there are many ways to order words within sentences. The author's syntax choices reflect his or her style.

Display these sentences:

- You begin to get used to marvelous days if there are too many of them, and begin to think they're supposed to happen.
- If you have too many marvelous days, you begin to get used to them, to think that all days are supposed to be like that.

Prompt students to identify the sentence structure of each example, identifying the differences in word order, meaning, emphasis, and effect between the sentences.

Direct students to compare the two displayed sentences to the first sentence in the memoir they have just read:

- Too many marvelous days in a row and you begin to get used to it, to think that's the way it's supposed to be.

Ask why the author might have chosen that syntax. *(It sounds informal, puts the emphasis on "marvelous days," and has an intriguing word order.)*

PRACTICE AND APPLY

As students draft their analyses, tell them to use what they have learned about syntax when they discuss the author's style.

English Language Support

Write Informational Texts Adapt the collection opener strategy, Learning Circles, to help students prepare to write their analyses for the Performance Task.

1. Organize students into groups of three, with these roles: one student should record similes, another examples of personification, and the third observations about syntax.
2. Have students then listen to the selection and make their notes.
3. Let students share their findings. Remind them to ask clarifying questions and build on each other's comments.

Analyze Text: Memoir

RI 3

RETEACH

Tell students that a **memoir** is a kind of nonfiction writing in which the writer recalls actual events he or she experienced. Review and discuss these features of a memoir:

- **First-person point of view:** The writer uses first-person pronouns, such as *I, me,* and *mine,* so readers can see events through his or her eyes.
- **Informal language:** The sentences sound like someone having a conversation.
- **Personal feelings and reactions:** The words describe how the person feels about the experience.
- **A changed attitude or new understanding:** The writer tells about the importance of an experience—how the experience leads to new ideas or insights that are significant to the writer.

Have students identify one or more of the listed features in each of these sentences:

- The first time I saw the little yellow house, I said to myself, "Someday I'm going to live there."
- Above all else, I felt at peace and grateful just to be alive.
- When that roller coaster began to plummet, I thought for sure I'd black out.

INDEPENDENT READING

Students can apply the skill to another memoir from the school or classroom library. You might suggest the following: *An American Childhood* by Annie Dillard or *Red Scarf Girl* by Ji-li Jiang.

Tell students to read the memoir, or a portion of it, and to identify examples of the features discussed in the lesson. Ask students to record each example in a graphic organizer, such as a Spider Map. Then, ask them to include descriptions of the effectiveness of each feature and an explanation of how it shapes, or is shaped by, the events of the narrative.

INTERACTIVE GRAPHIC ORGANIZER
Spider Map

from Polar Dream

Memoir by Helen Thayer

Why This Text

Students may read a memoir without a complete understanding of the way elements of the text interact. Memoirs such as this one by the renowned explorer Helen Thayer may use figurative language or an introspective writing style that becomes clear only after the reader's examination of explicit textual evidence. With the help of the close-reading questions, students will develop an understanding of how the particular elements of a memoir are woven together to reveal the thoughts and emotions of the writer.

Background Have students read the background and the information about the author. Introduce the selection by telling students that Thayer has had a lifetime of adventures, including walking 4,000 miles across the Sahara Desert, kayaking 2,200 miles in the Amazon, and studying wild wolves for six months in the Canadian Yukon, actually living alongside a wolf den to study the pack's daily life. Tell them she has been honored by the White House and the National Geographic Society and was named "One of the Great Explorers of the 20th Century."

SETTING A PURPOSE Ask students to pay close attention to how this true story is told. How soon into the memoir did students begin to recognize that the writer was giving her own observations about an event that really happened to her?

Standards Support

- cite multiple pieces of textual evidence
- analyze interactions between elements of an informational text
- determine the meaning of words and phrases, including figurative language, and analyze the impact of specific word choice on meaning and tone
- determine an author's point of view or purpose in a text

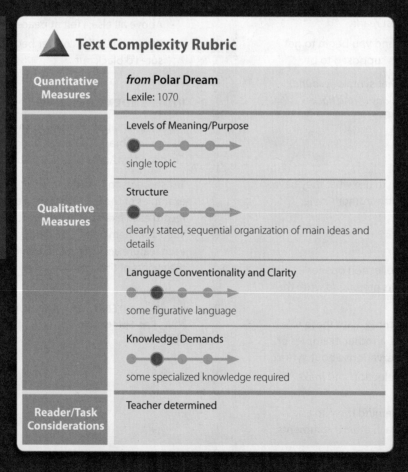

Text Complexity Rubric

Quantitative Measures	***from* Polar Dream** Lexile: 1070
Qualitative Measures	**Levels of Meaning/Purpose** single topic
	Structure clearly stated, sequential organization of main ideas and details
	Language Conventionality and Clarity some figurative language
	Knowledge Demands some specialized knowledge required
Reader/Task Considerations	Teacher determined

Strategies for CLOSE READING

Analyze the Meanings of Words and Phrases

Students should read this memoir carefully all the way through. Close-reading questions at the bottom of the page will help them focus on a thorough analysis of the meanings of words and phrases, including figurative language and word choice, and of the author's style. As they read, students should record comments or questions about the text in the side margins.

WHEN STUDENTS STRUGGLE . . .

To help students analyze the meanings of words and phrases, especially of figurative language, have them work in small groups to fill out a chart such as the one shown below as they analyze the memoir.

CITE TEXT EVIDENCE For practice in "unpacking" the meaning of figurative language in a text and the comparison created by each figure of speech, have students cite specific textual evidence to complete the chart.

Comparison	Example	Effect
Simile:	". . . my nerves were as tight as violin strings . . ." (line 87)	creates a vivid image of her taut nerves about to snap
Metaphor:	"My hands were blistered clubs . . ." (lines 1–2)	creates a vivid image of cold, swollen hands
Personification:	". . . she was a tender, attentive mother caring for her cubs." (lines 128–129)	likens the polar bear to a human mother

---

Background Helen Thayer *is a decorated explorer and adventurer. Her achievements include being the first woman to walk across the Sahara Desert, kayaking 1,200 miles across two rivers in the Amazon, and walking 1,600 miles across the Gobi Desert in Asia. In 1988, at the age of 50, she became the first woman to walk and ski to the North Pole without a snowmobile or dogsled. She wrote about her adventure in Polar Dream.*

from
Polar Dream

Memoir by Helen Thayer

CLOSE READ
Notes

1. **READ ▶** As you read lines 1–64, begin to collect and cite evidence.

- Circle the metaphor in the second sentence, and explain the meaning of it in the margin.
- Underline items Thayer wears to stay warm.
- Write in the margin why it's important for Thayer to stay hydrated.

A I woke at 5:30 A.M. after a restless night's sleep. My hands were blistered clubs and hurt every time I touched something. Overnight enormous blood blisters had formed to reach all the way down to the second joint of each finger except my left little finger, which had somehow escaped freezing. I knew I had to keep the blisters intact so that my hands wouldn't become raw and bleeding. It would be better to use my heavy mitts as much as possible even though they were clumsy. I thought back to the previous morning, remembering the crazy repacking of my sled with gear ending up in all the wrong
10　places as I just stood there not wanting to offend anyone. I decided what is done is done. One learns one's lessons the hard way sometimes and, besides, if that was to be the only problem of the whole expedition, then I would consider myself lucky.

Reaching over I painfully and slowly unzipped the tent door to inspect the new day. Just like yesterday. The wind had dropped. I looked out at cold, clear skies and a light northerly wind. Another

Her hands are unresponsive and feel wooden because of painful blisters.

45

---

1. **READ AND CITE TEXT EVIDENCE**

A **ASK STUDENTS** to read their margin notes to a partner and then write one response that explains the meaning of the metaphor in lines 1–2, citing specific textual evidence. *Students should explain that Thayer's hands are so cold, swollen, and unresponsive that she compares them to "blistered clubs," using a metaphor to create a striking image that appeals to the reader's sense of sight and touch.*

FOR ELL STUDENTS Have students reread lines 14–23. Point out the weather vocabulary: *wind* (line 15), *cold, clear* (line 16), *another beautiful . . . day* (lines 16–17), *snowstorm* (line 18), and *frost* (line 21). Have students define these words by using context clues, or by drawing them or using gestures.

beautiful Arctic day. Charlie was up and looking at his empty bowl. I
crawled out of my sleeping bag, creating a minor snowstorm as I
brushed against the frost-covered tent roof while I pulled on my
20 jacket. I'm normally a morning person but there was something about
the intense cold, the tent frost down my neck, and my sore hands that
made that morning most unappealing. But it was time to greet
Charlie and start the day.

Stepping out of the tent, still in my insulated blue camp booties, I
checked the thermometer, minus 41 degrees. I looked around for
bears or tracks and saw none, but I was surprised to notice that the
shore ice with its jagged blocks and pinnacles ended only one hundred
feet from my tent. In the settling light of last evening it had looked as
if I was at least four hundred yards from the closest rough shore ice. It
30 was my first lesson in the **sly** nature of the changing Arctic light and
the way it affected depth perception.

Charlie was bouncing up and down at the end of his chain
looking well rested. I hugged him good morning as his soft tongue
wiped across my face. I poured what looked like a pound of dog food
into his bowl, which he attacked with gusto.

Now for my stove. I simply had to light it that morning. I needed
water for the next leg of my journey and a hot breakfast would get my
day started off right. I carefully put a pair of woollen gloves over my
liners and with clenched teeth I forced my cruelly protesting fingers
40 to push the stove tube into the gasket at the top of the fuel bottle.
Success. I lit it, put snow and ice into my two-quart pan, and soon had
warm water. To conserve fuel, I heated water only to a temperature at
which I could still put my finger into it.

It was only six o'clock, so I decided to have a leisurely breakfast of
a bowl of granola, milk powder, coconut flakes, raisins, and butter
mixed with warm water. I sat on my sled to enjoy the full effect of my
first breakfast of the expedition only to find that after the third
spoonful it was frozen. So much for leisurely breakfasts! I added more
warm water and ate the rest as fast as possible. Then I melted enough
50 ice to fill two vacuum bottles with water and a carbohydrate powder.

The dry Arctic air holds little moisture, causing quick dehydration
of the body, which, in turn, causes early fatigue and reduces the
body's ability to keep warm, so fluid would be just as important as

[margin note] ¹sly:
clever; tricky

[margin note] Thayer wants
to stay
hydrated so
she can be
warm and
energized.

46

---

food to keep my energy reserves up. I put my day's supply of crackers,
cashews, walnuts, and peanut butter cups in my day food bag along
with the two vacuum bottles and slipped everything down into the
front of the sled bag. Then, remembering Charlie's appetite for
crackers, I added a few more.

B Last to be packed was the tent. I was completely **engrossed** in
60 finding a way to twist the tent ice screws out of the ice so that my
hands wouldn't scream in protest when suddenly I heard a deep, long
growl coming from the depths of Charlie's throat. In a flash I looked
at him and then in the direction in which he was staring. I knew what
I would see even before I looked. A polar bear!

It was a female followed by two cubs coming from Bathurst
Island,¹ slowly, purposefully, plodding through the rough shore ice
toward me. They were two hundred yards away. With a pounding
heart I grabbed my loaded rifle and flare gun and carefully walked
sideways a few steps to Charlie, who was snarling with a savagery that
70 caught my breath. Without taking my eyes off the bear, I unclipped
Charlie from his ice anchor and, again walking sideways, I led him to
the sled where I clipped his chain to a tie-down rope. The bear, now
only 150 yards away, wasn't stopping. Her cubs had dropped back but
she came on with a steady measured stride while I frantically tried to
D remember all the Inuit² had told me. Keep eye contact, move sideways

[margin note] engrossed:
absorbed;
focused

¹ **Bathurst Island:** an uninhabited island that is part of the Canadian Arctic Archipelago.
² **Inuit:** a group of people belonging to the Eskimo family who live throughout the
Canadian Artic.

---

2. **◄ REREAD AND DISCUSS** Reread lines 59–64. In a small group,
discuss whether Thayer seems prepared for the situation that occurs.

3. **READ ►** As you read lines 65–103, continue to cite textual
evidence.

• Underline what Thayer was told to do if a polar bear approached her.
• Circle figurative language that describes how Thayer feels during the
encounter with the polar bear.
• In the margin, explain what this figurative language conveys about
Thayer.

47

Critical Vocabulary: sly (line 30) Have students share their
definitions of *sly*. Ask them to provide two or more synonyms
of the word *sly*, leading them to recognize that a synonym is a
word that has the same (or nearly the same) meaning as that
of another word. *Students should be able to cite the words* clever,
tricky, *and* crafty, *among others.*

FOR ELL STUDENTS Point out the words *perception* (line 31),
conserve, temperature (line 42), *fluid* (line 53), and *energy* (line
54). Explain, or ask a volunteer to explain, the meaning of each
of the words. Point out that many Spanish-speaking students
might recognize that these words are cognates for the Spanish
words *percepción, conservar, temperatura, fluido,* and *energia.* Lead
students to recognize that many scientific or technical terms have
cognates in many languages.

2. **REREAD AND DISCUSS USING TEXT EVIDENCE**

B **ASK STUDENTS** to appoint a reporter for each group to cite
textual evidence and line numbers about the level of Thayer's
preparedness for the situation with the polar bear. *Students
should cite evidence from lines 59–64 to support their position.*

3. **READ AND CITE TEXT EVIDENCE**

C **ASK STUDENTS** to read their margin notes to a partner and
then produce one response that best describes how Thayer feels
during her encounter with the polar bear. *Students should cite the
simile that Thayer uses in lines 87–88 to convey the tension and
anxiety she feels during her confrontation with the bear.*

Critical Vocabulary: engrossed (line 59) Have students share
their definitions of *engrossed*. Why does she use the word to
provide the backdrop for the imminent encounter with the
bear? *She may want to show that she is surprised by the situation
that is about to occur.*

"Don't wound a bear, you'll make it even more dangerous...."

or slightly forward, never backward, stay calm, don't show fear, stand beside a tent, sled, or other large object to make my five feet three inches appear as large as possible. Don't shoot unless forced to. Don't wound a bear, you'll make it even more dangerous, and never run.

80   Repeating to myself, "Stay calm, stay calm," I fired a warning shot to the bear's left. The loud explosion of the .338 had no effect. On she came. I fired a flare, landing it a little to her right. Her head moved slightly in its direction but she didn't stop. I fired another flare, this time dropping it right in front of her. She stopped, looked at the flare burning a bright red on the white ice, then looked at me. She was only one hundred feet away now.

Thayer is tense and nervous.

C By this time my nerves were as tight as violin strings and my heart could have been heard at base camp. The bear began to step around the flare, and I dropped another flare two feet in front of her. Again

90   she stopped, looked at the flare and at me. Then she fixed her tiny black eyes on Charlie, who was straining at the end of his chain, snapping and snarling trying to reach her. She looked back at her cubs. I could sense her concern about Charlie's snarling, **rabid** act and her cubs. She waited for her cubs to catch up, then moved to my left in a half circle. In spite of my sore fingers I fired two more flares in quick succession, trying to draw a line between her and me. She stopped, then moved back toward my right. I fired two more flares and again she stopped. She seemed to want to cross the line of flares but was unsure of the result and of Charlie, so she elected to stay back.

rabid:
raging; uncontrollable

48

100   She kept moving right in a half circle, still one hundred feet away. Finally, with a last long look she plodded north with her two new cubs trotting behind her, their snow-white coats contrasting with their mother's creamy, pale yellow color.

F   The whole episode lasted fifteen minutes but seemed years long. I was a nervous wreck. My hands were shaking as I stood still holding my rifle and flare gun, watching the trio slowly move north. But in spite of the mind-numbing fear that still gripped me, I could feel deep down inside a real satisfaction. I now knew that I could stand up to a

E 110   bear in the wild, stay calm enough to function and still remember the words of wisdom from the Inuit. With Charlie's help I had passed my first test. The bear had been completely silent as it had approached and moved around me on paws thickly padded with fur on the undersides. I was thankful for Charlie's warning. Now he had stopped growling and snarling but still stood rigid, watching the bears as they zigzagged in and out of the rough ice hunting for the seals that lived in the cold waters beneath the ice. He seemed to hardly notice the giant hug I gave him. He was still on guard.

The bears were only about four hundred yards away but I decided to continue packing my tent and move around to stay warm, still

120   keeping a wary eye on the bears. I was getting cold. My fear and flowing adrenaline had kept me warm but I was beginning to shiver

Charlie made noise when the polar bear approached; Thayer had not heard her. Charlie keeps watch even after the immediate threat of the bear has passed.

4. ◀ REREAD Reread lines 65–86. The writer could have used many short sentences to retell the advice she received. What is the effect of retelling all the advice she received in three sentences?

Retelling the advice in this way creates the effect that she is thinking quickly and trying to retrieve any bit of advice that will help her.

5. READ ▶ As you read lines 104–129, continue to cite textual evidence.
   - Underline the emotions Thayer feels after the polar bear leaves.
   - Make notes in the margin about why Thayer is grateful to Charlie.
   - Circle words that describe the polar bear.

49

WHEN STUDENTS STRUGGLE . . .

To help students understand the interactions between particular elements in a text, such as how ideas influence individuals or events, or how individuals influence ideas or events, ask them to reread lines 65–103. Invite students to work in small groups to discuss how the advice given to Thayer by the Inuit about how to react, especially to remain calm, probably saved her life.

Critical Vocabulary: rabid (line 93) Have students explain *rabid* as Thayer uses it here. Why does she use the word to describe Charlie's actions toward the polar bear and her cubs? *Thayer probably wants to emphasize how savage polar dogs can be if provoked.*

4. **REREAD AND CITE TEXT EVIDENCE**

D **ASK STUDENTS** to reread the three sentences in lines 75–79, observing their sentence type and length to analyze the author's style. *Students should point out that all three sentences are imperative, showing her quick recall of the Inuit advice about what not to do if confronted by a polar bear, and that sentences 1 and 3 seem to have combined short, choppy sentences into a single sentence, conveying Thayer's quick thinking as she retrieves the advice that could now save her life.*

5. **READ AND CITE TEXT EVIDENCE** Remind students that in a memoir, the author expresses his or her point of view, as well as personal thoughts and emotions.

E **ASK STUDENTS** to read their margin notes to a partner and then create a response about Thayer's feelings toward Charlie, showing why she is grateful to him. *Students should cite explicit textual evidence from lines 110–111 and 113–117.*

now. I finished packing and stood around until ten o'clock, keeping warm, until I was sure the bears had disappeared and weren't circling back to me. If I stayed out from the coast, keeping away from the rough ice, I hoped to make up the time I had lost. But as I started out I still thought about the bears. Even as frightened as I had been, it was a thrill to see a bear and her cubs in their natural environment. She was unafraid of me, powerful and dangerous, yet graceful. And she was a tender, attentive mother caring for her cubs.

6. **◀ REREAD** Reread lines 104–129. How does the author's specific word choice convey the importance of this experience to her? Support your answer with explicit textual evidence.

"Shaking" and "mind-numbing fear" are vivid words that emphasize the danger she faces. Thayer's use of words like "satisfaction" and "thrill" convey the pride she feels in how she handled the situation.

SHORT RESPONSE

Cite Text Evidence Analyze the way Thayer uses a particular style to convey the meaning of events in the text. Include examples of words and phrases as they are used in the text, such as figurative language and specific word choice. Be sure to review your reading notes and **cite text evidence** in your response.

At the beginning of the essay, Thayer uses a metaphor and specific descriptive details to convey the harsh conditions she faces. When the polar bear arrives, she groups a series of sentences together in a way that reveals the speed of her thinking. However, once the polar bear moves on, she describes the "thrill" she felt and "satisfaction" she experiences.

50

---

6. **REREAD AND CITE TEXT EVIDENCE**

F **ASK STUDENTS** to identify the author's specific word choice in describing how she felt after the experience with the polar bear. How does her word choice convey her ideas and emotions through specific language? *Students should cite textual evidence from lines 104–129 to support the idea that Thayer adapts her word choice and writing style to express her thoughts about (and pride in) her response to this episode.*

SHORT RESPONSE

Cite Text Evidence Students should cite specific textual evidence to support their analysis of Thayer's writing style to convey the meaning of events. Students should:

- analyze words, phrases, figurative language, and word choice.
- assess whether her style supports her meaning and tone.
- cite specific evidence from the text to support their reasons.

TO CHALLENGE STUDENTS . . .

For more context about the Arctic, the polar region at the northernmost part of the Earth, students can conduct print, online, or multimedia research to write a report about this frigid place and the skills needed to survive there.

ASK STUDENTS to do some preliminary research to find an aspect of the topic that interests them. Possible topics for their research might include:

- The Dangers Faced by Polar Explorers
- How Our Changing Climate Is Affecting the Arctic
- The Daily Life of the Inuit
- How Polar Bears Survive in the Arctic

With the class, discuss the following elements of a research report after students have chosen a topic:

- Plan Your Research

  Write questions about your topic.

  Research your topic and take notes.

  Organize your notes.

  Write an outline based on your notes.
- Write your Report

  Keep your purpose and audience in mind.

  Write a first draft, revise your report, and proofread it.
- Publish and Share

  Make a final copy of your report.

  Publish and share it.

ASK STUDENTS what they hope to discover as they research their report. How is the information they find similar to, yet different from, the autobiographical account of the Arctic shared by Thayer?

DIG DEEPER

With the class, return to Question 2, Reread and Discuss. Have students share the results of their discussion.

ASK STUDENTS whether they were pleased with the outcome of their group discussions. Have each group share its feelings about Thayer's preparedness for the situation with the polar bear. Encourage groups to tell whether they thought that Thayer had portrayed the event accurately. How did her style of writing, including her specific word choice, use of figurative language, and of varying sentence types and lengths, affect the telling of the event?

- Encourage each group to explain what the majority opinion of the group was concerning Thayer's level of preparedness. What compelling evidence did the group cite from the memoir to support this opinion?

- Guide students to tell whether there was any convincing evidence cited by group members holding a different opinion. If so, why didn't it sway the group's position?

- Have groups explain whether or not they found sufficient evidence to support their opinion that she was prepared (or ill-prepared) for the encounter with the bear. Did everyone in the group agree as to what made the evidence sufficient? What conflict-resolution techniques did the group use to resolve any differences of opinion?

- After students have shared the results of their group's discussion, ask whether any other group had expressed an opinion that differed from their own. Ask if the other group's opinion had merit. If so, why didn't it persuade the group to change its position?

ASK STUDENTS to return to their Short Response answer and revise it based on the class discussion.

CLOSE READING NOTES

from **The Tempest**

Soliloquy by William Shakespeare

Why This Text?

Reading this soliloquy by one of the most famous characters in Shakespearean drama exposes students to the language and dramatic techniques of a literary giant. This lesson helps students meet the challenge of interpreting Shakespearean vocabulary, grammar, sentence structure, and allusions.

▶ View It!

Professional Development Podcast:

Text Complexity

Key Learning Objective: The student will be able to identify elements of Shakespearean language, interpret meaning, and analyze a soliloquy.

RL 1 Cite textual evidence.
RL 2 Determine a central idea.
RL 4 Determine meanings of words and phrases.
RL 5 Analyze how a soliloquy's form or structure contributes to its meaning.
SL 1 Engage in collaborative discussions.
SL 6 Adapt speech to a variety of contexts and tasks.

▲ Text Complexity Rubric

Quantitative Measures	*from* **The Tempest** **Lexile:** N/A
Qualitative Measures	**Levels of Meaning/Purpose** ●━●━●━●▶ multiple levels of complex meanings
	Structure ●━●━●━●▶ complex, unfamiliar story concepts
	Language Conventionality and Clarity ●━●━●━●▶ archaic, unfamiliar language
	Knowledge Demands ●━●━●━●▶ cultural and literary knowledge essential to understanding
Reader/Task Considerations	• Teacher determined • Vary by individual reader and type of text • See the Text X-Ray for suggested Reader/Task Considerations.

English Language Support Before teaching, use the Text X-Ray for an overview of the text's complexity. The Text X-Ray and the supports and scaffolds in the Teacher's Edition will help you guide students of different skill levels.

Meaning Making
Language Development
Effective Expression
Content Knowledge
Foundational Skills

Text Complexity: Qualitative Measures

Levels of Meaning/Purpose

●——●——●——●——→

multiple levels of complex meaning

Help students determine meanings.
- Teacher's Edition side notes, pp. 146, 147
- English Language Support, p. 145
- Strategies for Annotation, p. 147
- Determine Meanings, p. 147

To reteach how to determine meanings, see
- Determine Meanings, p. 148a

 Use It! **Level Up Tutorial:** Elements of Poetry

***ZOOM IN ON* DETERMINING MEANING** Tell students that Shakespeare often **inverts,** or reorders, words in some sentences for effect.

- Write these lines on the board:
  ". . . to the dread rattling thunder / Have I given fire." (lines 12–13)
  "But this rough magic / I here abjure." (lines 18–19)
- Tell students that it is easier to understand these lines when rephrased in subject-verb-object order. Model how to rephrase the first example: I have given fire to the dread rattling thunder.
- Have pairs write sentences that restate the second example in subject-verb-object order. Define unfamiliar words as needed.

Structure

●——●——●——●——→

complex, unfamiliar story concepts

Help students analyze the form of a Shakespearean soliloquy.
- Teacher's Edition side notes, pp. 145, 146, 147
- Analyze Form, p. 147

To teach additional aspects of poetic form, see
- Analyze Form, p. 148a

 Use It! **Level Up Tutorial:** Rhythm

***ZOOM IN ON* ANALYZING A SOLILOQUY** Read aloud Analyze Form on page 147. Emphasize that a **soliloquy** shares the thoughts of one character trying to resolve a conflict or make a decision. Have pairs use these questions to analyze Prospero's thoughts:

- To whom is Prospero speaking in the first nine lines? Why is he talking to this audience? (*He speaks to many weak spirits because they have helped him work his magic.*)
- What does Prospero think back upon in lines 9–18? What do the images in these lines reveal about him? (*He thinks about all that he has done with the aid of magic. He is powerful.*)
- What decision does Prospero make? Why is his decision important? (*Prospero decides to give up magic after one last act; it is important because it will be a change in his life.*)

Language Conventionality and Clarity

•──•──•──● ——▶

archaic, unfamiliar language

Help students acquire familiarity with speaking, reading, and discussing Shakespeare's poetry.

- Teacher's Edition side note, p. 146
- English Language Support, p. 146
- Performance Task, p. 148

ZOOM IN ON **PRETEACH VOCABULARY** Write these words on the board: *curfew* (line 8); *bedimmed* (line 9); *mutinous* (line 10); *promontory* (line 14); *potent* (line 18); *abjure* (line 19). Have pairs of students look up each word in a dictionary or other reference work. Then read each word in context and ask students to determine the best meaning for each. Suggest that students write the chosen definitions on sticky notes attached to the page.

Knowledge Demands

•──•──•──● ——▶

cultural and literary knowledge essential to understanding

Support English learners in building the cultural and literary background necessary for understanding the soliloquy.

- Teacher's Edition Background note, p. 145

A&E For more background, students can view the video "Biography: William Shakespeare" in their eBooks.

- Student Edition footnotes, p. 146

ZOOM IN ON **BUILDING CULTURAL AND LITERARY KNOWLEDGE** To provide context for the speech, read aloud the Background on page 145, along with the Background notes in the Teacher's Edition. Invite students to ask questions. Then explain the following:

- line 1: *Ye* is the archaic term for "you" and indicates direct address.
- line 6: *Whereof* means "of which."
- line 11: *Twixt* means "between." *Azured vault* means "blue sky."
- line 17: *Oped* is "opened."

Suggested Reader/Task Considerations

Consider the following before assigning this soliloquy to students.

- Do students have the skills to comprehend this soliloquy?
- Will students be able to manage Shakespeare's language?

ZOOM IN ON **SUPPORTING COMPREHENSION**

- To support students' comprehension, first play the audio version of the soliloquy several times, pausing to discuss confusing words or phrases.
- Display lines 1–12 (through "Set roaring war"). Read them aloud, and model how to paraphrase their meaning. (*You magical creatures who have helped me control the sun, wind, and weather . . .*) Ask pairs of students to use the same strategy for lines 12–18 ("*to the dread . . . so potent art.*" Sample paraphrase: *I have caused lightning and earthquakes, uprooted trees, and raised the dead with my magic.*), and then for lines 18–25. ("*But this rough magic . . . drown my book.*" Sample paraphrase: *But now I will give up magic. Once I have cast a musical spell on these people, I'll destroy my magic staff and book.*) Clarify students' responses as needed.

Background Have students read the background to this excerpt and the information about the playwright. Share this additional information about this soliloquy:

- Shakespeare makes allusions to Roman mythology. He often borrowed from earlier sources, and some lines in this soliloquy are nearly identical to lines in the Roman poet Ovid's *Metamorphoses*. Educated members of Shakespeare's audiences would have recognized the literary allusions.

- Prospero begins his soliloquy as the play nears its end. He has just sent his servant, the spirit Ariel, to bring back those who are under his spell. Prospero said, "Go release them, Ariel. / My charms I'll break, their senses I'll restore, / And they shall be themselves."

SETTING A PURPOSE Direct students to use the Setting a Purpose prompt to focus their reading. Remind them to generate questions as they read.

Analyze Form

RL 5

Tell students that Prospero is the main character in *The Tempest*. Point out that a **soliloquy** is a speech given by a character alone on the stage. In a soliloquy, the character reveals thoughts and plans.

 ASK STUDENTS to reread the Background section and suggest what goal Prospero has had throughout most of the play. Why might Shakespeare have chosen to have Prospero give a soliloquy toward the end of the play? *(By the end of the play, Prospero has used his magic to right the wrong that was done to him by Antonio and Alonso. Now, Shakespeare uses the soliloquy to reveal Prospero's thoughts about his actions and reveal how events have changed him.)*

A&E BIO

Background *The Tempest, from which this excerpt is taken, is believed to be the last play Shakespeare wrote alone. In* The Tempest, *Prospero, the duke of Milan and a powerful magician, was exiled from Italy and left to die at sea by his brother, Antonio, and Alonso, the king of Naples. After twelve years, Fortune finally sends Antonio and Alonso within Prospero's reach. He conjures a powerful storm, the tempest, causing his enemies to shipwreck on his island. Prospero then seeks to use his magic to make these lords restore him to his rightful position.* **A**

from
The Tempest

Soliloquy by William Shakespeare

William Shakespeare *(1564–1616) is generally considered the greatest playwright in the English language. From about 1592 on, he performed in and wrote plays in London. The location most closely associated with him is the Globe Theatre, shown here. Most of Shakespeare's early plays are about historical figures, although he also wrote more light-hearted comedies. Later, Shakespeare penned his famous tragedies, including* Hamlet *and* Macbeth.

SETTING A PURPOSE In *The Tempest*, Prospero, who has learned to cast spells from a book of magic, rules over a mystical island. As you read, think about what Prospero plans to do with his power and what that means for his character.

from The Tempest **145**

English Language Support

Read Closely Have students use the audio feature in their eBooks to listen to the speech before or as they read it for the first time.

- Reread aloud these sets of lines, summarizing each: lines 1–8, 8–18, 18–25. *(He addresses the spirits that have helped him work magic. He says he has brought darkness at noon, stirred up violent weather, caused earthquakes, and opened graves. Then he says that he is through with magic. Once his last deed is done, he will break his magic staff and destroy his magic book.)*

- Summarize what Prospero is saying, and model how to restate the first eight lines in modern English. Work with students to rewrite lines 8–18. Have groups of students paraphrase the remaining lines and share their rewrites with the class.

- Assign two or three students one of these sets of lines to rewrite in modern English: 1–8, 8–18, 18–25. Encourage them to discuss their differences in phrasing and to come to a consensus about a final version to share with the class.

TEACH

CLOSE READ

 For more context and historical background, students can view the video "Biography: William Shakespeare" in their eBooks.

Determine Meanings
(LINES 1–8)

RL 1,
RL 4

Tell students that language is always changing and is not the same today as it was when Shakespeare wrote. Point out that in lines 1–8, Prospero is speaking to elves and other invisible spirits. His grammar, vocabulary, and word order are "Shakespearean."

B **CITE TEXT EVIDENCE** Tell students to reread lines 1–8 and cite the lines that might be stated this way in modern English: "You airy spirits leave no footprints on the sand as you chase the waves that come ashore." *(And ye that on the sands with printless foot / Do chase the ebbing Neptune, and do fly him / When he comes back)* Reread the lines aloud to help students appreciate the connection between rhythm and image.

Analyze Form **(LINES 22–25)**

RL 1,
RL 5

Tell students that after recalling the magical power he has used, Prospero says, "I'll break my staff." Explain that a staff is a stick, like a magic wand.

C **CITE TEXT EVIDENCE** Have students reread lines 22–25 and cite the words that show Prospero has undergone an important change. *(He says about his staff that he'll "Bury it certain fathoms in the earth" and also says, "I'll drown my book." He's giving up his powers by destroying his staff and his book of spells.)*

COLLABORATIVE DISCUSSION Have students take turns rereading segments of the soliloquy that show Prospero's special powers. Have them share ideas about what his final words reveal about him and his plans.

ASK STUDENTS to share any questions they generated in the course of reading and discussing the selection.

---

from **The Tempest**
ACT 5, Scene 1

Prospero. Ye elves of hills, brooks, standing lakes and groves,
And ye that on the sands with printless foot
Do chase the ebbing Neptune,[1] and do fly him
When he comes back; you demi-puppets that
5 By moonshine do the green sour ringlets make
Whereof the ewe not bites; and you whose pastime
Is to make midnight mushrooms, that rejoice
To hear the solemn curfew; by whose aid,
Weak masters[2] though ye be, I have bedimmed
10 The noontide sun, called forth the mutinous winds,
And 'twixt the green sea and the azured vault
Set roaring war—to the dread rattling thunder
Have I given fire, and rifted Jove's stout oak[3]
With his own bolt; the strong-based promontory
15 Have I made shake, and by the spurs plucked up
The pine and cedar; graves at my command
Have waked their sleepers, oped, and let 'em forth
By my so potent art. But this rough magic
I here abjure. And when I have required
20 Some heavenly music—which even now I do—
To work mine end upon their senses that
This airy charm[4] is for, I'll break my staff,
Bury it certain fathoms in the earth,
And deeper than did ever plummet sound
25 I'll drown my book.

COLLABORATIVE DISCUSSION What does Prospero plan to do with his source of power? What does that tell you about Prospero's character? Share your ideas with other group members.

---

[1] **ebbing Neptune:** Neptune was the mythical Roman god of water and the sea; "ebbing Neptune" suggests waves flowing away from shore. Like tiny seabirds on a beach, the elves chase the ocean waves as they flow away from the shore, and "fly" or run from them as they flow back to shore.

[2] **Weak masters:** supernatural spirits that do not work powerful evil.

[3] **rifted Jove's stout oak:** Jove was the mythical Roman king of the gods for whom the oak tree was sacred. Jove was identified with thunderbolts, too. Here the image is of lightning splitting the oak.

[4] **airy charm:** magical music.

English Language Support

Word Study Display these words: *brooks, foot; mushrooms, noontide.* Say each word aloud, emphasizing the different sounds made by the same two letters—*oo*. Have students repeat the words several times.

- Write the following on the board: *shook, boot, moon, book, loot, forsook, tooth, look, drool.* Pronounce each one and clarify the meaning of those that may be unfamiliar to students.

- Then have students work with a partner to sort the words into two categories according to which sound the *oo* makes.

Determine Meanings

RL 4

The English language we use today is different from the language used by writers in the 1600s. To understand a Shakespearean play, you need to analyze how Shakespeare uses the language of his time to create rhythm and meaning. These elements all appear in the excerpt from *The Tempest*.

Grammar — Shakespeare used familiar pronouns such as *you, yourself, your,* and *yours,* but he also used other forms of *you: thou, thee, thy, thine,* and *ye.* Shakespeare used *my* or *mine* before a noun, but we no longer say phrases such as *mine eyes.*

Word Order — The positions of words and phrases in Shakespearean language can sound strange to modern ears. Prospero says:

> **the strong-based promontory**
> **Have I made shake, and by the spurs plucked up**
> **The pine and cedar;**

A modern English speaker might use this sentence structure: "I have made the strong-based promontory shake, and plucked up the pine and cedar by the spurs."

Vocabulary — Shakespeare's vocabulary included words that modern English speakers either no longer use or use differently. What is a "strong-based promontory"? It's the strong rocky base that holds the "spurs," or roots, of pine and cedar trees.

Blank Verse — Shakespeare wrote many of his plays, including *The Tempest,* in **blank verse,** or unrhymed iambic pentameter. In blank verse, the final words of the lines do not rhyme, and each line consists of ten syllables alternating unstressed and stressed.

Analyze Form

RL 5

In a drama, a **soliloquy** is a speech given by a character alone on a stage. It is different from a **monologue,** which is a speech that is often directed to another character.

In soliloquies, characters seem to be thinking aloud, revealing thoughts, feelings, and plans. It is almost as if the characters are talking to themselves. In lines 18–19 of his soliloquy, Prospero announces his plan with the words, "But this rough magic / I here abjure." He is saying that he will no longer work his magic.

CLOSE READ

Determine Meanings

RL 4

Have students find an example of each element of Shakespearean language in the soliloquy.

Make these points about blank verse:

- The term *blank verse* describes any unrhymed poetry that has lines with a regular rhythm.
- Shakespearean blank verse has lines with five stressed syllables, often in this pattern: duh-DAH, duh-DAH, duh-DAH, duh-DAH, duh-DAH. This pattern is called iambic pentameter.
- Iambic pentameter is said to be most like natural English speech. Poets who use it usually introduce variations, so that the lines don't all sound alike.

Have students read aloud a ten-syllable line to listen for a pattern of stresses. Direct them to the soliloquy's last line and ask why it varies from iambic pentameter. *("I'll drown my book" has only four single-syllable words. It stands out as a forceful final statement.)*

Analyze Form

RL 5

Point out lines 18–19: "But this rough magic I here abjure." Help students recognize its significance:

- It is the only short sentence in the soliloquy, signaling an abrupt change.
- It follows descriptions of Prospero's powers.
- It leads to the close of the soliloquy and a major change for Prospero.

Strategies for Annotation   ✏️ 🗐 *Annotate it!*

Determine Meanings

RL 4

Share these strategies for guided or independent analysis of the soliloquy:

- Highlight in yellow words that are no longer used in modern spoken English.
- Underline groups of words that would be positioned differently in modern English sentences.
- Add a note to restate the meaning in modern English.

The pine and cedar; graves at my command

Have waked their sleepers, oped, and let 'em forth

<u>By my so potent art.</u> But this rough magic

> With my powerful magic, I've commanded graves to open and the dead to come out.

PRACTICE & APPLY

Analyzing the Text

Possible answers:

1. *You fairies that by moonlight make the sour-tasting grassy rings that grazing sheep avoid.*

2. *solemn curfew; A curfew is a set time at night when one thing ends and others begin. Here, the "solemn curfew" is midnight.*

3. *He has dimmed the sun at noon, made stormy winds blow, and caused a terrible, destructive storm at sea. He has added lightning to thunder, and cut apart a stout oak tree with a lightning bolt. His spells have literally shaken the earth and caused the dead to rise from their graves.*

4. *"By my so potent art" means "using my powerful magic."*

5. *Blank verse gives the soliloquy its rhythm and makes it less like conversational dialogue and more like a poem. Prospero speaks like a poet reciting his lines with strong emotion.*

6. *In lines 1–8, Prospero might make fanciful gestures with his hands as he playfully describes the elves and fairies. In lines 9–18, he might take a bold posture and gesture more wildly as he forcefully describes the violent and powerful things he has done by magic. In lines 19–25, his voice may grow softer and he may take on a gentler, thoughtful appearance as he says that he is giving up magic forever—a significant admission for such a powerful man.*

7. *Words about sight, sound, and touch that describe characters and events, such as fairies playing with waves, lightning and thunder, shaking earth, and heavenly music, help readers imagine the scene that Prospero is describing.*

FOR STANDARD ENGLISH LEARNERS

Pronunciation Some students may have difficulty voicing the initial /th/ sound in words such as *this*; instead, they may pronounce the sound as /d/, saying *dis*. Write these lines from the soliloquy on the board: "To work mine end upon their senses that / This airy charm is for . . ." (lines 21–22). Read the lines aloud several times, emphasizing the /th/ sounds. Have students repeat the lines until they pronounce the words confidently.

Analyzing the Text

RL 2, RL 4, RL 5, SL 1, SL 6

Cite Text Evidence   Support your responses with evidence from the text.

1. **Interpret** In lines 4–6, Prospero refers to "green sour ringlets." These rings were said to be a poisonous trail made by fairies dancing in the night. (Today, a circle of mushrooms that sprouts overnight is still called a fairy ring.) How would you restate Prospero's words in modern English?

2. **Interpret** What words in lines 5–8 help you understand when fairies and other magical creatures were free to come out?

3. **Cause/Effect** In lines 9–18, Prospero vividly describes the powerful things he has accomplished with magic. What are some of the effects of his spells?

4. **Interpret** What does Prospero mean in line 18, when he says, "By my so potent art"?

5. **Analyze** Shakespeare wrote Prospero's soliloquy in blank verse. How does this form contribute to the meaning of the text?

6. **Draw Conclusions** How might an actor playing Prospero use his voice and gestures to convey the meanings of the text in these three main sections: lines 1–8, lines 9–18, lines 19–25?

7. **Evaluate** This excerpt from *The Tempest* includes many examples of imagery—the words and phrases that appeal to the five senses. Evaluate the impact the imagery has on your understanding of the text.

PERFORMANCE TASK

Speaking Activity: Dramatic Reading
Divide the lines of this soliloquy among the members of a small group so that each participant has several lines that express one idea or related ideas.

- Together, discuss and analyze the Shakespearean vocabulary and sentence structure.
- Use your analysis to rewrite Prospero's soliloquy in your own words.
- Then, as a group, deliver your version of the soliloquy to the class.

Assign this performance task.

PERFORMANCE TASK

Speaking Activity: Dramatic Reading Have students work in small groups. Suggest they use footnotes with the soliloquy, published versions of *The Tempest*, or glossaries of words commonly used by Shakespeare to help them. Have them practice their readings with a partner. As they perform, remind them to adapt their speech to changing meanings and words in the passage.

Analyze Form

TEACH

Tell students that Prospero's soliloquy sounds like a poem because of its rhythmical pattern. Display these terms and definitions:

meter: the pattern of stressed and unstressed syllables in a line of poetry
foot: a unit of meter with one stressed syllable
iamb: a two-syllable foot with the second syllable stressed
tetrameter: a line with four feet
pentameter: a line with five feet
iambic tetrameter: four iambs in a line
iambic pentameter: five iambs in a line

Help students contrast the two iambic meters by showing foot divisions and stressed syllables in lines of poetry. Prompt students to use the listed terms to tell about the rhythms they hear:

As NIGHT | drew ON | and, FROM | the CREST

Of WOOD | ed KNOLLS | that RIDGED | the WEST

When I | have SEEN | the HUN | gry O | cean GAIN

Ad VAN | tage ON | the KING | dom OF | the SHORE

Emphasize that although a poem may have an identifiable meter, poets introduce variations in rhythms to connect sound to meaning and to avoid singsong sameness.

PRACTICE AND APPLY

Show students the symbols ´ and ˘. Explain that these symbols can be used above syllables to mark the pattern of stresses they hear.

Tell students to identify the feet and stresses in the following lines from Prospero's soliloquy: line 2, line 5, line 15, line 24.

And ye | that on | the sands | with print | less foot

By moon | shine do | the green | sour ring | lets make

Have I | made shake, | and by | the spurs | plucked up

And deep | er than | did ev | er plum | met sound

Determine Meanings

RETEACH

Tell students that William Shakespeare is often called the greatest playwright who ever wrote in English, and his plays are still being performed. Point out that because Shakespeare wrote in an older form of English, readers may need footnotes and other help to clarify meaning. As readers become more accustomed to Shakespeare's language, they can also figure out likely meanings.

Display well-known quotations from Shakespeare's plays in order to help students make modern paraphrases of Shakespearean English. For example:

- "What's in a name? that which we call a rose by any other name would smell as sweet." *(Who cares what something is called? A rose would still smell sweet if it had a different name.)*

- "Lord, what fools these mortals be." *(Wow! These human beings sure are foolish.)*

- "Neither a borrower, nor a lender be; For loan oft loses both itself and friend." *(Don't borrow or lend money. A loan that's not paid back can end a friendship.)*

PRACTICE AND APPLY

Have students find this famous quotation in the soliloquy they have just read:

I'll break my staff,
Bury it certain fathoms in the earth,
And deeper than did ever plummet sound
I'll drown my book.

Guide students to make a line-by-line paraphrase. *(I'll destroy my magic wand. I'll bury it deep underground. And I'll throw my book of magic spells into the deep sea.)*

English Language Support

Read Closely Discuss the meanings of the following: *staff* (scepter or wand), *fathom* (unit of depth measurement equivalent to six feet), *plummet* (a lead weight on a string, dropped into water to "sound," or measure, the depth). Then provide these sentence frames to guide students' paraphrasing in the Practice and Apply activity.

- I will destroy my _____ and bury it _____. *(magic wand; very deep underground)*

- I will throw my magic book _____. *(into the deep sea)*

Allied with Green

Short Story by Naomi Shihab Nye

Why This Text?

"Allied with Green" is an example of the type of complex text that students are increasingly expected to read and analyze. It is driven mainly by language and imagery rather than plot. Students determine the meaning of the story's figurative language and analyze the author's style and the effects it creates.

▶ **View It!**

Professional Development Podcast:

Text Complexity

Key Learning Objective: The student will be able to determine the theme of a short story and to analyze word choice and style.

RL 1 Cite textual evidence.
RL 2 Determine and analyze theme.
RL 3 Analyze how elements of a story interact.
RL 4 Determine the meanings of words and phrases.
RL 6 Analyze points of view.
W 1 Write arguments.
W 4 Produce clear and coherent writing.
W 10 Write routinely.
SL 1 Engage in collaborative discussions.
L 1b Choose among compound, complex, and compound-complex sentences to signal differing relationships among ideas.
L 4c Consult reference materials to determine pronunciation or clarify meaning.

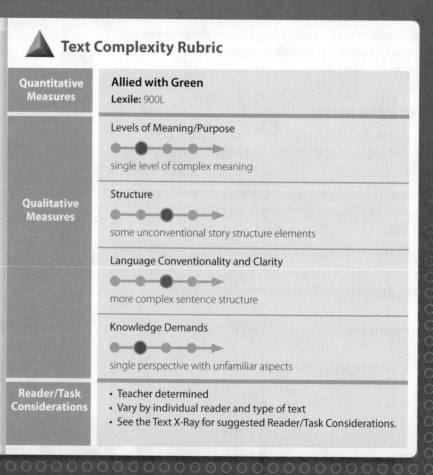

▲ **Text Complexity Rubric**

Quantitative Measures

Allied with Green
Lexile: 900L

Qualitative Measures

Levels of Meaning/Purpose

single level of complex meaning

Structure

some unconventional story structure elements

Language Conventionality and Clarity

more complex sentence structure

Knowledge Demands

single perspective with unfamiliar aspects

Reader/Task Considerations

• Teacher determined
• Vary by individual reader and type of text
• See the Text X-Ray for suggested Reader/Task Considerations.

English Language Support Before teaching, use the Text X-Ray for an overview of the text's complexity. The Text X-Ray and the supports and scaffolds in the Teacher's Edition will help you guide students of different skill levels.

Meaning Making · Effective Expression · Foundational Skills · Content Knowledge · Language Development

Text Complexity: Qualitative Measures

Levels of Meaning/Purpose

single level of complex meaning

Help students determine the meanings of words and phrases.

- Teacher's Edition side notes, pp. 150, 151, 152, 153
- When Students Struggle, p. 150
- Strategies for Annotation, p. 151
- Determine the Meanings of Words and Phrases, p. 153

To teach point of view, see

- Analyze Point of View, p. 156a

▶ *Use It!* **Interactive Whiteboard Lessons:** Point of View; Figurative Language and Imagery

ZOOM IN ON DETERMINING MEANING Explain that **personification**, or giving human characteristics to something inanimate, is a key element of this short story. The author uses this device to express her message to readers.

- Organize students into small groups, assigning each group one of these passages: lines 15–17; lines 34–38; lines 55–58; lines 74–77.
- Have students identify and discuss the examples of personification that appear in their assigned lines. They should answer these questions: *In what way is "green" (plant life) described as being like a person? How might thinking of green as a person change what people do?*
- Have each group share its examples with the class. As a class, discuss the idea that the author emphasizes through all of the examples.

Structure

some unconventional story structure elements

Help students use elements of the short story to determine theme.

- Teacher's Edition side notes, pp. 149, 151, 152, 153
- English Language Support, pp. 149, 152
- Strategies for Annotation, p. 153
- Determine Theme, p. 153

To reteach determining theme, see

- Determine Theme, p. 156a

▶ *Use It!* **Level Up Tutorial:** Theme

ZOOM IN ON DETERMINING THEME Explain that a **theme** is the message about life or human behavior that the author wants to express. Explain that ideas that are repeated or emphasized often point toward the theme. Have students work with a partner to reread the story, noting repeated phrases or images as well as ideas or events that are described in detail. Ask pairs to share their examples. Record the examples on the board and guide students to consider ideas that they have in common to develop a statement of theme.

Language Conventionality and Clarity

more complex sentence structure

Teach unfamiliar vocabulary in context.

- Teacher's Edition Critical Vocabulary notes, pp. 150, 151, 152, 155
- English Language Support, p. 155
- Applying Academic Vocabulary, p. 152
- Strategies for Annotation, p. 155
- Vocabulary Strategy: Using a Glossary, p. 155

Support students' understanding of sentence structure.

- Teacher's Edition side notes, p. 156
- English Language Support, p. 156
- Language Conventions: Sentence Structure, p. 156

ZOOM IN ON **DETERMINING MULTIPLE MEANINGS** Explain that many words have more than one meaning. To understand an author's intended meaning, readers must consider a word's context. Point out *tend* in line 102. Write these definitions for *tend* on the board: *to usually act in a certain way; to move in a certain direction; to take care of; to serve.*

- Have pairs choose the definition closest to the meaning of *tend* in the text and identify nearby words and phrases that helped them determine the definition. (*Tend means "care for or look after." The words* water *and* dig *and the final sentence support this meaning.*)
- Ask pairs why *tend* is "a more important verb than people realize." (*Possible response: For a plant [or person] to grow, it must be tended, which means cared for. Tending is the foundation of relationships.*)

Knowledge Demands

single perspective with unfamiliar aspects

Support English learners in understanding the context of the story.

- Teacher's Edition Author note, p. 149

For more historical background, students can view the video "Greening Lower Manhattan" in their eBooks.

ZOOM IN ON **BUILDING CONTEXT** Develop an understanding of references in the text.

- Point out the footnote on page 149. Explain that *xeriscape* (line 9) comes from the Greek word for "dry," *xeros*. This type of landscaping saves water and reduces use of chemicals. Plants used in xeriscaping thrive in local conditions and so need less "tending."
- Note the reference to Joni Mitchell (line 52). In her song "Big Yellow Taxi," "paradise" is paved over and trees displayed in museums. Its chorus says, "you don't know what you've got till it's gone."

Suggested Reader/Task Considerations

Consider the following before assigning this short story to students.

- Do students have the skill to infer ideas and connections that are not explicitly stated?
- Will students be interested in the topic of this short story?

ZOOM IN ON **SUPPORTING COMPREHENSION**

- Display lines 39–44. Using a Think Aloud, model how to make these inferences: Lucy's father is also a supporter of green; his attitude may have influenced Lucy's.
- Have students share what they know about gardening or farming, discussing what people must do to raise plants. As students read, have them note how Lucy approaches these tasks and think about what theme her attitude expresses.

Naomi Shihab Nye Have students read the information about the author. Point out that Nye is an accomplished poet as well as a writer of fiction, and her background as a poet is evident in the story. Encourage students to pay attention to the author's use of language and images.

SETTING A PURPOSE Direct students to use the Setting a Purpose question to focus their reading. Remind them to also generate their own questions as they read.

Determine Theme
(TITLE; LINES 1–2)

RL 1,
RL 2

Tell students that the **theme** of a story is a message about life or human nature that the author wants to convey. Often, readers must **infer,** or make a good guess about, the theme from evidence in the text. Explain that authors sometimes reveal the theme in the story's title, as well as in the words and actions of characters.

A CITE TEXT EVIDENCE Have students read the title and lines 1–2. Ask what it means to be "allied" and what "allied with green" might suggest about the story's theme. *(To be allied means to be mutually supportive or working together. The title suggests that the character is an ally or supporter of green.)* Ask students to cite evidence in lines 1–2 that supports this inference. *(When asked what she believes in, Lucy writes "the color green.")*

English Language Support

Culturally Responsive Instruction In a class discussion, help students connect to the character's viewpoint.

ASK STUDENTS where Lucy sees green and why those places are significant. What does she believe would happen to the hospital without green? Why? Have small groups discuss the importance of green spaces in their lives and share highlights of their conversations.

Naomi Shihab Nye (b. 1952) *was born to a Palestinian father and an American mother. During her adolescence, she lived in St. Louis, Missouri; Jerusalem; and San Antonio, Texas; and she has traveled extensively as an adult. Influenced by her heritage and the cultural diversity of the places she has known, Nye has written books of poetry as well as fiction for younger audiences.*

A Allied with Green

Short Story by Naomi Shihab Nye

SETTING A PURPOSE As you read, consider the author's use of the word *green*. How is she using the term to describe something that Lucy, the story's main character, feels very strongly about?

F or her paper on "What I Believe In," Lucy writes first "the color green."

That's how everything starts. A tiny shoot of phrase prickling the mind . . .

Then she runs around for a few days doing other things but noticing the green poking up between buildings, on sides of roads, in front of even the poorest homes, how pots of green lined on rickety front porches, hanging baskets of green on light posts downtown, the new meticulous xeriscape[1] beds of 10 puffy green grasses and plants alongside the river, are what seem to keep everything else going. If people could not see

(t) ©Michael Nye; (c) ©Irish_design/Shutterstock

---
[1] **xeriscape** (zîr´ ĭ-skāp´): landscaping that saves water and protects the environment.

English Language Support

Read Closely Display lines 5–13, highlighting each use of *green*.

- Note that in line 10, *green* is an adjective; other times, it is a noun. Ask what the noun *green* means. *(anything that grows)*
- Ask why green "seems to keep everything else going." *(People depend on plants.)* Discuss what this suggests about the theme. *(People should appreciate the green in their lives.)*
- Ask why Nye repeats the word *green*. *(to emphasize the story's focus)* Have groups predict Nye's message about green.

CLOSE READ

Determine the Meanings of Words and Phrases

RL 1, RL 4

(LINES 15–17)

Explain that an author's **style** is his or her manner of writing—*how* something is said rather than *what* is said. Point out that this author's style includes frequent use of **figurative language,** comparisons or expressions that are not literally true. One example of figurative language is **personification,** or the assigning of human traits to animals, objects, or ideas.

B **CITE TEXT EVIDENCE** Ask students to reread lines 15–17 and cite the author's use of personification. *(The author assigns feelings to the color green, for example, "Green has had a terrible summer" and "green has had many second thoughts.")*

Ask how this use of personification reveals the narrator's feelings about plants. *(It shows that the narrator feels close to, or allied with, green (plants), as if she understands their feelings, as someone might understand the feelings of a friend.)*

CRITICAL VOCABULARY

addiction: Lucy was supposed to write a paper about addiction and she wrote about trimming plants.

ASK STUDENTS why Lucy considers trimming plants to be an addiction. *(Lucy feels that she is addicted to plants, or "green," because she loves plants and feels we are all dependent on them, the way an addict is dependent on a substance.)*

median: The author says that Lucy's father plants trees on medians as an apology.

ASK STUDENTS to explain what he is apologizing for and why he chooses medians for his planting. *(He is apologizing for driving on the highway every day. Since the median runs down the middle of the highway, he is trying to at least make the space a bit more beautiful.)*

green from the windows of the hospital, the hospital might fall down. She believes this.

Once she starts making a list, it will not stop.

Green has had a terrible summer. Threatened by the longest drought and highest heat in recorded history, green has had many second thoughts. **B**

Lucy's family could only water with a sprinkler on Wednesday evenings between eight and ten. When she and 20 her mom wash lettuce, blueberries, peaches, they carry the plastic tubs of fruit water outside to pour onto a plant. It's ritual now. It's holy water. The city had a water waster hotline. It made the national news. You could turn people in for excessive watering.

Last semester, when asked to write a paper on **addictions,** Lucy wrote about trimming and got a C. Her teacher scrawled across the top of the paper, "What is this?" But Lucy often feels happiest with pruning shears in her hand, heading toward an overgrown jasmine vine.

30 It's a clear task, trimming. The longer you've done it, the more you know how it encourages green, in the long run. Also, you can have fine ideas while trimming. Queen's crown, germander, plumbago. *Snip, snip, snip.*

She knew it had been mentioned before, but thought she ought to include how cities assault their green for two reasons: money and greed. Later, feeling remorseful, or sickened by the new view, they name everything for green—Oak Meadows, Lone Pine. You could find it almost anywhere now.

Lucy's father demonstrated against developments when he 40 was in college. She had a faded black and white picture of him holding a NO! sign, his hair bushy and wild. Highways slashing through green space—he now drives one of those highways almost every day, feeling guilty. He plants free trees in scrappy **medians,** as an apology. Sometimes people steal them. When he planted four little palms in pots as a gift to Freddy's Mexican Restaurant, they got plucked from the soil overnight. Obviously some people were desperate for green. And surely, with all the population issues now, some developments were necessary, but look at what happened 50 before you knew it—hills sheared, meadows plucked, fields erased, the world turns into an endless series of strip centers— yo, Joni Mitchell! Joni sang about parking lots when the world

addiction
(ə-dĭk´shən) *n.* An *addiction* is a habit one is dependent on.

median
(mē´dē-ən) *n.* A *median* is a dividing area between opposing lanes of traffic on a highway or road.

WHEN STUDENTS STRUGGLE . . .

Explain that figurative language is key in this story. Have students use a chart like the one below to track the use of figurative language and analyze its meaning in lines 11–13. Have them continue filling in the chart as they read.

Expression	Meaning	Purpose
"the hospital might fall down"	The view of green plants keeps patients' spirits up.	to show the importance of plants in people's lives

 LEVEL UP TUTORIALS For additional support, assign the following *Level Up* tutorial: **Figurative Language**

had probably half the number it has now. Her dad told her that. She likes Joni Mitchell.

The boulevard wakes up when a strip of green is planted down its center.

The sad room smiles again when a pot of green is placed on a white tablecloth.

No one goes to Seattle to see the concrete.

An exhausted kid says, I'm going outside—sick of her mother's voice, she knows she will feel better with bamboo.

In Dallas people run around the lake or refresh themselves at the **arboretum**.

San Antonians send their kids to summer digging classes at the botanical gardens. The kids come home with broccoli. After a while.

Patience is deeply involved with green.

It's required.

So, why don't people respect green as much as they should?

This was the serious question growing small fronds and tendrils at the heart of Lucy's paper. She knew her teacher might turn a snide nose up at it. Oh, blah blah, isn't this rather a repeat of what you wrote last semester?

People took green for granted. They assumed it would always be skirting their ugly office buildings and residences

arboretum
(är´bə-rē´təm) *n.*
An *arboretum* is a place where many trees are grown for educational or viewing purposes.

CLOSE READ

Determine Theme
RL 1, RL 2

(LINES 59–66)

Tell students they can infer a story's theme by analyzing statements made by a narrator or character.

C **CITE TEXT EVIDENCE** Have students reread lines 59–66, cite examples that reveal theme, and ask how they reveal theme. *("No one goes to Seattle to see the concrete." "An exhausted kid . . . will feel better with bamboo." People "refresh themselves at the arboretum." They show people need green, so it must be protected.)*

Determine the Meanings of Words and Phrases
RL 2, RL 4

(LINES 69–71)

Remind students that the author includes figurative language, which she uses to develop the theme.

D **ASK STUDENTS** to reread lines 69–71 and identify the figurative expression. Ask what comparison it makes and how this supports the theme. *(The phrase "the serious question growing small fronds and tendrils" compares Lucy's question to a plant. It supports the theme by reinforcing her belief in the value of plants.)*

> **CRITICAL VOCABULARY**

arboretum: The author says that in Dallas people refresh themselves in the arboretum.

ASK STUDENTS why an arboretum is refreshing. *(An arboretum provides a sanctuary from city life.)*

Strategies for Annotation

Determine the Meanings of Words and Phrases
RL 4

Have students reread lines 69–71 and use their eBook annotation tools to do the following:

- Underline the example of figurative language.
- Use two different colors (yellow and green) to highlight the two things being compared.
- In a note, explain the meaning of the comparison.

So, why don't people respect green as much as they should?

This was the serious question growing small fronds and tendrils at the heart of Lucy's paper.

The question is compared to a plant—"growing small fronds and tendrils."

CLOSE READ

For more context and historical background, students can view the video "Greening Lower Manhattan" in their eBooks.

Determine the Meanings of Words and Phrases

RL 2, RL 4

(LINES 98–105)

Point out that the story concludes with a final figurative expression that also sums up the theme.

Ⓔ ASK STUDENTS to reread lines 98–105 and explain what the author means by "carry a bucket" in line 105. *(to tend and care for green plants)* Ask how this supports the story's theme. *(It suggests that we all must do our part to protect this valuable resource.)*

> #### CRITICAL VOCABULARY
>
> **obituary:** The author tells us that Lucy clipped Robert Isabell's obituary, or death notice, from the newspaper and kept it on her desk.
>
> **ASK STUDENTS** what Lucy might have learned from Isabell's obituary and why she kept it on her desk. *(She might have learned important facts about his life and accomplishments. She kept it because she admired him and felt inspired by him.)*

COLLABORATIVE DISCUSSION Have small groups of students discuss the author's use of the word *green.* Encourage them to write notes as they talk. Then have each group share their ideas with the class and discuss others' reactions to the author's word choice.

ASK STUDENTS to share any questions they generated in the course of reading and discussing the selection.

English Language Support

Listen Actively Remind students to listen actively, think about what the other person says, and ask clarifying questions. Provide these sentence stems:

- What do you mean when you say____?
- Can you give me an example of ____?
- Why do you think that _____?
- Can you say more about ____?

---

and so they didn't give it the attention it deserved. Somewhat like air. Air and green, close cousins.

Lucy truly loved the words *pocket park.*[2]

80 She loved community gardeners with purple bandannas tied around their heads. She loved their wild projects— rosemary grown so big you could hide in it.

She loved roofs paved with grass.

She loved the man in New York City—Robert Isabell— who planted pink impatiens on the metal overhang of his building. He had started out as a florist, at seventeen, in Minnesota—green state in the summer, not so green in December. Then he moved to New York City and became a major party planner, incorporating flowers, lighting, tents, fabrics, to create magical worlds of festivity. He didn't attend

90 his own parties. He disappeared once he got everything set up. Sometimes he hid behind a giant potted plant to see what people liked. Lucy found his **obituary** in the newspaper, clipped it out, and placed it on her desk. She wished she could have worked for him just to learn how he put flowers together on tables, how he clipped giant green stalks and placed them effectively around a tent to make Morocco, Italy, the French Riviera. Transporting. Green could take you away.

Ⓔ Save you. But you had to care for it, stroke it, devote yourself to it, pray to it, organize crews for it, bow down to it.

100 You had to say the simple holy prayer, rearranging the words any way you liked best—"Dig, Grow, Deep, Roots, Light, Air, Water, Tend."

Tend was a more important verb than most people realized.

You had to carry a bucket.

obituary
(ō-bĭch´ōō-ĕr´ē) *n.* An *obituary* is a public notice of a death.

COLLABORATIVE DISCUSSION What is unusual about the author's use of the word *green,* and why does she use it that way? Talk about your ideas with other group members.

---
[2] **pocket park:** a small park accessible to the general public.

APPLYING ACADEMIC VOCABULARY

affect	ensure

THINK-PAIR-SHARE Have pairs discuss the questions below. Encourage them to include the academic vocabulary words *affect* and *ensure.* Ask volunteers to share their responses with the class.

- How do the imagery and figurative language in the story **affect** your understanding of its theme?
- Why is it important for the main character to **ensure** that green plants are valued and protected?

Determine Theme

RL 2

In short stories like "Allied with Green," authors often use the characters to share a theme with the reader. A **theme** is a message about life or human nature. In works of fiction, themes are the "big ideas" that readers infer based on evidence from the text. The following statements are examples of themes that might be found in short stories:

- A person can gain more by giving than by taking.
- We may not appreciate what we have until it is gone.

Often the theme of a story is not stated directly. It's usually implied. You have to analyze the text to see what it reveals about the theme. To determine the theme, it is helpful to

- look at the title to see if it contains a significant idea
- analyze the characters' words and actions, especially how characters change
- evaluate whether the setting has special meaning to a character
- look for important statements by the narrator or a character

Determine the Meanings of Words and Phrases

RL 4

An author's **style** is his or her manner of writing—*how* something is said rather than *what* is said—and it often corresponds to the genre of the writing. Style can be described with words such as *formal, journalistic, literary, flowery,* and *plain.*

Readers can analyze an author's style by making observations about the author's word choice and descriptive details, among other elements. An author may use **imagery**—words and phrases that appeal to the senses—to help readers imagine how things look, feel, smell, sound, and taste.

An author's style may also include **figurative language,** comparisons and expressions that are not literally true but give meaning in imaginative ways. One form of figurative language is **personification,** the giving of human qualities to animals, objects, or ideas. The author of "Allied with Green" uses personification to give human qualities to the color green and other objects.

Review "Allied with Green." How would you describe the style in which it's written?

Allied with Green **153**

TEACH

CLOSE READ

Determine Theme

RL 2

Review that theme is a message about human nature or life. Discuss the list of tips and then have students review the story and cite examples for each tip.

- **Title:** *The title suggests that a character in the story is an ally, or supporter, of green.*
- **Character's words and actions:** *"For her paper on 'What I Believe In,' Lucy writes first 'the color green.'"* (lines 1–2)
- **Setting:** *The importance of the setting is shown in the way Lucy notices green wherever she goes (lines 5–11) and in how much pleasure she gets from tending her plants. (lines 30–33)*
- **Important statements by narrator:** *"You had to carry a bucket." (line 105)*

Discuss what the examples suggest about the theme. *(The theme has to do with Lucy's belief in the value of green, growing plants and her love of tending them.)*

Determine the Meanings of Words and Phrases

RL 4

Review that style is an author's manner of writing and that an author's word choice can help readers analyze the style of a work. Review the definitions of imagery, figurative language, and personification. Discuss what Naomi Shihab Nye's frequent use of these elements reveals about her style. *(Her style can be described as literary or poetic.)*

Strategies for Annotation   🖉 📖 *Annotate it!*

Determine Theme

RL 2

Have students review the story and use their eBook annotation tools to do the following:

- Highlight in yellow a character's words and actions that support the theme.
- Highlight in green important statements by the narrator.
- In a note, draw conclusions about the theme based on this evidence.

For her paper on "What I Believe In," Lucy writes first "the color green."

That's how everything starts. A tiny shoot of phrase prickling the mind . . .

Then she runs around for a few days doing other things

Lucy sees, thinks about, and interacts with plants. It is central to her life, to all life.

PRACTICE & APPLY

Analyzing the Text

RL 1, RL 2, RL 3, RL 4, RL 6

Possible answers:

1. *The phrase means "a few words that are the start of an idea for a school paper." A tiny shoot, the beginning of a green plant, is compared to the beginning of an idea. The phrase "the color green" is what "prickles" Lucy's mind.*

2. *It shows that Lucy is a sensitive, perceptive person who cares very much about the importance of green plants.*

3. *Nye compares water used to wash fruit and reused to water plants to holy water in a religious service. The water is precious and used in a kind of ritual to keep plants alive.*

4. *Her teacher, who didn't appreciate Lucy's previous paper on trimming plants, is likely to "turn a snide nose up at" this one and say that Lucy hasn't come up with new ideas.*

5. *The narrator is making the point that development is a destructive force ("cities assault their green"; "Highways slashing through green space"; "hills sheared, meadows plucked, fields erased"). She is also making the point that people are often ambiguous about preserving green spaces—cities develop for greed and money, then people feel remorseful. Even Lucy's father feels a bit guilty about his lack of 100% commitment.*

6. *Plants give life even to inanimate things, like a boulevard and a room.*

7. ***Imagery:*** *"a faded black and white picture . . . his hair bushy and wild";* ***Figurative Language:*** *"It's holy water"; "You had to carry a bucket."* ***Personification:*** *"Green has had a terrible summer"; "green has had many second thoughts"; "The sad room smiles."*

8. *People must respect and care for green plants of all kinds because "green" refreshes and sustains human life.*

FOR STANDARD ENGLISH LEARNERS

Remind students that words such as *never, nothing, not, no, hardly, scarcely,* and *barely* should not appear together in the same sentence. Have them correct these examples of double negatives and watch for similar errors in their essays.

- We don't have no green in our neighborhood. *(We don't have any green in our neighborhood.* or *We have no green in our neighborhood.)*
- The park hasn't barely any grass. *(The park has barely any grass.* or *The park hasn't any grass.)*
- There isn't nothing more peaceful than a garden. *(There is nothing more peaceful than a garden.* or *There isn't anything more peaceful than a garden.)*

Analyzing the Text

RL 1, RL 2, RL 3, RL 4, RL 6, W 1, W 4, W 10

Cite Text Evidence   Support your responses with evidence from the text.

1. **Interpret** In lines 3–4, the author uses the phrase "a tiny shoot of phrase prickling the mind" to describe how everything starts. What does the phrase mean?

2. **Infer** Once Lucy decides on the topic for her school assignment, she can't help but notice the green around her. What does this tell you about her character and how she feels about her topic?

3. **Interpret** Reread lines 18–22 to find what the narrator compares to holy water. What does that comparison suggest?

4. **Predict** Lucy chooses to write about the color green for her school assignment. Based on her teacher's reaction to her paper from last semester, what will her teacher's reaction to this topic probably be?

5. **Draw Conclusions** Reread lines 34–51. What point is the narrator making about developments?

6. **Analyze** What does the personification in lines 55–58 help the reader understand?

7. **Analyze** Use a chart like this one to list examples of imagery, figurative language, and personification that contribute to Naomi Shihab Nye's style.

Elements	Examples
Imagery	
Figurative Language	
Personification	

8. **Draw Conclusions** What is the theme of this story?

PERFORMANCE TASK

Writing Activity: Argument Look back through "Allied with Green" to take notes on the points Lucy makes in favor of green. Adapt those ideas to develop a three- to four-paragraph argument in support of or against her position.

- Introduce your opinion.
- Specify support for your opinion with reasons and examples.
- Acknowledge a possible argument from an opponent and refute it.
- Conclude with a statement that summarizes your opinion and ties your ideas together.

Assign this performance task.

PERFORMANCE TASK

W 1, W 4, W 10, SL 1

Writing Activity: Argument Have individual students take notes and decide their position. Review the steps for writing an argument, emphasizing the need to support claims with clear reasons and evidence. Have pairs review each other's drafts and offer suggestions for revision, paying attention to the organization of the draft. Then, have pairs with opposing views take turns reading aloud their essays, followed by a group discussion about the issues.

Critical Vocabulary

addiction   median   arboretum   obituary

Practice and Apply Answer each question with *yes* or *no*. With your group, use examples and reasons to explain your answer.

1. Could someone have an **addiction** to chocolate? Why or why not?

2. Could a single-lane road have a **median?** Why or why not?

3. Is an **arboretum** like a garden? Why or why not?

4. Is an **obituary** like a biography? Why or why not?

Vocabulary Strategy: Using a Glossary

A **glossary** is a list of specialized terms and their definitions. A glossary can exist on its own, or it can be part of a larger text. A text may have more than one glossary if it refers to multiple types of specialized terms that a reader is not assumed to know. Here are more useful details about glossaries.

- When a printed book contains a glossary, words are listed in the back of the book in alphabetical order.
- A digital, or electronic, glossary allows readers to click on a word in the text to see its definition and hear its pronunciation.
- A glossary may contain information about a word's pronunciation and part of speech.

Notice the parts of this glossary entry for the word *median*.

median (mēˊdē-ən) *n.* A *median* is a dividing area between opposing lanes of traffic on a highway or road.

Practice and Apply This literature program contains multiple glossaries. Use the table of contents and the glossaries to answer the following questions.

1. In which glossary would you expect to find a listing for the Critical Vocabulary words that are highlighted in each selection?

2. Which glossary would you use to learn definitions for the literary terms that are used in the instruction?

3. According to the glossary, what is the part of speech for the word *obituary*?

PRACTICE & APPLY

Critical Vocabulary

Possible answers:

1. *Yes, because the word* addiction *can be used generally, as well as to name a medical condition.*

2. *No, a median runs through the center of a road; it can't run through a single lane.*

3. *Yes, an arboretum is like a garden because plants are on display in both; in an arboretum, the plants are trees.*

4. *Yes, an obituary tells about the life of a person, giving biographical information about someone who has just died.*

Vocabulary Strategy: Using a Glossary

Answers:

1. *Glossary of Critical Vocabulary*

2. *Glossary of Literary and Informational Terms*

3. *noun*

English Language Support

Exchange Information and Ideas Have students answer both sets of Practice and Apply questions with a partner. Have them join small groups to compare their answers before sharing them with the class.

Strategies for Annotation   ✎ 🗐 *Annotate it!*

Using a Glossary

Have students locate the entry for *median* in the Glossary of Critical Vocabulary. Encourage them to use their eBook annotation tools to do the following:

- Highlight the entry word in yellow.
- Highlight the pronunciation in blue.
- Highlight the part of speech in green.
- Underline the definition.
- In a note, use the word in a sentence that illustrates its meaning.

median (mēˊdē-ən) *n.* A **median** is a dividing area between opposing lanes of traffic on a highway or road.

After the accident, one car had stopped on the median.

Language Conventions: Sentence Structure

L 1b

- Review the definitions of **compound sentence** and **coordinating conjunction,** and use the first chart to discuss the two ways to join independent clauses to form a compound sentence.
- Review the definitions of **complex sentence** and **subordinating conjunction.** Use the second chart to discuss how to join an independent clause and a subordinate clause to form a complex sentence.
- Then review the definition of a **compound-complex sentence** and the two examples.

Possible answers:

1. *Compound sentence: He planted four little palms in pots, but they were stolen. Compound-complex sentence: He planted four little palms in pots, but they were stolen because people were desperate for green.*

2. *Compound sentence: A pot of green is placed on a white tablecloth, and a sad room seems to smile. Compound-complex sentence: When a pot of green is placed on a white tablecloth, a sad room seems to smile, and everyone feels welcome.*

Assess It Online!

Online Selection Test
- Download an editable ExamView bank.
- Assign and manage this test online.

Language Conventions: Sentence Structure

L 1b

When you combine two independent clauses, you make a **compound sentence.** There are two basic ways to combine clauses to make a compound sentence: (1) with a **coordinating conjunction,** such as *and, but,* and *or;* (2) with a semicolon.

Independent Clauses	Urban parks are calm places. City dwellers need them.
Compound Sentence	Urban parks are calm places, and city dwellers need them.
Independent Clauses	The color green suggests life. People are drawn to green.
Compound Sentence	The color green suggests life; people are drawn to green.

When you combine a subordinate clause with an independent clause, you make a **complex sentence.** A subordinate clause begins with a **subordinating conjunction,** such as *after, although, as, because, before, even though, if, since, so that, though, unless, until, when, where,* and *while.*

Independent Clause	Gardens give many rewards.
Subordinate Clause	although gardening requires patience
Complex Sentence	Although gardening requires patience, gardens give many rewards.

A **compound-complex sentence** combines two or more independent clauses and one or more subordinate clauses. Note the three clauses in each example:

> When trees grow on city sidewalks, people must take care of them, or the trees will fail to thrive.

> People love the pocket park because it was green and quiet; they found peace there.

Practice and Apply The following independent clauses are taken from "Allied with Green." For each independent clause, add more clauses to make a compound sentence and a compound-complex sentence. Then explain how each sentence type signals a different relationship between ideas.

1. He planted four little palms in pots.

2. A pot of green is placed on a white tablecloth.

English Language Support

Connect Ideas Explain that the sentence structures described above convey ideas accurately by showing the relationship that connects them.

- Display the following: *1. Soon they were bigger than the pots. 2. It cheers up the whole room.* Work with students to create two compound sentences by combining these independent clauses with the Practice and Apply sentences and a conjunction. *(Sample response: A pot of green is placed on a white tablecloth, and it cheers up the whole room.)*

- Display these sentences: *Plants add oxygen to our air. Plants bring color into our lives. They bloom in the spring and summer.* Have pairs combine two clauses to form compound and complex sentences, and all three to form a compound-complex sentence. *(Plants add oxygen to our air, and they bring color into our lives. Plants bring color into our lives when they bloom. . . . Plants add oxygen to our air, and they bring color into our lives when they bloom. . . .)*

- Have pairs write and share three sentences about the story: one compound, one complex, and one compound-complex.

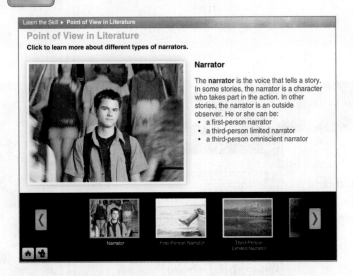

INTERACTIVE WHITEBOARD LESSON
Analyze Point of View

RL 3,
RL 6

TEACH

Tell students that **point of view** is the vantage point from which a story is told. The writer's choice of a **narrator,** or the voice that tells the story, determines the point of view. When a story is told from the **first-person point of view,** the narrator is a character in the story and uses first-person pronouns. In a story told from the **third-person point of view,** the narrator is not a character and uses third-person pronouns.

Share and discuss these steps for analyzing point of view:

Step 1: Look at the Pronouns Does the narrator use first-person or third-person pronouns?

Step 2: Identify the Narrator Is the narrator an outside observer, or a character in the story?

Step 3: Analyze the Effects What do I learn about the narrator? What do I learn from the narrator about events and other characters? What is this narrator unable to tell me?

COLLABORATIVE DISCUSSION

Have students work in pairs to use the three steps above to analyze the point of view of "Allied with Green." Suggest that students pay particular attention to what we learn about Lucy from the narrator. Ask: What does the narrator want us to think about Lucy? Suggest that students take notes during the discussion, and have each pair share their analysis with the class. *(The narrator uses third-person pronouns, so the point of view is third person. The narrator uses beautiful imagery, descriptions of "green," and Lucy's feelings about "green," suggesting that the narrator shares Lucy's point of view.)*

Determine Theme

RL 2

RETEACH

Review with students that a **theme** is a big idea about life that the author of a story wants to convey. Emphasize that the theme is not the same as what the story is about. For example:

- "Allied with Green" is about a girl who is writing a paper on the importance of green.
- The theme of "Allied with Green" can be stated as *People must respect and care for green plants because "green" refreshes and sustains human life.*

Tell students that the theme of a story is often not stated and must be figured out from evidence in the story, such as the characters' words and actions and what the narrator tells us.

Read aloud each of the following lines from "Allied with Green." Discuss with students what each line reveals about the theme.

- "No one goes to Seattle to see the concrete." (Line 59)
- "So, why don't people respect green as much as they should?" (Line 69)
- ". . . Green could take you away. Save you. But you had to care for it, stroke it, devote yourself to it . . ." (Lines 97–99)

 LEVEL UP TUTORIALS Assign the following *Level Up* tutorial: **Theme**

INDEPENDENT READING

Students can apply the skill to another short story of their own choosing. Have students work independently to identify ways in which the author reveals the theme. Suggest that students take notes to record evidence that helps them infer the theme.

Big Rocks' Balancing Acts

Expository Essay by Douglas Fox

Why This Text?

This essay takes an interesting approach to presenting complex technical concepts through the words and experiences of real scientists who are studying them. As they analyze the text, students will learn to understand how it is organized and to use organizational patterns to support comprehension.

Key Learning Objective: The student will be able to analyze elements of an expository essay and its structure.

For practice and application:

The Hidden Southwest:
The Arch Hunters
Essay by James Vlahos

Close Reader selection
"The Hidden Southwest: The Arch Hunters"
Informational Text by James Vlahos

RI 1   Cite textual evidence.
RI 2   Determine central ideas; provide an objective summary.
RI 3   Analyze the interactions in a text.
RI 4   Determine meanings of words and phrases.
RI 5   Analyze the structure an author uses to organize a text.
RI 6   Determine an author's purpose.
W 7   Conduct short research projects.
SL 4   Present claims and findings in a focused, coherent manner.
L 1a   Explain the function of phrases.
L 4b   Use Latin affixes and roots.
L 6   Acquire and use general academic and domain-specific words.

▲ Text Complexity Rubric

Quantitative Measures	**Big Rocks' Balancing Acts** **Lexile:** 1060L
Qualitative Measures	**Levels of Meaning/Purpose** single purpose and topic
	Structure more than one text structure; organization is complex but mostly explicit
	Language Conventionality and Clarity some unfamiliar academic and domain-specific words
	Knowledge Demands somewhat complex science concepts
Reader/Task Considerations	• Teacher determined • Vary by individual reader and type of text • See the Text X-Ray for suggested Reader/Task Considerations.

English Language Support

Before teaching, use the Text X-Ray for an overview of the text's complexity. The Text X-Ray and the supports and scaffolds in the Teacher's Edition will help you guide students of different skill levels.

Meaning Making · Language Development · Effective Expression · Content Knowledge · Foundational Skills

Text Complexity: Qualitative Measures

Levels of Meaning/Purpose

single purpose and topic

Help students identify central ideas in an expository essay.

- Teacher's Edition side notes, pp. 157, 162, 163, 165
- When Students Struggle, p. 158
- Analyze Structure: Essay, p. 165

To teach distinguishing between facts and opinions, see

- Analyze Texts: Fact and Opinion, p. 168a

 Use It! **Interactive Whiteboard Lesson:** Main/Central Idea and Details

ZOOM IN ON **IDENTIFYING CENTRAL IDEAS** Explain that finding the **central idea** of a text is key to understanding it. Display and read lines 88–108. Have pairs discuss the central idea using these sentence frames:

- In this section, the author explains _____. *(how balanced rocks were created)*
- Important details include _____ and _____. *(the rocks couldn't have rolled from anywhere; water destroys weaker rock, leaving the strong rock behind; the Mojave Desert was once covered in lakes; the rocks have been there for 15 to 20 thousand years)*
- The central idea of this section is _____. *(that water carved these rocks, which means they have been there for a very long time)*

Structure

more than one text structure; organization is complex but mostly explicit

Help students analyze the structure of an expository essay.

- Teacher's Edition side notes, pp. 157, 158, 159, 160, 161, 162, 163, 164, 165
- English Language Support, pp. 158, 159, 164
- Strategies for Annotation, pp. 162, 165
- Analyze Structure: Essay, p. 165

To reteach analyzing an essay, see

- Analyze Structure: Essay, p. 168a

 Use It! **Level Up Tutorials:** Chronological Order; Cause-and-Effect Organization; Comparison-Contrast Organization

ZOOM IN ON **ANALYZING STRUCTURE** Review the signal words for each pattern of organization on page 165. Explain that an author may use more than one **organizational structure** to convey relationships among ideas, events, or objects.

- Display lines 69–87. Ask students to identify two organizational patterns in the passage and find two signal words for each pattern. *(Chronological order signal words:* earlier this year, now, now and then, several minutes later; *spatial order signal words:* away from, end of, above, on top of.)*
- Have small groups discuss how each organizational pattern helps communicate important ideas. Ask volunteers to share responses.

Language Conventionality and Clarity

some unfamiliar academic and domain-specific words

Teach unfamiliar vocabulary in context.

- Teacher's Edition Critical Vocabulary notes, pp. 160, 161, 163, 167
- English Language Support, p. 167
- Applying Academic Vocabulary, p. 161
- Vocabulary Strategy: Latin Roots, p. 167

Support students' reading and discussion of the selection.

- Teacher's Edition side note, p. 164
- English Language Support, pp. 163, 166

Help students understand prepositional phrases.

- Teacher's Edition side note, p. 168
- Strategies for Annotation, p. 168
- Language Conventions: Prepositional Phrases, p. 168

ZOOM IN ON **UNPACKING SENTENCES** Explain that a prepositional phrase is a group of words that adds details by using a preposition (such as *near, by,* or *at*) and a noun. Provide several examples of prepositional phrases, pointing out the preposition in each. Then display this sentence and ask volunteers to underline the prepositional phrases and circle or highlight each preposition.

> "Unlike a lot of the other balanced rocks they've seen, this one is on the side of a small mountain, in a place where it could have landed after rolling from somewhere higher up." (lines 113–115)

To check for understanding, ask:

- Where is this balanced rock located?
- Why is it different from others?

Knowledge Demands

somewhat complex science concepts

Support English learners in understanding the scientific context of the essay.

- Teacher's Edition Author note, p. 157
- Content-Area Connection, p. 160
- Performance Task, p. 166

ZOOM IN ON **BUILDING SCIENTIFIC CONTEXT** Note the scientific use of metric measurements in lines 35, 36, 117, and 165. Because the metric system is the primary measurement system outside the United States, ask students familiar with it to compare or estimate the sizes and distances noted in these lines:

- Lines 35–36: The rocks may be as tall as 15 feet and weigh more than 30,000 pounds.
- Line 117: The rock has moved only about an inch.
- Line 165: A 3-kilometer shift would be nearly 2 miles.

Suggested Reader/Task Considerations

Consider the following before assigning this essay to students.

- Can students make connections between what they learn in this selection and their studies in other classes?
- Do students need support to complete the Performance Task?

ZOOM IN ON **SUPPORTING COMPREHENSION**

- This essay may tie into students' earth science curriculum. If so, ask what they know about rocks before the class reads the essay. After reading, have students discuss what information from the essay might apply in their science class.
- Emphasize that summary presentations should include only the most important ideas about the topic. Meet with students individually to help them organize and express their ideas before presenting.

Douglas Fox Have students read the information about the author. Tell students that James Brune, the geologist mentioned in the essay, published an article in the journal *American Scientist* in 2007 titled "Gauging Earthquake Hazards with Precariously Balanced Rocks."

SETTING A PURPOSE Direct students to use the Setting a Purpose prompt to focus their reading. Remind them to write questions they have while reading.

Analyze Structure: Essay
RI 3, RI 5
(LINES 1–2)

Explain that this selection is an **expository essay,** a short work of nonfiction that presents or explains information and ideas. Point out that all writers, whether they are writing fiction or nonfiction, want to grab readers' interest at the beginning. Direct students to lines 1–2.

A **ASK STUDENTS** what image the first sentence creates in their minds. Talk about why the author chose to begin the article in this way. *(The sentence describes a person leaning out of a flying airplane taking photos. The image is both a little startling and intriguing. It makes readers wonder what taking pictures from airplanes has to do with rocks.)*

Analyze Language
RI 1, RI 4
(LINES 12–15)

Call attention to the words in quotation marks. Explain that these words are not dialogue, as in a story. In expository text, a **quotation** relates a real person's exact words. Note that the bracketed words were added by the author for clarity.

B **CITE TEXT EVIDENCE** Have students cite Richard Brune's exact words and tell what effect the quotation has on the text. *(The speaker's exact words are, "It's not that bad. From 1,000 feet you've probably got at least nine or 10 seconds before you really have to pull the rip cord." The quotation gives the text a personal "eyewitness" feel. It also gives the reader an idea of what Brune is like.)*

Douglas Fox *is a science, environmental, and technology writer who lives in northern California. His pursuit of science stories has led him to many exotic places, including Australia, Mauritius, Papua New Guinea, and Antarctica. In addition to writing, Fox sometimes takes photos for his stories, which have appeared in many scientific journals, magazines, and books.*

Big Rocks' Balancing Acts

Expository Essay by Douglas Fox

©John Hoffman/Shutterstock; Text: Reprinted with permission from the Oct. 19, 2011, Science News for Kids.

SETTING A PURPOSE In this article, you'll get familiar with a curiosity in nature. As you read, think about what makes these rock formations so unique and what people can learn from them. Write down any questions you have while reading.

Richard Brune was pretty dizzy the first time he shot photos while leaning out of a flying airplane.

The plane's door had been removed so Brune could ride with one leg outside. As the tiny propeller plane zigzagged over the desert, Brune leaned out over empty air. The 80 mile-per-hour headwind pummeled his face. He looked through his camera and snapped pictures of the rocky desert hundreds of feet below.

10   He got woozy after a few seconds, unsure which way was up. He learned to avoid that feeling by keeping his eyes on the shifting, slanting horizon whenever he could. And just in case he tumbled out of the plane, he wore a parachute. "It's not that bad," says Brune, who has done plenty of skydiving. "From 1,000 feet you've probably got at least nine or 10 seconds [of falling] before you really have to pull the rip cord."

Big Rocks' Balancing Acts **157**

FOR STUDENTS WITH DISABILITIES

To ensure that students with cognitive disabilities can successfully comprehend this scientific text, use one or more of these strategies:

- Preview the selection, using a Think Aloud strategy to predict what readers will learn based on each of the headings and other text features.
- Summarize key ideas in each section before students read it.
- Provide one or two questions for each section that will help students focus on and identify important ideas.
- Have students listen to the audio text as they follow along in their books.

Analyze Structure: Text Features

RI 5

(PHOTO AND CAPTION; HEADING)

Tell students that photographs and captions are **text features,** elements that help organize or call attention to important information. Photographs and captions can clarify or add to the information in the text.

 ASK STUDENTS how the photograph and caption contribute to the text. *(The photograph gives a good visual example of a balanced rock and what little support it has. The caption tells how long the rock has been in that spot.)*

Point out the **heading** and tell students that this is another text feature that authors use to help organize information. A heading helps readers understand what the section is about.

ASK STUDENTS what they expect to read about in this section, based on the heading. *(The section will probably explain something about Richard Brune's "odd hobby" of photographing balanced rocks.)*

English Language Support

Explain that each heading introduces a main idea related to the topic of the essay and that the text following the heading will develop that idea. Tell students that rewording the heading as a question will help them to focus on the most important details in that part of the text.

- Have students work with a partner to write the heading as a question. *(Possible responses: What is the odd hobby? What is odd about this hobby?)*

- As students read this passage, remind them to look for answers to their questions.

It is estimated this balanced rock has occupied this spot in the Mojave Desert for 15,000 to 20,000 years.

Brune wasn't flying over the desert in southern California to be a daredevil. He was taking pictures of balanced rocks. Big, balanced rocks. Really awkward ones. The kind of rock that looks like it would tip over, roll down a hill and flatten a
20 car if someone were silly enough to lean against it.

ODD HOBBY

Richard and his dad, James Brune, have a passion for balanced rocks. James is a geologist, someone who studies the history and movement of the Earth as recorded in rocks, at the University of Nevada in Reno. He has spent 20 years looking for balanced rocks across the deserts of Nevada and California.

Richard, his son, isn't officially a scientist, but he is good with airplanes, parachutes, cameras, computers—all kinds of gadgets. When he was younger, he would camp in the
30 desert while his dad did scientific work there. Richard, now 46, has helped his dad study balanced rocks for 15 years, photographing them from the air and then hiking into the desert with his dad to find them.

"We've found literally thousands of these rocks," says James. Some of them stand up to 5 meters tall and weigh 15,000 kilograms—real car crushers!

©Douglas Fox

WHEN STUDENTS STRUGGLE . . .

To guide students' comprehension, have them work in pairs to fill out a chart, like the one to the right, for each section of the text. Tell students to pause after they read each section and ask themselves, "What is this section mostly about?" Have students reread the text if they need to, and restate the important ideas in their own words.

 LEVEL UP TUTORIALS For additional support, assign the following *Level Up* tutorial: **Main Idea and Supporting Details**

It sounds like an odd hobby, but James, the geologist, is serious about these rocks. He has also studied earthquakes for many years, and he believes that balanced rocks can tell us something important about earthquakes.

STANDING STRONG

An earthquake's tremors can topple balanced rocks. So if you look at these rocks across California, you should find clues about where sizable earthquakes have happened.

In places that haven't experienced large earthquakes, you should find really delicate rocks—ones you could tip over with a finger. But in places that have seen more serious quakes, the only rocks left standing in the balance should be those that are far harder to tip over.

Geologists find these rocks so interesting because they could give clues about the severity of earthquakes over thousands of years. In parts of California, records collected by scientists go back only about 150 years. Historical data on tremor intensities are important when determining how strong a bridge or dam needs to be to survive earthquakes.

HOW OLD IS OLD?

All of this depends, of course, on finding out how long the balanced rocks have been standing.

It's a basic question, really: How quickly does the land change? Maybe you've wondered it yourself. Have you ever walked down a path, kicked a rock and wondered how long that rock had stood there before you knocked it down the hill? Maybe it was there for one year. Maybe 100 years. Perhaps even 10,000 years.

Or maybe you sat on a boulder and wondered who else had sat there. Was the boulder there when the first pioneers rolled their wagons by 200 years ago? Or maybe even when the very first humans arrived in North America 15,000 years ago?

Believe it or not, scientists have clever ways to figure this stuff out.

Earlier this year, Richard Brune went to the Mojave Desert in southern California to find out how long some balanced rocks have been standing.

The desert slopes gently away from a mountain of globby shaped granite rocks. Gravel and lots of prickly plants cover

Section Heading	Important Ideas
Odd Hobby	James Brune is a geologist, a scientist who studies rocks. Richard, his son, works with him taking photographs. They've been studying balanced rocks for 15 years. James believes that we can learn about earthquakes from these rocks.

CLOSE READ

Analyze Structure: Essay (LINES 44–54)

RI 1, RI 3, RI 5

Explain that authors use different **patterns of organization,** or ways of structuring the ideas and information in expository writing. An author might use one pattern throughout an essay, or different sections might follow different patterns. One pattern of organization is **cause and effect,** in which text is organized to show the relationship between causes and effects.

E **ASK STUDENTS** to reread lines 44–48 and identify the two causes and their effects in the paragraph. *(cause: no large earthquakes have occurred; effect: delicate, easy-to-tip balanced rocks can be found; cause: strong earthquakes have occurred; effect: only more solidly grounded rocks are found)*

English Language Support

Read aloud lines 41–43. Tell students that recognizing the cause-and-effect relationship in these sentences will help them figure out later causes and their effects. Have pairs use the following sentence frame to restate the relationship between the events:

Because of_____, balanced rocks_____. *(earthquakes; fall over)* Suggest that students use the sentence frame to help them express other cause-and-effect relationships in the text.

Explain that sometimes an author uses a signal word or phrase, such as *because, so,* or *as a result,* to indicate a cause-and-effect relationship.

F **CITE TEXT EVIDENCE** Ask students to reread lines 49–54. Have students cite the signal word or phrase and the cause-and-effect relationship it indicates. *(signal word: "because"; cause: balanced rocks can give clues about the history of earthquakes; effect: geologists are interested in studying balanced rocks)*

Analyze Structure: Essay (LINES 92–95)

RI 3,
RI 5

The author presents another cause-and-effect relationship in lines 92–95. In this case, there is no signal word, and the relationship is implied.

G **ASK STUDENTS** to closely reread lines 92–95 and to explain the cause-and-effect relationship. *(cause: river water "chews away the weaker types of rock"; effect: the stronger types of rock are left behind, sometimes balancing on thin foundations)*

CRITICAL VOCABULARY

gully: Brune walks along the bottom of a gully, looking for balanced rocks.

ASK STUDENTS why balanced rocks would occur on the edge of a gully. *(A gully is formed by running water. The water forms a ditch by washing away sand or lightweight soil. That leaves the rocks behind.)*

bedrock: The author explains how the balanced rocks were probably formed from the bedrock beneath the desert floor.

ASK STUDENTS to relate the process in their own words. *(River water flows over the solid bedrock and cuts paths by wearing away the softer rock, leaving only the harder, stronger rock behind.)*

gradual: The process of water wearing away rock is a gradual one.

ASK STUDENTS to explain why the author uses *gradually* instead of *slowly*. (*Slowly* means simply "not quick or fast." *Gradually* suggests something happening in steps, or little by little.)

---

the ground. Richard has parked his Jeep at the end of a bumpy dirt road. He now walks on the sandy bottom of a winding **gully** with Dylan Rood, a geologist from Lawrence Livermore National Laboratory in California.

Speckled granite rocks stacked like giant brown marshmallows tower above the gully on both sides. Now and 80 then, Richard and Rood spot a rock balanced on top of the stack, like a milk jug standing upside down.

> ## " Speckled granite rocks stacked like giant brown marshmallows tower above the gully. "

"Be careful," says Richard, as Rood approaches one rock. "That one could go off easily. It wouldn't take much."

Several minutes later, Rood climbs to another rock, this one the size of a TV, sitting on top of the marshmallows. "Woohoo!" he hollers to Richard. "Just with a thumb I can move it."

CARVED BY WATER

People often assume that rocks become balanced after falling on top of each other. But that wasn't the case for these 90 marshmallow stacks—there's nowhere the balanced rocks could have rolled from above.

G Instead, scientists think these balanced rocks were probably carved by water. As rivers cut gullies into the granite **bedrock** beneath the desert floor, water chews away the weaker types of rock, leaving only the stronger behind.

Imagine a house built of strong bricks and held together by weak cement—bedrock often has these strong and weak parts, although they aren't always visible. If the house is continuously exposed to running water, the cement will 100 **gradually** wear away. But the bricks will remain. And some of the bricks will be left stacked or balanced on top of each other—like the granite marshmallows in the gully.

gully
(gŭl´ē) *n.* A *gully* is a deep ditch cut in the earth by running water.

bedrock
(bĕd´rŏk´) *n. Bedrock* is the solid rock that lies under sand, soil, clay, and gravel.

gradual
(grăj´ōō-əl) *adj.* If something is *gradual*, it advances little by little.

160 Collection 3

CONTENT-AREA CONNECTION

Science and Geography Explain that the Mojave Desert, the site of James Brune's research, lies in southern California, southern Nevada, and northwestern Arizona. In addition to balanced rocks, it contains other rock formations and desert features.

Activity Form small mixed-ability groups to find out more about the Mojave Desert. Ask each group to create a poster highlighting the important facts they discover about this region. Suggest that each student in a group be responsible for researching one aspect, such as landforms, climate, vegetation, and animal life. Have students organize their posters with headings and use text features such as bulleted lists to present their information clearly. Encourage students to include illustrations and noncopyrighted images as well. Let groups present and display their posters.

Rood thinks that most of these rocks were carved out during the last Ice Age.[1] "There was a lot more water," he says. "There were big lakes all over the Mojave Desert." If that's true, it would mean these rocks have been standing like bowling pins in the desert for 15,000 to 20,000 years—four or five times longer than the pyramids of Egypt!

SUNBURNED ROCK

Rood and Richard plan to test this age estimate. Late one
110 afternoon, a couple of days after their walk through the marshmallow gully, they find a refrigerator-sized boulder that looks ready to roll downhill.

Unlike a lot of the other balanced rocks they've seen, this one is on the side of a small mountain, in a place where it *could* have landed after rolling from somewhere higher up. But Richard and Rood have a way of knowing that it didn't. They can tell, in fact, that it's sitting within a few centimeters of where it was eroded out of the surrounding bedrock.

Rood points out a vein of brownish quartz crystals,
120 several fingers thick, that runs through the bedrock a few meters behind the rock. That layer runs for 30 meters before disappearing. It is tilted, like the hour hand of a wall clock at 8 o'clock—but otherwise straight as an arrow. That same layer of quartz runs through the boulder. It is perfectly lined up with the layer in the bedrock. It would be a pretty unlikely **coincidence** if the boulder just rolled down the mountain and landed that way. This rock has to be sitting in its original birthplace.

Rood hangs a tape measure down the boulder, which is
130 6 feet tall.

He hammers a small piece off of the boulder every few inches from top to bottom. Back at the lab, he'll test these bits of rock to see how long each part of the boulder has been exposed to sunlight.

Rood measures this by using an accelerator-mass spectrometer, a monster machine the size of an 18-wheeler. He'll use this machine to measure tiny amounts—a few quadrillionths of a gram—of a rare radioactive form of the element beryllium.

coincidence
(kō-ĭn′sĭ-dəns) *n.*
A *coincidence* is a sequence of events that although accidental seems to have been planned.

---
[1] **Ice Age:** a time in history when thick sheets of ice covered large areas of land.

CLOSE READ

Analyze Structure:
Essay (LINES 109–112)

RI 1,
RI 3,
RI 5

Explain that even though an article or essay might have one overall pattern of organization, individual paragraphs or sections might use a different pattern. Information in this paragraph (lines 109–112) is organized in **chronological,** or time, order.

H CITE TEXT EVIDENCE Ask students to reread lines 109–112. Have students cite the words and phrases that indicate the passage of time or the order of events. *(The phrases "Late one afternoon" and "a couple of days after their walk" indicate when the event is occurring and that it happens after the walk in the gully that was described previously.)*

CRITICAL VOCABULARY

coincidence: The author describes how Rood and Richard know that the boulder did not roll or fall from somewhere else.

ASK STUDENTS to describe the coincidence that would have to have occurred for the boulder to simply roll or fall into position. *(The boulder, with its brownish "stripe" of quartz crystals, would have had to roll to a stop in just a certain way to line up exactly with the quartz crystals in the bedrock.)*

APPLYING ACADEMIC VOCABULARY

affect	ensure

THINK-PAIR-SHARE Have students turn to a partner to discuss the questions below. Ask them to include the academic vocabulary words *affect* and *ensure* in their responses. Then have volunteers share their responses with the class.

- How does flowing water **affect** bedrock?
- How does the slow process of erosion in the Mojave Desert **ensure** that balanced rocks will remain for many years?

Analyze Structure:

RI 3,
RI 5

Essay (LINES 140–148)

Tell students that some causes have multiple effects. Here, Fox describes a cause-and-effect relationship related to how long a rock is exposed to sunlight. The second effect is not stated directly, but is implied.

(I) ASK STUDENTS to closely reread lines 140–148 and to explain the cause and the two effects. *(cause: the sun's rays hit the rock; effect 1: beryllium-10 develops in its outer layer; effect 2: the presence or absence of beryllium-10 allows scientists to determine how long the rock has been exposed to sunlight)*

Analyze Language

RI 1,
RI 4

(LINES 140–148)

Tell students that authors of expository text may use **figurative language,** or words used in a way that is different from the literal meaning. They do this to help make complex technical concepts clear to readers.

(J) CITE TEXT EVIDENCE Have students reread lines 140–148 and cite two examples of figurative language. Ask them to tell what each means and identify the author's purpose in using it. *("the rock is getting sunburned": The author compares the process of beryllium-10 forming in a rock to a person getting sunburned to help readers relate a complex process to something familiar. The expression "before running water chews it out of the desert floor" helps readers visualize how running water eats away at the rock.)*

This is one section of an accelerator-mass spectrometer, an enormous instrument scientists can use to analyze and collect data about rock samples.

140   This rare form, called beryllium-10, is created when cosmic rays from space hit the rock and split apart larger atoms of oxygen and nitrogen. You might say that when this happens, the rock is getting sunburned. As long as the rock is sitting out in the open, the cosmic rays are hitting it and beryllium-10 is forming in the outer 2 or so centimeters of the rock. But while the rock is buried underground—before running water chews it out of the desert floor—it's shaded from cosmic rays, so no beryllium-10 develops.

OLDEST PLACES

By measuring the sunburn—that is, the amount of
150 beryllium-10 in the rock fragments—scientists can tell how long ago the rock emerged from the surrounding bedrock.

©James King-Holmes/Photo Researchers, Inc./Science Source

162 Collection 3

Strategies for Annotation   🖉 🗐 *Annotate it!*

Analyze Structure: Essay

RI 3,
RI 5

Have students use their eBook annotation tools to analyze the text. Ask students to do the following:

- In lines 140–148, highlight in yellow each cause.
- Highlight in green each effect.
- In notes, write down any implied effects.
- Reread the text to make sure you fully understand the cause-and-effect relationship.

happens, the rock is getting sunburned. As long as the rock is sitting out in the open, the cosmic rays are hitting it and beryllium-10 is forming in the outer 2 or so centimeters of the rock. But while the rock is buried underground—before running water chews it out of the desert floor—it's shaded from cosmic rays, so no beryllium-10 develops.

Rood has already used this method, called exposure dating, on one balanced rock in the Mojave Desert. He found that it had been freestanding for 18,000 years—about what he expected if the rock was carved out during the last Ice Age.

Scientists have used exposure dating all over the world. Deserts, usually the oldest places, change the slowest because there is little water to alter the landscape. Once a rock is standing, it can stay still for a long time because there is
160 hardly any water to erode it or wash it away. And during the winter, ice doesn't form inside cracks in the rock and slowly pry it apart.

In places with lots of water, things change quickly. Over the past 150 years, the Missouri River has shifted its winding path by three kilometers in some places, leaving its mark in the landscape.

Antarctica probably has the oldest, most unchanging landscapes on Earth. Ice covers most of the continent, but a few small areas remain ice-free. In one such place, called the
170 Olympus Range, you can sit on boulders that haven't moved in five or six million years! The rocks survived because Antarctica is a desert: It is so cold that it receives hardly any rain or snow. The continent was once warmer and wetter, but when it became cold and dry, it stayed that way.

ROCK TIPPING

Here in California, Rood and Richard need to know not only how long their **precariously** balanced rocks have been standing but also how hard they are to knock over.

These are tough questions. The best way to find out how firmly in place a rock is—simply push it over. But toppling
180 a rock that's been balanced for 18,000 years is sort of like chopping down one of the oldest redwood trees. No one wants to do it.

Once, though, Richard and James Brune had a chance to topple some rocks. They heard about a businessman who was building some houses in the desert and planned to knock over some balanced rocks that were in the way.

The Brunes convinced the developer to let them do it for him. They fastened a steel cable to each rock and used a gadget to measure exactly how much pulling was needed to bring
190 down the boulder. "It was kind of fun," admits James. "They

precarious
(prĭ-kâr´ē-əs) *adj.*
If something is *precarious*, it is dangerous and unstable.

CLOSE READ

Analyze Structure:
Essay (LINES 156–162; 167–174)

RI 1, RI 2,
RI 3, RI 5

Tell students that lines 156–162 describe a cause and three effects. Note that sometimes an effect is named first, and then the cause is identified.

K CITE TEXT EVIDENCE Have students identify the cause and its effects in this paragraph by citing the text. *(cause: in a desert, "there is little water to alter the landscape"; effect 1: change occurs very slowly; effect 2: a rock "can stay still for a long time"; effect 3: "ice doesn't form inside cracks in the rock and slowly pry it apart")*

Explain that identifying the cause-and-effect organization of a paragraph can help students determine the **central idea**—the most important idea in the paragraph or section of text.

L CITE TEXT EVIDENCE Ask students to reread lines 167–174 and cite an example of a word that reveals the cause-and-effect structure. *(The word* because *in the sentence "The rocks survived because Antarctica is a desert" reveals a cause-and-effect structure.)* What is the central idea of this paragraph, and how does the above sentence support it? *(The central idea is that Antarctica has the oldest, most unchanging landscapes on Earth. The sentence about Antarctica being a desert reinforces this idea, showing why the landscape is unchanging.)*

CRITICAL VOCABULARY

precarious: Some of the rocks are precariously balanced.

ASK STUDENTS to describe a rock that is *not* precariously balanced. *(A rock that is not precariously balanced would have a good, solid foundation under it. It would not be easily tipped over or rolled.)*

English Language Support

Improve Reading Fluency Explain that when reading informational text aloud, students must pronounce terms correctly and read at a steady pace.

- Display lines 156–174. Have volunteers highlight punctuation marks that indicate pauses and identify unfamiliar words. Pronounce each one as students repeat after you.

- Read each paragraph aloud, with students echo reading. Have students continue practicing with a partner, taking turns until their reading is smooth and accurate.

CLOSE READ

Analyze Structure: Essay (LINES 193–204)

RI 3, RI 5

Once again, in lines 193–204, Fox uses an example to support the statement he makes in the first sentence in lines 193–194.

(M) ASK STUDENTS to explain what "less destructive" method Richard has found. Ask what pattern of organization the author uses to describe this method. *(Richard first takes photographs, then loads the photos into a computer and makes a virtual model. He can then run a computer program to learn how much force it takes to tip the rock, without actually moving it. The author uses chronological order in this description.)*

English Language Support

Remind students that certain words and phrases signal the type of organization that an author uses. Display lines 193–204.

- Have students consult the chart on page 165 of their text to answer the following questions: What signal word from the chart appears in this part of the text? *(then)* What type of organization does it signal? *(chronological)*

- Have students work with a partner to find other signal words that show this pattern of organization. *(begins, back at home)*

COLLABORATIVE DISCUSSION Have small groups of students review the aspects of geological research described in the essay and discuss what surprised them. Have each group summarize the main points of their discussion and share their conclusions with the class.

ASK STUDENTS to share any questions they generated in the course of reading and discussing the selection.

---

were 7 or 8 feet high and weighed many tons." And each landed with a satisfying thud.

(M) Richard has also found less destructive ways to pull on rocks. Out in the Mojave Desert with Rood, he takes out a camera and begins photographing from all sides the refrigerator-sized boulder they're studying.

Back at home, he'll load the photos into a computer that will stitch the pictures into a three-dimensional model of the rock—a virtual rock.

200   Richard can then run that virtual rock through a computer program that shakes and knocks the rock down many times. By tipping that virtual rock they can ensure that the other one—the real rock—has a fighting chance to stay standing for another 18,000 years.

COLLABORATIVE DISCUSSION What surprising details does the author reveal about how geologists conduct their research? Discuss your ideas with a small group of classmates.

TO CHALLENGE STUDENTS . . .

Analyzing Media The opening scene and the author's frequent use of quotations from scientists suggest that this essay could make a compelling documentary film.

ASK STUDENTS to work in small groups to discuss how they would create a documentary based on this essay. Tell students to consider the following:

- Camera angles: Which scenes would they shoot close-up? Which would be long shots, or "big picture" shots?

- Sound elements: What music would be effective? Where would they include interviews? Voice-overs?

- What special effects might enhance the film?

Analyze Structure: Essay

RI 2, RI 3, RI 5

"Big Rocks' Balancing Acts" is an **expository essay,** which presents or explains information or ideas. To ensure that informational texts are clear to readers, writers choose a **pattern of organization,** a particular arrangement of ideas and information. Facts and details can be organized in a variety of ways. This chart shows a few common patterns of organization:

Pattern	What It Shows or Highlights	Signal Words or Phrases
chronological order	the order in which actions or events occur	*first, second, then, at the same time*
cause-and-effect order	the relationship between events and their causes	*because, and so, as a result, therefore*
compare-and-contrast order	the similarities and differences of two or more subjects	*like, by contrast, similarly, as opposed to, however*
spatial order	the arrangement of details according to their physical position or relationship	*top, bottom, above, in front of*

A pattern of organization may be used to organize an entire piece of writing or single paragraphs within a longer work. Reread lines 113–118. Identify the pattern of organization within that paragraph and the words or phrases that signal the organization.

Being able to identify patterns of organization can help readers find a writer's main, or central, idea, which is the most important idea in an essay. Often, the **central idea** is not directly stated but is implied by supporting details. As you read, use these strategies to identify and understand central ideas in an expository essay:

- Identify the specific topic of each paragraph or section.
- Examine the details the author includes in that section.
- Look for words that signal an organization.
- Ask what idea or message the details convey about the topic.

Where in "Big Rocks' Balancing Acts" does the author introduce the topic and central idea of the essay?

CLOSE READ

Analyze Structure: Essay

RI 2, RI 3, RI 5

Guide students to understand and distinguish among the four organizational patterns shown in the chart. Provide this additional information:

- Chronological order means time order. An essay that relates events usually uses this pattern.
- Causes and effects help us understand how and why things happen. Essays that explain concepts or processes may use this pattern.
- To compare and contrast, the author needs at least two events or objects that have something in common.
- Authors use spatial order when they describe a place.

Emphasize that an author might organize a single paragraph in an essay using one of these patterns, even though the rest of the essay follows a different pattern. Have students reread the paragraph in lines 113–118 and identify the pattern and the words that signal it. *(compare-and-contrast; signal words: "Unlike," "But")*

Help students understand that the author introduces the topic, balancing rocks, at the end of the introduction, after describing Richard Brune's daring picture-taking. He introduces the central idea at the end of the next section, "Odd Hobby," when he explains that studying balanced rocks "can tell us something important about earthquakes." *(lines 39–40)*

Strategies for Annotation

✏️ 🗐 *Annotate it!*

Analyze Structure: Essay

RI 3, RI 5

Share these strategies for guided or independent analysis:

- In paragraphs that describe cause-and-effect relationships, highlight in yellow the cause.
- Highlight in green the effect or effects.
- Reread the text to make sure you have found all of the cause-and-effect relationships and that you understand them fully.
- In a note, explain the ideas in your own words.

Imagine a house built of strong bricks and held together by weak cement—bedrock often has these strong and weak parts, although they aren't always visible. If the house is continuously exposed to running water, the cement will gradually wear away. But the bricks will remain. And some

Analyzing the Text

RI 1, RI 2,
RI 3, RI 4,
RI 5, RI 6

Possible answers:

1. The author uses spatial order in these lines as he describes the appearance of a particular rock and its surroundings. The measurements and the position words, such as "tilted," "straight," and "perfectly lined up," help reveal the pattern.

2. Geologist James Brune and his son Richard have been studying balanced rocks to learn about earthquakes.

3. Balanced rocks give clues about the severity of earthquakes in a region over thousands of years because delicate rocks remain only where no earthquakes have occurred. These clues are helpful in the construction of bridges or dams because builders know more about the likelihood and severity of tremors in the area.

4. The author compares bedrock to bricks held together with weak cement to help readers visualize how the action of water on rock wears away the weak parts and leaves bricks, or a stack of rocks, behind. The stacked rocks are compared to marshmallows to help readers visualize their shapes.

5. The author uses informal language and addresses readers directly, helping them to connect to their own experiences and curiosity.

6. These rocks have been balancing for a long time and should be left alone for the sake of natural beauty and for further study.

English Language Support

Read Closely Explain to students that before they can develop a research question, they must learn more about their topic.

- Have students read general information about their topic in an encyclopedia or other reference work.
- Have them work with a partner to identify the focus of their research. Provide these questions to help them zero in on what they want to learn: What is most interesting about my topic? What is most important about my topic? What should people know about my topic?
- Have pairs explain their focus and their research questions. Encourage students to work together to refine the question(s).

---

 eBook *Annotate It!*

Analyzing the Text

RI 1, RI 2, RI 3,
RI 4, RI 5, RI 6,
W 7, SL 4

Cite Text Evidence   Support your responses with evidence from the text.

1. **Recognize and Analyze** Under the heading "Sunburned Rock," examine lines 119–130. What pattern of organization is evident in these paragraphs? What details help you to recognize it?

2. **Summarize** Reread from the beginning of the essay to the end of the section "Odd Hobby." In your own words, describe the most important idea the author of this expository essay wants readers to understand.

3. **Cite Evidence** Reread the section "Standing Strong." Why is it worthwhile to study balanced rocks?

4. **Analyze** Reread lines 96–102. What comparisons does the author make, and how are they helpful for readers?

5. **Draw Conclusions** Reread lines 57–68. What might be the author's reason in using the pronoun *you* and presenting information in this way?

6. **Analyze** What important idea from the essay is in the concluding sentence?

PERFORMANCE TASK

Speaking Activity: Summary Presentation Choose a concept or term about geology from "Big Rocks' Balancing Acts" (for example: *earthquake tremors, granite, bedrock, accelerator-mass spectrometer, erosion, Ice Age,* or *geology* itself). Think of a question related to that term to explore, such as *"How many ice ages have taken place on Earth?"* Research your topic and present a brief summary of the information you find.

- Find at least two informational print or online articles on the topic. Make sure these sources are credible.
- List the most important ideas you want to present.
- Begin your summary with an introduction that specifies your topic clearly, establishes your central idea, and hooks listeners into listening further.
- Explain the central idea or ideas from your research.

Assign this
performance task.

PERFORMANCE TASK

W 7,
SL 4

Speaking Activity: Summary Presentation Have students work individually or in pairs. Encourage students to spend time shaping their initial question so their research can be focused and efficient. Provide these tips for students' oral delivery: familiarize yourself with the material—do not simply read the summary aloud; practice delivering your summary in a room by yourself; if making eye contact makes you uncomfortable, look just over the heads of your audience.

Critical Vocabulary

gully	bedrock	gradual	coincidence	precarious

Practice and Apply Identify the vocabulary word that is tied in meaning to the italicized word in each question. Give your reasons.

1. Which word goes with *patience*? Why?
2. Which word goes with *drill*? Why?
3. Which word goes with *cliff*? Why?
4. Which word goes with *rainstorm*? Why?
5. Which word goes with *chance*? Why?

Vocabulary Strategy: Latin Roots

A **root** is a word part that came into English from an older language. You can check a print or digital dictionary to learn about roots; the entry for a word often gives details about the word's origin. Roots from Latin appear in many English words. This sentence comes from "Big Rocks' Balancing Acts":

> If the house is continuously exposed to running water, the cement will gradually wear away.

The word *gradually* contains a root, *grad*, from the Latin word *gradus*, which means "step" or "stage." You can see the root meaning in the different meanings of the word *grade*, which have to do with steps, stages, or levels. The root meaning also appears in the word *gradually*, which describes actions taken step by step. In the example sentence, the cement doesn't disappear all at once, but wears away in stages. By recognizing the root *grad*, you can make a good guess about the meanings of longer words that include it.

Practice and Apply Read each sentence. Identify the word with the Latin root *grad*. Tell what each word means. Use a print or digital dictionary to check your ideas.

1. After learning camera settings, we graduated to taking nature photos.
2. The hill has a gradient that is perfect for sledding.
3. Until astronomers understood that planets orbit the Sun, they had trouble explaining the retrograde motion of planets during part of the year.
4. The art appears to be red, but a closer look shows gradations of color.
5. Weathering and erosion slowly cause the degradation of mountains.
6. Some products last forever in landfills, while others are biodegradable.

Critical Vocabulary

Possible answers:

1. *gradual; Waiting for something to occur in stages requires patience.*
2. *bedrock; You need a drill to cut through bedrock.*
3. *precarious; Something that might fall from the edge of a cliff is balanced in a precarious way.*
4. *gully; Rain and flowing water can carve a gully in the earth.*
5. *coincidence; A coincidence happens by chance.*

Vocabulary Strategy: Latin Roots

Possible answers:

1. *graduated: moved on to the next step*
2. *gradient: amount of slope*
3. *retrograde: moving backward or in a direction opposite to what is expected*
4. *gradations: series of stages*
5. *degradation: the opposite of building up; breaking down*
6. *biodegradable: able to be broken down by bacteria or other life forms*

English Language Support

Use Knowledge of Morphology On the board, display a web with the root *grad* and its definition: "step" or "stage."

- Read each Practice and Apply sentence aloud. Then have students work with a partner to identify the word in each sentence that contains the root *grad*. Record the words in the web and work with students to define them using the root meaning and context clues.

- Assign pairs of students one or more of the Practice and Apply sentences. Have them identify the word that contains the root *grad* and define it using context clues and the meaning of the root. Then have partners add their word(s) and definition(s) to the class web.

- Have students read the Practice and Apply sentences and identify each word that contains the root *grad*. Write the words in the web and discuss their meanings. Then call on students to use each word in an original sentence.

Language Conventions: Prepositional Phrases

L 1a

Point out to students that prepositions, such as the examples shown, are common words that they use every day.

With the class, examine each of the following sentences. Guide students to identify the prepositional phrase, what the phrase modifies, and what it tells.

- One of the windows is open. *(modifies "One" and tells* which*)*
- The hinge on the door squeaks like a rusty gate. *(modifies "hinge" and tells* which*; modifies "squeaks" and tells* how*)*
- She stuffed her cold hands into her pockets and squeezed her fists into tight balls. *(modifies "stuffed" and tells* where*; modifies "squeezed" and tells* how *or to what extent)*

Possible answers:

- *Balanced boulders stand like bowling pins in the desert.*
- *The rocks were carved by water and have remained standing for a long time.*
- *In lands with little water, people can sit on ancient boulders.*

Assess It Online!

Online Selection Test
- Download an editable ExamView bank.
- Assign and manage this test online.

Language Conventions: Prepositional Phrases

L 1a

A **preposition** is a part of speech that relates one word to another. These are just a few common prepositions: *about, across, against, at, before, beside, between, by, for, from, in, like, next to, of, on, on top of, over, through, to,* and *with.*

A **phrase** is a group of related words that acts like a single word in a sentence. A **prepositional phrase** acts like a **modifier,** a word that changes the sense of another word in a sentence. A prepositional phrase includes a preposition, its object (the noun or pronoun that follows the preposition), and any modifiers. These examples show how the prepositional phrase always modifies or relates to another word in a sentence, telling which one, where, when, how, why, or to what extent.

modifies

The scientists fly over the southern California desert.

(The prepositional phrase *over the southern California desert* modifies *fly* and tells *where.*)

modifies

The scientists have a passion for balanced rocks.

(The prepositional phrase *for balanced rocks* modifies *passion* and tells *what kind.*)

modifies   modifies

One of them shoots photos from the plane.

(The prepositional phrase *of them* modifies *One* and tells *which.* The prepositional phrase *from the plane* modifies *shoots* and tells *where.*)

Writers use prepositional phrases to add information to their sentences. This sentence from "Big Rocks' Balancing Acts" has five prepositional phrases:

And some of the bricks will be left stacked or balanced on top of each other—like the granite marshmallows in the gully.

Practice and Apply Use these prepositional phrases to build sentences that tell about information in "Big Rocks' Balancing Acts." Try to use more than one phrase in a sentence.

- in the desert
- with little water
- on ancient boulders
- by water
- like bowling pins
- for a long time

Language Conventions: Prepositional Phrases

L 1a

Have students locate lines 3–8 of the essay and use their eBook annotation tools to do the following:

- Underline each prepositional phrase.
- Highlight the preposition in yellow.
- Highlight in green the word the phrase modifies.
- In a note, write what the phrase tells about the modified word.

The plane's door had been removed so Brune could ride with one leg outside. As the tiny propeller plane zigzagged over the desert, Brune leaned out over empty air. The 80 mile-per-hour headwind pummeled his face. He looked through his camera and snapped pictures of the rocky desert hundreds of feet below.

Analyze Texts: Fact and Opinion

TEACH

Tell students that most informational writing contains both facts and opinions. Explain that a **fact** is a statement that can be proved, or verified. An **opinion** is a statement that expresses a writer's belief, feelings, or thoughts; it cannot be proved. In general, facts are more reliable than opinions. However, some informational writing includes the opinions of experts, which are based on their experience and knowledge of the subject matter.

- Display the following text (lines 103–105):
  Rood thinks that most of these rocks were carved out during the last Ice Age. "There was a lot more water," he says. "There were big lakes all over the Mojave Desert."
- Explain that the first sentence is an opinion because it expresses the scientist's belief about when the balanced rocks were established. The word *thinks* is a clue. However, the opinion is based on his expert knowledge of the subject.
- The second and third sentences are facts that can be proved by consulting scientific sources.
- Point out that the opinions expressed by the geologist Rood are not necessarily those of the author Douglas Fox.

PRACTICE AND APPLY

Display lines 37–40 of the essay. Have students identify a fact, an author's opinion, and an expert opinion, and give reasons for their answers.

Fact: *"He has also studied earthquakes for many years."*

Author's Opinion: *"It sounds like an odd hobby."*

Expert Opinion: *"He believes that balanced rocks can tell us something important about earthquakes."*

Reasons: *The fact can be verified by checking the scientist's research and publications. The author's opinion is what Douglas Fox expresses about studying rocks as a hobby. The expert opinion is based on his many years of studying earthquakes.*

Tell students to be careful to distinguish between facts and opinions when they do research for their summary presentations in the Performance Task.

Analyze Structure: Essay

RETEACH

Remind students that an expository essay presents or explains information or ideas. Explain that an author chooses one or more patterns of organization as a way to structure the information. Review the patterns in the chart shown in the skill lesson "Analyze Structure: Essay." Provide the following examples of topics that might use each type of organization. Talk about why each pattern of organization "fits" the topic.

- An expository essay tells about events before, during, and after a natural disaster in **chronological,** or time, order.
- An expository essay explores the **causes and effects** related to using more and less fertilizer on vegetable plants.
- An expository essay **compares and contrasts** life in New York City and in Los Angeles.
- An expository essay describes an award-winning school building using **spatial** order.

LEVEL UP TUTORIALS Assign one or more of the following *Level Up* tutorials: **Chronological Order; Cause-and-Effect Organization; Comparison-Contrast Organization**

INDEPENDENT READING

Students can apply their knowledge of patterns of organization to help them understand other pieces of expository text. For example, stop and ask students to identify the patterns in paragraphs or sections of a textbook they are using in class. Remind students to look for signal words as clues.

The Hidden Southwest: The Arch Hunters

Essay by James Vlahos

Why This Text

Students may read an essay without a complete understanding of the author's central idea and details that support it. Essays such as this one by James Vlahos may have more than one complex central idea, and a pattern of organization that is clarified only with careful study. With the help of the close-reading questions, students will determine the central ideas by examining the evidence, enabling them to develop a cohesive understanding of an informational text.

Background Have students read the background information that describes the rock formations in Canyonlands National Park in Utah. The landscape has been carved by erosion and weathering into an intricate maze of deep narrow canyons and other odd landforms such as mesas, buttes, and rock arches. Introduce the selection by sharing a description from Edward Abbey's book *Desert Solitaire*, in which he depicts the rocks in Canyonlands as "monolithic formations of sandstone."

SETTING A PURPOSE Ask students to pay close attention to the central ideas in this essay and to the interactions among individuals, ideas, and events in the text. How soon into the essay does Vlahos present the essay's central idea?

Standards Support

- cite several pieces of textual evidence
- determine two or more central ideas in a text
- analyze the interactions among individuals, events, or ideas in a text
- analyze the structure an author uses to organize a text

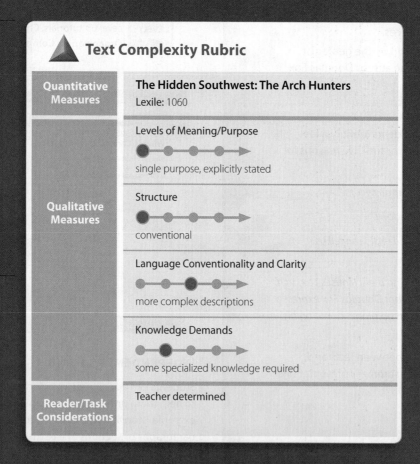

Text Complexity Rubric

Quantitative Measures

The Hidden Southwest: The Arch Hunters
Lexile: 1060

Qualitative Measures

Levels of Meaning/Purpose
single purpose, explicitly stated

Structure
conventional

Language Conventionality and Clarity
more complex descriptions

Knowledge Demands
some specialized knowledge required

Reader/Task Considerations
Teacher determined

Strategies for CLOSE READING

Determine the Central Idea

Students should read this essay carefully all the way through. Close-reading questions at the bottom of the page will help them focus on a thorough analysis of the central idea of the essay and on the details that support it. As they read, students should record comments or questions about the text in the side margins.

WHEN STUDENTS STRUGGLE . . .

To help students follow the central idea of the essay, they should work in a small group to fill out a chart such as the one shown below as they analyze the essay.

CITE TEXT EVIDENCE For practice in finding the central idea the writer develops over the course of the text, ask students to examine the details and evidence that support the central idea.

> *Central Idea: Rock arches are natural wonders that attract curious explorers.*
>
> *Detail 1: Generations of explorers have been astounded by rock arches.*
>
> *Detail 2: Rock arches are almost as iconic as Old Faithful and Half Dome.*
>
> *Detail 3: People notice rock when it takes "flight in the sky," flouting physical laws.*
>
> *Detail 4: The author and two other explorers search for the rock arch and are ecstatic when they find it.*

The Hidden Southwest:
The Arch Hunters
Essay by James Vlahos

CLOSE READ
Notes

1. **READ ▶** As you read lines 1–22, begin to collect and cite text evidence.

- Circle the repeated statement in lines 1–10.
- In the margin, state in your own words the central (or main) idea the repeated statement expresses.
- Underline the supporting details in lines 1–22 that develop the central idea.

Ⓐ Ⓑ The rock arch is lost. It's around here somewhere but could be anywhere; we've searched all morning and gotten nowhere. Picking my way through boulders and gnarled junipers, I reach the scalloped rim of a high mesa and peer over the edge. My stomach drops.

This part of Canyonlands National Park is known as the Needles District, a name too tidy to describe the slickrock chaos erupting from the valley below. There are knobs, blobs, towers, and fins, an array containing every shape of sculpted rock save the one we're seeking. The arch is lost.

10 Two men join me on the overlook. The first wears a plaid Western shirt neatly tucked into blue Levi's. Leathery, all limbs and no body fat, he steps **nimbly** to the precipice. "Did you talk to Alex Ranney?" he is saying.

The writer cannot find the rock arch he is searching for.

nimbly: *gracefully*

51

1. **READ AND CITE TEXT EVIDENCE** Explain that the central idea is usually stated at the beginning or end of an essay, a paragraph, or a section of text; however, in this essay, the central idea of the first section (lines 1–10) is restated at the end, also.

Ⓐ **ASK STUDENTS** to evaluate the effectiveness of the repetition of the sentence "The rock arch is lost" in lines 1–10. *Students should note that the repetition stresses the importance of the goal of the arch hunters to find the rock arch.*

Critical Vocabulary: nimbly (line 13) Have students explain "nimbly," as Vlahos uses it here. Why might the arch hunter need to step nimbly? *to keep from falling off the overlook*

FOR ELL STUDENTS Explain that a compound word is usually two words joined together to make one word. "Canyonlands" (line 6) and "slickrock" (line 7) are compound words.

ASK STUDENTS to look for other compound words in the text and cite them in the margin.

"I did," replies the second man. Wearing a khaki shirt, shorts, and mirrored sunglasses, he looks like a refugee from a Kalahari game drive.

"Did you get any more clues?" asks Western Shirt.

"Nope, Ranney was elusive," replies Sunglasses.

20 "Tight-lipped."

"Totally. He said, 'I want you to be able to find it yourself and get the thrill of discovery.'"

The rock formation we seek is a quadruple arch known as Klingon Battle Cruiser. The first recorded sighting wasn't until 1994 by Ranney, a canyoneer from Tucson, Arizona. Not on any map or trail, it has probably been glimpsed by fewer than a dozen people in the history of the park. Tom Budlong (Western Shirt) and Tom Van Bebber (Sunglasses) desperately want to add their names to the list. These guys are no casual tourists. Rather, they are arch hunters.

30 Few sights are as celebrated in—or as iconic of—the American West as the natural rock arch. Arches have astounded generations of desert wanderers, from Teddy Roosevelt, who camped below Rainbow Bridge in 1913, to Edward Abbey, who memorably **venerated** them in *Desert Solitaire*. America's spans are internationally recognizable wonders on par with Old Faithful and Half Dome, their shapes burned into the collective consciousness by countless photographs and films.

Rock shouldn't take flight in the sky; when it does, in scorn of known physical laws, people take notice. Arches National Park,
40 America's best known repository of spans, draws more than 800,000 visitors each year from around the world. Yet despite such obvious attraction, few consider searching outside park boundaries—even

venerate:
celebrate

2. ◀ REREAD Reread lines 1–22. Use the central idea and the supporting details to write a summary of the first two paragraphs.

The writer and two other men cannot find the rock arch they are looking for in Canyonlands National Park.

3. READ ▶ As you read lines 23–45, continue to cite textual evidence.

• Circle the specific reason the arch hunters are in the park.

• Underline the details that suggest that a rock arch is an extraordinary sight.

52

---

though the Colorado Plateau has the highest density of rock arches worldwide. There are at least 2,000 stone spans scattered throughout the Four Corners states.

Budlong and Van Bebber belong to the world's **preeminent**, and perhaps only, arch-hunting club—NABS, the Natural Arch and Bridge Society. Its 110 members scour the globe by plane, boat, 4x4, and foot.
50 They prowl Antarctic islands, Algerian sands, and the canyons of the American Southwest. True explorers, they live for the moment of discovery: rounding a canyon bend to spot a miracle of natural engineering that perhaps nobody else in the world has ever seen.

In the case of Klingon Battle Cruiser, that moment of revelation is proving hard to come by. Van Bebber had invited me along on a week's worth of arch hunting, hoping I might catch the fever. This is not an encouraging start. He examines a map, scratches his chin, and sighs, "It's probably just right below us."

I leave the pair to study their charts and hike several hundred yards along the rim. Looking down at an expanse of tawny rock, I
60 realize I am gazing *through* it—through a yawning window at the tiny green dots of trees in the valley below. Nearby, I see three additional **portals**. "Over here!" I shout.

I step carefully from the canyon rim onto the top of the arch and feel a swirl of vertigo. After it subsides I take a second step, then a third, following a rock catwalk into blue sky. Reaching the apex I rotate slowly around, a full 360 degrees, the canyon bottom hundreds of feet straight below.

Worldwide, arches number in the tens of thousands, and probably no place is better suited to their formation than the Colorado Plateau.
70 The sandstone is porous and erosive. The geological strata are such that harder layers lie atop weaker ones; the softer rock erodes from

preeminent:
superior to all others

Budlong and Van Bebber strive to discover what no one else has seen.

portals:
entrances

4. ◀ REREAD AND DISCUSS Reread lines 23–45. With a small group discuss the reasons why adventurers seek out rock arches.

5. READ ▶ As you read lines 46–88, continue to cite textual evidence.

• In the margin, paraphrase the reason why the writer says Budlong and Van Bebber are true explorers.

• Circle the sentences that show that the narrator has found the arch.

• Underline the sentences in lines 77–88 that reveal an unexpected discovery.

53

---

2. **REREAD AND CITE TEXT EVIDENCE**

B **ASK STUDENTS** to cite textual evidence that shows the central idea of the first two paragraphs and the details that support it. How might the repetition of the first sentence suggest that this is the central idea? *By repeating the statement that "The rock arch is lost," Vlahos is suggesting the importance of this idea. Students should cite evidence from lines 1–2 and 8–10.*

3. **READ AND CITE TEXT EVIDENCE** Vlahos states that when rock takes "flight in the sky . . . people take notice."

C **ASK STUDENTS** to cite details that suggest that a rock arch, which stands high in the sky, is an awesome sight. *Students should cite details from lines 23–24 and 30–45.*

Critical Vocabulary: venerate (line 33) Have students share their definitions of *venerate*. Ask how *venerate* fits into Vlahos's discussion of rock arches, which extend for miles. *The spans of rock arches are so huge that people have honored them.*

4. **REREAD AND DISCUSS USING TEXT EVIDENCE**

D **ASK STUDENTS** to appoint a reporter for each group to explain the arch hunters' motivations. *Students should cite evidence from lines 23–28, 30–35, and 38–45.*

5. **READ AND CITE TEXT EVIDENCE**

E **ASK STUDENTS** to read their margin notes to a partner and then write one response that best paraphrases Vlahos's assessment of Budlong and Van Bebber as being "true explorers." *Students should cite evidence from lines 46–52, and 54–59.*

Critical Vocabulary: preeminent (line 46) Ask students why Vlahos uses this word to support his claim that Budlong and Van Bebber are "true explorers". *He wants to show that they belong to the foremost arch-hunting club—perhaps the only one.*

Critical Vocabulary: portals (line 62) Have students explain the meaning and importance of *portals*.

below to leave an arch standing above. And finally, the plateau is in the midst of a rapid geological uplift. Cliff walls push higher while at the same time rivers and meltwater carve deeper and faster. The twin forces produce the critical fins and cracks.

A day after finding Klingon Battle Cruiser, I stand at the base of an **undulating** mass of slickrock, a natural staircase of narrow benches and tilted slopes. With Van Bebber's outstretched palms providing a necessary toehold on blank rock, I scramble up to the first
80　shelf. After walking along it until I find a low-angle passage, I clamber to the next level of the staircase, and the next. A few hundred yards upslope is my goal: the massive triangular portal of Cleft Arch. The only visible route up to the fourth and final bench, however, is too steep. Frustrated, I follow the shelf south and round a corner to make a startling discovery. Tucked under an overhang, invisible until I'm right upon it, is an Anasazi ruin with three well-preserved walls of neatly stacked stone. Arch hunting, I'm learning, often yields much more than the arches themselves.

undulating:
moving up and down like a wave

The sandstone, geological strata, and geological uplift cause rock arches to form in the Colorado Plateau.

6.　**◀ REREAD**　Reread lines 70–75. Write an explanation in the margin of the cause-and-effect connection between events in these lines.

SHORT RESPONSE

Cite Text Evidence　What is the central idea of the essay? Consider the important details the writer conveys about rock arches in the text. Review your reading notes, and **cite text evidence** in your response.

The central idea of the essay is that rock arches are natural wonders that attract curious explorers. Rock arches "take flight in the sky... in scorn of physical laws" so it is no wonder that they have "astounded generations of desert wanderers." The author, along with Budlong and Van Bebber, expend great effort to find a rock arch and express excitement when they do.

54

6.　**REREAD AND CITE TEXT EVIDENCE**　Vlahos explains the process of rock-arch formation at the end of his essay, relating cause-and-effect events.

F　**ASK STUDENTS**　to read their margin notes to a partner and then explain the cause-and-effect relationship between the Colorado Plateau and the formation of rock arches. *Students should cite textual evidence from lines 70–75. The Colorado Plateau is probably the place best suited to the formation of rock arches.*

Critical Vocabulary: undulating　(line 77) Ask students for examples associating the word with natural disasters.

SHORT RESPONSE

Cite Text Evidence　Students should:

- explain what the central idea is of the essay.
- give reasons for their point of view.
- cite details and evidence from the text to support their viewpoint.

TO CHALLENGE STUDENTS . . .

For more context about rock arches, Canyonlands, and other national parks, students can research rock arches in national parks online.

ASK STUDENTS　what they have learned about unusual rock formations and about the natural beauty of our national parks. *Students should report on the facts they have learned and the impression they were left with.*

DIG DEEPER

With the class, return to Question 4, Reread and Discuss. Have students share the results of their discussion.

ASK STUDENTS　whether they were satisfied with the outcome of their small-group discussions. Have each group share the reasons they cited to explain the motivations of adventurers who seek out these unusual rock formations. What compelling evidence did the group cite to support their opinion?

- Guide students to tell whether there was any convincing evidence cited by group members who did not agree with the reasons given by the majority of the group. How did the group handle this difference of opinion?
- Have groups explain how they decided whether or not they had found enough textual evidence to support their ideas or opinion. Did everyone in the group agree as to what made the evidence sufficient? How did the group use conflict-resolution techniques to resolve disagreements?
- After students have shared the results of their group's discussion, ask whether they think another group shared any reasons they wished they had brought to the table.

ASK STUDENTS　to return to their Short Response answer and to revise it based on the class discussion.

ANCHOR TEXT # Ode to enchanted light

ANCHOR TEXT # Sleeping in the Forest

Poem by Pablo Neruda

Poem by Mary Oliver

Why These Texts?

Poetry can capture the beauty and awe of nature in a unique way, allowing the reader to see aspects of the world in a new way. This lesson focuses on different forms of poetry and the different ways in which poets express personal thoughts and feelings.

Key Learning Objective: The student will learn how to analyze poetic form and how poets use figurative language to express feelings and ideas.

For practice and application:

Poems About Nature

Close Reader selection
Poems About Nature
Poetry by Leslie Marmon Silko,
Victor Hernandez Cruz, and Gwendolyn Brooks

RL 1 Cite textual evidence.
RL 2 Determine a theme or central idea.
RL 4 Determine the meaning of words and phrases.
RL 5 Analyze how a poem's form contributes to its meaning.
RL 6 Analyze points of view of narrators in a text.
W 3 Write narratives.
W 10 Write routinely.
SL 1 Engage in collaborative discussions.

▲ Text Complexity Rubric

	Ode to enchanted light Lexile: N/A	Sleeping in the Forest Lexile: N/A
Quantitative Measures		
Qualitative Measures	Levels of Meaning/Purpose multiple levels of meaning	Levels of Meaning/Purpose multiple levels of meaning
	Structure Complex structures, such as sonnets, villanelles, etc.	Structure free verse, no particular patterns
	Language Conventionality and Clarity figurative, less accessible language	Language Conventionality and Clarity figurative, less accessible language
	Knowledge Demands moderately complex theme	Knowledge Demands experience includes unfamiliar aspects
Reader/Task Considerations	• Teacher determined • Vary by individual reader and type of text • See the Text X-Ray for suggested Reader/Task Considerations	

English Language Support Before teaching, use the Text X-Ray for an overview of the text's complexity. The Text X-Ray and the supports and scaffolds in the Teacher's Edition will help you guide students of different skill levels.

Meaning Making

Language Development

Effective Expression

Content Knowledge

Foundational Skills

Text Complexity: Qualitative Measures

 Levels of Meaning/Purpose

Help students determine meaning.

- Teacher's Edition side notes, pp. 170, 172, 174
- English Language Support, pp. 169, 170
- Close Read Screencasts, p. 169
- Determine Meaning, p. 174

To teach how to determine theme, see

- Determine Theme, p. 174a

▶ *Use It!* **Interactive Whiteboard Lesson:** Theme/Central Idea

***ZOOM IN ON* COMPARING POEMS** Remind students that when they compare, they look for ways that things are the same or different.

- Write the following on the board: *unlike, however, but, in contrast, on the other hand*. Explain that each shows a relationship between ideas that are different.
- Write these words on the board: *the same as, similar to, both, like, in common*. Explain that they show similarities between things.
- Have students work with a partner to write one sentence describing a difference between the two poems and another explaining a similarity, focusing on the view of nature presented in each poem.

▲ **Structure**

Help students analyze the form of odes and other lyric poems.

- Teacher's Edition side notes, pp. 170, 171, 172, 173
- When Students Struggle, p. 172
- Strategies for Annotation, pp. 171, 173
- Analyze Form, pp. 171, 173

To teach how to analyze narrator, see

- Analyze Narrator, p. 174a

 Understanding Form

▶ *Use It!* **Interactive Whiteboard Lesson:** Form in Poetry

***ZOOM IN ON* ANALYZING POETIC FORM** Tell students that a poem's **form** includes its rhythm, line length, rhyme, whether it is divided into stanzas, and even its punctuation.

- Model how to analyze poetic form. Read aloud the sentence in lines 5–11 of "Sleeping in the Forest" while students follow along in their books. Ask students why such a long sentence fits the poem's topic. (*This uninterrupted flow fits with the speaker's long and peaceful sleep.*) Point out that the poem is not broken into stanzas, just as the speaker's sleep is unbroken.
- Next, have pairs discuss why "Ode" is divided into stanzas. Have them consider the topic of each stanza and how those topics relate to each other. Ask volunteers to share their insights.

▲ Language Conventionality and Clarity

Help students discuss poetry.

- Teacher's Edition side note, p. 172
- English Language Support, p. 169

ZOOM IN ON **FIGURATIVE LANGUAGE** Explain that poets use **figurative language**, including metaphors, similes, and personification, to express a theme. Display these examples: *The world is / a glass overflowing / with water* (Neruda, lines 13–15); *I thought the earth / remembered me, she / took me back so tenderly* (Oliver, lines 1–3).

- Identify the figure of speech in each. *(metaphor; personification)*
- Ask pairs to compare the view of the natural world that each image expresses. *(Possible responses: The image from "Ode" celebrates nature's abundance. The image from "Sleeping" shows "mother earth" as a place of security and comfort. Both poets present nature positively, but Oliver expresses a personal link with nature.)*

▲ Knowledge Demands

Support English Learners in understanding background.

- Teacher's Edition Background note, p. 169

ZOOM IN ON **BUILDING LITERARY BACKGROUND** Share information about the poets with students:

- Both poets are known for their nature poems. One critic notes that Neruda's nature poems let us "examine a particular plant, a stone, a flower . . . at leisure." Poet Maxine Kumin describes Mary Oliver as standing "on the line between earth and sky."
- Explain that Neruda wrote in Spanish. Locate his original "Oda a la luz encantada" and have a Spanish speaker read it aloud. Discuss differences in sound and rhythm between the versions.

▲ Suggested Reader/Task Considerations

Consider the following before assigning these poems to students.

- Will students be able to remember details and make connections between the texts?
- Will students need support to answer any questions about the material?

ZOOM IN ON **SUPPORTING COMPREHENSION**

- Have small groups each compare one feature of the two poems: overall view of nature; sensory images; figurative language; and structure. Each group should share its findings in a whole-class discussion.
- If students find the questions on page 174 challenging, organize them in mixed-ability groups, assigning one question to each group. Have groups write answers to their questions and share with the class.

TEACH

CLOSE READ

Background Have students read the background and information about the poets. Tell students that, although these poets use different poetic forms and styles to write about nature, both express an appreciation for nature that causes us to consider our own feelings about nature and our relationship with it.

SETTING A PURPOSE Direct students to use the Setting a Purpose prompt to focus their reading. Remind them to write down questions as they read.

English Language Support

Read Closely Before discussing each poem, read it aloud as students listen and follow along. Point out that unless there is a mark of punctuation, readers should not pause at the end of a line.

- Have student pairs practice reading each poem aloud with expression. Remind them to pay attention to punctuation marks.
- After students complete the activity, ask them what words and lines in each poem stand out when they read it aloud. Discuss what impression the poem creates when they listen to it.

English Language Support

Analyze Language Tell students that a poem's title can introduce the topic or show the poet's views on the subject.

- Read the title of Neruda's poem aloud. Write the word *enchanted* on the board. Explain that in this context, it means "magical."
- Ask students what the use of the word *enchanted* suggests to them about Neruda's view of nature. *(He sees nature as magical, offering something that is beyond what can be easily explained.)*
- Tell students to look for "magical" images as they read the poem.

Background *The topic of nature is popular with poets around the world and throughout history. Two of the most important poets of the 20th century, Pablo Neruda and Mary Oliver, continue this tradition with their poems in this lesson. Neruda's poem "Ode to enchanted light" was written originally in Spanish. Its Spanish title is "Oda a la luz enchantada."*

Ode to enchanted light

Sleeping in the Forest

Poem by Pablo Neruda   Poem by Mary Oliver

Pablo Neruda (1904–1973) *was the pen name of Ricardo Eliecer Neftalí Reyes Basoalto. Born in a small town in Chile, Neruda began writing poetry as a child. While a student, he met Gabriela Mistral, a famous poet. She encouraged Neruda to continue writing. Neruda went on to write hundreds of poems and gain a worldwide reputation. He was awarded the Nobel Prize for Literature in 1971 for his lifetime of work.*

Mary Oliver (b. 1935) *was born in Maple Heights, Ohio. She spent a great deal of time in her younger years writing, reading, and walking through the woods where she grew up. Today, Oliver always walks with a notepad so she can write down her thoughts immediately. Oliver's first book of poems was published in 1962. Since then she has written many books and won many awards for her poetry.*

SETTING A PURPOSE As you read, think about how each poet portrays a meaningful experience in nature. Beyond the subject matter, how are the poems similar? How are they different? Write down any questions you have while reading.

Compare Texts **169**

Close Read Screencasts

 Close Read

Modeled Discussions

Have students click the *Close Read* icons in their eBooks to access two screencasts in which readers discuss and annotate the following key lines from each poem:

- "A cicada sends . . ." ("Ode to enchanted light" lines 10–12)
- "I thought the earth . . ." ("Sleeping in the Forest" lines 1–5)

As a class, view and discuss at least one of these videos. Then have students work in pairs to do an independent close read of an additional passage—the last stanza from "Ode to enchanted light" (lines 13–15) or the last seven lines in "Sleeping in the Forest" (lines 12–18).

Analyze Form: Ode (LINES 1–15)   RL 1, RL 5

Explain that an **ode** expresses appreciation for its subject. It usually deals with serious themes and may follow set rules for structure, rhyme, and rhythm.

A CITE TEXT EVIDENCE Have students identify evidence that this poem is an ode. *(It expresses appreciation for natural light shining through leaves. Phrases such as "shining / on every leaf" and "a glass overflowing" express an abundance of natural beauty.)*

Determine Meaning (LINES 3–5)   RL 1, RL 4

Explain that **figurative language** compares things in a way that is not literally true, to emphasize ideas or create an emotional effect. Note that a **simile** is a type of figurative language that compares using *like* or *as*.

B CITE TEXT EVIDENCE Ask students to identify the simile in lines 3–5. *("light / like a green / latticework of branches")* Ask students to identify the comparing word (*like*), explain what is being compared, and tell how this simile affects the poem's meaning. *(The light is compared to a green crisscross pattern, creating the "enchanted" image of dappled, dancing light.)*

🔲 Text in FOCUS   English Language Support

Understanding Form (Line 15)

Have students view the **Text In Focus** video on this page of their eBook to understand line breaks in poetry and to learn how to use punctuation cues to aid comprehension. Then have students use **Text In Focus Practice** to apply what they have learned.

Ode to enchanted light
by Pablo Neruda
translated by Ken Krabbenhoft

Under the trees light
has dropped from the top of the sky,
light
like a green
5 latticework of branches,
shining
on every leaf,
drifting down like clean
white sand.

10 A cicada sends
its sawing song
high into the empty air.

The world is
a glass overflowing
15 with water.

🔲 Close Read

🔲 Text in FOCUS

©vovan/Shutterstock

English Language Support

Analyze Language Direct students' attention to the first two lines: the speaker is located "under the trees" looking up. Explain that the images in the first stanza describe what the speaker sees from this perspective.

- Highlight the phrase "light like a green latticework of branches" in lines 3–5. Define the word *latticework*, and guide students to explain what is being compared in this simile. *(The light hits the branches and leaves to form a crisscross pattern.)*

- Discuss the simile in lines 3–5. Then have students find another simile in the poem. *("drifting down like clean white sand")* Ask what image this simile creates. *(Falling sand is soundless and soft; the light pours down in a silent, white stream.)*

- Have pairs identify the similes in the poem and explain their effect. Ask students to relate these images to the title of the poem. How is the light "enchanted"? *(The similes convey the speaker's perspective of looking up through the tree branches. The light is enchanted because it moves, shines, drifts, and transforms.)*

Analyze Form: Ode   RL 5

Pablo Neruda's poem is an **ode,** a poem that deals with serious themes, such as justice, truth, or beauty. An ode praises or celebrates its subject, which is usually a person, event, thing, or element in nature.

The word *ode* comes from the Greek word *aeidein*, which means to sing or chant. Originally, the ode was written to be accompanied by music and dance. A traditional ode is a long poem with a formal structure, and due to its dignified nature, its language is often formal as well. Many modern poets experiment with the form to make it fresh and interesting for modern readers. What do you notice about the length and arrangement of lines in Neruda's poem?

Analyzing the Text   RL 1, RL 4, RL 5

Cite Text Evidence   Support your responses with evidence from the text.

1. **Infer** What feelings are suggested in lines 1–9 of this poem? How does the poet suggest those feelings?

2. **Analyze** A cicada is an insect that makes a high-pitched, continual sound, usually in summer. Reread lines 10–12. What repeated first sounds, or **alliteration,** do you hear, and how are the sounds connected to the poem's meaning?

3. **Analyze and Evaluate** Does this poem meet the requirements of an ode? Why or why not?

Ode to enchanted light   **171**

PRACTICE & APPLY

Analyze Form: Ode   RL 5

Review the definition of an ode. Have students tell what subject the poet is praising in "Ode to enchanted light." Next, review that, when analyzing the form of a poem, students should pay attention to how the poem is laid out on the page—line lengths, line breaks, how the lines are grouped, and any patterns of rhythm and rhyme. Using the question as a prompt, discuss how the form of this poem impacts its meaning. (*The poem is a mix of long and short lines—some just one word long—and one long stanza followed by two shorter stanzas of equal length. The first stanza creates a cascading, tumbling feeling—as if the words are falling down the page in the same way that light is tumbling through the trees. The second stanza has a regular pattern of rhythm—almost like the sound of a cicada. Finally, in the last stanza, the longer middle line emphasizes the image of the "glass overflowing.")*

Analyzing the Text   RL 1, RL 4, RL 5

Possible answers:

1. *The lines suggest a feeling of calm, of being transfixed by the light dropping through the tree branches. The poet creates this feeling first with the setting, "Under the trees." Then, the phrase "a green/latticework of branches" compares the broken pattern of light to the crossed patterns of tree branches. This suggests a peaceful setting. He finishes the stanza with the image of the light as "drifting down like clean / white sand."*

2. *The /s/ sounds in "cicada sends / its sawing song" suggest the repetitious, raspy noise of a cicada itself.*

3. *Yes. The poem expresses an appreciation for how light enhances the beauty of sights and sounds in nature.*

Strategies for Annotation   Annotate it!

Analyze Form: Ode   RL 5

Have students use their eBook annotation tools to do the following:

- Count the number of lines in each stanza.
- Underline the repeating words.
- Highlight all repeating initial consonant sounds in yellow.
- Highlight repeating sounds within words in green.
- On a note, jot down any patterns in lines, stanzas, or rhythm.

Under the trees light

has dropped from the top of the sky,

light

like a green

latticework of branches,

> no set rhythmic pattern; suggests enchanting dance of light through branches of trees

Analyze Form: Lyric Poem (LINES 1–14)

RL 1,
RL 2
RL 5,
RL 6

Explain to students that a **lyric poem** is a poem that expresses the personal thoughts and feelings of a speaker. The **speaker,** or the person who is telling the poem, can be the poet or an invented character who has an experience that he or she is responding to.

A **CITE TEXT EVIDENCE** Ask students to reread lines 1–8, identify the speaker, and explain what he or she is communicating to the reader. Which words reveal the speaker's message? (*The poem begins with the word* I. *This suggests that the poet could be the speaker, recounting a very personal experience in the forest. The phrase "thought the earth remembered me," suggests that the poet is talking about an intimate companion—someone who is holding her like a mother might hold a baby in the "dark skirts" of her lap.*)

B **CITE TEXT EVIDENCE** Have students reread lines 9–14. Is the speaker comfortable in the natural world? What text evidence supports your answer? (*The speaker conveys the idea that, in the forest, the separation between her and the natural world dissolves. The speaker's thoughts are "light" and are in tune with the "small kingdoms" of animals.*)

Determine Meaning

RL 1,
RL 4

(LINES 9–11)

Remind students that poets often use figurative language to compare things, give emphasis to meaning, and create emotion.

C **ASK STUDENTS** to identify the figurative language used in lines 9–11 (*simile*) and explain its effect on the meaning of the poem. (*The poet compares two unlike things: her thoughts to flying moths. The simile describes how close to nature she feels, and how her thoughts come and go like moths flying.*)

COLLABORATIVE DISCUSSION Have partners reread the first two lines of each poem to one another and discuss their ideas about each speaker's relationship to nature. Remind students to cite evidence from the poems to support their ideas.

Sleeping in the Forest
by Mary Oliver

Close
Read

A

I thought the earth
remembered me, she
took me back so tenderly, arranging
her dark skirts, her pockets
5   full of lichens[1] and seeds. I slept
as never before, a stone
on the riverbed, nothing
between me and the white fire of the stars

B but my thoughts, and they floated   **C**
10   light as moths among the branches
of the perfect trees. All night
I heard the small kingdoms breathing
around me, the insects, and the birds
who do their work in the darkness. All night
15   I rose and fell, as if in water, grappling[2]
with a luminous doom. By morning
I had vanished at least a dozen times
into something better.

COLLABORATIVE DISCUSSION Read the first two lines of each poem and compare the images they present. What do these lines say about the speaker's relationship to nature? Share your ideas with the students in your class.

---
[1] **lichens** (lī´kənz): fungi that grow together with algae and form a crust-like growth on rocks or tree trunks.
[2] **grappling:** struggling.

WHEN STUDENTS STRUGGLE . . .

Guide students in understanding the rhythm of the poem. Discuss how the line lengths vary and how the punctuation occurs within the lines. Reread lines 14–18 aloud. Point out how the different line breaks and punctuation affect the rhythm. Then rewrite the poem, changing the line breaks. Reread the lines again.

ASK STUDENTS how reading the poem in this way changes the rhythm.

 LEVEL UP TUTORIALS For additional support, assign the following *Level Up* tutorial: **Rhythm.**

Analyze Form: Lyric Poem

RL 4, RL 5

"Sleeping in the Forest" is a **lyric poem,** a short poem in which a single speaker expresses personal thoughts and feelings. Lyric poetry is a broad category that includes traditional forms such as odes and sonnets, as well as **free verse,** a form that does not use formal structure or rhyme schemes. In fact, in ancient times, lyric poems were created to be sung. Although they aren't sung today, lyric poems do have some elements in common with songs, including

- a sense of rhythm and melody
- imaginative word choice, or **diction**
- the creation of a single, unified impression

What is the single, unified impression conveyed in this poem?

Analyzing the Text

RL 1, RL 4, RL 5

> Cite Text Evidence   Support your responses with evidence from the text.

1. **Interpret** Reread the last sentence in the poem. What might the speaker mean by "something better"?

2. **Analyze** Reread lines 5–7. What is compared to "a stone / on the riverbed"? Where else does that image appear in the poem?

3. **Analyze and Evaluate** Identify examples of each of the elements of a lyric poem that appear in "Sleeping in the Forest." Do you think Oliver's poem is a good example of a lyric poem? Why or why not?

PRACTICE & APPLY

Analyze Form: Lyric Poem

RL 4, RL 5

Review the elements of lyric poetry with students and discuss the question. *(The single impression is of someone blissfully lying on the forest floor at night, absorbing the sounds, sights, and feelings of the forest. It's an image of a child sleeping in his or her mother's arms.)* Then ask students to tell whether the poem is traditional or free verse. Have students provide an explanation for their answer. *(The poem is free verse. The arrangement of words and lines does not follow any fixed rules for number of lines, line length, or pattern of rhythm and rhyme.)*

Analyzing the Text

RL 1, RL 4, RL 5

Possible answers:

1. *Perhaps sleeping in the forest enriches the speaker so that she is a better person, at one with nature. Perhaps spending a night in the forest has sent the speaker into another realm, better than the world of daylight.*

2. *The sleeping speaker is compared to a stone on the riverbed; both lie still. The image of being in water is reinforced by these words elsewhere in the poem: "floated"; "rose and fell, as if in water."*

3. *The poem is intimate, expressing the speaker's thoughts and feelings about nature and life, as inspired by a blissful experience sleeping in a forest one night. While the poem is free verse and has no end rhymes, it does have a steady rhythm, suggestive of the breathing of an infant. Word choices such as "the white fire of the stars" and "small kingdoms breathing" are imaginative. It gives an impression of a child sleeping in its mother's arms.*

Strategies for Annotation

 Annotate it!

Analyze Form: Lyric Poem

RL 4, RL 5

Share these strategies for guided or independent analysis:

- Highlight in blue imaginative word choices.
- On a note, jot down how the arrangement of lines creates rhythm and how the rhythm changes throughout the poem.

> I heard the small kingdoms breathing
> around me, the insects, and the birds
> who do their work in the darkness. All night
> I rose and fell, as if in water, grappling
> with a luminous doom. By morning

> The changing rhythm is like the in-and-out/rising-and-falling of gentle breathing while sleeping.

PRACTICE & APPLY

Determine Meaning
RL 1, RL 4

Discuss the examples of simile, metaphor, and personification. Then, ask students to reread "Ode to enchanted light" before answering the question. *(This is a simile. It uses the word* like *to compare the light to "clean white sand.")* Ask students to find additional examples of figurative language in each poem. Discuss the impact each one has on meaning and emotion.

Analyzing the Text
RL 1, RL 4, RL 5, RL 6

Possible answers:

1. *"The world is a glass overflowing with water" is a metaphor. The image suggests that the world, like overflowing water, is clear, sparkling, fresh, life-giving, and abundant.*

2. *The earth is personified as a woman wearing dark skirts with pockets. Perhaps the poet is making a connection to the familiar concept of Mother Nature or an earth goddess from mythology, who lovingly cradles and nurtures the speaker during sleep.*

3. *In Neruda's poem, "drifting down like clean / white sand" is part of a simile comparing the light dropping through the trees to drifting sand. In Oliver's poem, "but my thoughts, and they floated / light as moths among the branches / of the perfect trees," is a simile comparing the speaker's thoughts to floating moths. One image conveys downward motion; the other conveys a feeling of floating upward.*

4. *In "Ode to enchanted light," the speaker's vision of light is the subject of the poem. Light is enchanting, or magical. In "Sleeping in the Forest," the speaker is in darkness, seeing only "the white fire of the stars." The phrase "luminous doom" suggests a negative or worrisome connection to something light or glowing.*

Determine Meaning
RL 1, RL 4

Through **figurative language,** words are used in an imaginative way to express ideas that are not literally true. The most common types are

 a comparison between two unlike things using the word *like* or *as* (*friendship as sturdy as a tree*)

 a comparison of two things that are basically unlike but have some qualities in common; a metaphor does not contain the word *like* or *as* (*a forest of confused thoughts*)

 the giving of human qualities to an animal, object, or idea (*the trees stood guard*)

In the poem "Ode to enchanted light," the poet Pablo Neruda states that light is "drifting down like clean / white sand." What type of figurative language does this phrase represent?

Analyzing the Text
RL 1, RL 4, RL 5, W2, W 10

Cite Text Evidence Support your responses with evidence from the texts.

1. **Interpret** Reread lines 13–15 of "Ode to enchanted light." What type of figurative language is represented here, and what is the comparison being made? What feelings does this evoke in the reader?

2. **Analyze** What is personified in lines 1–5 of "Sleeping in the Forest"? Why might the poet have chosen to use this personification?

3. **Compare** Reread lines 8–9 of "Ode" and lines 9–11 of "Sleeping in the Forest." What similarities do you observe in the poets' use of language?

4. **Analyze** How do the images of light differ in these two poems?

PERFORMANCE TASK

Writing Activity: Poem Write a four-stanza poem to describe an experience with nature.

• Base the poem on your own experiences or on an imagined one.

• Experiment with figurative language.

• Consider expressing a theme or message about nature.

• As you create your poem, try reading it aloud to help you refine your choices of words or effects.

Assign this performance task.

PERFORMANCE TASK
W 3, W 10

Writing Activity: Poem Have students work independently. Tell students to do the following: decide on the main message they want to convey; read and listen to other types of poems to help them choose a form that suits their message; decide who the speaker will be; choose words carefully, using imaginative words and figurative language; and use imagery.

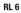

INTERACTIVE WHITEBOARD LESSON
Determine Theme

RL 2,
SL 1

TEACH

Explain that the **theme** of a poem is the main message about life or human nature that a poet communicates to the reader. The theme is often implied, rather than directly stated. Readers can identify the theme by paying attention to the words and details in a poem and by asking themselves, "What big message about life is the poet trying to tell me?"

Use the Interactive Whiteboard Lesson "Theme/Central Idea" to help students identify and explore theme in poetry.

Review the steps for identifying theme:

1. Examine clues in the text. What does the title tell you? How does the poet use figurative language to convey a message?

2. Use the clues to determine the theme.

COLLABORATIVE DISCUSSION

Have students work in groups to apply the steps to the example texts in the Interactive Whiteboard Lesson. Have students compare their results in a group discussion.

FOR STUDENTS WITH DISABILITIES

If students struggle with orally communicating their thoughts in group discussion, allow them to use their tablets to share their ideas about the possible themes of the poems. Alternatively, have them record their insights on paper for a partner to read aloud.

Analyze Narrator

RL 6

TEACH

Explain that the **speaker** of a poem is the voice that "talks" to the reader. Tell students that, in a lyric poem, the speaker can be the poet, but doesn't have to be. They can identify the speaker by paying attention to the words and details in the poem.

Reread lines 1–5 of "Sleeping in the Forest." Tell students that the phrase "I thought the earth remembered me, she took me back so tenderly" suggests that the speaker is an adult who is doing something he or she has done before, and that he or she has feelings of intimacy, familiarity, and safety with the earth.

Point out that because the poem is told in the first-person singular—using pronouns such as *I, me,* and *my*—it is possible that the speaker is the poet, recounting an actual experience in the forest. Explain further, however, that as with many poems, it is almost impossible to tell who the speaker is for certain.

PRACTICE AND APPLY

Have students identify other details that help them understand who the speaker is and what the poem reveals about the speaker.

Have students discuss the following questions with a partner:

- Is there just one speaker? How do you know?
- What words and details suggest who the speaker is?
- What are the thoughts and feelings of the speaker? Do they change throughout the poem?
- Have you had similar experiences? How did they make you feel? How might you describe the experience in a poem?

English Language Support

Read Closely Adapt the collection opener strategy, Learning Circles, to help students analyze the speaker in "Sleeping in the Forest."

1. Form small groups of three and have members choose their roles: one should record details and words that identify the speaker; one should note lines that show the speaker's thoughts and feelings; and the third should analyze whether or not the speaker changes during the poem.

2. Have students listen to the poem or reread it and make their notes.

3. Have group members share and discuss what they have learned about the speaker. Remind them to ask clarifying questions and build on each other's comments.

Problems with Hurricanes

Victor Hernández Cruz

Prayer to the Pacific

Leslie Marmon Silko

Tornado at Talladega

Gwendolyn Brooks

Why These Texts

Because poetry, both in its form (lines and stanzas rather than sentences and paragraphs) and in its use of language (sound devices, imagery, and figurative language), is so different from prose, some students may have difficulty understanding it. With the help of the close-reading questions, students will analyze three poems, using the questions to enhance their comprehension. This close reading will lead students to develop a deeper understanding of not only the specific poems but also poetry in general.

Background Have students read the background information about nature being an inspiration for poets. Tell them that these three poems are all lyric poems—short poems in which a single speaker expresses his or her personal thoughts and feelings. In these poems, nature has been an inspiration to each of the poets. Their varied heritages have colored their styles and their individual responses to nature, but each adds insights into the world we live in.

SETTING A PURPOSE Ask students to read each poem carefully and slowly, noting how the poem sounds as well as what it says. Remind them to pay close attention to the author's tone and use of figurative language.

Standards Support

- cite evidence from the text
- determine the meaning of words and phrases, including figurative language
- analyze how a poem's form contributes to its meaning

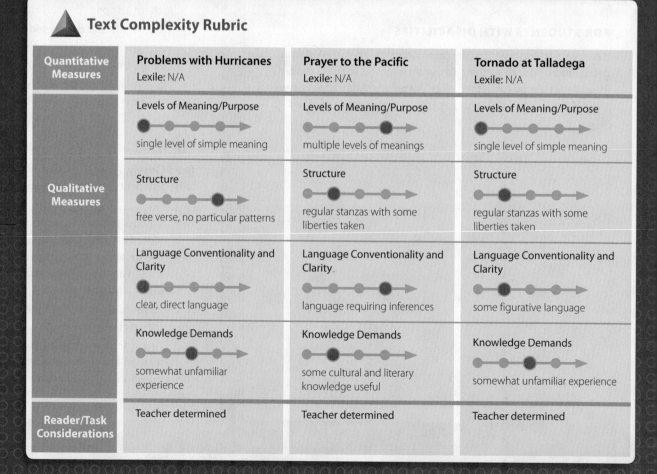

▲ Text Complexity Rubric

	Problems with Hurricanes	Prayer to the Pacific	Tornado at Talladega
Quantitative Measures	Lexile: N/A	Lexile: N/A	Lexile: N/A
Qualitative Measures	Levels of Meaning/Purpose single level of simple meaning	Levels of Meaning/Purpose multiple levels of meanings	Levels of Meaning/Purpose single level of simple meaning
	Structure free verse, no particular patterns	Structure regular stanzas with some liberties taken	Structure regular stanzas with some liberties taken
	Language Conventionality and Clarity clear, direct language	Language Conventionality and Clarity language requiring inferences	Language Conventionality and Clarity some figurative language
	Knowledge Demands somewhat unfamiliar experience	Knowledge Demands some cultural and literary knowledge useful	Knowledge Demands somewhat unfamiliar experience
Reader/Task Considerations	Teacher determined	Teacher determined	Teacher determined

Strategies for CLOSE READING

Determine Meaning

Students should read each poem carefully and slowly. Close-reading questions at the bottom of the page will help them determine the meaning of figurative language to better understand the poems. As they read, students should jot down comments or questions about the text in the margins.

WHEN STUDENTS STRUGGLE . . .

To help students cite text evidence in the poems, have them work in small groups to fill out a chart like the one shown below.

CITE TEXT EVIDENCE For practice in determining meaning, ask students to explain the meaning of the figurative language in the chart below.

Figurative Language	Meaning
If you are going out/ beware of mangoes/And all such beautiful/sweet things. ("Problems with Hurricanes," lines 32–35)	Very beautiful things can sometimes turn out to be dangerous.
Four round stones in my pocket I carry back the ocean/Thirty thousand years ago to suck and taste. ("Prayer to the Pacific," lines 15–16)	The ocean is very old and carries with it many mysteries.
Here, roots, ire, origins exposed / across this twig-strewn, leaf-strewn road they lie,/mute, and ashamed, and through. ("Tornado at Tallageda," lines 11–13)	Nature is powerful and can quickly demolish even a mighty tree.

Background *Nature has been an inspiration to poets and writers for thousands of years. Whether it's the soothing view of a sunset over the ocean or the startling sound of thunder in a rainstorm, nature can excite the senses and the imaginations of all people. The following three poems present different views on three aspects of nature.*

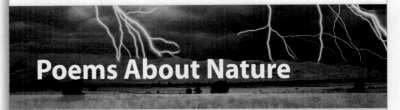

Poems About Nature

Problems with Hurricanes . . . . Victor Hernández Cruz
Prayer to the Pacific . . . . Leslie Marmon Silko
Tornado at Talladega. . . . . Gwendolyn Brooks

Victor Hernández Cruz *was born in Puerto Rico in 1949. When he was five, his family moved to New York City. He began writing at the age of 15. His lively, often humorous poems reflect his bilingual and bicultural heritage. Cruz is the author of numerous poetry collections and the recipient of many awards. .*

Leslie Marmon Silko *was born in Albuquerque, New Mexico, in 1948. She grew up on the Laguna Pueblo reservation. Her mixed ancestry (Laguna Pueblo, Mexican, and Caucasian) caused her a lot of pain, as she faced discriminatation from both the Native American and white communities. She would go on to write stories that explore how differences can be reconciled.*

Gwendolyn Brooks *was born in Kansas in 1917, but grew up in Chicago. She published her first poem when she was 14 years old. By the time she was 17, over one hundred of her poems were published in a poetry column in the Chicago Defender. She went on to become the first African American author to win the Pulitzer Prize.*

55

1. **READ ▶** As you read "Problems with Hurricanes," collect and cite textual evidence.

- In the first stanza, underline what the campesino says to worry about.
- Circle words the campesino uses to assess various ways of dying. In the margin, note the distinction he makes.
- In the margin, write why the campesino warns of "beautiful sweet things" (lines 34–35).

Problems with Hurricanes
by Victor Hernández Cruz

A campesino¹ looked at the air
And told me:
With hurricanes it's not the wind
or the noise or the water.
5   I'll tell you he said:
it's the mangoes, avocados
Green plantains and bananas
flying into town like **projectiles**.

projectile:
object thrown
with great
force

A   How would your family
10   feel if they had to tell
The generations that you
got killed by a flying
Banana.

The campesino
says that being
killed by the
water or wind
is honorable
but being
killed by a
flying fruit
would be
shameful.

Death by drowning has honor
15   If the wind picked you up
and slammed you
Against a mountain boulder
This would not carry shame
But
20   to suffer a mango smashing
Your skull
or a plantain hitting your
Temple at 70 miles per hour
is the ultimate disgrace.

¹ **campesino** (käm-pĭ-sē´-nō): a farm worker.

56

> *If you are going out*
> *beware of mangoes*
> *And all such beautiful*
> *sweet things.*

The campesino
warns the
speaker to
watch out for
appealing
things that
may seem
harmless.

B   25   The campesino takes off his hat—
As a sign of respect
toward the fury of the wind
And says:
Don't worry about the noise
30   Don't worry about the water
Don't worry about the wind—
If you are going out
beware of mangoes
And all such beautiful
35   sweet things.

2. **◀ REREAD** Reread the poem. What does the speaker suggest about nature in lines 32–35? What broader message about life might he be conveying?

The speaker suggests that nature can turn something as harmless as
a mango into a deadly object. The speaker may be conveying the
message that it is easy to be mindful of obvious dangers, but we
should also be wary of seemingly innocent things in our lives.

57

---

1. **READ AND CITE TEXT EVIDENCE**   The speaker tells readers that it would be shameful and disgraceful to die from being hit by a flying banana or mango.

   A   **ASK STUDENTS** whether or not they think the speaker is trying to be funny in lines 9–13. Have them support their answer with evidence from the text. *Students might say that they know the speaker is trying to be funny because he uses a funny example: bananas. Also, the idea of someone's legacy being ruined because he or she was hit by a flying banana is funny as well.*

   Critical Vocabulary: projectile (line 8) Have students share their definitions of *projectile*. Ask them to explain why they would not want to be hit by a projectile. *Students might say they don't want to be hit by a projectile because a projectile would be whizzing through the air and would probably hurt if it struck someone.*

2. **REREAD AND CITE TEXT EVIDENCE**   The poem talks about both the beauty and the unexpected power of nature.

   B   **ASK STUDENTS** how the campesino feels about nature and the power of storms. *The campesino respects nature and the power of storms. You can tell this because he takes off his hat as a sign of respect.*

3. **READ** ▶ As you read "Prayer to the Pacific," continue to cite textual evidence.

• In the margin, explain what Silko means when she calls the ocean "Big as the myth of origin" (line 5).
• Underline examples of personification in the poem.
• Circle the lines that have large gaps between words.

Prayer to the Pacific
by Leslie Marmon Silko

The ocean has many mysteries that cannot be known. We have many stories that tell how the world started, but no one can be certain of the truth.

I traveled to the ocean
    distant
        from my southwest land of sandrock
      to the moving blue water
    Big as the myth of origin.
5 Pale
pale water in the yellow-white light of
D   sun   floating west
      to China
10   where ocean herself was born.
Clouds that blow across the sand are wet.

Squat in the wet sand and speak to the Ocean:
    I return to you turquoise the red coral you sent us,
C   sister spirit of Earth.
15   Four round stones in my pocket I carry back the ocean
Thirty thousand years ago to suck and to taste.
    Indians came riding across the ocean
    carried by giant sea turtles.
Waves were high that day
20   great sea turtles waded   slowly out
        from the gray sundown sea.
Grandfather Turtle rolled in the sand   four times
    and disappeared
        swimming into the sun.

25 And so   from that time
    immemorial,
        as the old people say,
rain clouds drift from the west
        gift from the ocean.
30   Green leaves in the wind
Wet earth on my feet
    swallowing raindrops
        clear from China.

immemorial: *ancient; centuries old*

4. **◀ REREAD** Reread the poem and note the lines you circled. What is the effect of separating words within a line? What does it contribute to the meaning of the poem? Support your answer with explicit textual evidence.

It creates a sense of long, drawn-out movement. The water of the ocean is "floating" along, it isn't rushed. A turtle wading out to sea or rolling in sand will do so slowly because turtles move slowly. Gaps like the one in line 25 also suggest movement by the waves.

58   59

---

3. **READ AND CITE TEXT EVIDENCE**

C **ASK STUDENTS** why the author might have chosen to use personification in the poem. Have them note the poem's title. *The poem is a "prayer," and as such, it is directed to someone.* How does the author personify the ocean? *as a woman ("ocean herself"; "sister spirit")* What other things are personified? *Earth (who has a sister spirit), Grandfather turtle, and the ground swallowing raindrops.*

FOR ELL STUDENTS Clarify the meaning of the verb *squat.* Explain that in this context, it means to lower your body close to the floor by bending your knees.

4. **REREAD AND CITE TEXT EVIDENCE**

D **ASK STUDENTS** to read the poem quietly to themselves, resting at the separations within sentences, and pausing before each indented line. How does reading the poem as it is written affect its meaning? *Students may suggest that the poem becomes more of a spoken "prayer," and the pauses intensify the meaning.* Ask what visual effect the structure of the poem has. *Students may notice that some of the lines are arranged in a formation that resembles a wave.*

Critical Vocabulary: immemorial (line 26) The text says that *immemorial* has something to do with time. Have students share examples of other things that human beings have been doing since time immemorial (for example, *creating art, making music, waging war*). Then, ask students to share their definitions of *immemorial.*

5. **READ ▶** As you read "Tornado At Talladega," continue to cite textual evidence.

  • Underline examples of personification in the poem.
  • Circle examples of repetition.

Tornado at Talladega
by Gwendolyn Brooks

Who is that bird
reporting the storm?—
E after What came through
to do some landscaping.

5 Certain trees
stick across the road.
They are unimportant now.
F They cannot sass anymore.
Not one of these, the bewildered,
10 can announce anymore "How fine I am!"
Here, roots, **ire**, origins exposed,
across this twig-strewn, leaf-strewn road they lie,
mute, and ashamed, and through.

It happened all of a sudden.

15 Certain women and men and children
come out to stare.

ire:
rage; anger;
indignation

6. **◀ REREAD AND DISCUSS** Reread the poem. In a small group, discuss the way personification affects your perception of the trees.

SHORT RESPONSE

Cite Text Evidence How does each poet present nature in these poems? Review your reading notes and **cite text evidence** in your response.

Nature is shown as a powerful force in many ways. The speaker in Cruz's poem states that nature can make weapons of any object. Silko says one cannot fully comprehend all of the ocean's mysteries. Brooks presents a powerful image of trees destroyed by a tornado.

60

---

5. **READ AND CITE TEXT EVIDENCE**

  E **ASK STUDENTS** why the author describes the storm as something that "came through to do some landscaping." *The image conveys that the trees have been changed by the storm.*

6. **REREAD AND CITE TEXT EVIDENCE**

  F **ASK STUDENTS** to name some of the ways trees are affected by the storm. *They are "mute, and ashamed, and through."*

Critical Vocabulary: ire (line 11) Have students give examples of situations that would probably arouse their ire.

SHORT RESPONSE

Cite Text Evidence Students should:

• explain how each author presents nature.
• cite text evidence to support their answers.

TO CHALLENGE STUDENTS . . .

For more context and historical background, students can view the video "Science of a Hurricane" in their eBooks.

ASK STUDENTS to discuss the way the video treats the subject of hurricanes and the way the poet Cruz treats hurricanes in "Problems with Hurricanes." Remind students to cite specific passages from the poem and details from the video to support their claims. Students might address any of the following:

• the tone, or how the subject matter is treated. Is the tone of each piece serious, respectful, humorous, flippant, or something else?

• the author's use of figurative language, such as metaphor, simile, and personification in the poem as compared with the visual imagery that is present in the video. How does this use of language add to the meaning of the poem? What do the images in the video convey about hurricanes?

• the structure of the poem and the video clip.

• how they are similar to or different from other works about hurricanes that you are familiar with.

DIG DEEPER

With the class, return to the Short Response question. Have students share their answers.

ASK STUDENTS what additional information they can give about how each author they have studied dealt with the topic of nature in his or her poetry. Remind students to cite evidence from the text to support each of their points. Students should:

- consider the author's tone, or his or her attitude toward the subject. *The tone of "Problems with Hurricanes" is humorous until the very end, when it becomes serious. The tone of "Prayer to the Pacific" is reverent and serious. The tone of "Tornado at Talladega" is at various points humorous, awestruck, and sad.*

- consider the author's use of figurative language, such as similes, metaphors, and personification to express feelings. *In "Problems with Hurricanes," the author uses a simile—flying into town like projectiles—to describe the flight of fruit during a hurricane. In "Prayer to the Pacific" the author uses a simile to describe the ocean—big as the myth, or origin. In "Tornado at Talladega" the author uses a metaphor—landscaping—to describe the effect of the tornado.*

- consider how the author structures the poem. Look at where lines break and the gaps between words. *In "Problems with Hurricanes" the author places the word "But," line 19, on its own separate line to emphasize the difference between a death with honor and dying because a mango smashed into your head. In "Prayer to the Pacific" the author places large gaps between words when she wants the reader to slow down and feel the slow passage of time. In "Tornado at Talladega" the author emphasizes the suddenness and swiftness of a tornado's destruction by setting "It happened all of a sudden," line 14, totally apart from the rest of the poem.*

ASK STUDENTS to return to their Short Response answer and revise it based on the class discussion.

CLOSE READING NOTES

NATURE AT WORK

The FYI site provides links to online articles from a variety of magazines and newspapers. Help students choose a few articles to read to further their exploration of the topic Nature at Work.

NOVELWISE

Students can unlock the power of novels with this unique resource. Help students read through longer works with these tips:

- Find a Book
- Before You Read
- As You Read
- After You Read

Each book includes introductory material, worksheets, graphic organizers, and discussion guides.

ADDITIONAL TEXTS BY COLLECTION

Have students compare figurative language and imagery in three poems, citing text evidence to argue which poet most effectively uses these techniques to represent nature. Suggested poems include: "Sea Fever" by John Masefield; "Is the Moon Tired?" by Christina Rossetti; "On the Grasshopper and Cricket" by John Keats; "The Lake" by Edgar Allan Poe; "I Wandered Lonely as a Cloud" by William Wordsworth; and "The First Snowfall" by James Russell Lowell.

NONFICTION CONNECTIONS

Suggest that students increase their reading of informational texts. The nonfiction connections include

- speeches
- diaries
- true-life accounts
- newspaper articles
- political cartoons

Creating an Independent Reading Program

DAILY SCHEDULED TIME

Daily scheduled time for independent reading allows students to finish the books they select and helps them develop good independent reading habits.

- Schedule a time when students can read quietly, such as before the bell rings or at the end of class. Try to keep the same time each day.
- Ask students to pick a reasonable length of time to read. Appoint a student to monitor the time.

CLEAR EXPECTATIONS FOR IN- AND OUT-OF-CLASS READING

Clear expectations will help students develop lifelong reading habits.

- Work with students to create rules for silent reading time. Post the rules where they can be seen.
- Work with families to establish a homework reading policy and ensure that students read at home daily. Encourage parents to read with students, using a progress sheet to track home reading.
- Hold reading contests throughout the school year. Start with easily accomplished tasks, like reading for the most days in a row. As the year goes on, make the contests more challenging, like reading 5 news articles in a week or reading books of over 75 pages.
- Partner with school or municipal librarians to have them help students select books and fill out reading progress sheets.

COLLECTION **3**
PERFORMANCE TASK A

Interactive Lessons
To help you complete this task, use *Writing Narratives*.

Write a Personal Narrative

W **3a–e** Write narratives.
W **4** Produce clear and coherent writing.
W **5** Develop and strengthen writing.
W **10** Write routinely.

In this collection, you read about the strong and emotional connections that people have with different elements of nature. In particular, consider the experience that Eddy Harris recounts in the excerpt from his memoir, *Mississippi Solo*. Then think about your own interactions with nature. Write a personal narrative about a natural setting that is meaningful to you.

A successful personal narrative

- begins with a captivating lead that clearly establishes the situation
- contains a well-structured event sequence that unfolds naturally and logically
- uses descriptive details that offer insight on significant events and feelings
- creates vivid images in the reader's mind through the use of sensory language
- provides a conclusion that follows from and reflects on the narrated experiences and events

PLAN

Establish the Situation A personal narrative describes a true story from a person's life. Consider what made the sudden rainstorm on the Mississippi River memorable to Eddy Harris. Then think about memorable experiences you have had in a natural setting.

- Consider how the natural setting is important to you. Is it important now, or was it important in the past?
- Determine whether you have a story to tell about yourself and the setting.
- Identify the feelings you have about the setting.
- Think about how the experience with the natural setting changed your feelings or ideas.
- Specify the most important idea you want the reader to know.

myNotebook
Use the annotation tools in your eBook to mark up sensory language that you can use as inspiration later. Save each example to your notebook.

ACADEMIC VOCABULARY
As you share your experience, be sure to use the academic vocabulary words.

affect
element
ensure
participate
specify

PERFORMANCE TASK A

WRITE A PERSONAL NARRATIVE

W 3a–e, W 4, W 5, W 10, SL 4

Introduce students to the Performance Task by reading the introductory paragraph with them and reviewing the criteria for what makes a good personal narrative. Remind students that a personal narrative is a kind of autobiographical writing in which a writer uses vivid details to describe important events in his or her life.

PLAN

ESTABLISH THE SITUATION

Explain to students that they should choose an experience to write about that had a profound effect on them. Have students ask themselves:

- What specific details do I remember about the experience?
- What does the experience reveal about me, someone else, or human nature in general?
- Why would reading about this experience be interesting to others?

English Language Support

Plan a Personal Narrative Have students discuss their personal narrative plans with a partner using the following sentence frames and questions:

- The natural setting that is most memorable for me is _____.
- This place is memorable to me because _____.
- My experience in this setting caused me to change because _____.

- I want people to know _____ about this experience.
- After hearing your plan, I want to know more about _____.

Students can use their conversations to help them establish a situation for the narrative to explore.

PERFORMANCE TASK A

English Language Support

Understand Text Structure Point out that personal narratives usually follow a chronological organizational pattern, with events unfolding in the order in which they occurred. Remind students to list the events for their narratives in time order, using verb tenses that make the order of events clear, and plan transitions to link the events in a logical way for readers.

FOR STANDARD ENGLISH LEARNERS

Use Past-Tense Verbs Remind students that -ed is added to regular verbs to form the past tense. Provide the following examples for students to correct.

- Last summer we [hike, hiked] five miles through the woods.
- We [decide, decided] to camp near the lake.

Encourage students to monitor how they form past-tense verbs in their writing and formal speech.

PRODUCE

WRITE YOUR PERSONAL NARRATIVE

Explain to students that a personal narrative is written from the writer's point of view. Point out that they should use the pronouns *I*, *me*, and *my* when referring to themselves in the personal narrative. Remind students that first-person narrators know only their own thoughts and feelings, not those of others.

Discuss ways students might begin a personal narrative in a way that captivates and draws in an audience, reviewing suggestions such as the following:

- Include a funny or dramatic anecdote.
- Use vivid details and descriptions to paint a dramatic setting or first event.
- Use dramatic dialogue exchanged between the writer and another person in the narrative.

Organize Your Ideas In a personal narrative, you are the narrator, or the person telling the story. Organize your ideas about the personal narrative under the following categories.

- Setting
- Events
- Sensory Details
- Most Memorable Images
- Emotions and Reactions
- Conclusion

Interactive Lessons
For help in organizing your narrative, use the following lesson:
· Writing Narratives: Narrative Structure

Mentor Text Notice how in this example from *Mississippi Solo*, Eddy Harris uses descriptive words to appeal to the senses.

" The trees swooshed loudly as the leaves and branches brushed hard together. Branches fell. Rains came and poured down bucketfuls. "

Consider Your Purpose and Audience Think about what you want your audience to understand as you prepare to write.

PRODUCE

Write Your Personal Narrative Review the information in your notes as you begin your draft.

- Begin by clearly establishing the situation.
- Use first-person point of view to present the events in a clear and logical sequence.
- Write what you see, hear, smell, taste, and feel.
- Elaborate on your ideas, including descriptive details.
- Conclude by reflecting on what the experience meant to you.

my WriteSmart
Write your rough draft in *my*WriteSmart. Focus on getting your ideas down, rather than perfecting your choice of language.

Interactive Lessons
For help in drafting your narrative, use the following lesson:
· Writing Narratives: The Language of Narrative

Language Conventions: Connecting Ideas

A compound-complex sentence contains two or more main clauses and one or more subordinate clauses. Sentences like these can connect ideas and enhance descriptive detail. For example, read this description from *Mississippi Solo*.

" I tried to keep the stern pointed right into the flow *so* the canoe could ride the waves, *but* it didn't work. "

By using the words *so* and *but*, the writer has formed a compound-complex sentence to describe what could happen in attempting to move his canoe. Look for places in your narrative where you can add compound-complex sentences.

English Language Support

Use Language Effectively To emphasize the importance of using vivid sensory images in a personal narrative, review these examples from *Mississippi Solo*: lines 19–20, 25–30, and 62–70. Then have students create a three-column chart with these heads: (1) Sights, (2) Sounds, (3) Scents or Feelings. Have students list images for their own narratives that they want readers to experience. Then have partners brainstorm descriptive words and phrases that make each image come alive. Encourage students to include synonyms in their charts and explore how different word choices create precision and shades of meaning.

REVISE

Review Your Draft Work with a partner to determine if you have described your experience clearly and have used vivid details. Be sure to consider the following points.

Questions	Tips	Revision Techniques
Does my introduction clearly establish the situation and the setting?	**Underline** the opener.	**Add** an attention-grabbing statement. **Add** specific details to the setting to make it more precise.
Have I used the first-person point of view consistently?	**Check** that you have related events from your point of view.	**Change** any third-person pronouns to first-person pronouns.
Have I developed a plot line to make the personal narrative easy to follow?	**Note** whether the events are ordered in a logical sequence.	**Make** the order of events clear by adding such transition words as *next, finally, afterwards*.
Have I included effective descriptive details?	**Highlight** sensory details. **Note** which senses the details appeal to.	**Add** more and various sensory details that appeal to the senses.
Does my personal narrative reveal what an experience means to me?	**Underline** details that show why the experience is meaningful.	**Add** a clearly worded statement that reflects on what the experience means.

my WriteSmart

Have your partner or a group of peers review your draft in *my*WriteSmart. Ask your reviewers to note any words or phrases that could be replaced with more descriptive language.

Interactive Lessons
For help in revising your narrative, use the following lesson:
• Writing Narratives: Narrative Context

PRESENT

Create a Finished Copy Finalize your personal narrative and choose a way to share it with your audience. Consider these options:

- Present your personal narrative aloud to your class.
- Post your personal narrative as a blog entry on a personal or school website.
- Dramatize your personal narrative in a one-person performance.

PRODUCE

LANGUAGE CONVENTIONS

Have partners work together to brainstorm additional words and phrases they can use to form compound-complex sentences. For example:

after
even though
while
because

REVISE

REVIEW YOUR DRAFT

Have students answer each question in the chart to determine how they can improve their drafts. Invite volunteers to model their revision techniques.

PRESENT

CREATE A FINISHED COPY

Students can
- read aloud their narratives to the class, using different voices for characters and varying tone
- post their narratives as a blog entry on a personal or school website; respond to comments and questions from their readers
- dramatize their narratives in a one-person performance or dramatic monologue

WHEN STUDENTS STRUGGLE...

Write a Conclusion Make sure students understand that the events and details they include in their personal narrative should lead to a conclusion that explains the significance of the experience. Have students work with a partner to ask and answer the following questions.

- What did this experience teach you about life?
- What can other people learn from reading about your experience?
- How did the experience change your thoughts, your feelings, your goals, or your life?

After partners discuss the questions, have them write their answers and then choose the one they want to focus on in their narrative.

FOR STUDENTS WITH DISABILITIES

Evaluate Drafts After students review their drafts, allow partners or small groups to work together to suggest specific revisions for each other's drafts based on the techniques listed in the chart. After revisions have been made, have groups do a second review of each draft.

PERFORMANCE TASK A

USE THE SCORING RUBRIC

Have partners exchange final drafts of their personal narratives. Ask them to score their partner's narrative using the rubric. Then have students explain the reasons for the score given in each category, using the language of the rubric.

REFLECT ON THE PROCESS

Ask students to reflect on their writing process and on the final product they created for this assignment. Encourage them to think about what they learned, as well as what they might improve or do differently for future assignments. Have them write short responses to the following questions:

- Did you include descriptive details that made the natural setting come alive for readers?
- How well did you convey the most important idea you wanted readers to understand?
- What insights about your experience did you gain while writing this personal narrative?

PERFORMANCE TASK A RUBRIC
PERSONAL NARRATIVE

	Ideas and Evidence	Organization	Language
4	• The introduction engagingly and clearly establishes the natural setting and identifies the writer's experience in nature. • Descriptive details, realistic dialogue, and reflection strongly re-create the experience. • The conclusion summarizes the significance of the experience and leaves readers with an interesting thought.	• The organization is effective; ideas are arranged logically, and events are organized chronologically. • Transitions successfully connect ideas and show a naturally flowing sequence of events.	• The first-person point of view is used creatively and consistently. • Sensory language vividly describes people, places, and events. • Sentence beginnings, lengths, and structures vary and have a rhythmic flow. • Spelling, capitalization, and punctuation are correct. • Grammar and usage are correct.
3	• The introduction identifies the experience but could do more to present the natural setting and engage the reader. • Descriptive details and dialogue generally re-create the experience. • The conclusion summarizes most of the writer's ideas and feelings about the experience.	• The organization of ideas is generally logical; the sequence of events is occasionally confusing. • A few more transitions are needed to clarify the sequence of events and give it a more natural flow.	• The narrative occasionally shifts from the first-person point of view. • Sensory language describes people, places, and events but could be used more effectively. • Sentence beginnings, lengths, and structures vary somewhat. • Few spelling, capitalization, and punctuation errors occur. • Some grammatical and usage errors are repeated in the narrative.
2	• The introduction is ordinary; it mentions an experience in nature and hints at the setting. • A few descriptive details create lively scenes, but most details are ordinary; dialogue is lacking. • The conclusion only hints at the significance of the experience.	• The organization of ideas often doesn't follow a pattern, and the sequence of events is confusing in several places. • More transitions are needed throughout to clarify the sequence of events.	• The narrative frequently shifts from the first-person point of view. • The narrative lacks sensory language in several key parts. • Sentence structures barely vary, with some fragments or run-on sentences. • Spelling, capitalization, and punctuation are often incorrect. • Grammar and usage are incorrect in several places.
1	• The introduction does not focus on an experience or establish a setting. • Descriptive details and dialogue are unrelated or missing. • The narrative lacks a conclusion.	• The narrative is not organized; information and details are presented randomly. • Transitions are not used, making the narrative difficult to understand.	• The narrative lacks a consistent point of view. • Sensory language is not used. • Repetitive sentence structure, fragments, and run-on sentences make the writing confusing. • Spelling, capitalization, and punctuation are incorrect throughout. • Several grammatical and usage errors change the meaning of the writer's ideas.

TO CHALLENGE STUDENTS...

Add Dialogue Challenge students to add dialogue to their personal narratives. If their narratives already include dialogue, encourage them to revise the dialogue to more effectively convey events, descriptive details, and insights. Then have students compare their new version with their original version. Ask them to decide which version they prefer and explain why.

Write a Poetry Analysis

"Ode to enchanted light" and "Sleeping in the Forest" are lyric poems that convey an appreciation of nature. In this activity, you will analyze each poet's style by comparing and contrasting elements such as form, structure, and use of figurative language.

W 2a–f Write informative/explanatory texts.
W 4 Produce clear and coherent writing.
W 5 Develop and strengthen writing.
W 6 Use technology to produce and publish writing.
W 10 Write routinely.

A successful poetry analysis

- begins with clear thesis statement
- uses an effective organizational structure and transitions
- analyzes ideas and elements of the text and provides supporting textual evidence
- clearly explains how the poets use figurative language
- provides a conclusion that summarizes main points

PLAN

Identify Stylistic Elements Every poet has his or her own style. Reread each poem. Jot down stylistic elements of each poem as you read.

- Consider each poem's subject. What does the title reveal? What is the poet's attitude toward the subject?
- Study the form and structure of each poem. Note how the lines are organized and grouped. Think about the sound and rhythm. What effects do they create in the poem?
- Examine word choice. Are the words concrete or abstract? Do the word choices make the poem seem happy? sad? funny?
- Identify figurative language, and explain what it means.

ACADEMIC VOCABULARY

As you share your ideas, be sure to use the academic vocabulary words.

affect
element
ensure
participate
specify

Organize Your Ideas To organize and compare your ideas, use a Venn diagram to compare and contrast elements of each poet's style.

Ode to enchanted light — Both — Sleeping in the Forest

English Language Support

Plan a Poetry Analysis Make sure students understand that their analyses should express their own insights about the effectiveness of each poet's style. To help students focus on insights about the poems, have small groups discuss the following questions:

- What is the message of each poem?
- How does each poem make me feel?
- Which poem's message is most meaningful to me? Why?

WRITE A POETRY ANALYSIS

W 2a–f,
W 4, W 5, W 6,
W 9a, W 10, SL 4

Introduce students to the Performance Task by reading the introductory paragraph with them and reviewing the criteria for what makes a good poetry analysis. Remind students that when you analyze a poem, you look at its different parts to understand the poem's meaning and to appreciate the poet's craft.

PLAN

IDENTIFY STYLISTIC ELEMENTS

Suggest that students think about how to organize their analyses. Have students consider using

- a poem-by-poem organization that presents all the points about one poem and then all the points about the other
- a point-by-point organization that discusses each point and how it applies to both poems

English Language Support

Use Domain-Specific Words Review the meanings of these stylistic elements with students: form, structure, rhythm, figurative language. Then ask students to work in pairs to identify examples of these elements in each poem.

PERFORMANCE TASK B

English Language Support

Adapt Language Choices Have pairs exchange drafts of their thesis statements. Ask them to provide feedback to each other based on the following questions:

- Are the main points of my analysis stated clearly?
- Does my thesis statement engage the reader's attention?

Guide students as they work together to clarify and add interest to their statements.

PRODUCE

WRITE YOUR ANALYSIS

Suggest to students that they use their graphic organizers as a guide for writing the drafts of their analyses. Remind students to use separate paragraphs for each of their main points to make their analyses easier to understand. Point out that students can also add new ideas as they write.

Gather Evidence Use the annotation tools in your eBook to find supporting evidence from the poems. Save your evidence to *my*Notebook, in a folder titled *Collection 3 Performance Task*. Try to gather varied stylistic elements, such as figurative language.

Develop Your Thesis Statement A thesis statement identifies the main points of your analysis. It states what you want to say about the topic. A good thesis statement engages the reader's curiosity or gets the reader to ask questions.

> **PRODUCE**

Write Your Analysis Review the information in your Venn diagram as you begin your draft.

- Start with an engaging introduction that clearly identifies your topic and thesis statement.
- Arrange your information clearly and logically.
- Organize your main points in order of importance.
- Include supporting evidence from the poems.
- Maintain a formal style and use transitions to connect ideas.
- Conclude by summarizing your main points and offering an overall insight about each poet's style and its effects.

Language Conventions: Condensing Ideas

Sometimes a single word can connect one detail to another. Read this passage from the essay, "Big Rocks' Balancing Acts."

> *"* Geologists find these rocks so interesting because they could give clues about the severity of earthquakes over thousands of years. *"*

This passage could have been written as two sentences. Using *because* conveys the details more precisely.

✔ my WriteSmart

Write your rough draft in *my*WriteSmart. Focus on getting your ideas down, rather than perfecting your choice of language.

Interactive Lessons
For help in writing your draft, use:
• Developing a Topic
• Organizing Ideas

WHEN STUDENTS STRUGGLE . . .

Use an Outline If students have trouble organizing their analyses, particularly the comparison-and-contrast sections, have them work with partners to create outlines. The outline should list the thesis statement, the comparison and contrast of each stylistic element with supporting quotations, and the concluding section.

English Language Support

Understand Text Structure Remind students that the purpose of comparing and contrasting stylistic elements in the two poems is to help them develop their thesis statements. Advise students to organize their analyses so that they compare and contrast each stylistic element in turn. For example, students might first analyze the two poems' forms, then they might analyze each poem's use of figurative language, and so on. Have students discuss their Venn diagrams with a partner to help them determine how best to organize their drafts.

Review Your Draft Work with a partner or a group of peers to determine whether your analysis is effective. Be sure to consider the following points in each other's drafts.

my WriteSmart

Have your partner or a group of peers review your draft in *my*WriteSmart. Ask your reviewers to note whether the evidence you provide supports your main points.

Interactive Lessons
For help in revising your draft, use:
· Formal Style
· Introductions and Conclusions

Questions	Tips	Revision Techniques
Does my introduction have a thesis statement that explains the analysis?	**Underline** the thesis statement.	**Add** a sentence that clearly states the main point and sets up your analysis.
Do the key points presented in the analysis support the thesis statement?	**Highlight** key points throughout the analysis.	**Review** the poems' stylistic elements. **Add** evidence, such as quotations and concrete details.
Is the organization of my analysis easy to follow?	**Note** how the key points are organized.	**Revise** your points to show a comparison and contrast. **Relate** ideas with transitions.
Am I maintaining a formal style?	**Underline** any contractions in the analysis.	**Replace** contractions or other informal language with precise, formal vocabulary.
Does my conclusion summarize the thesis statement and offer an insight into the poems?	**Highlight** the sentence that restates the thesis.	**Reword** the conclusion to include the thesis statement. **Provide** an insight about the effects of each poet's style.

Create a Finished Copy Finalize your analysis and choose a way to share it with your audience. Consider these options:

- In a small group, take turns reading your analyses aloud.
- Post your analysis as a blog on a personal or school website.
- Send your analysis to a source that publishes literary reviews.

FOR STANDARD ENGLISH LEARNERS

Use Formal English Explain that students should use formal English in their analyses. Remind them to pay special attention to subject-verb agreement as they review their drafts. Guide students to recognize the differences between formal and informal English in the following examples: he say/he says, she be/she is, both is/both are.

PERFORMANCE TASK B

PRODUCE

LANGUAGE CONVENTIONS

Use Connecting Words As students plan their analyses, remind them to consider where they might use connecting words to help condense ideas and make their comparisons and contrasts stronger. Provide examples of words that show comparison or contrast, such as *in comparison, but, however, in contrast, while.* Work with students to brainstorm additional examples and post them on the board for easy reference.

REVISE

REVIEW YOUR DRAFT

Remind students that they don't have to worry about every little grammatical detail as they begin to revise. Suggest that they first focus on improving the content, organization, and style of their analyses. Point out that they can correct grammar, spelling, and punctuation as they prepare the final version of the analysis.

PRESENT

CREATE A FINISHED COPY

Students can present their analyses as literary reviews or as blogs on school or personal websites. Encourage others to read the analyses and to write comments about them. The authors can then respond to the comments.

English Language Support

Format Text Distribute or display the Student Model that accompanies *Interactive Lessons: Writing Informative Texts.* Direct students' attention to the way longer quotations from poetry support ideas. Point out that the lines of poetry are introduced by a colon, are indented, and are reproduced line for line. Tell students they can use this format as a model for how to support their key points using long quotations from the poems in their analyses.

PERFORMANCE TASK B

USE THE SCORING RUBRIC

Have students use the rubric to score the final draft of their own analysis. Then ask them to exchange analyses with a partner. Have them evaluate the scoring for each category and give reasons for their opinions.

REFLECT ON THE PROCESS

Tell students that reflecting on the process of planning and presenting this task will help them apply what they learned and improve their skills. Ask students to think about how well the organization of their analysis helped to communicate their points to the audience. Ask them to answer the following questions:

- What key points did you make?
- What examples from the poems best supported your key points?
- What original insight did you offer in your conclusion?
- How did your key points relate to the insight you offered?

PERFORMANCE TASK B RUBRIC
POETRY ANALYSIS

	Ideas and Evidence	Organization	Language
4	• The introduction is interesting; the thesis statement identifies the two poems and sets up a number of literary elements for comparison and contrast. • Specific, well-chosen quotations from the poems support the key points. • A satisfying concluding section summarizes the analysis and offers an original thought about the two poems.	• Key points and supporting text evidence are organized effectively and logically throughout the literary analysis. • The compare/contrast structure is clearly followed. • Transitions successfully show the relationships between ideas.	• The analysis has an appropriately formal style with precise language. • Sentence beginnings, lengths, and structures vary and flow well. Sentences show condensed ideas. • Spelling, capitalization, and punctuation are correct. • Grammar and usage are correct.
3	• The introduction could be more engaging; the thesis statement sets up a few elements for analysis. • A few more relevant quotations from the poems are needed to support key points. • The concluding section summarizes most of the analysis but doesn't leave the reader with a new idea to think about.	• The organization of key points and supporting text evidence is confusing in a few places. • The compare/contrast structure is not followed in some places. • A few more transitions could clarify the relationships between ideas.	• The style becomes informal. There is some imprecise language. • Sentence beginnings, lengths, and structures vary somewhat. Ideas could be condensed more. • Few spelling, capitalization, and punctuation mistakes occur. • Some grammatical and usage errors are repeated.
2	• The introduction is ordinary; the thesis statement only hints at the main comparisons and contrasting points of the analysis. • Quotations from the poems support some key points but are unclear or poorly chosen. • The concluding section restates the thesis statement but gives an incomplete summary of the analysis.	• Most key points are organized logically, but much of the supporting text evidence is out of place or used in a confusing manner. • There are many places where the compare/contrast structure is absent. • More transitions are needed throughout the literary analysis to connect ideas.	• The style is informal in many places, with too much vague and repetitive language. • Sentence structures barely vary, with some fragments or run-on sentences. • Spelling, capitalization, and punctuation are often incorrect. • Grammar and usage are incorrect in several places.
1	• The introduction is missing. • Examples and quotations from the poems are either irrelevant or missing. • The poetry analysis lacks a concluding section.	• A logical organization is not apparent; ideas are presented randomly. • There is no sense of comparing and contrasting ideas. • Transitions are not used, making the literary analysis difficult to understand.	• The style is inappropriate, and the language is inaccurate, repetitive, and too general. • Repetitive sentence structures, fragments, and run-on sentences make the writing confusing. • Spelling, capitalization, and punctuation are incorrect throughout. • Several grammatical and usage errors change the meaning of the writer's ideas.

182 Collection 3

FOR STUDENTS WITH DISABILITIES

Evaluate an Analysis Have small groups work together to score each other's analyses. Ask them to use the language of the rubric to cite reasons for each score. Remind students to compare each point on the rubric with an aspect of the analysis.

TO CHALLENGE STUDENTS ...

Compare and Contrast Speakers Have students select evidence from each poem that helps to describe the attitude, personality, or relationship to nature of the speaker of the poem. Students can focus on elements such as word choice, figurative language, imagery, and point of view. Ask students to compare and contrast the speakers and draw a conclusion about how the form of each poem suits or does not suit its speaker.

©PhotoSpin, Inc/Alamy; (bg) ©Corbis

Risk and Exploration

❝ All adventures, especially into new territory, are scary. ❞

—Sally Ride

STREAM TO START

Motivate students to read the collection texts, and spark their curiosity about the collection by playing the video and watching it in class. After students view the video, ask them to think about two things they hope to learn from reading about risk and exploration. Call on volunteers to share their responses.

PERFORMANCE TASK PREVIEW

Point out to students that they will complete one performance task at the end of the collection. The performance task will require them to further analyze the selections in the collection and to synthesize ideas about these analyses. Students will present their findings in a variety of products.

ACADEMIC VOCABULARY

> **► View It!**
> Professional Development Podcast:
> **Academic Vocabulary**

Students can acquire facility with the academic vocabulary words through frequent, repeated exposure as they analyze and discuss the selections in the collection. Academic vocabulary can be used in the instructional contexts shown below. This will enable students to incorporate the academic vocabulary words into their working vocabulary.

- Collaborative Discussion at the end of each selection
- Analyzing the Text questions for each selection
- Selection-level performance task
- Vocabulary instruction (for Critical Vocabulary and/or for Vocabulary Strategy)
- Language Conventions
- End-of-collection performance task for all selections in the collection

ASK STUDENTS to review the Academic Vocabulary word list for this collection. You may wish to pronounce each word aloud so students hear the correct pronunciation. Then, discuss the definitions and the related forms for each word. Remind students that they will encounter these five academic vocabulary words throughout the collection.

COLLECTION 4

Risk and Exploration

In this collection, you will encounter individuals who must confront a compelling question: How far is too far?

Stream to Start | hmhfyi.com | Channel One News®

COLLECTION
PERFORMANCE TASK Preview

After reading the selections in this collection, you will consider the risks of exploration in extreme conditions and present an argument on whether it is worth the costs.

ACADEMIC VOCABULARY

Study the words and their definitions in the chart below. You will use these words as you discuss and write about the texts in this collection.

Word	Definition	Related Forms
complex (kŏm´plĕks´) *adj.*	consisting of many interwoven parts that make something difficult to understand	complex number, complexity, complicate, complicated
potential (pə-tĕn´shəl) *adj.*	capable of doing or being something; having possibility	potent, potentiality, potential energy
rely (rĭ-lī´) *v.*	to depend on something or someone for support, help, or supply	reliable, reliability, reliance, reliant
stress (strĕs) *v.*	to put emphasis on something	stress fracture, stressed, stressed-out, unstressed, stressful
valid (văl´ĭd) *adj.*	convincing or having a sound reason for something	invalid, invalidation, validate, validation

184

▤ myNotebook

As students read, analyze, and discuss the texts in this collection, encourage them to create a *my*WordList folder in *my*Notebook to build their own personal word lists.

- **Annotate** Students can highlight vocabulary terms and other unfamiliar words and save each highlighted term to *my*Notebook.
- **Organize** Within *my*Notebook, students can drag each word into the *my*WordList folder.
- **Elaborate** Ask students to add details to the entry for each word, such as a definition, other forms of the word, and a sample sentence.

English Language Support

 View It!
Professional Development Podcast:
English Language Learners

ENGAGE WITH THE COLLECTION TOPIC

Draw students' attention to the title of the collection, Risk and Exploration. Discuss that risk, or the possibility of suffering harm, and exploration are often connected. People who explore by examining new things sometimes face danger.

ACCESS PRIOR KNOWLEDGE Ask students whether they have ever tried something new, and therefore, taken a risk. Discuss why even simple things like learning to ride a bike can be an exploration (of balance, for example) and a risk. Broaden the discussion by adding that people can also take risks when they explore new ideas.

SURVEY, QUESTION, PREDICT, READ, RESPOND, SUMMARIZE (SQP2RS)

Use this strategy to introduce informational texts in this collection to students.

- **First,** have students scan a text for 1–2 minutes prior to reading. Direct them to look at text features, such as images, graphics, or headings.
- **Then,** have students list several questions they think the text will answer. Also ask them to predict 1–3 things they think they will learn from reading the text.

- **Next,** have students read the text, looking for answers to their questions and noting whether their predictions were accurate. Once students have finished reading, have them discuss their findings with the class or in small groups.
- **Finally,** have students summarize the text orally or in writing.

Collection 4 Digital Resources for English Language Support

LANGUAGE WORKSHOP
Designated English Learners

You may use the digital Teacher Resources > Language Workshop to support English language learners in justifying opinions, condensing ideas, and participating in helpful discussions by paraphrasing key ideas.

 VIDEOS

This video will help students learn how to analyze an argument. Have students use **Text In Focus Practice** to apply the skills.

COLLECTION 4 DIGITAL OVERVIEW

Collection 4 Lessons	Media	Teach and Practice
**Student Edition	eBook**	**Video Links** (HISTORY, A&E, Channel One News)	**Close Reading and Evidence Tracking**
ANCHOR TEXT — Speech by John F. Kennedy "Remarks at the Dedication of the Aerospace Medical Health Center"	**Video HISTORY®** *JFK's New Frontier* / **Audio** "Remarks at the Dedication of the Aerospace Medical Health Center"	**Close Read Screencasts** • Modeled Discussion 1 (lines 4–13) • Modeled Discussion 2 (lines 31–42) • Close Read application PDF (lines 112–119)	**Text in Focus** • Analyzing an Argument (line 78) **Strategies for Annotation** • Trace and Evaluate an Argument • Using Context Clues
CLOSE READER — Online Essay by Joan Vernikos "Is Space Exploration Worth the Cost?"	**Video HISTORY®** *"Space Shuttle: The Last Mission"* / **Audio** "Is Space Exploration Worth the Cost?"		
Commentary by Philippe Cousteau "Why Exploring the Ocean Is Mankind's Next Giant Leap"	**Audio** "Why Exploring the Ocean Is Mankind's Next Giant Leap"		**Strategies for Annotation** • Analyze Structure: Sound Reasoning • Vocabulary Strategy: Prefixes
Science Article by Cheryl Bardoe from "Living in the Dark"	**Audio** from "Living in the Dark"		**Strategies for Annotation** • Determine Central Ideas and Details • Analyze Structure • Vocabulary Strategy: Greek Roots
CLOSE READER — Science Article by Elisabeth Rosenthal "Stinging Tentacles Offer Hint of Oceans' Decline"	**Audio** "Stinging Tentacles Offer Hint of Oceans' Decline"		
Poem by Georgia Douglas Johnson "Your World"	**Audio** "Your World"		
Collection 4 Performance Task: Present an Argument	fyi hmhfyi.com	**Interactive Lessons** Writing Arguments Giving a Presentation	

For Systematic Coverage of Writing and Speaking & Listening Standards	**Interactive Lessons** Using Textual Evidence Using Media in a Presentation

For foundational skills and reading intervention support: **READ180®**

Assess		Extend	Reteach
Performance Task	✓ **Assess It Online!**	**Teacher eBook**	**Teacher eBook**
Writing Activity: Research Report	Selection Test	**Compare and Contrast Two Versions of a Speech > Interactive Lesson >** Analyzing and Evaluating Presentations	**Trace and Evaluate an Argument > Level Up Tutorial >** Elements of an Argument
Speaking Activity: Informal Debate	Selection Test	**Hold an Informal Debate**	**Determine Meanings > Level Up Tutorial >** Tone
Writing Activity: Argument	Selection Test	**Analyze Technical Meanings**	**Analyze Structure: Cause-and-Effect Relationships > Level Up Tutorial >** Cause-and-Effect Organization > **Interactive Graphic Organizer >** Cause-and-Effect Chain
Writing Activity: Analysis	Selection Test	**Form in Poetry > Interactive Whiteboard Lesson >** Form in Poetry	**Determine Meanings: Imagery > Level Up Tutorial >** Imagery
Present an Argument	Collection Test		

Lesson Assessments Using Textual Evidence Using Media in a Presentation	**Standards Support and Enrichment**	For more instruction and practice in reading literary and informational texts, language, spelling, and speaking and listening, see Teacher Resources > Standards Support and Enrichment.
	For Designated English Language Instruction	To provide scaffolded support specific to the needs of English Learners during Designated English Language instruction, use the selection- and standards-aligned lessons found in Teacher Resources > Language Workshop.

Collection 4 Lessons	Key Learning Objective	Performance Task	Vocabulary Strategy
ANCHOR TEXT **Speech by John F. Kennedy** **"Remarks at the Dedication of the Aerospace Medical Health Center," p. 185A** **Lexile 1380L**	**The student will be able to . . .** trace and evaluate an argument.	Writing Activity: Research Report	Using Context Clues
Commentary by Philippe Cousteau **"Why Exploring the Ocean Is Mankind's Next Giant Leap," p. 193A** **Lexile 1360L**	**The student will be able to . . .** identify tone and evaluate the reasoning used to support a claim.	Speaking Activity: Informal Debate	Prefixes
Science Article by Cheryl Bardoe **from "Living in the Dark," p. 201A** **Lexile 1200L**	**The student will be able to . . .** analyze the structure of an informational text and paraphrase central ideas and details.	Writing Activity: Argument	Greek Roots
Poem by Georgia Douglas Johnson **"Your World," p. 213A**	**The student will be able to . . .** identify and analyze how imagery and extended metaphor can express a particular message or idea.	Writing Activity: Analysis	

Collection 4 Performance Task:

Present an Argument

Language Conventions	English Language Support	Differentiated Instruction	CLOSE READER Selection
Capitalization	• Determine Author's Purpose • Evaluate Argument • Use Context Clues • Use Capitalization • Modify to Add Details	**When Students Struggle:** Analyze Language	Online Essay by Joan Vernikos "Is Space Exploration Worth the Cost?" p. 192b **Lexile 1130L**
Adjective Clauses	• Analyze Structure • Determine Meanings • Condense Ideas with Clauses • Listen Actively	**When Students Struggle:** Trace an Argument **To Challenge Students:** Compare Two Arguments **For Standard English Learners:** Pronunciation **For Students with Disabilities:** Determine Meanings	
Verbal Phrases	• Use Context • Analyze Structure • Improve Reading Fluency • Word Study • Modify Sentences to Add Details • Prepare an Oral Presentation	**When Students Struggle:** Track Causes and Effects **For Students with Disabilities:** Use Audio Support **To Challenge Students:** Make Connections **For Standard English Learners:** Pronunciation	Science Article by Elisabeth Rosenthal "Stinging Tentacles Offer Hint of Oceans' Decline," p. 212b **Lexile 1370L**
	• Analyze Language • Review Concepts	**For Standard English Learners:** Analyze the Text	
Relative Pronouns	Plan to Present a Personal Narrative Use Academic Words Link Ideas Support Reasons with Evidence	**For Standard English Learners:** Adapt Speech **When Students Struggle:** Use a Graphic Organizer **For Students with Disabilities:** Practice on Camera **To Challenge Students:** Create a Promotional Video	

ANCHOR TEXT

Remarks at the Dedication of the Aerospace Medical Health Center

Speech by John F. Kennedy

Why This Text?

Students regularly encounter formal and informal arguments in media, in conversations, and in text materials. This lesson explores the argument developed in Kennedy's speech about the value of the space program.

▶ **View It!**

Professional Development Podcast:

Teaching Argument

Key Learning Objective: The student will be able to trace and evaluate an argument.

For practice and application:

Is Space Exploration Worth the Cost?

Online Essay by Joan Vernikos

Close Reader selection
"Is Space Exploration Worth the Cost?"
Online Essay by Joan Vernikos

RI 1 Cite text evidence.

RI 4 Analyze the impact of word choice on meaning and tone.

RI 5 Analyze the structure an author uses to organize a text.

RI 6 Determine an author's purpose.

RI 7 Compare and contrast a text to an audio, video, or multimedia version of the text.

RI 8 Trace and evaluate an argument.

SL 1 Engage effectively in a range of collaborative discussions.

SL 3 Delineate a speaker's argument and specific claims, evaluating the soundness of the reasoning and the relevance of the evidence.

W 2 Write informative/explanatory texts.

W 7 Conduct short research projects.

W 8 Gather relevant information.

L 2 Demonstrate command of conventions.

L 3 Use knowledge of language.

L 4 Determine the meaning of unknown words and phrases.

L 4a Use context as a clue to the meaning of a word or phrase.

L 4c Consult general reference materials.

L 4d Verify the preliminary determination of the meaning of a word or phrase.

▲ **Text Complexity Rubric**

	Remarks at the Dedication of the Aerospace Medical Health Center
Quantitative Measures	Lexile: 1380L

Levels of Meaning/Purpose

more than one purpose; implied, easily identified from context

Qualitative Measures

Structure

organization of main ideas and details complex; but clearly stated and generally sequential

Language Conventionality and Clarity

some unfamiliar, academic, or domain-specific words

Knowledge Demands

specialized knowledge required

Reader/Task Considerations
- Teacher determined
- Vary by individual reader and type of text
- See the Text X-Ray for suggested Reader/Task Considerations.

English Language Support

English Language Support Before teaching, use the Text X-Ray for an overview of the text's complexity. The Text X-Ray and the supports and scaffolds in the Teacher's Edition will help you guide students of different skill levels.

Meaning Making · Language Development · Effective Expression · Content Knowledge · Foundational Skills

Text Complexity: Qualitative Measures

Levels of Meaning/Purpose

more than one purpose; implied, easily identified from context

Help students to identify the author's purpose.

- Teacher's Edition side notes, pp. 185, 190
- English Language Support, p. 185
- Close Read Screencast, p. 185

To help students compare and contrast versions of a text, see

- Teacher's Edition side note, p. 190
- Compare and Contrast Two Versions of a Speech, p. 192a
- Speaking and Listening, p. 190

▶ *Use It!* Interactive Whiteboard Lesson: Author's Purpose and Perspective

ZOOM IN ON **UNDERSTANDING PURPOSE AND AUDIENCE** Explain that writers have a reason, or **purpose**, for writing a text. Writers choose words carefully so that their **audience** of readers or listeners will understand their message.

- Have students read the first three lines of the speech.
- Ask students to explain who was listening to the president's speech at that time.
- Ask students to discuss whether knowing the original audience affects how they will read the speech.

Structure

organization of main ideas and details complex; but clearly stated and generally sequential

Help students to trace and evaluate an argument.

- Teacher's Edition side notes, pp. 186, 187, 188, 189, 190
- English Language Support, pp. 186, 189
- When Students Struggle, p. 188
- Strategies for Annotation, p. 189
- Trace and Evaluate and Argument, p. 189

 Analyzing an Argument

To reteach argument, see

- Trace and Evaluate an Argument, p. 192a

▶ *Use It!* **Interactive Whiteboard Lesson:** Evaluating Arguments

ZOOM IN ON **TRACING AND EVALUATING AN ARGUMENT** Explain to students that in the speech the president wants to convince his audience about the importance of space exploration. Therefore, his speech is structured as an **argument** with logical reasoning. He includes a **claim,** or central idea, **reasons** that develop that claim, and **evidence** such as facts that elaborate on the reasons.

- Help students trace Kennedy's argument by using the following sentence frames:
  Claim: I think that _____.
  Reason: I believe this because _____.
  Evidence: This/The _____ supports my idea.

Language Conventionality and Clarity

some unfamiliar, academic, or domain-specific words

Teach unfamiliar academic vocabulary in context.

- Teacher's Edition Critical Vocabulary notes, pp. 186, 187, 188, 191
- Applying Academic Vocabulary, p. 187

Teach a vocabulary strategy.

- Vocabulary Strategy: Context Clues, p. 191
- English Language Support, p. 191
- Strategies for Annotation, p. 191

Guide students to apply capitalization and to modify sentences with additional details.

- Teacher's Edition side note, p. 192
- English Language Support, p. 192

ZOOM IN ON **PRETEACHING VOCABULARY** Have students work with a partner to look up the following words from the selection: *partisan* (line 5), *endeavor* (line 12), *frontier* (line 26), *competitor* (line 37), *instrument* (line 64), *setbacks* (line 98). Tell them that knowing these words will help them understand the speech.

- Ask students to prepare a list of the words with definitions to share with other students.

Knowledge Demands

specialized knowledge required

Help students to clarify the historical and political contexts of the speech.

- Teacher's Edition Background note, p. 185
- Performance Task, p. 190

ZOOM IN ON **BUILDING HISTORICAL CONTEXT** Read aloud the Background note with students following along in their texts. Provide additional information from the Teacher's Edition Background note. Add that many felt that the United States won the space race when American astronauts landed on the moon on July 20, 1969, nearly six years after President Kennedy was assassinated.

Suggested Reader/Task Considerations

Consider the following before assigning this argument to students:

- Will students understand the purpose for reading or listening to the speech?
- Do students have enough prior knowledge to understand the context of the speech?

ZOOM IN ON **SUPPORTING COMPREHENSION**

- Have students read the essay in pairs, reading short sections independently and then reading them aloud to each other. After reading each section, students should pause to briefly discuss what this section adds to their understanding of the topic.
- Have students consult a history book or the Internet to clarify historical details. Students can present their findings to the class.

Background Have students read the background and information about the author. Tell students that President Kennedy was known for giving memorable, powerful speeches. On the day of his inauguration in 1961, he famously stated, "Ask not what your country can do for you—ask what you can do for your country." In 1961, two years before this speech, Kennedy went before Congress and called for plans to send astronauts to the moon.

SETTING A PURPOSE Direct students to use the Setting a Purpose question to focus their reading. Remind students to generate questions as they read.

Determine Author's Purpose (LINES 1–13)

RI 1, RI 6

Explain to students that Kennedy prepared this speech for a specific **audience**—the group of people who listen to a speech or watch a performance. By identifying his audience, the speaker can select specific language and ideas that will appeal to the audience to achieve his **purpose,** or the reason he is giving the speech.

A **CITE TEXT EVIDENCE** Have students reread lines 1–13 and identify Kennedy's audience. What is Kennedy's likely purpose, and which words hint at this purpose? *(Kennedy is speaking to the Secretary, Governor, Vice President, Senator, members of Congress, members of the military, and assorted ladies and gentlemen. His purpose seems to be a call to action to do something new and pioneering. Phrases such as "It is an era which calls for action," "test the unknown and the uncertain," and "It is a time for pathfinders and pioneers" suggest this.)*

English Language Support

Explain to students that an author or speaker may have one or more purposes. For example, a speaker may want to entertain or inform, as well as persuade. Recognizing the speaker's purpose or purposes helps the audience understand how carefully to listen.

ASK STUDENTS to work in pairs to reread lines 1–13 and write words that give clues to Kennedy's purpose. Have students use a dictionary if needed to confirm the meaning of unknown words.

 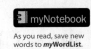

Background *In 1957, the country then known as the Soviet Union launched the first satellite to orbit Earth. The Soviet Union and the United States were bitter enemies at the time. After becoming the 35th president of the United States in 1961,* **John F. Kennedy** *was determined to equal the Soviet's knowledge of space. Well known for many accomplishments as president, Kennedy is also remembered as an inspirational speaker. He gave this speech the day before his assassination in November 1963.*

Remarks at the Dedication of the Aerospace Medical Health Center

Speech by John F. Kennedy

SETTING A PURPOSE As you read, pay attention to the points President Kennedy is making. Why does he think the United States should be involved with space research?

myNotebook

As you read, save new words to *myWordList*.

M r. Secretary, Governor, Mr. Vice President, Senator, Members of the Congress, members of the military, ladies and gentlemen:

For more than 3 years I have spoken about the New Frontier.[1] This is not a partisan term, and it is not the exclusive property of Republicans or Democrats. It refers, instead, to this Nation's place in history, to the fact that we do stand on the edge of a great new era, filled with both crisis and opportunity, an era to be characterized by achievement
10 and by challenge. It is an era which calls for action and for the best efforts of all those who would test the unknown and the

---

[1] **New Frontier:** term Kennedy used in his presidential campaign.

Close Read Screencasts

Modeled Discussions

Have students click the *Close Read* icons in their eBooks to access two screencasts in which readers discuss and annotate the following key passages:

- For more than 3 years . . . (lines 4–13)
- We have a long way . . . (lines 96–104)

As a class, view and discuss at least one of these videos. Then, have students work in pairs to do an independent close read of an additional passage—Kennedy's call to action and conclusion (lines 112–119).

For more context and historical background, students can view the video "JFK's New Frontier" in their eBooks.

Trace and Evaluate an Argument (LINES 31–42, 43–55)

RI 1,
RI 5,
RI 8

Explain that in an **argument** the speaker or writer states a claim supported by reasons and evidence.

B **CITE TEXT EVIDENCE** Ask students to reread lines 31–42 and cite the lines in which Kennedy states his claim. *(Lines 40–42)* Ask students to restate that claim in their own words. *(The study of medicine in space will make everyone's lives healthier and happier.)*

Tell students that to organize a text around a claim, a writer or speaker provides reasons and evidence that support the claim. **Reasons** explain a person's beliefs or actions. **Evidence** includes the facts, statistics, quotations, or anecdotes that support each reason.

C **CITE TEXT EVIDENCE** Ask students to reread lines 43–55, identify the first reason Kennedy uses to prove his claim, and cite the evidence he provides for support. *(Reason: Medical space research may open up new understanding of man's relation to his environment. Evidence: (1) Examinations of the astronaut's physical, mental, and emotional reactions can teach us more about the differences between normal and abnormal, about disorientation, and about changes in metabolism which could result in extending life span. (2) When you study the effects of exhaust gases on our astronauts, and you seek ways to reduce their toxicity, you are working on problems similar to those we face in our polluted urban centers.)*

CRITICAL VOCABULARY

metabolism: Kennedy believes that medical space research will teach us about "changes in metabolism" that happen during space travel.

ASK STUDENTS what system of an astronaut's metabolism Kennedy implies might be affected by space exploration. *(the pulmonary system, or lungs)*

---

uncertain in every phase of human endeavor. It is a time for pathfinders and pioneers.

I have come to Texas today to salute an outstanding group of pioneers, the men who man the Brooks Air Force Base School of Aerospace Medicine and the Aerospace Medical Center. It is fitting that San Antonio should be the site of this center and this school as we gather to dedicate this complex of buildings. For this city has long been the home of the pioneers
20 in the air. It was here that Sidney Brooks, whose memory we honor today, was born and raised. It was here that Charles Lindbergh and Claire Chennault,[2] and a host of others, who, in World War I and World War II and Korea, and even today have helped demonstrate American mastery of the skies, trained at Kelly Field and Randolph Field,[3] which form a major part of aviation history. And in the new frontier of outer space, while headlines may be made by others in other places, history is being made every day by the men and women of the Aerospace Medical Center, without whom there
30 could be no history.

B Many Americans make the mistake of assuming that space research has no values here on earth. Nothing could be further from the truth. Just as the wartime development of radar gave us the transistor, and all that it made possible, so research in space medicine holds the promise of substantial benefit for those of us who are earthbound. For our effort in space is not, as some have suggested, a competitor for the natural resources that we need to develop the earth. It is a working partner and a coproducer of these resources. And
40 nothing makes this clearer than the fact that medicine in space is going to make our lives healthier and happier here on earth.

C I give you three examples: first, medical space research may open up new understanding of man's relation to his environment. Examinations of the astronaut's physical, and mental, and emotional reactions can teach us more about the differences between normal and abnormal, about the causes and effects of disorientation, about changes in **metabolism**

metabolism
(mǐ-tăb´ə-lĭz´əm) *n.*
The *metabolism* of a living thing is all the processes that allow for growth and life.

---

[2] **Sidney Brooks . . . Charles Lindbergh . . . Claire Chennault** (shən´ôlt): Sidney Brooks was a young flyer killed in a training accident. Charles Lindbergh was the first transatlantic solo pilot, and Claire Chennault was an important figure in the development of air-war theories.

[3] **Kelly Field and Randolph Field:** airfields in the San Antonio area where many military pilots were trained.

English Language Support

Evaluate Argument Read lines 31–42 aloud. Model thinking about audience and wondering why Kennedy discusses objections before stating his claim in lines 40–42. Explain that Kennedy is talking to people who disagree with him; he compares space research to technology his audience considers useful to help them accept his ideas.

ASK STUDENTS How does this paragraph strengthen Kennedy's argument? *(by refuting a potential objection)*

which could result in extending the life span. When you
study the effects on our astronauts of exhaust gases which can
contaminate their environment, and you seek ways to alter
these gases so as to reduce their toxicity, you are working on
problems similar to those we face in our great urban centers
which themselves are being corrupted by gases and which
must be clear.

And second, medical space research may revolutionize
the technology and the techniques of modern medicine.
Whatever new devices are created, for example, to monitor
our astronauts, to measure their heart activity, their breathing,
their brain waves, their eye motion, at great distances and
under difficult conditions, will also represent a major advance
in general medical instrumentation. Heart patients may even
be able to wear a light monitor which will sound a warning if
their activity exceeds certain limits. An instrument recently
developed to record automatically the impact of acceleration
upon an astronaut's eyes will also be of help to small children
who are suffering miserably from eye defects, but are unable to
describe their **impairment**. And also by the use of instruments
similar to those used in Project Mercury, this Nation's private
as well as public nursing services are being improved, enabling
one nurse now to give more critically ill patients greater
attention than they ever could in the past.

And third, medical space research may lead to new
safeguards against hazards common to many environments.
Specifically, our astronauts will need fundamentally new
devices to protect them from the ill effects of radiation which
can have a profound influence upon medicine and man's
relations to our present environment.

Here at this center we have the laboratories, the talent,
the resources to give new **impetus** to vital research in the life
centers. I am not suggesting that the entire space program
is justified alone by what is done in medicine. The space
program stands on its own as a contribution to national
strength. And last Saturday at Cape Canaveral I saw our new
Saturn C-1 rocket booster,[4] which, with its payload,[5] when it
rises in December of this year, will be, for the first time, the
largest booster in the world, carrying into space the largest
payload that any country in the world has ever sent into space.

---

[4] **booster:** a rocket used to launch a spacecraft.
[5] **payload:** the load carried by a rocket or other vehicle.

impairment
(ĭm-pâr´mənt) *n.*
An *impairment* is an
injury or weakness.

Text in
FOCUS

impetus
(ĭm´pĭ-təs) *n.* The
impetus is the driving
force or motivation
behind an action.

APPLYING ACADEMIC VOCABULARY

stress	valid

THINK-PAIR-SHARE Discuss Kennedy's speech as a class using the
following questions. Guide students to include the academic vocabulary
words *stress* and *valid* in their contributions to the discussion.

- What ideas does Kennedy **stress** in his speech to support his claim?
- Is Kennedy's argument effective? Explain what **valid** evidence
  Kennedy provides to support his reasons.

TEACH

Trace and Evaluate an Argument (LINES 56–72, 79–88)

RI 1,
RI 5,
RI 8

Explain that to prove a claim a writer or speaker must
provide sufficient and credible reasons and evidence
that clearly relate to the claim.

D **ASK STUDENTS** to reread lines 56–72 and explain
how the second reason differs from the first reason.
*(The second reason focuses on medical technology
and techniques, while the first focuses on how medical
research in space might open up new understandings of
our relationship to our environment on Earth.)*

Explain that strong arguments address opposing
viewpoints. **Counterarguments** show that the speaker
or writer can disprove other viewpoints.

E **CITE TEXT EVIDENCE** Have students reread
lines 79–88 and cite evidence of a counterargument.
*(Kennedy anticipates the opposing view that medical
research in space doesn't justify the entire program. He
counters by stating that "the space program stands on
its own as a contribution to national strength.")*

CRITICAL VOCABULARY

impairment: Kennedy explains that medical
space research has led to new inventions that
automatically record physical reactions.

ASK STUDENTS how such monitoring would help
children who can't describe their impairments.
(Adults can't fix a problem until they can identify it.)

impetus: Kennedy expects the Aerospace Medical
Health Center to spur "vital research."

ASK STUDENTS why a new medical center might
serve as an impetus for such a purpose. *(A new
center would attract the best researchers and
equipment for research projects.)*

Text in
FOCUS   English Language Support

Analyzing an Argument (LINE 78)

Have students view the **Text In Focus** video on this
page of their eBook to learn how to analyze Kennedy's
argument. Then have students use **Text In Focus
Practice** to apply what they have learned.

Trace and Evaluate an Argument (LINES 89–96)

RI 1,
RI 5,
RI 8

Tell students that complex arguments can include more than one claim.

F **CITE TEXT EVIDENCE** Have students reread lines 89–96 and cite evidence of Kennedy's second claim. *(Claim: Despite "pressures in this country" to stop space exploration, the "space effort must go on.")* Then, ask students to determine the reason and evidence Kennedy offers to support this claim. *(Reason: The United States should be a leader. Evidence: "And in December," with the launch of the largest booster in the world, "the United States will be ahead.")*

CRITICAL VOCABULARY

tedious: Kennedy knows that there is hard work ahead in the U.S. space effort.

ASK STUDENTS to explain how the medical research that Kennedy proposes could be tedious. *(Medical research entails a good deal of detailed work, extreme precision, and dead ends.)*

COLLABORATIVE DISCUSSION Have students pair up and discuss specific language and techniques that Kennedy uses that would be inspirational to his specific audience. Ask students to consider and discuss the validity of Kennedy's points, explaining their reasons for their opinions. Then, have students share their conclusions with the class as a whole.

ASK STUDENTS to share any questions they generated in the course of reading and discussing the selection.

WHEN STUDENTS STRUGGLE

To guide students' comprehension of the reasons that Kennedy has cited to support his claim, have students work in pairs to fill out a chart like the one shown. For additional help, suggest that they look for signal words like *first*, *second*, and *third* to identify the reasons Kennedy uses in his argument.

 LEVEL UP TUTORIALS Assign the following *Level Up* tutorial: **Elements of an Argument**

F 90   I think the United States should be a leader. A country as rich and powerful as this which bears so many burdens and responsibilities, which has so many opportunities, should be second to none. And in December, while I do not regard our mastery of space as anywhere near complete, while I recognize that there are still areas where we are behind—at least in one area, the size of the booster—this year I hope the United States **Close Read** will be ahead. And I am for it. We have a long way to go. Many weeks and months and years of long, **tedious** work lie ahead. There will be setbacks and frustrations and disappointments. There will be, as there always are, pressures in this country

100   to do less in this area as in so many others, and temptations to do something else that is perhaps easier. But this research here must go on. This space effort must go on. The conquest of space must and will go ahead. That much we know. That much we can say with confidence and conviction.

Frank O'Connor, the Irish writer, tells in one of his books how, as a boy, he and his friends would make their way across the countryside, and when they came to an orchard wall that seemed too high and too doubtful to try and too difficult to permit their voyage to continue, they took off their hats and

110   tossed them over the wall—and then they had no choice but to follow them.

This Nation has tossed its cap over the wall of space, and we have no choice but to follow it. Whatever the difficulties, they will be overcome. Whatever the hazards, they must be guarded against. With the vital help of this Aerospace Medical Center, with the help of all those who labor in the space endeavor, with the help and support of all Americans, we will climb this wall with safety and with speed—and we shall then explore the wonders on the other side.

120   Thank you.

tedious
(tē´dē-əs) *adj.*
Something that is
tedious is boring.

COLLABORATIVE DISCUSSION Kennedy makes several points about why he thinks the United States should be involved with space research. Do you think the points he makes are valid? Does his speech inspire you to support space research? Discuss your ideas with a partner.

Claim: Medicine in space will make people's lives better.
SUPPORT:
Reason 1: understand man's relationship to his environment
Reason 2: revolutionize modern medicine
Reason 3: reduce environmental hazards

Trace and Evaluate an Argument

RI 5, RI 8

The speech you've just read is an **argument,** in which the speaker states a claim supported by reasons and evidence. A **claim** is the speaker's position on a problem or an issue. The strength of an argument relies not on the claim but on the support. **Support** consists of reasons and evidence used to prove the claim. **Reasons** are declarations made to explain an action or belief. **Evidence** includes specific facts, statistics, or examples.

To **trace,** or follow the reasoning of, an argument:

- Identify the claim, which may be stated directly or implied.
- Look for reasons and evidence that support the claim.
- Pay attention to the way the author connects the claim, reasons, and evidence.
- Identify **counterarguments,** which are statements that address opposing viewpoints. A good argument anticipates opposing viewpoints and provides counterarguments to disprove the opposing views.

Some arguments have more than one claim, which might only be determined after careful examination of the text. To trace the argument in Kennedy's speech:

Divide the speech into sections: lines 1–30, 31–78, 79–104, 105–120.

Examine each section for a part of the argument.

Summarize the two claims suggested in lines 31–78 and 79–104.

To **evaluate** an argument, or decide whether it makes sense and is convincing:

- Consider whether the evidence logically supports the claim.
- Examine the logic to ensure the ideas make sense and are in a proper order.
- Consider whether the opposing view has been adequately addressed.
- Identify persuasive techniques such as appeals to emotion.

CLOSE READ

Trace and Evaluate an Argument

RI 5, RI 8

Help students understand the terms and divide the speech into sections. Once students have examined the sections, have them summarize the claims. *(In lines 31–78, Kennedy gives examples to support his claim that medical space research makes life on Earth better. In lines 79–104, Kennedy gives examples that support his claim that space research increases our national strength.)*

English Language Support

Ask students to work in pairs. Have them use this sentence frame to create claim summaries:

In lines _____, Kennedy gives examples to support his claim that _____.

To help students evaluate an argument, make sure they understand how to judge logical relationships between ideas:

- Explain that there must be a clear and reasonable connection between the claim and its support.
- Explain that writers and speakers can use different organizational patterns to make their arguments clear and coherent. For example, they can use order of importance, going from the least to the most important reason (or the reverse), or cause-and-effect relationships, showing how one event or action either leads to or results from another.

Strategies for Annotation 🖊 🗎 *Annotate it!*

Trace and Evaluate an Argument

RI 1, RI 5, RI 8

Share these strategies for guided or independent analysis:

- Highlight in yellow the claims that Kennedy makes.
- Underline each reason and the evidence that supports it. On a note, list the types of evidence that Kennedy relies on.
- Highlight in blue opposing claims Kennedy anticipates. Summarize his counterarguments in a note.
- On a note, record words or phrases that express an inspiring tone.

Research in space medicine may benefit people on Earth.

Many Americans make the mistake of assuming that space research has no values here on earth. Nothing could be further from the truth. Just as the wartime development of radar gave us the transistor, and all that it made possible, so research in space medicine holds the promise of substantial benefit for those of us who are earthbound. For our effort

Analyzing the Text
RI 1, RI 4,
RI 5, RI 8

Possible answers:

1. *These words support his position that the United States needs to be a pioneer in space research and that the members of his audience are the pioneers in that field. He compliments them by associating them with leaders in their field and implies that they are making history.*

2. ***Opposing Viewpoints:*** *(1) Space research has no value on Earth. (2) Research in space medicine competes for natural resources that are needed to develop Earth.*
   Kennedy's Counterarguments: *(1) Research holds the promise of substantial benefit. The wartime development of radar spurred the development of the transistor. (2) Space is a partner and coproducer of resources, and space medicine is going to make people's lives healthier and happier.*

3. *Kennedy speaks of "small children who are suffering miserably from eye defects." This language elicits sympathy from his listeners, which may lead them to accept his argument.*

4. *The focus has shifted from the ways in which medical space research improves life on Earth to the way the space program contributes to national strength. Lines 87–90 state the new focus. Kennedy has shifted his focus in order to make another claim and to appeal to national pride.*

5. *Kennedy repeats "Whatever the" at the beginning of sentences in lines 113–115. In lines 115–117, he repeats "with the help of." The repetition reinforces a belief in success, no matter how difficult the task may be, if we stay committed to the program.*

6. *Kennedy establishes an effective, coherent, and logical argument. His claim about the need for medical space research is clearly supported with three reasons, each of which is supported by relevant evidence. The second claim about continuing the space program is also supported by a clear reason (the American leadership role) and evidence (the U.S. is rich and powerful).*

Speaking and Listening
RI 7,
SL 3

Have students listen to and analyze an audio version of Kennedy's speech while they reread the text of the speech. The audio speech can be found in their eBook. See Compare and Contrast Two Versions of a Speech on page 192a for further instruction on comparing two versions of a speech.

---

eBook *Annotate It!*

Analyzing the Text
RI 1, RI 4, RI 5,
RI 7, RI 8, W 2,
W 7, W 8, SL 3

Cite Text Evidence   Support your responses with evidence from the text.

1. **Interpret** Kennedy refers to his audience as *pathfinders* and *pioneers* and mentions the *New Frontier*. Why might Kennedy use these words?

2. **Cite Evidence** Using a chart like the one shown, identify two opposing viewpoints that Kennedy anticipates in lines 31–42 and cite Kennedy's counterarguments to those viewpoints.

Opposing Viewpoints	Kennedy's Counterarguments

3. **Draw Conclusions** Reread lines 64–68. How does Kennedy describe the children who might benefit from medical space technology? What might Kennedy be trying to accomplish through his choice of language?

4. **Draw Conclusions** Examine lines 79–88. Describe Kennedy's shift in focus. Why might Kennedy make this shift in his argument?

5. **Cite Evidence** Examine lines 112–119. Identify phrases that Kennedy repeats. What ideas is he emphasizing with this repetition?

6. **Evaluate** Considering the audience and purpose of Kennedy's speech, is his argument convincing? Do his conclusions arise logically from the reasons and evidence he has cited?

Speaking and Listening

Listen to an audio version of President Kennedy delivering the speech you have just read. How is hearing the speech different from reading it? With a partner or small group, choose two sections of the speech and discuss how the delivery of the speech conveys the meaning of the words.

PERFORMANCE TASK

Writing Activity: Research Report
Research a recent or planned space mission for medical research by NASA (National Aeronautics and Space Administration).

- Identify one mission and write a brief description of its purpose and outcome.
- Explain whether or not it is in keeping with Kennedy's views about space research.
- Share your findings with the class.

Assign this
performance task.   ✔my WriteSmart

PERFORMANCE TASK
W 2,
W 7,
W 8

Writing Activity: Research Report Have students work in pairs or small groups.

- Direct students to reread the speech to review Kennedy's position on medical space research.
- Have students review how to use search terms to gather information effectively.

Critical Vocabulary

L 4a, L 4c, L 4d

metabolism	impairment	impetus	tedious

Practice and Apply Choose the response that best answers each question. Then discuss with a partner why the other choices are incorrect.

1. If a person's **metabolism** were not functioning properly, what symptom might be present?
   a. toned muscles
   b. labored breathing
   c. tanned skin
   d. shiny hair

2. Which condition would be considered an **impairment?**
   a. sensitive taste buds
   b. a slight limp
   c. 20/20 vision
   d. a photographic memory

3. Which would NOT serve as an **impetus** to study harder?
   a. a chance to play on a team
   b. a mention on the honor roll
   c. a reward from a parent
   d. a speech on physical fitness

4. Which task might be the most **tedious?**
   a. walking your dog
   b. redecorating your room
   c. shopping for groceries
   d. planning a party

Vocabulary Strategy: Using Context Clues

When you encounter an unfamiliar word, look at its **context**—or the surrounding words, phrases, or sentences—to try to understand its meaning. Look at the following example:

> We have a long way to go. Many weeks and months and years of long, *tedious* work lie ahead.

The work described as "tedious" is also described as "long" and lasting for "many weeks and months and years." Work that lasts a very long time has the potential to be difficult, boring, or tiring. Checking the word's meaning in the dictionary confirms that *tedious* means "tiresome" or "boring."

Practice and Apply Reread Kennedy's speech and find the following words: *host, substantial, impairment, profound.* Look at the surrounding sentences for clues to each word's meaning. Then fill out a chart like the one shown.

Word	Context Clues	Guessed Definitions	Dictionary Definition
host (lines 21–24)			
substantial (lines 31–36)			
impairment (lines 64–68)			
profound (lines 73–78)			

Critical Vocabulary

L 4a, L 4c, L 4d

Answers: **1.** *b;* **2.** *b;* **3.** *d;* **4.** *c*

Vocabulary Strategy: Using Context Clues

Word	Context Clues	Guessed Definitions	Dictionary Definition
host	follows a list of names; followed by "of others"	a lot; many	a great number
substantial	modifies "benefit," something Kennedy wants to emphasize	great; significant	considerable in importance
impairment	children unable to describe impairment are suffering from "eye defects."	injury; damage	condition of being damaged or injured
profound	modifies "influence," something Kennedy wants to emphasize	great	deep or far-reaching

English Language Support

Use Context Clues Have students work in pairs. Provide each pair with a chart with the first two columns completed. Have them reread the lines in the speech that contain each word and find the context clues that are shown in the chart. Then ask them to use the clues to complete the Guessed Definitions column before confirming the definitions in a dictionary.

Strategies for Annotation 🖊 📋 *Annotate it!*

Using Context Clues

L 4a

Have students locate the sentences containing *host, substantial, impairment,* and *profound* in Kennedy's speech. Encourage students to use their eBook annotation tools to do the following:

- Highlight each word.
- Reread the surrounding sentences, looking for clues to the word's meaning. Underline any clues you find, such as examples, synonyms, or antonyms.
- Review your annotations and try to infer the word's meaning.

space research has no values here on earth. Nothing cou[ld] further from the truth. Just as the wartime developmen[t] radar gave us the transistor, and <u>all that it made possible</u>, so research in space medicine holds the promise of substantial <u>benefit</u> for those of us who are earthbound. For our effort

> substantial: "great" or "significant"?

PRACTICE & APPLY

Language Conventions: Capitalization

Tell students that the examples in the chart are just a few of the types of proper nouns that need capitalization. Invite volunteers to supply other organizations, events, and/or documents as examples. *(Possible answers: Library of Congress, Boy Scouts of America, Memorial Day, Fourth of July, United States Constitution)*

Answers:

1. *the State of the Union*

2. *Martin Luther King Jr. Day*

3. *Apollo 11 Flight Plan*

4. *NASA; National Aeronautics and Space Administration*

English Language Support

Use Capitalization Use these sentences to introduce or review other common capitalization rules:

- A spacecraft flies very fast. (first word in sentence)
- Of course, I have never been in space. (the pronoun *I*)
- During his life, President Kennedy gave many speeches. (titles before names)
- The first Monday in September is when we observe Labor Day. (weekdays, months, and holidays)

ASK STUDENTS to work in pairs to write sentences using the rules that they have learned. Then ask them to rewrite the sentences using no capitalization. Have them exchange sentences with another pair and challenge them to capitalize the sentences correctly.

Language Conventions: Capitalization L 2, L 3

In your writing, you will need to apply the rules of capitalization to **proper nouns**—the names of specific people, places, and things—including organizations, historical documents, and events. In the following example, note which proper nouns are capitalized.

> In "Remarks at the Dedication of the Aerospace Medical Health Center," President Kennedy honored the Brooks Air Force Base School of Aerospace Medicine. He also mentioned that Americans demonstrated "mastery of the skies" in World War I, World War II, and the Korean War.

Note that when writing a title, the articles *and* and *the* remain lowercase, as do the prepositions *at* and *of*. The chart below shows three types of proper nouns that require capitalization. When events or organizations are abbreviated, their abbreviations are also capitalized.

Capitalization of Proper Nouns		Abbreviations
Organizations	American Library Association	ALA
	World Health Organization	WHO
Events	World War II	WW II
	Presidents' Day	
Documents	Bill of Rights	
	Declaration of Independence	

Practice and Apply These sentences include proper nouns that lack correct capitalization. In each sentence, indicate which proper nouns should be capitalized. Consult reference materials for terms or titles that are unfamiliar to you.

1. Each January, the President of the United States delivers a speech called the state of the union.

2. Once a year, we observe Martin Luther King Jr. day to celebrate the great civil rights leader.

3. In 1969, Apollo 11 was the first manned space mission to land on the Moon. The details of the mission are preserved in a document called the Apollo 11 flight plan.

4. In 2011, five top scientists were selected by nasa, the national aeronautics and space administration, to investigate discoveries on the planet Mars.

English Language Support

Modify to Add Details Explain that just as correct capitalization makes ideas clear to readers, so do specific details. Explain that **prepositional phrases,** consisting of a preposition with a noun, pronoun, gerund, or clause, can add details about time, manner, place, or cause. Prepositions such as *in, from, on,* and *with* show how nouns in a sentence are related.

- Model adding the prepositional phrase "to Congress" to the first Practice and Apply item. Point out that "of the United States" and "of the union" are also prepositional phrases. Help students write two sentences that include prepositional phrases.

- Have students work in pairs to make a list of prepositions. Tell them to use their lists to add one prepositional phrase to each Practice and Apply item. Explain that they may need to revise the sentences to add their phrases.

- Tell students to write four sentences about Kennedy's speech that include prepositional phrases. Ask them to underline the phrases they use and remind them to use correct capitalization.

Compare and Contrast
Two Versions of a Speech

TEACH

Point out that the sound of a speaker's voice can be a powerful tool of persuasion. The delivery of a speech can affect how the ideas are received. Have students listen to the audio version of Kennedy's speech and ask them to note the following:

- **Tone** is the attitude a writer or speaker has toward a subject. In speaking, tone can be conveyed by the sound of the voice. For example, a speaker might state a phrase in a manner that is playful, casual, mournful, or insistent, indicating the tone.
- **Emphasis** is the stress a speaker places on certain words or main points of an argument. A raised voice or a lowered voice creates emphasis. Gestures, such as a loud clap of hands, can be used as well, often indicating a speaker's strong emotion.
- **Pace** is the speed at which someone delivers a speech. It can create a certain rhythm, captivating listeners to follow the flow of ideas.

PRACTICE AND APPLY

Audio Clip: 10 minutes

Suggest students listen to the speech more than once, pausing when necessary to determine what vocal techniques help to support Kennedy's argument and recording them in a chart like the one shown below.

Technique	Evidence from Speech
Tone	
Emphasis	
Pace	

After students listen to the speech, have them hold a discussion to compare and contrast the print and audio texts of the speech. Ask students to explain how hearing the speech is different from reading it and how the delivery of the speech conveys the meaning of the words, citing passages from the speech to support their answers. *(Accept all reasonable responses.)*

 INTERACTIVE LESSON Have students complete the tutorial in this lesson: **Analyzing and Evaluating Presentations**

Trace and Evaluate an Argument

RETEACH

Review the terms *claim, reasons, evidence, opposing claims,* and *counterargument.* Then, give an example of a claim, such as "Animal dissection in middle schools should be banned."

- Ask students to provide examples of types of reasons and evidence that might be used to support the claim. *(Sample Reason: The practice can have a negative impact on students performing the dissections.)*
- Provide the following opposing claim: "Animal dissection is an important way for students to learn about biology." Ask: How could you counter this viewpoint? *(Sample Answer: Save dissections for college students majoring in biology or medical school students.)*

 LEVEL UP TUTORIALS Assign the following *Level Up* tutorial: **Elements of an Argument**

INDEPENDENT READING

Students can apply the skill to a current magazine or newspaper editorial. Have students work independently to outline the claim, support, opposing claim, and counterargument. Ask: Does the writer include enough support to prove the claim? Does he or she do an adequate job of anticipating possible objections?

Is Space Exploration Worth the Cost?

Online Essay by Joan Vernikos

 For more context and historical background, students can view the video "Space Shuttle: The Last Mission" in their eBooks.

Why This Text

Students often finish reading the text of an argument without a complete grasp of the author's ideas and evidence. Arguments like this one by Joan Vernikos may have difficult language or complex reasoning that becomes clear only with careful study. With the help of the close-reading questions, students will trace and evaluate her argument on the risks and rewards of space exploration. This close reading will lead students to develop a coherent understanding of Vernikos's argument.

Background Have students read the background and information about the author. Introduce the selection by telling students that Dr. Joan Vernikos strongly believes that knowledge gained from space exploration can greatly benefit humans here on Earth. An expert on stress and healthy aging, she wrote one of her most popular books—*Sitting Kills, Moving Heals*—using information gained from astronauts' experiences in space to remedy sedentary earthbound lifestyles.

SETTING A PURPOSE Ask students to pay attention to the reasons Vernikos uses to support her position. How soon into the essay can they begin to identify her position?

Standards Support

- cite several pieces of textual evidence
- determine central ideas in a text
- trace and evaluate an argument
- assess an author's claims and reasoning

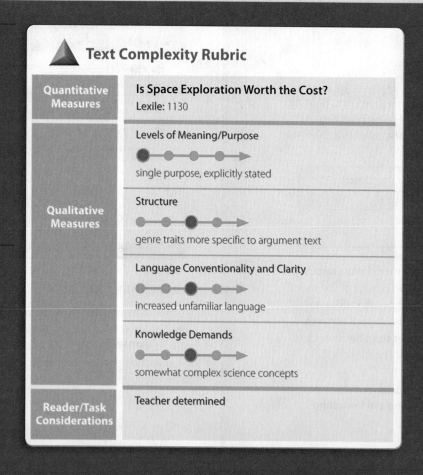

Text Complexity Rubric

Quantitative Measures

Is Space Exploration Worth the Cost?
Lexile: 1130

Qualitative Measures

Levels of Meaning/Purpose

single purpose, explicitly stated

Structure

genre traits more specific to argument text

Language Conventionality and Clarity

increased unfamiliar language

Knowledge Demands

somewhat complex science concepts

Reader/Task Considerations

Teacher determined

Strategies for CLOSE READING

Trace and Evaluate an Argument

Students should read this argument carefully all the way through. Close-reading questions at the bottom of the page will help them focus on a thorough analysis of the argument. As they read, students should jot down comments or questions about the text in the side margins.

WHEN STUDENTS STRUGGLE . . .

To help students follow the reasons Vernikos cites to support her claim, have students work in small groups to fill out a chart like the one shown as they analyze the essay.

CITE TEXT EVIDENCE For practice in tracing an argument, ask students to cite the evidence Vernikos uses to support each reason.

CLAIM: Human space exploration is worth the cost.

SUPPORT:

Reason 1: Humans may need to populate other planets in the future, and only trained astronauts can adequately prepare for this.

Reason 2: Knowledge gained from human space exploration greatly benefits many aspects of life on Earth.

Reason 3: Monetary returns on space investments far outweigh the costs.

Reason 4: The creativity of our nation's youth in fields such as science and engineering must propel the U.S. into a leadership role in space exploration.

Background *Beginning in 1981, NASA launched American astronauts into outer space through the Space Shuttle Program. However, budget cuts forced NASA to discontinue the shuttle program in 2011. For years, scientists and economists have debated whether NASA should carry out human space travel in the future. As Director of NASA's Life Sciences Division, Dr. Joan Vernikos studied the harmful effects of weightlessness on astronauts.*

Is Space Exploration Worth the Cost?

Online Essay by Joan Vernikos

CLOSE READ
Notes

1. **READ ▶** As you read lines 1–31, begin to collect and cite evidence.

- Circle the question at the beginning of the essay.
- In the margin, explain what Vernikos says about the human spirit in lines 5–7.
- Then, underline the main idea in each of the next two paragraphs.

A Why explore? Asked why he kept trying to climb Everest, English mountaineer George Mallory reputedly replied, "Because it was there." Exploration is intrinsic to our nature. It is the contest between man and nature mixed with the primal desire to conquer. It fuels curiosity, inspiration and creativity. The human spirit seeks to discover the unknown, and in the process explore the physical and psychological potential of human **endurance**.

There have always been the few risk-takers who ventured for the rest of us to follow. Because of earlier pioneers, air travel is now
10 commonplace, and space travel for all is just around the corner. Economic and societal benefits are not immediately evident, but they always follow, as does our understanding of human potential to overcome challenges. Fifty years after Sputnik,[1] space remains the next frontier.

Humans seek to test their limits and explore the mysterious.

endurance:
ability to withstand difficulties over time

---

[1] **Sputnik:** the world's first artificial satellite was put into orbit around Earth by the Soviet Union on October 4, 1957. Its launch marked the start of the space age.

63

---

1. **READ AND CITE TEXT EVIDENCE** Students' goals in reading lines 1–31 are to begin to grasp Vernikos's position on space exploration and to identify her main ideas.

A **ASK STUDENTS** to infer Vernikos's answer to the title's question based on the information she introduces in the first and second paragraphs. *Students may point to her positive discussion of humans' enduring and "intrinsic" need to explore, as well as her references to specific "economic and societal benefits" of space exploration to infer that Vernikos supports the idea that space exploration is worth the cost.*

Critical Vocabulary: endurance (line 7) Ask students to share their definitions of *endurance*. Ask how endurance fits into Vernikos's discussion of exploration. *Vernikos believes that exploration of the unknown tests the limits of humans' physical and mental abilities.*

B Without risking (human) lives, robotic technology such as unmanned missions, probes, observatories, and landers enables space exploration. It lays the groundwork, and does the scouting. But as I heard former astronaut Thomas Jones often say, "only a (human) can experience what being in space feels like, and only a (human) can
20 communicate this to others." It is (humans) who repair the Hubble telescope.[2] It is (humans) who service the International Space Station (ISS). Mercury astronauts were the first to photograph Earth from space with hand-held cameras. Earth scientists in orbit on the ISS may view aspects of global change that only a trained eye can see. In addition, studying astronauts in the microgravity of space has been the only means of understanding how gravity affects (human) development and health here on Earth. It is highly probable that, in this century, (humans) will settle on other planets. Our ability to explore and sustain (human) presence there will not only expand
30 Earth's access to mineral resources but, should the need arise, provide alternative habitats for humanity's survival.

(At what cost?) (Is there a price to inspiration and creativity?)
C Economic, scientific and technological returns of space exploration have far exceeded the investment. Globally, 43 countries now have

---
[2] **Hubble telescope:** a space telescope launched in April of 1990 by the United States, the Hubble telescope orbits Earth and provides clear pictures for astronomical study. It was named for the astronomer Edwin Powell Hubble.

---

2. ◀ **REREAD** Reread lines 15–31. Circle every use of the word *human* in this paragraph. What idea is Vernikos emphasizing by repeating this word? What opposing viewpoint does she refute?

It is not enough to send unmanned missions into space. Humans must actually go into space if we are to keep expanding our knowledge. She is addressing the opposing viewpoint that it is cheaper and safer to explore space with robotic technology.

3. **READ** ▶ As you read lines 32–55, continue to cite text evidence.
- Circle the questions at the beginning of the first paragraph.
- Underline the claim Vernikos makes about the benefits of space exploration in lines 32–47.
- Underline the claim in lines 48–55 and paraphrase it in the margin.

64

Astronaut Susan L. Still in the Spacelab Module during a mission aboard the Space Shuttle Columbia.

their own observing or communication satellites in Earth orbit. Observing Earth has provided G.P.S.,[3] meteorological forecasts, predictions and management of hurricanes and other natural disasters, and global monitoring of the environment, as well as **surveillance** and intelligence. Satellite communications have changed
40 life and business practices with computer operations, cell phones, global banking, and TV. Studying humans living in the microgravity[4] of space has expanded our understanding of osteoporosis and balance disorders, and has led to new treatments. Wealth-generating medical devices and instrumentation such as digital mammography and outpatient breast biopsy procedures and the application of telemedicine to emergency care are but a few of the social and economic benefits of manned exploration that we take for granted.

D Space exploration is not a drain on the economy; it generates infinitely more wealth than it spends. Royalties on NASA patents and
50 licenses currently go directly to the U.S. Treasury, not back to NASA. I firmly believe that the Life Sciences Research Program would be self-supporting if permitted to receive the return on its investment. NASA has done so much with so little that it has generally been assumed to have had a huge budget. In fact, the 2007 NASA budget of $16.3 billion is a minute fraction of the $13 trillion total G.D.P.[5]

---
[3] **G.P.S.:** an abbreviation for Global Positioning System, a system for determining one's position on Earth by comparing radio signals received from different satellites placed into orbit by the United States Department of Defense (DOD).
[4] **microgravity:** also called *zero gravity* or *weightlessness*, microgravity is the near absence of gravity.
[5] **G.D.P.:** an abbreviation for Gross Domestic Product, the total market value of all the goods and services that are produced inside a country during a specified period.

---

surveillance:
close observation

New technology developed by NASA has made much more money than it has cost the government.

4. ◀ **REREAD AND DISCUSS** With a small group, discuss whether the evidence Vernikos cites to defend the cost of space exploration is sufficient (lines 48–55). Cite text evidence in your discussion.

5. **READ** ▶ Read lines 56–67. Underline the opposing viewpoint Vernikos references, and restate it in the margin.

65

---

2. **REREAD AND CITE TEXT EVIDENCE**

B **ASK STUDENTS** to evaluate the effectiveness of the repetition of "human." *The repetition emphasizes the role humans play and refutes the idea that robotic space exploration is adequate.*

FOR ELL STUDENTS Explain that the prefix **un** in *unmanned* means "not." The mission does not include humans but rather robots or mechanical beings.

ASK STUDENTS to look for other uses of the prefix *un* and cite them in the margin.

3. **READ AND CITE TEXT EVIDENCE** Vernikos claims that the "social and economic benefits" of manned exploration outweigh the costs.

C **ASK STUDENTS** to find and cite specific examples of these benefits in the text and in their margin notes. *Students should cite examples in lines 34–47.*

4. **REREAD AND DISCUSS USING TEXT EVIDENCE**

D **ASK STUDENTS** to appoint a reporter for each group to cite specific text evidence and line numbers to support their position about the sufficiency of Vernikos's evidence. *Students should cite evidence from lines 48–50 and 54–55.*

5. **READ AND CITE TEXT EVIDENCE**

ASK STUDENTS to read their margin notes to a partner and then create one response that best states the opposing viewpoints in lines 56–67 and uses specific textual evidence. *Students should emphasize that NASA generates "more wealth than it spends."*

Critical Vocabulary: surveillance (line 39) Ask students what examples of surveillance they can associate with cell phones. *Students should be able to point to apps that enable them to locate their lost phones.*

legitimate:
logical

Some say
there are
more
important
things than
space
exploration.

Education is
the most
important
aspect.

E "What's the hurry?" is a **legitimate** question. As the late Senator William Proxmire said many years ago, "Mars isn't going anywhere." Why should we commit hard-pressed budgets for space exploration when there will always be competing interests? However, as Mercury, 60 Gemini and Apollo did 50 years ago, our future scientific and technological leadership depends on exciting creativity in the younger generations. Nothing does this better than manned space exploration. There is now a national urgency to direct the creative interests of our youth towards careers in science and engineering. We need to keep the flame of manned space exploration alive as China, Russia, India, and other countries forge ahead with substantial investments that challenge U.S. leadership in space.

6. **◀ REREAD** Reread lines 56–67 and continue to cite text evidence.
- Underline the counterargument Vernikos addresses.
- Then circle the pieces of evidence you find most convincing.
- Make notes in the margin to justify your choices.

SHORT RESPONSE

Cite Text Evidence Explain whether or not Vernikos convinced you that space exploration is worth the cost. Review your reading notes, and evaluate the strength and reasonableness of the claims and evidence offered. Be sure to **cite text evidence** from the essay in your response.

Vernikos did convince me that space exploration is worth the cost.
Her claim that what we learn from space exploration improves life
for all of us on Earth was supported by strong evidence, including
new medical treatments, faster and better communication, and
better weather forecasting. Her claim that space exploration
doesn't actually cost much is supported well by the minute fraction
of the G.D.P. that is spent on it.

66

6. REREAD AND CITE TEXT EVIDENCE

E **ASK STUDENTS** to cite text evidence that shows how Vernikos appeals to the reader's patriotism. *By citing China, Russia, India, and other countries, she uses an emotional appeal of competitive and patriotic pride.*

Critical Vocabulary: legitimate (line 57) Ask students to explain *legitimate* as Vernikos uses it here. *She probably wants to appear fair-minded and open to considering all sides of an issue.*

SHORT RESPONSE

Cite Text Evidence Student responses will vary, but they should cite evidence from the text to support their positions. Students should:
- explain whether or not they agree with Vernikos's argument.
- cite specific evidence from the text to support their reasons.

TO CHALLENGE STUDENTS . . .

For more context and an additional expert opinion on the future of space travel, students can search online for video clips in which Buzz Aldrin expresses his views on the future of space exploration.

ASK STUDENTS where Aldrin thinks U.S. space exploration should be headed in the future and whether his views on space travel are similar to or different from those of Vernikos. *Aldrin believes that the U.S. should continue to invest in space exploration. Students should recognize that both Vernikos and Aldrin believe that other nations, such as China, will leap ahead of the United States in exploring space and that this is not a positive development for the U.S.*

DIG DEEPER

With the class, return to Question 4, Reread and Discuss. Have students share the results of their discussion.

ASK STUDENTS whether they were satisfied with the outcome of their small-group discussions. Have each group share what their majority opinion was. What compelling evidence did the group cite from the article to support this opinion?

- Encourage students to tell whether there was any compelling evidence cited by group members holding the minority opinion. If so, why didn't it sway the group's position?
- Have groups explain how they decided whether or not they had found sufficient evidence to support their opinion. Did everyone in the group agree as to what made the evidence sufficient? How did the group resolve any conflicts or disagreements?
- After students have shared the results of their group's discussion, ask whether another group shared any findings they wished they had brought to the table.

ASK STUDENTS to return to their Short Response answer and to revise it based on the class discussion.

*my*SmartPlanner Create lesson plans and access resources online.

Why Exploring the Ocean Is Mankind's Next Giant Leap

Commentary by Philippe Cousteau

Why This Text?

Students regularly encounter opinions and persuasive language in texts, speech, and media. This lesson guides students to evaluate the strength of an argument and focuses attention on language that reveals an author's attitude.

Key Learning Objective: The student will be able to evaluate the reasoning used to support a claim and identify tone.

RI 1 Cite textual evidence.
RI 2 Determine central idea.
RI 4 Determine meanings of words and phrases.
RI 5 Analyze structure.
RI 8 Assess argument and claims for sound reasoning.
W 7 Conduct short research projects.
W 8 Gather information from multiple print/ digital sources.
SL 1 Engage in collaborative discussions.
SL 3 Delineate a speaker's argument and specific claims.
SL 4 Present claims and findings in a focused, coherent manner.
L 1a Explain function of phrases and clauses.
L 4b Use Latin affixes as clues to meaning.
L 6 Acquire and use grade-appropriate academic vocabulary.

 Text Complexity Rubric

	Why Exploring the Ocean Is Mankind's Next Giant Leap Lexile: 1360L
Quantitative Measures	
	Levels of Meaning/Purpose more than one purpose; implied, easily identified from context
Qualitative Measures	**Structure** organization of main ideas and details is complex but mostly explicit; may exhibit disciplinary traits
	Language Conventionality and Clarity some unfamiliar, academic, or domain-specific words
	Knowledge Demands some specialized knowledge required
Reader/Task Considerations	• Teacher determined • Vary by individual reader and type of text • See the Text X-Ray for suggested Reader/Task Considerations.

English Language Support Before teaching, use the Text X-Ray for an overview of the text's complexity. The Text X-Ray and the supports and scaffolds in the Teacher's Edition will help you guide students of different skill levels.

Meaning Making · Effective Expression · Foundational Skills · Content Knowledge · Language Development

Text Complexity: Qualitative Measures

Levels of Meaning/Purpose

more than one purpose; implied, easily identified from context

Help students determine meaning.
- Teacher's Edition side notes, pp. 195, 196, 197, 198
- English Language Support, p. 195
- Determine Meanings, p. 197

To reteach how to determine meanings, see
- Determine Meanings, p. 200a

 Use It! *Level Up* Tutorial: Tone

***ZOOM IN ON* EVALUATING TONE** Explain that tone shows the author's feelings about a topic. The words, phrases, and details the author includes convey the tone.

- Read aloud lines 18–25 and work with students to identify words that show how the author feels about the shuttle program.
- Help students express that the author feels that even though the program was a source of pride, it may not have been worth the cost.

Structure

organization of main ideas and details is complex but mostly explicit; may exhibit disciplinary traits

Help students analyze reasoning.
- Teacher's Edition side notes, pp. 193, 194, 195, 196, 197, 198
- English Language Support, p. 193
- When Students Struggle, p. 194
- Strategies for Annotation, p. 197
- Analyze Structure: Sound Reasoning, p. 197

 Use It! *Level Up* Tutorials: Elements of an Argument, Analyzing Arguments; **Interactive Whiteboard Lesson**: Evaluating Arguments

***ZOOM IN ON* ANALYZING STRUCTURE** Define the term **reasoning** as "speaking or writing about a topic in a logical way."

- Introduce the term **logical fallacy.**
- Explain that a text that has logical fallacies may not be persuasive. Define **circular reasoning** *(repeating an idea with no evidence)*, **either/or fallacy** *(suggesting that there are only two choices in a situation instead of more)*, and **overgeneralization** *(making statements that are too broad)* as types of logical fallacies.
- Guide students to look for examples of logical fallacy in the text.

Language Conventionality and Clarity

some unfamiliar, academic, or domain-specific words

Teach unfamiliar academic vocabulary in context.
- Teacher's Edition Critical Vocabulary notes, pp. 194, 195, 199

Help students use prefixes.
- English Language Support, p. 199
- Strategies for Annotation, p. 199
- Vocabulary Strategy: Prefixes, p. 199

Guide students to use adjective clauses.
- Teacher's Edition side note, p. 200
- English Language Support, p. 200
- Language Conventions: Adjective Clauses, p. 200

ZOOM IN ON **USING PREFIXES** Explain that a **prefix** is a word part added before a word or a root.

- Read lines 35–38 aloud with students following along. Write *disservice* on the board and circle *dis-*. Tell students that it means "opposite of." Model determining the meaning of the word using the prefix.
- Write *co-invented* (line 38) on the board and circle *co-*. Have student pairs determine the meaning of the prefix *co-* and the full word's meaning.
- Have students look for prefixes while reading to help them determine word meanings.

Knowledge Demands

some specialized knowledge required

Help students understand and explore the topic.
- Teacher's Edition Background note, p. 193
- Content-Area Connection, p. 195
- Performance Task, pp. 198, 200a
- English Language Support, pp. 198, 200a

ZOOM IN ON **BUILDING CONTEXT** Discuss the title of the commentary. Point out that the phrase *giant leap* refers to famous words of American astronaut Neil Armstrong as he stepped onto the moon, "That's one small step for a man, one giant leap for mankind."

- Discuss with students what the author reveals about his attitude toward the ocean. Does he think it is important? What does the title show that he wants to prove with his commentary?

Suggested Reader/Task Considerations

Consider the following before assigning this text:
- Are students aware of comprehension strategies that they can use to read the text?
- Can students use analytical thinking skills to understand reasoning used in the text?

ZOOM IN ON **SUPPORTING COMPREHENSION**

- Have students complete K-W-L charts to support comprehension. Before reading, ask volunteers to share what they already know about ocean exploration and what else they want to know about it; after reading, have them share what they learned.
- Introduce Cousteau's claim—that more ocean exploration is needed. Have pairs use sticky notes as they read to label each of Cousteau's reasons for this claim, and ask which reason each pair considers strongest.

TEACH

CLOSE READ

Background Have students read the background and information about the author. Supplement the information by telling students that Philippe Cousteau Jr. is continuing the family tradition of environmental activism. Philippe's grandfather was Jacques-Yves Cousteau (1910–1997), a French naval officer who became an ocean explorer. He helped to invent diving equipment, underwater cameras, and other technologies for undersea exploration. His books and appearances in movies and on TV brought public awareness to the wonders of the oceans. He continued working with his son, the author's father, filmmaker and environmentalist Philippe Cousteau Sr. (1940–1979).

SETTING A PURPOSE Direct students to use the Setting a Purpose text to focus their reading. Remind them to generate questions as they read.

Analyze Structure: Sound Reasoning (LINES 1–15)

RI 5, RI 8

Point out that the title includes a reference to Neil Armstrong's famous words, spoken as he became the first human to walk on the moon. Armstrong's words: "That's one small step for [a] man, one giant leap for mankind."

A **ASK STUDENTS** to reread the title and lines 1–15 and tell what the title and text reveal about Philippe Cousteau's **claim,** or position on an issue. *(Cousteau believes that space exploration has overshadowed ocean exploration, and it is time for that to change. The new "giant leap" will be the exploration of the oceans.)*

Background *Today, concerns over the ocean environment and potential economic and technological benefits are spurring greater interest in deep-sea exploration.* **Philippe Cousteau** *(b. 1980) is the grandson of Jacques Cousteau, the explorer whose 1960s television show revealed undersea wonders. Philippe Cousteau shares his grandfather's passion for ocean conservation, and he reports regularly on environmental and humanitarian stories from around the world.*

Why Exploring the Ocean Is Mankind's Next Giant Leap

Commentary by Philippe Cousteau

SETTING A PURPOSE As you read, consider whether Philippe Cousteau's reasons for further ocean exploration are valid. Write down any questions you may have while reading.

"Space . . . the final frontier." Not only has this classic phrase dazzled the many millions of fans of the Star Trek franchise, some could argue it has defined a big part of the American ideal for the last 50 years. The 1960s were dominated by the race to the moon and Americans were rightfully proud to be the first nation to make it there.

However, another incredible feat happened in 1960 that is largely forgotten today. For the first time in history, on January 23, 1960, two men, Lt. Don Walsh and Jacques Piccard,
10 descended to the deepest part of the ocean, the bottom of the Challenger Deep in the Mariana Trench located in the western Pacific Ocean. While this feat made international news, the race to the depths of this planet was quickly overshadowed by the race to the moon—and no one has ever gone that deep since.

English Language Support

Analyze Structure Introduce the text with the SQP2RS strategy.

- First, have students scan the text before reading, looking for words that signal contrasts. *(however, while, but, not, despite)*
- Then have students list questions about comparisons and contrasts. Have them predict things they may learn from the text.
- Next, students should read to answer questions and check predictions. They may use the eBook annotation tools to underline contrast words and highlight phrases discussing contrasting ideas.
- Finally, have students summarize the text.

of the American ideal for the last 50 years. The 1960s were dominated by the race to the moon and Americans were rightfully proud to be the first nation to make it there.

However, another incredible feat happened in 1960 that is largely forgotten today. For the first time in history, on

Analyze Structure: Sound Reasoning (LINES 41–56)

RI 1,
RI 8

Point out that Cousteau is making the claim that the end of the space shuttle program is an opportunity for a valuable ocean-exploration program. He supports this claim with **reasons,** logical statements given to support a claim.

B CITE TEXT EVIDENCE Tell students to reread lines 41–56 to name the two main reasons Cousteau gives to support his claim. *(We have (1) "a golden opportunity" and (2) "a pressing need" to explore the oceans.)*

Point out that a solid persuasive argument contains **evidence,** or facts, examples, quotations, experiences, and other pieces of information that support the claim.

C CITE TEXT EVIDENCE Ask students to reread lines 49–51 and identify a piece of evidence in this paragraph that supports one of Cousteau's reasons for ocean exploration. *(The reason that we have a "golden opportunity" is supported by the evidence of "critical medical advances," such as AZT derived from a reef sponge.)*

CRITICAL VOCABULARY

diplomat: The author says that the space shuttle program led to diplomatic firsts. The adjective *diplomatic* describes international relations.

ASK STUDENTS what diplomatic events occurred as a result of the space shuttle trips to the International Space Station. *(Astronauts from different countries worked together on the ISS.)*

sustain: Forms of energy that are sustainable can be used without harming the environment.

ASK STUDENTS how the author feels about sustainable forms of energy. *(He believes that sustainable energy sources are a worthwhile goal.)*

And for the last 50 years, we have largely continued to look up. But that trend may be changing.

In July 2011, the space shuttle program that had promised to revolutionize space travel by making it (relatively) affordable and accessible came to an end after 30 years. Those three decades provided numerous technological, scientific and **diplomatic** firsts. With an estimated price tag of nearly $200 billion, the program had its champions and its detractors. It was, however, a source of pride for the United States, capturing the American spirit of innovation and leadership.

With the iconic space program ending, many people have asked, "What's next? What is the next giant leap in scientific and technological innovation?"

Today a possible answer to that question has been announced. And it does not entail straining our necks to look skyward. Finally, there is a growing recognition that some of the most important discoveries and opportunities for innovation may lie beneath what covers more than 70 percent of our planet—the ocean.

You may think I'm doing my grandfather Jacques Yves-Cousteau and my father Philippe a disservice when I say we've only dipped our toes in the water when it comes to ocean exploration. After all, my grandfather co-invented the modern SCUBA system and "The Undersea World of Jacques Cousteau" introduced generations to the wonders of the ocean. In the decades since, we've only explored about 10 percent of the ocean—an essential resource and complex environment that literally supports life as we know it, life on earth.

We now have a golden opportunity and a pressing need to recapture that pioneering spirit. A new era of ocean exploration can yield discoveries that will help inform everything from critical medical advances to **sustainable** forms of energy. Consider that AZT, an early treatment for HIV, is derived from a Caribbean reef sponge, or that a great deal of energy—from offshore wind, to OTEC (ocean thermal energy conservation), to wind and wave energy—is yet untapped in our oceans. Like unopened presents under the tree, the ocean is a treasure trove of knowledge. In addition, such discoveries will have a tremendous impact on economic growth by creating jobs as well as technologies and goods.

diplomat
(dĭp´lə-măt´) *n.*
A *diplomat* is a person appointed by a government to interact with other governments.

sustain
(sə-stān´) *v.* If things *sustain,* they remain in existence.

194   Collection 4

WHEN STUDENTS STRUGGLE...

To help students follow Cousteau's argument, tell them to fill in an outline as they read to track the claim, reasons, and evidence. Have students work in pairs and use an outline with three sections labeled "Thesis," "Key Point," and "Support." In the "Thesis" section, have students write Cousteau's claim *(People should devote time and resources to ocean exploration).* In the "Key Point" section, have students list reasons. In the "Support" section, have students list evidence that supports the reasons.

 LEVEL UP TUTORIALS For additional support, assign the following *Level Up* tutorials: **Elements of an Argument; Analyzing Arguments**

A submersible, a craft designed for deep-sea research, glides just above the ocean floor.

In addition to new discoveries, we also have the opportunity to course correct when it comes to **stewardship** of our oceans. Research and exploration can go hand in glove[1]
60 with resource management and conservation.

Over the last several decades, as the United States has been exploring space, we've **exploited** and polluted our oceans at an alarming rate without dedicating the needed time or resources to truly understand the critical role they play in the future of the planet. It is not trite to say that the oceans are the life support system of this planet, providing us with up to 70 percent of our oxygen, as well as a primary source of protein for billions of people, not to mention the regulation of our climate.

70 Despite this life-giving role, the world has fished, mined and trafficked the ocean's resources to a point where we are actually seeing dramatic changes that are seriously impacting today's generations. And that impact will continue as the world's population approaches 7 billion people, adding strain to the world's resources unlike any humanity has ever had to face before.

In the long term, destroying our ocean resources is bad business with devastating consequences for the global economy, and the health and sustainability of all

D **steward**
(stoo′ərd) *n.* A *steward* is a person who supervises and manages something.

exploit
(ĕk′sploit′) *v.* If you *exploit* something, you use it selfishly.

E

---
[1] **hand in glove:** in close combination with something else.

CONTENT-AREA CONNECTION

W 1, W 7

Ocean Energy In lines 45–56, Philippe Cousteau discusses some ways the ocean can help provide energy. Wind energy is used to make electricity by wind flowing over the blades of a turbine. The ocean is a good place for wind turbines because there are strong winds over some parts of the oceans.

Activity Have pairs research ocean wind farms and why people do or do not want them. Have them write a two-paragraph argument discussing the pros and cons of wind farms, including a claim, reasons, and evidence. Invite volunteers to share their research with the class.

CLOSE READ

Analyze Structure: Sound Reasoning (LINES 57–69)

RI 1, RI 8

Cousteau presents another reason to support his claim that we should prioritize ocean exploration.

D **CITE TEXT EVIDENCE** Have students reread lines 57–69, identify the reason he gives, and cite evidence that supports this reason. *(Reason: Ocean exploration will help us improve resource use and conservation. Evidence: Oceans have become increasingly polluted. Oceans provide oxygen and food and regulate climate.)*

Determine Meanings

RI 4

(LINE 70)

Tell students that authors of arguments may use words that appeal to the emotions.

E **ASK STUDENTS** what impact the words *life-giving role* (line 70) have. *(to show we owe our lives to oceans)*

English Language Support

Help students analyze the emotional effect of the words *life-giving role*. Lead students to connect the idea that life is important with the idea that oceans help people stay alive. Therefore, the role of oceans is valuable.

CRITICAL VOCABULARY

steward: Cousteau says that we can improve our care of the oceans.

ASK STUDENTS why we should care about ocean stewardship. *(Because we've harmed the oceans, we're responsible for taking care of them.)*

exploit: Cousteau says that we've taken advantage of the oceans.

ASK STUDENTS how people exploit oceans. *(They fish from it, drill for oil from it, and ship goods on it.)*

Determine Meanings

RI 1,
RI 4

(LINES 87–93)

Tell students that Cousteau uses words to convey a tone of thrilled optimism about future ocean exploration.

F **CITE TEXT EVIDENCE** Have students identify words and phrases in lines 87–93 that convey Cousteau's attitude. Ask what effect these words are intended to have on readers. *("next big leap"; "exciting and bold"; "'wow' factor"; "dazzling technological feats"; "mystery of the unknown"; "scientific muscle"; "entrepreneurial spirit." All of these words have emotional impact and could inspire people to share the author's viewpoint.)*

Analyze Structure:
Sound Reasoning (LINES 94-96)

RI 8

Tell students that readers of persuasive writing evaluate how convincing the author has been.

G **ASK STUDENTS** to reread the next-to-last paragraph (lines 94–96) and tell what the author implies will happen if people don't "take the plunge." *(He is suggesting that if we don't invest in exploring oceans, they won't "continue to provide life to future generations.")* Ask for ideas about how valid this suggestion is based on reasons and evidence in the commentary. *(Sample answer: This argument is valid because it shows that our future is tied to the health of the world's oceans.)*

COLLABORATIVE DISCUSSION Have small groups review the text to note statements in which Cousteau tells what he believes should be done. Have students write the reasons and evidence he provides to support his claim, and why his argument is or is not convincing.

ASK STUDENTS to share any questions they generated in the course of reading and discussing the selection.

80 creatures—including humans. Marine spatial planning, marine sanctuaries, species conservation, sustainable fishing strategies, and more must be a part of any ocean exploration and conservation program to provide hope of restoring health to our oceans.

While there is still much to learn and discover through space exploration, we also need to pay attention to our unexplored world here on earth. Our next big leap into the unknown can be every bit as exciting and bold as our pioneering work in space. It possesses the same "wow" factor:
90 alien worlds, dazzling technological feats and the mystery of the unknown. The United States has the scientific muscle, the diplomatic know-how and the entrepreneurial[2] spirit to lead the world in exploring and protecting our ocean frontier.

Now we need the public demand and political will and bravery to take the plunge in order to ensure that the oceans can continue to provide life to future generations.

Today is a big step in that direction and hopefully it is just the beginning.

COLLABORATIVE DISCUSSION What does Philippe Cousteau want you to realize after reading this commentary? What does he want you to do? Is his evidence convincing? Talk about your ideas with other group members.

---

[2] **entrepreneurial** (ŏn´trə-prə-nŏŏr´ē-əl): business-starting.

TO CHALLENGE STUDENTS . . .

Compare Two Arguments Have students complete a comparison and contrast analysis of Philippe Cousteau's argument for ocean exploration and John F. Kennedy's argument for space exploration. Students should work independently at first to analyze the arguments. Then, have students work in small groups to discuss their analyses. Students should answer questions similar to those below:

- Which argument is more persuasive and why?
- Which argument follows a clearer, more logical organizational structure?
- Are there any instances of **logical fallacy** (an error in reasoning that starts with a false assumption or mistaken belief) in either of the arguments? Explain.
- How do the arguments appeal to audience emotion, and how effective is this?

Analyze Structure: Sound Reasoning

RI 5, RI 8

Strong arguments use sound reasoning and evidence to support any claims. A carefully constructed written argument includes the following elements:

- **claim:** the writer's position on an issue or problem
- **reasons:** logical statements that explain an action or belief
- **evidence:** facts, examples, quotations, experiences, and other pieces of information that support the claim
- **counterargument:** reasons and evidence given to disprove an opposing viewpoint

An argument may appear to be persuasive, but it may be based on faulty reasoning. A **logical fallacy** is an error in reasoning that often starts with a false assumption or mistaken beliefs. Here are a few logical fallacies:

Logical fallacy	Definition	Example
Circular reasoning	Repeating an idea rather than providing evidence.	I am too tied to my cell phone because I can't put it down.
Either/or fallacy	A statement that suggests there are only two choices available in a situation that really offers more than two options.	Either the city should provide recycling bins or throw out the Recycling Act.
Overgeneralization	A generalization that is too broad.	A ballet dancer would be a natural at gymnastics.

Assess the reasoning in an argument by determining whether

- the argument presents a clear claim
- the reasons make sense and are presented in a logical order
- the evidence is valid and adequately supports the claim
- there are no instances of logical fallacies or faulty reasoning

Determine Meanings

RI 4

The **tone** of a written work expresses the author's attitude toward his or her subject. For example, the tone can be described as angry, sad, or humorous. An author's choice of words, phrases, and details signal the tone of the work.

This sentence from Philippe Cousteau's commentary includes words that reveal his attitude about ocean exploration:

> **We now have a golden opportunity and a pressing need to recapture that pioneering spirit.**

What words in this sentence show an enthusiastic tone?

CLOSE READ

Analyze Structure: Sound Reasoning

RI 5, RI 8

After reviewing the elements of a well-constructed argument, have students state Cousteau's claim. *(We should invest in exploring and protecting the oceans.)*

After reviewing the logical fallacies in the chart:

- Have students look through the commentary to find the author's references to the space program.
- Have students decide if Cousteau's reasoning is sound or if it uses an either/or fallacy. *(An either/or choice between exploring the ocean or space is implied, when it's possible other options exist. However, there's no logical fallacy because he isn't focused on the choice. He's using comparisons to the space program to structure his argument.)*

Determine Meanings

RI 4

Review that writing that is intended to persuade often has words that appeal to the emotions. Philippe Cousteau has strong feelings about his subject, which he shares with readers through his choice of words.

Have students identify words that convey an enthusiastic tone in the excerpted sentence. *("golden opportunity," "pressing need," "pioneering spirit")*

Strategies for Annotation

🖊️ 🗐 *Annotate it!*

Analyze Structure: Sound Reasoning

RI 5, RI 8

Use this excerpt from lines 46–53 and share these strategies for guided or independent analysis:

- Highlight in yellow the reason the author gives for why ocean exploration is important.
- Underline evidence that supports the reason.
- On a note, comment about how persuasive the argument seems.

exploration can yield discoveries that will help inform everything from critical medical advances to sustainable forms of energy. Consider that AZT, an early treatment for HIV, is derived from a Caribbean reef sponge, or that a great deal of energy—from offshore wind, to OTEC (ocean

> AZT point is good evidence; No specific evidence of energy production, just types of energy.

Analyzing the Text

RI 1, RI 2, RI 4, RI 5, RI 8

Possible answers:

1. *Cousteau compares space exploration with ocean exploration to express that exploring the ocean inspires the same innovation and leadership as space exploration.*

2. *The author states his claim in the last sentence. Ocean exploration will lead to discoveries and innovations.*

3. *Cousteau cites medical advances, untapped energy sources, and discoveries in the ocean that will lead to economic growth. The support seems plausible, but predictions are not the same as factual evidence.*

4. *The author's tone is urgent, as shown in words such as* exploited, polluted, alarming rate, critical role, life support system, strain to the world's resources unlike any humanity has ever had to face before, *and* devastating consequences.

5. *The author looks back to the space program and ahead to an ocean program to show positive similarities: innovation, pioneering spirit, excitement, new technologies with far-reaching benefits. He also looks back to the harm caused by our neglect of the oceans and ahead to a devastating future that would result if we continued our neglect.*

6. *The author notes that others may prefer to invest in the space program but says we "need to pay attention to our unexplored world here on Earth." His commentary supports shifting attention to the oceans, though he doesn't directly address objections such as financial costs.*

English Language Support

Expressing Opinions Explain that expressing opinions effectively requires certain skills, including

- using phrases such as *Can you explain what you mean by . . . ?* and *That's interesting, but I think that . . .*
- supporting your ideas with detailed and relevant evidence from the text and your own knowledge
- using words such as *can, may, possibly, likely, could, should,* and *might* to express opinions and shades of meaning

FOR STANDARD ENGLISH LEARNERS

Pronunciation Explain that speaking clearly is important in a debate. Some students may have difficulty voicing the /r/ in initial consonant clusters and the /r/ in words with r-controlled vowels. They may omit the /r/ in a word such as *trench*, saying *t'ench* instead, or the /r/ at the end of *for*, saying *fo'.* Write this sentence on the board: *Further <u>exploration</u> of the Mariana <u>Trench</u> opens the <u>door</u> <u>for great</u> discoveries.* Read the sentence aloud, emphasizing the /r/ sounds. Have students echo your reading several times.

---

eBook *Annotate It!*

Analyzing the Text

RI 1, RI 2, RI 4, RI 5, RI 8, W 7, W 8, SL 1, SL 4

Cite Text Evidence   Support your responses with evidence from the text.

1. **Compare** What comparison does the author develop in the first five paragraphs, and what is his purpose?

2. **Interpret** Reread lines 26–34. Which sentence presents the author's claim? Assess the clearness of the claim by restating it in your own words.

3. **Assess Reasoning** Reread lines 45–56. Do the examples of support seem valid? Explain.

4. **Infer** Reread lines 61–84. What is the author's tone? Which words and phrases in the paragraphs reveal that tone?

5. **Analyze** How does the author describe both past events and future events to persuade readers to agree with him?

6. **Evaluate** Examine lines 85–93. How sound is the author's reasoning here? Explain your assessment.

PERFORMANCE TASK

Speaking Activity: Informal Debate Philippe Cousteau begins by mentioning the 1960 exploration of the Mariana Trench. Would further exploration of this deep-sea region be worthwhile? Divide your group into two teams to informally debate that question.

In an informal debate, speakers from each side take turns presenting and supporting valid claims and countering opposing claims. The whole group can decide on the rules to follow. You may want to use a moderator, for example, and have a time limit for each speaker.

- First, research the Mariana Trench and any attempts to explore it in recent years.
- Investigate the potential for benefits in exploring the region.
- Identify the potential risks involved. Find out if any issues or problems have been reported.
- Listen well to any opponent's points to help you prepare your responses.

Assign this performance task.

PERFORMANCE TASK

W 7, W 8, SL 1, SL 4

Speaking Activity: Informal Debate Guide students to reliable sources of information about the Mariana Trench. Suggest that students

- take notes in three categories: Facts, Benefits, Risks
- develop a proposition to debate

See the lesson **Hold an Informal Debate** in Extend and Reteach for additional instructional ideas on holding a debate.

Critical Vocabulary

L 4b, L 6

diplomat   sustain   steward   exploit

Practice and Apply Choose the situation that is the better match with the meaning of the vocabulary word. Give your reasons.

1. **diplomat** **a.** Leaders discuss policy with leaders of other countries.
   b. Political leaders are chosen on Election Day.

2. **sustain** **a.** Laws limit the kinds of fish that can be caught.
   b. Fishing boats overfish local fishing stocks.

3. **steward** **a.** The city ignores its local fishing industry.
   b. Citizens rely on their city to clean up polluted areas.

4. **exploit** **a.** Young children attend school for six hours a day.
   b. Young children work long hours in factories.

Vocabulary Strategy: Prefixes

A **prefix** is a word part added before a word or a root. Readers can use their knowledge of prefixes to analyze words and find familiar parts and relationships. This chart shows two common prefixes.

Prefix	Meaning	Example Words
dis-	not, lack of, opposite of	dishonest, disgrace, disinfect, discourage, dispute, distract
ex-	not, out, away from	exchange, exhale, exclude, expose, extract, external

Notice the words with prefixes in this sentence from Cousteau's commentary:

> You may think I'm doing my grandfather Jacques Yves-Cousteau and my father Philippe a disservice when I say we've only dipped our toes in the water when it comes to ocean exploration.

You can see that *disservice* has the prefix *dis-*. A disservice is the opposite of a helpful service. The word *exploration* has the prefix *ex-* before a Latin root; the original meaning of the Latin word is "to search out."

Practice and Apply Complete each word with the prefix *dis-* or *ex-*. Check a print or digital dictionary to make sure the word makes sense.

1. People have always ___**ploited** natural resources.

2. Marine animals that are ___**posed** to pollutants may become ill.

3. Overfishing may cause some fish to become ___**tinct**.

4. There are ___**tinct** actions to take to protect oceans.

Critical Vocabulary

L 4b, L 6

Answers: 1. *a;* **2.** *a;* **3.** *b;* **4.** *b*

Vocabulary Strategy: Prefixes

1. *exploited*

2. *exposed*

3. *extinct*

4. *distinct*

FOR STUDENTS WITH DISABILITIES

Students may struggle with the multiple (but related) meanings of the prefixes *dis-* and *ex-*. Have students work with a partner to discuss the meanings of the Example Words in the chart in their texts. Then have them write completion sentences using three Example Words from each row, e.g., A *(dishonest)* person will not tell the truth. Remind them to try to include context clues in the sentences. Then have them exchange sentences with another pair and complete each other's sentences.

English Language Support

Using Affixes Explain that using different prefixes with the same root word can result in very different meanings, even though all are related to the meaning of the root word. Have students use a dictionary and work in mixed-ability groups to discuss how the meaning of a root word below changes with the addition of prefixes:

- *cover (dis-, un-, re-)*
- *tract (ex-, re-, de-, con-)*
- *pose (dis-, ex-, im-, com-)*

Assign one root word per group, and have groups share their findings with the class.

Vocabulary Strategy: Prefixes

L 4b, L 6

Have students use their eBook annotation tools to analyze words with *dis-* and *ex-* on page 196:

- Highlight the word.
- Underline the target prefix.
- On a note, give a meaning for the word that includes a meaning for the prefix.
- Check their ideas in a print or digital dictionary. Adjust the note as needed.

While there is still much to learn and <u>dis</u>cover through space <u>ex</u>ploration, we also need to pay attention to our un<u>ex</u>plored world here on earth. Our next big leap into the unknown can be every bit as exciting and bold as our pioneering work in space. It possesses the same "wow" factor:

> discover:
> to reveal, as in "the opposite of cover"

Language Conventions: Adjective Clauses

L 1a

Use the example sentences in the instructional segments of the lesson to clarify that an adjective clause modifies a noun or a pronoun, just as a single adjective does:

- However, another incredible feat happened in 1960 that is largely forgotten today. (modifies the noun *feat*)
- Lt. Don Walsh and Jacques Piccard descended to Challenger Deep, which is the deepest part of the ocean. (modifies the proper noun *Challenger Deep*)
- Jacques Piccard, who was a Swiss engineer, developed underwater vehicles. (modifies the proper noun *Jacques Piccard*)
- More people know about the astronauts who traveled to the moon than about these two explorers. (modifies the noun *astronauts*)

Sample answers for Practice and Apply:

1. *Scientists who want to learn about weather patterns study the ocean.*

2. *Ocean exploration will be the next giant leap that will bring new technologies to everyone.*

3. *Discoveries about ocean life will affect everyone who lives on planet Earth.*

4. *Our pioneering spirit, which led us to the moon, is still strong.*

Language Conventions: Adjective Clauses

L 1a

An **adjective** is a part of speech that modifies a noun or a pronoun. It answers the question *What kind? Which?* or *How many?* A **clause** is a group of words that has a subject and a predicate—the two main parts of a complete sentence. An **adjective clause** acts like an adjective to modify a noun or pronoun in the rest of the sentence.

In an adjective clause, the subject is often a **relative pronoun**—a pronoun that relates, or connects, adjective clauses to the words they modify in a sentence. Relative pronouns include *who, whom, whose, which,* and *that.* Notice the relative pronoun in this sentence from "Why Exploring the Ocean Is Mankind's Next Giant Leap":

> However, another incredible feat happened in 1960 that is largely forgotten today.

The relative pronoun *that* introduces the adjective clause *that is largely forgotten today.* The clause modifies the noun *feat*, answering the question *What kind of feat?*

When you write, you can use adjective clauses to tell more about a noun or a pronoun in a sentence. The adjective clause is underlined in each of these sentences.

> Lt. Don Walsh and Jacques Piccard descended to Challenger Deep, which is the deepest part of the ocean. (The adjective clause tells more about *Challenger Deep.*)

> Jacques Piccard, who was a Swiss engineer, developed underwater vehicles. (The adjective clause tells more about *Jacques Piccard.*)

> More people know about the astronauts who traveled to the moon than about these two explorers. (The adjective clause tells more about *astronauts.*)

Practice and Apply Use the relative pronoun in parentheses to introduce an adjective clause that tells about the underlined noun or pronoun. Write the new sentence.

1. Scientists study the ocean. (who)

2. Ocean exploration will be the next giant leap. (that)

3. Discoveries about ocean life will affect everyone. (who)

4. Our pioneering spirit is still strong. (which)

English Language Support

Condense Ideas with Clauses Explain that adjective clauses tell more about a noun and condense ideas to create precise sentences. Write these sentences on the board, omitting the relative pronoun for each.

1. (*whose*) Philippe Cousteau knows a lot about ocean trenches. His father and grandfather explored the ocean.
2. (*which*) Some scientists study the sea. Others find it uninteresting.
3. (*who*) Leaders pass fishing laws. They care about saving fish stocks.
4. (*that*) The submarine is no longer working. It was tested yesterday.

- Model combining the first pair of sentences using the relative pronoun *whose.* Provide the relative pronoun for each of the remaining sentence pairs, and guide students to work in small groups to condense them.
- Display the relative pronouns *whose, which, who,* and *that,* and have pairs work to condense the sentences.
- Ask students to condense the sentences using adjective clauses. Have them underline each adjective clause once and the noun or pronoun it tells about twice.

Hold an Informal Debate

SL 1, SL 3, SL 4

TEACH

To help students prepare for the Performance Task, offer information about debates. Display these terms and definitions:

- **proposition**: A positively worded statement, or claim, that can clearly be supported or opposed.
- **affirmative speaker**: A debater who supports the proposition.
- **negative speaker**: A debater who opposes the proposition.
- **case**: A group of arguments on either the affirmative or negative side.
- **rebuttal**: A speech that attacks the opponent's stated arguments and evidence.

Explain that debaters need to research the facts and learn about differing viewpoints on the issue. Each team must prepare to rebut the arguments and evidence of the opposing side.

Explain that an informal debate is organized more loosely than a formal debate, but debaters still follow rules for speaking and listening. Display and discuss the following:

When speaking, remember to

- choose words that help you convey a convincing tone
- speak loudly, calmly, and clearly
- rebut politely, without sarcasm or personal attacks

When listening, remember to

- take notes about the points made
- listen for reasons and evidence that can be disputed
- not interrupt

PRACTICE AND APPLY

Direct students to line 22 of Cousteau's commentary, in which he notes opposing viewpoints about the space shuttle program.

Ask the group to come up with a proposition that would belong in a debate on this issue. *(Example: The space shuttle program was worth its $200 billion cost.)* Assign the role of a champion or a detractor to each student. Have students demonstrate making affirmative and negative statements that could belong in a debate.

English Language Support

Listen Actively Have students work with a partner to write their affirmative and negative statements and practice presenting them. As students speak, support listeners in asking questions to clarify meaning. As necessary, help students who are presenting to answer the questions.

Determine Meanings

RI 4

RETEACH

Display a short descriptive sentence, such as "The door is shut." Have students read it using different tones of voice, such as annoyed, playful, worried, angry, hopeful, pleased. Explain that just as a tone of voice expresses feelings, written words express an author's feelings about a subject. Tell students that examples of tones in a written work include angry, humorous, admiring, annoyed, urgent, and enthusiastic.

Point out that an author chooses words carefully to convey just the right tone. Display these two sentences for students to compare. Prompt students to identify the words with emotional impact and name the tone in each.

- The dark, mysterious ocean holds hidden dangers. *(threatening, advising)*
- The ocean depths startle us with amazing things. *(surprised, intrigued)*

 LEVEL UP TUTORIALS Assign the following *Level Up* tutorial: **Tone**

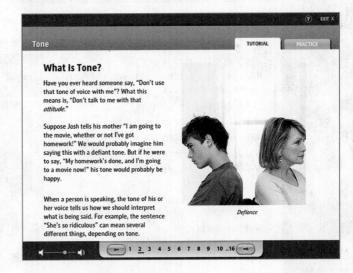

INDEPENDENT READING

Show students typical persuasive texts, such as editorials, blogs, and advertisements. Have students identify words that appeal to emotion and use an adjective to describe the general tone.

Living in the Dark

Science Article by Cheryl Bardoe

Why This Text?

Nonfiction articles help us learn about our world. Understanding how an author structures an article and learning to determine central ideas and details will help students critically analyze texts. This lesson examines text structure and asks students to identify and paraphrase central ideas and important details.

View It!

Professional Development Podcast:

Informational Text

For practice and application:

Stinging Tentacles Offer Hint of Oceans' Decline

Newspaper Article by Elisabeth Rosenthal

Close Reader selection

"Stinging Tentacles Offer Hint to Oceans' Decline," *Science Article by Elisabeth Rosenthal*

Key Learning Objective: The student will be able to analyze the structure of an informational text and paraphrase central ideas and details.

RI 1	Cite textual evidence.
RI 2	Determine central ideas in a text; provide an objective summary.
RI 3	Analyze interactions between individuals, events, and ideas.
RI 4	Determine technical meanings.
RI 5	Analyze the structure an author uses.
RI 6	Determine an author's purpose.
W 1	Write arguments to support claims.
W 4	Produce clear and coherent writing appropriate to purpose and audience.
W 8	Gather relevant information and paraphrase the data and conclusions.
W 10	Write routinely.
L 1a	Explain the function of phrases.
L 4a	Use context.
L 4b	Use Greek roots.
L 4c	Consult reference materials to clarify meaning.
L 4d	Verify meaning.
L 6	Acquire and use academic and domain-specific words.

▲ Text Complexity Rubric

Quantitative Measures

Living in the Dark
Lexile: 1200L

Qualitative Measures

Levels of Meaning/Purpose

more than one purpose; implied

Structure

mostly implied cause-and-effect structure; simple graphics, supplementary to understanding

Language Conventionality and Clarity

fairly straightforward sentence structure; many unfamiliar domain-specific words

Knowledge Demands

complex science concepts

Reader/Task Considerations

- Teacher determined
- Vary by individual reader and type of text
- See the Text X-Ray for suggested Reader/Task Considerations.

English Language Support
Before teaching, use the Text X-Ray for an overview of the text's complexity. The Text X-Ray and the supports and scaffolds in the Teacher's Edition will help you guide students of different skill levels.

Meaning Making

Language Development

Effective Expression

Content Knowledge

Foundational Skills

Text Complexity: Qualitative Measures

Levels of Meaning/Purpose

more than one purpose; implied

Help students determine central ideas and details.

- Teacher's Edition side notes, pp. 202, 205, 206, 209, 210
- English Language Support, p. 205
- Strategies for Annotation, p. 202
- Determine Central Ideas and Details, p. 209

▶ *Use It!* **Interactive Whiteboard Lesson:** Main/Central Idea and Details

Interactive Graphic Organizer: Main Idea Chart

ZOOM IN ON **DETERMINE CENTRAL IDEAS AND DETAILS** Display the Interactive Graphic Organizer: Main Idea Chart. Explain that a **central idea** is a key idea of a section of text. **Details** are information included to help readers understand the central idea.

- Instruct students to complete a graphic organizer with central ideas and details for each part of the article.
- Then have pairs write a **paraphrase** of the central idea and the most important details for each part.
- Finally, have students write clear, coherent, and concise summaries of what they learned with the support of their graphic organizers and paraphrases.

Structure

mostly implied cause-and-effect structure; simple graphics, supplementary to understanding

Help students analyze the cause-and-effect structure of the article.

- Teacher's Edition side notes, pp. 201, 203, 204, 205, 207, 208, 209, 210
- English Language Support, p. 203
- When Students Struggle, p. 204
- Strategies for Annotation, p. 209
- Analyze Structure, p. 209

To reteach structure, see

Analyze Structure: Cause-and-Effect Relationships, p. 212a

▶ *Use It!* **Level Up Tutorial:** Cause-and-Effect Organization

ZOOM IN ON **ANALYZING CAUSE-AND-EFFECT STRUCTURE** Tell students that the article is organized around **cause-and-effect relationships.** They should consider what happens in the article and why to understand these relationships.

- Introduce signal words for causes: *due to, because of*, and *since*. Then discuss signal words for effects: *as a result, therefore,* and *led to.*
- Work with the class to write sentences on the board using the signal words, clarifying meanings as necessary.
- Have students make note of signal words they notice as they read each section of the article.

Language Conventionality and Clarity

fairly straightforward sentence structure; many unfamiliar domain-specific words

Teach unfamiliar vocabulary in context.

- Teacher's Edition Critical Vocabulary notes, pp. 202, 203, 204, 206
- English Language Support, pp. 201, 212a
- Applying Academic Vocabulary, p. 203
- Strategies for Annotation, p. 69
- Analyze Technical Meanings, p. 212a

Help students use Greek roots and analyze sentence structure.

- Teacher's Edition side notes, pp. 208, 211, 212
- English Language Support, pp. 207, 212
- Strategies for Annotation, p. 211
- Vocabulary Strategy: Greek Roots, p. 211
- Language Conventions: Verbal Phrases, p. 212

ZOOM IN ON **UNPACKING WORDS** Preview the meanings of the Greek roots *hydro, therm/thermo, photo, logy, syn/sym, geo, scope, tecto, micro,* and *bio*. Write the definitions on the board.

- Model using roots to help understand the word *hydrothermal* (line 43).
- As students read the article, have them write a list of words that contain the roots.
- Have students stop at the end of each section and work with a partner to define the words using the root meanings.

Knowledge Demands

complex science concepts

Support English learners in understanding the scientific context of the article.

- Teacher's Edition Background note, p. 201
- Performance Task, p. 210

Help students understand evidence.

- Teacher's Edition side note, p. 207

ZOOM IN ON **BUILDING SCIENTIFIC KNOWLEDGE** Have students work in pairs to research the technology of submarines. Challenge them to explain why scientists are able to send mini-subs deep into the ocean.

- Ask each pair to create a one-page poster with brief sentences (and illustrations) summarizing their collected information.
- Have them share the posters with the class.

Suggested Reader/Task Considerations

Consider the following before assigning this article to students.

- Will the students remain motivated to read the text?
- Will the difficulty of the concepts interfere with comprehension?

ZOOM IN ON **SUPPORTING MOTIVATION**

- Have students create questions based on the article's subheads. For example, *Where does a whale go when it falls?* As students read, have them note answers to their questions.
- In small groups, have students draw a diagram of the ocean, showing what features and life forms exist at various depths. Each group should review the text to make sure all key details are included in the diagram.

TEACH
CLOSE READ

Background Have students read the background and information about the author. Tell students that even with early submarine technology scientists were able to travel only a limited distance into the oceans' depths. In the 1970s, however, new technologies set deep-sea exploration on a remarkable trajectory. Explain that scientists often have to reevaluate their theories and beliefs based on new evidence. This article provides a good example of that process.

SETTING A PURPOSE Direct students to use the Setting a Purpose prompt to focus their reading. Remind them to write down their own questions as they read.

Analyze Structure   RI 5
(HEADING ABOVE LINE 1)

Explain to students that authors often use text features such as **headings** to organize information. The heading that precedes a section of an article can give readers an idea of what the section is about. Suggest that students turn headings into questions to help figure out what information will follow.

(A) **ASK STUDENTS** what they think this first section of the article will be about based on the heading. (*The heading suggests that the section will tell what happens when a whale "falls," or dies and drops to the bottom of the ocean.*)

Background *For many years, it was nearly impossible to study life at the bottom of our oceans. Therefore, very little was known about deep-sea habitats. But recent 20th-century technological advances have allowed scientists to begin to discover surprising forms of life in the ocean depths. In her writing,* **Cheryl Bardoe** *likes to draw back the curtain to reveal how scientists explore the unknown. She presently lives in Chicago, Illinois, where she once worked at the city's famous Field Museum of Natural History.*

from
Living in the Dark

Science Article by Cheryl Bardoe

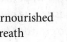

(l) ©Cathryn Montoya; (r) ©TsuneoMP/Shutterstock; (bg) ©Willyam Bradberry/Shutterstock

SETTING A PURPOSE As you read, notice how scientific study has altered past beliefs about Earth's oceans. Write down any questions you have while reading.

When a Whale Falls   **A**

Imagine the moment when a great blue whale, undernourished and exhausted from migrating, grunts out its last breath somewhere in the Pacific Ocean.

Then, as the pressure of the surrounding water squeezes the last air reserves from the whale's lungs, this massive creature begins to sink.

It plunges 700 feet (200 meters) through the ocean's top layer, the warm "sunlight zone" where algae kick-start life's food chain with photosynthesis. It drops another 2,600
10 feet (800 meters) through the cold twilight zone, where no plants live and fish have extra-large eyes to catch the faintest glimmers of sun. It descends down, down, down through 3,300 feet (1 kilometer) or more of the midnight zone. Here, temperatures hover close to freezing; deep-sea creatures must

from Living in the Dark **201**

English Language Support

Use Context Display lines 7–9, and highlight the word *photosynthesis*. Model using context and word parts (e.g., *photo-*, meaning "light") to define photosynthesis as the way plants convert sunlight into chemical energy.

- Preview lines 1–46, listing words students find difficult on the board. Have pairs use the context strategy and a dictionary to define these terms. Have pairs share their definitions and ask and answer basic questions about them.

- Have students use the context strategy to define the science terms *habitat* (line 25), *bacteria* (line 31), and *ecosystem* (line 39). Have

them discuss their definitions, asking and answering questions about how they used the strategy. Students should listen carefully so that they can use the strategy effectively.

- Have pairs skim the article to find challenging words. Have them list each word with its line number and use the strategy to write a definition for each word, confirming their ideas with a dictionary. Ask them to share their work with the class in a discussion including detailed questions and answers.

Determine Central Ideas and Details (LINES 24–32)

RI 2,
RI 3

Explain to students that **paraphrasing,** or restating information in your own words, is an effective strategy to help them understand complex ideas in a text.

B **ASK STUDENTS** to reread lines 24–32 and paraphrase the description of the whale fall. *(Sample answer: A variety of deep-sea creatures come to feed upon the fallen whale body. Some eat the outside flesh, and others eat the carcass from within. The whale fall becomes a habitat for all these diverse creatures.)*

CRITICAL VOCABULARY

cache: The author describes the whale carcass as a "cache of resources" for a variety of deep-sea creatures.

ASK STUDENTS what the author's use of this phrase suggests. *(The phrase conveys that the wealth of food provided by the whale carcass is hidden or inaccessible. It suggests a hidden or buried treasure.)*

geyser: The author chose to use the more familiar word *geyser* as a way to help readers understand hydrothermal vents.

ASK STUDENTS how a hydrothermal vent is like a geyser. *(It leaks natural gas into the ocean, the way a geyser shoots hot water and steam into the air.)*

---

flash their own lights to break the darkness; and the weight of the water feels like about 500 bowling balls pressing in on every square inch of the whale's carcass.

The tiny flecks of dead plankton that are called marine snow may drift for months before reaching the ocean floor. 20 But this great blue whale plummets so quickly that scavengers barely get a nibble. Its 160-ton carcass thumps down nearly intact, depositing as many nutrients as several thousand years' worth of marine snow—all in one fell swoop.

B This **cache** of resources, called a whale fall, will become the center of a unique habitat. First, it attracts deep-sea scavengers. Hagfish—unsightly creatures also called slime eels—wriggle inside the carcass and begin to eat it from the inside out. Squat lobsters, sleeper sharks, and crabs tear at the whale's flesh and scatter crumbs into nearby sediments. Then 30 mollusks colonize those sediments. Meanwhile, fantastical worms, slugs, and bacteria bore into the whale's bones to feast on fatty marrow.

Finally come bacteria that transform the chemicals leaking out of the decaying bones into food for themselves and others. Much as plants use energy from the sun to make their own nourishment, these "chemosynthetic" bacteria use energy from chemical reactions to create the basic building blocks of life. Within months this whale carcass may support more than 40,000 creatures; it might keep this chemosynthetic ecosystem 40 going for up to a century.

The living things that take up residence on this whale fall are similar to those that live near undersea **geysers** (called hydrothermal vents) or cracks that leak natural gas into the ocean (called cold seeps). Together, these three habitats have completely changed how scientists think about the basic rules for life.

cache
(kăsh) *n.* A *cache* is an amount of something that has been hidden away.

geyser
(gī´zər) *n.* A *geyser* is a natural hot spring that shoots hot water and steam into the air.

Life Where Life Isn't Possible

For most of human history, the ocean's secrets have been beyond reach. Gazing across the water's rippling surface, who could have guessed what truly lay beneath? In the 1840s, 50 British naturalist Edward Forbes dredged the Aegean Sea[1] 100 times to find out. The deeper his device went, the less it

---

[1] **Aegean Sea** (ĭ-jē´ən sē): an arm of the Mediterranean Sea between Greece and Turkey.

Strategies for Annotation 🖉 📄 *Annotate it!*

Determine Central Ideas and Details

RI 2

Share these strategies for guided or independent analysis.

- As you read, highlight in yellow central ideas.
- Underline the details that support them.
- Use the text you've annotated to paraphrase, or restate the information in your own words.

This cache of resources, called a whale fall, will become the center of a unique habitat. First, it attracts deep-sea scavengers. Hagfish— unsightly creatures also called slime eels—wriggle inside the carcass and begin to eat it from the inside out. . . . Then mollusks colonize those sediments. Meanwhile, fantastical worms, slugs, and bacteria bore into the whale's bones to feast on fatty marrow.

dragged up, and Forbes concluded that nothing at all lived below 1,600 feet (500 meters) deep. This theory fit perfectly with what others had observed on land. If the extreme climates of the Arctic and high mountain peaks snuffed out life, then the cold, dark, deep sea must be empty too.

> ❝ **Within months this whale carcass may support more than 40,000 creatures.** ❞

Over the next century, people challenged this theory. Corals were hauled up from 2,500 feet (750 meters) deep; starfish and oysters were gathered from 7,500 feet
60 (2,300 meters). One expedition collected 4,700 new species from as deep as 16,000 feet (5,000 meters)—that's more than three miles underwater! Because photosynthesis isn't possible at such depths, scientists decided that marine snow provided the base of the food chain for these animals. Sure, they acknowledged, life was possible in the deep sea. But scientists assumed that life forms living off such scraps would be **meager**. And so they continued to believe that life couldn't survive in the most extreme ocean-floor conditions.

Then everything changed.
70 In 1977, a team of geologists squeezed into the research mini-sub called *Alvin*, hoping to confirm whether geysers (like Old Faithful in Yellowstone National Park) existed on the ocean floor. The hydrothermal vents were there, all right. So was a "Garden of Eden,"[2] as the scientists called it, of mussels, anemones, and 7-foot (2-meter) worms with crimson, feather-like plumes. The stunned researchers gathered samples and called biologists at the Woods Hole Oceanographic Institute (WHOI) in Massachusetts.

meager
(mē´gər) *adj.* If something is *meager*, it is small or deficient in quantity.

[2] **Garden of Eden:** the garden that was the first home of Adam and Eve according to the Bible.

from Living in the Dark **203**

APPLYING ACADEMIC VOCABULARY

complex	rely

THINK-PAIR-SHARE Have students work in pairs to discuss the following questions. Guide students to include the academic vocabulary words *complex* and *rely* in their discussion. Remind them that paraphrasing portions of the text in their own words is one way to understand the concepts.

- How is the life in the **complex** deep-sea environment connected?
- What evidence in the text describes ways the creatures **rely** on each other to survive?

Analyze Structure
RI 1,
RI 3,
RI 5

(LINES 62–68)

Explain that writers of science articles often use a **cause-and-effect** structure to show relationships between events and concepts. This helps readers understand how the first event, the **cause,** leads to one or more **effects. Signal words,** such as *because, since,* and *therefore,* help readers identify cause-and-effect relationships.

ⓒ **CITE TEXT EVIDENCE** Have students reread lines 62–68. Ask students to explain the cause-and-effect relationship and to cite the words that signal it. *(Cause: Photosynthesis isn't possible at very great ocean depths. Effects: Scientists believed that marine snow [flecks of dead plankton] was the main source of food there. They also assumed that only "meager" life forms could survive. Signal words: "Because," "And so.")*

English Language Support

Read aloud lines 62–68 with students following along. Ask students to point out any cause-and-effect signal words and then answer the question in pairs, writing their ideas in a flowchart graphic. Then have them use their charts to persuade others with phrases such as *I think that …* or *I agree with X, but ….* about how the ideas are related.

CAUSE: Photosynthesis is not possible deep in the ocean.

EFFECT: Scientists thought marine snow was the only food.

EFFECT: Scientists thought the life forms would be small.

CRITICAL VOCABULARY

meager: The author uses the word *meager* to describe how few life forms scientists expected to find on the ocean floor.

ASK STUDENTS why the scientists believed that life forms on the ocean floor would be meager. *(Scientists assumed that there wasn't enough food available to sustain a multitude of life forms.)*

Analyze Structure

RI 1,
RI 3,
RI 5

(LINES 79–86)

Remind students that a cause-and-effect pattern of organization shows the relationship between events or ideas.

D **CITE TEXT EVIDENCE** Have students reread lines 79–86. Ask students to cite the causes of scientists' ideas about life on Earth being "suddenly turned upside down." *("Scientists had found an ecosystem that didn't rely on the sun for energy"; creatures were "thriving in a place that would be toxic for any other known organism.")*

> **CRITICAL VOCABULARY**
>
> **tectonic:** The author introduces a geological term, *tectonic plates*, to help explain what hydrothermal vents are and how they occur.
>
> **ASK STUDENTS** what other kinds of geological events might result from the shifting of tectonic plates. *(earthquakes, volcanoes)*

English Language Support

Improve Reading Fluency Remind students that it is important to match their reading pace to the content of what they are reading. More complex explanations need to be presented more slowly and with pauses that are indicated by commas so that listeners have time to comprehend the information. Model how to read lines 87–114 at a steady pace and with correct pauses as students follow along. Then have pairs of students listen to each other read the lines aloud. Encourage students to provide feedback about the pace of reading and correct pauses.

On the sea floor, a spider crab, mussels, and worms are revealed by the light of a submersible vehicle.

 80 "It was predicted that vents would exist," explains Santiago Herrera, a biologist currently working at WHOI. "What wasn't predicted was that there would be anything living there." Scientists had found an ecosystem that didn't rely on the sun for energy. Not only that, but its inhabitants were thriving in a place that would be toxic for any other known organism. Ideas about the origins and requirements for life on Earth were suddenly turned upside down.

Hydrothermal Vents

You can often find undersea volcanic activity where Earth's **tectonic** plates are pulling apart. As the planet's crust stretches thin, molten rock breaks through to create new
90 crust. Meanwhile, water soaks into the crust through nearby cracks, dissolving rocks and heating up to temperatures of 660 degrees Fahrenheit (350 degrees Celsius) before rising again through a "chimney" on the ocean floor. When the mineral-rich, super-hot water from the geyser meets the oxygen-rich, frigid water of the deep sea, a chemical reaction is triggered that forms hydrogen sulfide. This smells like rotten eggs and looks like black smoke spewing into the ocean.

tectonic
(tĕk-tŏn´ĭk) *adj.*
If something is *tectonic*, it relates to the deformation of Earth's rocky crust.

©J. MacDonald/National Oceanic And Atmospheric Administration (NOAA)

WHEN STUDENTS STRUGGLE . . .

Help students understand the complex processes described in the text by using a graphic organizer like the one shown. Direct students to reread lines 87–93. Have students work in pairs to fill out the chart to show the chain of causes and effects that creates a hydrothermal vent. Explain that each new effect the author mentions becomes the cause of the next one. When they have finished, have students use the chart to paraphrase the process.

 LEVEL UP TUTORIALS For additional support, assign the following *Level Up* tutorial: **Cause-and-Effect Organization**

Scientists now know that some bacteria release energy by breaking down these sulfides spewing from the geysers. These same bacteria then harness that energy to turn carbon dioxide and oxygen from the ocean water into sugars—that is, food energy. Ta-da! Here's the foundation for an entire deep-sea food chain.

These chemosynthetic bacteria may be food for other creatures themselves, or may live in symbiosis[3] with other deep-sea dwellers. The giant tube worms, for example, have no mouths or stomachs, but get their food by hosting billions of bacteria within their bodies. Many clams and mussels living near these vents get their food the same way.

Hydrothermal vents have been a constant source of surprises, ranging from the single-celled microbe that actually lives *inside* a vent (and tolerates temperatures of 250 degrees Fahrenheit, or 120 degrees Celsius) to the white crab with such furry arms that it was dubbed the "yeti crab."

Cold Seeps

Scientists discovered a second type of deep-sea chemosynthetic habitat in 1984. This time, bacteria were breaking down the hydrogen sulfide and methane that oozed from cracks in the ocean floor near Monterey Bay, California. Scientists have since identified three sources for these "cold seep" communities: large deposits of oil or natural gas beneath the seabed; deep trenches created by one tectonic plate sinking below another; and undersea landslides or erosion that expose chemical deposits in the seabed.

Cold seep communities play a major role in shaping Earth's climate, Herrera says. "If they did not exist, a lot of methane would end up in the atmosphere." Without bacteria breaking down methane from the ocean floor, this greenhouse gas[4] would escape from the ocean and make Earth warmer.

Cold seep habitats develop like those at hydrothermal vents do, but with different species. Chemosynthetic bacteria arrive first, forming large white mats on the sea floor. Crabs and shrimp come to scavenge dead bacteria, and mussels arrive that live with symbiotic bacteria. Over time, the

---

[3] **symbiosis** (sĭm´bē-ō´sĭs): a relationship between two living things that benefits both of them.
[4] **greenhouse gas:** a gas in the atmosphere that traps heat.

from Living in the Dark **205**

CLOSE READ

Determine Central Ideas and Details (LINES 98–103)
RI 2, RI 3

In lines 98–103, the author describes the key process that creates the deep-sea food chain.

(E) ASK STUDENTS to reread lines 98–103 and paraphrase the chemical process that creates the deep-sea food chain. *(Possible answer: Bacteria around the geysers break down sulfides. They use the energy this releases to turn carbon dioxide and oxygen into sugars, which form the basis of the food chain.)*

English Language Support

Have students work in mixed-ability pairs to choral read lines 98–103. Then have them make a list of possible words to include in a paraphrase of the chemical process, confirming definitions in a dictionary as necessary. Next have them write their paraphrases independently. Finally, ask them to read each other's paraphrases and offer suggestions for revisions.

Analyze Structure
RI 1, RI 3, RI 5
(LINES 129–138)

In the section "Cold Seeps," the author provides a range of information about a deep-sea chemosynthetic habitat discovered in 1984. She organizes this information in a number of paragraphs showing cause-and-effect relationships, in which one event brings about, or causes, another.

(F) CITE TEXT EVIDENCE Have students reread lines 129–138 and cite the cause-and-effect structure of the paragraph. *(cause: chemosynthetic bacteria arrive; effect: large white mats form on the sea floor; effect: crabs and shrimp come to scavenge on dead bacteria, and mussels arrive; effect: carbonate produced by the bacteria gives tube worms a better grip; effect: tube worms build up branches; effect: other organisms live in the tube worm branches)*

TEACH

CLOSE READ

Determine Central Ideas and Details

RI 2,
RI 3

(HEADING; LINES 139–155)

Remind students that readers can use headings in a text to help identify central ideas.

G **ASK STUDENTS** to reread lines 139–155 under the heading "Whale Bones, Stepping Stones" and to paraphrase the explanation of how whale bones act as stepping stones. *(Some species travel long distances from one deep-sea habitat to another. Scientists think that they may use whale falls as "stepping stones," or stops along the way, on this journey.)*

Analyze Language

RI 4,
L 4a

(LINES 152–153)

Point out that the scientist Craig Smith uses the word *specialists* in an unusual way. Explain that students can use context clues, or the words and phrases surrounding a word that provide hints, to determine the word's meaning.

H **ASK STUDENTS** to reread lines 152–153 and to use context to determine what Smith means by "specialists." Ask how this differs from the ordinary use of the word. *(In this context, specialists refers to species that are particularly well suited for life in a certain type of habitat. The context clues "in each habitat" and "Some species" hint that the meaning has to do with animal species and not "human experts in a field," which is a more common meaning. The overall topic of the paragraph also hints at a discussion about animals and not human "specialists.")*

> **CRITICAL VOCABULARY**
>
> **decompose**: The author describes what happens to the fat found in whale bones.
>
> **ASK STUDENTS** to describe what happens when the fats in the whale bones are decomposed. *(The bacteria that decompose the fat give off hydrogen sulfides, which attract species that live off the sulfides.)*

206 Collection 4

---

chemosynthetic bacteria produce a hard material called carbonate, which offers tube worms a firmer ground to grip than the muddy sea floor. Then tube worms build up their hard, protective branches, providing living space for even more organisms.

G ### Whale Bones, Stepping Stones

So far, whales are the only animals we know of that can affect
140 life on the ocean floor the same way shifting tectonic plates do. Besides their hefty size, whales are unique in that fats make up 60 percent of their bone weight. (For comparison, humans are born with almost no fat in their bones.) In life, this bone fat helps whales float and store energy. In death, these fats are **decomposed** by bacteria that give off hydrogen sulfide—sound familiar? Once the chemosynthetic community that lives off these sulfides is in full swing, whale falls host an average of 185 different species—the highest number yet observed in such deep-sea communities.
150 Whale falls might explain how species travel across vast ocean spaces from one hydrothermal vent or cold seep to the next. "There are specialists in each habitat, but there is also overlap," says Craig Smith, a professor at the University of Hawaii, who discovered the first whale fall in 1987. "Some species may use whale falls as stepping stones."

Smith says that seeing the same kinds of communities at hydrothermal vents, cold seeps, and whale falls shows us how connected the oceans really are. "The connectivity is across widespread spaces from seemingly isolated habitats."

At the Whims of the Waves

160 Thirty-five years have passed since the discovery of the first hydrothermal vent—but study of the deep sea has really just begun. The main obstacle is getting there.

Fieldwork in the ocean requires tremendous resources. For starters, scientists need a ship and a crew. Reaching a field site may take weeks at sea. Then scientists need high-tech equipment to open a window onto the watery world. Even if everything comes together, success is at the whims of weather and waves. Herrera remembers one expedition where an unmanned, remotely operated vehicle (called an ROV) drifted
170 into the wrong place at the wrong time and was destroyed

decompose
(dē´kəm-pōz´) *v.*
When things *decompose*, they decay and break down into their basic parts.

206 Collection 4

FOR STUDENTS WITH DISABILITIES

Students may have difficulty with the scientific concepts and descriptions in the selection. Have pairs of students listen to small chunks of the text in the audio recording while they follow along in the eBook. Have them pause and discuss what they have understood before listening to the same chunk of text again to confirm their ideas.

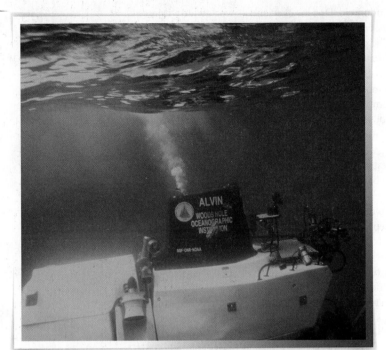

The *Alvin* submersible begins its descent under water.

by the ship's propellers. "Every time you put something overboard on a ship," he says, "it's basically a miracle that you get it back."

Under such conditions, scientists must balance the thrill of discovery with persistence and patience. Smith knows what that's like. His team discovered the first whale fall at the tail end of the last *Alvin* dive on a research trip. "Within ten minutes of *Alvin's* return, we knew what we had," he says, "but we had to wait a year to get back and investigate it."

180   Fortunately, improvements in technology are giving scientists more ocean access than ever. In 2010, Herrera sailed to the Coral Triangle, near Indonesia. This is the most diverse marine ecosystem on the planet, and scientists wonder if the deep-sea communities underlying the coral reefs there might be the reason. Herrera was one of only a few scientists on the ship, but video footage of his ROV dives was transmitted to Massachusetts, Maryland, and Washington, plus Canada

from Living in the Dark   **207**

CLOSE READ

Analyze Structure   RI 5

(PHOTO AND CAPTION ABOVE LINE 171)

Explain that visual elements such as photos can add or clarify information. Captions help explain visuals.

🅘 **ASK STUDENTS** what the photo shows and why the author might have included it. *(It shows the submersible* Alvin *beginning its descent; it clarifies what the submarine looks like and how small it is.)*

Cite Evidence (LINES 174–179)   RI 1

Explain that the author draws a **conclusion,** a statement based on evidence and experience, about exploration: "scientists must balance the thrill of discovery with persistence and patience."

🅙 **CITE TEXT EVIDENCE** Have students reread lines 174–179 and cite text evidence that supports the author's conclusion. *(Smith's team discovered the first whale fall at the bottom of the ocean, but he had to wait a year before he could return and investigate.)*

English Language Support

Have students reread lines 174–179 and express their opinion about whether the evidence provided is enough to support the conclusion. Coach them to use sentence frames such as these to express their ideas:

- The author might include more information about _____ to support her conclusion.
- The author provides strong evidence that supports her conclusion that _____ .

English Language Support

Word Study Review some of the ways the phoneme /sh/ is spelled.

- *ss* as in *pressure* (line 4)
- *s* as in *sure* (line 64)
- *ti* as in *national* (line 72)
- *ci* as in *specialists* (line 152)
- *sh* as in *ship* (lines 171, 172, 186)
- *ce* as in *ocean* (line 181)
- *si* as in *tension*
- *ch* as in *machine*

Have volunteers read aloud the sentence in which each example word is used while other students follow. Write the example words on the

board and say each word aloud, emphasizing the /sh/ sound. Then discuss the *si* and *ch* words, which do not have text examples, but represent other ways that the phoneme /sh/ is spelled.

ASK STUDENTS to work with a partner to confirm the pronunciation of each example word in a dictionary.

CLOSE READ

Explain to students that cause-and-effect patterns of organization are not always explicit, or clearly stated. Sometimes readers need to infer the relationship based on evidence in the text.

 CITE TEXT EVIDENCE Have students closely reread lines 190–200. Ask what cause-and-effect relationship they can infer and what evidence supports their inference. *(Because of the amazing discoveries made on this expedition, and because there is so much left to discover, scientists will return to study the area. Evidence: "The goal . . . was to . . . identify places worth returning to"; "saw far more than they expected"; "We suspect this is one of the areas of highest biodiversity on Earth"; "Scientists will definitely be going back")*

COLLABORATIVE DISCUSSION Have groups of students discuss the recent discoveries about the ocean and scientists' reactions to them. Encourage students to write notes as they talk. Then, have each group share their ideas with the class.

ASK STUDENTS to share any questions they generated in the course of reading and discussing the selection.

FOR STANDARD ENGLISH LEARNERS

Pronunciation Remind students that it is important to speak clearly in discussions so that other students can more easily take notes. Discuss negative constructions with the following examples. Read each example aloud and ask students to choose the correct negative construction. Then ask students to choral read each sentence with the correct answer.

- I was sure the scientists [wouldn't never/would never] believe that life exists at the bottom of the ocean. *(would never)*
- [Nobody can/Can't nobody] tell what will be discovered in the next deep sea exploration. *(Nobody can)*

---

and Indonesia. Dozens of scientists worldwide witnessed and discussed the dives as if they were all present on the ship.

190 The goal of this expedition was to explore unseen waters and identify places worth returning to for in-depth research. Scientists saw far more than they expected. Monitoring video from most exploratory dives means watching hours of flat and empty (which is to say, boring) seabed scroll by, hoping to spot something exciting. But on this expedition, Herrera says, "we were never bored because we were constantly seeing amazing species. We suspect this is one of the areas of highest biodiversity[5] on Earth." Scientists will definitely be going back—just as soon as they can find the money to fund 200 another expedition.

To date, scientists have identified more than 1,300 species in deep-sea chemosynthetic habitats. These organisms have introduced us to completely new ways of life and expanded our view of how adaptable life can be. Yet they raise as many questions as they answer. Smith predicts that scientists will find life popping up in even more surprising locations: "We haven't exhausted the list of processes that create these kinds of ecosystems."

The oceans cover 70 percent of Earth's surface, yet less 210 than 5 percent of this resource has been explored. "This is definitely worth investing your whole life to study," Herrera says.

COLLABORATIVE DISCUSSION The author tells how scientists react to evidence that challenges ideas they had long accepted as possibilities. How have scientists reacted to the discoveries of deep-sea habitats? Talk about your ideas with other group members.

---

[5] **biodiversity:** the range of living things within an environment.

TO CHALLENGE STUDENTS . . .

Make Connections The article "Living in the Dark" illustrates how scientists sometimes must change their beliefs and assumptions in the light of new evidence.

ASK STUDENTS to discuss in small groups other examples of scientists re-evaluating their beliefs, such as in the study of outer space or in medical research. Direct students to analyze the cause of each re-evaluation and what additional effects it might have. Suggest that students do some brief research to prepare for the discussion.

Analyze Structure

RI 3, RI 5

Science writing usually presents relationships between events or ideas. Events can show **cause-and-effect relationships,** in which one event brings about, or causes, the other. The event that happens first is the **cause;** the one that follows is the **effect.**

Readers of science writing can grasp cause-and-effect relationships by thinking about what happens and why. One of the main clues readers can look for are **signal words.** Words or phrases that signal causes are *due to, because of,* or *since.* Words or phrases that signal effects are *as a result, therefore,* and *led to.* Sometimes the cause-and-effect relationship is not obvious, and readers must look deeper for **implied** causes and effects. This involves making inferences based on clues in the text.

Organizing information into a chart can help you to connect causes and effects. This chart shows a cause-and-effect chain based on ideas in the section "Cold Seeps" of the excerpt from "Living in the Dark."

Cause	Effect	Effect	Effect
cold seep communities form	bacteria break down hydrogen sulfide and methane	methane can't escape from ocean floor	potential global warming is reduced

Reread lines 1–13 from the section "When a Whale Falls." Organize the information into a chart that shows a cause-and-effect chain.

Determine Central Ideas and Details

RI 2, RI 3

Paraphrasing is the restating of information in your own words. When you read science texts, you may encounter complex ideas and new vocabulary. To check your understanding, use paraphrasing to restate the language in the text. For example, reread lines 33–40 of the excerpt from "Living in the Dark." Then read this paraphrase of the sentence comparing green plants and deep-sea bacteria:

> **Plants make their own food using the sun's energy, but these "chemosynthetic" bacteria use chemical energy to make food.**

Look back at lines 33–40 again. Tell what a "chemosynthetic ecosystem" is in your own words.

CLOSE READ

Analyze Structure

RI 3, RI 5

To help students understand how to identify cause-and-effect relationships, explain that it is sometimes easier to identify the effect first and then examine the text for the causes. Also point out that the cause is not always the first event mentioned in the text. To understand the cause-and-effect relationship, readers need to think about how the events are related.

Have students study the sample cause-and-effect chain. Then, direct them to reread lines 1–13 and create a similar chain to show the cause-and-effect relationship. *(cause: the whale becomes undernourished and exhausted from migration —> effect: the whale dies —> effect: water pressure squeezes the last air from the whale's lungs —> effect: the whale carcass begins to sink)*

Determine Central Ideas and Details

RI 2, RI 3

Remind students that they can paraphrase, or use their own words, to help them understand confusing or complex parts of a text. Have students study the sample paraphrase and compare it to the author's original text. Next, have students reread lines 33–40 and paraphrase the explanation of "chemosynthetic ecosystem." *(Possible answer: A chemosynthetic ecosystem is a community of life forms that depend directly and indirectly on the whale carcass for food.)*

Strategies for Annotation   ✎ 🖯 *Annotate it!*

Analyze Structure

RI 3, RI 5

Share these strategies for guided or independent analysis:

- Highlight in yellow the effects.
- Underline causes the author gives for those effects.
- Use your annotations to help you paraphrase the cause-and-effect relationships.

In life, this bone fat helps whales float and store energy. In death, these fats are decomposed by bacteria that give off hydrogen sulfide—sound familiar? Once the chemosynthetic community that lives off these sulfides is in full swing, whale falls host an average of 185 different species—the highest yet observed in such deep-sea communities.

PRACTICE & APPLY

Analyzing the Text

RI 1, RI 2,
RI 3, RI 5,
RI 6

Possible answers:

1. *The carcass on the ocean bottom supports animals that feed on the whale's flesh. Bacteria give off hydrogen sulfide as they decompose the fats in the whale's bones. Hydrogen sulfide, in turn, powers a chemosynthetic community that can live for up to a century.*

2. *cause: water soaks into cracks in Earth's stretched crust —> effect: water dissolves rocks, becomes very hot, and rises through a chimney formation —> effect: minerals in hot water meet oxygen in frigid water —> effect: hydrogen sulfide forms*

3. *The three habitats are whale falls, hydrothermal vents, and cold seeps. All the habitats are on the ocean floor. All are sources of chemosynthetic ecosystems—varied life forms that don't depend on sunlight for food. At the bottom of each food chain in these habitats are bacteria that produce food from sulfides.*

4. *The bacteria that make food energy from sulfides may become food for other living things, or they may live inside the bodies of other living things and produce food there.*

5. *Until scientists found thriving communities around hydrothermal vents, they believed that life in the deep ocean would be meager. Scientists thought that photosynthesis was the basis for every food chain, and that deep-sea life would depend on marine snow for food. At the vents, they found an entirely new kind of food chain, built on chemicals, in an area that would be toxic to most organisms on Earth.*

6. *The author has quoted biologist Santiago Herrera throughout the article, so another quotation brings the article to a close. In addition, his comment captures the excitement that the author wants to convey about exploration of the deep sea.*

Analyzing the Text

RI 1, RI 2, RI 3,
RI 5, RI 6, W 1,
W 4, W 8, W 10

Cite Text Evidence   Support your responses with evidence from the text.

1. **Cause-Effect** What are the major effects of a giant whale's death on ocean life?

2. **Cause-Effect** Reread lines 87–97. Note the cause-and-effect connections in that paragraph. Paraphrase the information in the form of a chart that shows the cause-and-effect chain. Label the first box as "Cause" and complete it with this entry:
   Water soaks into cracks in Earth's stretched crust.

3. **Compare** What are the three types of habitats described in this article, and how are they alike?

4. **Interpret** Reread lines 104–109. How would you paraphrase the information in the first sentence of this paragraph?

5. **Cite Evidence** Reread lines 79–86 from the section "Life Where Life Isn't Possible." What ideas were "suddenly turned upside down," and why?

6. **Evaluate** Why might the author have decided to end the article using the scientist's quotation?

PERFORMANCE TASK

Writing Activity: Argument
Think about Santiago Herrera's statement at the end of the excerpt from "Living in the Dark." Why does he have that opinion? Why might someone else have a different opinion? Do you agree with Herrera's statement? Use your answers to those questions to write a one- to three-paragraph argument.

- In your introduction, state your opinion, or claim, clearly.
- In the rest of the essay, present valid reasons for your opinion and support them with evidence from the text and other sources that you can rely on.
- Try to present and refute one counterargument to your claim.

PERFORMANCE TASK

W 1, W 4,
W 8, W 10

Writing Activity: Argument Have students work independently to plan and write the argument.

- Direct students to reread Herrera's statement (lines 210–212) and the questions posed in the Performance Task.
- Have students decide on their opinion and take notes from the text to support it.

Assign this
performance task.

- If students have trouble coming up with a counterargument, suggest that they work with a partner, each arguing a different side of the question.

Critical Vocabulary

| cache | geyser | meager | tectonic | decompose |

Practice and Apply Complete each sentence to show that you understand the meaning of the vocabulary word.

1. It's wise to keep a **cache** of . . .

2. Scientists study **geysers** to learn . . .

3. If you ate a **meager** meal, you . . .

4. Everywhere on Earth, **tectonic** . . .

5. Bacteria will **decompose** . . .

Vocabulary Strategy: Greek Roots

A **root** is a word part that came into English from an older language. You can check a print or digital dictionary to learn about roots; the entry for a word often gives details about the word's origin. Roots from ancient Greek are often called **combining forms** because they are combined to form words, especially terms in science and technology.

In the excerpt from "Living in the Dark," you read about Earth's tectonic plates. What do tectonic plates have to do with the meaning of the Greek root *tecto*, "building"? The movements of the plates are responsible for building continents, mountains, and oceans.

Practice and Apply Read each phrase and identify the word made from Greek combining forms. Refer to the chart for the root's meaning. Then define the phrase. Use a print or digital dictionary to check your ideas.

1. hydrothermal vents

2. photosynthesis in green plants

3. microscopic organisms

4. symbiotic bacteria

5. hydrogeological events

PRACTICE & APPLY

Critical Vocabulary

Possible answers:

1. *It's wise to keep a **cache** of canned food in case the power goes out.*

2. *Scientists study **geysers** to learn about what is below Earth's surface.*

3. *If you ate a **meager** meal, you would still be hungry.*

4. *Everywhere on Earth, **tectonic** forces are moving continents.*

5. *Bacteria will **decompose** dead organic matter, such as fallen leaves.*

Vocabulary Strategy: Greek Roots

Possible answers:

1. **hydrothermal:** *hydrothermal vents are "heated water" openings in the sea floor.*

2. **photosynthesis:** *photosynthesis in green plants is the use of "light" to "put together" chemicals and make food.*

3. **microscopic:** *microscopic organisms are too "small" to "see" with the naked eye.*

4. **symbiotic:** *symbiotic bacteria live "together with other life forms" in an interdependent connection.*

5. **hydrogeological:** *hydrogeological events have to do with "water" and "earth," or the actions of groundwater.*

Strategies for Annotation 🖉 🗂 *Annotate it!*

Vocabulary Strategy: Greek Roots

Have students locate words in the article that include Greek roots. Encourage them to use their eBook annotation tools to do the following:

- Highlight each word in yellow.
- Underline surrounding words or phrases that help in determining the meaning.
- In a note, explain the connection between the Greek roots and the surrounding text.

Much as plants use energy from the sun to make their own nourishment, these "chemosynthetic" bacteria use energy from chemical reactions to create the basic building bl of life. . . .

> "Syn" means "together." The bacteria make food when chemicals come together.

Language Conventions: Verbal Phrases

L 1a

Tell students that we use verbal phrases frequently when we speak or write. Ask students to think about how often they use the word *to*. Often, they are using it as part of a verbal phrase: *I have to run to the store; You need to find that homework assignment.* Point out that verbal phrases can appear at any point in a sentence. For example, in the third sample sentence, *To breathe, whales come to the surface,* the order could be changed to *Whales come to the surface to breathe.*

Possible answers:

1. *Deep-sea scientists want to learn about communities on the sea floor.*

2. *To see in darkness, fish of the deep sea have extra-large eyes.*

3. *Crabs and shrimp come to the ocean floor to scavenge dead bacteria.*

4. *Scientists need equipment to detect undersea vents, seeps, and whale falls.*

5. *To explore new worlds is the goal of a deep-sea expedition.*

✓ Assess It Online!

Online Selection Test
- Download an editable ExamView bank.
- Assign and manage this test online.

Language Conventions: Verbal Phrases

L 1a

A **verbal** is a verb form that is used as a noun, an adjective, or an adverb. An **infinitive** is a verbal that begins with *to* and has the base form of a verb. The infinitive is underlined in each of these sentences.

- Our plan is <u>to sail</u>. (The infinitive acts like a noun and tells what *our plan* is.)
- There may be whales <u>to photograph</u>. (The infinitive acts like an adjective to modify *whales* and tell *what kind*.)
- <u>To breathe</u>, whales come to the surface. (The infinitive acts like an adverb to modify *come* and tell *why*.)

A **verbal phrase** is made of a verbal and any other words that complete its meaning. The **infinitive phrase** is underlined in each of these sentences. The whole phrase in each sentence acts the same way as the infinitive alone.

- Our plan is <u>to sail tomorrow</u>.
- There may be whales <u>to photograph from the boat</u>.
- <u>To breathe the air they need</u>, whales come to the surface.

Note the infinitive phrase in this sentence from "Living in the Dark":

Meanwhile, fantastical worms, slugs, and bacteria bore into the whale's bones <u>to feast on fatty marrow</u>.

The infinitive phrase acts like an adverb to modify the verb *bore*. It tells why bacteria bore into the whale's bones.

Practice and Apply Read each group of words and the question in parentheses. Add an infinitive phrase to answer the question and complete a sentence using the words. Refer to the excerpt from "Living in the Dark" for ideas to include.

1. deep-sea scientists want (What do they want?)

2. fish of the deep sea have extra-large eyes (Why do they have such eyes?)

3. crabs and shrimp come to the ocean floor (Why do they come?)

4. scientists need equipment (What kind of equipment?)

5. the goal of a deep-sea expedition (What is the goal?)

English Language Support

Modify Sentences to Add Details Read aloud the definitions of *verbal, infinitive, verbal phrase,* and *infinitive phrase*. In the second set of example sentences, have students identify the part of speech for each example infinitive phrase. *(to sail tomorrow—noun; to photograph from the boat—adjective; to breathe the air they need—adverb)* Explain that infinitive phrases help a writer provide details about the topic.

- Read each Practice and Apply item aloud. Help students develop an answer to each question. Have pairs use the answers to write complete sentences that use infinitive phrases.

- Have students complete the Practice and Apply items on their own. Then have pairs rewrite each sentence with the infinitive phrase in one or more different positions.

- Have students complete the Practice and Apply items and then work in pairs to underline the infinitive phrases in their sentences. Monitor their work, and distinguish between infinitive phrases and prepositional phrases beginning with the word *to* as necessary.

Analyze Technical Meanings

TEACH

Informational texts often contain **technical language,** or language that has meaning specific to a technical field, such as oceanography or astrophysics. Provide students with the following strategies for determining the meaning of technical language:

- **Use context clues** in the surrounding text to help determine a word's meaning. For example, lines 35–37 of "Living in the Dark" state, "Much as plants use energy from the sun to make their own nourishment, these 'chemosynthetic' bacteria use energy from chemical reactions . . ." The writer provides clues to the meaning of *chemosynthetic* by comparing it to how plants use energy from the sun.
- **Use familiar word parts** For example, if you can identify a Greek or Latin root, such as *hydro* ("water") or *bio* ("life"), in a term you don't know, it will give you an idea of what the term means.
- **Look it up in a dictionary** or science-specific resource. Use print or online dictionaries, encyclopedias, or glossaries to confirm your understanding of a technical term.

PRACTICE AND APPLY

Have students in small groups find and read a science article about a subject they are interested in. Direct them to record unfamiliar technical language in a chart like the one shown. Have students write what they think the word means in the middle column, look up the meaning in a reference source, and write that definition in the last column.

Unfamiliar Word	Your Definition	Reference Definition

English Language Support

Prepare an Oral Presentation Have students reread their science article and take notes about the most important ideas. Then have them plan a short oral presentation summarizing the most interesting ideas in their article using complete sentences and key words. Encourage them to practice the presentation with a partner before delivering it to a small group.

Analyze Structure: Cause-and-Effect Relationships

RETEACH

Review with students that writers use a **cause-and-effect** pattern of organization to explain why something happened, what resulted from a specific action, or what relationship exists between events or ideas. Share these strategies with students:

- Look for headings that indicate cause and effect, such as "When a Whale Falls."
- To find effects, read to answer "What happened?" To find causes, read to answer "Why did it happen?"
- Look for signal words and phrases, such as *because, since, due to,* and *therefore.*
- Don't assume that the first event *caused* the second event.
- Use a graphic organizer to record cause-and-effect relationships as you read.

 LEVEL UP TUTORIALS Assign the following *Level Up* tutorial: **Cause-and-Effect Organization**

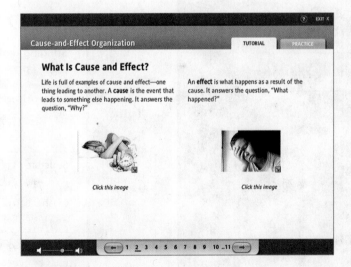

INDEPENDENT READING

Students can apply the skill to another science article of their own choosing. Have them use a graphic organizer such as the Cause-and-Effect Chain to record cause-and-effect relationships as they read. Have small groups discuss the relationships they found.

 INTERACTIVE GRAPHIC ORGANIZER Have students complete the Cause-and-Effect Chain.

Stinging Tentacles Offer Hint of Oceans' Decline

Newspaper Article by Elisabeth Rosenthal

Why This Text

Students may have difficulty understanding long newspaper articles in which central ideas are developed over several pages. When an article includes unfamiliar scientific concepts, this problem may become acute. With the help of the close-reading questions, students will analyze the cause-and-effect relationships that the author uses to organize her writing. This close reading will lead students to understand the article's central ideas and how those ideas influence individuals featured in the article.

Background Have students read the background and information about the author and the article. Introduce the article by reminding students that oceans are vast—covering about 70 percent of Earth's surface—but fragile. Much industrial and consumer pollution ends up in oceans. No international body effectively controls the fishing industry, and overfishing is rampant. Oceans, which are key to the planet's climate system, are also sensitive to climate change.

SETTING A PURPOSE Ask students to pay attention to the cause-and-effect relationships in the article. How does the author use them to organize her writing?

Standards Support

- cite several pieces of textual evidence
- determine central ideas in a text
- analyze interactions between individuals, events, and ideas
- determine the meaning of words and phrases
- analyze the structure an author uses to organize a text

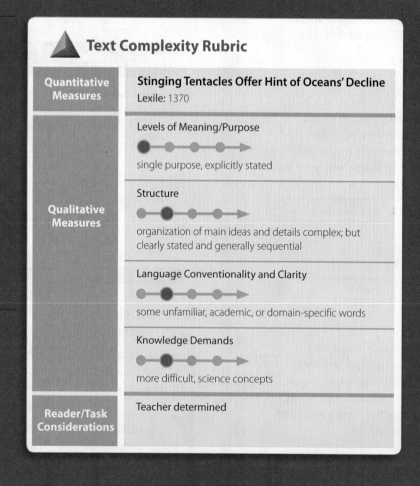

Text Complexity Rubric

Quantitative Measures	**Stinging Tentacles Offer Hint of Oceans' Decline** Lexile: 1370
Qualitative Measures	**Levels of Meaning/Purpose** single purpose, explicitly stated
	Structure organization of main ideas and details complex; but clearly stated and generally sequential
	Language Conventionality and Clarity some unfamiliar, academic, or domain-specific words
	Knowledge Demands more difficult, science concepts
Reader/Task Considerations	Teacher determined

Analyze the Structure of a Newspaper Article

Students should read this article carefully all the way through. Close-reading questions at the bottom of the page will help them focus on a thorough analysis of the structure of the article. As they read, students should jot down comments or questions about the text in the margins.

WHEN STUDENTS STRUGGLE . . .

To help students analyze the structure of "Stinging Tentacles Offer Hint of Oceans' Decline," have them work in small groups to fill out a chart like the one shown below.

CITE TEXT EVIDENCE For practice in analyzing the structure of a newspaper article, ask students to cite text evidence for a cause-and-effect chain.

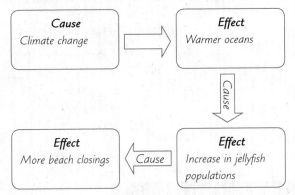

Cause
Climate change

Effect
Warmer oceans

Cause

Effect
More beach closings

Cause

Effect
Increase in jellyfish populations

Background Elisabeth Rosenthal *(born 1956)* is a medical doctor and an award-winning journalist. Before Rosenthal was named science editor for the New York Times, *she worked as a reporter in Beijing, China, where she broke landmark stories on health in China. In this article, she writes about swarms of jellyfish in the waters off the coast of Barcelona, Spain, and explains what their growing numbers tell us about the health of the world's oceans.*

Stinging Tentacles Offer Hint of Oceans' Decline

Newspaper Article by Elisabeth Rosenthal

CLOSE READ
Notes

1. **READ ▶** As you read lines 1–17, begin to collect and cite evidence.
   - Circle the central idea in the third paragraph, and underline the details that support it.
   - In the margin, restate the central idea of this paragraph.
   - Circle the central idea in lines 15–17, and paraphrase the idea in the margin.

August 3, 2008

BARCELONA, Spain—Blue patrol boats crisscross the swimming areas of beaches here with their huge nets **skimming** the water's surface. The yellow flags that urge caution and the red flags that prohibit swimming because of risky currents are sometimes topped now with blue ones warning of a new danger: swarms of jellyfish.

In a period of hours during a day a couple of weeks ago, 300 people on Barcelona's bustling beaches were treated for stings, and 11 were taken to hospitals.

A From Spain to New York, to Australia, Japan and Hawaii, jellyfish
10 are becoming more numerous and more widespread, and they are showing up in places where they have rarely been seen before, scientists say. The faceless marauders are stinging children blithely bathing on summer vacations, forcing beaches to close and clogging fishing nets.

skimming:
gliding across water

The jellyfish population is exploding. They show up where they were rarely seen before.

67

---

1. **READ AND CITE TEXT EVIDENCE** Explain to students that beach patrols often use flags to warn bathers of potential hazards, such as riptides and dangerous waves.

A **ASK STUDENTS** to discuss the cause-and-effect relationships described in the third paragraph. *Students should recognize that there are two causes—there are more jellyfish, and they are showing up where they were rarely seen before—and three effects—children are stung, beaches close, and fishing nets are clogged. Students may point out that in this paragraph the central idea is the cause of the supporting details.*

Critical Vocabulary: skimming (line 2) Have students model the gerund *skimming*, and ask volunteers to use the word in sentences with a marine context. *We saw pelicans skimming the waves.*

Jellyfish
invasions are a
sign of
unhealthy
oceans.

But while jellyfish invasions are a nuisance to tourists and a hardship to fishermen, for scientists they are a source of more profound alarm, a signal of the declining health of the world's oceans.

"These jellyfish near shore are a message the sea is sending us saying, 'Look how badly you are treating me,'" said Dr. Josep-María Gili, a leading jellyfish expert, who has studied them at the Institute of Marine Sciences of the Spanish National Research Council in Barcelona for more than 20 years.

The explosion of jellyfish populations, scientists say, reflects a combination of severe overfishing of natural predators, like tuna, sharks and swordfish; rising sea temperatures caused in part by global warming; and pollution that has depleted oxygen levels in coastal shallows.

pronounced:
observable,
evident

These problems are **pronounced** in the Mediterranean, a sea bounded by more than a dozen countries that rely on it for business and pleasure. Left unchecked in the Mediterranean and elsewhere, these problems could make the swarms of jellyfish menacing coastlines a grim vision of seas to come.

"The problem on the beach is a social problem," said Dr. Gili, who talks with admiration of the "beauty" of the globular jellyfish. "We need to take care of it for our tourism industry. But the big problem is not on the beach. It's what's happening in the seas."

Jellyfish, relatives of the sea anemone and coral that for the most part are relatively harmless, in fact are the cockroaches of the open waters, the ultimate maritime survivors who thrive in damaged environments, and that is what they are doing.

Within the past year, there have been beach closings because of jellyfish swarms on the Côte d'Azur in France, the Great Barrier Reef of Australia, and at Waikiki in the United States.

In Australia, more than 30,000 people were treated for stings last year, double the number in 2005. The rare but deadly Irukandji jellyfish is expanding its range in Australia's warming waters, marine scientists say.

While no good global database exists on jellyfish populations, the increasing reports from around the world have convinced scientists that the trend is real, serious and climate-related, although they caution that jellyfish populations in any one place undergo year-to-year variation.

"Human-caused stresses, including global warming and overfishing, are encouraging jellyfish surpluses in many tourist destinations and productive fisheries," according to the National Science Foundation, which is issuing a report on the phenomenon this fall and lists as problem areas Australia, the Gulf of Mexico, Hawaii, the Black Sea, Namibia, Britain, the Mediterranean, the Sea of Japan and the Yangtze estuary.

Causes:
overfishing,
rising sea
temperatures,
pollution
Effects:
business and
tourism
suffering,
beaches
closing,
jellyfish
stinging
people.

2. ◀ **REREAD** Reread lines 9–17. Review the central ideas in the two paragraphs and write a summary of the text so far. Include essential supporting details.

Jellyfish are all over beaches and appearing in places where they have never been seen before. They are stinging children, forcing beaches to close, and getting caught in fishing nets. Scientists think their invasion means that the oceans are not healthy.

3. **READ** ▶ As you read lines 18–59, analyze the cause-and-effect pattern of organization.

- Circle the causes of events and underline the effects of each cause.
- Record notes in the margin about how one or more events, or causes, bring about one or more other events, or effects.

4. ◀ **REREAD** Reread Dr. Gili's statements in lines 18–19 and 33–36. Paraphrase his comments in your own words.

Gili says that the jellyfish are close to the shore because the condition of the ocean is poor. He says that the big problem is not with tourism at the beach but in the declining quality of the ocean.

2. **REREAD AND CITE TEXT EVIDENCE**

B **ASK STUDENTS** to discuss the cause-and-effect relationship identified in lines 16–17. How does this relationship connect to the ones you discussed in Question 1? *Students should recognize that the author identifies a primary cause—the declining health of the oceans—which leads to the proliferation of jellyfish, which leads to beach closings and clogged fishing nets.*

3. **READ AND CITE TEXT EVIDENCE**

C **ASK STUDENTS** to discuss how the causes they circled in lines 23–27 relate to the cause-and-effect relationship they discussed in Question 2. *Students should understand that these are the causes of the declining health of the ocean.*

Critical Vocabulary: pronounced (line 28) Have students suggest synonyms of the adjective *pronounced*. *striking, marked, clear, noticeable*

4. **REREAD AND CITE TEXT EVIDENCE**

D **ASK STUDENTS** what Dr. Gili's main argument is. *He thinks that the big problem is "what's happening in the seas"; that is, how the oceans are being badly treated by people.* How does Dr. Gili view the jellyfish problem? *He argues that increased jellyfish populations near shore send the message that we're damaging the oceans. So the jellyfish invasions are a symptom of the main problem. However, he recognizes that they also create social problems, like downturns in the tourism industry.*

FOR ELL STUDENTS Challenge your students by pointing out the words *relatives* and *relatively*. Have a volunteer explain their meaning and guess why they may share the same root.

> "Though the stuff of horror B-movies, jellyfish are hardly aggressors."

Boats check on jellyfish at sea. If jellyfish end up on the beaches they will be collected there.

lethal:
deadly

60 In Barcelona, one of Spain's most vibrant tourist destinations, city
(E) officials and the Catalan Water Agency have started fighting back,
trying desperately to ensure that it is safe for swimmers to go back in
the water.
(F) Each morning, with the help of Dr. Gili's team, boats monitor
offshore jellyfish swarms, winds and currents to see if beaches are
threatened and if closings are needed. They also check if jellyfish
collection in the waters near the beaches is needed. Nearly 100 boats
stand ready to help in an emergency, said Xavier Duran of the water
agency. The constant squeal of Dr. Gili's cellphone reflected his de
70 facto role as Spain's jellyfish control and command center. Calls came
from all over.
  Officials in Santander and the Basque country were concerned
about frequent sightings this year on the Atlantic coast of the
Portuguese man-of-war, a sometimes **lethal** warm-water species not
previously seen regularly in those regions.
  Farther south, a fishing boat from the Murcia region called to
report an off-shore swarm of Pelagia noctiluca—an iridescent
purplish jellyfish that issues a nasty sting—more than a mile long. A

5. **READ** ▶ As you read lines 60–97, continue to cite evidence.
  • In the margin, list the steps Dr. Gili takes to protect the beaches.
  • Underline the dangers the jellyfish pose for humans.

chef, presumably trying to find some advantage in the declining
80 oceans, wanted to know if the local species were safe to eat if cooked.
Much is unknown about the jellyfish, and Dr. Gili was unsure.
  In previous decades there were jellyfish problems for only a couple
of days every few years; now the threat of jellyfish is a daily headache
for local officials and is featured on the evening news. "In the past few
years the dynamic has changed completely—the temperature is a little
warmer," Dr. Gili said.
  Though the stuff of horror B-movies, jellyfish are hardly
aggressors. They float haplessly with the currents. They discharge
their venom automatically when they bump into something warm—a
90 human body, for example—from poison-containing stingers on
mantles, arms or long, threadlike tendrils, which can grow to be yards
long.
  Some, like the Portuguese man-of-war or the giant box jellyfish,
can be deadly on contact. Pelagia noctiluca, common in the
Mediterranean, delivers a painful sting producing a wound that lasts
weeks, months or years, depending on the person and the amount of
contact.
  In the Mediterranean, overfishing of both large and small fish has
left jellyfish with little competition for plankton, their food, and fewer
100 predators. Unlike in Asia, where some jellyfish are eaten by people,
here they have no economic or **epicurean** value.

epicurean:
relating to the enjoyment of food

6. ◀ **REREAD AND DISCUSS** Reread lines 64–86. With a small group,
evaluate the efforts of Dr. Gili's team in the struggle to protect the
beaches. Is this a long-term solution or a short-term solution to the
problem? Cite text evidence in your discussion.

7. **READ** ▶ As you read lines 98–117, continue to cite text evidence.
  • Circle the central ideas attributed to Purcell and Gili.
  • Then in the margin, summarize what the two experts see as the major
    causes for the jellyfish invasion.

70

71

---

5. **READ AND CITE TEXT EVIDENCE**

(E) **ASK STUDENTS** to paraphrase how the Catalan Water
Agency is "fighting back" against jellyfish. *The agency works with
Dr. Gili's team to monitor jellyfish swarms, determine whether
beaches need to be closed, and collect jellyfish near beaches. These
measures are designed to make the sea safe for swimmers.*

Critical Vocabulary: lethal (line 74) Have students share their
definitions of *lethal*, and ask volunteers to use the adjective in
sentences about other sea animals. *Sharks can be dangerous, but
remarkably few shark-human encounters prove lethal.*

6. **REREAD AND DISCUSS USING TEXT EVIDENCE**

(F) **ASK STUDENTS** in each group to explain their reasoning.
*Students should realize that the team's efforts are short-term
solutions because they focus on the immediate problem—jellyfish
swarms—and not on the underlying cause of the problem—
declining ocean health.*

7. **READ AND CITE TEXT EVIDENCE**

(G) **ASK STUDENTS** to outline one of the cause-and-effect
relationships described by Dr. Purcell. *Global warming leads to
warmer seas, which allows jellyfish to breed "better and faster."*

Critical Vocabulary: epicurean (line 101) Have students give
the meaning of the base word *epicure. someone with refined
tastes in food* Have students give the meaning of the suffix
-an. characteristic of So what is the definition of *epicurean*?
characteristic of a person who has refined tastes in food

G The warmer seas and drier climate caused by global warming work to the jellyfish's advantage, since nearly all jellyfish breed better and faster in warmer waters, according to Dr. Jennifer Purcell, a jellyfish expert at the Shannon Point Marine Center of Western Washington University.

Global warming has also reduced rainfall in temperate zones, researchers say, allowing the jellyfish to better approach the beaches. Rain runoff from land would normally slightly decrease the salinity 110 of coastal waters, "creating a natural barrier that keeps the jellies from the coast," Dr. Gili said.

Then there is pollution, which reduces oxygen levels and visibility in coastal waters. While other fish die in or avoid waters with low oxygen levels, many jellyfish can thrive in them. And while most fish have to see to catch their food, jellyfish, which filter food passively from the water, can dine in total darkness, according to Dr. Purcell's research.

Global warming helps jellyfish breed faster. Reduced rainfall lets them get to the coast. Jellyfish can live in polluted water.

8. **READ ▶** As you read lines 118–144, continue to cite text evidence.
- Underline what happens to Mirela Gómez after she is stung.
- Underline what Dr. Nogué says about the effect of the stings.
- Circle what Antonio López says about jellyfish.

Residents in Barcelona have forged a prickly coexistence with their new neighbors.

H 120 Last month, Mirela Gómez, 8, ran out of the water crying with her first jellyfish sting, clutching a leg that had suddenly become painful and itchy. Her grandparents rushed her to a nearby Red Cross stand. "I'm a little afraid to go back in the water," she said, displaying a row of angry red welts on her shin.

Francisco Antonio Padrós, a 77-year-old fisherman, swore mightily as he unloaded his catch one morning last weekend, pulling off dozens of jellyfish clinging to his nets and tossing them onto a dock. Removing a few shrimp, he said his nets were often "filled with more jellyfish than fish."

130 By the end of the exercise his calloused hands were bright red and swollen to twice their normal size. "Right now I can't tell if I have hands or not—they hurt, they're numb, they itch," he said.

Dr. Santiago Nogué, head of the **toxicology** unit at the largest hospital here, said that although 90 percent of stings healed in a week or two, many people's still hurt and itched for months. He said he was now seeing 20 patients a year whose symptoms did not respond to any treatment at all, sometimes requiring surgery to remove the affected area.

toxicology: the study of poisons

72

73

---

8. **READ AND CITE TEXT EVIDENCE**

H **ASK STUDENTS** to discuss the chain of events demonstrated by the experience of Mirela Gómez. *Students should note that the girl went to the beach with her grandparents, where she was stung by a jellyfish, which made her cry and run out of the water. The girl's distress convinced her grandparents to take her to a first-aid stand. Now Mirela is "a little afraid" to go back in the water.* Why might the author have included this anecdote in her article? *This story is a good example of how increasing jellyfish populations can hurt the tourism industry, which is one of the central ideas of the article.*

Critical Vocabulary: toxicology (line 133) Have students give the meaning of the base word *toxic*. *poisonous, or relating to poison* Have students give the meaning of the suffix *-logy*. *science* Explain that this suffix is usually preceded by a connective vowel, in this case *o*. So what is the definition of *toxicology*? *the science of poisons and their effects*

FOR ELL STUDENTS Challenge students to interpret the meaning of the adjective *angry* in the context of this text (line 124).

CLOSE READ
Notes

The sea, however, has long been central to life in Barcelona, and
140 that is unlikely to change. Recently when the beaches were closed,
children on a breakwater collected jellyfish in a bucket. The next day,
Antonio López, a diver, emerged from the water. "There are more
every year—we saw hundreds offshore today," he said. "You just have
to learn how to handle the stings."

9. **◀ REREAD** Reread lines 139–144. Restate what Antonio López says
in your own words.

*People will have to put up with jellyfish because more and more of
them are showing up in the ocean.*

SHORT RESPONSE

Cite Text Evidence Briefly summarize the growing problem of jellyfish as it is
presented in this article. Review your notes, and be sure to **cite text evidence**
as you explain the causes and effects of the growing population of jellyfish.

*Jellyfish are all over the beaches and appearing in places where they
have never been seen before. They are stinging children, forcing
beaches to close, and getting caught in fishing nets. Scientists think
that jellyfish invasions are a sign that oceans are not healthy. In the
past, jellyfish problems lasted for only a few days. Today, they are a
constant problem due to warmer waters, reduced rainfall, and
pollution—conditions that allow jellyfish to thrive. Since the jellyfish
seem to be here to stay, people will have to learn to live with them
and their stings.*

74

9. **REREAD AND CITE TEXT EVIDENCE**

① ASK STUDENTS why the author might have ended her
article with López's statement. *Students should recognize that the
diver's statement is one of resignation, or even pessimism. He doesn't
believe that society will address the underlying cause of the jellyfish
problem—declining ocean health. So his advice is simply to accept
the fact that there will be more and more jellyfish and to get used to
the stings. By ending the article with this quote, the author seems to
be saying that it is hard to disagree with Lopez's view.*

SHORT RESPONSE

Cite Text Evidence Students' responses should include text
evidence that supports their positions. They should:

- give examples of problems caused by growing jellyfish
  populations.
- explain what is causing the increase in jellyfish populations.
- describe possible responses to the problem.

TO CHALLENGE STUDENTS . . .

For greater understanding, students can research how increasing
jellyfish populations may affect the ocean's chemistry and
ecosystems.

ASK STUDENTS what some of the "feedback loops" are that
scientists believe exacerbate the jellyfish problem. *Students may
describe a feedback loop involving the climate system. Scientists
have discovered that ocean bacteria, which play a crucial role
in recycling the nutrients of dead organisms, have a hard time
with jellyfish. Instead of absorbing dead jellyfish's carbon, the
bacteria breathe it back out as carbon dioxide, thus increasing the
atmospheric concentrations of this greenhouse gas . . . leading to
greater climate change and more jellyfish. Alternatively, students
may describe a feedback loop involving the food chain. Jellyfish
consume large amounts of plankton, which means less food for
small fish. If populations of small fish decline, so will populations of
their predators, including many of the marine animals that prey on
jellyfish. So, the more jellyfish there are, the fewer jellyfish predators
will survive.*

DIG DEEPER

With the class, return to Question 3, Read. Have students share
their margin notes about causes and effects.

ASK STUDENTS to follow the cause-and-effect chains back as far
as they can.

- What is the primary cause of the jellyfish problem? *Students
  should understand that scientists have identified three main
  causes for surging jellyfish populations: climate change (warmer
  seas and less runoff), overfishing (of jellyfish predators), and
  pollution (which jellyfish can thrive in). Each of these factors,
  students should realize, is caused by humans.*

- What are the obstacles to long-term solutions to the jellyfish
  problem? *Since modern society is the source of the three main
  causes of increased jellyfish populations, the solutions would
  have to come from people. Governments would need to curb
  ocean pollution, crack down on overfishing, and enact measures
  to reduce greenhouse gas emissions. So the obstacles are
  political.*

ASK STUDENTS to return to their Short Response answer and
revise it based on the class discussion.

Your World

Poem by Georgia Douglas Johnson

Why This Text?

Poetry can open up the mind to new ideas and inspire readers to action. This lesson focuses on how poets use imagery and figurative language to convey an inspiring message.

Key Learning Objective: The student will be able to identify and analyze how imagery and extended metaphor can express a particular message or idea.

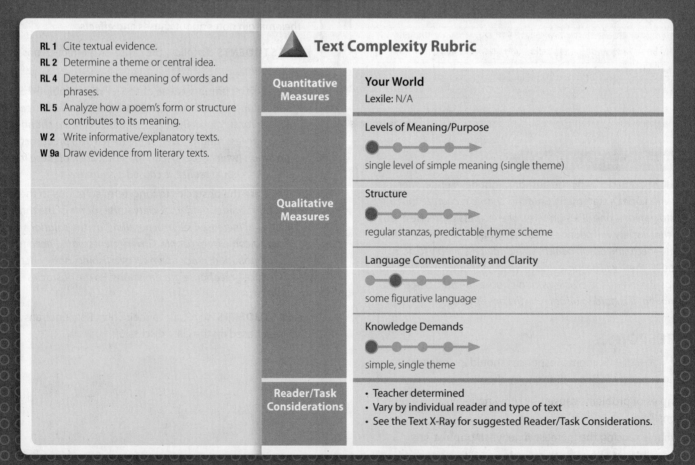

RL 1 Cite textual evidence.
RL 2 Determine a theme or central idea.
RL 4 Determine the meaning of words and phrases.
RL 5 Analyze how a poem's form or structure contributes to its meaning.
W 2 Write informative/explanatory texts.
W 9a Draw evidence from literary texts.

Text Complexity Rubric

Quantitative Measures

Your World
Lexile: N/A

Qualitative Measures

Levels of Meaning/Purpose

single level of simple meaning (single theme)

Structure

regular stanzas, predictable rhyme scheme

Language Conventionality and Clarity

some figurative language

Knowledge Demands

simple, single theme

Reader/Task Considerations

- Teacher determined
- Vary by individual reader and type of text
- See the Text X-Ray for suggested Reader/Task Considerations.

English Language Support

Before teaching, use the Text X-Ray for an overview of the text's complexity. The Text X-Ray and the supports and scaffolds in the Teacher's Edition will help you guide students of different skill levels.

Meaning Making

Language Development

Effective Expression

Content Knowledge

Foundational Skills

Text Complexity: Qualitative Measures

Levels of Meaning/Purpose

single level of simple meaning (single theme)

Help students interpret figurative language.
- Teacher's Edition side notes, pp. 213, 214
- English Language Support, p. 213
- Determine Meanings, p. 214

To reteach determining meanings, see
- Determine Meanings: Imagery, p. 214a

 Use It! Level Up Tutorial: Imagery

ZOOM IN ON FIGURATIVE LANGUAGE Explain that **figurative language** gives meanings other than the literal, or real, meanings of words. Tell students that this poem includes an **extended metaphor:** Two things that are not like each other are compared over many lines. The poet also uses **imagery** to show how things look, feel, smell, sound, and taste to make the comparison.

- Hold up a pencil. Say: *This is a pencil, but if a writer mentions a pencil figuratively, the pencil might mean "the power to tell people things."* Write on the board, "The words flowed merrily through the pencil's narrow point." Ask students what the pencil is being compared to in the metaphor. *(a stream with a strong current)*

Structure

regular stanzas, predictable rhyme scheme

Guide students to analyze the structure of a poem.
- Form in Poetry, p. 214a
- English Language Support, p. 214a

 Use It! Interactive Whiteboard Lesson: Form in Poetry

ZOOM IN ON STRUCTURAL ELEMENTS Tell students that looking at the **form** of a poem—lines, stanzas, and line breaks—can help them identify pace, mood, rhythm, and tone.

- Have student pairs look at the poem's structure and write complete sentences about the number of stanzas, the number of lines, and how the lines are divided among stanzas.
- Then have them read the poem aloud and express their opinions in a discussion about how the form of the poem affects the pace, mood, rhythm, and tone. Remind them to justify their opinions with examples from the poem and relevant background knowledge. For example, a stanza break may slow down the pace, a single word on a line may create a serious mood or reflective tone, and lines with matching lengths and stressed syllables may create an urgent rhythm.

Language Conventionality and Clarity

some figurative language

Guide students to express ideas and interpretations independently.

- Performance Task, p. 214

▶ *Use It!* **Level Up Tutorial:** Tone

ZOOM IN ON **INTERPRETING TONE** Explain that students will work independently on a poetry analysis for the Performance Task. Analyses should include insights about tone. Tell students that the **tone** of the poem is the speaker's attitude toward the subject and is conveyed through the poet's word choices.

- Have partners take turns reading the poem and listing words that convey the poet's tone *(sighted, distant, throbbed, burning)*.
- Then have them discuss their ideas about tone with another pair, taking notes so they can use ideas in their analyses.

Knowledge Demands

simple, single theme

Help students understand the context of the poem.

- Teacher's Edition Background note, p. 213

ZOOM IN ON **CLARIFYING CONTEXT** Familiarize students with the **context** of the poem before they read it.

- Read aloud the Background and Setting a Purpose notes (p. 213). Explain that the people who moved to Harlem during the Harlem Renaissance expressed their ideas about their lives through many different types of art.
- Discuss how moving to a new place can motivate people to think about their lives and how to improve them.

Suggested Reader/Task Considerations

Consider the following before assigning this poem to students:

- Will students be motivated by the style of writing in the poem?
- Will students be able to make inferences that connect the ideas in the poem?

ZOOM IN ON **SUPPORTING COMPREHENSION**

- Before reading the poem, have a discussion about how readers' experiences lead them to interpret poems in different ways.
- Tell students that connecting ideas that the writer is presenting with experiences in their own lives will help them understand the poem.

Background Have students read the information about the poet. Tell students that in the early 1900s the need for workers in northern factories of the United States caused a mass migration of African Americans from the South. Many settled in Harlem, a neighborhood of New York City. There, writers, artists, and musicians worked to establish a proud cultural identity. The neighborhood was transformed from a deteriorating area to a thriving middle-class community. This movement was called the Harlem Renaissance.

SETTING A PURPOSE Direct students to use the Setting a Purpose prompt to focus their reading. Remind students to write down questions they have as they read.

Determine Meanings

RL 1, RL 4

(LINES 1–4, 5–8)

Explain that **figurative language** communicates meanings beyond the literal meanings of words. Poets often use figurative language to compare things, emphasize ideas, or give an emotional effect. One type of figurative language is extended metaphor. An **extended metaphor** compares two essentially unlike things at some length and in several ways.

 CITE TEXT EVIDENCE Have a volunteer reread lines 1–4 aloud. Explain that these first few lines of the poem introduce an extended metaphor that unifies the entire poem. Have students cite details that reveal the metaphor and what it might represent. *("In the narrowest nest" is a clue to the extended metaphor. The poet may be using* nest *as a metaphor for the speaker's home.)*

Explain that another type of figurative language is **imagery**—the use of words and phrases that convey how things look, feel, smell, sound, and taste.

 ASK STUDENTS to reread lines 5–8 aloud. Have them describe what they imagine as they read the lines and identify words and phrases that appealed to their senses. *(Possible answer: The words "sighted the distant horizon" and "sky-line encircled the sea" create the visual image of the point where the sky meets the sea.)*

COLLABORATIVE DISCUSSION Have partners discuss their questions and what the poem teaches about risk taking. Have them share their ideas with the larger group.

Your World

Poem by Georgia Douglas Johnson

Georgia Douglas Johnson *(1880–1966) was one of the most famous African American women writers of the early 1900s. She is associated with the Harlem Renaissance—an African American literary and cultural movement of the 1920s and 1930s. Johnson wrote four volumes of poetry as well as plays and fiction.*

SETTING A PURPOSE Sometimes a poem contains a message designed to inspire. As you read, consider the poet's message and how it may inspire others to take risks.

Your world is as big as you make it
I know, for I used to abide
In the narrowest nest in a corner
My wings pressing close to my side.

5 But I sighted the distant horizon
Where the sky-line encircled the sea
And I throbbed with a burning desire
To travel this immensity.

I battered the cordons[1] around me
10 And cradled my wings on the breeze
Then soared to the uttermost reaches
With rapture, with power, with ease!

COLLABORATIVE DISCUSSION In what ways does this poem teach a lesson about risk-taking? Share your ideas with other group members.

---

[1] **cordons** (kôr´dnz): lines or borders stretched around an area, indicating that access is restricted.

©Ikon Images/SuperStock

Your World **213**

English Language Support

Analyze Language Display the poem and read it aloud as students follow. Invite volunteers to highlight words and phrases that express how things look, feel, smell, sound, or taste—a technique called **imagery.**

ASK STUDENTS to work in pairs to reread the poem and discuss how the imagery helps them understand it. Remind students to support their opinions with evidence from the poem, to include counterarguments, and to acknowledge new information in order to persuade their partner during the conversation.

PRACTICE & APPLY

Determine Meanings   RL 4

Review the information about figurative language. Remind students that in this poem one of the things being compared in the metaphor is the speaker herself. Discuss the examples of imagery that give clues to this extended metaphor. Ask students to describe what they see, hear, feel, smell, or taste as they read the lines. Then, work with students to identify other examples of imagery that help develop the metaphor. *(Examples of imagery and clues to the metaphor include "narrowest nest," "My wings pressing close to my side," "cradled my wings," and "soared to the uttermost reaches.")* Discuss the impact each one has on meaning and emotion.

Analyzing the Text   RL 1, RL 2, RL 4

Possible answers:

1. *Words that appeal to the senses include "sky-line encircled the sea" (sight); "throbbed" (touch); "burning desire" (touch).*

2. *The speaker means that she broke through the barriers that were holding her back.*

3. *The poet makes a comparison between the speaker and a trapped bird.*

4. *The theme of "Your World" might be life is what you make of it. If you set your dreams high, you can reach them.*

FOR STANDARD ENGLISH LEARNERS

Remind students that an analysis is written in the present tense. Explain that it is important to write complete sentences, including a subject and a verb, so that readers will understand their ideas. Then, provide the following examples for students to correct by including a form of the verb *be*.

- This _____ a poem with an extended metaphor. *(is)*
- The poet's ideas about life _____ interesting. *(are)*
- Feelings _____ shown by the words in the comparisons. *(are)*

Have students exchange their analyses with a partner to review them for incomplete sentences.

Determine Meanings   RL 4

In the poem "Your World," the poet conveys a comparison of two unlike things through the **speaker,** or the voice that "talks" to the reader. Because this figurative comparison is carried through the entire poem, it is called an **extended metaphor,** a figure of speech that compares two essentially unlike things at some length and in several ways.

The poet also uses **imagery,** words and phrases that appeal to the senses, to engage the reader and develop the extended metaphor. In these two lines, the descriptions encourage readers to use their senses:

> line 6: Where the sky-line encircled the sea
> line 10: And cradled my wings on the breeze

Look back at the poem. Find additional examples of imagery and lines that give clues about the extended metaphor.

Analyzing the Text   RL 1, RL 2, RL 4, W 2, W 9a

   Cite Text Evidence   Support your responses with evidence from the text.

1. **Interpret** What words in the second stanza appeal to the senses?

2. **Interpret** What does the speaker mean when she says, "I battered the cordons around me"?

3. **Compare** Through the extended metaphor, what comparison does the poet make?

4. **Draw Conclusions** A poem's **theme** is a message about life or human nature that the poet shares with the reader. What is the theme of "Your World"?

PERFORMANCE TASK

Writing Activity: Analysis Think about the extended metaphor in this poem. Write at least one paragraph analyzing the extended metaphor. These questions may help you organize your thoughts and writing:

- What words and phrases show the comparison throughout the poem?
- Why might the poet have chosen this comparison?
- What feelings are suggested by the comparison?

Assign this performance task.

PERFORMANCE TASK   W 2, W 9a

Writing Activity: Analysis Have students work independently. Direct them to

- create a chart listing text evidence that develops the metaphor
- use the chart to draft their paragraphs
- organize their ideas in a logical way
- conclude by restating their main ideas and insights

INTERACTIVE WHITEBOARD LESSON
Form in Poetry

RL 5

TEACH

Explain to students that the **form** of a poem is the way in which the words and lines are arranged on the page.

- A **line** is the core unit of a poem.
- A **stanza** is a group of lines. Each stanza may contain a complete idea that contributes to the overall meaning.
- The place where a line ends is called a **line break.**

Explain that a line break does not always signal the end of a sentence or thought. A line break can occur in the middle of a sentence or phrase to create emphasis or a meaningful pause. Poets use a variety of line breaks to convey a wide range of effects, such as pace, mood, rhythm, and tone.

- **Pace** is how fast or slow a poem is read. Short sentences speed up a poem's pace; longer sentences slow it down.
- **Mood** is the feeling or atmosphere that the poet creates.
- **Rhythm** is a pattern of stressed and unstressed syllables in a line of poetry. Rhythm brings out the musical quality of language, emphasizes ideas, and creates mood.
- A poem's **tone** is the speaker's attitude toward the subject.

PRACTICE AND APPLY

Display "Your World" on the board or on a device. Work with students to analyze its form. Have students

- tell how many lines and stanzas the poem has
- describe how each thought begins and ends
- explain the effects created by the poem's line breaks

English Language Support

Review Concepts Have students work independently to prepare to present the poem to each other in a small group.

- Encourage students to focus on speaking clearly and pausing at correct points.
- Then, after each student presents the poem, prompt and support others in the group to ask questions about how each thought begins and ends, and what effects are created by the line breaks. If necessary, give students example questions such as, *What thoughts begin and end in the second stanza?*

INTERACTIVE WHITEBOARD LESSON
Determine Meanings: Imagery

RL 4

RETEACH

Review that figurative language is a way of using words to express ideas that are not literally true, and that **imagery** is a type of figurative language that consists of words and phrases writers use to create pictures in the reader's mind. Imagery draws on **sensory details,** or words and phrases that appeal to the reader's senses of sight, hearing, smell, taste, and touch.

Have volunteers suggest sensory words for each sense, such as *dazzling, luminous,* and *vivid* for sight. List the words on the board, and discuss how each word appeals to that sense.

Then, work with students to analyze the imagery in "Your World." Have students reread the poem. Then, have students identify words and phrases that appeal to their senses. Ask:

- How did you feel?
- What did you imagine as you read?
- How does this imagery affect meaning?

LEVEL UP TUTORIALS Assign the following *Level Up* tutorial: **Imagery**

INDEPENDENT READING

Individual students or partners can apply the skill to another poem they have read. Have students identify specific words and phrases that appeal to the senses and describe how these details appeal to the senses.

RISK AND EXPLORATION

The FYI site provides links to online articles from a variety of magazines and newspapers. Help students choose a few articles to read to further their exploration of the topic Risk and Exploration.

NOVELWISE

Students can unlock the power of novels with this unique resource. Help students read through longer works with these tips:

- Find a Book
- Before You Read
- As You Read
- After You Read

Each book includes introductory material, worksheets, graphic organizers, and discussion guides.

ADDITIONAL TEXTS BY COLLECTION

Suggest students read the following:

- from *Gulliver's Travels* by Jonathan Swift

Have students read the selection and summarize the events narrated. Then have them retell part of the story in some other form, such as a song or graphic novel. Display their creations around the room or publish them on a class website.

NONFICTION CONNECTIONS

Suggest that students increase their reading of informational texts. The nonfiction connections include

- speeches
- diaries
- true-life accounts
- newspaper articles
- political cartoons

Creating an Independent Reading Program

PARENT AND FAMILY COMMUNICATION

Regular communication between teachers, students, and families builds support for independent reading.

- Send home short progress notes at regular intervals. Ask students to draft notes about what they read and learned and what they liked about the book.
- Include a parent form with the student note so that parents or guardians can record any questions or comments they may have, as well as the number of minutes or hours their student reads. Request that they sign, date, and return the note.
- Encourage students to read a few pages from their book to family members, or encourage family members to read the book aloud with their student.

RECORDING BOOKS AND TEXTS READ

Using a system for recording materials read will help students remember and analyze their choices.

- Prepare a reading log or digital spreadsheet for students to use. Have them keep the logs in their reading folders or on their digital device. If you are partnering with school or municipal librarians, give them a copy of the log.
- In addition to logging the title and author of the books read, ask students to record when they started and finished the book, whether it was easy or difficult, and what they liked or disliked.
- Remind students to log their progress whenever they finish reading a book.
- Go over the log with students during their individual reading conferences.

Interactive Lessons

To help you complete this task, use:
• *Writing Arguments*
• *Giving a Presentation*

PERFORMANCE TASK

Present an Argument

Persuasive speeches such as John F. Kennedy's "Remarks at the Dedication of the Aerospace Medical Health Center" can have powerful effects. In the following activity, you will draw from Kennedy's speech and other texts to prepare and present an argument. You will try to persuade others whether major exploration is worth the risk.

A successful argument

- contains an engaging introduction that establishes the claim
- supports key points with reasoning and relevant evidence pulled from a variety of solid, credible sources
- uses language that effectively conveys ideas and adds interest
- concludes by forcefully summing up the claim

W 1a–e Write arguments.
W 4 Produce clear and coherent writing.
W 5 Develop and strengthen writing.
W 7 Conduct short research projects.
W 8 Gather relevant information.
SL 4 Present claims and findings.
SL 5 Include multimedia components and visual displays.
SL 6 Adapt speech to a variety of contexts and tasks.

fyi
hmhfyi.com

Visit hmhfyi.com to explore your topic and enhance your research.

PLAN

Choose Your Position Think about the texts you read in this collection and the various points made by the writers concerning risk and exploration. Then choose a position either for or against major exploration based on the risks involved, and write out your claim in a statement.

Gather Information Focus on the selection(s) that have information you can cite to support your position. Jot down important details that support your claim. Consider the following:

- What are your reasons for taking the position you took?
- What evidence can you use as quotes to support your claim?
- What might others say to oppose your claim? How would you try to convince them to agree with you?
- What do you want your audience to understand?

myNotebook

Use the annotation tools in your eBook to find evidence that supports your claim. Save each piece of evidence to your notebook.

ACADEMIC VOCABULARY

As you plan and present your speech, be sure to use the academic vocabulary words.

complex
potential
rely
stress
valid

PRESENT AN ARGUMENT

W 1a–e, W 4, W 5, W 7, W 8, SL 4, SL 5, SL 6

Introduce students to the Performance Task by reading the introductory paragraph with them and reviewing the criteria for what makes a good argument. Remind students that an argument needs to be written well, in the same way that an essay does, but that the delivery of the argument is of equal importance in persuading an audience.

PLAN

GATHER INFORMATION

Remind students that organizing information as they research will make it easier for them to write their arguments. Point out that students can arrange all the evidence for a particular reason together in a file, or they can color code the information within their notes to support a particular reason.

English Language Support

Plan to Present an Argument Point out that understanding opposing sides of an argument can help students support their own position on the issue. Have pairs list reasons and evidence from collection texts that support arguments for and against exploration. Then have students use these sentence frames to discuss their presentation plans with a partner:

- The risks of exploration are/aren't worth the benefits because _____.

- I agree with your point that _____; however, I still think that _____ because _____.
- I will look for results of explorations that show _____.
- What other types of evidence do you think I should look for?

Encourage students to use the conversations to focus their research and develop their arguments.

English Language Support

Use Academic Words Remind students to include academic language in their arguments. Provide the following sentence starters as examples:

This example clearly illustrates how _____.

The report indicates that _____.

PRODUCE

DRAFT YOUR ARGUMENT

Remind students that they should keep their audience in mind as they write and that they should try to be persuasive. Point out that as they write students should hear their arguments in their head to make sure they are sounding both logical and convincing to the people they will be addressing.

English Language Support

Link Ideas Have partners identify places in their drafts where adding connecting words and phrases could help show relationships between the claim, reasons, and evidence. Review additional examples of linking words and their function. For example:

Next (shows a sequence)
For example (introduces evidence)
As a result (shows an effect)
On the other hand (contrasts ideas)

WHEN STUDENTS STRUGGLE . . .

Use a Graphic Organizer If students have trouble organizing their reasons and evidence, suggest that they prepare graphic organizers showing their central claim, reasons for the claim, and evidence that supports each reason. Then have small groups discuss how relevant to the reason each piece of evidence is.

Do Further Research Research additional print and digital sources to find solid, credible evidence for your argument.

- Search for facts, quotes, and statistics that support your claim.
- Try to find sources that don't agree with you. Develop a counterargument to address an opposing view.

Organize Your Ideas Think about how you will organize your speech. This can help you to present your ideas coherently.

Mentor Text Read this passage from President Kennedy's speech, which shows how word choices can engage the audience.

> " It is an era which calls for action and for the best efforts of all those who would test the unknown and the uncertain in every phase of human endeavor. It is a time for pathfinders and pioneers. "

Interactive Lessons
For help in incorporating evidence, use:
- Writing Arguments: Creating a Coherent Argument
- Writing Arguments: Persuasive Techniques

PRODUCE

Draft Your Argument Use the information you have gathered to help you write your argument.

- Introduce your claim. Begin with an attention-grabbing comment or an unusual or funny quote, statistic, or story.
- Organize your reasons and evidence logically. For example, will it work better to start with your weakest or strongest argument?
- Be sure to include quotes and other data from your sources.
- Use words and phrases such as *because, therefore,* and *for that reason* to make your argument clearer and more cohesive.
- Conclude your argument. Summarize your main points in a restatement, and connect them to your introduction.

*my*WriteSmart

Write your rough draft in *my*WriteSmart. Focus on getting your ideas down, rather than perfecting your choice of language.

Language Conventions: Using Pronouns for Cohesion

Cohesive writing flows smoothly from one sentence to another. Using pronouns is a cohesive way to avoid unnecessary repetition. Read the following quotation from the speech "Remarks at the Dedication of the Aerospace Medical Health Center."

> " For this city has long been the home of the pioneers in the air. It was here that Sidney Brooks, whose memory we honor today, was born and raised. "

Notice how the pronoun *It* refers to the noun *city*, in the first sentence. This helps to connect an idea in one sentence to an idea in another.

English Language Support

Support Reasons with Evidence Review types of evidence and point out each in the Student Model found in *Digital Lessons*: Writing Arguments.

- *facts*: information that can be proven, such as the date of an event
- *examples*: specific instances that illustrate an idea
- *quotations*: statements about a topic, usually by an expert in the field
- *statistics*: numerical data, such as the number of exploration accidents

Encourage students to include at least one piece of each type of evidence in their drafts.

Prepare Visuals Select multimedia resources to create charts, graphs, or pictures that clarify and strengthen your claim. Make sure that all visuals are large enough to be read easily.

Practice Your Argument Present your argument aloud. Try speaking in front of a mirror, or make a recording of your presentation and listen to it. Then practice with a partner.

Evaluate Your Argument Work with your partner to determine whether your argument is effective.

myWriteSmart

Have your partner or a group of peers review your draft in myWriteSmart. Ask your reviewers to note any reasons that do not support the claim or lack sufficient evidence.

Interactive Lessons
For help in practicing your delivery, use:
• Giving a Presentation: Delivering a Presentation

Questions	Tips	Revision Techniques
Did I clearly state my claim?	**Highlight** the claim.	**Revise** the existing claim to make your position more clear.
Is my claim supported logically?	**Underline** the reasons. **Highlight** your evidence.	**Add** more reasons, if your argument lacks support. **Replace** weak evidence with stronger examples, facts, or quotes.
Is the style of my argument formal enough?	**Underline** any use of informal language, such as contractions.	**Focus** on specific words to improve. **Write** out any contractions to sound more precise.
Is my response to an opposing claim understandable?	**Highlight** any counterarguments. **Note** the wording of your response.	**Use** transitions to set off your counterargument from an opposing claim.
Does the conclusion have a strong restatement?	**Underline** the conclusion.	**Add** a restatement of the claim, if needed, to clarify. **Make** your point forcefully.

Deliver Your Speech Finalize your argument and present it to the class.

PERFORMANCE TASK

PRODUCE

LANGUAGE CONVENTIONS

Point out how the quotation from Kennedy's speech uses the relative pronoun *whose* to add information about Sidney Brooks. Have students review their drafts to look for places where they could clarify their arguments by using pronouns to refer back to nouns or noun phrases.

REVISE

PRACTICE YOUR ARGUMENT

Whether they practice in front of a mirror or with a partner, students should evaluate both content and delivery. Talk with students about a well-organized argument that is mumbled or delivered hesitantly as opposed to a well-delivered argument that is based on bad reasoning or weak evidence. Help students to recognize the importance of both parts of the task.

PRESENT

DELIVER YOUR SPEECH

Students may present their arguments directly to the class, or they may post videos of their presentations on a school or class website. Remind students to use appropriate eye contact, adequate volume, and clear pronunciation.

FOR STANDARD ENGLISH LEARNERS

Adapt Speech Remind students of the differences between formal speech and informal conversation. As they practice their responses, encourage them to pay special attention to words containing the digraph *th* in initial, medial, and final positions. Speaking slowly and clearly can help them focus on following the rules of standard English to pronounce the digraphs.

FOR STUDENTS WITH DISABILITIES

Practice on Camera To help students focus on the delivery of their arguments, have them record videos of themselves practicing the speech. Remind them to look at the camera and use voice effectively by varying pitch and tone for emphasis. Then have them view the video with a peer to help them identify ways to revise their arguments and improve their delivery.

PERFORMANCE TASK

USE THE SCORING RUBRIC

Let students use the rubric to score their own presentations. Then have partners evaluate each other's score. Students should use language from the rubric to provide feedback in each category.

REFLECT ON THE PROCESS

Tell students that taking the time to reflect on the planning and presentation processes in this task will help them apply what they learned and improve their skills. Ask students to think about how well their arguments persuaded the audience. Then have them answer the following questions:

- How well did your visuals support and strengthen your claim?
- Which of your reasons was most convincing?
- What evidence did you use to address opposing views?

PERFORMANCE TASK RUBRIC
ARGUMENT

	Ideas and Evidence	Organization	Language
4	• The introduction grabs the audience's attention; the claim clearly states the speaker's position on an issue. • Logical reasons and relevant evidence support the claim. • Opposing claims are anticipated and effectively addressed with counterarguments. • The concluding section effectively summarizes the claim.	• The reasons and evidence are organized logically and consistently throughout the speech. • Transitions logically connect reasons and evidence to the presenter's claim.	• The speech reflects a formal style. • Sentence beginnings, lengths, and structures vary and have a rhythmic flow. • Sentences show cohesion through the use of pronouns to avoid repetition of nouns. • Grammar, usage, and mechanics are correct.
3	• The introduction could do more to grab the audience's attention; the speaker's claim states a position on an issue. • Most reasons and evidence support the speaker's claim, but they could be more convincing. • Opposing claims are anticipated, but counterarguments need to be developed more. • The concluding section restates the claim.	• The organization of key reasons and supporting evidence is logical in some places. • A few more transitions are needed to clarify the relationships between ideas.	• The style becomes informal in a few places. • Sentence beginnings, lengths, and structures vary somewhat. • Could use more pronouns to avoid wordiness in sentences and improve cohesion. • Some grammatical and usage errors are present.
2	• The introduction does not grab the audience's attention; the speaker's claim identifies an issue, but the position is not clearly stated. • The reasons and evidence are not always logical or relevant. • Opposing claims are anticipated but not addressed logically. • The concluding section includes an incomplete summary of the claim.	• The organization of reasons and evidence is confusing in some places, and it often doesn't follow a pattern. • Several more transitions are needed to connect reasons and evidence to the presenter's claim.	• The style becomes informal in several places. • Sentence structures rarely vary, and some fragments or run-on sentences are present. • Sentences lack cohesion. • Grammar and usage are incorrect in several places, but the speaker's ideas are still clear.
1	• The introduction is confusing. • Supporting reasons and evidence are missing. • Opposing claims are neither anticipated nor addressed. • The concluding section is missing.	• A logical organization is not used; reasons and evidence are presented randomly. • Transitions are not used, making the speech difficult to understand.	• The style is inappropriate for the speech. • Repetitive sentence structure, fragments, and run-on sentences make the speech hard to follow. • Several grammatical and usage errors change the meaning of ideas.

TO CHALLENGE STUDENTS ...

Create a Promotional Video Challenge students to adapt their arguments to develop a video that seeks public support for a specific exploration project. Students should employ audio and visual elements that help convince the audience of the merits of the exploration program.

The Stuff of Consumer Culture

“ We live much of our lives in a realm I call the *buyosphere*. ”

—Thomas Hine

STREAM TO START

Motivate students to read the collection texts, and spark their curiosity about the collection by playing the video and watching it in class. After students view the video, ask them to think about two things they hope to learn from reading about consumer culture. Call on volunteers to share their responses.

PERFORMANCE TASK PREVIEW

Point out to students that they will complete one performance task at the end of the collection. The performance task will require them to further analyze the selections in the collection and to synthesize ideas about these analyses. They will share their findings in a multimedia presentation.

ACADEMIC VOCABULARY

View It!

Professional Development Podcast:
Academic Vocabulary

Students gain facility with the academic vocabulary words through frequent, repeated exposure as they analyze and discuss collection texts. Use academic vocabulary in the instructional contexts listed below to help students incorporate these words into their working vocabulary.

- Collaborative Discussion following each selection
- Analyzing the Text questions for each selection
- Selection-level Performance Task
- Vocabulary instruction (for Critical Vocabulary and/or for Vocabulary Strategy)
- Language Conventions
- End-of-collection Performance Task for all selections in the collection

ASK STUDENTS to review the Academic Vocabulary words for this collection. Pronounce each word aloud so students hear the correct pronunciation. Then, discuss the definitions and related forms for each word. Remind students that they will encounter these five words throughout the collection.

The Stuff of Consumer Culture

In this collection, you will take a look at our consumer culture and consider the question: How much is enough?

Stream to Start

hmhfyi.com

Channel One News®

COLLECTION
PERFORMANCE TASK Preview

At the end of this collection, you will research and write an informative essay about consumerism, using information from the selections in the collection as your starting point. Then you will create a multimedia presentation of your essay to share with others.

ACADEMIC VOCABULARY

Study the words and their definitions in the chart below. You will use these words as you discuss and write about the texts in this collection.

Word	Definition	Related Forms
attitude (ăt´ĭ-tōōd´) n.	a way of thinking or feeling about something or someone	attitudes, attitudinal, attitudinize
consume (kən-sōōm´) v.	to buy things for your own use or ownership	consumed, consumer, consumer good, consuming, consumption
goal (gōl) n.	the object toward which your work and planning is directed; a purpose	goals
purchase (pûr´chĭs) v.	to buy	purchasable, purchaser, purchasing, purchasing power
technology (tĕk-nŏl´ə-jē) n.	the application of science and engineering as part of a commercial or industrial undertaking	technologic, technological, technologist

myNotebook

As students read, analyze, and discuss the texts in this collection, encourage them to create a *my*WordList folder in *my*Notebook to build their own personal word lists.

- **Annotate** Students can highlight vocabulary terms and other unfamiliar words and save each highlighted term to *my*Notebook.
- **Organize** Within *my*Notebook, students can drag each word into the *my*WordList folder.
- **Elaborate** Ask students to add details to the entry for each word, such as a definition, other forms of the word, and a sample sentence.

COLLECTION 5 DIGITAL OVERVIEW

my SmartPlanner | **eBook** | **myNotebook** | **WriteSmart** | **fyi** hmhfyi.com

Collection 5 Lessons	Media	Teach and Practice
**Student Edition	eBook**	▶ **Video Links** HISTORY A&E ① Channel One News	**Close Reading and Evidence Tracking**
ANCHOR TEXT Informational Text by Jeanne E. Arnold from *Life at Home in the Twenty-First Century*	▶ **Video HISTORY®** "The Story of US: The Rise of Television" ◀ **Audio** from *Life at Home in the Twenty-First Century*	**Close Read Screencasts** • Modeled Discussion 1 (lines 23–31) • Modeled Discussion 2 (lines 134–142) • Close Read application PDF (lines 173–183) **Text in Focus** • Understanding Complex Text (line 8) **Strategies for Annotation** • Analyze Structure: Cause and Effect • Cite Evidence • Domain-Specific Words
CLOSE READER Essay by Andres Padilla-Lopez "Teenagers and New Technology"	◀ **Audio** "Teenagers and New Technology"	
Informational Text by Thomas Hine "Always Wanting More" from *I Want That*	◀ **Audio** "Always Wanting More" from *I Want That*	**Strategies for Annotation** • Determine Meaning • Synonyms and Antonyms
CLOSE READER Essay by Lourdes Barranco "Labels and Illusions"	◀ **Audio** "Labels and Illusions"	
Poem by X. J. Kennedy "Dump" Poem by Gary Soto "How Things Work"	◀ **Audio** "Dump" ◀ **Audio** "How Things Work"	**Strategies for Annotation** • Analyze Poetry: Form • Determine Theme
Short Story by Charles Yu "Earth (A Gift Shop)"	◀ **Audio** "Earth (A Gift Shop)"	**Strategies for Annotation** • Analyze Stories: Science Fiction • Determine Theme • Verifying Meaning
CLOSE READER Short Story by Shinichi Hoshi "He—y Come On Ou—t!"	◀ **Audio** "He—y Come On Ou—t!"	
Collection 5 Performance Task: Create a Multimedia Presentation	**fyi** hmhfyi.com	**Interactive Lessons** Conducting Research Using Media in a Presentation

For Systematic Coverage of Writing and Speaking & Listening Standards	**Interactive Lessons** Writing a Narrative Producing and Publishing with Technology

English Language Support

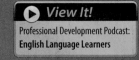
▶ View It!
Professional Development Podcast:
English Language Learners

ENGAGE WITH THE COLLECTION TOPIC

Draw students' attention to the collection title, The Stuff of Consumer Culture. Explain that *stuff* has two meanings: the essence or substance of something, or a bunch of objects, usually not worth much. Tell students that both meanings apply here. This collection explores why people keep buying things—in other words, what drives the consumer culture— as well as what actual things they buy.

ACCESS PRIOR KNOWLEDGE Ask students why this topic is important to think about. Discuss what society does with all of its "stuff." What is the attitude of the American culture toward buying more "stuff"?

FIVE-WORD SUMMARY

Use this strategy to help students determine the central ideas of the texts in this collection.

- Have students read a paragraph and create a list of what they consider its five most important words—the words that best explain and clarify the paragraph's main idea.
- Then, have pairs discuss their individual lists. Tell each pair to develop a single list of the five most important words, selecting only words from their individual lists. Remind students that they should discuss and defend their word choices as they work to synthesize their lists.

- Next, gather pairs into groups of four and have them share, discuss, and defend their word choices. Ask groups to work together to synthesize their lists, forming a single list of the text's five most important words.
- Finally, have students individually summarize the paragraph, including each of the five key words on their group's final list and underlining each of those words.

❯ Collection 5 Digital Resources for English Language Support

LANGUAGE WORKSHOP
Designated English Learners

You may use the digital Teacher Resources > Language Workshop to support English learners in evaluating a writer's claim, using verbs to express inferences, and participating in discussions to identify and evaluate information and evidence.

 VIDEOS

This video will help students learn strategies for understanding complex text. Have students use **Text In Focus Practice** to apply the skills.

Collection 5 Lessons	Key Learning Objective	Performance Task	Vocabulary Strategy
ANCHOR TEXT **Informational Text by Jeanne E. Arnold Lexile 1640L** from *Life at Home in the Twenty-First Century,* p. 221A	**The student will be able to . . .** identify cause-and-effect patterns of organization in an informational text and draw conclusions from the text and graphs.	Writing Activity: Informative Essay	Domain-Specific Words
Informational Text by Thomas Hine Lexile 1240L "Always Wanting More" from *I Want That* p. 233A	**The student will be able to . . .** identify features of an author's style and make inferences using textual details and their own knowledge.	Speaking Activity: Discussion	Synonyms and Antonyms
Poem by X. J. Kennedy "Dump," p. 241A **Poem by Gary Soto** "How Things Work," p. 241A	**The student will be able to . . .** analyze a poem's form and identify theme and irony.	Writing Activity: Literary Analysis	
Short Story by Charles Yu Lexile 1010L "Earth (A Gift Shop)" p. 249A	**The student will be able to . . .** identify elements of science fiction and analyze a story to determine its theme.	Writing Activity: Narrative	Verifying Meaning

Collection 5 Performance Task:

Create a Multimedia Presentation

For foundational skills and reading intervention support: SYSTEM 44 READ180

Assess		Extend	Reteach
Performance Task	✓ *Assess It Online!*	**Teacher eBook**	**Teacher eBook**
Writing Activity: Informative Essay	Selection Test	**Cite Evidence: Understanding Statistics**	**Cite Evidence > Level Up Tutorial >** Reading Graphic Aids
Speaking Activity: Discussion	Selection Test	**Determine Central Ideas and Details > Interactive Whiteboard Lesson >** Main/Central Ideas and Details	**Determine Meaning > Level Up Tutorial >** Author's Style
Writing Activity: Literary Analysis	Selection Test		**Determine Theme > Level Up Tutorial >** Theme **Compare Forms in Poetry > Level Up Tutorial >** Elements of Poetry
Writing Activity: Narrative	Selection Test	**Analyze Stories: Setting > Interactive Whiteboard Lesson >** Setting	**Analyze Stories: Science Fiction**
Create a Multimedia Presentation	Collection Test		

Lesson Assessments Writing a Narrative Producing and Publishing with Technology	**Standards Support and Enrichment**	For more instruction and practice in reading literary and informational texts, language, spelling, and speaking and listening, see Teacher Resources > Standards Support and Enrichment.
	For Designated English Language Instruction	To provide scaffolded support specific to the needs of English Learners during Designated English Language instruction, use the selection- and standards-aligned lessons found in Teacher Resources > Language Workshop.

ANCHOR TEXT

from Life at Home in the Twenty-First Century

Informational Text by Jeanne E. Arnold

Why This Text?

In the social sciences, researchers gather and analyze data and present their findings. As students read more academic texts, they can build their understanding of how research is documented. In this lesson, students analyze organization and draw conclusions from it.

 View It!

Professional Development Podcast:

Text Complexity

Key Learning Objective: The student will be able to identify cause-and-effect patterns of organization in an informational text and draw conclusions from the text and graphs.

For practice and application:

Close Reader selection
"Teenagers and New Technology"
Essay by Andres Padilla-Lopez

Text Complexity Rubric

Quantitative Measures	*from* **Life at Home in the Twenty-First Century** Lexile: 1640L
Qualitative Measures	**Levels of Meaning/Purpose** more than one purpose; implied, easily identified from context **Structure** sophisticated graphics, essential to understanding the text; may also provide information not otherwise conveyed in the text **Language Conventionality and Clarity** increased unfamiliar, academic, or domain-specific words **Knowledge Demands** complex social sciences and statistical concepts
Reader/Task Considerations	• Teacher determined • Vary by individual reader and type of text • See the Text X-Ray for suggested Reader/Task Considerations.

RI 1 Cite text evidence.
RI 2 Determine central ideas.
RI 3 Analyze interactions between ideas in a text.
RI 4 Determine meanings of words and phrases; determine technical meanings.
RI 5 Analyze organizational structure.
W 2 Write informative/explanatory texts.
W 7 Conduct short research projects.
W 8 Gather relevant information from multiple print and digital sources.
L 3a Eliminate redundancy.
L 4a Use context as a clue to the meaning of a word or phrase.
L 6 Acquire and use accurately grade-appropriate words.

Language Conventions	English Language Support	Differentiated Instruction	CLOSE READER Selection
Eliminate Redundancy	• Analyze Structure • Understand Cohesion • Listen Actively • Select Affixes • Condense Ideas	**For Students with Disabilities:** Strategies for Analyzing Text **When Students Struggle:** Conclusions and Statistics **To Challenge Students:** Group Discussion	Essay by Andres Padilla-Lopez "Teenagers and New Technology," p. 232b **Lexile 1040L**
Noun Clauses	• Improve Reading Fluency • Use Transitions • Read Closely • Express Opinions • Use Nouns	**For Standard English Learners:** Pronunciation	Essay by Lourdes Barranco "Labels and Illusions," p. 240b **Lexile 1030L**
	• Read Closely • Culturally Responsive Instruction • Exchange Ideas	**When Students Struggle:** • Analyze Structure • Analyze Poetry: Form **For Standard English Learners:** Pronunciation	
Spelling	• Analyze Language • Word Study • Use Modal Expressions • Support Opinions • Write Text Accurately	**For Students with Disabilities:** Strategies for Discussion **To Challenge Students:** Analyze Theme	Short Story by Shinichi Hoshi "He—y Come On Ou—t!" p. 258b **Lexile 860L**
	Plan a Multimedia Presentation Select Language Resources Understand Text Structure Understand Cohesion	**For Standard English Learners:** Use Possessive Pronouns **When Students Struggle:** Integrate Multimedia Elements **For Students with Disabilities:** Expand the Completion Time **To Challenge Students:** Discuss Point of View	

English Language Support Before teaching, use the Text X-Ray for an overview of the text's complexity. The Text X-Ray and the supports and scaffolds in the Teacher's Edition will help you guide students of different skill levels.

Meaning Making

Language Development

Effective Expression

Content Knowledge

Foundational Skills

Text Complexity: Qualitative Measures

Levels of Meaning/Purpose

more than one purpose; implied, easily identified from context

Help students identify evidence in support of central ideas in informational text.

- Teacher's Edition side notes, pp. 222, 223, 226, 227, 228, 229
- English Language Support, p. 228
- When Students Struggle, p. 223
- Close Read Screencasts, p. 221
- Strategies for Annotation, p. 227
- Cite Evidence, p. 229

Guide students to identify central ideas.

- Teacher's Edition side note, p. 222
- English Language Support, p. 222

To reteach Cite Evidence, see

- Cite Evidence, p. 232a

To teach understanding statistics, see

- Cite Evidence: Understanding Statistics, p. 232a

 Use It! **Level Up Tutorials:** Reading for Details, Reading Graphic Aids

***ZOOM IN ON* IDENTIFYING EVIDENCE** Tell students that **evidence** in an informational text may include facts found in a graphic aid, such as a **line graph**. Display the graph from page 223.

- Explain what the points on the graph represent, using the first one as an example.
- Then have pairs use the data from the graph to fill in a two-column chart with the headings "Number of Televisions" and "Number of Families." Have them compare charts in small groups and return to the graph to resolve discrepancies.
- As a class, discuss what conclusions can be drawn from this statistical information. *(Possible responses: Few families have more than five televisions, but many have more than one. Owning multiple televisions is common.)*

Structure

sophisticated graphics, essential to understanding the text; may also provide information not otherwise conveyed in the text

Help students analyze the structure of informational text.

- Teacher's Edition side notes, pp. 221, 223, 224, 225, 226, 229
- English Language Support, p. 221
- Strategies for Annotation, pp. 224, 229
- Analyze Structure: Cause and Effect, p. 229

 Use It! **Interactive Whiteboard Lesson:** Patterns of Organization

***ZOOM IN ON* ANALYZING STRUCTURE** Tell students that sometimes one **cause** may have **multiple effects**. Display lines 32–49. Point out that this paragraph develops the importance of television in Americans' lives by showing how it affects the way they use the space in their homes. Have students identify these effects. *(Possible responses: Because television is so important to Americans, they organize their living space around it: seating faces the television; televisions are positioned as the focal point of a room; builders and architects design around the television.)*

Language Conventionality and Clarity

increased unfamiliar, academic, or domain-specific words

Teach unfamiliar vocabulary in context.

- Teacher's Edition Critical Vocabulary notes, pp. 224, 225, 226, 227, 228, 231
- Teacher's Edition side note, p. 225
- English Language Support, p. 225
- Applying Academic Vocabulary, p. 225
- Strategies for Annotation, p. 231
- Vocabulary Strategy: Domain-Specific Words, p. 231

Support students' analysis of the selection through their reading, discussion, and writing.

- Teacher's Edition side notes, pp. 228, 232
- English Language Support, pp. 230, 232
- Language Conventions: Eliminate Redundancy, p. 232

***ZOOM IN ON* UNPACKING SENTENCES** Display the sentence in lines 75–81. Work with students to highlight subjects *(viewing, coding)* and verbs *(accounts, reveals)* in the independent clauses. Note that information in parentheses is helpful but not essential to the meaning of the sentence. Ask pairs these questions:

- How much of people's TV viewing is attentive and focused? *(11 percent)*
- How much TV do people watch every day? *(an average of 46 minutes)*
- How did researchers gather information? *(by analyzing 380 hours of videotape)*

Knowledge Demands

complex social sciences and statistical concepts

Support English learners in understanding terms and concepts related to the content of the text.

- Teacher's Edition Background note, p. 221

 For more background on the history of television, students can view the video "AMERICA The Story of Us: The Rise of Television" in their eBooks.

***ZOOM IN ON* BUILDING SCIENTIFIC CONTEXT** Help students build understanding of technical terms in the text.

- In line 2, *analog* and *digital* describe ways to record and process data. Analog technology, such as cassettes and VCRs, reads data recorded in sequence on tape. Digital technology (DVDs, mp3s) reads data recorded as ones and zeroes instead.
- In line 25, *collective* refers to the people sharing a particular space.
- In line 42, *spatial distribution* means "location."
- In line 77, *coding* describes sorting and analyzing research data.

Suggested Reader/Task Considerations

Consider the following before assigning this text to students.

- Will students struggle to comprehend this informational text?
- Do students need support in order to understand the graphics included in the text?

 Understanding Complex Text

***ZOOM IN ON* SUPPORTING COMPREHENSION**

- Have students read one section at a time. Divide the paragraphs in each section among mixed-ability groups; each group should use the Five-Word Summary strategy to determine its paragraph's main idea. Record main ideas on the board and have students use them to summarize the text's most important points.
- Before students read, preview the line graph and battleship curve, explaining how each is to be read and what each displays. Note that lines 151–172 provide additional explanation of the battleship curve.

Background Share the following with students:

- Although archaeologists study what is left behind by past cultures, the study cited in this text is of families in present-day Los Angeles, California.

- *CRT* stands for "cathode ray tube," a kind of vacuum tube used in electronic devices. CRTs were in heavy, bulky monitors used for TV sets and computers.

SETTING A PURPOSE Direct students to use the Setting a Purpose prompt to focus their reading. Remind students to generate questions as they read.

Analyze Structure: Cause and Effect (LINES 1–8)

RI 1, RI 5

Tell students that this informational text uses a **cause-and-effect structure** to organize the author's ideas about how television has changed American life.

A CITE TEXT EVIDENCE Have students reread lines 1–8 and cite three major areas affected by broadcast communication. *(economic decisions, political outcomes, and moral reasoning)* Invite students to share familiar examples of TV programs and advertisements that could have an impact in each of the areas cited.

English Language Support

Read aloud lines 4–8. Explain that to identify a cause-and-effect relationship, readers can ask whether one thing **affects** another or if one thing happens **because** of another. Work with students to complete these sentences:

- Broadcast communication **affects** _____. *(economic decisions, political outcomes, and moral reasoning)*

- **Because** broadcasting affects many aspects of life, _____. *(TV advertisers spent over $50 billion during the recession)*

English Language Support

English Language Support (LINES 1–8)

Understanding Complex Text Have students view the **Text In Focus** video on this page of their eBook to learn strategies for comprehending this complex text. Then have students use **Text In Focus Practice** to apply what they have learned.

HISTORY VIDEO

Background *It's hard to imagine, but less than 100 years ago, television as we know it didn't exist. Then in 1927, Philo T. Farnsworth successfully transmitted an image onto a remote screen. By the early 1950s, TV purchases skyrocketed. Today almost every home in the United States has at least one. This excerpt from* Life at Home in the Twenty-First Century *describes what a team of archaeologists uncovered about TVs when they examined the daily lives of 32 California families.*

from

LIFE at HOME in the TWENTY-FIRST CENTURY

Informational Text by Jeanne E. Arnold

SETTING A PURPOSE Perhaps no other technology is more widely shared as the television. As you read, keep track of how the popularity of this consumer good has changed over time. How will archaeologists of the future track its significance? Write down any questions you have while reading.

myNotebook

As you read, mark up the text. Save your work to *my*Notebook.
- Highlight details
- Add notes and questions
- Add new words to *my*WordList

Television and Daily Life

In North America, and in as few as three generations, mass media broadcast by analog and digital signal has all but replaced oral history and become the primary conveyor of culturally shared ideas. Broadcast communication, particularly television-streamed content, figures so prominently in economic decisions, political outcomes, and moral reasoning that even at the height of the last U.S. recession, TV advertising expenditures exceeded $50 billion.

Television is now so intricately woven into the fabric of the
10 American family experience that few children born during the last two decades will be able to imagine a social world that

Text in FOCUS

(r) ©joingate/Shutterstock

Close Read Screencasts

Close Read

Modeled Discussions

Have students click the *Close Read* icons in their eBooks to access two screencasts in which readers discuss and annotate the following key passages:

- "One set is typically located . . . how we orient our bodies" (lines 23–31).

- "Archaeologists rely on seriation . . . determines the relative age of each layer" (lines 134–142).

As a class, view and discuss at least one of these videos. Then, have students work in pairs to do an independent close read of an additional passage—"In the complex story . . . CRT use plummeted" (lines 173–183).

Determine Central Ideas (LINES 24–28)

RI 2

Tell students that archaeologists study the roles that objects play in people's lives. In this study of how families use TV sets, the author points out that a TV set plays a significant role in daily social life.

B **ASK STUDENTS** to reread the sentence that begins with the words *The set used by the collective* in lines 24–28. Discuss the author's main idea—that TV is "an agentive participant." Ask students to restate that idea in their own words. *(The TV set is more than an object made by people; it changes how people live with one another.)*

Cite Evidence (LINES 32–38)

RI 1,
RI 2

Point out that the paragraph running from lines 32 to 49 tells about living spaces that include TV sets.

C **CITE TEXT EVIDENCE** Have students reread lines 32–38 and cite text that describes what photographs of living rooms reveal. *(The photos "repeatedly reveal spaces organized around televisions.")* Ask what point the author is making. *(When people gather in their living room, they don't look at one another when talking. Their attention is on the TV set.)*

---

has not been partly shaped by the imagery, discourse, and ideas originating from television programming. In fact, many twenty-first century children are born in the physical presence of a TV: most labor, delivery, and recovery rooms in the U.S. now feature large, wall-mounted flat-panel sets. That TVs are witness to such intimate and emotionally bonding experiences speaks volumes about televisions and the American way of being.

20   Currently, 99 percent of U.S. households own a TV, and more than 50 percent own three or more. All of the families in our study have at least one TV, and most have two or more. One set is typically located in a large space used by all family members, such as the living room, family room, or den. The set used by the collective is a compelling example of an object that is not merely a tangible product of otherwise invisible cultural forces but rather an agentive[1] participant in the daily production of social lives. The introduction of a new TV to a living room, for example, shapes the decisions underlying

30   where we locate our furniture, where we direct our gaze, and how we orient our bodies.

At some deeper cognitive level, our relationship to the TV—which includes a relationship to the object itself but also our personal experiences centering on TV media— even shapes the ways that we relate to our built spaces. Our photographs of living room assemblages[2] repeatedly reveal spaces organized around televisions rather than spaces with other primary affordances, such as face-to-face conversation. For all of its influence on the design and organization of

40   space, the TV may as well be a hearth,[3] which until quite recently in human history exerted the most influence on the spatial distribution of social interactions and activities inside homes. Indeed, families often locate the TV immediately adjacent to a wood-burning stove or fireplace, and new homes feature recessed fireplace-like nooks designed for television sets. The TV has ascended to the rank of essential major appliance (alongside the refrigerator, clothes washer, and dryer) around which builders and architects imagine the designs of residential spaces.

---

[1] **agentive:** having the power to cause an effect.
[2] **assemblages:** collections of people or things.
[3] **hearth:** the brick or cement floor of a fireplace that extends into a room.

English Language Support

Understand Cohesion Tell students that language features often link one sentence or idea to another. Display lines 20–31.

- Read aloud the first two sentences, noting that *three* and *two* are used as pronouns to refer to the noun *TV*. Reread the sentences, adding *TVs* after *three* and *two* to clarify the connections.
- Explain that an action in one sentence may be restated as a noun phrase later. Have pairs locate the action referred to by the phrase "The introduction of a new TV to a living room." *("One set is typically located in a large space used by all family members")*

- Explain that paraphrasing ideas, events, or actions allows a writer to show connections between parts of the text without repeating the same words over and over. Highlight "The set used by the collective" and "The introduction of a new TV to a living room." Have students review the paragraph to identify the earlier text that is paraphrased by each phrase. Then have students share their responses. *("One set . . . in a large space used by all family members"; "One set is typically located in . . . the living room")*

LOS ANGELES HOUSEHOLDS AND TV OWNERSHIP

NUMBER OF TELEVISIONS

Source: Center on Everyday Lives of Families (CELF)

This graph is based on data about TV ownership among 32 California families. The data was gathered by researchers from the University of California, Los Angeles (UCLA), and Connecticut College.

Families now also routinely equip various bedrooms with televisions. Fully 25 of the 32 CELF[4] families (78 percent) have a TV in the parents' bedroom, and 14 families (47 percent) place a TV in one or more of the bedrooms used by children. Researchers at the Kaiser Family Foundation surveyed 1,051 U.S. households with young children and found that 43 percent place a TV in at least one child's bedroom.

The same Kaiser-funded project reveals that 87 percent of children age four to six years are able to turn on the TV without assistance. Most two- and three-year-olds can do the

---

[4] **CELF:** the Center on the Everyday Lives of Families at the University of California at Los Angeles, which studies how families approach the challenges of everyday life.

WHEN STUDENTS STRUGGLE...

Students may struggle with the statistical figures that the author uses to support his conclusions. Suggest that students track the statistics and conclusions by filling in a graphic organizer as shown here. Students can also use the chart to track conclusions to figures presented in the graphs in this selection.

Conclusion	Statistics
Our relationship to TVs shape how we arrange our living spaces.	• 25 of 32 families: TVs in parents' bedroom • 14 of 32 families: TVs in children's bedrooms

CLOSE READ

For more context and historical background, students can view the video "AMERICA The Story of Us: The Rise of Television" in their eBooks.

Cite Evidence (GRAPH)   RI 1, RI 2

Explain that **graphic aids** are diagrams, graphs, maps, and other visual tools that are printed, handwritten, or drawn in a text. Explain that line graphs such as the one on this page can indicate trends. Point out that the **horizontal axis** of the graph shows the increasing number of TV sets, left to right, and the **vertical axis** shows the increasing number, or frequency, of households, bottom to top.

D ASK STUDENTS to reread the information in the line graph and explain the patterns the line graph reveals about the 32 households studied. *(Every household had at least one TV. Only two households had just one TV set. At the other extreme, two households had six or seven TV sets.)*

Analyze Structure: Cause and Effect (LINES 50–65)   RI 1, RI 3, RI 5

Tell students that the researchers gathered data about the number of TV sets per household, the locations of those sets, and the TV-related activities of young children.

E CITE TEXT EVIDENCE Have students reread lines 50–65 and cite text evidence that explains what societal phenomenon has resulted in thousands of studies of the effects of TV on children. *(More than 40 percent of families place a TV "in at least one child's bedroom," and "American children learn how to operate and engage with the TV at a very young age." As a result, TV has an impact on children's lives. The studies are designed to find out more about that impact.)*

 LEVEL UP TUTORIALS For additional support, assign the following *Level Up* tutorial: **Reading for Details.**

CLOSE READ

Analyze Structure: Cause and Effect (LINES 66–98)

RI 1,
RI 3,
RI 5

Point out that the researchers took notes on the activities of individual family members and also videotaped families they were studying. They then examined the videos to code the behaviors they saw. They were looking for evidence of the impacts of television viewing, which have been debated.

F **CITE TEXT EVIDENCE** Have students reread lines 66–98, cite examples of what has been debated, and explain what the researchers discovered to support both sides of the debate. *(The debate asks whether TV viewing leads to "reduced social interaction" or whether families use TV time "as a platform for togetherness." Researchers found that, on weekdays, an "average daily total of just 46 minutes" is spent on "attentive, focused TV viewing"—which is less than predicted. They also found that when family members watch together, it's "usually a social experience." However, they also found that "kids view solo" more than adults, and "children in families that have TVs in one or more bedroom spaces are more likely to watch TV alone.")*

> **CRITICAL VOCABULARY**
>
> **observation:** Tell students that when scientists make observations they use a coding system so that they can gather data in a systematic way.
>
> **ASK STUDENTS** what kinds of coding might have been used for the video observations. *(There may have been a list of activities, and researchers checked off the ones they observed families engage in.)*

---

same (82 percent), and the majority of children belonging to both age groups are capable of changing the channel. Suffice it to say that American children learn how to operate and engage with the TV at a very young age, a fact that has motivated more than 4,000 studies addressing the impacts of TV on children, education, and the social lives of families.

These impacts, however, are debated. Some researchers associate TV viewing with reduced social interaction, while others report the opposite and even see evidence for families' use of TV time as a platform for togetherness. Research based on our unique observational data sets is new to the discussion and actually lends support to both generalizations, reflecting the complex relationship Americans have with television. For example, our study shows that families are not actively engaging with TV as much as we might otherwise predict. Attentive, focused TV viewing accounts for only 11 percent of all primary person-centered scan sampling **observations**, and the careful coding of 380 hours of videotape (derived from our observational videography) reveals that families engage with TV media on weekday afternoons and evenings for an average daily total of just 46 minutes (although the TV may be turned on for much longer periods). Furthermore, families' viewing is usually a social experience: during about two-thirds of observations where a child or adult watches TV, at least one other family member is present.

However, children are slightly more likely than their parents to watch TV alone. Kids view solo in about 17 percent of the cases where we record TV viewing as the primary activity, mothers and fathers watch alone in only 6 percent and 13 percent of the cases, respectively. We also found that children much more frequently watch TV in a bedroom (34 percent of primary TV observations, alone or with others) than either of their parents (9 percent for mothers and 10 percent for fathers). Indeed, the socially isolating potential of TV appears higher among families that have more than one TV set in the home. Children in families that have TVs in one or more bedroom spaces are more likely to watch TV alone than children in families that do not have a TV in a child's or parents' bedroom.

observation
(ŏb´zər-vā´shən) *n.*
An *observation* is the act of watching something.

Strategies for Annotation ✎ 🖹 Annotate it!

Analyze Structure

RI 1,
RI 2,
RI 5

Have students use their eBook annotation tools to cite information about the effects of television in the paragraphs that begin "These impacts, however, are debated" (lines 66–98).

- Highlight in yellow references to *less social interaction* as a result of TV use.
- Highlight in green references to *more social interaction* as a result of TV use.
- Underline the researchers' summarizing statements about both effects.

These impacts, however, are debated. Some researchers associate TV viewing with reduced social interaction, while others report the opposite and even see evidence for families' use of TV time as a platform for togetherness. Research based on our unique observational data sets is new to the discussion and actually lends support to both generalizations, reflecting the complex relationship Americans have with television.

> **Some researchers associate TV viewing with reduced social interaction.**

The Material Legacy of TV

The **proliferation** of video media technology since the debut of network television in 1946 has had a profound influence on American lifestyles. Indeed, few Americans can imagine everyday life without access to TV. Television is so entrenched in popular culture that we are surprised when we meet people who do not have at least one set. In 1947, U.S. households owned 44,000 TVs, just one set per 3,275 people. During the early 2000s, people purchased about 31 million TVs annually in the U.S., or one new TV for every nine Americans each year.

Of course, sales figures do not reflect the number of sets already found in what archaeologists regard as systemic context (here, the home): the behavioral system in which artifacts[5] participate in everyday life. The full inventory of TVs emerges only when the count includes the sets purchased in years past and still in the house. Only some older TVs are replaced. As is true for most artifacts, the life history of each individual television is entangled in the changing ways that families use them, the availability of similar artifacts in the home, and the desire for newer forms of visual media technologies.

Eventually the life history of a TV, or at least the portion of the life history that overlaps with family use, comes to an end. At that point, the artifact exits the systemic context and enters an archaeological context, a state in which interaction is primarily with the natural environment, such as the city dump. The Environmental Protection Agency estimates that

proliferation
(prə-lĭf´ər-rā´shən) *n.*
A *proliferation* is the fast growth of something.

---
[5] **artifacts:** objects made by humans.

Life at Home in the Twenty-First Century **225**

APPLYING ACADEMIC VOCABULARY

technology	purchase

THINK-PAIR-SHARE Have students turn to a partner to discuss the following questions. Guide students to include the academic vocabulary words *technology* and *purchase* in their responses. Ask volunteers to share their responses with the class.

- How does **technology** influence family life?
- What are the reasons that families **purchase** new **technologies**?

CLOSE READ

Analyze Structure: Cause and Effect (LINES 115–119)
RI 1, RI 3, RI 5

Tell students that when archaeologists study artifacts they look for evidence about how the objects got to a particular place and how and why people used them.

G **CITE TEXT EVIDENCE** Tell students to reread lines 115–119 and cite one of the reasons that consumers get rid of older TV sets. *(People may replace older TVs because of "the desire for newer forms of visual media technologies.")*

Determine Meanings
RI 4
(LINES 120–125)

Tell students that the author uses the technical terms *systemic context* and *archaeological context*.

H **ASK STUDENTS** to reread lines 120–125 and contrast the two contexts. *(Systemic context is how and where an artifact is used; archaeological context is where it goes after it is thrown out.)*

English Language Support

Display lines 109–125. Highlight the definition of *systemic context* in lines 110–112 and the information about archaeological context in lines 122–125.

- Have pairs explain the ideas in these lines and share their explanations.
- Then have students discuss the difference between the two contexts, based on what they've learned.

CRITICAL VOCABULARY

proliferation: There has been a proliferation of video media technology ever since Americans were first exposed to TV programs.

ASK STUDENTS why the proliferation of this technology has had a "profound influence on American lifestyles." *(With increasing numbers of TVs in their homes, Americans watch more TV and make it an important part of daily life.)*

Analyze Structure: Cause and Effect (LINES 130–142)

RI 3, RI 5

Point out and read aloud the sentence in lines 141–142: *Frequency seriation thus determines the relative age of each layer.*

I **ASK STUDENTS** to reread lines 130–142 and include the word *because* in an explanation of what that sentence in lines 141–142 means. *(Because styles of artifacts change over time, archaeologists look at layers of buried trash to see which layers have shared styles of artifacts. They can use changing styles to tell which layers are older or younger than others.)*

Cite Evidence (LINES 143–150)

RI 1, RI 2

Explain that students can make judgments based on evidence and reasoning, or **draw conclusions,** as they read informational text like this. Point out that text evidence about archaeologists digging in landfills today and in the future can help them draw conclusions about evidence of TV use.

J **CITE TEXT EVIDENCE** Have students reread lines 143–150 and draw a conclusion about TV owners' preferences based on evidence in garbage layers forming today. *(People preferred color CRT TV sets through the 1980s, but people today prefer flat-screen TVs. The evidence that supports this is that today's landfills will have few black-and-white sets and significantly more color CRT sets. The increasing number of flat screens will show that their popularity has just taken off.)*

CRITICAL VOCABULARY

municipal: Trash may be dumped in municipal landfills.

ASK STUDENTS what landfills have to do with municipal services. *(Sanitation is one of the responsibilities of city and town governments.)*

during the mid-2000s, Americans discarded an average of 1.5 billion pounds of TVs each year, in the range of 25 to 27 million sets annually, of which only 4 to 4.5 million were collected for domestic recycling.

An Archaeology of TVs

130 The rate at which TV technology evolves and the sheer volume of television sets people discard both suggest that this artifact will be particularly useful for teasing out discrete generations of household refuse from the materially complex and jumbled strata[6] that constitute our **municipal** landfills. Archaeologists rely on seriation—the sequencing of functionally similar artifacts based on stylistic differences—as a method for ascertaining relative chronology[7] at archaeological sites. Although seriation cannot be used to pinpoint a specific date, it places older and younger materials in order based 140 on the simple assumption that object styles change over time. Frequency seriation thus determines the relative age of each layer.

We expect 1980s-era landfill strata to contain high proportions of black-and-white TVs and color CRT TV sets, but very low proportions of rear-projection TVs and no flat panels. Garbage layers forming today will contain few black-and-white sets, numerous color CRT sets, and (assuming a continued low rate of recycling) an increasing number of flat panels, assuming that household disposal of any particular 150 TV may postdate its purchase by a decade or more.

Archaeologists often use battleship curves to depict frequency seriation patterns. These graphs are particularly useful for showing changes in the proportion of different technological styles of artifacts over time. Interpretation of the curves is straightforward: the width of a horizontal bar for each year represents a percentage of a total count (see right axis opposite). In 1990, for example, 22.6 million TVs were purchased in the U.S. Only 6 percent were black-and-white sets, whereas 46 percent were color CRT models 160 less than 19 inches in size and another 46 percent were large color CRT models. Just 2 percent were the new rear-projection models, and flat panels had not yet debuted.

municipal
(myōō-nĭs´ə-pəl) *adj.*
If something is *municipal*, it relates to a city or town.

---

[6] **strata:** layers.
[7] **chronology** (krə-nŏl´ə-jē): the order of events in time.

FOR STUDENTS WITH DISABILITIES

Students may struggle with the factual density of this selection. Use one or more of these strategies to help them manage the text:

- Preview main ideas by reading the first paragraph under each heading together and discussing what students will learn in that part of the text.
- Have students read the text with a partner, pausing periodically to discuss important ideas or record questions for class discussion.
- Choose key passages for students to read and discuss in small groups.
- Listen to the audio recording as a class, pausing at intervals to point out key ideas that students can write in their notes.

DISPOSAL RATE OF TELEVISIONS

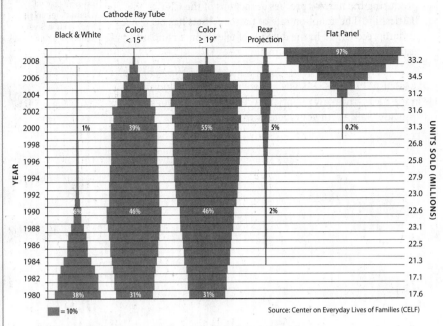

	Cathode Ray Tube					UNITS SOLD (MILLIONS)
YEAR	Black & White	Color < 15"	Color ≥ 19"	Rear Projection	Flat Panel	
2008					97%	33.2
2006						34.5
2004						31.2
2002						31.6
2000	1%	39%	55%	5%	0.2%	31.3
1998						26.8
1996						25.8
1994						27.9
1992						23.0
1990	6%	46%	46%	2%		22.6
1988						23.1
1986						22.5
1984						21.3
1982						17.1
1980	38%	31%	31%			17.6

■ = 10%   Source: Center on Everyday Lives of Families (CELF)

This battleship curve is a graphic aid used by archaeologists to record an artifact's patterns of use across a period of time. Here, the battleship curve indicates periods of popularity and fading use of different styles of TVs.

The shape of each battleship curve is particularly telling, providing an at-a-glance account of changes in the popularity of an artifact style or type over the course of its history. After the artifact's introduction, curves typically become gradually wider as the artifact style becomes more popular. As newer styles enter the material system, the first curve **tapers** and eventually terminates altogether. The maximum widths 170 and rates of tapering (in both directions) summarize the popularity, rapidity of change in preference or supply, and persistence through time.

In the complex story of U.S. television consumption, several well-defined patterns emerge. Black-and-white TV sets persisted until the early 2000s, long after color CRT sets began dominating household assemblages, and rear-projection units enjoyed a long lifespan but never gained popularity. When

taper
(tā´pər) *v.* When things *taper*, they gradually get thinner.

CLOSE READ

Cite Evidence

RI 1,
RI 2,
RI 3

(LINES 151–172; GRAPH)

Tell students that the author helps readers understand how to interpret this graph of "battleship curves," so named because the step-like shapes, or curves, resemble the head-on profiles of battleships. Explain that the text that accompanies a graph, the title and caption, and the label for each vertical axis enable readers to understand the information shown.

Ⓚ **CITE TEXT EVIDENCE** Have students study the graph and reread lines 151–172. Have students cite data in the text or graph as they answer the following:

- What does the width of a horizontal bar represent? *(Its width "represents a percentage of a total count" of TVs purchased for a particular year.)*

- The text says that in 1990, "46 percent were color CRT models less than 19 inches in size." Where is that data on the graph? *(In the second battleship, between four and five squares make up the width of the bar for 1990.)*

- In the period shown, what was the most popular and longest-lasting TV set purchased? *(Color CRT TV sets that were equal to or greater than 19 inches were popular from the 1980s into the mid-2000s.)*

- Why is the battleship for Rear Projection sets so thin? *(Fewer were sold than other kinds of TV sets.)*

CRITICAL VOCABULARY

taper: As newer styles of TVs become available, the battleship curves of older styles taper.

ASK STUDENTS what a tapering curve indicates in the graph. *(That style of TV became less popular.)*

Strategies for Annotation   🖉 ▤ Annotate it!

Cite Evidence

RI 1,
RI 2,
RI 3

Have students use their eBook annotation tools to cite text evidence that connects data from the graph to the text. For example, in lines 173–177:

- Highlight in yellow the text that interprets data from the Black & White column of the graph from 1980–2001.

- Highlight in green information that reflects the percentages of 39% and 55% in 2000. Highlight in blue text that summarizes data showing usage no greater than 10%.

- Add a note showing data from the graph that indicates the persistence of black-and-white TV sets.

In the complex story of U.S. television consumption, several well-defined patterns emerge. Black-and-white TV sets persisted until the early 2000s, long after color CRT sets began dominating household assemblages, and rear-projection units enjoyed a long lifespan but never gained popularity. When

1990–2008, B&W TVs account for between 6% and about 1% of sets in landfills

Cite Evidence (LINES 173–183)

RI 1,
RI 3

Point out that in the last paragraph of this excerpt the author sums up the patterns shown in the battleship curve.

 CITE TEXT EVIDENCE Have students tell what is significant about the adoption rate of flat-panel sets and cite evidence from the battleship graph that supports their conclusion. *(The rate is "unprecedented in the domain of television technology." In the graph, between 1999 and 2008 (less than 10 years), flat-screens in landfills soared from less than 1% to nearly 100% (97%). That means flat-panel sets replaced earlier models faster than replacements had ever occurred before.)*

> **CRITICAL VOCABULARY**
>
> **precipitous**: Sales of color CRT models declined precipitously.
>
> **ASK STUDENTS** to show on the graph where the precipitous decline began. *(Sudden tapering of the second and third battleships starts in 2006.)*

English Language Support

Discuss the meaning of the word *precipitous*. Then direct students' attention to lines 177–183. Ask them what other words in these sentences emphasize the same idea as *precipitous*. *(steep, plummeted)* What does the author want readers to understand about the trend she is describing? *(The changeover from CRT models to flat-panel televisions was dramatic and quick.)*

COLLABORATIVE DISCUSSION Have students work in small groups to discuss the clues that TV sets in landfills will provide archaeologists and the conclusions archaeologists are likely to draw from these clues. Suggest that students find evidence in the text about what happens to TV sets after they are no longer used and what "frequency seriation" is.

ASK STUDENTS to share any questions they generated in the course of reading and discussing the selection.

---

significantly better TV technology emerged in the form of flat-panel models, color CRT models declined **precipitously**, producing the narrow profiles at the tops of the CRT battleships. The adoption rate of flat-panel sets has been steep and unprecedented in the domain of television technology, expanding as CRT use plummeted.

180

precipitous (prĭ-sĭp´ĭ-təs) *adj.* When something is *precipitous*, it is very steep, like a cliff.

COLLABORATIVE DISCUSSION When future archaeologists study life in the past—the early twenty-first century—what clues will TV sets provide? Talk about your ideas with other group members.

TO CHALLENGE STUDENTS . . .

Group Discussion In lines 50–99, the author points out that research has caused some debate about TV's impact on the family, with some researchers concluding that TV isolates family members from each other, while other researchers conclude that TV actually brings families together. Have students work in small groups to discuss the implications of these findings. How is TV shaping family life? What are the qualitative costs and benefits of TV use for families? Have students cite evidence from the selection to support their claims and conclusions.

Analyze Structure: Cause and Effect

RI 2, RI 5

The **structure** of a text is the way it is put together. Authors of informational texts organize their central ideas in paragraphs, and may organize the paragraphs in sections with **headings.** Within the sections, you can identify **patterns of organization,** a particular arrangement of ideas and information. For example, a **cause-and-effect** pattern of organization shows one or more events (causes) leading to one or more other events (effects).

This chart shows a single cause leading to multiple effects, based on details in the first four paragraphs of the section "Television and Daily Life" in the informational text you've just read.

> **CAUSE:** There is at least one TV in 99 percent of U.S. households.

> **EFFECT:** Media broadcast is the main conveyor of culturally shared ideas.

> **EFFECT:** Living spaces are organized and designed around a TV set.

> **EFFECT:** Oral history and face-to-face conversation are reduced.

Restate one of these cause-and-effect connections, using the phrase *as a result.*

Cite Evidence

RI 1, RI 2

Graphic aids are diagrams, graphs, maps, and other visual tools that are printed, handwritten, or drawn. In informational texts, graphic aids organize, simplify, and summarize information. Here are a few types of graphic aids:

- Line graphs show numerical quantities across time and can indicate trends. The **vertical axis** of a graph indicates frequency. The **horizontal axis** shows the categories being considered.
- Bar graphs use horizontal and vertical bars to show or compare categories of information.
- Picture graphs convey information through symbols instead of lines and bars.

As you read, you can use evidence from both the text and the graphic aids to **draw a conclusion**—make a judgment based on evidence and reasoning.

Reread lines 157–162. Examine the graph on page 227. What conclusion can you draw from the text and the graph about flat-panel TV sets?

TEACH

CLOSE READ

Analyze Structure: Cause and Effect

RI 2, RI 5

Tell students that science texts are often organized in cause-and-effect patterns because scientists look for answers to the question *Why?* Answers to *why* questions are causes. A cause can lead to one effect or many effects or be part of a cause-and-effect chain, in which one effect becomes the cause of another effect. *(Sample responses: At least one TV is found in almost every household; as a result, American culture is spread by media broadcast. Living spaces are organized and designed around TV sets as a result of the presence of at least one TV in 99 percent of households. Oral history and face-to-face conversation are reduced as a result.)*

Cite Evidence

RI 1, RI 2

Review different types of graphic aids with students. Explain that each time students encounter a graphic aid they should look for its title, read any captions to determine what information is being presented, and examine any labels on the axes. Point out that the axes do not always show the same things and can vary not only between types of graphs, but also between different applications of the same type of graph. *(Sample answer: For the first few years that flat-panel TVs were available, not many people bought them. But they then became popular faster than any previous types of TVs.)*

Strategies for Annotation

Analyze Structure: Cause and Effect

RI 2, RI 5

Using lines 94–99 as an example, share these strategies for guided or independent analysis:

- Highlight in yellow information about causes.
- Highlight in green information about effects.
- In a note, summarize the cause-and-effect connection.

10 percent for fathers). Indeed, the socially isolating potential of TV appears higher among families that have more than one TV set in the home. Children in families that have TVs in one or more bedroom spaces are more likely to watch TV alone than children in families that do not have a TV in a child's or parents' bedroom.

> One possible effect of a TV in a child's bedroom is greater social isolation.

Analyzing the Text

RI 1,
RI 2,
RI 5

Possible answers:

1. *Because consumers depend so much on television-streamed content to make decisions, advertisers spend tens of billions of dollars to influence these viewers.*

2. *The authors have studied families to observe the influences of TV in the home. As scientists, they want to gather numerical data about how people actually behave around their TV sets.*

3. *Through most of human history, the hearth was the place where families gathered for warmth, food, and social activity. A modern TV set is like a hearth because it has become a central spot in the home for family activities.*

4. *The most important findings have to do with the complex relationship that Americans have with television. The authors found support for opposing views: TV is a way for families to be together, and TV is a way for children to be alone. They also discovered that people are actively watching TV for less time than one might predict.*

5. *The details in this section show that in the early 2000s people purchased about "31 million TVs annually in the U.S." The data also suggests that American consumers at this time did not exhibit good recycling habits when it came to discarding TVs.*

6. *Twelve households owned only two TVs. This is notable because it is the largest number of households of the 32 represented in the graph. It suggests that most homes own two TVs only.*

7. *Flat-panel TVs will continue to be most popular, with wide bands extending up through several years. Then, a new TV technology will likely be introduced. As it grows in popularity, its bands will widen as the bands for flat panels narrow.*

8. *Archaeologists look for how artifacts are arranged when buried. By counting the discarded objects and measuring where they lie in an ancient trash mound or a more recent landfill, archaeologists can tell how popular the objects were and how long ago they were used. TVs are artifacts because they are objects that reveal the culture of the people who used them.*

English Language Support

Listen Actively Have students take turns presenting their completed essays in small groups. Ask group members to discuss what they learn from each essay about new television technology and what questions they still have.

Analyzing the Text

RI 1, RI 2, RI 5,
W 2, W 7, W 8

Cite Text Evidence   Support your responses with evidence from the text.

1. **Cite Evidence** Reread the first paragraph. What causes more than $50 billion of TV advertising expenditures?

2. **Infer** What information about American families were the archaeologists gathering?

3. **Compare** Reread lines 39–46. According to the author, in what ways is a TV like a hearth?

4. **Summarize** Reread lines 66–99. What are the most important findings in this study of the impacts of TV?

5. **Infer** According to the details in "The Material Legacy of TV" section, during the mid-2000s, 25–27 million American-owned sets were discarded, but only 4–4.5 million were collected in domestic recycling. What might these figures suggest about the purchasing habits of American consumers?

6. **Analyzing Graphics** Of the 32 households represented in the graph on page 223, what number of households own only two TVs? What makes that figure worth noting?

7. **Predict** Look at the graph of battleship curves. How do you think the graph might change in the years ahead?

8. **Draw Conclusions** What do archaeologists look for as they study artifacts, and what does TV have to do with artifacts?

PERFORMANCE TASK   my WriteSmart

Writing Activity: Informative Essay You've just read that a number of different types of televisions have been available through the years. Find out about a new development in TV technology and write about it in a brief informational essay.

- Use digital or print sources about consumer electronics to research your topic.
- Take notes as you try to answer questions like: Who invented this technology and when? How does it work? How could it change how people watch TVs? Why would consumers want to purchase it?
- Use your notes to create an outline of your ideas.
- Share your completed essay with a partner or group that has written about other new features of TVs. Discuss the different features and consumers' attitudes toward them.

Assign this
performance task.

PERFORMANCE TASK

W 2, W 7, W 8

Writing Activity: Informative Essay Have students do preliminary research by scanning sources about consumer electronics to find information about recent TV types.

- Students may jot down questions based on the products described.
- They may then review their questions for one or two that can lead to more research.
- Have them pick a topic that has enough information for an essay.

Critical Vocabulary

observation	proliferation	municipal
taper	precipitous	

Practice and Apply Complete each sentence to show that you understand the meaning of the bold word.

1. The scientist counted each **observation** of . . .

2. We've recently had a **proliferation** of . . .

3. An example of a **municipal** service is . . .

4. To draw lines that **taper,** you . . .

5. A change that occurs in a **precipitous** way is . . .

Vocabulary Strategy: Domain-Specific Words

The subject areas of *Life at Home in the Twenty-First Century* are sociology and archaeology. Sociology is the study of human societies. Archaeology is the study of the things left behind by past societies. When you read about any area of study, you will encounter **technical language,** terms and phrases used by specialists in a certain field or domain. Note the term *social interactions* in this quotation:

> For all of its influence on the design and organization of space, the TV may as well be a hearth, which until quite recently in human history exerted the most influence on the spatial distribution of *social interactions* and activities inside homes.

One way to figure out the meaning is by looking at its two parts: *social* has something to do with living with other people; *interactions* are the ways people communicate with each other. But often with technical language, you need to use a print or digital dictionary to confirm the meaning. For more highly specialized terms, you might have to use resources specific to the field, such as a manual of nautical terms for language about sailing.

Practice and Apply Compare your ideas with other group members as you find and define these terms: *observational data sets* (line 70); *observations* (line 76); *systemic context* (lines 110–111).

PRACTICE & APPLY

Critical Vocabulary

Possible answers:

1. *The scientist counted each observation of a family member turning on a TV.*

2. *We've recently had a proliferation of cicadas, which seem to be in every tree.*

3. *An example of a municipal service is trash collection.*

4. *To draw lines that taper, you start with a thick marker and switch to a thin one.*

5. *A change that occurs in a precipitous way is so sudden that people are unprepared for it.*

Vocabulary Strategy: Domain-Specific Words

Possible answers:

Observational data sets *are the sets of numbers that researchers recorded as they observed family members interacting with their TV sets.* Observations *are acts of watching something and noting what is observed.* Systemic context *refers to the place and ways an object is used. Archaeologists examine systemic context to understand how an artifact was used in everyday life.*

English Language Support

Select Affixes Note that *interaction* is the noun form of the verb *interact* (the suffix *-tion* makes a word a noun).

- Have students choose the correct word to complete this sentence: I need to [*organize, organization*] my room.

- Have students find three nouns ending in *-tion* in the passage and then write sentences using each verb.

Strategies for Annotation ✎ 🖥 *Annotate it!*

Vocabulary Strategy: Domain-Specific Words

Have students use their eBook annotation tools to examine the context for domain-specific terms. Ask students to do the following:

- Highlight in yellow the target term.
- Highlight in green context clues.
- Note a likely meaning.
- See if the meaning makes sense in context; adjust note as needed.
- Consult a specialized dictionary, if needed.

Of course, sales figures do not reflect the number of sets already found in what archaeologists regard as systemic context (here, the home): the behavioral system in which artifacts participate in everyday life. The full

Likely: The way in which an artifact is actually used.
Actual: The living society that artifacts were once a part of.

Language Conventions: Eliminate Redundancy

L 3a

Review the common redundancies shown in the chart by having students tell why the underlined words are unnecessary. Offer support as needed for Practice and Apply by directing students to identify words that repeat the same meaning.

Possible answers:

1. *Television sets are now essential appliances in our homes, like refrigerators and stoves.*

2. *Most American toddlers can turn on the TV and change a channel without assistance.*

3. *Although many people believe that watching TV is a solitary activity, some researchers have evidence that families use TV to spend time together.*

4. *The enormous number of TV sets that we discard will provide future archaeologists with clues about how we lived.*

Language Conventions: Eliminate Redundancy

L 3a

When you write to inform and explain, your goal is to be clear and concise. Watch out for **redundancy,** the use of unnecessary words. Reread your sentences to make sure that every word has a purpose.

This list shows common redundancies; the unnecessary words are underlined.

- each <u>and every</u> person
- never before <u>in the past</u>
- the <u>true</u> facts
- may <u>possibly</u> exist
- big <u>in size</u>
- prepared <u>in advance</u>
- <u>entirely</u> complete
- connect <u>together</u>

Avoid using words that repeat what you've already said. Compare these two sentences:

> **Television has an impact on our behaviors and actions, affecting everything from what we purchase to what we talk about in our conversations.**

> **Television has an impact on our behaviors, from what we purchase to what we talk about.**

You can tell that the second sentence is stronger because it makes its point in fewer words. In the first sentence, *behaviors* and *actions* are synonyms; *impact* and *affecting* express the same meaning; and *in our conversations* repeats the meaning of *what we talk about.*

Practice and Apply Rewrite each sentence to eliminate the redundancy.

1. Television sets are now essential items in our homes, as basic to our living spaces as refrigerators, stoves, and other necessary appliances.

2. Most American toddlers can turn on the TV without assistance or help from an adult and are also capable of changing a channel from one to another.

3. Although many people hold the belief and opinion that watching TV is a solitary activity, some researchers have evidence that families use the time in front of a TV as a way of spending time together.

4. The TV sets that we discard are enormous in number and will surely provide clues about how we live to archaeologists of the future looking back into the past.

English Language Support

Condense Ideas Explain to students that unnecessary words can make a sentence harder to read and sometimes confusing.

- Read each phrase in the chart on Student Edition page 232. Explain to students why the underlined words are unnecessary. Then write this sentence on the board: *I want each and every one of you to prepare in advance a report with the true facts about television.* Have students work with a partner to rewrite it without the unnecessary words. (*I want each of you to prepare a report with the facts about television.*)

- Discuss the reason that each underlined word or phrase in the chart is unnecessary. Then have pairs identify the unnecessary words in the Practice and Apply sentences. Work together to rewrite the sentences.

- Have students rewrite the Practice and Apply sentences and then meet with a partner to compare their versions. Call on pairs to read their sentences aloud.

Cite Evidence: Understanding Statistics

RI 1, RI 2, RI 3

TEACH

Tell students that because scientific research involves collecting, organizing, and interpreting data, researchers provide **statistics,** or numerical information, in their reports. Together, reread lines 87–94 of the excerpt from *Life at Home in the Twenty-First Century* to identify the statistics and discuss the comparisons the researchers are pointing out.

> **Kids view solo in about 17 percent of the cases where we record TV viewing as the primary activity, mothers and fathers watch alone in only 6 percent and 13 percent of the cases, respectively. We also found that children much more frequently watch TV in a bedroom (34 percent of primary TV observations, alone or with others) than either of their parents (9 percent for mothers and 10 percent for fathers).**

Explain that the term *statistics* also refers to the methods that researchers use to collect and analyze data. Remind students that these researchers' observations were made based on 32 families. Ask whether the conclusions drawn about those families could be applied to most American families. During the discussion, make these points about statistics:

- For studies about large populations, researchers choose a **sample** of a population to study. The sample must be chosen so that it is representative of the larger population.
- If the researchers choose a **random sample,** they choose in a way that all possible samples have an equal **probability,** or chance, of being selected. A random sample reduces the likelihood of bias.
- When studying causes and effects, researchers use statistical methods to determine the probability that a particular outcome would have occurred by chance and does not have the cause under study.

PRACTICE AND APPLY

Have students examine the numerical data in another segment of this informational text or in another informational text. Tell students to explain the pattern by writing a summarizing sentence or drawing a graphic. Direct students to write two thoughtful questions about how the statistics were gathered and analyzed.

Cite Evidence

RI 1, RI 2

RETEACH

Review that **graphic aids** are visual tools that accompany text. Review the following graphic aids:

- **diagram:** a kind of drawing that shows the parts of an object or the steps in a process
- **map:** a kind of drawing showing part of the surface of Earth
- **graph:** a kind of drawing that shows numerical relationships

Review common kinds of graphs:

- **circle graph, or pie chart:** a graph that shows percentages
- **line graph:** a graph that shows changes over time
- **bar graph:** a graph that compares size or number
- **pictograph:** a graph in which icons stand for quantities

Use either of the graphs in the excerpt from *Life at Home in the Twenty-First Century* to review strategies for understanding graphs:

- Read the **title** to see what the graph shows.
- Look at the **labels** on the **horizontal** and **vertical axes.**
- Read any **captions.**
- Draw conclusions about the patterns shown.

 LEVEL UP TUTORIALS Assign the following *Level Up* tutorial: **Reading Graphic Aids**

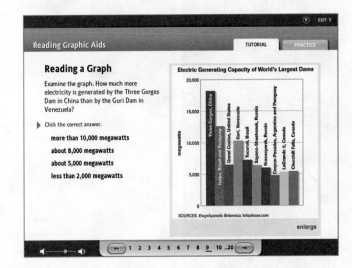

INDEPENDENT READING

Guide students to informational texts that contain graphs. Have partners choose a graph to examine. Ask students to write two or more observations about details or patterns in the graph.

Teenagers and New Technology

Magazine Article by Andres Padilla-Lopez

Why This Text

Students may be overwhelmed by magazine articles with complex, multi-part structures. If the article includes an array of supporting evidence—personal anecdotes, numerical data, and graphs—students may find themselves even more at a loss. With the help of the close-reading questions, students will analyze the evidence presented in the article. This close reading will lead students to understand the structure of the article, including the cause-and-effect relationships used to organize its sections.

Background Have students read the background and information about the article. Introduce the article by pointing out that communication technologies have, from time to time, upset the social order. In 1946, for example, U.S. households owned about 40 million radios—and only 50,000 televisions. Within a few years, television would supplant radio in the American household, and everyone would have something to say about the social and cultural consequences.

SETTING A PURPOSE Ask students to pay attention to the cause-and-effect relationships in many paragraphs. How does the author use them to organize his writing?

Standards Support

- cite multiple pieces of text evidence
- determine central ideas in a text
- determine the meaning of words
- analyze the structure used to organize a text
- determine an author's point of view

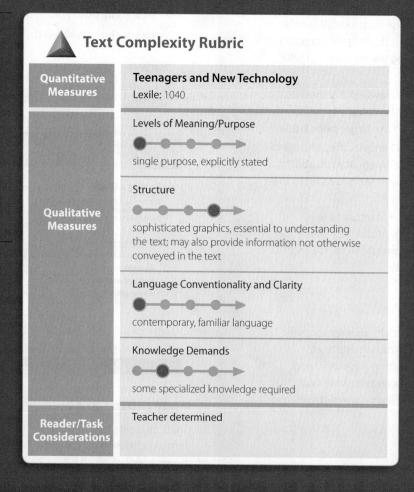

Text Complexity Rubric

Quantitative Measures	**Teenagers and New Technology** Lexile: 1040
Qualitative Measures	Levels of Meaning/Purpose single purpose, explicitly stated
	Structure sophisticated graphics, essential to understanding the text; may also provide information not otherwise conveyed in the text
	Language Conventionality and Clarity contemporary, familiar language
	Knowledge Demands some specialized knowledge required
Reader/Task Considerations	Teacher determined

Strategies for CLOSE READING

Analyze the Structure of a Magazine Article

Students should read this article carefully all the way through. Close-reading questions at the bottom of the page will help them focus on a thorough analysis of the structure. As they read, students should jot down comments or questions about the text in the margins.

WHEN STUDENTS STRUGGLE . . .

To help students analyze the structure of "Teenagers and New Technology," have them work in small groups to fill out a chart like the one shown below.

CITE TEXT EVIDENCE For practice in analyzing the structure of a magazine article, ask students to cite text evidence for some of the cause-and-effect relationships.

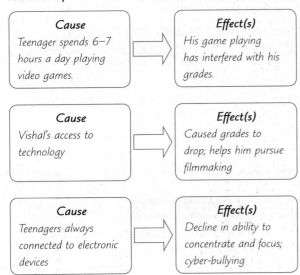

Cause	Effect(s)
Teenager spends 6–7 hours a day playing video games.	His game playing has interfered with his grades.

Cause	Effect(s)
Vishal's access to technology	Caused grades to drop; helps him pursue filmmaking

Cause	Effect(s)
Teenagers always connected to electronic devices	Decline in ability to concentrate and focus; cyber-bullying

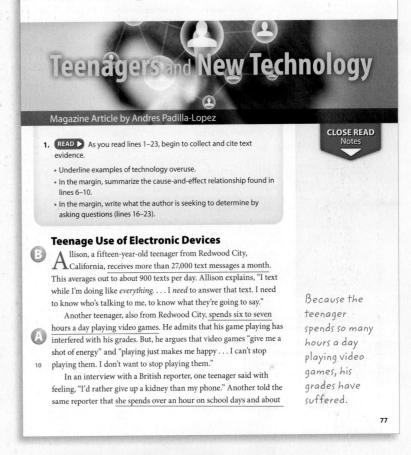

Background *The world's first text message was sent on December 3, 1992. Neil Papworth sent the message "Merry Christmas" from his personal computer to the phone of Richard Jarvis. Technology has come quite a long way since then. The social networking site Facebook has over one billion active users; 2.4 billion people around the world use text messaging as a means of communication; and 30.2 percent of the world's population now use the Internet. Maybe it's important to ask: What are the effects of our obsession with new technology?*

Teenagers and New Technology

Magazine Article by Andres Padilla-Lopez

CLOSE READ
Notes

1. **READ ▶** As you read lines 1–23, begin to collect and cite text evidence.

   • Underline examples of technology overuse.
   • In the margin, summarize the cause-and-effect relationship found in lines 6–10.
   • In the margin, write what the author is seeking to determine by asking questions (lines 16–23).

Teenage Use of Electronic Devices

B   Allison, a fifteen-year-old teenager from Redwood City, California, receives more than 27,000 text messages a month. This averages out to about 900 texts per day. Allison explains, "I text while I'm doing like *everything*. . . . I *need* to answer that text. I need to know who's talking to me, to know what they're going to say."

A   Another teenager, also from Redwood City, spends six to seven hours a day playing video games. He admits that his game playing has interfered with his grades. But, he argues that video games "give me a shot of energy" and "playing just makes me happy . . . I can't stop playing them. I don't want to stop playing them."

10   In an interview with a British reporter, one teenager said with feeling, "I'd rather give up a kidney than my phone." Another told the same reporter that she spends over an hour on school days and about

Because the teenager spends so many hours a day playing video games, his grades have suffered.

77

1. **READ AND CITE TEXT EVIDENCE** Tell students that this magazine article, like many, is organized in sections with subheadings. The subheadings tell you what a particular section is about and may be important clues about the article's overall structure.

A **ASK STUDENTS** to further explore the cause-and-effect relationship described for the Redwood City teenager. What causes him to spend so many hours playing video games each day? *Students should note that playing video games makes him happy and gives him "a shot of energy" (lines 8–9). So, students can now describe a causal chain: playing video games makes teenager happy* ➞ *he plays the games 6–7 hours each day* ➞ *his grades have suffered.*

The author is asking the reader to examine the benefits of technology.

double that time on weekends hanging out with some 450 Facebook friends.

So, how do *you* use electronic devices? Are your Facebook friends the same as your real-life friends, or do they include people you've never met? Are the friends you've never met more interesting than your real-life friends? Do you feel lost without your cell phone? Must 20 you answer every text message immediately? Are you itching to get out of class to play video games? Or perhaps you worry about the amount of time you spend on your electronic devices. Maybe you think that texting and Facebook are a waste of time.

Facts and Figures

The numerical data is more specific than the generalizations.

Recent studies estimate that 93 percent of teenagers between the ages of 12 and 17 years of age regularly go online to use the Internet. Studies also show that 75 percent of all teenagers own cell phones. Half of that 75 percent sends fifty or more texts a day. One in three sends 100 or more texts per day. Some teenage cellphone users don't even use their phones to make actual phone calls—except to their

Teenagers and the Internet

(D) 74% have their own computer
63% of Internet users go online daily
(C) 27% use phones to go online
73% are on a social network

Contact with Friends Every Day

54% text message
38% call on a cell phone
30% talk on a landline phone
24% instant message
11% e-mail
25% use a social network site

Note that if you add up the percents, you find that many teenagers must use various methods of contacting friends daily.

Landline phones are being surpassed in popularity by cell phones.

2. ◀ REREAD Reread lines 1–15. What are the similarities of the structure of each of the first three paragraphs? Support your response with explicit textual evidence.

Each paragraph begins with the introduction of a teenager and then follows up with an explanation of how each teen is addicted to technology—"a fifteen-year-old teenager" who receives "about 900 texts per day" is followed by "another teenager, also from Redwood City" who plays video games "six to seven hours a day."

3. READ ▶ As you read lines 24–35 and study the bar graphs, continue to cite evidence.

- Underline text that contains numerical data, and circle text that makes a generalization. In the margin, note a difference between these two kinds of information.
- What conclusion can you draw about landline phones from the information in the graphs? Note your conclusion in the margin.
- In the margin, make an inference about the reason teenagers may make "actual phone calls" to their parents.

4. ◀ REREAD Review the graphs. What conclusion can you draw about why significantly more teenagers use text messaging than e-mail to communicate with their friends? Support your answer with explicit evidence from the graphs.

More teenagers probably use text messaging to communicate with their friends because it can be done on a phone, instead of being done at a computer. Only 27 percent of teenagers use their phone to go online. Since e-mail requires the user to be online, we might be able to assume that the 54 percent of teens who communicate via text message have easier access to their phones than their computers.

2. **REREAD AND CITE TEXT EVIDENCE**

(B) **ASK STUDENTS** to summarize each of the first three paragraphs. *Cause-and-effect relationships define the teenagers' experiences. Allison gets more than 27,000 texts a month and needs to answer each one. A teenager plays video games 6 to 7 hours a day because they make him happy. Another has over 450 Facebook friends and spends hours each weekend hanging out with them.*

3. **READ AND CITE TEXT EVIDENCE**

(C) **ASK STUDENTS** to discuss the first bar graph. What conclusion can you draw about phones from this graph? *Students should understand that only about a quarter of teenagers use phones to go online.* What kind of phones are these teenagers using? *Students should realize that people use cell phones or smart phones to connect to the Internet.*

FOR ELL STUDENTS Explain that in this context, *itching* means "having a restless desire" rather than "having a skin irritation."

4. **REREAD AND CITE TEXT EVIDENCE**

(D) **ASK STUDENTS** to discuss whether the first bar graph gives evidence about why more teenagers communicate with friends by text message than by e-mail. *Students should realize that text messaging is done by phone, while e-mail is done (online) by computer or phone. The first bar graph shows that few teenagers use their phones to go online, but 74 percent of them own a computer. It also shows that 63 percent of teenage Internet users go online each day. The graph doesn't say how many teenagers are Internet users, but it does say that 73 percent of teenagers belong to a social network. So, the first graph would seem to indicate that plenty of teenagers have computers, use the Internet, and go online daily to communicate by e-mail if they wish to. The reason(s) for their preference for text messaging must lie elsewhere.*

232d Collection 5

> " Scientists wonder about the long-term effects on a teenager's still-developing brain. "

connected to electronic devices. Educators notice a decline in students' ability to concentrate on any one thing for an extended period of time. Scientists wonder about the long-term effects on a teenager's still-developing brain. What do the instant **gratification** and rapid stimulation offered by electronic media do to a teenager's brain? Scientists also fear that yielding to one distraction after another develops an inability to focus. Parents worry about the presence of predators on social networking sites. They are also alarmed by the threat of cyber-bullying. Teenagers, like Vishal and Allison, ask themselves if their slipping grades and inability to concentrate on school tasks are worth it.

(F) 50

(H)

On the other hand, supporters argue that today's powerful cell phones offer teenagers new worlds of opportunity. They stress that understanding new technology is essential to future success. They recognize that tools, such as texting and Facebook, meet needs common to all teenagers, such as defining their personal identity and establishing their independence. These technologies provide new avenues for teenagers to do the things teenagers have always wanted to do: flirt, boast, gossip, complain, tease, and get news. Some educators see new technologies as an exciting way of connecting with students. Others view them as a tool for personalizing education and encouraging individual students' interests.

(G)

60

gratification:
reward

The information is mostly against the overuse of technology.

These statements support the use of technology.

Parents may not know how to send text messages.

30   parents. Instead, they use texting to communicate. And, as all cell phone owners know, today's phones enable you to do much more than just texting. They allow users to take and share pictures, play games, listen to music, swap videos, and access the Internet and social networking sites such as Facebook and Twitter. The average teenager has 201 Facebook friends!

The Pros and the Cons

One high school student from California **aptly** sums up the conflicting attitudes held by both adults and teenagers about the use of digital devices. Vishal is a bright seventeen-year old with a passionate interest in filmmaking. As he puts it, technology is "bad

40   for me as a student" because it has caused his grades to go down. On the other hand, he says, it is good for me as a learner." Vishal's access to technology has distracted him and made it difficult for him to concentrate on his assigned schoolwork, but it has also helped him to pursue in depth his interest in filmmaking.

(E)

Currently educators, scientists, parents, and even some teenagers themselves worry about the long-term effects of always being

aptly:
appropriately

6. ◀ **REREAD** Reread lines 36–57. Explain how the cause-and-effect pattern of organization is used in this section to connect ideas. Support your answer with explicit textual evidence.

    The author explicitly lists the effects of technology. An "inability to focus" and a "decline in students' ability to concentrate on any one thing for an extended period of time" are both directly attributed to "the use of digital devices." Vishal's access to technology—a cause—has "distracted him and made it difficult for him to concentrate "—an effect.

7. **READ** ▶ As you read lines 58–71, continue to cite textual evidence.

    • Circle positive effects of using digital devices.
    • In the margin, explain which position, pro or con, the author emphasizes now.

5. **READ** ▶ As you read lines 36–57, continue to cite textual evidence.

    • Underline negative effects of using digital devices.
    • Circle positive effects of using digital devices.
    • In the margin, explain what positions, pro or con, the author seems to emphasize.

---

5. **READ AND CITE TEXT EVIDENCE**

    (E) **ASK STUDENTS** to weigh the negative and positive effects of using digital devices. *On the negative side, students should cite Vishal's admission that technology distracts him and makes it hard for him to concentrate on schoolwork; educators' observation that students' ability to concentrate is declining; scientists' fear that technology causes an "inability to focus"; and parents' worries about online predators and cyber-bullies. On the positive side, there are only Vishal's assertions that technology is good for him "as a learner" and that it has helped him pursue filmmaking.*

    Critical Vocabulary: aptly (line 36) Have students give the definition of the base word *apt*. *"well suited or intelligent"* Have them give the definition of the suffix *-ly*. *"in a certain manner"* So what is the meaning of *aptly*? *"in a suitable or intelligent manner"*

6. **REREAD AND CITE TEXT EVIDENCE**

    (F) **ASK STUDENTS** to describe the general cause-and-effect pattern. *There is only one cause—technology, or more precisely, the overuse of electronic devices—and several effects. However, the author implies some causal chains. For example, electronic devices give users "instant gratification and rapid stimulation," which may affect teenagers' brains in the long term (lines 50–51).*

7. **READ AND CITE TEXT EVIDENCE**

    (G) **ASK STUDENTS** to paraphrase positive effects of digital devices. *Technology lets teenagers define their identities, establish independence, and socialize. It helps teachers connect with students, personalize lessons, and encourage students.*

    Critical Vocabulary: gratification (line 50) Have students suggest synonyms of *gratification* that would work in this context. *fulfillment, pleasure, enjoyment*

Wherever you stand on the various issues raised, there is no doubt
70 that electronic devices are here to stay. How we use these devices,
whether we choose to have them work for us or against us, is up to us.

8. ◀ **REREAD AND DISCUSS** Reread lines 58–71. With a small group,
draw several conclusions about the ways that teens can use
technological devices to work for them instead of against them. Cite
explicit textual evidence in your discussion.

SHORT RESPONSE

Cite Text Evidence What types of information does the author include to
show the ways in which teens use technological devices? What overall insight
does the reader gain on the use of these devices? Review your reading notes,
and be sure to **cite evidence from the text** in your response.

> The article presents a variety of information to show the ways that
> teens use or misuse technology. The article quotes examples of the
> negative effects of technology overuse: "Allison, a fifteen-year old
> teenager from Redwood City, California, receives more than 27,000
> text messages a month." Statistics provide insight into the cause of
> the problem: "75 percent of all teenagers own cell phones." The
> author also uses bar graphs to illuminate the various ways in which
> teens use technology—e-mail, instant message, and social network
> sites. The reader gains insight into "how we use these devices" and
> "whether we choose to have them work for us or against us."

82

TO CHALLENGE STUDENTS . . .

For deeper understanding, students can research negative and
positive effects of using electronic devices in cars.

ASK STUDENTS to discuss some of the negative effects of using
electronic devices in cars. *Students should understand that talking
on a cell phone while driving is dangerous. The driver, distracted, is at
risk of not seeing other cars, traffic lights, or pedestrians until it is too
late to avoid crashing. Researchers have compiled statistics showing
that driving while talking on a cell phone is about as dangerous as
driving while drunk. Interestingly, the effect is the same for hands-
free phones as for handheld phones. The problem, scientists say, is
not that we're holding a cell phone but that our brains are focused
on the conversation, not the road.*

Have students discuss some of the positive effects of new
technology in cars. *Students should recognize that cell phones are
useful in case of breakdowns or emergencies. People can summon
assistance immediately, and lives might be saved. Many smart
phones have GPS, which helps drivers get places without becoming
lost. Cell phones and other electronic devices are also a way to keep
children occupied during long drives, which means fewer distractions
for the driver.*

---

8. **REREAD AND DISCUSS USING TEXT EVIDENCE**

H **ASK STUDENTS** in each group to start by considering their
responses to Question 7. How can teens use digital devices to
achieve each of these positive outcomes? *Students may note, for
example, that by texting and using Facebook, teens are able to define
their identities. Students could also mention that by flirting and
gossiping online, teens can socialize much as their parents did, but
with new technology. Finally, students may say that computers,
smart phones, and tablets let them pursue their interests, further
their education, and connect with teachers.*

SHORT RESPONSE

Cite Text Evidence Students should:

- describe the types of information included in the article.
- give examples of evidence from anecdotes, statistics, and graphs.
- explain what insight they gained from the article.

DIG DEEPER

1. With the class, return to Question 1, Read. Have students share their underlined examples.

ASK STUDENTS to discuss the term *technology overuse*.

- What is the nature of the problem this article explores? *Students should realize that the author examines the consequences of teenagers' overuse of electronic devices. The new technology isn't a problem if teenagers don't dedicate excessive amounts of time to it.*

- What evidence—explicit or implied—does the author present of "technology overuse"? *Students should note that receiving 900 text messages a day will necessarily consume a large part of Allison's waking hours. On average, she will "need" to answer a text almost every minute. Similarly, students will probably deem six to seven hours of daily video games as "overuse," especially since the Redwood City teenager says that he can't stop playing them. However, students may feel that the third teenager is not overusing her devices. She has a large number of Facebook friends but spends only one to two hours online with them each day.*

2. With the class, return to Question 3, Read. Have students share their responses to the question.

ASK STUDENTS to discuss the data presented here.

- Have students analyze the numerical data and the generalizations presented in lines 24–35. *Students should recognize that the generalizations are supported by logic and experience. We all know people who use their phones mainly or exclusively to text, and of course it is true that smart phones can take pictures, play games, and listen to music. The numerical data, on the other hand, comes from "studies" that, although not cited, carry greater authority. The author implies that the studies are reputable, so readers should consider the data seriously.*

ASK STUDENTS to return to their Short Response answer and revise it based on the class discussion.

CLOSE READING NOTES

Always Wanting More
from I Want That!

Informational Text by Thomas Hine

Why This Text?

This nonfiction text presents a familiar economic topic—shopping. The text lets students examine how an author combines facts and reflection. This lesson focuses on the language an author uses to express ideas and viewpoints and on inferences readers can make.

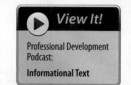

View It!

Professional Development Podcast:

Informational Text

Key Learning Objective: The student will be able to identify features of an author's style and make inferences using textual details and prior knowledge.

For practice and application:

Labels and Illusions

Essay by Lourdes Barranco

Close Reader selection
"Labels and Illusions"
Essay by Lourdes Barranco

RI 1 Cite text evidence.
RI 2 Determine central idea.
RI 4 Determine meanings of words and phrases.
RI 5 Analyze the structure an author uses to organize a text.
RI 8 Evaluate specific claims in a text.
SL 1 Engage in collaborative discussions.
L 1a Explain the function of phrases and clauses.
L 4d Verify the preliminary determination of the meaning of a word or phrase.
L 5b Use synonym/antonym relationships to understand words.
L 6 Acquire and use grade-appropriate academic vocabulary.

▲ Text Complexity Rubric

Quantitative Measures	**Always Wanting More *from* I Want That!** Lexile: 1240L

Levels of Meaning/Purpose

more than one purpose; implied, easily identified from context

Structure

organization of main ideas and details is complex, but clearly stated and generally sequential

Qualitative Measures

Language Conventionality and Clarity

increased unfamiliar language

Knowledge Demands

somewhat complex social science, social studies concepts

Reader/Task Considerations
- Teacher determined
- Vary by individual reader and type of text
- See the Text X-Ray for suggested Reader/Task Considerations.

English Language Support
Before teaching, use the Text X-Ray for an overview of the text's complexity. The Text X-Ray and the supports and scaffolds in the Teacher's Edition will help you guide students of different skill levels.

Meaning Making

Language Development

Effective Expression

Content Knowledge

Foundational Skills

Text Complexity: Qualitative Measures

Levels of Meaning/Purpose

more than one purpose; implied, easily identified from context

Help students make inferences about important ideas in informational text.

- Teacher's Edition side notes, pp. 233, 234, 235, 236, 237
- English Language Support, pp. 233, 236
- Strategies for Annotation, p. 234
- Make Inferences, p. 237

To teach how to determine central ideas and details, see

- Determine Central Ideas and Details, p. 240a

▶ *Use It!* **Interactive Whiteboard Lesson:** Main/Central Idea and Details

ZOOM IN ON **MAKING INFERENCES** Remind students that when they **make inferences,** they use details in the text as well as their own knowledge to draw logical conclusions. Write the word *progress* on the board and define it as "moving forward by inventing new things." Then have students read lines 33–52 with a partner.

- Ask students what inference they can make about the impact of progress on people's buying habits. *(Progress makes it harder to fulfill the ideals of comfort and modernity, keeping them just out of reach, which means that people must buy more in their effort to attain them.)*
- Have students identify specific details that support their inference.

Structure

organization of main ideas and details is complex, but clearly stated and generally sequential

Help students use the elements of style, tone, and voice to determine the meaning of informational text.

- Teacher's Edition side notes, pp. 233, 235, 236, 237
- English Language Support, p. 233
- Strategies for Annotation, p. 237
- Determine Meaning, p. 237

To reteach determine meaning, see

- Determine Meaning, p. 240a

▶ *Use It!* **Level Up Tutorial:** Author's Style

ZOOM IN ON **ANALYZING TONE** Tell students that an author's tone or attitude may change throughout a text. Explain that although Thomas Hine's **tone** is often ironic, it changes in lines 65–74. Display the paragraph and highlight these words and phrases: "massive deficit," "exploit the low-wage workers," "enough resources," "clean air and clean water," "sustain." Ask students how they would describe the author's tone based on his language here. *(He has a serious attitude toward this part of this topic.)* Have them discuss why this tone is appropriate for this part of the text. *(He is talking about global issues and the negative impact that consumerism can have on people, the environment, and the economy.)*

Language Conventionality and Clarity

increased unfamiliar language

Teach unfamiliar academic vocabulary in context.

- Teacher's Edition Critical Vocabulary notes, pp. 234, 235, 236, 239
- Applying Academic Vocabulary, p. 235
- Strategies for Annotation, p. 239
- Vocabulary Strategy: Synonyms and Antonyms, p. 239

Support students' analysis of the selection.

- English Language Support, p. 238

Help students recognize and use noun clauses.

- Teacher's Edition side note, p. 240
- English Language Support, p. 240
- Language Conventions: Noun Clauses, p. 240

ZOOM IN ON **IDENTIFYING CONNOTATIONS** Tell students that many words convey feelings or ideas that go beyond their dictionary definition. Point out the word *consume* in line 27. Explain that it has several definitions, including "to eat," "to use up," or "to buy." It also suggests doing these actions greedily, hastily, or without thinking. A **synonym** such as *buy* would not convey quite the same ideas. Ask students how the **connotation** of *consume* reinforces the point the author is making. *(The author shows how people buy things they don't need just for the sake of buying; they consume material objects greedily.)*

Knowledge Demands

somewhat complex social science, social studies concepts

Support English learners in understanding necessary background information.

- Teacher's Edition Background note, p. 233
- Teacher's Edition side note, p. 236

ZOOM IN ON **BUILDING CONTEXT** After students read, share these statistics from a four-week study of the behaviors of American consumers (based on a 2014 Gallup poll). Discuss how they relate to Hine's central ideas.

- 58% of shoppers said they bought more than they had planned.
- 38% made a purchase on the spur of the moment.
- 31% went shopping for fun.
- 27% bought something that cost more than a week's pay.

Suggested Reader/Task Considerations

Consider the following before assigning this informational text to students.

- Can students draw on their prior knowledge to understand the author's key points?
- Are students able to pose questions that help them evaluate the validity of the author's claims?

ZOOM IN ON **SUPPORTING COMPREHENSION**

- Before students read, ask these questions: *What is your attitude toward shopping? Where do you shop most frequently? Do you ever buy things you don't need? Why?* Have students make connections to their own attitudes and experiences as they read.
- Have students read in pairs, pausing at intervals to ask questions about the author's claims. Provide these sentence stems: *What does the author mean by _____? What evidence does the author provide to support his belief that _____? Do you agree/disagree with the author's statement that _____?*

Background This excerpt comes from the book *I Want That! How We All Became Shoppers*. In the book, Hine traces the history of shopping back to before shopping existed, in prehistoric times, to show that humans have always been motivated to acquire things. He has said his style of writing is intended to replicate the experience of shopping, as if the reader is shopping in his store of ideas. Hine invites readers to watch for surprises in his books, just as a shopper might find surprises in the aisles of a store.

SETTING A PURPOSE Direct students to use the Setting a Purpose questions to focus their reading. Remind students to generate questions as they read.

Determine Meaning
(LINES 1–13)

RI 1, RI 4

Tell students that an author's **style** of writing involves *how* something is said rather than *what* is said. An author's **word choices** reveal how the author feels about the topic. This attitude is called **tone.**

 CITE TEXT EVIDENCE Have students cite words and phrases in lines 1–13 that reveal an amused, even ironic tone. (*People who seek a simpler life are "a distinct market segment." He uses quotation marks around the word* authentic *to show that the products designed for this market are not real at all. It's ironic that people are told "what they need to buy to achieve a simpler life."*)

Make Inferences (LINES 1–13)

RI 1

Tell students that when readers make an **inference** they use what the author says along with what they know to make a logical guess about what is not directly stated.

 ASK STUDENTS to reread the first paragraph and tell what they can infer about the reasons why people of the past and present seek a simpler life. (*In the past, wealthy rulers sought simplicity because they were bored by their possessions. People today who are not pleased by their possessions think a simpler life will bring more satisfaction.*)

English Language Support

Define these words and phrases to help students make a valid inference: *distinct market segment* ("specific group of buyers"); *abundance* ("plenty; more than enough of something"); *austerity* ("lack of luxury; a plain lifestyle").

Background *A writer on history, culture, and design,* **Thomas Hine** *coined the word* populuxe *as the title of his first book. The word has become commonly used to describe the enthusiasms of post-World War II America. Hine was born in a small New England town near Boston. He lived in a house that was built in 1770, a very different setting from the modern world he writes about now.*

Always Wanting More
from I WANT THAT!

Informational Text by Thomas Hine

SETTING A PURPOSE What keeps people in our consumer society always wanting more? And when is having more enough? As you read, consider how Thomas Hine answers these questions.

A
B

Throughout most of history, few people had more than a couple of possessions, and as a consequence, people were very aware of each object. Life was austere. The ability to be bored by a material surfeit[1] was a rare privilege. There are many stories of kings and emperors who sought a simpler life, if only briefly. Now, that emotion has become widespread, and those who wish to simplify are identified as a distinct market segment. Whole lines of "authentic" products have been created to serve this market, and magazines are published to
10 tell people what they need to buy to achieve a simpler life. In our age of careless abundance, austerity is a luxury, available

(t) ©James Chan, Ph.D.; (b) ©IMG_191 LLC/Shutterstock

---

[1] **surfeit** (sûr´fĭt): an excessive amount.

English Language Support

Improve Reading Fluency Explain that **tone,** which is the writer's attitude toward the topic, affects the way a passage is read aloud.

- Read aloud lines 1–13, emphasizing the sarcastic tone in lines 8–13 to express Hine's attitude about people who buy things to simplify lives that are complicated from buying things.
- Break the paragraph into lines 1–3; 3–8; 8–13. Read aloud each set of lines, pausing to allow students to repeat them.
- Have students practice using an ironic tone by reading the last set of lines to a partner.

Make Inferences

RI 1

(LINES 20–22)

Tell students that an important idea in economics is the difference between needs and wants. Needs are the basic things that everyone requires to live. Wants are the things that people desire.

C ASK STUDENTS what the sentence in lines 20–22 seems to say about human nature in societies with a high standard of living. *(People are never satisfied with just meeting their needs, and no matter how many wants are met, they can still come up with new ones.)*

CRITICAL VOCABULARY

superfluity: The author points out that superfluity might be a sign of a high standard of living.
ASK STUDENTS why superfluity makes some people uneasy. *(It seems wasteful to have more stuff than you need.)*

intangible: People enjoy owning objects, but they often seek satisfaction from intangibles too.
ASK STUDENTS what examples of intangibles are given in the text, and why they are called intangibles. Have students suggest other intangibles people value. *(The examples are comfort and modernity. They're intangibles because they're qualities or ideas—you can't see or touch them. Other intangibles are learning, friendship, progress, and beauty.)*

---

only to multimillionaires, the occasional monk, and the really smart shopper.

   "The standard of life is determined not so much by what a man has to enjoy, as by the rapidity with which he tires of any one pleasure," wrote Simon Patten, the pioneering economist-philosopher of consumption, in 1889. "To have a high standard of life means to enjoy a pleasure intensely and tire of it quickly." Patten's definition of the standard of life was based

20 on **superfluity:** He expected that people would always have more than they need and would never have all they might want. That was a novel idea in Patten's time, and it is one that still makes many people uneasy. In material terms, it seems terribly wasteful, a misuse of the resources of a finite world. And in psychological terms, it seems to trap us in a cycle of false hope and inevitable disappointment. We work in order to consume, and we consume in order to somehow compensate for the emptiness of our lives, including our work. Indeed, there is some evidence that people who feel least fulfilled

30 by their work are the most avid shoppers, while those who love their work find shopping a burden, though they don't necessarily buy less.

   Our materialism is oddly abstract, a path toward an ideal. The things we acquire are less important than the act of acquiring, the freedom to choose, and the ability to forget what we have and to keep on choosing. We don't aspire, as people in China did during the 1970s, to "Four Musts": a bicycle, a radio, a watch, and a sewing machine. We aspire instead to such **intangibles** as comfort and modernity,

40 qualities for which standards change so rapidly that the buying can never stop. "Progress is our most important product," Ronald Reagan used to say during his tenure as spokesman for General Electric. And in 1989, after the Berlin Wall fell, multitudes throughout Eastern Europe disappointed intellectuals in the West by behaving as if freedom was the same thing as going shopping. Even China moved on in the 1980s to the "Eight Bigs": a color television, an electric fan, a refrigerator, an audio system, camera, a motorcycle, a furniture suite, and a washing machine. Now China is moving

50 beyond the specific "Bigs" and aspires to more, a quest that will never end. A large super-store chain is opening stores there.

superfluity
(soo´pər-floo´ĭ-tē) *n.*
Superfluity is overabundance or excess.

intangible
(ĭn-tăn´jə-bəl) *n.*
An *intangible* is something that is hard to describe because it cannot be perceived by the senses.

English Language Support

Use Transitions Explain that transitions are words and phrases that show how ideas are connected. Transitions can show sequence *(first, next, last)*, contrast *(instead, on the other hand)*, similarity *(and, in addition)*, and other relationships.

- Read aloud the sentence in lines 28–32. Work with students to identify the transition word that signals a contrast between people who do and do not love their work. *(while)* Help them paraphrase this idea in simpler language, using *while*. *(People who don't like their jobs love to shop, while people who love their jobs don't like to shop.)*

- Have pairs review lines 33–52 and identify the transition word that contrasts people in China and America. *(instead, line 39)* Have them rephrase the idea using *meanwhile, however,* or *on the other hand*. Invite pairs to share their sentences.

- Have students review lines 14–52 and identify all the transitions they find. Then have them share their findings in pairs and explain the connection made by each transition. Finally, have students work independently to write original sentences expressing ideas from the text, using these transitions: *on the contrary, in addition, moreover.*

It is amazing to think that from the dawn of time until the time of Adam Smith,[2] a bit more than two centuries ago, people believed that wanting and having things was a drain on wealth, rather than one of its sources. That doesn't mean, however, that they didn't want things or that they didn't, at times, go to great lengths to attain them.

60 Now, as I move, mildly entranced, behind my cart at a super store, grabbing items I feel for a moment that I need, I am assumed to be increasing the prosperity not merely of my own country, but of the entire world. Indeed, in the wake of the World Trade Center attacks, Americans were **exhorted** not to sacrifice, as is usual in wartime, but to consume.

There are those who disagree. Can the massive deficit that the United States runs with other countries, which is driven by our hunger for ever more low-priced goods, be sustained indefinitely? Does our appetite for inexpensive goods from overseas exploit the low-wage workers who make them, or 70 does it give them new opportunities? And more profoundly, are there enough resources in the world to provide everyone with this kind of living standard and still have enough clean air and clean water? How many super-store shoppers can one planet sustain?

exhort
(ĭg-zôrt´) v. If you exhort, you make an urgent appeal to others.

---

[2] **Adam Smith:** a Scottish economist who lived in the 18th century.

APPLYING ACADEMIC VOCABULARY

attitude	consume	goal

THINK-PAIR-SHARE Have students turn to a partner to discuss the following questions. Guide students to include the academic vocabulary words *attitude, consume,* and *goal* in their responses. Ask volunteers to share their responses with the class.

- According to the author, what accounts for the **attitude** of modern **consumers** toward the consumption of goods?
- What is the **goal** of the modern superstore?

CLOSE READ

Determine Meaning RI 4
(LINES 53–64)

Tell students that the term **voice** refers to an author's unique style of expression.

D **CITE TEXT EVIDENCE** Have students reread lines 53–64 and cite evidence of the author's voice. *(He says, "It is amazing to think" to express his own surprise at how ideas about wealth have changed only in the last two hundred years. He tells about his own experience at a super store: He is "mildly entranced" and "grabbing items I feel for a moment that I need.")* What does this reveal about the author's personality? *(He is playful, humorous, and sometimes sarcastic.)*

Determine Central Idea RI 2
(LINES 65–74)

Tell students that on this page the author explores contrasting ideas about prosperity and consumption.

E **ASK STUDENTS** to reread lines 65–74 and tell what point the author is making. *(The author raises questions about whether spending money on things as a way to increase wealth and prosperity is valid. The questions ask whether a high standard of living can really last for Americans and for the rest of the planet.)*

> **CRITICAL VOCABULARY**
>
> **exhort:** After an attack on the United States, Americans were exhorted to shop.
>
> **ASK STUDENTS** why Americans were exhorted to shop. *(The government encouraged them to consume to keep the economy prosperous.)*

FOR STANDARD ENGLISH LEARNERS

Some students may have difficulty pronouncing initial *th* (as in *this*) and final *t* (as in *doesn't*). Read lines 53–58 aloud, emphasizing correct pronunciation of *that, than, they, them, doesn't,* and *didn't*. Then have students practice reading the paragraph aloud in pairs as you circulate to check their pronunciation.

Determine Meaning
RI 1,
RI 4

(LINES 78–81)

Point out that the word *buyosphere* in line 80 has been invented by the author.

 CITE TEXT EVIDENCE Have students reread lines 78–81 and name examples of places in the buyosphere. Ask for ideas about what the word suggests to readers and why the author made this word choice. *(The buyosphere is made of "big box stores, boutiques, malls, Main Streets, Web sites, and other retailers." The author chose this word to be both comical and startling, suggesting a scientific concept, like the biosphere or atmosphere, that defines the sphere in which we live as defined by the buying of things.)*

Make Inferences
RI 1

(LINES 86–89)

Tell students that the author is reflecting on what he has observed in superstores.

G **ASK STUDENTS** to reread lines 86–89. Have students discuss why the author uses the phrase "perverse tribute." *(We live in a world of plenty, but instead of showing gratitude, we're bored. We lack emotional connections to the things we own.)*

> **CRITICAL VOCABULARY**
>
> **apathy:** The author says that a superstore provokes apathy rather than amazement.
>
> **ASK STUDENTS** why the author contrasts apathy with amazement. *(to point out that we should be amazed by a superstore rather than indifferent to it)*

COLLABORATIVE DISCUSSION Have students form small groups to review the text for references to the past, present, and future. Suggest that they think about how modern consumers are like and different from those in past ages. In what ways may future consumers change, and why?

ASK STUDENTS to share any questions they generated in the course of reading and discussing the selection.

These are serious questions that need to be addressed, but those who raise such issues have rarely considered the power of objects and the fundamental role that acquiring and using objects has played since prehistoric times. In this story, the big box stores, boutiques, malls, Main Streets, Web sites, and other retailers that constitute the buyosphere[3] represent the fulfillment of an ancient dream. The local super store is a wonder of the world. Never before have so many goods come together from so many places at such low cost. And never before have so many people been able to buy so many things.

Nevertheless, we yawn at a super store rather than marvel at it. That such a store could provoke **apathy** instead of amazement is a perverse tribute to the plenitude of our consumer society and the weakness of the emotional ties that bind us to the many objects in our lives. Never before has so much seemed so dull.

And even if a super store is not the noblest expression of personal liberty or the highest achievement of democracy, we should consider that it does provide a setting for exercising a kind of freedom that has threatened tyrants and autocrats for thousands of years. We go to a super store to acquire things that prove our own power. It is a place where people really do get to choose.

apathy
(ăp'ə-thē) *n. Apathy* is indifference or the lack of interest or concern.

COLLABORATIVE DISCUSSION The author presents ideas about wanting and having things in the past, the present, and the future. What does he say about how wanting and having things change over time? Talk about your ideas with other group members.

---

[3] **buyosphere:** a term the author uses to describe all the places that modern consumers buy things.

English Language Support

Read Closely Use the collection opener strategy, Five-Word Summary.

- Have students read a passage and list its five most important words—those that best explain and clarify the main idea.
- Then have pairs discuss their lists to draft one list of the five most important words. Form groups to share, discuss, and defend these word choices before synthesizing the words into a final list of five.
- Have students summarize the text individually, including and underlining each of the five words on their group's final list.

Determine Meaning

RI 4

Often, a written work is a reflection of an author's **style,** a manner of writing that involves how something is said rather than what is said. An author can share ideas or express viewpoints by using stylistic elements like these:

- **Word choice** is an author's use of words. Well-chosen words help an author to express ideas precisely and artistically. Word choice is part of **diction,** which involves the use of vocabulary and word order. An author's word choice can be formal or informal, serious or humorous.
- **Tone** is the author's attitude toward a subject. Like word choice, a tone can convey different feelings. The tone of a work can often be described in one word, such as *playful, serious,* or *determined.*
- **Voice** is an author's unique style of expression. The use of voice can reveal an author's personality, beliefs, or attitudes.

Consider the word choices in this sentence from "Always Wanting More," which describes the author's feelings about being part of a consumer culture:

> **Now, as I move, mildly entranced, behind my cart at a super store, grabbing items I feel for a moment that I need, I am assumed to be increasing the prosperity not merely of my own country, but of the entire world.**

The tone in this sentence could be described as self-mocking, meaning the author is making fun of himself. What word choices are examples of this?

Make Inferences

RI 1

To grasp an implied or unstated idea in a text, readers can make an **inference**—a logical guess based on facts and a person's own knowledge. The chart shows an inference made from a section of the text you've just read.

Textual Detail	Knowledge	Inference
"And in 1989, after the Berlin Wall fell, multitudes throughout Eastern Europe disappointed intellectuals in the West by behaving as if freedom was the same thing as going shopping."	The Berlin Wall separated East Germany, which was under Communist control, from West Germany, which had a democratic form of government and greater freedom.	The fall of the Berlin Wall signaled freedom for East Germans. They focused on purchasing things that they had not been able to get before.

What inference can you make about the reason "intellectuals in the West" were disappointed?

CLOSE READ

Determine Meaning

RI 4

Explain that readers can deepen their appreciation of a text's style by observing how the author uses sentence fragments or long sentences, for example, or precise adjectives and vivid verbs. Explain that every writer has a different *voice* because every writer uses language in his or her own way. Voice is what allows a reader to "hear" a personality in a selection.

After students read the boldfaced sentence, have them find words that convey a self-mocking tone and explain why the author has this attitude. *(Possible answers: The phrases "mildly entranced" and "grabbing items I feel for a moment that I need" show that the author behaves like every other unthinking shopper, under the influence of an ancient urge to acquire.)*

Make Inferences

RI 1

Review that readers use what is directly stated in text to draw conclusions. After students read the example in the chart, ask them what it means to "make an inference."

To help students answer the question below the chart, discuss what is directly stated in the text and what students know about "intellectuals in the West." *(Possible answer: Intellectuals in the West had hoped that East Germans would express their new freedom in a "high" way, such as expressing political and personal freedoms. The intellectuals were disappointed when the East Germans focused on the "low" activity of shopping.)*

Strategies for Annotation Annotate it!

Determine Meaning

RI 4

Share these strategies for guided or independent analysis:

- Highlight in yellow words and phrases that help you hear the author's voice.
- On a note, write words that seem to describe the author.

Now, as I move, mildly entranced, behind my cart at a super store, grabbing items I feel for a moment that I need, I am assumed to be increasing the prosperity not m[erely of my] own country, but of the entire world. Indeed, in th[...]

> witty, honest, playful, doesn't act superior or take himself too seriously

Analyzing the Text
RI 1, RI 2,
RI 4, RI 5

Possible answers:

1. *"Those who wish to simplify are identified as a distinct market segment" and "tell people what they need to buy to achieve a simpler life" are ironic; the point of simplifying is to remove oneself from the market. The word* authentic *is in quotes to show the author means the opposite; the contradiction "austerity is a luxury" and the list "multimillionaires, the occasional monk, and the really smart shopper" show the absurdity of the trend.*

2. *The author's tone might be described as serious. Words such as "trap us in a cycle of false hope and inevitable disappointment" and "emptiness of our lives" suggest an earnest, serious attitude about the issue of shopping.*

3. *The serious questions have to do with the negative effects of Americans' desire to consume: the continuation of the U.S. trade deficit; the effects of low wages on overseas workers; and the misuse of natural resources.*

4. *The author is making the point that we are so accustomed to abundance that we don't realize how amazing a superstore is; we find superstores boring.*

5. *The first paragraph introduces the idea that through most of history only kings and emperors had the "rare privilege" of owning more things than they needed. The last paragraph points out that now most people have as much economic power as "tyrants and autocrats."*

6. *Hine's writing style includes somewhat formal vocabulary:* material surfeit, misuse of the resources of a finite world, *such intangibles as* comfort and modernity. *But he incorporates his own experiences in an informal, friendly way. His tone is occasionally serious, but mostly playful, as he points out the absurdities of consumer culture. It's human nature to acquire things, he says, so we can't help ourselves even though we'll never be satisfied.*

English Language Support

Express Opinions Help students prepare for discussion:

- Have them work in pairs to record evidence that supports Hine's claims, including direct quotations as well as other details. Have pairs exchange their lists and comment on ideas that are the same or different.

- Have them state whether they agree or disagree with Hine and why. Remind them to be aware of how their word choices affect the audience. Point out that *certainly*, *must*, and *should* have a stronger impact than *probably*, *might*, and *could*.

Analyzing the Text
RI 1, RI 2, RI 4,
RI 5, RI 8, SL 1

Cite Text Evidence   Support your responses with evidence from the text.

1. **Interpret** A contrast between what is expected and what actually happens is called **irony.** Authors who use irony are often adding a humorous touch in expressing their ideas. In the first paragraph, what words and phrases does the author use to show an ironic tone?

2. **Analyze** An author may express more than one kind of tone in a piece of writing. Reread lines 26–32. What word would you use to describe the author's tone here? What words or phrases contribute to this tone?

3. **Summarize** Reread lines 65–78. How would you summarize the "serious questions" that the author refers to?

4. **Infer** Reread lines 85–90. What point is the author making when he says that we "yawn at a superstore"?

5. **Compare** Reread to compare the ideas in lines 1–13 with the ideas expressed in lines 91–97. What does an ordinary person in modern times now have in common with the kings and emperors of the past?

6. **Analyze** Based on this informational text, what are your impressions of the writing style of Thomas Hine? Explain how the author's word choice, tone, and voice support his style and express his ideas about consumerism.

PERFORMANCE TASK

Speaking Activity: Discussion
In small groups, prepare for a class discussion about the claims, or positions, that Thomas Hine shares about our consumer culture.

- First, identify a list of the claims.
- Consider the following questions: How well does the author support his claims? Are there any I would challenge? How does my own experience as a consumer connect to these claims?

- With your other group members, discuss responses to the questions.
- Participants who disagree with Hine's ideas can present their own views. Be sure to support points with evidence.
- For the class discussion, each small group might choose a reporter to present your responses to the questions.

Assign this performance task.

PERFORMANCE TASK
RI 8,
SL 1

Speaking Activity: Discussion Before students divide into small groups, you may want to guide the whole group in identifying the author's claims by

- asking students to note the author's beliefs about the reasons for and results of shopping
- emphasizing that a belief may be supported by facts and reasons, but it may also be disputed

Critical Vocabulary

L 4d, L 5b, L 6

superfluity   intangible   exhort   apathy

Practice and Apply Answer each question with *yes* or *no*. With your group, use examples and reasons to explain your answer.

1. Would you want a **superfluity** of luck?

2. Do **intangibles** bring success?

3. Can advertising **exhort**?

4. Is **apathy** like sympathy?

Vocabulary Strategy: Synonyms and Antonyms

Synonyms are words with similar meanings, such as *chilly* and *cool*. **Antonyms** are words with opposite meanings, such as *chilly* and *warm*. Identifying synonyms and antonyms can help readers understand the meanings of unfamiliar words. Note the synonyms in this sentence from "Always Wanting More":

> We aspire instead to such *intangibles* as comfort and modernity, *qualities* for which standards change so rapidly that the buying can never stop.

Intangibles are like qualities—both are things that cannot be seen or touched, but still have value.

Note the antonyms in this quotation:

> That such a store could provoke *apathy* instead of *amazement* is a perverse tribute to the plenitude of our consumer society . . .

Apathy is the opposite of amazement—apathy is a lack of interest.

Practice and Apply Identify the synonym or antonym for the bold word in each sentence. Use it to make a logical guess about the meaning of the bold word. Verify the meaning in a print or digital dictionary.

1. We live in a **finite** world where resources are limited.

2. The abundance of products makes us forget that we didn't always have such **plenitude.**

3. It is ironic that **austerity** should seem like luxury to wealthy consumers.

4. We were told not to **sacrifice**, as is usual in wartime, but to consume.

5. Individual freedoms have always threatened tyrants and **autocrats.**

PRACTICE & APPLY

Critical Vocabulary

L 4d, L 5b, L 6

Possible answers:

1. *Yes, if I had a superfluity of luck, I'd be extremely lucky.*

2. *Yes, intangibles like good health and intelligence can help a person achieve goals.*

3. *Yes, advertising exists to exhort consumers to buy.*

4. *No, apathy is not having any feelings, and sympathy is having kind, caring feelings for someone.*

Vocabulary Strategy: Synonyms and Antonyms

1. limited *(synonym); a finite world has limits.*

2. abundance *(synonym); plenitude is having plenty.*

3. luxury *(antonym); austerity means living with less.*

4. consume *(antonym); to sacrifice is to give up something.*

5. tyrants *(synonym); autocrats control the people they rule.*

 INTERACTIVE VOCABULARY TUTOR
WordSharp Context Clues: Synonym and Restatement
WordSharp Context Clues: Antonym and Contrast

English Language Support

Synonyms and Antonyms Tell students that a thesaurus is a language resource that will help them find synonyms for unfamiliar words. For each Practice and Apply item, allow students to work in pairs using a thesaurus to identify familiar synonyms for the boldfaced word. They may also use a dictionary to identify a familiar antonym for each boldfaced word. Have students list these synonyms and antonyms following their guesses for each item.

Strategies for Annotation   🖊 📖 *Annotate it!*

Vocabulary Strategy: Synonyms and Antonyms

L 4d, L 5b, L 6

Have students use their eBook annotation tools to identify synonyms and antonyms in lines 33–34:

- Underline the word *abstract*.
- Highlight in yellow a synonym for *abstract*.
- Highlight in green a word part that is an antonym for *abstract*.
- Note the meaning for *abstract*. Check your idea in a print or digital dictionary. Adjust the note as needed.

Our materialism is oddly abstract, a path toward an ideal. The things we acquire are less important than the

abstract: not concrete or not material

Language Conventions: Noun Clauses

L 1a

Use the example sentences in the chart on this page to clarify the varied functions of a noun:

- The noun *choices* is the simple subject because it tells what the sentence is about.
- A noun that is a direct object receives the action of a transitive verb. The noun *things* receives the action of the verb *purchase*.
- The noun *Mom* is the object of the preposition *for*.
- A predicate noun follows an intransitive verb. Intransitive verbs include all forms of *to be*. The noun *superstore* follows the verb *is*.

Have students offer similar explanations for the functions of the listed noun clauses.

After students read the strategy for distinguishing noun clauses from other subordinate clauses, have them apply the strategy—replacing the whole clause with the pronoun *someone* or *something*—to each noun clause in the chart.

Possible answers to Practice and Apply:

1. *"Why we always want more things"* functions as the subject of the sentence.

2. *"how we live today"* functions as a predicate noun.

3. *"what we already have"* functions as the object of the preposition *of*.

4. *"that more is better"* functions as the direct object of the verb *believe*.

5. *"where all this shopping is leading us"* functions as the object of the preposition *about*.

Language Conventions: Noun Clauses

L 1a

A **clause** is a group of words that has a subject and a predicate—the two main parts of a sentence. A **noun clause** is a subordinate clause that is used as a noun; it cannot stand alone and make sense. As the chart shows, the function of noun clauses can vary depending on the specific sentence.

Function	Noun	Noun Clause
subject	Shoppers' <u>choices</u> are amazing.	<u>That shoppers have so many choices</u> is amazing.
direct object	We purchase <u>things</u>.	We purchase <u>whatever we want</u>.
object of preposition	Buy the dress for <u>Mom</u>.	Buy the dress for <u>whoever can wear it</u>.
predicate noun	This place is a <u>superstore</u>.	This place is <u>where we shop</u>.

These pronouns may introduce noun clauses: *that, what, who, whoever, which, whose*. These conjunctions may introduce noun clauses: *how, when, where, why, whether*.

The listed pronouns and conjunctions also introduce other kinds of subordinate clauses. To identify a noun clause, think about how the clause functions in the sentence. Ask: Can I replace the whole clause with a noun or the pronoun *someone* or *something*? If the substituted word fits, you've identified a noun clause.

The noun clause is underlined in this quotation from "Always Wanting More":

> He expected <u>that people would always have more than they need and would never have all they might want</u>.

The noun clause functions as a direct object of the verb *expected*. The pronoun *something* could replace the clause and fit in the sentence: "He expected something."

Practice and Apply Identify the noun clause in each sentence. Tell how you know it is a noun clause.

1. Why we always want more things is an interesting question.

2. We see new products and buy them; this is how we live today.

3. Sometimes we buy more of what we already have.

4. Perhaps we believe that more is better, but we're never content.

5. It's time to step back and think about where all this shopping is leading us.

English Language Support

Use Nouns Discuss with students the explanations of noun clauses on this page. Answer any questions that they have. Then display the Practice and Apply sentences on the board.

- Read each of the Practice and Apply sentences aloud, replacing the noun clause with the word *something*. Work with students to identify the clause that has been replaced.

- Guide students to identify the noun clause in each sentence using these questions: (1) *What is an interesting question?* (2) *What is this?*

(3) *What do we buy more of?* (4) *What do we believe?* (5) *What do we need to think about?* Explain that the answers to these questions are the noun clauses.

- Have pairs of students discuss whether or not the noun clause in each sentence could be easily replaced by single nouns and what that tells them about the function or usefulness of noun clauses. Invite them to share an original sentence that contains a noun clause.

Determine Central Ideas and Details

RI 1,
RI 2,
RI 5

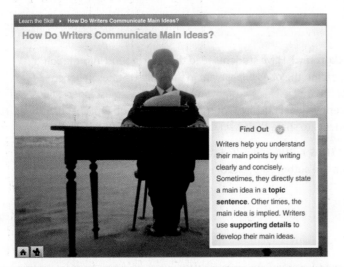

Learn the Skill ▸ How Do Writers Communicate Main Ideas?

How Do Writers Communicate Main Ideas?

Find Out

Writers help you understand their main points by writing clearly and concisely. Sometimes, they directly state a main idea in a **topic sentence**. Other times, the main idea is implied. Writers use **supporting details** to develop their main ideas.

TEACH

Tell students that to understand an informational text, readers look at its **structure.** Informational texts are often organized in paragraphs that present **main ideas** and **supporting details.**

With students, reread lines 14–32 of the selection. Then, ask these questions to help them identify the topic and supporting details:

- What is the topic of this paragraph—a few words that tell what it is about? *(consumption; a high standard of life)*
- What is a problem with superfluity "in material terms"? *(It's wasteful and "a misuse of the resources of a finite world.")*
- What is wrong with superfluity "in psychological terms"? *(It's a trap. "We work . . . to consume . . . we consume to compensate for the emptiness of our lives, including . . . work.")*

Consider the details and state a main-idea sentence that sums up the author's point about the topic. *(A high standard of life brings problems because people have too much but are never satisfied.)*

PRACTICE AND APPLY

Have students reread the third paragraph of "Always Wanting More," which begins on line 33. Have them work in pairs to write a topic, note supporting details, and state the main idea. *(Main idea: The act of acquiring, the freedom to choose, and the ability to forget what we have are more important than the actual things we buy. Details: China once only aspired to "Four Musts." That changed to "Eight Bigs" as it grew. Now, a super-store chain is opening there. When the Berlin Wall fell, people expressed "freedom" by shopping.)*

Determine Meaning

RI 1,
RI 4

RETEACH

Review the concept of *style* by displaying these two sentences and asking how they are alike and how they differ:

- Americans sure seem to love their gadgets, and they're willing to spend, spend, spend to own them.
- U.S. household expenditures on electronic devices have shown steady annual increases.

Point out that although the sentences' meanings are similar, the **style**—how each is written—differs. Help students to identify differences in **word choices.** Point out that the **voice** of the author is what the reader "hears." The voice in the first sentence is chatty and casual. In the second, the voice is more formal.

Tell students that a related feature of style is **tone.** The tone of a text reveals the author's attitude toward the topic and may be described with just one word, such as *concerned* or *lighthearted.*

Ask students for a word to describe the author's tone in this selection. *(Samples: humorous, sarcastic, concerned)*

LEVEL UP TUTORIALS Assign the following *Level Up* tutorial: **Author's Style**

Author's Style

TUTORIAL   PRACTICE

What Is Style?

What makes an abstract painting of a national monument so different from a realistic painting? How can you tell that a song on the radio is by Taylor Swift and not Alicia Keys?

The way a painter uses color and texture or the way a musician uses melody and rhythm is unique to each artist. Just as each artist or musician has an identifiable style, so does every individual writer.

Like artists and musicians, writers have their own unique styles.

1 2 3 4 5 6 7 8 9 10 ..17

INDEPENDENT READING

Provide another informational text in which the author's voice comes through. After reading, ask small groups to write one or two sentences about the author's style. Have students discuss supporting evidence and reasons for their statements.

Labels and Illusions

Essay by Lourdes Barranco

Why This Text

Students often have difficulty with a text that requires them to make inferences and identify and interpret elements of a writer's style. This essay is such a text. With the help of the close-reading questions, students will interpret irony, make inferences based on text evidence, and analyze the author's word choice and tone. The results of their close reading will help students develop a thorough understanding of what the text says both explicitly and implicitly.

Background Have students read the background information describing the obesity problem in the United States. Tell them that this article examines how marketing strategies, especially deceptive labeling, have contributed to the problem. Encourage students to share their own examples of deceptive labeling.

SETTING A PURPOSE Tell students to pay close attention to what the author suggests or implies as well as what she says directly.

Standards Support

- cite multiple pieces of textual evidence
- make inferences
- determine the central idea of a text
- determine the meanings of words and phrases as they are used in the text
- analyze the impact of a specific word choice on meaning and tone

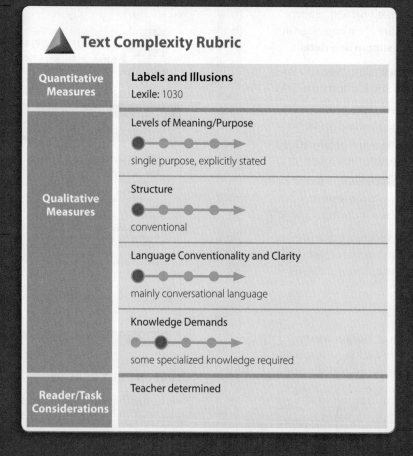

Text Complexity Rubric

Quantitative Measures

Labels and Illusions
Lexile: 1030

Qualitative Measures

Levels of Meaning/Purpose

single purpose, explicitly stated

Structure

conventional

Language Conventionality and Clarity

mainly conversational language

Knowledge Demands

some specialized knowledge required

Reader/Task Considerations

Teacher determined

Strategies for CLOSE READING

Make Inferences

Students should read the essay carefully, thinking about what the author is implying as well as what she says directly. Close-reading questions will help students collect and cite text evidence to support their inferences. As they read, students should summarize their inferences in the margin.

WHEN STUDENTS STRUGGLE . . .

To help students make inferences, have them work in small groups to fill out a chart like the one shown below.

CITE TEXT EVIDENCE For practice making inferences, ask students to make inferences based on the text evidence below.

Text from the Article	Inferences
"The labeling of these food and drink items seems whimsical, if not completely inaccurate." (lines 16–17)	"Whimsical" implies that the labels are not serious, let alone accurate.
"To make the problem worse, marketers working in the clothing industry have created strategies for making us think we are thinner than we actually are." (lines 37–39)	Marketers are more interested in selling products than in labeling them accurately.

Background *Obesity is a leading cause of preventable death in America. Between the 1980s and the 2000s, childhood obesity rates tripled in the United States. This increase can be directly attributed to an increase in snacking and portion sizes and a decrease in physical activity. Children who are obese are significantly more likely to be obese as adults. A nationwide initiative to combat obesity through education and a focus on increasing physical activity may hold the key to battling this epidemic.*

Labels and Illusions

Essay by Lourdes Barranco

CLOSE READ
Notes

1. **READ ▶** As you read lines 1–17, begin to cite text evidence.
- Underline phrases that describe what marketers do.
- In the margin, make an inference about the effect of certain marketing strategies on obesity.

A Let's face it, these days we all are worried about the expanding size of American waistlines. Some of us worry about our own waistlines; others are concerned with the rise in obesity among Americans in general. One thing we should examine more closely is how marketers—the people who **devise** strategies to make us buy certain products—are contributing to the rise of obesity in our country.

devise:
come up with

B Marketers have developed some fanciful food labeling strategies to make us think we are consuming less food, when in fact we are not.
10 For example, you might order a medium soft drink in a fast food restaurant (seemingly a wise move if you're trying to eat less). You later discover that the same size soft drink has magically transformed itself into a "large" drink in another restaurant. Which size soda did you actually drink: a medium or a large? Perhaps you ask for a small order of french fries in a restaurant, and when you get it, it seems huge. The labeling of these food and drink items seems whimsical, if not completely inaccurate. What's going on?

Some marketing strategies may contribute to obesity through misleading labeling.

83

1. **READ AND CITE TEXT EVIDENCE** Remind students that they have underlined phrases that describe what marketers do.

A **ASK STUDENTS** to use details and phrases in lines 1–17 to infer the effects of some marketing strategies. *Possible response: Marketing strategies contribute to obesity by making us think we are eating less than we actually are.*

Critical Vocabulary: devise (line 5) Have students share their definitions of *devise*. Ask them when they have devised a plan or a solution to a problem. *Answers will vary Possible response: getting a friend to a surprise birthday party.*

For those of us trying to eat reasonable portions, an additional problem can arise from our own inability to judge the size of our meals. Consider the following optical illusion, first documented in 1875: the Delboeuf [del bœf] effect. Start with two dots of equal size. Then surround one dot with a large circle and the other with a small circle. Guess what happens—suddenly the second dot, the one surrounded by the small circle, looks much larger than the first dot, even though they are the same size.

What does this have to do with the amount of food we eat? Koert van Ittersum, a professor of marketing at Georgia Tech, and Brian Wansink, director of the Food and Brand Lab at Cornell, found out. They performed a series of experiments to measure the effect of the Delboeuf illusion on people's perception of portion size. They served two groups of people the same size portion but on different-size plates. People who were served on larger plates thought that they had been served a small portion. People served on smaller plates thought that they had been served a large portion. The research showed that

Both studies show that the size of the surrounding circle affects the perception of the size of what is in it.

our eyes can deceive us about the amount of food we're actually eating.

To make the problem worse, marketers working in the clothing industry have created strategies for making us think that we are thinner than we actually are. A common dilemma faced by people of all ages is trying to determine which size of an article of clothing fits them. Their confusion is understandable. Depending on the store, a pair of slacks labeled size 8, 6, or 4 might fit the same woman. A sweater labeled extra large or medium might fit a large man.

What causes these differences? The answer is "vanity sizing," the practice of labeling clothes as smaller sizes than they really are. In other words, a dress that is really a size 8 may be labeled a size 2. By using vanity sizing, clothing manufacturers flatter people into thinking that they are not as large as they may actually be. Apparently, this encourages people to purchase the items of clothing. Remember, the marketers who devise these labels are people who want you to buy their company's products.

---

2. **◀ REREAD** Reread lines 8–17. A contrast between what is expected and what actually occurs is called *irony*. The use of irony can create strong effects, including humor. What words and phrases add an ironic tone to this paragraph?

The words "fanciful" and "whimsical" and the phrase "magically transformed itself" add an ironic tone to the paragraph. The words "fanciful" and "whimsical" add a slightly humorous tone to the paragraph because food labels aren't usually thought of as having a personality. When we realize how many "strategies" have been put into these simple labels and the harmful effects they have, these labels are no longer "fanciful."

---

3. **READ ▶** As you read lines 18–36, continue to cite textual evidence.
- Underline the results of each experiment.
- In the margin, explain how the results of the Delboeuf effect compare to those of the van Ittersum/Wansink experiment.

4. **◀ REREAD** Reread lines 18–36. State the main idea of this section and explain how both experiments support it.

The Delboeuf effect provides insight into why people in the van Ittersum/Wansink experiment were deceived into thinking they had more or less food, depending on the size of the plate. Both the Delboeuf effect and the van Ittersum/Wansink experiment support the main idea of this section, "The research showed that our eyes can deceive us about the amount of food we're actually eating."

5. **READ ▶** As you read lines 37–58, continue to cite textual evidence.
- Underline phrases that suggest that "vanity sizing" makes people feel good.
- Circle the conclusion that sums up the central idea of this essay.
- In the margin, restate what consumers can do to counteract the influence of marketers.

---

2. **REREAD AND CITE TEXT EVIDENCE** Remind students that irony occurs when the author's meaning is the opposite of what he or she actually says.

B **ASK STUDENTS** to find a phrase in lines 8–17 in which the author means the opposite of what she actually says. *magically transformed (line 12)*

3. **READ AND CITE TEXT EVIDENCE**

C **ASK STUDENTS** to explain how the results of the van Ittersum/Wansink experiment show that the Delboeuf effect does influence people's perception of how much they are eating. *The van Ittersum/Wansink experiment proves that the way food is presented affects our perception of how much we are eating.*

FOR ELL STUDENTS Explain that the word *reasonable* can mean "capable of thinking clearly," but in this context it means "conforming with common sense."

4. **REREAD AND CITE TEXT EVIDENCE** Encourage students to describe the Delboeuf effect and to compare that description with the results of the van Ittersum/Wansink experiment.

D **ASK STUDENTS** to state the main idea of each paragraph on page 84. *The Delboeuf effect shows that factors affect how people perceive the size of their meals. The van Ittersum/Wansink experiment supported this claim.*

5. **READ AND CITE TEXT EVIDENCE** Have students identify any phrases that help them understand what *vanity sizing* means.

E **ASK STUDENTS** to explain the concept of "vanity sizing" and why it might be useful to clothing manufacturers. *Vanity sizing is the practice of labeling larger articles of clothing with smaller sizes. It flatters people by making them think that they are not as large as they really are and, thereby, increases sales.*

Consumers
should be
suspicious of
labels and use
common sense.

F   What can consumers do? First, we should ignore the labels "small," "medium," and "large" as they apply to food and drink. We're probably buying a lot more than we need. We should also be skeptical of clothing labels. We may not be as trim and physically fit as the label would lead us to believe. To stay healthy and avoid obesity, we must rely on our own good sense and on our knowledge of what characterizes a healthy person.

6. **◄ REREAD**   Reread lines 52–58. An author may use more than one kind of tone in an essay. What word would you use to describe the author's tone in this paragraph? What words and phrases reflect this tone?

The author's tone in this paragraph is serious. She tells readers to be "skeptical" or even to "ignore" labels, and recommends that readers rely on their "knowledge" of what being healthy means and their "own good sense" instead of being misled by labels.

SHORT RESPONSE

Cite Text Evidence   Summarize the central idea of this essay and the most effective information the author includes to support it. **Cite text evidence** and relevant reading notes in your response.

The author gives factual information to support her position that marketers "devise strategies to make us buy certain products." By showing us the way the Delboeuf effect works and how easily "our eyes can deceive us about the amount of food we're actually eating," it's easy to see how easily consumers are manipulated. By using phrases such as "devise strategies" to describe what marketers do, and "flattered" and "fooled" to describe how consumers are manipulated, the argument that obesity and marketing are linked is quite persuasive.

86

6.   **REREAD AND CITE TEXT EVIDENCE**   Tell students that some adjectives that may describe tone are *playful, sarcastic, serious, cheerful,* and *reverent.*

F   **ASK STUDENTS** to find words or phrases that suggest the author's tone. *Possible responses:* should ignore, be skeptical, to stay healthy, we must, our own good sense.

FOR ELL STUDENTS   Point out to Spanish-speaking students that *skeptical* has a cognate, *escéptico.*

SHORT RESPONSE

Cite Text Evidence   Students' responses will vary, but they should cite evidence from the text to support their answers. They should:

- summarize the central idea of the essay.
- cite the author's most convincing information.
- cite specific evidence from the text to support their ideas.

TO CHALLENGE STUDENTS . . .

To extend students' understanding of this essay, have them research the practice of vanity sizing.

ASK STUDENTS to research at least five articles on the subject and summarize their findings in an essay. Encourage them to include charts, graphs, and other visual representations. Their essays should address:

- what vanity sizing is.
- the purpose of vanity sizing.
- why vanity sizing is appealing to some people.
- the extent to which markets target vanity sizing to specific groups.
- why some retailers and dress designers argue that vanity sizing is a myth.
- why vanity sizing is or is not an effective marketing strategy.

DIG DEEPER

With the class, return to the Short Response question. Have students share and discuss their answers.

ASK STUDENTS to note how their responses are alike and how they are different.

- Have students discuss in more depth how inaccurate labeling is linked to the problem of obesity in the United States.
- Summarize the strategies marketers use to make us think that we are eating less than we actually are.
- Ask students to give personal examples that illustrate their experience of faulty labeling or labeling inconsistencies.
- Have students discuss what they can infer the author thinks of marketers who use these strategies and of us if we fall for these strategies.

ASK STUDENTS to return to their response to the Short Response question and revise it based on their discussion.

COMPARE TEXTS

Dump

Poem by X. J. Kennedy

How Things Work

Poem by Gary Soto

Why These Texts?

An understanding of and appreciation for poetry can enhance students' experiences with other related forms, including the lyrics in popular music. This lesson focuses on the poetic form in two poems and how theme and irony contribute to a poem's meaning.

▶ **View It!**

Professional Development Podcast:
Text-Dependent Analysis

Key Learning Objective: The student will be able to analyze a poem's form and to identify theme and irony.

RL 1 Cite textual evidence.
RL 2 Determine theme.
RL 4 Determine the meanings of words and phrases; analyze the impact of rhymes and other repetitions of sounds on a verse or stanza of a poem.
RL 5 Analyze how a poem's form contributes to its meaning.
W 2 Write informative/explanatory texts.
W 4 Produce clear and coherent writing.
W 10 Write routinely over extended time frames.

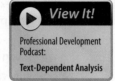

Text Complexity Rubric

	Dump	How Things Work
Quantitative Measures	**Dump** Lexile: N/A	**How Things Work** Lexile: N/A
Qualitative Measures	Levels of Meaning/Purpose — single level of complex meaning	Levels of Meaning/Purpose — single level of complex meaning
	Structure — regular stanzas with some liberties taken	Structure — free verse, no particular patterns
	Language Conventionality and Clarity — some figurative language	Language Conventionality and Clarity — contextual ambiguous language
	Knowledge Demands — moderately complex theme	Knowledge Demands — moderately complex theme
Reader/Task Considerations	• Teacher determined • Vary by individual reader and type of text • See the Text X-Ray for suggested Reader/Task Considerations.	

English Language Support

Before teaching, use the Text X-Ray for an overview of the text's complexity. The Text X-Ray and the supports and scaffolds in the Teacher's Edition will help you guide students of different skill levels.

Meaning Making

Language Development

Effective Expression

Content Knowledge

Foundational Skills

Text Complexity: Qualitative Measures

▲ Levels of Meaning/Purpose

Help students determine the themes of poems.

- Teacher's Edition side notes, pp. 242, 243, 247
- English Language Support, p. 241
- Strategies for Annotation, p. 247
- Determine Theme, p. 247

To reteach how to determine theme, see

- Determine Theme, p. 248a

 Use It! **Level Up Tutorial:** Theme

ZOOM IN ON **DETERMINING THEME** Explain that analyzing words and phrases can reveal a work's **theme,** or message. Display stanza 3 from "Dump." Discuss these questions:

- Think about "discarded hopes." What did the dump objects once mean to the people who owned them? *(The items were meant to fulfill people's dreams and make them happy.)*
- What words and phrases in the stanza show that these objects could not live up to their promise? *("hard facts," "rout," "jerked inside-out")*
- Based on the text details, what does the dump **symbolize,** or stand for? *(Possible response: a place to get rid of the things that remind a person of his or her failure to achieve happiness)*

▲ Structure

Help students compare and contrast the form and other elements of two poems.

- Teacher's Edition side notes, pp. 242, 243, 244, 245, 246, 247
- English Language Support, p. 248
- When Students Struggle, pp. 243, 245
- Strategies for Annotation, pp. 244, 246
- Analyze Poetry: Form, pp. 244, 246
- Compare Forms in Poetry, p. 247

To reteach how to compare forms in poetry, see

- Compare Forms in Poetry, p. 248a

 Use It! **Level Up Tutorials:** Rhythm, Elements of Poetry

ZOOM IN ON **COMPARING FORMS** Explain that a poem's form may be created through the use of **rhythm, end rhyme,** and **stanza** or **sentence length.**

- Assign small mixed-ability groups one of the poems. Group members should take turns reading the poem aloud while listening students take notes on what they hear, including rhyming words, a steady rhythm or beat, the use of stanzas, and long or short sentences.
- Ask each group to summarize the structure of their assigned poem and then share their findings with the class.
- Record key ideas from the groups on the board and use them to contrast the forms of the two poems.

▲ Language Conventionality and Clarity

Teach unfamiliar vocabulary in context.

- Applying Academic Vocabulary, p. 242

Support students' analysis of the poems through their reading, discussion, and writing.

- Teacher's Edition side notes, p. 245
- English Language Support, pp. 243, 248
- Performance Task, p. 248

ZOOM IN ON **DEFINING MULTIPLE-MEANING WORDS** Tell students that some words in "Dump" have more than one definition. The poet wants readers to consider these multiple meanings in order to understand his poem on multiple levels. Display these words: *brink* (line 1), *petrified* (line 18), *lightened* (line 22).

- Have pairs use a dictionary to find all relevant meanings of each word. *(brink: the edge of a deep slope, or the point at which something begins; petrified: dead and frozen in position, or paralyzed with fear; lightened: lit up with light, or made less heavy, or relieved of cares or worries)*
- As a class, discuss which meaning fits the literal sense of the poem. Then analyze how the other definitions work to change and enrich the meaning of the line.

▲ Knowledge Demands

Support English learners in understanding the poems' context.

- Teacher's Edition Background note, p. 241
- Content-Area Connection, p. 241

ZOOM IN ON **BUILDING BACKGROUND** Share this information about both poets.

- X. J. Kennedy's poems are praised for their vibrant use of rhyme and rhythm and captivating subjects. Kennedy believes strongly that poetic form is significant and worth readers' attention.
- Gary Soto's advice to aspiring poets is to read as much as they can, starting with modern works and moving back to the classics. He credits his high school reading as the catalyst for his career choice.

Suggested Reader/Task Considerations

Consider the following before assigning these poems.

- Will students be interested in the content of these poems?
- Do students have enough knowledge of the elements of poetry to understand the analysis of form?

ZOOM IN ON **SUPPORTING COMPREHENSION**

- Spark students' interest by discussing what ideas they think a poem entitled "Dump" will explore. Then read aloud the first sentence of "How Things Work": "Today it's going to cost us twenty dollars / To live." Ask students to predict the direction of this poem as well.
- Preteach terms related to the structure of these poems, such as *meter, rhythm, rhyme scheme,* and *free verse.* Encourage students to draw on their prior knowledge to add details to each definition.

TEACH

CLOSE READ

Background Have students read the background and information about the poets. Explain that students are going to read two poems that reflect on people's everyday experiences and relationships with material things. The first poem commemorates the dump, a place where people discard old, used, broken, or unwanted items. The second poem shares a perception about people's everyday spending and its effects on others' ability to spend.

SETTING A PURPOSE Direct students to use the Setting a Purpose prompt about our consumer society to focus their reading. Remind students to write down questions they have as they read.

Background *Writers and poets alike often use their writing to make statements about important topics like consumerism. X. J. Kennedy and Gary Soto each examine our consumer society in their respective poems "Dump" and "How Things Work."*

DUMP

Poem by X. J. Kennedy

How Things Work

Poem by Gary Soto

(bg) ©Don Farrall/Getty Images; (tl) ©Ulrich Mueller/Shutterstock; (tr) ©archideaphoto/Shutterstock; (tc) ©canikiligi/Shutterstock; (bc) ©X. J. Kennedy; (b) ©The Associated Press/AP Images

X. J. Kennedy (b. 1929) *has won many awards for his poetry collections, including the Robert Frost Medal. Kennedy has published numerous books for young people, including collections of poetry and novels. Traditional in form, Kennedy's poems often include narrative, wit, and humor, but he also explores themes about serious topics, such as growing up and loss.*

Gary Soto (b. 1952) *never dreamed about writing as a child. But after reading a book of poetry in college, he began to write his own poems and dedicated himself to the craft. While Soto has written poetry and novels for adults, he is probably best known as a writer for young adults and children. From his point of view, he is writing about the feelings and experiences of most American kids.*

SETTING A PURPOSE As you read, think about what each poet is saying about our consumer society and how that society works.

CONTENT-AREA CONNECTION

Science/Ecology Tell students that dumps are open spaces filled with garbage, usually away from areas where people live. Dumps create many problems, however: they are at risk of catching on fire, they pollute the soil and groundwater, and they attract rodents and insects. Although people may think *landfill* is just another name for *dump*, landfills are more carefully managed and environmentally friendly.

Activity Have students work in pairs to research the science and architecture of landfills. Ask them to make a handout explaining how a landfill works and the way it is constructed. Encourage them to include other facts that they think are important to know. Have pairs then share their handouts in small groups and discuss what their research has helped them to realize about the problem of waste in America.

Analyze Poetry:
Form (LINES 1–20)

RL 1,
RL 4,
RL 5

Explain to students that the **form** of a poem is its arrangement of words and lines on the page. A poem's form gives it rhythm and emphasizes meaning. Explain that **traditional** forms of poetry have a fixed set of rules for

- the number of lines the poem has
- how the lines are divided into **stanzas,** or groups
- the pattern of end rhymes, called **rhyme scheme**
- the pattern of stressed and unstressed syllables, called **meter,** with each unit of meter called a **foot**

A **CITE TEXT EVIDENCE** Have students reread lines 1–20 aloud. Ask students to cite evidence that reveals whether or not the poem has a traditional form. (*The poem has a traditional form. It has a fixed rhyme scheme, such as the end rhyming words* pour / store *and* find / mind *in the first stanza. Each stanza has a fixed number of four lines. In general, it has a fairly regular meter, with the second syllable in each foot being stressed:* Here **lie** dis**card**ed **hopes.** *The word* over *is likely pronounced as one syllable: o'er.*)

Determine the Meanings of Words and Phrases

RL 4

(LINES 13–14)

Explain to students that poets often use irony as a way to express disapproval of something or to emphasize a point. **Irony** is a contrast, or difference, between what is expected to happen and what actually happens.

B **CITE TEXT EVIDENCE** Ask students to reread lines 13–14 and identify evidence of the irony in these lines. How is this an example of irony? (*"Roof shingles bought on sale / That rotted on their roof" is ironic because the speaker probably thought he or she was saving money but then lost that money when the shingles rotted and had to be thrown out.*)

Dump
by X. J. Kennedy

A The brink over which we pour
Odd items we can't find
Enough cubic inches to store
In house, in mind,

5 Is come to by a clamber
Up steep unsteady heights
Of beds without a dreamer
And lamps that no hand lights.

Here lie discarded hopes
10 That hard facts had to rout:
Umbrellas—naked spokes
By wind jerked inside-out,

Roof shingles bought on sale **B**
That rotted on their roof,
15 Paintings eternally stale
That, hung, remained aloof,

Pink dolls with foreheads crushed,
Eyes petrified in sleep.
We cast off with a crash
20 What gives us pain to keep.

APPLYING ACADEMIC VOCABULARY

attitude	consume

THINK-PAIR-SHARE Have students turn to a partner to discuss the following questions. Guide students to include the academic vocabulary words *attitude* and *consume* in their responses. Ask volunteers to share their responses with the class.

- What is the speaker's **attitude** in "Dump" about how people **consume** things?
- Is the speaker's **attitude** in "How Things Work" the same or different?

As we turn now to return
To our lightened living room,
The acrid smell of trash
Arises like perfume.

25 Maneuvering steep stairs
Of bedsprings to our car,
We stumble on homecanned pears
Grown poisonous in their jar

And nearly gash an ankle
30 Against a shard of glass.
Our emptiness may rankle,[1]
But soon it too will pass.

---
[1] **rankle:** to cause constant irritation.

Dump **243**

Analyze Poetry: Form (LINES 25–28)

RL 1,
RL 5

Explain to students that an iamb is a metrical foot made up of an unstressed syllable followed by a stressed syllable. This creates the rhythm of duh-DAH, duh-DAH. Tell students that poets may vary the rhythm to stress ideas.

C CITE TEXT EVIDENCE Ask students to reread lines 25–28 and cite an example of a break in the iambic rhythm. Have them explain how it affects the meaning of the poem. *(The rhythm of "homecanned pears" and "in their jar" calls for each syllable to be stressed rather than every other syllable, breaking the pattern and emphasizing how familiar, comforting items made at "home" have now grown toxic.)*

Determine Meanings of Words and Phrases (LINES 29–32)

RL 1,
RL 4

Explain to students that the **tone** of a poem expresses the speaker's attitude, or how he or she feels toward a subject. Tell students that the tone of a poem can have a powerful impact on meaning.

D CITE TEXT EVIDENCE Ask students to reread the last stanza, lines 29–32. Have students identify words and phrases that help the reader understand how the speaker feels. *(Lines 31 and 32 convey a tone of sarcasm about how quickly our feeling of loss of material things passes, implying that we move on to consume more stuff that we'll end up throwing away, too.)*

WHEN STUDENTS STRUGGLE . . .

Demonstrate meter by reading the poem aloud, clapping on stressed syllables. (Note that in the first line, *over* is pronounced as one unstressed syllable, as "o'er.") Read aloud each stanza, clapping the beat. Note sections such as "homecanned pears" where the rhythm temporarily changes.

ASK STUDENTS to reread a stanza on their own, clapping out the beats to identify the rhythm.

 LEVEL UP TUTORIALS For additional support, assign the following *Level Up* tutorial: **Rhythm.**

English Language Support

Culturally Responsive Instruction Encourage a class discussion to help students connect to the poem's topic.

ASK STUDENTS to list the objects that are found in this dump. What other items would be included in a landfill today that are not mentioned in the poem? Have them think about what they might take to a dump or landfill. How do they think they would feel after getting rid of these things? Why?

Analyze Poetry: Form

RL 5

Review the features of a traditional poem. Have students describe the rhyme scheme and meter of "Dump." Discuss how these contribute to the rhythm, meaning, and mood of the poem. *(The iambic meter creates a singsong rhythm, giving the poem a familiar nursery-rhyme feeling, which contrasts with the sad images of "discarded hopes" and "Eyes petrified in sleep." This creates an ironic, biting tone that shows that the poet regrets the way we toss out so much of the things that are supposed to give life meaning.)*

Analyzing the Text

RL 1,
RL 4,
RL 5

Possible answers:

1. *There are eight stanzas with four lines each. This form gives the poem a quick pace and regular chanting rhythm, thus creating a light contrast to the darker ideas of loss and emptiness throughout the poem.*

2. *Roof shingles bought on sale*

   That rotted on their roof,

   Paintings eternally stale

   That, hung, remained aloof,

3. *Stanzas 2, 5, and 6 break from the* abab *rhyme scheme, disrupting the reader and creating a feeling that a visit to the dump can be unsettling and jarring.*

4. *The poem's form creates its rhythm and emphasizes the meaning of certain words, contributing to the irony that familiar items of consumer comfort have turned dangerous and toxic in the dump.*

🖉 🗒 **eBook** *Annotate It!*

Analyze Poetry: Form

RL 5

The **form** of a poem is its structure, including the arrangement of words and lines. The poem "Dump" has a **fixed,** or **traditional, form** because it follows fixed rules:

- The poem is divided into **stanzas** that include the same number of lines.
- The poem has a pattern of end rhymes, called a **rhyme scheme.** A rhyme scheme is noted by assigning a letter of the alphabet, beginning with *a*, to each line. Lines that rhyme are given the same letter. For example, in the first stanza, the end words are *pour, find, store,* and *mind.* The stanza's rhyme scheme is *abab.*

The **meter** of a poem is the regular pattern of stressed and unstressed syllables. Each **foot,** or unit of meter, includes one stressed syllable. "Dump" has these characteristics of meter:

- Most lines have the same number of feet.
- Each metrical foot is the kind called an iamb—an unstressed syllable followed by a stressed syllable: duh-DAH, duh-DAH.

Because a meter that follows a rigid pattern can sound as singsong as a nursery rhyme, poets often choose to work more loosely with meter. Listen for the meter in stanza 3:

> Here lie discarded hopes
> That hard facts had to rout:
> Umbrellas—naked spokes
> By wind jerked inside-out,

Analyzing the Text

RL 1, RL 4, RL 5

Cite Text Evidence Support your responses with evidence from the text.

1. **Identify Patterns** How many stanzas does the poem have? How many lines are in each stanza? Why might the poet have chosen to organize the poem this way?

2. **Identify Patterns** Choose and copy a stanza from the poem. Use stress marks to identify the stressed syllables in each line of the stanza.

3. **Analyze** Which stanzas vary from the *abab* rhyme scheme? What impact does this variation have on the poem's meaning?

4. **Analyze** How does the poem's form contribute to its meaning?

Strategies for Annotation   🖉 🗒 *Annotate it!*

Analyze Poetry: Form

RL 1,
RL 5

Have students use their eBook annotation tools to identify the rhyme scheme in "Dump." Ask students to do the following:

- Highlight the words at the end of each line to show the rhyme scheme, using a different color for each rhyming pair.
- Review your highlights. On a note, use the letters *a* and *b* to indicate the rhyme scheme.
- Continue in the same way for the remaining stanzas.

> The brink over which we pour
>
> Odd items we can't find
>
> Enough cubic inches to store
>
> In house, in mind,
>
> (lines 1–4)

Rhyme scheme, first stanza: *abab*

Analyze Poetry:
RL 1,
RL 5

Form (LINES 1–9)

Review with students that the form of a poem is the way in which the words and lines are arranged on the page, and that traditional forms follow fixed rules for number of lines, rhyme scheme, and meter. Then, explain that other forms of poems do not have these rules. These poems are called **free verse**. Free verse often sounds like everyday conversational speech. Remind students that analyzing the lines of a poem can help them identify its form.

 CITE TEXT EVIDENCE Ask students to reread lines 1–9 and cite examples from the text that show it is written in free verse. (*The lines of the poem are different lengths, and there is no rhyme scheme. None of the end words in any of the lines rhyme, and sentences often end in mid-line. For example,* Today it's going to cost us twenty dollars / To live. Five for a softball. Four for a book.) Ask students to point to examples of incomplete sentences—or fragments—and explain how these affect the poem. (*Sentence fragments such as "Five for a softball" and "Four for a book" give the poem a conversational tone. When people speak to each other, they often speak in fragments as ideas come to mind.*)

FOR STANDARD ENGLISH LEARNERS

Pronunciation Display lines 2 and 5. Highlight these words: *softball, task, left.*

- Pronounce each word, emphasizing the final consonant in these clusters (*ft, sk, ft*). Have students repeat the words after you several times.

- Then say the lines, taking similar care to make the last consonants audible. Ask students to repeat the lines to a partner. Circulate to check accuracy of pronunciation.

COLLABORATIVE DISCUSSION Have students work initially with a partner to analyze the poems and answer the questions. Then, have pairs join the larger group to discuss their ideas.

ASK STUDENTS to share any questions they generated in the course of reading and discussing the poems.

How Things Work
by Gary Soto

Today it's going to cost us twenty dollars
To live. Five for a softball. Four for a book,
A handful of ones for coffee and two sweet rolls,
Bus fare, rosin[1] for your mother's violin.
5   We're completing our task. The tip I left
For the waitress filters down
Like rain, wetting the new roots of a child
Perhaps, a belligerent cat that won't let go
Of a balled sock until there's chicken to eat.
10   As far as I can tell, daughter, it works like this:
You buy bread from a grocery, a bag of apples
From a fruit stand, and what coins
Are passed on helps others buy pencils, glue,
Tickets to a movie in which laughter
15   Is thrown into their faces.
If we buy a goldfish, someone tries on a hat.
If we buy crayons, someone walks home with a broom.
A tip, a small purchase here and there,
And things just keep going. I guess.

COLLABORATIVE DISCUSSION Both poems have speakers who share thoughts about their surroundings or situations. Which speaker expresses stronger reactions to the situation? What degree of control does either speaker appear to have over what they describe? Discuss your responses with other group members.

---

[1] **rosin** (rŏz´ĭn): a sticky substance that comes from tree sap and is used to increase sliding friction on certain stringed instruments' bows.

WHEN STUDENTS STRUGGLE . . .

Point out that "How Things Work" has a much different form than "Dump." Reread the first eight lines of each poem aloud with students. Emphasize the predictable rhythm and rhyme scheme of "Dump" and the unpredictable, almost stop-and-go flow of ideas in "How Things Work." Then, have students work with partners to take turns rereading the sections of each poem to each other.

ASK STUDENTS to describe how they feel after reading and listening to each poem.

 LEVEL UP TUTORIALS For additional support, assign the following *Level Up* tutorial: **Elements of Poetry.**

Analyze Poetry: Form
RL 5

Review the information about free verse, and have students discuss their answers to the questions.

(Possible answers:

- *The poet expresses the idea that one person's spending allows another to spend. Free verse allows him to explain this in a simple, clear way.*
- *The varying line lengths, sentence fragments, and random punctuation give the poem its form. This seems more like regular conversation.)*

Analyzing the Text
RL 1, RL 4, RL 5

Possible answers:

1. *The reader would pause after the first line and then emphasize "To live," as if the speaker is startled by the realization that money is a requirement "to live."*

2. *The tip for the waitress is compared to rain; it "filters down like rain, wetting the new roots of a child." The figurative comparison suggests that the waitress will use the money for things her child needs and that money "passed on" nourishes other things.*

3. *The reader should pause briefly after each comma, a bit longer after the period, and then stress "I guess" to show the speaker's doubt about "how things work."*

4. *The lines are different lengths, containing many phrases to give it rhythm and emphasize the meaning that one person's spending enables another to spend.*

5. *The form creates a feeling of thoughts tumbling out of the speaker's mind, as if the speaker is figuring out "how things work" and explaining it at the same time.*

Analyze Poetry: Form
RL 5

A poem's **form** is its structure and the way its words and lines are arranged. Some forms are also defined by poetic devices, such as rhyme, rhythm, and meter. A poem's form is closely linked to its meaning, which makes the poem's form important to its message.

The poem "How Things Work" is written in a form called **free verse,** which has natural rhythms rather than regular patterns of rhyme, rhythm, meter, or line length. A poet may choose free verse to make the language similar to natural speech.

Still, the sounds of words and the rhythms within lines matter in free verse. The poet has made choices about where to break lines, how to punctuate each line, and which words and phrases will best convey particular sound-meaning connections.

To analyze free verse, ask questions such as the following:
- What ideas is the poet expressing? How does the use of free verse support those ideas?
- What rhythms do the line lengths and the punctuation in the poem create? How do these poetic devices add to my understanding of the poem?

Analyzing the Text
RL 1, RL 4, RL 5

Cite Text Evidence   Support your responses with evidence from the text.

1. **Interpret** Reread the first sentence of the poem in lines 1–2. Where would you pause, and what words would you stress to give that sentence meaning and feeling?

2. **Interpret** In lines 5–7, what does the speaker compare to rain, and what does that comparison help readers picture?

3. **Interpret** Reread the last two lines of "How Things Work." Where might be the best places to pause? What words should you stress to help convey the poem's meaning?

4. **Analyze** Review lines 14–19 and examine how the poet arranges the words and lines. Describe the variations in line lengths. What is the poet trying to explain, and how does the form support those ideas?

5. **Analyze** How does the poem's form contribute to its meaning?

Strategies for Annotation   Annotate it!

Analyze Poetry: Form
RL 1, RL 5

Share these strategies for guided or independent analysis:
- Highlight in yellow words that are emphasized in each line.
- On a note, write how the emphasis on these words affects rhythm and meaning.

Today it's going to cost us twenty dollars

To live. Five for a softball. Four for a book,

A handful of ones for coffee and two sweet rolls,

Bus fare, rosin for your mother's violin.

> Rhythm stops and starts like real thoughts. The emphasized words show the speaker is surprised and maybe appalled by how much life costs.

Determine Theme

RL 2, RL 4

Poems like "Dump" and "How Things Work" often have a **theme,** or a lesson about life or human nature that the poet shares with the reader. A theme usually is developed over the course of a poem, rather than stated directly at the beginning or end. Readers can infer a poem's theme by thinking about the title, the imagery, the form, and the language the poet uses to describe the subject.

Poets might give clues about the poem's theme through the **tone,** or the speaker's attitude toward the subject. One way they may convey the tone is through the use of **irony,** or the use of language to say the opposite of what is meant.

How can you tell that the speaker in "Dump" is using an ironic tone in these lines?

> **The acrid smell of trash**
> **Arises like perfume.**

Pay attention to text details as you dig deeper into the poems. Use text clues to determine the themes in each poem and to analyze how those themes are developed through the tones.

Compare Forms in Poetry

RL 2, RL 5

You have read two poems on a shared subject—the things we own. Each poet describes an everyday activity and reflects on it in a unique way. The poem's form is the way the poet organizes ideas, including the arrangement of words and lines.

To compare the forms of these poems, analyze the structure that each poet uses. Use a chart like this to help you make comparisons between the two poems.

Elements to Think About	"Dump"	"How Things Work"
form of poem		
setting		
lines and stanzas		
sensory and figurative language		
tone		
theme		

PRACTICE & APPLY

Determine Theme

RL 2, RL 4

Review the information about theme and how a poet can convey a theme through tone and irony. Then, have students answer the question. *(Possible answers: Saying that an "acrid smell" is like "perfume" is ironic because this is the opposite of what the speaker means. The acrid smell of trash isn't like perfume—it stinks.)*

Compare Forms in Poetry

RL 2, RL 5

Have partners work together to analyze the structure of each poem and fill in the chart. As a group, discuss how the differences in form affect the meaning of each poem.

Sample answers:

Elements to Think About	"Dump"	"How Things Work"
form of poem	traditional	free verse
setting	the dump	a walk in town or the city, after having a coffee and rolls at a restaurant
lines and stanzas	8 stanzas; 4 lines each	no stanzas; 19 lines
sensory and figurative language	"by a clamber," "steep unsteady heights"	"Like rain, wetting the new roots of a child"
tone	light rhythm but dark images; ironic	frustrated but resigned
theme	We are part of the toxic cycle of acquiring and discarding things.	Life is unfortunately a chain of events linked by money.

Strategies for Annotation

 Annotate it!

Determine Theme

RL 2, RL 4

Share these strategies for guided or independent analysis:

- Highlight in yellow examples of ironic tone.
- Highlight in blue text clues that convey theme.
- Use a note to explain the theme of the poem.

As far as I can tell, daughter, it works like this:

You buy bread from a grocery, a bag of apples

From a fruit stand, and what coins

Are passed on helps others buy pencils, glue,

Tickets to a movie in which laughter

Is thrown into their faces.

> Theme: It's sad that life is a chain of money.

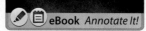

PRACTICE & APPLY

Analyzing the Text

RL 1, RL 2,
RL 4, RL 5

Possible answers:

1. The theme is that the value people put on material things lasts for only a short time.

2. It's sort of sad that money makes things work.

3. Both poems address the same subject: how the things we buy and own are such important parts of our lives. The speaker in each poem describes personal reactions to experiences with things that are purchased.

4. The tone in both poems is ironic. In "Dump" the speaker seems disgusted by the junk at the dump but will buy more stuff that will become junk. The lines "Tickets to a movie in which laughter / Is thrown into their faces" in "How Things Work" are ironic because the speaker is saying the opposite of what he means: Laughter suggests pleasure, but not if it's "thrown" into your face.

5. In both poems, the speakers sum up what they have observed about consumerism in an ironic tone to cast some doubt on the subject. The last two lines of "Dump" tell that people dislike the feeling of "emptiness" when they have fewer things, but the feeling soon passes as they refill empty spaces with new stuff—our lives have become an endless cycle of acquiring and discarding. The last two lines of "How Things Work" convey a similar message—money connects us all in a possibly unfortunate, endless cycle.

6. The repetitious rhythm and end rhymes in "Dump" suggest lighthearted feelings, which contrast with the negative descriptions and serious message of the poem. This contrast disturbs readers, which might be why the poet chose this form. The speaker in "How Things Work" is talking to his or her daughter. The poet may have chosen the form of free verse because its natural rhythms suggest an everyday conversation. It's a sweet, natural conversation with a child about a serious subject.

7. Sample response: At the dump, we clamber up / steep unsteady heights / to the brink. / Beds without a dreamer. / Lamps that no hand lights. / We can't find enough cubic inches / in our house, our mind / to store odd items.

English Language Support

Exchange Ideas Remind students that to **compare** is to show similarities; to **contrast** is to explain differences. Invite them to use these sentence frames to explain their ideas to a partner before they write their literary analysis.

• One way the two poems differ is _____.
• One way the two poems are similar is _____.

Analyzing the Text

RL 1, RL 2, RL 4,
RL 5, W 2, W 4,
W 10

Cite Text Evidence Support your responses with evidence from the poems.

1. **Draw Conclusions** What is the theme of "Dump"?

2. **Draw Conclusions** What is the theme of "How Things Work"?

3. **Compare** In what ways do the poems "Dump" and "How Things Work" seem most alike?

4. **Compare** Reread lines 14–15 of "How Things Work." In what way is the tone similar to the tone in "Dump"?

5. **Compare** Reread the last two lines of each poem. How are the speakers' statements alike, and what message, or theme, do they leave the reader with?

6. **Evaluate** Why might the poet have chosen regular meter and rhyme to express the ideas in "Dump"? Why might the poet have chosen free verse for "How Things Work"?

7. **Connect** Reread lines 1–8 of "Dump." How might those ideas be expressed in language like that in "How Things Work"?

PERFORMANCE TASK

Writing Activity: Literary Analysis Write a one-page analysis of the poems. In your analysis, compare and contrast the views and experiences of consuming expressed in each poem.

• Complete the graphic organizer from the Compare Forms in Poetry section. Use the completed chart to organize your ideas.

• Include words and lines from the poems to support the key points and ideas in your analysis.

• Organize your analysis clearly, using a compare-contrast structure.

• Sum up each speaker's central idea, or theme, and the tone, or attitude toward the subject.

Assign this performance task.

PERFORMANCE TASK

W 2,
W 4,
W 10

Writing Activity: Literary Analysis Have students work independently. Direct them to

• use the chart to draft their analysis
• organize their ideas in a logical way
• conclude by restating their main idea and insights

Determine Theme

RETEACH

Explain that the **theme** of a poem is the message a poet communicates. Discuss the topic and theme of the poem "Dump." Explain that while the topic is a look at the things left at a dump, the theme is a message about that topic: how we participate in an endless cycle of acquiring things that temporarily give us meaning, which we eventually throw away.

Point out that the theme is often implied rather than directly stated. Readers can identify the theme by paying attention to the words and details in a poem and by asking themselves, "What big message about life is the poet trying to tell me?"

Review the following steps for identifying the theme:

1. Examine clues in the text. What does the title tell you? How does the poet use words and details to convey a message?
2. Use the clues to figure out the message.

Together, consider the details and state a main-idea sentence that sums up the author's message. *(A high standard of life brings problems because people have too much but are never satisfied.)*

 LEVEL UP TUTORIALS Assign the following *Level Up* tutorial: **Theme**

English Language Support

Exchange Ideas To help students determine the theme of a poem they have read in this lesson, use a Think-Pair-Share strategy.

- Have students return to the poem and take notes about details and images that will help them complete the first step above.
- Invite them to meet with a partner to share their notes. Ask them to make inferences about the poem's theme and write a theme statement expressing their idea.
- Call on pairs to read their theme statements aloud.

PRACTICE AND APPLY

Have students work with a partner to apply the steps to another poem of their choosing. After their analysis, have students share their ideas about theme with other pairs of students in the class.

Compare Forms in Poetry

RETEACH

Review that the **form,** or structure, of a poem is the arrangement of the words and lines on the page. Remind students that **traditional** forms follow a set of rules that apply to their rhythmic pattern, line length, or rhyme scheme, while in **free verse** the poet decides on the form. Poets choose a form of poetry that works best for the thoughts and ideas they want to express.

Review these steps for comparing form:

1. Examine the line lengths and stanzas. Compare the number of lines per stanza and how the stanzas are organized. Note the emphasis created by the line breaks in each form.
2. Look for patterns of rhythm. Analyze line length and rhyming words, and identify any patterns of stressed and unstressed syllables (meter).
3. Compare the effects each form has on the poem's meaning.

 LEVEL UP TUTORIALS Assign the following *Level Up* tutorial: **Elements of Poetry**

INDEPENDENT READING

Have partners apply the steps to another pair of poems of their choosing. Encourage students to find examples of both traditional and free-verse poetry. Suggest they fill out a Compare and Contrast graphic organizer as they do their analyses. Have pairs read their poetry choices aloud to a group and explain their analyses in a group discussion.

Earth (A Gift Shop)

my **Smart**Planner Create lesson plans and access resources online.

Short Story by Charles Yu

Why This Text?

Science fiction offers readers opportunities to explore how works of imagination can draw attention to social issues and provoke thought and debate. This lesson leads students to analyze a science fiction story and think about the big ideas in it.

Key Learning Objective: The student will be able to identify elements of science fiction and analyze a story to determine its theme.

For practice and application:

Close Reader selection
"He-y Come On Ou-t!"
Short Story by Shinichi Hoshi

RL 1 Cite textual evidence.

RL 2 Determine theme.

RL 3 Analyze story elements.

RL 4 Determine the meanings of words and phrases.

W 3 Write narratives to develop imagined experiences or events.

W 4 Produce clear and coherent writing.

W 10 Write routinely over extended time frames.

L 2b Spell correctly.

L 4d Verify the preliminary determination of word meaning by checking the context and a dictionary.

L 6 Acquire and use accurately grade-appropriate words.

▲ Text Complexity Rubric

Quantitative Measures	Earth (A Gift Shop) Lexile: 1010L
Qualitative Measures	**Levels of Meaning/Purpose** single level of complex meaning
	Structure less familiar story concepts
	Language Conventionality and Clarity contemporary, familiar language
	Knowledge Demands clearly fantastical perspective
Reader/Task Considerations	• Teacher determined • Vary by individual reader and type of text • See the Text X-Ray for suggested Reader/Task Considerations.

English Language Support Before teaching, use the Text X-Ray for an overview of the text's complexity. The Text X-Ray and the supports and scaffolds in the Teacher's Edition will help you guide students of different skill levels.

Meaning Making

Language Development

Effective Expression

Content Knowledge

Foundational Skills

Text Complexity: Qualitative Measures

Levels of Meaning/Purpose

single level of complex meaning

Help students determine the theme of a science fiction short story.

- Teacher's Edition side notes, pp. 250, 251, 252, 253, 254, 255
- English Language Support, p. 252
- Strategies for Annotation, p. 251
- Determine Theme, p. 255

▶ *Use It!* **Level Up Tutorial:** Theme

ZOOM IN ON DETERMINING THEME Discuss how **science fiction** stories often convey a message about what the future holds if people do not change their ways. One way authors develop such a **theme** is by describing a future society that readers can compare with their own.

- Have pairs use details from the story to explain these elements of the narrator's world: education, recreation/fun, art.
- Discuss how the fictional future compares with our present society.
- Then ask pairs to complete this theme statement: If humans continue to _____, then _____. *(Possible response: If people continue to waste Earth's resources and rely too much on technology, then people in the future society will care only about buying things and not about learning, imagining, and creating.)*

Structure

less familiar story concepts

Help students analyze the elements of a science fiction story.

- Teacher's Edition side notes, pp. 249, 250, 252, 253, 254, 255
- English Language Support, pp. 249, 253
- Strategies for Annotation, p. 255
- Analyze Stories: Science Fiction, p. 255

To teach how to analyze setting, see

- Analyze Stories: Setting, p. 258a

To reteach how to analyze science fiction, see

- Analyze Stories: Science Fiction, p. 258a

▶ *Use It!* **Interactive Whiteboard Lesson:** Setting

ZOOM IN ON ANALYZING SCIENCE FICTION Direct students to return to lines 106–110 in their eBooks:

- Have them highlight details that develop understanding of the setting of the story. *("no one can go outside on Earth anymore because it's 170 degrees Fahrenheit"; "laboratory-synthesized Summer in a Bottle")*
- Then ask them to explain how these details illustrate elements of the **science fiction** genre. *(The setting shows how human technology has changed Earth's environment; consumers in the future society have something in common with today's shoppers: they enjoy products that smell good.)*

Language Conventionality and Clarity

contemporary, familiar language

Teach unfamiliar vocabulary in context.

- Teacher's Edition Critical Vocabulary notes, pp. 250, 251, 257
- Applying Academic Vocabulary, p. 252
- Strategies for Annotation, p. 257
- Vocabulary Strategy: Verifying Meaning, p. 257

Help students analyze language and style.

- Teacher's Edition side note, p. 249
- English Language Support, pp. 249, 250

Support students' discussion of the story as well as their own writing.

- Teacher's Edition side notes, pp. 254, 258
- English Language Support, pp. 254, 258
- Language Conventions: Spelling, p. 258

ZOOM IN ON **USING CONTEXT** Tell students that the author uses many phrases that mean something other than what the words say. Explain that these **idioms** can often be defined from **context**. Have students return to the story and work together to define these expressions, using clues from the surrounding text:

- Line 28: "pooled our resources" (*"shared what we had"*)
- Line 63: "raised the bar" (*"increased expectations; made it more difficult"*)
- Line 135: "going down that road" (*"considering that idea—that the name should be accurate"*)
- Line 152: "swing by" (*"visit"*)

Knowledge Demands

clearly fantastical perspective

Support English learners in understanding background on the author.

- Teacher's Edition Author's note, p. 249

ZOOM IN ON **BUILDING BACKGROUND** Point out the illustration on page 252. Explain that the message on the tote bag refers to similar ones that appear on T-shirts and other items in many gift shops. These items make fun of tourists' need for souvenirs to prove they went somewhere, as well as their high expectations that a vacation will change their lives. Then explain that the story is an audio brochure. The narrator is trying to "sell" Earth to tourists to get them to visit and, more importantly, to buy things. Encourage students to look for the advertising techniques that the narrator uses and note how they create a humorous effect.

Suggested Reader/Task Considerations

Consider the following before assigning this short story to students.

- Will students be able to **infer** the ironic purpose of the author?
- Will students be engaged by the author's style?

ZOOM IN ON **SUPPORTING COMPREHENSION**

- Define *irony* as saying one thing but meaning another. Explain that the narrator wants to make Earth appealing to potential visitors, but the text reveals its flaws. Point out that in lines 28–41, the narrator and friends collect music and art in a museum for tourists, but people in the future society are too ignorant to appreciate it.
- Read lines 1–15 lines aloud to introduce the narrator's casual, conversational style. Have pairs read the rest of the story aloud.

Charles Yu Tell students that in his writing Yu likes to play with ideas about science fiction itself and the blurry boundary between science fiction and real life. He uses humor to explore the question "Are we real?"

SETTING A PURPOSE Direct students to use the Setting a Purpose prompt to focus their reading. Remind them to generate questions as they read.

Analyze Stories: Science Fiction (LINES 9–11)

RL 1,
RL 3

Explain that **science fiction** uses scientific ideas and imagination to explore possibilities of the past or future.

(A) **CITE TEXT EVIDENCE** Have students reread lines 9–11 and cite evidence that this story is set in the future. *(The story happens after "the fossil fuels ran out and all of the nation-states collapsed and a lucky few escaped Earth and went out in search of new worlds to colonize.")*

English Language Support

Define *setting* as when and where a story takes place. Note that science fiction stories often occur in the future.

- Display these phrases: "Earth: The Planet"; "Earth: A Bunch of Civilizations"; "Earth: Not Much Going On Here Anymore." Guide students to label each as *past, present,* or *future.*

- Ask what additional information lines 14–15 reveal about the setting. *(The events occur much, much farther into the future than the era named "Earth: Not Much Going On Here Anymore.")*

Determine the Meanings of Words and Phrases (LINES 14–15)

RL 1,
RL 4

Tell students that **style** is *how* an author writes rather than *what* an author writes. Point out that Yu's style includes sentence fragments and informal word choices.

(B) **CITE TEXT EVIDENCE** Direct students to reread lines 14–15 and give ideas about why the author chose to write in this style, citing examples of the author's choices that reveal his style. *(The phrases "pretty long" and "really long" and the sentence fragments "Followed by another pretty long time" and "Which was then followed by a really long time" convey an informal, humorous tone and help readers hear the narrator's conversational voice.)*

Charles Yu (b. 1976) *wrote his first short story in college, but he didn't write another one until years later after he graduated from law school. During the day, he works as a lawyer for a visual effects company in southern California. He does most of his writing at night, after he has spent time with his family and his children have gone to bed. Yu has written two short story collections and a novel.*

Earth (A Gift Shop)

SPECIAL OFFER

10%

OPEN

Short Story by Charles Yu

SETTING A PURPOSE As you read this science fiction story, think about the author's portrayal of Earth's future and how he creates this portrayal.

Come to Earth! Yes, that Earth. A lot of people think we're closed during construction, but we are not! We're still open for business.

Admittedly, it's a little confusing.

First, we were Earth: The Planet. Then life formed, and that was a great and good time.

And then, for a little while, we were Earth: A Bunch of Civilizations!

Until the fossil fuels ran out and all of the nation-states
10 collapsed and a lucky few escaped Earth and went out in search of new worlds to colonize.

Then, for what seemed like forever, we were Earth: Not Much Going On Here Anymore.

And that lasted for a long time. Followed by another pretty long time. Which was then followed by a really long time.

(t) ©Michelle Jue; (bc) ©vertical/Shutterstock; (br) ©elisekurenbina/Shutterstock; (bg) ©Comstock/JUPITER IMAGES/Getty Images; (bl) ©gpory/Shutterstock

English Language Support

Analyze Language Display lines 1–15. Explain that a variety of sentence structures create a conversational voice for the narrator.

- Read lines 1–3 aloud, and guide students to identify the fragment.

- Ask pairs to identify fragments in lines 1–15 and rewrite them as complete sentences. Have them explain how complete sentences change the narrator's voice.

- Ask pairs to identify fragments, exclamations, and informal word choices in lines 1–15 and share their findings.

Analyze Stories: Science Fiction (LINES 28–41)   RL 3

Point out that the author imagines a future Earth that has been turned into a museum.

C **ASK STUDENTS** to reread lines 28–41 and tell what the objects in the museum reveal about future Earth. *(After the collapse of civilizations, people are uneducated and can't recognize or appreciate art. They mix opera with a TV talk show and know nothing about a painting except that it was important.)*

Determine Theme   RL 1, RL 2
(LINES 51–60)

Tell students that a **theme** is a message about life or human nature that the author shares with the reader. Explain that in this segment of the story the narrator is describing what human beings value.

D **CITE TEXT EVIDENCE** Have students reread lines 51–60 to note the words that reveal what is most important to humans at this time in the future. Ask what point the author might be making. *(After only five years of schooling, kids "join the leisure force as full-time professional consumers." Humans who visit Earth still want "credit accounts" and "lifelong loyalty rewards programs." The author is pointing out that to be human is to buy things.)*

CRITICAL VOCABULARY

enterprising: The narrator says that human beings are an enterprising species. **ASK STUDENTS** what they would expect enterprising people to do. *(open a business, invent a product, make money)*

mandatory: The narrator says that five years of schooling are mandatory. **ASK STUDENTS** how education in the future has changed, according to the narrator. *(In the future, students don't have to attend school beyond fourth or fifth grade.)*

Then, after a while, humans, having semi-successfully established colonies on other planets, started to come back to Earth on vacation. Parents brought their kids, teachers brought their classes on field trips, retirees came in groups of 20 twenty or thirty. They wanted to see where their ancestors had come from. But there was nothing here. Kids and parents and teachers left, disappointed. *That's it?* they would say, or some would even say, *It was okay I guess, but I thought there would be more.*

So, being an **enterprising** species and all, some of us got together and reinvented ourselves as Earth: The Museum, which we thought was a great idea.

 We pooled our resources and assembled what we could find. To be sure, there was not a whole lot of good stuff left after the collapse of Earth: A Bunch of Civilizations! One of 30 us had a recording of Maria Callas singing the Violetta aria in *La Traviata*.[1] We all thought it sounded very pretty, so we had that playing in a room in the museum. And I think maybe we had a television playing episodes of *The Tonight Show Starring Johnny Carson*. The main attraction of the museum was the painting we had by some guy of some flowers. No one could remember the name of the guy or the painting, or even the flowers, but we were all pretty sure it was an important painting at some point in the history of paintings and also the 40 history of people, so we put that in the biggest room in the center of everything.

But parents and teachers, being humans (and especially being descendants of the same humans who messed everything up in the first place) thought the whole museum was quite boring, or even *very* boring, and they would say as much, even while we were still within earshot, and we could hear them saying that to each other, about how bored they were. That hurt to hear, but more than that what was hurtful was that no one was coming to Earth anymore, now 50 that it was a small and somewhat eclectic museum. And who could blame them? After the collapse of civilization, school just has never been the same. By the time kids are done with their five years of **mandatory** schooling, they are eight or even nine years old and more than ready to join the leisure force as full-time professional consumers. Humans who went

enterprising
(ĕn′tər-prī′zĭng) *adj.*
An *enterprising* person is someone who accepts challenges and takes initiative.

mandatory
(măn′də-tôr′ē) *adj.*
If something is *mandatory*, it is required.

---

[1] **Violetta aria in *La Traviata*:** a song from the famous opera by Giuseppe Verdi in which the character Violetta sings joyfully about love.

English Language Support

Word Study Display these words: *great, teachers, ready.* Point out that the same vowel pair makes three different sounds: long *a*, long *e*, short *e*.

- List these additional words: *instead, break, breakfast, team, streak, steak, treat, heading, measly.* Have students repeat each word.
- Have pairs sort the words according to the sound that *ea* makes and read their lists aloud. *(long a: break, steak; long e: team, streak, treat, measly; short e: instead, breakfast, heading)*

> " After the collapse of civilization, school just has never been the same. "

elsewhere have carried on that tradition from their days on Earth. They are ready to have their credit accounts opened, for their spending to be tracked, to get started in their lifelong loyalty rewards programs. Especially those humans who are
60 rich enough to be tourists coming back here to Earth.

Eventually one of us realized that the most popular part of the museum was the escalator ride. Although you would think interstellar[2] travel would have sort of raised the bar on what was needed to impress people, there was just something about moving diagonally that seemed to amuse the tourists, both kids and adults, and then one of us finally woke up and said, well, why not give them what they want?

So we did some research, in the few books we had left, and on the computer, and the research confirmed our **hypothesis**:
70 Humans love rides.

So Earth: The Museum was shuttered for several years while we reinvented ourselves and developed merchandise and attractions, all of the things we were naturally good at, and after another good long while, we finally were able to reopen as Earth: The Theme Park and Gift Shop, which did okay but it was not too long before we realized the theme park part of it was expensive to operate and kind of a hassle, really, as our engineering was not so good and we kept making people sick or, in a few cases, really **misjudging** g-forces,[3] and word got
80 out among the travel agencies that Earth: The Theme Park and Gift Shop was not so fun and actually quite dangerous, so we really had no choice but to drop the theme park part and that is how we became Earth: The Gift Shop.

Which was all anyone ever wanted anyway. To get a souvenir to take home.

We do have some great souvenirs.

hypothesis
(hī-pŏth´ ĭ-sĭs) *n.*
A *hypothesis* is an explanation or theory for something that can be tested for validity.

misjudge
(mĭs-jŭj´) *v.* If you *misjudge* something, you form an incorrect opinion about it.

---
[2] **interstellar:** between stars.
[3] **g-forces:** the amount of force someone experiences when he or she accelerates at the same rate as every unit of his or her mass.

Earth (A Gift Shop) **251**

Determine Theme   RL 2
(LINES 71–83)

Tell students that the narrator's description of how Earth is reinvented shows what human beings value.

E **ASK STUDENTS** to reread lines 71–83 to sum up what readers learn about Earth's transformations. *(After Earth: The Museum was closed because it was too boring, humans on Earth developed merchandise and attractions in Earth: The Theme Park and Gift Shop. But because they no longer had engineering skills, the rides were too dangerous. Earth became just a gift shop instead.)* What theme do these details suggest? *(The details suggest that of all the money-making ventures that people in the future have made of Earth, the best was to make it solely a place to buy things instead of experiences.)*

CRITICAL VOCABULARY

hypothesis: The narrator says that research confirmed the hypothesis that people love rides. **ASK STUDENTS** what is ridiculous about using the word *hypothesis* here. *(The narrator is suggesting that their research was scientific, but their knowledge of science was limited.)*

misjudge: The author says that the ride designers misjudged g-forces. **ASK STUDENTS** why misjudging g-forces would be a problem. *(People would be thrown off the rides or injured because of poor planning.)*

English Language Support

Use Modal Expressions Remind students that they must use clues in the text to infer themes, or messages about people and life conveyed through the story. Encourage them to use their eBook annotation tools to highlight details that suggest themes. Then have students discuss and justify the themes they identify.

• Display the words *can* and *may*. Model their use in discussing a theme: *People thought the museum was boring. This <u>may</u> mean that when people do too much shopping, they forget how to think.*

• Have students write the words *possibly, likely, could,* and *would* in their notebooks. Review their meanings. Then have pairs review lines 57–60 for clues that suggest a theme. Ask them to write sentences that use one of the modal expressions to explain how the story details suggest a theme.

• Have students write the words *potentially, certainly, should,* and *might.* Then ask them to review the first three pages of the story to identify clues to themes. Have them form pairs to discuss and justify their ideas, using the modal expressions.

CLOSE READ

Determine Theme RL 2

(LINES 88–92)

Tell students that an idea about human values presented earlier is repeated in the first catalog item in lines 88–92.

F **ASK STUDENTS** to reread the description after number 1 (lines 88–92) and tell what point is being made about human "progress." *(Humans moved past the Age of Learning, later seen as boring, into the Age After the Age of Learning, in which learning was no longer valued—people preferred ignorance.)*

English Language Support

Tell students that a yawn is often seen as a sign of boredom. Guide them to understand the point that the author is making in these lines by having them complete these sentences with a partner:

- People in the story's present age are bored by _____. *(the Age of Learning)*
- This reaction shows that _____. *(learning/knowledge is no longer important to them)*

Analyze Stories: RL 1, RL 3
Science Fiction (LINES 87–113)

Tell students that future worlds depicted in science fiction have many similarities with the world of the present.

G **CITE TEXT EVIDENCE** Have students reread lines 87–113 and note details that are really about our world today, not the future. Ask for ideas about the author's purpose in listing these "top-selling items." *(The distant future is unlikely to still have karaoke, DVDs, and video games. The author is poking fun at what we purchase today and our shallowness, making the point that today's consumer society is just as likely to be thriving centuries into the future. Saying that a "beautiful painting of a nature scene" is "almost like a photograph" points out that we've lost our appreciation of both nature and art.)*

I WENT TO EARTH
And all I got was this cheesy tote-bag

G
F
Our top-selling items for the month of October:

1. *History: The Poster!* A 36" × 24" color poster showing all of the major phases of human history. From the Age Before

90 Tools, through the short-lived but exciting Age of Tools, to the (yawn) Age of Learning, and into our current age, the Age After the Age of Learning.

2. *War: The Soundtrack.* A three-minute musical interpretation of the experience of war, with solos for guitar and drums. Comes in an instrumental version (for karaoke lovers).

3. *Art: The Poster!* Beautiful painting of a nature scene. Very realistic-looking, almost like a photograph. Twenty percent off if purchased with History: The Poster!

100 4. *God, the Oneness: A Mystical 3-D Journey.* 22-minute DVD. Never-before-seen footage. Comes with special glasses for viewing.

5. *Science: The Video Game.* All the science you ever need to bother with! Almost nothing to learn. So easy you really don't have to pay attention. For ages three to ninety-three.

6. *Summer in a Bottle.* Sure, no one can go outside on Earth anymore because it's 170 degrees Fahrenheit, but who needs outside when they have laboratory-synthesized Summer

APPLYING ACADEMIC VOCABULARY

attitude	consume	purchase

THINK-PAIR-SHARE Have students turn to a partner to discuss the following questions. Guide students to include the academic vocabulary words *attitude*, *consume*, and *purchase* in their responses. Ask volunteers to share their responses with the class.

- What is the narrator's **attitude** toward the tourists who visit Earth to **purchase** things?
- What does the story seem to say about the human drive to **consume**?

in a Bottle? Now comes in two odors: "Mist of Nostalgia" or
"Lemony Fresh."

110   7. *Happiness: A Skin Lotion.* At last you can be content and
moisturized, at the same time. From the makers of Adventure:
A Body Spray.

Other strong sellers for the month include Psychologically
Comforting Teddy Bear and Shakespeare: The Fortune
Cookie. All of the items above also come in ring tones,
T-shirts, cups, and key chains.

And coming for the holidays, get ready for the latest
installment of Earth's greatest artistic work of the last century:

120 *Hero Story: A Hero's Redemption (and Sweet Revenge),* a
computer-generated script based on all the key points of the
archetypal[4] story arc that we humans are.

Which brings us back to our original point. What was our
original point? Oh yeah, Earth: The Gift Shop is still here. Not
just here, but doing great! Okay, maybe not great, but okay,
we're okay. We would be better if you came by and shopped
here. Which is why we sent you this audio catalog, which we
hope you are reading (otherwise we are talking to ourselves).
Earth: The Gift Shop: The Brochure. Some people have said

130 the name, Earth: The Gift Shop, is a bit confusing because it
makes it seem like this is the official gift shop of some other
attraction here on Earth, when really the attraction is the
gift shop itself. So we are considering changing our name to
Earth (A Gift Shop), which sounds less official but is probably
more accurate. Although if we are going down that road, it
should be pointed out that the most accurate name would
be Earth = A Gift Shop, or even Earth = Merchandise, since
basically, if we are being honest with ourselves, we are a theme
park without the park part, which is to say we are basically

140 just a theme, whatever that means, although Earth, an Empty
Theme Park would be an even worse name than Earth = A
Gift Shop, so for now we're just going to stick with what we've
got, until something better comes along.

So, again, we say: Come to Earth! We get millions of
visitors a year, from near and far. Some of you come by
accident. No shame in that! We don't care if you are just
stopping to refuel, or if you lost your way, or even if you just

---

[4] **archetypal:** having the qualities of an original model or prototype. Common
archetypes include the hero, the trickster, the wise old man, and the Earth
mother.

FOR STUDENTS WITH DISABILITIES

To ensure that all students have access to the ideas brought out in
discussion, implement one or more of these strategies:

- Write key points on the board.
- Conduct discussions in a circle to enable all students to look at each
other when they are speaking.
- Scan notes from discussion and send them to students electronically.

CLOSE READ

Analyze Stories: Science Fiction (LINES 118–122)   RL 3

Point out that the narrator describes the greatest
artistic work of the previous century in this imagined
future Earth.

H **ASK STUDENTS** to reread lines 118–122 and give
their own ideas about whether this work deserves to
be called artistic. *(The "greatest artistic work" is a script
about the "archetypal story arc that we humans are,"
generated by a computer using "key points." Literature
developed by computers might be called artistic, but
there's no real human creativity involved.)*

English Language Support

Display lines 118–122 and paraphrase what the
sentence is saying. Make sure students understand
that *artistic* means "showing imagination, creativity,
and skill" and that a computer produces this "artistic"
work. Ask students whether a computer can show
imagination and creativity. Lead them to understand
that the author is using irony in this passage to show
what will pass for great works of art or literature in the
future, when people are too lazy to do creative work.

Determine Theme   RL 1, RL 2
(LINES 123–143)

Tell students that the narrator offers different names
for Earth and even tells what the theme of Earth is.

I **CITE TEXT EVIDENCE** Have students reread
the paragraph that begins on line 123 and cite the
different names for Earth. Ask them what the narrator
points out about a theme and how that idea is
connected to the theme of this story. (Earth: The
Gift Shop *which might change to* Earth (A Gift Shop) *or*
Earth = A Gift Shop *or* Earth = Merchandise. *The
narrator says that "we are a theme park without the
park part, which is to say we are basically just a theme."
The theme of the story has to do with our planet
becoming a place to shop.)*

TEACH

CLOSE READ

Analyze Stories: Science Fiction (LINES 155–162)

RL 3

Tell students that the narrator's "audio catalog" is coming to a close, with a final attempt to appeal to the emotions of potential tourists.

J ASK STUDENTS to reread the sentences in which the narrator repeats the word *home*, beginning on line 155, and tell how effective the narrator seems to be at selling the idea of visiting Earth. *(The narrator is not very persuasive. He or she advertises Earth as home to humans but also mentions that it might not be home anymore, since humans left it thousands of years ago.)*

Determine Theme (LINES 161–162)

RL 1, RL 2

Review that the theme of a story is the "big idea" about life or human nature that it conveys.

K CITE TEXT EVIDENCE Have students identify the two sentences that best point to the theme of this story. *("I was a human on Earth. Even if all I did was shop there.")* Ask how students would recast that theme in their own words. *(In the end, the future Earth will be nothing more than a place for human beings to shop.)*

COLLABORATIVE DISCUSSION Have students work in small groups. Suggest that they contrast *what* the author wants to point out and *how* he points it out.

ASK STUDENTS to share any questions they generated in the course of reading and discussing the selection.

English Language Support

Support Opinions Review with students ways that they can build on others' comments and express their own in collaborative discussion:

Show agreement: I agree that _____.

Express disagreement: That's a good point, but _____.

Add details or new insights: In addition, I think that _____.

---

150 want to rest for a moment and eat a sandwich and drink a cold bottle of beer. We still have beer! Of course, we prefer if you come here intentionally. Many of you do. Many of you read about this place in a guidebook, and some of you even go out of your way and take a detour from your travels to swing by the gift shop. Maybe you are coming because you just want to look, or to say you were here. Maybe you are coming to have a story to tell when you get back. Maybe you just want to be able to say: I went home. Even if it isn't home, was never your home, is not anyone's home anymore, maybe you just want to say, I touched the ground there, breathed the air, looked at the moon the way people must have done nine or ten or a hundred 160 thousand years ago. So you can say to your friends, if only for a moment or two: I was a human on Earth. Even if all I did was shop there.

COLLABORATIVE DISCUSSION In what ways is this a serious story? In what ways is it not at all serious, and why did the author choose to do both with his portrayal of Earth's future? Talk about your ideas with other group members.

TO CHALLENGE STUDENTS...

Analyze Theme Suggest that students consider the central idea in the selection "Always Wanting More" from earlier in Collection 5 and compare that idea to the theme of "Earth (A Gift Shop)." Have small groups hold an informal debate to explain how each author makes his point or develops his theme, and make a case about which author's approach is more effective. Make sure that students cite evidence from both texts to make their cases.

Analyze Stories: Science Fiction

RL 3

Written works that come from an author's imagination fall in the broad category called fiction. In **science fiction,** an author explores unexpected possibilities of the past or the future. The author combines knowledge of science and technology with a creative imagination to present a new world. "Earth (A Gift Shop)" has elements found in other science fiction stories:

Elements of Science Fiction
- descriptions of how humankind's technologies have altered planet Earth
- colonization of other planets
- impossible events and settings like those in a fantasy story
- a future world with many features and issues common in today's world

Science fiction writers create fantasy worlds, but they often include familiar elements to make these worlds seem believable. Characters usually speak and behave the way real people do. They often have the same goals and motivations as real people, but they pursue them in fantasy worlds set in the future, the past, or a time completely separate from history.

Choose one of the elements in the list and tell how it is shown in "Earth (A Gift Shop)."

Determine Theme

RL 2

A **theme** is a message about life or human nature that the author shares with the reader. In works of fiction, themes are the "big ideas" that readers can infer based on the story the author tells.

While the topic of a science fiction story might be time travel, its theme might be about humans' responsibility for future generations. The following are examples of themes found in science fiction:

Themes in Science Fiction
- Technological advances will make us smarter and happier.
- Technological advances will cause us to lose control over our lives.
- Tampering with biological systems brings ruin.
- Humanity will survive only if we conquer our urge for war.

To identify the theme in a science fiction text, look at the details the author presents. Do certain characters make significant statements about science and technology? Is technology presented as a positive force that benefits mankind, or is it shown as a potentially threatening force? Consider these questions in the context of "Earth (A Gift Shop)."

Earth (A Gift Shop) **255**

CLOSE READ

Analyze Stories: Science Fiction

RL 3

Discuss what is meant by the phrase "unexpected possibilities of the past or future." Then, review how science fiction is like and different from fantasy stories: Impossible events and imaginary characters are in both kinds of fiction, but science fiction often explores the effects of science and technology.

After students read the list of elements of science fiction, have them review "Earth (A Gift Shop)" to find an example of each element. *(Sample answers: Humankind's technologies have altered planet Earth to make it unlivable—the temperature outside is 170 degrees Fahrenheit. Wealthy human beings left Earth to colonize other planets, though some come back as tourists. The main impossible event is that the whole planet can be turned into a museum, theme park, or gift shop. The author is exaggerating today's consumer culture by imagining a future Earth that exists solely for the purpose of shopping.)*

Determine Theme

RL 2

Use the examples of themes in science fiction to emphasize that the theme of a story is not the same as its topic. Remind students that in "Earth (A Gift Shop)" the human drive to make technology has turned the setting—planet Earth—into a place filled with not much more than things to purchase. Encourage students to keep this in mind as they share ideas about the theme of "Earth (A Gift Shop)."

Strategies for Annotation   *Annotate it!*

Analyze Stories: Science Fiction

RL 3

Share these strategies for guided or independent analysis:
- Highlight in yellow details showing an element of science fiction stories.
- Add a note to tell about the element.

could blame them? After the collapse of civilization, school just has never been the same. By the time kids are done with their five years of mandatory schooling, they are eight or even nine years old and more than ready to join the leisure force as full-time professional consumers. Humans who went

> a future world where buying things is more important than learning— like today's world?

Earth (A Gift Shop) **255**

Analyzing the Text
RL 1, RL 2, RL 3, RL 4

Possible answers:

1. *"Earth (A Gift Shop)" is science fiction because the author imagines a future world with issues that are similar to those on Earth today. Technologies have altered planet Earth, causing fossil fuels to run out and nation-states to collapse. Some humans are able to leave to colonize other planets, so interplanetary travel is common.*

2. *The narrator uses* we and us *to refer to the people left behind on Earth, and* all of us *to refer to those who live on Earth now.*

3. *Descriptions that convey ideas about today's consumer culture include language familiar in ads: "Never-before-seen footage," "For ages three to ninety-three," "be content and moisturized." Things commonly offered today—"ring tones, T-shirts, cups, and key chains"—are still offered. There's an unrealistic, comical suggestion that many basic consumer technologies have not advanced at all in the far-distant future.*

4. *The sequence of names is "Earth: The Planet"; "Earth: A Bunch of Civilizations!"; "Earth: Not Much Going On Here Anymore"; "Earth: The Museum"; "Earth: The Theme Park and Gift Shop"; "Earth: The Gift Shop." Future names could be "Earth (A Gift Shop)" or "Earth = A Gift Shop" or "Earth = Merchandise." The author uses the name changes to suggest that the whole planet has been just a brand for centuries. The name changes show how widespread marketing and merchandising are on Earth—in the future and now.*

5. *Our preoccupation with consuming and with merchandise is destroying our civilization and replacing deep values with superficial ones.*

6. *The author uses humor to show that he disapproves of modern consumer culture. His language has an ironic, disrespectful tone. For example, to point out the loss of knowledge, the narrator uses the ridiculous example that the main attraction of the museum was "the painting we had by some guy of some flowers."*

PERFORMANCE TASK
W 3, W 4, W 10

Writing Activity: Narrative Help students develop a plan for a fictional narrative in a brief form, such as "flash fiction" or a "short short." Have students

- freewrite or brainstorm to answer the questions *Who? Where and when? What if . . . ?*
- imagine the problem or conflict that characters face

- list possible main events that will lead from the conflict to the climax to the resolution

See the lessons in Extend and Reteach for ideas for additional instruction in plot and setting.

Assign this performance task.

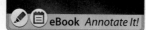

Analyzing the Text
RL 1, RL 2, RL 3, RL 4, W 3, W 4, W 10

Cite Text Evidence Support your responses with evidence from the text.

1. **Identify** What elements of science fiction does the story "Earth (A Gift Shop)" have?

2. **Infer** To whom might the narrator be referring when using the pronoun *we* throughout the story?

3. **Cite Evidence** In the list of "top-selling items," what are some descriptions that convey ideas about today's consumer culture?

4. **Draw Conclusions** The narrator tells how "Earth: The Planet" has undergone several name changes. What point might the author be making?

5. **Draw Conclusions** What is the theme of this story?

6. **Analyze** How does the narrator's use of language reveal the author's attitude toward the story topic?

PERFORMANCE TASK

Writing Activity: Narrative In the science fiction world of "Earth (A Gift Shop)," humans no longer live on Earth. What would it be like to vacation in that world? How and why might someone have had to escape Earth to find a home on another planet? Pick a part of that plot to expand into a fictional narrative of your own.

- Create an outline of your story, including the narrator, characters, setting, and plot events with a conflict and resolution.
- List the gadgets or technologies that the characters will encounter.
- Include a theme that leaves readers with a message about technology.
- Use your plan to draft and then revise a 2–3-page fictional narrative.

Critical Vocabulary

L 4d, L 6

enterprising   mandatory   hypothesis   misjudge

Practice and Apply Use your own knowledge and experiences to answer each question.

1. Who is an **enterprising** person you know? What makes him or her enterprising?

2. What is **mandatory** at your school? Why?

3. What **hypothesis** can you make about human nature? Why is it a hypothesis?

4. When have you **misjudged** someone or something? How did you find out the truth?

Vocabulary Strategy: Verifying Meaning

When you come across an unfamiliar word in a text, there are a number of steps you can take to verify the word's correct meaning.

Step 1	Step 2	Step 3	Step 4
Determine the likely meaning using **context,** the surrounding words and sentences.	Substitute the likely meaning for the word in the sentence to see if it makes sense.	Look up the word in a print or digital dictionary to verify the likely meaning.	Determine which definition after the entry word best fits with the context.

Use the steps to consider and verify the meaning of *enterprising* in this sentence from "Earth (A Gift Shop)":

> So, being an *enterprising* species and all, some of us got together and reinvented ourselves as Earth: The Museum, which we thought was a great idea.

The context shows that being enterprising has to do with a great idea and inventing something again, so it might mean "creative" or "cooperative." Both of those meanings make sense in the sentence. The dictionary offers this definition: "Showing initiative and willingness to take on new projects." To be enterprising is to be willing to take on the project Earth: The Museum.

Practice and Apply Find the sentence with the word *eclectic* in line 50 of "Earth (A Gift Shop)." Complete the four steps in the chart to verify the meaning for this context. Then restate the sentence using the dictionary meaning you have identified.

Critical Vocabulary

L 4d, L 6

Possible answers:

1. *My uncle is enterprising because he came to this country as a teenager, and within ten years he had his own business.*

2. *Attendance is mandatory. Students are not allowed to move to the next grade unless they have come to school for a certain number of days each year.*

3. *Based on my personal experiences, I have the hypothesis that most people cannot keep secrets. It's a hypothesis because I haven't done the research yet to prove it.*

4. *I misjudged the distance from the high diving board to the pool. When I got up there, I turned around and came down.*

Vocabulary Strategy: Verifying Meaning

Sample restatement of sentence with eclectic:

That hurt to hear, but more than that, what was hurtful was that no one was coming to Earth anymore, now that it was a small museum with items from various sources.

Strategies for Annotation   *Annotate it!*

Vocabulary Strategy: Verifying Meaning

L 4d, L 6

Have students use their eBook annotation tools and the steps for verifying meaning to do the following:

- Highlight in yellow the word *eclectic.*
- Highlight in green clues to meaning in the surrounding words and sentences.
- Note one or more likely meanings.
- Decide which meaning makes sense in the context.

the whole museum was quite boring, or even *very* boring, and they would say as much, even while we were still within earshot, and we could hear them saying . . . how bored they were. . . . now that it was a small and somewhat eclectic m

> eclectic
> Possible meaning from context: "boring" Dictionary definition: "Made up of elements from a variety of sources." This makes more sense in the context of the paragraph before this one.

Language Conventions: Spelling

L 2b

Review that homophones are words that sound alike but have different spellings and meanings. If students find that they often misspell particular homophones, suggest that they keep a list with a meaning clue beside each.

Answers:

1. *It's, their*

2. *effect, capitals*

3. *peace, principal*

4. *aisles, scents*

Language Conventions: Spelling

L 2b

When you proofread your writing for accuracy, always check that every word is spelled correctly. If you are using a computer, the spellcheck feature catches most misspellings—but not all. Be especially attentive to **homophones,** words that sound alike but have different meanings and spellings. These descriptions of souvenir items come from "Earth (A Gift Shop)":

> **painting of a nature scene**
> **never-before-seen footage**

The words *scene* ("something to view") and *seen* (a form of the verb *to see*) are homophones. Knowing that a word has one or more homophones helps you check for correct meaning-spelling matches. You can verify the spelling and meaning of a homophone in a digital or print dictionary.

Some commonly misspelled homophones are *threw/through, right/write/rite, their/there/they're,* and *your/you're.*

This chart shows other commonly misspelled homophones.

affect (to cause a change) **effect** (result)	**cents** (pennies) **scents** (smells) **sense** (feeling; intelligence)	**peace** (calm state) **piece** (part)
aisle (pathway) **I'll** (I will) **isle** (island)	**cereal** (of grain) **serial** (in a series)	**principal** (chief) **principle** (standard; belief)
capital (city; money) **capitol** (lawmakers' building)	**currant** (small raisin) **current** (present time; flow of water)	**rain** (precipitation) **reign** (period of control) **rein** (strap for horse)
cite (quote; summon to court) **sight** (what is seen) **site** (location)	**it's** (it is) **its** (belonging to it)	**wait** (stay) **weight** (heaviness)

Practice and Apply Correct one or more spelling errors in each sentence.

1. Its time for tourists to visit there old planet, Earth.

2. One affect of the collapse of civilizations was the end of national capitols, such as Paris and Washington, D.C.

3. Earth is at piece now, and our principle activity is selling things.

4. Walk through the isles of the gift shop and sniff the sense "Mist of Nostalgia" and "Lemony Fresh."

English Language Support

Write Text Accurately List these homophones on the board: *threw/through, right/write/rite, their/they're/there, your/you're, it's/its.* Say them all aloud together.

- Work with students to write a meaning clue beside each of the homophones on the board.
- On the board, write sentences similar to this one, using each set of homophones at least once: *I saw [their, they're, there] house.* Have students work in pairs to choose the correct word for each sentence.

- Have students choose one homophone from each of the five sets on the board. Have them write original sentences using the homophones and read them aloud to a partner. Have partners write the homophones down and check the accuracy of their spelling against the sentences.

INTERACTIVE WHITEBOARD LESSON

Analyze Stories:
Setting

RL 3,
W 3

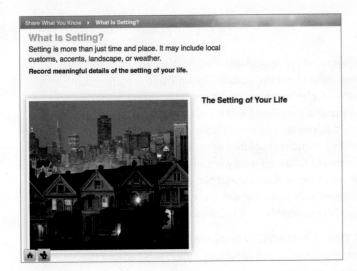

TEACH

Prepare students for the Performance Task by focusing attention on the setting of their stories. Review that the **setting** is the time and place of the story action.

Explain that writers include details of the setting, showing features such as the landscape, weather, season, time of day or night, living conditions, and the way that people dress and talk. Emphasize that in a science fiction story the setting is especially significant. The writer provides details to help readers know that the characters are not on Earth, for example, or that events are taking place in a future time.

Display the following influences of settings in fiction. For each one, ask students to name stories in which setting plays that role.

- affects how characters act and feel
- creates the story conflict
- conveys a mood, such as peacefulness or fear
- suggests a theme or has symbolism

COLLABORATIVE DISCUSSION

Encourage students to visualize a setting they might use in their story. Have students write two or three sentences to describe it. Each writer may find ideas for clarifying or enhancing the sentences by reading them aloud and listening as other group members tell what they picture.

Analyze Stories:
Science Fiction

RL 3

RETEACH

Remind students that any story that comes from the author's imagination is called fiction. Explain that within the broad category of fiction are varied kinds of stories, including science fiction. As you make the following points about **science fiction,** encourage students to give examples from stories they have read or viewed:

- The story may be set in the future.
- The characters may not all be human.
- The plot may involve actual recent technologies and scientific discoveries.
- The story may deal with the effects of technology on individuals, societies, and planet Earth.
- The story may deal with humans' place in the universe.

Tell students that science fiction is most like another kind of fiction, fantasy, because both often involve imaginary worlds and impossible events. Explain that the main difference is the connection to science and technology in science fiction. Offer these descriptions of stories, and have students tell which ones are science fiction, and why:

- A group of human astronauts sets up permanent settlements on Mars. *(science fiction)*
- Human civilizations vanish as Earth's resources are used up. *(science fiction)*
- Mice that talk and act like people live in an underground city. *(fantasy)*
- A killer virus is released by a laboratory worker seeking revenge against a boss. *(science fiction)*
- A brother and sister discover their supernatural ability to read people's minds. *(fantasy)*
- A robot programmed to protect a house refuses to let anyone leave. *(science fiction)*

PRACTICE AND APPLY

Have students look through "Earth (A Gift Shop)" for elements it shares with other science fiction. Tell students to complete each of these sentences with information from the story:

- *The setting for the story "Earth (A Gift Shop)" is . . .*
- *The narrator tells how planet Earth . . .*
- *Human beings who colonized other planets may . . .*

He—y, Come On Ou—t!

Short Story by Shinichi Hoshi

Why This Text

Some stories are so complex the theme must be inferred from details in the text. Other stories are relatively simple in their structure and plot, with a message that is directly stated. "He—y, Come On Ou—t!" is an uncomplicated tale with the feel of an allegory, and although the message is clear, students may have difficulty seeing how it points to a greater truth, one that is not limited to the scope of the story. With the help of the close-reading questions, students will understand what the author is saying about preserving not only the earth but also the truth for future generations.

Background Have students read the background and information about the author. Explain that the name Hoshi means "star" in Japanese, and it is not the pseudonym readers may assume it is given his favorite setting, outer space. But Hoshi's stories are not simply "science fiction": they defy category, blending together dystopic visions of the future with elements of folklore, fantasy, social criticism, and humor. Hoshi's universal themes have earned him a worldwide audience, and his stories have been translated into more than 20 languages. Today his cautionary tales seem more relevant than ever.

SETTING A PURPOSE Ask students to pay attention to the way the author uses details of setting, plot, character, and dialogue to convey the story's theme.

Standards Support

- cite textual evidence
- determine a theme or central idea in a text
- analyze how particular elements of a story interact
- determine the meanings of words and phrases as they are used in text

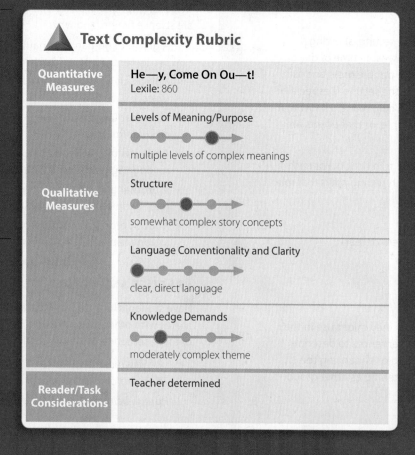

Text Complexity Rubric

Quantitative Measures

He—y, Come On Ou—t!
Lexile: 860

Qualitative Measures

Levels of Meaning/Purpose

multiple levels of complex meanings

Structure

somewhat complex story concepts

Language Conventionality and Clarity

clear, direct language

Knowledge Demands

moderately complex theme

Reader/Task Considerations

Teacher determined

Strategies for CLOSE READING

Determine Theme

Students should read this story carefully all the way through. Close-reading questions at the bottom of the page will help them use details in the text to determine the story's "message," or theme. As they read, students should jot down comments or questions about the text in the margins.

WHEN STUDENTS STRUGGLE . . .

To help students determine theme in "He—y, Come On Ou—t!," have them work in small groups to fill out a chart like the one shown below.

CITE TEXT EVIDENCE For practice in using details in the text to make inferences about the theme, have students analyze each of the following details from the story.

Detail	What It Reveals
" . . . a small shrine had been swept away by a landslide." (lines 3–4)	This image of destruction provides an intriguing setting for the story.
"You might bring down a curse on us. Lay off." (line 24)	This dialogue shows that some people are afraid of acting on a situation without a full understanding of it.
"the scientist . . . [s]uggesting the thing had a perfectly plausible explanation, said simply, 'Fill it in.'" (lines 54–57)	Scientists may "cover up" the truth because they don't want to lose face.
"The concessionaire had his cohorts mount a loud campaign . . . 'Perfect for the disposal of such things as waste from nuclear reactors.'" (lines 81–84)	People out to make a profit may not consider the consequences of some of their actions.
"Young girls whose betrothals had been arranged discarded old diaries in the hole." (lines 114–115)	Memories and experiences are equated with toxic waste.

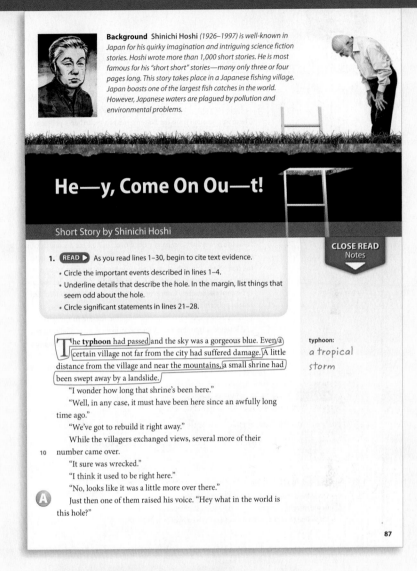

Background Shinichi Hoshi *(1926–1997) is well-known in Japan for his quirky imagination and intriguing science fiction stories. Hoshi wrote more than 1,000 short stories. He is most famous for his "short short" stories—many only three or four pages long. This story takes place in a Japanese fishing village. Japan boasts one of the largest fish catches in the world. However, Japanese waters are plagued by pollution and environmental problems.*

He—y, Come On Ou—t!

Short Story by Shinichi Hoshi

CLOSE READ
Notes

1. **READND** As you read lines 1–30, begin to cite text evidence.
   - Circle the important events described in lines 1–4.
   - Underline details that describe the hole. In the margin, list things that seem odd about the hole.
   - Circle significant statements in lines 21–28.

The **typhoon** had passed and the sky was a gorgeous blue. Even a certain village not far from the city had suffered damage. A little distance from the village and near the mountains, a small shrine had been swept away by a landslide.

"I wonder how long that shrine's been here."

"Well, in any case, it must have been here since an awfully long time ago."

"We've got to rebuild it right away."

While the villagers exchanged views, several more of their
10 number came over.

"It sure was wrecked."

"I think it used to be right here."

"No, looks like it was a little more over there."

Just then one of them raised his voice. "Hey what in the world is this hole?"

typhoon:
a tropical
storm

87

1. **READ AND CITE TEXT EVIDENCE** In line 14, one of the villagers discovers a hole in the ground.

Ⓐ ASK STUDENTS about the reaction of the other villagers to the hole. Why do they gather around it? *They are curious about it because it seems odd.* What explanation is suggested in line 20? *Someone wonders if it's a fox's hole.*

Critical Vocabulary: typhoon (line 1) Have students explain the meaning of *typhoon*. What can they infer about the severity of the typhoon from the first paragraph? *It was a bad storm with a wide reach.*

It is totally
dark.
It is very deep.

It doesn't
produce
an echo.

There is no
indication
where it
came from.

B Where they had all gathered there was a hole about a meter in diameter. They peered in, but it was so dark nothing could be seen. However, it gave one the feeling that it was so deep it went clear through to the center of the earth.

20 There was even one person who said, "I wonder if it's a fox's hole." "He—y, come on ou—t!" shouted a young man into the hole. There was no echo from the bottom. Next he picked up a pebble and was about to throw it in.

"You might bring down a curse on us. Lay off," warned an old man, but the younger one energetically threw the pebble in. As before, however, there was no answering response from the bottom. The villagers cut down some trees, tied them with rope and made a fence which they put around the hole. Then they repaired to the village.

"What do you suppose we ought to do?"

30 "Shouldn't we build the shrine up just as it was over the hole?"

A day passed with no agreement. The news traveled fast, and a car from the newspaper company rushed over. In no time a scientist came out, and with an all-knowing expression on his face he went over to the hole. Next, a bunch of gawking curiosity seekers showed up; one could also pick out here and there men of shifty glances who appeared to be **concessionaires**. Concerned that someone might fall into the hole, a policeman from the local substation kept a careful watch.

One newspaper reporter tied a weight to the end of a long cord and lowered it into the hole. A long way down it went. The cord ran

40 out, however, and he tried to pull it out, but it would not come back up. Two or three people helped out, but when they all pulled too hard, the cord parted at the edge of the hole. Another reporter, a camera in

concessionaire:
businessperson

---

2. **◄ REREAD** Reread lines 1–30. Which details about the setting seem realistic? Which details suggest an otherworldly setting?

Typhoons and landslides may occur and buildings may be damaged during an actual natural disaster. However, the creation of a hole with "no echo from the bottom" suggests an otherworldly setting.

3. **READ ►** As you read lines 31–74, continue to cite text evidence.
- Circle the sentences that show the scientist's thoughts.
- In the margin, paraphrase the significant statement in line 58.
- Underline the concessionaire's offers to the mayor in lines 59–68.

88

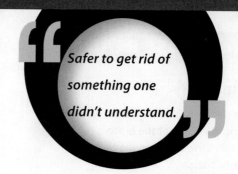

> *Safer to get rid of something one didn't understand.*

hand, who had been watching all of this, quietly untied a stout rope that had been wound around his waist.

C The scientist contacted people at his laboratory and had them bring out a high-powered bull horn, with which he was going to check out the echo from the hole's bottom. He tried switching through various sounds, but there was no echo. The scientist was puzzled, but he could not very well give up with everyone watching him so

50 intently. He put the bull horn right up to the hole, turned it to its highest volume, and let it sound continuously for a long time. It was a noise that would have carried several dozen kilometers above ground. But the hole just calmly swallowed up the sound.

In his own mind the scientist was at a loss, but with a look of apparent **composure** he cut off the sound and, in a manner suggesting that the whole thing had a perfectly plausible explanation, said simply, "Fill it in."

D Safer to get rid of something one didn't understand.

The onlookers, disappointed that this was all that was going to

60 happen, prepared to disperse. Just then one of the concessionaires, having broken through the throng and come forward, made a proposal.

"Let me have that hole. I'll fill it in for you."

"We'd be grateful to you for filling it in," replied the mayor of the village, "but we can't very well give you the hole. We have to build a shrine there."

"If it's a shrine you want, I'll build you a fine one later. Shall I make it with an attached meeting hall?"

Before the mayor could answer, the people of the village all

70 shouted out.

composure:
being calm
and in control
of yourself

It is better to
take attention
away from
something
than it is to
admit it is
beyond com-
prehension.

89

---

2. **REREAD AND CITE TEXT EVIDENCE** Point out that the setting of the story starts to change in lines 16–19.

B **ASK STUDENTS** to cite the line that signals a shift from a realistic setting to a more otherworldly setting. *Students may cite "However, it gave one the feeling that it was so deep it went clear through to the center of the earth."*

3. **READ AND CITE TEXT EVIDENCE** Explain that in lines 45–51 the scientist does a series of things in the hope of getting some answers.

C **ASK STUDENTS** to name the scientist's actions in the correct sequence. *The scientist contacts people at his lab; he instructs them to bring out a high-powered bull horn; he switches through various sounds; he turns it up to its highest volume; he sounds it continuously for a long time.* What is he hoping to find? *He is hoping to find an echo.*

Critical Vocabulary: concessionaire (line 36) Have students compare their definitions for *concessionaire*.

Critical Vocabulary: composure (line 55) Have students explain the meaning of *composure*. What is behind the scientist's "apparent composure"? What is he unwilling to show the others? *He doesn't want to show that he has failed to find an explanation. He is trying to appear confident.*

FOR ELL STUDENTS Encourage students to guess the meaning of *bull horn*. Have a volunteer identify the meaning of each of the words. Then have another volunteer guess the meaning of *bull horn* and why it is called that.

"Really? Well, in that case, we ought to have it closer to the village."

"It's just an old hole. We'll give it to you!"

So it was settled. And the mayor, of course, had no objection.

(E) The concessionaire was true to his promise. It was small, but closer to the village he did build for them a shrine with an attached meeting hall.

About the time the autumn festival was held at the new shrine, the hole-filling company established by the concessionaire hung out
80 its small shingle at a shack near the hole.

The concessionaire had his cohorts mount a loud campaign in the city. "We've got a fabulously deep hole! Scientists say it's at least five thousand meters deep! Perfect for the disposal of such things as waste from nuclear reactors."

Government authorities granted permission. Nuclear power plants fought for contracts. The people of the village were a bit worried about this, but they **consented** when it was explained that there would be absolutely no above-ground contamination for several thousand years and that they would share in the profits. Into the
90 bargain, very shortly a magnificent road was built from the city to the village.

Trucks rolled in over the road, transporting lead boxes. Above the hole the lids were opened, and the <u>wastes from nuclear reactors</u> tumbled away into the hole.

consent:
agree

> 4. **◀ REREAD** Certain statements in a story will hint at a theme. What theme is suggested by the statement you paraphrased in line 58?
>
> *The statement suggests that it is not wise to make decisions without a full understanding of what is involved.*
>
> 5. **READ ▶** As you read lines 75–136, continue to cite textual evidence.
> - Underline all the things that people throw into the hole.
> - Make notes in the margin about how the hole is affecting people's behavior.
> - Circle details in lines 126–136 that recall an episode earlier in the story.

90

> *The hole showed no signs of filling up.*

From the Foreign Ministry and the Defense Agency boxes of unnecessary <u>classified documents</u> were brought for disposal. Officials who came to supervise the disposal held discussions on golf. The lesser functionaries, as they threw in the papers, chatted about pinball.
100 The hole showed no signs of filling up. It was awfully deep, thought some; or else it might be very spacious at the bottom. Little by little the hole-filling company expanded its business.

<u>Bodies of animals</u> used in contagious disease experiments at the universities were brought out, and to these were added the <u>unclaimed corpses of vagrants</u>. Better than dumping all of its garbage in the ocean, went the thinking in the city, and plans were made for a long pipe to carry it to the hole.

The hole gave peace of mind to the dwellers of the city. They concentrated solely on producing one thing after another. Everyone
110 disliked thinking about the eventual consequences. People wanted only to work for production companies and sales corporations; they had no interest in becoming junk dealers. But, it was thought, these problems too would gradually be resolved by the hole.

Young girls whose betrothals had been arranged discarded <u>old diaries</u> in the hole. There were also those who were inaugurating new love affairs and threw into the hole <u>old photographs of themselves taken with former sweethearts</u>. The police felt comforted as they used the hole to get rid of accumulations of expertly done **counterfeit** bills.
120 Criminals breathed easier after throwing <u>material evidence</u> into the hole.

Whatever one wished to discard, the hole accepted it all. The hole cleansed the city of its filth; the sea and sky seemed to have become a bit clearer than before.

The hole lets people get rid of anything.

It gives people peace of mind.

People don't need to think about trash or waste.

People don't need to think of the consequences of their actions.

counterfeit:
fake

91

---

4. **REREAD AND CITE TEXT EVIDENCE** Have students note the unusual structure, style, and word choice in line 58.

(D) **ASK STUDENTS** to analyze why the phrase stands out. *It is in a paragraph of its own; it uses the pronoun* one, *which makes it seem like a general rule.* Why might the author want to call attention to this line? *It might be an important part of the story.*

5. **READ AND CITE TEXT EVIDENCE** Explain that in this section, people get rid of waste materials by throwing them into the hole.

(E) **ASK STUDENTS** to name a kind of waste that could pose a public health hazard. *Students may suggest nuclear waste, dead animals, or corpses of vagrants.*

Critical Vocabulary: consent (line 87) Have students explain the meaning of *consent*. What was offered to the villagers to get them to consent to the building of a nuclear plant? *Students may suggest official assurances of safety and a share of the profits.*

Critical Vocabulary: counterfeit (line 118) Have students explain the meaning of *counterfeit*. Why would counterfeit bills be something people would want to get rid of? *They are illegal to print; if large caches are found, there can be serious penalties.*

FOR ELL STUDENTS Explain that a betrothal is the act of getting engaged to marry someone. Then encourage students to guess why girls with arranged betrothals would throw their diaries into the hole.

Aiming at the heavens, new buildings went on being constructed one after the other.

One day, atop the high steel frame of a new building under construction, a workman was taking a break. Above his head he heard a voice shout:

"He—y, come on ou—t!"

130 But, in the sky to which he lifted his gaze there was nothing at all. A clear blue sky merely spread over all. He thought it must be his imagination. Then, as he resumed his former position, from the direction where the voice had come, a small pebble skimmed by him and fell on past.

F The man, however, was gazing in idle reverie at the city's skyline growing ever more beautiful, and he failed to notice.

6. ◀ **REREAD AND DISCUSS** Reread lines 126–136. With a small group, discuss your interpretation of the story's ending. Review your reading notes and cite text evidence in your discussion.

SHORT RESPONSE

Cite Text Evidence A story's theme is the central idea about life that the writer conveys. What is the theme of "He—y, Come On Ou—t!"? Review your reading notes and **cite text evidence** in your response.

The theme of the story is that humans will face consequences if they behave foolishly. In spite of a warning, a young man tosses a pebble into a hole that appears mysteriously. More people gather around the hole, but no one has figured out quite what it is. However, it is decided that the hole should be filled and a shrine should be built over it because it is "safer to get rid of something one didn't understand." Characters carelessly fill the hole with all sorts of garbage, and the village seems to prosper as a result. However, the incident at the conclusion of the story suggests that all of the garbage they have disposed of is about to come back upon them.

92

TO CHALLENGE STUDENTS . . .

Tell students that in this story Shinichi Hoshi presents a bleak picture of a world where people are eager to "bury" unpleasant things—including cadavers and nuclear waste—without thinking about the consequences of their actions, or their legacy for future generations.

ASK STUDENTS to work with a partner or small group to list the items people throw into the hole and tell who benefits and who is hurt as a result. Point out that there can be immediate and long-term effects: for instance, the act of throwing away a diary can immediately benefit the diarist who has something to hide. On the other hand, if nothing of the truth remains, future generations will have nothing to learn from.

- Point out that throwing away some things may serve the immediate interests of a few but in the process may damage the lives of many. For instance, the practice of burying nuclear waste and other toxic substances can have deleterious effects on the population at large for a very long time.
- Have groups research the issue of nuclear waste. They can explore storage and disposal in the United States and other countries, health effects, and what to do in the event of contamination.
- Students can research the meltdown at Japan's Fukushima nuclear reactor in 2011—one of the worst nuclear disasters of all time—and compare it with the incidents at Three Mile Island (1979) and Chernobyl (1986).
- Students may want to speculate about what Hoshi, who died in 1997, might have thought about the disaster that did so much damage to his home country.

6. **REREAD AND DISCUSS USING TEXT EVIDENCE**

F **ASK STUDENTS** to discuss details in the final sentence (lines 135–136). Who is the man? What is he doing? *He is a construction worker; he is looking up at the city's beautiful skyline.* What doesn't he see? *He doesn't see a small pebble falling past him.* Where have students encountered the same image? *At the beginning of the story a young man throws a pebble in the hole (lines 24–25).*

SHORT RESPONSE

Cite Text Evidence Students should:

- draw conclusions about the theme from details in the text.
- identify plot elements that contribute to the story's message.
- analyze the impact of images, word choice, and dialogue on meaning.
- interpret the conclusion and what it reveals about the author's attitude toward the subject.

DIG DEEPER

1. With the class, return to Question 3, Read. Have students share their responses.

   ASK STUDENTS to think about the way the author uses each of the characters to exemplify a particular kind of self-interest.

   • Have students describe the actions of the scientist, the curiosity-seekers, the newspaper reporters, the concessionaires, the police, and the mayor. How does each one react to the hole? What do they want to do with it?

   • Have students draw conclusions about their motives. What might each stand to gain from the situation?

   • Have students share ideas about who wields the most influence in the village. How do the businessmen get people to agree to their plans? How does the author reveal his attitude toward them?

   • Have students share ideas about the scientist's role. How does he get people to believe in what he is saying? What is the author's attitude toward the scientist?

2. With the class, return to Question 6, Reread and Discuss. Have students share their responses.

   ASK STUDENTS to share their interpretations of the end of the story.

   • Have students discuss the significance of the line "He—y, come on ou—t!" (line 129). Who is speaking these words? Where else in the text have they seen them? Why did the author choose this as the title of the story?

   • Have students draw conclusions about the pebble. Was it the same pebble that was thrown into the hole by the young man in line 25? Where did it come from?

   • Have students describe the workman's attitude toward the pebble. Why did he "fail to notice" it as it fell? What was he looking at instead?

   • Have students discuss the author's vision of the future. How does he see our present mistakes backfiring on us?

   ASK STUDENTS to return to their Short Response answer and revise it based on the class discussion.

CLOSE READING NOTES

THE STUFF OF CONSUMER CULTURE

The FYI site provides links to online articles from a variety of magazines and newspapers. Help students choose a few articles to read to further their exploration of the topic The Stuff of Consumer Culture.

NOVELWISE

Students can unlock the power of novels with this unique resource. Help students read through longer works with these tips:

- Find a Book
- Before You Read
- As You Read
- After You Read

Each book includes introductory material, worksheets, graphic organizers, and discussion guides.

ADDITIONAL TEXTS BY COLLECTION

Suggest that students read the following:

- "The World Is Too Much With Us" by William Wordsworth

Read the poem aloud to students. Then have them analyze the form, focusing on rhyme scheme and meter to see if they can identify a pattern. How does the structure of the poem give them clues to what the theme is?

NONFICTION CONNECTIONS

Suggest that students increase their reading of informational texts. The nonfiction connections include:

- speeches
- diaries
- true-life accounts
- newspaper articles
- political cartoons

Creating an Independent Reading Program

TEACHER GUIDANCE ON TEXT SELECTION AND PROGRESS

Students can benefit from the teacher's knowledge of literary and informational texts, while teachers can evaluate students' progress.

- As students delve into their books, ask them if the selection seems easy, hard, or about right.
- Individually, have each student read a page aloud. Keep track of miscues, and ask the student a few comprehension questions.
- Make recommendations based on your assessment. If the student is struggling, suggest easier texts to build skills. If the student isn't challenged, suggest other selections that require more effort.
- Have students set a goal for reading: for example, a set number of pages per day, or a certain number of new vocabulary words. They can track their goals using progress forms or journals.

STUDENT-TEACHER CONFERENCING

One-on-one conferences help teachers track students' progress and help students get suggestions for improvement and further reading.

- Ask students why they chose the work and how they reacted to it. Did they enjoy it and, if so, why? What new information did they learn? What was easy or hard about the book? What did they do when they got to a word they didn't know?
- Listen carefully and give feedback as needed. Make additional recommendations to encourage further reading. If a student likes a selection, suggest works in the same series or by the same author.
- If students are ready to begin post-reading logs or activities, ask them if they have questions or need clarification before they start.

Interactive Lessons
To help you complete this task, use:
• *Conducting Research*
• *Using Media in a Presentation*

PERFORMANCE TASK

Create a Multimedia Presentation

This collection focuses on the proliferation of consumerism and how it has affected American culture and our environment. In this activity, you will research a topic related to consumerism. You will draw from *Life at Home in the Twenty-First Century,* other texts in the collection, and your research findings to write an informative essay about the topic you chose. Then you will prepare and give a multimedia presentation on that topic.

A successful multimedia presentation

- uses technology to share information through text, graphics, video, music, and/or sound
- organizes ideas logically in a way that is interesting and appropriate to purpose and audience
- presents findings in a focused manner, with relevant facts, definitions, and examples
- emphasizes salient points from a variety of sources and media
- concludes with a section that summarizes the findings presented

W 2a–f Write informative/ explanatory texts.
W 4 Produce clear and coherent writing.
W 5 Develop and strengthen writing.
W 6 Use technology to produce and publish writing.
W 7 Conduct short research projects.
W 8 Gather relevant information.
W 10 Write routinely.
SL 4 Present claims and findings.
SL 5 Include multimedia components in presentations.
SL 6 Adapt speech to a variety of contexts and tasks.

fyi
hmhfyi.com

Visit hmhfyi.com to explore your topic and enhance your research.

PLAN

myNotebook

Use the annotation tools in your eBook to find evidence that supports your points. Save each piece of evidence to your notebook.

Determine Your Topic Review the texts in the collection. Think about the points each author makes about consumerism. Brainstorm a list of possible topics, such as how TV ads influence consumers or how purchasing behavior in reality TV might affect consumerism. Choose a topic that will interest you and others.

- Transform your topic into a research question you want to answer, such as *What kinds of TV ads influence teenage consumers?* or *How does reality TV change people's attitudes toward and increase consumerism?*
- Make sure your question is open-ended and cannot be answered in a single word.
- Generate further questions that will help you find evidence.

ACADEMIC VOCABULARY

As you plan and present your presentation, be sure to use the academic vocabulary words.

attitude

consume

goal

purchase

technology

Collection Performance Task **259**

PERFORMANCE TASK

W 2a–f, W 4,
W 5, W 6,
W 7, W 8,
W 10, SL 4,
SL 5, SL 6

CREATE A MULTIMEDIA PRESENTATION

Introduce students to the Performance Task by reading the introductory paragraph with them and reviewing the criteria for what makes a good multimedia presentation. Remind students that a good multimedia presentation needs to combine strong information and well-organized multimedia to support that information.

▶ *View It!*

Professional Development Podcast:
Performance Tasks

PLAN

DETERMINE YOUR TOPIC

Explain to students that as they assemble their multimedia presentations, they will be looking for different types of sources that answer their research questions. As students consider what point they want to make about consumerism, encourage them to think about how graphics, music, sound effects, and video can engage their audience and support their ideas.

English Language Support

Plan a Multimedia Presentation Make sure students understand that their presentations should focus on a specific topic related to consumerism. Have pairs brainstorm a list of possible topics. Remind them to look for evidence in the collection texts that supports points that the authors make about consumerism. Then have partners share their topic ideas using the following questions:

What will be the topic of your presentation?

What interests you about this topic? Why?

What information from the collection texts relates to your topic?

What questions do you have about this topic?

What information will you look for in your research?

What multimedia elements will engage and inform your audience?

Students can use their conversations to help them focus their research and plan their presentations.

English Language Support

Select Language Resources Encourage students to use their knowledge of morphology to change word forms as they summarize information from their notes. Discuss the differences among the following sentence pairs:

- Teenagers said they would <u>probably</u> text instead of call. / Teenagers showed a higher <u>probability</u> of texting versus calling.
- Teenagers' technology use was more <u>frequent</u> on the weekends. / Teenagers used technology more <u>frequently</u> on the weekends.
- The <u>emphasis</u> in the article was that the benefits of technology use outweigh any negative effects. / The article <u>emphasized</u> that the benefits of technology use outweigh any negative effects.

PRODUCE

DRAFT AN INFORMATIVE ESSAY

Remind students to use their outlines as a guide for their drafts. Explain that beginning each paragraph with one main idea will help ensure a logical presentation of information. As students write, tell them to select ideas that they will clarify with multimedia elements.

WHEN STUDENTS STRUGGLE

Integrate Multimedia Elements Let partners help each other determine how to integrate multimedia elements effectively. As one partner reads aloud a draft of the essay, have the other note important or interesting ideas, facts, and details. After they both read their drafts, have them use their notes to discuss ways in which multimedia elements might improve their presentations. Encourage students to suggest ideas for text revisions along with appropriate visuals and other multimedia elements.

Gather Information In the collection's texts, look for information related to the topic you chose. Take notes on key points, observations, and events that will help you understand your topic, answer your questions, and support your ideas.

Do Research Use print and digital resources to find additional information that addresses your research question.

- Search for credible sources. Use keywords or subject searching in the library to find books related to your topic. Use a search engine to find Internet sources.
- Take notes on facts, details, and examples that explain and support your main points.
- Identify multimedia components, such as graphics, maps, videos, or sound that could emphasize your main points.

Organize Your Ideas Think about how you will organize your information. Create an outline showing the information you will present in each paragraph. Make sure each idea follows from the previous idea and leads into the next idea.

> **I.** Use Roman numerals for main topics.
>   A. Indent and use capital letters for subtopics.
>   1. Indent and use numbers for supporting facts and details.
>   2. Indent and use numbers for supporting facts and details.
> **II.** Use Roman numerals for main topics.
>   B. Indent and use capital letters for subtopics.
>   1. Indent and use numbers for supporting facts and details.

Consider Your Purpose and Audience Think about your audience as you prepare your presentation. Your goal is to use multimedia to get your points across most effectively to this particular audience.

Interactive Lessons
For help in doing your research, use the following lesson:
· Conducting Research: Taking Notes

PRODUCE

Draft an Informative Essay Use your notes and your outline to draft an informative essay that you can use to create your presentation.

- Begin with an attention-grabbing introduction that defines your topic. Include an unusual comment, fact, quote, or story.
- Organize your information into paragraphs of related ideas.

Write your rough draft in *my*WriteSmart. Focus on getting your ideas down, rather than on perfecting your choice of language.

English Language Support

Understand Text Structure Have partners exchange outlines and discuss how each idea, fact, or detail supports a main idea. Help them organize outlines more logically or add details. Then have them list transitions to link their ideas:

Transition	Purpose
also, next, in addition, for example	to introduce a fact or an example
so, because, as a result, since	to show cause or effect
similarly, in contrast, however, instead	to compare or contrast

- Include supporting facts, details, and examples.
- Make sure your ideas transition logically.
- Write a conclusion that follows from and supports your main ideas and leaves the reader with a lasting impression.

Prepare Your Presentation Think about what you want your presentation to look like. Choose a presentation tool to create a slideshow.

- Use text from your essay that explains each topic and subtopic. Revise the text to keep your presentation brief and clear.
- Integrate multimedia components that emphasize your main points. Each component should have a clear purpose.
- Check that all text and visuals are large and clear enough that everyone in the audience can see them.

Interactive Lessons
For help in planning your presentation, use the following lesson:
• Using Media in a Presentation: Using Presentation Software

REVISE

Practice Your Presentation Try speaking in front of a mirror, or make a recording of your presentation and listen to it. Then practice your presentation with a partner.

- Speak clearly and loudly.
- Maintain eye contact. Look directly at your audience.
- Use gestures and facial expressions to emphasize ideas.

Evaluate Your Presentation Use the chart on the following page to determine whether your presentation is effective.

- Check that your ideas are clearly and logically presented.
- Verify that your text includes specific and accurate information.
- Examine your audio and visual components to make sure they are relevant and well integrated.

✓ myWriteSmart

Have a group of peers review your draft and your multimedia elements in *my*WriteSmart. Ask your reviewers to note any ideas or visuals that are unclear or not in a logical sequence.

Interactive Lessons
For help in refining your presentation, use:
• Using Media in a Presentation: Building and Practicing Your Presentation

PRESENT

Deliver Your Presentation Finalize your multimedia presentation. Then choose a way to share it with your audience. Consider these options:

- Use your presentation to give a news report about your topic.
- Create and share a video recording of your presentation.

FOR STANDARD ENGLISH LEARNERS

Use Possessive Pronouns Remind students to follow the rules of standard English in their presentations. For example, some students may use the pronoun *they* instead of *their* in informal conversation. Help them identify places in their presentations where they should use *their*, not *they*, to indicate possession. Review by using the following example:

Children are more likely than *their* parents to watch TV alone.

PERFORMANCE TASK

English Language Support

Understand Cohesion Remind students that when a pronoun refers back to a noun, the noun and pronoun must agree in number. Display the following examples:

- Does <u>a teenager's</u> technology use affect *his* or *her* ability to concentrate?
- The study examined how <u>teenagers'</u> use of technology affects *their* brains.

REVISE

PRACTICE YOUR PRESENTATION

Suggest that partners critique each other's multimedia presentations, evaluating both the information and the multimedia that accompanies it. Partners should offer and discuss suggestions for improvement.

PRESENT

DELIVER YOUR PRESENTATION

Students can

- present news reports about their topics, making sure to include answers to these questions: *who, when, what, where, why,* and *how.*
- make video recordings of their presentations, which can be presented to the class or uploaded onto a school website for others to watch.

FOR STUDENTS WITH DISABILITIES

Extend the Completion Time Let students divide their work into manageable chunks and complete the task over an extended period. They may practice the introduction, body, and conclusion at different times. They may also record sections separately and edit their videos to combine the sections. Consider modifying schedules so that students can deliver presentations at a time when they work more productively, such as early in the day or following an activity period.

PERFORMANCE TASK

USE THE SCORING RUBRIC

Assign three students to score each presentation, with each student focusing on one of the three rubric categories. Ask students to write a brief explanation of the reasons for their score.

REFLECT ON THE PROCESS

Tell students that taking the time to reflect on the planning and presentation processes in this task will help them apply what they have learned and improve their skills. Ask students to think about how well their presentations informed the audience. Then have them briefly respond to the following questions:

- What were the best sources of information on your topic?
- What multimedia elements of your presentation were most effective?
- How engaging was the delivery of your presentation?

PERFORMANCE TASK RUBRIC
MULTIMEDIA PRESENTATION

	Ideas and Evidence	Organization	Language
4	• The introduction is appealing and informative. • The topic is well developed with relevant facts, concrete details, interesting quotations, and examples from reliable sources. • The conclusion capably summarizes the information presented.	• The organization is effective and logical throughout the essay. • Text, visuals, and sound are combined in a coherent manner. • Transitions successfully connect related ideas.	• The language reflects a formal style. • Sentence beginnings, lengths, and structures vary and have a rhythmic flow. • Grammar, usage, and mechanics are correct.
3	• The introduction could do more to grab the reader's attention; the introduction states the topic. • One or two key points could use more support in the form of relevant facts, concrete details, quotations, and examples from reliable sources. • The concluding section summarizes the information presented.	• The organization is confusing in a few places. • Text, visuals, and sound are mostly combined in a coherent manner. • A few more transitions are needed to connect related ideas.	• The style becomes informal in a few places. • Sentence beginnings, lengths, and structures vary somewhat. • Some grammatical and usage errors are repeated in the presentation.
2	• The introduction is only partly informative; the topic and purpose are unclear. • Most key points need more support in the form of relevant facts, concrete details, quotations, and examples from reliable sources. • The concluding section partially summarizes the information presented.	• The organization is logical in some places but often doesn't follow a pattern. • Text, visuals, and sound are combined in a disorganized way. • More transitions are needed throughout to connect related ideas.	• The style becomes informal in several places. • Sentence structures barely vary, and some fragments or run-on sentences are present. • Grammar and usage are incorrect in several places, but the speaker's ideas are still somewhat clear.
1	• The introduction is missing. • Facts, details, quotations, and examples are from unreliable sources or are missing. • The conclusion is missing.	• A logical organization is not used; information is presented randomly. • Text, visuals, and sound are missing. • Transitions are not used, making the presentation difficult to understand.	• The style is inappropriate for the presentation. • Repetitive sentence structure, fragments, and run-on sentences make the presentation hard to follow. • Several grammatical and usage errors change the meaning of ideas.

TO CHALLENGE STUDENTS . . .

Discuss Point of View Challenge students to discuss their points of view about consumerism in small groups. Encourage students to support points of view with evidence from their own research as well as from other student presentations.

©Mohd Shahnizan Hussin/Shutterstock

Guided by a Cause

❝ The fullness of our heart comes in our actions. **❞**

—Mother Teresa

STREAM TO START

Motivate students to read the collection texts and spark their curiosity about the collection by playing the video and watching it in class. After students watch the video, ask them to think about two things they hope to learn from reading about people who have taken up a cause. Call on volunteers to share their responses.

PERFORMANCE TASK PREVIEW

Point out to students that they will complete two performance tasks at the end of the collection. The performance tasks will require them to further analyze the selections in the collection and to synthesize ideas about these analyses. Students will present their findings in a variety of products.

ACADEMIC VOCABULARY

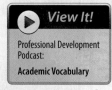

View It!

Professional Development Podcast:

Academic Vocabulary

Students can acquire facility with the academic vocabulary words through frequent, repeated exposure as they analyze and discuss the selections in the collection. Use academic vocabulary in the instructional contexts listed below to help students incorporate these words into their working vocabulary.

- Collaborative Discussion at the end of each selection
- Analyzing the Text questions for each selection
- Selection-level Performance Task
- Vocabulary instruction (for Critical Vocabulary and/or for Vocabulary Strategy)
- Language Conventions
- End-of-collection Performance Task for all selections in the collection

ASK STUDENTS to review the Academic Vocabulary word list for this collection. You may wish to pronounce each word aloud, so students hear the correct pronunciation. Then, discuss the definitions and the related forms for each word. Remind students that they will encounter these five academic vocabulary words throughout the collection.

COLLECTION 6

Guided by a Cause

In this collection, you will consider the question: What inspires people to take action to improve their world?

 Stream to Start

 fyi hmhfyi.com

 Channel One News®

COLLECTION

PERFORMANCE TASK Preview

At the end of this collection, you will have the opportunity to:

- research and write an informative essay about a dramatic and deadly fire that destroyed a New York City factory in 1911
- participate in a panel discussion on what commitment to a cause can mean

ACADEMIC VOCABULARY

Study the words and their definitions in the chart below. You will use these words as you discuss and write about the texts in this collection.

Word	Definition	Related Forms
contrast (kən-trăst´) v.	to show differences between two or more things that are being compared	contrasted, contrasting, contrastive
despite (dĭ-spīt´) prep.	in spite of; even though	despiteful
error (ĕr´ər) n.	a mistake	erroneous, erroneously, errorless
inadequate (ĭn-ăd´ĭ-kwĭt) adj.	not enough or sufficient to fulfill a need or meet a requirement	adequate, adequately, inadequacy, inadequately
interact (ĭn´tər-ăkt´) v.	to act upon each other	interaction, interacting, interactive, interactively

⊟ myNotebook

As students read, analyze, and discuss the texts in this collection, encourage them to create a *my*WordList folder in *my*Notebook to build their own personal word lists.

- **Annotate** Students can highlight vocabulary terms and other unfamiliar words and save each highlighted term to *my*Notebook.
- **Organize** Within *my*Notebook, students can drag each word into the *my*WordList folder.
- **Elaborate** Ask students to add details to the entry for each word, such as a definition, other forms of the word, and a sample sentence.

English Language Support

 View It!
Professional Development Podcast:
English Language Learners

ENGAGE WITH THE COLLECTION TOPIC

Draw students' attention to the title of the collection, Guided by a Cause. Explain that *cause,* as it is used in this title, refers to a principle or movement that someone works for or commits to. Tell students that this collection looks at the events that inspire people to take up a cause and the results of their efforts.

ACCESS PRIOR KNOWLEDGE Ask students to identify some causes that they or people they know feel strongly about. Discuss how being involved in promoting a cause can affect a person's life and outlook.

THINK-WRITE-PAIR-SHARE

Use this strategy to encourage collaborative discussion about texts in this collection.

- **First,** display a question about an aspect of a text students have read or are in the process of reading.
- **Then,** tell students to examine the text and consider possible responses to the question. Have them write individual answers to the question.
- **Next,** pair students and ask them to share their thoughts with their partners, reminding pairs to ask each other

clarifying questions as they discuss their individual ideas. Once discussion has ended, have students revise their written responses to reflect any of their ideas that may have changed during discussion.

- **Finally,** have students share their answers with the entire class.

 Collection 6 Digital Resources for English Language Support

LANGUAGE WORKSHOP
Designated English Learners

You may use the digital Teacher Resources > Language Workshop to support English learners in crafting proposals, improving cohesion, and participating in discussions to identify relevant information.

 VIDEOS

These videos will help students learn how to understand statistics and complex data and how to identify chronological order. Have students use **Text In Focus Practice** to apply those skills.

Collection 6 Lessons	Media	Teach and Practice

Media

Video Links HISTORY A&E Channel One News

Teach and Practice

Close Reading and Evidence Tracking

Student Edition | eBook

ANCHOR TEXT

History Writing by Albert Marrin from *Flesh & Blood So Cheap: The Triangle Fire and Its Legacy*

History Writing by Zachary Kent from *The Story of the Triangle Factory Fire*

- ▶ **Video HISTORY®** *America The Story of Us: The Triangle Shirtwaist Fire*
- 🔊 **Audio** from *Flesh & Blood So Cheap*
- 🔊 **Audio** from *The Story of the Triangle Factory Fire*

Close Read Screencasts
- Modeled Discussion 1 *Flesh & Blood So Cheap* (lines 45–55)
- Modeled Discussion 2 *The Story of the Triangle Factory Fire,* (lines 20–28)
- Close Read application PDF *Flesh & Blood So Cheap,* (lines 197–206) *The Story of the Triangle Factory Fire,* (lines 33–41)

Text in Focus
- Identifying Chronological Order (line 71)

Strategies for Annotation
- Determine Central Idea and Details
- Analyze Structure: Chronological Order
- Analyze Presentations of Information
- Latin Roots

CLOSE READER

History Writing by Lynne Olsen from "The Most Daring of [Our] Leaders"

Speech by John Lewis "Speech from the Democratic National Convention"

- ▶ **Video HISTORY®**
- 🔊 **Audio** from "The Most Daring of [Our] Leaders"
- 🔊 **Audio** "Speech from the Democratic National Convention"

Historical Novel by Margaret Peterson Haddix from *Uprising*

CLOSE READER

Short Story by ZZ Packer from "Doris Is Coming"

- 🔊 **Audio** from *Uprising*
- 🔊 **Audio** from "Doris Is Coming"

Strategies for Annotation
- Analyze Point of View
- Compare and Contrast: Genres
- Analogies

ANCHOR TEXT

Personal Essay by Craig Kielburger "Craig Kielburger Reflects on Working Toward Peace"

CLOSE READER

Online Article by David Karas "Difference Maker: John Bergmann and Popcorn Park"

- ▶ **Video HISTORY®** *"The Fight to End Child Labor"*
- 🔊 **Audio** "Craig Kielburger Reflects on Working Toward Peace"
- 🔊 **Audio** "Difference Maker: John Bergmann and Popcorn Park"

Close Read Screencasts
- Modeled Discussion (lines 7–14)
- Close Read application PDF (lines 138–145)

Text in Focus
- Understanding Data (line 53)
Strategies for Annotation
- Analyze Text: Personal Essay
- Multiple Meanings

Documentary directed by Judy Jackson "It Takes a Child"

EXEMPLAR

Poem by Nikki Giovanni "A Poem for My Librarian, Mrs. Long"

- 🔊 **Audio** "A Poem for My Librarian, Mrs. Long"

Strategies for Annotation
- Determine Meaning: Style

Short Story by D'Arcy McNickle "Train Time"

- 🔊 **Audio** "Train Time"

Strategies for Annotation
- Analyze Stories: Character Development
- Using a Dictionary

Collection 6 Performance Tasks:
A Write an Informative Essay
B Participate in a Panel Discussion

fyi hmhfyi.com

Interactive Lessons
A Writing Informative Texts
A Conducting Research

B Participating in Collaborative Discussions

For Systematic Coverage of Writing and Speaking & Listening Standards

Interactive Lessons

Writing Informative Texts
Giving a Presentation

For foundational
skills and reading
intervention support: READ180

Assess		Extend	Reteach
Performance Task	✅ *Assess It Online!*	**Teacher eBook**	**Teacher eBook**
Speaking Activity: Summary	Selection Test	**Primary and Secondary Sources > Interactive Whiteboard Lesson >** Primary and Secondary Sources	**Analyze Presentations of Information**
Writing Activity: Narrative	Selection Test		**Analyze Point of View > Level Up Tutorial >** Third-Person Point of View **Compare and Contrast: Genres > Level Up Tutorial >** Prose Forms
Speaking Activity: Argument	Selection Test	**Trace an Argument > Interactive Whiteboard Lesson >** Elements of an Argument	**Analyze Text: Personal Essay**
Media Activity: Photo Documentary	Selection Test	**Camera Shots and Shot Selection**	**Elements of a Documentary**
Writing Activity: Poem	Selection Test	**Determine the Meanings of Words and Phrases**	**Determine Meaning: Style > Level Up Tutorial >** Author's Style
Writing Activity: Character Analysis	Selection Test	**Analyze Story Elements: Setting > Interactive Whiteboard Lesson >** Setting	**Analyze Stories: Characterization > Level Up Tutorial >** Methods of Characterization
A Write an Informative Essay **B** Participate in a Panel Discussion	Collection Test		

Lesson Assessments Writing Informative Texts Giving a Presentation	**Standards Support and Enrichment** **For Designated English Language Instruction**	For more standard instruction and practice, see Teacher Resources > Standards Support and Enrichment. To provide support for English Learners during Designated English Language instruction, use the lessons found in Teacher Resources > Language Workshop.

Collection 6 Lessons	Key Learning Objective	Performance Task	Vocabulary Strategy
ANCHOR TEXT **History Writing by Albert Marrin** **Lexile 900L** from *Flesh & Blood So Cheap: The Triangle Fire and Its Legacy*, p. 265A **History Writing by Zachary Kent** **Lexile 1110L** from *The Story of the Triangle Factory Fire*, p. 265A	**The student will be able to . . .** determine central ideas and details, analyze chronological order, and analyze authors' writings on the same topic.	Speaking Activity: Summary	Latin Roots
Historical Novel by Margaret Peterson Haddix **Lexile 800L** from *Uprising*, p. 283A	**The student will be able to . . .** analyze points of view in a text and compare and contrast different genres.	Writing Activity: Narrative	Analogies
ANCHOR TEXT **Personal Essay by Craig Kielburger** **Lexile 1080L** "Craig Kielburger Reflects on Working Toward Peace," p. 307A	**The student will be able to . . .** identify and analyze elements of a personal essay and determine an author's point of view.	Speaking Activity: Argument	Multiple Meanings
Documentary directed by Judy Jackson "It Takes a Child," p. 317A	**The student will be able to . . .** analyze the purpose of a documentary and understand the features used in it.	Media Activity: Photo Documentary	
EXEMPLAR **Poem by Nikki Giovanni** "A Poem for My Librarian, Mrs. Long," p. 321A	**The student will be able to . . .** analyze a poet's style and determine a theme.	Writing Activity: Poem	
Short Story by D'Arcy McNickle **Lexile 670L** "Train Time," p. 327A	**The student will be able to . . .** analyze methods of characterization and flashback in a short story.	Writing Activity: Character Analysis	Using a Dictionary

Collection 6 Performance Tasks:

A Write an Informative Essay
B Participate in a Panel Discussion

Language Conventions	English Language Support	Differentiated Instruction	CLOSE READER Selection
Capitalization	• Read Closely • Analyze Language • Select Affixes • Understand Cohesion • Word Study • Support Opinions	**For Students with Disabilities:** Cause and Effect **For Standard English Learners:** • Past Perfect Tense • Pronunciation **When Students Struggle:** Restate Main Ideas	History Writing by Lynne Olsen "The Most Daring of [Our] Leaders," p. 282b **Lexile 1190L** Speech by John Lewis "Speech from the Democratic National Convention," p. 282b **Lexile 890L**
Phrases	• Understand Text Structure • Improve Reading Fluency • Support Opinions • Analyze Point of View • Analyze Dramatic Irony • Culturally Responsive Instruction	**When Students Struggle:** • Track Causes and Effects • Analyze Plot **To Challenge Students:** Discuss the Role of Women **For Standard English Learners:** Past Tense Verbs	Short Story by ZZ Packer from *Doris Is Coming*, p. 306b **Lexile 880L**
Dangling Modifiers	• Understand Text Structure • Select Affixes • Read Closely • Express Opinions • Modify to Add Details • Interact via Written English	**When Students Struggle:** Track Elements of Personal Essays	Online Article by David Karas "Difference Maker: John Bergmann and Popcorn Park," p.320b **Lexile 1130L**
	• View Closely • Analyze Language • Select Affixes • Use Subject-Specific Terms	**For Students with Disabilities:** Use Audio	
Combining Sentences with Phrases	• Analyze Language • Use Nouns and Noun Phrases • Connect Ideas	**When Students Struggle:** Determine Meaning: Style	
Misplaced Modifiers	• Understand Cohesion • Read Closely • Connect Ideas • Modify to Add Details	**When Students Struggle:** Characterization **To Challenge Students:** Character's Point of View	
A Participles as Adjectives	**A** Write Informative Texts Understand Text Structure Condense Ideas **B** Plan a Collaborative Discussion Link Ideas Support Opinions Prepare to Practice and Present	**A For Standard English Learners:** Use Simple Past Tense **When Students Struggle:** Add Facts and Details **For Students with Disabilities:** Listen to the Essay **To Challenge Students:** Conduct Additional Research **B For Standard English Learners:** Form Negatives **When Students Struggle:** Practice Speaking Techniques **For Students with Disabilities:** Videotape the Discussion **To Challenge Students:** Gather Additional Evidence	

ANCHOR TEXT

from Flesh & Blood So Cheap: The Triangle Fire and Its Legacy

ANCHOR TEXT

from The Story of the Triangle Factory Fire

*my***SmartPlanner** Create lesson plans and access resources online.

History Writing by Albert Marrin

History Writing by Zachary Kent

Why These Texts?

This lesson guides students to compare two examples of history writing on the same topic and to understand how an author's perspective shapes his or her presentation of history.

▶ **View It!**

Professional Development Podcast:

Informational Text

Key Learning Objective: The student will be able to determine central ideas and details, analyze chronological order, and analyze authors' writings on the same topic.

For practice and application:

Close Reader selections

"The Most Daring of [Our] Leaders"
History Writing by Lynne Olsen

"Speech from the Democratic National Convention"
Speech by John Lewis

RI 1 Cite text evidence.
RI 2 Determine central ideas.
RI 3 Analyze interactions between individuals, events, and ideas.
RI 5 Analyze structure.
RI 6 Determine author's point of view or purpose.
RI 9 Analyze how authors shape presentations.
W 2 Write informative/explanatory texts.
W 7 Conduct short research projects.
W 8 Gather information from print and digital sources.
SL 4 Present claims and findings.
SL 6 Adapt speech to contexts and tasks.
L 2 Demonstrate command of the conventions of capitalization.
L 4b Use Latin affixes and roots as clues to meaning.
L 4d Verify the meaning of a word or phrase.

▲ Text Complexity Rubric

	from Flesh & Blood So Cheap Lexile: 900L	*from* The Story of the Triangle Factory Fire Lexile: 1110L
Quantitative Measures		
Qualitative Measures	Levels of Meaning/Purpose single purpose and topic	Levels of Meaning/Purpose single purpose and topic
	Structure conventional organization of main ideas and details; traits common to informational texts	Structure organization somewhat complex but generally sequential
	Language Conventionality and Clarity clear and direct, but some unfamiliar academic language and longer descriptions	Language Conventionality and Clarity less straightforward sentence structure; some unfamiliar academic language
	Knowledge Demands some simple historical concepts	Knowledge Demands some simple historical concepts
Reader/Task Considerations	• Teacher determined • Vary by individual reader and type of text • See the Text X-Ray for suggested Reader/Task Considerations.	

TEXT X-RAY

English Language Support Before teaching, use the Text X-Ray for an overview of the text's complexity. The Text X-Ray and the supports and scaffolds in the Teacher's Edition will help you guide students of different skill levels.

Meaning Making

Language Development

Effective Expression

Content Knowledge

Foundational Skills

Text Complexity: Qualitative Measures

▲ Levels of Meaning/Purpose

Help students analyze the perspective from which information is presented.

- Teacher's Edition side notes, pp. 267, 268, 269, 271, 273, 275, 276, 279
- English Language Support, pp. 265, 271, 273
- Close Read Screencasts, p. 265
- Strategies for Annotation, p. 279
- Analyze Presentations of Information, p. 279

To reteach how to analyze presentations of information, see

- Analyze Presentations of Information, p. 282a

 Use It! **Level Up Tutorials:** Author's Perspective

ZOOM IN ON COMPARING PERSPECTIVES Explain that the details authors include in a text give insight into their **perspectives** on a topic.

- Have small groups reread each selection and highlight or record the direct quotations.
- Have groups discuss what these quotations reveal about each author's perspective on the Triangle fire. Provide these sentence frames:
  The quotations in the [first/second] selection mainly focus on _____.
  They help readers understand _____.
  For example, the author quotes ____, who says _____.
  The author includes these details to show _____.

▲ Structure

Help students determine central ideas, details, and their organization.

- Teacher's Edition side notes, pp. 266, 267, 268, 269, 270, 271, 272, 274, 275, 276, 277, 278
- English Language Support, pp. 266, 269, 270, 275, 276
- When Students Struggle, p. 270
- Strategies for Annotation, pp. 272, 274, 278
- Determine Central Idea and Details, p. 274
- Analyze Structure: Chronological Order, p. 278

 Identifying Chronological Order

 Use It! **Level Up Tutorial:** Main Idea and Supporting Details

ZOOM IN ON DETERMINING CENTRAL IDEA AND DETAILS After students have read the first selection, have them complete these steps in mixed-ability groups:

- Assign several paragraphs to each group. Have students identify the **topic** of each paragraph, examine its specific details, and determine and state its **main idea** in a sentence.
- Ask groups to take turns sharing their main idea sentences. Write each sentence on the board in order.
- Discuss how all the statements relate to the **central idea** of the selection.

▲ Language Conventionality and Clarity

Teach unfamiliar vocabulary in context.

- Teacher's Edition Critical Vocabulary notes, pp. 266, 268, 270, 272, 275, 277, 281
- English Language Support, p. 266
- Applying Academic Vocabulary, p. 269
- Strategies for Annotation, p. 281
- Vocabulary Strategy: Latin Roots, p. 281

Support students' analysis of the selections.

- Teacher's Edition side notes, pp. 277, 282
- English Language Support, pp. 271, 273, 276, 277, 279, 282
- Language Conventions: Capitalization, p. 282

Provide students with practice in selecting affixes.

- English Language Support, p. 269

ZOOM IN ON **ANALYZING LANGUAGE** Write these sentences on the board:

> "Wind gusts made eerie sounds, like the howling of great beasts in pain. . . ." (lines 92–93, *Flesh & Blood*)
> "In 1933 President Franklin Roosevelt named Frances Perkins secretary of labor." (lines 52–53, *The Story*)

Explain that an **objective** viewpoint simply states facts, while a **subjective** viewpoint includes an opinion or judgment. To identify viewpoint, students should watch for emotional language. Guide students to find words that express emotion or judgment in the two quotations. *(The first is subjective, as shown by the words* eerie, howling, beasts, *and* pain. *The second is objective; it simply states facts.)*

▲ Knowledge Demands

Support English Learners in understanding the context.

- Teacher's Edition Background note, p. 265
- Content-Area Connection, p. 267

To teach primary and secondary sources, see

- Primary and Secondary Sources, p. 282a

 For more context and historical background, students can view the video "AMERICA The Story of Us: The Triangle Shirtwaist Fire."

▶ *Use It!* **Interactive Whiteboard Lesson:** Primary and Secondary Sources

ZOOM IN ON **BUILDING UNDERSTANDING OF CONTEXT** Discuss these terms:

- In *Flesh & Blood* line 122, *union organizers* are people who recruit workers to join a union, an organization that protects workers' rights.
- In *The Story* line 17, *manslaughter* is a lesser charge than murder; although many workers died, the owners did not intend to kill them.
- In *The Story* line 27, *Capital* refers to wealthy businessmen.

▲ Suggested Reader/Task Considerations

Consider the following before assigning these history selections to students.

- Might students struggle with the graphic descriptions in the first selection?
- Will students be able to follow the action as it is described in lines 108–222 of the first selection?

ZOOM IN ON **SUPPORTING COMPREHENSION**

- Give students an overview of the text to assess whether the fates of the workers are too gruesome. As an alternative, summarize lines 108–222 and have them read lines 1–107 and 223–265.
- After discussing key ideas from the first part of the selection, work with students to highlight words and phrases in lines 108–222 that tell where and when the action in each paragraph takes place.

TEACH

CLOSE READ

Background Have students read the background and information about the authors. Offer additional information about the allusion in the title of Albert Marrin's book:

- The quotation "flesh and blood so cheap" comes from a poem of social protest, "The Song of the Shirt" by English poet Thomas Hood (1799–1845).
- The first stanza of the poem has the lines "With fingers weary and worn, / With eyelids heavy and red, / A woman sat in unwomanly rags / Plying her needle and thread— / Stitch! stitch! stitch! / In poverty, hunger, and dirt."
- The fifth stanza includes the lines "O God! that bread should be so dear, / And flesh and blood so cheap!"

SETTING A PURPOSE Direct students to use the Setting a Purpose questions to focus their reading. Remind students to generate questions as they read.

English Language Support

Read Closely Read the title of Marrin's book aloud and explain to students that it is a reference to a poem written in the nineteenth century.

- Share the image of the seamstress from the first stanza of the poem, using the information in the Teacher's Edition Background note. Discuss how that image connects to the topic of the selection students are about to read.
- Then write the lines from the fifth stanza on the board. Define *dear* and *cheap* for students. Invite volunteers to explain what the poet means. Then ask students what the author's use of this line from the poem for the title of his book suggests about his view of the factory fire that killed so many workers. *(Possible response: He is sympathetic to the workers and may think that their employers did not place much value on their lives.)*

Background *An event can be so dramatic and so haunting that it compels the generations that follow it to dissect its details and to trace its impact. A deadly disaster occurred in New York City in 1911 at a company in the ten-story Asch Building. Known today as the Brown Building, it is now a National Historic Landmark. These history writings are detailed accounts of what happened and the long-term effects.*

The Triangle Factory Fire

(l) ©Photodisc/Getty Images; (r) ©Underwood & Underwood/Corbis

from Flesh & Blood So Cheap: The Triangle Fire and Its Legacy
History Writing by Albert Marrin

Albert Marrin (b. 1936) *taught social studies in a junior high school and then became a college teacher. But he realized that he missed telling stories as he had as a teacher. That's when Marrin decided to write history for young adults. He has now produced more than thirty nonfiction books, for which he has won numerous awards.*

from The Story of the Triangle Factory Fire
History Writing by Zachary Kent

Zachary Kent *is the author of over fifty books for young readers. He writes primarily about history and has written biographies of various noted figures, including Abraham Lincoln and Charles Lindbergh.*

SETTING A PURPOSE As you read, think about how each writer presents information on the same event. How are the pieces similar? How are they different? Write down any questions you have while reading.

myNotebook

As you read, mark up the text. Save your work to *my*Notebook.
- Highlight details
- Add notes and questions
- Add new words to *my*WordList

Close Read Screencasts

Modeled Discussions

Have students click the *Close Read* icons in their eBooks to access two screencasts in which readers discuss and annotate the following key passages:

- *Flesh & Blood So Cheap*, lines 45–55
- *The Story of the Triangle Factory Fire*, lines 20–28

As a class, view and discuss the videos. Then, have students work in pairs to do an independent close read of two additional passages:

- *Flesh & Blood So Cheap*, lines 197–206
- *The Story of the Triangle Factory Fire*, lines 33–41

Determine Central Idea and Details (LINES 1–30)

RI 1,
RI 2

Tell students that lines 1–30 present specific facts, or **details,** about the type of work being done and the materials used on each of the top three floors of the building. The author is preparing readers to visualize the setting and understand the dangers to come.

Ⓐ **CITE TEXT EVIDENCE** Have students identify the main activity on each of the three floors, including details that reveal the danger of fire. (*On the eighth floor, the cutters cut fabric called lawn, which "burned as easily as gasoline." On the ninth floor, workers sewed at tables so close together that there was "only a narrow aisle" between rows. On the tenth floor, the shirtwaists were inspected, packed, and shipped. The tenth floor "also held the showroom and owners' offices."*)

English Language Support

Display lines 1–30. Highlight these phrases: "On the eighth floor" in line 2, "to the ninth floor" in line 22, and "to the tenth floor" in line 28. Work with students to pick out important details that tell about the work done on each floor in the sentences following each highlighted phrase.

CRITICAL VOCABULARY

flammable: The cotton fabric called lawn and the tissue paper that separated the fabric layers were both flammable.

ASK STUDENTS why the author is pointing out that these things were flammable. (*They will catch fire and burn easily, contributing to the spread of the fire.*)

---

from **Flesh & Blood So Cheap**
by Albert Marrin

Ⓐ The Triangle Waist Company occupied the top three floors of the Asch Building. On the eighth floor, forty cutters,[1] all men, worked at long wooden tables. Nearby, about a hundred women did basting[2] and other tasks. Paper patterns hung from lines of string over the tables. Although cutters wasted as little fabric as possible, there were always scraps, which they threw into bins under the tables. Every two months or so, a rag dealer took away about a ton of scraps, paying about seven cents a pound. He then sold them back to cotton mills to remake into new cloth. The last pickup was in January.

10

On March 25, the cutters prepared for their next day's work. Since it was Saturday, everyone would leave early, at 4:45 P.M. Workers from other firms had already left; Triangle employees had to stay longer to fill back orders. Carefully, cutters spread "lawn" (from the French word *lingerie*) on their tables 120 layers thick. Lawn was not just *any* cotton fabric. Sheer and lightweight, it was beautiful and comfortable—and burned as easily as gasoline. Each layer was separated from the others by a sheet of equally **flammable** tissue paper.

20

After cutting, the various pieces would go by freight elevator to the ninth floor for sewing and finishing. There, eight rows of sewing machine tables, holding 288 machines in all, occupied the entire width of the room. Only a narrow aisle separated one row from another; the tables were so close together that chairs touched back to back between the rows. From time to time, workers would take the finished shirtwaists[3] to the tenth floor for inspection, packing, and shipping. This floor also held the showroom and owners' offices.

30

By 4:40 P.M., the cutters had finished their work. With five minutes to go, they stood around, talking until the quitting bell rang. Although it was against the rules, some lit cigarettes, hiding the smoke by blowing it up their jacket sleeves. On the floor above, workers had begun to walk toward the lockers to

flammable
(flăm´ə-bəl) *adj.*
If something is *flammable,* it is easy for it to catch on fire and burn.

---

[1] **cutters:** people who cut cloth in a clothing factory.
[2] **basting:** stitching.
[3] **shirtwaists:** women's blouses that resemble men's shirts.

©Photodisc/Getty Images

English Language Support

Analyze Language Display lines 1–3, and highlight the word *cutters.* Have a volunteer read the definition in the footnote. Explain that this is one of the terms specific to the domain of clothing production that the author uses to convey precise information about his topic.

- Display lines 1–20 and these headings: *Materials, Workers, Jobs.* Using three different colors, work with students to highlight terms that fit each category. Discuss their meanings.

- Have pairs list domain-specific terms in lines 1–30. Have them compare lists with another pair and collaborate to organize the

words into categories, looking up definitions as needed. Ask them to write a sentence for each category that shows how the words relate to each other. Prompt them with this example: *One of the fabrics used was a special cotton called lawn.*

- Ask pairs of students to list domain-specific terms in lines 1–30. Then have them use these words to summarize the work done at the Triangle Waist Company.

get their coats and hats. They looked forward to Sunday and family visits, boyfriends, dances, and nickelodeons.[4] Although they had no inkling of what was about to happen, many had only minutes to live.

We will never know for sure what started the Triangle Fire. Most likely, a cutter flicked a hot ash or tossed a live cigarette butt into a scrap bin. Whatever the cause, survivors said the first sign of trouble was smoke pouring from beneath a cutting table.

Cutters flung buckets of water at the smoking spot, without effect. Flames shot up, igniting the line of hanging paper patterns. "They began to fall on the layers of thin goods underneath them," recalled cutter Max Rothen. "Every time another piece dropped, light scraps of burning fabric began to fly around the room. They came down on the other tables and they fell on the machines. Then the line broke and the whole string of burning patterns fell down." A foreman ran for the hose on the stairway wall. Nothing! No water came. The hose had not been connected to the standpipe.[5] Seconds later, the fire leaped out of control.

Yet help was already on the way. At exactly 4:45 P.M., someone pulled the eighth-floor fire alarm. In less than two minutes, the horse-drawn vehicles of Engine Company 72 arrived from a firehouse six blocks away. The moment they arrived, the firefighters unloaded their equipment and prepared to swing into action. As they did, the area pumping station raised water pressure in the hydrants near the Asch Building. Other units soon arrived from across the Lower East Side with more equipment.

Meanwhile, workers on the eighth floor rang furiously for the two passenger elevators. Safety experts have always advised against using elevators in a fire. Heat can easily damage their machinery, leaving trapped passengers dangling in space, to burn or suffocate. Despite the danger, the operators made several trips, saving scores of workers before heat bent the elevators' tracks and put them out of action.

Those who could not board elevators rushed the stairway door. They caused a pileup, so that those in front could not open the door. Whenever someone tried to get it open, the crowd pinned her against it. "All the girls were falling on me

---

[4] **nickelodeons:** early movie theaters that charged five cents for admission.
[5] **standpipe:** a large pipe into which water is pumped.

CONTENT-AREA CONNECTION

Science Point out phrases on page 267 that describe fire, and discuss the impression of energy and movement they convey. Explain that fire is a form of energy; it creates heat and light as a result of a chemical reaction.

Activity Have small groups research fire and how it works. Suggest that they begin by listing research questions such as these: *What chemical reaction produces fire? What causes smoke? What are flames? What does a fire need to keep burning? What can put out a fire most effectively? Why does a fire spread?* Ask groups to report on the facts they learn, using visual displays or posters to illustrate important principles.

CLOSE READ

  For more context and historical background, students can view the video "AMERICA The Story of Us: The Triangle Shirtwaist Fire" in their eBooks.

Analyze Presentations of Information (LINES 40–44)
RI 1, RI 6

Point out that history writers offer their interpretations along with factual information.

B **CITE TEXT EVIDENCE** Have students closely reread lines 40–44 and cite details in which the author interprets his research. (*"We will never know for sure what started the Triangle Fire." He describes the "most likely" cause based on survivors' reports.*)

Determine Central Idea and Details (LINES 45–71)
RI 2

Tell students that **central ideas,** or main ideas, are the most important ideas in a text. To identify the main idea in a paragraph, readers should pay attention to what all the sentences tell about.

C **ASK STUDENTS** to reread lines 45–71. Have students summarize this section by stating the main idea of each paragraph in a sentence. (*Cloth and paper burst into flames that were out of control in seconds. Firefighters quickly arrived at the building. Scores of workers managed to escape in two passenger elevators before heat destroyed the tracks.*)

Text in FOCUS English Language Support

Identifying Chronological Order (LINE 71)

Have students view the **Text In Focus** video on this page of their eBook to learn how to identify the chronological order of events recounted in the text. Then have students use **Text In Focus Practice** to apply what they have learned.

Analyze Presentations of Information (LINES 89–96)   RI 6

Explain that a history author's **point of view** may be **subjective** at times, revealing the author's opinions and beliefs. This may be done through the author's word choice and through the details the author emphasizes.

D **CITE TEXT EVIDENCE** Have students reread lines 89–96. Ask students to cite especially vivid descriptive details and explain why the author includes those details. (*"Wind gusts made eerie sounds, like the howling of great beasts in pain." The author believes the event was horrifying and wants readers to share the terror and panic experienced by the victims.*)

Determine Central Idea and Details (LINES 100–104)   RI 2

Point out that the author is using quotations from survivors to support his main ideas.

E **ASK STUDENTS** what Mary Bucelli's words, in lines 100–104, reveal about the situation. (*Her words support the idea that there was no plan for escaping a fire, and no one knew what to do. The workers panicked and thought only of saving themselves.*)

CRITICAL VOCABULARY

reign: The author says that confusion reigned.

ASK STUDENTS what caused confusion to reign. (*The workers had not had fire drills, so they didn't know what to do. Confusion took control.*)

FOR STUDENTS WITH DISABILITIES

Tell students that this part of the text conveys the confusion that the workers in the factory felt as they tried to escape the fire. To help students understand these events, have them listen to the audio recording of lines 94–139 as they follow along in their texts. Then, using a cause-and-effect diagram such as this one, guide them to identify what happened to the workers on the ninth floor.

---

and they squeezed me to the door," Ida Willensky recalled. "Three times I said to the girls, 'Please, girls, let me open the door. Please!' But they would not listen to me." Finally, cutter Louis Brown barged through the crowd and forced the
80   door open.

Workers, shouting, crying, and gasping for air, slowly made their way downstairs. There were no lights in the stairway, so they had to grope their way in darkness. A girl fell; others fell on top of her, blocking the stairs until firefighters arrived moments later. Yet everyone who took the stairway from the eighth floor got out alive, exiting through the Washington Place doors. Those on the ninth floor were not so lucky.

D 90   New Yorkers say that March comes in like a lion (with cold wind) and leaves like a lamb (with April's warm showers). Now, as fire raged on the eighth floor, the elevator shafts became wind tunnels. Wind gusts made eerie sounds, like the howling of great beasts in pain, while sucking flaming embers upward. On the ninth floor, embers landed on piles of finished shirtwaists and cans of oil used to make the sewing machines run smoothly. Instantly, the air itself seemed to catch fire.

Had there been fire drills, surely more would have survived. Unfortunately, confusion **reigned**. Workers had to make life-and-death decisions in split seconds amid fire,
100   smoke, and panic. It was everyone for themselves. "I was
E   throwing them out of the way," Mary Bucelli said of the women near her. "No matter whether they were in front of me or coming from in back of me, I was pushing them down. I was only looking out for my own life." Mary joined others who ran to the Greene Street stairway. They made it down to the street or up to the tenth floor and the roof, before flames blocked this escape route.

Others headed for the elevators and stairway on the Washington Place side of the building. Forcing open the
110   doors to the elevator shaft, they looked down and saw an elevator starting what would be its last trip from the eighth floor. "I reached out and grabbed the cables, wrapped my legs around them, and started to slide down," recalled Samuel Levine, a sewing machine operator. "While on my way down, as slow as I could let myself drop, the bodies of six girls went falling past me. One of them struck me, and I fell on top of the elevator. I fell on the dead body of a girl. Finally I heard

> **reign**
> (rān) *v.* If some things *reign* over something else, it means they dominate it.

Firefighters in a horse-drawn fire engine race to respond to the fire at the Triangle Waist Company.

F

120 the firemen cutting their way into the elevator shaft, and they came and let me out."

Those who reached the ninth-floor stairway door found it locked. This was not unusual, as employers often locked doors to discourage latecomers and keep out union organizers. "My God, I am lost!" cried Margaret Schwartz as her hair caught fire. Nobody who went to that door survived, nor any who reached the windows.

With a wave of fire rolling across the room, workers rushed to the windows, only to meet more fire. Hot air expands. Unless it escapes, pressure will keep building, eventually blowing a hole even in a heavy iron container

130 like a boiler. Heat and pressure blew out the eighth-floor windows. Firefighters call the result "lapping in"—that is, sucking flames into open windows above. That is why you see black scorch marks on the wall above the window of a burnt-out room.

G

With fire advancing from behind and flames rising before them, people knew they were doomed. Whatever they did meant certain death. By remaining in the room, they chose death by fire or suffocation. Jumping ninety-five feet to the ground meant death on the sidewalk. We cannot know what

140 passed through the minds of those who decided to jump. Yet

Flesh & Blood So Cheap **269**

APPLYING ACADEMIC VOCABULARY

contrast	despite	inadequate

THINK-PAIR-SHARE Have students turn to a partner to discuss the following questions using the academic vocabulary words *contrast*, *despite*, and *inadequate*. Ask volunteers to share responses with the class.

- Why did so many people die **despite** firefighters' efforts?
- How was the tragedy intensified by **inadequate** safety measures?
- **Contrast** the situations on the different floors. Which floor had the most survivors? Why?

CLOSE READ

Analyze Presentations of Information (LINES 120–125) RI 6

Tell students that an **author's perspective** is the combination of ideas, feelings, values, and beliefs that influence the way the author presents information.

F **CITE TEXT EVIDENCE** Have students reread lines 120–125 and cite the reason that the ninth-floor stairway door was locked. (*"This was not unusual, as employers often locked doors to discourage latecomers and keep out union organizers."*) Ask students why the author might have included this detail. (*He wants to show how little power workers had at that time.*)

Determine Central Idea and Details (LINES 130–132) RI 2

Marrin continues describing events on the ninth floor.

G **ASK STUDENTS** what the information about "lapping in" in lines 130–132 helps readers understand. (*Flames were sucked into open windows above the eighth floor, so fire on the ninth floor grew.*)

English Language Support

Read lines 130–132 aloud. To help students understand the concept of "lapping in," draw a simple diagram showing the flames traveling from lower windows to upper windows. Have pairs write a sentence explaining what this detail helps them understand about the situation on the ninth floor.

English Language Support

Select Affixes Explain that affixes change a word's meaning and part of speech. Have students choose the correct form of each word in parentheses:

Employers (usual) locked the doors. (*usually*)

Locked doors made (survive) impossible. (*survival, surviving*)

Due to the (expand) of the hot air, pressure built up inside the building. (*expansion*)

Death was a (certain) for many workers. (*certainty*)

Flesh & Blood So Cheap **269**

Determine Central Idea and Details (LINES 152–177)

RI 2

Point out that the two paragraphs in lines 152–177 tell about the work of firefighters.

H **ASK STUDENTS** to closely reread lines 152–177, determine what each paragraph is mainly about, and state each main idea in a sentence. *(Firefighters brought water, but they couldn't use it on the windows with people near them. Firefighters brought life nets, but these failed due to the tremendous force of the falling bodies.)*

English Language Support

Model how to identify the main idea of lines 152–162, using the strategy in the When Students Struggle note on this page. Then have pairs follow the same steps to identify the main idea of lines 163–177. Prompt them as needed.

> #### CRITICAL VOCABULARY
>
> **portable**: Water streamed from portable towers.
>
> **ASK STUDENTS** why the towers had to be portable. *(so that they could be carried on the fire wagons)*

---

their thinking, in those last moments of life, may have gone like this: If I jump, my family will have a body to identify and bury, but if I stay in this room, there will be nothing left.

A girl clung to a window frame until flames from the eighth floor lapped in, burning her face and setting fire to her hair and clothing. She let go. Just then, Frances Perkins reached the scene from her friend's town house on the north side of Washington Square. "Here they come," onlookers shouted as Engine Company 72 reined in their horses. "Don't jump; stay there." Seconds later, Hook and Ladder Company 20 arrived.

Firefighters charged into the building, stretching a hose up the stairways as they went. At the sixth-floor landing, they connected it to the standpipe. Reaching the eighth floor, they crawled into the inferno on their bellies, under the rising smoke, with their hose. Yet nothing they did could save those at the windows. Photos of the **portable** towers show streams of water playing on the three top floors. (A modern high-pressure pumper can send water as high as one thousand feet.) Plenty of water got through the windows, but not those with people standing in them. A burst of water under high pressure would have hurled them backward, into the flames.

Hoping to catch jumpers before they hit the ground, firefighters held up life nets, sturdy ten-foot-square nets made of rope. It was useless. A person falling from the ninth floor struck with a force equal to eleven thousand pounds. Some jumpers bounced off nets, dying when they hit the ground; others tore the nets, crashing through to the pavement. "The force was so great it took men off their feet," said Captain Howard Ruch of Engine Company 18. "Trying to hold the nets, the men turned somersaults. The men's hands were bleeding, the nets were torn and some caught fire" from burning clothing. Officers, fearing their men would be struck by falling bodies, ordered the nets removed. The aerial ladders failed, too, reaching only to the sixth floor. Desperate jumpers tried to grab hold of a rung on the way down, missed, and landed on the sidewalk.

People began to jump singly or in groups of two or three, holding hands as they stepped out the windows. William G. Shepherd, a reporter for United Press, watched the "shower of bodies" in horror.

portable
(pôr′tə-bəl) *adj.*
If something is *portable*, it can be carried or moved easily.

WHEN STUDENTS STRUGGLE . . .

Guide students in these steps to develop statements of main ideas:

- Reread one paragraph.
- Think of a good title for the paragraph. It should name the paragraph topic—what most or all of the sentences tell about.
- Think about the details in the paragraph. Ask: What is most important to know about the paragraph topic?
- Write a sentence that answers that question.
- Use a graphic organizer like the one shown to record topics and main ideas.

Paragraph Title (Topic)	Main Idea
Life Nets	The firefighters' rope nets were not strong enough to hold the falling bodies.

LEVEL UP TUTORIALS For additional support, assign the following *Level Up* tutorial: **Main Idea and Supporting Details.**

I saw every feature of the tragedy visible from outside the building. I learned a new sound—a more horrible sound than any description can picture. It was the sound of a speeding, living body on a stone sidewalk.

Thud—dead, thud—dead, thud—dead, thud—dead.
190 *Sixty-two thud—dead. I call them that, because the sound and the thought of death came to me each time, at the same instant. . . . Down came the bodies in a shower, burning, smoking—flaming bodies, with the disheveled hair trailing upward. . . .*

On the sidewalk lay heaps of broken bodies. A policeman later went about with tags, which he fastened with wires to the wrists of the dead girls. . . . The floods of water from the firemen's hose that ran into the gutter was actually stained red with blood.

Onlookers saw many dreadful sights, none more so than the end of a love affair. A young man appeared at a window. Gently, he helped a young woman step onto the windowsill,
200 held her away from the building—and let go. He helped another young woman onto the windowsill. "Those of us who were looking saw her put her arms around him and kiss him," Shepherd wrote. "Then he held her out into space and dropped her. But quick as a flash he was on the windowsill himself. . . . He was brave enough to help the girl he loved to a quicker death, after she had given him a goodbye kiss."

Meanwhile, others managed to reach the fire escape. It had not been designed for a quick exit. FDNY[6] experts later declared that those on the three top floors of the Asch
210 Building could not have made it to the ground in under three hours. In reality, they had only minutes.

People crowded onto the fire escape. As they walked single file, flames lapped at them through broken windows. Worse, the human load became too heavy for the device to bear. Bolts that fastened it to the building became loose. It began to sway, then collapsed at the eighth floor, tumbling dozens into the courtyard. "As the fire-crazed victims were thrown by the collapse of the fire escape, several struck the sharp-tipped palings,"[7] the New York *Herald* reported. "The
220 body of one woman was found with several iron spikes driven

---
[6] **FDNY:** the Fire Department of New York City.
[7] **palings:** fences with stakes.

CLOSE READ

Analyze Presentations of Information (LINES 182–196)   RI 5

Tell students that history researchers use **primary sources,** firsthand accounts by people who witnessed or took part in an event. In lines 182–196, this author includes an excerpt from an eyewitness account, an example of a primary source.

I **ASK STUDENTS** to reread lines 182–196 and explain why the author included this excerpt. *(It is a vivid description of the horror of that day, and it helps put the reader in the scene.)*

English Language Support

Display Shepherd's account and read it aloud. Then have pairs identify words and phrases that describe what he heard and saw. Have students discuss how this description affects their understanding of the event and why.

Determine Central Idea and Details (LINES 207–219)   RI 2

Clarify that a fire escape is a metal stairway on the exterior of a building, accessible from windows.

J **ASK STUDENTS** to reread lines 207–219 and summarize the most important information about the fire escape. *(The fire escape collapsed under the weight of the people, but its design would not have allowed people to reach the ground in time anyway.)*

English Language Support

Understand Cohesion Explain that transitional words and phrases link ideas, point out examples, show a contrast, identify a time relationship, or add information. Transitions make writing flow more smoothly. Display lines 207–211.

• Have students read the lines. Work with them to identify words or phrases that lead into a new thought or link back to an earlier detail. *(meanwhile, later, in reality)* Discuss the meaning of each.

• Have students identify transitional expressions in the lines. Then have them take turns reading the passage aloud to a partner, with the transitions and without. Ask them to explain the function of each transition they identified.

• Ask students to identify transitions in the paragraph. Then have them volunteer others with which they are familiar, such as *for instance.* Have students then work in pairs to write two or three sentences explaining an aspect of the fire and its consequences using those transitional expressions.

Determine Central Idea and Details (LINES 223–239)

RI 1,
RI 2

Explain that Marrin has previously described events on the eighth and ninth floors. Beginning on line 223, he describes what happened on the tenth floor.

(K) CITE TEXT EVIDENCE Have students reread lines 223–239 and cite a sentence that states the main idea. *("The tenth floor was the best place to be.")* Ask students to cite details that support that idea. *(People there "survived by dashing up the stairs to the roof." In the next building, "students lowered the ladders, climbed down, and helped survivors to safety." "Only one person from the tenth floor died.")*

CRITICAL VOCABULARY

inspection: Fire Chief Croker made an inspection of the building.

ASK STUDENTS what he was probably doing to make his inspection. *(looking at the burned-out rooms, studying the fire escape and stairwells, examining the site for evidence of how the fire started)*

FOR STANDARD ENGLISH LEARNERS

Past Perfect Tense Some students may use the past perfect tense when the simple past is correct. Discuss the sentence in lines 234–237, clarifying that "had caught" describes an event that happened before "it was necessary" and "many of them had blackened faces." Have pairs write several sentences using the past perfect tense to show the sequence of events in the fire. Invite them to share their sentences.

This is a photograph of the gutted tenth floor of the Asch Building that was taken in the aftermath of the fire.

entirely through it." Others crashed through the skylight into the room below, where they died on the cement floor.

(K) The tenth floor was the best place to be. Those who worked there, or reached it from the floor below, survived by dashing up the stairs to the roof. When they arrived, they found the roof fifteen feet lower than its Washington Place neighbor's, a building shared by New York University and the American Book Company.

230 Luckily, Professor Frank Sommer was teaching his law class in a room that overlooked the Asch Building. When Sommer realized what was happening, he led his class to the roof of their building. There they found two ladders left by painters during the week. Students lowered the ladders, climbed down, and helped survivors to safety. For some women, said Sommer, "it was necessary to beat out the flames that had caught their clothing, and many of them had blackened faces and singed hair and eyebrows." Yet only one person from the tenth floor died. Seeing flames licking up from the ninth floor, she panicked and jumped out a window.

240 By 5:15 P.M., exactly thirty-five minutes after flames burst from beneath a cutting table, firefighters had brought the blaze under control. An hour later, Chief Croker made his **inspection**. He found that the Asch Building had no damage

inspection
(ĭn-spĕk´shən) *n.*
An *inspection* is an official examination or review.

©Bettmann/Corbis

Strategies for Annotation ✎ 📖 *Annotate it!*

Determine Central Idea and Details

RI 2

Have students use their eBook annotation tools to annotate lines 223–239.

- Highlight the sentence that states the main idea.
- Underline details that support that main idea.

The tenth floor was the best place to be. Those who worked there, or reached it from the floor below, survived by dashing up the stairs to the roof. When they arrived, they to its structure. Its walls were in good shape; so were the floors. It had passed the test. It was fireproof.

The woodwork, furniture, cotton goods, and people who worked in it were not. Of the 500 Triangle employees who reported for work that day, 146 died. Of these, sixteen men were identified. The rest were women or bodies and body
250 parts listed as "unidentified." The Triangle Fire was New York's worst workplace disaster up to that time. Only the September 11, 2001, terrorist attacks on the twin towers of the World Trade Center took more (about 2,500) lives.

Chief Croker was no softie; he was used to the horrors that came with his job. But this was different. As he explored the top three floors of the Asch Building, he saw sights "that utterly staggered him," the New York *World* reported. "In the drifting smoke, he had seen bodies burned to bare bones, skeletons bending over sewing machines." Those sights sent
260 him down to the street with quivering lips.

Next morning, March 26, Chief Croker returned for another look. The only creatures he found alive were some half-drowned mice. He picked one up, stroked it gently, and put it in his pocket. The chief would take it home, he said. "It's alive. At least it's alive."

Analyze Presentations of Information (LINES 254–265)

RI 1,
RI 6

Tell students that a history author uses **portrayals**, descriptions of historical figures, to reveal his or her perspective on events.

CITE TEXT EVIDENCE Have students cite details about Chief Croker and explain why the author includes them. (*"Chief Croker was no softie; he was used to the horrors that came with his job." The author quotes a newspaper report that said Croker was "utterly staggered." The author says, "Those sights sent him down to the street with quivering lips," and describes Croker gently stroking a half-drowned mouse. The author wants to show that even a hardened professional had difficulty coping with the enormity of this disaster.*)

English Language Support

To help students understand the portrayal of Chief Croker, work with them to define these words: *softie* ("someone who is weak or overly emotional"), *staggered* ("overwhelmed, horrified, or astonished"), *quivering* ("shaking or trembling"). Have them explain in their own words how Chief Croker was affected by what he saw and what his reaction tells readers about the scene.

English Language Support

Word Study Write these words from pages 272 and 273 on the board: *firefighters, fireproof, woodwork, workplace*. Explain that these are all **compound words,** words formed from two or more other words. Tell students that often they can define compound words if they know the meanings of the individual words that make them up. Remind them that context clues also help. Model the strategy using the word *woodwork,* saying: *The two words tell me that woodwork is something worked, or made, out of wood. From lines 246–247, I learn that the woodwork is in the* building and burned with the flames. I think woodwork *means "the wood that trims doors and windows."*

- Have pairs of students use the same strategy to define the remaining compound words on the board. Discuss their meanings.
- Then have pairs return to lines 1–39. Ask them to list the compound words they find in this passage. (*pickup, everyone, lightweight, shirtwaists, showroom, boyfriends*) Have them define each word using their knowledge of the individual words and context clues.

Determine Central Idea and Details RI 2

Guide students to review the text to find details that support the main idea shown in the partial outline. *(Possible details: no-smoking rules were not enforced; aisles were too narrow; water hose was not connected to standpipe; doors to stairwells were locked; fire drills had never been held; fire escape was unsound)*

Analyzing the Text RI 1, RI 6

Possible answers:

1. *The fire began on the eighth floor, where most of the workers escaped by elevators or stairs. On the ninth floor, some used a stairway to escape, but the other stairway was locked. These workers jumped to their death or died in the fire. On the tenth floor, workers climbed the stairs to the roof and found safety.*

2. *The author is giving a reason for the disorder and panic that led to so much loss of life. The lack of fire drills meant that workers had no idea what to do.*

3. *The author suggests that people jumped from windows so that their bodies would be identified.*

4. *The author believes the firefighters did what they could and acted heroically but that their equipment was not sufficient and the situation was hopeless.*

5. *It is most important to understand that this disaster could have been prevented.*

6. *The story is still told because of the lessons learned as a result of that disaster.*

Determine Central Idea and Details RI 2

The **central idea,** or main idea, in a piece of history writing is the most important idea about the topic. It may be stated explicitly in a sentence, or it may be implied. The main idea is often suggested by smaller key ideas, each developed in a paragraph or a longer section of the work.

Main ideas are supported by **details,** facts and other pieces of information that build upon or clarify the main ideas. When you read history writing, notice the details that answer basic questions, such as, *When and where does the event take place? Who is involved? What are the causes and the immediate and long-term effects?*

As you read, you can keep track of key ideas and details by taking notes in outline form. Restate the main ideas of paragraphs or sections, numbered in Roman numerals. Below each idea, list the supporting details.

> The Triangle Waist Company Fire
> I. The Triangle factory was a dangerous firetrap.
>   A. Paper scraps hung from the rafters.
>   B. There were always scraps under the tables.
>   C.

Once you have completed an outline for the entire text, look to see how all the main ideas and details help to develop the main idea of the entire text. What other details from *Flesh & Blood So Cheap* could you add to this outline?

Analyzing the Text RI 1, RI 6

Cite Text Evidence Support your responses with evidence from the text.

1. **Summarize** Review the text to find details about the different floors of the building. What is important to understand about these locations?

2. **Cause/Effect** Reread lines 97–100. Why does the author give a detail about fire drills?

3. **Draw Conclusions** According to the author, why might workers have jumped from the windows?

4. **Cite Evidence** What does the author seem to think of the firefighters' efforts during this disaster?

5. **Evaluate** What is most important to understand about this event?

6. **Connect** Why is the story of the Triangle Fire still being told?

Strategies for Annotation Annotate it!

Determine Central Idea and Details RI 2

Have students locate lines 127–132. Share these strategies for guided or independent analysis:

*   Select a paragraph or section.
*   Highlight the stated main idea.
*   Underline details that support that main idea.

rushed to the windows, only to meet more fire. Hot air expands. Unless it escapes, pressure will keep building, eventually blowing a hole even in a heavy iron container like a boiler. Heat and pressure blew out the eighth-floor windows. Firefighters call the result "lapping in"—that is, sucking flames into open windows above. That is why you

from **The Story of the Triangle Factory Fire**

by Zachary Kent

In the days following the fire, city officials sifted through the charred rubble at the Asch Building and tried to fix the fault for the tragedy. Fire Chief Croker angrily stated, "There wasn't a fire escape anywhere fronting on the street by which these unfortunate girls could escape." Doors that opened inward instead of outward, overcrowding in work areas, and blocked exits also were to blame. Fire Marshal William Beers stunned New Yorkers by soon declaring, "I can show you 150 loft buildings far worse than this one."
10 Lillian D. Wald of the Joint Board of Sanitary Control also reported on the general situation. "The conditions as they now exist are hideous. . . . Our investigators have shown that there are hundreds of buildings which invite disaster just as much as did the Asch structure."

Accused of ignoring their employees' safety, Triangle owners Blanck and Harris were charged with manslaughter. During the three week trial angry citizens packed the courtroom. Outside, in the **corridors**, women screamed, "Murderers! Murderers! Make them suffer for
20 killing our children!" Lawyers argued that Blanck and Harris kept all of the Triangle doors locked during the workday, therefore causing many of the deaths. Weighing the evidence, however, the jury returned a verdict of not guilty. "I cannot see that anyone was responsible for the disaster," explained juror H. Houston Hierst. "It seems to me to have been an act of the Almighty."[1] The New York *Call* viewed the matter differently. "Capital can commit no crime," it angrily declared, "when it is in pursuit of profits."

Furious New Yorkers refused to let the issue rest.
30 In October 1911 the city established a Bureau of Fire Prevention to inspect safety standards in other buildings. Five months earlier the New York State legislature created a special Factory Investigating Commission. Through the

corridor
(kôr´ĭ-dər) *n.*
A *corridor* is a narrow hallway or passageway.

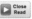
Close Read

---

[1] **an act of the Almighty:** a term that refers to events or actions that are beyond the control of human beings.

The Story of the Triangle Factory Fire **275**

Analyze Structure: Chronological Order

RI 5

(LINES 39–41)

Point out that the author is describing what happened after the fire, which occurred on March 25, 1911.

 ASK STUDENTS to reread lines 39–41 and tell how long it took New York State lawmakers to pass safety laws for workers. (*Laws were passed within three years after the fire.*)

English Language Support

To help students answer the question, remind them that the fire took place in March 1911. Have them reread lines 39–41 and locate the year by which the new laws were passed. Then have students identify the word in line 40 that tells them what the author thinks about this length of time. (*quickly*)

Analyze Presentations of Information (LINES 41–42)

RI 1, RI 6

Review that an **author's perspective** is the combination of ideas, feelings, values, and beliefs that influence the way the author presents information.

 CITE TEXT EVIDENCE Have students reread lines 41–42 and cite evidence that reveals what the author values. (*"New York State's Industrial Code, the finest in the nation."*) Ask if the statement reveals an objective or subjective point of view. (*subjective, because it is the author's opinion*)

New York City garment workers take part in a May Day parade in 1916.

next four years Commission investigators crawled and pried through the rooms and cellars of factories and tenement houses[2] all across the state. They examined workers' filthy living conditions and witnessed the dangers of crippling machinery and long work hours in dusty, dirty firetraps.

C 40   As a result of the Commission's shocking findings, New York State quickly passed thirty-three new labor laws by 1914. These laws formed the foundation of New York   D

_____
[2] **tenement houses:** very run-down city apartments where the poor and immigrants often live.

276   Collection 6

©Library of Congress Prints & Photographs Division

English Language Support

Analyze Language Remind students that authors choose the words that best convey their meaning and create the effect that they want. Display lines 32–38 on the board.

- Highlight the word *crawled* in line 34. Discuss the meaning of the word, "moved along very slowly on hands and knees." Then work with students to explain what this word helps them understand about the investigators' efforts. (*It shows how carefully and thoroughly the investigators inspected the buildings.*)

- Highlight the words *crawled* and *pried* in line 34. Discuss their meanings. Then ask pairs of students to write a sentence explaining what idea the author conveys by his use of those two verbs.

- Highlight these words: *crawled, pried, filthy, crippling,* and *firetraps.* Have pairs of students explain the effect of each word on readers' understanding of the investigators' efforts and the workers' living conditions.

State's Industrial Code, the finest in the nation. Soon other states followed New York's example and **enacted** protective labor laws.

One Factory Commission investigator had witnessed the fateful Triangle fire. Frances Perkins said, "We heard the fire engines and rushed . . . to see what was going on. . . . We got there just as they started to jump. I shall never forget the frozen horror which came over us as we stood with our hands on our throats watching that horrible sight, knowing that there was no help."

In 1933 President Franklin Roosevelt named Frances Perkins secretary of labor. She and other social reformers dedicated their lives to insuring worker safety throughout the country. "They did not die in vain and we will never forget them," vowed Perkins. From the ashes of the tragic Triangle factory fire came help for millions of United States laborers today.

enact
(ĕn-ăkt´) *v.* If you *enact* something, you make it into a law.

COLLABORATIVE DISCUSSION You've now read two accounts of a disaster that occurred a century ago. If a similar fire were to start in a garment factory of today, how might the events be the same or different? Talk about your thoughts with other group members.

FOR STANDARD ENGLISH LEARNERS

Pronunciation Some students may struggle with the pronunciation of the /v/ sound in words such as *protective* (line 43), *lives* (line 54), *vain* (line 55), and *never* (line 55), instead pronouncing it as /f/ or /b/. Write this sentence on the board and have students repeat it after you and then to each other:

The very tragic events of that day resulted in laws that would protect lives in the future.

CLOSE READ

Analyze Structure: Chronological Order

RI 5

(LINES 45–51)

Tell students that history texts may sometimes refer back in time to earlier events. Readers must pay close attention to determine the time period being referenced.

E **ASK STUDENTS** to closely reread lines 45–51 and determine when Frances Perkins made the comments that are quoted and what those comments refer to. *(When she was working on the Factory Commission, sometime in the years after the fire, Perkins recalled what she had seen on that day.)*

> **CRITICAL VOCABULARY**
>
> **enact**: States enacted protective labor laws.
>
> **ASK STUDENTS** what happens before a law is enacted. *(Lawmakers debate it and then vote on it.)*

COLLABORATIVE DISCUSSION Have students work in groups to discuss the question. Remind students to cite evidence from both texts about the effects of the Triangle Factory Fire.

ASK STUDENTS to share any questions they generated in the course of reading and discussing the selections.

English Language Support

Support Opinions As students prepare for discussion, remind them that they should support their own opinions with reasons and evidence to persuade others to agree with them. They should also listen actively and ask questions to help them understand the points that other students make. Provide these sentence stems:

- I think that ___ because ___.
- Could you please repeat what you said about ___?
- What I think you mean is ___. Is that correct?
- Could you give me an example to show what you mean about ___?
- I agree with you that ___, but I also think that ___.
- ___ is another example of what you were talking about.

Analyze Structure: Chronological Order

RI 5

Help students understand the terms. Review the types of text clues that signal sequence, and discuss how these can help readers track events in a piece of history writing. Clues to chronological order in the lesson excerpt are *"October 1911,"* *"Five months earlier,"* and *"Through the next four years."*

Analyzing the Text

RI 1, RI 2, RI 5

Possible answers:

1. *Before the Triangle Factory Fire, factories in New York City were dirty, overcrowded firetraps. Exits were blocked, and fire escapes didn't exist or didn't work. The workers had no legal protections for their safety.*

2. *Citizens pushed lawmakers to make buildings safer. New York City established a bureau to inspect safety standards. New York State had investigators report on safety conditions in factories and tenements. Within three years after the fire, the state passed thirty-three new labor laws to make working conditions safer.*

3. *Angry citizens wanted the factory owners to be punished. Jurors believed the fire was not the fault of the owners. The jurors might have found no legal proof of responsibility, or they might have been swayed by the power of the business owners, as suggested by the newspaper the* New York Call.

4. *The author is making the point that a disaster can have a positive result. Although the Triangle Factory Fire was a great tragedy, it led to some beneficial changes in labor and safety laws.*

---

eBook *Annotate It!*

Analyze Structure: Chronological Order

RI 5

A **pattern of organization** is the particular arrangement of ideas and information. Authors of history texts often use the **chronological order** organization to arrange events by their order of occurrence—what happens first, next, then, and finally. When reading history texts, pay attention to dates, times, and words and phrases that signal sequence, such as *before, meanwhile, later,* and *after that.*

Identify the clues to the chronological organization in this paragraph from *The Story of the Triangle Factory Fire:*

> Furious New Yorkers refused to let the issue rest. In October 1911, the city established a Bureau of Fire Prevention to inspect safety standards in other buildings. Five months earlier the New York State legislature created a special Factory Investigating Commission. Through the next four years Commission investigators crawled and pried through the rooms and cellars of factories and tenement houses all across the state.

Analyzing the Text

RI 1, RI 2, RI 5

Cite Text Evidence   Support your responses with evidence from the selection.

1. **Infer** What was true of factories in New York City before the Triangle fire?

2. **Summarize** What changes occurred in the aftermath of the tragedy? Within what time period did the changes happen?

3. **Compare** Reread lines 15–28. How and why did the jurors' viewpoint differ from that of angry citizens?

4. **Infer** Reread the last sentence. Despite the horror and loss of life caused by the fire, how might it have been a useful experience, according to the author?

Strategies for Annotation   *Annotate it!*

Analyze Structure: Chronological Order

RI 5

Have students locate lines 29–33. Share these strategies for guided or independent analysis:

- Highlight in yellow words and phrases that signal chronological order.
- Underline the event that happened first.

> Furious New Yorkers refused to let the issue rest.
> In October 1911 the city established a Bureau of Fire
> Prevention to inspect safety standards in other buildings.
> Five months earlier the New York State legislature created a
> special Factory Investigating Commission. Through the
> next four years Commission investigators crawled and pried

Analyze Presentations of Information

RI 3, RI 6, RI 9

History writing is nonfiction that presents events and people of the past. What makes this type of writing interesting is how it presents interactions between people and events. History writing often combines features of a narrative text (a true story with a setting, characters, and a plot) and an informational text (paragraphs of main ideas and factual details).

History writers base their work on factual research. However, two history writers might write about the same event in different ways. How writers shape their presentations of key information can depend on individual points of view. **Author's perspective** is the unique combination of ideas, values, feelings, and beliefs that influence the way a writer looks at a topic.

In comparing the perspectives of two or more authors writing about the same event, look for clues like these in the texts:

Tone	**Tone** is the author's attitude toward his or her subject. Would you describe the writing as serious? Lively? Angry? Notice any emotions the writer expresses while presenting the facts and how the emotions contribute to the overall effect of the writing.
Point of view	Analyze the author's presentation of information to determine his or her point of view. When writing from a **subjective** point of view, an author includes personal opinions, feelings, and beliefs. When writing from an **objective** point of view, the author focuses on factual information and leaves out personal opinions.
Direct statements	Be aware of any statements or comments that seem to come directly from the author. In particular, watch for ideas that may be repeated or restated. What light do these statements shed on the writer's interpretation of facts?
Emphasis	Determine how each author presents his or her ideas about the topic. Do the writers emphasize different evidence? Do they put forth different interpretations of facts?
Portrayals	Pay attention to how the historical figures are portrayed. Think about why that person is included and what makes him or her memorable.

In the excerpt from *Flesh & Blood So Cheap*, read how author Albert Marrin describes Chief Croker (lines 261–265). Next, read the description of Croker by author Zachary Kent in lines 1–7 from *The Story of the Triangle Factory Fire*. Then, compare these two passages. What similarities and differences do you notice in the history writers' descriptions? What do these details reveal about each author's perspective?

The Story of the Triangle Factory Fire **279**

Analyze Presentations of Information

RI 3, RI 6, RI 9

Review the definition of *author's perspective* and the elements shown in the chart. After students have studied the chart, discuss why interpretation is such an important part of a history writer's work and why readers should be sensitive to an author's perspective.

(Possible answers regarding the two presentations of Chief Croker: Both passages tell about the aftermath of the fire and Croker's reaction. Both include quotations from the chief. Marrin describes Croker's picking up a half-drowned mouse, stroking it gently, and taking it home because "At least it's alive." This story shows that the fire was so terrible, even the hardened chief was overcome with emotion. Marrin has a more subjective, emotional perspective than Kent, who describes Croker's anger at the lack of safety in the building. Kent's more objective point of view focuses on the chief's professionalism and the causes and effects of the fire.)

English Language Support

Exchange Ideas Guide students to work in small groups to answer the questions on page 280. Each group should answer one question. When all the groups are finished, they can take turns presenting their answers to the class. Encourage students to provide their classmates with useful feedback.

Strategies for Annotation ✐ 🖻 *Annotate it!*

Analyze Presentations of Information

RI 3, RI 6

Share these strategies for guided or independent analysis using lines 97–101 from *Flesh & Blood So Cheap*:

- Highlight in yellow text that reveals the author's interpretation of facts.
- Underline words with emotional impact.
- In a note, write a word that labels the tone.

Had there been fire drills, surely more would have survived. Unfortunately, confusion reigned. Workers had to make life-and-death decisions in split seconds amid smoke, and panic. It was everyone for themselves. "I was throwing them out of the way," Mary Bucelli said of the

urgent, serious, grim

PRACTICE & APPLY

Analyzing the Text

RI 1, RI 2, RI 3, RI 6, RI 9

Possible answers:

1. *The Story of the Triangle Factory Fire would be a better source for research on the effects because it covers the short-term and long-term effects of the fire.*

2. *Frances Perkins witnessed the Triangle Factory Fire and was horrified by it. She never forgot that unsafe working conditions led to the tragedy, and she used that knowledge when she became secretary of labor under President Franklin Roosevelt.*

3. *Both authors used primary sources, information published at the time of the event. They quoted from eyewitness accounts, news reports, and editorials.*

4. *These lines are an example of Marrin's perspective. The author's description is evidence of a dramatic tone ("a wave of fire rolling across the room"). The point of view is objective, giving factual information about the action of heat.*

5. *The phrases "filthy living conditions," "dangers of crippling machinery," "long work hours in dusty, dirty firetraps" all reveal the author's feelings of disgust at the conditions.*

6. *Both authors emphasize the importance of safe working conditions. Today, we have fire drills, and our buildings have smoke alarms and fire and safety inspections. These regulations are the result of laws designed to prevent tragedies like the Triangle Factory Fire.*

7. *The emphasis in the excerpt from Flesh & Blood So Cheap is on the causes of the fire and the events during the fire. The author includes graphic details to convey the panic and horror. In the excerpt from The Story of the Triangle Factory Fire, the author focuses on the aftermath of the tragedy and on the effects it had on safety regulations in workplaces.*

Analyzing the Text

RI 1, RI 2, RI 3, RI 6, RI 9, W 2, W 6, SL 4, SL 6

Cite Text Evidence   Support your responses with evidence from the texts.

1. **Cause/Effect**   Which of the two texts would you use to research the effects of the Triangle Fire? Why?

2. **Compare**   Look back at both texts to find mention of Frances Perkins. Why is she an important person to know about?

3. **Infer**   What kinds of sources did both authors use in researching this topic?

4. **Analyze History Writing**   Read lines 126–130 from *Flesh & Blood So Cheap*. Are these lines an example of author Albert Marrin's perspective? Explain why or why not.

5. **Analyze Tone**   Read lines 36–38 from *The Story of the Triangle Factory Fire*. What clues do you see in these lines to Zachary Kent's attitude about the conditions that are described?

6. **Connect**   What idea presented by both authors is most relevant to us today? Why?

7. **Analyze Key Information**   The two historical writings cover different aspects of the same event. Briefly review each text for its key details. Then tell what each selection emphasizes.

PERFORMANCE TASK

Speaking Activity: Summary Presentation   The Triangle Factory Fire raised issues about inadequate workplace safety, labor rights, and factory jobs. Despite great progress in improving working conditions since 1911, these issues are still in the news. Give a summary presentation about a current event that shares features with the Triangle Factory Fire.

- Use online and print resources to learn about a recent event.

- Use several sources to get varied viewpoints and interpretations of the event.

- Summarize the event by telling what happened, describing the people involved, and discussing any issues surrounding the event.

- End your presentation by telling how this event is similar to and different from the Triangle Factory Fire.

- After rehearsing, deliver your presentation to classmates.

PERFORMANCE TASK

W 2, W 7, W 8, SL 4, SL 6

Assign this performance task.

Speaking Activity: Summary Presentation   Guide students to reliable sources of current events, and suggest that they not limit themselves to events in the United States. Students' presentations should include

- a summary of the event with answers to the questions *what, where, when, who,* and *how*

- examples of causes, immediate effects, and future effects

- comparisons and contrasts with the Triangle Factory Fire

   INTERACTIVE LESSON   Have students complete the tutorials in this lesson: **Giving a Presentation**

Critical Vocabulary

flammable	reign	portable
inspection	corridor	enact

Practice and Apply Complete each sentence to show that you understand the meaning of the bold word.

1. If a cleaning fluid is **flammable,** you should . . .

2. Fear and worry **reign** when . . .

3. A **portable** desk is one that . . .

4. An **inspection** of a restaurant is done to . . .

5. A **corridor** is the same as . . .

6. If a rule is **enacted,** it . . .

Vocabulary Strategy: Latin Roots

A **root** is a word part that came into English from an older language. Roots from the ancient language of Latin appear in many English words. This chart shows three common Latin roots:

Latin Root	Meaning	Example Words
spec	"to look at"	inspect, spectacle, aspect
struct	"to build"	construct, destructive, instruction
dic	"to say or tell"	dictate, predict, contradiction

Note the words with Latin roots in this sentence from *Flesh & Blood So Cheap*:

> An hour later, Chief Croker made his inspection. He found that the Asch Building had no damage to its structure.

The root meaning of *spec*, "to look at," is in the word *inspection*, "the act of looking closely." The root meaning of *struct*, "to build," is in the word *structure*, "something that is built." Finding a Latin root in an unfamiliar word can help to unlock the word's meaning. A print or digital dictionary can help confirm the meaning.

Practice and Apply Find the words with Latin roots in each sentence. Give a meaning for the word that includes the meaning of the Latin root.

1. Fire obstructed the doorways, so there was no prospect of escape.

2. Nobody could have predicted the destruction caused by the fire.

3. From the perspective of the jurors, their verdict was fair.

Critical Vocabulary

Possible answers:

1. *If a cleaning fluid is flammable, you should never use it near heat or a spark.*

2. *Fear and worry reign when people learn that a war is about to begin.*

3. *A portable desk is one that is small and light enough to carry around with you.*

4. *An inspection of a restaurant is done to make sure that food is being prepared safely.*

5. *A corridor is the same as a hallway.*

6. *If a rule is enacted, it is put into effect, and people must follow it.*

Vocabulary Strategy: Latin Roots

Possible answers:

1. obstructed *means "blocked, or built against something";* prospect *means "what you can expect, or look toward in the future."*

2. predicted *means "told about ahead of time";* destruction *means "the opposite of building."*

3. perspective *means "viewpoint, or the way you look at something";* verdict *means "the jury's decision, or what the jury says."*

 INTERACTIVE VOCABULARY TUTOR WordSharp
Word Structure: Latin Roots

Strategies for Annotation ✐ 📋 *Annotate it!*

Vocabulary Strategy: Latin Roots

Have students use their eBook annotation tools to identify a word with a Latin root in the sentence that begins in line 30 of *The Story of the Triangle Factory Fire.*

- Highlight in yellow a word with a Latin root in the chart above.
- Underline the root.
- In a note, write a meaning for the word that is connected to the meaning of the root.
- Check the meaning in a print or digital dictionary.

In October 1911 the city established a Bureau of Fire
Prevention to <u>inspect</u> safety standards in other buildings.
Five months earlier the New York State legislature created

"to look into"

Language Conventions: Capitalization

L 2

Review the examples in the chart. Before assigning Practice and Apply, ask students to offer additional examples.

Answers:

1. *capitalize* Waist Company, Italian

2. *capitalize* Engine Company, *lowercase* firehouse

3. *lowercase* operator, *capitalize* Finally, *lowercase* firemen

4. *capitalize* On, March, *lowercase* professor, *capitalize* Building

5. *capitalize* New, World, Chief

GRAMMAR NOTES: Level One
Lesson 14: Using Capital Letters

Online Selection Test
- Download an editable ExamView bank.
- Assign and manage this test online.

Language Conventions: Capitalization

L 2

When you proofread your writing, check to see that you have used capital and lowercase letters correctly. This chart shows general rules.

Capitalize	Examples
First words of sentences and quotations	A fire started. One man called, "Everyone out now!"
People and titles	Mayor Sanchez, General Robert E. Lee, Fire Chief Croker
Geographical names such as cities, continents, regions, streets, roads	New York, East River, Fifth Avenue
Organizations and buildings	League of Women Voters, International Monetary Fund, Empire State Building, Eiffel Tower
Time periods such as days, months, holidays, events, and eras (but not seasons)	Friday, May 3; the Fourth of July; the Triangle Factory Fire; the Jurassic Period
Documents and publications	Declaration of Independence, *Harper's Weekly, The Boston Globe*
Adjectives formed from proper nouns	North American cities, Japanese food, Mexican folklore

When you're unsure of which capitalization rule applies, a digital or print manual for usage and style can come in very handy to jog your memory of these rules.

Practice and Apply Some capital letters should be lowercase, and some lowercase letters should be capitalized. Find and fix the errors.

1. Most of the workers at the Triangle waist company were young women, including many italian immigrants.

2. The horse-drawn vehicles of engine company 72 arrived from a Firehouse six blocks away.

3. Sewing machine Operator Samuel Levine recalled, "finally I heard the Firemen cutting their way into the elevator shaft, and they came and let me out."

4. on that Saturday in march, Frank Sommer, a Professor of law, was teaching his class in a room that overlooked the Asch building.

5. The new York *world* reported on chief Croker's reaction to viewing the horrible scene.

English Language Support

Understand Capitalization Read each rule aloud. Then have volunteers read the examples. Make sure students understand why some words in the examples are not capitalized.

- Display lines 1–11 of *Flesh & Blood So Cheap* on the board and work with students to identify the rule for each capitalized word. (*The, On, Nearby, Paper, Although, Every, He, The: first words of sentences; Triangle Waist Company: name of a business organization; Asch Building: name of a building; January: name of a month*)

- Have small groups record the rules in a two-column chart. Then have them look for examples in the selections that illustrate each rule. Have them record the examples in the right column, with line numbers. Encourage them to find as many as they can. Ask groups to share their charts with the class.

- Display lines 20–28 from page 275 on the board. Ask pairs of students to explain how the rules of capitalization apply to these lines.

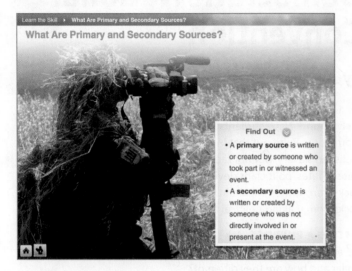

INTERACTIVE WHITEBOARD LESSON
Primary and Secondary Sources

RI 5,
RI 6

TEACH

Tell students that the two selections about the Triangle Factory Fire are secondary sources and that each includes quotations from primary sources. Offer these definitions and examples:

- A **primary source** is created by someone who took part in or witnessed an event. Examples include eyewitness accounts, speeches, diaries, autobiographies, photos, and video footage.
- A **secondary source** is created by someone not directly involved in or present at the event. Examples include informational books, textbooks, encyclopedia articles, and essays and articles written after the event.

Explain that when students do research for their Performance Task presentations they will be doing what authors Albert Marrin and Zachary Kent did: reviewing multiple sources, both primary and secondary. Discuss the main purposes of each kind of source:

- Primary sources provide personal, subjective views of the event and a sense of time and place.
- Secondary sources provide an overview and factual details. The points of view are often both subjective and objective.

COLLABORATIVE DISCUSSION

Help students locate either author's book or another secondary source on the Triangle Factory Fire. Have students find references to primary sources that were consulted and discuss how and why the author incorporated the primary source material into the text.

Analyze Presentations of Information

RI 6,
RI 9

RETEACH

Review that the term **author's perspective** refers to beliefs, opinions, and ideas that affect how an author presents information. Explain that paying attention to clues about an author's perspective helps readers make thoughtful judgments about the information in the text.

Display the two sentences shown below, and ask students to compare and contrast them. During discussion, guide students to note that each author has a different perspective. Discuss the **tone** (author's attitude toward the topic), **word choices** (including connotations), and **emphasis** (what details are given importance) in each sentence.

- If workers at the Triangle factory had practiced fire drills, they would not have become panic-stricken victims of this horrific disaster.
- The Triangle Factory Fire happened so quickly that many workers never had a chance to escape.

PRACTICE AND APPLY

Have students locate each of the passages listed below in their text. Ask: What is each author's perspective in the passage? How do the passages differ in tone, word choice, and emphasis?

- Lines 120–125, from *Flesh & Blood So Cheap*
- Lines 20–22, from *The Story of the Triangle Factory Fire*

English Language Support

Read Closely Adapt the collection opener strategy Think-Write-Pair-Share to help students complete the Practice and Apply activity.

- Read aloud the description of the activity, clarifying the terms *tone, word choice,* and *emphasis* as needed.
- Tell students to read each passage, noting ideas about each of the listed elements, before they write their answers.
- Next, pair students and ask them to share their thoughts with their partners, reminding pairs to ask each other clarifying questions as they discuss their individual ideas. Once discussion has ended, have students revise their written responses to reflect any of their ideas that may have changed during discussion.
- Have students share their answers with the entire class.

from "The Most Daring of [Our] Leaders"

By Lynne Olson

Why These Texts

Students may be surprised when they read about the many changes that have occurred in recent U.S. history. Over the last few decades, much has changed in the United States for African Americans. With the help of the close-reading questions, students will analyze how two texts present information about key events in the civil rights movement. This close reading will lead students to compare and contrast the two presentations.

Speech from the Democratic National Convention

By John Lewis

Background Have students read the background and author information. Point out that in 1865 the Thirteenth Amendment abolished slavery, but not racial prejudice. Throughout the United States, politicians devised legal structures to segregate blacks from whites, maintain white privileges, and prevent blacks from making political and economic gains.

SETTING A PURPOSE Ask students to pay attention to the presentation of information in the two texts. How are they similar and how are they different?

Standards Support

- cite multiple pieces of text evidence
- determine central ideas in a text
- analyze interactions between individuals, events, and ideas
- determine the meaning of words
- analyze the structure of a text
- determine an author's purpose
- analyze how two authors write about history

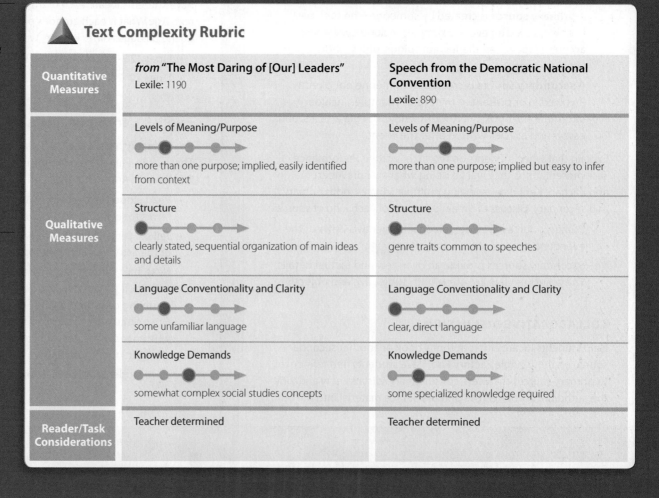

▲ Text Complexity Rubric

	from "The Most Daring of [Our] Leaders"	Speech from the Democratic National Convention
Quantitative Measures	Lexile: 1190	Lexile: 890
Qualitative Measures	Levels of Meaning/Purpose more than one purpose; implied, easily identified from context	Levels of Meaning/Purpose more than one purpose; implied but easy to infer
	Structure clearly stated, sequential organization of main ideas and details	Structure genre traits common to speeches
	Language Conventionality and Clarity some unfamiliar language	Language Conventionality and Clarity clear, direct language
	Knowledge Demands somewhat complex social studies concepts	Knowledge Demands some specialized knowledge required
Reader/Task Considerations	Teacher determined	Teacher determined

Analyze Presentations of Information

Students should read both texts carefully all the way through. Close-reading questions at the bottom of the page will help them focus on a thorough analysis of the presentation of information. As they read, students should jot down comments or questions about the text in the margins.

WHEN STUDENTS STRUGGLE . . .

To help students analyze how the authors present information, have them work in small groups to fill out a chart like the one shown below.

CITE TEXT EVIDENCE For practice in analyzing the presentation of information, ask students to cite text evidence for the first two rows of the chart and then write their impressions for the last row.

from "The Most Daring of [Our] Leaders"	Speech from the Democratic National Convention
Point of View	Point of View
Third-person: ". . .the students . . . formed a central committee . . ." (lines 50–51)	First-person: ". . . when my seatmate, Albert Bigelow, and I tried to enter . . ." (lines 10–11)
Author's purpose	Author's purpose
To document how Diane Nash and other Fisk students organized sit-ins at lunch counters and restaurants of Nashville's downtown stores	To attest that the U.S. has made great progress since the author's 1961 "Freedom Ride" but that people still need to vote and "speak out"
Effect on reader	Effect on reader
This text gives a clear, chronological account of what happened. It's a good presentation of history.	This speech is stirring and hopeful. It convinces you to keep fighting, to "stand up."

Background *From the 1880s until the 1960s, "Jim Crow" laws in many American states enforced segregation between white people and black people. When the U.S. Supreme Court overturned the "separate but equal" doctrine in 1954, it was the beginning of a period of upheaval and marked the beginning of the civil rights movement. Civil rights activists participated in nonviolent forms of protest, such as sit-ins at lunch counters, and engaged in acts of civil disobedience, such as riding buses into the Deep South to challenge segregation at interstate terminals.*

from
"The Most Daring of [Our] Leaders"
By Lynne Olson

Speech from the
Democratic National Convention
By John Lewis

Lynne Olson *writes books of nonfiction. Before she started writing books full-time, she worked as a journalist for the Associated Press and as the White House correspondent for the Baltimore Sun. Her book Freedom's Daughters was the first book to take an in-depth look at women's roles in the civil rights movement. The portion of Freedom's Daughters that you will read here tells of the experiences of Diane Nash, a young woman from Chicago who attended Fisk University in Nashville, Tennessee, in 1959. In Nashville, both Diane Nash and John Lewis were influenced by Reverend James Lawson's teachings on the philosophy of nonviolence.*

John Lewis *was born in Alabama in 1940. He was a student at Fisk University when the civil rights movement gained momentum. As a college student, he studied the philosophy of nonviolence. In 1960, he helped plan a lunch counter sit-in in Nashville that went on peacefully for a month and then ended in the beating and arrest of the protesters. Eventually these protests were successful, and Nashville became the first major city in the South to desegregate its lunch counters. Lewis has served as the U.S. Representative of Georgia's Fifth Congressional District since his election to Congress in 1986. In his Speech to the Democratic National Convention, delivered in Charlotte, North Carolina, in 2012, Lewis talks about the progress America has made since he made an earlier trip to Charlotte in 1961.*

95

1. **READ ▶** As you read lines 1–55, begin to collect and cite text evidence.

• Underline Nash's and the Fisk students' reactions to segregation. Explain in the margin how the other students' reactions influenced Nash.

• In the margin, note the central idea of the section. Circle three details that support the main idea.

from "The Most Daring of [Our] Leaders"
History Writing by Lynne Olson

epiphany:
discovery

Nash's moment of **epiphany** came at the Tennessee State Fair in 1959. She had gone to the fair on a date, and wanted to use the ladies' room. She found two—one marked WHITE WOMEN, the other COLORED WOMEN—and for the first time in her life suffered the degradation of Jim Crow. This was no longer an intellectual exercise: She was being told in the most searing way imaginable that *she* was beyond the pale, unfit to use the same facilities as white women. Outraged by the experience, she was even more upset that her date, a Southerner, did not share her fury. Neither did most of her

10 fellow Fisk students. They did not seem to care that they could shop at downtown stores but not eat at the stores' lunch counters, or that they had to sit in the balcony to see a movie. The more Nash found out about segregation in Nashville, the more she felt "stifled and boxed in." In the rest of the country, Nashville had the reputation of being more racially progressive than most Southern cities. Blacks could vote in Nashville. The city's schools and buses were integrated. Blacks served on the police force, fire department, City Council, and Board of Education. But segregation still firmly ruled in theaters, restaurants, hotels, and libraries, and Diane Nash, a deep-dyed

20 moralist, decided then and there that Nashville was in a "stage of sin." She couldn't believe that "the children of my classmates would have to be born into a society where they had to believe that they were inferior." Above all, she could not believe that her classmates were willing to let that happen.

Since they did not seem to share her anger, she looked elsewhere for support. Paul LaPrad, a white exchange student at Fisk, told her about a black minister named James Lawson, who was training college students in the use of nonviolence as the framework for an all-out attack on segregation. For Lawson, who had spent three years

30 in India studying the principles of Gandhi, nonviolence was more than just a protest technique: It was the means by which he ordered his life. The young minister talked about the power of nonviolent confrontation with evil, about overcoming the forces of hate and transforming society through love and forgiveness. At first, Nash was skeptical. How could such high-flown idealism be harnessed as a weapon against gun-toting sheriffs and club-swinging racists? Even after attending several of Lawson's workshops, she still was sure "this stuff is never going to work." But since, as she said, it was "the only game in town," she kept going back, and after weeks of studying

40 theology and philosophy, of reading Thoreau and other advocates of passive resistance, of discussion and arguments with the workshop's other participants, the intense young woman from Chicago was finally captured by Lawson's vision. She was particularly drawn to his belief that to be effective, these young would-be activists would have to transcend self-hatred and a sense of inferiority, that they would have to learn to love themselves. Having been raised in a **milieu** that downplayed her blackness, she now found herself part of a group "suddenly proud to be called 'black.' Within the movement . . . we came to a realization of our own worth . . ."

50 In the late fall of 1959, the students at Lawson's workshops formed a central committee to act as the decision-making body for the group. Nash, who had impressed everyone with her clear-eyed thinking and the intensity of her developing commitment to nonviolence, was named to the committee. More and more, the students were turning to her as one of their main leaders.

Nash is upset by their indifference, and inspired to take action. Their apathy led Nash to like-minded people.

Upset with Nashville's segregation laws, Nash becomes involved in nonviolent practices.

milieu:
environment

2. **◀ REREAD** Reread lines 26–49. Why was Nash drawn to the idea of the activists learning "to love themselves"? Support your answer with explicit textual evidence.

In the past, Nash had "downplayed her blackness," so the idea of African Americans recognizing their "own worth" and learning to be "proud to be called 'black'" was an important idea for her.

---

1. **READ AND CITE TEXT EVIDENCE** Explain to students that segregation had been part of southern life for many generations. People took it for granted.

Ⓐ ASK STUDENTS to compare and contrast Nash's opinion of segregation with that of her fellow students at Fisk University. *Students should understand that Nash, who was from the northern city of Chicago, where segregation was not as severe, was "outraged" by the experience of being relegated to second-class citizenship. On the other hand, her classmates were used to segregation, "did not seem to care," and basically just went about their lives.* What did Nash think of her classmates' reaction? *She found it even more upsetting than the segregation itself.*

Critical Vocabulary: epiphany (line 1) Have students share their definitions of *epiphany*. What made Nash's moment at the state fair an epiphany? *It was an epiphany because she experienced something that made her realize the true meaning of segregation.*

2. **REREAD AND CITE TEXT EVIDENCE**

Ⓑ ASK STUDENTS why black Americans raised in the South might have a "sense of inferiority." *Students should realize that southern blacks encountered segregation every day of their lives. To survive, they might adapt, unconsciously accepting their position as second-class citizens.* Why might Nash also have had a "sense of inferiority"? *She was raised in Chicago, where segregation wasn't so bad, but it was an environment that "downplayed her blackness."* What mental change did Nash and other activists have to accomplish? *they had to learn to be proud of their blackness instead of downplaying it or hating themselves.*

Critical Vocabulary: milieu (line 46) Have students suggest synonyms of the noun *milieu*. *setting, background, location*

FOR ELL STUDENTS Ask students to infer the meaning of the idiomatic phrase *clear-eyed thinking* (line 52). *It means "perceptive thinking," "smart thinking," or "thinking that is not muddled."*

> **What am I *doing*? And how is this little group of students my age going to stand up to these powerful people?**

C The committee had chosen the lunch counters and restaurants of Nashville's downtown stores as the target of the students' first protest, scheduled for February 1960. For the next several months, the
D students underwent rigorous training to prepare for the upcoming
60 sit-ins, and on February 13, 124 students left a Nashville church and made their way to the lunch counters of several downtown stores. There, they took their seats and asked for service. The men wore suits and ties, the women, dresses, stockings, and high heels. They were poised and polite and gave little outward sign of the fear many of them felt. Diane Nash, for one, was terrified—a terror that would never leave her, no matter how many sit-ins and protests she would participate in afterward.

As frightened as the students were during that first sit-in, however, they had to struggle to keep from laughing at the stunned, panicky
70 reactions of white store workers and **patrons**, who acted, Nash recalled, as if these well-dressed young people were "some dreadful monster . . . about to devour them all." Waitresses dropped dishes, cashiers broke down in tears, an elderly white woman almost had a seizure when she opened the door of a store's "white" ladies' room and found two young black women inside.

patron:
customer

---

3. **READ** ▶ As you read lines 56–106, continue to cite textual evidence.
   • Underline activists' preparations and actions in the sit-ins.
   • Circle how white store workers, patrons, and the city reacted to the sit-ins.
   • In the margin, summarize why Nash was made the head of the committee.
   • In the margin, explain how this section is organized.

98

There were no arrests and no violence. After a couple of hours, the students left the stores, jubilant that their first foray had gone without a hitch. A second sit-in was planned for the following week. In the meantime, several members of the students' Central Committee came
80 to Nash and asked her to head the group. She was hardworking and outwardly fearless, and she did not seem to have the ego problems that a lot of the men had. "Because she was a woman and not a man, I think Diane never had to go around and do any posturing," said Bernard Lafayette, an American Baptist College student and one of the Nashville movement's leaders. But Nash had no desire to become the recognized head of this movement. Like most young women of that time, she had been raised to stay in the background. The men pressured her into accepting, however, and when she returned to her dorm room, she was so frightened by what she had done that she
90 could hardly keep her legs from collapsing under her. "This is Tennessee," she told herself. "We are going to be coming up against . . . white Southern men who are forty and fifty and sixty years old, who are politicians and judges and owners of businesses, and I am twenty-two years old. What am I *doing*? And how is this little group of students my age going to stand up to these powerful people?"

Once again, she managed to damp down her fear. She joined the other students in the second sit-in, which was as quietly successful as the first. Nevertheless, the city was losing its patience. Nashville
100 officials, deluged by complaints from store owners that the sit-ins were causing whites to stay away from downtown, warned the students not to continue. If the warning wasn't heeded, they made clear, the kids could forget about being treated with kid gloves any longer. Worried about the possibility of violence and arrests, the ministers connected with the movement urged the students to reconsider their plans for another demonstration on February 27.

She was "hard-working," "fearless," and without ego. Committee members pressured her into accepting.

This section is organized chrono-logically: planning the protests; the first sit-in; the second sit-in; Nash becoming a leader.

---

4. ◀ **REREAD AND DISCUSS** Reread lines 56–67. In a small group, discuss why the students prepared so intensely for the sit-ins, and why they dressed up for the first protest.

5. **READ** ▶ As you read lines 107–123, continue to cite textual evidence. Underline police actions in the February 27 demonstration.

99

---

3. **READ AND CITE TEXT EVIDENCE**

C **ASK STUDENTS** to find and summarize text evidence of how the activists prepared for and carried out the two sit-ins. *Students should mention the following: the committee chose their first targets (lines 56–57); students underwent training (lines 59–60); students, "poised and polite," undertook the first sit-in (lines 62–64); students left the stores (lines 76–77); the second sit-in was planned (line 78); and Nash and other students successfully carried out the second sit-in (lines 97–99).*

Critical Vocabulary: patron (line 70) Have students share their definitions of *patron*, and ask volunteers to use the noun in sentences. *Example: White patrons were astonished to see blacks seating themselves at the lunch counter.*

4. **REREAD AND DISCUSS USING TEXT EVIDENCE**

D **ASK STUDENTS** to infer reasons for the "rigorous training." *Students should recognize that the sit-in students would possibly be met with violence from customers, store employees, or the Nashville police. Earlier, Nash wondered how nonviolence could work against "gun-toting sheriffs and club-swinging racists" (lines 35–36). For the sit-in to succeed, students would need training in nonviolent methods of demonstration.*

5. **READ AND CITE TEXT EVIDENCE**

E **ASK STUDENTS** to find and summarize evidence for the police's role during the Woolworth's sit-in. *Students should note the following: the police were absent when the students were being beaten up (line 115); when the police arrived, they left the attackers alone and instead told the students to leave the lunch counter (lines 116–119); the police arrested the students who were practicing nonviolence for "disorderly conduct" (lines 120–122).*

With their numbers swelling, the young people refused. In the middle of another snowstorm, more than three hundred of them poured into downtown Nashville. No sooner had some of them sat
110 down at the Woolworth's lunch counter than the ministers' fears proved justified. The demonstrators were met by an opposing force of cursing young white toughs, who yanked them from their stools and threw them to the floor, beat them with fists and clubs, kicked them, spat on them, extinguished lighted cigarettes on their backs and in

E their hair. The police were nowhere in sight, and when they finally arrived, they approached not the white attackers, but the bruised and shaken demonstrators, who were spattered with mustard and ketchup,

F spit and blood. "Okay, get up from the lunch counter or we're going to arrest you," one of the cops barked. When no one obeyed, the
120 students were ordered to their feet, arrested for disorderly conduct, and marched out, through a gauntlet of hostile whites, to police paddy wagons. When they looked over their shoulders at the lunch counter, they saw a new wave of students quietly moving in to take their place.

6. ◀ **REREAD** Reread lines 107–123. Explain why the "ministers' fears proved justified" during the sit-in at the Woolworth's lunch counter. In what respect could this sit-in be regarded as a victory? Support your response with explicit textual evidence.

This time the young people were cursed at, beaten, and kicked. The police arrested the demonstrators, not their attackers. Despite the violence and lack of police support, the students didn't give up: "they saw a new wave of students quietly moving in to take their place."

100

7. **READ ▶** As you read lines 1–44 of John Lewis's speech, continue to cite textual evidence.

• Underline what happened when the Freedom Riders got off the buses, and note in the margin what you can infer about their journey (lines 1–16).
• In the margin, explain the parallels between the Freedom Riders and voting.

Speech from the Democratic National Convention
Speech by John Lewis

I first came to this city in 1961, the year Barack Obama was born. I was one of the 13 original "Freedom Riders." We were on a bus ride from Washington to New Orleans trying to test a recent Supreme Court ruling that banned racial discrimination on buses crossing state lines and in the stations that served them. Here in Charlotte, a young African-American rider got off the bus and tried to get a shoe shine in a so-called white waiting room. He was arrested and taken to jail.

On that same day, we continued on to Rock Hill, South Carolina,
10 about 25 miles. From here, when my seatmate, Albert Bigelow, and I

G tried to enter a white waiting room, we were met by an angry mob that beat us and left us lying in a pool of blood. Some police officers came up and asked us whether we wanted to press charges. We said, "No, we come in peace, love and nonviolence." We said our struggle was not against individuals, but against unjust laws and customs. Our goal was true freedom for every American.

Since then, America has made a lot of progress. We are a different society than we were in 1961. And in 2008, we showed the world the true promise of America when we elected President Barack Obama. A
20 few years ago, a man from Rock Hill, inspired by President Obama's

H election, decided to come forward. He came to my office in Washington and said, "I am one of the people who beat you. I want to apologize. Will you forgive me?" I said, "I accept your apology." He started crying. He gave me a hug. I hugged him back, and we both started crying. This man and I don't want to go back; we want to move forward.

As the Freedom Riders got closer to New Orleans, they were in more danger.

101

---

6. **REREAD AND CITE TEXT EVIDENCE**

F **ASK STUDENTS** to discuss how the participants in the Woolworth's sit-in might have perceived the day's events. *Students should understand that the sit-in students probably didn't feel that they had won a decisive or even symbolic victory. They had been beaten up; the police hadn't helped them or even apprehended their attackers; instead, the police had arrested the protesters themselves, who were the victims of violence. Still, the students could possibly see cause for hope—the nonviolence movement was gaining adherents, and it was putting intense public attention on segregation.*

FOR ELL STUDENTS Explain that the word *swelling* (line 107) refers to numbers—the numbers got greater.

7. **READ AND CITE TEXT EVIDENCE**

G **ASK STUDENTS** to make and support inferences about the journey of the Freedom Riders. *Students can infer that at least some southern police wanted to enforce the law or even sympathized with the Freedom Riders. Several officers asked Lewis and his companion if they wanted to press charges against their attackers. Students can also infer that as the Freedom Ride continued south and gained media attention, the response of whites grew more violent. A Freedom Rider was arrested in Charlotte; Lewis and Bigelow were beaten up in Rock Hill.*

The Riders were engaged in nonviolent protest to achieve equality, leading to the freedom to vote without restrictions.

Brothers and sisters, do you want to go back? Or do you want to keep America moving forward? My dear friends, your vote is precious, almost sacred. It is the most powerful, nonviolent tool we
30 have to create a more perfect union. Not too long ago, people stood in unmovable lines. They had to pass a so-called literacy test, pay a poll tax. On one occasion, a man was asked to count the number of bubbles in a bar of soap. On another occasion, one was asked to count the jelly beans in a jar—all to keep them from casting their ballots.

Today it is unbelievable that there are officials still trying to stop some people from voting. They are changing the rules, cutting polling hours and imposing requirements intended to suppress the vote.

I've seen this before. I've lived this before. Too many people struggled, suffered and died to make it possible for every American to
40 exercise their right to vote.

And we have come too far together to ever turn back. So we must not be silent. We must stand up, speak up and speak out. We must march to the polls like never before. We must come together and exercise our sacred right.

8. ◀ REREAD AND DISCUSS Reread lines 17–26. With a small group, discuss the anecdote Lewis relates about the man from Rock Hill. In what way did this incident allow both men "to move forward"? Cite text evidence in your discussion.

SHORT RESPONSE

Cite Text Evidence Compare and contrast the texts by Olson and Lewis. What is similar and different in the two accounts? Review your reading notes and be sure to **cite text evidence** in your response.

Olson writes about Nash's experiences so that readers understand the historical importance of her actions. Lewis shares his thoughts and feelings about his experiences to emphasize that people should learn from the past and guard against repeating similar injustices today.

102

8. REREAD AND DISCUSS USING TEXT EVIDENCE

(H) ASK STUDENTS to compare and contrast the encounters between the two men, from the original beating in Rock Hill to the hug in Washington. *The Rock Hill man took part in a violent crime. He must have come to realize how wrong his actions were, for he was "inspired" by the election of the first black President to visit Lewis. He must have felt a lot of guilt. Lewis, although he believed in the nonviolence movement, may have felt resentment and anger at his attackers. To move forward, the man needed forgiveness, while Lewis needed to hear and accept the man's apology.*

SHORT RESPONSE

Cite Text Evidence Students' responses should include text evidence that supports their positions. They should:

- explain how the texts are similar and different.
- give examples of differences of perspective.
- give examples of differences of purpose.

TO CHALLENGE STUDENTS . . .

For more context and historical background, students can view the video "Class of the 20th Century: 1963–1968" in their eBooks.

ASK STUDENTS what view Dr. Martin Luther King expresses about violent acts. *Dr. King says that nothing can be accomplished by violence and that violence only leads to more problems in society.* In what ways do the actions of Diane Nash and John Lewis reflect the views of Dr. King? *Both Nash and Lewis performed nonviolent acts to stand up for their beliefs and improve society.*

DIG DEEPER

With the class, return to Question 3, Read. Have students share their underlined texts about the activists' preparations.

ASK STUDENTS to discuss the activists' clothing and demeanor during the sit-in.

- What was the importance of the men's "suits and ties" and the women's "dresses, stockings, and high heels"? *Students should recognize that the protesters wanted to send a message to white owners, employees, and customers. Segregation essentially told blacks that they were "inferior" and thus "unfit to use the same facilities" as whites. By dressing their best, the students were countering with their own message: they were equal and deserved equal treatment.*

- Why was it important for the students to be "poised and polite"? *Again, the students wanted to send a message. By behaving politely in a dangerous situation, they showed that they were equal, not inferior, to white patrons. Also, they were practicing nonviolence, so poise and politeness were probably parts of their strategy.*

ASK STUDENTS to return to their Short Response answer and revise it based on the class discussion.

from **Uprising**

Historical Novel by Margaret Peterson Haddix

Why This Text?

Students will often encounter works of historical fiction in their personal reading or in their reading at school. Understanding how an author uses elements of storytelling to bring a historical event to life will help students become more astute readers. This lesson also asks students to compare historical fiction and nonfiction texts to understand the important differences between the genres.

Key Learning Objective: The student will be able to analyze points of view in a text and compare and contrast different genres.

For practice and application:

Close Reader selection
"Doris Is Coming"
Short Story by ZZ Packer

RL 1 Cite textual evidence.

RL 2 Provide an objective summary.

RL 3 Analyze story elements.

RL 4 Determine the meaning of words and phrases.

RL 6 Analyze point of view.

RL 9 Compare and contrast fictional and historical accounts of the same event.

W 3 Write a narrative based on a historical event.

W 4 Produce clear and organized writing.

W 5 Revise, edit, and rewrite to strengthen writing.

W 9 Draw evidence from literary and historical texts to support analysis, reflection, and research.

W 10 Write routinely for longer/shorter time frames.

L 1a Explain the function of phrases and clauses.

L 5 Demonstrate understanding of figurative language.

L 5b Use an analogy to better understand words.

▲ Text Complexity Rubric

Quantitative Measures	*from* **Uprising** Lexile: 800L
Qualitative Measures	**Levels of Meaning/Purpose** single level of simple meaning (single theme)
	Structure some unconventional story structure elements
	Language Conventionality and Clarity increased, clearly assigned dialogue
	Knowledge Demands unfamiliar, multiple perspectives
Reader/Task Considerations	• Teacher determined • Vary by individual reader and type of text • See the Text X-Ray for suggested Reader/Task Considerations.

English Language Support Before teaching, use the Text X-Ray for an overview of the text's complexity. The Text X-Ray and the supports and scaffolds in the Teacher's Edition will help you guide students of different skill levels.

Text Complexity: Qualitative Measures

Levels of Meaning/Purpose

single level of simple meaning

Help students analyze the point of view from which the selection is told.

- Teacher's Edition side notes, pp. 283, 286, 287, 290, 291, 293, 295, 296, 297, 298, 302, 303
- English Language Support, pp. 286, 287, 290, 291, 293, 295, 297, 298, 300
- Strategies for Annotation, pp. 287, 299, 303
- Analyze Point of View, p. 303

To reteach how to analyze point of view, see

- Analyze Point of View, p. 306a

▶ *Use It!* **Level Up Tutorial:** Third-Person Point of View

ZOOM IN ON ANALYZING POINT OF VIEW Tell students that a story is usually told through first-person (an "I" narrator) or third-person **point of view**. A third-person narrator is not part of the story; his or her view of events may be **limited** to what one character knows or **omniscient** ("all-knowing").

- Display lines 447–449. Guide students to identify clues that tell them what the point of view is and then identify the specific point of view. (Jane, she, *and* he *show that the narrator is third-person; details about Jane's thoughts but not the man's reaction show that the point of view is limited to only what Jane experiences.*)
- Ask students how this point of view helps them understand events and characters. (*It provides a close-up account of events.*)

Structure

some unconventional story structure elements

Help students compare and contrast the treatment of the same event in historical fiction and history writing.

- Teacher's Edition side notes, pp. 284, 285, 288, 289, 292, 294, 297, 300, 301, 303
- English Language Support, pp. 283, 285, 288, 294, 301
- When Students Struggle, pp. 284, 293
- Strategies for Annotation, pp. 290, 296
- Compare and Contrast: Genres, p. 303

To reteach how to compare and contrast genres, see

- Compare and Contrast: Genres, p. 306a

▶ *Use It!* **Level Up Tutorial:** Prose Forms

ZOOM IN ON COMPARING AND CONTRASTING GENRES Give students practice **comparing** and **contrasting** accounts of the same event in works of different genres.

- Have students identify details about the fire in lines 97–107 of *Flesh & Blood*, and record them on the board. (*There had been no fire drills so no one knew what to do. People were pushing trying to get to an exit. Those who made it to the Greene Street stairs survived.*)
- Have groups read lines 525–544 in *Uprising*, noting facts from the first selection that also appear in this account. (*There is mass confusion; there have been no fire drills so no one knows what to do.*)
- Then have groups discuss how the treatment of these facts differs in the two selections. (*Haddix reveals facts through the behaviors, feelings, and dialogue of the characters instead of simply stating them.*)

Language Conventionality and Clarity

increased, clearly assigned dialogue

Teach unfamiliar vocabulary in context.

- Teacher's Edition Critical Vocabulary notes, pp. 284, 285, 287, 288, 291, 292, 295, 298, 305
- English Language Support, p. 292
- Applying Academic Vocabulary, p. 286
- Strategies for Annotation, p. 305
- Vocabulary Strategy: Analogies, p. 305

Help students understand figurative language.

- Teacher's Edition side notes, pp. 289, 299
- English Language Support, p. 289

Guide students to recognize verbal phrases.

- Teacher's Edition side notes, p. 306
- English Language Support, p. 306
- Language Conventions: Phrases, p. 306

ZOOM IN ON **ANALYZING FIGURATIVE LANGUAGE** Tell students that **figurative language** compares two unlike things to make a description more vivid. Write "The flames kept dividing, devouring stack after stack of shirtwaists, racing each other down the tables" on the board.

- Explain that *devouring* means "eating greedily." Ask students to describe the effect of this comparison on their understanding of the fire. *(The fire is gobbling up the clothing on the tables; there is nothing left; the fabrics are feeding the fire.)*
- Then ask them what the phrase "racing each other" helps them to visualize. *(This phrase shows the speed with which the fire is traveling.)*

Knowledge Demands

unfamiliar, multiple perspectives

Support English Learners in building historical and cultural context.

- Teacher's Edition Author's note, p. 283
- Content-Area Connection, p. 302

ZOOM IN ON **BUILDING UNDERSTANDING OF CONTEXT** Discuss these terms that appear in the selection:

- In line 15, "closed shop" means that everyone who works there must be a union member.
- In line 136, "Yiddish" refers to the language spoken by Jewish people from Central and Eastern Europe.
- In line 312, "finishing school" is a place where wealthy girls learned social skills.

Suggested Reader/Task Considerations

Consider the following before assigning this fictional excerpt.

- Will students be able to understand the relationship among the parts of the excerpt?
- Will students be able to make connections to other nonfiction works they have read on the same subject?

ZOOM IN ON **SUPPORTING COMPREHENSION**

- Have students listen to each section, pausing to discuss where the action takes place, what is happening, and what the characters are doing in each section.
- Have students record details about the fire. Review *Flesh & Blood So Cheap* to have students identify facts also used in *Uprising*.

CLOSE READ

Margaret Peterson Haddix Tell students that nearly a decade before the Triangle fire, a fire at the Iroquois Theater in Chicago killed over 500 people because they couldn't get out of the building. Building codes for public spaces were changed in response to that tragedy. After the Triangle fire, positive and lasting reforms occurred in worker safety. When details of the fire and conditions in the Asch Building became public, people across the country protested for safer working conditions. Reforms made after the Triangle fire are still followed in today's workplaces.

SETTING A PURPOSE Direct students to use the Setting a Purpose prompt to focus their reading. Remind students to generate questions as they read.

Analyze Point of View
RL 6

(LINES 7–10)

Explain that in fiction the **narrator** is the voice that tells the story. The author's choice of a narrator is called the **point of view,** which gives readers a specific perspective on the story. In *Uprising*, the author uses **third-person limited,** which has the following characteristics:

- The narrator is not a character and is outside the story.
- The narrator uses third-person pronouns, such as *he, she, him, her, their.*
- The reader sees the story events and other characters through the eyes of one character, who is often the main character of the story.

Explain that lines 7–10 are italicized to indicate internal dialogue, meaning this is what Yetta is thinking.

 ASK STUDENTS what the internal dialogue in lines 7–10 reveals about Yetta. *(It reveals that Yetta is hard on herself and expects more accomplishment.)*

Margaret Peterson Haddix (b. 1964) *grew up on a farm in Ohio. While her father was a farmer and her mother a nurse, Haddix always wanted to be a writer. Her inspiration was her father, who was always telling her stories. Haddix has now written more than a dozen books for young adults. Asked why she likes writing for young audiences, Haddix replies that teenagers are naturally great characters in books—often more interesting than adults.*

from Uprising

Historical Novel by Margaret Peterson Haddix

SETTING A PURPOSE This fiction excerpt is based on the real-life event of the Triangle Factory Fire. As you read, think about how the author has used facts and her own imagination to make the events of the fire come to life.

Yetta

Yetta was listening for the bell on the time clock, waiting to finish her day. It was a Saturday afternoon in March, and the spring breezes were back. She'd heard them rattling the windows when the machines were shut down for lunch; she knew that as soon as she stepped outside, they'd tease at her hair and tug at her hat. This year, the breezes seemed to carry a slightly different message: *Another year past and what do you have to show for yourself? So you can read English a little bit better, so you handed out a few suffrage[1] flyers—do you*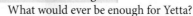
10 *think that that's enough?*

What would ever be enough for Yetta?

---

[1] **suffrage:** the right or privilege of voting.

(t) ©The Backstage Studio/Adams Literary; (l) ©SuperStock/SuperStock; (r) ©Lewis Hine/Kheel Center/Cornell University

---

English Language Support

Understand Text Structure Explain each of the three parts of this story tells how one character experiences the Triangle Factory Fire. Display lines 1–10. Tell students that this paragraph introduces Yetta. Explain that the italicized words show what Yetta is thinking.

- Have students echo read the paragraph. Work with them to identify where Yetta is and what her thoughts show about the way she is feeling.

- Have students reread the paragraph. Point out that Yetta is talking to herself, addressing herself as "you." Ask: *What is the tone of her thoughts? (critical)* Then have pairs skim page 284 to find an additional example of Yetta's thoughts.

- Explain that the italicized text is called internal dialogue. Have students read the top of page 284, which is dialogue that Yetta is speaking. Ask them to discuss the differences between external and internal dialogue and why the author includes both in the selection.

CLOSE READ

Compare and Contrast:

RL 1,
RL 3,
RL 9

Genres (LINES 23–26)

Explain to students that **historical fiction** is a type of story that is set in the past and includes real places and events. Authors base the stories on facts and research, but they use their imaginations to create scenes, dialogue, and sometimes even characters to tell the story.

B CITE TEXT EVIDENCE Have students reread lines 23–26. What does the author's description of the characters' actions reveal about the real-life working conditions at the factory? *(Yetta and Jennie both stand up and stretch "cramped muscles," unhunch "rounded shoulders," and stamp their feet to wake up "feet that had gone numb on the sewing machine pedal." This suggests that the work the women did was physically demanding and potentially damaging to their bodies.)* Have students reread lines 21–30 of the excerpt from *Flesh & Blood So Cheap* and note how that description of the working conditions compares to this description. *(The description in the informational text does not describe the effect the conditions have on the workers' bodies, as does the historical fiction, but it allows readers to visualize the working conditions that make Yetta and Jennie feel the way they do.)*

CRITICAL VOCABULARY

mischievous: The author describes the little dance Jennie does as mischievous.

ASK STUDENTS why Jennie's dance might be considered mischievous. *(because dancing in the factory might not be allowed; because Jennie is teasing Yetta about Jacob, who had asked Yetta to go dancing with him)*

"I think they set the clocks back again," the girl beside her muttered. "It's got to be past quitting time!"

"And that's why we need a strong union, why we need a closed shop," Yetta muttered back.

The girl rolled her eyes at Yetta.

"Don't you ever give up?" she asked over the clatter of the machine.

20 "No," Yetta said, but she grinned at the girl, and the girl grinned back, and Yetta thought maybe, just maybe, they'd inched just a little closer to the solidarity[2] Yetta longed for. This girl's name was Jennie, and she was new.

The bell finally rang, and Yetta and Jennie both stood up and stretched, reviving cramped muscles, unhunching rounded shoulders, stamping feet that had gone numb on the sewing machine pedal. **B**

"I'm going dancing tonight," Jennie said, **mischievously** tapping out a rhythm on the floor. "What are you doing?"

"Um . . . I don't know," Yetta said. "I haven't decided yet."

30 Bella and Jane had been nagging her to go visit Rahel and the new baby, a little boy they'd named Benjamin. Bella and Jane had already gone once, but Yetta had had a cold then and only sent her regrets.

Well, really, I wouldn't want the baby getting sick because of me, Yetta told herself. *Maybe I'm not well enough, even yet. . . .*

"I bet that cutter who watches you all the time would take you dancing," Jennie said. "All you have to do is just . . ." She pantomimed cozying up to an invisible man, gazing up adoringly at the invisible man's face, fluttering her eyelashes.

40 Yetta blushed.

"There's not a cutter who watches me all the time," she said, but she couldn't help glancing toward Jacob's table. Jacob hadn't said a word to her about dancing since she'd turned down his invitation, all those months ago. But he did seem to find lots of reasons to walk past her sewing machine, to ride in the same elevator with her, morning and evening. Even halfway across the room, she could instantly pick out his figure in the cluster of cutters standing around laughing and talking and smoking. Jacob was bent over the table, smoothing

50 out the layers of lawn fabric ready to be cut first thing Monday morning. There had to be at least a hundred and twenty layers

mischievous
(mĭs´chə-vəs) *adj.*
If someone is *mischievous*, the person is naughty.

---

[2] **solidarity:** unity, especially in the case of workers joining together in a union.

WHEN STUDENTS STRUGGLE …

To be sure students understand the series of events in a rapidly developing plot, it can help to break down each action in the series. In lines 69–86, the author describes the quick spread of the fire and Yetta's realization of the danger.

Have students reread lines 69–86. In pairs, have them fill out a cause-and-effect chain like the one shown. Explain that the chain will help them understand what is happening leading to Yetta's realization. Have students paraphrase the events. Ask students to use this strategy as they read or reread the selection.

 LEVEL UP TUTORIALS For additional support, assign the following *Level Up* tutorial: **Plot: Sequence of Events.**

of the gauzy fabric spread across the table, each one separated
from the others by sheer tissue paper. Jacob handled it all
so gently, almost lovingly. Above his head, the tissue-paper
patterns dangled from wires, so when he stood up it was like
watching someone across a forest, half hidden by hanging
moss and low branches.

Suddenly Jacob and the other cutters jumped back. One
of the men sprinted over to a shelf on the wall and seized a
60 red fire pail. Jerkily, he raced back and threw the pail of water
under one of the tables, at the huge bin of fabric scraps left
over from days and days of cutting out shirtwaists.

"Not again! Those cutters and their cigarettes," Yetta said
scornfully. It was clear what had happened: One of them had
dropped a match or a cigarette butt or a still-burning ember
into the scrap bin. At least someone was smart enough to keep
buckets of water around, if the cutters couldn't be stopped
from smoking.

But then there was a flash, and Yetta saw the flame jump,
70 from under the table to the top of it. More men grabbed
buckets, desperately pouring water onto the flames, but
there'd been only three buckets on that shelf, so they had to
run across the room for more.

The water was nothing to the fire. The flames raced
the length of the lawn fabric; they sprang up to the
dangling paper patterns and danced from one to the next,
the patterns writhing³ down to ash and spitting off more
flames. In seconds the fire had gone from being something
to scoff at under a table to a voracious beast ready to engulf
80 the entire room.

Beside Yetta, Jennie began to scream.

"Stop it! This is a fireproof building!" Yetta yelled at
Jennie.

*But we're tinder,*⁴ she remembered.

Yetta slammed her hands against Jennie's shoulders and
screamed, "Go!"

The aisle between the sewing machine tables was narrow,
and the wicker baskets where they stacked the shirtwaists kept
snagging their skirts. And other girls were blocking the aisle,
90 some screaming and hysterical like Jennie'd been. One girl

---

scorn
(skôrn) *n. Scorn* is
disrespect or disdain.

---

³ **writhing:** twisting.
⁴ **tinder:** material that burns easily.

Uprising **285**

Cause		Effect		Effect		Effect
fire spreads to table top		*water won't put out fire*		*fire burns up fabric and spreads quickly*		*Jennie screams, but Yetta tells her not to worry.*

CLOSE READ

Compare and Contrast: Genres (LINES 63–68)

RL 1, RL 9

Remind students that this is a fictionalized account
of the Triangle Factory Fire that they read about
earlier in Collection 6. Point out that lines 31–44 of
the excerpt from *Flesh & Blood So Cheap* describe how
the fire started. In lines 63–68 of *Uprising*, the author
depicts the same event.

C **CITE TEXT EVIDENCE** Have students reread
lines 31–44 of *Flesh & Blood So Cheap* and then reread
lines 63–68 of *Uprising*. Ask students to cite evidence
of the similarities between the two accounts and
how the author's description of the scene in *Uprising*
reveals it to be historical fiction. *(The cutters are
smoking in each account, and the fire starts beneath
a cutting table; in* Uprising, *Yetta is commenting on
the cutters and what their smoking caused, as well as
the fact that some of them had sense enough to keep
water nearby.)*

English Language Support

Remind students that *Flesh & Blood So Cheap* is a
nonfiction account. Explain that when they compare
the texts, they should look for details that are the
same and different.

- Read aloud the lines from *Flesh & Blood So Cheap*.
  Record the sequence of events on the board and
  point out the author's statement that it is not clear
  exactly how the fire started.

- Next, read aloud lines 63–68 from this selection.
  Record the significant details from this account on
  the board next to the first set of facts.

- Have pairs work to compare and contrast the
  information presented in each account.

CRITICAL VOCABULARY

scorn: The author uses the word *scornfully* to
convey how disgusted Yetta is about the cutters
and their smoking in the factory.

ASK STUDENTS why Yetta feels such disdain at the
cutters starting a small fire that she looks at them
scornfully. *(because it's dangerous and seems like it's
something the cutters do too often)*

Analyze Story Elements

RL 3

(LINES 91–103)

Explain to students that authors reveal information about characters through text details such as dialogue (what the characters say out loud), actions, internal thoughts, and interactions with other characters. In this section, the author depicts two different sides of Yetta's character.

D **ASK STUDENTS** to reread lines 91–103 and describe what change in Yetta's character is depicted. *(At first she's trying to help others escape, but when she sees the woman fall out of the eighth-story window, she panics and freezes, realizing she might die.)*

English Language Support

Read Closely Display lines 107–117. Remind students that the third-person narrator tells what the main characters do and what they think and feel. Ask pairs to read the passage and answer these questions:

- What does the word *shoved* mean? Why do Jacob and Yetta have to "shove forward"? *(Shoved means "pushed forcefully"; they have to "shove forward" because of the crowds of people blocking their way.)*

- What does the word *relieved* mean? Why does Yetta feel relieved when she sees Mr. Bernstein pull out the hose? *(Relieved means "feeling less anxiety"; she feels that Mr. Bernstein is taking control of the situation.)*

- What happens when the hose is turned on? *(No water comes out.)*

Discuss students' responses. Then have them explain how this scene shows how the characters' problem is becoming more serious.

D fainted right at Yetta's feet. Yetta reached down and slapped her, jerked her up.

"No time for that!" Yetta screamed. "You'll die!"

Across the room, Yetta saw a spark land in a woman's hair. In seconds, the woman's whole pompadour[5] was aflame. Everyone was screaming, but Yetta thought she could hear this woman's screams above all the others. The woman lurched across the room, slammed into one of the windows. No— slammed through. She'd thrown herself out the window.

100 *We're on the eighth floor*, Yetta thought numbly, and now it was her turn to freeze in panic and fear. Sparks were flying throughout the room now, landing everywhere. Anyone could be next.

Hands grabbed Yetta from behind.

"Yetta, come on!"

It was Jacob.

> **❝ Sparks were flying throughout the room now, landing everywhere. ❞**

Jacob and Yetta shoved forward, toward the Washington Place stairs, pulling along Jennie and the girl who'd fainted. Yetta glanced back once more and was relieved to see that
110 Mr. Bernstein, the factory manager, had had some of the men pull a fire hose out of the Greene Street stairwell. He stood over the worst of the flames, pointing the hose confidently.

No water came out.

"Turn it on! Turn it on!" Mr. Bernstein was screaming. Yetta wasn't sure if she could hear him or if she was just reading his lips. "Where is the water?" he screamed again.

Not a drop. He flung down the hose and ran.

---

[5] **pompadour:** a woman's hairstyle.

APPLYING ACADEMIC VOCABULARY

despite	inadequate	interact

THINK-PAIR-SHARE Have partners discuss the following questions. Guide students to include the academic vocabulary words *despite*, *inadequate*, and *interact* in their responses. Ask volunteers to share their responses with the class.

- In what ways were the safety measures **inadequate** in the case of a major fire?

- How do the characters and the fire **interact** throughout the story?

- How do the characters continue with their efforts to escape **despite** the terrifying obstacles?

Now Mr. Bernstein was rushing through the crowds of girls, some still heading toward the cloakroom[6] to get their hats.

"Don't worry about your hats!" he screamed. "Just get out!"

He was slapping and punching the girls, beating them as though he blamed them for the fire. No—he was goading them toward the doors, toward the elevators and the fire escape. He was only slapping the hysterical girls, like Yetta had done with the girl who'd fainted. He was trying to save their lives.

We are on the same side now, Mr. Bernstein and me, Yetta **marveled**.

She shoved against a girl who'd dropped her purse, who'd seen her coins roll under the table.

"Don't stop for that!" Yetta screamed. "It's not worth it! Save your life!"

She and Jacob together pulled the girl up, lifting her past the table, toward the door. There were already dozens of other girls crowded around the door, screaming in Yiddish and English and what Yetta now recognized as Italian. "Open it! Open it!" "Oh, please, for the love of God!" "*Madonna mia, aiutami!*"

But it was locked.

Some of the girls were pounding on the elevator door, too, screaming for the elevator operator to come to them. Miraculously, the elevator door opened, and the crowd surged forward, sobbing and praying and screaming.

"Just wait—just wait—I'll come right back!" the operator hollered.

The doors were closing, but Yetta shoved Jennie forward, shoving her on top of the girls already in the elevator. Saving her, at least.

"*Will* he come back?" Yetta asked Jacob, and Jacob shrugged.

Yetta couldn't just stand there and wait. She wasn't going to stand still while the flames raced toward her, while others pressed their faces against a door that might never open. She grabbed Jacob's hand and pulled him along, circling around the fire. She looked back once and saw that someone had managed to open the door to the Washington Place stairs;

marvel

(mär′vəl) *v.* If you *marvel* at something, you are surprised or astonished by it.

---

[6] **cloakroom:** a room where coats are hung up.

CLOSE READ

Analyze Point of View
RL 1, RL 6

(LINES 118–129)

The author describes the actions of one of the managers of the factory from Yetta's perspective.

E **CITE TEXT EVIDENCE** Have students reread lines 118–129, and ask them to identify why Yetta thinks she and Mr. Bernstein were on the same side. *(Possible answer: He slapped and punched some of the hysterical girls to make them keep moving toward the doors, which is similar to what Yetta did to a couple of the women who were panicking.)*

English Language Support

Read aloud line 128. Clarify that Yetta is a union organizer and Mr. Bernstein is a manager who would be against her trying to start a union in the factory. Discuss what they are both trying to do in this part of the text.

CRITICAL VOCABULARY

marvel: The author uses the word *marveled* to described Yetta's reaction to what Mr. Bernstein was doing.

ASK STUDENTS how Yetta feels about her realization that she and Mr. Bernstein are "on the same side now." *(Yetta is a union organizer, and Mr. Bernstein probably fought against her efforts to start a union. When lives are on the line, she is surprised to see that they can work together for the same goal.)*

Strategies for Annotation
Annotate it!

Analyze Point of View
RL 6

Share these strategies for identifying point of view:

- Highlight in blue the phrases that reveal Yetta's point of view.
- Highlight in yellow the actions Yetta takes.
- Add a note that describes Yetta's perspective on the actions of the other women.

Yetta couldn't just stand there and wait. She wasn't going to stand still while the flames raced toward her, whi pressed their faces against a door that might never o grabbed Jacob's hand and pulled him along, circling the fire. She looked back once and saw that someone had managed to open the door to the Washington Place stairs;

Yetta sees that what the others are doing isn't going to be effective.

CLOSE READ

Compare and Contrast: Genres (LINES 161–165)

RL 1,
RL 9

Remind students that *Uprising* is based on factual details of the Triangle Factory Fire.

F **CITE TEXT EVIDENCE** Have students read lines 91–96 of the excerpt from *Flesh & Blood So Cheap* and then reread lines 161–165 of *Uprising*. Ask students to cite details that are similar in each account of the spreading fire. (*"cans of oil," "the oiled floor," "finished shirtwaists," "fabric scraps," "the air itself seemed to catch fire,"* and *"the air itself seemed to be on fire."*) Point out the similar detail in both accounts of the air seeming to be on fire. Ask students what would likely be the source of this detail that makes it a fact and not an image from the author's imagination. (*The image that the air "seemed to be on fire" likely came from an interview or account of someone who was on the ninth floor and survived the fire.*)

English Language Support

Display both passages and have students work together to pick out words and phrases that describe similar ideas.

CRITICAL VOCABULARY

singe: The author describes what happens when a spark of flame lands on Yetta's arm.

ASK STUDENTS to describe why Yetta was horrified when the spark singed her arm. (*Sample answer: She'd watched the fabrics in the factory go up in flames so quickly she feared the spark was going to light her clothes ablaze.*)

---

the door opened in, toward the crowd. Maybe it hadn't been locked after all. Maybe it was just the weight of the crowd
160   pushing forward, pinning it shut.

But it was too late to go back now. Flames were shooting across the path they'd just crossed, speeding across the oiled floor, licking up shirtwaists and fabric scraps and wicker baskets. The air itself seemed to be on fire, the flames living on fabric dust.

F

"Fire escape," Yetta moaned to Jacob, and it was so hot now that her words felt like flames themselves, painful on her tongue.

"No good," Jacob mumbled back. "Doesn't go all the way
170   to the ground."

So they didn't head for the window near the airshaft, where people were climbing out one at a time, onto the rickety metal railing. What was left?

"Greene Street stairs," Jacob whispered.

Those were back by the table where the fire had started, where it now burned the fiercest. But there was a partition wall blocking off the stairs and the elevator from the rest of the room. On a normal workday that was where the guard sat, inspecting purses and glaring at the girls as if he thought they
180   were all thieves. Today, maybe that partition was enough to keep the fire away from the stairs.

Yetta and Jacob raced on, skirting the flames, still pulling along hysterical, senseless workers who didn't seem to know where to go. They passed a desk where the bookkeeper, Miss Lipshutz, was shouting into the mouthpiece of a telephone, "Please! Somebody listen! Somebody's got to tell the ninth floor! Hello? Somebody—please!"

A spark landed on the sleeve of Yetta's shirtwaist, and she watched in horror as it sputtered and shimmered and burned
190   straight through. She could feel it **singeing** her skin.

Jacob slapped his bare hand onto Yetta's sleeve, starving the flame.

'*A dank,*'" Yetta whispered, but there was no time for him to say, "You're welcome," because they were at the doorway to the partition now, shoving their way behind it.

No flames here.

singe
(sĭnj) *v.* If you *singe* something, you slightly burn it.

---

7 **a dank** (ä dänk): "thank you" in the Yiddish language.

English Language Support

Improve Reading Fluency Display lines 161–190. Discuss with students the action that is occurring in this part of the text. Work with them to identify the words and phrases that the author uses to create a mood of terror and excitement. Read the passage aloud, communicating that same feeling through your vocal expression. Then reread one paragraph at a time, modeling how to speed up the pace or add intensity to the words where appropriate. Have students echo read each paragraph after you, repeating as necessary in order to achieve fluency.

Girls were still standing by the freight elevator door, the only elevator they were normally allowed to use. They were pounding on the closed door like they thought that was their only chance. It was so hot behind the partition that Yetta could barely breathe.

Can people melt? she wondered. In her mind she saw wax dripping down from Sabbath[8] candles. *My life, melting away . . .*

"Stairs!" Jacob screamed at the girls by the elevator door.

He jerked open the stairway door and it opened out, making another obstacle in the tiny vestibule. Yetta and Jacob shoved the girls through the doorway and scrambled in behind them. The stairway was airless and close and still hot, but there were no sparks flying through the air. Through the window in the stairwell, Yetta could see the workers scrambling down the fire escape, teetering precariously on the metal railings, struggling past the metal shutters.

"Hurry!" Yetta screamed at the girls around her. They were sobbing hysterically, clutching the railing, clutching each other. They were yammering away in some language Yetta didn't recognize, or maybe it wasn't a language at all, just witless jabbering.

> ## " They were sobbing hysterically, clutching the railing, clutching each other. "

"The fire!" one of them managed to say. "What if it's everywhere?"

"There's no smoke coming from down there!" Yetta screamed at them, pointing at the landings below them. "Go down to the ground! You'll be safe! The flames are going up, not down!"

Up.

---

[8] **Sabbath:** the day of worship in the Jewish and other religions.

CLOSE READ

Analyze Figurative Language (LINES 202–204)
RL 4, L 5

Explain that a **metaphor** compares two unlike objects or ideas. Have students reread lines 202–204, in which the author employs a candle metaphor.

H **ASK STUDENTS** why the author chose to use a candle metaphor for Yetta's life. *(Possible answer: Yetta is caught in a fire, picturing religious candles melting. She had seemed afraid about the direction of her own life earlier in the story. Now, she is afraid that her life will melt away like the wax in a candle.)*

Compare and Contrast: Genres (LINES 205–213)
RL 1, RL 9

Point out that the author of *Uprising* is describing details that were also recounted in lines 5–7 of the the excerpt from *The Story of the Triangle Factory Fire.*

I **CITE TEXT EVIDENCE** Have students reread lines 5–7 of the history writing and lines 205–213 of *Uprising.* Ask students to cite examples of how Haddix took these details and expanded them into fiction. *(The history writing briefly mentions this detail: "Doors that opened inward instead of outward, overcrowding in work areas, and blocked exits also were to blame." In* Uprising, *the author has added details that expand on this to make the story come to life: Jacob "jerked open the stairway door and it opened out, making another obstacle in the tiny vestibule.")*

English Language Support

Analyze Language Explain that **figurative language** often makes a comparison that helps readers visualize characters, settings, or events more clearly.

- Tell students that in lines 202–204 Yetta is comparing her life to a candle that is melting into nothing. Discuss how the comparison helps readers know what is happening in the story.

- Explain that personification is a type of figurative language that describes something that is not human as if it is. Have students pick out words in lines 161–165 that make the flames seem human. Discuss what is conveyed about the fire by the personification. *(The fire is "licking up" the shirtwaists and "speeding" across the oiled floor, "living on fabric dust." The personification makes the fire seem more dangerous.)*

- Discuss the personification in lines 161–165. Ask students to look on page 290 to find another example. Have them explain what is personified and what picture the language creates in their minds. *(The inferno is "eating up the air." This conveys that it is getting harder to breathe and that the fire is everywhere.)*

Analyze Point of View

RL 6

(LINES 237–243)

Explain that authors use italicized text to show characters' thoughts. In third-person limited point of view, readers can see the interior thoughts of only the primary character the author has chosen.

J **ASK STUDENTS** to reread lines 237–243 and ask them why Yetta feels compelled to warn the workers on the ninth floor. *(Sample answer: Her friend Bella is on the ninth floor, but Yetta also feels responsible for her fellow workers because she is a union organizer.)*

English Language Support

Support Opinions Have students reread lines 237–243. Discuss what Yetta is about to do when she remembers that no one has told the ninth floor about the fire. What does she decide she must do? Why? What is Jacob's reaction to her decision? Why?

ASK STUDENTS to discuss the consequences of Yetta's action and why she makes the choice that she does. Provide these sentence frames:

- I think Yetta _____.
- I agree with ____, but I also think _____.
- I haven't thought about it that way because _____.

Encourage students to reflect on decisions that they have made in the past to help them understand Yetta's action. Point out that a person's ethical code may help a person figure out what to do in a particular situation.

Yetta glanced up to the landing above her, remembering what the bookkeeper had been screaming into the phone: *Somebody listen! Somebody's got to tell the ninth floor!*

230   They didn't know. One flight up, on the ninth floor, where two hundred and fifty girls worked, where Yetta had worked before the strike, where Bella worked now—up there, they had no idea there was an inferno raging beneath them, eating up the air, climbing higher and higher and higher.

Almost on their own, Yetta's feet had already started slapping down the stairs, once she finally got the jabbering girls moving. But now she stopped.

Bella, she thought. My other friends. *My sisters. My comrades. My union.*

"What are you doing?" Jacob screamed, already three 240 steps down.

"Somebody has to tell the ninth floor!" she screamed back. "I have to!"

She turned around and began clattering up the stairs.

Strategies for Annotation

Compare and Contrast: Genres

RL 9

Share these strategies for guided or independent analysis:

- Historical fiction authors base their stories on the facts of an event.
- In the excerpt, highlight in yellow the information that likely can be verified by researching the facts of the Triangle Factory Fire.
- Underline the text that appears to be fiction.

Yetta glanced up to the landing above her, remembering what the bookkeeper had been screaming into the phone: *Somebody listen! Somebody's got to tell the ninth floor!*

They didn't know. One flight up, on the ninth floor, where two hundred and fifty girls worked, where Yetta had worked

Jane

"Papa's taking us shopping! Papa's taking us shopping!" Harriet chanted, bouncing up and down joyously in the elevator on the way to Mr. Blanck's office at the Triangle factory.

"Hush. Everybody knows that," Millicent said scornfully.

250   "She's just excited," Jane said mildly. She patted Harriet's shoulder, trying to calm her down, and gave Millicent and the elevator operator a sympathetic smile. Harriet's chanting was a bit maddening. But, as always, it was hard to know the best way to handle the girls. Miss Milhouse would have scolded Harriet soundly; she would have taken it as her personal mission to **stifle** the little girl's exuberant personality. And she would have praised Millicent to the skies for her tidiness, her aversion to noise and mess, her ability to sit or stand still practically forever without squirming or exclaiming.

Personally, Jane thought Millicent was in danger of
260   becoming a priggish bore. And she worried that someday somebody *would* **stifle** Harriet's exuberance.

"Make it be like a stream," Bella had advised her, when Jane had asked for help. "You don't want to chop her off— *bam!*" She'd slammed the side of her right hand against her left palm. "But make it go a good way."

"You mean, I should try to channel her enthusiasm into positive outlets?" Jane asked.

After Jane explained what "channel," "enthusiasm," "positive," and "outlets" meant, Bella grinned and nodded:
270   "Yes, yes, exactly! You say what is in my heart for that girl!"

Now, as the elevator zoomed upward, Harriet began tugging on the elevator operator's jacket.

"Mister, you didn't know we were going shopping, did you? Papa's taking us as a treat, because our mama went to Florida for the—what's it called?—social season. And she took the car with her, on the train, so we had to take a taxi cab to get here, and the taxi cab's still waiting outside, for us to come back. Except Madam'selle Michaud's not going shopping with us, just Papa, and—"

280   "Harriet," Jane said warningly.

"She's okay," the elevator operator said. "You're the Blanck girls, right? The boss's daughters?"

stifle
(stī´fəl) *v.* If you *stifle* something, you hold it back.

CLOSE READ

Analyze Point of View
RL 1, RL 6

(LINES 248–261)

Explain that this section is told from the point of view of the governess for the children of one of the factory owners, Mr. Blanck. Define a governess as a woman hired by families to educate and train the children. Note that shifting points of view allows Haddix to explore more deeply a character mentioned only in passing in an earlier part of the story and tells the same story from another perspective.

(K) CITE TEXT EVIDENCE Have students reread lines 248–261 and cite evidence of Jane's relationship with her boss at the Blanck household. What does this evidence reveal about Jane's job? *(Here, the author is noting how Miss Milhouse usually reacts to the two Blanck girls. The details are not in italicized print, so they are not shared as Jane's actual thoughts. The author as narrator is telling them to the reader. The author notes that Miss Milhouse would have scolded Harriet and praised Millicent. It's clear, however, that Jane likes "Harriet's exuberance" and thinks Millicent is "in danger of becoming a priggish bore." This suggests that Jane and her boss do not see eye to eye when it comes to dealing with the children, which might make Jane's job difficult for her.)*

CRITICAL VOCABULARY

stifle: The author describes Miss Milhouse's actions as holding back young Harriet's lively personality.

ASK STUDENTS why Jane might be concerned about Harriet being stifled. *(Jane might worry that negative feedback from Miss Milhouse will make Harriet less energetic and curious.)*

English Language Support

Analyze Point of View Display lines 249–261 and explain that the narrator is third-person limited in each part of the text, but uses different language to show the different backgrounds and personalities of each character.

- Read the passage aloud. Tell students that in order to be a governess, Jane must have some education herself. Ask them what words in this passage suggest that Jane is educated. Work with students to define these words, such as *exuberant, aversion, priggish*.

- Have students read the passage to a partner. Then ask them to draw

inferences about Jane's background based on the language used to express her thoughts. Encourage them to support their inferences with specific evidence.

- Display lines 541–545 in addition to lines 249–261. Explain that the second excerpt reflects Bella's thoughts. Have partners compare the language used in each passage and make inferences about each girl's background. Call on pairs to share their inferences and supporting evidence.

Analyze Story Elements

RL 1,
RL 3

(LINES 293–315)

Explain that authors use **dialogue,** written conversations between characters, to bring characters to life and reveal each character's personality.

Ⓛ CITE TEXT EVIDENCE Have students reread lines 293–315. What is Jane's attitude toward Harriet's questions? Ask students to cite specific evidence in the passage to support their answer. *(Jane tries to answer Harriet's questions directly and logically, saying "There are scientific reasons" that the elevator would not go through the roof. Then, when Harriet keeps asking more questions, Jane realizes she doesn't have the answers and says they'll have to research the answer at a bookstore. This suggests Jane does not want to just dismiss or mislead Harriet the way Millicent does.)*

English Language Support

Demonstrate a reproving look to help students understand Jane's reaction to Millicent's comments in lines 283–285. Discuss why Jane feels this way.

CRITICAL VOCABULARY

reprove: Jane gives Millicent a reproving look, suggesting Jane doesn't like what the girl has said.

ASK STUDENTS for examples of when a student might receive a reproving look from an adult or an authority figure. *(Sample answers: when someone says something that embarrasses a parent; when someone treats a sibling poorly)*

"Our papa and Uncle Isaac own the whole factory," Millicent bragged. "They employ more than seven hundred people."

"Millicent!" Jane shot the girl a **reproving** look. *Remember what I've told you about bragging?* she wanted to scold. But she'd always hated Miss Milhouse correcting her in front of other people, so she'd vowed not to do that to Millicent or Harriet. It was just really tempting at times like this. *First thing Monday morning, I need to have a little talk with both girls . . . .*

290 The elevator was gathering speed. Harriet clutched Jane's hand.

"What if the elevator goes all the way through the roof?" she asked.

"Silly, that would never happen," Millicent scoffed.

"Why not?"

"Because—because it wouldn't be proper," Millicent said.
300 She lowered her voice, as if that would keep the elevator operator from hearing. "If we went through the roof, the people below us could see up our skirts."

The elevator operator's face turned red, he was trying so hard not to laugh.

Jane sighed.

"There are scientific reasons the elevator would never go through the roof," she said. "Because of how the elevator's made, how it works."

"How does it work?" Harriet asked.

310 Oops. Jane had been afraid she'd ask that. Somehow elevator mechanics had not been in the curriculum at Jane's finishing school.

"Next week we can go to the bookstore and find a book that explains it all," Jane said. "Or maybe you can find one with your papa."

"The elevator runs on a cable," the operator said. "The cable goes up to gears, and those are on the roof. Maybe sometime you can ask your papa to show you the gearbox. But if you want to go to the roof, you have to use the Greene Street
320 stairs. That's the only way to get there."

"Thank you," Jane said, smiling gratefully at the operator. He was a pimply boy, maybe a little younger than her. A year ago, he would have been completely invisible to her, but now she wondered about his life. Which country had he come

reprove
(rĭ-pro͞ov´) *v.* If you *reprove* someone, you express disapproval.

English Language Support

Word Study Tell students that both possessive nouns and contractions have apostrophes. Help students distinguish between them with these examples:

- Write "The elevator operator's face turned red" (line 303) on the board. Explain that the 's shows possession. Tell students they can check by asking whose face turned red.
- Then write "Because of how the elevator's made, how it works." (lines 307–308) Explain that the 's is a contraction; the apostrophe replaces

the letter *i* in *is*. Tell students they can check by rereading the sentence with the full verb form to see if it makes sense.

- Have students identify each of the underlined words as a possessive noun or a contraction.

1. The car's waiting outside for us. *(contraction)*

2. The car's engine was making a funny noise. *(possessive)*

from? Did he bring his family with him, or was he all alone? Was he supporting a widowed mother and a younger brother and sister or two on his salary as an elevator operator? Did Mr. Blanck and Mr. Harris pay him more or less than they paid their sewing machine operators?

330   "Tenth floor," the operator announced, bringing the elevator to a halt and sweeping open the barred door. "Where your papa the boss works."

    He had the slightest hint of mockery in his voice, just enough for Jane to hear. He even gave her a conspiratorial wink, which was much too forward, but somehow Jane didn't mind. She winked back, and stepped out onto the polished wood floor of a spacious reception area.

    "Miss Mary! Miss Mary!" Harriet cried, running over to one of the desks.

340   "Oh, sweetie, Miss Mary's busy right now," said the short, frazzled-looking woman behind the desk. "The switchboard operator didn't come in today, so Miss Mary has to do all her typing *and* connect every call that comes in. The eighth floor can't even call the ninth floor without my help."

    Harriet inspected the telephone switchboard behind the woman's desk, the wires hanging slack.

    "So if you plug in this wire here, then—"

    "Oh, sweetie, don't touch," Miss Mary said, gently pushing Harriet's hand away. "I really don't have time—I'll explain

350 it to you some other day." She looked up at Jane. "You're the governess, right? You can just take them into Mr. Blanck's office, and then go tell him they're here."

    "Where is Mr. Blanck?" Jane asked.

    "Oh, he was just down on the ninth floor—no, wait, back in the storeroom? I'm sorry, I'd look for him myself, but—" The harried secretary gestured at the papers strewn across her desk, the bill poking out from her typewriter.

    A contraption beside the typewriter buzzed, and Miss Mary looked over at it expectantly.

360   "What's that?" Harriet whispered.

    "Oh, it's the new telautograph," Miss Mary said. "'The latest in business machinery,' is how it's advertised. Looks like there's a message coming from the eighth floor. They write something on a pad of paper downstairs, and this pen is supposed to write the same thing on this pad right here."

    "Like magic," Harriet breathed.

CLOSE READ

Analyze Point of View   RL 6
(LINES 333–337)

The author describes this silent exchange between Jane and the elevator operator strictly from Jane's point of view.

Ⓜ **ASK STUDENTS** to reread lines 333–337 and explain why Jane gladly returns the elevator operator's wink. *(Even though Jane works for a wealthy family, she feels she has more in common with the elevator operator, and this is a way to let him know that she is more like him than the boss's daughters.)*

English Language Support

To help students understand the exchange between Jane and the elevator operator, explain that the word *forward* has several meanings. Read lines 333–337 aloud and act out the wink for students, exaggerating the gesture to help them pick up the attitude it suggests.

- Then write these words and phrases on the board: "in front," "being ahead of a trend," "bold."
- Ask students which meaning best fits *forward* as it is used in this sentence. *(bold)*

WHEN STUDENTS STRUGGLE...

In this section, the author reveals some important factual information about what was happening on the tenth floor as the fire was burning two floors below. Have students reread lines 338–366. Ask them to look for information that indicates why there was a lack of communication between the eighth, ninth, and tenth floors when the fire started. Have students record the information in a simple chart like the one shown.

ASK STUDENTS who or what is to blame for the communication problems. *(Possible answers: the phones and telautograph didn't work right; Miss Mary didn't keep up with her switchboard duties; the fire burned up the phone and telautograph lines.)*

Communication Problems
"The eighth floor can't even call the ninth floor without my help."
"Looks like there's a message coming from the eighth floor."
"The pen didn't move."
"It'd be magic if it ever worked right."

LEVEL UP TUTORIALS For additional support, assign the following *Level Up* tutorial: **Conflict.**

Compare and Contrast: Genres (LINES 388–400)

RL 1,
RL 9

Remind students that historical fiction has the advantage of allowing the author to take factual information and embellish the story to make it more engaging to the reader.

(N) CITE TEXT EVIDENCE Have students reread lines 21–27 from the history writing *Flesh & Blood So Cheap* and then read lines 388–400 of *Uprising*. How does the author's description of the pressing department on the tenth floor in *Uprising* make the facts presented in *Flesh & Blood So Cheap* more compelling? (*The* Uprising *author makes the packed room seem even more difficult to work in with hot irons and dangerous gas tubes overhead. The author also describes the workers as looking weary.*)

English Language Support

Tell students that the author of *Uprising* includes details that reinforce the ideas brought out in *Flesh & Blood,* writing about how hard the workers' jobs were and how difficult the conditions were. Have pairs of students identify details in lines 389–400 that help them to understand the factory setting more clearly.

The pen didn't move.

"It'd be magic if it ever worked right," Miss Mary snorted. "Probably isn't anything anyhow, just the girls downstairs
370 playing with it on their way out the door."

Miss Mary turned back to her typing, and Jane shooed the girls toward Mr. Blanck's office.

"I want to go see the showroom!" Harriet said, skipping down the hall. "Madam'selle Michaud, you'll love it! You can see all the latest fashions before Paris!"

"That's because even Paris doesn't know as much about fashion as our papa," Millicent said, agreeing with her younger sister for once.

"Some other time," Jane said. "Miss Mary said to wait in
380 his office, remember?"

They turned in at a doorway, but the sign on the door said Isaac harris, not max blanck.

"Uncle Isaac!" Harriet called.

A man behind a desk waved, but there was another man with him, a dapper-looking gentleman holding up samples of delicate embroidery.[9] Jane flashed an apologetic look at Mr. Harris and pulled the girls away.

(N) "Look, you can see into the pressing department from here," Harriet said, pointing past a break in the wall into
390 a vast open space, where rows and rows of weary-looking workers stood over ironing boards. Each one of the irons was connected to the ceiling by an odd array of tubes.

"Is Papa afraid those workers are going to steal his irons?" Harriet asked. "Is that why the irons are tied up?"

Jane didn't have the slightest idea, so she was glad that Millicent answered first.

"No, silly. The gas comes down those tubes and heats the irons," Millicent said. "Papa says we must never ever go in there, because one of those irons could blister our skin in
400 an instant."

And does he care at all about the workers operating the irons? Jane wondered bitterly. *Some of them look no older than Millicent!*

"Quick, now," she told the girls. "Into the office. Wait right there."

---

[9] **embroidery:** decorative needlework in cloth.

English Language Support

Analyze Language Tell students that they can write more precise sentences by condensing ideas using compound verbs.

- Write "She winked back, and stepped out onto the polished wood floor of a spacious reception area." (lines 336–337) on the board. Have students identify the compound verb. (*winked, stepped*) Then write these sentences: *She winked back. She stepped out onto the polished wood floor of a spacious reception area.* Point out that the second version is choppy and does not show a connection between ideas.

- Have students work in small groups to condense the ideas in these sentences:

The girls looked up as she came into the room. The girls smiled at her. (*The girls looked up and smiled at her as she came into the room.*)

The manager had enough fabric for the job. The manager did not have any fabric left over. (*The manager had enough fabric for the job but did not have any left over.*)

> ❝ **Papa says we must never ever go in there, because one of those irons could blister our skin in an instant.** ❞

She was infected suddenly with some of Miss Mary's franticness, or maybe she was just tired of hearing the admiring tone in the girls' voices every time they mentioned their papa. Or maybe it was the sight of the **haggard** workers
410 hunched over their irons, girls who looked entirely too young, who would probably look entirely too old after just a year or two on the job. Regardless, Jane was ready to be done working for the day, ready to be out in the fresh air, arm in arm with Bella and Yetta. She was pretty sure that she and Bella had finally convinced Yetta to go with them to visit Rahel and Rahel's new baby. It would probably be a touching family reunion.

Yes, Yetta will be so much happier if she'll just forgive her sister for getting married, Jane thought. *My father and I, on the*
420 *other hand . . .*

She hadn't forgotten her promise to Mr. Corrigan to write her father a letter. She'd written him many, many letters, actually—she'd just torn them all up.

What is there to say?

Jane pulled the door shut on Millicent and Harriet, catching barely a glimpse of Mr. Blanck's imposing mahogany desk, of the lovely arched windows behind the desk. Harriet was scrambling into the huge leather chair.

"Harriet! A young lady would never put her feet up on the
430 desk!" she heard Millicent cry out, in scandalized horror.

Jane decided to let Millicent wage that battle on her own. Secretly, she was thinking, *Oh, Harriet, maybe you should go on being the kind of girl who puts her feet on desks. Better that, than hiding under them . . .*

She scurried down the hall, back to the double elevator doors. She decided to look for Mr. Blanck on the ninth floor first. She knew that was where Bella worked, and it'd be good

haggard
(hăg´ərd) *adj.* If you're *haggard*, you are worn out and exhausted.

Uprising **295**

CLOSE READ

Analyze Point of View   RL 6
(LINES 406–414)

Explain that third-person limited point of view allows the author to explore the character's thoughts and dreams without putting them into dialogue form with another character. In this section, the author is limited to doing this for Jane only.

Ⓞ ASK STUDENTS to reread lines 406–414 and explain why the sight of the workers hunched over their irons agitated Jane and made her want to leave quickly. *(Jane identified with the factory workers and had good friends who worked in the factory, so the sight of the workers reminded her that she is still like them even though she works for the wealthy owner of the factory. She wants to leave quickly because the weekend means free time to do what workers want with their friends and families.)*

> **CRITICAL VOCABULARY**
>
> **haggard:** This is the second time Jane has observed the worn-out workers and wondered how young they were.
>
> **ASK STUDENTS** why Jane is concerned with the age of the haggard-looking workers. *(because some of them are about the same age as Millicent, the boss's daughter, who has a much easier life and will not be ground down by work at such a young age)*

English Language Support

Understand Cohesion Remind students that most pronouns take the place of a noun or other pronoun, called the **antecedent.** However, some pronouns replace an implied, not stated, antecedent. Display lines 431–434.

• Highlight the word *her* in line 431. Have students work in pairs to identify the antecedent, reminding them to use context clues if more than one antecedent is possible. *("Her" could refer to Jane or Millicent, but the context concerning the "battle" makes it clear that Millicent is the antecedent.)*

• Highlight the pronoun *that* in line 433. Explain that its antecedent is not a specific noun, but a situation. Ask which lines make clear what *that* refers to. *("That" refers to the phrase "being the kind of girl who puts her feet on desks." Jane contrasts the boldness of putting one's feet on desks with the shyness of "hiding under them.")*

• Have students read lines 431–434 and identify the pronouns. Have pairs note or describe the antecedent for each pronoun and discuss how the pronouns serve to link the sentences together.

Analyze Story Elements

RL 1,
RL 3

(LINES 468–470)

Remind students that authors often include details that reveal traits or qualities about a character without directly stating the traits or qualities. Students can use these details to **infer**, or make good guesses, about the characters.

P **CITE TEXT EVIDENCE** Have students reread lines 468–470 and make an inference about Jane's relationship with Bella. Ask students to cite evidence to support their inferences. *(The author shows Jane's thoughts about Bella: "No wonder Bella felt so overwhelmed, coming here from her tiny little village in Italy." This suggests that Jane is empathetic to her friend and can relate to Bella's feelings about the factory.)*

---

if she could warn Bella that she'd be a few minutes late getting out to the street, especially if it took her a long time to find
440   Mr. Blanck.

Passing Miss Mary's desk, Jane was surprised to notice that the woman had vanished, leaving the telephone receiver hanging off the hook.

That's odd. She seemed like such a conscientious sort . . . .

A different elevator operator came up this time, a swarthily handsome Italian man.

If Bella's precious Pietro looks anything like that, no wonder she can't forget him! Jane thought. Then she had to hide her face so he didn't see her giggling at her own wickedness.
450   The elevator buzzed annoyingly. Again and again and again.

"Eighth floor's going crazy," the elevator operator growled. He scowled at the panel of lights that kept flashing at him as he shut the door behind Jane and the elevator began its descent. "Hold on a minute! I'm coming! I'm coming!"

"They've probably all got spring fever," Jane said. "And it's Saturday."

"Yeah, yeah," the operator grumbled, letting her out on the ninth floor. "But do they gotta take it out on me?"
460   The ninth floor was not what Jane expected. After the cleanliness and elegance of the tenth floor, she wasn't prepared for this dim, dirty space with the tables and the machines and the girls packed in so tightly together. The room was huge, but the tables stretched from one side of the building to the other. By the windows, there wasn't even space to walk around the tables. And shirtwaists and shirtwaist parts were piled everywhere, mountains of fabric by each machine.

P *No wonder Bella felt so overwhelmed, coming here from her tiny little village in Italy,* Jane thought.
470   Jane herself felt a little overwhelmed.

"Excuse me. Do you know where I could find Mr. Blanck or Bella Rossetti?" she asked the girl at the nearest sewing machine.

The girl looked up blankly, and said something that might have been "I don't speak English" in some other language. Just then a bell sounded, and the machines stopped and hundreds of girls sprang up from their machines all at once. It spooked Jane a little, the darkness of the room and the foreign jabbering and the girls moving like machines, themselves. But

---

Strategies for Annotation

Compare and Contrast: Genres

RL 9

Share these strategies for comparing nonfiction and historical fiction texts:

- Reread the paragraph.
- Highlight in yellow details that might have come from a nonfiction article source like *Flesh & Blood So Cheap*.
- Add a note offering your opinion about whether *Uprising* uses the facts of the Triangle Factory Fire fairly or unfairly.

The historical accounts say that the working conditions at the factory were hideous. Adding fiction details to show this seems very fair.

The ninth floor was not what Jane expect[ed]
cleanliness and elegance of the tenth floor, she
for this dim, dirty space with the tables and machines and
the girls packed in so tightly together. The room was huge,
but the tables stretched from one side of the building to the
other. By the windows, there wasn't even space to walk around

480 then one of the girls stepping out of the cloakroom began to sing, "Ev'ry little movement has a meaning of its own"—one of those popular songs that you heard everywhere, nowadays. Some of the other girls joined in, and they all seemed so light-hearted suddenly. Saturday afternoon and the sun was shining and work was over; these girls looked happier than anyone Jane had ever seen at a formal ball.

Then, two tables away, Jane spotted Bella heading down the aisle between the tables and laughing and talking to the girls around her.

490 "Jane! What are you doing here?" Bella shouted over to her.

> **Just then a bell sounded, and the machines stopped and hundreds of girls sprang up from their machines all at once.**

"Looking for you and Mr. Blanck," Jane said.

"Well, we wouldn't be together!" Bella called back merrily.

Jane worked her way through the crowd toward her friend. She explained about Millicent and Harriet and the shopping, and how long it would take her to get down to the sidewalk. Then Bella said, "Oh, wait, you have to meet my friends—this is Annie and Dora and Josie and Essie and Ida. And come here—" She pulled her back down the aisle between the tables. 500 "This is my boss, Signor Carlotti. This is my friend, Jane Wellington, Signor Carlotti, and she knows proper Italian *and* proper English."

"Hello," Signor Carlotti said.

"I am a factory inspector," Jane said, suddenly inspired to lie. "If I were to interview the girls in this factory, would they tell me that you treat them with respect? Are you fair to all your workers?"

Uprising **297**

CLOSE READ

Compare and Contrast: Genres (LINES 480–486)
RL 1, RL 9

Explain that authors of historical fiction often use a wide range of sources when they write a story. They often add historical details not only about the event they are writing about, but also about the time period of the event. They use these details to give a broader view into the society of the time.

Q CITE TEXT EVIDENCE Ask students to reread lines 480–486 and to cite an example of a cultural detail that likely came from sources about the time period. Have students describe how this detail enhances the story. *(The author includes a line from a song and explains through Jane's perspective that it was "one of those popular songs that you heard everywhere, nowadays." This shows that popular music seemed as important to young people of this time period as it is today. This makes it easier to relate to the young women in the factory.)*

Analyze Story Elements (LINES 504–507)
RL 3

Remind students that Jane is fond of Bella and is looking forward to spending time with her.

R ASK STUDENTS to reread lines 504–507. Why might Jane decide to lie to Bella's boss? *(Jane is in a good mood and may have decided to lie to Bella's boss in a playful way to not only poke fun at him but also to make a point about treating her friend fairly.)*

English Language Support

Express Opinions Tell students that looking at a character's actions, words, and thoughts can help them form an opinion about his or her traits. Explain that their opinions need to be supported with text details.

- Read aloud lines 497–502. Then work with students to express an opinion about Bella. Provide this sentence frame: Bella may be described as ___ because she ____. *(friendly; introduces Jane to many friends in the factory)*

- Have students reread lines 484–486. Invite them to express an opinion about Jane, using the words *likely* or *possibly*. Have them justify the opinion using a direct quotation. *(Jane may be from a wealthy family because she compares the girls to people she has "seen at a formal ball.")*

- Have small groups discuss Bella's and Jane's characters. Then ask them to write their ideas about each character, using words such as *certainly/definitely*, *should/would*, and *in my opinion* and citing direct quotations from the text in support. Invite groups to read their analyses to the class.

Analyze Point of View

RL 3,
RL 6

(LINES 516–521)

Explain to students that **dramatic irony** occurs when the reader knows something that a character in a story does not know. Because third-person limited point of view only permits the author to reveal one character's thoughts and perspective, it allows the author to create situations of dramatic irony.

S **ASK STUDENTS** how lines 516–521 create dramatic irony in the story. *(Jane thinks she hears Yetta calling out to convince the girls to form a union—"her dearest wish"—but the reader knows that Yetta is trying to save the girls from the fire on the eighth floor—again, Yetta's "dearest wish" at the time.)*

CRITICAL VOCABULARY

wistful: The author uses the word *wistful* to describe Bella's response to Jane's comment.

ASK STUDENTS why Bella might feel wistful about her boss treating her better. *(because Bella's boss probably doesn't treat her or the other girls all that well, and a change in his attitude is something Bella may have hoped for since she started working there)*

At the first word out of her mouth, Signor Carlotti's face changed—first, to awe at her upper-class accent, then to fear.

510 "Oh, er—yes! Yes! Of course!" Signor Carlotti exclaimed.

It was all Jane and Bella could do, not to double over giggling as they walked away.

"Maybe he really will change how he treats you, Monday morning!" Jane whispered.

"Oh, do you think so?" Bella asked **wistfully**.

S Across the room, strangely, Jane heard Yetta's voice now. She couldn't make out the words, but Yetta seemed to be calling out in great excitement, from the midst of the crowd of girls getting ready to leave. Maybe she was talking them

520 into another strike. Maybe this one would work—maybe Yetta would get her dearest wish.

"Doesn't Yetta work on the eighth floor?" Jane asked.

Before Bella could answer, screams came suddenly from the back of the room. Screams—and a great burst of light.

wistful
(wĭst′fəl) *adj.* If you're *wistful*, you are thoughtful and longing for something.

298   Collection 6

English Language Support

Analyze Dramatic Irony Explain that **dramatic irony** is when readers know something the characters do not. Here, readers know what Yetta, Jane, and Bella are doing as well as events on different floors, but the characters don't know each other's actions or what is happening elsewhere in the factory.

• Display lines 241–243. Then read aloud the highlighted lines on this page. Guide students to make the connection between what Yetta decides to do and what Jane and Bella hear. Have pairs of students write a sentence explaining why Jane and Bella don't know what Yetta is doing.

• Tell students that dramatic irony occurs elsewhere in this selection. Direct their attention to lines 450–457. Have them reread this passage with a partner and explain the dramatic irony. *(The workers on the eighth floor are frantically calling for the elevator as a way to escape from the fire, but the characters think they are just anxious to leave work for the day.)*

• Have students work in small groups to identify additional instances of dramatic irony in the text. Have them explain why each example is dramatic irony. Then discuss how the use of this device affects the mood of the selection.

Bella

Bella couldn't tell what had happened. It was just like her first day of work, when everyone else was yelling and running and knocking over baskets and trampling shirtwaists they didn't bother to stop and pick up. And, for a moment, just like on that first day, Bella couldn't understand the words everyone

530 else kept saying. The English part of her brain shut off, the Yiddish words in her brain evaporated, even the Italian she heard around her sounded garbled and foreign.

Then she smelled smoke, and the words made sense.
"Fire!"
"*S'brent!*"
"*Fuoco!*"
Jane clutched her shoulders.
"Where do we go? What do we do?" Jane asked. "We always had fire drills at school—where have they told you to

540 go in the event of a fire?"

Bella didn't know what a fire drill was. People were crowded in all around her, shoving and pushing from behind, blocking the way in front of her. The tables on either side of the aisle seemed to be closing in on her. She was penned in, just like a goat or a pig.

No better than an animal, Bella thought, and somehow this seemed all of piece with not being able to read and wanting only food and Signor Carlotti spitting on her and Signor Luciano cheating her. *I bet back home your family*

550 *slept with goats and chickens in the house,* Signora Luciano had sneered at her once, and Bella hadn't even understood that that was an insult. But now she'd seen how other people lived; she'd seen what Jane and Yetta expected out of life. She refused to think of herself as a hog in a pen waiting to be slaughtered.

"This way!" she said, grabbing Jane's hand and scrambling up on top of the nearest table.

From there, she could see the fire. It was blowing in the back window, one huge ball of flame rolling across the

560 examining tables stacked with shirtwaists. The flames kept dividing, devouring stack after stack of shirtwaists, racing each other down the tables.

Where are they trying to get to? Bella wondered.

Uprising **299**

CLOSE READ

Compare and Contrast: Genres (LINES 568–570)

RL 1,
RL 3,
RL 9

The author's dramatic depiction of Bella and Yetta trying to escape the fire both brings the horrible real-life event to life and adds a human element to the facts of the tragedy.

Ⓤ **CITE TEXT EVIDENCE** Have students reread lines 568–570. Then, direct them back to the historical account *Flesh & Blood So Cheap* to look for nonfiction evidence of what is described here in *Uprising*. *(Lines 72–75 from* Flesh & Blood So Cheap *depict workers piled up at the doors.)*

Ask students to cite details that were added by the author of *Uprising* that bring this part of the story to life and to describe the impact of these details. *(The author adds that Bella "looked around frantically," which is probably how everyone on this floor is acting at this moment—frantic. These details heighten the suspense, adding a sense of true desperation felt by the characters in the fictional account.)*

English Language Support

Read Closely Have students reread lines 574–585. Remind them that important ideas are revealed by a character's actions. Have students respond to these questions before gathering in groups to compare their answers:

- What does Bella do as she and Jane struggle to escape?
- What do these actions show about her character?

The first flame leaped from the examining table to the first row of sewing tables.

"It's coming toward us!" Jane screamed behind her. "Where do we go?"

Ⓤ Bella looked around frantically. Girls were packed in around the doors and elevators. Only a handful seemed to
570 remember that there was another way out.

"The fire escape!" Bella screamed back, grateful for that day so long ago, before the strike, when she'd actually seen where the fire escape was.

The aisles were still crowded. Bella leaped from one table to the next, and somehow Jane managed to follow. Bella leaped again, suddenly surefooted. Except for the smoke burning her eyes and throat, she could have been back in the mountains near Calia, jumping from rock to rock.

"I've got to—make sure—Harriet and Millicent—are—
580 all—right," Jane panted behind her, as they cleared another table. She began coughing, choking on the smoke.

Bella bent down and snatched up a pile of shirtwaist sleeves. She held two over her mouth and handed the others to Jane.

"Here. So you can breathe."

They kept racing across the tables. And it really was a race, because the flames were speeding toward the fire escape window too. Through the smoke, Bella could barely make out the progress of the fire. *The flames are going to get there first—*
590 *no, we are!—no, look how fast the fire's moving . . . .*

They reached the end of the tables and jumped down to the floor. The flames were reaching for Bella's skirt, so she lifted it up as she ran for the fire escape. She had one leg out the window, balanced on the metal railing, when Jane grabbed for her arm.

"Wait—is that safe?" Jane asked.

She'd actually stopped to peer down at the rickety stairs, at the flames shooting out the eighth-floor window, at the eighth-floor shutters that seemed to be blocking the path of all
600 the other girls already easing their way down.

"Safe?" Bella repeated numbly. Anything seemed safer than where they were now. But she pulled back a little, reconsidering. She shifted her weight back from the foot that was on the fire escape to the knee perched on the windowsill. And in that moment, the fire escape just . . . fell away.

English Language Support

Read Closely Explain that punctuation marks such as ellipses and dashes are used for specific purposes. Review the function of each mark.

- Display and read aloud lines 579–581. Have students repeat the lines with the same intonation and tempo. Then ask pairs to write a sentence explaining the purpose of the dashes. *(to show that Jane can hardly speak)*
- Display lines 589–590. Ask students to write an explanation of what idea or feeling the ellipsis and dashes communicate. Have them share their work with another student. *(The dashes show how*

Bella's thoughts are racing; they show how frantically her mind is working as she tries to outrun the flames. The ellipsis shows that Bella's thoughts trail off because she has no more time to think.)

- Ask students to choose a passage that includes dashes and one that includes ellipses. Have them practice reading each in a way that illustrates the purpose of the punctuation. Then have them write an explanation of the function of the dashes and ellipses. Finally, ask them to read the passages and their explanations to the class.

> ## " She'd actually stopped to peer down at the rickety stairs, at the flames shooting out "

"*Madonna mia!*" Bella cried. Jane grabbed her, pulling her back in through the window. "The other girls—"

Jane shook her head, maybe meaning, *Don't ask,* maybe meaning, *I saw it all, them falling, I can't even begin to tell*
610 *you how awful it was . . . .* Bella tried to remember who'd been ahead of her on the fire escape—Dora? Essie? Ida? All of them? The boot of the girl immediately in front of Bella had had a fancy silver buckle, the kind of thing a girl would have been proud of, the kind of thing she would have gone around showing off, making sure her skirt flounced up to display it as much as possible. Had Bella seen that buckle before?

"Bella! Where's another exit?" Jane cried out.

But Bella couldn't think about anything but a fancy silver buckle.

620 Suddenly Yetta was there.

"Greene Street stairs!" Yetta was screaming. "Go!"

Bella grabbed her friends' hands and took off running again. But Yetta pulled her hand back.

"You go on!" she screamed. "I still have to—"

The rest of Yetta's words were lost in the crackle of advancing flames.

The smoke rose and fell and shifted. One minute, Bella could see ahead of her, a straight path to the partition by the door. The next minute, she was groping blindly forward,
630 tripping over people who had fallen. She'd dropped the shirtwaist sleeves she'd been using to cover her mouth and nose. She grabbed up another stack, but just before she pressed it to her face she noticed that these shirtwaist sleeves were already burning. She dropped them to the floor, and began to sag toward the floor herself.

But she was still holding Jane's hand. Jane yanked her back up.

Uprising **301**

CLOSE READ

Compare and Contrast: Genres (LINES 606–616)   RL 9

Have students reread lines 212–223 of the selection *Flesh & Blood So Cheap.*

Ⓥ **ASK STUDENTS** to reread lines 606–616 of this story and to tell how the fire escape collapse might have been depicted differently if the author were telling the story from Jane's perspective looking out the window. *(Sample answer: Because Jane was at the window and saw the fire escape fall, the author could have described some of the brutal deaths depicted in the nonfiction account.)*

English Language Support

Read Closely Display lines 620–637.

- Tell students that words and phrases that signal time can help them understand the order of events and characters' actions. Have pairs highlight words and phrases related to time in this part of the text. *(Suddenly, again, "still," One minute, The next minute, just before, began, still)*

- Then have partners take turns explaining the sequence of events involving the three characters using some of these key words.

TO CHALLENGE STUDENTS . . .

Discuss the Role of Women Remind students that *Uprising* is told through the eyes of three different women. Point out that most of the employees of the Triangle Waist Company were women. Ask students to work in a small group to discuss what the details in *Uprising* might reveal about the role of women in America in the early 1900s. Ask students to cite details from the story that reveal the women characters' attitudes toward work, colleagues, and their personal lives. Ask groups to consider and discuss how attitudes and roles have changed since this time.

Analyze Story Elements

RL 1,
RL 3

(LINES 659–671)

The author depicts a dilemma for Bella: does she save her friend Jane or does she save herself?

W CITE TEXT EVIDENCE Ask students to reread lines 659–671 and note whom Bella saves. Have them review the "Bella" section for evidence to support their answers. (*Bella saves herself because earlier she says she refuses to die like an animal in the fire.*)

COLLABORATIVE DISCUSSION Have groups of students discuss the depictions of the Triangle Factory Fire in *Uprising, Flesh & Blood So Cheap,* and *The Story of the Triangle Factory Fire* to identify where the author of *Uprising* combines fact and fiction. Ask students to discuss how the combination of fact and fiction enhances their understanding about the real-life event. Encourage students to write notes as they talk. Then, have students share their thoughts with the class.

ASK STUDENTS to share any questions they generated in the course of reading and discussing the selection.

FOR STANDARD ENGLISH LEARNERS

Remind students that when they talk or write about events that occurred in the past, they need to use past tense forms of verbs. Review the formation of the past tense by adding the suffix -*ed*, providing examples. Then have partners take turns saying these statements with the correct past tense verb.

- The author <u>include</u> the fact about the fire escape when she wrote her novel.

- She also <u>add</u> fictional dialogue to bring her characters to life.

"The stairs—" Jane gasped.

They stumbled forward. Bella pulled her wool skirt
640 up over her head, blocking out the smoke and the flames.
Immodest, she thought, an English word she'd just learned.
She didn't care.

Jane grabbed a bucket of water from a nearby shelf and
flung it toward the fire, and some of it splashed back onto
Bella. None of it seemed to reach the fire. Or, if it did, it didn't
make any difference. The flames kept shooting forward. There
were no more buckets left on the shelf, only some tipped over
empty on the floor.

"The girls will be so scared," Jane breathed, and Bella
650 knew she meant Harriet and Millicent, waiting in their
father's office upstairs. "I've got to—"

She stopped, looking down.

"My skirt," she said.

A ring of flames was dancing along the bottom of her
skirt. She stepped forward and the flames flared.

"We'll put it out," Bella said.

Jane began rushing toward a vat by the stairs.

"Water—"

"No, no! That's machine oil, sewing machine oil!" Bella
660 screamed, pulling her back. The dark oil was bubbling over,
running down the sides of the vat. The fire was beginning to
race along the streams of oil. Bella had to jump past it. And
then Jane was on one side of the flames, Bella on the other.

"Jane!" Bella screamed.

"Go on!" Jane screamed back. "Go get the girls! Make sure
they're safe up there!"

"But you—"

"I'll go another way!" Jane said. "I'll meet you later!"

Bella whirled around. The pathway to the stairs was
670 closing in. In a second it would be gone.

Bella ran forward.

COLLABORATIVE DISCUSSION How has the author combined fact and fiction in this novel excerpt? Talk about your ideas with other group members.

CONTENT-AREA CONNECTION

History and Geography Yetta and Bella both use words from languages other than English. Explain that like many who worked in the fabric industry in the early 1900s, they are immigrants. Direct students' attention back to lines 468–469, which reveal that Bella comes from Italy. Tell students that Yetta, who is Jewish, may have come from Russia.

Activity Display a K-W-L chart. Discuss what students already know about twentieth-century immigration patterns, drawing from their studies in other classes as well as ideas from this selection. As a class, generate questions about immigration during this time period. For example, from which countries did immigrants come in the first decade of the 1900s? What were their reasons for coming to the United States? Where did they settle once they were here? Then assign questions to pairs or small groups of students to answer, using print or digital resources. Use the information they acquire to complete the chart.

Analyze Point of View

RL 3, RL 6

In a work of fiction, the **narrator** is the voice that tells the story. The author's choice of narrator is called the **point of view**. Authors deliberately choose a point of view in order to give readers a certain perspective on the story. The three types of point of view are shown in this chart.

Point of View in Narratives		
First Person	**Third-Person Limited**	**Third-Person Omniscient ("All-Knowing")**
• Narrator is a story character. • Narrator uses first-person pronouns such as *I, me, mine, we, our.* • Reader sees events and characters through narrator's eyes.	• Narrator is not a character and is outside the story. • Narrator uses third-person pronouns such as *he, she, him, her, their.* • Reader sees events and characters through one character's eyes.	• Narrator is not a character and is outside the story. • Narrator uses third-person pronouns such as *he, she, him, her, their.* • Reader is shown different characters' thoughts and feelings.

In the novel excerpt you've just read, the author has made an unusual choice in point of view. By presenting events through the eyes of multiple characters, the author:

- shows what the characters think of one another as they interact
- shows characters in different places at the same time
- builds suspense by shifting back in time when the reader already knows about the danger to come

Which point of view has the author chosen, and what impact does this have on how the reader experiences the story?

Compare and Contrast: Genres

RL 9

Historical fiction is set in the past and includes real places and events. The author researches the topic as a nonfiction author does, but uses imagination as well as facts to create imaginary scenes and dialogue between characters. Sometimes the fictional story will depict real people and imaginary characters interacting and experiencing real historical events.

To compare and contrast two forms of writing, notice how the details of real events appear in the fictional story. For example, read lines 15–20 from the nonfiction excerpt *Flesh & Blood So Cheap*. Then read lines 51–57 from the novel *Uprising*. How has the author of the fictional story used factual details differently from the author of the nonfiction selection?

Uprising **303**

CLOSE READ

Analyze Point of View

RL 3, RL 6

Help students understand the different points of view that authors use. Have students reread lines 221–228. Ask them how this is an example of third-person limited narration. *(This part of the story is told from Yetta's perspective. We are able to see her thoughts and the events through her eyes. The author also uses the third-person pronoun* her.*)* Discuss answers to the questions. *(Possible answers: The author has chosen to tell the story through the eyes of three different characters experiencing the same event. In each section, the author uses third-person limited to give us a unique look into one character's experience.)*

Compare and Contrast: Genres

RL 9

Explain to students that one of the reasons historical fiction is such a popular genre is that it combines facts about an event with the art of storytelling. To compare and contrast a historical account and a fictional account of the same event, have students reread the lines from the two selections. Discuss which passage engaged students more and what they think are the pros and cons of the two genres. Then, discuss students' answers to the final question in the lesson. *(The author of* Uprising *has provided the same information about the cotton fabrics being separated by sheer tissue paper. She has added a character, Jacob, who is working with the fabric and has added a figurative description of tissue paper patterns like "hanging moss and low branches.")*

Strategies for Annotation **Annotate it!**

Analyze Point of View

RL 6

Have student locate lines 571–578. Share these strategies for guided or independent analysis:

- Highlight in yellow words and phrases that reveal the author's use of point of view.
- Underline any pronouns that are also clues to the point of view.
- Write a note identifying the type of point of view and through whose eyes the passage is being told.

The aisles were still crowded. Bella leaped from one table to the next, and somehow Jane managed to follow. Bella leaped again, suddenly surefooted. Except for the smoke burning her eyes and throat, she could have been back in the mountains near Calia, jumping from rock to rock.

> 3rd-person-limited; seeing events through Bella's eyes and thoughts

PRACTICE & APPLY

Analyzing the Text
RL 2, RL 3, RL 6, RL 9

Possible answers:

1. At the end of the excerpt, Yetta, Jane, and Bella are all trying to escape from the fire on the ninth floor. Bella makes it toward the Greene Street stairs, but Jane is cut off by the fire and must find another way. After pointing her friends toward that exit, Yetta has held back for some reason not yet known.

2. During each account, we find out something about each character's background and goals. This makes the characters come alive to the reader and seem more sympathetic. Yetta is Jewish, a union organizer who believes in fair treatment of workers. Jane was educated at a finishing school, she works as a governess, and her friendship with Yetta and Bella is helping her to understand class differences. Bella is an Italian immigrant and has struggled with prejudice; she has a boyfriend named Pietro. The girls all seem like real people, and although they come from different backgrounds, they have hopes and dreams for the future—boyfriends, better jobs, fairer treatment. But now none of that matters; they all have one common goal—to escape with their lives.

3. Jane brings her charges to the tenth floor, with its big offices and fancy desks. Mr. Blanck's daughters have a governess and a mother who travels to Florida for the social season. Jane is overwhelmed by the contrast with the "dim, dirty space" on the ninth floor and the packed working conditions the girls must endure. We hear her thoughts such as "No wonder Bella felt so overwhelmed . . . " that show she is not happy seeing the difficult working conditions.

4. Although the nonfiction account shows that the fire escape's collapse was part of the real-life event, the image of the fancy silver buckle is from the author's imagination. It shocks the reader, just as it shocks the character Bella. The author uses details like this to bring readers into the scene and into the minds of the characters.

5. On the tenth floor, Harriet points out the pressing department through a "break in the wall into a vast open space, where rows and rows of weary-looking workers stood over ironing boards." The author then uses dialogue between Harriet and Millicent to describe the irons and the gas heating system. This is a natural way to work information into any story.

6. The dialogue in historical fiction has two purposes: to move the narrative along, as in any fiction story, and to provide factual information. The dialogue in the excerpt from Uprising is like natural conversation. The quotations in the nonfiction work stand alone and provide supporting evidence for the author's main ideas.

Analyzing the Text
RL 2, RL 3, RL 6, RL 9, W 3, W 4, W 5, W 9, W 10

Cite Text Evidence Support your responses with evidence from the text.

1. **Summarize** At the end of this novel excerpt, where is each character going and why?

2. **Compare** How does the shifting point of view help you understand the similarities and differences among the three characters?

3. **Cite Evidence** How does the author use the chapter entitled "Jane" to show contrasts between the business owners and the workers?

4. **Analyze** Reread lines 590–618. Then look back to lines 212–222 of the excerpt from *Flesh & Blood So Cheap.* Why might the author of *Uprising* have introduced the fancy silver buckle?

5. **Evaluate** Find a passage in which the author provides facts about the setting. How effectively does the author make this information seem part of a fictional work? Explain.

6. **Synthesize** How is dialogue in this historical novel different from the quotations in the nonfiction excerpt from *The Story of the Triangle Factory Fire*?

PERFORMANCE TASK

Writing Activity: Narrative Suppose that a short chapter follows the three that you have read. In this chapter, the point of view remains third-person limited, but events are seen through the eyes of a different character. Write that new chapter.

- Choose a character already introduced, such as Jacob or Harriet.
- Read closely to learn about the character's likely goals, experiences, and interactions with other characters.

- Reread the nonfiction excerpts about the Triangle Fire to gather more factual details.
- Write a draft of your chapter.
- Read it aloud to a partner, and make revisions based on your listener's suggestions.

Assign this performance task.

PERFORMANCE TASK
W3, W4, W5, W9, W10

Writing Activity: Narrative Have students work independently to write a narrative. Direct students to choose a character to serve as narrator. Have them make notes on the character's actions, dialogue he or she may have, and any other details that will help shape the narrative. Remind students to reread the nonfiction accounts of the event and make notes on usable details. Have students revise and edit their drafts based on feedback from a partner.

Critical Vocabulary

L 5b

mischievous	scorn	marvel	singe
stifle	reprove	haggard	wistful

Practice and Apply Use each bold word in your answer to the question. Explain your reasoning.

1. Would someone smile with **scorn** or have a **wistful** smile while thinking about an unreachable goal?

2. Would someone have a **haggard** expression while behaving in a **mischievous** way?

3. What might a **reproving** look **stifle**?

4. Would you rather **marvel** at a campfire or have it **singe** you?

Vocabulary Strategy: Analogies

Verbal analogies are comparisons between two pairs of words. The relationship between the first pair of words is the same as the relationship between the second pair. For example, if the first pair of words is *big* and *little*, the second pair might be *tall* and *short*, because both words in each pair are antonyms. The analogy is stated, "*Big* is to *little* as *tall* is to *short*." It is written with colons in this pattern: **big : little :: tall : short**. This chart shows common relationships in verbal analogies.

Relationship	Example
Word : Antonym	heavy : weightless :: troubled : joyful
Word : Synonym	rush : haste :: mistake : error
Part : Whole	finger : hand :: branch : tree
Object : Description	blanket : warm :: sun : bright
Object : Action or Use	ruler : measure :: hammer : pound

Practice and Apply Choose the word that best completes each analogy. Give the reason for your choice.

1. obstacle : barrier :: goal : (achieve, difficulty, destination)

2. basket : wicker :: sweater : (wool, container, jacket)

3. partition : separate :: doorway : (build, enter, elevator)

4. flame : inferno :: snowflake : (fire, blizzard, cooling)

5. respectfully : scornfully :: generously : (selfishly, admiringly, humorously)

Critical Vocabulary

L 5b

Possible answers:

1. *Someone would have a wistful smile while thinking about an unreachable goal. Smiling wistfully suggests the thought "I wish I could have that but I can't." A scornful smile suggests the thought "That isn't worth having."*

2. *Someone behaving in a mischievous way is having fun and probably has a lively expression, not a haggard one. A haggard expression shows tired, worn-out feelings.*

3. *A reproving look is one that shows disapproval, so it might stifle misbehavior.*

4. *I'd rather marvel at a campfire, enjoying its amazing warmth and color. I wouldn't want it to singe me by burning my skin.*

Vocabulary Strategy: Analogies

Possible answers:

1. *obstacle : barrier :: goal : destination; it's a synonym for goal, just as barrier is a synonym for obstacle.*

2. *basket : wicker :: sweater : wool; a sweater is made of wool, just as a basket is made of wicker.*

3. *partition : separate :: doorway : enter; you enter a space through a doorway, just as you separate a space with a partition.*

4. *flame : inferno :: snowflake : blizzard; a snowflake is part of a blizzard, just as a flame is part of an inferno.*

5. *respectfully : scornfully :: generously : selfishly; selfishly is an antonym for generously, just as scornfully is an antonym for respectfully.*

Vocabulary Strategy: Analogies

L 5b

Have students locate analogies in the selection. Remind students that elements of figurative language such as metaphors and similes are types of analogies. Encourage students to use their eBook annotation tools to do the following:

- Highlight each analogy they find.
- Look for and underline the specific things that are being compared.

so gently, almost lovingly. Above his head, the tissue-paper patterns dangled from wires, so when he stood up it was like watching someone across a forest, half hidden by hanging moss and low branches.

Language Conventions: Phrases

L 1a

Tell students that participial phrases and gerunds can help make writing compelling to read. They can enhance descriptions and provide vivid action. Writers and storytellers rely on such evocative use of language to draw in readers and listeners. Use the following as a comparative example:

The programmers worked long hours to finish the beta version of the software.

This conveys information about what the programmers were doing, but the writing is dull.

Glued to their keyboards and typing frantically, the programmers logged endless hours to finish the beta version of the software.

With the addition of participial phrases, the second sentence pops off the page and engages the reader.

Possible answers:

1. *"Pouring water onto the flames" is a gerund phrase because it functions as a noun, naming what was started. (The phrase is the direct object of the verb* started.*)*

2. *"Blinded by the smoke" is a participial phrase because it functions as an adjective, modifying* workers.

3. *"Attacking everything in its path" is a participial phrase because it functions as an adjective, modifying* beast.

4. *"Leaping out a window" is a gerund phrase because it functions as a noun, naming what was done. (The phrase is the object of the preposition* by.*)*

✓ Assess It Online!

Online Selection Test
· Download an editable ExamView bank.
· Assign and manage this test online.

Language Conventions: Phrases

L 1a

A **verbal** is a verb form used as a noun, an adjective, or an adverb. A **participle** is a verbal that functions as an adjective to modify a noun or pronoun.

Verb	Present Participle	Past Participle	Adjective Use
hurry	(is) hurrying	(has) hurried	a hurrying crowd; a hurried job
pay	(is) paying	(has) paid	the paying viewers; a paid bill;
sing	(is) singing	(has) sung	all of us singing; the sung tunes

A **participial phrase** is made of a participle and any other words that complete its meaning. The participial phrase is underlined in each of these sentences. The whole phrase functions as an adjective.

> Yetta listened for the bell <u>signaling the end of work</u>. (participial phrase modifies the noun *bell*)

> <u>Hunched over their machines</u>, the workers grew tired. (participial phrase modifies the noun *workers*)

> <u>Reading this historical novel</u>, we learned about a tragic fire. (participial phrase modifies the pronoun *we*)

A **gerund** is another verbal. It is formed from the present participle of a verb, the form with the ending *-ing*. A gerund functions as a noun in a sentence.

Verb	Gerund	Noun Use
hurry	hurrying	I don't like hurrying.
pay	paying	Take a ticket after paying.
sing	singing	Singing lifts the spirits.

A **gerund phrase** is made of a gerund and any other words that complete its meaning. The gerund phrases are underlined in this sentence. Each whole phrase functions as a noun.

> The factory workers began <u>screaming in fear</u> and <u>running for their lives</u>, but <u>escaping the flames</u> was not possible.

Practice and Apply Identify the verbal phrase in each sentence. Tell how you know it is a gerund phrase or a participial phrase.

1. Men grabbed buckets and started pouring water onto the flames.

2. Blinded by the smoke, workers could not find their way.

3. The fire was like a wild beast, attacking everything in its path.

4. Some people met their death by leaping out a window.

English Language Support

Understand Phrases Explain that participles and gerunds may take the same form but serve different functions. If a verbal phrase functions as an adjective, then it is a **participial phrase.** If a verbal phrase can be replaced by words such as *who/whom/what/that*, it is a **gerund phrase.**

· Write sentences 1 and 4 on the board. Underline the verbal phrase in each, and ask students if it can be replaced with *who/whom* or *what/that*. Guide them to recognize each as a gerund phrase that functions as a noun.

· Display the Practice and Apply sentences. With students' help, highlight the verbal phrases. Have pairs work to identify each as a participial or gerund phrase.

· Write this sentence stem on the board: _____, Millicent and Harriet began _____. Have pairs of students add a participial phrase to the beginning of the sentence and a gerund phrase to the end. Invite them to share their sentences. *(Possible response: Bored with looking for their father, Millicent and Harriet began playing hide-and-seek.)*

Analyze Point of View

RETEACH

The author of *Uprising* tells a fictionalized story of the Triangle Factory Fire through the eyes of three characters—Yetta, Jane, and Bella—each with her own unique perspective on the events. The author tells each character's story using the same point of view: third-person limited.

An author may employ multiple points of view for a number of reasons. He or she may want to show how the events affect characters in different ways. Another reason may be to give the reader a diverse perspective on the story's events. Others may want to explore a unique way of telling a complex story.

 LEVEL UP TUTORIALS Assign the following *LevelUp* tutorial: **Third-Person Point of View**

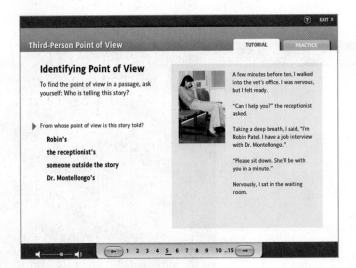

INDEPENDENT READING

To explore the effect of using multiple points of view, have students fill in a comparison-and-contrast chart like the one shown below. What did each character uniquely think, see, and feel as the fire raged? What did all three characters experience that was similar? When they're done, have students meet in a small group to share their observations.

Yetta	Jane	Bella

Compare and Contrast: Genres

RETEACH

Review **historical fiction** with students. Remind them that historical fiction authors base their stories on research and facts. Authors use their imaginations and storytelling tools to create the narrative, inventing characters and dialogue that could reasonably make sense based on the facts. Point out that historical fiction should never be considered an authoritative source—it is intended primarily to be a compelling read.

Point out that although historical fiction is based on information that might be found in informational texts, historical fiction shares common elements with other types of fiction, including character, plot, setting, conflict, and a theme.

 LEVEL UP TUTORIALS Assign the following *LevelUp* tutorial: **Prose Forms**

INDEPENDENT READING

Have students find another example of historical fiction and a corresponding informational text about the same event. Direct students to look for specific factual information found in the nonfiction selection that appears or is somehow referenced in the fiction piece. Have students consider the following questions:

- Does the author of the historical fiction piece remain true to the facts?
- Are there instances during which the author of the fiction piece takes too much liberty with the facts?

Have students present their observations to the class.

Doris Is Coming

Short Story by ZZ Packer

Why This Text

"Doris Is Coming" is a short story about an African American girl who goes to a local soda fountain and sits at the counter. Students may not think this is a particularly exceptional undertaking unless they know that the story is set in the South in the 1960s, when groups of young black people risked their lives sitting at Whites-Only lunch counters in order to challenge racial segregation. Studying a fictional character from the same period and in the same setting will help students understand the thoughts and feelings of people who went through the experience in real life.

Background Have students read the background and information about ZZ Packer. Explain that in a sit-in, a group of students would go to a lunch counter and ask to be served; if they were not, they would refuse to move until they were. If they were arrested, a new group would take their place. Although the students were always nonviolent and respectful, they were often brutalized by local law officials and violent segregationists.

SETTING A PURPOSE Ask students to pay attention to the way the author uses story elements such as setting to convey the story's theme.

Standards Support

- cite textual evidence
- analyze how particular elements of a story interact
- compare and contrast a fictional portrayal and a historical account of the same period

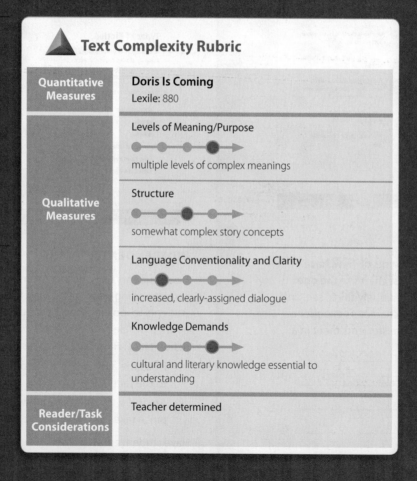

Text Complexity Rubric

Quantitative Measures	**Doris Is Coming** Lexile: 880
Qualitative Measures	Levels of Meaning/Purpose multiple levels of complex meanings
	Structure somewhat complex story concepts
	Language Conventionality and Clarity increased, clearly-assigned dialogue
	Knowledge Demands cultural and literary knowledge essential to understanding
Reader/Task Considerations	Teacher determined

Strategies for CLOSE READING

Compare and Contrast Genres

Students should read this story carefully all the way through. Close-reading questions at the bottom of the page will help them use details in the text that will help them to understand the story in its historical context. As they read, students should jot down comments or questions about the text in the margins.

WHEN STUDENTS STRUGGLE . . .

To help students compare "Doris Is Coming" with nonfiction works on the same subject, have them work in small groups to fill out a chart like the one below.

CITE TEXT EVIDENCE For practice in comparing and contrasting genres, have students find examples in "Doris Is Coming" that correspond to the nonfiction examples in "The Most Daring of [Our] Leaders."

"The Most Daring of [Our] Leaders"	*Doris Is Coming*
"This was no longer an intellectual exercise: She was being told in the most searing way imaginable that she was beyond the pale, unfit to use the same facilities as white women." (lines 5–8)	*"Without looking up she said, 'Sorry. We don't serve colored people.'"* (line 17)
"But segregation still firmly ruled in theaters, restaurants, hotels, and libraries" (lines 18–19)	*"The waitress frowned, confused, but when she finally got it, she laughed. 'Seriously though,' the waitress said, turning solemn. 'I can't serve you.'"* (lines 21–23)
"She was particularly drawn to his belief that to be effective, these young would-be activists would have to transcend self-hatred and a sense of inferiority, that they would have to learn to love themselves." (lines 43–46)	*"When Doris closed her book, about to leave, she said, 'I just want you to know I'm leaving now. Not because you're making me or because I feel intimidated or anything . . . Next time I'll want some food, all right?'"* (lines 60–64)

Background ZZ Packer (born 1973) is an award-winning writer of short fiction. She nicknamed herself ZZ because her given name, Zuwena (Swahili for "good"), was hard for teachers to pronounce. Recognized as a talent at an early age, Packer's first significant publication was in Seventeen magazine, when she was 19. "Doris Is Coming" is a short story about a young African American girl growing up Louisville, Kentucky, in the early 1960s.

Doris Is Coming

Short Story by ZZ Packer

CLOSE READ
Notes

1. **READ ▶** As you read lines 1–23, begin to collect and cite text evidence.

- Underline parts of the text that describe the setting.
- In the margin, summarize what the main character is doing in lines 1–14.
- In the margin, note the conflict that arises in lines 15–23.

A She walked from Stutz's and up along Fourth Street. When she got to Claremont, the street where she lived, she kept going, past Walnut and Chestnut and all the other streets named after trees. She hit the little business district, which was still lit for New Year's, the big incandescent bulbs on wires like buds growing from vines, entwining the trees and lighting the shop facades. When she walked farther, she felt, for the first time, some purpose other than solitude motivating her. She rushed, and did not know why, until she found it, Clovee's Five and Dime. As soon as she saw it, she knew what she was doing.

10　It was warm inside, and she made her way to the soda fountain, even warmer from the grill's heat. A white man stood at the ice cream machine and whirred a shake. Two white men sat at the counter and talked in low, serious tones, occasionally sucking up clots of shake through a straw.

She walks past the street where she lives to the business district and goes into Clovee's to the soda fountain, where there are several white men.

103

1. **READ AND CITE TEXT EVIDENCE** In lines 1–14 the girl is rushing toward a destination.

A **ASK STUDENTS** to cite evidence marking her route. What is her starting point? Where does she end up? What familiar streets does she pass along the way? *She starts out at Stutz's and walks along Fourth Street. She passes Claremont and hits the business district. She ends up at Clovee's Five and Dime.*

FOR ELL STUDENTS Many students may not know what a *Five and Dime* was. Explain that it was a large store selling a variety of inexpensive items—originally for five cents or a dime.

There was one waitress, hip propped against the side of the counter, wiping the countertop with a rag that had seen cleaner days. Without looking up she said, "Sorry. We don't serve colored people."

B "Good." Doris said. "I don't eat them." She remembered Helen telling her that this was the line someone used during a sit-in, and
20 Doris was glad to have a chance to use it.

The waitress frowned, confused, but when she finally got it, she laughed. "Seriously though," the waitress said, turning solemn. "I can't serve you."

The two men talking looked over at her and shook their heads. They began talking again, occasionally looking over at Doris to see if she'd left.

"What if I stay?"

C The waitress looked to the man making the shake, eyes pleading for help. "I don't know. I don't know. I just don't make the rules and I
30 feel sorry for you, but I don't make 'em."

The man walked over with a shake and gave it to the waitress, who bent the straw toward herself and began to drink it. "Look," the man said to Doris, "I wouldn't sit here. I wouldn't do that."

"You wouldn't?"

"I wouldn't if I were you."

She sat. Shaking, she brought out her World History book. She'd made a book cover for it with a paper bag, and she was glad she'd done it because she was sweating so much it would have slipped from her hands otherwise. She set it on the counter, opened it, as if she did
40 this everyday at this very shop, and tried to read about the Hapsburgs, but couldn't.

It occurred to her that other students who did sit-ins were all smarter than she; they'd banded together, and had surely told others

2. **◄ REREAD AND DISCUSS** With a small group, discuss Doris's "joke"—what it means, what it tells you about Doris, and how it advances the plot (lines 15–23).

3. **READ ►** As you read lines 24–47, continue to cite textual evidence.
    • Circle the actions that reveal Doris's feelings.
    • Underline what the waitress and the man say to Doris.
    • In the margin, summarize the developing situation.

---

of their whereabouts, whereas she had foolishly come to Clovee's all
D by herself. She stared at her book and didn't dare look up, but from the corner of her eye she noticed when the two men who'd been talking got up and left.

The man at the ice cream machine made himself some coffee and beckoned the waitress to him. When he whispered something to her,
50 she swatted him with the rag, laughing.

Once Doris felt the numbness settle in her, she felt she could do it. She tried at the Hapsburgs again.

The waitress said, "Student? High school?"

"Yes, Ma'am. Central."

"My daughter's over at Iroquois."

E "We played them last Friday." Doris didn't know what the scores were, didn't care, but had heard about the game over the intercom.

"Well." The waitress started wiping the counter again. Going over the same spots.

60 When Doris closed her book, about to leave, she said, "I just want you to know I'm leaving now. Not because you're making me or because I feel **intimidated** or anything. I just have to go home now."

The waitress looked at her.

"Next time I'll want some food, all right?"

"We can't do that, but here's half my shake. You can have it. I'm done."

The shake she handed over had a lipstick ring around the straw, and a little spittle. Doris knew she wouldn't drink it, but she took it anyway. "Thanks, ma'am."

The waitress looks at Doris and thinks of her own daughter, who is about the same age.

intimidate:

threaten; frighten

4. **◄ REREAD** Reread lines 42–47. What mistake does Doris see she's made? Cite text evidence in your answer.

She'd put herself in harm's way by thinking she could go it alone. Others had "banded together, and had surely told others of their whereabouts, whereas she had foolishly come" on her own.

5. **READ ►** As you read lines 48–79, continue to cite textual evidence.
    • In the margin, explain the connection the waitress makes with Doris.
    • Circle details that show Doris is in control of her actions and emotions.
    • In the margin, make an inference about how Doris feels about her experience (lines 70–79).

---

2. **REREAD AND DISCUSS USING TEXT EVIDENCE** Explain that in line 18 Doris uses the line "I don't eat them" to respond to the waitress's comment about serving "colored" people.

B **ASK STUDENTS** to discuss evidence showing that Doris was prepared to say this. *Doris was "glad to have a chance to use it."* What was the joke intended to do? *It was intended to lighten the mood and to catch the workers off-guard.* What inference can be made from the fact that the joke had been used before? *There was always the possibility of violence at a lunch counter sit-in.*

3. **READ AND CITE TEXT EVIDENCE** Point out that the waitress seems uncomfortable with the store's policy.

C **ASK STUDENTS** what she says and does in lines 28–30 that reveals her attitude. *She looks at the man making the shake with "eyes pleading for help"; she tells Doris that "I just don't make the rules and I feel sorry for you . . ."*

4. **REREAD AND CITE TEXT EVIDENCE** In lines 45–47 Doris "stared at her book and didn't dare look up."

D **ASK STUDENTS** to make an inference about how she feels based on this behavior. *Students may say she feels threatened and vulnerable; the two men who leave seem menacing.*

5. **READ AND CITE TEXT EVIDENCE** In this section, Doris has a conversation with the waitress.

E **ASK STUDENTS** to think about the fact that Doris "didn't care" what the scores were. Why not? *She was too excited by the fact that they were having a real conversation; the scores were inconsequential.*

Critical Vocabulary: intimidate (line 62) Have students explain the meaning of *intimidate*. What situations might make someone feel intimidated? *Students may suggest being the new kid in school or talking to a celebrity.*

Doris seems to be a bit numb, as though she can't believe what she's just done. She also seems happy and relaxed, thinking about her family at home.

F 70   Outside Clovee's Five and Dime, the world was cold around her, moving toward dark, but not dark yet, as if the darkness were being adjusted with a volume dial. Whoever was adjusting the dial was doing it slowly, consistently, with infinite patience. She walked back home and knew it would be too late for dinner, and the boys would be screaming and her father wanting his daily beer, and her mother worried sick. She knew that she should hurry, but she couldn't. She had to stop and look. The sky had just turned her favorite shade of barely lit blue, the kind that came to windows when you couldn't get back to sleep but couldn't quite pry yourself awake.

6. **◀ REREAD** Reread lines 51–79. How have the characters' perspectives changed? Cite explicit textual evidence in your response.

At first, the waitress tried to get Doris to leave. Then they actually have a conversation, which is courageous under the circumstances. The waitress offers Doris her shake, and Doris thanks her.

SHORT RESPONSE

Cite Text Evidence   Think about the texts in this Collection that describe the real experiences of Diane Nash and John Lewis during sit-ins in the 1960s. What references to historical details do you find in the story? In what ways are Doris's fictional experiences different from the real experiences of Nash and Lewis? **Cite text evidence** in your response.

Although Doris experienced resistance when she sat at the lunch counter, it was not as violent as the response Nash and Lewis faced. The fact that Doris was refused service at the lunch counter was based on historical accounts of similar events. While some people may have sympathized with Nash and Lewis, the behavior of the waitress is most likely fictional. It is also unlikely that the actual nonviolent protesters would have attempted a sit-in alone.

106

---

6. **REREAD AND CITE TEXT EVIDENCE**   Have students think about Doris's sense of euphoria in lines 70–79.

F   **ASK STUDENTS** to explain why she feels so happy. How did the conversation with the waitress help change her mood? *The waitress made an effort to connect with Doris, and Doris found the strength to stand up for herself.*

SHORT RESPONSE

Cite Text Evidence   Students should support their positions with evidence from this selection and two nonfiction selections describing the real experiences of Diane Nash and John Lewis. They should:

- compare and contrast the fiction and nonfiction stories with respect to character, setting, and point of view
- examine how the author uses historical details to tell a story
- determine which story details are fact-based and which are made-up

TO CHALLENGE STUDENTS . . .

Tell students that the lunch counter sit-ins of the 1960s began in Greensboro, North Carolina, when a non-violent sit-in at a segregated lunch counter sparked a movement that spread throughout the region, forcing many establishments to change their segregationist policies.

ASK STUDENTS to research this important part of civil rights history through photography, videos, and articles. They can find online exhibits of photos and interviews with important participants in the events. Have students prepare short presentations about facts that they have discovered.

DIG DEEPER

With the class, return to Question 6, Reread. Have students share their responses.

ASK STUDENTS to think about how the perspectives of Doris and the waitress change at the end of the story.

- Why does the waitress start a conversation with Doris? *She may be aware that segregation is unjust; in telling Doris that she "doesn't make the rules" she shows she is conflicted about Clovee's policy. Students may also point out that the waitress seems to wait for the two men to leave before she can talk to Doris, suggesting she may feel intimidated by their presence.*

- Why does this change the dynamic between the two characters? How does this lead to a change in their perspectives? *The waitress asks Doris a friendly question, to which Doris gives a brief but polite reply; this gives the waitress the opportunity to take the next step ("My daughter's over at Iroquois"), which creates a connection between herself and Doris, resulting in a real conversation between two equals—an event neither one of them is likely to forget. Their brief exchange made it possible for them to imagine a different kind of world.*

ASK STUDENTS to return to their Short Response answer and revise it based on the class discussion.

ANCHOR TEXT

Craig Kielburger Reflects on Working Toward Peace

Personal Essay by Craig Kielburger

Why This Text?

Students regularly read personal essay writing in print and digital media on their own and at school. Recognizing elements of personal essays helps students focus on an author's reasons for writing, giving them a deeper understanding of the topic. This lesson guides students to identify and analyze elements of personal essays and to determine an author's perspective.

Key Learning Objective: The student will be able to identify and analyze elements of a personal essay and determine an author's point of view.

For practice and application:

Difference Maker:
John Bergmann and Popcorn Park
Newspaper Article by David Karas

Close Reader selection
"Difference Maker: John Bergmann and Popcorn Park,"
Online Article by David Karas

RI 1 Cite textual evidence.
RI 2 Determine central ideas.
RI 3 Analyze interactions between ideas.
RI 4 Determine the meaning of words and phrases.
RI 5 Analyze structure.
RI 6 Determine author's point of view.
RI 8 Trace and evaluate an argument.
W 1 Write arguments.
W 9b Apply grade 7 Reading standards.
W 10 Write routinely over extended time frames.
SL 4 Present claims and findings.
L 1c Correct dangling modifiers.
L 4 Determine the meaning of multiple-meaning words..
L 4a Use context as a clue to meaning.
L 4c Consult a dictionary to clarify the precise meaning of a word.
L 4d Verify preliminary determination of meaning.
L 6 Acquire and use grade-appropriate general academic vocabulary.

▲ Text Complexity Rubric

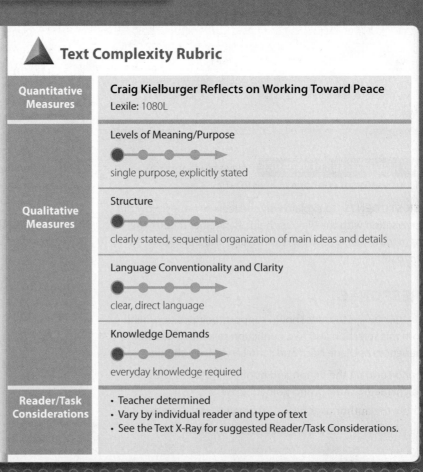

Quantitative Measures	**Craig Kielburger Reflects on Working Toward Peace** Lexile: 1080L
Qualitative Measures	**Levels of Meaning/Purpose** ●─●─●─●─▶ single purpose, explicitly stated
	Structure ●─●─●─●─▶ clearly stated, sequential organization of main ideas and details
	Language Conventionality and Clarity ●─●─●─●─▶ clear, direct language
	Knowledge Demands ●─●─●─●─▶ everyday knowledge required
Reader/Task Considerations	• Teacher determined • Vary by individual reader and type of text • See the Text X-Ray for suggested Reader/Task Considerations.

English Language Support Before teaching, use the Text X-Ray for an overview of the text's complexity. The Text X-Ray and the supports and scaffolds in the Teacher's Edition will help you guide students in different proficiencies and skill levels.

Text Complexity: Qualitative Measures

Levels of Meaning/Purpose

single purpose, explicitly stated

Help students determine the author's perspective in this essay.

- Teacher's Edition side notes, pp. 308, 309, 312, 313
- English Language Support, p. 309
- Close Read Screencasts, p. 307
- Determine Author's Point of View, p. 313

 Understanding Data

ZOOM IN ON ANALYZING PERSPECTIVE Explain that readers can infer the **author's perspective** on a topic by looking at details in the text. Display lines 54–58.

- Discuss with students why the author mentions Gandhi, what opinion he expresses, and what image stirs up a feeling in readers. *(He wants to show that, like Gandhi, he is concerned with social justice for children; he states the opinion that he learned his best lessons from children; the image of the girl with no legs creates an emotional response.)*

- Ask pairs to explain what they learn about the author's perspective from these details. *(He believes that efforts to change the world must begin with changing the lives of children.)*

Structure

clearly stated, sequential organization of main ideas and details

Help students analyze the elements of a personal essay.

- Teacher's Edition side notes, pp. 307, 308, 310, 311, 313
- English Language Support, pp. 307, 308, 311
- When Students Struggle, p. 310
- Strategies for Annotation, p. 313
- Analyze Text: Personal Essay, p. 313

To teach how to trace an argument, see

- Trace an Argument, p. 316a

To reteach how to analyze a personal essay, see

- Analyze Text: Personal Essay, p. 316a

▶ *Use It!* **Interactive Whiteboard Lesson:** Elements of an Argument
Level Up Tutorials: Prose Forms, Author's Purpose

ZOOM IN ON ANALYZING A PERSONAL ESSAY Explain that sometimes the **purpose** of a personal essay is stated; at other times, readers must infer the purpose from the way the author **structures** the essay and the **detail**s that he or she includes, such as personal experiences and facts.

- Have students reread the last paragraph of Kielburger's essay. Ask them to work with a partner to state his purpose, based on this paragraph and their reading of the essay.

- Then have students explain how the author's structure or organization supports their view of his purpose. Ask them to pick out the passage that they think most clearly conveys the author's reason for writing and explain their choice.

Language Conventionality and Clarity

clear, direct language

Teach unfamiliar vocabulary in context.

- Teacher's Edition Critical Vocabulary notes, pp. 308, 309, 311, 312, 315
- Applying Academic Vocabulary, p. 309
- Strategies for Annotation, p. 315
- Vocabulary Strategy: Multiple Meanings, p. 315

Support students' analysis of the selection through their reading, discussion, and writing.

- Teacher's Edition side notes, pp. 312, 316
- English Language Support, pp. 311, 312, 314, 316
- Language Conventions: Dangling Modifiers, p. 316

ZOOM IN ON **DETERMINING MEANING** Remind students that many words have more than one meaning. Context clues around a **multiple-meaning word** may indicate which definition the author intends. Display this sentence: "Collectively, we have all it takes to create a just and peaceful world" (lines 134–135).

- Point out the word *just*. Explain that it has several meanings. Ask students to use a digital or print dictionary to identify the definitions of *just*.
- In small groups, have students come to a consensus on which definition fits the context. (*"fair"*) Have them explain their choice.

Knowledge Demands

everyday knowledge required

Support English learners in building the background necessary to understand the personal essay.

- Teacher's Edition Background note, p. 307

HISTORY For more context and historical background, students can view the video "The Fight to End Child Labor" in their eBooks.

ZOOM IN ON **BUILDING CONTEXT** Tell students that since 1995, Kielburger's organization Free the Children has provided these life-changing services, equipment, and supplies to people around the world:

- $16 million in medical supplies
- clean water, health care, and sanitation to over a million people
- the construction of over 650 schools
- educational opportunities for 55,000 children daily

Invite students to learn more about Free the Children and Kielburger's other philanthropic organizations by visiting their websites.

Suggested Reader/Task Considerations

Consider the following before assigning this essay to students.

- Will students develop an interest in the topic as a result of reading the essay?
- Do students feel confident about managing the demands of the text?

ZOOM IN ON **SUPPORTING COMPREHENSION**

- Before students read, ask them to reflect on a problem in the world that they would like to solve. Explain that Craig Kielburger was so concerned about the hardships endured by children around the world that he decided to do something about it. Have students read to find out what he did.
- Read the first paragraph aloud to students to introduce them to Kielburger's writing style. Then have students take turns reading the essay aloud with a partner and pausing at intervals to ask questions or discuss important ideas.

CLOSE READ

For more context and historical background, students can view the video "The Fight to End Child Labor" in their eBooks.

Background Have students read the background information about Craig Kielburger and his founding of the organization Free the Children. Explain that along with his brother Marc, Kielburger has started other organizations and efforts to bring positive change to the world. Me to We aims to help people from all over become "world changers." An event called We Day ties to a yearlong activism effort called We Act.

SETTING A PURPOSE Direct students to use the Setting a Purpose prompt to focus their reading. Remind them to write down questions as they read.

Analyze Text:
Personal Essay (LINES 1–6)

Tell students that a **personal essay** is a short work of nonfiction that reflects the writer's experiences, feelings, and personality. Explain that using first-person point of view and casual, informal language are two common elements of a personal essay.

A **CITE TEXT EVIDENCE** Have students reread lines 1–6, and ask them how they know the essay is written using first-person point of view. *(The use of the pronouns* I, our, *and* my *indicate first-person point of view.)* Then, ask them to point out language the author uses that sounds informal and conversational. *(Possible responses: "I dreamed of being Superman"; "snatch up all of the bad people"; "I would spend hours flying across the park")*

English Language Support

Make sure that students understand the allusion to Superman in line 1. Explain that he is a fictional superhero who has the ability to fly, has x-ray vision, and is dedicated to saving people and catching criminals. Direct students' attention to the word *flying* in line 4. Guide them to understand that the author is using it metaphorically to create a connection to Superman. Discuss its meaning in the paragraph. *("running very quickly")*

 HISTORY VIDEO

Background *In 1995, when* **Craig Kielburger** (b. 1982) *was only twelve years old, he founded Free the Children, an international organization whose goal is to help young people achieve their fullest potential. Almost two million youths are now involved in education and development programs in 45 countries. Kielburger has received wide recognition, recently becoming one of the youngest recipients of the Order of Canada.*

Craig Kielburger Reflects on Working Toward Peace

Personal Essay by Craig Kielburger

SETTING A PURPOSE In this essay, Kielburger calls for a fairer, more just world. As you read, pay attention to how he describes his experiences as a young activist.

When I was very young I dreamed of being Superman, soaring high above the clouds and swooping down to snatch up all of the bad people seeking to destroy our planet. I would spend hours flying across the park, stopping momentarily to kick a soccer ball in my path or to pat my dog, Muffin, who ran faithfully at my heels.

   One day, when I was twelve years old and getting ready for school, I reached for the newspaper comics. On the front page was a picture of another twelve-year-old boy from Pakistan, with a bright red vest and his fist held high. According to the article, he had been sold into bondage[1] as a weaver and forced to work twelve hours a day tying tiny knots to make carpets. He had lost his freedom to laugh and to play. He had lost his

A

10

---

[1] **bondage:** the state of being held as a slave.

Craig Kielburger Reflects on Working Toward Peace **307**

Close Read Screencasts ▶ Close Read

Modeled Discussions

Have students click the *Close Read* icon in their eBook to access a screencast in which readers discuss and annotate lines 7–14, a key passage that discusses an important moment of discovery in the author's life.

As a class, view and discuss the video. Then, have students work in pairs to do an independent close read of an additional passage—the author's conclusion (lines 138–145).

(t) ©David Livingston/Getty Images; (c) ©Katrina Brown/Shutterstock

Analyze Text: Personal Essay (LINES 15–31)

RI 3,
RI 5

Note that in a personal essay the author shares insights from life experiences.

B **ASK STUDENTS** to review lines 15–31. Point out that Kielburger says the newspaper article about the boy murdered in Pakistan "changed my life forever." Ask students to summarize the issues that galvanized him to start Free the Children. *(He became deeply concerned about child labor in poverty-stricken areas.)*

Determine Author's Point of View (LINES 36–48)

RI 1,
RI 6

Explain that an author's **perspective** is the unique combination of ideas, values, feelings, and beliefs that influences the way the writer looks at a topic. Identifying emotional words and descriptions can help readers determine an author's perspective.

C **CITE TEXT EVIDENCE** Ask students to review lines 36–48 to identify statements with a strong emotional impact and explain what they tell about Kielburger's values. *(Statements like "I dream of a day when . . . children do not have to die" and "This is less money than Americans spend on cosmetics" show that Kielburger feels that people who can spend money on luxuries could use that money to help the less fortunate.)*

CRITICAL VOCABULARY

syringe: A young girl spends her days pulling apart used syringes she collects from hospitals.

ASK STUDENTS why separating used syringes might be dangerous. *(They have sharp needles; and may contain hazardous substances or bacteria.)*

■ Text in FOCUS   English Language Support

Understanding Data

Have students view the **Text In Focus** video on this page of their eBook for help in comprehending the statistics and data the author cites to support his argument. Then have students use **Text In Focus Practice** to apply what they have learned.

---

freedom to go to school. Then, when he was twelve years old, the same age as me, he was murdered.

B I had never heard of child labor and wasn't certain where Pakistan was—but that day changed my life forever. I gathered a group of friends to form an organization called Free the Children.

20 Over the past four years, in my travels for Free the Children, I have had the opportunity to meet many children around the world—children like Jeffrey, who spends his days in a Manila garbage dump, alongside rats and maggots, where he sifts through decaying food and trash, trying to salvage a few valuable items to help his family survive. He dreams of leaving the garbage dump one day.

I have met children like eight-year-old Muniannal, in India, with a pretty ribbon in her hair, but no shoes or gloves, who squats on the floor every day separating used **syringes** gathered from hospitals and the streets for their plastics.
30 When she pricks herself, she dips her hand into a bucket of dirty water. She dreams of being a teacher.

I have met children in the sugarcane fields of Brazil who wield huge machetes close to their small limbs. The cane they cut sweetens the cereal on our kitchen tables each morning. They dream of easing the hunger pains in their stomachs.

Poverty is the biggest killer of children. More than 1.3 billion people—one-quarter of the world's population— live in absolute poverty, struggling to survive on less than one dollar a day. Seventy percent of them are women and
40 children. I dream of a day when people learn how to share, so that children do not have to die.

C Every year, the world spends $800 billion on the military, $400 billion on cigarettes, $160 billion on beer, and $40 billion playing golf. It would only cost an extra $7 billion a year to put every child in school by the year 2010, giving them hope for a better life. This is less money than Americans spend on cosmetics in one year; it is less than Europeans spend on ice cream. People say, "We can't end world poverty; it just can't be done." The 1997 United Nations Development Report carries
50 a clear message that poverty can be ended, if we make it our goal. The document states that the world has the materials and natural resources, the know-how, and the people to make a poverty-free world a reality in less than one generation.

syringe
(sə-rĭnj´) *n.* A *syringe* is a medical instrument used to inject fluids into the body.

English Language Support

Understand Text Structure Display lines 19–25 on the board and read the passage aloud. Point out that the author begins the paragraph with an example and ends with an important statement.

- Work with students to identify the example in the paragraph. Then have them read aloud the important statement. Discuss what the statement makes readers realize and think about.

- Have students analyze the structure of the paragraph. Ask them why this is or is not an effective method of organizing ideas.

Gandhi[2] once said that if there is to be peace in the world it must begin with children. I have learned my best lessons from other children—children like the girls I encountered in India who carried their friend from place to place because she had no legs—and children like José.

I met José in the streets of San Salvador, Brazil, where 60 he lived with a group of street children between the ages of eight and fourteen. José and his friends showed me the old abandoned bus shelter where they slept under cardboard boxes. They had to be careful, he said, because the police might beat or shoot them if they found their secret hideout. I spent the day playing soccer on the streets with José and his friends—soccer with an old plastic bottle they had found in the garbage. They were too poor to own a real soccer ball.

D

> "Gandhi once said that if there is to be peace in the world it must begin with children."

We had great fun, until one of the children fell on the bottle and broke it into several pieces, thus ending the game. 70 It was getting late and time for me to leave. José knew I was returning to Canada and wanted to give me a gift to remember him by. But he had nothing—no home, no food, no toys, no **possessions**. So he took the shirt off his back and handed it to me. José didn't stop to think that he had no other shirt to wear or that he would be cold that night. He gave me the most precious thing he owned: the jersey of his favorite soccer team. Of course, I told José that I could never accept his shirt, but he insisted. So I removed the plain white T-shirt I was wearing and gave it to him. Although José's shirt was 80 dirty and had a few small holes, it was a colorful soccer shirt

possession
(pə-zĕsh´ən) *n.*
A *possession* is
something you own.

---
[2] **Gandhi:** Mohandas Karamchand Gandhi (more commonly called Mahatma Gandhi), an Indian leader whose belief in justice inspired many people around the world.

Craig Kielburger Reflects on Working Toward Peace **309**

APPLYING ACADEMIC VOCABULARY

| interact |

THINK-PAIR-SHARE Have students turn to a partner to discuss the following question. Guide students to include the academic vocabulary word *interact* in their responses. Ask volunteers to share their responses with the class.

- How would you describe the author's **interactions** with children in areas of poverty? What might people learn from **interacting** with others who live such very different lives?

TEACH

CLOSE READ

Determine Author's Point of View (LINES 59–77)

RI 1,
RI 6

Explain to students that one way readers can recognize an author's perspective is by paying attention to details and examples the author chooses to share from his or her experiences.

D **CITE TEXT EVIDENCE** Ask students to review lines 59–77 and explain how they can identify how the author feels about the experience he had with José and a group of street children in Brazil. *(Describing the game of soccer as "great fun" and pointing out that José gave Kielburger "the most precious thing he owned" show that the author feels warmly toward José and the other children and was deeply impressed by the experience.)*

English Language Support

Remind students that the author's perspective is the way he or she looks at an issue or experience. If a writer uses positive words, readers can infer that he or she views the experience positively; negative words suggest that the writer's perspective is not favorable.

- Have pairs highlight words in lines 68–77 that show the author's feelings about what he is doing or about the people around him.
- Ask pairs to share their words and then decide whether they show positive or negative feelings. *(Possible response: Words such as "great fun," "shirt off his back," "most precious thing," and "favorite" suggest positive feelings.)*

CRITICAL VOCABULARY

possession: The author tells how a poor boy in Brazil gave him a T-shirt, the boy's favorite possession.

ASK STUDENTS to tell what it shows when someone like José, who has very little, is willing to give a new friend one of his few possessions. *(It shows that he thinks sharing is more important than owning things.)*

Analyze Graphics

RI 2,
RI 5

(PHOTOGRAPH)

Remind students that a **graphic aid** is a visual tool, such as a chart, diagram, graph, or photograph. Explain that graphic aids present readers with information in a visual way.

E **ASK STUDENTS** to examine the photograph and point out what they can tell from the image about Craig Kielburger's appearance and personality. *(Possible answer: He appears to be young; his facial expression makes him seem friendly and relaxed; he is dressed casually, so he doesn't seem to be too concerned about wanting to appear businesslike or professional.)* Then, ask students to describe what the image tells them about what Kielburger is doing. *(Possible answer: The podium and microphone indicate that he is giving a speech or talk to an audience and perhaps interacting with them; the projected images suggest that he is speaking about an effort that young people are working on together.)*

310 Collection 6

©Arthur Mola/AP Images

WHEN STUDENTS STRUGGLE . . .

To guide comprehension about elements of personal essays, have students work independently or with a partner to complete a chart like the one shown to identify ideas the author shares. Then have students share their charts with a larger group.

LEVEL UP TUTORIALS For additional support, assign the following Level Up tutorial: **Author's Purpose.**

Thoughts the author shares	What he wants others to understand
José, who had nothing, taught him about sharing.	Life would be better for everyone if we all learned to share.
Many young people see life as depressing.	

and certainly much nicer than mine. José grinned from ear to ear when I put it on.

I will never forget José, because he taught me more about sharing that day than anyone I have ever known. He may have been a poor street child, but I saw more goodness in him than all of the world leaders I have ever met. If more people had the heart of a street child, like José, and were willing to share, there would be no more poverty and a lot less suffering in this
100 world. Sometimes young people find life today too depressing. It all seems so hopeless. They would rather escape, go dancing or listen to their favorite music, play video games or hang out with their friends. They dream of true love, a home of their own, or having a good time at the next party. At sixteen, I also like to dance, have fun, and dream for the future. But I have discovered that it takes more than material things to find real happiness and meaning in life.

One day I was the guest on a popular television talk show in Canada. I shared the interview with another young person
110 involved in cancer research. Several times during the program this young man, who was twenty years old, told the host that he was "gifted," as indicated by a test he had taken in third grade. Turning my way, the host **inquired** whether I, too, was gifted. Never having been tested for the gifted program, I answered that I was not.

When I returned home my mother asked me, "Are you certain you aren't gifted?" I realized that I had given the wrong answer. I was gifted, and the more I reflected, the more I concluded that I had never met a person who was not special
120 or talented in some way.

Some people are gifted with their hands and can produce marvelous creations in their **capacity** as carpenters, artists, or builders. Others have a kind heart, are compassionate, understanding, or are special peacemakers; others, again, are humorous and bring joy into our lives. We have all met individuals who are gifted in science or sports, have great organizational skills or a healing touch. And, of course, some people are very talented at making money. Indeed, even the most physically or mentally challenged person teaches all of us
130 about the value and worth of human life.

inquire
(ĭn-kwīr´) v. If you *inquire* about something, you ask about it.

capacity
(kə-păs´ĭ-tē) n. A person's *capacity* is his or her role or position.

CLOSE READ

Analyze Text: Personal
Essay (LINES 94–107; 116–130)

Remind students that in a personal essay an author often shares personal experiences from which he or she gained insight or learned a lesson.

F **ASK STUDENTS** to review lines 94–107 and consider how Kielburger's interactions with people different from himself have enriched his life. *(Possible answer: From spending time with José and being so impressed with the boy's generosity, Kielburger learns that happiness and meaning in life do not come from material possessions.)*

Point out to students that a personal essay may be a blend of storytelling, facts, and wisdom.

G **CITE TEXT EVIDENCE** Ask students to reread lines 116–130 and identify elements of storytelling, facts, and wisdom. *(In lines 116–120, Kielburger concludes a story about being on a talk show and then presents the wise statement that he "had never met a person who was not special or talented in some way." He follows this up with facts that describe particular talents that people might have.)*

CRITICAL VOCABULARY

inquire: The author tells how a talk show host inquired about whether Kielburger was gifted.

capacity: The author uses capacities to discuss different roles or positions people have.

ASK STUDENTS to tell what questions the talk show host might have inquired of the author in his capacity as the founder of Free the Children. *(He might have asked how Kielburger got the idea.)*

English Language Support

Select Affixes Display lines 121–130 and read the passage aloud.

- Explain that *marvelous* (line 122) is the adjective form of the verb *marvel*, "to wonder at." Ask pairs to create a synonym by adding a suffix to *wonder*. *(wonderful, wondrous)*
- Highlight *creations* (line 122) and have pairs use affixes to form related words. Then have students rewrite this sentence using

one of their words in place of *creations*: We can all produce amazing creations. *(Possible response: Everyone has the power to be creative.)*

- Highlight *capacity, organizational,* and *value*. Ask pairs to rewrite the sentence in which each word appears, using a different form of the word created by adding or removing an affix.

Determine Author's Point of View (LINES 131–137)

RI 6

Explain that to determine an author's perspective students can look for **opinions,** or ideas that cannot be proved, that the author shares and examine the author's **tone,** or attitude toward a subject.

(H) ASK STUDENTS to reread lines 131–133 and note the author's opinion that God "gave each and every person special talents or gifts, but he made no one gifted in all areas." Have students reread lines 134–137 and tell what these lines reveal about the author's perspective. *(Possible answer: His perspective is that we have to pool our talents to bring about happiness.)*

Analyze the Meanings of Words and Phrases

RI 1, RI 4

(LINES 138–145)

Explain that an author's perspective can also be determined by examining the tone, or attitude toward a subject, that the author uses.

(I) CITE TEXT EVIDENCE Have students reread lines 138–145, cite details that reveal the author's tone, and explain the tone. (*"each of us has the power to be Superman," "I dream of the day," and "when all children … are free to be children" show that the tone is optimistic.*)

CRITICAL VOCABULARY

exploitation: The author uses the word *exploitation* to describe one of the world's "worst evils."

ASK STUDENTS to identify examples the author provides to show how children are exploited. *(Jeffrey has to sift through a garbage dump; Muniannal has to separate dangerous used syringes.)*

COLLABORATIVE DISCUSSION Have partners take notes on the children Kielburger describes and why he tells about them, citing evidence from the text.

ASK STUDENTS to share any questions they generated in the course of reading and discussing the selection.

I think that God, in fact, played a trick on us. He gave each and every person special talents or gifts, but he made no one gifted in all areas.

H

Collectively, we have all it takes to create a just and peaceful world, but we must work together and share our talents. We all need one another to find happiness within ourselves and within the world.

I realize, now, that each of us has the power to be Superman and to help rid the world of its worst evils—

140 poverty, loneliness, and **exploitation**. I dream of the day when Jeffrey leaves the garbage dump, when Muniannal no longer has to separate used syringes and can go to school, and when all children, regardless of place of birth or economic circumstance, are free to be children. I dream of the day when we all have José's courage to share.

I

exploitation
(ĕk´sploi-tā´shən) *n.*
Exploitation is the unfair treatment or use of something or someone for selfish reasons.

COLLABORATIVE DISCUSSION What is Craig Kielburger's purpose in describing the particular children he has met? Talk about your ideas with other group members.

English Language Support

Read Closely Adapt the collection opener strategy, Think-Write-Pair-Share, to help students prepare for their collaborative discussion. First, read aloud the discussion question. Clarify that *purpose* refers to a reason for doing something. Tell students that they need to explain why the author includes descriptions of the children. Next, tell students to reread the selection, using sticky notes to mark details and record ideas about the author's purpose. Then, pair students to share what they have written. Finally, have students participate in their group discussion.

Analyze Text: Personal Essay

RI 3, RI 5

A **personal essay,** like "Craig Kielburger Reflects on Working Toward Peace," is a nonfiction essay in which an author expresses an opinion or provides some insight based on personal experiences. Authors have different purposes for writing a personal essay. Often it is to make others aware of an important issue or topic by connecting the topic to the author's own life.

Personal essays often include the following elements:
- descriptions of personal experiences in which the author gained significant insight or learned a lesson
- first-person point of view, using the pronouns *I* and *we*
- a mixture of storytelling, personality, facts, and wisdom
- casual language that seems like a conversation with the reader

Review Kielburger's personal essay, and find an example of each element.

Determine Author's Point of View

RI 6

The author of a personal essay has a **perspective,** the unique combination of ideas, values, feelings, and beliefs that influence the way he or she looks at a topic. In his essay, Kielburger shows how he looks at himself, others, and his role in the world. To understand an author's perspective, note these features in the essay:
- statements of the author's **opinions**—personal ideas that cannot be proven true
- details and examples from the author's experiences
- words and descriptions that have emotional impact
- the writer's **tone,** or attitude toward a subject, such as humorous or serious

As you read personal essays, you can figure out the author's perspective by completing a chart such as this one.

Statement, Detail, or Tone	What It Reveals About Kielburger
"that day changed my life forever" (line 17)	He is affected by the stories and hardships of others.

Reread lines 20–41. What does the last sentence of each paragraph reveal about Kielburger's perspective?

Craig Kielburger Reflects on Working Toward Peace **313**

CLOSE READ

Analyze Text: Personal Essay

RI 3, RI 5

Help students understand what a personal essay is. Discuss each part of the definition: it is nonfiction, it is an essay, and it shares an opinion or an insight that comes from the author's personal experiences.

Discuss the elements often included in personal essays. Have students point out examples of each element from the selection. *(Examples: Kielburger retells his personal experience of reading about a Pakistani child laborer and how it changed his life. Throughout, Kielburger uses the first-person pronoun I. Kielburger tells stories, such as his exchange of T-shirts with José. He interjects his own personality by sharing his amazed reaction to José's generosity. He includes facts and figures about the toll of poverty throughout the world ["more than 1.3 billion people . . . live in absolute poverty"]. He shares his wisdom in his insight that all people are "gifted." He begins with a casual description of his childhood fascination with Superman.)*

Determine Author's Point of View

RI 6

Discuss the author's perspective as a blend of his ideas, values, feelings, and beliefs. Have students explain what the text reveals about him. *(Possible answer: Each paragraph ends with a reference to a child's dream. Kielburger concludes with a dream of his own, showing that like all children he dreams of a better future.)*

Strategies for Annotation 🖊 🗐 *Annotate it!*

Analyze Text: Personal Essay

RI 3, RI 5

Share these strategies for guided or independent analysis:
- Highlight in yellow a personal insight the author shares.
- Highlight in green first-person pronouns.
- Indicate where the author shares a personal experience by highlighting the beginning in pink.
- Underline words and phrases that are conversational and casual.

I have learned my best lessons from other children—children like the girls I encountered in India who carried their friend from place to place because she had no legs—and children like José.

I met José in the streets of San Salvador, Brazil, where

he lived with a group of street children between the ages of eight

Analyzing the Text

RI 1, RI 2,
RI 3, RI 5,
RI 6

Possible answers:

1. *Kielburger was the same age as the murdered Pakistani boy, who had lived as a slave. The sudden awareness of injustice against a boy like him caused Kielburger to act like his hero, Superman, and try to save the world.*

2. *Kielburger is compassionate because he cares about children who are struggling and suffering. He is hopeful because he believes that poor people's lives can improve. He is motivated because he started his own organization and became an activist.*

3. *Kielburger gives facts and figures to support his claim that poverty can be ended. He probably hopes that readers will consider spending money on poor people instead of on luxury items like cosmetics and ice cream.*

4. *Kielburger says that he—and everyone else in the world—is gifted. The gifts are unique talents that people can share with one another, such as the ability to build things, play sports, heal others, or make money. His purpose is to emphasize the great potential of every person and the connectedness of everyone in the world.*

5. *The essay introduction and conclusion both refer to Superman. In the introduction, Kielburger presents Superman as a child's fantasy hero. In the conclusion, he says that everyone has the power to be a real "Superman" and end real evils in the world.*

6. *It is valid because if people behaved less selfishly and shared what they had the world would be a better place. Selfishness about things, land, and beliefs are what cause fights, wars, and injustice. It's not valid because world suffering can't be reduced by people acting like street children and sharing what they have; that's too simple a view of how economies work in the real world.*

English Language Support

Express Opinions Review these ideas with students before they begin to prepare their arguments:

- Tell them that direct quotations can be used as evidence to support their claim. Suggest that they work with a partner to reread the essay and highlight interesting and powerful statements that they might be able to use.

- Explain that they need to adjust their language choices to reflect their purpose, which is to convince readers to agree with their opinion about the essay. Review words that they might use to express their opinions, such as *may, possibly,* and *could.*

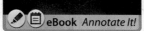 **eBook** *Annotate It!*

Analyzing the Text

RI 1, RI 2, RI 3,
RI 5, RI 6, RI 8,
W 1, W 9b, W 10,
SL 4

Cite Text Evidence Support your responses with evidence from the text.

1. **Cause/Effect** Why did the story about the murdered boy have such a strong impact on Kielburger?

2. **Infer** What words would you use to describe Kielburger, and why are those descriptions fitting?

3. **Analyze** Reread lines 37–54. Why does Kielburger provide this information? What effect might he hope this section has on the reader?

4. **Draw Conclusions** What is Kielburger's purpose in saying that he is gifted?

5. **Analyze** How does Kielburger connect the introduction and conclusion of his essay?

6. **Evaluate** Reread lines 94–108. Is Kielburger's statement about "the heart of a street child" valid? Why do you think that?

PERFORMANCE TASK

Speaking Activity: Argument Has this essay persuaded you that global poverty can be ended? Why or why not? Present an oral argument in which you give your opinion of Craig Kielburger's essay.

- Consider questions such as, *Does Kielburger do enough to convince you? Does his choice of evidence effectively support his point of view? If not, why is it inadequate and what additional evidence might he have included?*

- Take notes on the evidence that Kielburger uses to support his claim about ending poverty.

- As you draft your speech, be sure to include an interesting introduction that clearly states your claim.

- Use the evidence you found in the text to support your claim.

- Include a conclusion that summarizes your opinion.

- Practice your speech aloud, using appropriate eye contact, adequate volume, and clear pronunciation.

- Deliver your speech and have a group of peers evaluate it.

Assign this performance task.

PERFORMANCE TASK

RI 1, RI 8,
W 1, W 9b,
W 10, SL 4

Speaking Activity: Argument Have students work independently. Direct them to

- organize their argument in a logical way
- be sure they have clearly stated their claim
- include reasons and evidence from the text that support their ideas

Critical Vocabulary

L 4, L 4c, L 6

syringe   possession   inquire

capacity   exploitation

Practice and Apply Identify the vocabulary word that is tied in meaning to the italicized word in each question. Give your reasons.

1. Which word goes with *needle*?

2. Which word goes with *answer*?

3. Which word goes with *underpaid*?

4. Which word goes with *ownership*?

5. Which word goes with *skill*?

Vocabulary Strategy: Multiple Meanings

The definition of a word often depends on its **context,** the words and sentences that surround it. Note the word *capacity* in these two sentences:

> A. The only tickets left were "Standing Room Only" because the theater was filled to capacity.

> B. Some people are gifted with their hands and can produce marvelous creations in their capacity as carpenters, artists, or builders.

To figure out the meaning in each sentence, first use context to make a logical guess. Then you can use a print or digital dictionary to look up and choose the appropriate definition.

The word *capacity* has many meanings. The context helps you make a logical guess about which one fits in each sentence. In sentence A, *capacity* means "a maximum number." In sentence B, from Kielburger's essay, *capacity* means "a position or role." These meanings can be confirmed in a dictionary.

Practice and Apply Use context to give a likely meaning for the italicized word in each sentence. Check your idea in a print or digital dictionary.

1. A. Kielburger read an *article* in the newspaper.
   B. Remember to put the correct *article* before a noun.

2. A. Kielburger met children at work in fields of *cane*.
   B. The man tapped the *cane* on the sidewalk as he walked.

3. A. The United Nations published a *document* about ending poverty.
   B. Students learn to *document* their sources when doing research.

PRACTICE & APPLY

Critical Vocabulary

L 4, L 4a, L 4c, L 4d, L 6

Possible answers:

1. syringe: *A needle is part of a syringe, which is a medical instrument that injects or draws out fluids.*

2. inquire: *When you inquire, or ask, you get an answer.*

3. exploitation: *Workers who are underpaid are being used unfairly, which is an example of exploitation.*

4. possession: *Something that you own, or possess, is a possession.*

5. capacity: *If you have the capacity to do something, you have the skill to do it.*

Vocabulary Strategy: Multiple Meanings

1. A. *a written account*
   B. *the word* the, a, *or* an

2. A. *sugarcane*
   B. *a walking stick*

3. A. *a published report*
   B. *to cite the source of a quotation or piece of information and to make a bibliography of sources used in research*

Strategies for Annotation   ✏️ 🗐 *Annotate it!*

Multiple Meanings

L 4, L 4a, L 4c, L 4d, L 6

Have students review lines 101–107 to identify the intended meaning of *material*. Have them use the eBook annotation tools to do the following:

- Highlight the word *material* in yellow.
- Reread the surrounding words and sentences, looking for clues to the word's meaning. Underline the clues.
- Use the annotations to infer the word's meaning as used in the text.
- Use a print or digital dictionary to confirm which meaning the author intends, and make a note of that meaning.

They would rather escape, go dancing or listen to th [material: *adj.* Of or concerned with the physical as opposed to the spiritual or intellectual.] music, <u>play video games</u> or hang out with their frien of true love, <u>a home of their own</u>, or having a good ti party. At sixteen, I also like to dance, have fun, and dream for the future. But I have discovered that it takes more than material things to find real happiness and meaning in life.

PRACTICE & APPLY

Language Conventions: Dangling Modifiers

L 1c

Discuss the terms and guide students to recognize how a dangling modifier does not connect to a specific word in a sentence. As you examine each example of a dangling modifier, point out that the modifier is intended to connect to a word that follows it but that no such word is present in the sentence.

Answers:

1. *Correct*

2. *Possible answer: To bring attention to child poverty, Kielburger took the first step of forming an organization.*

3. *Correct*

4. *Possible answer: Separating used syringes for plastic parts, the little girl is likely to harm her health.*

5. *Possible answer: Sharing their few possessions, the poor have generous hearts.*

6. *Possible answer: Finding poverty everywhere in the world, we cannot imagine ending the problem.*

Language Conventions: Dangling Modifiers

L 1c

A **modifier** is a word or a group of words that changes, or modifies, the meaning of another word in a sentence. Some modifiers are phrases used as adjectives and adverbs to describe or give more detail. A **dangling modifier** is a modifier that modifies a word not clearly stated in the sentence. It often appears at the start of a sentence.

In the following examples, take note of the sentences with a dangling modifier and their corrected versions.

Dangling modifier	Working long hours, there is little time for play. (Who is working long hours?)
Correct	Working long hours, these children have little time for play. (The phrase modifies *children*.)
Dangling modifier	Sold into bondage, the opportunity to go to school was lost. (Opportunity wasn't sold into bondage.)
Correct	Sold into bondage, the young laborer lost the opportunity to go to school. (The phrase modifies *laborer*.)
Dangling modifier	To help children in poverty, their stories must be told. (Who helps?)
Correct	To help children in poverty, Craig Kielburger tells their stories. (The phrase modifies *Craig Kielburger*.)

Practice and Apply Identify the correctly written sentences. Fix the sentences with dangling modifiers.

1. Shocked by the article about a murdered child weaver, Kielburger felt a strong desire to make a change.

2. To bring attention to child poverty, the first step was forming an organization.

3. To support his family, one boy hunts for items in a garbage dump.

4. Separating used syringes for plastic parts, harm to the little girl's health is likely.

5. Sharing their few possessions, generous hearts are found among the poor.

6. Finding poverty everywhere in the world, it's hard to imagine ending the problem.

English Language Support

Modify to Add Details Display the chart of examples above. Discuss how the second sentence in each set corrects the error in the first.

- Work with students to read sentences 1, 4, and 5 in the Practice and Apply activity, identify each participial phrase, and find the word being modified. Then have pairs determine whether the modifier is dangling or not. Prompt them by pointing out where the phrase is in relationship to the word it modifies.

- Write sentences 2, 4, 5, and 6 on the board. Discuss with students why the modifier would be labeled as dangling in each. Explain

that, in some cases, they must add new words or change the word order to correct the problem. Assign one sentence each to pairs to correct, providing guidance as needed. Then have pairs read their new sentences aloud.

- Have students return to the drafts of their speeches and add one or more participial phrases to modify a noun or pronoun.

Trace an Argument

TEACH

Explain to students that an argument is speaking or writing that expresses a position on a problem and supports it with reasons and evidence.

Use the Interactive Whiteboard Lesson "Elements of an Argument" to build background for and teach the skill. Guide students through the Share What You Know screens and the first Learn the Skill section (screens 1–10.)

PRACTICE AND APPLY

After completing the Practice and Apply screens of the IWB lesson, have partners review "Craig Kielburger Reflects on Working Toward Peace" and identify examples of claims the author presents and evidence he uses to support each claim.

English Language Support

Interact via Written English Give students practice in written interaction as they complete the Practice and Apply activity. Assign mixed-ability pairs sections of the text to review. Have each pair identify one claim and one piece of supporting evidence. Provide these sentence frames to help them state their answers: *Kielburger believes that ___. To support this idea, he says that ___.* Then have pairs exchange papers with another pair. Students should read the other pair's answer and respond to it, using these sentence frames as appropriate: *We (agree/disagree) that Kielburger claims that ___. A better way to state Kielburger's claim is ___. Another fact that supports his claim is ___.*

Analyze Text: Personal Essay

RETEACH

Review with students that in a personal essay the author expresses an opinion or shares an insight based on his or her personal experiences. Often the author's purpose for writing a personal essay is to make others aware of an important issue.

Use a graphic organizer like the one shown to discuss elements of personal essays. Guide students to add examples of each element from "Craig Kielburger Reflects."

Element	Example from text
• includes descriptions of personal experiences that resulted in a lesson or insight for the author	Craig's story about his television appearance that leads to his realization about people being "gifted"
• uses first-person point of view	"One day I was a guest"; "I shared"; "Turning my way"; "my mother asked me"
• presents a mix of storytelling, personality, facts, wisdom	His recounting of his realization shows his hopeful, optimistic personality.
• uses casual, conversational language	

Have students focus on a particular section of text, such as lines 108–137. Students can work independently or in pairs. Have students discuss their responses with a larger group.

INDEPENDENT READING

Students can use the organizer to identify examples of each element from another personal essay they may have read or are reading on their own. Allow them to share their findings.

English Language Support

Read Closely Display and review the chart above with students, making sure they understand each element. Have them take turns reading the examples in the right column.

- Have pairs then complete the chart, returning to the essay to find examples of the last characteristic. Tell them that a conversational style doesn't necessarily include slang or common expressions but uses words that are familiar and easy to understand.
- Call on pairs to share their examples. Discuss how this style of writing helps the author fulfill his purpose.

MEDIA *from* **It Takes a Child**

Documentary

Why This Media?

Students regularly encounter documentaries on television, online, and in classrooms. By learning to identify and analyze the different features in documentaries, students will become critical viewers—better able to understand the purposes of documentaries and how they convey information.

Key Learning Objective: The student will be able to analyze the purpose of a documentary and understand the features used in it.

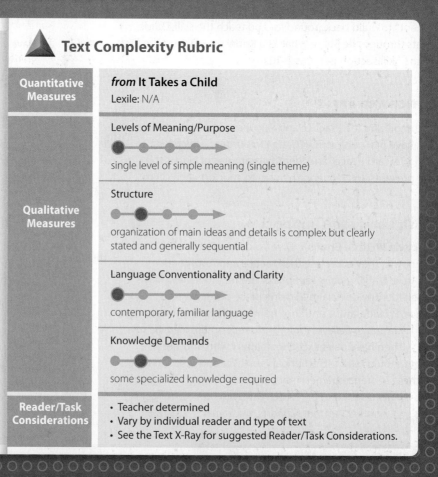

RI 6 Determine point of view or purpose.

RI 7 Compare and contrast a text to an audio, video, or multimedia version.

SL 2 Analyze the main ideas and supporting details presented in diverse media.

SL 3 Delineate a speaker's argument and claims.

SL 4 Present claims and findings.

SL 5 Include multimedia and visuals in presentations.

Text Complexity Rubric

Quantitative Measures

from **It Takes a Child**
Lexile: N/A

Qualitative Measures

Levels of Meaning/Purpose

single level of simple meaning (single theme)

Structure

organization of main ideas and details is complex but clearly stated and generally sequential

Language Conventionality and Clarity

contemporary, familiar language

Knowledge Demands

some specialized knowledge required

Reader/Task Considerations

- Teacher determined
- Vary by individual reader and type of text
- See the Text X-Ray for suggested Reader/Task Considerations.

English Language Support

Before teaching, use the Text X-Ray for an overview of the text's complexity. The Text X-Ray and the supports and scaffolds in the Teacher's Edition will help you guide students of different skill levels.

Meaning Making

Language Development

Effective Expression

Content Knowledge

Foundational Skills

Text Complexity: Qualitative Measures

Levels of Meaning/Purpose

single level of simple meaning (single theme)

Help students understand the message and purpose of a documentary.

- Teacher's Edition side note, p. 319
- English Language Support, p. 317

To teach camera shots and shot selection, see

- Camera Shots and Shot Selection, p. 320a

▶ *Use It!* **Interactive Whiteboard Lesson:** Author's Purpose and Perspective

ZOOM IN ON **DETERMINING MEANING AND PURPOSE** Remind students that the filmmaker's **message** is conveyed through the **narration** and other spoken words, **images**, and **sound effects**. Organize students into mixed-ability pairs. Have them watch the documentary once and then play it again, pausing at logical points to respond to these questions:

- What important ideas are presented?
- How do the images support the ideas?
- What does the filmmaker want the audience to understand about the children and their situations?

Afterward, have students write a statement expressing the overall message and purpose of the documentary.

Structure

organization of main ideas and details is complex but clearly stated and generally sequential

Help students analyze the elements of a documentary.

- Teacher's Edition side note, p. 319
- Interpret Information, p. 317
- Analyze Media, p. 319

To reteach elements of a documentary, see

- Elements of a Documentary, p. 320a

▶ *Use It!* **Level Up Tutorial:** Analyzing Visuals

ZOOM IN ON **ANALYZING MEDIA** View the first minute and thirty seconds of the clip with students. Have students identify the techniques explained on Student Edition page 319.

- Have pairs watch the video and answer this question: Which element of the documentary is most effective in conveying the purpose?
- Have pairs share their responses, citing how the use of the technique supports their ideas. *(Possible response: The images are most powerful in achieving Kielburger's purpose. Even without narration, it is clear to viewers that children shouldn't be in those conditions.)*

Language Conventionality and Clarity

contemporary, familiar language

Teach unfamiliar vocabulary in context.

- Applying Academic Vocabulary, p. 318

Guide students to discuss and write about a documentary.

- Teacher's Edition side note, p. 318
- English Language Support, p. 319

ZOOM IN ON **IDENTIFYING WORD ORIGINS** Tell students that the word *documentary* is related to the word *document*, which comes from a Latin word that means "example or proof."

- Have students write two sentences explaining how the documentary offers examples or proof.
- Then have them find *document* in a dictionary and identify other related words. Discuss each word they find. *(Possible responses: documentation, documentarian, documentable)*

Knowledge Demands

some specialized knowledge required

Support English learners in understanding necessary background information.

- Teacher's Edition Background note, p. 317
- As You View, p. 318

ZOOM IN ON **BUILDING BACKGROUND** Tell students that according to a 2012 International Labor Office report there were 168 million child laborers worldwide. Explain that this number reflects a one-third decrease in child labor since 2000. About four percent of these children are in bondage or forced labor; the rest work in home industries or on family farms. The problem will not be solved until families can survive without their children's income. Programs that offer cash incentives to keep children in school are among those that have achieved some success.

Suggested Reader/Task Considerations

Consider the following before assigning this documentary to students.

- Will students be able to use viewing strategies to understand the filmmaker's methods and message?
- Will students comprehend the more subtle elements of the film?

ZOOM IN ON **SUPPORTING COMPREHENSION**

- Watch the first minute of the documentary with students. Draw their attention to the effect of the music and opening images on the audience's understanding of setting; the ideas brought out by the narration; and the purpose of Craig Kielburger's comments.
- After viewing, return to the closing sequence. Ask students to describe Craig's expression and body language in this part. Discuss why this is an effective ending for the clip. *(Possible response: The disbelief on Craig's face and the way in which he moves away convey the horror he feels. This emphasizes that child labor is wrong.)*

TEACH

CLOSE READ

Background Have students read the background information about *It Takes a Child*. Remind students that when Craig Kielburger was only twelve years old he founded Free the Children, an organization whose goal is to help young people achieve their fullest potential. Point out that Kielburger became interested in the plight of children after reading about a 12-year-old boy in Pakistan who had been sold into bondage. Explain that although many countries have laws forbidding the use of children as laborers, other countries do not have these laws or are very lax in the enforcement of these laws. Discovering this, young Craig was inspired to show the world the sad realities of child labor in some parts of the world. This documentary tells about the trip he made to South Asia to view child labor up close.

SETTING A PURPOSE Direct students to use the Setting a Purpose information and prompt to focus their viewing. Remind students to generate questions as they read and view.

English Language Support

View Closely Provide students with these sentence stems to help them listen actively and note important ideas during their first viewing of the video.

- *From what is said during the documentary, I learn_____.*
- *From the images in the documentary, I learn _____.*
- *One question I have is _____.*
- *I will watch the video a second time to _____.*

Have students share their notes from their first viewing of the documentary in small groups and discuss their purpose in watching it a second time.

Background *When child activist Craig Kielburger was twelve years old, he became interested in the plight of child laborers. Inspired by the story of twelve-year-old Iqbal, a child labor activist who had been murdered in South Asia, Kielburger realized that a child could make a difference in the world. Kielburger then traveled to South Asia to see child labor first hand. With the help of a film crew, he documented his journey so that the world could see what he himself had witnessed.*

MEDIA ANALYSIS

from It Takes a Child

Documentary directed by Judy Jackson

SETTING A PURPOSE The documentary you are about to view features some of the adults and children Craig Kielburger spoke with during his trip to South Asia. It also shows workplaces he visited and what he observed there.

As you view the film clip, think about why Kielburger decided to make this journey and what he wanted to find out. Notice the ways that filmmaking and news reporting come together to help you understand Kielburger's reasons for traveling to South Asia. Write down any questions you have during viewing.

©Bullfrog Films

English Language Support

Analyze Language Explain that the clip includes both an unseen narrator's voice as well as that of Craig Kielburger, whom they will see.

- Watch the first minute of the clip with students. Work with them to compare the language used by the narrator and Kielburger, guiding them to see that Kielburger's is more conversational. Discuss the purpose of the narration in this first part of the film. *(It gives important background information.)* View the rest of the clip, pausing frequently to discuss what other important ideas are brought out by the narrator.

- Have students watch the clip in pairs. Ask them to note the difference in the language used by the narrator and by Kielburger. Ask students to explain why each style of expression is appropriate for the speaker and purpose. *(The narrator is communicating facts and other types of information. Kielburger's speech is conversational because he is talking to the audience and to the others in the film.)*

AS YOU VIEW Tell students that they will be watching a documentary. A **documentary** is a nonfiction film that gives information about important or noteworthy people, places, or events. Explain that documentary filmmakers use special kinds of filmmaking techniques in order to present information in a way that will have an impact on viewers. Point out that some of these techniques include the following:

- **interviews,** or the spoken words of people in the documentary
- **footage,** or sections of film that give specific information about the subject
- **voice-over narration,** or the spoken words of an unseen narrator who tells about the subject

Have students read the As You View paragraphs to help them focus their viewing and to understand how a documentary filmmaker makes choices about which techniques to use. Then, as students watch the video clip, have them keep track of examples of the documentary filmmaker's techniques, note how each is used in this film, and note the impact each technique has on the viewer.

COLLABORATIVE DISCUSSION Have students work with a partner to list the interviews and images that the filmmaker presents. Then, have students discuss each one and the impact it had on them as they watched the film clip. Students can tell which technique had the most impact on them and give reasons for their thinking.

ASK STUDENTS to share any questions they generated in the course of viewing and discussing the documentary.

FOR STUDENTS WITH DISABILITIES

Students may struggle to hear some parts of the documentary, particularly the interviews conducted in busy settings with background noise. For these parts of the film, pause and explain what Kielburger and others just said or provide a transcript of the comments made.

MEDIA

Format: Documentary

Running Time: 2:54 minutes

AS YOU VIEW Documentary filmmakers gather factual material about their subjects, much like news reporters do, and use film to tell a true story about their subjects. The filmmakers then use various techniques to convey the information in a way that will have an impact on the viewers.

As you view the documentary clip, consider how the director's choice of scenes affects the impact of the words spoken in the interviews. As needed, pause the video and write notes about what impresses you and about ideas you might want to talk about later. Replay or rewind the video so that you can clarify anything you do not understand.

©Bullfrog Films

COLLABORATIVE DISCUSSION With a partner, discuss how the film presents an inside view into child labor conditions. Which of the interviews and images had the most impact? Why? Discuss the concepts the film conveys and how it conveys them. Cite specific evidence from the documentary to support your ideas.

APPLYING ACADEMIC VOCABULARY

contrast	interact

THINK-PAIR-SHARE Have students turn to a partner to discuss the following questions. Guide students to include the academic vocabulary words *contrast* and *interact* in their responses. Ask volunteers to share their responses with the class.

- How do Kielburger and the children in the documentary **interact**?
- When you **contrast** your life with the lives of the children in the documentary, what differences are apparent?

Analyze Media

A **documentary** is a nonfiction film that gives viewers information about important people, major events, significant discoveries, or historical places. Documentaries use features to help viewers understand the information.

Features of a Documentary	Strategies for Viewing
Interviews are usually filmed specifically for a documentary. Filmmakers may interview: • experts on the subject • people who knew the person • people who were involved in an event	Think about why the filmmaker chose this person for an interview. Does the person: • have special knowledge about the subject? • present another side of the story?
Footage is filmed material that gives information about a subject. Documentary filmmakers combine different types of footage to tell their subject's story. Footage can include film clips, news reports, photographs, and interviews about a subject.	Think about why the particular footage was chosen. Does it: • show details of a historical time? • create an emotional response? • reveal the filmmaker's perspective or point of view?
Voice-over narration is the voice of an unseen speaker that is heard on a documentary. The voice-over can provide important facts about the subject. It can also help explain the footage.	Listen to the voice-over narration for additional information about the footage. Does the voice-over change from one speaker to another? What points made by voice-overs seem most important to the subject?
Sound effects can be used for a variety of purposes.	Follow the music cues. Do they signal a change in the documentary's setting or mood? Listen for sound effects, such as screeching tires or bombs exploding. Do they help you better understand what is happening? Listen to the dialogue. Does it help you better understand the subjects?

Think about how these features interact with each other in the clip from *It Takes a Child* to tell the story of Craig Kielburger's commitment to the cause of exposing the injustices of child labor.

English Language Support

Select Affixes As they write or discuss responses to the Strategies for Viewing questions, students should use affixes correctly to avoid confusing their readers or listeners. Write this sentence on the board and work with students to revise it with correct affixes: "The interviewer was probable try to show how children might be reluctant to work collect plastic to make money for their family." *(The interviewer was probably trying to show how children might be reluctant to work collecting plastic to make money for their family.)* Then have students work with a partner to write or discuss answers to the remaining questions.

CLOSE READ

Analyze Media

Help students understand the different kinds of features, or techniques, used by documentary filmmakers to convey information.

- Discuss the strategies for viewing for each kind of feature. Have students name one example of each type of feature from the documentary. *(Possible answers: Kielburger interviews a man who supervises a girl worker. There is film clip footage of Kielburger sitting with a group of children, asking them questions and clearly connecting with them on a personal level. A woman narrates the documentary, although the narration also includes sections of 15-year-old Craig talking about his trip. There is music from some of the places where Kielburger travels.)*

- Have students answer the corresponding questions about the strategies for viewing. *(Possible answers: The interview with the supervisor gives viewers knowledge about the work conditions of the girl with the syringes. The film clip of Kielburger shows the setting where he traveled and how close he became with the children he was interviewing. The music gives viewers a sense of the foreign cultures where Kielburger traveled.)*

- Point out that after filmmakers shoot the scenes and record the sounds, they assemble and edit the scenes and sounds to help convey the documentary's message. Explain that part of that editing process is deciding which techniques work best. Ask students how effectively the filmmakers of Craig Kielburger's trip wove the techniques together to tell Craig's story. How easy was it for students to understand the message of the documentary?

English Language Support

Guide students to work in small groups to answer the questions on page 320. Each group should answer one question. When all the groups are finished, they can take turns presenting their answers to the class. Encourage students to provide their classmates with useful feedback.

Analyzing the Media

RI 6, RI 7, SL 2, SL 3

Possible answers:

1. The central idea of the documentary is that children in some parts of the world are forced to do hard work and that this practice is unjust. The documentary shows several scenes of actual children doing child labor, such as the little girl who is sorting through used medical syringes.

2. The filmmaker's purpose is to inform and to persuade the viewer that the practices of child labor are unjust. The footage and interviews about the girl with the syringes seem startling and sad. The interview with the man about the girl makes the example more startling because he seems so uninformed as to the dangers of her task.

3. **Interview:** Kielburger's interview with the man about the girl with the syringes shows how indifferent people in these countries are to the dangers of this type of child labor. **Footage:** Footage of Kielburger observing child laborers shows how closely he was able to research the subject. **Voice-over:** A female narrator's voice tells details about Kielburger's trip, and Kielburger's voice, as a fifteen-year-old, describes what he wanted to do and his reactions. **Sound effects:** We hear music from India stopping at important points to emphasize the seriousness of the content. Then, it softly and dramatically starts up again.

4. The opening footage, with scenes and music from some of the places Kielburger visits, gives viewers a sense of the cultures in these places.

5. The woman's and Craig's voice-overs contribute details about why and how Craig traveled to India, including Craig's feelings about the trip. The interviews with the little girl with the syringes and the man provide specific details about that situation and show the man's indifference to or ignorance of the dangers the girl faces.

6. In his essay, Craig shares additional details about the girl who was sorting syringes. We learn that she was eight years old when he met her and that she, like Craig and the other children he met, had a dream. Her dream was to be a teacher. The film clip shows the reality of the awful conditions she works in. It also shows twelve-year-old Craig's sad reaction when he talks to the man about the little girl's work and its dangers. Together, the documentary and the essay show that Craig not only investigated the issues in person, but that he followed up by sharing his findings and experiences. He was guided by a cause not only to investigate unfair child labor, but also to try to convince others of the need for action.

Analyzing the Media

RI 6, RI 7, SL 2, SL 3, SL 4, SL 5

Cite Text Evidence Support your responses with evidence from the media.

1. **Infer and Summarize** What is the **central idea,** or most important idea about a topic, that the documentary presents? Describe the scenes that take place in the film and how those scenes support the central idea.

2. **Analyze** Identify the filmmaker's purpose or purposes in making the documentary. What key parts of the film convey the purpose or purposes?

3. **Infer** Think about the features the filmmaker uses in the documentary. Fill out a chart like this one and tell how they clarify the issues presented.

Feature	How It Clarifies Issues

4. **Analyze** How does the opening introduce the setting? What combination of features work together in the opening to present a sense of the place Kielburger is visiting and to help you understand the setting?

5. **Compare** Compare and contrast the information in the narrator voice-over and in the interviews. What information does each feature contribute?

6. **Evaluate** Think about your reading of the personal essay by Craig Kielburger in this collection. How do the ideas presented in the documentary help clarify the points made in the essay, and how do both relate to the collection topic, "Guided by a Cause"?

PERFORMANCE TASK

Media Activity: Photo Documentary What does it take to be committed to a cause despite great obstacles? Let people know about a person in your school or community who works on an important social cause. Create a photo documentary to tell that person's story.

- Take photos of the person involved in his or her work, or use photos that already exist.

- Choose some of the documentary features you learned about to help you create your documentary.

- Interview your subject and include quotations in your documentary or record a soundtrack of the interview with music.

- Present your documentary to a group of classmates. Then discuss their reactions to it.

Assign this performance task.

PERFORMANCE TASK

SL 4, SL 5

Media Activity: Photo Documentary Have students develop their documentaries about a school or community worker. Students should

- choose the worker and gather or take photos of that person at work
- create a set of questions that will reveal his or her social cause
- record the interview or use quotations
- decide whether to add music and sound effects
- present the documentary to the class

Camera Shots and Shot Selection

TEACH

Explain to students that filmmakers use different kinds of camera shots in their documentaries. A **camera shot** is a single continuous view taken by a camera. Each camera shot is chosen by a filmmaker to create a specific effect on viewers. When all the camera shots are completed, the filmmaker reviews them all and decides which ones to put together to create the entire film. Putting together a variety of camera shots allows the filmmaker to emphasize different ideas. It also adds variety to the film, making it more interesting to watch.

Discuss the following camera shots with students:

- An **establishing shot** introduces viewers to the location of the scene, usually by presenting a wide view of an area. A filmmaker will choose this kind of shot to establish the setting. In the Kielburger documentary, the first footage establishes the setting in a city in India, with evidence of poverty and more traditional forms of transportation.
- A **close-up** shot shows a close view of a person or object. A filmmaker will use this kind of shot to make viewers feel like they know the character. The filmmakers of *It Takes a Child* show close-ups of children's smiling faces, showing how young and innocent they are.
- A **long shot** gives a wide view of a scene, showing a person and his or her surroundings. A filmmaker uses this kind of shot to allow viewers to see the "big picture" and to show the relationship between the characters and the environment. The long shot of the boat on the river shows one of the common forms of transportation in this part of India.
- A **point-of-view** shot shows what a character sees through his or her eyes. A filmmaker uses this kind of a shot to help viewers identify with a character. Point-of-view shots of the syringes show the dangerous reality of the job done by the little girl.

PRACTICE AND APPLY

Have students view *It Takes a Child* again. Ask them to identify other examples of these camera shots and to tell their effects on viewers. Have students discuss how each shot makes the documentary more interesting and effective.

Elements of a Documentary

RETEACH

Remind students that documentary filmmakers use different kinds of techniques to help viewers understand the information they want to convey. Review the following techniques with students:

- **Interviews** are question-and-answer sessions that are usually filmed specifically for a documentary. Filmmakers may interview experts on a subject, the people involved in an event or situation, or others who are close to those people.
- **Footage** is filmed material that gives information about a subject. Footage can include film clips, news reports, photographs, and interviews about a subject.
- **Voice-over narration** is the voice of an unseen speaker that is heard over a documentary. The voice-over can provide important facts about the subject or help explain the footage.
- **Sound effects** can be used for various purposes. Music can be used to create a mood or to give clues about the setting. Sound effects like cars driving give a sense of the setting. Dialogue can give viewers a better sense of the people in a documentary.

English Language Support

Use Domain-Specific Terms Have pairs of students review the techniques by taking turns to read aloud each term and its explanation. Then ask them to use each term in a sentence, either restating an idea from the explanation in their own words or relating the technique to the documentary they just watched. Invite pairs to read their sentences aloud.

INDEPENDENT VIEWING

Have students view another documentary and name the kinds of techniques the filmmaker uses. Have students discuss the purpose of these techniques and their effects on viewers.

Difference Maker: John Bergmann and Popcorn Park

Newspaper Article by David Karas

Why This Text

Students may have difficulty discerning the author's purpose and point of view in a newspaper article. When the article profiles a noteworthy character with a compelling story, figuring out the author's perspective becomes more challenging. With the help of the close-reading questions, students will analyze the author's statements, examples, and descriptions of the subject. This close reading will lead students to understand the author's purpose, as well as the remarkable subject.

Background Have students read the background information about Popcorn Park Zoo and John Bergmann. Introduce the article by reviewing the life histories of different kinds of domestic animals. Pets like cats, dogs, and canaries can hope to live out their lives in the homes of their owners. But other domestic animals—cast-offs from circuses, zoos, theme parks, and laboratories—face an uncertain future.

SETTING A PURPOSE Ask students to pay attention to the author's statements about—and descriptions of—Bergmann. What do they reveal about the author's purpose and point of view?

Standards Support

- cite multiple pieces of text evidence
- determine central ideas in a text
- analyze individuals, events, and ideas
- determine the meaning of words
- determine an author's purpose or point of view

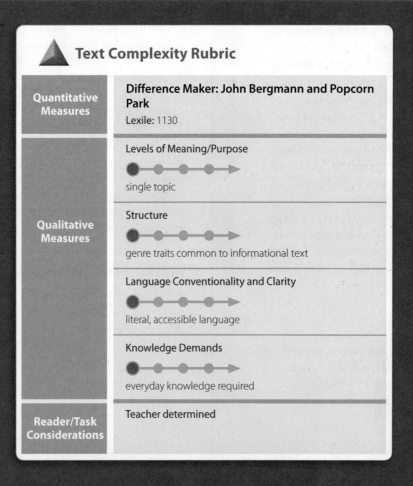

Text Complexity Rubric

Quantitative Measures

Difference Maker: John Bergmann and Popcorn Park
Lexile: 1130

Qualitative Measures

Levels of Meaning/Purpose
single topic

Structure
genre traits common to informational text

Language Conventionality and Clarity
literal, accessible language

Knowledge Demands
everyday knowledge required

Reader/Task Considerations
Teacher determined

Strategies for CLOSE READING

Determine Author's Purpose and Point of View

Students should read this article carefully all the way through. Close-reading questions at the bottom of the page will help them focus on a thorough analysis of the author's purpose. As they read, students should jot down comments or questions about the text in the margins.

WHEN STUDENTS STRUGGLE . . .

To help students determine the author's purpose in "Difference Maker," have them work in small groups to fill out a chart like the one shown below.

CITE TEXT EVIDENCE For practice in determining an author's purpose, ask students to cite text evidence for each cell in the left column of the chart and then interpret the evidence in the adjoining cell of the right column.

Statement of opinion	What it reveals
Bergmann "seems to have found his dream job." (line 98)	The author understands how lucky Bergmann is; maybe the author is a little envious.
Bergmann "chuckles as he lifts up the towels that cover the papers in his office—which is in a barn." (lines 2–3)	The author thinks Bergmann is a kind, unassuming man.
Animals "treat Bergmann like a rock star." (lines 24–25)	The author has a sense of humor and uses it to make a point.
"It took many nights of comfort and coaxing to help him again become comfortable" (lines 54–55)	The author admires Bergmann's compassionate attitude toward animals.

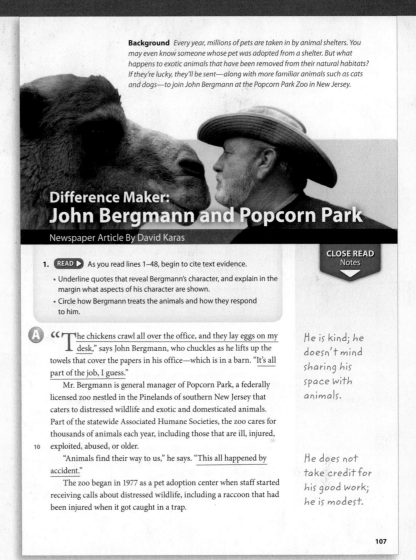

Background *Every year, millions of pets are taken in by animal shelters. You may even know someone whose pet was adopted from a shelter. But what happens to exotic animals that have been removed from their natural habitats? If they're lucky, they'll be sent—along with more familiar animals such as cats and dogs—to join John Bergmann at the Popcorn Park Zoo in New Jersey.*

Difference Maker:
John Bergmann and Popcorn Park
Newspaper Article By David Karas

CLOSE READ
Notes

1. **READE ▶** As you read lines 1–48, begin to cite text evidence.
   - Underline quotes that reveal Bergmann's character, and explain in the margin what aspects of his character are shown.
   - Circle how Bergmann treats the animals and how they respond to him.

A "The chickens crawl all over the office, and they lay eggs on my desk," says John Bergmann, who chuckles as he lifts up the towels that cover the papers in his office—which is in a barn. "It's all part of the job, I guess."

Mr. Bergmann is general manager of Popcorn Park, a federally licensed zoo nestled in the Pinelands of southern New Jersey that caters to distressed wildlife and exotic and domesticated animals. Part of the statewide Associated Humane Societies, the zoo cares for
10 thousands of animals each year, including those that are ill, injured, exploited, abused, or older.

"Animals find their way to us," he says. "This all happened by accident."

The zoo began in 1977 as a pet adoption center when staff started receiving calls about distressed wildlife, including a raccoon that had been injured when it got caught in a trap.

He is kind; he doesn't mind sharing his space with animals.

He does not take credit for his good work; he is modest.

107

1. **READ AND CITE TEXT EVIDENCE** Explain to students that the article contains numerous quotes from Bergmann, and that such quotes can be informative at more than one level.

A **ASK STUDENTS** to find and cite quotes that tell the reader something about Bergmann. *Students should mention the article's opening sentence, "The chickens crawl all over the office, and they lay eggs on my desk."* What does this quote tell us about the chickens? *They have free run of Bergmann's office and do what chickens do—walk around and lay eggs.* What does the quote tell us about Bergmann? *It shows that he is the kind of person who welcomes animals into his life. He doesn't care if they mess up his office or lay eggs on his desk.*

As new animals came in, more cages were built, and piece by piece the zoo was born.

Today, more than 200 animals call the zoo home—including African lions, tigers, mountain lions, a camel, emus, wallabies, monkeys, bears, and, of course, the peacocks that roam the property and greet the more than 75,000 annual visitors in the parking lot.

On a recent morning, Bergmann made his rounds to the different cages, greeting the animals individually and calling them by name.

The routine is a familiar one for the animal residents, who treat Bergmann like a rock star. Chickens hitch a ride on the back of his golf cart, and tigers twice his size rise to greet him and gain his attention.

He is humble. He does not say that the animals love him.

"You are around [the animals] a lot," he says of his occupation. "I guess there is some realization [by them] that you have done something for them."

B Bergmann has bonded with each of the animals in his care, but Bengali is a special case. The Bengal tiger came to the zoo from Texas, where he had been rescued from an abusive, neglectful environment.

emaciated:
extremely thin

"He was **emaciated** . . . you could see all his ribs and bones," Bergmann recalls. "The way he looked, it was like he didn't have a will to live."

The staff slowly nursed Bengali back to health. He underwent surgeries to repair broken teeth and other ailments. His largest challenge, though, was getting back up to his proper weight—400 pounds—from 180 pounds.

It was when Bengali met an old lioness in the shelter next to his, Bergmann says, that he truly began to come alive. Each day, Bengali

108

walked the fence to catch a glimpse of his new friend, until he finally built up the energy to walk his entire habitat.

"When he went out, he saw her, and he just got so excited," Bergmann said, smiling.

Today, when Bergmann visits, the massive tiger **chuffs** at him—a greeting—and rubs against the fence.

But helping animals recover from conditions like this isn't achieved by sticking to an eight-hour workday.

C "It is sometimes a 24/7 job," Bergmann says. "Dante [a tiger] is feeling uncomfortable, [so] you stay here through the night."

Dante, much the opposite of Bengali, became afraid of a lioness in a neighboring cage after his companion died. It took many nights of comfort and coaxing to help him again become comfortable with his enclosure.

D Bergmann credits his family with accommodating his unpredictable schedule—and his habit of occasionally bringing animals home with him to give them a little extra care and attention.

chuff:
make a sharp puffing sound

Staying up with Dante is similar to how parents sit through the night with a child who has nightmares.

2. **◄ REREAD** Reread lines 31–48. Why does Karas include the story of Bengali? Support your answer with explicit textual evidence.

The story reveals Bergmann's connection to the animals. Bergmann nursed Bengali back to health, which made him very happy. Bengali returns Bergmann's affection—he "chuffs" when he sees Bergmann.

3. **READ ►** As you read lines 49–90, continue to cite textual evidence.
   - Write two examples in the margin of how the zoo resembles a family, and underline sentences that support your answer.
   - Circle how animals become residents of Popcorn Park.

109

Critical Vocabulary: emaciated (line 34) Have students share their definitions of *emaciated*. Explain whether you would describe an animal that should weigh 400 pounds but weighs only 180 pounds as emaciated. *An animal that is severely underweight must be described as emaciated.*

FOR ELL STUDENTS Explain to students that the phrase *made his rounds* means "went from place to place (as part of work)." Ask volunteers to name some jobs that involve making rounds. *Hospital doctors make daily rounds; delivery trucks make rounds.*

2. **REREAD AND CITE TEXT EVIDENCE**

B **ASK STUDENTS** to tell the story of Bengali in their own words. *He came from a place where he had been abused and neglected. Bergmann and his staff worked hard to make Bengali healthy. Bengali wasn't happy until he became friends with an old lioness. Bengali and Bergmann are glad when they see each other.*

3. **READ AND CITE TEXT EVIDENCE**

C **ASK STUDENTS** to find and cite passages about the zoo that remind them of family situations. *Students should note Bergmann's staying up all night with Dante (lines 51–56), his working seven days a week and not realizing it (lines 64–66), his comparison of the zoo to a retirement home (lines 74–75), and the home cooking for one of the animals (lines 85–87).*

Critical Vocabulary: chuff (line 47) Have students share their definitions of *chuff* and use the verb in an original sentence.

60 "My whole family has grown up with this," he says. His son, a veterinarian, works at the zoo, and his daughter, a teacher, uses animal themes in her lesson plans.

At the end of the day, Bergmann considers himself lucky.

"A lot of times you work seven days a week, and you don't even know it," he says. "You are doing what you love. You enjoy helping the animals out."

The staff has seen a wide range of animals find their way to Popcorn Park.

70 Porthos, a lion, was found in a converted horse stall with the floor caked with excrement. Doe, a deer, is so old she has gray eyelashes. And Princess, a camel, has a talent for picking the winner of sporting events.

"We take them when no one else wants them," Bergmann says, admitting that the zoo can sometimes resemble a retirement home for older creatures living out their senior years in peace.

The zoo also has a large kennel, which has high adoption rates for the household pets there. Many come from states with severely overcrowded animal shelters, where animals would not be held long before being put down.

The animals are treated like family, including when it comes to their food preferences.

80 The zoo runs primarily on donations, Bergmann says, which help offset the cost of its 42 staff members, including veterinarians and animal control officers, who provide constant care for the animals.

And that doesn't include supplies and specialty food items needed to accommodate the picky eaters among the menagerie.

On a recent afternoon, the aroma of homemade mashed potatoes filled the zoo's kitchen. The meal was for one of the animals that enjoyed variety at lunchtime.

And, honoring the zoo's namesake, visitors can purchase air-popped popcorn to share with some of the farm and domesticated

90 animals that have less-rigid diets.

---

4. ◀ **REREAD AND DISCUSS** Reread lines 57–90. In a small group, discuss the ways Popcorn Park is different from other zoos.

5. **READ** ▶ As you read lines 91–119, continue to cite textual evidence.
   • Underline what Bergmann wants people to learn from the zoo.
   • Circle examples of Bergmann's compassionate character.

110

" *He didn't belong here. . . . All we did was keep him company when he was here.* "

Ⓔ Beyond helping animals in need, Bergmann says that the zoo has a larger mission.

"I always hope, and I always think, [that visitors] walk out of here with more compassion for animals than they walked in here with," he says. "I always thought that was a [large part] of our mission, that we would change the minds of people to have more compassion for animals."

While he seems to have found his dream job, Bergmann says he has trouble with one aspect of his work: saying goodbye to the

100 animals that die.

Sonny, an elephant, had been brought to the United States from Zimbabwe to be trained for circus work. After he resisted his training, he was sent to a New Mexico zoo, from which he escaped several times.

Rather than putting him down, in 1989 the zoo sent a letter to other facilities across the country to see if anyone might give a new home to the troubled creature.

"We were the only one that raised our hand," Bergmann says.

It took extensive care and much training, but Sonny finally

110 adapted to his new surroundings at Popcorn Park and lived there a dozen more years, dying in 2001.

A local funeral home donated its services to host a ceremony for Sonny, and Bergmann delivered a eulogy.

"He didn't belong here," he said, remembering his friend. "All we did was keep him company when he was here."

111

---

4. **REREAD AND DISCUSS USING TEXT EVIDENCE**

Ⓓ **ASK STUDENTS** in each group to present the differences they found. *Students should mention the following differences: Popcorn Park is very much a family operation (lines 57–60), working at Popcorn Park is "doing what you love" (lines 64–66), Popcorn Park takes old and unwanted animals (lines 73–75), Popcorn Park has a kennel from which visitors can adopt household pets (lines 76–77), Popcorn Park's budget mainly comes from donations (line 80), and visitors can feed some of the animals at Popcorn Park (lines 88–90).*

5. **READ AND CITE TEXT EVIDENCE**

Ⓔ **ASK STUDENTS** what Bergmann says about the zoo's "larger mission." *He hopes to "change the minds of" visitors when they go to the park and leave with "more compassion for animals" (lines 95–97).*

FOR ELL STUDENTS Spanish speakers will probably recognize a cognate for *eulogy (line 113): elogio,* meaning "a statement of praise." Point out that the English word *eulogy* often refers to a statement of praise given at a funeral.

For Bergmann, it was bittersweet to see Sonny leave Popcorn Park.
F "It is very sad that he is not with us any longer," Bergmann says,
holding back tears as he adds a comforting thought. "But he is with
his herd again."

6. ◀ **REREAD** Reread lines 116–119. What does Bergmann mean when
he says that Sonny is "with his herd again"?

*He means that Sonny has joined all of the other elephants who have
died. He also is implying that being in a zoo didn't make Sonny any
less of an elephant than those in the wild.*

SHORT RESPONSE

Cite Text Evidence What is the author's purpose in writing this newspaper
article? How does Karas portray Bergmann? Review your reading notes, and
be sure to **cite text evidence** in your response.

*Karas shows how one man's efforts can be the difference between
life and death for many animals—those that are "ill, injured,
exploited, abused, or older." He shows that the animals are well
cared for at Popcorn Park: "Many come from states with severely
overcrowded animal shelters, where animals would not be held long
before being put down." Karas portrays Bergmann as a sensitive,
humble, and kind man—he does this in part by using Bergmann's own
words: "You are doing what you love." He writes that the animals
greet Bergmann like a "rock star," showing that the animals feel as
strongly for him as he does for them.*

112

TO CHALLENGE STUDENTS . . .

For more context, students can research zoos in the United States.

ASK STUDENTS how the mission of zoos has changed over
the last hundred years. *Students should recognize that a century
ago zoos were designed to showcase exotic animals to the public.
Zoos were a spectacle. Scientists—and wealthy hunters and
collectors—used to travel the world in search of new species and
biological wonders. Many of the animals encountered by these
expeditions were shot and preserved, their skins becoming parts of
museum collections. Others, however, were captured, cared for, and
transported back to major U.S. cities, where they were incorporated
into zoological parks. The public flocked to see such incredible beasts
as gorillas, yaks, and kangaroos.*

*In recent decades, many animal species have become endangered
in their native habitats. Zoos have responded by transforming
themselves into conservation centers. Instead of simply showcasing
exotic animals, they now work together to establish and maintain
breeding populations of threatened species. Some zoos even fund
conservation efforts in other countries. The goal of many modern
zoos is to re-introduce species to their native habitats.*

---

6. **REREAD AND CITE TEXT EVIDENCE**

F **ASK STUDENTS** how elephants live in the wild. *Students
should understand that elephants are intelligent, long-living, social
animals that live in large family groups, or herds, that roam vast
distances.* How do elephants live in zoos? *They might live in small
groups of two or three. Their enclosures are rarely more than a
few acres.*

SHORT RESPONSE

Cite Text Evidence Students' responses should include text
evidence that supports their positions. They should:

- describe Karas's purpose(s) in writing the article.
- give examples that show the author's purpose.
- describe Karas's portrayal of Bergmann.

DIG DEEPER

1. With the class, return to Question 1, Read. Have students share what they have circled.

   ASK STUDENTS to discuss what Bergmann's relationship with the animals reveals about his character.

   - Can we learn anything about Bergmann from how he treats the animals at the zoo? If so, what? *Bergmann greets each animal "by name," which shows that in his eyes they are individuals. This aspect of his character is reinforced by the author's observation that Bergmann "has bonded" with each of the zoo's animals. He knows each animal's history, problems, and personality.*

   - Can we learn anything about Bergmann from how the animals treat him? If so, what? *The animals really seem to like Bergmann. They treat him "like a rock star." The chickens ride with him on his golf cart. Tigers rise to greet him and get his attention. So the animals trust Bergmann, which indicates that his affection is genuine—his kind words are backed up by real actions.*

2. With the class, return to Question 5, Read. Have students share what they have circled.

   ASK STUDENTS to discuss how the story of Sonny reveals Bergmann's compassionate character.

   - Why didn't other zoos want to take the elephant? *Sonny was a "troubled creature," unhappy and unruly, perhaps because he wasn't reared in captivity. He was brought from Zimbabwe to the United States to do "circus work," but he "resisted his training" and ended up at a zoo in New Mexico. He didn't like life at the zoo either, because he tried to escape several times.*

   - How would you characterize Bergmann's relationship with Sonny? *Bergmann was realistic, for he knew that Sonny belonged back in Africa: "He didn't belong here." But Bergmann and his staff gave Sonny the care and training he needed, and eventually Sonny became a "friend," another member of the Popcorn Park family.*

   ASK STUDENTS to return to their Short Response answer and revise it based on the class discussion.

CLOSE READING NOTES

EXEMPLAR
A Poem for My Librarian, Mrs. Long

Poem by Nikki Giovanni

Why This Text?

Poetry often reflects on the personal experiences of the writer. Analyzing a poet's style deepens the readers' understanding of those experiences. This lesson focuses on how poets use stylistic techniques to express a central idea.

Key Learning Objective: The student will be able to analyze a poet's style and to determine a theme.

RL 1 Cite textual evidence.
RL 2 Determine theme.
RL 4 Determine the meanings of words and phrases.
RL 5 Analyze how a poem's form contributes to its meaning.
W 3 Write narratives.
W 4 Produce clear and coherent writing.
W 10 Write routinely over extended time frames.
L 1a Explain the function of phrases and clauses.
L 1c Place phrases and clauses within a sentence.

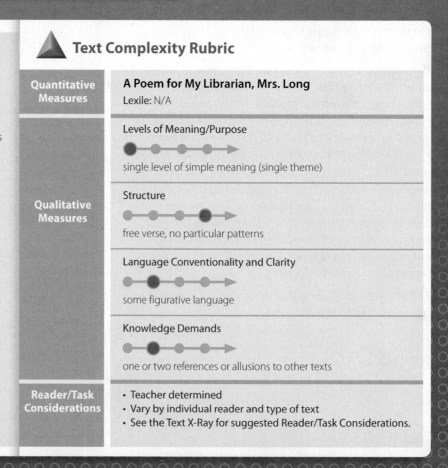

▲ Text Complexity Rubric

	A Poem for My Librarian, Mrs. Long
Quantitative Measures	Lexile: N/A
Qualitative Measures	**Levels of Meaning/Purpose** single level of simple meaning (single theme)
	Structure free verse, no particular patterns
	Language Conventionality and Clarity some figurative language
	Knowledge Demands one or two references or allusions to other texts
Reader/Task Considerations	• Teacher determined • Vary by individual reader and type of text • See the Text X-Ray for suggested Reader/Task Considerations.

English Language Support
Before teaching, use the Text X-Ray for an overview of the text's complexity. The Text X-Ray and the supports and scaffolds in the Teacher's Edition will help you guide students of different skill levels.

Meaning Making

Language Development

Effective Expression

Content Knowledge

Foundational Skills

Text Complexity: Qualitative Measures

Levels of Meaning/Purpose

single level of simple meaning (single theme)

Help students determine the theme of the poem.

- Teacher's Edition side notes, pp. 321, 322, 323, 324
- English Language Support, p. 323
- Determine Theme, p. 324

▶ *Use It!* **Interactive Whiteboard Lesson:** Theme/Central Idea

ZOOM IN ON **DETERMINING THEME** Explain that a poet may convey more than one **theme**, or message, in a poem. After students have read Giovanni's poem, have them return to these lines: 26–27, 38–40, 44–46. Ask pairs to discuss the ideas brought out in these lines and the theme they support, using these sentence frames:

- The stereoscope in the library let the speaker _____. *(visit faraway places in her dreams)*
- The speaker would sit on her gray glider with her books and _____. *(dream of a faraway world)*
- The library with its books and stereoscope helped the speaker understand that _____. *(there was a world beyond the one she lived in)*
- The poet is saying that _____. *(books and knowledge open up our lives to new experiences)*

Structure

free verse, no particular patterns

Help students analyze the elements of a poet's style.

- Teacher's Edition side notes, pp. 321, 322, 323, 324
- English Language Support, p. 321
- When Students Struggle, p. 323
- Strategies for Annotation, p. 324
- Determine Meaning: Style, p. 324

To reteach elements of style in poetry, see

- Determine Meaning: Style, p. 326a

▶ *Use It!* **Level Up Tutorials:** Author's Style, Elements of Poetry

ZOOM IN ON **ANALYZING STYLE** Tell students that every writer has his or her own **style,** or way of expressing ideas.

- Have small groups of students look for and discuss the elements of style explained in the chart on Student Edition page 324.
- Then have them characterize Giovanni's style based on their discussion. Have them write one or more adjectives that describe her unique way of writing in this poem.
- Ask groups to volunteer their adjectives and explain why they chose them. Work together to select the best words to describe Giovanni's style.

Language Conventionality and Clarity

some figurative language

Teach unfamiliar vocabulary in context.

- Applying Academic Vocabulary, p. 322

Support students' discussion and writing about the poem.

- Teacher's Edition side notes, pp. 323, 326
- English Language Support, pp. 325, 326
- Language Conventions: Combining Sentences with Phrases, p. 326

Guide students' analysis of allusions.

- Teacher's Edition side notes, p. 322

To teach how to determine the meaning of allusions, see

- Determine the Meanings of Words and Phrases, p. 326a

ZOOM IN ON **ANALYZING CAPITALIZATION** Point out that an important element of Nikki Giovanni's style in this poem is the use of lowercase letters rather than capital letters for proper names and addresses.

- Display lines 8–27. Work with students to highlight words that should be capitalized. Then rewrite the lines with correct capitalization.
- Have pairs discuss these questions: How does the capitalization change their impression of the poet's style? *(The style becomes more formal and less like the thoughts of someone retracing happy memories.)* What happens to the name of Mrs. Long when the other names are capitalized? *(It no longer stands out; it loses its place of importance.)*

Knowledge Demands

one or two references or allusions to other texts

Support English learners in understanding the historical context of the poem and the poet's background.

- Teacher's Edition Background note, p. 321

ZOOM IN ON **BUILDING CONTEXT** Read lines 41–43 aloud, pointing out how these lines show the speaker's affection for her grandmother. Then tell students that Nikki Giovanni's grandmother was very influential in her life. She credits her grandmother with helping her to value her African American roots; this pride led her to advocate for change in the status of black Americans through her poetry, particularly in the 1960s. By 1970, Giovanni was recognized as a leading literary voice.

Suggested Reader/Task Considerations

Consider the following before assigning this poem to students.

- Will students understand the allusions made throughout the poem?
- Will students need support in order to complete the Performance Task?

ZOOM IN ON **SUPPORTING COMPREHENSION**

- Before students read the poem, remind them that an allusion is a reference to a well-known person, work of art, book, or event. Explain that some of the poet's allusions may be unfamiliar because they refer to people or things from the 1940s and 1950s. Display the poem. Highlight the allusions and, using the footnotes and Teacher's Edition notes, explain each one.
- Suggest that students use a web diagram to help them gather ideas for their poems. Then, as they begin writing first drafts, circulate around the room to help them organize and express their ideas.

CLOSE READ

Background When Nikki Giovanni was growing up in the early 1950s, life for African Americans was very different than it is today. There were many laws that required the separation of blacks and whites. During the time of the Civil Rights Movement, Giovanni became inspired to begin writing poetry. In this poem, the speaker considers the obstacles faced by her Jim Crow–era librarian in obtaining a diverse selection of books to open the wider world to young people.

SETTING A PURPOSE Direct students to use the Setting a Purpose prompt to focus their reading.

Determine Theme (TITLE)   RL 2

Tell students that the theme of a poem is a message about life or human nature that the poet wants to convey. Often, readers must infer, or make a good guess about, the theme from evidence in the text. Explain that authors sometimes reveal the theme in the poem's title.

(A) ASK STUDENTS to reread the title and explain how it might reveal the poem's theme. *(Possible answer: The poet is writing about Mrs. Long, her local or school librarian, who must have helped her find books to borrow when the poet was a troubled little girl. The theme might have to do with the power of books—and people who love books—to change the lives of young people.)*

Determine Meaning: RL 4, RL 5
Style (LINES 1–7)

Explain to students that **style,** or manner of writing, involves *how* something is said rather than *what* is said. Discuss the literary elements that contribute to style:

- **structure:** line lengths, breaks, rhyme scheme, punctuation
- **figurative language:** using words and phrases to express ideas in an imaginative way
- **sound devices:** ways of using words for the sound qualities they create

(B) CITE TEXT EVIDENCE Have students reread lines 1–7 aloud with you and identify elements of style. *(The line structure gives the poem a conversational feel; the repeating sound of words ending in -ing gives the poem rhythm. There is little punctuation, making it feel fluid.)*

Nikki Giovanni (b. 1943) *has been one of the best-known American poets since publishing her first book of poetry in 1968. Giovanni grew up in the racially segregated South. When Giovanni attended college, she became a part of a movement of African American writers who were finding new ways to express pride in their distinct culture. In addition to her poetry collections, Giovanni is also an award-winning children's author.*

A Poem for My Librarian, Mrs. Long

(YOU NEVER KNOW WHAT TROUBLED LITTLE GIRL NEEDS A BOOK)

Poem by Nikki Giovanni

AS YOU READ In the poem, Nikki Giovanni looks back at her childhood and the people who most influenced her. As you read, think about how Giovanni's childhood experiences shaped her dreams and her writing.

(t) ©Monica Morgan/Wireimage/Getty Images; (b) Terry Vine/Stone/Getty Images

At a time when there was no tv before 3:00 P.M.
And on Sunday none until 5:00
We sat on front porches watching
The jfg[1] sign go on and off greeting
5   The neighbors, discussing the political
Situation congratulating the preacher
On his sermon

---

[1] **jfg:** a brand of coffee that was popular in Knoxville, Tennessee; an old electrically lit sign for the coffee is a famous landmark in Knoxville, Tennessee.

A Poem for My Librarian, Mrs. Long   **321**

English Language Support

Analyze Language Explain that some poets use punctuation differently from the way it is used in prose. Display lines 1–7 on the board. Read the lines aloud, repeating them as needed.

- Ask students what they notice about the punctuation. Discuss how the absence of punctuation affects the way the poem is read.
- Ask students to discuss what feeling the lack of punctuation conveys. *(Possible answers: harmony, peace, unity)*

CLOSE READ

Determine the Meanings of Words and Phrases

RL 4

(LINES 8–17)

Explain that in lines 8–17 Giovanni makes **allusions,** or references, to several jazz musicians popular at the time: Nat King Cole, Matt Dennis, Ella Fitzgerald, and Sarah Vaughan. In particular, she alludes to a hit song sung by Vaughan called "Black Coffee."

 ASK STUDENTS to reread lines 8–17 and explain what the allusions reveal about the young Nikki Giovanni. *(These allusions reveal that she loved music. The rhythms of jazz and the words in popular songs may have inspired her love for rhythm and words, which she later shared in her poetry.)*

Determine Meaning:

RL 1, RL 4

Style (LINES 28–33)

Point out that Giovanni's style includes frequent use of figurative language. One example is her use of an **idiom,** or an expression that has a meaning different from the meaning of its individual words.

 CITE TEXT EVIDENCE Ask students to reread lines 28–33 and identify the idiom. Have students explain its meaning in the poem. *(The phrase "hat in hand" is an idiom. It suggests begging and showing respect for someone more powerful. This reveals the powerless position that African Americans had in the southern United States at this time. It shows the speaker's appreciation for Mrs. Long for going to a library in a white neighborhood to borrow the books the girl wanted.)*

Determine Theme

RL 2, RL 4

(LINES 34–40)

Tell students that they can infer the theme of a poem by analyzing the words and actions of the speaker.

 ASK STUDENTS to reread lines 34–40. Ask them what these lines reveal about the poem's theme. *(The speaker tells that because of Mrs. Long she was able to get access to the books she wanted. This supports the idea that the girl is giving thanks to Mrs. Long.)*

There was always radio which brought us
Songs from wlac in nashville and what we would now call
10 Easy listening or smooth jazz but when I listened
Late at night with my portable (that I was so proud of)
Tucked under my pillow
I heard nat king cole and matt dennis, june christy and
      ella fitzgerald
15 And sometimes sarah vaughan sing black coffee
Which I now drink
It was just called music

There was a bookstore uptown on gay street
Which I visited and inhaled that wonderful odor
20 Of new books
Even today I read hardcover as a preference paperback only
As a last resort

And up the hill on vine street
(The main black corridor) sat our carnegie library[2]
25 Mrs. Long always glad to see you
The stereoscope[3] always ready to show you faraway
Places to dream about

Mrs. Long asking what are you looking for today
When I wanted *Leaves of Grass* or alfred north whitehead
30 She would go to the big library uptown and I now know
Hat in hand to ask to borrow so that I might borrow
Probably they said something humiliating since southern
Whites like to humiliate southern blacks

But she nonetheless brought the books
35 Back and I held them to my chest
Close to my heart
And happily skipped back to grandmother's house
Where I would sit on the front porch
In a gray glider and dream of a world
40 Far away

---

[2] **carnegie library:** a library built with money donated by the businessman Andrew Carnegie.

[3] **stereoscope:** an optical instrument with two eyepieces used to create a three-dimensional effect when looking at two photographs of the same scene.

APPLYING ACADEMIC VOCABULARY

despite	interact

THINK-PAIR-SHARE Have students turn to a partner to discuss the following questions. Guide students to include the academic vocabulary words *despite* and *interact* in their responses. Ask volunteers to share their responses with the class.

- Why did Mrs. Long continue to go uptown to get books **despite** the negative **interactions** she most likely encountered?
- How would you describe the speaker's **interaction** with Mrs. Long?

I love the world where I was
I was safe and warm and grandmother gave me neck kisses
When I was on my way to bed

But there was a world
45 Somewhere
Out there
And Mrs. Long opened that wardrobe
But no lions or witches[4] scared me
I went through
50 Knowing there would be
Spring

COLLABORATIVE DISCUSSION Notice how the poet talks about
familiar and faraway places. How does the poem itself travel
to a faraway place? How does it keep the reader grounded in
familiarity? Talk about your ideas with other group members.

---

[4] **wardrobe . . . lions or witches:** refers to *The Lion, the Witch and the Wardrobe*
by C. S. Lewis; in the book, the characters visit a make-believe land, called
Narnia, via the wardrobe, or closet, in a spare room.

WHEN STUDENTS STRUGGLE . . .

Have students use a chart to help them analyze stylistic techniques.

Technique	Example from the Poem
structure	varying line lengths; unconventional punctuation
figurative language	idiom: line 31
sound devices	repeating sounds: lines 3–6

LEVEL UP TUTORIALS For additional support, assign the
following *Level Up* tutorial: **Elements of Poetry.**

CLOSE READ

Determine Meaning: Style (LINES 41–51)
RL 4, RL 5

Tell students that another element that contributes
to Giovanni's style is the structure of the lines and
stanzas. Explain that Giovanni uses varying line
lengths and stanzas to create a rhythm that sounds
like everyday speech. Reread lines 41–51 aloud.

F **ASK STUDENTS** to tell how the line lengths and
stanzas contribute to the poem's meaning. *(Shorter
to longer line lengths help build ideas and link them
together. Different stanzas show movement from
one idea or event to another. The rhythm of the lines
captures the emotions of the speaker.)*

Determine Theme
RL 1, RL 2

(LINES 44–51)

Point out that Giovanni concludes with a final symbol
that contributes to the poem's theme. Explain that a
symbol is a person, a place, an object, or an activity
that stands for something beyond itself. For example,
an olive branch is often seen as a symbol of peace.

G **ASK STUDENTS** to reread lines 44–51. Have
students analyze the lines, identify the symbol, and
explain what it means. *(Spring is a symbol for new
beginnings. In these lines, it means moving into the
future or bigger world with optimism.)*

English Language Support

Guide students through the last stanza of the poem,
making sure they understand the allusion to *The
Lion, the Witch and the Wardrobe* and the idea that
characters emerged into a new world through the
wardrobe, or closet. Ask students what the speaker's
entrance into a new world is. *(books)* Then have them
identify the word she uses to describe that new world.
(spring)

COLLABORATIVE DISCUSSION Have students work
with a partner to identify the way the poet creates both
faraway and familiar places. Then, have partners join the
group and share their ideas in a broader discussion.

CLOSE READ

Determine Meaning: Style   RL 4, RL 5

Discuss the definition of *style* and the ways in which a poet or author's style can be described. Explain that analyzing the words and phrases in a poem can help readers identify a poet's style.

Review the definitions of stylistic techniques listed in the chart, discussing how Nikki Giovanni uses these techniques in "A Poem for My Librarian, Mrs. Long." Ask students to explain what those uses reveal about her style.

Then, have students identify the stylistic technique in lines 8–17. (*Possible answers: The first word in each line is capitalized, and most proper nouns are lowercase. There is no end punctuation and only a few internal commas. As a result, the poem looks informal and suggests speed—as if we are seeing the poet's rush of thoughts and memories.*)

Determine Theme   RL 2

Review the definition of *theme*. Emphasize that the theme of a poem is not always directly stated. Discuss how the theme is conveyed in "A Poem for My Librarian, Mrs. Long." Then, have students reread the poem and answer the question.

(*Possible response: As a child, the poet was a "troubled little girl" who found help and dreams at the local public library. There, Mrs. Long, the librarian, welcomed the girl, was always glad to see her, and encouraged her reading. Mrs. Long gave the girl what she needed—support as well as books. Mrs. Long opened "that wardrobe" so that the girl could enter another world.*)

Determine Meaning: Style   RL 4, RL 5

Style is the particular way in which a poet or author writes—not *what* is said but *how* it is said. It is made up of many elements, including word choice, stanza and line length, figurative language, sound devices, and form. Style can be described with words such as *formal, whimsical, flowery,* and *plain.*

By making careful use of word choices and techniques, a poet can craft poetry with a signature style. For example, "A Poem for My Librarian, Mrs. Long," written by Nikki Giovanni in the form of **free verse**, presents irregular rhythm and rhyme and language that flows like everyday speech. The poet conveys meaning through a variety of stylistic techniques, including:

Punctuation/ Capitalization	Poets might use these in unconventional ways to draw attention or prompt readers to look at something differently.
Stanza and Line Length	In free verse, poets can vary the lengths of stanzas or lines to suit the stylistic effects the poet wants to achieve.
Figurative Language	Using simile and metaphor allows a poet to play creatively with language.
Sound Devices	Along with rhythm and rhyme, a poet can choose from a range of devices, often to create a mood or convey certain meanings.

Read lines 8–17 of "A Poem for My Librarian, Mrs. Long." Identify the stylistic technique you see.

Determine Theme   RL 2

A **theme** is a message about life or human nature that a writer or poet shares with the reader. In poetry, themes are not always stated directly. The reader of a poem can infer a theme by thinking about the poem as a whole and looking at what is said, what is suggested, and how the words, sounds, and ideas come together.

In the poem you've just read, the poet is also the speaker, reflecting on her childhood experiences. After giving details about everyday activities, she turns her attention to her love of books. The poem is dedicated to Mrs. Long, the librarian who likely endured adversity so that the young girl could have access to the books she wanted.

What seems most important to understand about the poet's relationship with Mrs. Long?

Strategies for Annotation   Annotate it!

Determine Meaning   RL 1, RL 4

Share these strategies for guided or independent analysis:

- Highlight in yellow examples of figurative language.
- Highlight in blue examples of sound devices.

But there was a world

Somewhere

Out there

And Mrs. Long opened that wardrobe

But no lions or witches scared me

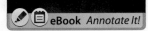
Analyzing the Text

RL 1, RL 2, RL 4,
RL 5, W 3, W 4,
W 10

Cite Text Evidence   Support your responses with evidence from the text.

1. **Cite Evidence** What words would you use to describe the poet as a child? Why would those words fit?

2. **Infer** Reread lines 28–33. What does the poet now understand about Mrs. Long?

3. **Interpret** An **allusion** is a reference to a famous person, place, event, or work of literature. The final stanza of this poem makes an allusion to C. S. Lewis's famous fantasy novel *The Lion, the Witch and the Wardrobe*, in which young characters help end a witch's curse of endless winter. Why might the poet have ended the poem with this allusion?

4. **Analyze** How does the poet's use of punctuation and capitalization contribute to the poem's meaning?

5. **Evaluate** The **tone** of a poem expresses the poet's attitude toward a subject. These are some words that can be used to describe tone: *awed, ironic, thoughtful, grateful, hopeful, angry*. Do any of those words seem to fit this poem? Choose one word, or think of another, that describes the poem's tone, and tell why that word fits the poem.

6. **Analyze** How would you describe Nikki Giovanni's style based on the stylistic techniques she employs in "A Poem for My Librarian, Mrs. Long"?

7. **Draw Conclusions** What could be the theme of this poem?

PERFORMANCE TASK

Writing Activity: Poem Mrs. Long acted generously to a child, and that child never forgot it. Think back to an experience or a connection with someone who acted generously to you. Free-write about your memory—noting phrases, sentences, quotations, and anything else that comes to mind.

Use your written ideas to write a poem in free verse form. Look back at the poem you've just read for ideas about how to:

- convey the sights, sounds, and smells you remember
- portray the person you remember
- tell about your feelings then and now

PRACTICE & APPLY

Analyzing the Text

RL 1, RL 2,
RL 4, RL 5

Possible answers:

1. *She was imaginative because she liked to dream of faraway places. She was intelligent because she read challenging books, like Walt Whitman's* Leaves of Grass *and the philosopher Alfred North Whitehead. She was loving because of her affectionate relationship with her grandmother. She was hopeful because she knew that somewhere out in the world she would find "spring."*

2. *As an adult, the poet realizes the humiliation Mrs. Long went through to bring a child books that were available only in "the big library uptown." Mrs. Long had to ask to borrow the books "hat in hand"—acting deferential and probably enduring humiliation from the white librarians.*

3. *Because the poem deals with the importance of books in childhood, it ends fittingly with an allusion to a popular children's book. The poet might have included this particular book because it's about children who find a magical world behind a wardrobe, which the poet compares to the world made available by Mrs. Long.*

4. *The punctuation and capitalization are used in unconventional ways, or not at all, to draw attention to certain words and phrases and to emphasize ideas.*

5. *The tone of the poem seems dreamy, as the poet moves from memory to memory, as if thinking aloud.*

6. *The poet's style is whimsical yet thoughtful.*

7. *Childhood experiences with loving adults shape a person and are never forgotten.*

English Language Support

Use Nouns and Noun Phrases Tell students that they can bring their subjects to life with adjectives, prepositional phrases, and participial phrases. Display this sentence: *My white-haired, smiling grandmother, perfumed with cookie dough and sweet cinnamon spice, opened her heart and her home to me.*

- Work with students to highlight the adjectives and participial phrase that modify the noun *grandmother*. Ask what picture of the grandmother these words create.

- Then have students write a sentence in a similar pattern about the subject of their poem. Encourage them to add prepositional and participial phrases to modify their nouns. Invite them to read their sentences to a partner.

Assign this
performance task.

PERFORMANCE TASK

W 3, W 4,
W 10

Writing Activity: Poem Have students work independently. Tell students to

- choose a person and an experience to write about
- decide on the main message they want to convey
- choose their words carefully, using only words that are necessary and that enhance meaning

Language Conventions: Combining Sentences with Phrases

L 1a,
L 1c

Review the definitions of types of phrases. Then, display the following sentences:

Mrs. Long wanted to help young Nikki. Mrs. Long would go to the big library uptown.

Explain that students can combine these two sentences using a participial phrase to show a stronger connection between the ideas and to give the sentence a smoother, less choppy rhythm.

Wanting to help young Nikki, Mrs. Long would go to the big library uptown.

Discuss how the combined sentence connects the two ideas more closely. Then, use the examples in the chart to help students understand how to combine two sentences using different types of phrases.

Possible answers:

1. *Sitting on their front porches, families greeted their neighbors. Families sat on their front porches, greeting their neighbors.*

2. *To the young girl visiting the bookstore, new books smelled wonderful. The new books at the bookstore smelled wonderful to the young girl.*

3. *The library was located on Vine Street in the black neighborhood. The library was located in the black neighborhood, on Vine Street.*

4. *Because of her love of poetry, the girl asked the librarian for* Leaves of Grass. *Loving poetry, the girl asked the librarian for* Leaves of Grass.

5. *Mrs. Long borrowed the book from the uptown library, probably facing prejudice there. To borrow the book from the uptown library, Mrs. Long probably faced prejudice.*

6. *The poet says that Mrs. Long opened a wardrobe to help a child find a new world. The poet says that, by opening a wardrobe, Mrs. Long helped a child enter a new world.*

Language Conventions: Combining Sentences with Phrases

L 1a, L 1c

By using phrases to combine sentences, you can vary the length of your sentences and make your writing sound mature. The following are types of phrases you can use to combine sentences.

- A **prepositional phrase** begins with a preposition, such as *at, about, for, from, in,* or *of.*
- An **infinitive phrase** begins with an infinitive verb (*to* + verb).
- A **participial phrase** begins with the past or present participle of a verb, such as *walked* or *walking.*
- A **gerund phrase** begins with a gerund, or *-ing* word. A gerund phrase always functions as a noun, rather than an adjective or an adverb.

The chart below provides an example for how to use each phrase type to combine sentences.

Phrase Type	Two Sentences	Combined Sentence
Prepositional phrase	The poet remembers her childhood. She has vivid memories.	The poet has vivid memories of her childhood.
Infinitive phrase	The stereoscope showed pictures of faraway places. The girl dreamed about the places.	The stereoscope showed the girl pictures of faraway places to dream about.
Participial phrase	The girl held borrowed books close to her heart. She skipped home with them.	Holding her borrowed books close to her heart, the girl skipped home.
Gerund phrase	The poet remembers her librarian. She feels grateful for the librarian's help.	Remembering her librarian's help makes the poet feel grateful.

Practice and Apply Combine the two sentences with a phrase of your choice.

1. Families sat on their front porches. They greeted their neighbors.

2. The young girl visited the bookstore. New books smelled wonderful.

3. The library was located in the black neighborhood. It was on Vine Street.

4. The girl loved poetry. She asked the librarian for *Leaves of Grass.*

5. Mrs. Long borrowed the book from the uptown library. She probably faced prejudice there.

6. The poet says that Mrs. Long opened a wardrobe. Mrs. Long helped a child enter a new world.

English Language Support

Condense Ideas Review the types of phrases listed in the chart. Discuss how the combined sentences show clear connections between ideas.

- Work together to complete the first Practice and Apply item. Then assign the other items to pairs or small groups. Have them combine their sentences and explain their new sentences to the class.

- Have students complete the activity independently and then compare answers with a partner.

Determine the Meanings of Words and Phrases

RL 4

TEACH

Explain that an **allusion** is a reference to a famous person, place, event, or other work of literature. Then, discuss the following points:

- Poets use allusions to help them convey meaning in a single word or two.
- In order to understand an allusion, the reader must understand the meaning of the reference.
- No reader can recognize every allusion. It is sometimes necessary to do research in order to understand the reference.

Guide students to interpret examples such as the following:

- My mom is no Scrooge, but she almost never buys things she doesn't need. *(Scrooge is a character from* A Christmas Carol, *by Charles Dickens, who is stingy and mean. A Scrooge refers to a person who is miserly.)*
- That girl has a Mona Lisa smile. *(Leonardo Da Vinci's* Mona Lisa *is a painting of a woman that is known for her mysterious smile. A Mona Lisa smile is one that is very hard to understand.)*

PRACTICE AND APPLY

Students can apply the skill to identify and analyze some of the allusions in "A Poem for My Librarian, Mrs. Long" that they have not already explored. Have students answer the following questions about each allusion:

- What does the allusion refer to?
- What do you need to know about the allusion to understand its meaning in the poem?

Have students record their responses in a three-column chart like the one shown.

Allusion	What It References	Meaning in Poem
jfg		
gay street		
vine street		
wardrobe		

Determine Meaning: Style

RL 4, RL 5

RETEACH

Discuss with students their favorite types of music. Have students name different recording artists and discuss how each artist has a unique sound. Point out that this unique sound is the singer's or musician's own style—the way that the artist sings or plays music.

Review that in literature **style** is an author's unique way of writing; it is *how* something is written rather than *what* is written. Remind students that the following literary elements are part of an author's style:

- **punctuation/capitalization:** using unconventional ways to draw attention or prompt readers to look at something differently
- **stanza and line length:** varying lengths of lines and stanzas to create different effects
- **figurative language:** using simile and metaphor to play creatively with language
- **sound devices:** using different techniques to create mood or convey meaning

Reread the poem aloud. Work with students to identify elements of style in the poem.

LEVEL UP TUTORIALS Assign the following *Level Up* tutorial: **Author's Style**

INDEPENDENT READING

Individual students can apply these skills to analyze another poem of their choosing. After their analysis, have students discuss the styles of other poets with a partner or small group.

Train Time

Short Story by D'Arcy McNickle

Why This Text?

This short story offers students an opportunity to analyze in depth a character with complex motivations as well as a moral dilemma set in an often-overlooked episode in our country's history. The story's sophisticated structure includes the use of flashback, and the lesson guides students to understand and analyze this literary technique.

Key Learning Objective: The student will be able to analyze methods of characterization and flashback in a short story.

RL 1 Cite text evidence.
RL 2 Determine theme or central idea.
RL 3 Analyze how elements of a story interact.
RL 4 Determine the meaning of words and phrases.
RL 6 Analyze points of view of different characters or narrators.
W 1 Write arguments to support claims.
W 4 Produce clear and coherent writing.
W 9a Apply *Grade 7* Reading standards to literature.
W 10 Write routinely for a range of tasks, purposes, and audiences.
L 1c Place phrases and clauses within a sentence, correcting misplaced modifiers.
L 4c Consult reference materials to determine or clarify meaning.
L 6 Acquire and use general academic words and phrases.

▲ Text Complexity Rubric

Quantitative Measures	**Train Time** Lexile: 670L
Qualitative Measures	**Levels of Meaning/Purpose** single, but somewhat complex, theme
	Structure somewhat complex story concepts; several shifts in chronology, e.g., flashback and flash forward
	Language Conventionality and Clarity fairly accessible language, but some longer descriptions and less straightforward sentence structure
	Knowledge Demands single perspective, with a moderately complex theme; some cultural and historical knowledge useful
Reader/Task Considerations	• Teacher determined Vary by individual reader and type of text • See the Text X-Ray for suggested Reader/Task Considerations.

English Language Support Before teaching, use the Text X-Ray for an overview of the text's complexity. The Text X-Ray and the supports and scaffolds in the Teacher's Edition will help you guide students of different skill levels.

Meaning Making

Language Development

Effective Expression

Content Knowledge

Foundational Skills

Text Complexity: Qualitative Measures

Levels of Meaning/Purpose

single, but somewhat complex, theme

Help students analyze character development.
- Teacher's Edition side notes, pp. 328, 330, 331, 332, 333
- English Language Support, p. 329
- When Students Struggle, p. 328
- Strategies for Annotation, p. 333
- Analyze Stories: Character Development, p. 333

To reteach how to analyze characterization, see
- Analyze Stories: Characterization, p. 336a

 Use It! **Level Up Tutorial:** Methods of Characterization

ZOOM IN ON **ANALYZING CHARACTER DEVELOPMENT** Review the four methods of **characterization** as described on Student Edition page 333. Write these words on the board: *conscientious, principled, stubborn.* Discuss the meaning of each with students. Then organize students into small groups.

- Assign each group one of the adjectives. Have them reread the story to find details that support that trait for each character.
- Have groups share their work with the class.

Structure

somewhat complex story concepts; several shifts in chronology, e.g., flashback and flash forward

Help students analyze the use of flashback and other story elements.
- Teacher's Edition side notes, pp. 327, 329, 330, 331, 332, 333
- English Language Support, p. 331
- Analyze Stories: Flashback, p. 333

To teach how to analyze the setting of a story, see
- Analyze Story Elements: Setting, p. 336a

 Use It! **Interactive Whiteboard Lesson:** Setting

ZOOM IN ON **ANALYZING FLASHBACK** After reading, define **flashback** as an event included in a story that happened before the story's main action. Have partners use these questions to analyze the author's purpose for including a flashback in this story:

- How do the flashback details about Eneas's relationship with his grandparents and his view of his living situation help readers see the situation from the children's viewpoint? *(Possible response: The flashback shows that Eneas is devoted to his grandparents. This helps readers feel sympathy for the children and anger that they are being torn from their homes.)*
- What does the author accomplish by including the flashback? *(Possible response: The author wants readers to understand the children's and families' perspective; although the plan seemed beneficial, in fact, it caused great heartache and hardship.)*

Language Conventionality and Clarity

○—●—○—○—→

fairly accessible language, but some longer descriptions and less straightforward sentence structure

Teach unfamiliar vocabulary in context.

- Teacher's Edition Critical Vocabulary notes, pp. 328, 329, 330, 332, 335
- Applying Academic Vocabulary, p. 330
- Strategies for Annotation, p. 335
- Vocabulary Strategy: Using a Dictionary, p. 335

Support students' comprehension and response to the story.

- Teacher's Edition side notes, pp. 332, 336
- English Language Support, pp. 327, 331, 334, 336
- Performance Task, p. 334
- Language Conventions: Dangling Modifiers, p. 336

ZOOM IN ON USING CONTEXT Display these words: *bellowing* (line 9); *earnestly* (line 29); *stifling* (line 39); *pondered* (line 81); *shirking* (line 122); *remorse* (line 185).

- Model using context clues to define *bellowing*. Explain that the word *steer* refers to male cattle raised for beef. Since the characters have heard a sound, *bellowing* must refer to the roar that a large livestock animal makes.
- The have students use the same strategy to define the other words, confirming the definitions in the dictionary.

Knowledge Demands

●—●—○—○—→

single perspective with a moderately complex theme; some cultural and historical knowledge useful

Support English Learners in understanding the historical context of the story.

- Teacher's Edition Background note, p. 327

ZOOM IN ON UNDERSTANDING CONTEXT The predominant belief about Native Americans during the 1800s reform movement was that they needed to blend in with the rest of society. Share these facts:

- Reformers began building schools near reservations. However, since children returned home at night, their community ties remained strong. Eventually, distant boarding schools were built, ending students' daily contact with their families.
- At these schools, children were not allowed to speak their own language or wear their own clothes. Ironically, one effect of the boarding schools was to create unity among groups of Native Americans, which led to a successful activism movement in the 1970s.

Suggested Reader/Task Considerations

Consider the following before assigning this short story to students.

- Will students be able to make inferences about characters' traits from the details in the story?
- Will students be overly challenged by the Analyzing the Text questions on page 334?

ZOOM IN ON SUPPORTING COMPREHENSION

- Model how to infer the Major's traits from the details in lines 124–133. Say: *In this paragraph, the Major makes his proposal to Eneas. The details show that the Major is determined; he is a problem solver; and he sees things from Eneas's perspective.*
- Have students work in mixed-ability groups to answer the questions. Assign one question to each group and have them share their responses with the class.

CLOSE READ

Background Have students read the background and information about the author. Tell students that in addition to his writing, D'Arcy McNickle was respected as a scholar and activist. He was the first director of the Chicago Newberry Library's Center for the History of the American Indian, which now is named after him. McNickle was an administrator in the U.S. Bureau of Indian Affairs and a founding member of the National Congress of American Indians. Although he sold his allotment of reservation land to finance his education at Oxford, McNickle remained a strong voice in support of Native American rights and culture.

SETTING A PURPOSE Direct students to use the Setting a Purpose question to focus their reading. Remind students to generate their own questions as they read.

Analyze Story Elements: Mood (LINES 1–16)

RL 1, RL 4

Tell students that the **mood** is the feeling or atmosphere that a writer creates for the reader. Descriptive words, imagery, and dialogue can all help to establish the mood.

(A) **CITE TEXT EVIDENCE** Ask students to reread lines 1–16 and describe the mood the author establishes at the beginning of the story. Have students cite supporting evidence in the text. *(The mood is one of expectancy: "everybody stood waiting, listening"; "all stood waiting and gazing eastward"; "boys pushed forward to the edge of the platform." There is also a sense of confusion, as shown by the dialogue about whether anyone had heard the train whistle.)*

Background *In the late 1800s, social reformers in the United States believed they could help move Native Americans into mainstream society by re-educating Native American children away from their families. Author* **D'Arcy McNickle** *(1904–1977) was forced to go to a boarding school. McNickle went on to college where he became interested in literature and writing. In his stories, he gained a reputation for vivid descriptions of how the larger mainstream culture affected traditional Native American ways.*

Train Time

Short Story by D'Arcy McNickle

SETTING A PURPOSE As you read, think about the moral problem that the main character is faced with. What is that problem, and how does he deal with it?

(A) On the depot platform everybody stood waiting, listening. The train has just whistled, somebody said. They stood listening and gazing eastward, where railroad tracks and creek emerged together from a tree-choked canyon.

Twenty-five boys, five girls, Major Miles—all stood waiting and gazing eastward. Was it true that the train had whistled?

"That was no train!" a boy's voice explained.

"It was a steer bellowing."

10 "It was the train!"

Girls crowded backward against the station building, heads hanging, tears starting; boys pushed forward to the edge of the platform. An older boy with a voice already turning heavy stepped off the weather-shredded boardwalk and stood wide-legged in the middle of the track. He was the doubter. He had heard no train.

©Flirt/SuperStock

English Language Support

Understand Cohesion Explain that indefinite pronouns do not name a specific person, place, or thing. Tell students that these words often end in *body*, *one*, or *thing*, although words such as *some*, *all*, *several*, and *many* are also indefinite pronouns. Display lines 1–4.

- Have students locate the indefinite pronoun in line 1. *(everybody)* Then have them read line 5. Ask them who *everybody* is. *(twenty-five boys, five girls, Major Miles)*

- Ask students to identify the indefinite pronouns in lines 1 and 2. *(everybody, somebody)* Discuss how these pronouns change the

focus from the characters to their actions. Ask what idea is emphasized and what mood this creates. *(The idea of waiting is emphasized, creating a mood of suspense, expectancy.)*

- Have students identify the indefinite pronouns as well as the personal pronouns in lines 1–4. Ask them to identify antecedents for these pronouns, suggesting that they look further in the text. Then have them explain why the author started his story this way. How does the use of these pronouns affect the readers' focus on the scene?

Analyze Stories: Character Development (LINES 28–36)

RL 1,
RL 3

Explain that authors make characters seem real through **characterization,** methods of revealing the characters' **traits,** or qualities. Two key methods of characterization are through the narrator's comments and through the character's own words, actions, and thoughts.

B CITE TEXT EVIDENCE Ask students to reread lines 28–36 and to cite what the narrator tells us directly about the Major. Then, ask what we can infer about the Major from his own actions and thoughts. (*The narrator tells us that the Major is a "man of conscience" and does things "earnestly." From the Major's "soldier bearing," we learn that he is dutiful. The "words [that] tumbled about in his mind" show that he believes in what he is doing and is frustrated at the children's reactions.*)

CRITICAL VOCABULARY

exasperate: The author tells us that the Major was exasperated.

ASK STUDENTS to explain why the Major feels that way. (*The Major feels exasperated because he has achieved what he sees as a worthy goal—sending the children to boarding school. But they resist his efforts rather than appreciate them.*)

conscience: Major Miles is described as a "man of conscience."

ASK STUDENTS what they would expect from a person of conscience. (*Possible answer: I would expect such a person to have strong ideas about what is right and to live up to them.*)

Major Miles boomed, "You! What's your name? Get back here! Want to get killed! All of you, stand back!"

The Major strode about, soldierlike, and waved
20 commands. He was **exasperated**. He was tired. A man driving cattle through timber had it easy, he was thinking. An animal trainer had no idea of trouble. Let anyone try corralling twenty to thirty Indian kids, dragging them out of hiding places, getting them away from relatives and together in one place, then holding them, without tying them, until train time! Even now, at the last moment, when his worries were almost over, they were trying to get themselves killed!

B Major Miles was a man of **conscience**. Whatever he did,
30 he did earnestly. On this hot end-of-summer day he perspired and frowned and wore his soldier bearing. He removed his hat from his wet brow and thoughtfully passed his hand from the hair line backward. Words tumbled about in his mind. Somehow, he realized, he had to vivify[1] the moment. These children were about to go out from the Reservation and get a new start. Life would change. They ought to realize it, somehow—

"Boys—and girls—" there were five girls he remembered. He had got them all lined up against the building, safely away from the edge of the platform. The air was stifling with end-
40 of-summer heat. It was time to say something, never mind the heat. Yes, he would have to make the moment real. He stood soldierlike and thought that.

"Boys and girls—" The train whistled, dully, but unmistakably. Then it repeated more clearly. The rails came to life, something was running through them and making them sing.

C Just then the Major's eye fell upon little Eneas and his sure voice faltered. He knew about little Eneas. Most of the boys and girls were mere names; he had seen them around
50 the Agency with their parents, or had caught sight of them scurrying behind tipis and barns when he visited their homes. But little Eneas he knew. With him before his eyes, he paused.

He remembered so clearly the winter day, six months ago, when he first saw Eneas. It was the boy's grandfather, Michel Lamartine, he had gone to see. Michel had contracted to cut wood for the Agency but had not started work. The Major had gone to discover why not.

---

[1] **vivify:** to make more lively.

exasperate
(ĭg-zăs´pə-rāt´) *v.*
If you *exasperate* someone, you make the person very angry.

conscience
(kŏn´shəns) *n.*
Conscience is the conforming to or living up to one's own sense of what is right.

WHEN STUDENTS STRUGGLE . . .

To guide students in understanding the author's use of characterization, have them work in pairs to fill out a chart like the one shown. Explain that from supporting evidence in the text they can make inferences about the Major's character traits. Supporting evidence can include what the narrator tells us as well as what the Major himself says, does, and thinks. Model how to begin filling out the chart, and have students continue completing it as they read the rest of the story.

Character Traits	Supporting Evidence
wants to do the right thing	*"man of conscience"*
proud	*"soldier bearing"*

LEVEL UP TUTORIALS For additional support, assign the following *Level Up* tutorial: **Methods of Characterization.**

It was the coldest day of the winter, late in February, and the cabin, sheltered as it was among the pine and cottonwood of a creek bottom, was shot through by frosty drafts. There was wood all about them. Lamartine was a woodcutter besides, yet there was no wood in the house. The fire in the flat-topped cast-iron stove burned weakly. The reason was apparent. The Major had but to look at the bed where Lamartine lay, twisted and shrunken by rheumatism.[2] Only his black eyes burned with life. He tried to wave a hand as the Major entered.

"You see how I am!" the gesture indicated. Then a nerve-strung voice faltered. "We have it bad here. My old woman, she's not much good."

Clearly she wasn't, not for wood-chopping. She sat close by the fire, trying with a good-natured grin to lift her **ponderous** body from a low seated rocking chair. The Major had to motion her back to her ease. She breathed with an asthmatic[3] roar. Wood-chopping was not within her range. With only a squaw's hatchet[4] to work with, she could scarcely have come within striking distance of a stick of wood. Two blows, if she had struck them, might have put a stop to her laboring heart.

"You see how it is," Lamartine's eyes flashed.

The Major saw clearly. Sitting there in the frosty cabin, he pondered their plight and at the same time wondered if he would get away without coming down with pneumonia.[5] A stream of wind seemed to be hitting him in the back of the neck. Of course, there was nothing to do. One saw too many such situations. If one undertook to provide **sustenance** out of one's own pocket there would be no end to the demands. Government salaries were small, resources were limited. He could do no more than shake his head sadly, offer some vague hope, some small sympathy. He would have to get away at once.

Then a hand fumbled at the door; it opened. After a moment's struggle, little Eneas appeared, staggering under a full armload of pine limbs hacked into short lengths. The boy was no taller than an ax handle, his nose was running, and

ponderous
(pŏn′dər-əs) *adj.*
If something is *ponderous*, it is very heavy.

sustenance
(sŭs′tə-nəns) *n.*
Sustenance is the food needed to live.

---

[2] **rheumatism** (rōō′mə-tĭz′əm): a disease causing stiffness in the joints and muscles.

[3] **asthmatic** (ăz′măt′ĭk): characterized by labored breathing and coughing.

[4] **squaw's hatchet**: a small hand ax used by Native American women to cut small things.

[5] **pneumonia** (nŏŏ-mōn′yə): a disease causing inflammation of the lungs.

Train Time **329**

CLOSE READ

Analyze Stories: Flashback (LINES 47–57)

RL 3

Explain that the author interrupts the scene at the depot with a **flashback,** a description of events that took place at an earlier time. A flashback can give the reader insight into the characters' current situation.

C ASK STUDENTS to reread lines 47–57. Ask what time period the flashback refers to and why the author includes it. (*It refers to a winter day six months ago when the Major first saw Eneas. It explains how he knew Eneas and why he feels differently about him.*)

Tell students to pay attention to what other insights the rest of the flashback (lines 58–166) gives into the scene at the depot.

CRITICAL VOCABULARY

ponderous: The author describes the old woman's body as "ponderous."

ASK STUDENTS why he might have chosen this word instead of *heavy* or *huge*. (Ponderous *conveys how hard it was for the woman to move.*)

sustenance: The Major felt that he could not provide sustenance for the Lamartine family.

ASK STUDENTS why it might not have been wise for the Major to provide sustenance. (*There were so many poor families in need of food that he could never provide for them all.*)

English Language Support

Read Closely Display lines 80–90. Read the paragraph aloud.

- Discuss the method of characterization the author uses in this paragraph to reveal the Major's traits. (*The author shows what the Major is thinking.*) Then write these phrases on the board: *eager to help; unwilling to get involved.* Have students choose the one that describes the Major based on his thoughts.

- Model how to use a Read Aloud/Think Aloud strategy to make an inference about the Major's character based on lines 80–82.

(*The Major is almost as concerned for himself as he is for the couple.*) Then have students use the same strategy to make inferences about the Major from lines 84–90. (*Possible response: The Major is not influenced by emotion; rather, he is very practical and logical as shown by his acceptance that he can't help everyone.*)

- Have students write a short paragraph describing what they learn about the Major from his thoughts. Remind them to include details from the text that support their analysis.

Analyze Stories: Character Development (LINES 99–118)   RL 1

Remind students that authors often provide clues to a character's traits through the character's own words and actions.

D **CITE TEXT EVIDENCE** Have students reread lines 99–118. Ask what we learn about the Major from this portion of the text and why the Major acted "against his own principles" in helping the family. *(This text provides further evidence that the Major is a "man of conscience" who wants to do the right thing. He is also capable of being touched by the devotion and loyalty that Eneas displays: "Something about the boy made the Major forget his determination to depart." This causes him to go against his principles, which oppose paying out of his own pocket to provide sustenance for the Indian families.)*

Analyze Stories: Flashback (LINES 124–133)   RL 1, RL 3

Remind students that the author interrupted the scene at the depot with a flashback to the previous winter. Point out that while the flashback scene continues, in line 124 the action flashes forward in time.

E **CITE TEXT EVIDENCE** Ask students to reread lines 124–133 and to identify the evidence that signals the shift in time. Ask what has happened to the Major during that time. *(Evidence: "some weeks later." During those weeks, the Major has figured out a plan for helping Eneas and his family.)*

CRITICAL VOCABULARY

inexplicable: The Major inexplicably changed his mind about helping Eneas's family.

ASK STUDENTS what might cause a person to behave inexplicably. *(an experience or event that has a strong impact and causes the person to change long-held beliefs, such as the impact that meeting Eneas had on the Major)*

---

he had a croupy cough.[6] He dropped the wood into the empty box near the old woman's chair, then straightened himself.

A soft chuckling came from the bed. Lamartine was full of pride. "A good boy, that. He keeps the old folks warm."

D Something about the boy made the Major forget his determination to depart. Perhaps it was his wordlessness, his uncomplaining wordlessness. Or possibly it was his loyalty to the old people. Something drew his eyes to the boy and set him to thinking. Eneas was handing sticks of wood to the old woman and she was feeding them into the stove. When the firebox was full a good part of the boy's armload was gone. He would have to cut more, and more, to keep the old people warm.

The Major heard himself saying suddenly: "Sonny, show me your woodpile. Let's cut a lot of wood for the old folks."

110   It happened just like that, **inexplicably**. He went even farther. Not only did he cut enough wood to last through several days, but when he had finished he put the boy in the Agency car and drove him to town, five miles there and back. Against his own principles, he bought a week's store of groceries, and excused himself by telling the boy, as they drove homeward, "Your grandfather won't be able to get to town for a few days yet. Tell him to come see me when he gets well."

That was the beginning of the Major's interest in Eneas.
120   He had decided that day that he would help the boy in any way possible, because he was a boy of quality. You would be shirking your duty if you failed to recognize and to help a boy of his sort. The only question was, how to help?

E When he saw the boy again, some weeks later, his mind saw the problem clearly. "Eneas," he said, "I'm going to help you. I'll see that the old folks are taken care of, so you won't have to think about them. Maybe the old man won't have rheumatism next year, anyhow. If he does, I'll find a family where he and the old lady can move in and be looked after.
130   Don't worry about them. Just think about yourself and what I'm going to do for you. Eneas, when it comes school time, I'm going to send you away. How do you like that?" The Major smiled at his own happy idea.

inexplicable
(ĭn-ĕkˈsplĭ-kə-bəl) *adj.* If something is *inexplicable*, it is difficult to understand.

---

[6] **croupy cough:** an illness that causes a loud barking cough.

APPLYING ACADEMIC VOCABULARY

contrast	despite	error

THINK-PAIR-SHARE Have students turn to a partner to discuss the following questions. Guide students to include the academic vocabulary words *contrast*, *despite*, and *error* in their responses. Ask volunteers to share their responses with the class.

- **Contrast** the Major's viewpoint with that of the families on the Reservation. Why does he feel he is right **despite** the attitudes of the families?

- Do you think he has made an **error** in judgment? Why or why not?

> He had decided that day that he would help the boy in any way possible.

There was silence. No shy smiling, no look of gratitude, only silence. Probably he had not understood.

"You understand, Eneas? Your grandparents will be taken care of. You'll go away and learn things. You'll go on a train."

The boy looked here and there and scratched at the ground with his foot. "Why do I have to go away?"

140 "You don't have to, Eneas. Nobody will make you. I thought you'd like to. I thought—" The Major paused, confused.

"You won't make me go away, will you?" There was fear in the voice, tears threatened.

"Why, no Eneas. If you don't want to go. I thought—"

The Major dropped the subject. He didn't see the boy again through spring and summer, but he thought of him. In fact, he couldn't forget the picture he had of him that first day. He couldn't forget either that he wanted to help him. Whether 150 the boy understood what was good for him or not, he meant to see to it that the right thing was done. And that was why, when he made up a quota[7] of children to be sent to the school in Oregon, the name of Eneas Lamartine was included. The Major did not discuss it with him again but he set the wheels in motion. The boy would go with the others. In time to come, he would understand. Possibly he would be grateful.

Thirty children were included in the quota, and of them all Eneas was the only one the Major had actual knowledge of, the only one in whom he was personally interested. With each 160 of them, it was true, he had had difficulties. None had wanted to go. They said they "liked it at home," or they were "afraid" to go away, or they would "get sick" in a strange country; and the parents were no help. They, too, were frightened and uneasy. It was a tiresome, hard kind of duty, but the Major knew what was required of him and never hesitated.

---

[7] **quota:** a predetermined, fixed amount of something or people.

Train Time **331**

Analyze Stories: Flashback (LINES 146–153)

RL 1, RL 2, RL 3

Explain that once again the action of the story flashes forward in time. Although we are still in the flashback scene, lines 146–153 bring us closer to the opening scene at the depot.

F ASK STUDENTS to reread lines 146–153. Have students identify the time shift and summarize what has occurred during that period. *(The time shift is signaled by "He didn't see the boy again through spring and summer." During that time, the Major has decided that the best way to help Eneas is to include him in a group of children being sent away to school.)*

Analyze Stories: Character Development (LINES 149–165)

RL 1, RL 3

Point out that in lines 149–151 the Major thinks, "Whether the boy understood what was good for him or not, he meant to see to it that the right thing was done."

G CITE TEXT EVIDENCE Ask students what they can infer about the Major's character from this statement. *(He is stubborn. He is so certain that he is right, he is unable to see that others may hold different opinions.)* Ask students to continue rereading lines 151–165 and cite additional evidence to support their inference. *("The Major did not discuss it with him again but he set the wheels in motion"; "In time to come, he would understand. Possibly he would be grateful"; "None had wanted to go"; ". . . the Major knew what was required of him and never hesitated.")*

English Language Support

Understand Cohesion Tell students that transitional expressions, such as *for instance, as a result, next, in addition,* and *consequently,* help readers know how ideas are connected. Display lines 146–156.

- Work with students to highlight transitional words and phrases. *("In fact" in line 147, "And that was why" in line 151, "In time to come," in line 155)* Using a Read Aloud/Think Aloud strategy, guide students to see the function of each transition. *("in fact": to add emphasis; "and that was why": to highlight cause/effect; "in time to come": to point ahead)*

- Have students work in pairs to identify transitional words and expressions. Have them alternate reading the sentences with the transitions and without them. Ask them to explain how the meaning of each sentence is affected if the transition is omitted.

- Have students write three sentences summarizing the ideas conveyed in lines 146–156. Then ask them to include three transitions that link the ideas in their sentences. Call on volunteers to read their summaries aloud.

Analyze Stories:
Flashback (LINES 166–170)

RL 1,
RL 2,
RL 3

Explain that here, almost at the end of the story, the author ends the flashback and brings us back to the depot.

 CITE TEXT EVIDENCE Have students reread lines 166–170 and cite evidence that shows the end of the flashback. *("this moment of going away")* Ask them to summarize the insight the flashback gives into this scene. *(The flashback has given insight into why the Major feels that he is doing a good thing for Eneas and the other children, despite the contrast with their own feelings. It has also shown why the Major has taken such an interest in Eneas and believes that he is "a boy who, with the right help, would blossom and grow strong.")*

Determine Meanings of Words and Phrases

RL 4

(LINES 181–188)

Explain that D'Arcy McNickle uses vivid **imagery,** or words that appeal to the senses, in his description of the approaching train.

ASK STUDENTS to reread lines 181–188 and to identify examples of imagery. Ask what effect is created by the imagery. *(Examples: "pounding near"; "headlong flying locomotive"; "Whoo-oo, whoo-oo"; "roar of rolling steel." The imagery creates the effect of tremendous speed and of time passing too quickly.)*

> **CRITICAL VOCABULARY**
>
> **ignorance**: The Major believed that he was freeing the children from ignorance by sending them away.
>
> **ASK STUDENTS** to explain why he believed that. *(He believed they were ignorant of mainstream learning and culture. He was sending them to school to be educated.)*

COLLABORATIVE DISCUSSION Have small groups discuss the Major's successes and failures. Remind them to take notes as they talk and to cite evidence for their ideas. Have each group share their conclusions with the class.

The difference was, that in the cases of all these others, the problem was routine. He met it, and passed over it. But in the case of Eneas, he was bothered. He wanted to make clear what this moment of going away meant. It was a breaking
170 away from fear and doubt and **ignorance**. Here began the new. Mark it, remember it.

His eyes lingered on Eneas. There he stood, drooping, his nose running as on that first day, his stockings coming down, his jacket in need of buttons. But under that shabbiness, the Major knew, was real quality. There was a boy who, with the right help, would blossom and grow strong. It was important that he should not go away hurt and resentful.

The Major called back his straying thoughts and cleared his throat. The moment was important.
180 "Boys and girls—"

The train was pounding near. Already it had emerged from the canyon, and momentarily the headlong flying locomotive loomed blacker and larger. A white plume flew upward—*Whoo-oo, whoo-oo.*

The Major realized in sudden sharp remorse that he had waited too long. The vital moment had come, and he had paused, looked for words, and lost it. The roar of rolling steel was upon them.

Lifting his voice in desperate haste, his eyes fastened on
190 Eneas, he bellowed: "Boys and girls—be good—"

That was all anyone heard.

ignorance
(ĭg´nər-əns) *n.*
Ignorance is the condition of being uneducated or uninformed.

COLLABORATIVE DISCUSSION What has the Major succeeded in doing? What has he failed to do? Talk about your ideas with other group members.

TO CHALLENGE STUDENTS . . .

Character's Point of View In "Train Time," we learn a great deal about the Major's thoughts, beliefs, and motivations. But what about Eneas? What is he thinking as he stands on the platform waiting for the train? What would he like to say to the Major? to his grandparents?

ASK STUDENTS to discuss these questions in a group and to compose a brief monologue for Eneas. Remind students to review the story for evidence to support their ideas. Have volunteers deliver their monologues to the class.

Analyze Stories: Character Development

RL 2, RL 3

The **characters** in a work of fiction are the people, animals, or imaginary creatures who take part in the action. The way that the author creates and develops the characters is called **characterization**. Authors use four basic methods of characterization:

Methods of Characterization

- making direct comments about a character through the voice of the narrator
- describing the character's physical appearance
- presenting the character's speech, thoughts, and actions
- presenting information about the character through the thoughts, speech, and actions of other characters

With these methods, the author helps readers identify **character traits,** which are the qualities of appearance and personality that make a character seem real. Readers can infer character traits from the character's words, actions, thoughts, appearance, and interactions with other characters.

Reread lines 53–118 of "Train Time," the paragraphs in which the Major first meets Eneas. Tell how the author uses each of the four listed methods of characterization to show Eneas to readers and to develop his character.

Analyze Stories: Flashback

RL 3

In a literary work, a **flashback** is an interruption of the action to show events that took place at an earlier time. A flashback provides information to help readers understand a character's current situation. To follow a narrative, readers pay attention to language that signals shifts in time. For example:

the author shifts back in time, using flashback	"Stanley thought back to last month, when he first saw his new home."
the author ends the flashback, shifting ahead to the present time of the story	"Now, just one month later, Stanley felt as if he had never lived anywhere else."

In which sentence of "Train Time" does the author first lead readers back in time?

CLOSE READ

Analyze Stories: Character Development

RL 2, RL 3

Review the term *characterization* and the four methods. Have students reread lines 53–118 of "Train Time" and identify examples of each method and what the examples reveal about Eneas. *(Possible answers: Narrator's direct comments: "Perhaps it was his wordlessness, his uncomplaining wordlessness. Or possibly it was his loyalty to the old people." These examples reveal that Eneas is loyal, kind, patient, and tolerant. Physical appearance: "The boy was no taller than an ax handle, his nose was running, and he had a croupy cough." Character's actions: " . . . staggering under a full armload of pine limbs . . . He dropped the wood into the empty box near the old woman's chair, then straightened himself. . . . Eneas was handing sticks of wood to the old woman." These reveal that Eneas is barely able to do the chores, but he is determined to help others. Thoughts, speech, and actions of other characters: "Lamartine was full of pride. 'A good boy, that. He keeps the old folks warm.'" This reveals Eneas's devotion to the older people.)*

Analyze Stories: Flashback

RL 3

Review the term *flashback* and the examples. Point out that the flashback in "Train Time" begins in lines 53–54: "He remembered . . . when he first saw Eneas." Explain that students should think about why the author included the flashback and what it reveals.

Strategies for Annotation *Annotate it!*

Analyze Stories: Character Development

RL 2, RL 3

Share these strategies for guided or independent analysis:

- Highlight in yellow the narrator's comments about Eneas.
- Highlight in blue descriptions of Eneas's appearance.
- Highlight in pink descriptions of Eneas's actions.
- Highlight in green a character's speech, thoughts, or actions that reveal something about Eneas.

. . . little Eneas appeared, staggering under a full armload of pine limbs hacked into short lengths. The boy was no taller than an ax handle, his nose was running, and he had a croupy cough. He dropped the wood into the empty box near the old woman's chair, then straightened himself. Lamartine was full of pride. "A good boy, that. He keeps the old folks warm."

PRACTICE & APPLY

Analyzing the Text

RL 1, RL 2,
RL 3, RL 6

Possible answers:

1. *They will be taken to a boarding school in Oregon, where they will learn to fit into mainstream culture.*

2. *From the Major's actions, we can tell that he is used to being obeyed. ("Major Miles boomed, 'You! . . . Get back here! . . . All of you, stand back!'") From his thoughts, we can tell that he is somewhat blind to others' feelings. (He had to drag the children out of hiding, yet he felt that he was doing the right thing and they should be grateful.)*

3. *The Major's point of view is that he is helping the children by offering them an education. However, the children feel that they are being sent away against their will. Their parents are "frightened and uneasy."*

4. *The flashback (lines 53–156) happens six months earlier, when the Major meets Eneas and decides that the boy and his grandparents need help. The flashback helps develop the conflict between the Major and the Indians.*

5. *The Major feels that he is improving the children's lives. The reader sees that the children's lives will change, but not necessarily for the better. They are being taken from their homes, families, and culture.*

6. *The setting is an Indian reservation in the late 1800s. At that time, government officials believed that the best way to help Native American families was to send the children away to school. This helps the reader understand why the Major believed he was doing the right thing.*

7. *In the end, the Major is not able to complete the speech he wanted to give about the importance of the moment. This shows how pointless that message would have been.*

English Language Support

Connect Ideas Explain to students that interesting writing includes a variety of sentence structures.

- Review how to combine two clauses to form a compound sentence. Have students locate two sentences in their analyses with related ideas. Work with them to combine their sentences.

- Review complex sentences. Have students work with a partner to reread their analyses and find places where they can create a complex sentence by turning one sentence into a subordinate clause.

- Review compound, complex, and compound-complex sentences. Encourage students to rewrite sentences if they do not have examples of each type.

Analyzing the Text

RL 1, RL 2, RL 3,
RL 6, W 1, W 4,
W 9a, W 10

Cite Text Evidence Support your responses with evidence from the text.

1. **Predict** What is going to happen to the children waiting for the train?

2. **Cite Evidence** Reread lines 17–27. What does this section tell you about Major Miles? What method(s) of characterization was used to convey that information?

3. **Infer** How does the Major's point of view differ from the other characters' points of view?

4. **Analyze** What section of the story is told as a flashback? What does the flashback reveal about the plot and characters?

5. **Analyze** What might the reader understand about the situation that the Major appears not to understand?

6. **Connect** How does the **setting**—the time and place of the action—affect the reader's understanding of the characters?

7. **Draw Conclusions** Why might the author have decided to end the story as he did?

PERFORMANCE TASK

Writing Activity: Character Analysis
In "Train Time," the Major does not think he is doing anything wrong—or does he? Write two or three paragraphs to describe the character of the Major.

- Answer these questions to help organize your ideas: What does the Major value? What actions does he take? How does the Major seem to feel about Reservation Indians?

- Include quotations from the story to support your ideas about the Major.

- Discuss the different ways the author reveals the Major's character traits.

Assign this performance task.

PERFORMANCE TASK

RL 1, RL 3,
RL 6, W 1,
W 4, W 9a,
W 10

Writing Activity: Character Analysis Before students begin writing their character analyses, remind them of the various methods authors use to reveal character traits. Have students

- meet in groups to discuss the questions in the Performance Task
- work independently to write their analyses

Remind students to cite evidence from the text to support their ideas.

Critical Vocabulary

L 4c, L 6

exasperate	conscience	ponderous
sustenance	inexplicable	ignorance

Practice and Apply Answer each question with *yes* or *no*. With your group, use examples and reasons to explain your answer.

1. If someone was **exasperated,** could you tell?

2. Should you trust a person of **conscience**?

3. Could an action be **ponderous**?

4. Is **sustenance** unnecessary?

5. Could a person behave in an **inexplicable** way?

6. Is **ignorance** the same as ignoring someone?

Vocabulary Strategy: Using a Dictionary

When you find an unknown word in a text, you can first use **context,** or the words and sentences around the word, to try to determine its meaning. Note the word *conscience* in this sentence from "Train Time": *Major Miles was a man of* conscience. There are no helpful context clues to the meaning of *conscience.* If you look it up in a dictionary, you might find these definitions:

> **1a.** An awareness of morality in regard to one's behavior; a sense of right and wrong that urges one to act morally: *Let your conscience be your guide.* **b.** A source of moral or ethical judgment or pronouncement: *a document that serves as the nation's conscience.* **c.** Conformity to one's own sense of right conduct: *a person of unflagging conscience.*

Definition **1c** best matches the meaning of *conscience* in the sentence.

A dictionary entry has additional information about a word, including a word's **pronunciation** and **part of speech**. The letters and symbols in parentheses show the word's pronunciation, followed by an italicized abbreviation of the part of speech. The pronunciation key in a dictionary can help you determine how to pronounce a word.

Practice and Apply Find these words in "Train Time": *bearing* (line 30), *tipis* (line 51), *gesture* (line 88). Use a print or digital dictionary to identify the definition that matches the context and the part of speech. Then use the pronunciation key to say the word.

PRACTICE & APPLY

Critical Vocabulary

L 4c, L 6

Possible answers:

1. *Yes, because the exasperated person would be sighing, eye-rolling, and showing other signs of being annoyed.*

2. *Yes, because a person of conscience is principled and is likely to value honesty.*

3. *Yes, because a person could walk heavily, taking ponderous footsteps.*

4. *No, because sustenance, such as nourishment, is essential to life.*

5. *Yes, because people can do things for no apparent reason.*

6. *No, because ignorance is a lack of knowledge or education; ignoring someone means not paying attention.*

Vocabulary Strategy: Using a Dictionary

Possible answers:

bearing: n. (noun), *posture, how one carries oneself*

tipis: n. (noun), *tepees, dwellings made of a conical framework of poles covered with bark or skins*

gesture: n. (noun), *a motion of the limbs*

Strategies for Annotation 🖉 🗐 *Annotate it!*

Using a Dictionary

L 4c, L 6

Have students locate the paragraph with the word *routine* (lines 166–171). Encourage them to use their eBook annotation tools to do the following:

- Highlight in yellow the word *routine*.
- Underline surrounding words and phrases that are likely clues to its meaning.
- Write a note that is a guess at the meaning based on the clues.
- Use a dictionary to confirm the meaning, writing the definition that best fits in this passage.

The difference was, that in the cases of all these others, the problem was routine. He met it, and passed over it. But in the case of Eneas, he was bothered. He wante~~~~ what this moment of going away meant.

> **routine**
> guess: ordinary
> dictionary: having no special quality; ordinary

PRACTICE & APPLY

Language Conventions: Misplaced Modifiers

L 1c

Review the definition of a modifier and the steps for correcting a misplaced modifier. Explain that a modifier can be a clause, as in the first example shown; a phrase, as in the second example; or a single word. Also point out that there can be more than one way to correct a misplaced modifier. For example, the second example could be rewritten as, *"The Major believed that, in the future, the children would thank him."*

Possible answers:

1. *Major Miles, fulfilling his duty, made a list of thirty children's names.*

2. *Of all the children, little Eneas was the only one the Major knew.*

3. *Major Miles was sure that the children leaving the reservation would have better lives.*

4. *The children who were leaving their families had tears and fearful faces.*

5. *At the school in Oregon, Eneas would give up the only culture he had known.*

6. *Coming down the tracks was the train that would change the children's lives forever.*

Assess It Online!

Online Selection Test
- Download an editable ExamView bank.
- Assign and manage the test online.

Language Conventions: Misplaced Modifiers

L 1c

A **modifier** is a word or a group of words that changes, or modifies, the meaning of another word in a sentence. A **misplaced modifier** is in the wrong place in a sentence and can confuse a reader. As you review your writing, follow these steps to identify and fix misplaced modifiers.

- Find the modifier.
- Identify what word the modifier was intended to modify.
- Place the modifier as close as possible to the word, phrase, or clause it is supposed to describe.

In the following examples, note the underlined modifier and the word or phrase it was intended to modify.

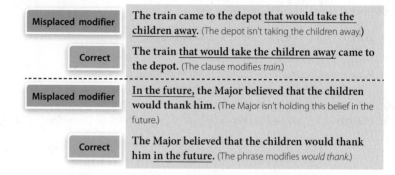

Practice and Apply Each sentence has a misplaced modifier. Find and fix the error.

1. Major Miles made a list of thirty children's names fulfilling his duty.

2. Little Eneas was the only one of all the children the Major knew.

3. Leaving the Reservation, Major Miles was sure that the children would have better lives.

4. The children had tears and fearful faces who were leaving their families.

5. Eneas would give up the only culture he had known at the school in Oregon.

6. The train was coming down the tracks that would change the children's lives forever.

English Language Support

Modify to Add Details Review the instruction and the examples on the Student Edition page, drawing students' attention to the forms that modifiers can take.

- Write the first Practice and Apply sentence on the board. Work with students to identify the modifier. *(fulfilling his duty)* Then discuss which word it tells about. *(Major Miles)* Have pairs rewrite the sentence with the modifying phrase in the correct position. Follow the same steps with the second sentence.

- Display the Practice and Apply sentences. Call on volunteers to highlight the modifying phrase or clause in each sentence. Together, identify which word or words each modifies. Then have pairs rewrite each sentence correctly. Have them read their rewritten sentences aloud.

- Have pairs of students take turns reading the Practice and Apply sentences aloud and explaining how to correct the placement of the misplaced modifier.

Analyze Story Elements: Setting

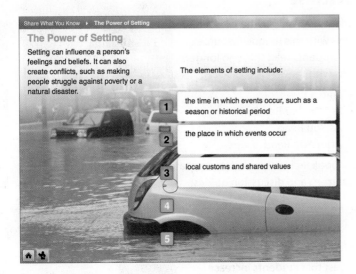

Share What You Know ▸ The Power of Setting

The Power of Setting

Setting can influence a person's feelings and beliefs. It can also create conflicts, such as making people struggle against poverty or a natural disaster.

The elements of setting include:

1. the time in which events occur, such as a season or historical period

2. the place in which events occur

3. local customs and shared values

4.

5.

TEACH

Explain that in addition to time and place, the **setting** of a story can include elements of culture, social class, weather, and landscape, thus transporting the reader into the world of the story.

Discuss how the setting can affect the plot of a story in a number of ways:

- The setting can influence characters by determining their living conditions and shaping their personalities, goals, and dreams.
- The setting can create obstacles to resolving the conflict, such as dangerous weather conditions or a difficult time period such as a war.
- Setting can also serve as a symbol. A **symbol** is a person, a place, an object, or an activity that stands for something beyond itself. A story's setting can represent an important idea, such as a garden standing for hope.
- Finally, the setting can affect the **theme** of the story. The theme is a message about life or human nature that the author wants to share with the reader.

Work with students to identify the setting of "Train Time" and analyze its effect on the plot. *(It contributes to the conflict between the Major and the families.)*

INDEPENDENT READING

Students can apply the skill to another short story of their own choosing. Have them analyze the setting(s). Suggest that they use a chart to record ways in which the setting impacts the plot.

Analyze Stories: Characterization

RETEACH

Discuss the four basic methods of **characterization** authors use.

METHOD	EXAMPLE
direct comments through the voice of the narrator	*Cinderella was always kind and patient, no matter how badly she was treated.*
description of physical appearance	*Her filthy rags and work-roughened hands could not disguise her delicate beauty.*
the character's speech, thoughts, and actions	*"I wish I could go to the ball, but there is so much cleaning to do!" she sighed.*
other characters' speech, thoughts, and actions	*"I must find her," the prince declared. "She is the sweetest, kindest woman I've ever met."*

Discuss what inferences a reader can make about Cinderella from each example.

LEVEL UP TUTORIALS Assign the following *Level Up* tutorial: **Methods of Characterization**

INDEPENDENT READING

Students can apply the skill to another short story, using a chart like the one above to record evidence and inferences.

English Language Support

Read Closely Give students practice in making inferences and expressing and justifying opinions about a character's traits.

- Work with students to express an opinion about Cinderella and identify supporting evidence: The word _____ describes Cinderella because she _____ . *(responsible; puts her work ahead of having fun)*
- Review the evidence about Cinderella's character. Then have pairs write an opinion about Cinderella using the words *possibly/likely* or *could/would* and explaining their supporting evidence.
- Ask pairs to choose another familiar character. Have them write a paragraph stating an opinion about one of the character's traits and supporting it with story evidence. Encourage students to express opinions with these words: *potentially/certainly/absolutely, should/might.*

GUIDED BY A CAUSE

The FYI site provides links to online articles from a variety of magazines and newspapers. Help students choose a few articles to read to further their exploration of the topic Guided by a Cause.

NOVELWISE

Students can unlock the power of novels with this unique resource. Help students read through longer works with these tips:

- Find a Book
- Before You Read
- As You Read
- After You Read

Each book includes introductory material, worksheets, graphic organizers, and discussion guides.

ADDITIONAL TEXTS BY COLLECTION

Suggest that students read the following:

- "Letter to the President General of the Daughters of the American Revolution" by Eleanor Roosevelt

After students read the letter, ask them what clues in the text hint at why the First Lady would have disagreed with the Daughters of the American Revolution enough to resign as a member.

NONFICTION CONNECTIONS

Suggest that students increase their reading of informational texts. The nonfiction connections include:

- speeches
- diaries
- true-life accounts
- newspaper articles
- political cartoons

Creating an Independent Reading Program

OPPORTUNITIES FOR SOCIAL INTERACTION

Discussing books with classmates allows students to share what they know and to learn about other books.

- In a small-group discussion, have students show the book, give the title and author, and then summarize it.
- If students read the same book, have them sit together and take turns reading aloud and discussing paragraphs or pages that made an impression on them.
- If students read different books on a similar topic, have them compare the books. One student should act as moderator to make sure everyone has an opportunity to share.
- At the end of the discussions, students should say whether they would recommend their books and why.

WRITING IN RESPONSE TO BOOKS AND TEXTS READ

Writing in response to texts gives students the opportunity to think more deeply about what they have read.

- Before group discussions, allow time for students to write notes about the book they would like to present.
- After the group discussions, encourage students to write a book review or retell the content in a different format, such as a graphic novel or a dramatic presentation.
- Throughout the school year, ask students to compare books they are reading with others they have read. What genres are they drawn to? Do they read about people and topics that have relevance to what they do in or outside of school? How do various books grab and hold their interest?

Write an Informative Essay

This collection focuses on important social causes. In the selections about the Triangle Factory Fire, you learned how a great tragedy led to public outcry to improve workplace conditions. In this activity, you will do additional research about a topic or person related to this fire. You will draw from the texts in the collection and your research findings to write an informative essay.

A successful informative essay

- clearly states the topic in a strong thesis statement
- organizes ideas and concepts logically
- supports central ideas with details from credible sources
- uses appropriate transitions to link ideas
- establishes and maintains a formal style
- provides a conclusion that follows from and supports the information presented

Mentor Text The opening phrases of these sentences help readers to follow the order of events in this passage from *Flesh & Blood So Cheap.*

> " At exactly 4:45 P.M., someone pulled the eighth-floor fire alarm. In less than two minutes, the horse-drawn vehicles of Engine Company 72 arrived from a firehouse six blocks away. The moment they arrived, the firefighters unloaded their equipment and prepared to swing into action. "

PLAN

Determine Your Topic Review the excerpts from *The Story of the Triangle Factory Fire, Flesh & Blood So Cheap,* and *Uprising.* Brainstorm a list of possible topics or people to research, such as the trial following the fire, the new labor laws, Frances Perkins, or Fire Chief Croker. Choose the topic that most interests you.

- Transform your topic into a research question you want to answer, such as *How did the fire impact workplace safety, and what was Frances Perkins' role in that? Why were fire precautions so inadequate during that time?*

W 2a–f Write informative/explanatory texts.
W 4 Produce clear and coherent writing.
W 5 Develop and strengthen writing.
W 6 Use technology to produce and publish writing.
W 7 Conduct short research projects.
W 8 Gather relevant information.
W 10 Write routinely.

fyi
hmhfyi.com

Visit hmhfyi.com to explore your topic and enhance your research.

myNotebook
Use the annotation tools in your eBook to record details from the selections that support your topic. Save each detail to your notebook.

ACADEMIC VOCABULARY

As you plan and draft your essay, be sure to use the academic vocabulary words.

contrast
despite
error
inadequate
interact

PERFORMANCE TASK A

WRITE AN INFORMATIVE ESSAY

W 2a–f, W 4, W 5, W 6, W 7, W 8, W 9b, W 10

Introduce students to the Performance Task by reading the introductory paragraph with them and reviewing the criteria for what makes a good informative essay. Remind students that a good informative essay includes evidence that supports the main points the writer makes.

PLAN

DETERMINE YOUR TOPIC

Remind students that their topic questions are likely to change as they do more research into their chosen topics. Explain that students should be open to adjusting their topics and questions as they find additional information that intrigues them or that takes them in a different direction. Point out that flexibility is an important part of the planning phase for any writing task that involves research.

English Language Support

Write Informative Texts Make sure students understand that their informative essays should focus on a specific topic or person related to the Triangle Factory Fire. Then have pairs use the sentence frames and questions to discuss their writing plans:

- *I think _____ is interesting because _____.*
- *I will research more information about _____ to see how it relates to _____.*
- *I will also find examples of _____ to tell my reader more about _____.*
- *I like your idea, but I think it might be hard to find information about _____. Maybe you can try _____ instead.*

Students can use their conversations to help them focus their research and develop their essays.

PERFORMANCE TASK A

PLAN

DO RESEARCH

Remind students that when researching on the Internet they will find websites with information that is not credible or reliable. To evaluate a website's reliability, students should answer these questions:

- Who created the site?
- What are the site's stated goals?
- Does the site provide credits?
- Are there more reliable sources with information about the topic?

PRODUCE

WRITE YOUR ESSAY

Remind students to use their outlines as a guide for their first draft. Point out that each main idea should be supported by the details and evidence included in their outlines. Suggest that students center each paragraph on one main idea as they write.

FOR STANDARD ENGLISH LEARNERS

Use Simple Past Tense Remind students that in formal English, the simple past tense does not use the helping verb *had*. Have students rewrite each sentence using simple past tense.

- The workers [had ran] from the fire. *(ran)*
- The fire [had spread] rapidly. *(spread)*

WHEN STUDENTS STRUGGLE...

Add Facts and Details If students have trouble outlining, suggest that they work with partners to add facts and details for each paragraph in their outline. To start, have them write the question that each paragraph will answer. Then they can add facts and details from their research notes that help answer that question.

- Make sure your question is open-ended.
- Generate further questions that will help you find specific evidence.

Gather Information Look for information in the selections that relates to your topic. Take notes on key points, observations, and events that will help you gain a better understanding of your topic, answer your questions, and support your main points.

Do Research Use print and digital sources to find additional information that addresses your research question.

Interactive Lessons
For help in doing your research, use
- Conducting Research: Types of Sources

- Use keywords or subject searching in the library to find print sources. Find credible Internet sources.
- Use evidence to explain and support your main points.
- Check that the information you find is supported by the information you read in the collection.

Organize Your Ideas Organize your essay by creating an outline showing the information you will present in each paragraph. Make sure each idea follows logically from the previous idea and leads into the next idea.

Consider Your Purpose and Audience What does the audience already know? What background information will they need? Keep this in mind as you prepare to write.

PRODUCE

Write Your Essay Use your notes and your outline as you begin your draft.

my WriteSmart
Write your rough draft in *my*WriteSmart. Focus on getting your ideas down, rather than on perfecting your choice of language.

- Begin with an attention-grabbing introduction.
- Organize your information into paragraphs of related ideas.
- Include facts, concrete details, definitions, and examples.
- Transition from one logical point to another, using words and phrases such as *because, despite, therefore,* and *as a result of.*
- Use a formal tone.
- Write a conclusion that supports your explanation.

Interactive Lessons
For help in drafting your essay, use
- Writing Informative Texts: Elaboration

English Language Support

Understand Text Structure Display the Student Model that accompanies *Interactive Lessons: Using Textual Evidence.* Read the informative essay aloud as students follow along. Ask students to explain how the writer presents information from experts. Then point out the quotations in paragraph 3. Explain that quotations from experts can make informative texts more engaging and authoritative. Post an annotated copy of the model for students to refer to as they write their own informative essays.

Language Conventions: Condensing Ideas

The more precisely worded the sentence, the more ideas a piece of writing can convey. For example, read this passage from *Flesh & Blood So Cheap*.

> "Workers, shouting, crying, and gasping for air, slowly made their way downstairs."

The passage might have read, "Workers slowly made their way downstairs. The workers were shouting. The workers were crying. The workers were gasping for air." Instead, the actions are condensed into a participial phrase, making it more precise.

REVISE

my WriteSmart

Evaluate Your Draft Use the chart to evaluate your essay.

Have a group of peers review your draft in *my*WriteSmart. Ask your reviewers to note any facts, details, or examples that do not support your thesis.

Questions	Tips	Revision Techniques
Is my thesis statement, or controlling idea, clear?	**Underline** the thesis statement.	**Revise** your thesis statement to explain what the essay will explore.
Is the essay organized by order of importance or in the order that key elements appear?	**Highlight** the key details. **Decide** whether they reflect a logical order.	**Rearrange** details in a logical order. **Use** transitions to connect the details.
Are my facts and details credible?	**Underline** the facts and details. **Check** that the evidence is from reliable sources.	**Add** facts and details from reliable sources.
Is the style of my essay formal?	**Highlight** any contractions and use of casual wording.	**Change** contractions. **Revise** any slang or casual expressions.
Does the conclusion restate my thesis?	**Underline** the restatement.	**Add** a sentence restating the thesis, if you need to. **Check** that it summarizes the main points.

PRESENT

Create a Finished Copy Post your essay as a blog on a personal or school website. Consider these additional options:

- Deliver your essay as a speech to the class.
- Organize a group discussion to share your ideas.
- Circulate a video recording of your essay.

Collection Performance Task A **339**

PERFORMANCE TASK A

PRODUCE

LANGUAGE CONVENTIONS

Make sure students understand that the participles in the example sentence act as adjectives modifying *workers*. Encourage students to look for places in their drafts where they can use participial phrases to condense ideas.

REVISE

EVALUATE YOUR DRAFT

Have students work with a partner to help them revise their essays. Pairs can exchange essays and take turns offering revision suggestions based on the chart.

PRESENT

CREATE A FINISHED COPY

To present their essays, students can

- present their essays orally to the class. Remind students to speak loudly and clearly, look directly at the audience, and use gestures and facial expressions to emphasize ideas.
- organize a group discussion to share ideas about their topics. Remind students to take turns and listen attentively as others speak.

English Language Support

Condensing Ideas To help students understand how to condense ideas in their essays, read the following aloud: *The article tells the story of a survivor. The survivor escaped by climbing down a ladder to a neighboring building.*

- Model the process by saying, "I can condense these two ideas by changing one sentence into a dependent clause: *The article tells the story of a survivor who escaped by climbing down a ladder to a neighboring building.*"

- Have partners work together to condense the ideas in the two sentences into one. Then ask them to write two sentences that condense the following ideas in two different ways: *She had no way to escape. The elevator had broken. The exit was locked.*

PERFORMANCE TASK A

USE THE SCORING RUBRIC

Have students use the rubric to score their own essays. Then have partners evaluate each other's score. Students should use the language of the rubric to provide feedback in each category.

REFLECT ON THE PROCESS

Tell students that reflecting on their writing process for this task will help them complete future assignments. Have students think about how well they informed their audience about their chosen topic and then answer the following questions:

- What was the most interesting piece of information you found when doing research?
- Which part of your essay was the most difficult to write? Why?
- How did writing your essay add to your understanding of the Triangle Factory Fire?

PERFORMANCE TASK A RUBRIC
INFORMATIVE ESSAY

	Ideas and Evidence	Organization	Language
4	• The introduction is appealing and informative; a thesis statement clearly identifies the topic in an engaging way. • The topic is well developed with relevant examples, concrete details, and interesting facts from the selections and other credible sources. • The concluding section capably summarizes the information presented.	• The organization is effective and logical throughout the essay. • Transitions successfully connect related ideas.	• The writing reflects a formal style, with strong, precise language. • Sentence beginnings, lengths, and structures vary and have a rhythmic flow. • Spelling, capitalization, and punctuation are correct. • Grammar and usage are correct.
3	• The introduction could do more to grab the reader's attention; the thesis statement identifies the topic. • One or two key points could be better supported with more relevant examples, concrete details, and facts from the selections and other credible sources. • The concluding section summarizes the information presented.	• The organization is confusing in a few places. • A few more transitions are needed to connect related ideas.	• The style is informal in a few places. • Language is too general in some places. • Sentence beginnings, lengths, and structures vary somewhat. • A few spelling, capitalization, and punctuation mistakes occur. • Some grammatical and usage errors are repeated in the essay.
2	• The introduction is only partly informative; the thesis statement only hints at a topic. • Most key points need more support in the form of relevant examples, concrete details, and facts. • The concluding section partially summarizes the information presented.	• The organization is logical in some places but often doesn't follow a pattern. • More transitions are needed throughout to connect related ideas.	• The style becomes informal in several places. • Overly general language is used in several places. • Sentence structures barely vary, with some fragments or run-on sentences present. • Spelling, capitalization, and punctuation are often incorrect. • Grammar and usage are incorrect in several places.
1	• The introduction is missing. • Examples, details, and facts are missing. • The essay lacks a concluding section.	• A logical organization is not used; information is presented randomly. • Transitions are not used, making the essay difficult to understand.	• The style is inappropriate for the essay. • Language is too general to convey the information. • Repetitive sentence structure, fragments, and run-on sentences make the writing difficult to follow. • Spelling, capitalization, and punctuation are incorrect throughout. • Several grammatical and usage errors change the meaning of the writer's ideas.

FOR STUDENTS WITH DISABILITIES

Listen to the Essay Let students make audio recordings of their drafts. Then have them review the recording with a peer to identify ways that they might improve their work.

TO CHALLENGE STUDENTS . . .

Conduct Additional Research Challenge students to research other factory tragedies, such as those that occurred in Bangladesh in 2012 and 2013. Ask students to compare and contrast the causes and effects of these tragedies with the Triangle Factory Fire. Invite students to share their findings with the class.

Participate in a Panel Discussion

In this collection, you read about problems in the world that inspire people to take action to solve those problems. In this activity, you will draw from the selections you read to take part in a panel discussion about what commitment to a cause can mean.

W 2a–f Write informative/explanatory texts.
W 4 Produce clear and coherent writing.
W 5 Develop and strengthen writing.
W 10 Write routinely.
SL 1a–d Engage in collaborative discussions.

A successful participant in a panel discussion

- makes a clear, logical generalization about the value of committing to a cause
- uses quotations and specific examples to illustrate ideas
- responds politely to the moderator and other group members
- evaluates other group members' contributions
- summarizes the discussion by synthesizing ideas

> **PLAN**

Get Organized Work with your classmates to prepare for the discussion.

- Form a small group and choose three texts from this collection, including "Craig Kielburger Reflects on Working Toward Peace," for the discussion of the importance of causes.
- Select one student to be the moderator. The rest of your classmates will be the audience when you hold the panel discussion.
- Set up a format for your discussion—a schedule that shows the order in which members will speak and for how long. The moderator will make sure members follow the schedule.
- Develop rules for the appropriate times for either the moderator or the audience to ask panel members questions.

Gather Evidence Work individually to analyze "Craig Kielburger Reflects on Working Toward Peace" and two other texts from the collection. Gather evidence about what it means to commit to a cause. Note specific details, examples, or quotations that illustrate your views. Then think about your own experiences. Ask yourself questions as you take notes.

ACADEMIC VOCABULARY

As you plan and draft your discussion points, be sure to use the academic vocabulary words.

contrast
despite
error
inadequate
interact

PERFORMANCE TASK B

PARTICIPATE IN A PANEL DISCUSSION

W 2a–f,
W 4, W 5,
W 10, SL 1a–d

Introduce students to the Performance Task by reading the introductory paragraph with them and reviewing the criteria for what makes a successful panel discussion. Remind students that in a successful discussion, panel members use quotations and examples to support their ideas and to respond to the ideas of others.

> **PLAN**

GET ORGANIZED

As groups select texts for discussion, they should identify the purpose of the cause each text describes. When they organize their panels, remind students that the moderator's role is to ask thought-provoking questions and to elicit well-supported responses.

English Language Support

Plan a Collaborative Discussion Explain that students will use evidence from three selections to support generalizations about the value of committing to a cause. To help each group choose texts, have two members review one half of the remaining collection texts while a second pair reviews the other. Then have students use the following sentence frames to share information with their groups:

[Text title] is about _____.

This text focuses on the cause of _____.

Examples that show reasons for addressing this cause include _____.

Responses to this cause include _____.

I think we [should/should not] discuss this text because _____.

After groups have selected the texts, they can use ideas from these conversations to help choose roles and gather information.

PERFORMANCE TASK B

English Language Support

Link Ideas Encourage students to think about the links among details, examples, and quotations as they gather information. Provide students with a list of transitional words and phrases that they might use to show a sequence of events, for example: *First, next, then, finally, after, at the end.*

PRODUCE

WRITE AND PRACTICE

Encourage students to make thorough, detailed outlines that include adequate and relevant support for their main ideas. Explain that they can use these outlines as a general guide during the discussion, but they might not have the time or opportunity to present all their evidence.

English Language Support

Support Opinions Have students practice using simple phrases to gain the floor or to ask for clarification during the discussion. For example:

I think that . . .

I agree with your idea that . . .

Would you please repeat your point about . . . ?

Would you share an example of . . . ?

- What sorts of problems motivate people to take action?
- What degree of positive change might one person or a group hope to accomplish?
- Are good intentions enough? How knowledgeable does a person need to be in order to take on an issue?
- What are the benefits or drawbacks of committing to a cause?
- How can working for change build character?

Use the annotation tools in your eBook to find evidence from the text to support your generalization. Save your evidence to *my*Notebook, in a folder titled *Collection 6 Performance Task.*

> myNotebook
>
> 📄 "Craig Kielburger Reflects on Working Toward Peace"
>
> "I had never heard of child labor and wasn't certain where Pakistan was—but that day changed my life forever."
>
> This sentence shows the turning point at which Craig Kielburger found his cause—working to end child labor.

During this time, the moderator should make a list of relevant questions to be asked during the panel discussion.

PRODUCE

Write and Practice Work individually to outline your ideas. Then practice with your group.

- State a clear generalization about the ways people in your assigned texts respond to a social problem.
- Write several central ideas that support your generalization.
- Match each piece of evidence with the idea it best supports.
- Prepare to "think on your feet" as you present your ideas to your group. The moderator will ask questions about your ideas and examples in order to prepare you for the real discussion.
- If you are the moderator, decide how to introduce and conclude the discussion. Write a statement telling the audience the topic and format. Write notes for a concluding statement. Be ready to alter your remarks if new ideas emerge in the discussion.

Interactive Lessons
For help in gathering evidence, use
· Preparing for Discussion

Write your outline in *my*WriteSmart. Focus on getting your ideas down, rather than on perfecting your choice of language.

Interactive Lessons
For help in planning and practicing the discussion, use
· Establishing and Following Procedure
· Speaking Constructively

342 Collection 6

English Language Support

Prepare to Practice and Present Advise students to organize their outlines in a way that lets them quickly locate information they'll need to make a point or answer a question. Emphasize that students should become sufficiently familiar with their topic to speak directly to others, glancing briefly at their outlines only as needed. Note that in a panel discussion, precise language and verbal and nonverbal techniques help participants engage and inform the audience. Before students practice their discussions, suggest the following strategies for reviewing their outlines:

- List your ideas and evidence in logical order. Highlight your strongest pieces of evidence to help you readily refer to them.
- Circle any words that you're not sure how to pronounce. Confirm pronunciations using a dictionary, and practice saying each word several times.

REVISE

Reinforce Your Ideas Based on the practice session and the rubric on the following page, make changes to your written response to the texts. Consider the following questions:

- Were you able to defend your generalization? If not, revise your response so that it better reflects your textual evidence and your central ideas.

- Were you able to answer the moderator's questions clearly and without hesitation? If not, you may need to adjust your response to find the information you need more easily.

- Did the moderator's questions help you see your text in a new light? If so, add new evidence to your response that you can share during the real discussion.

*my*WriteSmart

Have a partner or a group of peers review your outline in *my*WriteSmart. Ask your reviewers to note any information that isn't related to your viewpoint.

Interactive Lessons
For practice help, use
· Listening and Responding

PRESENT

Have the Discussion Now it's time to present your panel discussion before the rest of the class. Have your outline at hand for reference during the discussion.

- Begin by having the moderator introduce the topic, the panelists, and the basic format for the discussion. The moderator will then ask the first question and continue to facilitate the discussion in the agreed-upon format.

- Speak directly to the panel and audience. Refer to your notes as a reminder of your main points. Don't just read from them.

- Listen closely to all speakers so that you can respond fully.

- Maintain a respectful tone toward your fellow panel members, even when you disagree with their ideas.

- When all the panelists have made their statements and discussed ideas among themselves, the moderator should invite panelists and audience members to ask questions.

- Conclude by having the moderator summarize the discussion and thank the panelists for their participation.

Summarize Write a summary of the main points from the discussion. Then explain whether the discussion caused you to rethink your generalization, and why.

REVISE

REINFORCE YOUR IDEAS

Ask group members to provide specific feedback about how to improve questions and responses. Encourage students to simplify each response in order to express ideas clearly and concisely.

PRESENT

HAVE THE DISCUSSION

Remind panelists to speak loudly and clearly and to maintain eye contact with the moderator, other panelists, and audience members when they address them. When not speaking, panelists should model good listening behavior and direct their full attention to the speaker.

English Language Support

Support Opinions Remind students to acknowledge new information other panel members present and to use transitions to follow up with their own responses. Model an example: *I heard you say that experience is an important quality for people who commit to a cause. I hadn't thought about that before. However, I still think that believing in the cause is the most important quality. For instance, Craig Kielburger was only twelve when he began his fight against child labor, but he accomplished a lot.*

WHEN STUDENTS STRUGGLE . . .

Practice Speaking Techniques Before panelists begin, model strong speaking techniques. Demonstrate examples of employing eye contact, facial expressions, gestures, voice modulation, and inflection. Let students practice these techniques to emphasize important points for their discussions.

PERFORMANCE TASK B

USE THE SCORING RUBRIC

Let audience members use the rubric to score the performance of the panelists. Assign one student to evaluate the participation of a specific panel member. Students should then explain the scores they gave using language from the rubric.

REFLECT ON THE PROCESS

Explain that taking time to reflect on the preparation for and engagement in the discussion will help each student prepare for future assignments. After students think about the insights they gained from the process, have them answer the following questions:

- What were your strongest pieces of evidence?
- How did you elaborate on and respond to questions and comments from others?
- Which nonverbal techniques did you use effectively?

FOR STUDENTS WITH DISABILITIES

Videorecord the Discussion If a videocamera is available, give students the option of having their discussions recorded. They can use the videos to review and critique their performance.

PERFORMANCE TASK B RUBRIC
PANEL DISCUSSION

	Ideas and Evidence	Organization	Language
4	• The panelist clearly states a valid generalization and supports it with strong, relevant ideas and well-chosen evidence from the texts. • The panel member carefully evaluates others' evidence and reasoning and responds with insightful comments and questions. • The panelist synthesizes the analysis of the texts to help listeners understand the generalization.	• The panelist's remarks are based on a well-organized outline that clearly identifies the generalization and the supporting ideas and evidence. • The panelist concludes with a statement that reinforces the generalization and includes the ideas that have emerged from the discussion.	• The panelist adapts speech to the context of the discussion, using appropriately formal English to discuss the texts and ideas. • The panelist consistently quotes accurately from the texts to support ideas. • The panel member consistently maintains a polite and thoughtful tone throughout the discussion.
3	• The panelist states a generalization and supports it with relevant ideas and evidence from the texts. • The panel member evaluates others' evidence and reasoning and responds with appropriate comments and questions. • The panelist synthesizes some ideas and links to the generalization.	• The panelist's remarks are based on an outline that identifies the generalization, supporting ideas, and evidence. • The panelist concludes with a statement that reinforces the generalization.	• The panelist mostly uses formal English to discuss texts and ideas. • The panelist mostly quotes accurately from the texts to support ideas. • The panel member maintains a polite and thoughtful tone throughout most of the discussion.
2	• The panelist states a reasonably clear generalization and supports it with some ideas and evidence. • The panel member's response to others' comments shows limited evaluation of the evidence and reasoning. • The panelist does not synthesize ideas but simply repeats the generalization in a vague way.	• The panelist's remarks reflect an outline that may identify the generalization but does not organize ideas and evidence very effectively. • The panelist makes a weak concluding statement that does little to reinforce the generalization.	• The panelist uses some formal and some informal English to discuss the texts and ideas. • The panelist's quotations and examples sometimes do not accurately reflect the texts. • The panel member occasionally forgets to maintain a polite tone when responding to others' comments and questions.
1	• The panelist's generalization is unclear; ideas and evidence are not coherent. • The panel member does not evaluate others' evidence and reasoning. • The panelist does not synthesize ideas.	• The panelist does not follow an outline that organizes ideas and evidence. • The panelist's remarks lack any kind of conclusion or summary.	• The panelist uses informal English and/or slang, resulting in a lack of clarity. • The panelist's quotations and examples do not accurately reflect the texts. • The panel member does not maintain a polite tone when responding to others' comments and questions.

TO CHALLENGE STUDENTS . . .

Gather Additional Evidence Challenge students to find additional details, examples, and quotations that relate to insights they gained from their discussions. Encourage students to gather information about another cause from resources outside of the collection texts. Ask students to add a section to their discussion summaries that reflects this additional research.

TEACHER NOTE:

The page numbers to the left indicate pages in the Student Edition. Except for the entries below, the page numbers in the Student Edition and Teacher's Edition correspond.

Writing an Argument

Many of the Performance Tasks in this book ask you to craft an argument in which you support your ideas with text evidence. Any argument you write should include the following sections and characteristics.

Introduction

Clearly state your **claim**—the point your argument makes. As needed, provide context or background information to help readers understand your position. Note the most common opposing views as a way to distinguish and clarify your ideas. From the very beginning, make it clear for readers why your claim is strong; consider providing an overview of your reasons or a quotation that emphasizes your view in your introduction.

EXAMPLES

vague claim: Dogs need places to play.	**precise claim:** The city should create a large designated dog park.
not distinguished from opposing view: There are plenty of people who are afraid of dogs.	**distinguished from opposing view:** While some people consider it dangerous for dogs to run free, the facts show that dog parks are safe.
confusing relationship of ideas: Bored dogs get sick. Dog parks have lots of space.	**clear relationship of ideas:** By providing a large, safe area for dogs to run off-leash and play, dog owners throughout the city would also benefit.

Development of Claims

The body of your argument must provide strong, logical reasons for your claim and must support those reasons with relevant evidence. A **reason** tells why your claim is valid; **evidence** provides specific examples that illustrate a reason. In the process of developing your claim you should also refute **counterclaims,** or opposing views, with equally strong reasons and evidence. To demonstrate that you have

thoroughly considered your view, provide a well-rounded look at both the strengths and limitations of your claim and opposing claims. The goal is not to undercut your argument, but rather to answer your readers' potential objections to it. Be sure, too, to consider how much your audience may already know about your topic in order to avoid boring or confusing readers.

EXAMPLES

claim lacking reasons: A dog park would be a good thing because dogs would enjoy it and it would help the community.	**claim developed by reasons:** Among the benefits of a dog park are not only potentially healthier dogs and more well-adjusted pets, but also a stronger sense of community among dog owners.
omission of limitations: People who hate dogs and are opposed to this idea see no problems or safety issues, they just think the park is a waste of money.	**fair discussion of limitations:** We should not dismiss safety concerns. Planning for the park should include posted signs with rules of behavior, first aid facilities, and ongoing maintenance.
inattention to audience's knowledge: Socialization skills can't be taught in isolation, but issues of dominance are possible to teach with other dogs.	**awareness of audience's knowledge:** Readers unfamiliar with dog behavior may be surprised to learn that most injuries involving dogs happen in homes and on the street, not in well-planned dog parks.

Links Among Ideas

Even the strongest reasons and evidence will fail to sway readers if it is unclear how the reasons relate to the central claim of an argument. Make the connections clear for your readers, using not only transitional words and phrases, but also using clauses and even entire sentences as a bridge between ideas you have already discussed and ideas you are introducing.

EXAMPLES

transitional word linking claim and reason: The entire community will benefit from a dog park. First, dogs who are freed from always walking outside on leashes become better adjusted and better behaved, resulting in less aggressive behavior.

transitional phrase linking reason and evidence: A dog park must be large enough for dogs to run and not be crowded. In fact, evidence shows crowding can result in fights.

transitional clause linking claim and counterclaim: The benefits of the park are clear. Those opposed to the park plan, though, would say otherwise: They feel that there is too much potential for injuries to both people and pets.

Appropriate Style and Tone

An effective argument is most often written in a direct and formal style. The style and tone you choose in an argument should not be an afterthought—the way you express your argument can either drive home your ideas or detract from them. Even as you argue in favor of your viewpoint, take care to remain objective in tone—avoid using loaded language when discussing opposing claims.

EXAMPLES

informal style: The park will help dog owners all over the city, so the city should put out the cash.	**formal style:** Because the benefits of the park would reach dog owners throughout the city, it is logical for the city to provide the funding for the project.

continued

biased tone: It would be ridiculous to be against this plan.	**objective tone:** Arguments opposing the dog park plan have been refuted by statistics from reliable sources.
inattention to conventions: Let's make this park happen!	**attention to conventions:** This proposal, which will help provide humane treatment of pets at little cost, deserves City Council attention.

Conclusion

Your conclusion may range from a sentence to a full paragraph, but it must wrap up your argument in a satisfying way; a conclusion that sounds tacked-on helps your argument no more than providing no conclusion at all. A strong conclusion is a logical extension of the argument you have presented. It carries forth your ideas through an inference, question, quotation, or challenge.

EXAMPLES

inference: Humane treatment of dogs begins with community support.

question: Who doesn't want to live in a community that cares for its dogs humanely?

quotation: As our city's animal control warden says, "Dogs who run freely and play companionably are far less likely to be aggressive and cause injury to themselves or others."

challenge: Facilities of this type make the difference between a city that treats its dogs humanely and a city that ignores dogs' needs.

Writing an Informative Essay

Most of the Performance Tasks in this book ask you to write informational or explanatory texts in which you present a topic and examine it thoughtfully through a well-organized analysis of relevant content. Any informative or explanatory text that you create should include the following parts and features.

Introduction

Develop a strong **thesis statement.** That is, clearly state your **topic** and the **organizational framework** through which you will **connect** or **distinguish** elements of your topic. For example, you might state that your text will compare ideas, examine causes and effects, or explore a problem and its solutions.

EXAMPLE

Topic: street lighting
Sample Thesis Statements
Compare-contrast: To decide whether to install brighter street lamps or keep dimmer lights, consider the costs and the benefits of each type.
Cause-effect: While the causes of poor night-time visibility on city streets isn't difficult to guess, the effects can be many and devastating.
Problem-solution: Our town's poor nighttime visibility creates a growing problem with accidents, but through community action we can manage the issue.

Clarifying the organizational framework up front will help you organize the body of your text, suggest **headings** you can use to guide your readers, and help you identify **graphics** that you may need to clarify information. For example, if you compare and contrast the costs and benefits of installing brighter street lamps, you might create a chart like the one here to guide your writing. You could include the same chart in your paper as a graphic for readers. The row or column headings serve as natural paragraph headings.

	low lighting	bright lighting
Costs	Minimal maintenance of existing lights	Investment in all-new fixtures
Benefits	Old-fashioned charm	Increased visibility for motorists and pedestrians

Development of the Topic

In the body of your text, flesh out the organizational framework you established in your introduction with strong supporting paragraphs. Include only support directly relevant to your topic. Don't rely on a single source, and make sure the sources you do use are reputable and current. The table below illustrates types of support you might use to develop aspects of your topic. It also shows how transitions link text sections, create cohesion, and clarify the relationships among ideas.

Types of Support in Explanatory/ Informative Texts	Uses of Transitions in Explanatory/ Informative Texts
Facts and examples: One cause of poor lighting is inappropriate placement of lights; *for example, most pedestrian crosswalks currently have no extra lighting, increasing the risk to pedestrians from motor vehicles.*	*One cause* signals the shift from the introduction to the body text in a cause-and-effect essay. *For example* introduces the support for the cause being cited.

continued

Types of Support in Explanatory/ Informative Texts	Uses of Transitions in Explanatory/ Informative Texts
Concrete details: <u>On the other hand,</u> if residents want to preserve the surrounding darkness of night, they may want to explore other sources of lighting for pedestrian safety. *Hand-held flashlights, arm band lights, shoe reflectors, and strap-on head lighting are options.*	*On the other hand* transitions the reader from one point of comparison to another in a compare-contrast essay.
Statistics: <u>Turn to the city's accident statistics for evidence of pedestrian accidents that occur after dark: 54 accidents in the prior year.</u>	The entire transitional sentence introduces the part of a problem-solution essay that demonstrates the existence of a problem.

You can't always include all of the information you'd like to in a short essay, but you can plan to point readers directly to useful **multimedia links** either in the body of or at the end of your essay.

Style and Tone

Use formal English to establish your credibility as a source of information. To project authority, use the language of the domain, or field, that you are writing about. However, be sure to define unfamiliar terms to avoid using jargon your audience may not know. Provide extended definitions when your audience is likely to have limited knowledge of the topic.

Using quotations from reputable sources can also give your text authority; be sure to credit the source of quoted material. In general, keep the tone objective, avoiding slangy or biased expressions.

Informal, jargon-filled, biased language: People who think that navigating our city's streets as a pedestrian is a walk in the park obviously don't walk much. They have never had an SUV brush them off the crosswalk.

Extended definition in formal style and objective tone: Pedestrian safety refers to a variety of precautions. According to our city's official website, pedestrians can follow several tips for safe walking in low-light situations such as dusk, dawn, and night. Michael Keen, our city's safety expert, advises that as a pedestrian you should wear light clothing after dark, use a flashlight to light the walking path and to alert drivers, and never assume a car's driver will see you and stop for you, even if you have the Walk sign.

Conclusion

Wrap up your essay with a concluding statement or section that sums up or extends the information in your essay.

EXAMPLES

Articulate implications: Fifty-four pedestrian accidents in a year is an unacceptable number. If the city and its citizens can work together to provide necessary safety precautions and learn more about specific actions to encourage safety, we can significantly reduce the number of pedestrian accidents each year.

Emphasize significance: Pedestrian safety is everyone's responsibility. Safety islands, well-lit crosswalks, driver and pedestrian safety-awareness programs, and adequate street lighting are the city's responsibility. Pedestrians too have a responsibility—to dress so they are visible, to always look out for themselves, and to never assume a driver sees them. By working together toward awareness, we can significantly reduce pedestrian accidents in our city.

Writing a Narrative

When you are writing a fictional tale, an autobiographical incident, or a firsthand biography, you write in the narrative mode. That means telling a story with a beginning, a climax, and a conclusion. Though there are important differences between fictional and nonfiction narratives, you use similar processes to develop both kinds.

Identify a Problem, Situation, or Observation

For a nonfiction narrative, dig into your memory bank for a problem you dealt with or an observation you've made about your life. For fiction, try to invent a problem or situation that can unfold in interesting ways.

EXAMPLES

Problem (nonfiction)	Our family needed to train our newly chosen four-month-old West Highland White Terrier.
Situation (fiction)	One day, George, a nervous worrier, receives a mysterious gift in the mail.

Establish a Point of View

Decide who will tell your story. If you are writing a reflective essay about an important experience or person in your own life, you will be the narrator of the events you relate. If you are writing a work of fiction, you can choose to create a first-person narrator or to tell the story from the third-person point of view. The narrator can focus on one character or reveal the thoughts and feelings of all the characters. The examples below show the differences between a first- and third-person narrator.

First-person narrator (nonfiction)	Seven hundred fifty dollars: That's what it would cost me to go on the class trip to Washington, D.C. But it might as well have been a million dollars.

Third-person narrator (fiction)	Peter's fingers froze over the "What's new with you" prompt of his status page. The box was already filled out, waiting for him to press the Update key. "My mom found a new job!" said the box. Peter hadn't written those words. And, as far as he knew, his mother had stopped looking for work months ago.

Gather Details

To make real or imaginary experiences come alive on the page, you will need to use narrative techniques like description and dialogue. The questions in the left column in the chart below can help you search your memory or imagination for the details that will form the basis of your narrative. You don't have to respond in full sentences, but try to capture the sights, sounds, and feelings that bring your narrative to life.

Who, What, When, Where?	Narrative Techniques
People: Who are the people or characters involved in the experience? What did they look like? What did they do? What did they say?	**Description:** George, a friend I've known for as long as I can remember, is outgoing and loves being with people. But George has one quality that I find hard to understand. Even though he has no allergies, he is terribly afraid of certain foods and of getting sick from them. When we go out to eat together, he'll only eat fruit or a slice of meat. He'll never eat a sauce or any food like it. He'll say something like, "I don't know what's in their spaghetti sauce. It might not be good for me."

R6   Student Resources

continued

Who, What, When, Where?	Narrative Techniques
Experience: What led up to or caused the event? What is the main event in the experience? What happened as a result of the event?	**Description:** The next morning my brother and I ventured outside with Maggie. It was February and freezing cold. Maggie didn't like the wind and snow. She balked, stopping with a jerk when we walked. An hour later, our fingers and toes numb, our noses red and raw, Maggie cooperated. She had learned something, and we did too—we had a stubborn dog to train.
Places: When and where did the events take place? What were the sights, sounds, and smells of this place?	**Description:** In December, the air crisp but not yet bitingly cold, I thought ahead to winter break delights—sledding swiftly down the steepest hill, the smell of peppermint cookies, the crunch of ice when we skated.

Sequence Events

Before you write, list key events of the experience or story in chronological, or time, order. Place a star next to the point of highest tension—for example, the point at which a key decision determines the outcome. In fiction, this point is called the climax, but a nonfiction narrative can also have a climactic event.

To build suspense—the uncertainty a reader feels about what will happen next—you'll want to think about the pacing or rhythm of your narrative. Consider disrupting the chronological order of events by beginning at the end, then starting over. Or interrupt the forward flow of events with a flashback, which takes the reader to an earlier point in the narrative.

Another way to build suspense is with multiple plot lines. For example, the story about George's fear of foods involves a second plot line in which the narrator's aunt discovers what happened to her holiday fruitcake. Both plot lines intersect when the narrator shovels snow for a week, and as a result raises money for the class trip.

Use Vivid Language

As you revise, make an effort to use vivid language. Use precise words and phrases to describe feelings and action. Use telling details to show, rather than directly state, what a character is like. Use sensory language that lets readers see, feel, hear, smell, and taste what you or your characters experienced.

First Draft	Revision
My aunt usually sends a fruitcake to us, and I can't stand fruitcake.	Suddenly I thought of my aunt's usual holiday present—the dreaded fruitcake. [telling details]
I remembered my friend George and his dislike for certain foods.	My friend George and his fear of foods with mixed ingredients came to mind. I began to concoct a delicious scheme. [precise words and phrases]
George was afraid when he opened the box and saw a weird-looking cake.	George felt the heavy box from the unknown sender and shrieked when he saw the sticky mixture of dried fruit. [sensory details]

Conclusion

At the conclusion of the narrative, you or your narrator will reflect on the meaning of the events. The conclusion should follow logically from the climactic moment of the narrative. The narrator of a personal narrative usually reflects on the significance of the experience—the lessons learned or the legacy left.

EXAMPLE

Puppy class and its grueling weekly sessions with 12 yipping puppies had ended long ago. Maggie's performance wasn't stellar—she'd had to repeat the whole class to pass. But as I remembered the chill of that first morning walk in sub-zero winds, and the feeling of my numbed fingers, I thought what a smart dog she was after all. After repeated efforts, many crunchy biscuit treats, and lots of warm hugs, Maggie was trained. I proudly stroked her fur as she looked up at me with her knowing eyes.

Conducting Research

The Performance Tasks in this book will require you to complete research projects related to the texts you've read in the collections. Whether the topic is stated in a Performance Task or is one you generate, the following information will guide you through your research project.

Focus Your Research and Formulate a Question

Some topics for a research project can be effectively covered in three pages; others require an entire book for a thorough treatment. Begin by developing a topic that is neither too narrow nor too broad for the time frame of the assignment. Also check your school and local libraries and databases to help you determine how to choose your topic. If there's too little information, you'll need to broaden your focus; if there's too much, you'll need to limit it.

With a topic in hand, formulate a research question; it will keep you on track as you conduct your research. A good research question cannot be answered in a single word. It should be open-ended. It should require investigation. You can also develop related research questions to explore your topic in more depth.

EXAMPLES

Possible topics	Sailing—too broad Navigating waves—too narrow Sailing—in fair and foul weather
Possible research question	What is involved in learning to sail in all kinds of weather?
Related questions	What sailing equipment and techniques are essential? What knowledge of weather patterns is critical?

Locate and Evaluate Sources

To find answers to your research question, you'll need to investigate primary and secondary sources, whether in print or digital formats. **Primary sources** contain original, firsthand information, such as diaries, autobiographies, interviews, speeches, and eyewitness accounts. **Secondary sources** provide other people's versions of primary sources in encyclopedias, newspaper and magazine articles, biographies, and documentaries.

Your search for sources begins at the library and on the World Wide Web. Use **advanced search features** to help you find things quickly. Add a minus sign (–) before a word that should not appear in your results. Use an asterisk (*) in place of unknown words. List the name and location of each possible source, adding comments about its potential usefulness. Assessing, or evaluating, your sources is an important step in the research process. Your goal is to use sources that are credible, or reliable and trustworthy.

Criteria for Assessing Sources	
Relevance: It covers the target aspect of my topic.	• How will the source be useful in answering my research question?
Accuracy: It includes information that can be verified by more than one authoritative source.	• Is the information up-to-date? Are the facts accurate? How can I verify them? • What qualifies the author to write about this topic? Is he or she an authority?
Objectivity: It presents multiple viewpoints on the topic.	• What, if any, biases can I detect? Does the writer favor one view of the topic?

Incorporate and Cite Source Material

When you draft your research project, you'll need to include material from your sources. This material can be **direct quotations, summaries,** or **paraphrases** of the original source material. Two well-known **style manuals** provide information on how to cite a range of print and digital sources: the *MLA Handbook for Writers of Research Papers* (published by the Modern Language Association) and Kate L. Turabian's *A Manual for Writers* (published by The University of Chicago Press). Both style manuals provide a wealth of information about conducting, formatting, drafting, and presenting your research, including guidelines for citing sources within the text (called parenthetical citations) and preparing the list of Works Cited, as well as correct use of the mechanics of writing. Your teacher will indicate which style manual you should use. The following examples use the format in the *MLA Handbook.*

Any material from sources must be completely documented, or you will commit **plagiarism,** the unauthorized use of someone else's words or ideas. Plagiarism is not honest. As you take notes for your research project, be sure to keep complete information about your sources so that you can cite them correctly in the body of your paper. This applies to all sources, whether print or digital. Having complete information will also enable you to prepare the list of Works Cited. The list of Works Cited, which concludes your research project, provides author, title, and publication information for both print and digital sources. The following pages show the *MLA Handbook's* Works Cited citation formats for a variety of sources.

EXAMPLES

Direct quotation [The writer is citing a sailing manual.]	In high winds, you need to know how to tack into the wind. This is an essential skill. [Woods, 120]
Summary [The writer is summarizing the experiences of a sailing expert.]	Johnson fought winds so stiff that if he hadn't had an expert sailor with him to assist with the boom, he would have definitely capsized. [Johnson, 94]
Paraphrase [The writer is paraphrasing, or stating in her own words, material from page 48 of Gloria Schott's book.]	Learning key sailing terminology is essential. For example, as Schott explains, knowing what the preventer is and how to rig it can prevent the boom from swinging around and knocking someone overboard. [Schott, 48]

MLA Citation Guidelines

Today, you can find free websites that generate ready-made citations for research papers, using the information you provide. Such sites have some time-saving advantages when you're developing a Works Cited list. However, you should always check your citations carefully before you turn in your final paper. If you are following MLA style, use these guidelines to evaluate and finalize your work.

Books

One author

Lastname, Firstname. *Title of Book*. City of Publication: Publisher, Year of Publication. Medium of Publication.

Two authors or editors

Lastname, Firstname, and Firstname Lastname. *Title of Book*. City of Publication: Publisher, Year of Publication. Medium of Publication.

Three authors

Lastname, Firstname, Firstname Lastname, and Firstname Lastname. *Title of Book*. City of Publication: Publisher, Year of Publication. Medium of Publication.

Four or more authors

The abbreviation *et al.* means "and others." Use et al. instead of listing all the authors.

Lastname, Firstname, et al. *Title of Book*. City of Publication: Publisher, Year of Publication. Medium of Publication.

No author given

Title of Book. City of Publication: Publisher, Year of Publication. Medium of Publication.

An author and a translator

Lastname, Firstname. *Title of Book*. Trans. Firstname Lastname. City of Publication: Publisher, Year of Publication. Medium of Publication.

An author, a translator, and an editor

Lastname, Firstname. *Title of Book*. Trans. Firstname Lastname. Ed. Firstname Lastname. City of Publication: Publisher, Year of Publication. Medium of Publication.

Parts of Books

An introduction, a preface, a foreword, or an afterword written by someone other than the author(s) of a work

Lastname, Firstname. Part of Book. *Title of Book*. By Author of book's Firstname Lastname. City of Publication: Publisher, Year of Publication. Page span. Medium of Publication.

A poem, a short story, an essay, or a chapter in a collection of works by one author

Lastname, Firstname. "Title of Piece." *Title of Book*. Ed. Firstname Lastname. City of Publication: Publisher, Year of Publication. Page span. Medium of Publication.

A poem, a short story, an essay, or a chapter in an anthology of works by several authors

Lastname, Firstname. "Title of Piece." *Title of Book*. Ed. Firstname Lastname. City of Publication: Publisher, Year of Publication. Page range. Medium of Publication.

Magazines, Newspapers, and Encyclopedias

An article in a newspaper

Lastname, Firstname. "Title of Article." *Title of Book Periodical* Day Month Year: pages. Medium of Publication.

An article in a magazine

Lastname, Firstname. "Title of Article." *Title of Book Periodical* Day Month Year: pages. Medium of Publication.

An article in an encyclopedia

"Title of Article." *Title of Encyclopedia*. Year ed. Medium of Publication.

Miscellaneous Nonprint Sources

An interview

Lastname, Firstname. Personal interview. Day Month Year.

A video recording

Title of Recording. Producer, Year. Medium of Publication.

Electronic Publications

A CD-ROM

"Title of Piece." *Title of CD*. Year ed. City of Publication: Publisher, Year of Publication. CD-ROM.

A document from an Internet site

Entries for online source should contain as much information as available.

Lastname, Firstname. "*Title of Piece*." Information on what the site is. Year. Web. Day Month Year (when accessed).

Participating in a Collaborative Discussion

Often, class activities, including the Performance Tasks in this book, will require you to work collaboratively with classmates. Whether your group will analyze a work of literature or try to solve a community problem, use the following guidelines to ensure a productive discussion.

Prepare for the Discussion

A productive discussion is one in which all the participants bring useful information and ideas to share. If your group will discuss a short story the class read, first re-read and annotate a copy of the story. Your annotations will help you quickly locate evidence to support your points. Participants in a discussion about an important issue should first research the issue and bring notes or information sources that will help guide the group. If you disagree with a point made by another group member, your case will be stronger if you back it up with specific evidence from your sources.

EXAMPLES

> **disagreeing without evidence:** I don't think physical art is relevant today because nobody goes to museums.

> **providing evidence for disagreement:** I disagree that physical art is relevant today because so few people go to museums. For example, every large museum, such as the Metropolitan Museum of Art in New York, the Art Institute of Chicago, and the San Francisco Museum of Modern Art, has a website where the public can view art online. Current exhibitions are shown and previous exhibitions are archived for viewing. Why would someone need to go to a dark museum when images are so easy to view online? Even artists such as Julian Beever, who creates physical public art, have websites for the public to view their art. We can clearly view and compare multiple images of Beever's chalk art by clicking on his online gallery.

Set Ground Rules

The rules your group needs will depend on what your group is expected to accomplish. A discussion of themes in a poem will be unlikely to produce a single consensus; however, a discussion aimed at developing a solution to a problem should result in one strong proposal that all group members support. Answer the following questions to set ground rules that fit your group's purpose:

- What will this group produce? A range of ideas, a single decision, a plan of action, or something else?
- How much time is available? How much of that time should be allotted to each part of our discussion (presenting ideas, summarizing or voting on final ideas, creating a product such as a written analysis or speech)?
- What roles need to be assigned within the group? Do we need a leader, a note-taker, a timekeeper, or other specific roles?
- What is the best way to synthesize our group's ideas? Should we take a vote, list group members as "for" or "against" in a chart, or use some other method to reach a consensus or sum up the results of the discussion?

Move the Discussion Forward

Everyone in the group should be actively involved in synthesizing ideas. To make sure this happens, ask questions that draw out ideas, especially from less-talkative members of the group. If an idea or statement is confusing, try to paraphrase it, or ask the speaker to explain more about it. If you disagree with a statement, say so politely and explain in detail why you disagree.

SAMPLE DISCUSSION

JACK: How about you, Ella? Do you think physical art is relevant to people today? The rest of us say it is.

Question draws out quiet member

ELLA: Well, I don't know. We took a field trip to an art museum once to learn about the importance of art and the time periods of art, but none of the people I know go to museums otherwise. We also read about art and artists, like Julian Beever, but we can see his art online too.

Response relates discussion to larger ideas

JOSHUA: But don't we have the option of going to see physical art? I mean, we can go to a public space that has public art or to a museum and experience the art in person, right?

Question challenges Ella's conclusion

ELLA: Sure, but think of the possibilities for comparing images online versus in person. Someone can view and compare images by the same artist that are displayed in different museums by clicking online. How could they do that in person?

Response elaborates on ideas

VIVIAN: So you mean that people can view and compare more art online and the experience and the quantity is significant and worthwhile? I can see that, but is it more worthwhile than being physically present to view the actual work of art? There are things we can see and experience by examining the real object—things like texture in a painting or drawing—that might not be seen as well in an on-screen image.

Paraphrases idea and challenges it further based on evidence

Respond to Ideas

In a diverse group, everyone may have a different perspective on the topic of discussion, and that's a good thing. Consider what everyone has to say, and don't resist changing your view if other group members provide convincing evidence for theirs. If, instead, you feel more strongly than ever about your view, don't hesitate to say so and provide reasons related to what those with opposing views have said. Before wrapping up the discussion, try to sum up the points on which your group agrees and disagrees.

SAMPLE DISCUSSION

VIVIAN: OK, we just have a few more minutes. Do we want to take a vote?

Vivian and Jack try to summarize points of agreement

JACK: Sure. I think the three positions are NO, YES, and YES, BUT. . . . Does that sound right?

JOSHUA: Yeah, let's make a chart of these. I still say YES, physical art is relevant today. No BUT about it, because physical elements and experience are at the core.

Joshua maintains his position

ELLA: And I say YES, BUT. You've convinced me that physical art offers some experiences and close viewing possibilities, but I still think that easy, quick, universal access to online images removes barriers for viewing art for a lot of people today.

Ella and Jack qualify their views based on what they have heard

JACK: That makes sense. I'm changing my position from solid YES to YES, BUT. I think quick and easy access is important, though not always more important than slow and careful scrutiny of physical art and actually being there—like walking alongside sidewalk art.

VIVIAN: I'm with Joshua. I think being able to move around a work of art literally adds a whole new dimension to understanding art.

Vivian supports her position by making a new connection

Debating an Issue

The selection and collection Performance Tasks in this text will direct you to engage in debates about issues relating to the selections you are reading. Use the guidelines that follow to have a productive and balanced argument about both sides of an issue.

The Structure of a Formal Debate

In a debate, two teams compete to win the support of the audience about an issue. In a **formal debate,** two teams, each with two members, present their arguments on a given proposition or policy statement. One team argues for the proposition or statement and the other team argues against it. Each debater must consider the proposition closely and must research both sides of it. To argue convincingly either for or against a proposition, a debater must be familiar with both sides of the issue.

Plan the Debate

The purpose of a debate is to allow participants and audience members to consider both sides of an issue. Use these planning suggestions to hold a balanced and productive debate:

- **Identify Debate Teams** Form groups of six members based on the issues that the Performance Tasks include. Three members of the team will argue for the affirmative side of the issue—that is, they support the issue. The other three members will argue for the negative side of the issue—that is, they do not support the issue.
- **Appoint a Moderator** The moderator will present the topic and goals of the debate, keep track of the time, and introduce and thank the participants.
- **Research and Prepare Notes** Search texts you've read as well as print and online sources for valid reasons and evidence to support your team's claim. As with argument, be sure to anticipate possible opposing claims and compile evidence to counter those claims. You will use notes from your research during the debate.

- **Assign Debate Roles** One team member will introduce the team's claim and supporting evidence. Another team member will respond to questions and opposing claims in an exchange with a member of the opposing team. The last member will present a strong closing argument.

Hold the Debate

A formal debate is not a shouting match—rather, a well-run debate is an excellent forum for participants to express their viewpoints, build on others' ideas, and have a thoughtful, well-reasoned exchange of ideas. The moderator will begin by stating the topic or issue and introducing the participants. Participants should follow the moderator's instructions concerning whose turn it is to speak and how much time each speaker has.

Formal Debate Format

Speaker	Role	Time
Affirmative Speaker 1	Present the claim and supporting evidence for the affirmative ("pro") side of the argument.	5 minutes
Negative Speaker 1	Ask probing questions that will prompt the other team to address flaws in the argument.	3 minutes
Affirmative Speaker 2	Respond to the questions posed by the opposing team and counter any concerns.	3 minutes

continued

Speaker	Role	Time
Negative Speaker 2	Present the claim and supporting evidence for the negative ("con") side of the argument.	5 minutes
Affirmative Speaker 3	Summarize the claim and evidence for the affirmative side and explain why your reasoning is more valid.	3 minutes
Negative Speaker 3	Summarize the claim and evidence for the negative side and explain why your reasoning is more valid.	3 minutes

Evaluate the Debate

Use the following guidelines to evaluate a team in a debate:

- Did the team prove that the issue is significant? How thorough was the analysis?
- How did the team members effectively argue that you should support their affirmative or negative side of the proposition or issue?
- How effectively did the team present reasons and evidence, including evidence from the texts, to support the proposition?
- How effectively did the team rebut, or respond to, arguments made by the opposing team?
- Did the speakers maintain eye contact and speak at an appropriate rate and volume?
- Did the speakers observe proper debate etiquette—that is, did they follow the moderator's instructions, stay within their allotted time limits, and treat their opponents respectfully?

Reading Informational Texts: Patterns of Organization

Reading any type of writing is easier once you recognize how it is organized. Writers usually arrange ideas and information in ways that best help readers see how they are related. There are several common patterns of organization.

- main idea and supporting details
- chronological order
- cause-effect organization
- compare-and-contrast organization

1. Main Idea and Supporting Details

Main idea and supporting details is a basic pattern of organization in which a central idea about a topic is supported by details. The **main idea** is the most important idea about a topic that a particular text or paragraph conveys. **Supporting details** are words, phrases, or sentences that tell more about the main idea. The main idea may be directly stated at the beginning and then followed by supporting details, or it may be merely implied by the supporting details. It may also be stated after it has been implied by supporting details.

Sometimes you will come across a main idea that is a **factual claim**—a statement that can be verified by observation, a reliable source, or an expert's view. In some cases the main idea may be stated as a **commonplace assertion**—a statement that many people assume to be true, but is not necessarily so. In both cases, the details should support the statements.

Strategies for Reading

- To find a stated main idea in a paragraph, identify the paragraph's topic. The topic is what the paragraph is about and can usually be summed up in one or two words. The word, or synonyms of it, will usually appear throughout the paragraph. Headings and subheadings are also clues to the topics of paragraphs.
- Ask: What is the topic sentence? The topic sentence states the most important idea, message, or information the paragraph conveys about this topic. It is often the first sentence in a paragraph; however, it may appear at the end.
- To find an implied main idea, ask yourself: Whom or what did I just read about? What do the details suggest about the topic?
- Formulate a sentence stating this idea and add it to the paragraph. Does your sentence convey the main idea?

Notice how the main idea is expressed in each of the following models.

Model:
Main Idea as the First Sentence

When the nomads of Africa began using camels around AD 300, trade across the Sahara became easier. [Main idea] The donkeys, horses, and oxen that had been used previously could not travel far without stopping for food and water. Camels, on the other hand, could cover 25 miles in a day and often go for two weeks without water. [Supporting details]

Model:
Main Idea as the Last Sentence

The new trade routes passed through lands occupied by the Soninke people. These farming people referred to their chief as ghana. Soon the land came to be known as the kingdom of Ghana. The tribal chiefs taxed the goods that traveled across their territory. [Supporting details] By the eighth century, trade had made Ghana a rich kingdom. [Main idea]

Model:
Implied Main Idea

The West African savannas and forests south of the savanna were rich in gold. No salt was available there, though. In the Sahara, on the other hand, there was abundant salt but no gold. Traders brought salt south through the desert and traded it for gold mined from the forests.

> **Implied main idea:** Gold and salt were two important items that were traded in West Africa.

Practice and Apply

Read each paragraph, and then do the following:

1. Identify the main idea in the paragraph, using one of the strategies discussed on the previous page.
2. Identify whether the main idea is stated or implied in the paragraph.

Every day we are surrounded by technology and computerized devices. We sit at our computers for hours for all kinds of purposes—writing and researching topics for our assignments, watching movies, posting messages on our social network pages, listening to music, and more. We call friends on our mobile devices. We tweet. But what we do most frequently is text. E-mail used to be important for messages. Now, it's not fast enough to compete with texting.

When we view a news article or any other text, our eyes see the words, and we begin to read. The eye is the organ of vision, and its job is to send signals about visuals to the brain. Once the eyes transmit the words to the brain, the real actions involved in reading begin to happen. Many areas of the brain work together to decipher the written word, and signals travel with amazing speed to all those areas.

2. Chronological Order

Chronological order is the arrangement of events in the order in which they happen. This type of organization is used in short stories and novels, historical writing, biographies, and autobiographies. To show the order of events, writers use order words such as *before, after, next,* and *later* and time words and phrases that identify specific times of day, days of the week, and dates, such as *the next morning, Tuesday,* and *on July 4, 1776.*

Strategies for Reading

- Look in the text for headings and subheadings that may indicate a chronological pattern of organization.
- Look for words and phrases that identify times, such as *in a year, three hours earlier, in 202 BC,* and *the next day.*
- Look for words that signal order, such as *first, afterward, then, during,* and *finally,* to see how events or steps are related.
- Note that a paragraph or passage in which ideas and information are arranged chronologically will have several words or phrases that indicate time order, not just one.
- Ask yourself: Are the events in the paragraph or passage presented in time order?

Notice the words and phrases that signal time order in the first two paragraphs of the following model.

> **Model**
>
> ### A Butterfly Gets Its Wings
>
> How does a butterfly get its wings? During its life, the butterfly goes through different growth stages. There are four main stages altogether: 1) the egg, 2) the caterpillar, 3) the pupa, and 4) the adult. The ancient Greeks called this whole process *metamorphosis,* a word we still use today.
>
> At first, the butterfly is a single slimy egg, no larger than a fingertip. The baby insect grows within the egg until it is ready to hatch. For most types of butterflies, this first stage lasts about ten days. When the egg cracks open, a caterpillar crawls out.
>
> In the second stage, the caterpillar spends most of its time eating and growing. As the caterpillar becomes bigger, it sheds its spiky or fuzzy skin. This process is called *molting.* A caterpillar molts several times during its life. Once the caterpillar has shed its skin for the last time, it becomes a pupa.

Events

Order words and phrases

Time words and phrases

RI 2,
RI 3,
RI 5

PRACTICE AND APPLY POSSIBLE ANSWERS

1. *First paragraph: Every day we are surrounded by technology and computerized devices.*
   Second paragraph: We may think we read with our eyes, but really we read with our brains.

2. *In the first paragraph, the main idea is stated. In the second paragraph, the main idea is implied.*

PRACTICE AND APPLY
POSSIBLE ANSWERS

1. *"in the second stage"; "during its life"; "once"; "for the last time"; "in the third stage"; "immediately"; "then"; "after"; "finally"; "in a short time"*

2. *The four growth stages include the egg, the caterpillar, the pupa, and the adult.*

3. *A butterfly begins its life in the form of a single, slimy egg.*

In the third stage, the pupa immediately grows a hard shell called a *chrysalis*. Then, inside the chrysalis, the pupa goes through the changes that will make it a butterfly. The pupa's hormones turn its body into wings, antennas, and other butterfly parts. After all the changes are complete, the shell splits open. A butterfly is ready to make its entrance.

Finally, the adult butterfly breaks from the chrysalis. Its body, however, doesn't look quite right. It's all soft and wrinkly. As air and blood are pumped through the butterfly's body, it starts to look more like its usual self. In a short time, the butterfly is ready to try out its new wings. With a few flutters, it's off and away!

Practice and Apply

Refer to the preceding model to do the following:

1. List at least six words in the last three paragraphs that indicate time or order.
2. What does the writer call the four main parts in the life of a butterfly?
3. In what form does a butterfly begin its life?

3. Cause-Effect Organization

Cause-effect organization is a pattern of organization that shows causal relationships between events, ideas, and trends. Cause-effect relationships may be directly stated or merely implied by the order in which the information is presented. Writers often use the cause-effect pattern in historical and scientific writing. Cause-effect relationships may have several forms.

One cause with one effect

One cause with multiple effects

Multiple causes with a single effect

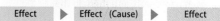

A chain of causes and effects

| Effect | ▶ | Effect (Cause) | ▶ | Effect |

Strategies for Reading

- Look for headings and subheadings that indicate a cause-effect pattern of organization, such as "Effects of Food Allergies."
- To find the effect or effects, read to answer the question, What happened?
- To find the cause or causes, read to answer the question, Why did it happen?
- Look for words and phrases that help you identify specific relationships between events, such as *because, since, had the effect of, led to, as a result, resulted in, for that reason, due to, therefore, if . . . then,* and *consequently.*
- Look closely at each cause-effect relationship. Do not assume that because one event happened before another, the first event caused the second event.
- Use graphic organizers like the diagrams shown to record cause-effect relationships as you read.

Notice the words that signal causes and effects in the following model.

Model

How a Tsunami Forms

Tsunami is a word that brings fear to people who live near the sea. Also known in English as a tidal wave, a tsunami is a huge ocean wave caused by an underwater volcanic eruption or earthquake.

An earthquake or the explosion of a volcano on the ocean floor creates massive waves of energy. These energy waves spread out in widening circles, like waves from a pebble dropped into a pond.

As the tsunami nears the shore, it begins to scrape along the ocean bottom. This friction causes the waves in the front to slow down. As a result, the waves traveling behind begin piling up and growing higher. This increase in height can happen very quickly—by as much as 90 feet in 10 or 15 minutes.

The effects of a tsunami can include the death of many people and the destruction of ships, buildings, and land along the shore. An especially dangerous situation may occur when the first part of a tsunami to hit the shore is the trough, or low point, rather than the crest of a wave. This trough sucks all the water away from the shore and may attract curious people on the beach. Within a few minutes, however, the crest of the wave will hit and may drown the onlookers. The most destructive tsunami ever recorded struck the Indonesian island of Sumatra, in 2004. It left more than 200,000 people dead.

Effect	
Signal words	
Cause	
Cause	
Effect	

Practice and Apply

1. Use the pattern of a chain of causes and effects, illustrated on page R18, to make a graphic organizer showing the causes and effects described in the text.

2. List three words that the writer uses to signal cause and effect in the last two paragraphs.

---

4. Compare-and-Contrast Organization

Compare-and-contrast organization is a pattern of organization that provides a way to look at similarities and differences in two or more subjects. A writer may use this pattern of organization to compare the important points or characteristics of two or more subjects. These points or characteristics are called **points of comparison.** The compare-and-contrast pattern of organization may be developed in either of two ways:

Point-by-point organization—The writer discusses one point of comparison for both subjects, then goes on to the next point.

Subject-by-subject organization—The writer covers all points of comparison for one subject and then all points of comparison for the next subject.

Strategies for Reading

• Look in the text for headings, subheadings, and sentences that may suggest a compare-and-contrast pattern of organization, such as "Plants Share Many Characteristics," to help you identify where similarities and differences are addressed.

• To find similarities, look for words and phrases such as *like, similarly, both, all, every, also,* and *in the same way.*

• To find differences, look for words and phrases such as *unlike, but, on the other hand, more, less, in contrast,* and *however.*

• Use a graphic organizer, such as a Venn diagram or a compare-and-contrast chart, to record points of comparison and similarities and differences.

Reading Informational Texts   **R19**

PRACTICE AND APPLY POSSIBLE ANSWERS

1. *Students should create a graphic organizer that shows a chain of causes and effects.*

   cause: earthquake or volcano occurs in ocean; effect (cause): waves spread out; effect (cause): tsunami scrapes along shore bottom; effect (cause): friction slows down front waves; effect (cause): the back waves grow higher; effect: enormous wave crashes ashore

2. *causes, as a result, the effects*

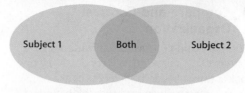

	Subject 1	Subject 2
Point 1		
Point 2		
Point 3		

Read the following models. As you read, use the signal words and phrases to identify the similarities and differences between the subjects and how the details are organized in each text.

Model 1

Living in Outer Space

Ten . . . nine . . . eight . . . The date is December 21, 1968.

Seven . . . six . . . five . . . alongside a launch gantry at Cape Kennedy, Florida, a huge Saturn V rocket stands fueled and ready for blastoff, hydrogen vapor steaming from its rocket motors.

Four . . . three . . . two . . . at the top of the rocket sits the *Apollo 8* command module, the capsule that will ferry astronauts Frank Borman, James A. Lovell Jr., and William A. Anders to the moon and back.

One . . . zero . . . Liftoff! The Saturn's powerful engines roar to life, and another exciting chapter in the history of the United States space program begins.

Today, that same *Apollo 8* command module is one of the most popular attractions at the Henry Crown Space Center at the Museum of Science and Industry in Chicago. For six days in 1968, this cone-shaped capsule was home to the first humans to leave the security of earth's orbit and venture out to visit another heavenly body.

Museum visitors, especially young people accustomed to space travel in the shuttle era, are often amazed at the cramped quarters within the capsule, and they wonder just how three adults lived for six days in such a compact environment. Space travel has come a long way since those pioneering days of the 1960s. Some of the main similarities and differences relate to living quarters and food.

Today's shuttle crews have both a flight deck and a lower crew-quarters deck in which to move around. The *Apollo* crews, however, were pretty much confined to their metal-and-fabric flight couches, although there was a little stretching room beneath the couches and around the hatch area that led to the lunar Excursion Module.

Mealtime is a highlight of anyone's day, including every astronaut's. Early space travelers were limited to puréed foods squeezed out of toothpaste tubes and juices in plastic bags. Shuttle crews, on the other hand, enjoy a much more appetizing diet. It's still not exactly fine dining, but at least the food is served on trays, is eaten with utensils, and includes healthy snacks, like fresh fruit.

At the end of a working "day" in space, all astronauts are ready for some rest. In *Apollo*, the crew simply drifted off to sleep on their couches. Aboard the shuttle, crew members sleep in special sleep restraints. Some sleep horizontally, while others opt for a vertical snooze. In zero gravity, position doesn't matter!

The United States has continued to develop the space program. The lessons learned during the first three decades of space flight are making life in the alien environment beyond earth's atmosphere much more pleasant for a new generation of space explorers.

Comparison words and phrases

Contrast words and phrases

Subjects

Model 2

To compare the two types of energy, we must first understand what energy is. Energy is the ability to do work. That doesn't just mean work as in homework or yard work. Energy comes in many forms, such as a rock falling off a cliff, a moving bicycle, or the stored energy in food. With all these forms, there are only two main types of energy, potential and kinetic. These are the energies of rest and motion.

> **Subjects**

Potential energy is the energy an object has stored up based on how high up it is or how much it weighs. For instance, suppose two kids weigh the same and climb a tree. If they are on different branches, the kid on the higher branch has more potential energy than the kid on the lower branch. However, if one kid weighs more than the other, and they both sit at the same height, the heavier kid has more potential energy than the lighter kid.

> **Comparison words and phrases**

> **Contrast words and phrases**

If the kids jump out of the tree, their potential energy becomes kinetic energy. This kind comes from the motion of an object. Kinetic energy increases with the speed of an object. When the kids jump, their speed increases as they fall. They have more kinetic energy when they are falling faster than they do when they first jump and are falling more slowly. Also, the more mass an object has, the more kinetic energy it has. Even if both kids jump at the exact same time, the one with more mass will always have more kinetic energy.

These two kids probably knew they were using a lot of energy, but they would probably be surprised to know how much work they had been doing.

Refer to the preceding models to answer the following questions:

1. Which model is organized by subject? Which model is organized by points of comparison?
2. Identify two words or phrases in each model that signal a compare-and-contrast pattern of organization.
3. List two points that the writer of each model compares and contrasts.
4. Use a Venn diagram or a compare-and-contrast chart to identify two or more points of comparison and the similarities and differences shown in one of the two models.

5. Problem-Solution Order

Problem-solution order is a pattern of organization in which a problem is stated and analyzed and then one or more solutions are proposed and examined. This pattern of organization is often used in persuasive writing, such as editorials or proposals.

Strategies for Reading

- Look for an explanation of the problem in the first or second paragraph.
- Look for words, such as *problem* and *reason*, that may signal an explanation of the problem.
- To find the solution, ask: What suggestion does the writer offer to solve the problem?
- Look for words, such as *propose, conclude,* and *answer,* that may signal a solution.

RI 2,
RI 3,
RI 5

PRACTICE AND APPLY POSSIBLE ANSWERS

1. *Model 1 is organized by points of comparison. Model 2 is organized by subject.*

2. *Possible answers: Model 1: "both," "although," "on the other hand," "while"; Model 2: "than," "both," "also," "same," "the larger of the two," "always"*

3. *Possible answers: Model 1: the size of the living quarters, the quality of the food, the shuttle's sleeping accommodations; Model 2: the relationship of height, weight, and speed to each type of energy*

4. *Students should create a Venn diagram or a compare-and-contrast chart. Possible answers:*
   Model 1: Apollo Crew (1968)—Living quarters: metal-and-fabric flight couches. Meals: pureed foods squeezed out of tubes and juice in plastic bags. Sleeping accommodations: slept on couches with no room to move or spread out. Shuttle crews (today)—Living quarters: separate flight deck and lower crew-quarters deck. Meals: food is served on trays, is eaten with utensils, and includes healthy snacks. Sleeping accommodations: use sleep restraints that allow crew to sleep horizontally or vertically.
   Model 2: Potential energy—based on height and weight; heavier objects have more potential energy. Kinetic energy—based on the motion of an object; energy increases with the speed of an object. Similarities—The heavier the object, the greater the energy.

Reading Informational Texts **R21**

PRACTICE AND APPLY
POSSIBLE ANSWERS

1. *Fargo does not have a large enough population to financially support a major-league franchise.*

2. *The writer proposes that the town of Fargo and nearby towns such as Moorhead, Grand Forks, and Aberdeen combine to help finance and support a new baseball team. The words "here's my plan" provide a clue to the reader.*

Model

I love baseball, but I won't be going to any major-league games, and I won't be rooting for the local major-league team. The reason is simple. There is no local major-league team in North Dakota. There's none in South Dakota or in Montana or even in Wyoming. The closest major-league team is the Minnesota Twins, and that's over 240 miles away!

The problem is that getting a major-league team costs money. Any city that wants a team has to have enough money to build a stadium. The city also has to have a big enough population to support the team. Fargo is the biggest city in North Dakota, and it only has about 91,484 people. That's not enough to support a major-league franchise. Sports stadiums often hold more people than Fargo has!

Even though the towns around here aren't exactly huge, there are a lot of die-hard baseball fans like my friends and me. So here's my plan. Why couldn't a couple of towns get together to build a stadium and start a team? For example, Moorhead, Minnesota, is right next to Fargo. They already share the same airport, and the metropolitan area has about 174,367 people. That might be enough to support a team. If it's not, then maybe Grand Forks, or even Aberdeen, could join in too.

People might say that there would be a problem naming a team that is supported by cities in two or three different states. I think baseball fans would be so happy to have a team, they wouldn't really care what it was called.

If enough people wrote to the Fargo and Moorhead city governments, maybe the idea could be put on the ballot. Major-league baseball is supposed to be our national pastime. Shouldn't we be a part of it too?

Practice and Apply

Reread the model and then answer the following questions:

1. According to the model, what is the cause of the problem?
2. What solution does the writer offer? What words are a clue?

Reading Arguments

1. Analyzing an Argument

An **argument** expresses a position on an issue or problem and supports it with reasons and evidence. Being able to analyze and evaluate arguments will help you distinguish between claims you should accept and those you should not. A sound argument should appeal strictly to reason. However, arguments are often used in texts that also contain other types of persuasive devices. An argument includes the following elements:

- A **claim** is the writer's position on an issue or problem.
- **Support** is any material that serves to prove a claim. In an argument, support usually consists of reasons and evidence.
- **Reasons** are declarations made to justify an action, decision, or belief—for example, "My reason for thinking we will be late is that the drive takes longer than five minutes."
- **Evidence** can be the specific references, quotations, facts, examples, and opinions that support a claim. Evidence may also consist of statistics, reports of personal experience, or the views of experts.
- A **counterargument** is an argument made to oppose another argument. A good argument anticipates the opposition's objections and provides counterarguments to disprove or answer them.

Claim	I think I should be allowed more time online.

| Reason | The Internet can provide opportunities for learning and enjoyment. |

| Evidence | The Internet can take you to faraway places and can bring art, music, and science right into your home. |

| Counter-argument | Some people think the Internet is bad for kids, but those people are looking at only the worst part of the Internet, not the best. |

Read the following editorial and use a chart like the one shown to identify the claim, reason, evidence, and counterargument.

Important Hours by Gina Maraini

"The Golden Years." That is what some people call old age. They think it is a time of peace and relaxation. But many old people spend time alone. Some cannot get out of their homes because of illness. "What can I do?" you ask. You can do more than you think to make an important contribution to an older person's life. Even spending an hour a week can mean a lot to an older neighbor who lives alone.

Some kids might say that they can only do good for an older person if they have lots of time and lots of patience. It's easy to talk yourself out of volunteering your time by saying, "I only have an hour a week. What good would that do?" Never underestimate just how much good you can do even in a little bit of time.

Sometimes things happen that seem unimportant to a kid but can really be a problem to an old person. If a small object like a pen or pencil slides under furniture, an older person often is not able to stoop down and pick it up. But they feel embarrassed to ask for help. So, the pen stays there. Sometimes it gets forgotten about and becomes lost. You can help that older person find these things. and by helping, you are reminding that person that he or she is not forgotten about either.

Sometimes it is hard for an older person to reach up high. Putting things away, like groceries, becomes a problem. Often the older person gets tired and gives up. You can help to put groceries and other heavy objects away. And by doing that, you are helping that older person feel like he or she can still keep up with life's challenges.

One of the most important things you can do for a senior citizen who lives alone is to give that person someone to talk to. Old people, who have lived long lives and had many experiences, have stories to tell that you can learn a lot from. And it is important for you to say so, too. That way, you can show the older person that he or she is contributing to your life.

PRACTICE AND APPLY POSSIBLE ANSWERS

Students should create a chart similar to the one on page R23. The chart should include details similar to the ones below.

Claim: *You can do more than you think to make an important contribution to an older person's life.*

Reason: *Even spending an hour a week can mean a lot to an older person.*

Evidence: *An older person may have trouble stooping down to pick up objects. You can help an older person find things. By helping, you are reminding the person that he or she is not forgotten.*

Evidence: *It can be hard for an older person to reach up high. By helping put away groceries and other heavy objects, you are helping the person feel that he or she can still keep up with life's challenges.*

Evidence: *Older people have lived a long life and have had many experiences. By listening to an older person's stories, you can show the person that he or she is contributing to your life.*

Counterargument: *It's easy to talk yourself out of volunteering your time by saying, "I only have an hour a week. What good would that do?" Never underestimate how much good you can do even in a little bit of time.*

PRACTICE AND APPLY POSSIBLE ANSWERS

Appeals by Association—bandwagon appeal: "join the leaders in your community and many of your neighbors who have already put their support behind Victor Velazquez"; testimonial: "Local business-woman Janice Wu is behind Victor Velazquez all the way . . ."
Emotional Appeals—appeals to pity, fear, or vanity: "a dinosaur who's stuck in the past or someone who's courageously facing the future"; "Why settle for Jill Jolsen, who hasn't lifted a finger to help this community?"
Word Choice—glittering generality: "once-in-a-lifetime chance to change this town"

You can make a real contribution to an older person's life. Even if you only have an hour to spend, you can help an older person feel cared about and important. Find ways to reach out, whether through volunteer organizations or just by being aware of who is alone in your neighborhood. And always remember: as much as you give, you get back so much more, simply by knowing the difference that you have made.

2. Recognizing Persuasive Techniques

Persuasive texts typically rely on more than just the **logical appeal** of an argument to be convincing. They also rely on ethical and emotional appeals and other **persuasive techniques**—devices that can convince you to adopt a position or take an action.

Ethical appeals establish a writer's credibility and trustworthiness with an audience. When a writer links a claim to a widely accepted value, the writer not only gains moral support for that claim but also establishes a connection with readers. For example, with the following appeal, the writer reminds readers of a value they should accept and links a claim to it: "Most of us agree that we should protect our natural resources, but we don't invest a lot of time or money to preserve them."

The chart shown here explains several other means by which a writer may attempt to sway you to adopt his or her position. Learn to recognize these techniques, and you are less likely to be influenced by them.

Persuasive Technique	Example
Appeals by Association	
Bandwagon appeal Suggests that a person should believe or do something because "everyone else" does	Every day more buyers are enjoying the conveniences of Internet shopping.
Testimonial Relies on endorsements from well-known people or satisfied customers	Todd Marshall, star of stage and screen, buys his shoes at Fine Footwear. Shouldn't you?
Snob appeal Taps into people's desire to be special or part of an elite group	Be among the first to enjoy the upgraded facilities at Spring Lake Fitness Center.
Appeal to loyalty Relies on people's affiliation with a particular group	Say *Yes!* to your community—support the campaign to build a new library!
Emotional Appeals	
Appeals to pity, fear, or vanity Use strong feelings, rather than facts, to persuade	We need to keep the homeless shelter open—think how you would feel if you had no place to go.
Word Choice	
Glittering generality A generalization that includes a word or phrase with positive connotations, to promote a product, person, or idea.	Buying handmade jewelry from the Hang Up helps support small-town America.

Practice and Apply

Identify the persuasive techniques used in this model.

Vote for Velazquez!

Whom do you want to represent you in congress—a dinosaur who's stuck in the past or someone who's courageously facing the future? Why settle for Jill Jolsen, who hasn't lifted a finger to help this community? Don't let her slick ads fool you. Instead, join the leaders in the community and many of your neighbors who have already put their support behind Victor Velazquez. Local businesswoman Janice Wu is behind Velazquez all the way—she says he will bring new jobs and fresh ideas that will really work. Don't miss this once-in-a-lifetime chance to change this town. Vote for Velazquez!

3. Analyzing Logic and Reasoning

While persuasive techniques may sway you to side with a writer, they should not be enough to convince you that an argument is sound. To determine the soundness of an argument, you really need to examine the argument's claim and support and the logic or reasoning that links them. To do this, it is helpful to identify the writer's mode of reasoning.

The Inductive Mode of Reasoning

When a person uses specific evidence to arrive at a **general principle,** or generalization, that person is using **inductive reasoning.** Similarly, when a writer presents specific evidence first and then offers a generalization drawn from that evidence, the writer is making an **inductive argument.** Here is an example of inductive reasoning.

Specific Facts
Fact 1 Turtles are the only reptiles that have a shell.
Fact 2 The green turtle, a sea turtle, can swim almost 20 miles an hour.
Fact 3 Snapping turtles have powerful, sharp-edged jaws and are aggressive when attacked.

Generalization
Turtles have a variety of protective strategies.

There are several types of inductive reasoning.

- **argument by cause and effect:** In this type of argument, the writer or speaker attempts to persuade by showing the causes that would lead to a desired or an undesired effect. **Example:** *If we don't see the movie today, we won't be able to see it on the weekend because the theater will be too crowded.*
- **argument by analogy:** In this type of argument, the writer or speaker compares familiar events and things to those that are unfamiliar in an attempt to persuade the audience to accept the new situation. **Example:** *You'll like this new movie because it has a plot that is similar to others you've seen.*
- **argument by authority:** In this type of

argument, the writer or speaker attempts to persuade by using an authoritative and reliable source as evidence. **Example:** *The movie critic gave the new movie three stars, so we should go see it.*

Strategies for Determining the Soundness of Inductive Arguments

Ask yourself the following questions to evaluate an inductive argument:

- **Is the evidence valid and sufficient support for the conclusion?** Inaccurate facts lead to inaccurate conclusions.
- **Does the conclusion follow logically from the evidence?** From the facts listed above, the conclusion that *all* turtles have a wide variety of protective strategies would be too broad a generalization.
- **Is the evidence drawn from a large enough sample?** Even though there are only three facts listed above, the sample is large enough to support the claim. If you wanted to support the conclusion that only turtles have a variety of protective strategies, the sample is not large enough.

The Deductive Mode of Reasoning

When a person uses a **general principle,** or generalization, to form a conclusion about a particular situation or problem, that person is using **deductive reasoning.** For example,

Being exposed to loud noise over a long period will damage a person's hearing.	General principle or generalization
▼	
I listen to my stereo at its highest setting for hours every day.	The situation being observed or considered
▼	
I will have some hearing loss.	Conclusion (also considered a deduction)

Similarly, a writer is making a **deductive argument** when he or she begins the argument with a claim that is based on a general principle

**PRACTICE AND APPLY
ANSWER**

The paragraph uses inductive reasoning based on argument by cause and effect.

and then presents evidence to support the claim. For example, a writer might begin a deductive argument with the claim "Many people have some hearing loss."

Strategies for Determining the Soundness of Deductive Arguments

Ask yourself the following questions to evaluate a deductive argument.

- **Is the general principle actually stated, or is it implied?** Note that writers often use deductive reasoning in arguments without stating the general principles. They assume that readers will recognize and agree with the principles. Be sure to identify the general principle for yourself.

- **Is the general principle sound?** Don't just assume the general principle is sound. Ask yourself whether it is really true.

- **Is the conclusion valid?** To be valid, a conclusion in a deductive argument must follow logically from the general principle and the specific situation.

The following chart shows two conclusions drawn from the same general principle.

All seventh-graders are going to the zoo next week.	
Accurate Deduction	**Inaccurate Deduction**
Laura is in the seventh grade; therefore, Laura is going to the zoo next week.	Laura is going to the zoo next week; therefore, Laura is in the seventh grade.

Laura may be going to the zoo with her family or friends.

Practice and Apply

Identify whether inductive or deductive reasoning is used in the following paragraph. If the mode of reasoning used is inductive, tell whether the paragraph uses argument by cause and effect, analogy, or authority.

In science class, I learned what different substances do for the human body. Protein aids growth and repairs muscles. Fruits and vegetables provide critical vitamins, and calcium strengthens bones. Carbohydrates supply energy to the body. Clearly, a balanced diet is important for good health.

Identifying Faulty Reasoning

Sometimes an argument at first appears to make sense but isn't valid because it is based on a fallacy. A **rhetorical fallacy** is a false or misleading statement. Learn to recognize these rhetorical fallacies.

Type of Fallacy	Definition	Example
Circular reasoning	Supporting a statement by simply repeating it in different words	I'm tired because **I don't have any energy.**
Either/or fallacy	A statement that suggests that there are only two choices available in a situation that really offers more than two options	**Either** we raise taxes, **or** we close the parks.
Oversimplification	An explanation of a complex situation or problem as if it were much simpler than it is	Getting a good grade in Mrs. Raimi's class depends on **whether she likes you.**
Overgeneralization	A generalization that is too broad. You can often recognize overgeneralizations by the use of words such as *all, everyone, every time, anything, no one,* and *none.*	You **never** get me anything I want.
Hasty generalization	A conclusion drawn from too little evidence or from evidence that is biased	She left after fifteen minutes. **She must not like us.**
Stereotyping	A dangerous type of overgeneralization. Stereotypes are broad statements about people on the basis of their gender, ethnicity, race, or political, social, professional, or religious group	**All rock stars** are self-centered.
Ad hominem or attacking the person	An attempt to discredit an idea by attacking the person or group associated with it. Candidates often engage in name-calling during political campaigns.	The **narrow-minded** senator opposes recycling.
Evading the issue	Responding to an objection with arguments and evidence that do not address its central point	Yes, I broke my campaign promise not to raise taxes, **but higher taxes have led to increases in police patrols and paved highways.**
False cause	The mistake of assuming that because one event occurred after another event in time, the first event caused the second one to occur	John didn't get his homework done because he had to take the dog for a walk.

PRACTICE AND APPLY POSSIBLE ANSWERS

Overgeneralization: *"Nobody gets rid of his or her trash properly and everyone writes graffiti on the walls."*
Explanation: The writer uses words such as nobody *and* everyone *to make broad generalizations about people.*

Hasty generalization: *"If the school seemed more worth caring about, students would take better care of it."*
Explanation: The statement presents a biased point of view based on one person's opinion.

False cause: *"The halls are dark and the walls are dingy because the maintenance staff has been on strike for several weeks."*
Explanation: The writer makes the assumption that one event (the strike) caused another (the condition of the building), but does not consider other possible causes.

Ad hominem or attacking the person: *"old-fashioned school board"*
Explanation: The writer uses negative language to discredit the board.

Either/or fallacy: *"Either we build a new school, or it will be destroyed in three years."*
Explanation: The statement does not take into account other alternatives.

Look for examples of logical fallacies in the following argument. Identify each one and explain why you identified it as such.

Dear Editors:

There has been a lot of talk about students' lack of concern for the appearance of our school. Nobody gets rid of his or her trash properly and everyone writes graffiti on the walls. But if the school seemed more worth caring about, students would take better care of it. Most of the school is very old. The halls are dark and the walls are dingy because the maintenance staff has been on strike for several weeks. The old-fashioned school board said that an entirely new building wasn't needed. So only a new gym was added. It is clean and bright because students have kept it that way. Either we build a new school, or it will be destroyed in three years.

4. Evaluating Persuasive Texts

Learning how to evaluate persuasive texts and identify bias will help you become more selective when doing research and also help you improve your own reasoning and arguing skills. **Bias** is an inclination for or against a particular opinion or viewpoint. A writer may reveal a strongly positive or negative bias on an issue by

- presenting only one way of looking at it
- overlooking key information
- stacking more evidence on one side of the argument than the other
- using unfairly weighted evidence, which is weak or unproven evidence that a writer treats as if it is more important than it really is
- using loaded language, which consists of words with strongly positive or negative connotations

EXAMPLE:

Barbara Larsen is the best choice for student council president because she has fresh ideas and fantastic people skills. (*Fresh* and *fantastic* have very positive connotations.)

Propaganda is any form of communication that is so distorted that it conveys false or misleading information. Some politicians create and distribute propaganda. Many logical fallacies, such as name-calling, the either/or fallacy, and false causes, are often used in propaganda. The following example shows an oversimplification. The writer uses one fact to support a particular point of view but does not reveal another fact that does not support that viewpoint.

EXAMPLE:

Since the new park opened, vandalism in the area has increased by 10 percent. Clearly, the park has had a negative impact on the area. (The writer does not include the fact that the vandalism was caused by people who were not drawn into the area by the park.)

Strategies for Assessing Evidence

It is important to have a set of standards by which you can evaluate persuasive texts. Use the questions below to help you assess the adequacy, accuracy, and appropriateness of facts and opinions that are presented as evidence.

- **Are the facts accurate?** Facts can be proved by eyewitness accounts, authoritative sources such as encyclopedias and experts, or research.
- **Are the opinions well informed?** Any opinions offered should be supported by facts, be based on research or eyewitness accounts, or come from experts on the topic.
- **Is the evidence sufficient?** Thorough, or sufficient, evidence leaves no reasonable question unanswered. If a choice is offered to the reader, enough evidence for making the choice should be given. If taking a side is called for, all sides of the issue should be presented.
- **Is the evidence biased?** Be alert to evidence that contains loaded language or other signs of bias.
- **Is the evidence relevant?** The evidence needs to apply to the topic and come from people, groups, or organizations that have important knowledge of, or credentials relating to, the topic.

- **Is it important that the evidence be current?** Where timeliness is crucial, as in the areas of medicine and technology, the evidence should reflect the latest developments in the areas.

Practice and Apply

Read the argument below. Identify the facts, opinion, and elements of bias.

Let your voice be heard. The students' league is hosting a demonstration against U.S. Representative Sharon Bullhorn on Saturday. Just last week, Representative Bullhorn voted against raising the minimum wage. Obviously Representative Bullhorn doesn't care about young people. If she did, she would have helped pass the much-needed minimum wage increase, so that preteens and teens could earn the money they deserve.

Strategies for Determining a Strong Argument

Make sure that all or most of the following statements are true:

- The argument presents a claim or thesis.
- The claim is connected to its support by a general principle that most readers would readily agree with. Valid general principle: *It is the job of a school to provide a well-rounded physical education program.* Invalid general principle: *It is the job of a school to produce healthy, physically fit people.*
- The reasons make sense.
- The reasons are presented in a logical and effective order.
- The claim and all reasons are adequately supported by sound evidence.
- The evidence is sufficient, accurate, and relevant.
- The logic is sound. There are no instances of faulty reasoning.
- The argument adequately anticipates and addresses reader concerns and counterclaims with counterarguments.

Practice and Apply

Use the preceding criteria to evaluate the strength of the following proposal.

Summary of Proposal

I propose that our school install video cameras in halls, lunchrooms, and other public areas to monitor students' activities.

Need

The halls and public areas of our school are not well supervised because of a shortage of security staff. Last month, three students were hurt in fights on school property.

Proposed Solution

Installing video monitors in the halls and public areas of the school will create a safe environment for students at a reasonable cost.

There is good evidence that video monitoring works. Westview School has monitored its students for over a year. In that time there has not been one incident of fighting or damage to property

People who are against video monitoring don't agree. They say that monitoring violates students' rights to privacy.

In my opinion, junior high students need to act like responsible adults. We need guidelines and monitoring to show us where the limits are and to help us learn to act responsibly on our own.

Not only does video monitoring work, but installing the equipment can lower supervisory costs in the long run. Only eight cameras would be needed, installed in the two main hallways, the lunchroom, and the auditorium. The total cost would be around $16,000. I believe the money can be found in the general school budget.

What idiot would not support video monitoring of students?

It would be a crime not to have video monitoring.

Most school officials only care about their jobs and not what's good for students. I say to those school officials who do care: Either install video cameras or wait for more students to be injured.

RI 8

PRACTICE AND APPLY
POSSIBLE ANSWERS

Facts: The Students' League is hosting a demonstration against Representative Sharon Bullhorn on Saturday. Last week, Representative Bullhorn voted against raising the minimum wage.
Opinion: "If she did [care], she would have helped pass the much-needed minimum wage increase, so that preteens and teens could earn the money they deserve."
Elements of bias: "Obviously Representative Bullhorn doesn't care about young people."

RI 8

PRACTICE AND APPLY

Students' responses will vary, but they should evaluate the strength of the claim, the evidence supporting the claim, and the counterarguments.

POSSIBLE ANSWERS

The writer presents a clear thesis and offers a logical and effective solution to help maintain a safe learning environment. The evidence the writer provides in support of video monitoring is adequate, accurate, and appropriate. He or she also anticipates counterclaims and addresses concerns about maintaining students' privacy. For the most part, this person's argument is strong. However, the writer's proposal is undermined at the end by faulty reasoning; specifically, the use of name-calling, generalization, and false cause. Ad hominem statements weaken what would otherwise be a strong proposal.

Grammar

Writing that has a lot of mistakes can confuse or even annoy a reader. A business letter with a punctuation error might lead to a miscommunication and delay a reply. Or a sentence fragment might lower your grade on an essay. Paying attention to grammar, punctuation, and capitalization rules can make your writing clearer and easier to read.

Quick Reference: Parts of Speech

Part of Speech	Function	Examples
Noun	names a person, a place, a thing, an idea, a quality, or an action	
Common	serves as a general name, or a name common to an entire group	poet, novel, love, journey
Proper	names a specific, one-of-a-kind person, place, or thing	Jackson, Pleasant Street, Statue of Liberty
Singular	refers to a single person, place, thing, or idea	shark, planet, flower, truth
Plural	refers to more than one person, place, thing, or idea	sharks, planets, flowers, truths
Concrete	names something that can be perceived by the senses	snake, path, Philadelphia, damage
Abstract	names something that cannot be perceived by the senses	intelligence, fear, joy, loneliness
Compound	expresses a single idea through a combination of two or more words	girlfriend, father-in-law, Christmas Eve
Collective	refers to a group of people or things	army, flock, class, species
Possessive	shows who or what owns something	Strafford's, Bess's, children's, witnesses'
Pronoun	takes the place of a noun or another pronoun	
Personal	refers to the person making a statement, the person(s) being addressed, or the person(s) or thing(s) the statement is about	I, me, my, mine, we, us, our, ours, you, your, yours, she, he, it, her, him, hers, his, its, they, them, their, theirs
Reflexive	follows a verb or preposition and refers to a preceding noun or pronoun	myself, yourself, herself, himself, itself, ourselves, yourselves, themselves
Intensive	emphasizes a noun or another pronoun	(same as reflexives)
Demonstrative	points to one or more specific persons or things	this, that, these, those

continued

Part of Speech	Function	Examples
Interrogative	signals a question	who, whom, whose, which, what
Indefinite	refers to one or more persons or things not specifically mentioned	both, all, most, many, anyone, everybody, several, none, some
Relative	introduces an adjective clause by relating it to a word in the clause	who, whom, whose, which, that
Verb	expresses an action, a condition, or a state of being	
Action	tells what the subject does or did, physically or mentally	run, reaches, listened, consider, decides, dreamed
Linking	connects the subject to something that identifies or describes it	am, is, are, was, were, sound, taste, appear, feel, become, remain, seem
Auxiliary	precedes the main verb in a verb phrase	be, have, do, can, could, will, would, may, might
Transitive	directs the action toward someone or something; always has an object	The storm **sank** the ship.
Intransitive	does not direct the action toward someone or something; does not have an object	The ship **sank.**
Adjective	modifies a noun or pronoun	**strong** women, **two** epics, **enough** time
Adverb	modifies a verb, an adjective, or another adverb	walked **out, really** funny, **far** away
Preposition	relates one word to another word	at, by, for, from, in, of, on, to, with
Conjunction	joins words or word groups	
Coordinating	joins words or word groups used the same way	and, but, or, for, so, yet, nor
Correlative	used as a pair to join words or word groups used the same way	both . . . and, either . . . or, neither . . . nor
Subordinating	introduces a clause that cannot stand by itself as a complete sentence	although, after, as, before, because, since, when, if, unless
Interjection	expresses emotion	wow, ouch, hurrah

Quick Reference: The Sentence and Its Parts

The diagrams that follow will give you a brief review of the essentials of a sentence and some of its parts.

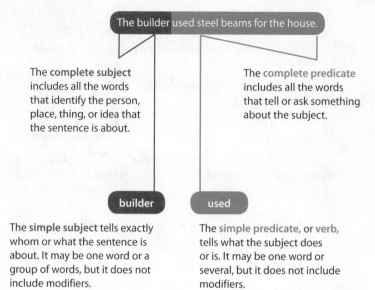

The **complete subject** includes all the words that identify the person, place, thing, or idea that the sentence is about.

The **complete predicate** includes all the words that tell or ask something about the subject.

The **simple subject** tells exactly whom or what the sentence is about. It may be one word or a group of words, but it does not include modifiers.

The **simple predicate,** or **verb,** tells what the subject does or is. It may be one word or several, but it does not include modifiers.

Every word in a sentence is part of a complete subject or a complete predicate.

subject

Verbs often have more than one part. A verb may be made up of a **main verb,** like *give,* and one or more **auxiliary,** or **helping, verbs,** like *will.*

A **direct object** is a word or group of words that tells who or what receives the action of the verb.

An **indirect object** is a word or group of words that tells to whom or for whom or to what or for what the verb's action is performed. A sentence can have an indirect object only if it has a direct object. The indirect object always comes before the direct object.

A **prepositional phrase** consists of a preposition, its object, and any modifiers of the object. In this phrase, *of* is the preposition and *comfort and convenience* is its object.

Quick Reference: Punctuation

Mark	Function	Examples
End Marks period, question mark, exclamation point	ends a sentence	We can start now**.** When would you like to leave**?** What a fantastic hit**!**
period	follows an initial or abbreviation **Exception**: postal abbreviations of states	Mrs**.** Dorothy Parker C**.** P**.** Cavafy, P**.**M**.**, A**.**D**.**, lb**.**, oz**.**, Blvd**.**, Dr**.** NE (Nebraska), NV (Nevada)
period	follows a number or letter in an outline	I**.** Volcanoes A**.** Central-vent 1**.** Shield
Comma	separates part of a compound sentence	I had never disliked poetry**,** but now I really love it.
	separates items in a series	She is brave**,** loyal**,** and kind.
	separates adjectives of equal rank that modify the same noun	The slow**,** easy route is best.
	sets off a term of address	Maria**,** how can I help you? You must do something**,** soldier.
	sets off a parenthetical expression	Hard workers**,** as you know**,** don't quit. I'm not a quitter**,** believe me.
	sets off an introductory word, phrase, or dependent clause	Yes**,** I forgot my key. At the beginning of the day**,** I feel fresh. While she was out**,** I was here. Having finished my chores**,** I went out.
	sets off a nonessential phrase or clause	Ed Pawn**,** the captain of the chess team**,** won. Ed Pawn**,** who is the captain**,** won. The two leading runners**,** sprinting toward the finish line**,** finished in a tie.
	sets off parts of dates and addresses	Mail it by May 14**,** 2010**,** to the Hauptman Company**,** 321 Market Street**,** Memphis**,** Tennessee.
	follows the salutation and closing of a letter	Dear Jim**,** Sincerely yours**,**

Mark	Function	Examples
	separates words to avoid confusion	By noon, time had run out. What the minister does, does matter. While cooking, Jim burned his hand.
Semicolon	separates items that contain commas in a series	We spent the first week of summer vacation in Chicago, Illinois; the second week in St. Louis, Missouri; and the third week in Albany, New York.
	separates parts of a compound sentence that are not joined by a coordinating conjunction	The last shall be first; the first shall be last. I read the Bible; however, I have not memorized it.
	separates parts of a compound sentence when the parts contain commas	After I ran out of money, I called my parents; but only my sister was home, unfortunately.
Colon	introduces a list	The names we wrote were the following: Dana, John, and Will.
	introduces a long quotation	Abraham Lincoln wrote: "Four score and seven years ago, our fathers brought forth on this continent a new nation. . . ."
	follows the salutation of a business letter	To Whom It May Concern: Dear Leonard Atole:
	separates certain numbers	1:28 P.M., Genesis 2:5
Dash	indicates an abrupt break in thought	I was thinking of my mother—who is arriving tomorrow—just as you walked in.
Parentheses	enclose less important material	It was so unlike him (John is always on time) that I began to worry. The last World Series game (did you see it?) was fun.

continued

Mark	Function	Examples
Hyphen	joins parts of a compound adjective before a noun	The not-so-rich taxpayer won't stand for this!
	joins parts of a compound with *all-*, *ex-*, *self-*, or *-elect*	The ex-firefighter helped rescue him. Our president-elect is self-conscious.
	joins parts of a compound number (to ninety-nine)	Today, I turned twenty-one.
	joins parts of a fraction	My cup is one-third full.
	joins a prefix to a word beginning with a capital letter	Which Pre-Raphaelite painter do you like best? It snowed in mid-October.
	indicates that a word is divided at the end of a line	How could you have any reasonable expectations of getting a new computer?
Apostrophe	used with *s* to form the possessive of a noun or an indefinite pronoun	my friend's book, my friends' books, anyone's guess, somebody else's problem
	replaces one or more omitted letters in a contraction or numbers in a date	don't (omitted *o*), he'd (omitted *woul*), the class of '99 (omitted *19*)
	used with *s* to form the plural of a letter	I had two A's on my report card.
Quotation Marks	set off a speaker's exact words	Sara said, "I'm finally ready." "I'm ready," Sara said, "finally." Did Sara say, "I'm ready"? Sara said, "I'm ready!"
	set off the title of a story, an article, a short poem, an essay, a song, or a chapter	I like Doctorow's "Another Place, Another Time" and Giovanni's "A Poem for My Librarian, Mrs. Long." I like Douglas Fox's essay "Big Rocks' Balancing Acts."
Ellipses	replace material omitted from a quotation	"When in the course of human events . . . and to assume among the powers of the earth. . . ."
Italics	indicate the title of a book, a play, a magazine, a long poem, an opera, a film, or a TV series, or the name of a ship	***Mississippi Solo***, ***Sorry, Wrong Number***, ***Newsweek***, the ***Odyssey***, ***Madame Butterfly***, ***Gone with the Wind***, ***Seinfeld***, ***Titanic***
Brackets	indicate a word or phrase that has been added to a quotation to make it clearer	"Spreading awareness [of the hurricane's damage] is an important part of our work."

Grammar **R35**

Quick Reference: Capitalization

Category	Examples
People and Titles	
Names and initials of people	Amy Tan, W. H. Auden
Titles used before a name	Professor Holmes, Senator Long
Deities and members of religious groups	Jesus, Allah, Buddha, Zeus, Baptists, Roman Catholics
Names of ethnic and national groups	Hispanics, Jews, African Americans
Geographical Names	
Cities, states, countries, continents	Philadelphia, Kansas, Japan, Europe
Regions, bodies of water, mountains	the South, Lake Baikal, Mount Everest
Geographic features, parks	Great Basin, Yellowstone National Park
Streets and roads, planets	318 East Sutton Drive, Charles Court, Jupiter, Pluto
Organizations, Events, Etc.	
Companies, organizations, teams	Ford Motor Company, Boy Scouts of America, St. Louis Cardinals
Buildings, bridges, monuments	Empire State Building, Eads Bridge, Washington Monument
Documents, awards	Declaration of Independence, Stanley Cup
Special named events	Mardi Gras, World Series
Government bodies, historical periods and events	U.S. Senate, House of Representatives, Middle Ages, Vietnam War
Days and months, holidays	Thursday, March, Thanksgiving, Labor Day
Specific cars, boats, trains, planes	Porsche, *Carpathia*, *Southwest Chief*, Concorde
Proper Adjectives	
Adjectives formed from proper nouns	French cooking, Spanish omelet, Edwardian age, Western movie
First Words and the Pronoun *I*	
First word in a sentence or quotation	This is it. He said, "Let's go."
First word of a sentence in parentheses that is not within another sentence	The spelling rules are covered in another section. (Consult that section for more information.)
First words in the salutation and closing of a letter	Dear Madam, Very truly yours,
First word, last word, and all important words in a title	*The Call of the Wild*, "Take Me Out to the Ball Game"

1 Nouns

A **noun** is a word used to name a person, a place, a thing, an idea, a quality, or an action. Nouns can be classified in several ways.

For more information on different types of nouns, see **Quick Reference: Parts of Speech,** page R30.

1.1 COMMON NOUNS

Common nouns are general names, common to entire groups.

1.2 PROPER NOUNS

Proper nouns name specific, one-of-a-kind people, places, and things.

Common	Proper
leader, park, forest, mountain	Sequoya, Sierra Nevada, Giant Forest, Mount Whitney

For more information, see **Quick Reference: Capitalization,** page R36.

1.3 SINGULAR AND PLURAL NOUNS

A noun may take a singular or a plural form, depending on whether it names a single person, place, thing, or idea or more than one. Make sure you use appropriate spellings when forming plurals.

Singular	Plural
tourist, city, mouse	tourists, cities, mice

For more information, see **Forming Plural Nouns,** page R61.

1.4 POSSESSIVE NOUNS

A **possessive noun** shows who or what owns something.

For more information, see **Forming Possessives,** page R62.

2 Pronouns

A **pronoun** is a word that is used in place of a noun or another pronoun. The word or word group to which the pronoun refers is called its **antecedent.**

2.1 PERSONAL PRONOUNS

Personal pronouns change their form to express person, number, gender, and case. The forms of these pronouns are shown in the following chart.

GRAMMAR PRACTICE ANSWERS

1. *Our class created a blog that tells about the books we've read.*
2. *When classmates write to us, we answer them.*
3. *If I find a comment from my teacher, I always answer him or her.*
4. *Every day there are more comments, and they are hard to ignore.*
5. *When you view the blog, you might enjoy the comments posted there.*

	Nominative	Objective	Possessive
Singular			
First person	I	me	my, mine
Second person	you	you	your, yours
Third person	she, he, it	her, him, it	her, hers, his, its
Plural			
First person	we	us	our, ours
Second person	you	you	your, yours
Third person	they	them	their, theirs

2.2 AGREEMENT WITH ANTECEDENT

Pronouns should agree with their antecedents in number, gender, and person.

If an antecedent is singular, use a singular pronoun.

> EXAMPLE: *Rachel wrote a **detective story**. It has a surprise ending.*

If an antecedent is plural, use a plural pronoun.

> EXAMPLES: ***The characters** have their motives for murder.*
> *Javier loves **mysteries** and reads them all the time.*

The gender of a pronoun must be the same as the gender of its antecedent.

> EXAMPLE: *The **man** has to use all his wits to stay alive and solve the crime.*

The person of the pronoun must be the same as the person of its antecedent. As the chart in Section 2.1 shows, a pronoun can be in first-person, second-person, or third-person form.

> EXAMPLE: ***You** want a story to grab your attention.*

Grammar Practice

Rewrite each sentence so that the underlined pronoun agrees with its antecedent.

1. Our class created a blog that tells about the books <u>they</u>'ve read.
2. When classmates write to us, we answer <u>him</u>.
3. If I find a comment from my teacher, I always answer <u>them</u>.
4. Every day there are more comments, and <u>it</u> is hard to ignore.
5. When you view the blog, <u>we</u> might enjoy the comments posted there.

2.3 PRONOUN FORMS

Personal pronouns change form to show how they function in sentences. The three forms are the subject form, the object form, and the possessive form. For examples of these pronouns, see the chart in Section 2.1.

A **subject pronoun** is used as a subject in a sentence.

> EXAMPLE: *All of my friends like our family dog. He is so friendly.*

Also use the subject form when the pronoun follows a linking verb.

> EXAMPLE: *The first puppy we chose was he.*

An **object pronoun** is used as a direct object, an indirect object, or the object of a preposition.

SUBJECT   OBJECT
He will lead them to us.
                OBJECT OF PREPOSITION

A **possessive pronoun** shows ownership. The pronouns *mine, yours, hers, his, its, ours,* and *theirs* can be used in place of nouns.

> EXAMPLE: *This money is mine.*

The pronouns *my, your, her, his, its, our,* and *their* are used before nouns.

> EXAMPLE: *We thanked the neighbors for their help.*

WATCH OUT! Many spelling errors can be avoided if you watch out for *its* and *their.* Don't confuse the possessive pronoun *its* with the contraction *it's,* meaning "it is" or "it has." The homonyms *they're* (a contraction of *they are*) and *there* ("in that place" or an expletive) are often mistakenly used for *their.*

TIP To decide which pronoun to use in a comparison such as "He tells better tales than (*I* or *me*)," fill in the missing word(s): *He tells better tales than I tell.*

Grammar Practice

Write the correct pronoun form to complete each sentence.

1. William Butler Yeats wrote the poem "The Song of Wandering Aengus," and it was published when (he, him) was in his early 30s.
2. This poem of (him, his) was published in 1899 in the collection *The Wind Among the Reeds*.
3. This collection contains 37 poems. All of (they, them) are written in Yeats's early style.
4. Yeats wrote many other poems. All of (their, his) dates of publication can be found by searching reputable online sources.
5. Yeats won the Nobel Prize in Literature in 1923 for (his, its) literary contributions.

2.4 REFLEXIVE AND INTENSIVE PRONOUNS

These pronouns are formed by adding *-self* or *-selves* to certain personal pronouns. Their forms are the same, and they differ only in how they are used.

A **reflexive pronoun** follows a verb or preposition and reflects back on an earlier noun or pronoun.

> EXAMPLES: *He likes himself too much. She is now herself again.*

Intensive pronouns intensify or emphasize the nouns or pronouns to which they refer.

> EXAMPLES: *They themselves will educate their children.*
> *You did it yourself.*

WATCH OUT! Avoid using *hisself* or *theirselves.* Standard English does not include these forms.

> NONSTANDARD: *Alex dedicated hisself to learning the magician's secrets.*
> STANDARD: *Alex dedicated himself to learning the magician's secrets.*

2.5 DEMONSTRATIVE PRONOUNS

Demonstrative pronouns point out things and persons near and far.

	Singular	Plural
Near	this	these
Far	that	those

2.6 INDEFINITE PRONOUNS

Indefinite pronouns do not refer to specific persons or things and usually have no antecedents. The chart shows some commonly used indefinite pronouns.

Singular	Plural	Singular or Plural	
another	both	all	none
anybody	few	any	some
no one	many	more	most
neither			

L 1

GRAMMAR PRACTICE ANSWERS

1. *he*
2. *his*
3. *them*
4. *their*
5. *his*

GRAMMAR PRACTICE ANSWERS

1. *Who has read or studied how the brain works?*

2. *Individuals who study the brain understand more about how we learn and think.*

3. *Nobody knows everything he or she can about the brain.*

4. *Each person's brain develops and forms new connections, but he or she isn't aware of these changes.*

5. *Scientists themselves often can't tell how their own brains change over time.*

TIP Indefinite pronouns that end in *one, body,* or *thing* are always singular.

> INCORRECT: *Did everybody play their part well?*

If the indefinite pronoun might refer to either a male or a female, *his or her* may be used to refer to it, or the sentence may be rewritten.

> CORRECT: *Did everybody play his or her part well?*
> *Did all the students play their parts well?*

2.7 INTERROGATIVE PRONOUNS

An **interrogative pronoun** tells a reader or listener that a question is coming. The interrogative pronouns are *who, whom, whose, which,* and *what.*

> EXAMPLES: *Who is going to rehearse with you?*
> *From whom did you receive the script?*

TIP *Who* is used as a subject; *whom* is used as an object. To find out which pronoun you need to use in a question, change the question to a statement.

> QUESTION: *(Who/Whom) did you meet there?*
> STATEMENT: *You met (?) there.*

Since the verb has a subject (*you*), the needed word must be the object form, *whom.*

> EXAMPLE: *Whom did you meet there?*

WATCH OUT! A special problem arises when you use an interrupter, such as *do you think,* within a question.

> EXAMPLE: *(Who/Whom) do you think will win?*

If you eliminate the interrupter, it is clear that the word you need is *who.*

2.8 RELATIVE PRONOUNS

Relative pronouns relate, or connect, adjective clauses to the words they modify in sentences. The noun or pronoun that a relative clause modifies is the antecedent of the relative pronoun. Here are the relative pronouns and their uses.

	Subject	Object	Possessive
Person	who	whom	whose
Thing	which	which	whose
Thing/Person	that	that	whose

Often, short sentences with related ideas can be combined by using a relative pronoun to create a more effective sentence.

> SHORT SENTENCE: *Yeats wrote "The Song of Wandering Aengus."*
> RELATED SENTENCE: *"The Song of Wandering Aengus" is a well-known poem in literature.*
> COMBINED SENTENCE: *Yeats wrote "The Song of Wandering Aengus," which is a well-known poem in literature.*

Grammar Practice

Write the correct form of each incorrect pronoun.

1. Whom has read or studied how the brain works?

2. Individuals whom study the brain understand more about how we learn and think.

3. Nobody knows everything they can about the brain.

4. Each person's brain develops and forms new connections, but they aren't aware of these changes.

5. Scientists theyselves often can't tell how their own brains change over time.

2.9 PRONOUN REFERENCE PROBLEMS

The referent of a pronoun should always be clear. Avoid problems by rewriting sentences.

An **indefinite reference** occurs when the pronoun *it, you,* or *they* does not clearly refer to a specific antecedent.

> UNCLEAR: *My aunt hugged me in front of my friends, and it was embarrassing.*
> CLEAR: *My aunt hugged me in front of my friends, and I was embarrassed.*

A **general reference** occurs when the pronoun *it, this, that, which,* or *such* is used to refer to a general idea rather than a specific antecedent.

> UNCLEAR: *Jenna takes acting lessons. This has improved her chances of getting a part in the school play.*

> CLEAR: *Jenna takes acting lessons. The lessons have improved her chances of getting a part in the school play.*

Ambiguous means "having more than one possible meaning." An **ambiguous reference** occurs when a pronoun could refer to two or more antecedents.

> UNCLEAR: *Tony talked to Fred and said that he could meet us later.*

> CLEAR: *Tony talked to Fred and said that Fred could meet us later.*

Grammar Practice

Rewrite the following sentences to correct indefinite, ambiguous, and general pronoun references.

1. When computer networks were first developed in the late 1950s and early 1960s, they didn't know how it would change worldwide communications.
2. Early networks were created for special purposes, and airlines and the U.S. Department of Defense used it.
3. Today people all around the world can use the Internet. This makes immediate communication possible.
4. With the Internet and wireless access, it can connect almost anyone anywhere.

3 Verbs

A **verb** is a word that expresses an action, a condition, or a state of being.

For more information, see **Quick Reference: Parts of Speech,** page R30.

3.1 ACTION VERBS

Action verbs express mental or physical activity.

> EXAMPLE: *Mr. Cho slept with the window open.*

3.2 LINKING VERBS

Linking verbs join subjects with words or phrases that rename or describe them.

> EXAMPLE: *When he awoke the next morning, his bed was wet from the rain.*

3.3 PRINCIPAL PARTS

Action and linking verbs typically have four principal parts, which are used to form verb tenses. The principal parts are the **present,** the **present participle,** the **past,** and the **past participle.**

Action verbs and some linking verbs also fall into two categories: regular and irregular. A **regular verb** is a verb that forms its past and past participle by adding *-ed* or *-d* to the present form.

Present	Present Participle	Past	Past Participle
jump	(is) jumping	jumped	(has) jumped
solve	(is) solving	solved	(has) solved
grab	(is) grabbing	grabbed	(has) grabbed
carry	(is) carrying	carried	(has) carried

An **irregular verb** is a verb that forms its past and past participle in some other way than by adding *-ed* or *-d* to the present form.

Present	Present Participle	Past	Past Participle
begin	(is) beginning	began	(has) begun
break	(is) breaking	broke	(has) broken
go	(is) going	went	(has) gone

L 1

GRAMMAR PRACTICE ANSWERS

1. *When computer networks were first developed in the late 1950s and early 1960s, developers didn't know how it would change worldwide communications.*
2. *Early networks were created for special purposes. The airlines and the U.S. Department of Defense used the early networks.*
3. *Today people all around the world can use the Internet. The Internet makes immediate communication possible.*
4. *The Internet and wireless access can connect almost anyone anywhere.*

3.4 VERB TENSE

The **tense** of a verb indicates the time of the action or the state of being. An action or state of being can occur in the present, the past, or the future. There are six tenses, each expressing a different range of time.

The **present tense** expresses an action or state that is happening at the present time, occurs regularly, or is constant or generally true. Use the present part.

> NOW: *That snow looks deep.*
>
> REGULAR: *It snows every day.*
>
> GENERAL: *Snow falls.*

The **past tense** expresses an action that began and ended in the past. Use the past part.

> EXAMPLE: *The storyteller finished his tale.*

The **future tense** expresses an action or state that will occur. Use *shall* or *will* with the present part.

> EXAMPLE: *They will attend the next festival.*

The **present perfect** tense expresses an action or state that (1) was completed at an indefinite time in the past or (2) began in the past and continues into the present. Use *have* or *has* with the past participle.

> EXAMPLE: *Poetry has inspired many readers.*

The **past perfect tense** expresses an action in the past that came before another action in the past. Use *had* with the past participle.

> EXAMPLE: *He had built a fire before the dog ran away.*

The **future perfect tense** expresses an action in the future that will be completed before another action in the future. Use *shall have* or *will have* with the past participle.

> EXAMPLE: *They will have read the novel before they see the movie version of the tale.*

TIP A past-tense form of an irregular verb is not used with an auxiliary verb, but a past-participle main irregular verb is always used with an auxiliary verb.

INCORRECT: *I have saw her somewhere before.* (*Saw* is the past-tense form of an irregular verb and shouldn't be used with *have.*)

CORRECT: *I have seen her somewhere before.*

INCORRECT: *I seen her somewhere before.* (*Seen* is the past participle of an irregular verb and shouldn't be used without an auxiliary verb.)

3.5 PROGRESSIVE FORMS

The progressive forms of the six tenses show ongoing actions. Use forms of **be** with the present participles of verbs.

> PRESENT PROGRESSIVE: *She is rehearsing her lines.*
>
> PAST PROGRESSIVE: *She was rehearsing her lines.*
>
> FUTURE PROGRESSIVE: *She will be rehearsing her lines.*
>
> PRESENT PERFECT PROGRESSIVE: *She has been rehearsing her lines.*
>
> PAST PERFECT PROGRESSIVE: *She had been rehearsing her lines.*
>
> FUTURE PERFECT PROGRESSIVE: *She will have been rehearsing her lines.*

WATCH OUT! Do not shift from tense to tense needlessly. Watch out for the following special cases.

- In most compound sentences and in sentences with compound predicates, keep the tenses the same.

  INCORRECT: *His boots freeze, and he shook with cold.*

  CORRECT: *His boots freeze, and he shakes with cold.*

- If one past action happens before another, do shift tenses.

  INCORRECT: *They wished they started earlier.*

  CORRECT: *They wished they had started earlier.*

Grammar Practice

Rewrite each sentence using a form of the verb(s) in parentheses. Identify each form that you use.

1. Some medical developments (begin) with the space age—for example, laparoscopy and robotics.
2. Both of these areas (grow) and (advance) the field of surgery.
3. In the 1990s "robotic assistants" (help) in surgery.
4. People (come) to expect simpler procedures because of these new techniques.
5. Some day other procedures that avoid cutting into tissue (develop).

Rewrite each sentence to correct an error in tense.

1. I seen a movie about the cobra and its natural enemy, the mongoose.
2. Most snakes hide and avoided people.
3. The cobra raised its head when it seeks out its next victim.
4. Both the male and female protected their eggs and will attack an approaching intruder.
5. The venom of a cobra was deadly and kills a human being within a few hours.

3.6 ACTIVE AND PASSIVE VOICE

The voice of a verb tells whether its subject performs or receives the action expressed by the verb. When the subject performs the action, the verb is in the **active voice.** When the subject is the receiver of the action, the verb is in the **passive voice.**

Compare these two sentences:

ACTIVE: *Virginia Hamilton wrote "The People Could Fly."*

PASSIVE: *"The People Could Fly" was written by Virginia Hamilton.*

To form the passive voice, use a form of *be* with the past participle of the verb.

WATCH OUT! Use the passive voice sparingly. It can make writing awkward and less direct.

AWKWARD: *"The People Could Fly" is a folk tale that was written by Virginia Hamilton.*

BETTER: *Virginia Hamilton wrote the tale "The People Could Fly."*

There are occasions when you will choose to use the passive voice because:

- you want to emphasize the receiver: ***The king was shot.***
- the doer is unknown: ***My books were stolen.***
- the doer is unimportant: ***French is spoken here.***

4 Modifiers

Modifiers are words or groups of words that change or limit the meanings of other words. Adjectives and adverbs are common modifiers.

4.1 ADJECTIVES

Adjectives modify nouns and pronouns by telling which one, what kind, how many, or how much.

WHICH ONE: *this, that, these, those*

EXAMPLE: *That bird is a scarlet ibis.*

WHAT KIND: *small, sick, courageous, black*

EXAMPLE: *The sick bird sways on the branch.*

HOW MANY: *some, few, ten, none, both, each*

EXAMPLE: *Both brothers stared at the bird.*

HOW MUCH: *more, less, enough*

EXAMPLE: *The bird did not have enough strength to remain perched.*

4.2 PREDICATE ADJECTIVES

Most adjectives come before the nouns they modify, as in the examples above. A **predicate adjective,** however, follows a linking verb and describes the subject.

EXAMPLE: *My friends are very intelligent.*

Be especially careful to use adjectives (not adverbs) after such linking verbs as *look, feel, grow, taste,* and *smell.*

EXAMPLE: *The bread smells wonderful.*

GRAMMAR PRACTICE ANSWERS

1. *Some medical developments began with the space age—for example, laparoscopy and robotics. (past tense)*
2. *Both of these areas have grown and have advanced the field of surgery. (present perfect tense)*
3. *In the 1990s "robotic assistants" helped in surgery. (past tense)*
4. *People have come to expect simpler procedures because of these new techniques. (present perfect tense)*
5. *Some day other procedures that avoid cutting into tissue will be developed. (future tense)*

ANSWERS

1. *I saw a movie about the cobra and its natural enemy, the mongoose.*
2. *Most snakes hide and avoid people.*
3. *The cobra raises its head when it seeks out its next victim.*
4. *Both the male and female protect their eggs and will attack an approaching intruder.*
5. *The venom of a cobra is deadly and kills a human being within a few hours.*

4.3 ADVERBS

Adverbs modify verbs, adjectives, and other adverbs by telling where, when, how, or to what extent.

> WHERE: *The children played outside.*
> WHEN: *The author spoke yesterday.*
> HOW: *We walked slowly behind the leader.*
> TO WHAT EXTENT: *He worked very hard.*

Adverbs may occur in many places in sentences, both before and after the words they modify.

> EXAMPLES: *Suddenly the wind shifted.*
> *The wind suddenly shifted.*
> *The wind shifted suddenly.*

4.4 ADJECTIVE OR ADVERB?

Many adverbs are formed by adding **-ly** to adjectives.

> EXAMPLES: *sweet, sweetly; gentle, gently*

However, **-ly** added to a noun will usually yield an adjective.

> EXAMPLES: *friend, friendly; woman, womanly*

4.5 COMPARISON OF MODIFIERS

Modifiers can be used to compare two or more things. The form of a modifier shows the degree of comparison. Both adjectives and adverbs have **comparative** and **superlative** forms.

The **comparative form** is used to compare two things, groups, or actions.

> EXAMPLES: *His father's hands were stronger than his own.*
> *His father was more courageous than the other man.*

The **superlative form** is used to compare more than two things, groups, or actions.

> EXAMPLES: *His father's hands were the strongest in the family.*
> *His father was the most courageous of them all.*

4.6 REGULAR COMPARISONS

Most one-syllable and some two-syllable adjectives and adverbs form comparatives and superlatives by adding **-er** and

-est. All three-syllable and most two-syllable modifiers have comparatives and superlatives formed with **more** or **most.**

Modifier	Comparative	Superlative
small	smaller	smallest
thin	thinner	thinnest
sleepy	sleepier	sleepiest
useless	more useless	most useless
precisely	more precisely	most precisely

WATCH OUT! Note that spelling changes must sometimes be made to form the comparatives and superlatives of modifiers.

> EXAMPLES: *friendly, friendlier* (Change *y* to *i* and add the ending.)
> *sad, sadder* (Double the final consonant and add the ending.)

4.7 IRREGULAR COMPARISONS

Some commonly used modifiers have irregular comparative and superlative forms. They are listed in the following chart. You may wish to memorize them.

Modifier	Comparative	Superlative
good	better	best
bad	worse	worst
far	farther *or* further	farthest *or* furthest
little	less *or* lesser	least
many	more	most
well	better	best
much	more	most

4.8 PROBLEMS WITH MODIFIERS

Study the tips that follow to avoid common mistakes.

Farther* and *Further Use *farther* for distances; use *further* for everything else.

Double Comparisons Make a comparison by using *-er/-est* or by using *more/most*. Using *-er* with *more* or using *-est* with *most* is incorrect.

> INCORRECT: *I like her more better than she likes me.*

> CORRECT: *I like her better than she likes me.*

Illogical Comparisons An illogical or confusing comparison results when two unrelated things are compared or when something is compared with itself. The word *other* or the word *else* should be used when comparing an individual member to the rest of a group.

> ILLOGICAL: *The narrator was more curious about the war than any student in his class.* (implies that the narrator isn't a student in the class)

> LOGICAL: *The narrator was more curious about the war than any other student in his class.* (identifies that the narrator is a student)

Bad vs. Badly *Bad,* always an adjective, is used before a noun or after a linking verb. *Badly,* always an adverb, never modifies a noun. Be sure to use the right form after a linking verb.

> INCORRECT: *Ed felt badly after his team lost.*

> CORRECT: *Ed felt bad after his team lost.*

Good vs. Well *Good* is always an adjective. It is used before a noun or after a linking verb. *Well* is often an adverb meaning "expertly" or "properly." *Well* can also be used as an adjective after a linking verb when it means "in good health."

> INCORRECT: *Helen writes very good.*

> CORRECT: *Helen writes very well.*

> CORRECT: *Yesterday I felt bad; today I feel well.*

Double Negatives If you add a negative word to a sentence that is already negative, the result will be an error known as a double negative. When using *not* or *-n't* with a verb, use *any-* words, such as *anybody* or *anything,* rather than *no-* words, such as *nobody* or *nothing,* later in the sentence.

> INCORRECT: *We haven't seen nobody.*

> CORRECT: *We haven't seen anybody.*

Using *hardly, barely,* or *scarcely* after a negative word is also incorrect.

> INCORRECT: *They couldn't barely see two feet ahead.*

> CORRECT: *They could barely see two feet ahead.*

Misplaced Modifiers Sometimes a modifier is placed so far away from the word it modifies that the intended meaning of the sentence is unclear. Prepositional phrases and participial phrases are often misplaced. Place modifiers as close as possible to the words they modify.

> MISPLACED: *We found the child in the park who was missing.*

> CLEARER: *We found the child who was missing in the park.* (The child was missing, not the park.)

Dangling Modifiers Sometimes a modifier doesn't appear to modify any word in a sentence. Most dangling modifiers are participial phrases or infinitive phrases.

> DANGLING: *Looking out the window, his brother was seen driving by.*

> CLEARER: *Looking out the window, Josh saw his brother driving by.*

Grammar Practice

Choose the correct word or words from each pair in parentheses.

1. When Ellis Island opened, it was the (larger, largest) port of entry to the United States.
2. In the 1980s, the facility underwent the (greatest, most greatest) restoration ever performed.
3. The restoration project (bad, badly) needed funds.
4. The project didn't have (no, any) funding until fundraising efforts began in 1982.
5. In 1990, the (grandly, grand) reopening was received (good, well).

L1

GRAMMAR PRACTICE ANSWERS

1. *largest*
2. *greatest*
3. *badly*
4. *any*
5. *grand; well*

GRAMMAR PRACTICE ANSWERS

1. *correct*

2. *Possible answer: The mother bear growled as we drove by in our car.*

3. *Possible answer: We took pictures of the bears while we were inside the camper.*

4. *correct*

5. *Possible answer: We had lots of film to tape our adventures.*

Grammar Practice

Rewrite each sentence that contains a misplaced or dangling modifier. Write "correct" if the sentence is written correctly.

1. We traveled to Yellowstone Park with many tourists.
2. Driving our car, the mother bear growled.
3. We took pictures of the bears in the camper.
4. My brother and I went for a hike, but we got lost.
5. Taping our adventures, we had lots of film.

5 The Sentence and Its Parts

A **sentence** is a group of words used to express a complete thought. A complete sentence has a subject and a predicate.

For more information, see **Quick Reference: The Sentence and Its Parts,** page R32.

5.1 KINDS OF SENTENCES

There are four basic types of sentences.

Type	Definition	Example
Declarative	states a fact, a wish, an intent, or a feeling	Charles Yu understands science fiction.
Interrogative	asks a question	Did you read "Earth (A Gift Shop)"?
Imperative	gives a command or direction	Read the story.
Exclamatory	expresses strong feeling or excitement	The story is great!

5.2 COMPOUND SUBJECTS AND PREDICATES

A compound subject consists of two or more subjects that share the same verb. They are typically joined by the coordinating conjunction **and** or **or.**

> EXAMPLE: *A short story or novel will keep you engaged.*

A compound predicate consists of two or more predicates that share the same subject. They too are usually joined by a coordinating conjunction such as **and, but,** or **or.**

> EXAMPLE: *The class finished all the poetry but did not read the short stories.*

5.3 COMPLEMENTS

A **complement** is a word or group of words that completes the meaning of the sentence. Some sentences contain only a subject and a verb. Most sentences, however, require additional words placed after the verb to complete the meaning of the sentence. There are three kinds of complements: direct objects, indirect objects, and subject complements.

Direct objects are words or word groups that receive the action of action verbs. A direct object answers the question **what** or **whom.**

> EXAMPLES: *The students asked many questions.* (Asked what?)
> *The teacher quickly answered the students.* (Answered whom?)

Indirect objects tell to whom or what or for whom or what the actions of verbs are performed. Indirect objects come before direct objects. In the examples that follow, the indirect objects are highlighted.

> EXAMPLES: *My sister usually gave her friends good advice.* (Gave to whom?)
> *Her brother sent the store a heavy package.* (Sent to what?)

Subject complements come after linking verbs and identify or describe the subjects. A subject complement that names or identifies a subject is called a **predicate nominative.** Predicate nominatives include **predicate nouns** and **predicate pronouns.**

> EXAMPLES: *My friends are very hard workers.*
> *The best writer in the class is she.*

A subject complement that describes a subject is called a **predicate adjective.**

> EXAMPLE: *The pianist appeared very energetic.*

6 Phrases

A **phrase** is a group of related words that does not contain a subject and a predicate but functions in a sentence as a single part of speech.

6.1 PREPOSITIONAL PHRASES

A **prepositional phrase** is a phrase that consists of a preposition, its object, and any modifiers of the object. Prepositional phrases that modify nouns or pronouns are called **adjective phrases.** Prepositional phrases that modify verbs, adjectives, or adverbs are **adverb phrases.**

> ADJECTIVE PHRASE: *The central character of the story is a villain.*

> ADVERB PHRASE: *He reveals his nature in the first scene.*

6.2 APPOSITIVES AND APPOSITIVE PHRASES

An **appositive** is a noun or pronoun that identifies or renames another noun or pronoun. An **appositive phrase** includes an appositive and modifiers of it. An appositive usually follows the noun or pronoun it identifies.

An appositive can be either **essential** or **nonessential.** An **essential appositive** provides information that is needed to identify what is referred to by the preceding noun or pronoun.

> EXAMPLE: *The book is about the author Naomi Shihab Nye.*

A **nonessential appositive** adds extra information about a noun or pronoun whose meaning is already clear.

Nonessential appositives and appositive phrases are set off with commas.

> EXAMPLE: *The book, an autobiography, tells how she began writing.*

7 Verbals and Verbal Phrases

A **verbal** is a verb form that is used as a noun, an adjective, or an adverb. A **verbal phrase** consists of a verbal along with its modifiers and complements. There are three kinds of verbals: **infinitives, participles,** and **gerunds.**

7.1 INFINITIVES AND INFINITIVE PHRASES

An **infinitive** is a verb form that usually begins with *to* and functions as a noun, an adjective, or an adverb. An **infinitive phrase** consists of an infinitive plus its modifiers and complements.

> NOUN: *To know her is my only desire.* (subject)
> *I'm planning to walk with you.* (direct object)
> *Her goal was to promote women's rights.* (predicate nominative)

> ADJECTIVE: *We saw his need to be loved.* (adjective modifying *need*)

> ADVERB: *She wrote to voice her opinions.* (adverb modifying *wrote*)

Because *to,* the sign of the infinitive, precedes infinitives, it is usually easy to recognize them. However, sometimes *to* may be omitted.

> EXAMPLE: *Let no one dare [to] enter this shrine.*

7.2 PARTICIPLES AND PARTICIPIAL PHRASES

A **participle** is a verb form that functions as an adjective. Like adjectives, participles modify nouns and pronouns. Most participles are present-participle forms, ending in *-ing,* or past-participle forms ending in *-ed* or *-en.* In the examples below, the participles are highlighted.

> MODIFYING A NOUN: *The dying man had a smile on his face.*

GRAMMAR PRACTICE POSSIBLE ANSWERS

1. *I read Jackie Robinson's autobiography to learn more about segregation in baseball.*

2. *Researching Robinson, I found out about the first African American baseball player in the United States.*

3. *Robinson played his entire major-league career with the same team, the Dodgers.*

4. *By stealing bases, Robinson became one of the most popular Dodgers.*

5. *Robinson became famous worldwide for earning a place in the Baseball Hall of Fame.*

MODIFYING A PRONOUN: *Frustrated, everyone abandoned the cause.*

Participial phrases are participles with all their modifiers and complements.

MODIFYING A NOUN: *The dogs searching for survivors are well trained.*

MODIFYING A PRONOUN: *Having approved your proposal, we are ready to act.*

7.3 DANGLING AND MISPLACED PARTICIPLES

A participle or participial phrase should be placed as close as possible to the word that it modifies. Otherwise the meaning of the sentence may not be clear.

MISPLACED: *The boys were looking for squirrels searching the trees.*

CLEARER: *The boys searching the trees were looking for squirrels.*

A participle or participial phrase that does not clearly modify anything in a sentence is called a **dangling participle.** A dangling participle causes confusion because it appears to modify a word that it cannot sensibly modify. Correct a dangling participle by providing a word for the participle to modify.

DANGLING: *Running like the wind, my hat fell off.* (The hat wasn't running.)

CLEARER: *Running like the wind, I lost my hat.*

7.4 GERUNDS AND GERUND PHRASES

A **gerund** is a verb form ending in *-ing* that functions as a noun. Gerunds may perform any function nouns perform.

SUBJECT: *Running is my favorite pastime.*

DIRECT OBJECT: *I truly love running.*

INDIRECT OBJECT: *You should give running a try.*

SUBJECT COMPLEMENT: *My deepest passion is running.*

OBJECT OF PREPOSITION: *Her love of running keeps her strong.*

Gerund phrases are gerunds with all their modifiers and complements.

SUBJECT: *Wishing on a star never got me far.*

OBJECT OF PREPOSITION: *I will finish before leaving the office.*

APPOSITIVE: *Her avocation, flying airplanes, finally led to full-time employment.*

Grammar Practice

Rewrite each sentence, adding the type of phrase shown in parentheses.

1. I read Jackie Robinson's autobiography. (infinitive phrase)
2. Robinson was the first major league African American baseball player in the United States. (participial phrase)
3. Robinson played his entire major league career with the same team. (appositive phrase)
4. Robinson went on to become one of the most popular Dodger players. (gerund phrase)
5. Today Robinson is famous worldwide. (prepositional phrase)

8 Clauses

A **clause** is a group of words that contains a subject and a predicate. There are two kinds of clauses: independent, or main, clauses and subordinate clauses.

8.1 MAIN AND SUBORDINATE CLAUSES

A **main (independent) clause** can stand alone as a sentence.

MAIN CLAUSE: *I read "Train Time."*

A sentence may contain more than one main clause.

EXAMPLE: *I finished dinner, and I read the story.*

In the preceding example, the coordinating conjunction *and* joins two main clauses.

For more information, see **Coordinating Conjunction,** page R31.

A **subordinate (dependent) clause** cannot stand alone as a sentence. It is subordinate to, or dependent on, a main clause.

EXAMPLE: *After I finished dinner, I read "Train Time."*

The highlighted clause cannot stand by itself. Note that a comma is added to the end of a dependent clause when it comes before a main clause.

8.2 ADJECTIVE CLAUSES

An **adjective clause** is a subordinate clause used as an adjective. It usually follows the noun or pronoun it modifies.

EXAMPLE: *Antonio and I are the actors who play the lead characters in our school's play.*

Adjective clauses are typically introduced by the relative pronouns *who, whom, whose, which,* and *that.*

For more information, see **Relative Pronouns,** page R40.

EXAMPLE: *The production, which is our school's big theatrical event, will take place in May.*

An adjective clause can be either essential or nonessential. An **essential adjective clause** provides information that is necessary to identify the preceding noun or pronoun.

EXAMPLE: *The drama club had to make a decision that three performances would be sufficient.*

A **nonessential adjective clause** adds additional information about a noun or pronoun whose meaning is already clear. Nonessential clauses are set off with commas.

EXAMPLE: *The club members, who had been discussing it for a long time, needed to come to an agreement about performance times and dates.*

8.3 ADVERB CLAUSES

An **adverb clause** is a subordinate clause that is used to modify a verb, an adjective, or an adverb. It is introduced by a subordinating conjunction.

For examples of subordinating conjunctions, see **Noun Clauses,** page R49.

Adverb clauses typically occur at the beginning or end of sentences.

MODIFYING A VERB: *When we need you, we will call.*

MODIFYING AN ADVERB: *I'll stay here where there is shelter from the rain.*

MODIFYING AN ADJECTIVE: *Roman felt as good as he had ever felt.*

TIP An adverb clause should be followed by a comma when it comes before a main clause. When an adverb clause comes after a main clause, a comma may not be needed.

8.4 NOUN CLAUSES

A **noun clause** is a subordinate clause that is used as a noun. A noun clause may be used as a subject, a direct object, an indirect object, a predicate nominative, or the object of a preposition. Noun clauses are introduced either by pronouns, such as *that, what, who, whoever, which,* and *whose,* or by subordinating conjunctions, such as *how, when, where, why,* and *whether.*

For more subordinating conjunctions, see **Quick Reference: Parts of Speech,** page R30.

TIP Because the same words may introduce adjective and noun clauses, you need to consider how a clause functions within its sentence. To determine if a clause is a noun clause, try substituting *something* or *someone* for the clause. If you can do it, it is probably a noun clause.

EXAMPLE: *I know whose woods these are.* ("I know *something.*" The clause is a noun clause, a direct object of the verb *know.*) *Give a copy to whoever wants one.* ("Give a copy to *someone.*" The clause is a noun clause, an object of the preposition *to.*)

GRAMMAR PRACTICE POSSIBLE ANSWERS

1. *Students who want school credit volunteer at animal shelters.*

2. *They help take care of dogs and cats when the shelters are understaffed.*

3. *The veterinarian tries to explain to students how they should care for sick animals.*

4. *Many people appreciate the students who donate their time each week.*

5. *When soccer season ends, I plan to work at the shelter.*

Grammar Practice

Add descriptive details to each sentence by writing the type of clause indicated in parentheses.

1. Some students volunteer at animal shelters. (adjective clause)

2. They help take care of dogs and cats. (adverb clause)

3. The veterinarian tries to explain to the students. (noun clause)

4. Many people appreciate the students. (adjective clause)

5. I plan to work at the shelter. (adverb clause)

9 The Structure of Sentences

When classified by their structure, there are four kinds of sentences: simple, compound, complex, and compound-complex.

9.1 SIMPLE SENTENCES

A **simple sentence** is a sentence that has one main clause and no subordinate clauses.

> EXAMPLE: *Sam ran to the theater.*
> *Max waited in front of the theater.*

A simple sentence may contain a compound subject or a compound verb.

> EXAMPLE: *Sam and Max went to the movie.* (compound subject)
> *They clapped and cheered at their favorite parts.* (compound verb)

9.2 COMPOUND SENTENCES

A **compound sentence** consists of two or more main clauses. The clauses in compound sentences are joined with commas and coordinating conjunctions (*and, but, or, nor, yet, for, so*) or with semicolons. Like simple sentences, compound sentences do not contain any subordinate clauses.

> EXAMPLES: *Sam likes action movies, but Max prefers comedies.*
> *The actor jumped from one building to another; he barely made the final leap.*

WATCH OUT! Do not confuse compound sentences with simple sentences that have compound parts.

> EXAMPLE: *The actor knew all the lines but didn't play the part well.*
> (Here *but* joins parts of a compound predicate, not a compound sentence.)

9.3 COMPLEX SENTENCES

A **complex sentence** consists of one main clause and one or more subordinate clauses.

> EXAMPLE: *One should not complain unless one has a better solution.*
> *Mr. Neiman, who is an artist, sketched pictures until the sun went down.*

9.4 COMPOUND-COMPLEX SENTENCES

A **compound-complex sentence** contains two or more main clauses and one or more subordinate clauses. Compound-complex sentences are, simply, both compound and complex. If you start with a compound sentence, all you need to do to form a compound-complex sentence is add a subordinate clause.

> COMPOUND: *All the students knew the answer, yet they were too shy to volunteer.*

> COMPOUND-COMPLEX: *All the students knew the answer that their teacher expected, yet they were too shy to volunteer.*

9.5 PARALLEL STRUCTURE

When you write sentences, make sure that coordinate parts are equivalent, or **parallel,** in structure.

> NOT PARALLEL: *Erin loved basketball and to play hockey.* (*Basketball* is a noun; *to play hockey* is a phrase.)

> PARALLEL: *Erin loved basketball and hockey.* (*Basketball* and *hockey* are both nouns.)

> NOT PARALLEL: *He wanted to rent an apartment, a new car, and traveling around the country.* (*To rent* is an infinitive, *car* is a noun, and *traveling* is a gerund.)

PARALLEL: *He wanted to rent an apartment, to drive a new car, and to travel around the country.*
(*To rent, to drive,* and *to travel* are all infinitives.)

10 Writing Complete Sentences

Remember, a sentence is a group of words that expresses a complete thought. In writing that you wish to share with a reader, try to avoid both sentence fragments and run-on sentences.

10.1 CORRECTING FRAGMENTS

A **sentence fragment** is a group of words that is only part of a sentence. It does not express a complete thought and may be confusing to a reader or listener. A sentence fragment may be lacking a subject, a predicate, or both.

FRAGMENT: *Waited for the boat to arrive.* (no subject)

CORRECTED: *We waited for the boat to arrive.*

FRAGMENT: *People of various races, ages, and creeds.* (no predicate)

CORRECTED: *People of various races, ages, and creeds gathered together.*

FRAGMENT: *Near the old cottage.* (neither subject nor predicate)

CORRECTED: *The burial ground is near the old cottage.*

In your writing, fragments may be a result of haste or incorrect punctuation. Sometimes fixing a fragment is a matter of attaching it to a preceding or following sentence.

FRAGMENT: *We saw the two girls. Waiting for the bus to arrive.*

CORRECTED: *We saw the two girls waiting for the bus to arrive.*

10.2 CORRECTING RUN-ON SENTENCES

A **run-on sentence** is made up of two or more sentences written as though they were one. Some run-ons have no punctuation within them. Others may have only commas where conjunctions or stronger punctuation marks are necessary. Use your judgment in correcting run-on sentences, as you have choices. You can change a run-on to two sentences if the thoughts are not closely connected. If the thoughts are closely related, you can keep the run-on as one sentence by adding a semicolon or a conjunction.

RUN-ON: *We found a place for the picnic by a small pond it was three miles from the village.*

MAKE TWO SENTENCES: *We found a place for the picnic by a small pond. It was three miles from the village.*

RUN-ON: *We found a place for the picnic by a small pond it was perfect.*

USE A SEMICOLON: *We found a place for the picnic by a small pond; it was perfect.*

ADD A CONJUNCTION: *We found a place for the picnic by a small pond, and it was perfect.*

WATCH OUT! When you form compound sentences, make sure you use appropriate punctuation: a comma before a coordinating conjunction, a semicolon when there is no coordinating conjunction, and a semicolon before a conjunctive adverb and a comma after it. A very common mistake is to use a comma alone instead of a comma and a conjunction. This error is called a **comma splice.**

INCORRECT: *He finished the job, he left the village.*

CORRECT: *He finished the job, and he left the village.*

11 Subject-Verb Agreement

The subject and verb in a clause must agree in number. Agreement means that if the subject is singular, the verb is also singular, and if the subject is plural, the verb is also plural.

11.1 BASIC AGREEMENT

Fortunately, agreement between subjects and verbs in English is simple. Most verbs show the difference between singular and plural only in the third person of the present tense. In the present tense, the third-person singular form ends in **-s.**

Present-Tense Verb Forms	
Singular	**Plural**
I sleep	we sleep
you sleep	you sleep
she, he, it sleeps	they sleep

11.2 AGREEMENT WITH *BE*

The verb **be** presents special problems in agreement, because this verb does not follow the usual verb patterns.

Forms of *Be*			
Present Tense		**Past Tense**	
Singular	**Plural**	**Singular**	**Plural**
I am	we are	I was	we were
you are	you are	you were	you were
she, he, it is	they are	she, he, it was	they were

11.3 WORDS BETWEEN SUBJECT AND VERB

A verb agrees only with its subject. When a prepositional phrase or other words come between a subject and a verb, ignore them when considering proper agreement. Identify the subject, and make sure the verb agrees with it.

> EXAMPLES: *A story in the newspapers tells about the 1890s.*
> *Dad as well as Mom reads the paper daily.*

11.4 AGREEMENT WITH COMPOUND SUBJECTS

Use plural verbs with most compound subjects joined by the word **and.**

> EXAMPLE: *My father and his friends play chess every day.*

To confirm that you need a plural verb, you could substitute the plural pronoun **they** for **my father and his friends.**

If a compound subject is thought of as a unit, use a singular verb. Test this by substituting the singular pronoun **it.**

> EXAMPLE: *Peanut butter and jelly [it] is my brother's favorite sandwich.*

Use a singular verb with a compound subject that is preceded by **each, every,** or **many a.**

> EXAMPLE: *Each novel and short story seems grounded in personal experience.*

When the parts of a compound subject are joined by **or, nor,** or the correlative conjunctions **either . . . or** or **neither . . . nor,** make the verb agree with the noun or pronoun nearest the verb.

> EXAMPLES: *Cookies or ice cream is my favorite dessert.*
> *Either Cheryl or her friends are being invited.*
> *Neither ice storms nor snow is predicted today.*

11.5 PERSONAL PRONOUNS AS SUBJECTS

When using a personal pronoun as a subject, make sure to match it with the correct form of the verb **be.** (See the chart in Section 11.2.) Note especially that the pronoun **you** takes the forms **are** and **were,** regardless of whether it is singular or plural.

> **WATCH OUT!** **You is** and **you was** are nonstandard forms and should be avoided in writing and speaking. **We was** and **they was** are also forms to be avoided.

> INCORRECT: *You was a good student.*
> CORRECT: *You were a good student.*
> INCORRECT: *They was starting a new school.*
> CORRECT: *They were starting a new school.*

11.6 INDEFINITE PRONOUNS AS SUBJECTS

Some indefinite pronouns are always singular; some are always plural.

Singular Indefinite Pronouns			
another	either	neither	one
anybody	everybody	nobody	somebody
anyone	everyone	no one	someone
anything	everything	nothing	something
each	much		

EXAMPLES: *Each of the writers was given an award.*
Somebody in the room upstairs is sleeping.

Plural Indefinite Pronouns			
both	few	many	several

EXAMPLES: *Many of the books in our library are not in circulation.*
Few have been returned recently.

Still other indefinite pronouns may be either singular or plural.

Singular or Plural Indefinite Pronouns		
all	more	none
any	most	some

The number of the indefinite pronoun *any* or *none* often depends on the intended meaning.

EXAMPLES: *Any of these topics has potential for a good article.* (any one topic)
Any of these topics have potential for good articles. (all of the many topics)

The indefinite pronouns *all, some, more, most,* and *none* are singular when they refer to quantities or parts of things. They are plural when they refer to numbers of individual things. Context will usually give a clue.

EXAMPLES: *All of the flour is gone.* (referring to a quantity)
All of the flowers are gone. (referring to individual items)

11.7 INVERTED SENTENCES

A sentence in which the subject follows the verb is called an **inverted sentence.** A subject can follow a verb or part of a verb phrase in a question; a sentence beginning with *here* or *there*; or a sentence in which an adjective, an adverb, or a phrase is placed first.

EXAMPLES: *There clearly are far too many cooks in this kitchen.*
What is the correct ingredient for this stew?
Far from the embroiled cooks stands the master chef.

TIP To check subject-verb agreement in some inverted sentences, place the subject before the verb. For example, change *There are many people* to *Many people are there.*

11.8 SENTENCES WITH PREDICATE NOMINATIVES

In a sentence containing a predicate noun (nominative), the verb should agree with the subject, not the predicate noun.

EXAMPLES: *The speeches of Martin Luther King Jr. are a landmark in American civil rights history.* (*Speeches* is the subject— not *landmark*—and it takes the plural verb *are.*)
One landmark in American civil rights history is the speeches of Martin Luther King Jr. (The subject is *landmark*—not *speeches*—and it takes the singular verb *is.*)

11.9 *DON'T* AND *DOESN'T* AS AUXILIARY VERBS

The auxiliary verb *doesn't* is used with singular subjects and with the personal pronouns *she, he,* and *it.* The auxiliary verb *don't* is used with plural subjects and with the personal pronouns *I, we, you,* and *they.*

SINGULAR: *She doesn't know Martin Luther King Jr.'s famous "I Have a Dream" speech.*
Doesn't the young woman read very much?

GRAMMAR PRACTICE ANSWERS

1. *learn*
2. *offers*
3. *think*
4. *go; hang*
5. *go*
6. *has*
7. *want*
8. *are*
9. *are*
10. *leaves*

PLURAL: *We don't have the speech memorized.*
Don't speakers usually memorize their speeches?

11.10 COLLECTIVE NOUNS AS SUBJECTS

Collective nouns are singular nouns that name groups of persons or things. *Team,* for example, is the collective name of a group of individuals. A collective noun takes a singular verb when the group acts as a single unit. It takes a plural verb when the members of the group act separately

> EXAMPLES: *Our team usually wins.* (The team as a whole wins.)
> *Our team vote differently on most issues.* (The individual members vote.)

11.11 RELATIVE PRONOUNS AS SUBJECTS

When the relative pronoun *who, which,* or *that* is used as a subject in an adjective clause, the verb in the clause must agree in number with the antecedent of the pronoun.

> SINGULAR: *I didn't read the **poem** about fireflies that was assigned.*

The antecedent of the relative pronoun *that* is the singular *poem*; therefore, *that* is singular and must take the singular verb *was.*

> PLURAL: *Mary Oliver and Pat Moran, who are very different from each other, are both outstanding poets.*

The antecedent of the relative pronoun *who* is the plural compound subject *Mary Oliver and Pat Moran.* Therefore *who* is plural, and it takes the plural verb *are.*

Grammar Practice

Locate the subject of each verb in parentheses in the sentences below. Then choose the correct verb form.

1. In our school, students have a chance to (learn, learns) many techniques and media for making art.

2. Our art program (offer, offers) many different types of classes throughout the year.

3. Many of the students (think, thinks) that the summer is a good time for taking art class.

4. Some (go, goes) to camp, work part-time jobs, or take classes during the summer months, while others just (hang, hangs) around.

5. For those who (go, goes) to school for art class, the experience will be worth the time.

6. Everyone (has, have) a chance to try new techniques, such as printmaking or computer manipulation of photographs and drawings.

7. Does anyone (want, wants) to discover creative ideas in art class?

8. Found objects, such as discarded wire or consumer by-products (is, are) useful for creating art with an environmental message.

9. There (is, are) many beautiful objects made from old things.

10. Each of the students (leave, leaves) art class having learned something special.

Vocabulary and Spelling

L 2b, L 4a–d, L 5a–c, L 6

The key to becoming an independent reader is to develop a tool kit of vocabulary strategies. By learning and practicing the strategies, you'll know what to do when you encounter unfamiliar words while reading. You'll also know how to refine the words you use for different situations—personal, school, and work.

Being a good speller is important when communicating your ideas in writing. Learning basic spelling rules and checking your spelling in a dictionary will help you spell words that you may not use frequently.

1 Using Context Clues

The context of a word is made up of the punctuation marks, words, sentences, and paragraphs that surround the word. A word's context can give you important clues about its meaning.

1.1 GENERAL CONTEXT

Sometimes you need to determine the meaning of an unfamiliar word by reading all the information in a passage.

The sweater was of inferior quality. It was torn and had several buttons missing.

You can figure out from the context that *inferior* means "poor or low."

1.2 SPECIFIC CONTEXT CLUES

Sometimes writers help you understand the meanings of words by providing specific clues such as those shown in the chart.

1.3 IDIOMS, SLANG, AND FIGURATIVE LANGUAGE

An **idiom** is an expression whose overall meaning is different from the meaning of the individual words. **Slang** is informal language in which madeup words and ordinary words are used to mean something different from their meanings in formal English. **Figurative language** is language that communicates meaning beyond the literal meaning of the words. Use context clues to figure out the meanings of idioms, slang, and figurative language.

Button your lip about the party. (idiom; means "keep quiet")

That's a really bad jacket; I want one. (slang; means "good-looking, excellent")

My brother had tried to make dinner. The kitchen was a battleground of dirty dishes, stains, spills, and potato peels. (figurative language; battleground, dirty dishes, stains, spills, and potato peels represent a messy scene)

Specific Context Clues		
Type of Clue	**Key Words/ Phrases**	**Example**
Definition or restate-ment of the meaning of the word	or, which is, that is, in other words, also known as, also called	Most chemicals are *toxic*, or **poisonous.**
Example following an unfamiliar word	such as, like, as if, for example, especially, including	*Amphibians*, such as **frogs and salaman-ders**, live in the pond by our house.
Comparison with a more familiar word or concept	as, like, also, similar to, in the same way, likewise	Like the rest of my *frugal* family, I always **save** most of the money I earn.

continued

Contrast with a familiar word or experience	unlike, but, however, although, on the other hand, on the contrary	I wish I had more *ingenuity* in making money instead of simply relying on the **same old** babysitting jobs.
Cause-and-effect relationship in which one term is familiar	because, since, when, consequently, as a result, therefore	Because the chemicals are *flammable,* the scientists wear special **fire-resistant** clothing.

2 Analyzing Word Structure

Many words can be broken into smaller parts. These word parts include base words, roots, prefixes, and suffixes.

2.1 BASE WORDS

A **base word** is a word part that by itself is also a word. Other words or word parts can be added to base words to form new words.

2.2 ROOTS

A **root** is a word part that contains the core meaning of the word. Many English words contain roots that come from older languages such as Greek, Latin, Old English (Anglo-Saxon), and Norse. Knowing the meaning of the word's root can help you determine the word's meaning.

Root	Meaning	Example
photo (Greek)	light	photography
therm (Greek)	heat	thermometer
cred (Latin)	believe	credit

continued

mot (Latin)	move	motion
hēadfod (Old English)	head, top	headfirst

2.3 PREFIXES

A **prefix** is a word part attached to the beginning of a word. Most prefixes come from Greek, Latin, or Old English.

Prefix	Meaning	Example
mal-	bad or wrong	**mal**function
micro-	small or short	**micro**scope
semi-	half	**semi**circle

2.4 SUFFIXES

A **suffix** is a word part that appears at the end of a root or base word to form a new word. Some suffixes do not change word meaning. These suffixes are:

- added to nouns to change the number of persons or objects
- added to verbs to change the tense
- added to modifiers to change the degree of comparison

Suffix	Meaning	Example
-s, -es	to change the number of a noun	lock + s = locks
-d, -ed, -ing	to change verb tense	stew + ed = stewed
-er, -est	to indicate comparison in modifiers	mild + er = milder soft + est = softest

Other suffixes can be added to the root or base to change the word's meaning. These suffixes can also determine a word's part of speech.

Suffix	Meaning	Example
-er	one who does	teacher
-able	capable of	readable
-ly	in what manner	slowly

2.5 CONTENT-AREA VOCABULARY

Knowing the meaning of Greek, Latin, and Anglo-Saxon word parts can help you figure out the meaning of content-area vocabulary.

Word Part	Meaning	Example
derm	skin	dermatologist
logy	study of	astrology
bio	life	biography
hydr	water	hydrant
hypo	below, beneath	hypodermic
vid/vis	to see	visual
fract	to break	fraction

Strategies for Understanding Unfamiliar Words

- Look for any prefixes or suffixes. Remove them so that you can concentrate on the base word or the root.
- See if you recognize any elements— prefix, suffix, root, or base—of the word. You may be able to guess its meaning by analyzing one or two elements.
- Think about the way the word is used in the sentence. Use the context and the word parts to make a logical guess about the word's meaning.
- Look in a dictionary to see whether you are correct.

Practice and Apply

Use the strategies in this section and the vocabulary lessons in this book to help you figure out the meanings of the following content-area words.

forefathers	vision	microfilm
biology	fracture	import
auditory	ecology	hypothermia

3 Understanding Word Origins

3.1 ETYMOLOGIES

Etymologies show the origin and historical development of a word. When you study a word's history and origin, you can find out when, where, and how the word came to be.

ge·om·e·try (jē-ŏm´ĭ-trē) *n.*, pl. **-tries** **1.** The mathematics of the properties, measurement, and relationships of points, lines, angles, surfaces, and solids. **2.** Arrangement. **3.** A physical arrangement suggesting geometric lines and shapes. [from Greek *geōmetriā*, from *geōmetrein*, to measure land].

3.2 WORD FAMILIES

Words that have the same root make up a word family and have related meanings. The following chart shows a common Greek root and a common Latin root. Notice how the meanings of the example words are related to the meanings of their roots.

Latin Root	*sens: "sense or feel"*
English	**sensory** relating to the senses
	sensitive responsive to sensations
	sensation a perception or feeling

continued

Greek Root	ast(e)r: "star"
English	**asteroid** a small object in outer space **asterisk** a star-shaped punctuation mark **astronomy** the study of outer space

3.3 FOREIGN WORDS

The English language includes words from diverse languages, such as French, Dutch, Spanish, Italian, and Chinese. Many words have stayed the way they were in their original languages.

French	Dutch	Spanish	Italian
ballet	boss	canyon	diva
vague	caboose	rodeo	cupola
mirage	dock	bronco	spaghetti

4 Synonyms and Antonyms

4.1 SYNONYMS

A **synonym** is a word with a meaning similar to that of another word. You can find synonyms in a thesaurus or a dictionary. In a dictionary, synonyms are often given as part of the definition of the word. The following word pairs are synonyms:

satisfy/please   occasionally/
                          sometimes

rob/steal   schedule/agenda

4.2 ANTONYMS

An **antonym** is a word with a meaning opposite that of another word. The following word pairs are antonyms:

accurate/incorrect   similar/different

fresh/stale   unusual/ordinary

5 Denotation and Connotation

5.1 DENOTATION

A word's dictionary meaning is called its **denotation.** For example, the denotation of the word *thin* is "having little flesh; spare; lean."

5.2 CONNOTATION

The images or feelings you connect to a word add a finer shade of meaning, called **connotation.** The connotation of a word goes beyond its basic dictionary definition. Writers use connotations of words to communicate positive or negative feelings.

Positive	Negative
slender	scrawny
thrifty	cheap
young	immature

Make sure you understand the denotation and connotation of a word when you read it or use it.

6 Analogies

An **analogy** is a comparison based on similarities between some things. Analogies can be used to explain unfamiliar words, subjects, or ideas in terms of familiar ones. An **analogy problem** shows a relationship between pairs of words. The relationship between the first pair of words is the same as the relationship between the second pair. Two relationships that analogy problems can express are part to whole and whole to part.

Part to Whole

handle : mug :: hilt : _____

a. hammer   **b.** jewelry   **c.** plate   **d.** sword

*Read this analogy as "handle **is to** mug as hilt **is to** _____."*

What is the relationship between a *handle* and a *mug*? (A *handle* is the part designed for holding a *mug*.)

A *hilt* is part of which item? (A *hilt* is the handle of a *sword.*)

Whole to Part

horse : mane :: pheasant : _____

a. bird **b.** feather **c.** paw **d.** animal

What is the relationship between a *horse* and a *mane*? (A *horse* has a *mane,* the long hair along the top and sides of its neck.)

Which item is part of a *pheasant*? (The bird called a *pheasant* has a *feather* covering.)

7 Homonyms, Homographs, and Homophones

7.1 HOMONYMS

Homonyms are words that have the same spelling and sound but have different meanings.

> *The snake shed its skin in the shed behind the house.*

Shed can mean "to lose by natural process," but an identically spelled word means "a small structure."

If only one of the meanings of a homonym is familiar to you, use context clues to help you define the word if it is used in an unfamiliar way.

7.2 HOMOGRAPHS

Homographs are words that are spelled the same but have different meanings and origins. Some are also pronounced differently, as in these examples.

> *Please close the door. (klōz)*
>
> *That was a close call. (klōs)*

If you see a word used in a way that is unfamiliar to you, check a dictionary to see if it is a homograph.

7.3 HOMOPHONES

Homophones are words that sound alike but have different meanings and spellings. The following homophones are frequently misused:

it's/its   they're/their/there

to/too/two   stationary/stationery

Many misused homophones are pronouns and contractions. Whenever you are unsure whether to write *your* or *you're* and *who's* or *whose,* ask yourself if you mean *you are* and *who is/has.* If you do, write the contraction. For other homophones, such as *fair* and *fare,* use the meaning of the word to help you decide which one to use.

8 Words with Multiple Meanings

Some words have acquired additional meanings over time that are based on the original meaning.

> *I had to be replaced in the cast of the play because of the cast on my arm.*

The word *cast* has two meanings here, but both have the same origin. All of the meanings of *cast* are listed in one entry in the dictionary.

9 Specialized Vocabulary

Specialized vocabulary refers to terms used in a particular field of study or work. For example, science and mathematics each has its own technical or specialized vocabulary. You can use context clues, dictionaries on specific subjects, atlases, or manuals to help you define these terms.

10 Using Reference Sources

10.1 DICTIONARIES

A **general dictionary** will tell you a word's definitions, spelling, syllables, pronunciation, parts of speech, and history and origin.

① **tan·gi·ble** (tăn´jə-bəl) *adj.* **②** **③**
④ **1a.** Discernible by the touch; palpable. **b.** Possible to touch. **c.** Possible to be treated as fact; real or concrete. **2.** Possible to understand or realize. **3.** *Law* Relating to or being property, such as land, objects, and goods. [Late Latin *tangibilis,* from Latin *tangere,* to touch.] **⑤**

① Entry word syllabication

② Pronunciation

③ Part of speech

④ Definitions

⑤ Etymology

A **specialized dictionary** focuses on terms related to a particular field of study or work.

10.2 THESAURI

A **thesaurus** (plural, *thesauri*) is a dictionary of synonyms. A thesaurus can be especially helpful when you find yourself using the same modifiers over and over again.

10.3 SYNONYM FINDERS

A **synonym finder** is often included in word processing software. It enables you to highlight a word and be shown a display of its synonyms.

10.4 GLOSSARIES

A **glossary** is a list of specialized terms, their definitions, and sometimes their pronunciations. Many textbooks contain glossaries, which are found at the back of the book. In fact, this text has three glossaries: the **Glossary of Literary and Informational Terms,** the **Glossary of Academic Vocabulary,** and the **Glossary of Critical Vocabulary.** Use these glossaries to help you understand how terms are used in this textbook. You can find electronic versions of many reference sources on the Internet, or in software programs at your school or library.

11   Spelling Rules

11.1   WORDS ENDING IN A SILENT *E*

Before adding a suffix beginning with a vowel or *y* to a word ending in a silent *e,* drop the *e* (with some exceptions).

> amaze + -ing = amazing
> love + -able = lovable
> create + -ed = created
> nerve + -ous = nervous

Exceptions: *change + -able = changeable; courage + -ous = courageous*

When adding a suffix beginning with a consonant to a word ending in a silent *e,* keep the *e* (with some exceptions).

> late + -ly = lately
> spite + -ful = spiteful
> noise + -less = noiseless
> state + -ment = statement

Exceptions: *truly, argument, ninth, wholly, awful,* and others

When a suffix beginning with *a* or *o* is added to a word with a final silent *e,* the final *e* is usually retained if it is preceded by a soft *c* or a soft *g.*

> bridge + -able = bridgeable
> peace + -able = peaceable
> outrage + -ous = outrageous
> advantage + -ous = advantageous

When a suffix beginning with a vowel is added to words ending in *ee* or *oe,* the final, silent *e* is retained.

> agree + -ing = agreeing   free + -ing = freeing
> hoe + -ing = hoeing   see + -ing = seeing

11.2   WORDS ENDING IN *Y*

Before adding most suffixes to a word that ends in *y* preceded by a consonant, change the *y* to *i.*

> easy + -est = easiest
> crazy + -est = craziest
> silly + -ness = silliness
> marry + -age = marriage

Exceptions: *dryness, shyness,* and *slyness*

However, when you add *-ing,* the *y* does not change.

> empty + -ed = emptied   but
> empty + -ing = emptying

When adding a suffix to a word that ends in *y* preceded by a vowel, the *y* usually does not change.

> play + -er = player
> employ + -ed = employed
> coy + -ness = coyness
> pay + -able = payable

11.3   WORDS ENDING IN A CONSONANT

In **one-syllable** words that end in one consonant preceded by one short vowel, double the final consonant before adding a suffix beginning with a vowel, such as

-ed or *-ing.* These are sometimes called 1+1+1 words.

dip + -ed = dipped   **set + -ing = setting**

slim + -est = slimmest   **fit + -er = fitter**

The rule does not apply to words of one syllable that end in a consonant preceded by two vowels.

feel + -ing = feeling   **peel + -ed = peeled**

reap + -ed = reaped   **loot + -ed = looted**

In words of more than one syllable, double the final consonant when (1) the word ends with one consonant preceded by one vowel and (2) when the word is accented on the last syllable.

be•gin´   per•mit´   re•fer´

In the following examples, note that in the new words formed with suffixes, the accent remains on the same syllable:

be•gin´ + -ing = be•gin´ning = beginning

per•mit´ + -ed = per•mit´ted = permitted

Exceptions: In some words with more than one syllable, though the accent remains on the same syllable when a suffix is added, the final consonant is nevertheless not doubled, as in the following examples:

tra´vel + er = tra´vel•er = traveler

mar´ket + er = mar´ket•er = marketer

In the following examples, the accent does not remain on the same syllable; thus, the final consonant is not doubled:

re•fer´ + -ence = ref´er•ence = reference

con•fer´ + -ence = con´fer•ence = conference

11.4 PREFIXES AND SUFFIXES

When adding a prefix to a word, do not change the spelling of the base word. When a prefix creates a double letter, keep both letters.

dis- + approve = disapprove

re- + build = rebuild

ir- + regular = irregular

mis- + spell = misspell

anti- + trust = antitrust

il- + logical = illogical

When adding *-ly* to a word ending in *l*, keep both *l's.* When adding *-ness* to a word ending in *n*, keep both *n's.*

careful + -ly = carefully

sudden + -ness = suddenness

final + -ly = finally

thin + -ness = thinness

11.5 FORMING PLURAL NOUNS

To form the plural of most nouns, just add *-s.*

prizes   dreams   circles   stations

For most singular nouns ending in *o,* add *-s.*

solos   halos   studios   photos   pianos

For a few nouns ending in *o,* add *-es.*

heroes   tomatoes   potatoes   echoes

When the singular noun ends in *s, sh, ch, x,* or *z,* add *-es.*

waitresses   brushes   ditches
axes   buzzes

When a singular noun ends in *y* with a consonant before it, change the *y* to *i* and add *-es.*

army—armies   **candy—candies**

baby—babies   **diary—diaries**

ferry—ferries   **conspiracy—conspiracies**

When a vowel (*a, e, i, o, u*) comes before the *y,* just add *-s.*

boy—boys   **way—ways**

array—arrays   **alloy—alloys**

weekday —weekdays   **jockey—jockeys**

For most nouns ending in *f* or *fe,* change the *f* to *v* and add *-es* or *-s.*

life—lives   **thief—thieves**

calf—calves   **shelf—shelves**

knife—knives   **loaf—loaves**

For some nouns ending in *f,* add *-s* to make the plural.

roofs   chiefs   reefs   beliefs

Some nouns have the same form for both singular and plural.

deer   sheep   moose   salmon   trout

For some nouns, the plural is formed in a special way.

man—men   goose—geese

ox—oxen   woman—women

mouse—mice   child—children

For a compound noun written as one word, form the plural by changing the last word in the compound to its plural form.

stepchild—stepchildren   firefly—fireflies

If a compound noun is written as a hyphenated word or as two separate words, change the most important word to the plural form.

brother-in-law—brothers-in-law

life jacket—life jackets

11.6 FORMING POSSESSIVES

If a noun is singular, add **'s.**

mother—my mother's car

Ross—Ross's desk

Exception: The **s** after the apostrophe is dropped after *Jesus', Moses',* and certain names in classical mythology (*Zeus'*). These possessive forms can thus be pronounced easily.

If a noun is plural and ends with **s,** add an apostrophe.

parents—my parents' car

the Santinis—the Santinis' house

If a noun is plural but does not end in **s,** add **'s.**

people—the people's choice

women—the women's coats

11.7 SPECIAL SPELLING PROBLEMS

Only one English word ends in **-sede:** *supersede.* Three words end in **-ceed:** *exceed, proceed,* and *succeed.* All other verbs ending in the sound "seed" are spelled with **-cede.**

concede   precede   recede   secede

In words with **ie** or **ei,** when the sound is long **e** (as in *she*), the word is spelled *ie* except after **c** (with some exceptions).

i before *e*	thief	relieve	field
	piece	grieve	pier
except after *c*	conceit	perceive	ceiling
	receive	receipt	
Exceptions:	either	neither	weird
	leisure	seize	

12 Commonly Confused Words

Words	Definitions	Examples
accept/ except	The verb *accept* means "to receive or believe"; *except* is usually a preposition meaning "excluding."	Did the teacher **accept** your report? Everyone smiled for the photographer **except** Jody.
advice/ advise	*Advise* is a verb; *advice* is a noun naming that which an *adviser* gives.	I **advise** you to take that job. Whom should I ask for **advice**?
affect/ effect	As a verb, *affect* means "to influence." *Effect* as a verb means "to cause." If you want a noun, you will almost always want *effect.*	How deeply did the news **affect** him? The students tried to **effect** a change in school policy. What **effect** did the acidic soil produce in the plants?
all ready/ already	*All ready* is an adjective meaning "fully ready." *Already* is an adverb meaning "before or by this time."	He was **all ready** to go at noon. I have **already** seen that movie.

continued

Words	Definitions	Examples
desert/ dessert	*Desert* (dĕz´ərt) means "a dry, sandy, barren region." *Desert* (dĭ-zûrt´) means "to abandon." *Dessert* (dĭ-zûrt´) is a sweet, such as cake.	The Sahara, in North Africa, is the world's largest **desert.** The night guard did not **desert** his post. Alison's favorite **dessert** is chocolate cake.
among/ between	*Between* is used when you are speaking of only two things. *Among* is used for three or more.	**Between** ice cream and sherbet, I prefer the latter. Gary Soto is **among** my favorite authors.
bring/take	*Bring* is used to denote motion toward a speaker or place. *Take* is used to denote motion away from such a person or place.	**Bring** the books over here, and I will **take** them to the library.
fewer/less	*Fewer* refers to the number of separate, countable units. *Less* refers to bulk quantity.	We have **less** literature and **fewer** selections in this year's curriculum.
leave/let	*Leave* means "to allow something to remain behind." *Let* means "to permit."	The librarian will **leave** some books on display but will not **let** us borrow any.
lie/lay	To *lie* is "to rest or recline." It does not take an object. *Lay* always takes an object.	Rover loves to **lie** in the sun. We always **lay** some bones next to him.
loose/lose	*Loose* (lo͞os) means "free, not restrained"; *lose* (lo͞oz) means "to misplace or fail to find."	Who turned the horses **loose**? I hope we won't **lose** any of them.
passed/ past	*Passed* is the past tense of *pass* and means "went by." *Past* is an adjective that means "of a former time." *Past* is also a noun that means "time gone by."	We **passed** through the Florida Keys during our vacation. My **past** experiences have taught me to set my alarm. Ebenezer Scrooge is a character who relives his **past.**
than/then	Use *than* in making comparisons. Use *then* on all other occasions.	Ramon is stronger **than** Mark. Cut the grass and **then** trim the hedges.
two/too/to	*Two* is the number. *Too* is an adverb meaning "also" or "very." Use *to* before a verb or as a preposition.	Meg had **to** go **to** town, **too.** We had **too** much reading **to** do. **Two** chapters is **too** many.
their/there/ they're	*Their* means "belonging to them." *There* means "in that place." *They're* is the contraction for "they are."	**There** is a movie playing at 9 P.M. **They're** going to see it with me. Sakara and Jessica drove away in **their** car after the movie.

Glossary of Literary and Informational Terms

Act An act is a major division within a play, similar to a chapter in a book. Each act may be further divided into smaller sections, called scenes. Plays can have as many as five acts or as few as one.

Adventure Story An adventure story is a literary work in which action is the main element. An **adventure novel** usually focuses on a main character who is on a mission and is facing many challenges and choices.

Alliteration Alliteration is the repetition of consonant sounds at the beginning of words. Note the repetition of the **b** sound in this line: The **b**oy's dog **b**egan **b**egging for **b**iscuits.

Allusion An allusion is a reference to a famous person, place, event, or work of literature.

Analogy An analogy is a point-by-point comparison between two things that are alike in some respect. Often, writers use analogies in nonfiction to explain unfamiliar subjects or ideas in terms of familiar ones.

See also Extended Metaphor; Metaphor; Simile.

Anecdote An anecdote is a short account of an event that is usually intended to entertain or make a point.

Antagonist The antagonist is a force working against the protagonist, or main character, in a story, play, or novel. The antagonist is usually another character but can be a force of nature, society itself, or an internal force within the main character.

See also Protagonist.

Argument An argument is speaking or writing that expresses a position on a problem and supports it with reasons and evidence. An argument often takes into account other points of view, anticipating and answering objections that opponents might raise.

See also Claim; Counterargument; Evidence.

Assonance Assonance is the repetition of vowel sounds within nonrhyming words. An example of assonance is the repetition of the *i* sound in the following line: Into the ink-filled jar she inserted the brush.

Assumption An assumption is an opinion or belief that is taken for granted. It can be about a specific situation, a person, or the world in general. Assumptions are often unstated.

Author's Message An author's message is the main idea or theme of a particular work.

See also Main Idea; Theme.

Author's Perspective An author's perspective is the unique combination of ideas, values, feelings, and beliefs that influences the way the writer looks at a topic. Tone, or attitude, often reveals an author's perspective.

See also Author's Purpose; Tone.

Author's Position An author's position is his or her opinion on an issue or topic.

See also Claim; Writer's Point of View.

Author's Purpose A writer usually writes for one or more of these purposes: to express thoughts or feelings, to inform or explain, to persuade, and to entertain.

See also Author's Perspective; Writer's Point of View.

Autobiography An autobiography is a writer's account of his or her own life. In almost every case, it is told from the first-person point of view. Generally, an autobiography focuses on the most significant events and people in the writer's life over a period of time.

See also Memoir.

Ballad A ballad is a type of narrative poem that tells a story and was originally meant to be sung or recited. Because it tells a story, a ballad has a setting, a plot, and characters. **Folk ballads** were composed orally and handed down by word of mouth from generation to generation.

Bias In a piece of writing, the author's bias is the side of an issue that he or she favors. Words with extremely positive or negative connotations are often a signal of an author's bias.

Biography A biography is the true account of a person's life, written by another person.

As such, biographies are usually told from a third-person point of view. The writer of a biography usually researches his or her subject in order to present accurate information. The best biographers strive for honesty and balance in their accounts of their subjects' lives.

Bibliography A bibliography is a list of related books and other materials used to write a text. Bibliographies can be good sources for further study on a subject.

See also Works Consulted.

Career Development Documents These documents include written business communications such as business letters, e-mails, and memos. In general, business correspondence is brief, to the point, clear, courteous, and professional.

Cast of Characters In the script of a play, a cast of characters is a list of all the characters in the play, usually in order of appearance. It may include a brief description of each character.

Cause and Effect Two events are related by cause and effect when one event brings about, or causes, the other. The event that happens first is the **cause**; the one that follows is the **effect.** Cause and effect is also a way of organizing an entire piece of writing. It helps writers show the relationships between events or ideas.

Character Characters are the people, animals, or imaginary creatures who take part in the action of a work of literature. Like real people, characters display certain qualities, or **character traits,** that develop and change over time, and they usually have **motivations,** or reasons, for their behaviors.

Central character: Central or main characters are the most important characters in literary works. Generally, the plot of a short story focuses on one main character, but a novel may have several main characters.

Minor characters: The less important characters in a literary work are known as minor characters. The story is not centered on them, but they help carry out the action of the story and help the reader learn more about the main character.

Dynamic character: A dynamic character is one who undergoes important changes as a plot unfolds. The changes occur because of the character's actions and experiences in the story. The changes are usually internal and may be good or bad. Main characters are usually, though not always, dynamic.

Static character: A static character is one who remains the same throughout a story. The character may experience events and have interactions with other characters, but he or she is not changed because of them.

See also Characterization; Character Traits.

Characterization The way a writer creates and develops characters is known as characterization. There are four basic methods of characterization.

- The writer may make direct comments about a character through the voice of the narrator.
- The writer may describe the character's physical appearance.
- The writer may present the character's own thoughts, speech, and actions.
- The writer may present thoughts, speech, and actions of other characters.

See also Character; Character Traits.

Character Traits Character traits are the qualities shown by a character. Traits may be physical (brown eyes) or expressions of personality (shyness). Writers reveal the traits of their characters through methods of characterization. Sometimes writers directly state a character's traits, but more often readers need to infer traits from a character's words, actions, thoughts, appearance, and relationships. Examples of words that describe traits include *courageous, humble, generous,* and *wild.*

Chronological Order Chronological order is the arrangement of events by their order of occurrence. This type of organization is used in fictional narratives and in historical writing, biography, and autobiography.

Claim In an argument, a claim is the writer's position on an issue or problem. Although an argument focuses on supporting one claim, a writer may make more than one claim in a text.

Clarify Clarifying is a reading strategy that helps readers understand or make clear what they are reading. Readers usually clarify by rereading, reading aloud, or discussing.

Classification Classification is a pattern of organization in which objects, ideas, and/or information are presented in groups, or classes, based on common characteristics.

Cliché A cliché is an overused expression. "Better late than never" and "hard as nails" are common examples. Good writers generally avoid clichés unless they are using them in dialogue to indicate something about a character's personality.

Climax The climax stage is the point of greatest interest in a story or play. The climax usually occurs toward the end of a story, after the reader has understood the **conflict** and become emotionally involved with the characters. At the climax, the conflict is resolved and the outcome of the plot usually becomes clear.

See also Plot.

Comedy A comedy is a dramatic work that is light and often humorous in tone, usually ending happily with a peaceful resolution of the main conflict.

Compare and Contrast To compare and contrast is to identify the similarities and differences of two or more subjects. Compare and contrast is also a pattern of organizing an entire piece of writing.

Conclusion A conclusion is a statement of belief based on evidence, experience, and reasoning. A valid conclusion is one that logically follows from the facts or statements upon which it is based.

Conflict A conflict is a struggle between opposing forces. Almost every story has a main conflict—a conflict that is the story's focus. An **external conflict** involves a character who struggles against a force outside him- or herself, such as nature, a physical obstacle, or another character. An **internal conflict** is one that occurs within a character.

See also Plot.

Connect Connecting is a reader's process of relating the content of a text to his or her own knowledge and experience.

Connotation A word's connotations are the ideas and feelings associated with the word, as opposed to its dictionary definition. For example, the word *mother,* in addition to its basic meaning ("a female parent"), has connotations of love, warmth, and security.

Consumer Documents Consumer documents are printed materials that accompany products and services. They usually provide information about the use, care, operation, or assembly of the product or service they accompany. Some common consumer documents are applications, contracts, warranties, manuals, instructions, labels, brochures, and schedules.

Context Clues When you encounter an unfamiliar word, you can often use context clues to understand it. Context clues are the words or phrases surrounding the word that provide hints about the word's meaning.

Counterargument A counterargument is an argument made to oppose another argument. A good argument anticipates opposing viewpoints and provides counterarguments to disprove them.

Couplet A couplet is a rhymed pair of lines. A couplet may be written in any rhythmic pattern: Follow your heart's desire/And good things may transpire.

See also Stanza.

Credibility Credibility is the believability or trustworthiness of a source and the information it provides.

Critical Essay *See* Essay.

Critical Review A critical review is an evaluation or critique by a reviewer, or critic. Types of reviews include film reviews, book reviews, music reviews, and art show reviews.

Database A database is a collection of information that can be quickly and easily accessed and searched and from which information can be easily retrieved. It is frequently presented in an electronic format.

Debate A debate is basically an argument—but a very structured one that requires a good deal of preparation. In school settings, debate usually is a formal contest in which two opposing teams defend and attack a proposition.

See also Argument.

Deductive Reasoning Deductive reasoning is a way of thinking that begins with a generalization, presents a specific situation, and then moves forward with facts and evidence toward a logical conclusion. The following passage has a deductive argument embedded in it: "All students in the math class must take the quiz on Friday. Since Lana is in the class, she had better show up." This deductive argument can be broken down as follows: generalization—All students in the math class must take the quiz on Friday; specific situation—Lana is a student who is in the math class; conclusion—Therefore, Lana must take the math quiz.

Denotation A word's denotation is its dictionary definition.

See also Connotation.

Description Description is writing that helps a reader to picture events, objects, and characters. To create descriptions, writers often use **imagery**—words and phrases that appeal to the reader's senses.

Dialect A dialect is a form of a language that is spoken in a particular place or by a particular group of people. Dialects may feature unique pronunciations, vocabulary, and grammar.

Dialogue Dialogue is written conversation between two or more characters. Writers use dialogue to bring characters to life and to give readers insights into the characters' qualities, traits, and reactions to other characters. In fiction, dialogue is usually set off with quotation marks. In drama, stories are told primarily through dialogue.

Diary A diary is a daily record of a writer's thoughts, experiences, and feelings. As such, it is a type of autobiographical writing. The terms *diary* and *journal* are often used synonymously.

Dictionary *See* Reference Works.

Drama A drama, or play, is a form of literature meant to be performed by actors in front of an audience. In a drama, the characters' dialogue and actions tell the story. The written form of a play is known as a script. A script usually includes dialogue, a cast of characters, and stage directions that give instructions about performing the drama. The person who writes the drama is known as the playwright or dramatist.

Draw Conclusions To draw a conclusion is to make a judgment or arrive at a belief based on evidence, experience, and reasoning.

Dynamic Character *See* Character.

Editorial An editorial is an opinion piece that usually appears on the editorial page of a newspaper or as part of a news broadcast. The editorial section of the newspaper presents opinions rather than objective news reports.

See also Op/Ed Piece.

Either/Or Fallacy An either/or fallacy is a statement that suggests that there are only two choices available in a situation when in fact there are more than two.

Emotional Appeals Emotional appeals are messages that create strong feelings to make a point. An appeal to fear is a message that taps into people's fear of losing their safety or security. An appeal to pity is a message that taps into people's sympathy and compassion for others to build support for an idea, a cause, or a proposed action. An appeal to vanity is a message that attempts to persuade by tapping into people's desire to feel good about themselves.

Encyclopedia *See* Reference Works.

Epic Poem An epic poem is a long narrative poem about the adventures of a hero whose actions reflect the ideals and values of a nation or a group of people.

Essay An essay is a short work of nonfiction that deals with a single subject. There are many types of essays. An **expository essay** presents or explains information and ideas. A **personal essay** usually reflects the writer's experiences, feelings, and personality. A **persuasive essay** attempts to convince the reader to adopt a certain viewpoint. A **critical essay** evaluates a situation or a work of art.

Evaluate To evaluate is to examine something carefully and to judge its value or worth. Evaluating is an important skill. A reader can evaluate the actions of a particular character, for example. A reader can also form opinions about the value of an entire work.

Evidence Evidence is a specific piece of information that supports a claim. Evidence can take the form of a fact, a quotation, an example, a statistic, or a personal experience, among other things.

Exaggeration An extreme overstatement of an idea is called an exaggeration. It is often used for purposes of emphasis or humor.

Exposition Exposition is the first stage of a typical story plot. The exposition provides important background information and introduces the setting and the important characters. The conflict the characters face may also be introduced in the exposition, or it may be introduced later, in the rising action.

See also Plot.

Expository Essay *See* Essay.

Extended Metaphor An extended metaphor is a figure of speech that compares two essentially unlike things at some length and in several ways. It does not contain the words *like* or *as.*

See also Metaphor.

External Conflict *See* Conflict.

Fable A fable is a brief tale told to illustrate a moral or teach a lesson. Often the moral of a fable appears in a distinct and memorable statement near the tale's beginning or end.

See also Moral.

Fact Versus Opinion A fact is a statement that can be proved, or verified. An opinion, on the other hand, is a statement that cannot be proved because it expresses a person's beliefs, feelings, or thoughts.

See also Generalization; Inference.

Fallacy A fallacy is an error—usually in reasoning. Typically, a fallacy is based on an incorrect inference or a misuse of evidence.

See also Either/Or Fallacy; Logical Appeal; Overgeneralization.

Falling Action The falling action is the stage of the plot in which the story begins to draw to a close. The falling action comes after the climax and before the resolution. Events in the falling action show the results of the important decision or action that happened at the climax. Tension eases as the falling action begins; however, the final outcome of the story is not yet fully worked out at this stage.

See also Climax; Plot.

Fantasy Fantasy is a type of fiction that is highly imaginative and portrays events, settings, or characters that are unrealistic. The setting might be a nonexistent world, the plot might involve magic or the supernatural, and the characters might have superhuman powers.

Farce Farce is a type of exaggerated comedy that features an absurd plot, ridiculous situations, and humorous dialogue. The main purpose of a farce is to keep an audience laughing. Comic devices typically used in farces include mistaken identity, wordplay (such as puns and double meanings), and exaggeration.

Faulty Reasoning *See* Fallacy.

Feature Article A feature article is a main article in a newspaper or a cover story in a magazine.

Fiction Fiction is prose writing that tells an imaginary story. The writer of a fictional work might invent all the events and characters or might base parts of the story on real people and events. The basic elements of fiction are plot, character, setting, and theme. Fiction includes short stories, novellas, and novels.

See also Novel; Novella; Short Story.

Figurative Language In figurative language, words are used in an imaginative way to express ideas that are not literally true. "Tasha's money is burning a hole in her pocket" is an example of figurative language. The sentence does not really mean that Tasha's pocket is on fire.

Instead, it means that Tasha is anxious to spend her money. Figurative language is used for comparison, emphasis, and emotional effect.

See also Metaphor; Onomatopoeia; Personification; Simile.

First-Person Point of View *See* Point of View.

Flashback In a literary work, a flashback is an interruption of the action to present events that took place at an earlier time. A flashback provides information that can help a reader better understand a character's current situation.

Foil A foil is a character who provides a striking contrast to another character. By using a foil, a writer can call attention to certain traits possessed by a main character or simply enhance a character by contrast.

Folklore The traditions, customs, and stories that are passed down within a culture are known as its folklore. Folklore includes various types of literature, such as legends, folk tales, myths, trickster tales, and fables.

See Fable; Folk Tale; Myth.

Folk Tale A folk tale is a story that has been passed from generation to generation by word of mouth. Folk tales may be set in the distant past and involve supernatural events. The characters in them may be animals, people, or superhuman beings.

Foreshadowing Foreshadowing occurs when a writer provides hints that suggest future events in a story. Foreshadowing creates suspense and makes readers eager to find out what will happen.

Form The structure or organization of a work of writing is often called its form. The form of a poem includes the arrangement of its words and lines on the page.

Free Verse Poetry without regular patterns of rhyme and rhythm is called free verse. Some poets use free verse to capture the sounds and rhythms of ordinary speech.

See also Rhyme.

Generalization A generalization is a broad statement about a class or category of people, ideas, or things based on a study of, or a belief about, some of its members.

See also Overgeneralization; Stereotyping.

Genre The term *genre* refers to a category in which a work of literature is classified. The major genres in literature are fiction, nonfiction, poetry, and drama.

Government Publications Government publications are documents produced by government organizations. Pamphlets, brochures, and reports are just some of the many forms these publications take. Government publications can be good resources for a wide variety of topics.

Graphic Aid A graphic aid is a text feature that is printed, handwritten, or drawn. Charts, diagrams, graphs, photographs, maps, and captions are examples of graphic aids.

Graphic Organizer A graphic organizer is a "word picture"—a visual illustration of a verbal statement—that helps a reader understand a text. Charts, tables, webs, and diagrams can all be graphic organizers. Graphic organizers and graphic aids can look the same. However, graphic organizers and graphic aids do differ in how they are used. Graphic aids help deliver important information to students using a text. Graphic organizers are actually created by students themselves. They help students understand the text or organize information.

Haiku Haiku is a form of Japanese poetry in which 17 syllables are arranged in three lines of 5, 7, and 5 syllables. The rules of haiku are strict. In addition to following the syllabic count, the poet must create a clear picture that will evoke a strong emotional response in the reader. Nature is a particularly important source of inspiration for Japanese haiku poets, and details from nature are often the subjects of their poems.

Hero A hero is a main character or protagonist in a story. In older literary works, heroes tend to be better than ordinary humans. They are typically courageous, strong, honorable, and intelligent. They are protectors of society who hold back the forces of evil and fight to make the world a better place. In modern literature, a hero may simply be the most important character in a story. Such a hero is often an ordinary person with ordinary problems.

Historical Documents Historical documents are writings that have played a significant role in human events. The Declaration of Independence, for example, is a historical document.

Historical Dramas Historical dramas are plays that take place in the past and are based on real events. In many of these plays, the characters are also based on real historical figures. The dialogue and the action, however, are mostly created by the playwright.

Historical Fiction A short story or a novel can be called historical fiction when it is set in the past and includes real places and real events of historical importance.

How-To Book A how-to book explains how to do something—usually an activity, a sport, or a household project.

Humor Humor is a quality that provokes laughter or amusement. Writers create humor through exaggeration, amusing descriptions, irony, and witty and insightful dialogue.

Hyperbole Hyperbole is a figure of speech in which the truth is exaggerated for emphasis or humorous effect.

Idiom An idiom is an expression that has a meaning different from the meaning of its individual words. For example, "to go to the dogs" is an idiom meaning "to go to ruin."

Imagery Imagery consists of words and phrases that appeal to a reader's five senses. Writers use sensory details to help the reader imagine how things look, feel, smell, sound, and taste.

Implied Main Idea *See* Main Idea.

Index The index of a book is an alphabetized list of important topics covered in the book and the page numbers on which they can be found. An index can be used to quickly find specific information about a topic.

Inductive Reasoning Inductive reasoning is the process of logical reasoning that starts with observations, examples, and facts and moves on to a general conclusion or principle.

Inference An inference is a logical guess that is made based on facts and one's own knowledge and experience.

Informational Text Informational text is writing that provides factual information. Examples include news reports, a science textbook, manuals, lab reports, and signs. Informational text also includes literary nonfiction, such as personal essays, opinion pieces, speeches, biographies, and historical accounts.

Internal Conflict *See* Conflict.

Internet The Internet is a global, interconnected system of computer networks that allows for communication through e-mail, listservs, and the World Wide Web. The Internet connects computers and computer users throughout the world.

Interview An interview is a conversation conducted by a writer or reporter in which facts or statements are elicited from another person, recorded, and then broadcast or published.

Journal A journal is a periodical publication issued by a legal, medical, or other professional organization. The term may also be used to refer to a diary or daily record.

Legend A legend is a story handed down from the past about a specific person, usually someone of heroic accomplishments. Legends usually have some basis in historical fact.

Limerick A limerick is a short, humorous poem composed of five lines. It usually has the rhyme scheme *aabba,* created by two rhyming couplets followed by a fifth line that rhymes with the first couplet. A limerick typically has a sing-song rhythm.

Loaded Language Loaded language consists of words with strongly positive or negative connotations intended to influence a reader's or listener's attitude.

Logical Appeal A logical appeal is a way of writing or speaking that relies on logic and facts. It appeals to people's reasoning or intellect rather than to their values or emotions. Flawed logical appeals—that is, errors in reasoning—are called logical fallacies.

See also Fallacy.

Logical Argument A logical argument is an argument in which the logical relationship between the support and claim is sound.

Lyric Poetry Lyric poetry is poetry that presents the personal thoughts and feelings of a single speaker. Most poems, other than narrative poems, are lyric poems. Lyric poetry can be in a variety of forms and cover many subjects, from love and death to everyday experiences.

Main Idea The main idea, or central idea, is the most important idea about a topic that a writer or speaker conveys. It can be the central idea of an entire work or of just a paragraph. Often, the main idea of a paragraph is expressed in a topic sentence. However, a main idea may just be implied, or suggested, by details. A main idea is typically supported by details.

Make Inferences *See* Inference.

Memoir A memoir is a form of autobiographical writing in which a writer shares his or her personal experiences and observations of significant events or people. Often informal or even intimate in tone, memoirs usually give readers insight into the impact of historical events on people's lives.

See also Autobiography.

Metaphor A metaphor is a comparison of two things that are basically unlike but have some qualities in common. Unlike a simile, a metaphor does not contain the words *like* or *as.*

See also Extended Metaphor; Figurative Language; Simile.

Meter In poetry, meter is the regular pattern of stressed (´) and unstressed (˘) syllables. Although poems have rhythm, not all poems have regular meter. Each unit of meter is known as a **foot** and is made up of one stressed syllable and one or two unstressed syllables.

See also Rhythm.

Minor Character *See* Character.

Monitor Monitoring is the strategy of checking your comprehension as you read and modifying the strategies you are using to suit your needs. Monitoring often includes the following strategies: questioning, clarifying, visualizing, predicting, connecting, and rereading.

Mood Mood is the feeling or atmosphere that a writer creates for the reader. Descriptive words, imagery, and figurative language all influence the mood of a work.

See also Tone.

Moral A moral is a lesson that a story teaches. A moral is often stated at the end of a fable.

See also Fable.

Motivation *See* Character.

Myth A myth is a traditional story that attempts to answer basic questions about human nature, origins of the world, mysteries of nature, and social customs.

Narrative Nonfiction Narrative nonfiction is writing that reads much like fiction, except that the characters, setting, and plot are real rather than imaginary. Narrative nonfiction includes autobiographies, biographies, and memoirs.

Narrative Poetry Poetry that tells a story is called narrative poetry. Like fiction, a narrative poem contains characters, a setting, and a plot. It might also contain such elements of poetry as rhyme, rhythm, imagery, and figurative language.

Narrator The narrator is the voice that tells a story. Sometimes the narrator is a character in the story. At other times, the narrator is an outside voice created by the writer. The narrator is not the same as the writer.

An **unreliable narrator** is one who tells a story or interprets events in a way that makes readers doubt what he or she is saying. An unreliable narrator is usually a character in the story. The narrator may be unreliable for a number of different reasons. For example, the narrator may not have all the facts or may be too young to understand the situation.

See also Point of View.

News Article A news article is writing that reports on a recent event. In newspapers, news articles are usually brief and to the point, presenting the most important facts first, followed by more detailed information.

Nonfiction Nonfiction is writing that tells about real people, places, and events. Unlike fiction, nonfiction is mainly written to convey factual information. Nonfiction includes a wide range of writing—newspaper articles, textbooks, instructional manuals, letters, essays, biographies, movie reviews, speeches, true-life adventure stories, advertising, and more.

Novel A novel is a long work of fiction. Like a short story, a novel is the product of a writer's imagination. Because a novel is considerably longer than a short story, a novelist can develop the characters and story line more thoroughly.

See also Fiction.

Novella A novella is a short prose tale, or short novel. It is longer than a short story and often teaches a moral, or satirizes a subject.

See also Short Story; Novel.

Ode An ode is a type of lyric poem that deals with serious themes, such as justice, truth, or beauty.

Onomatopoeia Onomatopoeia is the use of words whose sounds echo their meanings, such as *buzz, whisper, gargle,* and *murmur.*

Op/Ed Piece An op/ed piece is an opinion piece that typically appears opposite ("op") the editorial page of a newspaper. Unlike editorials, op/ed pieces are written and submitted by readers.

Oral Literature Oral literature consists of stories that have been passed down by word of mouth from generation to generation. Oral literature includes folk tales, legends, and myths. In more recent times, some examples of oral literature have been written down or recorded so that the stories can be preserved.

Organization *See* Pattern of Organization.

Overgeneralization An overgeneralization is a generalization that is too broad. You can often recognize overgeneralizations by the appearance of words and phrases such as *all, everyone, every time, any, anything, no one,* or *none.* An example is "None of the city's workers

really cares about keeping the environment clean." In all probability, there are many exceptions. The writer can't possibly know the feelings of every city worker.

Overview An overview is a short summary of a story, a speech, or an essay.

Paraphrase Paraphrasing is the restating of information in one's own words.

See also Summarize.

Pattern of Organization The term *pattern of organization* refers to the way ideas and information are arranged and organized. Patterns of organization include cause and effect, chronological, compare and contrast, classification, and problem-solution, among others.

See also Cause and Effect; Chronological Order; Classification; Compare and Contrast; Problem-Solution Order; Sequential Order.

Periodical A periodical is a magazine or another type of publication that is issued on a regular basis.

Personal Essay *See* Essay.

Personification The giving of human qualities to an animal, object, or idea is known as personification. For example, animals are personified when they have conversations with each other as if they were human.

See also Figurative Language.

Persuasion Persuasion is the art of swaying others' feelings, beliefs, or actions. Persuasion normally appeals to both the minds and the emotions of readers.

See also Emotional Appeals; Loaded Language; Logical Appeal.

Persuasive Essay *See* Essay.

Play *See* Drama.

Playwright *See* Drama.

Plot The series of events in a story is called the plot. The plot usually centers on a **conflict,** or struggle, faced by the main character. The action that the characters take to solve the problem builds toward a climax in the story. At this point, or shortly afterward, the problem is solved and the story ends. Most story plots have five stages: exposition, rising action, climax, falling action, and resolution.

See also Climax; Conflict; Exposition; Falling Action; Rising Action.

Poetry Poetry is a type of literature in which words are carefully chosen and arranged to create certain effects. Poets use a variety of sound devices, imagery, and figurative language to express emotions and ideas.

See also Alliteration; Assonance; Ballad; Free Verse; Imagery; Meter; Narrative Poetry; Rhyme; Rhythm; Stanza.

Point of View Point of view refers to how a writer chooses to narrate a story. When a story is told from the **first-person** point of view, the narrator is a character in the story and uses first-person pronouns, such as *I, me,* and *we.* In a story told from the **third-person** point of view, the narrator is not a character. Third-person narration makes use of pronouns such as *he, she, it,* and *they.* A writer's choice of narrator affects the information readers receive.

It is also important to consider whether a writer is writing from a **subjective** or an **objective** point of view. When writing from a subjective point of view, the writer includes personal opinions, feelings, and beliefs. When writing from an objective point of view, the writer leaves out personal opinions and instead presents information in a straightforward, unbiased way.

See also Narrator.

Predict Predicting is a reading strategy that involves using text clues to make a reasonable guess about what will happen next in a story.

Primary Source *See* Sources.

Prior Knowledge Prior knowledge is the knowledge a reader already possesses about a topic. This information might come from personal experiences, expert accounts, books, films, and other sources.

Problem-Solution Order Problem-solution order is a pattern of organization in which a problem is stated and analyzed and then one or more solutions are proposed and examined.

Prop The word *prop,* originally an abbreviation of the word *property,* refers to any physical object that is used in a drama.

Propaganda Propaganda is a form of communication that may use false or misleading information.

Prose The word *prose* refers to all forms of writing that are not in verse form. The term may be used to describe very different forms of writing—short stories as well as essays, for example.

Protagonist A protagonist is the main character in a story, play, or novel. The protagonist is involved in the main conflict of the story. Usually, the protagonist undergoes changes as the plot runs its course.

Public Documents Public documents are documents that were written for the public to provide information that is of public interest or concern. They include government documents, speeches, signs, and rules and regulations. Most public documents use text features, such as graphics, headers, or captions, to make sure readers can easily understand the information they communicate.

See also Government Publications.

Radio Play A radio play is a drama that is written specifically to be broadcast over the radio. Because the audience is not meant to see a radio play, sound effects are often used to help listeners imagine the setting and the action. The stage directions in the play's script indicate the sound effects.

Recurring Theme *See* Theme.

Reference Works Reference works are sources that contain facts and background information on a wide range of subjects. Most reference works are good sources of reliable information because they have been reviewed by experts. The following are some common reference works: encyclopedias, dictionaries, thesauri, almanacs, atlases, and directories.

Refrain A refrain is one or more lines repeated in each stanza of a poem.

See also Stanza.

Repetition Repetition is a technique in which a sound, word, phrase, or line is repeated for emphasis or unity. Repetition helps to reinforce meaning and create an appealing rhythm.

See also Alliteration; Sound Devices.

Resolution *See* Falling Action.

Review *See* Critical Review.

Rhetorical Questions Rhetorical questions are those that have such obvious answers that they do not require a reply. Writers often use them to suggest that their claim is so obvious that everyone should agree with it.

Rhyme Rhyme is the repetition of sounds at the end of words. Words rhyme when their accented vowels and the letters that follow have identical sounds. *Cat* and *hat* rhyme, as do *feather* and *leather.* The most common type of rhyme in poetry is called **end rhyme,** in which rhyming words come at the ends of lines. Rhyme that occurs within a line of poetry is called **internal rhyme.**

Rhyme Scheme A rhyme scheme is a pattern of end rhymes in a poem. A rhyme scheme is noted by assigning a letter of the alphabet, beginning with *a,* to each line. Lines that rhyme are given the same letter.

Rhythm Rhythm is a pattern of stressed and unstressed syllables in a line of poetry. Poets use rhythm to bring out the musical quality of language, to emphasize ideas, and to create moods. Devices such as alliteration, rhyme, assonance, and consonance often contribute to creating rhythm.

See also Meter.

Rising Action The rising action is the stage of the plot that develops the **conflict,** or struggle. During this stage, events occur that make the conflict more complicated. The events in the rising action build toward a **climax,** or turning point.

See also Plot.

Scanning Scanning is the process used to search through a text for a particular fact or piece of information. When you scan, you sweep your eyes across a page, looking for key words that may lead you to the information you want.

Scene In drama, the action is often divided into acts and scenes. Each scene presents an episode of the play's plot and typically occurs at a single place and time.

See also Act.

Scenery Scenery is a painted backdrop or other structures used to create the setting for a play.

Science Fiction Science fiction is fiction in which a writer explores unexpected possibilities of the past or the future, using known scientific data and theories as well as his or her creative imagination. Most science fiction writers create believable worlds, although some create fantasy worlds that have familiar elements.

See also Fantasy.

Screenplay A screenplay is a play written for film.

Script The text of a play, film, or broadcast is called a script.

Secondary Source *See* Sources.

Sensory Details Sensory details are words and phrases that appeal to the reader's senses of sight, sound, touch, smell, and taste. Note the sensory details in the following line. The morning sun shone brightly as a light breeze gently blew and rustled the poplar leaves. These details appeal to the senses of touch and smell.

See also Imagery.

Sequential Order Sequential order is a pattern of organization that shows the order of steps or stages in a process.

Setting The setting of a story, poem, or play is the time and place of the action. Sometimes the setting is clear and well defined. At other times, it is left to the reader's imagination. Elements of setting include geographic location, historical period (past, present, or future), season, time of day, and culture.

Setting a Purpose The process of establishing specific reasons for reading a text is called setting a purpose. Readers can look at a text's title, headings, and illustrations to guess what it might be about. They can then use these guesses to figure out what they want to learn from reading the text.

Short Story A short story is a work of fiction that centers on a single idea and can be read in one sitting. Generally, a short story has one main conflict that involves the characters and keeps the story moving.

See also Fiction.

Sidebar A sidebar is additional information set in a box alongside or within an article. Popular magazines often make use of sidebars.

Signal Words In a text, signal words are words and phrases that help show how events or ideas are related. Some common examples of signal words are *and, but, however, nevertheless, therefore,* and *in addition.*

Simile A simile is a figure of speech that makes a comparison between two unlike things using the words *like* or *as*: The calm lake was smooth as glass.

See also Figurative Language; Metaphor.

Sonnet A sonnet is a poem that has a formal structure, containing 14 lines and a specific rhyme scheme and meter. The sonnet, which means "little song," can be used for a variety of topics.

See also Rhyme Scheme.

Sound Devices Sound devices are ways of using words for the sound qualities they create. Sound devices can help convey meaning and mood in a writer's work. Some common sound devices include **alliteration, assonance, meter, onomatopoeia, repetition, rhyme,** and **rhythm.**

See also Alliteration; Assonance; Meter; Onomatopoeia; Repetition; Rhyme; Rhythm.

Sources A source is anything that supplies information. **Primary sources** are materials written by people who witnessed or took part in an event. Letters, diaries, autobiographies, and speeches are primary sources. Unlike primary sources, **secondary sources** are made by people who were not directly involved in an event or present when it occurred. Encyclopedias, textbooks, biographies, and most newspaper and magazine articles are examples of secondary sources.

Speaker In poetry the speaker is the voice that "talks" to the reader, similar to the narrator in fiction. The speaker is not necessarily the poet.

Speech A speech is a talk or public address. The purpose of a speech may be to entertain, to explain, to persuade, to inspire, or any combination of these purposes.

Stage Directions In the script of a play, the instructions to the actors, director, and stage crew are called the stage directions. Stage directions might suggest scenery, lighting, sound effects, and ways for actors to move and speak. Stage directions often appear in parentheses and in italic type.

Stanza A stanza is a group of two or more lines that form a unit in a poem. Each stanza may have the same number of lines, or the number of lines may vary.

See also Couplet; Form; Poetry.

Static Character *See* Character.

Stereotype In literature, characters who are defined by a single trait are known as stereotypes. Such characters do not usually demonstrate the complexities of real people. Familiar stereotypes in popular literature include the absent-minded professor and the busybody.

Stereotyping Stereotyping is a dangerous type of overgeneralization. It can lead to unfair judgments of people based on their ethnic background, beliefs, practices, or physical appearance.

Structure The structure of a work of literature is the way in which it is put together. In poetry, structure involves the arrangement of words and lines to produce a desired effect. One structural unit in poetry is the stanza. In prose, structure involves the arrangement of such elements as sentences, paragraphs, and events.

Style A style is a manner of writing. It involves how something is said rather than what is said.

Summarize To summarize is to briefly retell the main ideas of a piece of writing in one's own words.

See also Paraphrase.

Support Support is any information that helps to prove a claim.

Supporting Detail *See* Main Idea.

Surprise Ending A surprise ending is an unexpected plot twist at the end of a story. The surprise may be a sudden turn in the action or a piece of information that gives a different perspective to the entire story.

Suspense Suspense is a feeling of growing tension and excitement experienced by a reader. Suspense makes a reader curious about the outcome of a story or an event within a story. A writer creates suspense by raising questions in the reader's mind. The use of **foreshadowing** is one way that writers create suspense.

See also Foreshadowing.

Symbol A symbol is a person, a place, an object, an animal, or an activity that stands for something beyond itself. For example, a flag is a colored piece of cloth that stands for a country. A white dove is a bird that represents peace.

Synthesize To synthesize information means to take individual pieces of information and combine them in order to gain a better understanding of a subject.

Tall Tale A tall tale is a humorously exaggerated story about impossible events, often involving the supernatural abilities of the main character.

Teleplay A teleplay is a play written for television. In a teleplay, scenes can change quickly and dramatically. The camera can focus the viewer's attention on specific actions. The camera directions in teleplays are much like the stage directions in stage plays.

Text Features Text features are elements of a text, such as boldface type, headers, and subheadings, that help organize and call attention to important information. Italic type, bulleted or numbered lists, sidebars, captions, and graphic aids such as charts, tables, timelines, illustrations, and photographs are also considered text features.

Theme A theme is a message about life or human nature that the writer shares with the reader. In many cases, readers must infer what the writer's message is. One way of figuring out a theme is to apply the lessons learned by the main characters to people in real life.

> **Recurring themes:** Themes found in a variety of works. For example, authors from different backgrounds might express similar themes having to do with the importance of family values.
>
> **Universal themes:** Themes that are found throughout the literature of all time periods.

See also Moral.

Thesaurus *See* Reference Works.

Thesis Statement A thesis statement, or controlling idea, is the main proposition that a writer attempts to support in a piece of writing.

Third-Person Point of View *See* Point of View.

Title The title of a piece of writing is the name that is attached to it. A title often refers to an important aspect of the work.

Tone The tone of a literary work expresses the writer's attitude toward his or her subject. Words such as *angry, sad,* and *humorous* can be used to describe different tones.

See also Author's Perspective; Mood.

Topic Sentence The topic sentence of a paragraph states the paragraph's main idea; all other sentences in the paragraph provide supporting details.

Tragedy A tragedy is a dramatic work that presents the downfall of a dignified character or characters who are involved in historically or socially significant events. The events in a tragic plot are set in motion by a decision that is often an error in judgment on the part of the hero. Succeeding events are linked in a cause-and-effect relationship and lead inevitably to a disastrous conclusion, usually death. William Shakespeare's *Romeo and Juliet* is a famous tragedy.

Traits *See* Character.

Treatment The way a topic is handled in a work is referred to as its treatment. Treatment includes the form the writing takes as well as the writer's purpose and tone.

Turning Point *See* Climax.

Understatement Understatement is a technique of creating emphasis by saying less than is actually or literally true. It is the opposite of **hyperbole,** or exaggeration. Understatement is often used to create a humorous effect.

Universal Theme *See* Theme.

Unreliable Narrator *See* Narrator.

Visualize Visualizing is the process of forming a mental picture based on written or spoken information.

Voice The term *voice* refers to a writer's unique use of language that allows a reader to "hear" a human personality in the writer's work. Elements of style that contribute to a writer's voice can reveal much about the author's personality, beliefs, and attitudes.

Website A website is a collection of "pages" on the World Wide Web, usually devoted to one specific subject. Pages are linked together and accessed by clicking hyperlinks or menus, which send the user from page to page within a website. Websites are created by companies, organizations, educational institutions, branches of the government, the military, and individuals.

Word Choice The success of any writing depends on the writer's choice of words. Words not only communicate ideas but also help describe events, characters, settings, and so on. Word choice can make a writer's work sound

formal or informal, serious or humorous. A writer must choose words carefully depending on the goal of the piece of writing. For example, a writer working on a science article would probably use technical, formal words; a writer trying to establish the setting in a short story would probably use more descriptive words.

See also Style.

Workplace Documents Workplace documents are materials that are produced or used within a work setting, usually to aid in the functioning of the workplace. They include job applications, office memos, training manuals, job descriptions, and sales reports. Effective workplace documents include text features, such as graphics, headers, and captions, to help communicate information clearly.

Works Cited The term *works cited* refers to a list of all the works a writer has referred to in his or her text. This list often includes not only books and articles but also Internet sources.

Works Consulted The term *works consulted* refers to a list of all the works a writer consulted in order to create his or her text. It is not limited just to those cited in the text.

See also Bibliography.

Writer's Point of View A writer's point of view is the writer's opinion about a topic.

Using the Glossary

This glossary is an alphabetical list of vocabulary words found in the selections in this book. Use this glossary just as you would a dictionary— to determine the meanings, parts of speech, pronunciation, and syllabication of words. (Some technical, foreign, and more obscure words in this book are not listed here but are defined for you in the footnotes that accompany many of the selections.)

Many words in the English language have more than one meaning. This glossary gives the meanings that apply to the words as they are used in the selections in this book. Words closely related in form and meaning are listed together in one entry (for instance, *consumption* and *consume*), and the definition is given for the first form.

The following abbreviations are used to identify parts of speech of words:

adj. adjective   *adv.* adverb   *n.* noun   *v.* verb

Each word's pronunciation is given in parentheses. A guide to the pronunciation symbols appears in the Pronunciation Key below. The stress marks in the Pronunciation Key are used to indicate the force given to each syllable in a word. They can also help you determine where words are divided into syllables.

For more information about the words in this glossary or for information about words not listed here, consult a dictionary.

Pronunciation Key

Symbol	Examples	Symbol	Examples	Symbol	Examples
ă	pat	m	mum	ûr	urge, term, firm, word, heard
ā	pay	n	no, sudden* (sud'n)		
ä	father	ng	thing	**Symbol**	**Examples**
âr	care	ŏ	pot	v	valve
b	bib	ō	toe	w	with
ch	church	ô	caught, paw	y	yes
d	deed, milled	oi	noise	z	zebra, xylem
ě	pet	ŏŏ	took	zh	vision, pleasure, garage
ē	bee	ōō	boot		
f	fife, phase, rough	ŏŏr	lure	ə	about, item, edible, gallop, circus
g	gag	ôr	core		
h	hat	ou	out	ər	butter
hw	which	p	pop		
ĭ	pit	r	roar	**Sounds in Foreign Words**	
ī	pie, by	s	sauce	KH	*German* ich, ach; *Scottish* loch
îr	pier	sh	ship, dish	N	*French,* (bôn) bon
j	judge	t	tight, stopped	œ	*French* feu, œuf; *German* schön
k	kick, cat, pique	th	thin		
l	lid, needle* (nēd'l)	th	this	ü	*French* tu; *German* über
		ŭ	cut		

* In English the consonants *l* and *n* often constitute complete syllables by themselves.

Stress Marks

The relevant emphasis with which the syllables of a word or phrase are spoken, called stress, is indicated in three different ways. The strongest, or primary, stress is marked with a bold mark (´). An intermediate, or secondary, level of stress is marked with a similar but lighter mark (´). The weakest stress is unmarked. Words of one syllable show no stress mark.

Glossary of Academic Vocabulary

abnormal (ăb-nôr´məl) *adj.* not typical, usual, or regular; not normal

affect (ə-fĕkt´) *v.* to have an influence on or effect a change in something

aspect (ăs´pĕkt) *n.* a characteristic or feature of something

attitude (ăt´ĭ-tōod´) *n.* a way of thinking or feeling about something or someone

complex (kŏm´plĕks´) *adj.* consisting of many interwoven parts that make something difficult to understand

consume (kən sōom´) *v.* to buy things for your own use or ownership

contrast (kən-trăst´) *v.* to show differences between two or more things that are being compared

cultural (kul´chər-əl´) *adj.* of or relating to culture or cultivation

despite (dĭ-spīt´) *prep.* in spite of; even though

element (ĕl´ə-mənt) *n.* a part or aspect of something

ensure (ĕn-shŏŏr´) *v.* to make sure or certain

error (ĕr´ər) *n.* a mistake

evaluate (ĭ-văl´yoo-āt´) *tr.v.* to examine something carefully to judge its value or worth

feature (fē´chər) *n.* a prominent or distinctive part, quality, or characteristic

focus (fō´kəs) *v.* to direct toward a specific point or purpose

goal (gōl) *n.* the object toward which your work and planning is directed; a purpose

inadequate (ĭn-ăd´ĭ-kwĭt) *adj.* not enough or sufficient to fulfill a need or meet a requirement

interact (ĭn´tər-ăkt´) *v.* to act upon each other

participate (pär-tĭs´ə-pāt´) *v.* to be active and involved in something or to share in something

perceive (pər-sēv´) *v.* to become aware of something directly through any of the senses

potential (pə-tĕn´shəl) *adj.* capable of doing or being something; having possibility

purchase (pûr´chĭs) *v.* to buy

rely (rĭ-lī) *v.* to depend on something or someone for support, help, or supply

resource (rē´-sors´) *n.* something that can be used for support or help

specify (spĕs´ə-fī´) *v.* to state exactly or in detail what you want or need

stress (strĕs) *v.* to put emphasis on something

task (tăsk) *n.* an assignment or work done as part of one's duties

technology (tĕk-nŏl´ə-jē) *n.* the application of science and engineering as part of a commercial or industrial undertaking

text (tĕkst) *n.* a literary work that is regarded as an object of critical analysis

valid (văl´ĭd) *adj.* convincing or having a sound reason for something

Glossary of Critical Vocabulary

addiction (ə-dĭk´shən) *n.* An *addiction* is a habit one is dependent on.

anxiety (ăng-zī´ĭ-tē) *n. Anxiety* is an uneasy, worried feeling.

apathy (ăp´ə-thē) *n. Apathy* is indifference or the lack of interest or concern.

arboretum (är´bə-rē´təm) *n.* An *arboretum* is a place where many trees are grown for educational or viewing purposes.

avalanche (ăv´ə-lănch) *n.* An *avalanche* is a large mass of snow, ice, dirt, or rocks falling quickly down the side of a mountain.

bedrock (bĕd´rŏk´) *n. Bedrock* is the solid rock that lies under sand, soil, clay, and gravel.

cache (kăsh) *n.* A *cache* is an amount of something that has been hidden away.

capacity (kə-păs´ĭ-tē) *n.* A person's *capacity* is his or her role or position.

coincidence (kō-ĭn´sĭ-dəns) *n.* A *coincidence* is a sequence of events that although accidental seems to have been planned.

conscience (kŏn´shəns) *n. Conscience* is the conforming to or living up to one's own sense of what is right.

corridor (kôr´ĭ-dər) *n.* A *corridor* is a narrow hallway or passageway.

croon (krōōn) *v.* When someone *croons,* that person hums or sings softly.

cynic (sĭn´ĭk) *n.* A *cynic* is a person who has negative opinions about other people and what they do.

deck (dĕk) *n.* The *deck* is the platform on a ship or boat where people stand.

decompose (dē´kəm-pōz´) *v.* When things *decompose,* they decay and break down into their basic parts.

diplomat (dĭp´lə-măt´) *n.* A *diplomat* is a person appointed by a government to interact with other governments.

eloquence (ĕl´ə-kwəns) *n.* If someone behaves or speaks with *eloquence,* she uses persuasive, powerful expression.

enact (ĕn-ăkt´) *v.* If you *enact* something, you make it into a law.

enterprising (ĕn´tər-prī´zĭng) *adj.* An *enterprising* person is someone who accepts challenges and takes initiative.

ethereal (ĭ-thîr´ē-əl) *adj.* If something is *ethereal,* it is light and airy.

exasperate (ĭg-zăs´pə-rāt´) *v.* If you *exasperate* someone, you make the person very angry.

exhibition (ĕk´sə-bĭsh´ən) *n.* An *exhibition* is an organized presentation or show.

exhort (ĭg-zôrt´) *v.* If you *exhort,* you make an urgent appeal to others.

exploit (ĭk-sploit´) *v.* If you *exploit* something, you use it selfishly.

exploitation (ĕk´sploi-tā´shən) *n. Exploitation* is the unfair treatment or use of something or someone for selfish reasons.

flammable (flăm´ə-bəl) *adj.* If something is *flammable,* it is easy for it to catch on fire and burn.

frantic (frăn´tik) *adj.* If you do something in a *frantic* way, you do it quickly and nervously.

geyser (gī´zər) *n.* A *geyser* is a natural hot spring that shoots hot water and steam into the air.

gradual (grăj´ōō-əl) *adj.* If something is *gradual,* it advances little by little.

gully (gŭl´ē) *n.* A *gully* is a deep ditch cut in the earth by running water.

haggard (hăg´ərd) *adj.* If you're *haggard,* you are worn out and exhausted.

hypothesis (hī-pŏth´ĭ-sĭs) *n.* A *hypothesis* is an explanation or theory for something that can be tested for validity.

ignorance (ĭg´nər-əns) *n. Ignorance* is the condition of being uneducated or uninformed.

impairment (ĭm-pâr´mənt) *n.* An *impairment* is an injury or weakness.

impetus (ĭm'pĭ-təs) *n.* The *impetus* is the driving force or motivation behind an action.

inexplicable (ĭn-ĕk'splĭ-kə-bəl) *adj.* If something is *inexplicable,* it is difficult to understand.

inquire (ĭn-kwīr') *v.* If you *inquire* about something, you ask about it.

inspection (ĭn-spĕk'shən) *n.* An *inspection* is an official examination or review.

insulate (ĭn'sə-lāt') *v.* When you *insulate* something, you prevent the passage of heat through it.

intangible (ĭn-tăn'jə-bəl) *n.* An *intangible* is something that is hard to describe because it cannot be perceived by the senses.

inundate (ĭn'ŭndāt') *v.* To *inundate* is to give a huge amount of something.

judicious (jōō-dĭsh'əs) *adj.* If you are *judicious,* you have good judgment.

mandatory (măn'də-tôr'ē) *adj.* If something is *mandatory,* it is required.

maroon (mə-rōōn') *v.* To *maroon* is to abandon or leave someone in a place that is hard to get away from.

marvel (mär'vəl) *v.* If you *marvel* at something, you are surprised or astonished by it.

meager (mē'gər) *adj.* If something is *meager,* it is small or deficient in quantity.

median (mē'dē-ən) *n.* A *median* is a dividing area between opposing lanes of traffic on a highway or road.

metabolism (mĭ-tăb'ə-lĭz'əm) *n.* The *metabolism* of a living thing is all the processes that allow for growth and life.

mischievous (mĭs'chə-vəs) *adj.* If someone is *mischievous,* the person is naughty.

misjudge (mĭs-jŭj') *v.* If you *misjudge* something, you form an incorrect opinion about it.

moderate (mŏd'ər-ĭt) *adj.* When something is kept *moderate,* it is kept within a certain limit.

municipal (myōō-nĭs'ə-pəl) *adj.* If something is *municipal,* it relates to a city or town.

navigation (năv'ĭ-gā'shən) *n.* The *navigation* of a ship or boat is the act of guiding it along a planned course.

neural (nŏŏr'əl) *adj.* Anything that is *neural* is related to the nervous system.

neuron (nŏŏr'ŏn') *n.* A *neuron* is a cell in the nervous system that carries messages between the brain and other body parts.

neuroscience (nŏŏr'ō-sī'əns) *n.* *Neuroscience* is any of the sciences that study the nervous system.

neuroscientist (nŏŏr'ō-sī'ən-tĭst) *n.* A *neuroscientist* is a person who studies the brain and the nervous system.

obituary (ō-bĭch'ōō-ĕr'ē) *n.* An *obituary* is a public notice of a death.

observation (ŏb'zər-vā'shən) *n.* An *observation* is the act of watching something.

plantation (plăn-tā'shən) *n.* A *plantation* is a large farm or estate on which crops are raised.

ponderous (pŏn'dər-əs) *adj.* If something is *ponderous,* it is very heavy.

portable (pôr'tə-bəl) *adj.* If something is *portable,* it can be carried or moved easily.

porthole (pŏrt'hōl) *n.* A *porthole* is a circular window on a boat or ship.

possession (pə-zĕsh'ən) *n.* A *possession* is something you own.

precarious (prĭ-kâr'ē-əs) *adj.* If something is *precarious,* it is dangerous and unstable.

precaution (prĭ-kô'shən) *n.* A *precaution* is an action taken to avoid possible danger.

precipitous (prĭ-sĭp'ĭ-təs) *adj.* When something is *precipitous,* it is very steep, like a cliff.

proliferation (prə-lĭf'ər-rā'shən) *n.* A *proliferation* is the fast growth of something.

prowess (prou'ĭs) *n.* *Prowess* is the strength and courage someone has.

Glossary of Critical Vocabulary **R81**

reign (rān) *v.* If some things *reign* over something else, it means they dominate it.

reprove (rĭ-pro͞ov´) *v.* If you *reprove* someone, you express disapproval.

restrictive (rĭ-strĭk´tĭv) *adj.* When something is *restrictive*, it is limiting in some way.

scorn (skôrn) *n. Scorn* is disrespect or disdain.

sextant (sĕk´stənt) *n.* A *sextant* is an instrument used to determine location by measuring the position of the stars and sun.

shuffle (shuf´əl) *v.* When you *shuffle,* you move with short sliding steps.

singe (sĭnj) *v.* If you *singe* something, you slightly burn it.

snag (snăg) *v.* If you *snag* something, you catch it quickly and unexpectedly.

splinter (splĭn´tər) *v.* To *splinter* means to break up into sharp, thin pieces.

spyglass (spī´glăs´) *n.* A *spyglass* is a small telescope.

steward (sto͞o´ərd) *n.* A *steward* is a person who supervises or manages something.

stifle (stī´fəl) *v.* If you *stifle* something, you hold it back.

submerge (səb-mûrj´) *v.* When something *submerges,* it becomes covered by water.

superfluity (so͞o´pər-flo͞o´ĭ-tē) *n. Superfluity* is overabundance or excess.

sustain (sə-stān´) *v.* If things *sustain,* they remain in existence.

sustenance (sŭs´tə-nəns) *n. Sustenance* is the food needed to live.

swell (swĕl) *n.* A *swell* is a long, unbroken wave.

syringe (sə-rĭnj´) *n.* A *syringe* is a medical instrument used to inject fluids into the body.

taper (tā´pər) *v.* When things *taper,* they gradually get thinner.

tectonic (tĕk-tŏn´ĭk) *adj.* If something is *tectonic,* it relates to the deformation of Earth's rocky crust.

tedious (tē´dē-əs) *adj.* Something that is *tedious* is boring.

wistful (wĭst´fəl) *adj.* If you're *wistful,* you are thoughtful and longing for something.

Index of Skills

Key:

Teacher's Edition page numbers and subject entries are printed in **boldface** type.
Subject entries and page references that apply to both the Student Edition and the Teacher's Edition appear in lightface type.
There is no content from the Close Reader in this index.

A

abstract nouns, R30
Academic Vocabulary, 2, 53, 57, 62, 127, 131, 136, 175, 179, 184, **203**, 215, 220, 259, 264, 337, 341, R79. *See also* Glossary of Academic Vocabulary
act, of a play, R64. *See also* scenes
active voice, 55, R43
ad hominem, R27
adjective clauses, 200, R49, R50, R54
adjective phrases, R47
adjectives, 38, 200, R31, R43
  comparative forms of, R44
  compound, R35
  coordinate, 38
  infinitives as, R47
  as modifiers, 38, 88, 200, 306, 316, R43, R44
  participial phrases as, 306, R48
  predicate, R43
  prepositional phrases as, R47
  proper, 110, R36
  superlative forms of, R44
  verbals as, 212, 306, R47
adventure story, R64
adverb clauses, 88, R49
adverb phrases, R47
adverbs, 88, R31, R44
  comparative forms of, R44
  conjunctive, R51
  gerund phrases as, 326
  infinitive phrases as, 212, R47
  as modifiers, 88, 316, R44
  superlative forms of, R44
  verbals as, 212, 306, R47
affirmative speaker, 200a
alliteration, **39, 40,** 41, R64
allusion, 143, **321,** 325, **326a,** R64
almanacs, R73
analogies, 305, R58, R64. *See also* metaphors; simile
analogy problem, R58
analyzing, 142, 214, 248. *See also* Analyzing the Text; media analysis; poetry analysis; structural analysis
  arguments, **30a,** R23–R24
    presenting, 57–60, 215–218, 314
    writing, 127–130, 154, 210
  author's style, **137,** 141, **150,** 153, **233,** 237, **240a, 249,** 324, R5, **R75**
  character, 35, **93, 99, 101, 106, 110a,** 126, 153, **328,** 334
  details, 107
  form, 41, 75, 125, 147, 171, 173, 244, 246
  free verse, 246
  language, **32, 93,** 147, **157, 186, 206, 308, 321, 327**
  logic, R25–R26
  plot, 3, 4, 6, 7, 9, 10, 12, 13, 14, 18a

point of view, **156a,** 283, 287, 290, 291, 293, 295, 298, 299, 303, **306a**
presentations of information, 267, 268, 269, 271, 273, 275, 276
reasons/reasoning, R23, R25–R26
setting, 3, 4, 6, 7, 9, 10, 12, 13, 14, 18a, 258a, 336a
  stories, 15, 35, 68, 107, 255, 333
story elements, 286, 292, 296, 297, 302, 327
  symbols, 107
  text, 77, 141, 279, **308, 311,** 313
Analyzing the Media, 23, 27, 29, 92, 320
Analyzing the Text, 16, 36, 42, 50, 69, 73, 75, 76, 86, 108, 126, 142, 148, 154, 166, 171, 173, 174, 190, 198, 210, 214, 230, 238, 244, 248, 256, 274, 278, 280, 304, 314, 325
Anchor Text, 3A, 31A, 63A, 111A, 137A, 169A, 185A, 221A, 265A, 307A
anecdote, 23, 77, 132, R64
Annotate It!, **7, 12, 15,** 16, **17,** 21, 23, **26,** 27, **34, 35,** 36, **37, 41,** 42, **46, 49,** 50, **51, 67, 68,** 69, **70, 70a,** 73, 75, **79, 82, 85,** 86, **87, 95, 97, 105, 107,** 108, **109, 117, 118, 122, 125,** 126, **141,** 142, **144, 147,** 148, **151, 153,** 154, **155, 162, 165,** 166, **168,** 171, **173,** 174, **189,** 190, **191, 197,** 198, **199, 202, 209,** 210, **211,** 214, **224, 227, 229,** 230, **231, 234, 237,** 238, **239,** 244, 246, **247, 251, 255,** 256, **257, 272,** 274, 278, **279,** 280, **281, 287, 290, 296, 299, 303,** 304, **305, 313,** 314, **315, 324,** 325, **333, 334, 335**
antagonist, R64. *See also* protagonist
antecedents, R37–R38
antonyms, 239, 305, R58
apostrophe, R35, R62
appeals, R24
Applying Academic Vocabulary, 8, 20, 24, 33, 47, 65, 72, 78, 91, 94, 115, 139, 152, 161, 187, 225, 235, 242, 252, 269, 286, 309, 318, 322, 330
appositives, R47–R48
arguments, 189, R64. *See also* claims; debates; evidence
  analysis of, **30a,** R23
  claims in, 27, 197, R2, R23, R65
  comparing, 196
  conclusion in, R3
  counterarguments, **26,** 27, 189, 197, R23, R29, R66
  in debates, R14–R15, R67
  deductive, R25–R26, R67
  editorials as, 27
  elements of, 197, **316a,** R2–R3
  evaluating, **24, 25, 26,** 27, **186, 187, 188,** 189, **192a,** R28
  evidence for, 27, **186, 194,** 197, 216, R23, R29

facts in, 27
goal of, 30a
inductive, R25
introduction in, R2
logical, R71
opinions in, 27
persuasion in, 189, 197, R23–R29
point of view of, R73
reasons/reasoning in, 27, 189, 197, R23
support for, 189, R23–R24
tracing, **24, 25, 26,** 27, **186, 187, 188,** 189, **192a**
writing, 127–130, R2–R3
  artist's perspective, 92
Assess It!, 18, 38, 52, 70, 88, 110, 126, 144, 156, 168, 192, 200, 212, 232, 240, 258, 282, 306, 316, 326, 336
assonance, R64, R74
As You Read, 321
As You View, 28, 90, 91, 318
audience
  for argument, 57–59, 127–129, 215–217
  for fictional narrative, 54–55
  for informative essay, 338
  for media, 90, 92a
  for multimedia presentation, 259–261
  for personal narrative, 176–177
  for poetry analysis, 180–181
  for public art, 92
  for speeches, 185
  for summary presentation, 132–133
author's perspective, **269, 276,** 279, **282a, 308, 309, 312,** 313
author's purpose, **30a,** 43, 44, 47, 48, 49, **52a,** 73, 92, **185,** R64
autobiography, 141, R64. *See also* memoirs
auxiliary verbs, R31, R32, R53

B

ballad, R64
bar graph, 232a
base words, R56
bias, R28, R64
bibliography, R65. *See also* works cited; works consulted
biography, R64–R65
blank verse, 147
blog, 30, **30a**
boldface type, **78, 85, 88a,** R76
brainstorming, 53, 176, 259, 337

C

camera shot, 320a
capitalization, 192, 282
  of first words, 282, R36
  of geographical names, 110, 282, R36
  of organizations, 192, 282, R36
  of personal titles, 110, 282, R36
  in poems/poetry, 324

of pronoun *I*, 36
of proper adjectives, R36
of proper names, 110, R36
of proper nouns, 192
quick references for, R36
in quotations, 282
rules for, 192, 282, R30, R36
caption, 232a
career development documents, R65
case, in debates, 200a
cast of characters, 111, 125, R65
cause-and-effect relationships, **162, 163, 203,** 209
cause-effect organization, **159,** 165, **168a, 203, 204, 205, 207, 212a, 221, 223, 224, 225, 226,** 229, R4, R18–R19
central ideas, **21,** 23, **163,** 165, **202, 205, 206,** 209, **222, 235, 240a, 266, 267, 268, 269, 270, 271, 272,** 274, 320. *See also* main ideas
characterization, **38a, 110a, 328,** 333, **336a,** R65
  direct characterization, 110a
  indirect characterization, 110a
character analysis, 108
characters, 107, R65. *See also* characterization
  action of, 107, **153,** 333
  analysis of, 35, **93, 99, 101, 106, 110a,** 126, 153, 334
  antagonist, R64
  cast of, 125, R65
  central, R65
  development of, **118, 119, 328, 330, 331,** 333, **336b**
  dialogue of, 125, 303, R67
  dynamic, R65
  foil as, R69
  main, 53–55, **94,** 107, R65, R69, R73
  minor, R65
  motivations of, **97,** 107, **110a**
  mythical, 35
  narrator as, 54, 303, R71, R73, R75
  setting and, 93, 103, 105, 110a
  static, R65
  in stories, 107
  traits of, **96, 100,** 107, **110a, 328, 330, 331,** 333, R65
chronological order, **161,** 165, **168a, 275, 276, 277,** 278, R7, R16–R17, R65
circle graph, 232a
circular reasons/reasoning, 197, R27
Cite Text Evidence, **3, 5, 6, 7, 8, 9, 10, 12, 14,** 16, **20, 21, 22,** 23, **24, 25, 26,** 27, 29, 30, **31, 32, 33,** 36, **40,** 42, **43, 45, 47,** 50, **63, 65, 67,** 69, **72,** 73, 74, 75, 76, 77, **78, 81,** 86, 92, **94, 95, 96, 97, 98, 99, 100,** 103, **105, 106,** 108, **112, 113, 114, 115, 116, 118, 119, 121, 124,** 126, **137, 138, 139,**

object, R38
personal, R30, R37, R52
plural, R52
possessive, R39
predicate, R47
reference problems, R40
reflexive, R30, R39
relative, 200, R31, R40, R54
singular, R37–R40
subject, R38, R52–R53
pronunciation, 109, 155, 335, R59, R78
pronunciation key, R78
proofreading, 110, 258, 282
prop, R73
propaganda, R28, R73
proper adjectives, 110, R36
proper names, 110, R30
proper nouns, 192, R30, R37
proposition, 200a
prose, R68, R72, R73, R75
protagonist, R64, R69, R73
public documents, R73. *See also* government publications
punctuation, **321**, 324, **326a**, R33–R36
purpose of author. See author's purpose

Q
question mark, R33
questions, 23, R8, R74
quotation marks, R35
quotations
  capitalization in, 282
  direct, R9
  evidence and, 197, R23
  in informative essays, 131, 133, **157**
  in poetry analysis, 180–181

R
radio play, R73
random sample, 232a
reading arguments, R23–R29
  argument analysis, R23
  logical analysis, R25
  persuasive techniques, R24
  persuasive text evaluation, R28
  reasoning, R25–R27
reading informational texts, R16–R22
reading strategies, R23–R26, R25
reasoning
  circular, R27
  deductive, R25–R26
  evaluating author's, 197
  faulty, 197, R27
  inductive, R25
  sound, **193, 194, 195, 196,** 197
reasons, to support claims, **24, 186,** 189, **194,** R23
rebound response, 88
rebuttal, 200a
recurring theme, R76
redundancy, 232
reference aids, 109
references, 143, 325, R40, R64
reference sources, R59–R60, R73
reference works, R59–R60, R73
reflexive pronouns, R30, R39

refrain, in poem, R73. *See also* stanza
regular comparison, R44
regular verbs, R41
relative pronouns, 200, R31, R40, R54
repetition, 41, 141, R64, R73. *See also* alliteration; rhyme; sound devices
research
  for arguments, 57, 216
  for debates, R14
  drafts of project for, R9
  for multimedia presentation, 260
  online, 88a
  sources for, R8
  strategies for, R8
research report, 190
resolution, **14,** 15, 54, **67, 124,** 126, **336a,** R74. *See also* falling action
responses, 42, 88, 319, R69
response to literature, 42
review. *See* critical review
rhetorical fallacy, R27
rhetorical questions, R74
rhyme, R74
  author's purpose of, 73
  defined, 73
  end, 73, 244, R74
  free verse, 324, R69
  impact of, **72,** 73
  internal, R74
  nursery, 244
  patterns of, 246
  in stanzas, 244
rhyme scheme, **74,** 75, **76a,** 173, **242,** 244, R74
rhythm, 41, R74. *See also* meter
  free verse and, R69
  in lyric poems, 173
  in narratives, R7
  in poetry, **40,** 41, **42a,** 179, **214b,** 246, 324
rising action, **9,** 15, 54, **115, 120, 123, 124,** 126, **336a,** R74. *See also* plot
roots, 17, 87, 167, 211, 281, R56
rough draft. *See* drafts
run-on sentences, R51

S
sample, 232a
scanning, R74
scansion, 42a
scenes, 303, R64, R74. *See also* act, of a play
science fiction, **249, 250, 252, 253, 254,** 255, **258a,** R74. *See also* fantasy
scope, 211
screenplay, R74
script, 125, R65, R67, R74
search features, R8
secondary sources, **282a,** R8, R74–R75
semicolon, 18, R34, R51
sensory details, 55, 176, **214b,** R7, R70, R74. *See also* imagery
sentence fragments, 88, **137,** R51
sentences
  complements in, R46
  complete, 88, R51
  complex, 156, R50
  compound, 18, 156, R42, R50
  compound-complex, 156, R50

declarative, R46
exclamatory, R46
imperative, R46
interrogative, R46
inverted, R53
kinds of, R46
parts of, R32, R46
phrases and, R47
with predicate nominative, R53
predicates in, R46
run-on, R51
simple, 18, R50
structure of, 18, 23, 29, 156, R50–R51
topic, R16, R71, R76
sentence structure, 18, 156
sequence events, R7
sequential order, R74
setting, 15, 125, R74
  for action, R74
  analyzing, 3, 4, 6, 7, 9, 10, 12, 13, 14, 18a, 258a, 336a
  for character, **93, 103, 105,** 107, **110a,** 153
  for debate, R67
  details of, 15
  in drama, **113,** 125
  for fantasy, R68
  in fiction, R68
  in fictional narrative, 53–55
  in folk tales, 68
  in history writing, 279
  in myths, 35
  in personal narratives, 176
  plot and, 15, **336a**
  in poetry, 247
  in science fiction, 255
setting a purpose, R74
short stories, 53–56, 256, R74–R75. *See also* fiction
sidebar, **79,** 85, **88a,** R75
signal words, **159,** 165, **203,** R19, R75
silent *e,* R60
simile, **6, 72, 76a, 97, 139,** 141, **170,** 174, **299,** R75. *See also* figurative language; metaphors
simple predicate, R32
simple sentences, 18, R50
simple subject, R32
simple verbs, R32
singular nouns, R30, R37, R61
singular pronouns, R52
situation identification, R6
slang, R5, R55
soliloquy, **145,** 147–148
sonnets, **74,** 75, R75. *See also* rhyme scheme
sound devices, **321,** 324, **326a,** R73, R75. *See also* alliteration; assonance; meter; onomatopoeia; repetition; rhyme; rhythm
sound reasons/reasoning, **193, 194, 195, 196,** 197
sound effects, 319, **320a**
sources, R75. *See also* references
  primary, **282a,** R8, R73, R75
  reference, R59–R60
  for research, R8
  secondary, **282a,** R8, R74–R75
spatial order, 165, **168a**

speaker, 214, R75
  in arguments, 60, 189, 218, R25
  claim by, 189, 218
  debates by, R14–R15
  in lyric poems, **172,** 173, **174a**
  theme of, 247, 324
  voice-over narration of, **318,** 319, **320a**
speaking activity
  argument, 314
  demonstration, 86
  discussion, 76, 238
  dramatic reading, 69, 148
  informal debate, 198
  oral presentation, 280
  oral report, 166
  response to literature, 42
specialized dictionaries, R60
specialized vocabulary, R59
specific context clues, R55
speech, 215–218, **291a,** 335, R30–R31, R75
spell correctly, 110
spelling, 110, 258, R55–R63
SQP2RS, 184A
stage directions, **112, 114, 115,** 121, 125, R75
Standard English Learners, 9, 42, 45, 50, 54, 59, 114, 129, 133, 166, 142, 148, 154, 176, 181, 198, 208, 214, 235, 245, 261, 272, 277, 302, 338, 343
stanza, **40,** 41, **42a,** 76a, **214b,** 242, 244, **323,** 324, **326a,** R75. *See also* couplet; form
statements
  commonplace assertions as, R16
  concluding, 217, R5, R66
  direct, 279
  either-or fallacies as, 197, R27, R67
  facts as, 27, R68
  factual claims as, R16
  false, R27
  misleading, R27
  opinions as, 27
  paradoxes as, 75
  policy, R14
  thesis, R4, R76
static character, R65, R75
statistics, 232a
stereotype/stereotyping, R27, R75
Strategies for Annotation, 7, 12, 15, 17, 21, 23, 26, 27, 34, 35, 37, 41, 46, 49, 51, 67, 68, 70, 73, 75, 79, 82, 85, 87, 95, 97, 105, 107, 109, 117, 118, 122, 125, 141, 144, 147, 151, 153, 155, 162, 165, 168, 171, 173, 189, 191, 195, 197, 199, 202, 209, 211, 224, 227, 229, 231, 234, 237, 239, 244, 246, 247, 255, 257, 272, 274, 278, 279, 281, 287, 290, 296, 299, 303, 305, 313, 315, 324, 333, 335. See also **Annotate It!**
Stream to Start 2, 62, 136, 184, 220, 264
structural analysis
  cause-and-effect, **203, 204, 205, 208, 212a,** 221, 223, **224, 225, 226,** 229
  chronological order, 278
  essays, 165
  of informational texts, 240a
  news reports, **20, 21, 22,** 23

Index of Titles and Authors

Key:

Authors and titles that appear in the Student Edition are in lightface type.
Authors and titles that appear in the Close Reader are in **boldface** type.
Names of authors who appear in both the Student Edition and the Close Reader are lightface.
For these authors, Student Edition page references are lightface and Close Reader page references are **boldface**.

Student Edition Acknowledgments

"Allied with Green" from *There is No Long Distance Now: Very Short Stories* by Naomi Shihab Nye. Text copyright © 2011 by Naomi Shihab Nye. Reprinted by permission of HarperCollins Publishers.

"Always Wanting More" from *I Want That: How We All Became Shoppers* by Thomas Hine. Text copyright © 2002 by Thomas Hine. Reprinted by permission of HarperCollins Publishers.

Excerpt from *The American Heritage Dictionary of the English Language, Fifth Edition.* Text copyright © 2011 by Houghton Mifflin Harcourt. Adapted and reprinted by permission of Houghton Mifflin Harcourt Publishing Company.

"Another Place, Another Time" by Cory Doctorow from *The Chronicles of Harris Burdick* by Chris Van Allsburg. Text copyright © 2011 by Cory Doctorow. Illustrations copyright © 1984 by Chris Van Allsburg. Reprinted by permission of Houghton Mifflin Harcourt Publishing Company.

"Big Rocks' Balancing Acts" by Douglas Fox from *Science News for Kids*, October 19, 2011. Text copyright © 2011 by the Society for Science and the Public. Reprinted by permission of Science News for Kids.

"Dump" from *In a Prominent Bar in Secaucus: New and Selected Poems, 1955-2007* by X. J. Kennedy. Text copyright © 2007 by X. J. Kennedy. Reprinted by permission of Johns Hopkins University Press.

"Earth (A Gift Shop)" by Charles Yu from *Shadow Show*, edited by Sam Weller and Mort Castle. Text copyright © 2012 by Charles Yu. Reprinted by permission of Signature Literary Agency on behalf of the author.

Excerpt from *Flesh & Blood So Cheap: The Triangle Fire and Its Legacy* by Albert Marrin. Text copyright © 2011 by Albert Marrin. Reprinted by permission of Alfred A. Knopf, a division of Random House, Inc. Any third party use of this material, outside of this publication, is prohibited. Interested parties must apply directly to Random House, Inc. for permission.

"The Flight of Icarus" from *Stories of the Gods and Heroes* by Sally Benson. Text copyright 1940, renewed © 1968 by Sally Benson. Reprinted by permission of Dial Books for Young Readers, a division of Penguin Group (USA) Inc.

"How Things Work" from *A Fire in My Hand: Poems* by Gary Soto. Text copyright © 2006, 1999 by Gary Soto. Reprinted by permission of Houghton Mifflin Harcourt Publishing Company and BookStop Literary Agency, LLC, on behalf of the author. All rights reserved.

"Icarus's Flight" from *Mystery, So Long* by Stephen Dobyns. Text copyright © 2006 by Stephen Dobyns. Originally published by Penguin. Reprinted by permission of the author.

Excerpt from *Julianbeever.net.* Text copyright © by Julian Beever. Reprinted by permission of Julian Beever.

Excerpt from *Life at Home in the 21st Century: 32 Families Open Their Doors* by Jeanne E. Arnold, Anthony P. Graesch, Enzo Ragazzini and Elinor Ochs. Text copyright © 2012 by the Regents of the University of California. Reprinted by permission of the Regents of the University of California, Cotsen Institute and Jeanne Arnold. All rights reserved.

"Living in the Dark" by Cheryl Bardoe from *Muse*, Vol. 16, No. 2. Text copyright © 2012 by Cheryl Bardoe. Reprinted by permission of Cricket Magazine Group, a division of Carus Publishing Company.

"Magic and the Brain" by Susana Martinez-Conde and Stephen L. Macknik, from *Scientific American*, December 2008. Text copyright © 2008 by Scientific American, Inc. Reprinted by permission of Scientific American, Inc.

Excerpt from *Mississippi Solo* by Eddy Harris. Text copyright © 1988 by Eddy Harris. Reprinted by permission of Globe Pequot Press.

"Ode to Enchanted Light" from *Odes to Opposites* compiled by Ferris Cook. Originally published in Spanish as "Oda a la luz encantada" by Pablo Neruda, translated by Ken Krabbenhoft. Translation copyright © 1995 by Ken Krabbenhoft. Text copyright © 1995 by Pablo Neruda and Fundación Pablo Neruda. Text compilation copyright © 1995 by Ferris Cook. Reprinted by permission of Bullfinch and Agencia Literaria Carmen Balcells S.A. All rights reserved.

"Parents of rescued teenage sailor Abby Sunderland accused of risking her life" by Paul Harris from *The Observer*, June 13, 2010. Text copyright © 2012 Guardian News and Media Limited or its affiliated companies. Reprinted by permission of Guardian News Media.

Excerpt from *The People Could Fly: American Black Folktales* by Virginia Hamilton. Text copyright © 1985 by Virginia Hamilton. Reprinted by permission of Alfred A. Knopf, an imprint of Random House Children's Books, a division of Random House, Inc. Any third party use of this material, outside of this publication, is prohibited. Interested parties must apply directly to Random House, Inc. for permission.

"Poem for My Librarian, Mrs. Long" from *Acolytes* by Nikki Giovanni. Text copyright © 2007 by Nikki Giovanni. Reprinted by permission of HarperCollins Publishers.

"Reflections on Working Toward Peace" by Craig Kielburger from *Architects of Peace: Visions of Hope in Words and Images*, edited by Michael Collopy and Jason Gardner. Text copyright © 2000 by Michael Collopy. Reprinted by permission of New World Library.

"Rogue Wave" from *Rogue Wave and Other Red-Blooded Sea Stories* by Theodore Taylor. Text copyright © 1996 by Theodore Taylor. Reprinted by permission of the Theodore Taylor Estate and the Watkins/Loomis Agency.

"Ship of Fools" by Joanna Weiss from *The Boston Globe*, June 15, 2010. Text copyright © 2010 by Globe Newspaper Company. Reprinted by permission of PARS International on behalf of The Boston Globe. All rights reserved.

"Sleeping in the Forest" from *Twelve Moons* by Mary Oliver. Text copyright © 1972, 1973, 1974, 1976, 1977, 1978, 1979 by Mary Oliver. Reprinted by permission of Little, Brown and Company and Charlotte Sheedy Literary Agency on behalf of the author.

"The Song of Wandering Aengus" from *The Wind in the Reeds* by William Butler Yeats. Text copyright © The Estate of the Late William Butler Yeats. Reprinted by permission of United Agents, LLP, on behalf of The Estate of the Late William Butler Yeats.

"Sorry, Wrong Number" by Lucille Fletcher. Text copyright © 1948 by Lucille Fletcher. Reprinted by permission of William Morris Endeavor Entertainment, LLC.

Excerpt from *The Story of the Triangle Factory Fire* by Zachary Kent. Text copyright © 1989 by Children's Press, Inc. Reprinted by permission of Children's Press, an imprint of Scholastic Library Publishing, Inc. All rights reserved.

Excerpt from *Uprising* by Margaret Peterson Haddix. Text copyright © 2007 by Margaret Peterson Haddix. Reprinted by permission of Simon & Schuster Books for Young Readers, an imprint of Simon & Schuster's Children's Publishing Division and Adams Literary.

"Why Exploring the Ocean is Mankind's Next Giant Leap" by Phillippe Cousteau from *Light Years Blog*, March 13, 2012. Text copyright © Philippe Cousteau. Reprinted by permission of Philippe Cousteau.

Excerpt from "Women in Aviation" from *Red-Tail Angels* by Fredrick and Patricia McKissack. Text copyright © 1995 by Fredrick and Patricia McKissack. Reprinted by permission of Walker & Co.

"Your World" from *Share My World* by Georgia Douglas Johnson. Text copyright © 1962 by Georgia Douglas Johnson. Reprinted by permission of the Moorland-Spingarn Research Center, Howard University.

Close Reader Acknowledgments

Text copyright © 2011 by Houghton Mifflin Harcourt. Adapted and reprinted by permission from *The American Heritage Dictionary of the English Language, Fifth Edition*.

"Arachne" from *Greek Myths* by Olivia E. Coolidge. Text copyright © 1949 by Olivia E. Coolidge. Reprinted by permission of Houghton Mifflin Harcourt Publishing Company.

"Big Things Come in Small Packages" from *Don't Split the Pole: Tales of Down-Home Folk Wisdom* by Eleanora E. Tate. Text copyright © 1997 by Eleanora E. Tate. Reprinted by permission of Eleanora E. Tate.

Excerpt from *A Christmas Carol: Scrooge and Marley* by Israel Horovitz. Text copyright © 1979 by Israel Horovitz. Reprinted by permission of William Morris Endeavor Entertainment, LLC.

"Doris Is Coming" from *Drinking Coffee Elsewhere* by ZZ Packer. Text copyright © 2003 by ZZ Packer. Reprinted by permission of Riverhead Books, an imprint of Penguin Group (USA) Inc. and Canongate Books.

"Heartbeat" by David Yoo. Text copyright © 2005 by David Yoo. Reprinted by permission of Writers House, LLC, on behalf of the author.

"He—y, Come On O—ut!" by Shinichi Hoshi from *The Best Japanese Science Fiction Stories*. Text copyright © 1989 by Shinichi Hoshi. Reprinted by permission of Barricade Books.

Excerpt from "The Hidden Southwest: The Arch Hunters" by James Vlahos from Adventure.nationalgeographic.com. Text copyright © 2008 by National Geographic Society. Reprinted by permission of National Geographic Society.

Excerpt by Joan Vernikos from "Is Space Exploration Worth the Cost?" by Stephen Dubner from www.freakonomics.com, January 11, 2008. Text copyright © by Freakonomics, LLC. Reprinted by permission of William Morris Endeavor Entertainment LLC, on behalf of Freakonomics, LLC.

Excerpt from "John Bergmann runs a special zoo for older, exploited, and abused animals," retitled "Difference Maker: John Bergmann and Popcorn Park" by David Karas, October 25, 2012 from www.csmonitor.com. Text copyright © by The Christian Science Monitor. Reprinted by permission of David Karas.

Excerpt from Julianbeever.net. Text copyright © by Julian Beever. Reprinted by permission of Julian Beever.

"The Most Daring of Our Leaders" from *Freedom's Daughters: The Unsung Heroines of the Civil Rights Movement from 1830 to 1970* by Lynne Olson. Text copyright © 2001 by Lynne Olson. Reprinted by permission of Charles Scribner, an imprint of Simon & Schuster Children's Publishing Division.

Excerpt from *Polar Dream* by Helen Thayer. Text copyright © 1993 by Helen Thayer. Reprinted by permission of Millikan Swanson Weiss.

"Prayer to the Pacific" from *Storyteller* by Leslie Marmon Silko. Text copyright © 1981, 2012 by Leslie Marmon Silko. Reprinted by permission of Viking Penguin, a division of Penguin Group (USA) Inc. and Wylie Agency Inc.

"Problems with Hurricanes" from *Maraca: New and Selected Poems 1965–2000* by Victor Hernández Cruz. Text copyright © 1991 by Victor Hernández Cruz. Reprinted by permission of Coffee House Press.

Excerpt from *Stan Lee Presents A Christmas Carol by Charles Dickens*. Copyright © 2007 by Marvel Characters, Inc. Reprinted by permission of Marvel Entertainment.

"Stinging Tentacles Offer Hint to Oceans' Decline" by Elisabeth Rosenthal from *The New York Times*, August 3, 2008, www.nytimes.com. Text copyright © 2008 by The New York Times Company. Reprinted by permission of PARS International on behalf of The New York Times.

"Tornado at Talladega" from *Blacks* by Gwendolyn Brooks. Text copyright © 1945, 1949, 1953, 1960, 1963, 1968, 1969, 1970, 1971, 1975, 1981, 1987 by Gwendolyn Brooks. Reprinted by permission of Brooks Permissions.